AGAINST THE ODDS

The Public Life and Times of Louis Rasminsky

AGAINST THE ODDS

The Public Life and Times of Louis Rasminsky

BRUCE MUIRHEAD

UNIVERSITY OF TORONTO PRESS
Toronto Buffalo London

© University of Toronto Press Incorporated 1999
Toronto Buffalo London

Printed in Canada

ISBN 0-8020-0629-9 (cloth)

Printed on acid-free paper

Canadian Cataloguing in Publication Data

Muirhead, Bruce
Against the odds : the public life and times of Louis Rasminsky

Includes bibliographical references and index.
ISBN 0-8020-0629-9

1. Rasminsky, L. (Louis), 1908–1998.   2. Monetary policy – Canada – History –
20th century.   3. Bank of Canada – History.   4. Bank of Canada – Officials
and employees – Biography.   5. Bankers – Canada – Biography.   I. Title.

HG1552.R37M84 1999   332.1′1′092   C98-931629-9

University of Toronto Press acknowledges the
financial assistance to its publishing program of
the Canada Council for the Arts and
the Ontario Arts Council.

For Sandi, Ben, and Jacob

Contents

Preface

Louis Rasminsky was a humanitarian – a noun that is not applicable to many central bank governors. Admittedly, his primary concern, once he was appointed governor of the Bank of Canada, was to protect the value of the Canadian dollar. That, at times, meant relatively high interest rates, with concomitant adverse effects on Canadians, but it is also true that he never lost sight of their impact on ordinary people. He worried about higher rates of unemployment, about inequality of income, and about the dangers of foreign ownership of industry in Canada.

This humanitarian impulse came from his background – as a Jew when anti-semitism was widespread in Canada – as well as from his experience at the League of Nations during the Great Depression of the 1930s. His involvement in the negotiation and development of such international organizations as the International Monetary Fund and the United Nations was his attempt to make the world a better place, to learn from the disaster that had befallen it in the previous decade.

I owe a debt of gratitude to a number of people who helped in the researching and writing of this book. First, I would like to thank Corrine Miller, the archivist at the Bank of Canada, and her assistant, Helen Lafleur, for their unfailing help and advice. Corrine's knowledge of the Rasminsky Papers helped to speed up the process of reviewing tens of thousands of pages of documents. Similarly, when Louis Rasminsky emptied his private files, stored for years in various drawers and cabinets in his home, Corrine quickly made sense of them, putting the documents in an order that made their use easy. As well, the Bank's secretary, Ted Requard, kept a kindly eye on the project, while refraining from attempting to direct it in any way. Similarly, although the Bank provided funding for this project, it did not attempt to influence in any way my research and writing. I would also like to thank Steve High, a doctoral candidate at the University of Ottawa at the time, for research done in Geneva, in England, and in the United States. As well, his colleague Donald Wright helped in a smaller, but equally incisive way. My thanks also go to Jack Granatstein, whose counsel was crucial to the completion of this biography. In short, I owe him a debt that will be very difficult to repay. Thank you as well to John English, one of the 'anonymous' readers, as well as to two other truly unknown readers. Their criticisms and advice improved the flow of the text and also helped to clear up ambiguities and shortfalls.

I would also like to thank Gerry Hallowell, my editor at University of Toronto Press, for his unfailing advice and help in pushing this biography to completion. Through some difficult times he provided encouragement, which is gratefully acknowledged. Similarly, Emily Andrew, no longer with the Press, was my contact person who put a very human face on my dealings with UTP. John Parry, the copy editor for the biography, made the prose more intelligible and coherent. Finally, Lakehead University helped to ease the cost of publication somewhat through the provision of a grant. All the deficiencies and shortcomings of this book are, however, my own.

Last, but certainly not least, I would like to thank Louis Rasminsky for permitting me to write about his life. He placed no conditions, other than the right to approve the use of his private papers, on the direction that the biography would take. He was unfailingly helpful and submitted to more than twenty hours of my probing into his past. My one great regret is that he did not live to see the book in print.

PART ONE

The Centre Cannot Hold, 1908–1939

Chapter One

Montreal, Toronto, London

Louis Rasminsky was a man of honesty, integrity, and purpose. He was also a master at negotiation and achieved a type of result of which few others were capable. That genius was seen time and again throughout his more than four decades of service to both the League of Nations and the government of Canada and was a reflection of his obvious commitment and intelligence. At the League of Nations, his annual performance evaluations spoke to those attributes, and each year they became more laudatory. It was a similar story after he became a Canadian civil servant. Rasminsky was recruited to a very responsible position, and his career path moved quickly upward.

This ascent was an oddity in an overtly anti-semitic age, as it was in Canada during the years following his appointment as an official of the Bank of Canada's Foreign Exchange Control Board in 1940 and of the Bank itself in 1943. Anti-semitism seemed to be a factor in his being passed over for the post of senior deputy governor of the Bank in 1949 and for governor in 1955. The fact that he was made a deputy governor on 1 January 1955 was testament to his intelligence and his international reputation, which simply could not be overlooked. Though disappointed, perhaps, or unhappy, he was not embittered by the delays. Nor did he ever contemplate leaving the Bank even when passed over for higher office and when other, more luminous offers were made to him. Ultimately, Rasminsky overcame great odds to become governor in 1961 following the 'Coyne Affair' and in the process demonstrated great reserves of character. But that strength was not surprising, given his background and experience. The very fact of being Jewish, which had prevented him from becoming governor earlier, had long ago given him the ethical and moral fibre to deal with life.

Montreal was a tough city when Louis Rasminsky was born there on 1 February 1908. The family of his father, David, had immigrated to Canada in the 1870s to escape pogroms in Poland, while that of his mother, Etta, was a prominent one in St Catharines, Ontario. Indeed, Rasminsky's maternal grandfather was a learned man and had been accorded the honorary title of Reverend of the Jewish community in that city. Clearly, Rasminsky's father had found a better life in Canada; anti-semitism, while present in this country, lacked the more vicious aspects that sometimes characterized it in parts of Eastern Europe. However, as the twentieth century passed, the level of anti-semitism became more worrying for many Jews. Abbé Lionel Groulx, to become an important figure in the development of French-Canadian nationalism by the 1920s, was a confirmed anti-semite. In English Canada, the influential and prolific Goldwin Smith, as Gerald Tulchinsky has pointed out, 'was Canada's best-known Jew-hater in the late nineteenth century' and had helped to legitimize that attitude in the twentieth.[1]

Anti-semitism in Canada reflected a global trend that centred on both religious and secular aspects; in the popular press Jews were referred to as 'Christ-killers,' but they also controlled, according to the writings of anti-semites in Canada and Europe, the economy, judiciary, legislature, and press of various countries: 'This ... antisemitism was secular in mood, repudiating Jews not for traditional Christian reasons but because they were politically, socially and culturally alien. While reviving old images of the foes of Christendom, it also possessed a new and radical nationalistic dimension. The German economist Eugen Dühring went a significant step further by arguing that the Jews were a unique human species with distinctive physical and moral qualities – all of them negative.'[2]

Many Canadians would have agreed with that assessment. Indeed, some in the country's mainstream applauded the quotas that universities such as McGill, Queen's, and Toronto, among others, placed on Jewish students. As well, no matter how illustrious, Jewish graduands from some faculties found employment opportunities very limited. Doctors and dentists often had to find jobs in the United States, while humanities graduates were barred from the public service and also, by and large, from the staffs of universities. Anti-semitism was a fundamental aspect of Canadian society.

It was that type of atmosphere that led to the establishment of the Canadian Jewish Congress in March 1919, a resurgence of Canadian Zionism, and a revitalized Jewish community in the country. It also affected the young Rasminsky, who had moved to Toronto in 1913, making him very aware of his heritage and what it meant to be Jewish. While it set him apart from the Canadian mainstream, it also gave him the drive to succeed, to overcome the odds that were stacked against him as a Jew, instilling in him a personal morality and an ethical credo by which he lived.

As he passed into his early teenage years, he concentrated more and more on the issues and problems confronting Judaism, engaging in youthful and energetic debate over its future. He also wondered about his own – should he go to Palestine and work on a kibbutz, or join the struggle for a Jewish homeland? In 1927, while still at the University of Toronto, he wrote of some of his doubts to Rabbi Solomon Goldman in Cleveland, Ohio. The rabbi was impressed; his letter was 'as clear an exposition of the problem ... confronting young Jewish idealists as I have read in a long time.'[2] Which road to take?, Goldman asked Rasminsky in his reply. It was not an easy decision: 'The thinking young Jew finds himself at crossroads and the roads impassable.' Rasminsky had mentioned an alternative, on which Goldman commented: 'You offer the soundest solution to your problem, namely that of going to Palestine and working there with brain and brawn.' As well, Rasminsky had written of his own problems with the intensely theological orientation of the synagogue. However, that was necessary in a Christian country, the rabbi thought: 'In Palestine, Jewish life will fill every dale and mount every hill. In the diaspora, under the best circumstances, Jewish life will have to be concentrated in the synagogue. We will find it most difficult to maintain a Jewish culture, particularly in liberal countries, without some religious tinge.'

Obviously, Rasminsky took his faith seriously, and during the 1920s he increasingly immersed himself in its politics, an interest that was nurtured in his teens. Early on, his academic record had marked him as an outstanding student, which resulted in his selection as Harbord Collegiate's representative at a public speaking contest for city high schools. His subject, Theodore Herzl and the rise of Zionism, was ruled ineligible by the judges as being too 'political.' Quite probably an address on, for example, the imperial might of Great Britain would have been eminently acceptable, and this sort of reasoning demonstrated, to a young Jew, the prevailing double standard in Canada. However, Herzl's Zionism – a nationalist movement that was concerned with the idea of Jewish survival and the re-establishment of a Jewish homeland in the Middle East – was one against which the British were firmly ranged. Zionism also raised the spectre of dual loyalty among Jews to both Canada and to the state of Palestine. His second choice for the competition – the right of self-determination of peoples – resulted in his disqualification.[3]

The fact that he was chosen to represent Harbord Collegiate in the contest spoke to his academic achievement. Encouraged by his parents, he began to read widely in international economics and politics – an interest that stayed with him for the rest of his life. The young Rasminsky also found stimulation in the homes of some of his school friends. In his early teenage years he would often go to one of his friends' homes on Friday evenings and spend the time talking and debating with others his own age and with the chum's parents, who were very well educated.

Rasminsky's mother and father were interested in his education, monitoring his progress at school closely and encouraging him. He responded to this encouragement, and his report cards bear witness to his academic proficiency; his final marks between 1923 and 1925, when he entered the University of Toronto, were firsts in every subject, which ranged from composition to physics. Only the autumn of 1924 was marred with a geometry mark of 50 per cent (but bracketed with others such as 94 in French composition and algebra), which prompted his father to note, with some restraint, that 'outside of the Geometry mark the report is satisfactory.'[4]

He was his school's valedictorian in 1925, winning a number of scholarships against tough competition. One of the most satisfying was that received as a result of his excellent standing in the matriculation scholarship examination, where he pitted his knowledge against that of the brightest students in Ontario; in English, German, and history he stood first in the province. For the Jewish community around Harbord, it was a 'glorious success,' the first time that one of its members had scored so high.[5] For that effort, he also received a letter from the business manager and secretary treasurer of Toronto's board of education: 'I beg to inform you that the Board of Education at a meeting held on the 3rd. instant, passed the following resolution, viz: "That the congratulations of the Board be extended to Louis H. [sic] Rasminsky, Harbord Collegiate Institute, upon winning a scholarship at the recent examinations held by the Department of Education of the Province of Ontario."'[6]

As he moved into his late teens, he became more involved with the Jewish community in Toronto. He was a member of a group that patched up differences between Montreal's Young Judaeans and those in his city, which had split in 1921 over philosophical differences. By 1924, he was on the national executive, and two years later, he was vice-president of Toronto

Young Judaea – a group dedicated to strengthening the Zionist movement in Canada. It had committed itself to securing 'the recognition by Toronto Zionists and the Jewish community in general of the significance of Young Judaea work' and also believed that 'the future of the Canadian Zionist Movement is being menaced and undermined by the utter indifference of a younger generation that knew not Eastern Europe.'[7] It had undertaken a task that belonged also to 'older people as well – the burden of educating along Zionist lines their fellow Jewish youth. Herzl said the return to Zion must be preceded by a return to Judaism. If the young Canadian Jew is to return to Zion, he must first return to Judaism and he is often doing it in no uncertain fashion in Young Judaea.' The organization sponsored regular meetings to that end. Rasminsky and others participated in a Friday-evening lecture series; his first topic was 'Young Judaea – an Evaluation.'

Young Judaeans were particularly interested in post-biblical history, with a view to explaining the background of present-day Jewish life. Special attention was given to Jewish history and literature, current Jewish events, and Zionism. This sort of education was necessary, they believed, to provide some defences against the absorption of Jews into the surrounding Canadian culture and also against Jewish 'enemies within – apathy and short-sightedness.' It had to convince Jews who played 'a large part in positive and constructive Jewish movements in [North] America that the real problem that they must face if they have foresight and vision is the problem of the Jewish youth. Effective educational work cannot be done, without the support and cooperation of these people.'[8]

Rasminsky's career at the University of Toronto was most successful, and early on he was deemed a student to watch. Because of his high-school record, regulations permitted him to enter directly into the second year of the honours course in political science and economics, where he specialized in the latter. Why that subject? Even then, at the age of eighteen, he was interested in what he thought of as the public good and the public role in establishing and maintaining it – the difference in society that government could make if it used its powers judiciously. As he studied the department's curriculum, with its course headings like public finance and central banking, he later recalled, it was clear to him that this was where he should focus his energies.

With a first in almost every subject, his standing at the university was an enviable one: The department, as one of his professors, V.W. Bladen, wrote, did not 'scatter [firsts] about indiscriminately.' Moreover, since

Rasminsky had entered the program in second year, his 'achievement [became] very much greater.'[9] Bladen was at least part of the reason for Rasminsky's success at the university. He was, Rasminsky remembered, 'a good teacher and was concerned about his students and their abilities.'[10] Bladen was also a relative youngster in the department, having been appointed at the age of twenty-one in 1921. He was not content to teach the same subjects in the same way that they had been taught for the past fifty years.

One subject, in particular, that Bladen remembered was 'Advanced Economic Theory.' From the 1870s, it had consisted of a study of economics literature from Adam Smith to John Mill,

> plus some discussion of Marx and of the neo-Classical School, particularly of Jevons and Böhm-Bawerk ... I continued the tradition of lecturing on the classical literature, but I was conscious of the need to make this course much more than, and indeed very different from, the traditional 'History of Economic Thought.' The need was to educate economists, not historians of thought, and so from the very beginning, I was anxious to make this study of the classics increase my students' understanding of the modern literature and of the modern economy. I considered it necessary to induce them to read and think about some of the modern literature ... These were ... exciting years, years when one could not graduate students who had not been touched by the new wave of theory.[11]

The first time that Bladen taught the revamped course was in 1927, to a group that he called 'a vintage year,' which included Rasminsky and Wynne Plumptre. Certainly Rasminsky was stimulated by Bladen's approach, which gave the study of economics a new twist. Nor did the discussion and analysis end when the bell rang; Bladen recalled going to Plumptre's house 'to meet the group at one of their regular weekly meetings in their second year ... It was a very happy relationship, the young bachelor teacher and this brilliant group of students.' With teachers such as Bladen, Rasminsky thrived at the University.

His high position in the 'vintage class' demonstrated his keen and penetrating mind; the competition with his life-long friend Wynne Plumptre for the top place also demonstrated his focus and ambition. As J.L. Granatstein has pointed out, he was in a three-year battle with Plumptre to be head of the class. In 1926, Plumptre obtained 1.1, and Rasminsky, 1.2.[12] The following year, the standings were reversed, while in 1928 the two were tied in the top spot. Despite these standings, given the department's method of calculating the overall top student, its Massey scholarship went to Plumptre for study at Cambridge, while Rasminsky was left with nothing. He was disappointed, as his family did not have the means to send him to Oxford or Cambridge, to the London School of Economics, or to an Ivy League American university to take a postgraduate degree – then the usual route for academically talented and upwardly mobile young men.

At this juncture, he was the recipient of a bit of luck and an act of great thoughtfulness on the part of one of his teachers, Professor Gilbert Jackson.[13] Jackson took matters in hand and approached one of the leaders of the Jewish community to say that if Rasminsky had been an Anglican, he would have gone to the bishop, but since his student was Jewish, he had come to him. The professor told him that it would be a disgrace to the Jewish community if it did not give this young man an opportunity for further study. Within days, enough money had been donated to the University of Toronto's political economy department to establish a scholarship for study elsewhere, with Rasminsky as its first recipient. As a consequence, in the late summer of 1928 he was off to the London School of Economics (LSE) to study with some of the best and the brightest instructors and students in the world.

He had chosen LSE in large part because he had been entranced by a collection of essays written by Allyn Young, a Harvard professor then on a three-year leave at LSE. The book, *Economic Problems New and Old*,[14] was about money, the direction in which Rasminsky's interests lay. As well, LSE was in cosmopolitan and sophisticated London – he had little interest in what he considered to be dowdy and provincial Cambridge and Oxford.

The capital was an exciting city in the late 1920s – the centre of empire, of world finance, and of power. And before the Great Depression took hold, there was money to spend, and there were parties to attend. The environment was stimulating in every way for the young Rasminsky. His courses appealed to him – when time permitted that he attend – the theory of international trade, mercantilism, the tariff policy of the chief powers, and the problems of state sovereignty. He told Harold Innis, a former professor of his at Toronto, that Allyn Young in economic theory (a seminar for research students given by his putative thesis supervisor), Harold Laski in politics and sociology, and R.H. Tawney on industrial history were his 'staples.' He also sat in on Young's 'Principles of Economics,' which addressed themes such as forms of economic activity, the theory of production, costs and incomes, communal and competitive points of view, and modern schools of economic thought. Lionel Robbins was also one of his teachers, and the two would meet in official delegations in later years, with Robbins on the British side and Rasminsky on the Canadian.[15]

For a young man from Toronto, then a relative backwater, life in London was wonderful. The city, the people, the experience, and, most of all, the university were all stimulating. He wrote to Innis that 'one can worship at the shrine of Marx, Mill or Edmund Burke as one chooses. But this form of expression is rather unfair: one worships nothing at the LSE, or perhaps better, one changes the object of one's worship.'[16] Certainly Rasminsky would have agreed with Lionel Robbins's view: 'There was little or no teaching at the School ... which was not inspired by the spirit of search and discovery.'[17] Its traditions of 'friendliness' and 'informality' greatly appealed to the young Canadian.

However, his plans fell apart following his first term. Allyn Young succumbed to the British climate, dying of pneumonia, leaving Rasminsky high and dry. As a result, LSE lost some of its lustre, and his time there was saved only by the interest taken in him by Harold Laski and Theodor Gregory, a decent teacher but not at all inspiring, yet now his dissertation adviser. He and Laski became good friends, while he and Gregory would meet again in 1942. With a new supervisor, Rasminsky took as his thesis topic 'The Quest for Discrimination and Non-Discrimination in Trade Relations,' studying the development of the most-favoured-nation concept in trade. He chose the subject not necessarily because he had a burning desire to investigate the nitty-gritty of trade issues but because he needed a thesis topic and that one seemed to him as good as any others that he could think of.[18] It was a thesis never completed, and it is probably true that his heart was never in it. Instead, he heard the siren call of the League of Nations and spent the 1930s in Geneva.

Chapter Two

Geneva and the League of Nations

Geneva in 1930, headquarters of the League of Nations and of the International Labour Organization (ILO), was one of the most cosmopolitan cities in the world. The League itself was a thoroughly international body, though its effectiveness was impaired from the outset by the failure of the United States to join. The first secretary general, Sir Eric Drummond, had insisted that all officials were to act in independence of their own national authorities, and, with few exceptions, that attitude governed the secretariat as a whole.[1] For a young Canadian, the city and the League proved irresistible. Louis Rasminsky and his wife, Lyla, were to live in Geneva for nearly a decade while he worked for the League in a technical capacity, and the experience was to have a major influence on his thinking and his life.

It happened almost by chance, as seems to be the case with so many opportunities. One day in mid-1929, he was sitting in the LSE graduate lounge, when a staff member, L.G. Robinson, came in. He was then a lecturer in history and in 1932 became the first dean of postgraduate studies. However, as Rasminsky remembers, it seemed that his real job was to look after 'the moral welfare of graduate students.' Robinson took the only vacant seat in the room, which happened to be the one next to Rasminsky's. As they were having tea, Robinson turned to the Canadian and said that he knew that he was to leave for Canada at the end of the term. What, he inquired, did Rasminsky intend to do? University teaching in all probability, was the response. That was fine, but Robinson thought that it would be useful if the Canadian spent a few years on the continent before returning home. He had just received a notice that the League of Nations was looking for a graduate economist for its Economic and Financial Section, and there would be competitive examinations held in Berlin,

Copenhagen, London, and Paris. Rasminsky should put in for it. The young man applied, wrote the exam, and, in due course, was asked to present himself for an interview.

He was grilled by a panel led by his future chief, Alexander Loveday.[2] After questions dealing with monetary and economic policy, Loveday asked if he had any languages other than English. After some hesitation, Rasminsky said that he could read, write, and speak French. He had learned it in the classrooms of Toronto's Harbord Collegiate and practised it in Paris over the last few years when he could get there. At the hiring committee's prompting, he answered a few questions in French, to its satisfaction. What about others – German, for example? He could speak it well enough to get by, a result of the hours spent in Tubby Irwin's German class at Harbord Collegiate. Any others, the panel asked? Spanish, he replied, which he knew how to read, but not to speak.[3] The committee took him at his word. Based on this performance, it offered him the job; he had beaten out three hundred other candidates. Obviously, the committee saw something more than a reasonable proficiency in a few languages – a promise that would manifest itself during the 1930s.

His boyhood friend Lionel Gelber summed up the feeling of the Jewish community in Toronto when he sent congratulations: 'The usual phrases don't seem to apply in these circumstances. I mean, I can't say you do us honour; I can't say that you have again revealed the highest intellectual distinction; I can't even say your friends rejoice in a success wrested by sheer merit and mental power ... All these things are true, yet they will be said to you now a dozen times in various combinations and permutations. Frankly, I don't want to say them because what I feel is quite inexpressible. I will say this, though, and I mean it: that nothing has made me happier in a long time than the news you send me.'[4]

His old professor Gilbert Jackson told him that he had become 'something of a touchstone' in the halls of Baldwin House at the University of Toronto, which housed the department of political economy. 'When anyone applies for a scholarship now, someone generally says, "Well, he is quite a good man, of course, but he is not in the same class as Rasminsky."' That praise was doubled as a result of the new position.[5] As well, Norman Mackenzie and W.P.M. Kennedy, both professors of law at Toronto, wrote to him on receiving the news. Geneva, Mackenzie felt certain, would be most interesting. More important, the young man would experience international relations in their purest form – that would be most valuable, especially for a Canadian. However, he should be careful: 'A good many young idealists who go to Geneva become thoroughly disillusioned and somewhat cynical as a result of their experience there.' He did not, however, 'have fears ... on that score, for I know you have seen enough of the world to appreciate the difficulties in the way of international cooperation.'[6] He received similar advice from Kennedy, who hoped that he would 'stay with the League.'[7] Too many bright young men wanted to come back to the university, where 'in an enormous department they lose heart because promotion is like a snail and salary so low.'

His appointment was reason to celebrate in another way; his first action was to cable his girlfriend, Lyla Rotenberg, in Toronto: 'Have accepted job League of Nations at 13,700 Swiss francs [per year]. Will you marry me?' She replied: 'What is the exchange rate of the Swiss franc?'[8] Apparently, it was fine; they wed at her parents' home in Toronto on 15 July 1930, and the union was to last until her death in 1976. It was, he later recalled, 'the best thing [he] had ever done.' They moved to Geneva later that summer; he left behind an unfinished dissertation that never was completed.

The city and its primary tenant were special places in the 1930s. While some vilified the League of Nations as impotent and useless, that description could not be applied to its technical work. For a young economist, this was surely the place to be. For example, Rasminsky's department – the Economic and Financial Section – had several important functions. It was primarily a research group, whose work was designed 'to present a coherent world picture of economic and financial facts.'[9] As well, it provided the secretariat for the economic committee, the economic consultative committee, and all the technical subcommittees of the economic committee. It also staffed the secretariat for the technical committees set up to deal with economic questions and for all international economic conferences.

The section prepared various regular publications on financial and economic topics and supplied 'expert advice on banking, public finance, trade, etc., as well as on general economic trends and policies, as might be required by international economic and financial conferences and the financial and economic committees.' It provided documentation for the meetings of various committees and wrote the reports that gave effect to their decisions. The section ensured liaison with the more important international bodies, meetings, and congresses whose activities had a bearing on the economic work of the League.[10] And while its two subgroups – the financial section and the economic intelligence service – were separate during the 1930s, the distinction between them was blurred. 'Individual members of the Intelligence Service often were entrusted with work for the Financial Section, while members of the latter on occasion assisted in the research work of the Economic Intelligence Section.'[11]

In short, given the range of topics covered by his section and the work that he was doing, Rasminsky was exposed widely to ideas and people. He learned that he was not so much an economic theorist as one who was interested in the practical application of his craft. Certainly the League appreciated that orientation, which would yield him benefits in the years ahead. He also believed that what he was doing was useful and contributed something to people's understanding of their situation. He wrote to Mackenzie: 'It has struck me that those who are loudest in their criticism generally, have an eye only to the political work of the League and completely neglect the work of its technical organizations. I feel that it is precisely the technical work of the League that, removed as it is from political controversy and dispute, is able to be conducted along scientific lines and to achieve results immediately useful.'[12]

Each year officials conducted a series of studies of different sectors of economic activity, such as production, trade, money and banking, and public finance. These analyses were then brought together for the general reader in a survey covering all branches of activity, supplemented by statistical books of reference and a monthly statistical bulletin. According to League officials, the nature of that work was determined by a number of guiding principles. First among these was objectivity. As a memorandum prepared in the economic intelligence service pointed out, 'The figures are intended to speak for themselves. We are in no way concerned with policies or politics except insofar as this or that group of figures may by itself suggest success or failure and except insofar as the application of the policy modifies the mechanism within which the facts recorded take place.'[13] That work appealed to Rasminsky, as indeed did Geneva.

The city was small and very easy to move around, which helped Rasminsky and his wife establish and maintain friendships. Many of the contacts begun in Geneva lasted over the next sixty years and included some of the century's great economists. Indeed, the lure of Geneva attracted outstanding economists from all parts of the world. As Rasminsky and his colleagues often said, the quickest way of meeting any economist of note was to wait for him or her to arrive in Geneva. As another former high-ranking official of the League later noted, in the later 1920s and 1930s 'Geneva, and not London, Paris, Moscow, or Washington, was the clearing-house of the international affairs of the world.'[14]

For example, Jack Condliffe, a New Zealander who finished his career several decades later at the Stanford Research Institute, edited the League's *World Economic Survey*. He was succeeded as editor by the Oxford economist and future Nobel prize winner James Meade. The great Swedish economist from Stockholm University, Bertil Ohlin, was commissioned by the League to write a report, *The Course and Phases of the World Economic Depression*, which was completed in 1931. Rasminsky spoke with him regularly and helped him prepare his final report. It dealt with many of the subjects with which the young Canadian would concern himself later in life, such as the development of inflation. The report's mandate, as laid out by the Second Commission of the League's Eleventh Assembly, also had an impact on Rasminsky: 'When we consider the magnitude of the losses from which the world suffers during a period of economic stagnation similar to that through which the world is now passing, *it is impossible not to be impressed by the almost absolute failure of society ... to devise any means by which such disasters may be averted.*'[15]

Similarly, Gottfried Haberler, then professor of international economics at Harvard, was invited to update his theoretical volume on business cycles, *Prosperity and Depression.* Haberler spent two years in Geneva on the task, and Rasminsky, in the adjacent office, began every day with a lengthy conversation on economics and international finance. It was as good as any graduate seminar ever got. The ritual of the daily meeting was always the same; Rasminsky would walk in, Haberler would rise to shake his hand, wait for him to get comfortable, and then ask, 'Well, Rasminsky, what's new?'[16]

Rasminsky also kept in touch with an acquaintance from LSE days, the Hungarian Nicholas Kaldor (later Lord Kaldor); one of the first questions put Rasminsky's way following his appointment in Geneva came from Kaldor, who was applying for the post of junior lecturer at Queen's University in Kingston, Ontario. He wanted to know what Rasminsky thought about Canadian universities, Kingston as a place, and Queen's in particular. As well, did the salary of $2,000 'provide a livelihood?'[17] In the late 1920s, Kaldor had been the favourite pupil of Lionel Robbins and became, according to some, 'one of the most distinguished economists of the twentieth century, who will be recorded in the history of economic thought as a brilliant theoretician and applied economist, surpassed in originality only by [John Maynard] Keynes and [Sir Roy] Harrod among British economists this century.'[18]

Finally, there was Peggy Joseph, later Rasminsky's collaborator on the League's nutrition report and in 1933, when she turned up to work at the

ILO, 'the best woman economist I know,' at least according to Kaldor.[19] Rasminsky would have agreed with that high assessment.

The League was not the only drawing card for economists in Geneva, however, and the graduate school located down the road from the Palais des Nations, the École des Hautes Études internationale, invited guest lecturers for the summer period. Rasminsky was asked several times over the decade that he was in the city to lecture to students, and Jacob Viner, an enormously talented Canadian economist then teaching at the University of Chicago, was asked twice. A graduate of McGill with a PhD from Harvard, Viner had produced a thesis, 'Canada's Balance of International Indebtedness, 1900–1913: An Inductive Study in the Theory of International Trade,' which was the definitive work on the topic and was eventually published by Harvard University Press. Viner later became a very influential figure in American economic circles, as well as an adviser to the US Treasury. Indeed, one observer has noted that by 1945 Viner had become 'probably the [United States's] most distinguished international economist.'[20] His path would cross Rasminsky's throughout the rest of his life. In the war, for example, while Rasminsky was involved in the development of the International Monetary Fund, Viner called for creation 'of a workable international monetary system combining exchange stability and price-level stability.'[21] Viner also presented a report to Canada's Royal Commission on Banking and Finance in 1962, when Rasminsky was governor of the Bank of Canada. The young Canadian and his wife became good friends with the Viners and their two children.

As well, there were other friendships begun with League officials in different departments and with other residents of Geneva. Rasminsky's closest friend in the city was Rifat Tirana, an Albanian Muslim, educated at Beirut University. His wife, Rosamond (according to Rasminsky, the most beautiful woman in the world), was the daughter of William English Walling, one of the founders of the (US) National Association for the Advancement of Colored People, and of Rose Strunsky, a member of the distinguished German Jewish family.[22]

Throughout the decade, there were Canadians drifting through Geneva, some of whom Rasminsky came to know fairly well. Hume Wrong, a future undersecretary of state in the Department of External Affairs and ambassador to Washington, was the chief Canadian officer at Canada's League office in the later 1930s and became a good friend. Over an extended period in 1932, Wrong was in Geneva, and Rasminsky met with him formally and informally, both at the League and at the

Bavaria, a restaurant that was a favourite of the Rasminsky's. Similarly, Lester Pearson visited fairly frequently, and Rasminsky saw him whenever he was in the city. Later, Pearson was Canada's accredited representative in Geneva, though he never liked the place or the duties assigned to him.[23] Three decades later, their paths would cross closely, with Pearson as prime minister and Rasminsky as governor of the Bank of Canada.

Despite the variety of people in Geneva, the intellectual stimulation, and the challenge of working in an international environment, the Depression remained, and the grey cliffs that presented such a stunning backdrop to the city seemed to mirror the global condition. Deflation, tariff increases, import restrictions and quotas, grain-milling regulations, competitive exchange depreciations – indeed, the whole gamut of 'beggar-thy-neighbour' policies with which nations attempted to cope with the massive downturn in economic conditions – were endlessly discussed and analysed in Rasminsky's section and in other League departments dealing with economic matters. The League had become a focal point in the effort to resist the self-destructive acts in which so many countries were engaged, as well as in the attempt to bring about more international economic and political consultation and cooperation.

While the League was not successful in influencing the world's major countries to modify their economic behaviour, Rasminsky later claimed that 'we had some effect in slowing the rot and ... the activities of the League during this period – and the lessons learned – laid the foundation for the great development in international economic and financial cooperation which took place after the war, through the establishment of the International Monetary Fund, the World Bank, [and] the Food and Agriculture Organization.'[24] He was to play a major role in the creation of many of those institutions in 1944 and after. In short, Geneva was the centre of the international struggle against the Depression, and it was there that he received the 'internationalist' grounding that was to shape so much of his life.

Rasminsky's first job was to prepare papers for the gold delegation of the financial committee as well as help to research and write its final report. The gold delegation had been established by the League of Nations following a few years of discussion and agitation by interested parties on the question of gold. The League machinery had delegated some of its officials to join with certain outside members and form the gold delegation.[25] The delegation produced two interim reports in 1930 and 1931 and a final report in June 1932. Rasminsky's responsibility was for the chapter on the industrial consumption of gold; in the League's stimulating atmosphere even that subject could be interesting, or so he believed.

The committee's final report suggested that the real problem with gold was not its adequacy as an international means of payment but its distribution. In short, too much of the yellow metal was in the hands of the United States and a few European creditor countries. So far as its prospective adequacy, the delegation looked to the progressive development of the gold exchange standard to supplement gold reserves as a source of international liquidity. Following publication of the interim report in September 1930, 'the Gold Delegation continued to collect papers and to discuss principally the maldistribution of gold; but it was now working against the background of the collapse of world prices and world trade and anything it could say had little chance of relevance to the frantically urgent problems of economic policy every country had to face week by week.' R.S. Sayers called it 'a sad story, with no inspiring end.'[26]

Still, Rasminsky found the atmosphere in Geneva exhilarating, with the constant give and take of economic argument. Debate went on endlessly as Rasminsky and his colleagues tested ideas on topics such as deflation, how to prevent depressions, and even the Canadian economic situation and its special problems, given its proximity to the United States – no doubt a matter raised by Rasminsky.[27]

Life was good in those first heady years in the city, and Rasminsky's keen insight into the problems of the day and his work at the League earned him praise. Certainly his superiors valued his contributions, and the annual performance appraisals written about him by Alexander Loveday, the head of his section and a tough critic by anyone's measure, grew increasingly eloquent over the decade. His first, however, must have been especially welcome and set the tone for the rest; it recommended him for an annual increment of eight hundred Swiss francs. Loveday wrote that he had shown 'considerable power of independent thought and scientific analysis. He is a quick worker, but thorough and careful, moving easily from one subject to another.'[28]

As the Depression deepened and the lines of the unemployed lengthened, various international meetings were convened by desperate governments. An Imperial Economic Conference, held in Ottawa in the late summer of 1932, yielded very little. Similarly, a World Economic Conference, called by the British in 1933 to discuss competitive devaluations and trade problems and attended by over sixty countries, was not productive. Over the late spring and summer, nothing much was agreed to, and by autumn the conference disbanded and competitive devaluations continued as tariffs were manipulated for national reasons, to the benefit of none.

The League had been invited to participate in the deliberations of that international meeting, and Loveday's section produced several papers on aspects of the international situation. Rasminsky's contribution 'consisted of two long papers, one on price developments and the other on silver, the latter designed to debunk the views being vigorously advanced by the influential American Senator, Key Pittman, of the great silver producing state of Nevada, who felt that a large increase in the price of silver was all that was needed' to set the world to rights.[29]

Rasminsky's well-crafted and conceived paper was important for a reason that had little to do with the conference; it was thought much of by Clifford Clark, Canada's recently appointed deputy minister of finance, who was also in attendance. It confirmed his opinion, formed a few months earlier during a League committee meeting, that Rasminsky would be an extraordinary catch for the Canadian civil service. Seven years later, success would crown his efforts, but Clark's first few attempts to get Rasminsky into the service got nowhere. The League official had made it plain that he would not return to Canada for any job, but the possibility of being appointed secretary to the Royal Commission on Banking seemed too good to pass up. This body had been set up by the government of R.B. Bennett to investigate the functioning of the Canadian banking system and to ease the path towards establishment of a central bank. In the late spring of 1933, Rasminsky wrote to Norman Robertson, then stationed at Canada House in London, inquiring about his chances of being appointed to its staff.

Robertson, as well as Clark, was interested in securing Rasminsky for government service and, together with the deputy minister, pressed his case on Bennett. Like Clark, Robertson believed that Canada presented endless opportunity for a fertile mind such as Rasminsky's. Ultimately, however, their efforts failed. 'The Prime Minister ... had another nominee in mind. Clark [was] sorry and so am I that nothing has come of this opportunity to get you back in Canada ... where there is so much to be done that you could do better than anyone else I know.' The diplomat ended by promising to 'continue to keep an eye on the way things turn out, and will let you know of any development in the situation that may create another opportunity in which you might be interested.'[30] Wynne Plumptre, Rasminsky's friend and competitor from the University of Toronto, became the commission's assistant secretary.

Rasminsky had had his heart set on the royal commission, and rejection was disappointing. What did it mean for the future, Gelber asked from London? Were his chances of ever securing employment in Canada negligible, or would his chance come later? Gelber's next sentence read: 'There is always the thought that the executive offices are generally located on a higher storey!'[31] Rasminsky would come to fill those very nicely.

Soon after that failed initiative, Clark spoke again with Rasminsky about a possible position in his own department. He told the League official: 'I am asking the Civil Service Commission to create for me at once the position in the Department of which I spoke to you briefly ... Naturally, I am thinking of you in this connection and am wondering whether we cannot persuade you to come back to Canada at this time.'[32] The job description read as follows: 'Under direction, to make enquiries and investigations into problems of public finance and taxation as assigned; to study the working of existing types of taxation, their economic incidence, and their inter-relationships; to supervise the maintenance of information regarding taxation in other countries, especially as to methods of application and collection; and to perform other related work as assigned.'

Clark pointed out, almost apologetically, that the position centred around tax issues. However, there would be some work connected with establishment of the new central bank, and while Rasminsky might not 'fancy [himself] as a tax expert ... [there was] the possibility that you would slide over into the Central Bank when we get it set up.' Clark believed that the advertised post would attract 'a huge number of applications,' so he wanted Rasminsky to respond as quickly as possible. The starting pay was four thousand dollars per year minus the obligatory 10 per cent deduction extracted by the government during the Depression to help its financial situation. By November, the deputy minister had Rasminsky's reply; thanks but no thanks – the job of glorified tax man did not appeal to him at all.[33] Still, Clark would not concede defeat.

A further setback followed a few years later, as Rasminsky was turned down for another job. The position that he applied for at the tender age of twenty-six was that of assistant deputy governor of the newly established Bank of Canada; his applying was perhaps not unreasonable, given that the governor, Graham Towers, was only a decade older. Rasminsky had made inquiries of a few Canadians in Geneva in early 1935. J. Scott MacDonald, a diplomat in the city, was a fountain of information. When he returned to Ottawa, he sent Rasminsky a lengthy letter detailing the various parts of the Bank and the qualifications necessary to be considered for one of the positions.[34]

Rasminsky laid out his case in a letter of application to Clark. While at the League, he had specialized in banking, currency, and price movements, and he was familiar with both the theoretical aspects of those questions and the practical working of the central and commercial banking systems and the money markets of the principal countries of the world. As well, he had some administrative experience and knew about the problems connected with working in a large organization. His references constituted a who's who? of the world of the study of banking in the early 1930s – Jacob Viner, then an assistant secretary and economic adviser to the US secretary of the treasury; Parker Willis, formerly secretary of the US Federal Reserve Board and now professor of banking at Columbia; T.E. Gregory, professor of banking at the University of London; Per Jacobsson, economic adviser to the Bank for International Settlements in Basle, Switzerland; and Bertil Ohlin. He hoped, he wrote to Clark, that his application would 'receive serious consideration.'[35] It probably did, but Canada's domestic politics intruded on Rasminsky's hopes; the position of assistant deputy governor was to go to a French Canadian, L.P. Saint-Amour.

Rasminsky had also been contemplating academic life in Canada in a sort of absent-minded way, especially after the head of the University of Toronto's department of political economy, E.J. Urwick, had told him in early 1932 that he intended 'to get [Rasminsky] on [his] staff.' Far be it from Rasminsky to disabuse him of that notion. In truth, however, he was never really interested. That was just as well, because no firm offer ever came. Still, ever the optimist, the chair felt that Depression-imposed restrictions would be rescinded soon, writing to Rasminsky: 'The staff is still deficient and of course at the moment it is difficult to get any additions, but I still hope that the situation may have changed in a year or so, and in any case it is hardly conceivable that the Government will deliberately starve so important a Department as this, when many less important sections of the University are staffed twice as liberally.'[36]

Surely letters that Rasminsky received from department members throughout the early 1930s could only have solidified his intention to stay clear of academic entanglements. For example, Gilbert Jackson told him: 'Life must be much more exciting at your end just now than at our end.'[37] In Toronto, his big news was that Vincent Bladen's wife had broken her ankle while horseback riding and that another department member was away for a month on sick leave. As well, while Rasminsky was at the centre of the big questions of the day, such as Germany and Hitler, Japan and the Treaty of Versailles, the department was 'carrying on exactly as usual and with exactly the same objects that [it had] been doing for years past.' Later, the department's Donald MacGregor wrote that he would 'feel happier if there were more research and less talking' being done.[38]

There were two other considerations. Harold Laski, a professor at LSE, had told Rasminsky to think carefully if anything came up at Toronto: 'Are [there] people in economics at Toronto contact with whom ... will sharpen your own mind? Alternatively, can you see enough of people in Chicago, Columbia and Harvard, not to feel that you have buried yourself in a backwater?'[39] More to the point, however, Rasminsky was a Jew, and anti-semitism in Canada was a factor to weigh carefully. Laski made the telling point that if he went as an assistant professor, that could well be the top rank for him.

For a Jew such as Rasminsky, that dimension was real. In the 1930s, anti-semitism was part of the fabric of much of Canadian society; many people did not want to rent to Jews or to employ them. The Canadian Jewish Congress reported in 1937: 'During the past few years we have witnessed an amazing growth of antisemitism.'[40] Jews in many places were barred 'from hotels, beaches, golf courses and parks.' There were few in universities, and fewer in the civil service. Talent was passed over because of irrational prejudice. As O.D. Skelton, the powerful undersecretary of state for external affairs, wrote to W.L. Grant soon after Rasminsky's rejection of the tax job: 'When last in Geneva, I was much impressed by a young Canadian of Jewish extraction named Radziminsky [sic], ... now in the Economic Section of the League Secretariat. It struck me that he had the most vigorous and clear-cut intellectual equipment I had met in a young man for years. Clark ... was also impressed ... and made efforts to secure him for a minor post ... As it happened, Radziminsky was not prepared to take the post ... Even if he had been willing there would probably have been difficulties because of the prejudice in question.'[41]

Nor were conditions any better in universities. For example, some years earlier, though the situation still pertained in the 1930s, the principal of Queen's could publicly take pride in the fact that his university had only five Jews on staff: 'The presence of many Jews tended to lower the tone of Canadian Universities.'[42] Both McGill and the University of Toronto imposed quotas on Jewish students to restrict their numbers. In the case of the latter, dentistry, law, and medicine were especially regulated. As Cyril Levitt and William Shaffir have pointed out, 'From the 1930s through the Second World War, Jews found it difficult to enter certain professions ... At the University of Toronto School of Dentistry, a dexterity requirement was a favourite ploy for keeping Jewish students out; the small number who made it into the program often found themselves subjected to open abuse by anti-Semitic professors. Graduates of the University of Toronto Medical School found that their prestigious diplomas could not obtain internships for them, so an entire generation of Jewish medical students emigrated to the United States seeking hospital posts to hone their craft. Canada did not want them.'[43]

As well, physical violence against Jews was not rare in Canada; at the same time as Rasminsky was vaguely contemplating that his future might lie at the University of Toronto, Jews and gentiles bloodied each other at Toronto's Christie Pits in a vicious battle. The *Globe and Mail* reported in its lead headline in August 1939: 'Swastika Feud Battles in Toronto Injure 5 – Fists, Boots, Pipes Used in Bloor Street War.' The casualties were four Jews and one Christian.[44] Toronto was bad, but increasingly Montreal reminded some Jews of eastern Europe because of the prevailing anti-semitic climate.[45]

Despite his lack of interest in a university position, Rasminsky very much liked to interact with students and others whenever he returned to Toronto on leave, maintaining a rigorous schedule of meetings. On his first trip home in October 1932, for example, he was asked to lecture to a group of money, credit, and prices students at the university by one professor, and Gilbert Jackson put in a similar request. As well, he spoke to numerous Jewish organizations and other groups about the work of the League. His task, as he saw it, was to proselytize and to emphasize its strong side – the technical work undertaken.

That was an important job, as the League of Nations was the subject of much criticism in the 1930s. This irritated Rasminsky, and the review of a League document, the *World Economic Survey, 1931–32*, by the *Financial Post* focused his discontent. The newspaper had caustically referred to the League as merely an 'international debating society,' which drove Rasminsky to distraction. The report was 'fatuous.'[46] He wrote to Gilbert Jackson:

What irks me is that a journal of the standing and influence of the Toronto *Financial Post* should lend itself to the type of cheap, uncritical criticism of a scientific publication issued by the League which has not been banished from everything except the gutter-press of Europe. It is not that we object to criticism; on the contrary, we welcome it and often complain that the publications of our Section are not treated on their merits and subjected to the same sort of critical analysis and examination as the publications of a private individual. But the *Financial Post* article cannot claim to be criticism; it does not concern itself at all with the subject matter of the volume but is content with disparaging it because it happens to be issued under the imprimatur of the League.[47]

When the newspaper suggested that the international organization represented a 'burden' on Canada's taxpayers, Rasminsky cited a statistic – the country's total annual contribution to the League, including the secretariat, the International Labour Organisation (ILO), and the Permanent Court of International Justice, amounted to only $220,000 – a minuscule percentage of the League's total budget. Ignorance about the League among Canadians was remarkable. As he later told Loveday, 'The fault certainly lies somewhere in our organization.'[48]

The rejections and relative uncertainty about the future were enervating for Rasminsky, and what made the situation worse was the fact that he was increasingly troubled in 1935 by a slight swelling on the left side of his neck. His Swiss doctor suggested that it might respond to sunlight, so for at least one hour each day he exposed the cyst to what he hoped were the sun's healing rays. In London the Harley Street physicians whom he later consulted – Thomas Dunhill and Morley Fletcher – also felt that it was somehow related to stress, and they counselled time off to speed recovery. A month in the French and Swiss Alps helped to reinvigorate him, and he returned to Geneva in a different frame of mind. The cyst was eventually removed through surgery.

    That was quickly followed by a more serious problem with Lyla. In late 1935 and early 1936, she had become ill with peritoneal hypersensitivity, which made it increasingly difficult for her to digest food. As a result, she had lost weight to the point that her health was threatened. After careful inquiries, Rasminsky took her to the London clinic of Professor Dr J. Plesch – an expert in treating this illness. Later, Plesch was Albert Einstein's physician, and Keynes's. Unfortunately, this trip meant a long separation for Lyla from her husband and friends in Geneva. It was also tough on Rasminsky. As he wrote from Paris on his return journey to Geneva from the clinic in London: 'I hope that I will never again in my life go through a nightmare like that last half hour in London. Suddenly, in the clinic, it hit me like a blow that I was leaving you, practically alone, for a month.'[49]

His letters from the period demonstrate a desperation rarely seen again. They are peppered with references to 'another wasted day at the office' or 'if this banking thing is going to depend on me, it will never come out.' Was it possible, he asked his wife, that '[Dr] Dunlik's hand skipped a bit and he cut out part of my brain [during his cyst operation]?'[50] Nothing was right while his wife was away. Dinner parties with Scandinavians ('frightfully dull') were unsuccessful, as were lunches with some Dutch ('extraordinarily dull people').[51] Geneva was also dull, 'even for Geneva.' Just short of his twenty-eighth birthday, he wrote to Lyla about his unhappy state. He was 'quite convinced now that [he had] stayed here too long already and the sooner [he pulled] up stakes the better.' The League was 'no place for young men except those of cast-iron character who are able to resist the laziness inspired by the "cushiness" of the job. I feel that I've stopped growing here and certainly don't want to do Banks anymore.'[52]

An incident with their maid, Greta, a German, further unsettled Rasminsky, especially in his wife's absence. On her return to Geneva from a holiday in Germany, he had asked her 'whether she had found out if she was allowed to work for Jews ... She said she had told her family and all her friends she was working for Jews and they envied her. She said she sometimes felt that we didn't have any confidence in her on account of the German business, and I replied that we both liked her very much but that we sometimes felt ... that she was being subjected to anti-Jewish German influences – that if that was the case in the slightest degree it would of course be impossible for us to keep her in the house. She assured me that nothing could be farther from the truth.' One of the happiest days of his life must have been the letter from Plesch telling him that Lyla would be home in time for his twenty-eighth birthday.[53]

The incident with the maid demonstrated another facet of life in Europe that was of increasing concern for Rasminsky – that posed by the appointment of Hitler in January 1933 as chancellor of Germany. Rasminsky was intimately involved with the Jewish community in Geneva and in Europe more generally, and there were matters to address related to the more overt nature of the anti-semitism then prevailing on the continent. Certainly, German developments created tremendous unease, but there were also issues with the League that he did not like. For example, the decision to appoint the Briton James McDonald as the League's high commissioner for refugees rang alarm bells among Jews in Geneva and elsewhere. Rasminsky wired Stephen Wise, honorary president of the

American Jewish Congress (AJC), to encourage him to express the Congress's opposition to the appointment. McDonald was thought to be pro-German, while the candidate that the AJC supported, Raymond Fosdick, was pro-French. As Wise wrote back, it was too late: 'Now the only thing to do is to work with him, to make the best of a bad mess, for it is true that McDonald is pro-Hitler, though I believe he will prove civilized enough to oppose, though not too strenuously, the Nazi attitude to the German Jew.'[54]

Rasminsky had also never been happy with the political side of the League. By 1936, he found the atmosphere in Geneva 'stinking,' made that way in large part by the 'Spanish affair.'[55] In Spain, a vicious civil war raged, pitting the German-supported fascists of General Francisco Franco against democratic republicans. The League proved singularly unable to alter that course of events and could muster only a feeble attempt at mediation. Italian aggression, too, had provoked the League into imposing economic sanctions against that nation, designed to wear down the Italian economy. The Italian leader, Benito Mussolini, was intent on re-establishing the glory of the Roman Empire and had invaded the poor African country of Ethiopia in October 1935. By the following summer the entire country was his. The League's position was undermined in early 1936, however, by the the Hoare-Laval agreement, signed by the United Kingdom's foreign secretary, Sir Samuel Hoare, and Pierre Laval, the French prime minister and foreign minister. In short, the two proposed to appease Italy at Ethiopia's expense. It was, Rasminsky thought, a moral betrayal of everything that the League stood for. Faced with this fait accompli, the League's assembly rescinded the sanctions against Italy during the summer of 1937. 'Insatiable' described the appetites of Berlin and Rome; 'non-intervention [had] been stripped of its last rags.'[56]

Given all that had recently happened, but especially repeal of the sanctions, Rasminsky agreed with Rifat Tirana's assessment that the League had 'touched depths which even a year ago no one would have believed possible – there appear[ed] to be an acquiescing attitude on the part of most of the Secretariat being led ostensibly in that direction by [Secretary General Joseph] Avenol.' Many people had adopted the 'mentality of a civil servant and interest and passion in questions of a political and economic nature seemed to have died altogether.' The impression created under Avenol was 'of a tomb ... with everyone filling his coffin dutifully as required by the Staff rules ... Routine has been elevated to a first principle and pink slips ... continue to arrive at the rate of two or three a day! They are mostly about how to shut windows and lights, park the cars, how to be conceding to the demands of the Swiss authorities and so on *ad nauseam.*'[57]

While Rasminsky was saddened and worried by each failure of the League to deal with transgressions of one sort or another, he was also concerned about the decadence that more and more seemed to characterize life in Geneva. It appeared that the League fiddled while Europe smouldered. He identified with the sentiments of a friend describing the inauguration of the new Assembly Hall at the Palais des Nations in 1937 against the backdrop of the Italian and Spanish crises: 'It was impossible,' the friend wrote, 'not to feel that the Assembly Hall should be draped in black instead of radiant with a thousand concealed lights; that the music should be dirges instead of Jazz ... that the distinguished guests should be pouring ashes on their heads and rending their garmets instead of drinking and dancing ... And every detail of the party enhanced our feeling of disgust, of the BAD TASTE of the S.G. in letting it be done in the way that it was.'[58]

Still, that despair lay in the future, and Rasminsky, despite his occasional doubts about working for the League, his concern over his wife's health, his own health problems in 1935, a certain yearning for stimulation elsewhere, and his growing preoccupation with events in Germany, produced for Loveday work of a very high quality. He continued to edit the League publication *Money and Banking*, while also drafting the first volume of *Monetary Review*. As well, he wrote the price chapter for the study on production and prepared a special study by the Financial Committee of the problems involved in financial statistics. His chief considered 'his *Monetary Review* a first-class piece of work.'[59] Moreover, there was a tremendous opportunity offered to him in late 1936; he began an examination of the state of nutrition in Europe.

Rasminsky's work on the nutrition commission was a major focus of his attention from 1936 to the early 1940s, even after he had gone to work for the Canadian government. Nutrition had been on the League's agenda since 1925, when it began gathering together experts to establish what sorts of food people should eat. They reached agreement in 1935, whereupon the Australians, and especially Frank Macdougall, the economic adviser to the Australian government in London, suggested that food production was not the problem, but rather uncertain food distribution, caused by protective tariffs.

Macdougall was a powerful force behind the formation of the commission as an inspired way to get around protectionist elements in certain

European countries.[60] Australia, of course, was in the business of exporting wheat and other grains and found many potential markets closed off by high tariffs. If only European countries could be convinced of the importance to health of high-quality foods, rich in animal protein and vitamins, perhaps they would shift their agriculture from wheat to production of more meat, dairy products, fruits, and vegetables, thereby leaving room for the importation of wheat from Australia and other countries.

But there were other reasons for the nutrition commission's importance. Among certain countries of eastern Europe especially, nutrition was a real issue. Romania was a case in point. Doreen Warriner, a lecturer at University College, London, and also honorary secretary of the group that had published *Agricultural Dilemma*, had noted: 'There is no other country where the nutrition problem is so acute and where the solution is so easily attainable.'[61] While in that country, she had seen disease caused by malnutrition everywhere – 'rickets, gastero-enteritis, pellagra; and it has the highest infant mortality rate in Europe.' Pellagra was especially debilitating, caused by a deficiency of vitamins and minerals. Its result was extreme lethargy and an inability to work either hard or speedily. Warriner saw tremendous possibilities for educating Romanian consumers and producers about nutrition, especially as 'the soil and climate are magnificent for vegetables and fruit, poultry and milk derivatives.' Nor was it difficult to find suitable people for the task. As she noted, Dr Sabin Manuila, director of the Institute of Demography and Statistics in Bucharest, was 'a fanatic on nutrition, a medical man and statistician.'

Poland was similarly placed, at least in Warriner's mind. About one-third of its population was starving, and emigration seemed the fastest-growing industry. While Warsaw had appointed a nutrition official, he was 'the usual minor diplomat without interest.' Moreover, while the Polish statistical office was good, the ministries were 'hopeless.' If conditions were to be alleviated, then a first step might be to encourage the Poles to send a representative to the League's nutrition commission. Even relatively developed Britain had problems. Sir John Boyd Orr, director of the Imperial Bureau of Animal Nutrition and of the Rowett Institute – located in Aberdeen, Scotland, and one of the leading centres in Europe for the study of nutrition – pointed out in the *Observer* that 'more than fifty percent of children show definite signs of malnutrition, which will have their sequelae in poor physique and disabilities in later adult life.'[62]

The nutrition commission was the child of the League's mixed committee on the relationship of nutrition to health, agriculture, and economic policy. Lord Astor of Cliveden was named chair in September 1935, partly on the suggestion of Frank Macdougall, who reminded Rasminsky that the only successful revolutions were those made by conservatives.[63] However, Astor's appointment must have made the Cana-dian slightly uneasy; he was the centre of the so-called Cliveden set, a largely pro-German and anti-semitic group. Conservatives did dominate the committee. Among these were prominent Europeans, such as M.H. Queille, the former French minister of agriculture (according to Rasminsky, 'one of the greatest [protectionist] sinners'), Baron G. Acerbo, a former minister in the government of Benito Mussolini, Senator Casimir Fudakowski of Poland, and the Italian senator G. de Michelis.[64]

By the summer of 1936, the League had produced the *Interim Report on the Problem of Nutrition*, which described in detail the existing state of nutrition in various countries. It also attacked the 'root' of the problem: 'It is obvious,' the report pointed out, 'that the greatest single cause of defective nutrition in any community is poverty and the ignorance which is often associated with poverty.'[65] This document was the catalyst behind Rasminsky's appointment as a researcher of sorts to the mixed committee.

As the task of preparing papers for the committee and drafting the final report was entrusted to the Economic Intelligence Section, Loveday asked Rasminsky to become the League point man for the study 'in view of his exceptional capacities and all-round knowledge of economics.'[66] Despite protesting that he knew nothing of nutrition (with Loveday replying that no one else did either), Rasminsky took it on, partly because the prospect of substantial international travel beckoned. On his initiative, he was to visit eleven countries in Europe – Austria, Belgium, Czechoslovakia, Denmark, France, Hungary, the Netherlands, Poland, Romania, Sweden, and Yugoslavia – and to report on their state of nutrition. The clincher in this assignment was that Lyla was permitted to accompany him. The unfortunate aspect was that his leave home to Canada was to be postponed. Indeed, it was not until he left Europe just in advance of the German onslaught in Poland that he would be able to claim it. Macdougall was ecstatic about the appointment for two reasons: 'First, because I do not think it would be possible to find anybody on the staff of the League more fitted to bring well trained intelligence to bear on the problem, and secondly, because this should almost inevitably mean our doing a certain amount of work together which, I am sure, we shall both find pleasant.'[67]

Rasminsky travelled to London for a meeting at Lord Astor's home in St James' Square in late July 1936 to discuss the mechanics and strategy of the investigation. At Astor's suggestion, and with Macdougall's help, he also spoke with a number of others interested in the subject from a scientific, economic, and governmental point of view. He met with Macdougall and with Sir John Boyd Orr, who strongly urged him to visit his Aberdeen office in order to talk to two first-rate researchers, his deputy director, Francis Kelly, and Dr John Leitch, associated with the Rowett Institute.

The trip to Aberdeen was Rasminsky's introduction to the world of nutrition. As he had earlier written to Loveday, he was 'just beginning to find [his] way into the subject,' forming an impression 'of what people are doing and thinking.'[68] At Aberdeen, nutrition research was relatively advanced, as Orr and a team of researchers had investigated the diet of the industrial population of the city. As Rasminsky told a radio audience, 'They went into people's houses and saw how much of the different sorts of food they ate. When they compiled all their records they found that most of the people were getting enough to eat, but that their diet was lacking in certain of the protective foods.' In order to determine the longer-run effect on people, the researchers fed the same diet to a large number of rats. To another group of rats, they gave the same food, but with the addition of lettuce and milk. As Rasminsky said, the differences between the two groups were quite remarkable:

> The rats who were not getting the milk and lettuce were poor, miserable creatures. Their fur was thin and yellowish with bare patches in it. Their eyes were pink and the rats didn't have much energy. On the other hand, their brothers and sisters who got the additional milk and lettuce were the most beautiful, sleek, glossy rats that you ever saw. They were fat and their fur was beautifully snow-white with deep black patches in it. These rats were full of energy and jumped about in their cages the whole day long. Their eyes were bright and clear and they looked about as intelligent as it's possible for any rat to look. When I saw the difference between these two groups it made me feel that proper feeding alone could turn a [weak] C3 population into a [strong] A1 population.[69]

Certainly he left northern Scotland with a much better idea of what was entailed in the nutrition investigation and also imbued with some of the proselytizing zeal of his hosts.

He and Lyla departed on their two-month fact-finding excursion through

Europe in mid-October 1936, leaving behind as a contact person the economist Peggy Joseph, formerly of the ILO and one of the authors of its *Report on Workers' Nutrition and Social Policy*. She had been assigned by Loveday to collaborate with Rasminsky on the writing of the nutrition reports.

Each national nutrition committee, Rasminsky found, had a different mandate and composition. For example, in Holland it was manned by civil servants not given any latitude in dealing with any aspect of the investigation. As Rasminsky noted in a letter to a League colleague, René Charron, it was set up 'for the sole purpose of [only] giving effect to the Assembly resolution.' M. Stevens, head of the Dutch committee and of the agricultural and economic information department of the ministry of agriculture, told him that 'it was inconceivable that the Committee could have a nutrition policy.' The question of nutrition was being dealt with by certain departments in the Dutch government, and for his committee to have a policy, or even suggest a direction, 'would mean stepping on departmental toes, a possibility which he would not envisage.'[70] The idea of a bureaucratic turf war obviously repelled him. The Danish committee was made up of physiologists, while the Swedish one was also comprised of medical men, but there were hopes of extending it to include more representatives of economic, agricultural, and industrial interests.

On his return to Geneva, Rasminsky suggested to the Palais des Nations, in view of the diversity of the national committees, that at least a few months of preparation would be necessary by both League and national committees in order to establish common ground and make any sense at all out of the nutrition meeting scheduled to be convened in Geneva during 1937. He had been struck 'in every country by how little is actually known about the actual level of food consumption of the different income and occupational and geographic groups of the population.'[71]

He thought that circulating an agenda comprising very general points would be of some help. Among the matters included could be how various national committees were made up and their relationship to the government; a discussion by committees of such items as the level of nutrition in each country generally, according to income and class, and in agricultural areas; and finally, a discussion of the technique of education in nutrition used in different countries. Charron agreed with his analysis, especially in not provoking a reaction, responding that the chair of the French committee had told him that it was wise to rely on 'les voies lentes et imperceptibles de l'adaptation.'[72]

The nutrition trip throughout Europe had been a success, and Rasminsky's efforts were praised by his superiors in Geneva. He had stimulated thought and action along the lines of studies undertaken at the Imperial Bureau of Animal Nutrition and had convinced the Swedes and the Danes to improve their data collection and send information to him at the League. More important, at least to his mind, he had prevailed on the Czechoslovaks and the Romanians to collate their material for League use.

As he had discovered, the Romanians had quite good data on caloric intake for one thousand peasant families, and the officials with whom he had met had promised to put them in order for the nutrition committee meeting in Geneva. And that was crucial because 'the further East one [went] the more difficult [became] the economics of nutrition.'[73] In some eastern European countries, farmers ate nothing but potatoes and white bread, while in Romania, corn bread and white cabbage with a bit of meat at Christmas were the staples. At the same time, these farmers were producing milk, but they sold it to those better off. Indeed, they could not afford to give it to their children to drink.

As Rasminsky later told a radio audience, 'I don't suppose that ... you can imagine never eating eggs or vegetables or salad or milk. Yet many of these people had never even tasted these things.'[74] He believed that the Romanian meetings, held in November 1936, represented a break-through of sorts. On the trip he had helped as well to organize several new national committees and had worked to ensure that people who were really interested in the subject were placed on them. It was two months well spent.

Now the real work began. There were many aspects of the problem of nutrition to consider and analyse and some proselytizing to undertake among League delegations. In his list of countries, Rasminsky noted beside each what their attitude was towards the upcoming Geneva meeting. The Swedish and French delegates, for example, were 'unreservedly enthusiastic,' and the latter wanted 'to push [his] government.' Belgium was 'interested,' while Holland, through Stevens, was 'opposed.' The Danes were 'at first cold,' but had come around after further discussion. As for the others – countries where nutrition committees were not yet functioning – they were 'unreservedly enthusiastic and looking for guid-ance.'[75] That meant primarily eastern Europe, 'where the great bulk of the population [was] agricultural and feeds mainly on what it produces itself.'[76] Ominously, as Rasminsky reported to Loveday, in central and eastern Europe, many governments were interested in improved nutrition for purposes of military fitness; in some countries, two out of three conscripts were rejected because of poor physical condition.

Given the diversity of opinion demonstrated among nutrition commit-tees, Rasminsky suggested that the discussion in Geneva was not the place to go into the problem of agricultural protectionism or the general effects of commercial and economic policy on agriculture. That stance displeased the Dutch, who had told him that commercial policy must be fully explored; whatever malnutrition existed in Holland, they claimed, was the result primarily of difficulties in exporting dairy products. The Swedes were anxious that the League committee should outline the prob-able agricultural consequences of a general improvement in nutritional standards in Europe. The Poles meanwhile were insistent that the nutri-tion of the rural population should not be neglected but that nothing should be said suggesting that better nutrition would result from lower food prices as a result of freer trade in agricultural products. It was diffi-cult to balance the competing demands.

The result of these cross-currents was that Rasminsky was more than ever convinced that it would be impossible to reach any detailed agree-ment on the effect of agricultural protectionism on nutritional standards. The best that the mixed committee could hope for was to show the importance of tariff policy to nutrition and highlight it with a few exam-ples, such as demonstrating the inefficiency inherent in protecting ani-mal fodder with high tariffs and showing how costly it was to protect and subsidize consumption of dairy products.

Over the next few months in early 1937, Rasminsky and Peggy Joseph worked tirelessly on the *Final Report of the League of Nations Mixed Committee on Nutrition,* which was published in August 1937. In a world still wracked by depression, hunger, and poverty, it was a breath of fresh air. As the *New York Times* noted in an editorial, 'It will not be a best-seller, few may read it, but if the test is elemental human interest and bearing on the basic problems of our time, by all odds the most important book of the year is the 330-page report on "Nutrition."'[77] British newspapers were equally complimentary. The *New Statesman and Nation* remarked that it was 'the most authoritative and comprehensive study of the problem that we have yet had,'[78] while the *Times* called it 'remarkable.'[79]

All commentaries focused on the report's conclusion; it was not scar-city that caused malnutrition, but national policies and artificial barriers to agricultural trade. The link between nutrition and protectionism that Macdougall, Rasminsky, Joseph, and many other League experts were making was graphic. Nutrition was related to income and was part of the general economic problem, which could not be isolated from the broad factors of productivity, capital formation, credit policy, and general business-cycle policy. As Frank Macdougall told the League's assembly when delegations were discussing the findings of the nutrition commission:

> Our starting point must be must be the fact that all nations of the world, whether primarily agricultural or industrial, are determined for sound social, political or economic reasons, to maintain prosperous agricultural communities. This determination has led, especially during the depression, to severe restrictions upon world trade because, during that period, the consumption of food has been static or has in some cases even declined and the Governments of certain countries, particularly those of Europe, have found it necessary to defend the interests of their farmers by having recourse to many forms of restrictions upon imports. If, however, we approach this problem from the standpoint of Nutrition we find ourselves confronted by a far more favourable prognosis of the prospects of agriculture and world trade.

Farmers could then be convinced to grow what the committee called 'protective foods,' which would provide a high degree of natural protection against disease – for example, eggs, fresh vegetables and fruits, and milk. These items were relatively perishable and had to be produced within a short distance of their point of consumption. Such a change would, or so the Australians believed, help gradually to reorient production away from wheat, which they then would supply.[80]

The League was successful in terms of providing definite standards and showing how diets should be made up for health and efficiency. It was also active in giving publicity to the new knowledge about nutrition and had stimulated many governments to constructive action. League experts, primarily Rasminsky, continued to urge that nations establish national nutrition committees to ensure that their population, and particularly babies, younger people, and expectant mothers, were getting enough foods of the right type. They undertook studies on mortality rates of infants in different scenarios. As the League report pointed out: 'The mortality rate among the artificially fed infants was 56 times greater than that among those wholly breast-fed.' The differences were largely the result of deaths following respiratory infections and, to a lesser degree, gastro-intestinal and other infections. 'Thus, whereas only 4 out of 9,749 of the breast-fed infants died of respiratory infections, 82 out of the 1,707 artificially fed infants died from this cause.'[81]

At any rate, with Rasminsky's zeal and the backing of his superiors, no fewer than twenty countries established nutrition committees to pore over advice that flowed from the League during the next year. The first nutrition meeting, convened in Geneva between 22 and 26 February 1937, dealt with the topics suggested earlier by Rasminsky. Again, in August 1938, representatives from sixteen of those committees met in Geneva and spent the week discussing nutrition. The subject had gained prominence by late decade, largely on the basis of Rasminsky's efforts. Indeed, he wrote the nutrition commission's report, producing such a superior draft that, according to Loveday, it was 'accepted in a single session.'[82] Rasminsky, absent from Geneva when the report was tabled, was told by Peggy Joseph that even the drafting committee, normally a tough-minded body, was unstinting in its praise; its session of 6 July 1937 had been devoted to 'tributes' to him.[83]

Nor did the nutrition exercise stop there. Following his return to Canada in September 1939, Rasminsky travelled to South America to spread the nutrition gospel. The Argentines had asked for a League representative to enlighten them, and Rasminsky was the obvious choice, both because he was already in the western hemisphere and because of his wide-ranging knowledge of nutrition.[84] Given the situation, René Charron wrote to him: 'It only remains for me to wish you every success in what I know will be a hard task. I know that we can rely on you to do the best for the League in difficult circumstances.'[85] The only extra that Rasminsky insisted on for this mission was a fifty-thousand-dollar insurance policy against all risks, including war, payable directly to Lyla, not through the League. One could never be too careful. He had prepared well for the South American nutrition meetings, and the conference in Buenos Aires achieved all its objectives. Rasminsky produced a document for the League that would 'constitute an excellent first chapter to the whole report.'[86]

Rasminsky's work with nutrition ended at Buenos Aires. It had been an interesting three years researching and writing in an area of increasing importance. Indeed, the work that he had done on the issue formed a major element in the decision in 1945 to establish the Food and Agriculture Organization (FAO) as a specialized agency in Rome of the United Nations. When that was done, Rasminsky was there too, this time in the employ of the Canadian government.

Much changed in Europe with the gathering clouds of conflict throughout the mid- to late-1930s. Rasminsky had followed events in Germany closely since January 1933, when Hitler had been named as chancellor by the republic's aged president, Paul von Hindenburg. Elections on 5 March 1933 had given German totalitarian parties only 44 per cent of the vote, yet Hitler assumed dictatorial powers on 21 March. With Hindenburg's death in August 1934, Hitler proclaimed himself Reichs-führer; a plebiscite held on 19 August confirmed his new position, with 88 per cent of the electorate voting in his favour. Germany withdrew from the League of Nations on 14 October 1933.

No one could be left in any doubt as to the eventual result of his usur-pation of power, though the democracies, and especially Britain, later claimed to be. His world-view had been well-known since the publication in 1926 of *Mein Kampf*, which, after his accession to office, quickly became part of the German school curriculum. His plan was straightfor-ward. First, he would prepare his people for the approaching struggle and build up the armed forces in order to unite all people of German descent within, as he saw it, their historic homeland. The next step fore-saw creation of a Grosswirtschaftsraum, or large economic unified space, and Lebensraum, or living space, taking in all of Europe. Hitler would create a new world age – a Weltzeitalter – where Germans would lead.

On 7 March 1936, German forces remilitarized the Rhineland, com-mitting their first hostile act. More followed. On 12 March 1938, German troops occupied Austria. That September the British were instrumental in securing cession of the Sudetenland, a heavily German part of Czecho-slovakia, to the Reich in order to appease Hitler (a result of Prime Minis-ter Neville Chamberlain's trip to Munich and his 'peace in our time' return to Britain). And on 15 March 1939, German soldiers occupied Bohemia and Moravia. By month's end, Hitler had intimidated the Lithuanians into returning Memel, a city taken from Germany by the peace treaty of 1919. Finally, Berlin put pressure on Poland to return the Free City of Danzig (now Gdan'sk), also a casualty of the Treaty of Versailles. In this case, the Poles refused, and the British, stung by the Munich débâcle, announced their guarantee to Warsaw of intervention on behalf of Poland in the event of any act of German aggression. The seeds of war, sown some years before, were sprouting.

Rasminsky knew only too well that National Socialism was committed to a policy of anti-semitism. As Irving Abella and Harold Troper have noted, 'For the Nazis, anti-Semitism was far more than a tactical rallying cry to be muted when power was achieved and the practical problems of govern-ing the state confronted. On the contrary: power did not soften anti-Semitism, it legitimized it; power shifted anti-Semitism from speeches to policy, then from policy to law.'[87] On 7 April 1933, the first anti-Jewish law was passed in Germany, to be quickly followed by more than four hundred others. Rasminsky was appalled by what was happening. With the German take-over of Austria in March 1938, he was certain that war was 'absolutely inevitable ... and ... it may break out without warning.' Hitler was, common wisdom had it, 'preparing something big.' Rasminsky persuaded Lyla to take their baby, Michael, born in Geneva in November 1937, home to Canada. Switzerland was no place for Jews if Hitler's legions swept all before them. As Rasminsky wrote to his wife, 'If things are calm in Europe, your journey will still have been a precaution that in justice to our sweet son we had no right to avoid taking, even though the sacrifice is great.'[88] The reality of the situation was brought home to him on the return journey to Geneva from seeing Lyla off from Cherbourg. The only light cast was from tiny blue bulbs, one per compartment – obviously a wartime precaution. After all, the conductor told him, 'Tout Europe est en état d'alerte. Enfin, Verdun est à 45 kilomètres de Paris.'[89]

Rasminsky was also very active, helping others, and especially Jewish refugees, escape continental Europe for the safer confines of England. During the later part of the decade, he had devoted a sizeable portion of his salary to the purchase of rail and boat tickets for refugees' travel to London. One example of many was his donation through the offices of the Comité International pour le Placement des Intellectuels Réfugiés, providing money for a Hungarian refugee, Geza Krasnay, to escape to Britain. Europe was dangerous in 1939, and getting more so.

And while Lyla was safe and secure in the company of her family in Toronto, she too missed her husband and Geneva. They discussed, via the mails, the prospect of his securing employment in Ottawa, which did not appeal to her. They would be 'miserable' in Canada, though with Clifford Clark coming to Geneva for a meeting of the financial committee on 15 June, the opportunity for Rasminsky to inquire after possibilities in Canada seemed too good to pass up.[90] However, he was also considering a colleague's advice, that he should not leave because: '1) I'm too young to settle down in Canada, should remain a Musketeer for a while yet and; 2) if I leave now I'll probably be getting out of the League at its lowest ebb – it is likely to revive, people in USA are keen on our work and if it does, I'll get increased responsibility and opportunities.'[91]

The atmosphere in Geneva was gloomy, and there was much speculation as to what would happen to the League should war break out. Some of the rumours were truly unbelievable. One of these had Hitler agreeing not to invade Switzerland if the League closed down its Geneva offices and left the city immediately in case of war. While Rasminsky thought that fantastic, there was genuine and legitimate concern about the state of the League's finances, and another associated rumour that the organization would 'fold up' by midsummer because of its parlous condition.

Needless to say, that story, which spread like a grass fire in the last days of April, had an immediate and debilitating effect on League personnel. Conditions were so bad that Secretary General Avenol felt it necessary to issue an internal circular on 20 April designed to calm the situation: 'It has come to my knowledge that rumours of all sorts about the Secretariat as to the future of the League and the fate of its officials in the event of an outbreak of war in Europe ... I would appeal to all officials to preserve the dignity and calm which should characterize the members of an international organization and to refrain from doing or saying anything that might cause undue alarm as to the future of the Secretariat ... [Officials] may feel confident that everything that is possible will be done to safeguard their own interests and those of their families.'[92] In short, conditions were unstable.

Throughout Europe preparations were being made for war. For example, at lunch with the managing directors of three of Europe's largest banks – the Crédit Lyonnais, the Dutch Commercial Bank, and the Société de Banque Suisse – Rasminsky learned the location to which each had moved its securities (the French to the west coast, the Dutch to Amsterdam and the Swiss to Lausanne and Geneva). The Swiss director also said that his government had fortified its border with Germany, installing machine-gun posts every fifty yards or so. As Rasminsky wrote to Lyla, 'They will take their stand at the frontier and he claims that they can hold the Germans up for as long as two weeks, by which time, of course, the French will be there.'[93] That, as events transpired, would have been hollow comfort indeed.

As well, he heard of British preparations from Noel Frederick Hall, director for enemy economies in the ministry of economic warfare, 'which hasn't been created but is functioning just the same.' His job was to discover weak spots in Germany's economic organization to which pressure could be applied. With some incredulity, Rasminsky told Lyla: 'If half of what he says is true, the British preparation has been pushed very much further than anyone thinks, and the Germans are even more vulnerable economically than we believe.' However, Hall thought that war would not come, and that view was gaining ground among a certain group of people.[94]

There were also endless discussions about the Yugoslavian situation, what with differences of opinion between Croats and Serbs, and, more particularly as spring turned to summer, about the Polish condition and the possible German reaction to a move by Warsaw on Danzig, given the British guarantee to Poland. That situation was replete with 'ugly possibilities.' As Rasminksy wrote, it was unclear whether the British commitment to defend the Poles extended to Danzig, 'though it seem[ed] almost inconceivable that there isn't a clear understanding between the British and the Poles on this point.' From here, the analysis got more complicated:

> If Danzig proclaims its attachment to the Reich, without the German army doing anything, then one of two things must happen. Either the Poles, as a result of British pressure, do nothing – and in that case the whole British system of guarantees breaks down, for no small state could possibly place any faith in them; or the Poles send their troops into Danzig and probably precipitate a general war the immediate cause of which will have been 'a Polish attack on a German town which wanted to exercise its right of self-determination.' What a beautiful set-up for the German propoganda ministry.
>
> There is, of course, a third possibility – that ... the affair was handled through the League. Danzig ... is theoretically under League sovereignty. But I think this highly improbable. Pere Joseph [Avenol] would resist with the last ounce of his inertia.[95]

He also intended to ask Loveday for a raise in salary before he left for Canada. With a young family to support, his salary was stretched to the limit. Loveday protested that it would be too difficult to arrange such a thing yet was not willing to contemplate the possibility of losing Rasminsky. Still, others were being promoted – René Charron to director of the economic section, Francis Walters from head of the political section to deputy secretary general, and Thanassis Aghnides to under-secretary general.

While Rasminsky was genuinely pleased for those officials, he was also upset at being overlooked. He had already told his chief the salary he wanted, and if it was not definitely settled before he left for Canada, his intention was to take a job there. He told Loveday: 'I shall be very sorry if I am obliged to leave [Geneva] because I am unable to get what I conceive – all things considered – to be a fair remuneration for my services.'[96] He wrote to Lyla: 'I've got to take the bull by the horns sometime and as the political situation isn't stopping other people from getting on, why should it stop me?'

There had been 'a sounding' – something short of an offer – from McGill University that Rasminsky was using as pressure. His old professor at LSE, Lionel Robbins, had inspired the approach. He told Rasminsky that the department at McGill was 'on the move' and that Principal Cyril James was then in the United Kingdom looking for someone to 'put it on its feet.' James wanted Robbins for the job, but he would not take it and had sung Rasminsky's praises. The result, Robbins told Rasminsky, was that the principal wished to meet him, which he did on 16 July. While Rasminsky told Lyla that he was not really interested in the job, 'it would improve [his] bargaining position with Loveday if [he] got something like a firm offer from Montreal.'[97]

However, he was intrigued by the possibilities at McGill, especially after James expressed interest in him. The idea, the principal told him, was to let the entire faculty go – some members as they retired and others as their contracts expired. None, apparently, were very good. Then two new full professors would be appointed, with one heading up a new National Institute of Economics. The interview went very well, and when James learned that Rasminsky would be in Canada in September, he suggested that he come to Montreal to look the whole thing over.

The possibility was appealing for a number of reasons. First, the combination of the two jobs – that of professor and director of the institute – would be financially advantageous and intellectually rewarding. Second, the fact that the whole department was being so throughly reorganized would create a unique opportunity to start from scratch, with a minimum of vested interests, and build something up. As well, he thought that his future could lie in Canada. If war finally came, the dominion would play a crucial role in the British Empire. Even if war were somehow avoided, the country would still become more and more important. If he were offered the job, he would be able to immerse himself in academic work in Canada – an opportunity that would probably not arise again. Finally, for a Jew moving into semi-public life in Canada, if he could get in at the top, 'the anti-Jewish feeling that was so wide-spread in the country,' would be less significant for his career. That was something to think about. Even Robbins, when selling Rasminsky on the prospects, had discussed with him the depth of anti-semitism in Canada. As noted above, the university maintained strict quotas on Jewish students, and anti-semitic rhetoric had occasionally flowed from its hallowed halls.

Still, Rasminsky had qualms about a university career, much as he had earlier in the decade. Indeed, he wondered whether he would be very happy in such a setting. He did not have 'any great yearning for the academic life, which seems very much a dog eat dog affair, with murky eddies and crosscurrents of jealousy and bitterness.' Nor was he terrribly impressed with 'the intelligence of the academic economists.' And, as for Lyla, 'the real fact of the matter is that I don't want to leave Geneva. I love this place and can't imagine that [we] could be happier or as happy anywhere else.' Moving to Canada would be difficult for the family, and, he wrote Lyla, 'in my saner moments I don't know how we can even contemplate it.'[98] Given that, and the uncertainty surrounding his present position, he hoped only 'that I haven't got myself into a position regarding my salary from which I can't – if it is necessary – withdraw with dignity.'[99] He never did receive a much-deserved promotion.

And the work went on and on. He wrote papers on agricultural credits, briefs for the League's delegation on economic depressions, and analyses of medium-term credit to industry, while also doing work on exchange controls. None of this was stimulating, and he was missing Lyla and Michael. That, combined with Europe's political condition, made the general psychological depression in Geneva 'chronic.' Everyone's work was affected by the miasmal atmosphere, with many colleagues telling him that they had never done work as bad as what they were producing in League offices. What, he wondered, was it like to feel 'high-spirited, gay and hopeful.' It was a chore to get through each day, and he generally felt as if he 'were 100 years old.'[100]

He spent much of July in the company of the financial committee, whose members were discussing the issue of economic depressions – a subject that Rasminsky had been working on since February 1938. The council of the League had named a delegation on depressions to report on measures that might be employed to prevent or mitigate these catastrophes. Its appointment was the last of a series of efforts by the League's economic and financial departments to help clarify and solve the world's economic problems via consultation among experts on national economic problems common to a large number of countries.

Rasminsky had written: 'In the 20's and early 30's the League's approach to economic problems on the policy side had been mainly conceived in terms of restoring the mechanisms of international economic life – the reconstruction of an international currency system and the restoration of international trade.'[101] The early endeavours, reflected in the Brussels Conference of September–October 1920 and the Genoa Conference of 1922, had been generally successful, but later ones, such as the World Economic Conference of 1927, the Tariff Truce Conference of

1930, the proposals for a European Customs Union of 1930, and the World Economic Conference of 1933, were failures.[102]

He had written a two-hundred-page report for the depressions delegation, which had considered such ideas as monetary and fiscal policies, price and wage policy, and international economic policy.[103] This assignment sent him to England for two weeks in late July 1939 to discuss the problem with people in the British government. The interim final report, prepared by Rasminsky after war had been declared and while he was in the joint employ of the League and of the Canadian government, provided a first-rate analysis of the issues to which many Allied countries were by then turning their collective minds. Loveday told Avenol that the task was 'the most complex one with which any committee of the economics and finance organization has had to deal since the beginning of the League. Mr. Rasminsky's draft was in my opinion a piece of work of outstanding merit which was greatly appreciated by the Delegation.'[104] Certainly it had kept him awake at nights.

It was so complex in part because it was suggesting that the old ways of doing international business were discredited; new methods of organization were now necessary. Indeed, Rasminsky was proposing to rethink economic, social, and political relationships on a wide scale once the war was over. His position was a radical one, admirably laid out in a letter to Loveday:

> The point of view which I think should be stressed is, in fact, incorporated at various places in the document and no doubt it will be brought out still more strongly in the chapter on the right to work, which is not yet written. But I am very much afraid that in a very long document the basic approach may tend to become obscured in discussions of detail and I would like to see the basic approach stated very bluntly and concisely. I therefore repeat a suggestion ... namely that if you do publish the whole thing, including a revision of the stuff I prepared in Geneva, you should also publish as a separate little pamphlet a 20 or 25 page 'Statement of Policy.' This statement of policy should, in my view, be less an economic analysis than a manifesto. It should recognize what seems to be the basic fact which must condition the whole of our thinking about the economics of the post-war world, namely that this is in fact a revolutionary war and that the object of economic policy after the war will not be to make the institutions of a capitalist or semi-capitalist society work with a minimum of friction but to make sure that ... the fruits of production are widely distributed ... This point of view [must be] kept constantly in the foreground.[105]

Copies were also given in 1941 to Clifford Clark and Norman Robertson, now undersecretary of state for external affairs. Clark wrote: 'It is an exceedingly able piece of work – I agree with its economic conclusions; its political and social judgements are realistic; it is lucidly and forcefully written; and it is inspired throughout with a noble and lofty purpose ... What use will be made of it?' The deputy minister suggested to Graham Towers that he also might want to digest its contents. Robertson wanted to know its ultimate destination.[106]

But League officials still had to deal with League committees comprised of political appointees – a not-always-satisfying task, as Rasminsky had discovered. Nor was it any different when he was asked to fill in for a colleague on vacation, being the point man for a departmental draft report of dubious quality and accuracy written by the holiday-maker; he was 'left holding the bag ... acting as [a] whipping-boy for the committee.' Similarly, he was told by the coordinating committee to rewrite one of Loveday's own reports, which it had 'ripped to pieces.' As his chief had found that he had a luncheon appointment and was then otherwise engaged, he told Rasminsky to make the best of it. Even so, 'the report [didn't] amount to much, but it [was] adopted which seems to be the main thing in these parts.'[107] Then there were reports on taxation, continued work on nutrition, the Hungarian loan question, and more on credits to industry.

All that effort yielded a glowing appraisal from Loveday when it came time to grant the annual performance increment. Rasminsky had done 'exeptionally valuable work ... His work is always of a very high standard and he has the rare quality of being at once a first-class administrator and a first-class scientist.'[108] He had acted as secretary to the financial committee, to the coordinating committee, and to the delegation on economic depressions. He had worked on the preparation of the reports of the mixed committee on exchange control and of the financial committee on the general economic situation, as well as on those on medium-term industrial credit and agricultural credit. He was recommended for an annual increment.

His work during the spring of 1939 gained him praise from an unexpected quarter. During a trip to Geneva in early summer, Frank Macdougall told him that Lionel Robbins, recently returned to London from the Swiss city, was now 'going around everywhere talking in terms of the most extravagent admiration of [Rasminsky], saying [he was] by far the best person in Geneva and ranked head and shoulders above any of the young British economists.' It was unfortunate that Rasminsky could not bank that praise. But even here, told to his wife in a very private letter, his natural modesty got the better of him; following his recitation of Robbins's opinion, he noted, 'There, I've written it. I didn't think I would and I'm ashamed of myself for having done so, but I thought you would want to hear it.'[109]

He followed Lyla to Canada in mid-August 1939, having booked passage on one of the last liners leaving Le Havre before war broke out, arriving in Cobourg, Ontario, his mother-in-law's summer retreat, after war had been declared. He cabled Geneva offering to return, because he had said for years that when it happened it was the duty of every League official to be at his or her desk. His offer was refused; the secretary general decided that it was better for him to remain in Canada on League strength. Loveday wrote: 'There is a considerable amount of technical work for the Section that I want you to do and which can better be done on the other side of the Atlantic than here.'[110] As it turned out, he was extraordinarily lucky to be in a spot where he could get the variety of work that was to come his way.

The first part of his League work in North America was a fact-finding mission to La Paz, Bolivia, undertaken between 27 October and 9 November 1939, at the behest of the Bolivian government, concerning that country's financial situation. However, when he was asked to go, especially given the amount of time spent away from Lyla, he wrote to Loveday: 'I would not attempt to conceal from you that I am looking forward with anything but pleasure to going to Bolivia. From all accounts, the country is the most primitive on this continent with the possible exception of Paraguay.'[111]

The mission to La Paz was a part of a League policy to become more active in Latin America. As even the reluctant Rasminsky, who was on the front line in this effort, had told Loveday, the return per franc would be much greater than in Europe. As events transpired, he was greatly impressed by the natural beauty of the country and had a wonderful time in its capital city: 'La Paz and this country generally are the most interesting place I have been.' It was 'very, very beautiful – the Andes are so rugged and immense that they make our beloved Swiss and French Alps look like effete little upstarts.'[112]

Moreover, it was countries such as Bolivia that represented a fertile field for practical work. The level of public administration was very low, and many of those controlling the formation and execution of economic and financial policy were either incompetent or dishonest or both. As

Rasminsky pointed out, in the previous twelve years there had been forty ministers of finance, there was no capital accumulation in the country, and economic development was beyond the capabilities of its own resources, both human and financial. Foreign exchange was almost non-existent, the government was antagonistic towards foreign corporations wanting to exploit abundant tin reserves, and agriculture and manufacturing had almost hit historic lows. Very little was spent on education, and the rate of illiteracy was very high. In short, the Bolivians needed much help. It was all laid out in a twenty-nine-page report that Rasminsky sent to Loveday.[113] But more important, when Europe was impoverished by war and North and South America enriched by the same experience, then South America would be closer to the centre. He felt that 'the League should adapt itself to the long-run changes that are taking place.'[114]

The Bolivian request for a League investigation had been largely a political manoeuvre by competing factions in the country's political structure – a fact of which Rasminsky was only too well aware. He had asked Loveday for brief biographies of the chief protagonists, as well as 'the axes they are grinding,' but Geneva was too far removed from La Paz to be of much use.[115] On the one hand was the pro-German side, led by the minister of finance, Ferdnand Pou Mont, (who Rasminsky later called his Gilbert and Sullivan minister), and on the other hand, the pro-American side of Foreign Minister Ostria Gutierrez (the 'good' guy). The former attempted to hinder Rasminsky's investigation, while the latter did all in its power to facilitate the mission and secure League assistance. At stake was a subject of some importance – who should get the Bolivian output of tin. It had been going to Tacoma, Washington, for refining, but there was a move afoot to shift this export to Germany. Rasminsky's report, as well as the ascendancy in the struggle for power of the Gutierrez faction, served to continue the status quo.

Rasminsky's suggestion that the League undertake a more thorough study of the Bolivian situation fell a victim of the times; it was not practicable, given budgetary limitations. In Geneva, staff members were leaving, and a 'rather gloomy atmosphere' prevailed, what with 'so many empty offices and vacant chairs.' The League was even closing down the fourth floor of the Palais des Nations.[116] The Bolivian requests were quietly shelved.

Following his South American journey, Rasminsky began helping to prepare for a conference of North and South American fiscal committees in

Mexico City in June 1940 that would concern itself with the issue of double taxation, and where he would represent the League. This would, it was hoped, be the last in a series of conferences addressing the issue that began soon after the First World War. Discussion in 1920 in Brussels had highlighted the paralysing effect on commercial houses that resulted from their obligation to pay high taxes on the same profits in at least two countries, as well as the problem of double taxation with respect to interest and dividends. The gathering had led to a League of Nations study and, in 1923, a report analysing the economic effects of double taxation. High officials from a number of European countries had become involved, and they eventually prepared four model agreements on various aspects of double taxation. In October 1928, government representatives had met in Geneva and had developed three model agreements concerning taxation on income. Sixty tax treaties were ultimately signed.

Work had continued on into the 1930s, with the aim of eventually reducing the three model versions to one. Though the original goal was a multilateral agreement in this area, because of differences in legislation the contracting states were obliged to proceed bilaterally. The mandate of the Mexico City meeting of June 1940 was to attempt to secure enough consensus to unify points of view on the best solutions to common problems. As Rasminsky was to say in his opening address, 'It is to be hoped that our deliberations will open a path to the signing of agreements which will stimulate economic and commercial relationships among our countries ... It is of vital importance for each one of us to strengthen our internal economy by following equitable and healthy financial principles.'[117]

The Americans, while not League members, were wholeheartedly in favour of this initiative, wanting to negotiate tax treaties with their Latin American neighbours. One of them, Eldon King, deputy commissioner of the US Treasury's Bureau of Internal Revenue, had been very impressed on a visit to Geneva with the work of the fiscal committee. Indeed, a Swedish-American tax treaty was the direct consequence of a contact he had made there. In general, he was 'heartily in favour of the work done by the Fiscal Committee.' Rasminsky had made contact with King while in Washington, DC, on other business. He had also met with Henry Grady, assistant secretary of state, suggesting a meeting to iron out tax issues among countries of the western hemisphere. As well, Rasminsky had seen his friend Herbert Feis, of the State Department, mentioning the possibility of holding a meeting of fiscal committees in Latin America.

Everywhere, US officials were supportive of the proposal, and Rasminsky wrote to Loveday in late November, informing him: 'I think you can take it that the State Department would not consider that a Latin American meeting ... conflicted with any projects of their own under the Permanent Inter-American Committee for Economic Cooperation.' While senior staff members at the Inter-American Committee did not like the idea of League activity in the western hemisphere, they were prepared to turn a blind eye because they were not equipped to deal with technical questions such as taxation. Rasminsky also suggested that Geneva not attempt to cooperate with them in any way: 'There [was] nothing for us to cooperate with. Their economic and statistical departments are of no importance; the people in them are very pleasant but are not doing, nor would I guess capable of doing, really solid work – their work has no reputation of any sort. Cooperation with them is politically necessary at the moment, and this is the only reason I can conceive of for trying to effect it.'[118] The only true opposition to such a conclave might come from Sumner Welles, undersecretary of state, who was, Rasminsky told Loveday, 'close enough to the President to feel for the best place to put the stilleto.' Latin America was his career area, and he regarded that part of the world 'as his baby.' However, fears about this quarter proved groundless.[119]

Similarly, the Latin Americans were interested in the meeting, as Rasminsky discovered on his return trip from La Paz to the United States in November 1939. He had spent two days of the nearly four-day air trip back from Bolivia to Miami sitting beside Don Pedro Larranaga Montero, an important figure in the 'brains trust' of the newly elected president of Peru. Larranaga was on his way to Washington to represent Peru at an inter-American economic conference. As Rasminsky wrote, 'In the short intervals between the various installments of the story of his life, he showed a very keen interest in the problems of double taxation. It [was] true that his interest [was] that of a pickpocket who want[ed] to gang up with other pickpockets to divide the territory so that they will not all try to take everything away from the same victim ... But it is useful to know that this interest in the problem exists in Peru.'[120]

The Canadians also intended to go to Mexico City. Their interest was not altogether remarkable, given that Canada was a member of the fiscal committee in Geneva and that the country's income-tax commissioner from the Department of National Revenue, Fraser Elliott, had attended a number of meetings. However, as Rasminsky told Deperon back at League headquarters, 'I have been greatly heartened by the keen desire which many senior officials of the Canadian administration have expressed to me that League technical activities should be continued during the war and I think it highly desirable that Canadian participation in this work should be maintained so far as possible.'[121]

His own view was that such an effort, 'if you have the money,' would definitely yield benefits. It would help the Latin Americans with their tax problems, it would be of real service to the United States in gathering together the people they wanted to see to push on with their tax-treaty program, and it would be a good thing for the League. The meeting was held in Mexico City 3–15 June 1940, just as the German juggernaut rolled over France – a development that had Rasminsky on edge. As he told his wife, the news was terribly bad; 'one was almost afraid to go to sleep for fear of what one will read in the morning ... If it is necessary to believe in miracles to feel that we are going to win, I am prepared to believe in miracles.'[122]

Despite his frame of mind, he was a key figure at Mexico City. The event went off without a hitch, thanks in large part to his judicious efforts. For example, he coached the American Mitchell Carroll, the League expert on fiscal questions, to change the thrust of his opening remarks to address more adequately Mexican, rather than merely American, priorities. As well, Loveday and Rasminsky felt that Carroll should chair the conference as a whole, because of his knowledge of the questions under discussion. This might take delicate negotiation, because of the Mexican position as host country. Rasminsky wrote to Carroll suggesting that 'perhaps you would be content to leave the matter in my hands; if he [Luis Wiechers, head of Mexico's central bank] appears to feel at all strongly that the honour should be accorded to him as host, we should, I suppose, not get off to a bad start by not falling in with his idea.'[123] However, Rasminsky would use his powers of persuasion and did not expect this to be an issue, and indeed it was not. Carroll wrote to Loveday in its aftermath that 'Rasminsky ... took hold of the meeting and conducted it with such expertness that [he] won the admiration of everyone. Rasminsky's opening talk on the work of the League was an inspiring exposition of the activities and ideals of the technical sections and particularly your section, and his closing speech of gratitude was equally impressive.'[124]

Rasminsky also thought Mexico City a great success, even though 'such awful things were happening in Europe during those weeks that it was very difficult for me at any rate to feel that there was any reality behind the discussions.'[125] However, the meeting did useful work in bringing together the tax administrators of seven North and South American countries who were able to thresh out their difficulties. The talks were intended to be educational, and they met that objective. The Americans became actively involved with the Argentinians, Brazilians, and Peruvians in working towards tax agreements. As well, Rasminsky noted in a letter to Loveday, the Americans were now anxious to complete the tax negotiations with Canada that had started before the war.

There was even talk of having another meeting of this type at Lima sometime during 1941 to discuss a number of questions that had arisen as a result of the Mexico City conference. Among the issues the Mexicans wanted addressed was allocation of tax revenue among federal, state, and local jurisdictions. While Mexico was interested in developing a position on this matter, Rasminsky also told Loveday that 'this problem is a vitally important one here in Canada and was the subject of some very radical proposals in the recently published report of the Sirois – formerly Rowell – Royal Commission on Dominion-Provincial Relations.'[126] He sent a copy of the royal commission's final report to Deperon in Geneva.

The fiscal problem ended there for the time being, as prosecuting the war absorbed most of the energies of governments. Three years later a largely moribund League revived the suggestion of another meeting in Mexico City for its fiscal committee. Rasminsky, now a Canadian official, was asked by Associate Undersecretary of State for External Affairs Hume Wrong, for his opinion on whether or not Canada should attend. He had no strong views on the matter; three years away from the League had changed his perspective. As he told Wrong, it was very difficult 'to appraise the real value of such meetings ... or to point to any concrete results they accomplish.' The major point that he raised was that he thought it worthwhile to keep the League's technical organizations functioning and that it was important that Latin America know more about the League. The best he could suggest, he told Wrong, was to support the idea of having the fiscal committee meet in Mexico City the next summer without having Canada take any initiative.[127] By then, as it turned out, the League was for all intents and purposes dead, and a new organization, the United Nations, was on the drawing board.

But that lay in the future, and for the present Rasminsky's personal employment situation remained problematic. Given the world situation in the autumn of 1939, the League was obviously in the process of changing. Its (im)permanence was on everybody's mind. Rasminsky had earlier thought about other employment but, following his South American trip, was much more serious in considering alternatives. He realized that no one was in a position to proclaim definitively on the future of the League, but told his section head, Alexander Loveday, in early October: 'I shall have to decide on my own plans.'[128]

Certainly it seemed as if the League was falling apart. A colleague, Folke Hilgerdt, had written to him that suspicion and conspiracy were everywhere, the policy of senior administration was at best unclear, 'and the information given in Office Circulars [was] controversial to the extent that a mere description of the facts would imply disloyalty to certain of our superiors.'[129] All of the transit section's people were looking for employment elsewhere. While 'none of Loveday's "key men" appear to have resigned,' all were anxious about the future of the League. Rasminsky continued to follow up the McGill 'sounding,' sending Principal Cyril James a short biographical sketch at James's suggestion. Nothing came of it.

The solution to his potential problem came in the form of employment with the government of Canada. Rasminsky was courted at a special dinner held by Graham Towers and Clifford Clark and was offered the post of economic adviser to the Bank of Canada's Foreign Exchange Control Board (FECB) for the duration of the war, and he was also to be assistant to the chairman of the FECB. Moreover, Towers was willing that Rasminsky should also act as League correspondent and undertake special League missions when requested. Rasminsky cabled Loveday: 'Believe this arrangement advantageous all round my work would be in general economic policy and fit in well with your program.'[130]

The response was resounding silence, to the point that he was forced to cable again, 'Reply as Towers Clark anxious start immediately.'[131] He received in answer, 'Will reply cable when S[ecretary] G[eneral] returns.'[132] A week later, having still not heard, an increasingly concerned Rasminsky shot off 'If decision not yet taken could I know when expected? Please cable.'[133] Nine days later he had Loveday's reply: 'View expected importance [Depressions] Committee work would much prefer retain you fulltime. Contemplate asking you return Geneva second half this year. Subsequent movements for later decision.'[134] The depressions committee, Rasminsky believed, would never 'function effectively ... while the war continues.'[135] He would not return.

Rasminsky was not interested in staying on with the League by the spring of 1940. Rather, his preference was to resign. He had already offered to do so, and Loveday had refused to accept his offer. In a telegram acknowledging the obvious several months later, the head of the section told Rasminsky: 'I hope you will not commit yourself absolutely [to FECB] duration should circumstances so develop that your services required for longer period.'[136] As of April Fool's day 1940, Rasminsky reported to a new boss.

Loveday's approach to Rasminsky's requests demonstrated his reluctance to lose a first-rate official. In accounting for the lateness of his reply to the Canadian's many requests, Loveday later told him that in the early days of the war he had asked Hume Wrong about the possibility of Rasminsky's being employed by the Canadian government without abandoning his contract with the League. 'Wrong took up the question with the Canadian authorities and informed me that they regretted that it was against their regulations for any Government employee to receive two salaries or serve two masters. I thought, therefore, that the whole project, from the Canadian side, was off and it did not seem necessary for me to write again on the matter.'[137]

What remained for Rasminsky at the League were a few assignments, which decreased in number and importance as the war continued and the League weakened. He had one immediate task, however, and that was to scout out Princeton University in New Jersey as a possible site for certain League operations to continue, after its president, Harold Dodds, issued a formal invitation to that effect on 12 July 1940. Frank Aydelotte, director of the university's Institute for Advanced Study, had told the press that he and Dodds felt that 'the technical aspects of [the League's] work were much too valuable to be discontinued or even curtailed because of a war.'[138]

It was uncertain that the League would move the technical section, and the manoeuvring behind the scenes was an interesting study in international politics. Secretary General Avenol, a citizen of France, was opposed, primarily for reasons of difficult diplomatic relations between Vichy France and the United Kingdom. There was a 'battle royal' between proponents and opponents of the move. It was Loveday, most definitely in favour, who had asked Rasminsky to investigate conditions at Princeton and send him the information as soon as possible. The Canadian did so, considered the working facilities excellent, and strongly urged acceptance of the invitation. If senior administrators were reluctant, he suggested that the Rockefeller Foundation might favourably consider a request to finance the move if 'independent action' were desirable. The bonus was that he had been assured that 'Canadian authorities will cooperate fully if section established Princeton.'[139]

This was a most welcome piece of news to some officials in Geneva. It might now be possible to 'keep a small light alive on [the North American] side, in a kind of limited, non-Continental League, till better days come.'[140] In the end, it was decided that Loveday's economic and financial department – eight officials, accompanied by their wives and children, for a total of twenty-two persons – would relocate to Princeton for the duration of the war.

Despite his earlier intention to split his time between League and Canadian government business, the latter took increasing amounts of Rasminsky's time. When Loveday pleaded with him to come down to Princeton for a month at the end of 1940 to work on redrafting a section of the economic depressions report, he wrote back that it was not possible. He could not see his way clear to address Loveday's queries until early in the following year. By late February, he received another frantic letter from his former chief, saying, 'Geneva has cabled now for the third time about your leave ... I am also still awaiting news of your dates for coming here.'[141] Perhaps late March, was the reply.

Eventually Towers wrote, saying that Rasminsky would be there during the second week of April. However, Rasminsky continued to look over drafts of documents prepared by his former colleagues, and some of these, such as a paper on exchange stabilization, meshed nicely with his own developing interests. For example, Loveday's 'Lessons of Exchange Fluctuation, 1919–1939,' was a welcome addition to the literature on that subject, especially as Rasminsky received his copy in August 1943, in the midst of discussions over a proposed Anglo-American currency-stabilization fund.

His last 'official' act with the League was in December 1942, when he travelled to a League conference at Mont Tremblant, north of Montreal, to discuss the report of the depressions delegation and the international situation generally. Many of his old Geneva colleagues were there, such as Jack Condliffe, then based in London, and Alexander Loveday, both of whom gave Rasminsky long memoranda to read and comment on. As well, there were a number of national delegations in attendance, including a British and an American group. The only development of real interest, as far as he was concerned, was when those two delegations got into a violent conflict over southeast Asia – perhaps a harbinger of things to come. As Rasminsky wrote to his wife, 'The British here are pretty stand-pat and insensitive to the spirit of the times, while the Americans tend to take the position that British policy should be examined by the state of public opinion in the United States.'

Another US demand, so it was made clear, 'was for Europeans to get bag and baggage out of colonial areas and leave the natives to fend for themselves.' There was a sneaking suspicion, among some Europeans at least, that that would leave the field clear for American trade interests to move in to fill a post-colonial vacuum. Phillip Jessup, the US chairman of the meeting, asked Rasminsky to draft something designed to bring the conflicting views closer together. He did so, put it to the British and Americans at lunch, and got it accepted with certain minor amendments at the afternoon meeting. 'It was greeted with applause and acclamation ... Lord Hailey and the Dutchman didn't really like it but they felt they couldn't object so it becomes the unanimous view of the group.'[142]

Despite the disagreement evident at Mont Tremblant, however, Rasminsky did not believe that cooperation in a postwar world would be impossible. He had earlier commented on a memorandum written by L.C. Thompson-McCausland of the Bank of England. Its underlying assumptions were that Anglo–American harmony after the war would not be possible, that postwar American economic policy would be 'unintelligent,' and that the United Kingdom would play a role secondary to that of the United States in the international economic system.[143] The final point was probably true, but so what?

Moreover, Rasminsky did not believe that the United States would behave as the British thought. It seemed to him 'that the [Americans had] learned a good many economic lessons during the past few years; they [had] been frank to express their culpability for the great economic depression; and it will be a major disaster if, when they have finally come around to looking at economic problems from a world point of view, the UK starts to look at them from a narrow nationalist (or even imperialist) point of view.' He thought that there was much jealousy in the British position and that that was a poor basis from which to destroy the possibility of postwar cooperation that was so necessary for the well-being of all.

It was obvious that Rasminsky's days with the League were numbered; by the summer of 1942, Loveday had given up inviting him to Princeton discussions relating to League business. Rasminsky wrote tongue-in-cheek to Lyla on one occasion when such a gathering was being arranged: 'Is it or isn't it odd that he didn't ask me? Not that I would prefer Princeton to Cobourg that week-end, but I would like to feel offended if I properly can.'[144] He officially resigned from the League as of 30 June 1943. An important chapter in his life was over, with only one footnote remaining. Rasminsky was a member of the Canadian delegation to the founding conference of the United Nations in San Francisco in the spring of 1945 and so, to paraphrase Dean Acheson, 'present at the destruction' of the League as it was folded up and a new United Nations was born. Given his distance, he could watch it all with detached objectivity.

The League knew that it was losing an exceptional talent. The acting secretary general, the Irishman Sean Lester, wrote to him following his departure: 'In the discharge of your duties you proved yourself a very good economist and statistician. Owing to your exceptional ability and sound training you were able to turn easily and efficiently from one subject to another, and your work always showed outstanding merit.'[145] Loveday offered similar thoughts, telling Rasminsky: 'It is a sad severance, but in view of all the circumstances I think that you have probably taken the right decision ... May I repeat now my appreciation of what I have always felt was the exceptional excellence of your work.'[146] That was high praise from a hard-bitten warrior of international politics.

Rasminsky had obviously learned an enormous amount during his ten years of continuous, and three years of part-time, work with the League. The international expertise that he had gained would stand him in good stead over the course of his career with the Bank of Canada. Many of the issues discussed, formally or informally, during the 1930s returned to plague governments in the future. An old saying has it that one is not able to deal with the future unless one knows the past. Rasminsky did, and better than most.

PART TWO

War and Reconstruction, 1940–1961

Chapter Three

Ottawa and Wartime Controls

When Louis Rasminsky joined Canada's Foreign Exchange Control Board (FECB), it had been up and running for about seven months. The Board had been established by order-in-council on 15 September 1939 to conserve foreign exchange, and especially US dollars, in order to help finance the war effort. Rasminsky had been recruited by both the Bank of Canada's governor, Graham Towers, and the deputy minister of finance, Clifford Clark. He had been the guest of honour at a dinner hosted by the former – special treatment – and he was clearly destined for a senior position. When he was appointed in April 1940, it was as head of the economic and research division of the FECB. In June 1942, he was named chair of the Board's management committee, and on 9 September 1943 he became alternate chair – in effect, the person in charge of day-to-day operations. He fitted in easily, tackling involved and complex problems from investors and their lawyers, both Canadian and foreign.

While Rasminsky's knowledge of international finance was a definite advantage, it is probably true that his heart was never in the rather mundane shifting of paper and filling out of forms. He did not fit the description of foreign exchange detective, even though he did the job very well. His eye, conditioned by his experience at the League, was on the bigger picture. Certainly Graham Towers and Clifford Clark knew that; in all likelihood, the FECB appointment was a tactic designed to get Rasminsky quickly into Canadian service. As events transpired, only about 25 per cent of his time was spent on Board business.

It was while he was with the FECB that his natural talents came to the fore, especially in the area of international financial arrangements. He spent less time in Ottawa, and more in London and Washington, DC, where officials came to know him well and respect his judgment on a wide range of topics. He combined charm with an insight and intelligence that made people want to listen to him, as will be seen in chapter 4. Arguably, that was where his major contribution to the war effort lay – not in administering the FECB, but in negotiating with the British and Americans over the shape of elements of the postwar world.

Rasminsky was hired by Graham Towers. The position that he occupied at the FECB was that of assistant to the chairman – nominally Towers himself, but in practical terms Donald Gordon, the Bank's deputy governor and chairman (alternate) of the FECB. Rasminsky was also a member of the Board's important management committee, comprising senior men from the Board and chaired by Gordon, which developed policy and met regularly to discuss issues of pressing concern. The FECB was set up to deal with a wartime emergency – to control the outflow of foreign exchange.[1]

Exchange control was vitally important to the Canadian war effort. Indeed, without it the country would not have faced the postwar period with such equanimity. In the dark days before the implementation in April 1941 of the Hyde Park Agreement, which served to clear up Canada's economic difficulties with the United States, no stone was left unturned in the search for American money. The deficit, projected at a horrifying $478 million by April 1941, was a monster to be tamed.[2] Even with control, a Bank official and future governor, James Coyne, pointed out in early 1941 that 'all the conceivable measures that could be taken to rectify our exchange situation on current account would not be sufficient in combination to meet [the deficit with the United States].'[3]

Canada's hands were bound by wartime exigency. Its economy operated on the basis of 'a bilateral imbalance within a balanced North Atlantic triangle'; in happier times, a surplus with the United Kingdom could be used to cover a deficit with the United States as British pounds were exchanged for American dollars. In September 1939, however, sterling had been made inconvertible, and the old system collapsed. As a result, the more that Canada helped Britain against the Germans, the larger grew its deficit with the United States, which had to be paid for in gold or US dollars. And given British requirements in Canada, it was generally conceded early in the war that a very large increase in British purchases would take place. That would 'have a definite meaning in respect to importations from the United States, both because of the foreign content of certain munitions, etc. [about 30 per cent] which we will be selling to the United Kingdom [for inconvertible British pounds], capital requirements in connection with plant expansion, and finally the indirect effect arising from increased distribution of purchasing power in Canada.'[4] It was a 'double bind,'[5] and even though the Board raised the possibility – a suggestion that Rasminsky regarded as 'impossibly optimistic' – there was no way further to restrict imports from the United States *and* meet war-production targets. Nor would the United Kingdom agree, for its own good reasons, to build up dollar debt in Canada. As R.S. Sayers points out, 'This would be not only a dangerous form of indebtedness, but also an awkward precedent when talking to Sterling Area partners who would also have postwar requirements in the United States.'[6] The FECB's job was to ease that situation as much as possible.

When Canada imposed exchange controls on 16 September 1939, its dollar had gone to a 10 per cent discount in the New York free market, which was then the level adopted as the basis for a stabilized rate for transactions in Canada; its official mid-market rate was 1.10\frac{1}{2}$. It was also pegged against the pound sterling; on 16 September the rate was set at $4.43 to buy and $4.47 to sell. On that same morning, in an operation that would resemble the Overlord landings of 1944 in its complexity, about ten million copies of the necessary twelve forms in both English and French were printed in advance under absolute secrecy and distributed under seal to thirty-five hundred bank branches and four hundred customs posts across Canada. Arrangements were made with the telegraph companies for the simultaneous delivery to every one of those locations before the first(!) mail delivery on that day. As Joseph Schull describes it in his biography of Donald Gordon, all the presidents of the chartered banks were 'assembled' at the Bank of Canada building on Wellington Street in Ottawa and kept there until cabinet passed the order-in-council establishing the FECB. Towers had informed them of what was to happen, and once they were in on the secret no one was permitted to enter or leave. When the day dragged out long past the time that word should have been received, those waiting inquired as to what would happen if the order were not passed. 'That,' said the deputy governor, 'would be a serious matter ... You see, gentlemen, since secrecy is absolutely essential it would become my personal duty to slit all your throats.'[7] Happily, the cabinet reached agreement an hour later, and the bloodbath was averted.

The *Manual of Instructions to Authorized Dealers under the Foreign Exchange Control Act and Regulations* was a complex and complicated, indeed formidable, document. It is easy to imagine managers of local bank branches scratching their heads and, even with help from their regional offices, wondering how they could possibly interpret the language and in the process keep track of every American dollar in circulation in Canada. Running to more than one hundred pages, it included chapters on residential status (who was a Canadian?), rates of exchange, purchases of spot exchange (other than banknotes and coin), sales of spot exchange (other than banknotes and coin), transfers of Canadian dollars from residents to non-residents, export of goods, import of goods, and interest and principal payments on government and publicly issued corporate securities. All transactions were recorded on punch cards by FECB staff.

The initial resources of the Board consisted of the Exchange Fund, which had been created in 1935 out of gold revaluation profits when the price of the metal had been increased from US$20.67 per ounce to US$35, and had been held in suspense as a possible exchange-stabilization fund in case of need. In May 1940, an additional sum of $325 million was added when the FECB took over the gold and foreign exchange reserves of the Bank of Canada and purchased the remaining privately owned balances of foreign exchange. By February 1941, staff numbers had reached 553, most of them located in Ottawa.[8]

However, the number of people directly engaged in administering foreign exchange control does not give a complete picture of the cost in personnel of maintaining the system. Every day, literally thousands of transactions required a permit that was obtained at local bank branches; all purchases and sales of foreign exchange, all Canadian dollar payments to non-residents, and all securities transactions with non-residents were scrutinized. All receipts of US dollars by residents of Canada had to be sold to an authorized dealer as soon as they were received, and all requirements for US dollars on the part of residents of Canada had to be obtained from authorized dealers. Canadians were not allowed to dispose of any foreign exchange or engage in any transactions in foreign exchange without the authority of the Board. Control was also exercised over holdings of securities by residents and transactions in securities. All residents were required to register their holdings of foreign securities as of 15 September 1939, except those whose total holdings did not exceed $1,000. And the list of restrictions went on, overseen by FECB branches in Montreal, Toronto, Windsor, and Vancouver – it was a large operation, which reached into the furthest corners of the dominion.

The Board enforced its provisions by using any tool available, such as postal censorship. Most outgoing registered mail and about 1 per cent of ordinary mail were examined by postal censors for infractions of foreign exchange control. As a memorandum prepared by R.H. Tarr pointed out, 'Letters containing less than $1 are allowed to go forward. Those containing between $1 and $25 are normally returned to the sender unless a "gift travel' offence is indicated. Letters containing more than $25 and those containing less than that amount where "gift travel' offences are indicated, are referred to the Board, the currency involved being placed under seizure.'[9] As well, travellers leaving Canada were closely questioned at the border, and the Customs department had a period every two or three months where its officers searched those leaving the country. The chartered banks also kept records of all large transactions, of all $1,000 bills given out, and of large requests for $100 bills.

These methods yielded results. During 1943 and 1944, the number of attempted currency exports discovered by postal censorship where the amounts were returned to the senders was quite substantial. In 1943, the monthly average of letters returned was more than seven hundred, and the value of currency thus diverted was almost $5,000. The following year, the monthly average number was in excess of nine hundred, but the dollar value had fallen to approximately $4,400. Border checks also indicated some transgressions of the rules, and the FECB estimated that between 5 and 10 per cent of all travellers were smuggling amounts of American money out of the country. And the situation was worse with respect to Canadian currency being illegally taken out of the country. For example, in December 1943 – a representative month – Cdn$1.075 million was received by Canadian banks from American correspondents. Though the amounts represented a very small proportion of the Canadian war effort, they rankled for reasons relating to the pride of FECB officials. Postal censorship ended on 1 June 1945. Certainly Rasminsky agreed with a memorandum sent to him by an official: there was not 'much of a chance of continuing mail examination for foreign exchange control purposes in peacetime as a purely preventive measure since [senior postal administrators] felt that neither Parliament nor the general public would approve of any general examination of mail.'[10]

The Board would also take individuals or corporations to court if it thought such action advisable. Canadians who did not report their holdings of hard currency were special targets if the FECB became aware of their situation. For example, one individual in Fort William, Ontario, did not reveal the existence of an American bank account of some $38,000. The enforcement section wanted him charged with failure to declare foreign exchange in his possession; failure to sell; and illegal dealing in foreign exchange at various times since control.[11] In this case, moral suasion proved successful, and the courts were avoided.

Rasminsky also interpreted the cold language laid down in the FECB's manual for investors with questions, sometimes going to great lengths to explain Board policy in order to help them make sense of what might seem to be arcane bureaucratese. A typical example is an exchange between Rasminsky and Louis Stone, a member of the New York investment firm of Winslow, Douglas and McEvoy, which demonstrates the lengths to which Rasminsky and other Board members would go in explaining the rationale for a particular decision. Stone had visited Ottawa in October 1940 in order to view foreign exchange control in operation at first hand. Rasminsky was his contact in the Canadian capital, and the two had lengthy discussions on the subject, which continued even after Stone returned home. The American wrote to Rasminsky:

> I notice that Canadian Pacific 6/42 are selling on the New York Curb around 75 against 103 1/2 in Canada, a discount of about 28%. This issue is payable only in Canadian funds, but probably a substantial amount of the $12,500,000 outstanding total is held in the U.S. and the maturity is less than 18 months away. I do not know what the Board's policy is on such issues, but it seems to me that there are three general possibilities – 1: to allow payment at maturity in Canadian dollars convertible into U.S. dollars at the official rate, which means using a certain amount of your U.S. balances; 2: to allow payment in so-called 'black' Canadian dollars which can be sold in the free market and used for certain payments within Canada, involving an indirect weakening of the ultimate demand for official exchange; and 3: allow payment only in Canadian dollars restricted to replacement in Canadian securities, which might possibly be considered severe treatment.[12]

Rasminsky answered that the Board's policy regarding the payment of maturing Canadian obligations was to allow the debtor corporation to fulfil its contract in the currency specified. In the case of the Canadian Pacific Railway (CPR) 6 per cent bonds due on 15 March 1942, 'the Company would pay against representation at maturity the par value in Canadian funds. A non-resident recipient could re-invest in other Canadian securities, leave the money in Canada, or withdraw it by sale. in New York.'[13] However, given the shortage of US dollars in Canada in those pre–Hyde Park days, the Board's preference was to arrange with American bond-holders to leave their shares in Canada, to be exchanged for another security with a longer maturity. Stone's response was that there was 'no incentive for U.S. holders to switch them into similar longer term maturities payable only in Canadian funds, since the latter sell at an even greater dollar discount than the Canadian Pacific 6/42. Obviously, there must be some incentive.'[14] Would the Board not permit some exceptions to its rules?

Stone wanted the FECB to allow him to convert bonds into some other issue with a longer maturity, but payable in American rather than in Canadian dollars. Given that commitment, 'a substantial amount of repatriation can be effected, with a resultant saving in the amount of free exchange to be created on maturity of the Canadian Pacific 6/42.' The only cost would be the increase in the amount of interest payable in American dollars, so Stone thought, but that would be small compared with the amount of the principal saved. He concluded his letter with the observation that 'this 28% discount must be considered a rather discouraging indication of U.S. opinion as to Canada's ability to maintain its present exchange policy as far as March 1942. Any exception the Board might choose to make in this case would serve the double purpose of repatriating a near maturity and also improving the evident rating of Canada's position in the New York market.'

But that was not reason enough, as Rasminsky explained. By following the line suggested by Stone, the FECB would then have to apply this special ruling generally, which would lead to its losing control of some part of its foreign assets and increasing the amount of foreign exchange that it would subsequently have to put up to redeem outstanding obligations held by non-residents. Stone tried a few more times (Rasminsky called one effort an 'ingenious proposal'), stretching the correspondence well into 1941, but to no avail.[15] Foreign exchange control was vital to the Canadian war effort, and the profits of New York investment houses could not compete. Certainly it was necessary to soothe American concerns by reasoned argument, but not at the expense of the country's financial health.

This series of letters and replies was not atypical in Board operations; Rasminsky would attempt to make his correspondent see the situation from the Canadian perspective. He tried to make the institution approachable, keeping Canadians and others affected by its activities apprised of its motivations. As well, the Board applied its rules fairly and impartially, without regard to position or nationality; not even members of the FECB received preferential treatment when they travelled abroad on government business. For example, a 'Special Border Permit' spelled out how much foreign exchange Rasminsky was permitted on each trip out of the country; US$500 and Can$100. As the permit noted, 'Any authorized dealer of the Foreign Exchange Control Board is authorized to sell to the permit holder not more than $500 US per calendar month for the purpose for which the permit is issued.'[16] On the back are written his withdrawals.

Rasminsky's objective was an unbiased and objective organization, as was suggested in his replies to Stone. As well, he went to some lengths to explain to Donald Gordon his rationale for disagreeing with a point of view put forward by his immediate superior, Max Mackenzie, about corporate tax rates. He told Gordon:

> [The] study indicates that the recent increases in corporation taxes will, in the case of certain important companies, reduce the amounts available for distribution below the level of current distributions and necessitate a reduction in dividend rates if we stick to our present rates. Mr. Mackenzie recommends that, as a matter of administration, in cases where the non-resident interest does not exceed 25% and the deficiency of current earnings does not exceed 10%, we should approve a convertible dividend. Such approval would be coupled with an indication to the companies that our approval is not necessarily a precedent and a warning that they should 'put their house in order.' If the shortage is greater than 10% Mr. Mackenzie suggests that we should *negotiate* with the companies with a view to agreeing to conversion if *some* reduction is made in the dividend rate and give the same indication and warning as above.[17]

It was a bad precedent to set, Rasminsky thought, for reasons of both administration and principle. Since the inception of exchange control, the Board had been guided in its deliberations by general principles and did not enter into special bargains with individual applicants. That method had not only facilitated the task of administration but had also earned for the FECB its reputation for impartiality and consistency in rendering judgment. Rasminsky worried that, should Mackenzie's proposal be adopted, the Board would no longer be concerned with a purely accounting question, which could be answered with a 'yes' or a 'no,' in considering applications for the conversion privilege on dividend. It would be forced into the grey zone, anwering questions of 'more' or 'less,' where it would have to decide individual cases on their own merits and enter into negotiations with particular companies.

Was Rasminsky merely an inflexible bureaucrat who ignored subtlety and nuance? Certainly not. Above all else, he was even-handed and fair in his dealings, remaining single-minded in the consistency of his own administration and in how he applied the law to all. Jacques Kayalof, a member of a New York investment house, summed up the feelings of institutions in that city when he cabled to Rasminsky, on the termination of exchange control in December 1951: 'All controls are ... unpleasant, however, yours were an exception. Therefore, please accept our sincere thanks for fair and unbiased operation for twelve years.'[18]

The Board pursued every avenue in its search for foreign exchange, such as trying to recover hockey players' earnings (!), restricting royalty payments, and encouraging Canadian firms to recover income from foreign subsidiaries. It also encouraged some activities, becoming a tourism promoter in the United States for Canadian destinations. To that end, it focused on:

(1) the breaking down of rumours circulated in the USA designed to harm Canada's tourist business.

(2) assist[ing] in the preparation of numerous radio 'spots' and programmes, editorial and newspaper articles, and speeches. We were active in inspiring favourable editorial and news comment in Canadian and American newspapers and magazines. Many thousands of leaflets of various kinds were prepared, paid for and distributed.

(3) facilitat[ing] the entrance and exit of visitors to and from Canada and contribut[ing] to the removal of obstructions to their convenience and comfort. [The Board] originated the 'Be a Good Host' campaign.

(4) be[ing] very active in encouraging visitors to bring in US rather than Canadian dollars.[19]

The FECB's activities were successful, at least to the point that it 'increased Canada's income from tourists by ten per cent in 1941 and considerably more in 1942.'

Of course, tourist travel itself could not address the tremendous imbalance in the Canadian–American economic relationship, and in January 1941, the Board's senior personnel, including Rasminsky, attended a brainstorming session designed to develop measures to ease the situation. No figure was too small, and even ways to recover small amounts of money were explored. For example, rather than purchasing baled scrap from American suppliers, bringing light steel scrap bought in the United States to Canada for baling might save $1 million. As well, it was suggested that importation of coal, buses, tires, fruits, and vegetables – indeed, a host of products – be discouraged from American sources. Rasminsky wanted to restrict the amount of foreign exchange paid for films, as well as suggesting an effort to increase the Canadian portion of the haul on international shipments and closer supervision of amounts paid for telephone and telegraph charges, particularly on messages originating in the United States. Patents, copyrights, royalties, and syndicated newspaper material were also targeted.

Once the Hyde Park Agreement was in operation after April 1941, however, the intensity of the problem was greatly reduced.[20] The arrangement proved so salubrious to Canada as US military contracts were let – $200 million by mid-1941, $275 million in 1942, $301 million in 1943, and $314 million in 1944 – that American exchange began to pile up in Ottawa, attracting some critical attention by Washington. It was clear to the Americans that 'Hyde Park ... was doing more than had been intended and that they had better cancel orders placed through War Supplies Limited.' Success in the effort to reverse an untenable foreign exchange situation had brought in its wake some difficulty in North American economic relations.

In effect, it was too much of a good thing; in an understated way, Rasminsky described it as 'an interesting phase in foreign exchange control.'[21] In a change from the bleak days of 1940 and early 1941, Canada's cash reserves in gold and US dollars were now very healthy. On 31 December 1940, Canada's reserves of US dollars had been US$23 million; two years later, the figure stood at almost US$350 million. And therein lay the rub. Canadian–American negotiations were necessary in order to clear up misunderstandings about the nature of Canada's reserve position. The arrangement finally reached in late 1942 was that Washington would continue to place orders fairly freely through War Supplies, but its payments on account of such orders would be regulated so as to keep Canada's exchange holdings in gold and US dollars at an agreed figure. The Americans proposed a range of US$300–350 million, while Canada countered with US$400–430 million. Though the US negotiators insisted on their range, Canadian reserves of US dollars stood well above it for the rest of the war, even after termination of financial operations under the Hyde Park Agreement on 21 April 1944.[22] The Canadian government would later pursue a similar policy in return for an exemption from the US Interest Equalization Tax of 1963. Rasminsky, as governor of the Bank of Canada, would lead the negotiations.

The only problem was that the figure agreed to in late 1942 was lower than Ottawa would have liked and was less than the reserves then held. It was, however, greater than the official reserves before the war and would give Canada enough 'to come and go on in the immediate postwar period.' The goods ordered through War Supplies for which the United States did not pay would be those for which it had been paying under 'lend-lease' to other countries. Rasminsky noted that 'we shall now provide the other countries concerned with these goods directly under our own lend-lease plan.'[23] This scheme, called Mutual Aid, was a huge success.

Relations with the British were also under the purview of the FECB. The Board's new chair, Max Mackenzie, appointed after Gordon had gone to the Wartime Prices and Trade Board, followed his predecessor's procedure of writing to the Bank of England's George Bolton 'on a more or less personal basis' regarding 'troublesome cases concerning the status of individuals coming to Canada from England for permanent residence.'[24]

An example of the type of case that became increasingly common in Canada was the Canadian airman or soldier marrying a British woman. In one case in which the FECB took an interest, a Royal Air Force husband who was Canadian had been killed, and his widow and her children wished to immigrate to Canada. The FECB was involved because she had assets consisting of £4,000 of stock in Scottish Malayan Estates Limited, from which she normally obtained annual income of £180. In addition, she received pension and children's allowance of £190 per year. She had applied to the United Kingdom paymaster general's office for permission to have her pension and allowances for her children forwarded to her at her new address in Toronto. She had been told that this could not be done as she was a resident of England for purposes of foreign exchange control.

It was the Canadian understanding, however, that 'insofar as Canadian graduates of the British Commonwealth Air Training Plan are concerned, the Canadian authorities [would] pay pensions ... direct to dependents.' The Canadian authorities would then collect from the British. Presumably, the letter went on, 'if the pension is in the first instance paid by the Canadian authorities, there will be nothing to prevent the payment being made to any person in Canada,' regardless of the effects of Canadian and British controls. The FECB also believed that, 'any assets which the wife or children might receive from the husband's estate should be released for use in Canada and not made subject to your Control.'

There were also questions raised related to blocking the assets of former residents of enemy-occupied countries who were granted permanent entry into the United States, following the US declaration of war against Japan and the German declaration against the United States. The FECB prohibited the export from Canada of securities owned by residents of enemy-occupied countries or the use of any cash balances held in Canada by or on behalf of such people. It also prohibited the export of any US securities held for their account in Canada and the release to them of any US securities held for their account in the United States in the name of a Canadian bank or trust company. The reason for that policy, Rasminsky told James Ilsley, the dominion minister of finance, was 'the fear that the assets under our control might, if released to former residents of enemy-occupied countries, be used for purposes which would ... be of benefit to the enemy.'[25]

Still, it was not the Board's intention to leave such people destitute, so it transferred to the holders the income from their securities. As events transpired, the Canadian policy was much tougher than that of either the Americans or the British. That situation had prompted Rasminsky to write to Ilsley; did the minister wish to change it? He did. The Board's activities involved high-level diplomacy, hard-heartedness, compassion, and nastiness, applied in different measures at different times.

One of the major difficulties of Canada's wartime position was that the FECB was administering an exchange control in which the hardest of all currencies was Canadian dollars; the 'market' had in a sense decided that, because of the soundness of the currency, there was a tendency on the part of non-residents to accumulate Canadian dollars instead of converting them into convertible items. This situation, thought Rasminsky, was 'a perfect two-way hedge for anyone who had enough capital to immobilize it this way and it worries us since it is an over-hanging liability which we may be called upon to meet at a time when it suits us much less than it would to meet it now.' He went on: 'Some time ago, before the new arrangements with the United States were made, we took our courage in both hands as regards on large account of this type and told the people concerned that they must either convert now or lose the right of conversion. They chose the latter, which means that they are still taking a speculative position in Canadian dollars, though not against the Board.'[26]

The FECB was also in the front line with respect to ensuring that the sterling area received any Canadian dollars that legimately belonged to it. 'As you can imagine,' he wrote to Coyne, 'our toughest battles in this connection are with the Canadian subsidiaries of sterling area companies who resist our requests that they transfer their current earnings. On the whole we have been very successful, however, and have saved the Canadian tax-payer several millions of dollars by reducing the British deficit in this way.'

But that approach took some effort and diligence, especially because of the reluctance of some subsidiaries of sterling-area companies to patriate their Canadian-dollar profits, which would have helped those countries purchase Canadian exports without assistance. Though Mutual Aid was implemented in 1943, provision had been made in 1941 and 1942 for sterling-area access to Canada's market through a $700-million loan, followed by a gift of $1 billion to Britain. As a result, it fell to the FECB to ensure that any profits of any sterling-area company located in Canada were transferred to the appropriate exchange authority. Among other things, the Board 'required the subsidiaries of sterling area companies to file certain information with [it] which enabled [it] to ascertain that they were not piling up indebtedness on inter-company account to their parent organizations and that they were transferring their current earnings since the outbreak of war.'[27]

While the FECB had no legal authority to insist on such transfers, on the whole it was successful in persuading companies to conform to Canadian wishes. Still, there were transgressors, and Rasminsky and others took what action they considered necessary. For example, two interesting cases arose concerning the shares of two Australian subsidiaries located in Canada – Davis-Gelatine and Sunshine Waterloo Company. Rasminsky had checked the record and believed that these two were the only Canadian subsidiaries of sterling-area companies outside Britain that had earnings available for transfer. It was eventually determined that the former lay outside the purview of the FECB and Australian control, and the latter simply refused to cooperate. The Board had asked that profits be remitted to Australia, but in its reply the company noted that 'it is our sincere wish to cooperate to the fullest extent but it is with regret that we must advise you that it would be extremely difficult to comply at this time with your request to remit to Australia our accumulated profits.'[28] The firm also raised the question of the legal position of the Board in asking that funds be transferred.

Rasminsky had brought the situation to the attention of the Canadian Department of Finance, 'with the thought that in working out with the representatives of the Australian Government the allocation of supplies under the United Nations Mutual Aid Act you may think it worth while to suggest that that Government should take steps to cause the Canadian dollars referred to be placed at its disposal.' While in these cases the FECB did not have the legal right to compel companies to remit profits, in wartime moral suasion was often enough, and this was the course that Rasminsky recommended.

In this case, the minister of national revenue could invoke section 13 of the Income Tax Act and force the companies to distribute profits. As a memorandum written by the acting solicitor to the Treasury pointed out, however, 'It would be most difficult for the Minister to justify his taking action under Section 13 ... since his only reason for doing so would be the rather indirect one that dividends paid to sterling-area countries would relieve Canada to that extent from making a gift of Canadian dollars. Any such reason would undoubtedly be held an improper reason for the Minister to invoke under the Income War Tax Act.' The solicitor supported Rasminsky's 'moral suasion' approach.[29] By early 1944, in response at least in part to Rasminsky's concerns, the Australians did tighten their foreign exchange–control regulations in order 'to cover certain activities of overseas subsidiary companies controlled by persons in Australia.'[30]

Rasminsky was also involved in establishment of the Wartime Prices and Trade Board (WPTB), whose activities complemented those of the FECB. He had been part of a very small committee struck in September 1941, comprised of himself, Donald Gordon, and the Bank of Canada's deputy chief of research, Robert Beattie, designed to consider the necessary organization to administer an order-in-council setting maximum prices in Canada. It was set up in response to growing worry about inflation; during 1940–1, prices had risen about 17 per cent, and many in government remembered with some dismay the inflation that had characterized the First World War. The committee established guidelines on administration, structure, powers of a price controller, and enforcement procedures. It also addressed issues such as whether or not import prices should be pegged and the problem of export prices – how to maximize export income for the country and keep down the price on the portion of export commodities sold domestically. Various alternatives were discussed: '(a) a government export-import pool which would pay only the pegged price (or less) to all producers; (b) exchange rate adjustments to keep the Canadian dollar prices constant and; (c) subsidizing that part of export products consumed domestically to keep domestic prices down to the maximum.'[31]

Rasminsky also proposed alternatives to the price-ceiling plan, as he had concerns about the equity and fairness of the document then under discussion. He suggested that the government ration expenditure by allowing each Canadian family $1,500 a year to spend on essential items. As well, he suggested a number of points, including: '(a) public education respecting the real situation; (b) drastic curtailment of supply of certain [consumer] goods where [their manufacture] conflict[ed] with war programme; (c) increased excise taxes on items under (b); (d) increased income taxes; (e) freezing dividends; (f) pegging prices of goods which show signs of sharp increases.'

His suggestions were put over for discussion and were not acted on, but he did write a few memoranda on various issues. For example, he proposed a piecemeal approach to the price problem – that is, freezing the price structure of individual commodities. There was, he pointed out, no real sign of run-away inflation, or even of a price rise large enough to produce large-scale adjustments in basic wage rates. Moreover, price increases were only 'the symptoms of the evils we fear from inflation ... The evils themselves are the shortage of supplies in relation to purchasing power and the inequity involved if the necessary contraction of consumption is imposed by the price-rationing method. The mere act of price-freezing does nothing to deal with these basic problems.'[32] He went on to note:

> On the supply side, the real problem involves increasing output to its limits by making the most efficient possible use of available resources through standardization, conservation, concentration, etc. On the consumption side, the freezing of prices necessarily tends to increase consumption (by eliminating the restraining influence of the price increases which would otherwise take place) and hastens the necessity of direct consumer rationing. In my opinion, there is a greater chance that these 'real' problems will be dealt with successfully if we close in on major commodity groups one at a time than if we try to do everything at once. I fear that if we pursue the latter course – particularly if we freeze retail as well as wholesale prices – the entire time and thought of the price administration will be devoted to considering applications to price increases.
>
> The increases in real costs in Canada which are exerting pressure on the price ceiling are important; they are perhaps most concerned about the increased cost of labour, though I do not know that quantitatively this is a more important factor than the increased cost of transportation and increases due to the use of substitute materials, the reduced volume of production in certain lines and increases due to intermittent and slowed-down operations. There is still no coherent export price policy, which I think is quite a serious gap.

On 1 December 1941, the WPTB went into operation, regulating the cost of rent, clothing, food, and a host of other items – the price ceiling was in place. Between then and April 1945, costs rose only 2.5 per cent.

The issue of potential price increases, and Canadian pricing policy in general, also affected relations with the United States. As Rasminsky had asked in his memorandum, how should Canadian export commodities be priced? Because price freezing represented some cost to the Canadian taxpayer, should the export charge be higher in order to recoup some of the loss? This was a difficult question. Some correspondence was carried out among senior officials, such as the Bank of Canada's governor, Graham Towers; its deputy governor (and WPTB chairman), Donald Gordon; and the undersecretary of state for external affairs, Norman Robertson, about whether discussion should cover particular commodities rather than Canada's whole import–export price relationship with the United States.

Rasminsky was firmly of the opinion that the latter framework should prevail. The difficulty, he thought, was that discussions on those matters with the Americans in connection with individual items would almost certainly run in terms of what he called a 'just price.' The Americans would quite naturally try to apply the same criteria to Canadian goods as they would to domestic goods. If Canada put itself in a position where it would have to justify to the United States an increase in the price of any particular export on the basis of increased cost or of a fair return on the capital invested in producing it, 'our position is bound to be extremely weak. For domestic costs, including wages, have been frozen; the calculation of a fair return on capital is extremely difficult as we found under the original alternative formula for excess profits tax; and the premium on American funds which has in the past kept the export price from rising (and the disappearance of which the Americans admit would justify an increase in the American cost) has imposed costs on the Canadian economy in the form of higher Canadian dollar prices for imported goods which cannot be taken into account in an analysis of the position of one particular industry.'[33]

If Canada were to take the position that an increase in the export price of newsprint was justified because of higher costs, for example, then the Americans could well ask the Canadians if they were not subsidizing the newsprint producers on that part of their production that was sold at home. It was not a very strong argument to claim that the reason was that the bulk of the output was sold abroad. Rasminsky thought that the real point that should be made was this: 'If we had no price and wage ceiling in Canada and the price of export goods rose on the domestic market, the United States would have no basis whatever for insisting that we sell at lower prices to them than to our own people. But the price and wage ceiling involves certain costs to the Canadian Government. Those costs consist of (a) subsidies paid to domestic producers to get maximum production in the face of increased costs, (b) subsidies paid to importers to enable imported goods, which have risen in price, to sell at our ceiling levels, and (c) the foregoing of corporation taxes as a result of the price squeeze.'

Canada should argue that the Americans were asking it to incur money costs 'and make a present of them' to the United States by freezing export prices. If the price of newsprint were allowed to go up by US$3 per ton, the Canadian government would recover by far the greater part of this increase through the tax on excess profits and would have this money to help in keeping down domestic costs. With the price of newsprint thus stabilized, the money that accomplished that objective came from Canadian taxpayers, and the American consumers of the country's newsprint would get the benefit of Ottawa's costly wage and price policy without making any contribution to it.

Another general factor that justified higher prices for Canadian exports, even in cases where increases might not be warranted on the basis of a 'just price,' was the terms-of-trade question. With American prices rising rapidly and with Canada subsidizing imports in order to get essential supplies, the terms of trade were bound to turn against Canada. The US attitude in the case of newsprint put no limit whatever to the probable deterioration in Canada's terms-of-trade position.

And the price structure of the United States had risen more quickly than had Canada's; indeed, the American price position was deteriorating, as an FECB-commissioned study on a comparison of Windsor and Detroit's wage rates demonstrated. The findings had been sobering; the weekly earnings of hourly paid factory workers in Wayne County, Michigan, averaged $62.34 in December 1943 – more than twice the corresponding figures over the five years preceding 1939.[34] The average weekly earnings of industrial workers in some Canadian cities were nowhere near Wayne County's level, as suggested by the following figures: Windsor, $43.55; Fort William, $37.22; Vancouver, $33.89; Calgary, $30.51; London, $29.56; Edmonton, $29.52; Winnipeg, $28.70; Kitchener, $28.49; Ottawa, $27.92; Regina, $26.98; and Saskatoon $26.00.

The Americans were concerned about the impact of inflation on their war effort and were – or so Rasminsky believed as a result of a trip to

Washington, DC, and New York in April 1942 – contemplating 'an overall price ceiling along our lines.'[35] He reported that US tax programs designed to keep prices down had proved inadequate; if they were to keep prices from rising in the future even more than had been the case in the past, then new measures were necessary. The Americans implemented a price ceiling later that month.

There was another twist to continental economic relations that figured into the war effort – the pricing policies of US subsidiaries operating in Canada. Two arose in late 1942 – one concerning asbestos, and the other, pulpwood. What, the US Office of Price Administration (OPA) wanted to know, did the Canadians consider a fair price for raw asbestos mined in Canada by the subsidiary of a US firm? To that time, many foreign-owned concerns had been charging a discount of 5 per cent when selling to the parent corporation. The FECB had had occasion to review the export valuations of certain asbestos companies and found that in some cases exports were being made to affiliated companies in the United States at prices that were lower than those charged to unrelated companies and, in the Board's view, less than fair value and therefore involving an export of capital in the form of unrequited exports. The fair-valuation stipulation was based on an objective test – that is, transactions between companies dealing at arm's length.

The FECB drew this anomaly to the attention of the companies concerned, asking them to charge fair market value for their exports to affiliated companies. Rasminsky, who handled this very difficult matter, noted that it was the FECB's intention not to force any all-round increase in the export price of asbestos, or of any other product for that matter, but merely to discharge the duty laid on it to prevent the export of capital through the deliberate undervaluation of exports. Section 28 of the Foreign Exchange Control Order prohibited export of capital except under permit granted by the Board and deemed it an export of capital 'to export from Canada any property ... on terms which provide for the payment of price less than the fair value thereof.'

The Americans were anxious to control costs and saw this deliberate undervaluation as an attempt – a 'new technique' they called it – to increase Canadian export prices to the detriment of the US economy. Seymour Harris, director of the OPA's Office of Export–Import Price Control, told A.F.W. Plumptre and Monteath Douglas, both in Washington with the Canadian WPTB, that 'if the Canadian government should have recourse to this means of increasing the price for commodities which are for the most part sold in the United States market and are vital to the United States economy, the United States government, in turn, may very well fix dollars and cents ceilings on such commodities.' Canadian authorities 'may not relish' the end result.[36]

However, the OPA would wait until Rasminsky had given his views before deciding on what policy to recommend. While not insensitive to the delicacies of Canadian–American relations, Rasminsky maintained the Board's interpretation of the relevant section of the Foreign Exchange Control Order. He insisted on the fair valuation of a subsidiary's exports to the American parent corporation – a position supported by Clark and Towers and ultimately accepted by Washington.

Similarly, the case of pulpwood strained relations between the two allies. This situation was arguably worse than that relating to asbestos. The FECB had had to work out with individual American companies the valuation of their imports from Canada. Board officers visited mills in Wisconsin in order to determine a fair and equitable basis of valuing Canadian pulpwood then being exported at what Rasminsky called 'nominal prices, in some cases only slightly in excess of the cost of production, in all cases at values which, including the cost of transportation to the parent companies' mill, appeared to reflect a wood-pile cost at the mill in Wisconsin considerably less than what we had been led to believe was the current market value of inferior domestically produced wood in those areas.'[37]

One of the leading pulp manufacturers in Canada was selling pulp to its American parent at prices that at the time of imposition of the ceiling prices in the United States were US$20 to $30 per ton below those being obtained from unrelated customers. This situation was also covered by the Reciprocal Tax Convention signed between Canada and the United States on 1 January 1941. Under that agreement, the competent tax authority of either country could, when necessary, change the prices that would prevail between independent persons dealing at arm's length.

In short, Americans were getting Canadian wood cheaply. Negotiations were opened with the US mills in order to achieve a more equitable price for the resource, to which effort the mills, while putting up mild resistance, did not really object. Again, Rasminsky believed that the policy being pursued was fair and reasonable. Still, he wrote to Gordon, if there were 'considerations of high policy involved in connection with possible repercussions on our relationships with the United States which would cause the Board to alter its view and desist from further representations to the pulpwood people and other similar representations which we might in the future make,' he would be glad to get the deputy governor's input. In the event, the deputy minister of finance, Clifford Clark, allayed his concerns: 'I think our position is beyond reproach,' he wrote, 'and really do not see what considerations of high policy would be sufficient to justify the loss in taxes and exchange rightfully due us, that would otherwise take place.'[38] The matter ended there for both sides.

Rasminsky was also a member of a small, informal committee headed by William Mackintosh and including John Baldwin, Robert Bryce, John Deutsch, and Alex Skelton, whose task it was to consider problems such as those above as well as to plan for postwar developments. Postwar planning was, according to Donald Gordon, the head of the WPTB, vital, and the committee often met with Clark and Towers in order to consider proposals to deal with an always-threatening rise in the cost-of-living index.[39] Such troubles were bound to increase as the real supply of goods and services available for personal consumption fell. It was estimated that that decrease would be in the neighbourhood of 15 to 20 per cent in 1943, and already shortages in many lines were becoming apparent. Gordon was very concerned about the lack of personnel to work out and administer a much-enlarged rationing system. While the battles being fought around the world by the armed forces of various countries were of tremendous importance, there were others being waged more quietly on the home front designed to help ease a potentially troublesome economic situation.

Many of the issues that the FECB addressed during the war were discussed in study groups, organized by Rasminsky. The idea to hold such meetings had first been raised between Rasminsky and Gordon in early July 1941. The problem, both agreed, was two-fold – to keep up general spirits and enthusiasm so as to convince all staff members that they were participating in the war effort and to maintain the interest of those members of the staff actually involved. Rasminsky believed that perhaps twenty-five to thirty-five officials would be interested in attending such discussions. As events transpired, fifty-six responded favourably.[40]

To address the first point, he thought that a series of talks by FECB members could be given. He told Gordon: 'If [he] could get the Minister of Finance to give a talk this would be an admirable beginning.' The minister's speech might then be followed by what could only be described as a who's who of Canadian officialdom: W.C. Clark, 'Problems of War Finance'; L.D. Wilgress, 'The Effect of the War on Canada's Markets'; H.D. Scully, 'Import Controls and the Cooperation of the Customs Department in the Administration of Foreign Exchange Control'; N.A.

Robertson, 'The Economic Position of Canada vis-à-vis the US and the UK'; and H. Fortier, 'Censorship in Wartime, with particular reference to Foreign Exchange Control.'

By October, a questionnaire had been prepared for circulation among staff members, asking their opinions on how they would like to proceed. The responses gave some indication of preferences; for example, more than one-half of those who answered suggested subjects that were concerned primarily with problems of wartime economics, such as inflation, price control, priorities, and the practical problems being faced by other branches of government. The lectures, organized and arranged by Rasminsky, proved successful, and attendance remained high throughout the rest of the war. He remained a guiding spirit, as a summary of talks over a six-month period indicated: 'This would appear to be an appropriate time to express,' it noted, 'appreciation to Mr. Rasminsky for the time he was good enough to devote ... He was present at almost every meeting, and on numerous occasions steered us through difficulties which might otherwise have involved us all in lengthy but fruitless argument.'[41]

As the war turned in the Allies' favour, exchange control was slowly being relaxed. From May 1944, for example, travel restrictions were eased until US dollars were being provided for any reasonable travel expenditure. As well, applications for American currency for capital investment in new commercial ventures in the US-dollar area were approved where such investment was judged to have collateral advantages for Canada. Previously, exchange had been provided for capital purposes only when it was required to protect an existing investment. The government too took steps in the same direction by repealing certain sections of the War Exchange Conservation Act in 1944 and by abolishing the War Exchange Tax in 1945.

A footnote remained. William Lawson, whom Rasminsky had hired to work at the Board in 1941, but who had since joined the Canadian army, sent letters of inquiry about the possibility of being rehired. He was only twenty-five years old and a person of intelligence and integrity. Rasminsky wanted him back and took the unusual step of discussing the case with the governor before responding to Lawson at his address 'Somewhere in Germany.' He had 'the highest possible regard for [your] ability and since [you] left ... [had] nourished the hope that you would come back after the war. This hope has been shared by others here, including the Governor.'[42] Lawson did return, and in 1973 he became senior deputy governor. Rasminsky always said that one of the best decisions that he

ever made during his thirty-three years at the Bank of Canada was to
smooth the way for Lawson's return.

The war in Europe was over in May 1945 and in the Far East in August.
However, despite relaxations, foreign exchange control persisted, to help
with the restoration of a peacetime economy. While it was not finally abolished until 1951, it was greatly reduced in effect. Indeed, FECB management went to some lengths to define a new purpose for itself. In 1944,
Rasminsky had offered certain questions about the postwar organization
of the Board. What was to be the status of Canadian-dollar accounts of
non-residents and the unofficial market in Canadian dollars? Should the
unofficial market be done away with? Should the Board change its
arrangements for futures? Should it make a charge on purchases of US-
dollar futures and sales of sterling futures? What procedure was necessary
to control capital movements, and what changes, if any, should Board
personnel make in their own attitude towards various types of application?[43] All those matters and more were to be discussed with section
heads so that some sort of position could be put to government. As FECB
personnel well knew, however, the public would not be too tolerant of a
very active Board.

While Rasminsky and the Board were contemplating the future, a
different, more virulent challenge was issued by self-styled Independent
Conservative Frédéric Dorion, member of Parliament for Charlevoix-
Saguenay. As reported approvingly in *L'Action catholique* of 3 July 1944, at
the nomination meeting for his brother Noel, then a candidate in the
upcoming provincial election for Maurice Duplessis's Union Nationale,
Dorion had thundered against, among other things, the fact that the
Quebec government of Liberal Adélard Godbout had not prevented his
dominion counterparts 'from putting into the hands of Russian Jews the
Bank of Canada, the war information board and the national film
board.'[44] He cited Rasminsky by name.

Brooke Claxton, the Liberal MP for St Laurent–St George, took the
opportunity of a debate on the budget to demolish Dorion in a parliamentary address running over six columns, which even today translates
the dry language of Hansard into a ringing denunciation of anti-
semitism. Claxton centred on the personal attack on Rasminsky. He had
been, the MP said, 'born in Canada ... of the Jewish faith. Mr. Rasminski
was educated at the university of Toronto and the London school of economics. For many years he was on the economic staff of the League of
Nations. He is now an assistant to the governor of the Bank of Canada.
He is known in Canada and throughout the world as one of the outstand-

ing banking economists of the whole world. If the people of Ste-Anne de la Pocatière [Dorion's brother's provincial riding] could meet Mr. Rasminski they would find a gentleman who could speak French, who would delight and charm them with his knowledge of and love for their country, and who would impress them with the great services which he has given to our country.'[45]

Aside from Aboriginal people, we were all immigrants to Canada of one sort or another, Claxton went on, and when any Canadian joined in 'anti-Semitism of any kind, when we join in giving voice to racial theories of one kind or another, we point Hitler's sword at our own breasts ... Spiritually, the people who give way to racial prejudice, who breed intolerance by their own intolerance, who create injustice by being less than just, are walking in the footsteps not of Christ, but of all that Christianity and humanity stand and fight against in this war.'

Speaking for French Canada, Phillippe Picard of Bellechasse seconded Claxton's remarks. Faced with such an onslaught from both Liberals and members of the Co-operative Commonwealth Federation (Stanley Knowles in particular), Dorion at first said that he had been misquoted (which he had not been), and then he sat down. He did not renew his attack. Still, Dorion was merely giving voice to what many powerful and influential people probably believed. In that context, merit alone was not sufficient to ensure Rasminsky's promotion.

With V-E day in May 1945, the FECB began drastically to scale back its operations, though it was of some use during the 1947 exchange crisis, when Canada imposed restrictions on trade with the United States and on exportation of US dollars. However, generally speaking, between 1945 and 1951, controls were relaxed as Canada's exchange position improved, and restrictions on capital export and travel became much less onerous. The problem, from an administrative point of view, was that tough control was much easier to run than relatively light control, and the decisions being made by the FECB on various cases became increasingly difficult.

Things came to a head in December 1951. Rasminsky and his staff had had their daily meeting, where difficult decisions were made. At stake was an application by a Canadian firm to export capital to the United States. Much argument and disagreement ensued. As it was a particularly complex case, Rasminsky took it to Towers, going over the arguments for and against. In the midst of the conversation, he said to the governor, 'You know, the reason we're having so much difficulty with this is that it isn't absolutely certain that exchange control is needed at all.'[46] Towers agreed and later that afternoon met with Clifford Clark, who made a recommendation to the minister of finance, Douglas Abbott, that foreign exchange control be abolished. It was, and an order-in-council was passed marking the end of the FECB. It had been such an important part of the war effort and had also been of assistance in terms of helping Canada weather the 1947 exchange crisis. Still, no one missed it.

Chapter Four

The Road to Bretton Woods

While he was employed at the Bank of Canada and the Foreign Exchange Control Board (FECB), Louis Rasminsky also participated in a process that promised much for the future of global exchange stability. His contribution to the establishment of the International Monetary Fund (IMF) in 1946 was a large one; indeed, in some ways he can be seen as one of the 'keys' to its development and, to a lesser extent, to that of its twin, the International Bank for Reconstruction and Development (IBRD). In the case of the IMF, he was an important member of the Canadian delegation and acted as an interpreter between the Americans and British, discussing and arguing with John Maynard Keynes, the great British economist, honorary adviser to the Treasury, and leader of the British delegation to these talks. Similarly, he met frequently with the chief American representative, Harry Dexter White. Doubtless, without Rasminsky, there would still have been an IMF and an IBRD; what shape those institutions would have assumed in the absence of his counsel is moot. In all likelihood, the Fund would have been dominated by the United States even more than was the case at Bretton Woods.

Two plans emerged. Keynes, for the British, had developed the 'International Clearing Union' in late 1941, and White and the Americans, the 'International Stabilization Fund,' through a process that really began in early 1942.[1] James Meade, a close friend of Rasminsky's from Geneva days, but then in the employ of Britain's War Cabinet Office, later told him how Keynes came to espouse an internationalist point of view. The economist had written 'the first draft of the Clearing Union to show multilateralist people how foolish the logical implications of their ideas were ... [He] then got convinced by his own draft.'[2] Whatever the reason,

Keynes had firmly nailed his standard to the mast of international financial cooperation by early 1942.

For a person such as Rasminsky, shaped to a large degree by his experience as a member of the economic and financial section of the League of Nations, this cooperative ideal was welcome. As he later said, 'A large part of [his] intellectual life was invested in the idea of international collaboration and machinery that made collaboration possible.'[3] That approach had been conspicuously absent when, between 1929 and 1933, world industrial production had fallen by about 50 per cent, the value of global trade dropped by 75 per cent, and unemployment hit levels in North America and Europe never experienced again. Much of the blame for the horrendous state of affairs was laid at the feet of the 'beggar-thy-neighbour' policies pursued by governments as they unsuccessfully searched for the way out of depression. These policies, such as tariff increases, competitive exchange depreciations, import restrictions and quotas, and deflation had exacerbated the economic downturn. For those at the League who had had a ringside seat watching the agony of depression unfold and able to do little, it was a terrible sight. To be asked to participate in a process that would create a new institution endowed with sufficient resources, supported by at least two of the great powers, and which had the opportunity of persuading member states to follow established rules of behaviour was an irresistible offer. Rasminsky was especially attracted by the attempt to reconcile the desire for high employment with the avoidance of destructive external policies.

The two papers produced by the Americans and the British suggested that a new spirit animated international deliberations. Canadians seized on this approach as reflecting their country's basic postwar interests as well. As a country dependent on exports, Canada had to do what it could to further this sort of program on the international stage. Indeed, the Canadians were adamant that they be included in any discussions contemplated by the Americans and the British. Even the early meetings in May 1942 seemed important to Canada; while they might only be informal and exploratory, 'they may well lay the foundations for future action.'[4] But how to get invited to such an exclusive party? Perhaps the Americans would be prepared to suggest their inclusion. If so, that would make a most favourable entrance. If not, then a direct assault on the United Kingdom would be needed. As events transpired, neither nation had any serious objection to Canadian participation.

Not much transpired over the summer of 1942, though the British plan was given to the Americans in August. The first formal international talks were scheduled for October, comprising Britain, its dominions, and India. The Canadian position was clear – push self-interest, but at all costs, do what could be done to maintain Anglo–American cooperation.[5] As Roy Harrod has pointed out, 'The Canadians were keen that the British and Americans should think alike on postwar topics.'[6] The subject of postwar international economic and financial cooperation had been thoroughly canvassed at discussions of the joint economic committee of Canada and the United States set up as a wartime measure. At these meetings, according to Wrong, 'the conclusions had soon been reached that most postwar problems called for action in the international sphere, and that failure to tackle them by means of agreed action between the Governments concerned would lead to disastrous results.' As W.A. Mackintosh, a delegate to the October meetings in London and chair of the Canadian side of the Canadian–US joint economic committee, noted, multilateralism was the only solution to global problems.

Through the insight, intelligence, and persistence of delegates such as Wrong and Mackintosh, but especially Rasminsky, Canada did exert some influence on the process. Rasminsky became the consummate mediator between the British and US negotiators; he was also an expert economist possessed of superior technical skills. Harrod commented: 'Almost alone, outside the ranks of British and Americans, the Canadians seemed capable of understanding the international monetary problems as a whole. Their suggestions were intelligent and creative, and the British and Americans were always anxious to have them.'[7]

Rasminsky had already turned his mind towards these issues, having written extensively on world trade and its effect on employment during the 1930s. His work for the League's depressions delegation was an example of that interest, pointing out a possible direction: 'It was natural,' he wrote in 1939, 'that the League should have attempted to distill out of this experience some common wisdom, to observe what policies had been tried, which had failed and why, which had produced the results aimed at, and to attempt to determine what were the conditions of success in attempted to mitigate economic depressions.'[8] The League had early on tackled the problem of 'proper' policies designed to even out the peaks and troughs of capitalist economies, relying on a different approach from that of national governments. The League's emphasis, he thought, was on 'catholicity and many-sidedness, [an] avoidance of 'isms and panaceas, and [a] refusal to rely on any single line of attack.' That

ideal remained with Rasminsky throughout his life and was especially relevant during the ground-breaking discussions that took place between
October 1942 and July 1944.

The United Kingdom and the United States began considering forms of
international cooperation early in the war. Much of this activity centred
on trade issues, but the two nations were also investigating problems
caused by exchange instability and competitive devaluations. What sort of
institutions, officials wondered, would be able to work out exchange
problems successfully? – a seemingly intractable problem. In the financial
field, that meant, according to Rasminsky, addressing three issues: '(1)
avoiding competitive exchange rates and recognizing that the level of any
single country's exchange rate was properly a matter of international
concern; (2) avoiding bilateralism and blocked accounts in international
trade and making currency convertibility the norm, and; (3) [establish-
ing] a substantial fund [to accomplish these objectives] which would
enable countries which ran into temporary balance of payments difficulties to make both ends meet without resorting to unjustified currency
depreciation.'[9]

Nearly two months after the United States went to war, the (U.S.)
Council on Foreign Relations invited British and American delegates to
meet in New York to discuss the exchange problem. Rasminsky was also
asked to attend – the only non-Anglo-American present. An interesting
point arising from the conversations, according to the Canadian, was the
'internationalist' approach taken by the British delegation to problems of
the postwar world. Rasminsky noted with approval that even Keynes was
'shifting his ground because he [felt] that attempts at UK bilateralism
[would lead] to serious political friction with the United States.'

There was one irritant that Canadians would get to know well, if they
did not already. As Rasminsky told the Bank of Canada's governor, Graham Towers, in talk about postwar cooperation 'there was a marked tendency on the part of both the British and Americans to think entirely of
UK–USA action.'[10] It had been necessary 'on several occasions to put in a
word for Canada and other small countries.' As Towers could have said, it
was ever thus. That was the Anglo-Americans' attitude and could be seen
generally, from development of military policy to the Combined Boards.
They perceived the Second World War as *their* war and did not easily suffer demands from lesser belligerents such as Canada. This was also a
problem that worried participants in the talks of 23 October to 4 November 1942 in London, designed by the British to put their case to the

dominions and India with respect to a Clearing Union. All but Britain were unanimous in criticizing the sentiment expressed by the Clearing Union document, which implied that all countries other than the United Kingdom and the United States would be presented with a fait accompli.

The London conference included, as well as Canada and Britain, delegations from Australia, India, New Zealand, and South Africa. The British delegation was a talented one. Sir Frederick Phillips of the Treasury was in the chair, and Keynes of course was the key member, assisted by Sir Percivale Liesching of the Board of Trade, James Meade, the economist and future Nobel Prize winner, and the Treasury's Sir Wilfrid Eady. The delegation from Ottawa was comprised of Wrong, Mackintosh, and Rasminsky, whose inclusion drew the ire of one member of Parliament. The anti-semitic Social Credit MP for Westaskiwin in Alberta, Norman Jacques, had identified Rasminsky as a graduate of the London School of Economics, which had produced 'socialist trained experts to plan Canada's future.' Jacques took special exception to LSE, which he said had been 'founded by "British socialists with money supplied by German international finance for the purpose of training the bureaucracy of the future world socialist state to maintain the gold standard ... which [was] supported by the Soviet government."'[11] That was quite a mouthful.

The London meeting represented the first opportunity to question Keynes closely on his approach. The Clearing Union paper was the primary subject of discussion, but other issues were also discussed, such as control of prices of primary products, postwar relief, and statistics on national income and expenditure. While Anglo–American talks on these issues were a condition of Lend-Lease, they had not been possible earlier because the Americans were 'not far enough advanced with their own preparations and had other internal preoccupations.'[12] Therefore, as part of their 'strategy,' the British wanted to be on record as 'consulting' with the dominions and India. A common approach here, it was hoped in Whitehall, might bolster the case with Washington. A real difficulty, however, for the British was the US emphasis on commercial, as opposed to financial, policy; Congress was pressing for a new trade agreement with the United Kingdom that would include reductions in the British tariff and an assault on imperial preference. Washington took its initiative in conjunction with renewal of its Trade Agreements Act, which was to go before Congress in January 1943.

'The framing of a scheme,' Keynes proposed as he opened the conference, 'which aimed at achieving a high volume of exchange of goods and services between nations and which would, at the same time, serve to mitigate cyclical fluctuations should ... be placed at the forefront of any discussion about postwar economic problems ... There was a need for action of an essentially international character, that bilateralism should be avoided at all costs, and that currencies should be linked but not dependent upon gold.'[13] Or, as he later said, nations should be able 'to apply what we earn from our exports, wherever we may be selling them, to pay for whatever we may buy wherever we may buy it.'[14]

In order to reach that economic Valhalla, exchange stability was a prerequisite, and the key article of Keynes's proposal. 'A member country [could not] alter its exchange rates with other countries except on certain specified conditions.' The Clearing Union proposal also demanded that each country undertake unlimited obligation to provide other countries with such amounts of its currency as was required within the limits of the scheme. In other words, all would agree to accept 'bancor,' the name given to the plan's unit of account. The Clearing Union would be very large, reflecting the average of world trade between 1936 and 1938. Quotas would be determined by a country's average trade over that period; the Americans' would be $4.040 billion, or 19 per cent of the total; the British, US$4.973 billion, or 23 per cent; and the Canadians' US$1.161 billion, or about 5 per cent.

Keynes was, according to Rasminsky, 'very persuasive.'[15] For the better part of a week, the delegations questioned him. Rasminsky was especially active, asking a detatiled technical question here, and a political-strategic one there.[16] The discussions were very stimulating and, he wrote to Governor Towers, relatively non-confontational. Keynes was 'at his best and has been rude only once, (to [Sir Theodor] Gregory [representing India] – "I cannot answer incomprehensible questions").' Gregory had been the Cassel Professor of Economics at LSE for a decade after 1927, and also one of Rasminsky's professors.

The Canadian's contributions must have made his old teacher proud, as Rasminsky added to the high level of discussion with his detailed technical questions and observations about weaknesses in the plan. The margins of his personal copy of the Clearing Union document circulated by the British was filled with his cramped writing, pointing up questions to be raised or issues not clear. For example, with an eye on the United States, he suggested a formula giving some protection to creditor countries against the possibility that debtor countries would effect an all-round increase in quotas at the expense of creditors, which adjustment would make the whole scheme more palatable to the United States. This creditor–debtor debate pitted the United States against Britain and was a theme of the talks for two years. Rasminsky believed Keynes's proposal to impose a charge of 1 per cent on excess credit balances to be questionable, in so far as it would affect the only true creditor country in the post-war period, the United States. In what could be described as the understatement of the conference, he pointed out to the meeting of 27 October: 'This might be a very difficult provision to explain to the United States Congress.'[17]

Rasminsky's input was welcomed by Keynes, and he spoke often, to the point of becoming self-conscious. Indeed, as Hume Wrong noted, Rasminsky 'did most of the talking for [us], and did it very well.'[18] For his part, as he confided on 2 November to his diary of the London conference, 'For first time took very little part in discussion as I had talked so much last week.'[19] This reticence, however, was too much; the following day his diary records 'Vow of silence over.'

The talks were very satisfactory, at least to the British and Canadians. Rasminsky made the observation to Towers that 'the most interesting aspect of this preliminary general discussion was not so much what was said as what was not said. No one attacked the principle of the Clearing Union and there seemed to be general agreement that the idea was sound and should be given a trial.'[20] As well, there was a consensus that bold measures were called for, even if they did not fit in with established modes of thought. Keynes told the Canadians that their contributions had been 'particularly helpful.' Further, both he and Eady took Rasminsky aside following the meetings and 'particularly thanked [him] ... Eady pressed [Rasminsky] to come back to England for another visit,'[21] while Keynes asked him to Cambridge to continue the discussion – an invitation he was unable to accept.

Still, despite Rasminsky's hopeful view, there was some powerful opposition to the idea – the Bank of England, for example, remained implacably opposed. The Clearing Union was 'impracticably ambitious,' according to George Kershaw, the man in charge of the British Empire Division of the Bank, while the governor, Montagu Norman, was 'cynical about [it], regarding it as a politician's device to get something for nothing: The transition from war to peace, he told Rasminsky, [could] only be achieved through work and sweat and pains.'[22] Moreover, the pound 'was not compatible with [the] scheme.' The Bank's unequivocal opposition to the scheme was generated in part, Rasminsky thought, 'by personal hostility to Keynes.'[23]

The meeting was not all work, however, and Rasminsky spent some time observing life in London, especially as the Canadian delegation, unable to catch a flight home, was forced to remain there for the better part of a month. Despite the war and the blackout, life in the British capital was exciting. At times, it was also surprising. The rationing system was not particularly solid, he felt; anyone 'with money can eat as they wish.'[24] Food was surprisingly available, with his lunch on 24 October 'as good a meal as you could get anywhere in Ottawa[!]: assorted hors d'oeuvres, herring, shrimp salad, vegetable salad and cole slaw, [as well as] many other things [like] calf's liver and choice of vegetables (carrots and spinach) and choice of desserts (stewed figs). The waiter kept pressing food on us – wouldn't I have some apple flan as well as the figs! Didn't I want sugar on my figs? It was disturbing.' Dinner was no better, from a moral point of view – 'soup, roast lamb with macaroni and cold string beans and lettuce, apple-sauce.' There was, he observed, 'very little sign of austerity in the West End of London.' Still, the British spirit, he felt, was marvellous; there was complete confidence in victory, which, many felt, would happen quite soon, at least 'within a year or so.' He told Lyla in a letter: 'The thrilling news ... is [Montgomery's] great victory in Egypt [at Alamein] which has sent the country's temperature up 10 degrees. Everyone here is very excited – I suppose it is the best war news we have had yet.'[25]

By mid-1942 the US Treasury, with White at the helm, had prepared a document that laid out its position. The draft was shown to Keynes in July, though many more versions followed. In a memorandum accompanying a December draft of the 'Stabilization Fund of the United and Associated Nations,' White pointed out that while it was 'still too soon to know the precise form and magnitude of postwar monetary problems,' it was a certainty that nations would have to address three – 'to prevent the disruption of foreign exchanges, to avoid the collapse of some monetary systems, and to facilitate the restoration and balanced growth of international trade.'[26] White went on that 'the task of assuring the defeat of the Axis powers would be made easier if the victims of aggression, actual and potential, could have greater assurance that a victory of the United Nations will not mean in the economic sphere a repetition of the exchange instability and monetary collapse that followed the last war.'

The proposal issued in December 1942 was intended as a basis for discussion. It suggested that: '1. The fund shall consist of gold, currencies of member countries, and securities of member governments, which shall be used for the purpose of stabilizing the values of the currencies of member countries with respect to each other. 2. Each of the member countries shall be given a quota which shall represent its participation in the Fund. 3. The quota for each member country shall be determined by an agreed upon formula.'[27] As well, the fund would 'fix the rates at which it will exchange one member's currency for another, and the rates in local currencies at which it will buy and sell gold.' As in the Clearing Union proposal, 'the guiding principle in the fixing of such rates shall be the stability in exchange relationships.' The monetary unit of the fund would be the 'unitas,' consisting of 137 1/7 grains of fine gold, the equivalent of US$10. On 1 February 1943, it was officially communicated to London.

Both proposals were now on the table. Keynes's differed from White's in two important respects. First, the US plan contemplated an international stabilization fund holding resources of gold, securities, and local currencies. Keynes provided for an international clearing union with power to create credit, based on the willingness of the United States and other countries to accumulate credit balances representing claims against countries with debit balances. It would always have gold, marketable securities, and local currencies to cover all claims. Second, the American proposal provided for directors chosen by member countries on the basis of their contribution to the fund, which would give the United States the most votes. The British document provided for a board chosen by member countries on the basis of their quotas. The United Kingdom, with the largest volume of foreign trade, would have the greatest number of votes and the largest quota of debit balance; the United States could not accept that.[28]

As well, the Americans contemplated a much smaller fund, with defined national contributions. The Clearing Union proposal, based on the 'overdraft' principle, assigned to each country a limit on the amount of assistance that it could get through the Union, but the limit on the assistance that creditor countries would be required to give was determined by the sum of the drawing power of all other participants and could run into *very* large numbers. (To White, that was a total non-starter, as was Keynes's idea that voting power was to be in proportion to the right to borrow. Indeed, in a memorandum to the secretary of the Treasury, he underlined the offending portion and marked it with exclamation marks. Incredulity would not be too strong a word with which to describe the American reaction.) Finally, any country accumulating an excessive debt or credit balance would be required to take steps to adjust its economy to restore equilibrium in its international payments – again a difficult proposition for the US government.

These attitudes were complicated by relationships among officials that had deteriorated during 1942, even though that between the British prime minister, Winston Churchill, and the American president, Franklin Roosevelt, remained more or less warm.[29] Postwar British colonial policy was a major reason, for London had made no real commitments to free subjugated peoples, contrary to the objectives of the Atlantic Charter. In February 1943, the Canadians and the British held high-level discussions in order to explore the state of the Anglo–American relationship, which had soured because the Americans believed: '– that the UK was ruled by a reactionary aristocracy; – that the Empire, and especially the colonies and India, were ruled in the interests of a reactionary UK; – that there exists in the United States a widespread antipathy to the United Kingdom; – that recently the relations between the US and the UK have become more than normally strained; – that the difficulties in the way of close cooperation between the Governments of the UK and the US are therefore particularly great.'[30]

This state of affairs could slow the progress of the war and block new initiatives being considered that required Anglo–American cooperation, such as the Clearing Union and the Stabilization Fund. For Canadians, how London and Washington related to each other was much more than merely passing interest. Their suggestion to their British colleagues that, as a general rule, the United States and the United Kingdom should discuss only large issues of public policy in multilateral discussions was heartfelt; bilateral discussions between the two nations could be, and usually were, disastrous. Deputy minister Clark felt that the two would *never* agree if left to themselves; 'if the United States and the United Kingdom [were] left alone in a room together, trouble emerge[d] ... not trouble for others but trouble for themselves.'[31] This was where Canadian interpretation and mediation, self-serving though it might be, could be invaluable. In the case of postwar financial arrangements, it took the form of Canada's own plan, entitled 'Tentative Draft Proposals of Canadian Experts for and International Exchange Union,' which Rasminsky wrote.

For the present, however, the Canadians were concerned about the US Treasury proposals. They had some fifty questions for the Americans, most of which Rasminsky had prepared. Was the $5 billion suggested for the fund the appropriate size? (No – there was more danger in a fund that was too small than in one that was too large.) How precisely were quotas to be determined? What was the nature of the 'special reserve' referred to? Was two years not too short a period of office for the managing director? (Yes.) As all important decisions required a four-fifths majority and the United States would have 25 per cent of the voting strength, was this not disproportionate to Washington's contribution?[32] In short, the Canadians were concerned that a fund such as that contemplated by the United States would become a thoroughly American-dominated operation, which would exclude the input of smaller powers. Canada was not Costa Rica, as a Canadian paper pointed out, yet both countries would receive about the same clout in the new organization.

The issue of influence was too important to be left to the Americans and the British, or so it was felt in Ottawa. The Canadians, quarterbacked by Rasminsky, began to plot their own game strategy in anticipation of travelling to Washington to discuss White's plan. Their planning centred on combining some of the features of the two plans, basically changing certain aspects of the Keynes document to meet the views of the Americans. Rasminsky, encouraged by Clark, Robertson, Towers and Wrong, had been working on a paper of his own for some time. In those heady days in Ottawa, the idea that Canada was something more than a small dominion located on the northern slope of the planet was being felt in various departments. Officials such as Norman Robertson and Clifford Clark saw a country that was maturing into 'middle power' status – one that had a contribution to make to global affairs. While they sometimes ran afoul of Ottawa's political leadership – especially Prime Minister King, who was 'timid' about the prospects of 'mixing it up with the big boys' – the opportunity was too good to pass up.[33] Officials must, of course, bow to prime ministerial wishes, and the title of Rasminsky's plan, 'Draft Proposals of Canadian Experts for an International Exchange Union,' was suggestive of King's anxiety. The document was a reflection of his own confidence and that of some politicians, such as Minister of Justice Louis St Laurent.

By 24 March 1943, Rasminsky had distributed copies to members of the subcommittee of the economic advisory committee, which comprised a group of key economic officials, R.B. Bryce and W.A. Mackintosh of Finance, John Deutsch and Norman Robertson of External Affairs, and others. The essential revisions entailed placing a limit on the obligation to accumulate international currency – namely, the quota of each country – while also providing for a gold contribution by each member. Where the total size of the American fund was $5 billion, the Canadians wanted a $10-billion fund and a plan that would: 'i) stabilize exchange rates; ii) provide a convenient clearing mechanism to settle balances in international payments; iii) provide initial credits in foreign exchange to all countries in order to reduce the danger that economic and commercial policies in the period immediately after the war shall be largely determined by a deficiency of foreign exchange, and; iv) contribute to the re-establishment and development of a multilateral trading system and to restrain and reduce bilateralist trade and currency practices.'[34]

Perhaps as an indication of Rasminsky's importance in the process and his wide grasp of the technical issues involved, discussion of a Canadian plan took place at the Bank of Canada headquarters. The plan itself would be introduced in June 1943 at a meeting in Washington of a number of wartime allies.

In late April 1943, Rasminsky, Deutsch, Mackintosh, and A.F.W. Plumptre, the financial attaché at the Canadian legation in Washington, were in that city for talks with the Americans. It was significant that the United States chose to conduct its first official meetings on the subject with Canadian experts. The talks lasted five days and ranged over a variety of topics, on many occasions resembling a dialogue between Rasminsky, on the one hand, and Harry White and his aide Edward Bernstein, on the other hand.

On the question of the size of the fund, Bernstein felt that $5 billion accurately reflected postwar needs; as he noted, 'an examination of needs ... for the period 1936–38 indicate[d] that this sum would be adequate.' The American based his assessment on the fact that world net deficits on current account in 1936–8 amounted to about $2.5 billion. Rasminsky quickly retorted: 'One of the objects of the fund should be to avoid what happened during 1936–38.'[35] At any rate, Bernstein concluded, the fund's capacity was not limited to $5 billion; it could sell its own obligations, and it would have the power to borrow. Rasminsky remained unconvinced, especially when it seemed that political considerations weighed more heavily in the calculation than did economics. Clearly, the United States wanted to remain 'in control' of the fund; it was important for that nation that its quota not be made relatively smaller by others. And since a $2-billion contribution was thought to be the limit to which Congress would go, no more than a $5-billion total was to be permitted.

In other words, the size of the fund would bear a relationship not to the tasks at hand, but rather to American political realities. White in effect admitted as much: 'Some of us would have preferred a larger fund with a larger United States contribution. But attention must be paid to public opinion on the matter and its influence on Congress ... In order to ensure Congressional approval it is better not to try to put the United States contribution too high at the beginning.' The Canadians also grilled White on his easy assumption that the fund could borrow if need be. 'Would the country making a loan to the fund have some power of supervision over the country using the scarce currency thus provided?' The answer was that the *fund* would control the disbursement of money. And who would control the fund? These were political questions that did not yield readily to bureaucratic examination.[36]

Throughout the rest of the week, Rasminsky and the other Canadians continued to pound away at the US position. On the issue raised in article III(6) of the American document – that is, the fund's buying scarce currencies with gold – Rasminsky asked whether its gold reserves could satisfy this requirement. White promised to revise this article. The Canadians also raised a detailed technical question about contributing securities as part of the national involvement. Rasminsky told the Americans that it was one thing for a country to put up resources to finance its own needs and another if that country's resources could be used to acquire scarce currency in order to finance some other country's trade. He went on, 'There are relatively few countries whose securities are saleable in international markets. Canada is one of them. Hence Canada's securities are ones that are likely to be sold by the fund. If it should happen later that Canadian currency became scarce these securities would no longer be available for the acquisition of more Canadian currency. In order to maintain her exports, Canada would then have to be prepared to lend to the fund or to buy from the fund some less desirable obligation of another country.'[37]

The assistant secretary noted: 'You have given us something to think about ... In any case, III(6) will have to be re-written.'[38] Bernstein promised to rewrite article III(1), given Canadian concerns. Rasminsky's suggestion that the fund use exchange rates that existed one year earlier was also considered by the Americans. Later, rates as of 1 July 1943 were chosen. However, the United States was adamant in certain areas; it wished to retain a veto over a change in the value of gold – one of the main British objections.[39] The United States was not prepared to negotiate on this point.

And so it went. Unquestionably, the Canadians had some impact on US thinking, which the American secretary of the treasury acknowledged in a letter to Minister of Finance James Ilsley. He 'particularly wish[ed] to express [his] appreciation for the contributions to the discussions made by the technical experts that you sent to Washington. The many conversations they held with the experts of the United States were extremely helpful to us and, we hope, to them. As you will note we have embodied in the revised [Stabilization Fund] draft a large number of their suggestions.'[40] Clark sent a copy of the letter to Rasminsky.

The British had followed the North American meetings closely, and their embassy sent home a dispatch soon after the Canadians had departed. The telegram noted with some satisfaction that 'Canadian views on most points in line with ours.'[41] There was also a note that Clark had talked with the British ambassador 'as to what future procedure [the Canadians] should follow.' More discussions with the Americans were certain, but Clark recognized the perils of proceeding with White and company 'simply on the basis of their suggesting detailed amendments to S.F. and is considering if it would not be better to produce a Canadian draft embodying their views and not necessarily following S.F. or C.U. ... I am inclined to encourage him on this but would be glad to know at once if you disagree.'

Merely discussing the two plans point by point would lead only to long, fruitless, and barren arguments, which Clark thought would harden American views. Already, there were signs that most South American nations were adopting the US document as it stood, while smaller European allies such as Belgium and the Netherlands were also prepared to accept it, except for the US veto. The Canadians hoped to secure some 'substantial concessions' from the Americans as a result of the series of compromise proposals, which were, a British telegram noted, 'coherent and can be considered as a whole.' They were convinced 'that any such compromise plan will have to be based on the American scheme in form, embodying as many of the United Kingdom proposals as we can hope, by this means, to get the Americans to agree to.'[42]

The reply from London was fast; the Treasury believed the idea of a Canadian plan to be a good one, but only if put into effect 'at a later stage.'[43] This was precisely what Keynes had had in mind when, in his maiden speech in the House of Lords, he had called for new ideas and plans to be brought forward.[44] As the telegram pointed out, Keynes had wanted to produce a version of the stabilization fund that would be more satisfactory to the British, since the United States had refused to negotiate on the basis of the Clearing Union. In so far as his ideas commended themselves to the Canadians, 'it may well be better that new draft should be put forward by them rather than by us.' If London could work through Ottawa, so much the better; it would certainly circumvent US congressional hostility to all things British. It was, however, best for the two nations to stay in contact because 'it would be embarrassing if the

Canadian plan were to put forward a draft in which we did not agree, or if we were to put forward a fresh draft in which [they] did not agree. We should like therefore to collaborate closely with them and at this stage we feel that a certain delay may be useful rather than the reverse.' More probably, the British were concerned, and they admitted as much, that the 'finality and finished quality (flattery) of [a Canadian document] may prevent adequate discussion on their points.'[45] They also wanted to be satisfied about the US attitude to the Clearing Union before they abandoned their position and began operating on the basis that some form of the Stabilization Fund would ultimately be chosen.

Certainly the British had an overblown sense of their influence in Ottawa; Rasminsky had already written his own plan, which, with the prodding of Clark and Towers, was by then being considered by other officials. From Ottawa's perspective, it seemed important to synthesize the two plans so as to avoid being forced to take sides in any discussions, and a Canadian contribution could 'concentrate attention on the problems rather than the rival positions of the plans.'[46] As well, the entire financial initiative that had been launched by the Americans and the British was also in the Canadian interest. As matters then stood, since 'Canada [had] an almost embarrassingly high position in banking and financial circles in the United States and [was] not without reputation in Congress,' and the US Treasury did not command 'a great deal of support either in the country or in Congress,' then a 'Canadian plan would probably attract more support in the US than a Treasury plan.' It was not inconceivable that it would provide a much-needed push to the whole program.

On 3 June 1943, Rasminsky wrote Keynes a lengthy letter explaining the Canadian approach, which was based on the idea of a fund rather than the Clearing Union's banking principle, even though the latter was 'much neater and more beautiful.'[47] The Americans would never accept the overdraft idea on which the Keynes plan was based; in the United States, 'an overdraft was something akin to a crime.' Indeed, in the United States, customers' overdrafts were illegal in domestic banks. To make any plan acceptable to the US public, it was necessary to make it a common project, in which every country contributed to the fund and paid for the foreign exchange that it received. The Canadian plan increased the fund's resources from $5 billion to $12 billion, $8 billion of which was to be paid at once and $4 billion as required by way of mandatory loans.

As well, Rasminsky included an article that allowed the fund to borrow from members (which anticipated the General Arrangements to Borrow of the early 1960s). He knew that there would be a limit on the amount that the Americans would contribute. Also, it was possible that the United States would not behave like a good creditor – it might not create the conditions necessary for countries to balance their accounts so that they would not have to borrow extortionate amounts from Washington. The Americans had accepted that as a possibility by their insertion of a scarce-currency clause – if a currency were declared scarce, that declaration would absolve other countries of the need to avoid restrictions against that country. He told Keynes: 'In general I think it would be accurate to say that while we have adopted the American form our purposes have been to propose an institution with adequate resources to modify the rigidities of the American plan, to achieve a truly multilateral monetary organization and to make the operative sections workable.'

Rasminsky followed the American model in terms of capital subscription. However, he was not committed to that specific form and was prepared to rewrite his proposals in terms of the banking principle if that would contribute to the general agreement. As he later said, 'We do not care whether this new wine of international monetary collaboration is put into an old bottle called Stabilisation Fund or into a new bottle called Banking Principle. What we are mainly interested in is the wine itself: and in making sure that there is enough of it.'[48] He remarked: 'Our view is that the Fund to be established should be large enough to give all countries a real breathing-space after the war; large enough to give them time to go about their tasks of reconstruction and industrial re-equipment without having to consider wholesale import restrictions, export subsidies and similar measures in order to make both ends meet on international account.' As events would turn out, that was a forlorn hope, as the United States consistently opposed use of the Fund's resources for those purposes.

As well, the Canadians proposed an alternative to the American veto. The veto was so undemocratic that Rasminsky could not imagine that a group of countries could hold together long if such power were exercised in opposition to countries holding about 80 per cent of the voting strength. Finally, the Canadians had thrown their 'own' currency into the ring in competition with bancor and unitas – the monad, to which proposal Rasminsky appended the comment that all he could say in its favour was that it was no worse than the other two.

The United Kingdom soon pulled out all the stops in an attempt to convince the Canadians to publish their ideas *later* in the year. Transatlantic telegrams flew fast and furious. Both the British high commissioner in Ottawa and the United Kingdom's ambassador in Washington were given the task of squelching the Canadian plan. Clark's response was succinct 'he gave it as his considered opinion that our common objective, viz. ultimate acceptance by the Americans of a plan satisfactory in substance, is much more likely to be furthered if the Canadian plan is manifestly *not* the result of consultation with [the British].'[49] The deputy minister also expressed the opinion that early publication of the Canadian plan would help to break down the 'anti-everything attitude of New York bankers,' whom he described as being impressed with Canada's financial strength and competence 'and consequently likely to pay heed to Canadian view.'[50]

The high commissioner was instructed to pass along to the Canadians the message that there was 'no possibility of UK Government regarding [the Canadian plan] as acceptable.'[51] Its position remained that Canadian officials should make their points in the course of discussion and not produce a draft, since it would deflect attention from the Clearing Union. In conversation with Clark, he said that his government had been hoping that, at the right time, 'Canada might be able to play a decisive part in taking the initiative to bring about a synthesis between the two sets of proposals,' but June 1943, in its opinion, was not the right time.

Despite British objections, the Canadian plan was introduced at the meetings in Washington in June, 1943, to which the three original players and sixteen other countries sent delegations. White asked Rasminsky to make Canada's opening statement, but he declined in favour of Clark and Towers. The discussion that followed was 'diffuse and rambling and many [took] part.'[52] At the end of a very long afternoon, White asked Rasminsky to summarize the points made – a request greeted by the assembled delegations with 'hearty laughter all around.' Rasminsky then

> proceeded to make an analytical summary of the discussion which lasted for 15–20 minutes and which terminated in a spontaneous outburst of applause which lasted another 2. The meeting was then adjourned and hardly a person in the room didn't come up and say something nice. Clark was most enthusiastic. White said if he could do that sort of thing he would be well satisfied with himself. Pasvolsky patted me on the back. Robbins said a wonderful tour de force. And so on. Even the G[overnor], who is not wont, said that it was a very fine statement and pointed out that Morgenthau and I were the only ones who got any applause ... Even [the Canadian minister in Wash-

ington, Leighton] McCarthy had been hearing about me from all sides and especially from Sir Frederick Phillips, who was most enthusiastic.

While unofficially the British were 'kind about [the document],' officially they opposed Rasminsky's proposal, at least in terms of timing.[53] Keynes later told Mackintosh that even though he was distressed by its timing, the 'Canadian plan should ultimately be the plan accepted.'[54] When the Canadian scheme was published, he later wrote, 'I felt very doubtful ... whether the date for a new version had been rightly chosen. While in many respects, your draft was an improvement on the Stabilization Fund and more logical in clearing up doubtful matters, it did not, so far as we were concerned, go far enough in certain directions to form any certain basis for compromise. Indeed, it seemed to me that discussion had to go a little further before it was advisable to put any alternative down on paper in black and white.'[55] There was also the thought, shared by many in the British delegation, that the United States might feel that the Canadian draft represented what Britain would be willing to concede and would refuse to be persuaded that it did not. Obviously, the Canadians were not bound by any Whitehall program, and this easy assumption that the United Kingdom should dictate the course and pace of events rankled. In fact, Canadians had a much better grasp of the US political realities involved, while their technical experts, such as Rasminsky with his detailed understanding of economics, were more than the equal of the British.

Still, the British delegation could note with satisfaction that the Canadian plan distributed at the June meetings in Washington 'was produced but was not much discussed.'[56] Nor was it to be a factor in the future. For all intents and purposes, it died there, but not because it was not good enough; it was. It was simply a victim of superpower politics. However, the Canadian draft did 'help a bit between the Americans and the British, which remain[ed] a very difficult situation.'[57] And there was still hope, or so it seemed to Rasminsky, because the British had been well behaved and their delegation did 'not seem to share some of the [more extreme] views of [Whitehall] people.'

For Rasminsky, the discussions were significant for one other reason; while in Washington, he and Towers discussed his appointment to the Bank of Canada staff. On Wednesday afternoon, 16 June, the governor came to his hotel room, to hear Rasminsky make his case: '1) The maintenance of the connection with the League was pretty unrealistic; 2) [he] would like to join the B of C staff and; 3) [he] would like to work with him.'[58] There was never really any doubt, and a permanent job was his with a new title – executive assistant to the governor. So in summer 1943 he began a career with the Bank that was to span almost thirty years.

Following the June meetings (where a revised version of the Stabilization Fund had been presented on short notice), a new draft was published on 10 July and circulated to interested parties. This document reflected four items that the Americans believed essential if the plan were to have any chance of success: '1. The fund should be contributory; 2. Voting power should be in some rough way apportioned to contributions; 3. The liability of the participants should be limited, and not more than $2,000,000,000 to $3,000,000,000 should be expected from the U.S.A. as an initial contribution, and; 4. Agreement should be reached on initial exchange rates between the important countries.'[59]

For the better part of a year, from July 1943 to June 1944, the drafting continued, with more revisions coming primarily from the United States and the United Kingdom, with Canadian opinions sometimes thrown in for good measure. Given his role in the process, Rasminsky was invited to various conferences and meetings discussing the program and the institution. For example, in mid-August, the host Federal Reserve Board (FRB) of Chicago invited him to an international symposium on monetary stabilization sponsored by the FRBs of Chicago, Cleveland, Kansas City, Minneapolis, and St Louis. Of the approximately 180 participants, Rasminsky was one of two Canadians (Towers was the other) and was invited to the exclusive, fourteen-person breakfast hosted by Simeon Leland, chair of the board of the Chicago branch of the federal reserve system.

Anglo–American negotiations continued in an increasingly acrimonious atmosphere, with both sides needing the intervention of mediators. At one point, Rasminsky told Towers, he believed that things were so bad between the two 'that the British [were] psychologically prepared for a breakdown of the discussions ... [The Bank of England's L.C.] Thompson-McCausland spoke of the development of anti-American opinion in the United Kingdom as a reason why the British could not go too far in meeting American views.'[60] For his part, White talked to Rasminsky of his 'political difficulties' with Congress and how Keynes, who was 'very clever,' suddenly became 'very dense' at certain points in the discussions, claiming that he could not see how such and such could work.

Rasminsky was frequently a go-between, as both parties kept him informed. Keynes, for example, gave him a copy of British suggestions for the monetization of unitas, a very contentious point and not communicated to any other dominion, to the United States, or even to some other senior British officials. He was 'extremely anxious that [Rasminsky] should not communicate any views we might hold on [this question] to London or anyone else.'[61] Keynes valued Rasminsky's opinion and asked him if there were 'any prospect of your being able to pay a visit [to Washington where Keynes was visiting] in the course of the next week or two. I should greatly welcome a chance of keeping you in touch with the progress of our talks and ideas, and so I know would others in our party.'

The British and Americans met in Washington during September and October 1943, and by the latter month, progress seemed almost nonexistent to an outsider such as Rasminsky. At times, it appeared as if White and Keynes disagreed with each other just for the sake of disagreeing. Thompson-McCausland wrote to C.F. (later Lord) Cobbold – then a member of the Bank of England's Court and, from August 1945, its deputy governor – about the course of events: 'On Wednesday, Harry White spent much of the afternoon shouting' at Keynes and was 'inherently suspicious of [British] motives.'[62] Meanwhile Keynes had conceived a deep dislike for White and Bernstein 'and [showed] a growing determination not to let them get away with anything.' Where all this would lead was anyone's guess, especially as the American Bankers' Association (ABA) and the Department of State were more and more opposed to White's views, with State 'dislik[ing] him personally.'[63]

Thompson-McCausland believed that White would not break off the talks because he had 'the name of being vain, and will, I think, do a great deal to avoid the humiliation of a breakdown; the thought of Wall Street's glee would be very painful.' The ABA's opposition stemmed in part from the fact that there was no real banker involved in the negotiations, at least on the US side. (At Bretton Woods in July 1944, there was one banker on the American delegation.) From the September–October meetings, Thompson-McCausland wrote Cobbold: 'I have few enough claims, heaven knows, to express the banker's point of view but, believe it or not, I am the only one on either side who has worked in a bank – unless the F.R.B. people are included.'

When Roy Harrod in his Life of John Maynard Keynes writes that 'Harry White himself became mellow' under the influence of Keynes's sarcasm and wit, he is surely mistaken.[64] Indeed, the apparent lack of progress had more to do with the Keynes–White pyrotechnics than with lack of progress on substantive issues. At the end of the meeting on 16 October,

James Meade, of the British delegation, could write in his diary that 'one got the sense of a tremendous achievement which – touch wood – may really prove the first step towards important economic cooperation. The monetary discussions, (seriously marred, I fear, by Keynes' ill-manners) have greatly narrowed our differences.'[65]

The clash of personalities – or so some in the British delegation believed – led Keynes to put forward views with which others in the group did not agree and which they could not support. Indeed, the situation became so bad that Thompson-McCausland was given the job of telling Keynes to modify his approach. His opposition was 'bringing out the native timidity of the Morgenthau-White-Bernstein blood,' or so the British thought, which had the effect of making the Americans more obstinate. It looked as if Rasminsky's worried observation to Towers – that the British were prepared for a breakdown – might come true, especially after Keynes led off the final meeting 'with his most disarming smile.' London, he declared, did not consider the Stabilization Fund language 'to be a "decent Christian's mode of expression."' That was not, some in the British delegation thought, 'the happiest phrase in that company' – White and Bernstein were Jewish. The British economist ended his opening remarks 'by declaring with warmth and inadvertence that a counter-draft which the Americans had laid on the table was "simply the Talmud all over again."' The Talmud – the Jewish holy book – was Keynes's name for the Stabilization Fund draft of 10 July, in which White had made it clear that he did not contemplate further revisions.

Keynes and White argued over such things as the rigidity of exchange rates, with the former wanting some flexibility while the latter did not. As the American told Keynes, 'A degree of flexibility [would] vitiate the objective of the proposal. The difficulty in using objective criteria is that of measurement. Too great dependence on objective criteria might prevent the proper functioning of the consultation and approval provisions on exchange rates.' He maintained that 'changes in exchange rates must be dependent upon the judgement of the Fund.'[66] That was slight comfort to Keynes. Nor did White's attitudes about further discussion endear themselves to the British. The Americans refused to concede the British point that exchange devaluations often occurred in response to crisis conditions. The US refrain remained that the Fund would be responsive. There was also discussion over the size of the Fund; over the adverse feeling prevailing in London about giving up British gold to the Fund, with Keynes stating flatly that the gold contributions required of various countries would have to be scaled down; and over the British desire for a real international currency, not merely one for purposes of accounting – a position that White rejected.

Given such disagreements, Keynes invited Rasminsky down to Washington again to apprise him of his sense of where things were going, as well as to ask that he 'keep in touch' – which Rasminsky would gladly do, as he was 'anxious above all for Washington and London to agree.' At the conclusion of that round of Anglo–American discussions on 21 October, Liesching, Meade, and Thompson-McCausland returned to England via Canada 'to whisper results in the Canadians' ears' despite the Anglo–American agreement not to enter into discussions with other governments until they had agreed on the outstanding points themselves.[67] The British spent a good deal of time with Rasminsky.

But agreeing took time. At the end of November, the British treasury received another draft of the Stabilization Fund proposal; in December, London came up with its own draft, and in January 1944, a series of telegrams went out to the dominions informing them of progress. The Canadians circulated their own documents internally, drawing comparisons among the three plans. Rasminsky was particularly busy, writing numerous memoranda on the Stabilization Fund and on the development of another institution that had been proposed by White – the United Nations Bank for Reconstruction and Development, which was also to see light at Bretton Woods. The work, while satisfying, was difficult, the hours were long, and Rasminsky must have wondered if it would ever end. The Ottawa spring, however, brought him and his wife joy, with the birth of a daughter, Lola Rosamond, on 28 March.

By April 1944, the area of disagreement among experts had been narrowed so as to make possible publication in London, Moscow, Ottawa, and Washington of the 'Joint Statement by Experts on the Establishment of an International Monetary Fund.'[68] This document became the main working paper at Bretton Woods with respect to the IMF. Seventeen countries including Canada (the so-called agenda committee, though it did much more than that) gathered in Atlantic City, New Jersey, from 24 to 30 June 1944, just weeks after the Allied landings in Normandy, for preliminary conversations to smooth out bumps. The main conference, with forty-four delegations present, would convene in early July at Bretton Woods; this large resort, at a tiny whistle-stop in the White Mountains of New Hampshire, was far removed from the madding crowd, and also President Roosevelt's personal choice for the conference venue.[69]

In Atlantic City, US Treasury representatives were in a sour mood, even before the British appeared. As a general reflection of that situation, 'Treasury technicians were exceedingly defensive about [their] positions ... and were more interested in criticizing proposals from other delegations than in examining them for merit.'[70] As well, the Americans were suggesting one or two changes in the substance of matters vital to the British that had been agreed on only a few months earlier, after they had agreed not to propose any except by mutual consent, which was not possible, since the British delegation was still in mid-ocean. When the Americans had tried to bulldoze their way through, Rasminsky, who had become the unofficial adviser to both sides, as well as 'the Allied [dominions and India] spokesman,' had successfully resisted, persuading them 'not to put into general circulation the drafts of the changes they wanted before they discussed it with the British.'[71]

The British delegation arrived in Atlantic City on 23 June – a happy circumstance for Rasminsky – and it 'raised the intellectual level here very markedly. From the point of view of brainpower, [it] runs rings around everyone else ... It is just as well, since [the British] position is such that they must live on their wits for some time to come.'[72] Despite his admiration for its collective intelligence, however, Rasminsky discovered that it too had done a few ill-considered things – among them, drafting a number of changes to the 'Joint Statement,' which, if presented to the Americans, would surely antagonize them.[73] As a result, Rasminsky had to 'do exactly the same job on them as [he had done] on the Americans.' For example, the British delegation had been instructed to press for changes to the the exchange clauses of the Fund, agreement to which had only been reached some months earlier, through difficult negotiation.

As Lionel Robbins recorded in his diary for 23 June 1944: 'It was only on board ship [crossing to the United States] that I became fully aware of the fact that we had been instructed to press for still further modification of the exchange clauses of the Fund agreement ... I regret this very much.'[74] The following day, Keynes, in a meeting with Australia, Canada, and India, 'explained the work done on the boat, and the nature of the changes we intended to propose in regard to the Fund.' He was not surprised, Robbins wrote,

> when Rasminsky, who is leading for Canada, kicked off by saying that if we wanted to make the position of the Americans as difficult as possible we could not have chosen a better method than to put up the modification we have in mind for the exchange clause. We had already wrung from them last autumn such extensive concessions in this respect that they had been under

continuous public criticism ever since. In his view, it was quite hopeless to expect them to accept. This, of course, harmonises completely with what Dennis [Robertson] and I have said all along; but it was obviously something of a shock to the others. Rasminsky is so competent and so obviously distinterested that it would be difficult not to take him seriously.[75]

The British did listen to him seriously, but at times there was little that he could do to dissuade them from pursuing a course that conflicted with instructions issued by the British cabinet. Still, Rasminsky had an impact on the conference. As a member of the Brazilian delegation later noted, he was a good Anglo–American mediator: 'He could talk back to Keynes ... He was bold enough to discuss with him and contradict him, and had a much better view of the American position. Being a Canadian, linked sentimentally, emotionally and politically to the United Kingdom, but economically to the United States, he was in a wonderful position to be an interpreter.'[76] But he was much more than a mere mediator; he had credibility among the participants because of his obvious technical skills and impartial and objective approach.

In Atlantic City much hard work was put in. Even given all the previous work on the 'Joint Statement,' some seventy amendments were proposed. Despite Rasminsky's intervention, Keynes remained 'hot afoot' on some US phrasing: while the British emphasized exchange elasticity, the Americans pushed exchange stability; while the British stressed the rights of individual countries as against the Fund, the Americans emphasized the powers of the Fund as against individual countries; when Britain wanted the transitional period to be of uncertain (but longer) duration, the United States wanted the opposite.[77]

Discussions got quite heated on a number of occasions, as the minutes of a meeting in White's office with Keynes and the British demonstrate. Rasminsky's earlier hopes for success were dimmed, and some days the climate in the meetings reflected that outside the conference rooms in Atlantic City, 'pouring with rain and rather gloomy.'[78] He was not at all certain of final success – a thought echoed by Robbins in his diary.[79]

After the end of the Atlantic City sessions on 30 June, the delegations reconvened at Bretton Woods in early July. The Canadians went over the instructions issued by their cabinet. First, they were to oppose any flagrant manipulation of quotas for political reasons. They were not to support any upward adjustment of quotas on the basis of special pleading, and they were to use their influence to prevent an undignified scramble for quotas, to ensure that if the size of the Fund were increased, so must be the country's quota, and to make sure that the voting strength of the Commonwealth was not to be regarded as a unit.[80] The Canadians were to keep in mind Rasminsky's admonition that, in the matter of the appropriate quota size, member countries' contibutions to the Fund 'should not be regarded as something they are giving away but as a means for establishing a functioning world economy which is in the interests of every country.'[81]

The delegation was instructed to do what it could to get firm language regarding alteration of exchange rates and to oppose there being more than three permanent seats on the Fund, 'unless this system provides enough permanent seats to include Canada.' As well, it was to resist the US suggestion that members of the executive committee should be continuously available at Fund headquarters. That fight was lost, though Canada did achieve a minor victory, allowing for part-time directors.

The confusion at Bretton Woods, as George Bolton phrased it, was 'becoming so great that one has the feeling that we are living in a mad house.'[82] The American technical experts were now increasingly frustrated by the demands of the two US senators and eight US representatives, both Democrat and Republican, on the US delegation – politicians who, according to Bolton, sat on the heads of officials; Rasminsky, however, thought this idea of bipartisan political representation 'very clever.'[83] Bolton was also irritated with the Europeans, who were, he thought, not making much of an impression on anyone and, when they did, inevitably 'ranged themselves substantially behind State' and not the British. The battle over quotas and seats on the executive directorate was ferocious, while the Americans, at least according to the British delegation, were under instructions 'to preserve the maximum position for the South Americans,' in line with their good-neighbour policy. As well, the Soviet Union questioned its quota, which had been pegged, on the strength of its economy, at $800 million. It wanted $1.2 billion, which was eventually awarded.

The Canadian delegation was, in Rasminsky's words, 'playing quite a role here.'[84] Members were on the steering committee and on the agenda committee of the Bank commission, and Rasminsky was the reporter of the Fund commission, of which Harry White was chair and Keynes a member, as well as chair of the all-important drafting committee, consisting of the 'Big Five,' Mexico, and Canada, while Mackintosh had been appointed chair of the committee dealing with Fund operations. For Rasminsky, the drafting committee was of particular significance. It went over the language submitted, translating even garbled prose into readable English. Eventually, given the speed with which Keynes and White drove their charges, the committee was given the authority to draft the IMF document.

And the documentation relating to Bretton Woods was enormous. Drafts and redrafts, then more work, were sandwiched into a very short period of time in the summer of 1944. Ironically, speed was necessary because the Mount Washington Hotel where the delegates convened was booked in late July by the sworn enemy of the Fund initiative – the American Bankers' Association, for its annual convention. Even though things were 'in a pretty disorganized state,' Rasminsky wrote, 'on the whole, good progress [was] being made'; he had no doubt that 'agreement [will] be reached on the Fund.'[85]

His star was definitely in the ascendant at Bretton Woods, based on his work at previous conferences; on his tremendous intellect and skills; on the Canadian plan that he had submitted the previous year, which had demonstrated a wide command of the issues involved; and on his article 'International Credit and Currency Plans,' which had appeared in the July 1944 issue of the prestigious US periodical, *Foreign Affairs*. In terms of instant impact and notoriety, the last was very important. There, he had 'come out swinging' in favour of the Fund. His piece was a response to one written by John Williams, then an adviser to the Federal Reserve Bank of New York.

Foreign Affairs had published Williams's paper on the 'key currency' proposal, which was, Rasminsky said, 'a sort of rear-guard action by the Americans to maintain the supremacy of the US and the British on international monetary organizations' and that had the tacit approval of the chairman of the federal reserve system.[86] Rasminsky wrote: 'The proposal then under discussion at Bretton Woods was one contribution to ... reconstructing a functioning international economic system; and its potential usefulness is clearly conditional upon parallel action on cognate problems such as commercial policy and international long-range investment. In turn, tolerable international economic arrangements will not endure, and competitive currency depreciation, excessive trade restrictions, barter trade deals, rigid and stultifying exchange controls will not be avoided, unless the great industrial nations are successful in maintaining a high and reasonably stable level of domestic economic activity.'[87] Rasminsky wrote home that 'a great many people [had] complimented [him] on [his] Foreign Affairs article which seemed already to have been quite widely read.'[88] White had asked him for one hundred copies to distribute, while Keynes 'spoke of it in the highest terms.'

What had these final negotiations in the mountains of New Hampshire produced? Bretton Woods proposed a par-value system, which would provide for a system where currency stability would become the norm – currencies would be pegged against the US dollar, which in turn was convertible into gold at the rate of US$35 per ounce. The competitive devaluations of the 1930s might become just a faint memory, known better to historians than to economists.

In the judgment of many of the participants, part of the credit for what was accomplished at the conference could be laid at Rasminsky's feet and those of the other Canadians attending. As Keynes told the Ottawa *Citizen* during a post-conference trip to the Canadian capital, 'Canada played a very distinguished and dignified part all through Bretton Woods ... Your Mr. Rasminsky rendered most trojan service as chairman of the most important technical committee at the conference and his tremendous assistance in that connnection brought results which satisfied all concerned.'[89] As chair of the drafting committee, Rasminsky had *the* big role and was in charge of the language used.[90]

Edward Bernstein later said: 'At Bretton Woods, Rasminsky's major role was making sure that any continuing arguments between the United States and the United Kingdom didn't stop [the conference] from getting the International Monetary Fund [IMF] created.'[91] Aron Broches, then a member of the Netherlands delegation, said of Rasminsky that he was 'brilliant.'[92] Similarly, Burke Knapp of the US Federal Reserve Board and a member of the US delegation, noted that Rasminsky should have been named the IMF's first managing director, so great was his impact in 1944.[93] He was, according to Knapp, 'extremely highly qualified to head the Fund.' However, in the global postwar division of power, it was 'policy' that the Americans receive the presidency of the International Bank for Reconstruction and Development (IBRD), while a European was awarded the managing director's job.[94]

But there was a pay-off of sorts for Canada; because of the quality of its delegates, the country was 'listened to with great attention, not only by the big powers but also by the smaller countries, including the Europeans and Latinos.'[95] Rasminsky's old friend Rifat Tirana, now at the US State Department, also wrote to tell him of the 'paeans of praise on the work that you did at Bretton Woods' then making the rounds in his department.[96] The verdict among those who knew him and those who did not was that for all intents and purposes he was 'the cornerstone of the whole edifice.' And praise for Rasminsky came also from Louis St Laurent, in the privacy of the cabinet room, and from Clifford Clark, a tremendous supporter. Two years of international effort had led to a blue-print for the world's postwar monetary arrangements. But the Bretton Woods agreement would come into effect only if nations subscribing at least 65 per cent of the funds for the IMF and the IBRD approved it by the end of the next year. The events of 1945 would be momentous: Franklin Roosevelt's death, war's end in Europe, the founding of the United Nations, Labour's defeat of Churchill's Conservatives, and the dropping of the atomic bombs on Hiroshima and Nagasaki.

Louis Rasminsky led the ratification effort in Ottawa. In his defence of Bretton Woods to the House's Standing Committee on Banking and Commerce, he captivated Parliament with his explanation of the agreement. As was pointed out, 'For three days and three nights the hearings of a Commons committee went on, partly as a result of a Social Credit filibuster. Word went out that Rasminsky was turning to fascination a subject that had every possibility of being utterly boring to the uninitiated. Steadily the audience grew and seats in the House came to be at a premium.'[97] Several Social Credit members had become rather personal in their remarks about so-called experts in general, and about Rasminsky in particular. One, for example, Norman Jacques, the member of Parliament for Westaskiwin, told the House of Commons that Bretton Woods was nothing more than 'a deep laid plot ... to control the world politically, industrially and financially ... The world is being blackmailed by Shylock and Marx.'[98] Shylock was, of course, Shakespeare's Jewish villain in *The Merchant of Venice*. Jacques, who had earlier identified Rasminsky in the worst terms that he could muster – as a socialist-trained Jew from the London School of Economics – also had Rasminsky in mind here; 'I mean by Shylock the moneyed interests, high finance [and expecially so-called experts].'

Similarly, Victor Quelch, the member for the riding of Acadia and a leader of the anti–Bretton Woods faction in the House, had denounced the 'experts' for what he considered to be flawed advice. However, following Rasminsky's three-day presentation, Quelch apologized for intemperate remarks he had made about and to the official. He went on record as wishing 'to pay tribute to Mr. Rasminsky. I say that in view of the fact that in the House of Commons I was quite critical of certain experts. I want to make it quite plain that in so far as Mr. Rasminsky is concerned what I said in the House does not apply.'[99]

Later, the *Windsor Daily Star* could write that Rasminsky was a favourite with the working press. As well as being able to understand any problem of high finance, news people had discovered that he 'could make sense out of their questions, no matter how little they might know about the subject.' They needed 'only a pencil and notebook and ability to report accurately to have a clear and simple story.'[100] The Parliament of Canada confirmed Canada's acceptance of Bretton Woods just in time to sign before the deadline.

The approvals process in the United Kingdom and United States went ahead, though not without some speculation about failure. In the latter nation, banking opinion remained firmly opposed. Similarly, monetary conservatives and economic isolationists, continued to denounce the agreement. It was, according to one representative critic, 'totalitarian and collectivistic,' and more to the point, it was an infringement on private enterprise and personal liberty. As Orval Watts, the economic counsel to the Los Angeles Board of Trade, put it, 'Such an institution begins by conscripting part of the wealth of individuals in order to obtain capital. Merely to set it in operation ... involves an infringement on personal liberty.' The piece that he wrote was intended 'to show the restrictionism and ultimate insolvency resulting from any form of government-owned world bank or stabilization fund.'[101]

However, the Bretton Woods document swept all before it, especially as the US Treasury hired a New York public relations man, Randolph Festus, 'and devised one of the most elaborate and sophisticated campaigns ever conducted by a government agency in support of legislation.'[102] In the end, the Treasury had 'created a kind of Bretton Woods mystique which [was] felt but certainly not understood.'[103] A few months later, Harry White could confidently tell Rasminsky that approval was 'in the bag.'[104] Less than two months after Harry Truman became president, the covering legislation passed the House of Representatives on 7 June 1945, with only eighteen Republicans opposing, and the Senate approved it on 19 July, in a 61–16 vote.

In Britain, the announcement of the IMF met with a complete lack of interest. However, the *Times* had come out in opposition; there was, so some thought, 'a very critical spirit abroad in the House'; and the Bank of England remained opposed.[105] Rasminsky wrote to George Bolton a few days before Christmas 1944: 'I had thought ... I would make one final effort to make you see the light on Bretton Woods. But this being the season of good cheer, I imagine that such an effort would not be appreciated and I will let this chore stand over until later.'[106] However, caution was the byword in Britain, and the Americans were concerned when by mid-November 1945 only South Africa and Venezuela were prepared to ratify the Bretton Woods document. Many other countries were waiting to see if

Britain's new government would sanction the two institutions. The situation was salvaged only by provision of an American loan of US$3.75 billion to London. As a result, four days before the deadline, a battered Britain, the United States, and twenty-seven other countries signed the Bretton Woods accords on 27 December 1945.

Keynes, however, did not live to see the results of his contribution. He died of exhaustion and overwork in April 1946. It was a blow to the British, but also to the Canadians, who had used Keynes's keen mind to their own advantage. Rasminsky sent condolences to Lady Keynes, who remembered 'such pleasant moments together' and that her husband 'did like to work with you very much.'[107] Less than a year later, Harry White had quit the IMF and the US Treasury. He wrote to Rasminsky telling him of his intentions: 'I want you to learn from me rather than through the press that I am resigning from the Board.'[108] Rasminsky knew how much White wanted the IMF to succeed and also that he would watch it with keen interest as it progressed. With himself and Keynes gone, White told Rasminsky, 'Much depends on you because you have so much influence both with [the managing director] Mr. Gutt and many members of the Board.' With his retirement, the two great combatants of the IMF had departed the scene.

Before that happened, however, the Fund was undergoing a metamorphosis for the worse, many thought. Rasminsky believed that 1945 would provide the last opportunity for the exercise of courage and imagination in tackling problems of commercial policy and monetary organization. Indeed, it might well be 'that [that] opportunity has in fact already been missed; certainly the big objectives we all had in our minds a couple of years ago seem to be receding further and further out of sight.'[109] For example, Rasminsky had been 'greatly disturbed by the way [Bretton Woods] was run.'[110] While it was supposed to be an international conference, 'it was conducted as though it were a conference between the United States ... and the rest of the world.' He hoped that 'sooner or later the Americans [would] learn that they cannot participate in international negotiations on [that] basis.'

That was a forlorn wish, as developments at the inaugural meeting of the Fund and the Bank at Savannah, Georgia, in March 1946 suggested. There, according to Rasminsky, 'the outstanding general aspect ... was the very bad spirit which developed between the United States delegation ... and practically all other delegations. At a very early stage the Americans showed that they were quite determined to have their own way regarding all important issues and most unimportant issues that came before the meeting.'[111] That attitude was 'keenly resented by all the Europeans, all the British Dominions, and even by many of the Latin Americans.' What it added up to was that 'we have all been treated to a spectacle of American domination and domineeringness through their financial power which has to be seen to be believed.'[112] Keynes, especially, who had gone to Savannah expecting it to be a 'pleasant party,' was shocked by the American approach.[113]

The American insistence on having IMF headquarters in Washington, 'against the virtually unanimous wish of every other country is the chief example, but there are many others.' On the issue of locations, Rasminsky wrote, 'Every technical question was decided upon by reference to domestic US politics. The location of offices, for example, had to be Washington for the Fund as it is intended to sit between the Federal Reserve Board and the US Treasury, and New York for the Bank, where it can be supervised by the US S[ecurities] E[xchange] C[ommission].' The deciding factor in its location was Treasury Secretary Fred Vinson's unqualified support for Washington.[114] He went on: 'The foreign economic policy seems to be in the hands of the Treasury who are insensitive to other peoples' reactions and prepared to ram everything they want down everyone's throat.'

Another critical matter was whether executive directors should be full-time or part-time; at Bretton Woods, Canada had favoured part-time, and it had raised the issue again at Savannah. The United States would not budge; Rasminsky wrote: 'In ... conversation, it was simply impossible to reach Vinson's mind since it was completely closed. Last night, with the committee in deadlock on the issue, Ilsley, Clark, Towers and I went to see Clayton and White. I think that they heard franker talk from me than they had ever heard from a foreigner before in which I didn't mince words regarding what I thought of their attitude, what other people thought and what the consequences would be.'[115] Here, Rasminsky did have some influence on the Americans; the Fund eventually accommodated both part-time and full-time executive directors.

With the change in its structure, Rasminsky now doubted 'very much whether the Fund will succeed and I am certain that the life of the Managing Director would not be worth living.' Perhaps that was the US idea; as Edward Bernstein later related, in 1946, he had taken the French economic planner Jean Monnet to lunch. 'Who,' Monnet wanted to know, 'was to run the IMF?' Bernstein's reply – that it was to be the managing director – was met with a snort. 'No,' the Frenchman asked, 'who in the Treasury will run it?'[116]

All participants seemed chary of American policy. On 12 April 1946, Towers received a telegram from Cobbold apprising him of the fact that the British were very worried about the decisions taken at Savannah, 'particularly about location and function of Executive Director.'[117] They echoed Rasminsky's comment about the life of the managing director. Indeed, London thought that results of the Savannah conference were 'likely to prejudice the usefulness of the institution.' The British remained committed, however, and were prepared, at some considerable sacrifice, to put up a strong team for the executive. Who would become managing director? Camille Gutt was a serious contender and, if unanimously invited to serve, would accept. However, there were rumours that the Americans would oppose the Belgian; Cobbold went on, 'In speaking to Brand recently, Vinson observed that he thought we had agreed that a strong Canadian candidate would be best. We are very fearful lest Vinson is manoeuvring the rest of us into position where we have no candidate and will then produce either an American or a Latin American stooge thus completely dominating both the Fund and the Bank. If the Institutions are to retain any semblance of internationality we feel that this must be avoided at all costs.'

Vinson had asked Towers to let his name stand, and Keynes had given British approval. Towers had told Rasminsky and Ilsley of Vinson's approach and also 'that of all things in the world, this was the one he wanted least.'[118] Towers refused the offer, and even Harry Truman's telephone call to W.L. Mackenzie King to encourage Towers to accept the position was useless. Nor would Donald Gordon, another possibility, take on the job. He was head of the WPTB, and winding up its operations would be 'political dynamite.' The government could not let him go.[119] Camille Gutt was given the position as first managing director of the new organization. What the meetings and telegrams demonstrate, however, was concern over the degree of dependence that the IMF would have on the United States. In the eyes of the British and some Canadians, it did not bode well for the future.

Chapter Five

International Reconstruction

The years following 1945 were supposed to be the high-water mark of international cooperation. International institutions had been born out of a sense that the prewar way of doing things was discredited; 'beggar-thy-neighbour' policies, so prevalent in the 1930s, were to be a thing of the past. The International Bank for Reconstruction and Development (IBRD) was to ensure long-term development, the International Monetary Fund (IMF) was to guarantee exchange stability, the International Trade Organization (ITO) would ensure that 'proper' policies would be followed in trade matters, and the United Nations (UN) would oversee collective security and other matters. International regulation was to replace national self-centredness. It was Louis Rasminsky's job through the rest of the 1940s and 1950s to watch over that change for Canada, at the Bank of Canada and in the IMF and the IBRD.

However, the reality never quite lived up to the billing, as national problems intruded on governments, which continued to look to their own welfare first. The UN did not work well because of Soviet–American hostility, while the ITO charter was quickly 'marked off by reservations on the part of this and that nation.'[1] Indeed, indicative of the general mood, the *Economist* could note that at one point the charter seemed to contain 'five articles and 55 escape clauses.'[2] It died in 1949 when US President Harry Truman, certain of its defeat in Congress, did not submit it to legislators. The Fund also reflected that environment, as its lofty ambitions were ground down by the tenacity of postwar exchange problems. Rasminsky and others were forced to work in that debilitating atmosphere, made more difficult in the case of the IMF by an American intransigence and self-interest that had 'to be seen to be believed.'[3]

It appeared as if Keynes's warning, given at Savannah in March 1946, was coming true: he had 'evoked the assistance of the good fairies to watch over the Bretton Woods twins [the IMF and the IBRD] ... But a darker note had intruded; he hoped that the fairy Carabosse had not been forgotten lest coming uninvited she should curse the children. "You two brats," he visualized her as saying, "shall grow up politicians; your every thought and act shall have an *arrière-pensée*; everything you determine shall not be for its own sake or on its own merits but because of something else. If this should happen then the best that could befall – and that is how it might turn out – would be for the children to fall into an eternal slumber, never to waken or be heard of again in the courts and markets of mankind."'[4] The address – a not-very-oblique reference to American 'domineeringness' – was not well received by Fred Vinson, soon to be the US secretary of the treasury but then the chief American representative to the Savannah conference; he was 'full of resentment at Keynes' clever speech.'[5] In a sense, those Anglo–American skirmishes that had taken place between Keynes and White over the Fund's articles of agreement continued into the implementation phase. It was not an auspicious beginning.

Nor was the British situation much better. The Second World War was a wrenching experience, which in some ways had destroyed the United Kingdom as a great power. London had experienced a rapid shift from international creditor status to being a debtor country, forced to sell off US-dollar assets and incurring sterling liabilities to meet its wartime requirements. By 1945, it was destitute, reliant on the generosity of Canada and the United States. As one critic has commented, the decade following 'was one of the loneliest ... that Britain has lived through this century; relative to our allies, especially [North] America, it was also a time of poverty.'[6]

From Ottawa's perspective, that was not good; the country's international economic structure had been built around what J.B. Brebner had called 'a bilateral imbalance within a balanced North Atlantic triangle,' where a surplus in trade with the United Kingdom had paid for Canada's deficit with the United States. That system was now threatened by the continued inconvertibility of sterling and the creation of the sterling area as a closed trading bloc that largely excluded Canada. It was, many in Ottawa believed, an untenable situation.

As with international insitutions, Rasminsky was heavily involved in Canada's relations with Britain from the end of the war until he became governor of the Bank of Canada. He attended every meeting of the United Kingdom–Canada Continuing Committee (UKCCC), a high-level forum where senior officials exchanged views on commercial issues, from its inception in 1949 to 1961 – one of only two or three officials to do so. Similarly, during the 1950s he was the Bank of Canada's representative to the Interdepartmental Committee on External Trade Policy, which dealt on a number of occasions with the British case. Rasminsky became a sort of British conscience, encouraging that country to take the plunge into the murky waters of sterling convertibility and non-discrimination and in the process help to re-establish Anglo–Canadian trade. That, as events transpired, was a thankless job.

Rasminsky's expertise and interest did not, strictly speaking, lie with the sort of international organization designed to 'facilitate solutions of international economic, social and other humanitarian problems and promote respect for human rights and fundamental freedoms' that the United Nations would become. It was natural, however, given his background, that he should participate in the negotiations in San Francisco leading up to the establishment of the United Nations in mid-1945.[7] In an ironic twist, he was also asked by Hume Wrong of External Affairs to comment on a document received from Britain's Dominions Office relating to dissolution of the League of Nations in favour of a new world organization. Now, to paraphrase Dean Acheson, he was to be 'present at the destruction.'

In San Francisco, Rasminsky was assigned to Committee 3 of Commission II, which was considering the purpose and structure of the Economic and Social Council (ECOSOC), a sub-agency of the UN. He felt quite at home there, as the Council was to function much as had his old League of Nations section in Geneva. By early May 1945, delegations were pushing through the thick mud of international negotiation in earnest. While interest naturally centred around the negotiation of that part of the UN Charter connected with the maintenance of peace and its enforcement, some, such as Rasminsky, considered it an error to underestimate the importance of a UN technical capability. He was convinced that conflict was more likely if there were economic distress; indeed, he felt it to be 'almost inevitable unless countries managed to keep from treading on each others' toes in the economic policies they pursue[d].'[8] During the 1930s, he had had a ringside seat at the demise of international political cooperation, based in part at least on economic disagreements among League members. The UN and its associated agencies, along with the IBRD, the IMF, and the proposed ITO, would, he hoped, help to smooth out those differences.

By mid-May, Committee 3 had met seven times to discuss the relevant sections of the Dumbarton Oaks proposals, the great powers' UN blueprint, which had been drawn up by them in the late summer of 1944 at the beautiful estate near Washington, DC. For the Canadians, the document was contentious, taking it for granted that the four great powers, Britain, China, the United States and the USSR 'would control the destiny of the world.' The mechanism that would allow them to do so was the Security Council's veto – a central element of the proposed United Nations. Lester Pearson described it as 'leading to a farce.'[9] However, other than discussion, not much else had happened, and Rasminsky could see the process spinning far out into the future. Taking the bull by the horns, he put forward a redraft of the document under consideration relating to the purpose and structure of ECOSOC. His paper reflected what he had been saying in committee – that what had been written at Dumbarton Oaks 'did not reflect the vision of an organization Canada held.'[10] Nor, it would seem, did it represent the views of many others; as of 4 May – the last day for filing amendments to the Dumbarton Oaks proposals – more than seven hundred pages had been received.

With respect to that part under consideration by Committee 3, other delegations were prepared to withdraw their proposed amendments if the Canadian text were taken as a basis of discussion. Rasminsky asked the chair that the drafting committee 'be instructed to present to this committee at the earliest possible moment a re-draft of Chapter IX which will be based on the Dumbarton Oaks proposals and the Four Power amendments and take into consideration the lines of the Canadian proposals and incorporate all amendments put forward by other delegations.' The motion was approved unanimously.

What were Rasminsky's proposed amendments? In short, he felt that there should be an explicit obligation imposed on members to cooperate fully with each other. In the Dumbarton Oaks document, there was merely a statement that the organization should seek to accomplish that purpose. He also introduced as a basic purpose of the ECOSOC attainment of higher living standards and economic and social progress. Moreover, its role was made more significant – given more 'authority and prestige' – in Rasminsky's paper.[11] The eighteen nations that were to make up the Council were to be geographically representative and include some of major economic importance. Voting was to be by simple majority, with no veto. It was designed to follow up recommendations made by the UN General Assembly and was to receive reports from members of the UN and other agencies on the actions that they proposed taking to give effect to General Assembly recommendations. This provision was potentially useful, Rasminsky explained, 'both on account of the general antiseptic quality of light and because the requirement on countries to report on action taken provides some assurance that countries will not support a recommendation in the General Assembly if they mean the recommendation to be a dead letter so far as they themselves are concerned.'[12]

Finally, he proposed that the ECOSOC could set up any committee it thought necessary. As he noted, this Council should be 'the central organization for the achievement of the purposes of the United Nations in the field of Economic and Social cooperation.' And while its powers could be only those of coordination and recommendation, it would meet more frequently than the General Assembly, 'and we think it should have as much prestige and authority as is compatible with (a) the recommendatory character of its functions and (b) with the special position of the various functional agencies established by intergovernmental agreement.'

That was a throwback to Rasminsky's days with the League, when the most useful and worthwhile work was done by technical committees, though those efforts had been overshadowed by the focus on political events. The latter was of more immediate interest, and the personalities involved – foreign ministers and diplomats – ensured media coverage of that story, while the more mundane economic and social work done was largely unreported. Without public awareness of that aspect of the United Nations, there could not be the support necessary for the success of the work on economic and social problems.

But increasingly, it seemed to Rasminsky, the organization taking shape in San Francisco would not be up to the task. A lowest-common-denominator approach taken in negotiations compromised the UN even before it was off the drafting table. It would not be much of an improvement on the old League. Part of that outcome was a result of Soviet activity, and part because of the Americans and the British. Nobody, he thought, understood the USSR or even pretended to. Rasminsky complained that the Soviet delegation was 'completely unwilling to make any effort to understand the point of view of other countries or to make the slightest concession towards meeting it.' As a result, he was uncertain 'how far we are going to be able to get with the Canadian proposals for re-arrangement of Chapter IX ... as the Russians regard Dumbarton Oaks as Holy Writ, down to the last grammatical error on which mundane hands must not be laid.'[13]

Nor could Canada count on Britain and the United States to support its position. Rasminsky lamented that they were 'so acquiescent towards everything that the Russians want that they are creating what I fervently hope is a wrong impression of the distribution of power in the world.' As it turned out, it was the wrong impression, but at San Francisco, great-power cooperation was still alive and well, at least on the Western side. Moreover, the United States and the United Kingdom wanted the United Nations, and wanted the Soviet Union in it. Hence the emphasis on accommodation. As Rasminsky told Donald Gordon, the deputy governor of the Bank of Canada,

It was not easy to get the improvements made as the Russians resisted any change in the Dumbarton Oaks provisions and the British and Americans felt some obligation not to part company with their Russian partner. The Russians, as usual, were extremely difficult to negotiate with, being completely inflexible and quite obviously terrified at the personal consequences of changes which Moscow might not approve. They are riding very high on the wave of their wartime prestige and show little inclination to try to understand the point of view of other countries. It will certainly require the most conciliatory diplomacy on the part of the Western powers to avoid difficulties. On the other hand, I am among those who feel that we are entitled to expect the Russians to take a conciliatory attitude too and that there is nothing to be gained by buckling under to their wishes at every point.[14]

Drafting problems relating to Canada's amendments went on well into June, and ultimately most of its suggestions were not adopted. On the political side, what was being created represented in Rasminsky's opinion 'a definite retrograde step as compared with the Covenant of the League. The Covenant was based on the concept of International Law whereas what is being done here is based on the concept that the Great Powers are above the law. In fact, the Charter that is being created here is a three power alliance dressed up to look like international organization.'[15] 'It may be that this is the best that can be achieved at the present time and the general policy of our delegation has been not to jeopardize the unity of the Great Powers. The strain of sentimentality and idealism in the United States is such that American participation in world affairs is probably easier to accomplish through something that looks like international organization than through something that is frankly a power alliance. But it is difficult to have any enthusiasm for the Charter that is being drafted particularly in view of the great frictions that are already present among the Big Three.' Sometimes it was a difficult program to follow, and Rasminsky told a colleague in Canada's Foreign Exchange Control Board (FECB), Sidney Turk, that if there were any FECB business that he wished to write him about, it would 'be a pleasure to deal with simple problems again!'[16]

International cooperation, even on relatively unimportant questions, was elusive. Rasminsky could have said that it was 'déjà vu all over again.' Much like the League, the United Nations, it seemed, would be most useful for the technical side of operations. As he wrote to Clark, 'The arrangements for economic and social cooperation [are] ... the most successful and constructive part of the conference. The Dumbarton Oaks proposals [were] improved beyond recognition.'[17] The Canadians had been in the forefront of that campaign, and those changes had been accomplished against some pretty tough opposition. For Rasminsky, that was the only bright spot in an otherwise-disappointing conference.

As much as he might have wanted it to end, his role in the establishment of the UN was not yet finished. Delegations met in London following the San Francisco conference to finalize the process. The British were anxious to get the most capable person they could to take charge of the section preparing the draft document of ECOSOC. Would it be possible, they wondered, 'to spare Rasminsky for the work?'[18] Lester Pearson at External Affairs conveyed the request to the undersecretary of state, noting 'Officials of Preparatory Commission consider he would be best suitable person to get the work under way ... He would have major responsibility for shaping the form and activities of the Economic and Social Council. It is feared that if an able man is not proposed it may be necessary to accept an inferior nominee put forward by one of the other States.'

While Rasminsky found it impossible to go then, he was in the United Kingdom in January 1946 to attend the first session of the United Nations – meetings that did not improve his impressions of the fledgling organization caught up in a deepening Cold War. He congratulated Pearson on his 'near escape' from being named the UN's first secretary general: 'Now that it is clear that [Norway's Trygve] Lie is to be chosen as Secretary-General, I write you this note to offer my warmest congratulations on not having been elected. The job would have been a thankless and heart-breaking one. From what I have seen in San Francisco, and even more [in London], I would say that it was humanly impossible for anyone to make a success of it.'[19]

Still, Rasminsky did not object to being appointed the alternate to Paul

Martin on the ECOSOC. This was the least of several evils, Rasminsky thought, as the Council was capable of work and bore a resemblance to his old department at the League of Nations. He was happy to speak in favour of its first motion – that a conference be called to consider international action in the field of public health. That smacked of his own work on nutrition a decade earlier.

The road to the United Nations – begun so hopefully with the January 1942 Declaration of the United Nations; travelling through the Moscow Declaration of 30 October 1943, initialled by Britain, China, the United States, and the USSR; followed by the Dumbarton Oaks proposals of 9 October 1944 – had proved to be a *cul de sac* of sorts. As with the League, the political and diplomatic components of the organization were still-born, a result of the ideological hostility generated between the Soviet and American blocs. And while the technical organizations were reasonably free of that element, they also were at times subject to the whims of great-power diplomacy. It was a sad comment on the fundamental incompatibility of some nations' interests and represented, Rasminsky thought, a missed opportunity.

Rasminsky was obviously well-known to the British. He had dealt with many of their officials while at the League and as a Canadian public servant and had become good friends with a few. During the early postwar period, on behalf of the FECB and the IMF, he participated in discussions with British officials, as Canada did all in its limited power to help the United Kingdom return to the world of convertibility and non-discrimination, which it had of necessity abandoned with its declaration of war in September 1939.[20] He had been involved in Canada's financial talks with the British in 1946, when they had come to press their case for assistance. Canada had offered the huge sum of $1.25 billion, along with cancellation of the British debt of more than $600 million under the British Commonwealth Air Training Plan. That amount was added to an American loan of $3.75 billion. It was not enough, however, as Britain's problems proved almost intractable. Canadians were in close contact with London; if the United Kingdom were to experience economic and financial trouble, it could only reverberate unfavourably in Canada, or so they believed. Moreover, their own country was undergoing some difficult economic and financial times of its own, largely because of the amount of postwar assistance that it had offered some of its wartime Allies. Those problems resulted in certain measures designed to ease the situation, like the fifty-fifty arrangement, in which Ottawa had insisted that the British match their drawings on the Canadian loan with the sale to Canada of an equal amount of hard currency. Ottawa could not sustain the level of British drawings on the credit, which were then running at a much higher rate than had ever been anticipated.

The solution to Canada's difficulties lay in large part in getting the United States to recognize the magnitude of the British problem. Rasminsky and others were in continuous communication with the Americans over the summer and autumn, as Canada's economic position began to deteriorate. In June 1947, the same month that the US secretary of state, Gen. George Marshall, announced his plan for helping Europe, Rasminsky was in Washington with Graham Towers and Hume Wrong, Canada's ambassador there, to meet with Dean Acheson, Will Clayton, and J.D. Hickerson of the State Department to discuss Canada's emerging economic problem. As Rasminsky told the Americans, repeated rumours of a Canadian depreciation of its dollar were leading Canadian importers to anticipate payments due abroad, especially in the United States, while Canadian exporters were delaying receipt of payment. That made the situation worse. As well, as events then stood, about one-third of Canada's exports were sold against credits, while some 85 per cent of all imports involved cash payment.

The fact remained, however, that Canada was experiencing difficulty because of its high level of prosperity, which was reflected in high imports from the United States. As well, in 1946, the country had given away nearly $1 billion worth of merchandise, primarily to the United Kingdom. Total receipts from all current transactions with other countries in that year were $2.372 billion. Conversely, total expenditures that Canadians had to pay to non-residents were $2.883 billion, all of which amount was due and payable, as no other nation was giving Canada anything. The country was in the red to the tune of $511 million. As Graham Towers told the Canadian cabinet, 'Our experience ... is a vivid illustration of the fact that if a country wants to give things away without itself incurring foreign debt or using up its foreign cash reserves, *it must have a surplus in its current account transactions with the rest of the world equal to the value of its gifts.* In 1947, we had no surplus at all. We needed every cent of the value of our exports in order to pay our foreign bills. But as $511 millions of Canadian exports brought no payment to us, our reserves had to be used up in an amount equal to the value of such gifts.'[21]

The situation worsened further when sterling was made convertible on 15 July 1947, as required by the terms of the Anglo–American loan agreement. A British exchange crisis quickly followed, and London lost millions of its borrowed dollars, as some other nations simply cashed in their accumulated and abundant 'soft' pounds for scarce and 'hard' dollars. Under those circumstances, the United Kingdom found it impossible to maintain convertibility, which it abrogated a month later. The summer's events played a major role in the development of a similar setback in Canada in November 1947.

As that began to develop, Robert Bryce and Rasminsky were in London in September for discussions relating to possible solutions to an increasingly intractable Anglo–Canadian economic relationship. The talks quickly became unproductive, as the British adopted a leave-it-to-father attitude that grated on the Canadians. As a result, Rasminsky's contributions were 'blunt' and 'rather frigid.'[22] When the talks got around to Canada's import policy and the Treasury's Sir Wilfrid Eady's patonizing and ill-timed comment that 'it raised great political difficulties for the United Kingdom to be paying [Canada] United States dollars [under the fifty-fifty arrangements] at a time when [Canada] had no restrictions on imports from the United States,' Rasminsky's anger boiled over. Most people in Canada, he told Eady, would find it difficult 'to understand on what basis the United Kingdom would be entitled to express any views regarding our import policy and that there seem[ed] to be a fair amount of confusion regarding who was helping whom in the matter of exchange.' Later that afternoon, Sir Eric Machtig, the permanent head of the Dominions Office, telephoned Norman Robertson, Canada's high commissioner, and apologized for Eady's remarks.

Nor was Canada's treatment at the hands of certain Americans much better on occasion. As the country's exchange position deteriorated, Rasminsky and Towers went to Washington to negotiate a US-dollar loan from the Export–Import Bank, an agency of the US government. Towers had previously been led to believe by the bank's chair, William Martin, that it would be sympathetic, and a loan, easy to obtain. However, Martin was in Europe, and the Canadians had to deal with the acting chair, Herbert Gaston. He treated Towers as a delinquent debtor, which drove the governor into a near-frenzy and out of the room, to be followed soon by Rasminsky.

The situation was saved by an unofficial meeting between Rasminsky and his good friend from Geneva days, Rifat Tirana, now with the Export–Import Bank. Tirana suggested that he and another senior official meet with Rasminsky and Towers as if by chance to resolve the matter, and the solution would then be put to Gaston. The process worked, and on 4 November the two Canadians were back in the acting chair's office, accompanied by three Americans, including Tirana, to set the terms for the loan.[23] It fell short of Canadian requirements, however, but the country would make do; instead of $500 million over ten years, the Americans offered $300 million over five.

While discussions with the British and the Americans had been going on, Rasminsky and a number of other Canadian officials had also been involved in the preparation of an emergency program designed to address Canada's declining dollar reserves. It was announced by the minister of finance over the radio on 17 November 1947 and implemented by order-in-council. The Emergency Exchange Conservation Act was passed by Parliament on 5 December and given royal assent the following March. It imposed a wide range of import restrictions, covering many types of fruits and vegetables, packaged food, most textiles, sporting goods, and hardware. In addition, tourist allowances for Canadians visiting the United States would be reduced to $150 per year. As well, there were measures designed to bolster Canada's earnings, via such means as capital investment in export industries, and branch plants were encouraged to process more of their raw materials in Canada.

Rasminsky's involvement in the exchange crisis earned him dubious recognition in the House of Commons from the member of Parliament who would later appoint him governor of the Bank of Canada. As the emergency measures were being discussed, John Diefenbaker, then Conservative MP for Lake Centre (Saskatchewan), demanded that the minister of justice, James Ilsley, bring before Parliament the 'invisible incognitos' who were responsible for the 'usurpation of power.' He identified Clark, Rasminsky, and Towers, the financial advisers by whom the programs had been developed and who, Diefenbaker said, had had a wide variety of imports banned, placed on quota, or made subject to permit.[24] The only response of the minister of finance, Douglas Abbott, was rightly to label the charge 'nonsense.'

Rasminsky's 'foreign affairs' beat kept him in close contact with the Americans and the British as the exchange crisis disappeared, largely as an indirect consequence of the Marshall Plan. In operation by March 1948, the European Cooperation Adminstration (ECA), as the plan was formally known, was designed to grant US$13 billion over four years to certain countries in western Europe. As in the war's Lend-Lease, the Americans permitted off-shore purchases in Canada, which helped to clear up any lingering dollar problems. However, while Canada's condition improved, its economic relations with the British remained problematic.

Rasminsky attended the first meeting of the United Kingdom–Canada Continuing Committee (UKCCC) held in January 1949 in London. He was part of a team that had further talks in the spring with the United Kingdom and summer discussions with delegations from Britain and the United States – the so-called America–Britain–Canada (ABC) talks. Finally, to round out a hectic summer schedule, there was a meeting of Commonwealth finance ministers in London that followed closely on the heels of the ABC conference. These gatherings were all important, and Rasminsky played a major role, preparing briefs for the minister, Douglas Abbott, participating in strategy sessions, and contributing to the discussions themselves.

These meetings centred on yet another economic crisis that gathered steam during the first half of 1949, as well as Canadian questions relating to the British timetable for the introduction of sterling convertibility. Rasminsky found the talks, especially those of June and July, generally unsatisfactory, largely because of Abbott's reluctance to press the United Kingdom to move forward on convertibility and at least to acknowledge that Ottawa had a legitimate right to raise questions for discussion, such as convertibility's timetable. Certainly he recognized that London faced its own monumental difficulties, but he remained disappointed that senior members of the Canadian delegation were not more assiduous in putting the case for non-resident convertibility, given Canada's pre-war dependence on the British market. The country's interest in British recovery had been graphically demonstrated by its investment of billions of dollars, and it was entitled to urge the British to adopt as an objective an early return to the convertibility of sterling, or so Rasminsky believed.[25] But there were also good reasons for the British to undertake convertibility for their own interests. Rasminsky certainly agreed when one critic had noted: 'Behind the "protection" afforded by control, costs and prices tended to rise. The competitive power of countries with a system of restrictions was being reduced. "European industries tend to become flabby," and countries lose their position as key currencies.'[26]

While the conference was going on, Rasminsky was brought into the confidence of Bank of England officials, whom he knew well. They showed him a top-secret memorandum written by their governor, Lord Cobbold, outlining the steps that should be taken in order to improve the British condition. Among these were drastic reductions in food subsidies and in health and housing expenditures and changes in investment policies. Those measures, Rasminsky knew, would not appeal to the British electorate. As well, George Bolton made the startling admission that the

British crisis was primarily a domestic political one, caused by the Bank of England and the civil service. The bureaucracy had seized the opportunity presented by the falling off in sterling-area earnings resulting from the US recession and speculation against the pound 'to produce an atmosphere of crisis ... in the hopes that the government would agree to modify its social policies to a basis which the facts of the UK situation warranted.'[27] Rasminsky was appalled; it demonstrated a mind-set that was a negation of democracy – a usurpation of legitimate elected authority.

He thought that a large part of the British problem was the desire to preserve as much of the empire and sterling area as possible. Marshall Plan money was funding a good part of that effort; he wrote to Towers: 'By and large it is difficult not to feel confirmed in the conclusion that the British regard as one of the main advantages of ECA assistance that it enables them, while maintaining a certain standard of living and domestic investment, to build up a trading empire of their own and make sterling a strong currency over an important part of the world. As to what happens when ECA assistance comes to an end, I don't think the British have yet faced this.'[28] One can almost see Rasminsky's head moving from side to side as he was informed of British policy, at least as it was being developed in Whitehall. His comment to Towers summed up his impressions: 'I don't know whether the Civil Servants and the Bank people concerned really thought a programme along the above lines stood any chance of being accepted either in the UK or the USA.'

When the Commonwealth finance ministers' conference wound up on 18 July 1949, Rasminsky could see nothing to which he could point as a tangible result that would benefit any of the participants. A letter to Deputy Governor Donald Gordon demonstrated his depth of feeling: 'I shall not attempt to try to write an obituary notice of the Conference at this time. It was a pretty painful affair and has left me in a depressed frame of mind as regards the future.'[29] In reworking the final documents with British officials, he was able to get a substantial improvement in the statement of long-term objectives, with, as he pointed out, a more reasonable distribution of emphasis on the respective responsibilities of surplus and deficit countries. However, he was afraid that it was 'like the days in Geneva when everyone was in favour of peace, security and disarmament, but when they spoke of security they had in mind their own security, and when they spoke of disarmament, they had the other fellow in mind.' In short, the results were not encouraging, and Rasminsky surely agreed with the *Economist*'s caustic observation that, with respect to the final communiqué, 'the only thing to do was put into it everything that anyone had said.'[30]

From Canada's perspective, the negotiations went from bad to worse, and the ABC talks scheduled for Washington in September would, Rasminsky thought, 'represent the very last call for dinner.'[31] Obviously others believed that too, as the British took drastic action at the September meeting, devaluing sterling by 30 per cent, from US$4.02 to the pound to US$2.80. With the pound now worth 30 per cent less, Canada devalued its dollar by slightly more than 9 per cent in order to remain competitive in the British market. Rasminsky was not at the ABC discussions; instead he was attending the annual meeting of the IMF and the IBRD, also held in Washington in September. More about this is said below.

His months in Britain had left him shaken; nor were things much better on the continent. He had spent a week in Paris, visiting the Organization for European Economic Cooperation (OEEC), which had been set up to disburse ECA assistance, a week in Switzerland, at the Bank for International Settlements; and a few days in Italy. The continent was facing some of the same problems as Britain but chose, it seemed to him, to ignore them. France, Rasminsky told the board of directors of the Bank of Canada on his return to Ottawa, was living in a fool's paradise: 'The French [did] not admire British austerity.'[32] France was 'less disciplined' than Britain, and its government administrative apparatus less efficient and honest. As well, the French appeared to care not one whit what would happen to their increasing US-dollar deficit when ECA funding finished in 1952: 'They apparently believe that ... for one reason or another the United States should and will cover the French dollar deficit.' In that way, at least, they resembled the British.

On a gratifying personal note, Dag Hammarskjöld, then on the OEEC's executive committee, told the Canadian that it had wanted to ask him and John Williams, an adviser to the Federal Reserve Board of New York and an old adversary of Rasminsky's from Bretton Woods days, to come to Paris and spend five or six weeks 'just sitting around and talking' so that it could get their perspective on things.[33] When the Americans were approached about Williams, it was not possible to get him for an extended period of time, so the project was dropped; the OEEC felt that it could not ask Rasminsky to take the necessary leave under those circumstances.

Where possible in Britain and on the continent, Rasminsky had talked of freer trade and convertibility. His conditioning at the League and Canada's obvious interest helped to set his program. Obviously, the United Kingdom – Canada's biggest overseas trading partner – was reluctant to introduce sterling convertibility and non-discrimination because of its wrenching problems. And certainly the memory of the 1947 and 1949 crises remained fresh in British minds. A Conservative victory in the election of late 1951, following six years of the Labour party in power, suggested a change of policy. The new government had, after all, run on a platform of 'Set the People Free.'[34] Accordingly, Britain's 1952 announcement of the collective approach to freer trade and currencies, which promised introduction of convertibility in the near future, was seized on in Ottawa as representing the fulfilment of Canadian hopes. Forward movement, however, was disappointingly slow.

In Sydney, Australia, where he was attending a meeting of Commonwealth finance ministers in January 1954, Rasminsky wrote home to Towers that convertibility was off; it had 'no political sex appeal in the UK.'[35] When he put the case for convertibility to the British Treasury's Sir Leslie Rowan and the Board of Trade's Sir Frank Lee, they did not 'seriously ... challenge the case [he] made in favour of immediate action, nor did they disagree when [he] argued that if the UK [did] not act very soon, [it] may miss the boat entirely.' He went on: 'The only thing resembling an economic point they make is that European countries would feel that it was a very risky business to make sterling convertible in the present circumstances and that this belief would result in considerable pressure on sterling if it were convertible.'

The two British officials were not eager to implement convertibility. When Rasminsky inquired under what circumstances they would contemplate it, Rowan replied: 'When the US has started on the upgrade after the [1954] recession.' London's thinking was that '*if* the recession turn[ed] out to be short and shallow, and *if* the British are able to ride it through by moderate drawings on reserves and IMF without increasing import restrictions, and *if* the US does not backslide on import restrictions, but on the contrary, shows some progress, however modest, in its commercial policies, *then* the British Government will be in a strong, or at any rate stronger, position to deal with the political opposition to convertibility.' That was quite a mouthful and implied a confluence of circumstance that would be difficult to realize. The proceedings, he wrote to his wife, '[were] nothing more than a holding operation, ... though it is always useful to hear what people have to say and see how their attitudes have been developing.'[36]

His analysis was considerably harsher nine months later; it was now almost a certainty, he thought, that the British *would* 'miss the boat.' At the September 1954 meeting of Commonwealth finance ministers in

London, Britain's chancellor of the exchequer, R.A. Butler, was 'very touchy. [Rasminsky had] never seen him in worse form ... Butler didn't seem to know whether he was going forward or backward on the collective approach and of course when he vacillated the sterling area countries remembered all the difficulties and trotted them out.'[37] Walter Harris, Canada's new minister of finance, was at his first Commonwealth meeting, and Rasminsky thought it an ill-timed introduction to high-level international politics. He noted: 'The meeting was most unfortunate and the collective approach would be nearer if it had not been held.'

Convertibility remained on the horizon. A meeting of the UKCCC in London in June 1956 was nothing more than 'a reflection ... of the present passivity of British policy.'[38] It also showed 'how little on the ball is required for people to get to the top here.' Perhaps Rasminsky was being unfair. The Suez crisis had exploded the same year, and his British colleagues were scrambling to deal with its devastating economic and political fall-out, either beaten down with the sheer weight of problems or terribly overworked. The country had lurched from crisis to crisis since the war, politicians seemed powerless to provide direction, and officials were unable to suggest realistic solutions. At another UKCCC meeting in 1958, a mere five months before introduction of non-resident sterling convertibility in December, Rasminsky again appealed to the British to make some move towards the convertibility approach; 'hope deferred,' he quoted, 'turneth the heart sick.'[39] He left that conference with heartburn.

It was also true, however, that in the twelve years since the Canadian loan had been given, Canada had left Britain behind. During the 1950s, the country was one of the success stories of the industrialized world. Exports rose from $3 billion in 1948 to almost $5 billion in 1956, while commodity imports also increased. Prosperity abounded, jobs were abundant, and expectations for the future were limitless. If Canadians believed that, so too did others. As Rasminsky noted in New York in March 1953, 'The editors of some of your leading newspapers and periodicals seem to have entered into a friendly competition with each other to see who could produce the most glowing account of our present prosperity and future greatness.'[40] That circumstance was reflected in Canada's birth rate, one of the highest in the Western world. Despite the relative loss of the British market, Canada went from success to success. The fact that it did so via increasing dependence on the United States did not faze Canadians. Even Walter Gordon's Royal Commission on Canada's Economic Prospects, which reported in 1957 and warned against the perceived dangers of continentalization, also projected healthy increases over the next quarter century in the country's standard of living. So while support for British convertibility and non-discrimination had remained Canadian policy and Rasminsky might inquire about London's timetable, by the later 1950s it did not really matter. After all, the twentieth century now belonged to Canada.

The United Nations had floundered on Soviet–American hostility as wartime cooperation turned into Cold War belligerence. At times, Rasminsky must have thought that the IMF was also in danger of running aground, though not as a result of Cold War dynamics. To his mind, the United States seemed quite capable all by itself of compromising the organization. He had an interest in the IMF's international health, having been a midwife at its birth. Moreover, as of 8 March 1946, Rasminsky was Canada's executive director for the IMF, a position that he would hold until September 1962. His first act was to continue his quiet protest against the American insistence on full-time executive directors, which, Rasminksy believed, violated the original spirit in which the Fund was established; he returned his executive director's salary of US$17,000 per year. *Part-time* directors with responsibilities in their national capitals were key to the functioning of the IMF, or so Rasminsky felt. The Americans, initially on side with Canada, had changed their minds and their policy, in order to exert continuing influence over executive directors living in Washington for extended periods of time – part-time people working closely with other governments might prove too difficult to control. During his sixteen years on the managing board, he remained an unpaid, part-time director – one of only two.

Work began immediately; Rasminsky quickly became one of its most influential directors, committed to making it an international, as opposed to merely an American, success. For the first several years, at Gutt's request, Rasminsky was instrumental in preparing the Fund's annual report. It was not a happy exercise, as inconvertibility and exchange control prevailed the world over, the latter even in prosperous Canada. The reports reflected this reality, which Rasminsky captured in a letter home: 'Things are rapidly falling apart and will collapse unless something is done soon.'[41] The IMF seemed powerless against international economic and financial forces, and Rasminsky could only breathe a sigh of relief at US Secretary of State George Marshall's speech at Harvard University in June 1947 promising a European recovery program. Perhaps this would be the 'something.'

Rasminsky's drafting skills, honed in the hard school of the League of Nations, resulted in reports that concisely laid out the questions to be addressed by the new organization. The managing director, Camille Gutt, had found him indispensable and a good sounding-board for Fund issues, and he was always grateful for the months of work that the Canadian put in on IMF business, especially its annual reports. These documents highlighted the dismal economic and financial climate then prevailing in Europe. In that context it was very difficult, if not impossible, for the Fund to operate as had been anticipated. While possible cures could be prescribed, there were other increasingly intractable ailments; Anglo–American divergence on how the Fund should develop, so prevalent prior to 1944, continued into the postwar period. Its focus was American insistence on convertibility and non-discrimination, while the British practised the opposite – a difference that was damaging for international cooperation.

Rasminsky agreed that divergent policies animated London and Washington in their approach to the Fund and were not conducive to mutuality, even at the level of the managing board. As well, the internal organization of the Fund had prevented it from being a real force or from having a strong, continuing influence on the majority of its members. There were numerous examples in its early years, but one involved a crucial matter of principle, on which Rasminsky felt a favourable ruling by the IMF crucial, if the type of Fund that he had helped set up were ever to function.

At a managing board meeting, a number of executive directors had requested that a process be established allowing them to have private conversations with the managing director on issues of importance to their country and the Fund. Harry White, the American executive director, was implacably opposed and had placed a motion in the board's minutes that this not be allowed. To put it crudely, executive directors in private discussion might develop a position that would not be popular in Washington. White took exception to that, and Rasminsky took exception to White. Over the next several months, the Canadian lobbied other executive directors to get White's motion removed, putting a counter-motion to the board on 10 October 1946. It was met with general agreement but also with 'a violent and confused statement by Harry White condemning the approach to Governments by Executive Directors on the secrecy issue, and insisting that he could not accept the deletion from the minutes.'[42] Given the American's unreasonable attitude, Rasminsky believed further discussion pointless; he would, he said, report to Ottawa that 'the last remnants of secrecy were not to be salvaged.'

That stance, according to George Bolton, the British representative (and never a White supporter), brought 'an extraordinary volte-face from arrogance to humility which illustrates the unhappy confusion in which Harry White now finds himself. He apologised to Rasminsky ... and said that his only preoccupation was to ensure that the Managing Director should not be allowed to consult with any individual prior to his informing the whole Board.' The offending motion was removed, and the IMF lumbered on. This was an important episode, and one in which Rasminsky played a key role in securing the best internationalist result possible under the circumstances. His belief that the IMF must be independent of the United States was set in stone, and this outcome was one marker on the long road towards what he hoped was achievement of that end.

But while internal issues might occasionally raise temperatures among executive directors, for the most part the organization was almost somnolent between 1946 and 1951. There were reasons for this paralysis, among them that the United States did not want the Fund's resources to be involved in European reconstruction (which Washington believed lay more appropriately with its European Recovery Program) and that the postwar rehabilitation of the continent was turning out to be a much longer process than anticipated. Under the less-than-ideal conditions that prevailed, it is no wonder that Rasminsky's commitment, and that of other Canadians, to the IMF became less than complete.

Certainly that was what some Americans believed; J.P. Walsh, the third secretary at the US embassy in Ottawa, reported in mid-1950 to the State Department that 'Canadian enthusiasm for the International Monetary Fund [had] cooled considerably.'[43] Later, the embassy told Washington that Canadian idealism and enthusiasm for the Fund had 'tended to wither away in the face of postwar problems.'[44] There was a consensus of opinion in financial and government circles that Fund regulations with respect to fixed rates of currency and to the sale of gold were no longer realistic. As well, Rasminsky found its 'stinginess' in doling out its resources in time of need unhelpful. For example, there were no drawings on IMF resources in 1950, and only US$77 million in the two years following October 1949.[45] However, as early as May 1946, he had insisted, albeit with little success, that access to the Fund's resources should not be restricted unreasonably: 'If a member gives the necessary guarantees and carries out its undertakings in good faith, it must be able to use its quota with assurance ... The test to be applied should not primarily be quantitative but qualitative.'[46] Rasminsky's comment had been provoked by

White's categorical assertion that there was no 'automaticity' in Fund drawings – they would not be automatic – a position for which he was well known. Moreover, the Americans believed that any use of the Fund's resources must be temporary, as Frank Southard, the American executive director from 1949 to 1962, told the executive board: 'Any drawing must meet this basic test.'[47]

Canada had supported a Dutch resolution in the executive board and later tabled one of its own, which had called for easier access to resources. As well, the Australians had applied for $20 million worth of help, which the Americans had initially opposed. While the Americans later reversed their position, Rasminksy noted that 'Southard [had] given notice of a US proposal that the Fund should sell no more US dollars unless the purchasing country [gave] a firm commitment to repay within the maximum period of five years.'[48] Rasminsky did not like the Americans' attitude, their demands, or the process through which they pressed the Australians.

There were other irritants, and one in particular that affected Rasminsky personally. Through the muted prose of a memorandum written by Joseph Parkinson, Rasminsky's alternate at the Fund, comes a picture of an executive director furious with his US counterpart. The Canadian had attended the board meeting in September 1949, at the same time as the tripartite talks among Canada, the United Kingdom, and the United States were taking place in Washington.[49] The big news from the talks was the British intention to devalue sterling by approximately 30 per cent, from US$4.02 to US$2.80 to the pound. As a result, Ottawa would devalue the Canadian dollar, but only by about 9 per cent. Rasminsky had so informed a seemingly sympathetic Frank Southard on 18 September and had 'told of the considerations which [entered into the decision]: the world-wide character of the devaluations against the dollar, nearly all countries [matching Britain's 30 per cent devaluation against the US dollar]; the likelihood of falling prices in the US as a consequence, with resultant unfavourable repercussions on Canadian exports to dollar countries; possible long-run losses in the British market. If Canada did not move, she would stand almost alone beside the US ... which would mean enormous pressure on the Canadian rate. We would be driven off parity in the end, after losing substantial reserves.'[50] Southard was convinced by Rasminsky's arguments and briefed US Treasury Secretary Henry Snyder on the Canadian situation. As well, Louis St Laurent and the secretary of state for external affairs, Lester Pearson, had both travelled to Washington to sound out US opinion (which appeared favourable), before putting the question to cabinet.

From that point on, Parkinson records, 'misunderstandings seem to have developed.' On 19 September, when Canada tabled its proposal at the Fund, the US reaction was 'not sympathetic or even charitable.' Instead, Southard's response 'was grudging and reluctant ... He gave no indication that he understood or appreciated the difficulties Canada would face if it did not devalue [by at least 9 per cent].' Rasminsky was angry, tackling Southard after the meeting and demanding to know why his attitude had changed from Sunday to Monday: 'Southard seemed apologetic at first, but his real views soon came out. He began by saying that all he had wanted to do was to give a little encouragement to the Latins who were being unnecessarily stampeded into action to devalue by the behaviour of the Europeans and sterling area countries ... As an adviser to Snyder, and aware as he was of the political implications of the projected Canadian action, he had felt it his duty this morning ... to advise Snyder of the difficulties that would be created in the US if Canada were to desert the North American line-up.' Southard then told Rasminsky that Snyder had spoken with Canada's finance minister, Douglas Abbott, that morning and had put that case to him.

Rasminsky had a different story; Abbott had told him that the secretary of the treasury had been 'not unfavourable' to the Canadian need for a 9 per cent devaluation. When Rasminsky told the American that he would report Southard's version to Ottawa, he 'seemed most anxious that Rasminsky should not do this.' The US executive director ended the conversation by saying 'that everything he had said must be interpreted in the light of the fact that he was feeling unwell and had a temperature of 101.'[51] Indeed; he was not the only one.

As well, there were some personnel conflicts within the IMF, still a relatively small organization, that coloured perceptions. Many IMF officials had questioned the appointment of the American Andrew Overby as first deputy managing director on 9 February 1949. According to the careful language of J. Keith Horsefield, author of the Fund's official history, the functions of that position were 'never ... clearly defined ... From the point of view of the Fund ... the appointment of Mr. Overby had certain drawbacks. It was shortly followed by a further stiffening of the US attitude toward the use of the Fund's resources ... The coincidence [of Overby's appointment and the greater difficulty among Fund members in obtaining resources] had the unfortunate result of strengthening a suspicion in the minds of many members – perhaps particularly European members – that the Fund's policy was being dictated by the United States.'[52]

Overby was, many thought, merely an American plant to make the IMF better conform to American policy. Jean Monnet's observation of some years prior seemed to be coming true, as Overby did have a direct line to Henry Snyder. At the Fund and Bank meetings in Paris in September 1949, Rasminsky took the opportunity offered by a chance meeting in Towers's hotel room with William Martin of the US Treasury 'to give him some straight talk about US attitudes in the Fund and in particular about the way the US is giving reason for the belief that it is completely dominating the institution.'[53]

The British were also appalled by what they called 'the use made of the Fund to promote US political ends ... The most disturbing example has undoubtedly been the attack made since the Spring [of 1949] on the exchange rates of European members, in defiance of the provisions of the Articles which make it plain that the initiative for any change of rates rests exclusively with the member country concerned. Even when recognition of the existence of this initiative had been fought for and established (the only major point on which the US have not had their way), the US representatives used every available manoeuvre to avoid the clear intention of the Articles. It seems more than probable that, had the UK decision to devalue not been known to the Americans before the Annual Meeting in September, the occasion would have been used for an open attack on the sterling/dollar rate of exchange.'[54] The British document, ten pages long, is an extended rant over US practices in the IMF.

The British would have agreed with the Canadian analysis that some American officials connected with the Fund, but in particular White, Southard, and Overby, 'never at one time combined the qualities of technical competence, common sense and emotional stability.'[55] And since the US role was the dominant one, that complicated matters. Also making things more difficult was the way in which the IMF functioned; Gutt alluded to this in a letter to Rasminsky: 'We are an association in which every member has given up, in favour of the community, a part of his sovereign rights, in exchange for other advantages. But too many would prefer to stick to sovereign rights, and keep the advantages nevertheless.'[56] Given the conflict and tension that seemed to characterize the Fund by late in the decade, Gutt felt himself off balance 'as clearly as if I were on a shore and an undercurrent came and swept my feet away.'

He later told Rasminsky that he often wondered whether the unexpected appointment conferred on him at Savannah 'had been the right one.'[57] Gutt thought that his English was not up to the task, especially when it came to nuance, and he never considered himself an economist in a job where expert knowledge was required. He had been a good finance minister in Belgium because he had worked hard, knew the financial questions in general, and was lucky in choosing good advisers. However, he had attended too many conferences in his life not 'to know something of the ropes and be able to conduct and conclude a discussion in a satisfactory way.' He had the feeling that he had done little of that in Washington.

Rasminsky would have disagreed with Gutt's analysis of his own performance; he had earlier written that the managing director was 'a person of subtle intelligence [who had] adapted ... very successfully to the system of full-time directors.'[58] Rasminsky told him years later how much he had contributed to the establishment of the institution: 'I know that you had a very difficult time ... but in spite of the difficulties you did get the Fund started as a going concern and it has, I think, done a reasonably good job along the general lines laid out by you. Your years at the Fund were inevitably frustrating ones, partly because of the difficulties of starting a new organization and partly because the situation in Europe was not of a character that the Fund could do much to help by way of financial assistance. But I feel certain that if it had not been for your hard-headed approach to the Fund problems and your insistence that it should operate as a truly international institution there would have been no secure foundation on which to build, and the progress in later years would have been impossible.'[59] However, he would not have disagreed with Gutt's sense that the Fund was drifting, perhaps into irrelevance.

A part of that sense of foreboding lay in the Europeans' attitudes to the IMF and their growing isolationism. The continent's payment arrangements through the European Payments Union were now underpinning the mechanics of European isolationism in the monetary field: 'The fact that the administrative functions in connection with the European payments arrangements are exercised by the B[ank for] I[nternational] S[ettlements] plus the fact that central bankers and governments in most European countries are in profound disagreement, is undoubtedly leading to a shift away from the Fund towards the BIS.'[60] The reasons for this situation, Rasminsky thought, were several:

First, it gives central bankers a monthly reason for going to Switzerland ... Second, it provides an informal atmosphere in which inter-European central banking business can be transacted without fuss or fanfare. Third, it provides a place where European central bankers can meet without benefit of the presence of people from the Departments of Finance [especially in those] countries in which the central bank and Treasury do not always see eye to eye. And fourth – and not least – it provides a place where European central bankers can meet without benefit of the presence of Americans. These points – comfort and beauty, informality, the absence of Treasury officials and the absence of Americans are regarded as not inconsiderable advantages. The contrast with the International Monetary Fund as regards all of them is striking, and is reflected in a corresponding lukewarmness in the attitude of many of the European central banks toward the Fund.

Rasminsky hoped that the centre of European gravity in international monetary cooperation could be moved back to the Fund; indeed, he was intractably opposed to any 'European solutions.'[61] He did not know how that shift could be accomplished, and the Fund did seem to be caught between a rock and a hard place. In order to become more relevant in the European context, the IMF would have to take a more active role in the continent's rehabilitation. However, that was not possible, or so Gutt believed. He had explicitly ruled out providing assistance to *any* countries receiving Marshall Plan money in order not to create what he believed might be a wrong impression in the US Congress. The managing director was sensitive to the political realities involved. What, Rasminsky wondered, was the IMF's *raison d'être*? Serious self-examination must follow.

That did not happen, and at the Fund and Bank meetings held in Paris a year later it was business as usual. Moreover, European lack of interest in the Fund had increased, it seemed to Rasminsky, and the continent's horizons were shrinking. The French in particular set the tone. Even in areas of immediate importance to them, such as military cooperation through the North Atlantic Treaty Organization (NATO), created in April 1949 to counter the Soviet Union and the Eastern bloc, they were more than content to follow the American lead. NATO was not so much an example of international military cooperation against a common enemy as a great-power alliance, with the Americans in the role of director, placing various actors around the set. In a sense, the French were willing to fight to the last American, or at least to the last American dollar. Rasminsky, at a dinner and seated between the deputy governor of the Bank of France and one of its high officials, was left with the impression that all they were interested in was 'the crushing burden of taxation in France ... and how impossible it is for France to finance any additional military expenditures.'[62] The deputy governor went so far as to say 'that the social consequences of increased military expenditures here might be worse than occupation by the Russians.' To the Canadian, it brought back bad memories of pre-war France: 'Large sections of the French upper class are neutralist now just as they were appeasers before the last war.' A mere six years after the stunning events that had occurred at Bretton Woods, it seemed as if the spirit of international cooperation was non-existent, at least among certain people.

That was the context in which Canadian policy-makers discussed the possiblity of having their dollar float. The first mention of a fluctuating rate came in a Bank of Canada memorandum of January 1949 that outlined the case in favour:

1. It [was] undesirable that the exchange rate should be fixed by the Government, or should even appear to be so fixed; it is preferable to have a natural rate which could move up or down from time to time as economic conditions might require.
2. It has always been recognized that in the event of deflation or a substantial recession in the United States, it would almost certainly be necessary for the Canadian exchange rate to decline in order to facilitate whatever adjustments might be necessary in the Canadian economy ... It [would] be very difficult, however, for the authorities in charge of a fixed rate to recognize the appropriate time for such a move.
3. A freely moving rate would reduce the psychological atmosphere of restrictionism and control, particularly in the eyes of non-residents.[63]

As well, in some ways it seemed to be a natural end point following the 1946 appreciation to parity with the US dollar, the 1947 exchange crisis, and the devaluation of September 1949. The last event in particular had a marked effect on Canada. Following the devaluation, Canada's trade imbalance with the United States and its favourable balance with the rest of the world narrowed. In addition, a heavy capital inflow – a 'veritable flood of short-term capital'[64] – began from the United States, which resulted in a sharp increase in Canada's gold and US-dollar holdings, as Table 5.1 demonstrates. The inflow 'reflected a widespread view in Canada and abroad that, at a 9 per cent discount below the US dollar, the Canadian dollar was substantially undervalued.'[65] That understanding received some credibility when C.D. Howe, the powerful minister of trade and commerce, said in early June 1950: 'It is true ... that Canadian funds are at a 10 per cent discount, but that is a temporary situation. The historic position of the Canadian dollar is at par with the United States. How long that discount will continue, I don't know ... but it may not continue

TABLE 5.1
Canada's holdings of US dollars (millions)

Date	Position	Change
End 1949	1,117	—
30 May 1950	1,182	—
30 June 1950	1,255	73
31 July 1950	1,320	65
31 Aug. 1950	1,504	184
27 Sept. 1950	1,797	295

Source: LR76-522-2, 'Report on Washington Discussions,' 28–30 Sept. 1950.

for very long.'[66] The configuration of the tea leaves in the bottom of the cup gave force to the belief that the Canadian dollar would soon be revalued. Howe's statement merely confirmed what currency speculators already knew – namely, that

> several underlying forces in the balance of payments were contributing to the strength of the Canadian dollar. The Marshall Plan was now supplying Canada's overseas customers with US dollars for offshore purchases. Direct investment from the the United States had risen strongly in 1949 and then more than doubled in 1950, laying a foundation for a stronger trade-balance in the future. The long-term capital account as a whole improved by some $640 million between 1949 and 1950, partly reflecting the termination of the Canadian program of loans and credits for European reconstruction. And now, on top of this, came a favourable swing, largely speculative, of some $450 million on short-term capital account, so that the total capital account improved by more than $1 billion between the two years.

When all of that was added to the economic boom generated by the Korean War, which had begun the previous June, Canada's official gold and US-dollar reserves increased to record highs, standing at approximately $1.8 billion. This seemingly ideal situation carried with it a few undesirable elements. It had the potential to add to domestic inflationary pressures – during the summer and early autumn of 1950, Canadian authorities had had to purchase US$534 million – including about US$285 million in September alone – to prevent the Canadian dollar from moving off its peg. And given the mechanism through which that was done, tighter credit conditions were not possible. As Plumptre writes,

'In Canada, where international reserves are held not by the central bank but in the Exchange Fund, ... the government will normally obtain Canadian dollars for the purchase of foreign exchange by enlarging its regular sales of short-term securities. Such securities are sold in part to the the commercial banks and in part to the central bank. Thus, when the needs of the Exchange Fund are expanding, the commercial banks will find themselves with enlarged reserves at the central bank and also with enlarged holdings of short-term government securities. In short, the liquid position of the banking system and its ability to expand loans and investments will be increased.'[67]

As well, since most of the inward movement represented purchases of already-outstanding Canadian securities by US interests, it increased capital liabilities to the United States without correspondingly expanding the Canadian capacity to produce or to export. A rate that could float upward would discourage inward capital movements and would limit the ability of currency speculators to influence Canada's monetary system.[68]

By September 1950, the government concluded that it could no longer hold the existing rate without provoking an increase in inflation. It felt, however, that raising the dollar to parity would involve undue risk with respect to Canada's overall trading position. It had not forgotten that the 1946 return to parity with the US dollar had ultimately necessitated resort to emergency import controls in November 1947. The result was that the government had decided to free the dollar and let it find its own rate. As one critic later noted, 'Few commentators question that this was a good way, indeed the best way, for the economy to adjust to the capital inflow. With the higher value of the Canadian dollar, price increases were moderated, yet economic growth was strong and unemployment was low.'[69]

The fluctuating rate had some advantages for Canada. It did, for example, check the speculative inflow of foreign capital without having the undesirable effect of preventing the inflow of foreign capital of a permanent and productive nature. At the same time, it operated as a brake on any heavy outward movement of capital. An additional advantage of a flexible rate emerged in terms of a counterbalance to the inflationary influence in Canada of a rising US price level. The reaction to the float among the Canadian press and other informed commentators was almost unanimously favourable, and business leaders were overwhelmingly convinced that the country should not repeg the dollar under existing conditions. Many in fact felt it desirable to have the rates of all, or at least most, countries fluctuating freely *vis-à-vis* one another in a permanent system, as happened after 1973.

How did those who directed Canada's IMF policy react to this situation? An American report suggested that its three greatest supporters in Ottawa were Clifford Clark (whom it described as 'the head of the long-haired International Monetary Fund supporters'), Louis Rasminsky, and Graham Towers.[70] Certainly, Rasminsky remained firm in his defence of IMF principles. Still, as he later told the Fund's executive board,

> The exchange rate system established at Bretton Woods had not worked out ... in practice as had been hoped. The world circumstances had been different and in some ways more difficult than had been foreseen. What was in most people's minds when the Agreement was drafted was the experience of the 1930s and the dangers of competitive depreciation: the system set up provided against sudden and arbitrary changes in rates; it recognized the disruptive effects of sudden capital outflows and was on the whole friendly to exchange control. In point of fact, the world imbalance had turned out to be greater than the Fund could cope with and the dominant monetary movement throughout the whole period of Fund operation had been inflation rather than the reverse. There had been no tendency towards competitive exchange depreciation ... I did not know what the answer was in terms of the Fund system, but there were serious problems to be addressed.[71]

Enormous capital inflows, such as that experienced in Canada, which were very disruptive and difficult to control, represented a serious problem. Under the circumstances, with the potential damage to Canada's economy that defending a pegged rate represented, Rasminsky was in favour of the float. Sound economics dictated that position, and, while he might have been identified as a staunch Fund supporter, he remained comfortable with the decision.

Rasminsky was given the job of explaining the float to the Americans and the Fund, meeting with US Secretary of the Treasury Henry Snyder and with Camille Gutt of the IMF. When the broad lines of Canadian policy emerged from meetings of officials and ministers, Rasminsky had played a major role. He had been consulted by other government departments, and his opinion was respected in Ottawa. A series of telegrams from External Affairs suggests that his word was the decisive one, as departments such as Finance and External Affairs asked for and acted on it.[72] When Rasminsky presented the Canadian case to Snyder, it went very smoothly; the secretary listened 'attentively and sympathetically' and had no trouble with the float.[73]

With the Fund, things were not as clear-cut. Discussions of a floating

rate with Gutt had begun in Paris as early as 9 September 1950, when
Towers and Rasminsky, there for the annual meetings of the IMF and the
IBRD, had met with Gutt in his hotel room. According to Rasminsky, the
managing director failed to address the challenge posed to the Fund's
rules by a possible Canadian float. He and Towers were proposing the
most egregious breach of IMF rules, and Gutt 'was as nice as he could
be.'[74] Rasminsky deplored the response – he wanted argument and
gnashing of teeth: 'It was [Gutt's] clear duty to object and protest and
view with alarm ... [but] the poor man seems to have all the guts out of
him.' The managing director even went so far as to tell the Canadians
that he thought that a floating rate would be all right.

And that was the case. Almost alone among senior staff members, Rasminsky's good friend Edward Bernstein, now director of research at the
Fund, opposed the initiative. He argued that 'if the action was justified,
then world conditions were in fact too unstable for the Fund to work and
the best thing the staff members could do was go back and do something
in their own countries.'[75] Bernstein also felt that the floating rate would
be bad for Canada and would not solve its problems, which could be met
instead by direct controls over the inflow of capital. Canadians were, he
thought, 'doing great injury to the Fund without doing any lasting good
to [themselves], merely for the sake of immediate relief from the inward
pressure of speculative funds.' Parkinson told Rasminsky that 'Bernstein
acknowledged that Canada was not a pirate, but one could infer that he
thought Canada was embarking on a piratical pursuit.'[76] Bernstein's
monetary position was, some Canadians believed, 'questionable and ...
extreme.'[77]

At least part of the problem with the Canadian float was that feelings of
IMF staff members were hurt as a result of the perceived method by
which Canada informed the Fund of its policy. Senior staffers deeply
resented what they regarded as rather cavalier treatment by Canada in
giving so little notice and bringing the proposal before the Fund when it
was an accomplished fact.[78] That was not true, and Rasminsky reminded
them of the discussions on 9 September with Gutt; the fact that the
managing director had not informed his colleagues was not Ottawa's
problem.

The IMF's managing board met to consider the float and Canada's
request that the board take note of it on 30 September. Rasminsky made
the case and participated in a session to comment on an IMF staff paper,
'Canada: The Problem of Capital Imports.' The government, he suggested, had not undertaken the float without due consideration. Officials

had run models of alternative courses of action, such as creation of public debt in required amounts and direct control of the capital inflow, as suggested by IMF staff. However, the minister of finance had rightly rejected them:

> The objections to continuing to finance the inflow of capital through creating public debt without a corresponding increase in productive assets were: (a) the complete uncertainty as to the amounts which might be involved, (b) the foreign exchange cost, (c) the budgetary cost and (d) the loss of control of domestic monetary conditions and the creation of inflationary pressures. I described the objections to the proposal for capital import controls as being (a) technical - the difficulty of distinguishing between speculative and productive inflows, the problems, (including the problem of border control on Canadians,) that would be created by the emergence of a premium on Canadian dollars in the unofficial market which would be the inevitable result of our instructing our banks not to buy US dollars without reference to us, as we should be obliged to do, (b) substantive – the close and prevasive connections between the Canadian and American economic systems which had operated to the advantage of both countries; the fact that we might continue to want US assistance in developing our natural resources; and the difficulty of turning capital on and off like a tap or having an attitude friendly towards certain types of capital inflow and hostile to others, in view particularly of the difficulty referred to above in distinguishing between them, (c) psychological – the general trend of governmental and public opinion in Canada is away from controls and it would be difficult to explain using powers according to the preamble of the Foreign Exchange Control Act for the purpose of controlling capital exports, for the precisely opposite purpose.[79]

The managing board, comprised of appointees from those countries elected to it, adopted a different position from that of the staff and offered no word of criticism. Egypt, France, India, the Netherlands, the United Kingdom, the United States, and Venezuela all found Rasminsky's explanation convincing. They were so understanding that Gutt had to intervene at one point to protest that their general attitude – that Canada must decide its own policy – was a negation of the Fund concept; the Canadian government had responsibilities under the IMF agreement, too. That position did not carry the day, and Rasminsky obtained what his government wanted – the Fund took note of the Canadian action but did not approve it. The Canadian dollar quickly appreciated against the US currency; from a 10 per cent discount, it moved upward to US$1.04. It would float *de jure* until May 1962.

When two IMF officials travelled to Ottawa in late 1950, they received no satisfaction from the Canadian government when they asked for some sort of compromise on the dollar situation that they could use to bolster international confidence in the IMF. They returned to Washington, according to A.F.W. Plumptre of External Affairs, 'wondering whether Canada will ever again be a member of the Fund in good standing. They regard this as a severe blow - perhaps even a mortal blow - to the Fund; Canada has from the very beginning been regarded as one of its great sources of strength.'[80]

The Fund's analysis – that the Canadian dollar would float for some time – proved accurate; Rasminsky and Towers had advised Abbott not to return to a fixed parity soon. They believed that until international conditions were such that the Fund's objectives of convertibility and non-discrimination could be achieved by a number of major countries, it was not in Canada's power to accept the obligation of a fixed parity. However, that said, Canada was nearer to achieving the Fund's objectives than any other member, except the United States.[81] Those who were quick to criticize Canadian policy, they thought, should be aware of that fact.

There was little follow-up by the Fund, and in late autumn Rasminsky counselled External Affairs to take no further action. Certainly, it seemed, the government need not be overly concerned; support for the Fund had hit all-time lows, partly as a result of its attitude to helping out countries in need, which Rasminsky described as, 'niggardly and recalcitrant.'[82] American domination had much to do with that. The hard feelings seemed to have been forgotten a year later, however, when Ottawa withdrew all the restrictions on foreign exchange in December 1951 that had first been imposed in September 1939. The Fund staff had consultations with Rasminsky in March 1952, over the possibility that Canada should now fall under article VIII of the Fund agreement, which meant that it would fully subscribe to the IMF articles of agreement. (Article IV dealt with fixed exchange rates.) Rasminsky agreed and told Abbott that 'some of the staff would no doubt feel that an announcement that Canada was assuming the obligations [outlined in article VIII] would add to the Fund's prestige.'[83] The minister took his advice.

Rasminsky kept a weather eye on the Canadian exchange rate for the rest to the decade. He met regularly with the minister of finance to apprise him of the fluctuations of the Canadian dollar, the amount of long-term

TABLE 5.2
Canadian dollar, 1950–7

	Spot rates (Can$) for US dollars in Canada			Overall position of the Exchange Fund Account (gold and US$) (Can$million)
	High	Low	Close	
30 Sept. 1950	110	110	110	2,194
Oct.–Dec. 1950	107	$103^1/_4$	$105^{15}/_{16}$	2,038
1951	$107^{15}/_{16}$	$101^3/_{16}$	$101^3/_{16}$	1,746
1952	$101^1/_8$	$95^7/_8$	$97^1/_{32}$	1,846
1953	$99^{25}/_{32}$	$96^3/_4$	$97^3/_8$	1,786
1954	$98^3/_4$	$96^{11}/_{32}$	$96^{19}/_{32}$	1,910
1955	$100^1/_{16}$	$96^{15}/_{32}$	$99^{29}/_{32}$	1,810
1956	$99^{31}/_{32}$	$95^{21}/_{32}$	$95^{31}/_{32}$	1,890
Jan.–July 1957	$96^{11}/_{32}$	$94^{25}/_{32}$	$94^{13}/_{16}$	1,923

Source: LR76-518-9, LR, 'Exchange Fund Policy, 1950–57,' 16 Aug. 1957.

capital inflow, and the current-account deficit. He also advised the minister as to the state of the exchange fund account, which had been used in the past in support of the Canadian dollar. By virtue of the Currency, Mint and Exchange Fund Act, this fell under the Bank of Canada's purview, but the Bank acted on behalf of the minister of finance and took instructions from him.[84]

With a floating dollar, however, it was now Canadian policy to allow the exchange rate to be determined by the underlying forces of supply and demand in the exchange market. Any interventions by the exchange fund were directed towards what Rasminsky described as maintaining an 'orderly condition, i.e. to ensuring that reasonable amounts of exchange could be marketed at levels not differing substantially from those which had previously been quoted, that the movement in the exchange rate in the course of any day was not excessive, and that the transition from one level of rates to another brought about by market forces should be fairly gradual and not abrupt.'[85]

Table 5.2 demonstrates the dollar's movement over seven years. As Rasminsky wrote to Donald Fleming, the minister of finance in John Diefenbaker's first two governments, 'The sharpest exchange rate movement after the freeing of the Canadian dollar was that which took place between September 30, 1950, the last date [when] the US dollar was pegged at 110, and August 1952, when it reached $95^1/_2$, a fall of nearly fifteen cents in the value of the US dollar in less than two years. As the table demonstrates, movements in the exchange rate since that time have been on a much more modest scale.' Carefully managed, the dollar's travels through the twelve years of its float were relatively uneventful.

Louis Rasminsky wanted to be governor of the Bank of Canada. Since he had joined the Bank in 1943, he had established a reputation for integrity and intelligence, his skill at negotiating solutions to seemingly intractable problems had become well-known, he had maintained an unparalleled range of international financial contacts, and he had shown himself to be a very good manager. In short, all those qualities normally prized by nominating committees were a part of Rasminsky's character, and anyone of his accomplishment could contemplate the future with some equanimity. As a result, when Donald Gordon left the Bank in 1949 to become chairman of Canadian National Railways, Rasminsky believed that he stood a good chance to replace him as deputy governor – a cabinet appointment.

In a letter of 1946 to Lyla, he had written of a conversation with Towers that had a bearing on events three years later. If, the governor had then asked, he were appointed managing director of the IMF – a possibility then under consideration – would Rasminsky join him as his deputy? While the latter did not believe for a moment that the Fund would permit two Canadians in senior positions, the governor's query did allow him to raise the question of his future with the Bank:

> [Towers] said that the posts in the bank for which I was eligible are Governor and Deputy Governor. I said that I took it for granted that Gordon would become governor (to which he assented) and then asked whether, from the point of view of the Bank, there were any people who should be considered for the Deputy Governorship in preference to myself. He said no, there was no one. He then added that the only other person in the Bank who had a claim was Coyne ... As I told Towers, I had no doubt at all that Gordon would prefer Coyne to myself and what he wishes would certainly be endorsed by the Directors of the Bank and Government would have to have exceptionally strong reasons, which are not present, for opposing. I hinted to Towers, though I did not say so in that many words, that if Coyne were appointed Deputy Governor instead of me, I would ... leave the Bank.[86]

When Gordon moved on in 1949, Rasminsky remained as interested in the position as ever. However, the prevailing mood favoured James Coyne, who had been chosen in a close vote as senior deputy–designate by the nominating committee of the Bank's board. Rasminsky made short briefing notes to himself, to be put to the governor should the opportunity arise, which it did not. Still, the notes were an indication of how he viewed the situation.

He regarded himself as a 'contender' until the full board gave official sanction to Coyne; it could still reverse the decision of the nomination committee, and St Laurent's Liberals, or so Rasminsky believed, had made it clear that he was acceptable to them. He would be disappointed if not chosen. If the decision remained as it was, it raised the question in Rasminsky's mind as to his future with the Bank:

> The problem for me can be put in pretty concrete terms: is merit going to determine promotion and am I going to be able to contend with Coyne on approximately equal terms for the top job when Towers retires. In my opinion, on merit I should be able to, and this is evidently the situation as now regards the Deputy Governorship. The over-riding consideration in favour of Coyne as Deputy Governor is that Towers prefers him as his Deputy. As Coyne is clearly well-qualified, this is an important and valid consideration and gives no ground for complaint. But from my point of view the question is: is that preference also going to eliminate me now for the running as approximately equal contender with Coyne to succeed Towers?[87]

Coyne would have an edge if he were chosen as deputy, but Rasminsky hoped that certain things could be done to establish a status for him not too dissimilar, including: '(a) same salary as Coyne; (b) in FECB the line of authority to be Towers–Rasminsky with other arrangements (Executive Committee) as suggested by Towers. I to preside at Board meetings in Towers's absence; (c) I should attend meetings of Bank Directors; (d) I should generally attend Executive Committee of Bank; and (e) My title should be changed to Executive Assistant to Governor (singular) or some other and no one else in Bank to have same title.' That was not to be, however, and Coyne was named deputy when Gordon departed. When Coyne became governor, as of 1 January 1955, Robert Beattie, who had joined the Bank in 1935, became (senior) deputy, and Rasminsky, a deputy governor (a new position).

A Bank of England official, visiting Ottawa several years later, believed that the appointment of Rasminsky in 1949 had been stopped by cabinet: 'Quite a number of businessmen, bankers and bond dealers whom I met felt that Rasminsky ought to have been appointed Deputy Governor in 1949 instead of Coyne ... This fact very nearly happened according to someone whom I believe to be reliable ... The Secretary of the Cabinet, a friend of Rasminsky, attended the Cabinet meeting in 1949 at which the appointment of a Deputy Governor was considered. The officers of the Department of Finance had made it so clear whom they thought was the most suitable candidate that when the Secretary left the room to leave the ministers to deliberate alone, he wrote and posted a letter of congratulations to Rasminsky and was very surprised to hear next morning of Coyne's appointment.'[88] Whatever the veracity of that statement, antisemitism within the Canadian cabinet was a possible explanation of Rasminsky's being overlooked. Rasminsky has denied receiving a letter.

Michael Rasminsky, then twelve years old, remembers the pervading sense of gloom in the house on the day following the decision: 'One of my childhood memories ... [is that] on the day that Coyne's appointment as deputy governor was announced, my parents [were] going out to dinner and his being very, very shaken about something. And that was the day that that appointment was announced.'[89] It was behaviour so uncharacteristic of his father that the scene remained with the son.

There was a similar atmosphere in November 1954, when Coyne was chosen as Towers's successor. Even while that outcome was not unexpected, a number of observers believed that Rasminsky should have been appointed. Tom Kent of the *Winnipeg Free Press* wrote to him noting that he was 'on his record and in the opinion of many people, almost too good to be the third man in even the best of organizations.'[90] His old colleague from External Affairs, Douglas LePan, told him: 'Your reputation [in Washington] and elsewhere needs no further title to increase its lustre ... You are regarded in Washington as without peer in the field of foreign exchange.'[91]

Rasminsky was promoted to a new position created as of 1 January 1955; along with Ralph McKibbin he became a deputy governor. Douglas Fullerton suggests that this was done in order to persuade Rasminsky 'to stay on at the Bank.'[92] But if he was not appointed to the top post, why was he not given the job of senior deputy? Coyne later told Fullerton that 'the job entailed heavy adminstrative duties, and that Rasminsky's prospective continuing international involvement would require him to be away for a considerable amount of time.' However, it was more likely that Coyne simply preferred Beattie, with whom he was close.

Accusations of anti-semitism were levelled at the government, and there is probably some basis for them. Again a Bank of England official, on a fact-finding trip to Ottawa in November 1954, certainly thought so. He reported that 'Rasminsky's failure to reach the very top is widely attributed to antisemitism, which is surprisingly strong in Canada. I came across many examples of antisemitism and I have no doubt that it has seriously affected Rasminsky. There are, for example, many instances recorded in Hansard during the period in which Rasminsky was head of the Foreign Exchange Control Board of members of Parliament asked why it was that a Polish Jew was considered fit to manage the country's foreign exchange.'[93]

As well, an incident from the mid-1960s adds some credence to the speculation. At a lunch following a morning's official activity in Quebec City, Rasminsky, then governor, exchanged pleasantries with the son of former prime minister Louis St Laurent. Following their conversation, he asked the son to remember him to his father. As Michael Rasminsky remembers, 'St. Laurent *fils* came back after lunch ... with a message from Louis St. Laurent to say that one of the things that he had always felt very badly about was the fact that my father had not been appointed at that time, and intimated that it had been because of the issue of anti-semitism ... Obviously he was getting something off his conscience.'[94] John Diefenbaker, perhaps not the most credible witness, had a similar recollection of why Rasminsky had been passed over as governor; as prime minister, he appointed Rasminsky to the Bank's top position in 1961.

But if he was not chosen as either deputy in 1949 or as governor a half-decade later, his reputation was such that he was asked by the United Nations in the early 1950s to be an adviser on the establishment of the Bank of Israel. It was an enjoyable interlude with a number of trips to Lake Success in New York, where that bank's act was drawn up. It also resulted in a life-long friendship with its first governor, David Horowitz. And if his career seemed to have reached a relative impasse at the Bank, there were other offers. In 1953, he was courted by the University of Toronto and gave some thought to making the move. Sidney Smith, its president, asked him to become chair of the department of political economy following the death of Harold Innis. The department embraced economics, commerce and finance, political science, and sociology. Smith wanted to reinvigorate it, feeling that it had become 'too remote from issues of public economic policy ... [hoping] that [the new appointment] will bring the Department into closer touch with affairs and will ... speak out in public as occasion arises.' Rasminsky was also told that 'the courses offered are not thoroughly adapted to to-day's requirements for economics students.'[95]

It is doubtful, however, that his opinion of academic life had changed much since the 1930s, when he had contemplated making a move in that direction. He refused the offer of 1953 but remained involved in the search for an appropriate candidate. Smith pressed him to inquire whether Lionel Robbins was interested. He was not, and the president then asked Rasminsky to approach the latter's old friend, James Meade, at the London School of Economics, and make an offer. He also refused. Vincent Bladen, one of Rasminsky's old professors, was ultimately named chairman. That same year, Rasminsky was awarded an honorary doctorate by the University of Toronto. He had turned into a most illustrious alumnus.

The federal Department of External Affairs also actively recruited him for service. In mid-1955, Rasminsky received a letter from Jules Léger, the undersecretary of state, inquiring as to his availability. 'Mr. Pearson,' Léger wrote, 'took the opportunity of the Prime Minister's visit to Ottawa, last week, to discuss with him a certain number of diplomatic appointments, and in the course of the discussion your name was mentioned in connection with a senior post in Washington. The Prime Minister was very much attracted by this idea and Mr. Pearson has now asked me to approach you ... and obtain your reaction.'[96] The letter was followed up by a cable to Rasminsky in Istanbul, where he was attending the annual meeting of the IMF and the IBRD. While Rasminsky's immediate inclination was to turn it down, External Affairs continued to press him into 1956. In the end, however, as with all other attempts to pry him loose from the Bank, it was unsuccessful.

Louis Rasminsky was a very effective executive director of the IMF, and he had played a major role in the development of the Fund since 1946. He was well-respected by his fellow directors and regularly consulted by the managing director. However, his reputation also helped block any chance he might have had to become either the Fund's managing director or its deputy managing director. In a very real sense, the Americans knew him too well, thought him too familiar with the organization, and resented his unrelenting criticism of their IMF policy.

Both positions became open in 1951; the deputy managing director, Andrew Overby, was offered the job of assistant secretary of the US Treasury, while at the same time Camille Gutt was approaching the end of his five-year term as managing director. He was sixty-six years old and not keen to continue. The US embassy in Brussels passed along its information on his resignation: 'It would seem that Mr. Gutt has resigned because he feels that developments in the International Monetary Fund are not going according to his own outline for the effort of that organization ... Since the death of his wife by cancer two years ago and the loss of two of his three sons in the war, he has become a lonely and aloof man ... and is not interested in the lucrative salary which he receives as head of the International Monetary Fund.'[97] Many members believed it a propitious moment to appoint someone who could be counted on to breathe new life into the IMF; on its fifth birthday, it was too passive and too content to observe the big issues of the day from the sidelines. The British, for one, believed that it was 'flounder[ing] in the Doldrums,' with no effective leadership.[98] Similarly, the Canadians thought that 'this was not a spectacular period in the history of the Fund.'[99] That led to speculation over suitable candidates who would reinvigorate it.

There was another issue that required a strong guiding hand to resist American pressure. The Fund had been caught up in the Cold War in a way that some directors found distasteful. For example, in December 1950 Frank Southard had asked that the IMF consider restrictions on payments and transfers to China and North Korea and adoption of a form of foreign-funds control. The restrictions would be imposed for political and military purposes and did not arise from economic or financial necessity of the kind ordinarily envisaged in the Fund agreement. The People's Republic of China, in support of the North Koreans, had entered the Korean War and was, it seemed, pushing UN forces off the Korean peninsula. That offensive in the Far East had its US counterpart at IMF headquarters in Washington.

The Canadian alternate in Washington, Joseph Parkinson, was clearly unhappy with the request and uncertain how to proceed. Should the Fund, he asked Rasminsky, 'do no more than "take note" of the action of the United States'?[100] Rasminsky agreed with that stance, pending study of the whole question of whether or not the IMF even had jurisdiction over such issues. It was important, he thought, that the Fund not become 'associated in an active way with measures that were strictly political or part of national defense.' One of the 'brats' of Keynes's address at Savannah in 1946 *was* growing up a politician, as the Americans had their way.

The Americans, almost alone, were not unhappy with the way in which the Fund had evolved because they controlled so much of its apparatus and set so many of its precedents, which tended to alienate other countries. The United Kingdom was concerned about the over-abundance of Americans in senior positions, that made it difficult to create a genuinely international atmosphere. Moreover, as the Fund staff filled up with Americans, it was increasingly regarded as a US agency and less attractive in terms of career possibilities to non-Americans. Britain had also let the Americans know that it was not happy with the growing proportion of 'academic and theoretical economists who have not the practical experience which would give confidence in their advice to Governments.'[101]

The British were particularly keen to give the Fund a 'new look.' They had long attributed its failure to assume a dominant role in the international monetary field as resulting from the facts that it was controlled by Americans, reflected current US political policy, regarded its members with suspicion, and had an impossible management structure and procedures that were heavy-handed and indecisive.[102] To achieve reform meant replacing Overby with a more 'acceptable' candidate, as a first step. The British Treasury and the Bank of England favoured Rasminsky in early 1951.[103]

There was some thought that Rasminsky might be amenable to an approach, given the disappointment attendant on being passed over as senior deputy governor of the Bank of Canada in 1949. Before Ivar Rooth's appointment as managing director in 1951, a few in Whitehall considered nominating the Canadian for the top post. He was ambivalent about the job; while 'he has hitherto been unwilling to stand, for personal reasons, ... there are indications that if Gutt does not continue he would like to be given a chance of standing. He has, [however,] ... shown no definite keenness for the job ... His candidature would probably *not* be popular with the Americans.'[104] In any event, the British eventually settled on the Swede Ivar Rooth as 'their' candidate for managing director, which meant some tough negotiations with the Americans.[105] The latter eventually came around to that point of view, and Rooth took office on 3 August 1951.

With this appointment, attention now turned to that of the deputy managing director. The Americans, Sir Herbert Brittain, was told, 'have already indicated that the successor to Overby in the Fund should be either a Canadian or an American – no discriminating foreigners wanted.'[106] The British, initially cool to a North American for that position, realized that their options were limited; as Brittain noted in a minute, 'I agree that we are unlikely to avoid an American or Canadian. Indeed, as we had been instrumental in getting Rooth appointed we could hardly press for a European on this occasion.' The Bank of England's Sir George Bolton was asked whom he considered appropriate; he intended to suggest Rasminsky, who, or so the Treasury thought, 'would probably not accept.' Rasminsky fitted the British criteria for the job, other than the fact that he was Canadian; more important, he was 'not ... ultra-doctrinaire but would be a capable administrator who would assist Rooth in his efforts to liberalise the Fund.' As well, he could stand up to the Americans.

Accordingly, the British pushed a Rasminsky candidacy, even though he had as yet not indicated interest, nor had the British found out if the Bank of Canada would release him. That lacuna was corrected when Lord Cobbold, governor of the Bank of England, wrote to Towers asking: (a) Whether Rasminsky would be prepared to take it on (Towers did not know); (b) Whether you would be able to release him (Towers would if Rasminsky wanted to go); and (c) Whether there is any prospect of persuading the US authorities to accept a non-American candidate (Towers thought not).'[107] Cobbold ended by noting that his government felt that Rasminsky would be an extremely good choice.

British interest redoubled after the Americans proved unable to locate anyone whom they considered suitable to take Overby's place. The British ambassador in Washington, Sir Oliver Franks, was instructed by the Foreign Office to do all that he could 'to press the claims of Rasminsky.'[108] Rooth was also interested in the Canadian, wanting some international balance in the Fund's senior positions. The new managing director agreed with the British complaint that 'the United States [was] already too strongly represented in the important positions in the Fund and the Bank and that the Commonwealth has a good claim to provide the Deputy Managing Director of the Fund.' Rooth was also aware of the problems involved and the difficulty in overcoming the opposition of those who felt that Rasminsky's appointment might be undesirable in that he had represented Canada on the board. The British requested that their executive director 'canvass European Directors to obtain their support for our proposal ... Would you [also] suggest to [Southard] that the appointment of a Commonwealth candidate to this post would emphasize the international character of the Fund which already has American heads for five of its eight departments, and say that we should be particularly pleased to see a Canadian appointed and that we regard Rasminsky as suitable.'[109]

Southard was not impressed, according to A.M. Stamp, the United Kingdom's alternate executive director to the Fund, reacting to the suggestion of Rasminsky 'extremely violent[ly].'[110] Indeed, Southard maintained that he would not remain as US executive director if Rasminsky were appointed: 'He could think of nothing better calculated to ruin the Fund than Rasminsky's appointment. His reasons were Rasminsky's personality and behaviour towards the Americans on various occasions ... He said that these were personal reactions and that he had not discussed Rasminsky's name with his colleagues but felt that this opinion was shared by many of them.'[111]

Southard's assertion that members would not support Rasminsky was not true; the British believed that others would rally behind and, having counted heads, found that that was the case. Still, if the Americans could not be swayed, then Rasminsky's case was a non-starter. The only good that might come of it, or so Franks believed, was that 'the existence of Rasminsky's name as a candidate must mean that the United States will realise that any candidate they put forward must be a really good one.' In any event, the United States was intransigent, and Britain's draft-Rasminsky movement died. The American Merle Cochrane was appointed, remaining in that position until October 1962.

There was one other mention of Rasminsky during the decade as a possible candidate for managing director, this time in 1956. James Coyne had informally recommended to the IMF on behalf of Walter Harris, the minister of finance, that Rasminsky be put forward as managing director to succeed Rooth. The minister had told US Treasury Secretary George Humphrey that Rasminsky 'would make an admirable choice for Managing Director ... particularly if changes in its method of operations along the lines suggested could be brought into effect.'[112] Coyne was not putting Rasminsky's name forward 'on nationalistic grounds, and indeed will not make a formal nomination but I wanted to make our views known to the Secretary of the Treasury and yourself. Mr. Humphrey ... confirmed our previous understanding of United States views, that they would not consider it desirable for the Managing Director to be an American.' In any event, Rasminsky's candidacy as managing director was as still-born in 1956 as it had been a half-decade earlier. He was not interested in moving from the Bank of Canada, and other countries had taken to heart the informal dictum that the head of the IMF should be a European.

The various proposals by the British and Canadian governments on Louis Rasminsky's suitability for the positions of deputy managing director and managing director are testaments to his capability and competence. His chief liability, at least as seen from Washington, was that he was too intimately involved in all aspects of Fund policy development; he knew the Americans and the IMF too well. His well-defined sense of what the Fund should be doing and how it should do that, and his expert knowledge and range of contacts, were too great to allow the Americans to support him with any equanimity. They wanted the Fund to operate as an agency of Washington and recognized the difficulty of co-opting him. While it was true that Ivar Rooth fought to keep some distance between the IMF and the US Treasury, it was difficult for him as an outsider to do so. Rasminsky's reputation among staff and other executive directors was unparalleled, as was the independent turn of mind that he demonstrated. As an internal IMF memorandum from May 1956 noted, 'Discussions of major policy are tending to be concentrated into periods when both Rasminsky and [the German executive director Otmar] Emminger have found it possible to be in Washington for discussions. There is no doubt that the presence of these two ... has entirely changed the general atmosphere in the Board and raised the level of discussions to quite a different plane.'[113]

With Rasminsky not a serious candidate, the British wanted his reaction to a possibility they had in mind – Per Jacobsson, then at the Bank of International Settlements (BIS) in Basle, Switzerland. The venue chosen for the meeting was the BIS, and the British sent in their heaviest gun – the governor of the Bank of England. The Canadian had already told his alternate at the Fund, Jake Warren, how he would react: '1) J[acobsson] [is] a poor choice 2) that [Canada] thought the re-organization proposals should be proceeded with *before* the new M[anaging] D[irector] was chosen, even if this involved some delay and 3) if the US felt so far committed to J or for other reasons wanted to proceed with that name, we would wash our hands of it – not support but not oppose.'[114] Walter Harris agreed with the first two points, but not with the third.

When approached by Cobbold, Rasminsky spoke very frankly, basically reiterating the points made to Warren. According to the Canadian, the governor was 'pretty defensive' about Jacobsson, 'saying he didn't have all the qualities needed but he has some – glamour (!), a good entrée to European central banks, and he could talk down [head of IMF's research department Edward] Bernstein and [head of exchange-restrictions department Irving] Friedman. The last is the essential one, I'm sure.' Rasminsky continued: 'About half-way through the discussion I asked what his position was in relation to J. Cobbold said he had spoken to him ... and J was willing to discuss the matter. I said, well there's really no point in our continuing this discussion, is there? If the US and UK are agreed on J, that's that. I also said we could have wished we had been given an opportunity to say what we thought about J before he was approached. Cobbold said that the US and UK are now sounding out others because if there is strong opposition to J, he will not take the job.'[115] The following day, Rasminsky went to see Jacobsson at the latter's apartment. The hour was devoted to 'a discussion of J's references to Canada in the Annual Report of the B.I.S. The references were unbelievably sloppy and lacking in understanding of the Canadian situation.'

There were others who did not want Jacobsson. The French executive director, for example, in speaking for the Bank for International Settlements, thought that Jacobsson did not possess the right mix of administrative ability and temperament, though he did think him a man of influence in international financial circles.[116] As well, despite their championing of Jacobsson, some British seemed ambivalent; Rasminsky later wrote that '[the Bank of England's Maurice] Parsons is, or pretends to be, shocked by the nomination of J. He explains it by saying the British have, in effect, written off the Fund and are bored with the whole thing.' Edward Bernstein did not want him as managing director and resigned when Jacobsson was appointed. As he said years later, the Swede 'was no economist.'[117]

In the end, however, as Rasminsky had so clearly identified, Canadian opposition was of slight consequence if the Americans and the British were in favour; Per Jacobsson was appointed as managing director in November 1956. As events transpired, Rasminsky's objections were misplaced. Jacobsson was a good managing director, and he elevated the IMF to a new plane of activity.

By mid-decade, the IMF was in desperate need of reform, at least according to some directors, Rasminsky among them. The Canadians still wanted the system that Rasminsky had advocated in 1944, with executive directors residing in their home countries, employed by member governments, and attending Fund meetings as required. Instead, the United States had insisted on permanent directors, who had become, or so Rasminsky believed, 'professionals' who lived in Washington. Of sixteen directors and the same number of alternates, only those from Canada and West Germany had operating responsibilities in financial fields in their own countries. This arrangement had had, Rasminsky believed, a number of unfortunate consequences:

(i) It tended to diminish the authority of the Managing Director in relation to his own staff. The Board has tended to interfere in matters of internal administration, including appointments and promotions. It has been apparent to the staff that the Managing Director has not been master of his own administration, and this has inevitably affected the morale of the staff.

(ii) Discussions in the Fund Board have not been as fruitful or well-informed as would be the case if they were carried out by people who had some national operating responsibilities for the matters discussed.

(iii) With the Executive Directors in continuous session and with the Managing Director in a relatively weak position, countries have hesitated to discuss their own affairs with the head of the Fund before there was actual need to obtain Fund approval for some action or for use of Fund resources.[118]

Such changes as proposed by Rasminsky could be accomplished by agreement among the principal countries. Meetings of the board to discuss policy issues would be scheduled a limited number of times per year, and the executive directors representing the more important countries would be expected to come from their national capitals to attend. The system of alternates would continue, and they would deal with routine business. The internal administration of the Fund would be left to the managing director, who would be encouraged to cultivate relationships with member governments.

Rasminsky sounded out numerous colleagues on the Canadian proposals in June 1956 while visiting the BIS in Basle. As he told Coyne, he found 'the reception of our ideas most encouraging' among the Belgians, Dutch, French, Germans, and Italians.[119] For example, Wilfrid Baumgartner, then governor of the Bank of France but also the first choice of the United States and the United Kingdom for the managing director's position eventually secured by Jacobsson, was in favour of Rasminsky's ideas for reform: 'When I saw Baumgartner in Paris ... he expressed great enthusiasm for our ideas regarding the way the Fund should function, and said that he thought the attempt to find a successor to Rooth should be postponed until after these organizational proposals had been adopted. He also gave me clearly to understand that, if the Fund were reorganized along the lines we have in mind, he might well, towards the end of the year, be willing to re-consider his own previous negative attitude towards the job of Managing Director.'

As well, the Americans and the British did not disagree with the Canadian analysis. Even George Humphrey, the US secretary of the treasury, shared the view that the Fund had not worked particularly satisfactorily since 1946 and that the problem lay with the executive board. This was a major change of attitude on the part of the United States – it was Washington that had insisted on the IMF structure then in place. Cobbold was also in Canada's corner on this one, though he was unsure what to do. He wrote to Coyne: 'My personal belief ... is that with all the water which has gone under the bridge, it would not now be possible to change the system quickly or abruptly but it might later prove possible to work towards this system when the new Managing Director is in office.'[120] Rasminsky was adamantly opposed to that timetable; he wanted reform accomplished before a new managing director was appointed and captured by the status quo. Unfortunately for the Canadian, Cobbold's position was more representative, and Jacobsson, following his appointment, was given the job of responding to Rasminsky's initiative.

Jacobsson was not supportive. The new managing director favoured the system of permanent directors who would be familiar with the Fund's operation. He also believed it essential for him to be able to discuss cases with the managing board whenever necessary, which would not be possible if executive directors were resident elsewhere.[121] As Jacobsson told Rasminsky, 'I can only influence governments by the intermediary of the Executive Directors and if they are no good, I have no influence. Rasminsky tried to tell me that my influence would be greater if the members of the Board were less important as personalities. I do not think so ... Secondly, I stressed that there would always be a strong American influence. It would be stronger if there were no full Directors from other countries.'[122] While Rasminsky's proposals for IMF reform were not acted on in the way that he had hoped, he at least had Jacobsson's thanks for having put them forward. The Canadian proposals had 'served a useful purpose in high-lighting the need for greater contacts between the Fund and senior operating officials in member countries.' And so they had.

While the Canadian program was thwarted in terms of administrative reform, there were other areas where Rasminsky believed that other measures could make the IMF more relevant. One of these – access to the Fund's resources – was a difficult one on which to gain American agreement. Related to this matter was the question of global liquidity. As early as 1951, Camille Gutt had been aware of it and had submitted an outline called the 'Gutt Plan,' calling for a more pragmatic approach to access. The United States had been in favour, and at that time Rasminsky had believed that 'this ... reflect[ed] a genuine change of heart on the part of the United States and a desire to see the Fund play a more active role.'[123] However, the American conversion was not as dramatic as some had thought, and a half-decade later Rasminsky could write a memorandum noting that the Fund was 'still not playing the part it should in international affairs.'[124] He still wanted a stronger IMF – one that could more freely help members experiencing economic difficulty and that stood more firmly for convertibility and non-discrimination.

Over the next months, there was increasing discussion among IMF members about the Fund's becoming more active, especially in terms of adding to global liquidity. The annual meeting of September 1957 was the first time that that issue, and the IMF's ability to meet the type of emergency needs that had been one of the primary objects in its formation, were on the agenda. During the year, there had been a constant stream of applications for Fund drawings, mostly for amounts involving the gold and first credit tranches, but a few for amounts in excess of that. Out of its total resources of about US$9 billion in 1957, approximately US$3 billion had been drawn by the end of the year.[125] The largest beneficiary was the United Kingdom, which had received US$1.3 billion in 1956 to help deal with fall-out from the Suez crisis, but large advances had gone to France, India, and several other countries. As a result, there was some concern about a run on the IMF and talk about larger quotas. More and more, especially as American attitudes shifted, member governments realized that easy money could be obtained from the Fund provided that they were 'prepared to make the right sort of noises about their intentions to follow sound financial policies.'[126]

As well, global trade had expanded more quickly than global liquidity; between 1948 and 1965, the volume of world trade and payments was to rise by almost 300 per cent, while total reserves increased by slightly more than 50 per cent. Another potential problem lay in the changing composition of international reserves. In 1948, gold had accounted for 87 per cent of total reserves – in 1965, it had dropped to 69 per cent. World gold production had not been keeping pace with the great strides made in the global economy and was not adequate to meet the needs of the international system for reserves – a vital necessity, given the link between gold and the US dollar. As a result, a US initiative to increase Fund quotas was seen by most member governments to reflect their interests as well.

The first coordinated discussion took place at the annual meetings of the Fund and the Bank held in New Delhi, India, in October 1958. The Canadians believed that IMF resources should be increased through some sort of special mechanism. Rasminsky had told the July 1958 preparatory meeting in London for the Commonwealth Prime Ministers' Conference, that as early as Bretton Woods he had suggested that quotas in the aggregate were too small and that countries should pledge themselves to agree to a call-up of another 50 per cent. Based on his presentation, delegations were prepared to go along. A few months later, Per Jacobsson went on record as favouring a 50 per cent increase. By early December 1958, there was consensus.

As events transpired, however, a few countries, Canada among them,

TABLE 5.3
Proposals to IMF and IRBD executive board, Dec. 1958

Country	Quota (US$)	Proposed new quota (US$) or percentage increase
West Germany	$330 million	$787 million
Japan	$250 million	$500 million
Mexico	$90 million	$200 million
Cuba	$50 million	$115 million
Denmark	$68 million	$130 million
Norway	$50 million	$100 million
Turkey	$43 million	50 per cent
Israel	$7.5 million	$25 million
Burma	$15 million	50 per cent
Ceylon	$15 million	$64.5 million
Thailand	$12.5 million	50 per cent

Source: USNA, Department of Treasury Records, IMF, box 72, 'Quota Increases in the IMF: Special Increases for a Few Countries, 3 December 1958.'

wanted more than 50 per cent. At the executive board meeting of 12 December 1958, Rasminsky opened the discussion by stating that Canada deserved a 'special' increase in quota beyond 50 per cent to $550 million, from its present $300 million. Southard welcomed Canada's application; it 'would be very helpful to [the US government] to be able to present to the US Congress this evidence of [a] specially large contribution by ... Canada.'[127] Without such a move, American officials believed, their position was relatively exposed vis-à-vis Congress, especially given Britain's much-publicized reluctance to associate increased IMF resources with a definite move to convertibility though sterling convertibility for non-residents was introduced that same month).[128] There were put forward other requests for special increases in quotas (denominated in US$), which officials could use and did to bolster their case (see Table 5.3). Successful applicants included West Germany and Japan, reflecting their increasing importance in the global economy.[129]

Larger quotas had a purpose – they were to help countries weather the bumps associated with a return to convertibility and non-discrimination. Even before 1958, Rasminsky had launched his own campaign in the Fund's executive board, prevailing unsuccessfully on the British and the Germans to begin dismantling restrictions on trade.[130] For example, in the IMF record of 1955–6, Rasminsky was quoted as taking issue 'with the position of the staff that some Western European countries felt obliged to maintain a significant degree of restriction because of a sense of European solidarity, or to discriminate against dollar imports in view of the nature of the E[uropean] P[ayments] U[nion] settlement arrangements. He believed it was becoming increasingly clear that the basic reasons for continued discrimination were commercial policy considerations, including special export advantages gained by European countries through their regional or bilateral arrangements.'[131]

The West German rationale in favour of restriction, as presented to the managing board, was 'unconvincing and unacceptable,' at least according to Rasminsky's alternate at the Fund, Alan Hockin.[132] A complicating factor was West Germany's membership in the European Economic Community (EEC), or Common Market, formed in 1957. Rather than decreasing trade restrictions with non-member states, the EEC seemed to be doing the opposite. While Ottawa might protest its policy, it had little effect when the Common Market was supported and encouraged by Washington, which welcomed a Europe that was stronger economically as a bulwark against possible Soviet expansion.

Nor, Rasminsky thought, could British trade policy continue along the path followed since the end of the war. Non-resident convertibility had been introduced in December 1958, and at a UKCCC meeting six months later, he raised the second part of the mantra that he had so often intoned during the 1950s – non-discrimination. Were discriminatory policies being maintained for financial or for other reasons? He told British officials that he 'would have thought that the IMF could reach a decision in principle during the course of this year ... that convertibility should result in non-discrimination.'[133] A British summary of the meeting for distribution to its own officials noted: 'On non-discrimination, the Canadians, (especially, of course, Rasminsky) put forward their accustomed and indeed (in economic logic) well-founded logic. But they did not seek seriously to dispute our contention that while our objectives remained unchanged, we could not commit ourselves to a timetable in advance and that they must, in effect, trust our good faith and give us credit for what we had already done.[134] Rasminsky could have said that it was ever thus.

By 1959, both Rasminsky and Southard were pushing hard in the Fund against discrimination. The managing board was considering an IMF document, 'Discrimination,' and a draft for decision on discrimination for balance-of-payments reasons. The latter was the product of informal negotiations during September among directors on Southard's initiative. He had contacted the Canadians directly and had offered two alternatives – one directing members to reduce restriction and the other less forceful. Rasminsky preferred the first; indeed, he wanted the language strengthened, to make it categorical that discriminatory regimes must be dismantled; there was no longer any balance-of-payments reason for discrimination, especially with Britain and West Germany. To that end, and in anticipation of a meeting between the Canadian ambassador in Bonn and Otmar Emminger, Rasminsky told Frank Hooton, an official at Canada's embassy, that the ambassador should be briefed to emphasize that any discrimination was improper: 'The main practical consequence of European convertibility, so far as Canada is concerned is ... the fact that it eliminates any ... justification for discrimination.' When the ambassador made that point, 'he should do so not only with reference to Germany's own trade restrictions, but also with reference to the arrangements to patch up differences between the six EEC members and eleven others in Europe. The financial position of Europe is now so good that they should be removing trade restrictions generally, and not on a regional basis.'[135] That encouragement included Italy; the IMF was holding exchange consultations with that country in late 1959, and Rasminsky thought that appropriate language should suggest that Italy 'eliminate restrictions with all feasible speed and that the Fund expected that she would be able to do so within a short period of time.'[136]

In addressing an IMF board meeting called to discuss Southard's document, Rasminsky agreed that, with respect to dollar discrimination and the general issue of the dollar shortage, the Rubicon had been crossed – the so-called postwar transitional period was over. It was, he noted, 'proper and desirable that the Fund register its position along the lines that balance of payments reasons for discrimination have disappeared and hoped it would be clear that this applies to any type of discrimination – whether against the dollar area, the outer sterling area or elsewhere.'[137] While he had hoped for a much shorter statement about dollar discrimination – one that placed more 'emphasis on the principle than on the exceptions' – he recognized the necessity of accepting compromise in the hope of adopting the statement unanimously. It was so approved, but not before the French insisted that it be further watered down, against Rasminsky's forceful objections. They demanded that the resolution not prejudice the Fund's attitude with respect to discrimination for reasons other than balance of payments. His opposition, however correct it was, resembled Sisyphus in the underworld. Rasminsky had pushed his rock part way up the hill only to have it roll down again as another problem prevented him from reaching the top. It was a thankless job, which collided head-on with European determination to maintain discrimination as long as possible.

As to the transition to article VIII – that is, countries would accept the obligation not to impose exchange restrictions without prior approval of the IMF – Rasminsky believed that it should be administered strictly, and he would not like to see 'blanket approval of restrictions simply to induce members to enter Article VIII.'[138] He wanted article VIII maintained as a 'prestige term, an accolade bestowed by the Fund on high-class, truly convertible currencies, like the Canadian dollar; I would not like to see the currency of [article VIII] debased by the Fund recognizing a sort of conditional or limping convertibility.'[139]

As to the requirement of an effective par value as a prerequisite to article VIII, Rasminsky was less categorical, as indeed he needed to be, given that Canada's dollar floated. The par-value obligation was spelled out in article IV, and it contained no provisions allowing the Fund to grant exceptions. As Rasminsky told the executive board,

> The Fund had adopted an attitude of reasonable flexibility, as in the case of the Canadian dollar. He thought it should be noted that Canada had moved to Article VIII ... The Fund had even taken some initiative to favor free exchange markets as a method of getting rid of restrictions, and this had been successful. The Fund should avoid fashions in its attitude toward fluctuating rates. At present the Fund was flexible and looked at cases on their merits. [He] believed it was unwise for the Fund to go full circle and insist on par values as a prerequisite to a move to Article VIII, *even though this article did not mention par values.* This view did not mean that the Fund should not be concerned with par values but rather that it should not be concerned in the context of Article VIII. It might be argued that not having a par value was a suspicious circumstance in connection with capacity to maintain reasonable stability. But there were other suspicious circumstances, such as heavy import controls, capital controls, and so on.[140]

The board weighed in, with the French director, Jean de Largentaye, observing: 'As to the legal aspects of Fund consultations with members which were observing all the obligations of Article VIII, he could not accept the argument ... that such consultations were necessary in the light of the reference in Article I to collaboration to promote exchange stability, etc. This was not the first time that the Fund Staff had sought to use Article I as a means of establishing the powers of the Fund. Such efforts alienated members which otherwise were ready to cooperate with the Fund. It was in fact not easy to argue that regular consultations were needed to promote exchange stability when for 10 years there had been no consultation with one country, presumably Canada, which had allowed the exchange rate to fluctuate.'[141] As de Largentaye suggested, one could not always argue for purity when one had a floating dollar.

Ultimately, the North American campaign against discrimination waged in the IMF yielded little. The Europeans would liberalize only when it suited them. That was not until February 1961, when nine European countries finally eliminated the last of their restrictions on current payments and transfers.

It had been an interesting fifteen years since Rasminsky had first taken his seat at the IMF table. He had seen his career at the Bank of Canada sidetracked in 1949 and again in 1954. While he had on 1 January 1955 become a deputy governor – a position of some power and status in Ottawa – that had not been his objective. However, he resigned himself to the fact that he would not be governor and soldiered on as a senior member of the Bank of Canada team. That organization was, relatively speaking, terra incognita to him, as his work had been chiefly in the Fund and in conferences, discussions, and meetings abroad. Arguably, his greatest contribution had been in the IMF, with his attempts to 'internationalize' and 'de-Americanize' it. In that effort he was only partially successful. And the British, in his dealings with them, proved simply intransigent. While the work had been satisfying in many ways, it had also been frustrating. All of that was to change with the singular event of the so-called Coyne crisis of 1961. Louis Rasminsky was about to be appointed governor, almost against his will.

PART THREE

Two-Term Governor, 1961–1973

Chapter Six

Into the Breach

James Coyne was not a typical central banker, at least according to some. The US embassy in Ottawa, for example, believed as early as 1957 that 'Mr. Coyne sees fit to make subjective statements on various aspects of the economy, some of which seem to exceed the cautious pronouncements usually associated with central bankers.'[1] It commented again in mid-May 1959, suggesting: 'A conflict may be developing between the Canadian Department of Finance and the Bank of Canada over monetary policy.'[2] The embassy proved prescient when the governor gave his first controversial speech in late autumn 1959. So began the tortured tale that came close to devastating the Bank of Canada and resulted in Coyne's resigning as governor. It was this cataclysmic act in the history of the institution that propelled Louis Rasminsky into the limelight.

Strictly speaking, he was not in the direct line of succession; Robert Beattie was the statutory deputy governor, appointed in the same way as the governor, by the directors of the Bank, which action was then confirmed by order-in-council, and capable of acting for the governor when he was unavailable. Given Beattie's position, he was the logical choice as next in line, even though he and Coyne were of a similar age, both in their early fifties. Indeed, in its short history, the Bank had operated on the principle that the senior deputy would become governor. Coyne, the senior deputy, had succeeded Graham Towers on 1 January 1955, and if he had been reappointed to a second seven-year term in 1962, the job would have been his until the year end of 1968, when Rasminsky would have been sixty-one. In short, the so-called 'Coyne affair' created the break in Bank tradition that allowed Rasminsky to become governor.

Coyne was brilliant; most people at the Bank believed that. William Lawson, a close friend of the Coyne family (he was daughter Deborah Coyne's godfather) and senior deputy at the Bank from 1973 to 1984, said that Coyne was 'probably as brilliant as any one man [he had] ever met.'[3] He was also, many thought, arrogant beyond measure and completely convinced of the rightness of his convictions. Certainly he believed that his concern over developing inflation was correct and the tight money policy that resulted, necessary.[4]

The issue for John Diefenbaker's government was that Coyne's policy collided with its worry over increasing unemployment as the postwar boom slowed. The minister of finance, Donald Fleming, was explicit in the House of Commons in mid-1959: 'There is no tight money policy as far as this Government is concerned ... It is not the intention of the Canadian Government to inflict on the people of Canada a repetition of the tight money policy of our Liberal predecessors.'[5] A few lines of Hansard later, however, Fleming suggested that he had little control over monetary policy; it was not the responsibility of the government. As he told a questioner in the House, 'Monetary policy is a matter that Parliament has confided to the Bank of Canada.' A month earlier he had said: 'In the matter of monetary policy, this Parliament has placed the responsibility and ... power in the hands of the Bank of Canada. *The government does not exercise any sway in the field of monetary policy.*'[6] However, that was not the interpretation of many critics. If the issue of who had ultimate responsibility for monetary policy was unclear in the minister's mind, it was small wonder that it created such a crisis in Canada.

In this developing disagreement between governor and government, the fight was by no means as uneven as it appeared. The former was relatively autonomous, as laid out in the Bank of Canada Act of 1936 and its revisions. In the original act, the governor was given veto power over any action or decision of the Bank's board or its executive committee. If that power was exercised, the governor had, within seven days, to inform the minister of finance in writing of the circumstances. The minister must submit the matter to cabinet, which was then to confirm or disallow the veto.

This somewhat-unusual veto power was placed in the original Bank of Canada Act, which provided that the stock of the Bank should be sold to the public and that directors should be elected by the shareholders. The government therefore did not know who the directors of the Bank might be and considered it advisable to give veto power to its appointee, the governor. When the act was amended to provide for expropriation of the privately held shares and investment of total stock ownership in the government, the veto power was continued, with the addition of a proviso that disputes of this kind should be referred to cabinet.[7]

The veto was a powerful tool for any governor; as well, the original act had placed the bulk of the responsibility for the Bank's operation on the governor and the directors, with the government at arm's length. Still, ultimate authority for monetary policy was laid at the feet of the minister of finance and his or her cabinet colleagues. If an unresolvable conflict arose between the governor and the government, it would become the governor's duty to resign. The then-minister of finance, C.A. Dunning, noted in 1936: 'In the long run, the bank, in the performance of a vital sovereign function, must be responsible to the sovereign will expressed through a government. There cannot be two sovereigns in a single state.'[8] Later Prime Minister King had said: 'The last word is not with the Governor of the Bank, but with the Governor-in-Council which represents the House of Commons and which in turn represents the people of this country.' In 1941, the minister of finance, J.L. Ilsley, noted: 'The monetary policy which the Bank carries out from time to time must be the government's monetary policy, but the government must leave the carrying out of that policy, the choice of ways and means of executing it, to the management of the bank in whose judgement it has confidence.'[9]

Coyne did not dissent from the tradition of government responsibility. As well, the Bank of Canada Act gave the government a direct window into the Bank; it provided that the deputy minister of finance was an ex officio member of the Bank's board and of its executive committee. Though the deputy minister had no vote, it was his or her job to ensure that the minister was kept fully informed with regard to Bank policy and operations.

The system was predicated on cooperation between the governor of the Bank and the Department of Finance. While Clifford Clark was deputy minister and Graham Towers governor, close cooperation between the two was a reality. When the characters were changed to Ken Taylor, appointed deputy minister in 1951, and James Coyne at the Bank, the relationship was not so amicable. Taylor was not a strong deputy minister, while Coyne was a determined man, confident of his abilities and about the direction in which he wished to take the Bank. That strength led to the governor's injecting himself into what many considered to be the political process.

So, the Bank was a relatively autonomous institution, but not completely separate from government. It was not a department, was not dependent on government appropriations, controlled its own budget, and had its own board, which looked after such items as pensions and pay. There was good reason for this arm's-length distance from government, as the events of the early 1960s suggested. Its independence was crucial for Canada's domestic monetary policy, and it was also reassuring for investors abroad. Interest rates would not be subject to political exigencies, and the Canadian currency would be thereby protected. In the end, of course, there was provision for getting rid of a governor who consistently 'thwarted' government policy, but it was a tortuous and lengthy process. Indeed, it is arguable that the Bank's architects never anticipated that possibility. That, in sum, was where matters stood in 1961 as Coyne's Bank, or more particularly, Coyne, refused to budge.[10]

As the Bank began by mid-1959 to slow down the expansion of the money supply and increase interest rates, the stage was set for conflict. Fleming noted: 'April 27 [1960] was a grim day. Cabinet was called to meet in the morning. The Treasury bill rate had risen the previous Thursday and consequently the Bank of Canada rate rose to 4.98 per cent. Diefenbaker 'and [Secretary of State for External Affairs Howard] Green were in a tizzy. The Bank of Canada was blamed for the high interest rates and for withdrawing support from the bond market, so Coyne should be fired; no attempt should be made to defend him in the debate expected that afternoon. This nonsense vexed me sorely.'[11]

Fleming's autobiography, written a quarter-century after his run-in with Coyne, obscures the fact that his relationship with the governor was not close. Soon after Fleming had taken office, he had held a press conference to talk about monetary policy, 'which was widely interpreted as a rebuke to Mr. Coyne.'[12] As well, a few Conservatives had identified Coyne as a closet Liberal. George Hees, the minister of transport, for one, had denounced the governor as early as November 1957, claiming that he was in the Opposition camp. As well, as a former Bank official, George Watts, has observed, the Manitoban 'Coyne ... was a product of the atmosphere of the [*Winnipeg*] *Free Press*. This was not only the core of the Liberal Party but Liberal philosophy as well. Anyone formed in this mould would have very strong liberal philosophical ideas ... Unlike the relatively comfortable relationship that existed most of the time between his predecessor and the government, the change to the Diefenbaker regime must have placed him in a position which was alien to his background and unquestionably made things more difficult.'[13] The Conservative cabinet was not prepared to give Coyne the benefit of any doubt.

To further alienate the government, Coyne had advocated a certain perspective – what a former Bank of Canada official, George Freeman, has called a fierce Canadian nationalism – using his position as governor to warn the country of the dangers of continentalism.[14] It was ironic that the Conservatives should take exception to this message, given Diefenbaker's very pro-British and anti-continentalist views. But the *method* of Coyne's presentation had become almost as contentious as the substance. According to William Lawson, 'He annoyed almost everybody, including ... all the university academics across the country.' Coyne believed that those economists 'didn't matter.' The Bank's research department, where Lawson worked, felt very strongly about Coyne's approach. 'These guys were professional economists and they thought that the form of making the argument, whatever the merit of the argument was, was terribly important. You just had to argue these things in a respectable way.' While Lawson agreed with Coyne's pronouncements on the risks of the branch-plant economy, many dismissed it. And Lawson had a particular reason to dislike the approach – he was often sent to meetings of economists to defend the Bank's position.

Others believed that Coyne had simply gone too far. Earl Mulholland of the Bank of Montreal, for example, thought that 'Jimmy Coyne has overplayed his hand and has been dabbling too much in politics.'[15] E.R. Alexander of Sun Life Assurance felt that 'the feeling [was] almost universal that Coyne has gone much too far ... The Opposition in Parliament, while no doubt anxious to embarrass the Government as far as the available material will permit, shows no disposition to espouse Coyne's case on its merits.'[16]

Officials in the Bank prevailed on Beattie to intervene with Coyne, but to no avail. As Lawson said, 'Beattie was very, very able but he had ... one great fault; he admired Jim Coyne excessively.'[17] The governor had been his contemporary all through the University of Manitoba, and while Beattie was scholastically brilliant, 'Coyne was one notch higher.' As a result, it was never possible for Beattie, as Coyne's deputy, to restrain him. Lawson commented: 'We used to try very hard to work on Beattie to get him to moderate Jim Coyne, but he would respond by telling us how good Jim was.' And Beattie was never very approachable, being cold and distant with most people who worked at the Bank. George Freeman summed it up; people in the Bank 'didn't know what the hell was going on.'[18] The end result was tension so palpable that it could almost be cut with a knife.

However, the most serious issue for Coyne, because it was personal, was Diefenbaker's attack on his pension. In February 1960, following lengthy study, the Bank's board had approved a change in pension arrangements for the governor and his deputy. From now on, both would be eligible to receive one-half of their salaries – or in Coyne's case $25,000 per year, a large sum in 1960.[19] The change was implemented without being published in the *Canada Gazette*, and the minister of finance had not been formally notified. However, the Department of Justice had ruled in the past that such publication was unnecessary, and surely the minister should have been informed by his deputy or, in this case, the assistant deputy minister, A.F.W. Plumptre; the deputy minister was at a funeral on the day the pension issue was considered. Thirteen months later, when Fleming learned about the change, he was outraged. However, as J.L. Granatstein observes, 'The real reason for Fleming's anger was that after years of defending the governor against his colleagues, and with the economy in the doldrums and unemployment at its postwar peak, his patience was at an end.'[20] He wanted Coyne out.

The pension issue was the hot one with cabinet, and with the prime minister in particular. Despite his mood when apprised of the changes, Fleming initially defended the pension change in cabinet. On 1 May 1961, he told his colleagues: 'There was no real ground for an attack on the integrity of the Governor, who had not inspired the by-law amendments that had improved his pension position, and had retired from the Board meeting when this subject was discussed.'[21] He had other reasons for not wanting to renew the governor's appointment. However, on 2 May, Diefenbaker returned with a different interpretation; Coyne could have vetoed the pension change, and since he had not, he had been involved in the process. As a result, in a meeting in early June between Fleming and Coyne in which the minister asked for the governor's resignation, the pension issue dominated discussion.

The battle was now publicly joined, becoming more vicious with each passing day. According to Simon Reisman, then a senior official in Finance, 'Coyne had dug himself in behind the barricades on [the south side of Wellington Street] and refused to come out' despite encouragements from Finance.[22] The paper broadsides being exchanged across Wellington Street grew ever more numerous, to the point where George Freeman called it the battle of the duplicating machines. The Bank, with its photocopying technology, was better able to supply the guns, beating Finance's old mimeograph machine in the process.

Through many twists and turns, the public fight captivated the press and Canadians. Of course, given the government's ultimate power, it was an unequal contest; the bill declaring the office of governor of the Bank of Canada vacant passed in the House of Commons on 7 July, going to the Liberal-dominated Senate the following day. Coyne accepted an invitation to address its Banking and Finance Committee, and on 13 July 1961 the bill was rejected by the upper house. By all accounts, Coyne's performance before the committee was 'brilliant,' with not a dry Liberal eye in the room as he explained his position. Given the vindication bestowed by the not-guilty verdict rendered by the Senate, Coyne resigned immediately. The damage done to the Bank and especially to the government was incalculable.

A.F.W. Plumptre asks an obvious question; why did the government not leave Coyne in place until his term expired? After all, he had been governor since 1 January 1955 and his seven-year term would end on 31 December 1961. The answer was that the government had embarked on a policy of economic expansion and the June 1961 budget was to announce it. As the Conservatives felt that they needed the sympathetic cooperation of the Bank, which was not forthcoming because of Coyne's concern about inflation, he would have to be fired. 'In the economic circumstances prevailing,' Fleming later said, 'the implementation of the policy could not await the expiration of Mr. Coyne's term of office at the end of the year.'

But some officials at Finance also bore responsibility for the dismissal, at least according to Fleming. Writing to Plumptre years later, he remembered that he had been 'slow and reluctant to accept this view [that Coyne should be fired] but the verdict which you and Simon [Reisman] pronounced on the inadequacy of Mr. Coyne ... brought me to accept the view of my colleagues ... The last straw was supplied by yourself and Simon Reisman when after a stormy encounter with Mr. Coyne in the presence of other Ministers at a meeting in the Cabinet Chamber you expressed the opinion that Coyne was a very poor governor. Up till that time I had always been under the impression that you considered him able and that his policies were sound.'[23]

But who would replace Coyne? Donald Fleming had had his eye on Louis Rasminsky for some time. With his position on the international side of Bank affairs and as Canada's executive director of the International Monetary Fund, Rasminsky worked closely with the minister and had 'a very good relationship with Fleming.'[24] Rasminsky was also most acceptable to the government and to the Bank's board. He represented the reverse of James Coyne; he was as brilliant, but he was also 'a very orderly person ... [He] was thoughtful, careful, orderly – everything he did was measured.' As well, he did not go in for great displays of oratory. As Simon Reisman later put it, he 'was not a firecracker.'[25]

The cabinet had considered Rasminsky as a candidate at its meeting on 8 June 1961, following a representation of 2 June by two Bank directors that the deputy governor be appointed. While the government felt that it controlled the agenda, Fleming told cabinet: 'It was imperative that a successor take office as Governor before the presentation of the Budget. He suggested that he should approach Mr. Rasminsky to offer him the post. Mr. Rasminsky had been very co-operative at all times, and he enjoyed an international reputation as a brilliant central banker.'[26] During the discussion that followed, cabinet noted that, in considering Rasminsky as a possible successor, 'the government should not be influenced by the possibility of criticism by anti-semitic groups.' Though it decided that it was not appropriate to approach Rasminsky yet, he was clearly its choice.

Throughout the speculation that raged about him, however, Rasminsky made it very clear to the minister that there was only one governor, and that while Coyne occupied that position there could be no discussion of a successor, at least with him. That was the line he stuck to consistently, even in his regular meetings with the minister and despite a not-inconsiderable amount of pressure being applied in order to get him to commit himself. This pressure manifested itself in sometimes strange, even extreme, ways. Reisman was close to Fleming and saw him every day. On one such occasion early in June, the minister, knowing that his official was off to Paris with Rasminsky for a meeting of the Organization for Economic Cooperation and Development, asked Reisman to inquire whether Rasminsky would be amenable to an offer of the governor's position. During dinner that first evening in France, Reisman mentioned the minister's request to Rasminsky. His immediate response was that he did not want to talk about it. Reisman was surprised, since Rasminsky 'had not even heard the question.' When Reisman persisted, he was told: 'If you raise it again, [I shall] get up and leave right now.' They finished dinner, and the two men walked backed to the Hotel Athène where they were staying and parted company. Reisman later observed that he never really got over that. 'It was cold, it was preemptive, it was unfriendly. He never explained why he took that view. He never let me put the question ... I don't know what the hell got into him.'[27] On his return to Ottawa, he told the minister that the opportunity of sounding out Rasminsky never arose. The latter's attitude was consistent, however, with his personality and his view of the situation. There was only one governor.

On 13 June 1961, Fleming asked Rasminsky to come to his office. There, the minister told him that at an informal meeting that had been held in Quebec City on 11 June, the directors of the Bank had unanimously decided to appoint him as governor once Coyne's resignation had been received. The government was prepared to confirm the appointment immediately. Obviously, given what had gone on in the immediate past, the offer did not come as a surprise. Rasminsky merely repeated what he had told Reisman; there was only one governor, and, so far as he knew, Coyne was still it. However, Rasminsky did talk with Fleming about his own misgivings with respect to his qualifications for the office and the difficulties in assuming it under the present circumstances. He asked to be able to inform senior people at the bank, including Coyne, of the conversation. While the minister at first demurred, he later gave in to Rasminsky's wish. The first person whom Rasminsky consulted was Robert Beattie, who strongly urged him to take the job. The deputy also pledged his cooperation and support, which Rasminsky regarded as 'indispensable.'[28]

Ironically, the official rationale as to why his appointment as governor was not a realistic possibility in 1955 was now important in the choice. He had long specialized in the international aspects of banking and finance, and in 1954 this specialization had stood in his way. At that time the St Laurent government had wanted someone more closely associated with domestic finance to head the Bank. By 1961, with the Diefenbaker government following a policy of deliberate devaluation of the Canadian dollar and with the IMF questioning the propriety of the policy, Rasminsky's international knowledge and experience were invaluable.

The second reason, offered by the *Toronto Telegram*'s Peter Dempson, was that in 1954 being Jewish had been held against him. The columnist had then written: 'No Jew had ever headed any bank in Canada, and the chartered banks were said to have been opposed to his selection.'[29] By 1961, however, his appointment was now in line with Diefenbaker's Bill of Rights, which stated that there should be no discrimination because of race, creed, or colour. Canada itself had also changed somewhat since 1955, and while anti-semitism had not disappeared, it was less tolerated officially.

That was where matters stood until 14 July, the day after Coyne's resignation. Rasminsky had a meeting with Fleming at six p.m. and told him that he had consulted senior Bank staff and had come to the conclusion that accepting the position was the correct step. The question he had asked himself had evolved from 'Do you want this job in present circumstances?' to 'Do you have the right to refuse to do the job, if you are asked in present circumstances?' Still, he had some doubts, resulting from '(a) the possibility that there might be some misunderstanding between Government and [himself] regarding the role of the Bank and responsibilities for monetary policy, and (b) the existence of some opinion to the effect that the Government had moved to "take over" the Bank.'[30]

Rasminsky had drawn up a memorandum which he showed to the minister, who agreed completely with the principles enunciated. This document had been written at an after-hours meeting with Lawson. Rasminsky had scratched out the bulk of the memo on the back of an envelope, and Lawson, who could read his cramped scrawl, took it home and typed it out. The idea expressed on that piece of paper became a part of the Bank of Canada Act when it was revised in 1967. Indeed, in his testimony of 31 October 1966 to the House of Commons Committee on Finance, Trade and Economic Affairs, which was considering proposed changes in the act and related banking legislation, Rasminsky framed his remarks in terms of his statement of July 1961. What were its principles? The first was that 'in the ordinary course of events, the Bank has the responsibility for monetary policy.' The second condition on which Rasminsky would take the job was that 'if the Government disapproves of the monetary policy being carried out ... it has the right and the responsibility to direct the Bank as to the policy which the Bank is carrying out,' but it also had to follow certain procedures, as discussed below in chapter 7.[31]

In July 1961 he was also interested in the question of publicity and thought a judicious airing of his views and of the government's commitment to the explicit set of rules laid down would help recapture some of the ground that the Bank had lost and help stabilize financial markets. He wanted to release his memorandum to the press immediately on his accession to the governorship. The cabinet declined to authorize the press release according to Rasminsky's timetable.

Prime Minister Diefenbaker had a private, hour-long meeting with the governor on 17 July, in which he declaimed at some length on the disadvantages of publication. He told Rasminsky that 'the need I [Rasminsky] had felt to place certain views before the Government, before accepting the appointment, would be regarded as a reflection on the Government. [Diefenbaker] also said that I was, in the section dealing with responsibilities for monetary policy, putting forward an interpretation of the Bank of Canada Act which was not that of the Government.' Rasminsky replied that he was 'not putting forward an interpretation but stating what I thought the relations should be and that if the Government intended to maintain the position that they had no responsibility for monetary policy, I would not accept the Governorship. He said that this would not be their position.' In any event, the prime minister and the governor-designate reached a compromise; the latter would wait ten days to publish his memo.

In the conversation with Rasminsky, Diefenbaker raised two other points. First, on congratulating Rasminsky on his appointment (even though Rasminsky had not yet officially accepted the position), he said that 'his mind went back to 6½ years ago when I would have been appointed Governor except for one reason.' The reason, of course, was anti-semitism, and the Conservative cabinet had made public its position that it would 'not be influenced by the possibility of criticism by anti-semitic groups.'[32] When Rasminsky claimed that he did not believe that this was the reason behind his rejection in 1954, Diefenbaker told him that Louis St Laurent had said that 'he would find it impossible to defend [Rasminsky's] appointment in Quebec.'[33]

The second issue raised was the conduct of Les Mundy, the Bank's secretary. He had been a very visible supporter of Coyne, and Diefenbaker asked Rasminsky how he 'proposed to get rid of [him].' The governor's reply would be a comfort to Bank employees. He would not attempt to defend the judgment displayed in certain actions, 'but one had to make allowance for the emotional stress that people had been under in the Bank; that I felt certain that the Bank staff, including Mundy, wanted nothing more that to get down to the business of the Bank and develop a proper relationship with Government.' Rasminsky firmly told the prime minister that he was responsible for the administration of the Bank and that Diefenbaker could hold him responsible if things went wrong. The prime minister, Rasminsky noted with some understatement, 'accepted this formulation with evident reluctance.' There were others of whom the prime minister was very suspicious, including Ralph McKibbin, the deputy governor in charge of securities, who had initially been a strong Coyne supporter, and Beattie. Indeed, the *Ottawa Citizen* suggested in an article on 24 July that the latter 'may be replaced at the end of the year' when his term as the senior deputy expired.[34] Rasminsky's intention, however, was to heal the wounds; he asked Beattie to stay on and help him do that, which the deputy governor did, retiring in 1971.

Rasminsky also placed on record in his memorandum of July 1961 his views about the way in which monetary policy fitted into other public policies affecting the economic and financial welfare of the country. He took it as generally accepted that certain objectives were in the forefront of government considerations. Among these were high employment, price stability, and sustained economic growth. He went on: 'A flexible monetary policy is an essential element in the total blend of policies directed towards these ends. In a situation characterized by large unemployment and unused capacity, monetary policy should be directed to encouraging the use of credit. On the other hand, if the economy is approaching a condition of full stretch, policy should be directed towards discouraging the use of credit.'[35]

Too great a reliance on monetary policy, either as a restraining or a stimulating factor, would, however, lead to unsatisfactory and self-defeating ends. All arms of government would have to play a role in responding to the situation. What the new governor wanted to make explicit, as obvious as it might seem in retrospect, was the case for 'a careful and consistent meshing together of all the various aspect of financial policy ... while avoiding undue strains in particular sectors.' He did not want to become an unwitting Coyne, given the division of authority in Ottawa. The government had to see the need for close coordination of monetary, fiscal, debt-management, and other economic policies between itself (and especially Finance) and the Bank. If he were to become governor, Rasminsky wrote in his memorandum:

> I shall wish to play my full part in achieving the close working relationship with the Minister of Finance which is indispensable if the Bank is to discharge its responsibilities in a satisfactory way. I would hope to have frequent informal contacts with the Minister of Finance of the same character as I have had over the past years in my capacity of Executive Director of the International Monetary Fund and the International Bank. In addition, in order to ensure beyond doubt that continuing high importance is attached to maintaining lines of communication, and even though such precaution may now seem unnecessary, consideration should be given to setting up a routine procedure for regular meetings at fairly frequent intervals between the Minister of Finance and the Governor.

Those were the principles by which he would be guided in the discharge of his duties. These were agreed to by the Conservatives, and he was officially appointed by order-in-council on 24 July 1961. Rasminsky's memorandum, according to the *Globe and Mail*, when made public, cleared away 'any lingering doubts about the role of the Bank as an arm of Government, and as protector of the currency.'[36]

He had taken on a big job. Major repairs to the Bank's reputation were necessary. He would also have to continue to work out proper relations of mutual confidence with the government and remove the Bank from any continuing controversy. As well, he had to restore the Bank's position in the business and financial communities. He believed that he 'must again create the image and the reality of the Bank as a truly national institution removed from the hurly-burly of politics, which carries on its own business competently and is a source of objective and disinterested information and counsel to Government.'[37]

Rasminsky's memorandum was interesting also in that it wholeheartedly endorsed Coyne's position and repudiated Fleming's. Rasminsky understood clearly that in its day-to-day operations the Bank was independent of government influence. However, in the final analysis, and under specified conditions, Parliament was the ultimate arbiter of monetary policy. In a sense, he had returned the fulcrum to the position it held before the Diefenbaker government took office. As the *Regina Leader Post* pointed out, 'No old governor could have received a greater policy vindication from a new governor than has Mr. Coyne from Mr. Rasminsky.'[38]

The reaction to the appointment was unanimously positive. Among the articles written in support, and the letters that poured into the Bank, the Canadian Bankers' Association, that bastion of establishment opinion, was first off the mark in congratulating him. Robert Moon, the *Christian Science Monitor*'s Ottawa correspondent, noted that he was 'a Canadian banker not without honor in the foreign banking community, but virtually unknown in his own land.'[39] Moon thought the choice inspired. The Bank of England believed his selection 'a victory for common sense in the Canadian Government.'[40] Bruce Phillips, in a CBC news commentary, told Canadians: 'The appointment of Louis Rasminsky ... as the new governor of the bank draws a healing compress over the raw quivering wounds created by the Coyne fight with the government. From convulsion to calm in a week sums it up. By any reckoning, this is an excellent appointment. This man has a brilliant record and a brilliant reputation. He ranks as one of the world's outstanding figures in the field of monetary management.'[41]

The support was wider than the financial press or bank presidents; Rasminsky had now become a symbol for the Jewish community in Canada. Being elevated to the governorship meant a great deal in a country where anti-semitism on occasion raised its ugly head, and Ottawa's Jewish Community Centre held a dinner for the new governor in August.[42] There were now two Jewish senior officials in Canadian government service – Rasminsky and David Golden, deputy minister of defence production. There were, of course, many other Jews in the ranks immediately below them, and they would begin to make their mark during the decade.

Rasminsky's appointment settled part of the controversy – the pension issue remained. Rule 17, the controversial decision that allowed the governor to retire on one-half of his annual salary, had been suspended by the Bank's board in early summer. It was uncertain how to proceed. Just as the pension issue had caused trouble between Coyne and the minister of finance, in the aftermath of the crisis it provoked difficulties between Fleming and Rasminsky, admittedly on a different scale.

On 9 August, the minister telephoned the new governor to tell him that as he left a cabinet meeting the press had cornered him about Pension Rule 17. The minister had answered that the board of directors had suspended it, pending further study of the pension to be paid the governor. For Rasminsky, the important thing was that Coyne's pension had been raised again, and he was disappointed that Fleming had felt it necessary to reply.

The Bank situation was settling down, and the last thing that Rasminsky wanted was to revive 'old controversies and stir up matters once again.' Moreover, did the minister feel that he had the authority to discuss in public the actions taken by the Bank's directors, or did it fall more appropriately under the purview of that group, or the governor in their name? There might be situations in which it was fine for the minister to refer to actions of the directors, but in that case 'it should be on the basis of a considered statement made by him after the discussion with the Bank.' Rasminsky hoped that the minister 'did not regard his action in this case as in any sense normal,' and he did not leave any 'doubt in Mr. Fleming's mind that [he] was unhappy about what had taken place.'[43]

Rasminsky was so irritated by the extensive publicity given to Fleming's comments by the press that the next morning he phoned D.S. Maxwell, the assistant deputy attorney general. It was now 10 August, and on 24 July the Bank had requested a written opinion on the validity of Rule 17. He wanted it by the following day, when the executive committee of the board of directors was scheduled to meet. Maxwell's reply – that the request 'had been pretty vague and [that] he would require additional information before answering it' – irritated Rasminsky further. Specifically, the official wanted some guidance with respect to the relationship between the executive committee and the board. The governor 'did not quite see the relevance of this to the legal question raised' but would commit himself to forwarding anything that the department wanted as soon as possible. The conversation went on:

Mr. Maxwell then said that the question was a complicated one and he did not see what the urgency of getting an answer was. I said that I had not realized that the question was so complicated in view particularly of the fact that the Department of Justice had had to deal with it on previous occasions. To this he replied that on previous occasions the Department had dealt with only one aspect of the matter and the question raised now was much broader. On the question of urgency, he asked whether Coyne had applied for the pension. I said that though I did not see the relevance of this to the legal question which the Department had been asked, I would tell him that he had not. The urgency in my mind did not arise from this source but from the fact that publicity had been given to the matter and that it was one that the Trustees of the Pension Fund would wish in consequence to be in a position to deal with. Mr. Maxwell said that a reason for the delay in the Department had been the Minister's absence, that he was now back and that if possible he would be in touch with me before the meeting of the Executive Committee on August 11.

It appeared that if heat were applied in the proper place, an opinion could be served up in short time.

Bank directors were also offended by Fleming's off-the-cuff remarks. An editorial in the 11 August edition of the *Globe and Mail* questioning the director's intelligence was particularly disappointing. Fleming telephoned the governor that day to tell him that a director was coming over from his office to see Rasminsky. The governor had some sympathy; he reminded the minister 'that the feelings of the Directors had been badly bruised by recent events and that they were inevitably sensitive to the accusation that they were being treated as ciphers in the affairs of the Bank.'

What would Rasminsky have done if he had been pushed by the press, the minister inquired? That answer was simple. He would have 'declined to comment in any shape or form when asked the questions. The matter had been discussed in Parliament and if it was appropriate for the Government to make any statement on it at all that seemed to be the place where the statement should be made.' And since Fleming had raised a related question, Raminsky went on to say that he thought that the minister's clarification printed in the 10 August Ottawa *Journal* to the effect that Rasminsky 'was less interested in a fat pension than [he] was in serving the Bank' was ill-put. It raised inevitable comparisons between his attitude and Coyne's, 'and in so doing it tended to get me into the controversy which was contrary to my wishes.' It was also unfair to Coyne. It was probably a tough few days for Fleming; following the wrenching experience of the past several months, he was now being chastised by the new governor. At least this discussion went on behind closed doors.

That was where matters stood for some time, with no one prepared to cancel the suspension of Rule 17. There were various schemes put forward to revise it, but the matter continued to languish on the back burner. Rasminsky, the person now most affected by its suspension, was also unable to come to any firm conclusions as to what course to follow. He was 'afraid that almost anything that is done will revive the issue and [he] was most anxious to avoid this.'[44] Any change would have to appear in the *Canada Gazette* and would attract attention, and that would not be good for the Bank.

There were two ways of dealing with the problem. One was to do nothing, 'in the hope that with the lapse of time the whole issue will be forgotten and one will be able to deal with it objectively without the risk of attracting public attention.' The other way was to revoke the suspension of Rule 17. If that were the preferred course, it need not attract public attention, as it would not be necessary to put anything into the *Canada Gazette*. An alternative, which the governor believed to be 'absolutely beyond criticism,' would be to keep the existing five-year averaging period for his pension instead of adoting the three-year period suggested by some on the board. The only difference between the governor's pension and that of any other member of the staff would be that the former's would be payable immediately on retirement. It was important that the governor's position of independence should be protected through access to a pension. Still, this was a delicate matter that eventually became a non-issue; time healed all wounds, the country moved on, and the Bank of Canada gratefully shrank back into relative obscurity. Coyne's pension was restored.

But that did not mean that within the Bank the damage caused by the public battle was left to heal itself. As one young official in the research department later recalled, the carnage was extensive. Reflecting the sentiments of many employees, he 'felt a very strong loyalty to the institution and [Coyne] was the leader of the institution ... I probably accepted a good part of the righteousness of our position and also there was the sense in the institution of a kind of a siege going on.'[45]

It is, an old aphorism has it, an ill wind that does not blow somebody some good. And so it was in the Bank of Canada. The Coyne crisis was a staggering blow for an institution that prided itself on anonymity, as the institution's dispute with the prime minister became public. But it was also the event that allowed Louis Rasminsky, arguably one of the most 'successful' of the Bank's governors, to assume the chief post. He was also well equipped to address the domestic and international issues and problems that confronted the Bank and Canada during the 1960s and early 1970s. Under the circumstances then prevailing, a better choice could not have been made.

The young Louis Rasminsky, c. 1927.

Holidaying in Italy: Piazzo San Marco, Venice, 1932. On Rasminsky's right is Lyla
Rasminsky; on his left, Rosamond Rifat.

Dinner with Minister of Justice Louis St Laurent, United Nations San Francisco Conference, June 1945.

Rasminsky (far right), with Brooke Claxton (second from right), and Minister of Finance Douglas Abbott (second from left), in Ottawa, late 1940s.

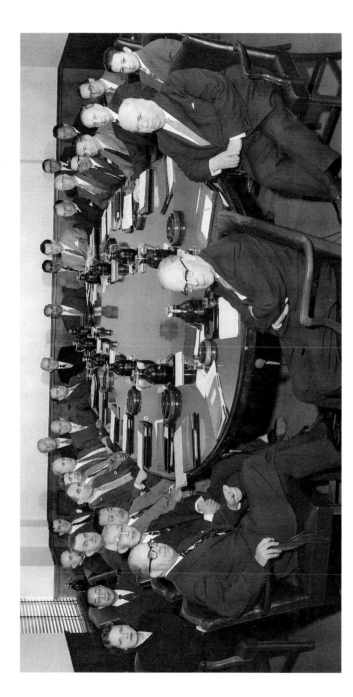

IMF executive board, August 1954. Managing director Ivar Rooth is at the head of the table. The US executive director, Frank Southard, is four down the table (clockwise) from Rooth; Rasminsky is three down from Southard, with his alternate in Washington, Jake Warren, sitting in the corner of the room. On Rasminky's left is the German director, Otmar Emminger, while the French executive director, Jean de Largentaye, is the sixth person around from Emminger. Merle Cochrane, the deputy managing director, is on Rooth's right.

En route to the Fund and Bank meetings in India, September 1958. From left: Wynne Plumptre, assistant deputy minister of finance; Donald Fleming, minister of finance; Mrs Fleming; Rasminsky; and Lyla Rasminsky.

The Rasminsky family in the early 1960s – Lola, Lyla, Louis, and Michael.

The official Bank of Canada photograph, taken on Rasminsky's appointment as governor.

At the Fund and Bank meetings in Washington, DC, October 1963. Slightly behind Rasminsky (pointing) is Simon Reisman.

Lyla and Louis Rasminsky, in the Altieri Palace after the Per Jacobsson Memorial Lecture, Rome, 9 November 1966.

On being made a companion of the Order of Canada in 1968, with Prime Minister Lester Pearson, Chief of Defence Staff General Jean Allard, and A.D.P. Heeney.

With Gerald Bouey at a meeting of the House of Commons Finance Committee, July 1969.

During intermission at a recital by renowned violinist Isaac Stern, 18 January 1982, in Ottawa. From left: Prime Minister Pierre Trudeau; Mrs Joan Comay, the wife of the first ambassador of Israel to Canada; Rasminsky; and H.E. Yeshaya Anug, the Israeli ambassador at the time.

At the inauguration of the Louis Rasminsky Fund for Social and Cultural Integration, May 1987. On his left is his daughter, Lola Weisstub; on his right, Bathsheva Levy, who was in charge of the fund.

Thomas D'Aquino Ross Tolmie Clark Davey Davie Fulton Bill Lawson Gordon Fairweather Gordon Robertson John Sigler Denis Coolican Jake Warren Roger Tassé Jean-Luc Pepin

Michel Gauvin Max Yalden Bob Bryce Anne Carver Jack Pickersgill Ronald Martland Beryl Plumptre Charles Ritchie Louis Audette Sylva Gelber Robert Stanfield Mitchell Sharp

André Bissonnette Louis Rasminsky Gerry Bouey David Golden Naomi Griffiths Simon Reisman Guy Roberge
(deceased)   (deceased)

The Round Table, 1991. Rasminsky was a member of the Round Table, which meets monthly at the Rideau Club, for many years.

Rasminsky in the 1990s, with his good friend Jerry Grey.

Chapter Seven

Rebuilding Confidence: First Term

Louis Rasminsky had always been an ordered man, which was reflected in his daily routine while he was at the Bank of Canada. He awoke at 8:00 a.m., had his breakfast in bed, read the morning paper, got dressed, then went off to work. On certain days, he would leave his home in Rockcliffe Park, the village surrounded by Ottawa where the city's well-off live, and walk with a few colleagues down Sussex Drive towards the Royal Canadian Mint, where he would be picked up by the Bank car. When he returned home in the evening, he would be met by his wife, have a drink, and talk with his family. That had been his routine for years, and his elevation to the governorship did not change it.

On his return from work, home became a sanctuary where the concerns of the day were left at the door, short of a small briefcase that went inside. His wife was very conscious of the weight of responsibility that her husband carried and made sure that nothing disturbed his time with her. He needed that sanctuary, as very quickly problems crowded into his life. The order and regulation of his private life contrasted sharply with the increasing disorder of international financial relationships and also with the increasing difficulty that Canada experienced in general as the 1960s wore on.

Still, as the Bank's *Annual Report* for 1961 notes, when Rasminsky took office, 'the level of economic activity in Canada was rising, but there was a great deal of unemployment and unused plant capacity and room for a large increase in employment.'[1] That was relatively good news for a governor at the beginning of his tenure. However, the world was increasingly competitive, and there were some disquieting signs on the horizon. An indication of that was the situation in which the United States found itself. Until the late 1950s, US economic power was thought to be so overwhelming that other countries would never be able to compete. By 1961, however, the global context had changed, the so-called dollar problem had disappeared, and the United States had to enhance its economic efficiency if it wanted to remain competitive with emerging economic giants such as Japan and West Germany. Something similar was also evident with Canada's other main trading partner, the United Kingdom, as it faced an uncertain future and struggled to remain in the economic race.

Rasminsky correctly noted in the *Annual Report* for 1961 that Canada could not 'escape this world trend, and the real determinant of our prosperity and welfare will be our ability to compete in a world of rapidly rising standards of economic productivity and efficiency.' That was a theme to which he would return during the twelve years of his mandate. For the present, however, pressing issues related to Bank organization and the changing nature of banking in the country remained. How the Bank of Canada responded under its new governor to both opportunities and problems would set the tone for the years ahead.

For the first while, Rasminsky did most of his public talking through the mechanism of the Bank's *Annual Report*; it seemed counterproductive to follow in Coyne's footsteps in terms of speech-making, even if it was intended to re-establish the position and reputation of the Bank in Canada and elsewhere. His first public address would be at a time and place of his own choosing, and not in the near future. As it was, a host of challenges remained that more than provided enough work and would, or so Rasminsky hoped, take the nation's mind off the upheavals of the recent past. A wonderful opportunity to effect just that result came with the establishment of the Royal Commission on Banking and Finance – the Porter Commission (1961–4).

It had been set up by the Diefenbaker government as a result of a request by the minister of finance to the Privy Council on 18 October 1961. Donald Fleming thought it desirable to undertake a broad review of the functioning of the Canadian financial system. The last such investigation, by the Macmillan Commission, had taken place in 1933, and in the meantime the Canadian economy, its financial resources, and its requirements had grown and changed greatly. The minister told his colleagues that economic growth was dependent on the adequacy and adaptation of the financial institutions through which funds were made available for expansion and development, and he wanted to ensure that these reflected current conditions in Canada.

The Porter Commission was asked to: '(a) enquire into and report upon the structure and methods of operation of the Canadian financial system, including banking and monetary systems and the institutions and processes involved in the flow of funds through the capital market; and (b) to make recommendations (i) for the improvement of the structure and operations of the financial system and, more particularly, (ii) concerning the Bank Act, the Bank of Canada Act, the Quebec Savings Banks Act, and other relevant federal legislation.'[2]

The first organizing meeting was held on 16 November 1961, and the Bank of Canada was invited to appear informally on 18 and 19 January 1962, and in a formal way later on. Getting ready for those sessions occupied the attentions of Bank officials for weeks on end. Many meetings were held, during which documents were prepared, and Rasminsky chaired as many of them as he was able. As Gerald Bouey has said, 'It was a great educational process for all of us, including the new governor.'[3]

Rasminsky worked shoulder to shoulder with other Bank officials, going through the drafts 'almost sentence by sentence.' That process was illuminating. Bouey, who had not been close to Rasminsky and did not know him well, became aware of how logical his mind was and how he prized intellectual honesty almost above all else; Rasminsky could not dismiss a 'respectable, intellectual argument' put forward by an official. The reputation that 'he was a prisoner of logical arguments' soon spread throughout the Bank. The give-and-take of the sessions was a valuable lesson for all and helped to prepare the governor for his testimony before the royal commission. It was, A.C. Lamb, a former deputy governor, recalled, 'classic Lou Rasminsky' and helped to draw the Bank together.[4]

What were his views as revealed in the briefs prepared for the Porter Commission? He did not shy away from the Bank's relations with government – the issue that had catapulted him into the governorship. While he had secured the cabinet's agreement in July 1961 to his demand for a clear delineation of who controlled monetary policy, he wanted that description entrenched in the Bank of Canada Act. As he had earlier suggested, the central bank had to be independent in its day-to-day operations. If it were not, then it became merely a department of government, 'which no country [had] found to be a satisfactory position for a central bank.'[5] Independence provided the assurance that the Bank would always act with its perception of the overall welfare of the Canadian currency in mind and with a longer-term perspective than would be the case if it were under close political control. That did not mean, however, that the Bank could completely ignore government over a period of time: 'the central bank [could not] pursue a policy that [was] at variance with the views of the elected representatives of the people on major issues. That would make it a state within a state, a negation of democracy.' Ultimately, the government must prevail, and it should have the right to insist on the monetary policy to be followed.

How should the issue be dealt with? Rasminsky emphasized the satisfactory nature of the Bank's current powers and its relationships with other policy-makers:

> These occasions [when disputes arise] are likely to be very rare and the question is whether statute should provide for them. We got along very well for 20 years without it, on the theory of joint responsibility. If it were not for the discussions of the last couple of years I would have said no revision in statute is necessary. My own experience since July 1961 does not suggest that revision is necessary. The monetary policy followed has been that of the central bank. Government has been informed and agreed, and has not disclaimed responsibility for monetary policy. But in view of these discussions, I think that while the conduct of monetary policy should remain in the hands of the central bank there is a case which the Commission should consider for amending the Statute to provide that the Government should have the power to give the Bank directives on monetary policy which are not inconsistent with other provisions of the Act. The purpose of this provision would be to strengthen the position of the central bank by making clear that Government as well as central bank is responsible for monetary policy.[6]

His point of view, accepted by the Porter Commission and encapsulating both his memorandum of July 1961 and his evidence given before the commission, was made official in an amendment to the Bank of Canada Act in 1967. It provided that in the ordinary course of events the Bank was responsible for monetary policy, though the government should be continuously informed as to Bank policy. If a conflict arose, earnest effort should be made to settle it through discussion. But what if no settlement emerged? Then the government had the right to direct the governor on the policy to be carried out. However, the directive had to be specific. As Rasminsky noted, 'The government couldn't simply say, "We'd like you to make money easier. We'd like you to get interest rates down." It had to be specific in terms, limited in duration, and published in the *Canada Gazette*, so that everybody would know. Then ... the Bank would have an obligation to carry it out ... If the Governor couldn't in good conscience [do that], he would have no choice but to [resign].'[7] The 1967 revision to the Bank Act gave effect 'to what all of us, Towers, Coyne, myself, always thought was the situation. Namely, that there was joint responsibility for monetary policy.'[8]

This system of dual responsibility was an article of faith with Rasminsky and was tested several times in the 1960s. He had seen at first hand what had happened to Coyne when the unwritten arrangement had been set aside over personality and politics. On several occasions during the 1960s, he had reason to clarify his position. One of those, in March 1964, he made in response to a speech by a secretary of state, Maurice Lamontagne, who had told the Montreal Junior Board of Trade that the government had 'put an end to the austerity program, reduced interest rates and increased the money supply.'[9] Rasminsky's letter to Finance Minister Walter Gordon was direct: 'I know that you agree that it would be most unfortunate if the impression were created that the Government had taken over the active direction of monetary policy, and I am sure that Mr. Lamontagne did not intend to give this impression ... The role of the Government in monetary policy has not been a directing one, and I think it would weaken the usefulness of the central bank if the public came to believe otherwise.'[10] In March 1968, the minister of finance, Mitchell Sharp, answered a question from the leader of the Ralliement Créditiste, Réal Caouette; 'Why,' the latter had asked, did the Department of Finance 'not use the Bank of Canada to create the credit matching that of production?'[11] Sharp's response – that the government had responsibility for monetary policy and that the Bank was the agency used to implement that policy – rang alarm bells at the Bank. Rasminsky's letter to protest the minister's interpretation went out the next day: 'I need hardly point out that this statement is not in accord with my understanding of the relationship between the Government and the Bank of Canada in the matter of responsibility for monetary policy.'[12] While the governor realized that the minister's answer was a quick response to a question put in the House, he believed it important to reiterate the relationship as embodied in the Bank of Canada amendments of 1967, given the unfortunate recent history in defining that relationship.

In late 1961 Rasminsky had also set up teams to look into other areas of concern to the Bank likely to be of interest to the Porter Commission. The commission received a list of these on 31 May 1962, and it invited Rasminsky to address the commission in early 1963. In wide-ranging testimony spread out over four days, the governor outlined, among other things, his views on inflation and his thoughts on the objectives and limitations of monetary policy. Inflation, he told the commission, was costly and destructive: 'Policies involving a persistent rise in prices at an appreciable rate would not make it any easier to achieve high employment and sustained growth over the longer run, to achieve continuing improvement in the basic efficiency and productivity of the economy, to achieve a balanced international position, or to satisfy the community's notions of equity in the distribution of income. In fact, the contrary is more likely to be true.' With respect to the effectiveness of monetary policy, and echoing what he had told John Diefenbaker in the summer of 1961, he said that it was only one tool of economic regulation. And while it was 'important enough to warrant a considerable effort to try to get it right and to make as much use of it as circumstances permit,' it was not a panacea. It could not carry the entire burden of regulating the general level of spending in the economy and maintaining what he called a satisfactory external financial condition. In short, it was best used as one ingredient in a mix of government policy – that is, fiscal policy and debt management – and it should contribute to 'sustained economic growth at high levels of employment and efficiency, internal price stability and the maintenance of a sound external financial position, an equitable sharing of economic benefits and burdens and a high degree of economic freedom.'[13]

Too much reliance on monetary policy 'either as a restraining or a stimulating factor would ... lead to unsatisfactory self-defeating results.'[14] Great strains in the economy would be created if it were left solely to the Bank to control an overheated economy without support from fiscal, debt-management, and other government economic policies. The result could well be intolerably high interest rates and disorganization in capital markets. The governor would have reason to emphasize this basic point throughout the decade. As well, Rasminsky noted, 'the precise part that monetary policy can appropriately play in stimulating economic expansion is necessarily influenced by the part being played by the concurrent fiscal, debt management and other economic policies of the Government.' In short, the Bank could not act alone.

Another subject on which he offered an opinion was the 6 per cent interest ceiling on chartered-bank loans then in effect, which had been the object of much public debate. George Freeman wrote the background information for the governor's testimony, which Rasminsky summarized for the commission:

On balance [the 6 per cent ceiling] has almost certainly worked against the interests of credit-worthy small borrowers in Canada in recent years rather than for them as intended. In relation to the amounts involved, loans to small borrowers generally cost more per dollar to administer and involve a greater element of risk than do loans to large borrowers. To be equally profitable to the lender, therefore, loans to most small borrowers must carry a somewhat higher gross rate of return than loans to large borrowers. In circumstances where the banks are not permitted to charge a higher rate on loans to small borrowers than they can readily obtain by lending their available funds to larger borrowers, therefore, the banks will not find it profitable to compete actively for the credit business of small firms and individuals, and indeed will have a positive incentive to cut back on volume of bank credit extended to such borrowers on a 6 per cent basis.

For many years, the chartered banks have found themselves in this position most of the time, and on occasion the situation has become even more acute for the small borrower when a temporary increase in market rates of interest has made a 6 per cent bank loan, for the time being, the cheapest form of credit available even to large borrowers ... The great majority of small business and personal borrowers have increasingly found themselves forced to turn to other lending institutions charging rates much higher than 6 per cent. Thus the main effect of this restriction on bank lending rates has been to shelter certain important areas of credit in Canada from chartered bank competition, thereby enabling non-bank lenders to charge the borrowing public unnecessary high rates of interest.[15]

The price of borrowing, if high enough, could fuel inflation and compromise the competitiveness of certain businesses. Also, the inability of banks to extend credit to clients, given the demand on their resources with the 6 per cent ceiling, could slow economic growth. Those were all considerations.

The ceiling had other adverse effects. Canada had one of the most open economies in the world and was easily buffeted by winds created elsewhere. The 6 per cent maximum did not necessarily reflect that reality. As he told commissioners, 'What is acceptable in the field of interest rate fluctuations in Canada must also be affected by the range of fluctuations in other countries, particularly in the United States on account of the closeness of our contact with them and the importance of capital flows.' Because Canada's current-account deficit limited on the country's economic and financial sovereignty, it was crucial that interest rates retain maximum flexibility in order to respond adequately to foreign forces. The limit had, the governor thought, outlived its usefulness.

The solution was obvious, at least to Rasminsky and the royal commission; the ceiling should go. The commission had pointed out that 'not even the major competitors of the banks opposed the removal of the rate ceiling and, in fact, most of them recommended its removal on grounds of equity.'[16] Walter Gordon, who remained minister of finance until November 1965, was opposed, however, feeling that the ceiling was too important to Canadians.[17] Rasminsky believed that too – it was too important *not* to remove it. As well, as he had noted, removing the ceiling did not mean increasing interest rates to more than 6 per cent – while that might happen, it was not pre-ordained. After Mitchell Sharp became minister in December 1965, the ceiling was rescinded.

The royal commission was a welcome diversion for the Bank of Canada, allowing the institution to catch its breath and define its role and place in Canadian society. It also provided a context in which to re-evaluate its organizational set-up, established in much simpler times. Did its structure reflect the more modern Canada that was developing? Was it well-equipped to deal with the issues and problems of the 1960s, or had it, administratively and operationally speaking, remained more suited to the 1930s?

Probably the latter was more true. An organization chart from the 1930s, when compared with the early 1960s, showed little difference, apart from the addition of a few deputy governors. In the intervening twenty-five years, Canada and the world had become more complex – a fact not reflected in the Bank's organization. As result, Rasminsky undertook administrative reforms with an eye to making the institution more 'professional.' As a part of that initiative, three new departments were created, making seven in all. As well, since it was becoming more and more difficult to keep track of programs under the informal procedures used in the past, he wanted the Bank to move to a systematic procedure for allocating its resources, both human and financial, in terms of the programs and missions that it wished to achieve. There were obvious advantages in 'the fact that such a system would force management to take conscious decisions regarding priorities and programme activities; it would bring about a definition of responsibilities for middle managers and departments and indicate what was expected of them; it would provide an opportunity for the decentralization of authority; it would provide the basis for the periodic appraisal of the extent to which programmes were being filled in the form of stocktaking and preparation for decisions on financial allocations.'[18]

Rasminsky thought that the more precise definition of responsibility and the decentralization of authority would be regarded as real advantages by middle management. They would also help to accomplish another objective that he had in mind – to break down the barriers that separated departments. In the securities department, for example, the deputy governor in charge, Ralph McKibbin, had traditionally run it as his own personal fiefdom. Under Rasminsky's prodding, that system slowly changed, and the Bank of Canada came to be run as a complete entity, not as a collection of departments.

Some of the change was propelled by the sheer physical growth of the Bank. The research department was broken up into several parts, including an international department, while the financial side of research was spun off into a new banking (later renamed monetary) and financial analysis department. Economic forecasting was also improved, and econometrics entered the Bank's language. As well, during Rasminsky's tenure, the institution became the first central bank in the world to allow private research groups to use certain of the computer-stored economic and financial statistics and computer programs that the Bank itself employed in analysing economic performance. It also began the publication of staff studies and in 1968 undertook a major revision of its monthly statistical bulletin to include topical articles on economic and financial subjects.

Later, Rasminsky brought in Harry Scott from Treasury Board to assess personnel administration at the Bank, which Scott found archaic; he advised the governor to implement the Hay rating system, which was done. As well, Scott wanted the Bank to recognize some sort of parity between jobs on the policy side, whence most senior managers had come, and those in operations, which had traditionally been neglected. In this area, Rasminsky was successful. Moreover, the entire reform process was made easier, and Bank capabilities were greatly enhanced, with introduction of computers in the 1960s.

Rasminsky was also very conscious of the changing nature of Canada. The June 1960 election in Quebec precipitated the so-called Quiet Revolution, and the Bank took its first tentative steps towards reflecting the reality of a resurgent Quebec. While it had had many francophone employees and a French-Canadian assistant deputy or deputy governor since its inception, the Bank of Canada had been, in its early years, an English-Canadian organization, both in temperament and in character. Under Rasminsky, it became 'sensitized' to the need to have francophones represented in adequate numbers in the professional ranks and a more congenial language environment for them. The Bank hired a languages professor from the University of Ottawa to conduct French lessons

TABLE 7.1
Language groups in the Bank's employ, 1962

	Women			Men		
	Applicants interviewed	Engaged	Proportion of engagements to interviews	Applicants interviewed	Engaged	Proportion of engagements to interviews
French Canadian	236	72	30.5	57	17	29.8
English	317	134	42.3	177	42	23.7
Total	553	206	37.3	234	59	25.2

Note: Proportion of French-Canadian engagements to total engagements is 35 per cent for females and 28.8 per cent for males.
Source: LR76-570-5-22, 7 Jan. 1963.

for all those interested. The program operated quietly for a number of years before it was overtaken by more 'official' bicultural and bilingual policies affecting federal institutions, which followed publication of two volumes of the reports of the Royal Commission on Bilingualism and Biculturalism in 1965 and 1967. As one deputy governor remembered, the Bank was 'forward looking in terms of bilingualism long before bilingualism became a major issue in the public service ... [It] was providing French lessons for its staff.'[19]

Rasminsky's bank also undertook a detailed examination of the number of French Canadians in the Bank's employ in 1962, to serve as the launching pad for new initiatives. Table 7.1 demonstrates the situation. As well, Rasminsky directed that the Bank trace percentages of francophones employed there between 1956 and 1962. For females in 1956 the figure had been 27 per cent, and in 1962, 36.6 per cent. Among males, the numbers were 18.9 per cent and 21.1 per cent, respectively. It was a snapshot of the situation in 1962; Rasminsky promised to increase those numbers, and he did so, especially in the professional ranks. The Bank pulled itself inside out as a result of its work for the Porter Commission, examining everything from the responsibilities of directors, through internal management, to staff organization and training. As Gerald Bouey later said, the governor, through his various initiatives, infused with Bank with new life; people 'all had a view of what [it] was there for, and what its objective was in a way that, I think, we never had under Coyne.'[20]

As Bank operations expanded, its physical space imposed limitations. Headquarters in Ottawa was a small square, unimposing structure built during the mid-1930s when the financial and monetary world had been much smaller. Some operations had been spun off to other locations, such as the building on Ottawa's King Edward Avenue, but these were clearly inadequate. Its agencies in cities across the country were also housed in buildings that were too small, and a major program, in which Rasminsky was a driving force, was implemented to modernize those existing and construct new ones.

The most spectacular result was realization in Ottawa of two towers that swallowed the old granite block, creating a unique and fascinating structure designed by Arthur Erickson and completed in 1980. There were others; Vancouver, for example, was awarded a new building, which became the object of some controversy when the Liberals won the 1963 federal election. The resolution of the issue required communication between the governor and the minister of finance. The location chosen by the Bank did not meet with the approval of a newly elected member of Parliament from Vancouver South – Arthur Laing, minister of northern affairs and natural resources. He wrote to Gordon, suggesting a different place, where the Bank's office tower would be nearer the offices of all the chartered banks and five blocks closer to the main post office. Laing thought that 'there [had] been an unfortunate cavalier attitude on the part of the Bank officials in regard to this matter. The implied threat that Vancouver must have a building at the very expensive site selected or no building at all seem[ed] poor advocacy for need.'[21]

While it was irritating to be forced to deal with essentially minor political questions, Rasminsky pressed Gordon to stand firm. The site, chosen in 1960 and the subject of various representations since then, was a good one; Vancouver's city council, the city's downtown business association, the BC, Vancouver, and New Westminster federations of labour, and other important groups in the province had urged that the Bank get on with construction. The Bank's view prevailed. The life of the governor was not all high policy-making and advising government on the thorny issues of the day.

But Louis Rasminsky's work did include a good deal of that. Two interconnected issues demanded attention in the spring and early summer of 1962 – should the dollar be repegged, and how should Ottawa deal with an exchange crisis that threatened the viability of the Canadian economy and currency? The second, in particular, was the first real test for Rasminsky and clearly demonstrated his single-minded determination to do what he thought was right. He had been governor for about ten months, and the crisis, though not totally unexpected, developed very quickly.

With respect to the first, in his memoirs Donald Fleming notes that the Conservatives announced a new policy in early 1961 – to 'endeavour to move the external value of our dollar to a "significant discount" [from the US dollar] for the benefit of our exporters, the benefit of Canadian producers in the domestic market, and the benefit of our tourist trade operators, all of whom were suffering from the severe disadvantages imposed by the premium' of the floating Canadian dollar, which then traded at US\$1.06.[22] Of great concern to the Conservatives was the wide spread of interest rates between Canada and other countries, and especially those then prevailing in the United States. A.F.W. Plumptre notes that the government 'wanted some action that would affect, and would be seen to affect, the value of the dollar.'[23] As Fleming told the House in his budget speech, 'It will be government policy to facilitate [a downward] movement [of the dollar].'[24]

To that end, it had proposed a number of policies designed to shift the currency downward, which were successful, as it fell to a discount of 3 per cent against the US dollar. The discount had increased by November to 4 per cent, and in February to 5 per cent, where it was unofficially pegged. The result was a significant decrease in Canada's current-account deficit; by early 1962, it had been reduced from about \$1.25 billion per year in 1961 to an annual rate of \$900 million. Merchandise trade in 1961 yielded a surplus of some \$180 million. Since the deficit in 1960 had been \$150 million, the overall swing was in the order of \$330 million. When the government's strategy became clear, Donald Marsh, then the assistant general manager of the Royal Bank of Canada, described this attempt to talk the rate down as the government's 'open mouth (or foot-in-mouth!) policy.'[25] To other countries, it smacked of unfairness, perhaps even of a competitive devaluation; Canada wanted to have its cake and eat it too.

Rasminsky suggested to Fleming that the International Monetary Fund (IMF) would want to hear about the new policy; indeed, it was on the agenda of a special executive board meeting held on 21 July 1961. There, the other directors made it clear that it was 'time Canada restored a fixed rate to its ... dollar.'[26] It fell to Rasminsky to put Canada's case to the board, where he outlined the potentially disruptive problems his country faced. However, opined the IMF's managing director, Per Jacobsson, Canada was taking unfair advantage of the situation, especially given that 'other countries [could] also ... say that they have difficulties [too].'

Moreover, the dollar's fall from a premium to a discount *vis-à-vis* US currency was an unhappy reminder to IMF members of Canada's float.

Later, the Americans took a swipe at the Canadian position, though they denied that the remarks were directed at this country. Robert Roosa, the US undersecretary of the treasury, denounced countries (of which Canada was then the only one) that had fluctuating exchange rates. In his view, 'there [were] two strong surviving attributes of the gold standard of earlier eras that must be continued ... One is that a fixed link must be preserved between gold ... and at least one national currency ... The second requirement ... is that leading countries maintain fixed (rather than variable) rates of exchange in relation to the dollar ... There must not be an escape hatch through which one country or another can seek temporary refuge from balance of payments disciplines by juggling its own exchange rate – beggaring its neighbours and disrupting the orderly processes of cost and price adjustment among the various products and services that are required for eventual balance of payments equilibrium.'[27]

Pressure from other governments had been building, and Canada had begun to review the effectiveness of the floating rate in early summer 1961. Soon after becoming governor Rasminsky had held discussions with a number of chartered-bank presidents, and among the topics covered were the advantages and disadvantages of a floating versus a fixed rate. Increasingly, the new governor favoured the latter. The results of those conversations could not have been of much help, however, at least in terms of developing some consensus; the range of opinion ran the gamut.[28] Rasminsky and Plumptre had also agreed that they should speak with Fleming about the floating rate before he left for the Fund's annual meeting in Vienna in September.

Why had senior policy-makers begun to re-examine the rate? To begin with, other countries had made it clear to Canada at meetings of the Organization for European Economic Cooperation (OEEC) in Paris and of the IMF in Washington that Canada's floating rate was 'a disturbing influence' in global financial affairs.[29] Times had changed since 1950, when Canada had been in a relatively favoured economic position; then other nations had been willing 'to put up with abnormal actions on [Canada's] part.' Eleven years later, that was not the case. In a 1961 report to a meeting of executive directors, IMF staff had suggested that 'Canada should re-establish an effective par value as soon as circumstances permit.'[30] This was the first time since 1956 that the issue had been raised officially.

Moreover, the fluctuating rate had not worked so well in the recent past, as Fleming's budget speech had suggested – a rate of US$1.06 was not helpful to the export side of the Canadian economy. Also of concern was its effect on Canada's reputation. A fixed rate was, by its nature, stable and secure – an impression that some officials now thought important to convey. As Plumptre wrote, 'At present there is far more doubt and uncertainty about the pace and direction of Canada's economic growth than there was a few years ago. The fact that the UK is negotiating with the EEC [for entry] has recently added a new and important uncertainty regarding our future.' Also, however misguided it might be, there was a business element demanding that the government show 'positive' leadership; perhaps a fixed rate would do that. In his memorandum, Plumptre suggested a rate of 95 US cents, with a two-cent spread on either side, even though the IMF's articles of agreement required that actual transactions in foreign exchange must not differ from parity by more than one per cent. Ottawa believed that while the Fund might at first resist the 4 per cent margin, it would in the end 'be only too glad to accept the wider spread if, in doing so, they could get Canada back into the fixed-rate fold.'[31] Other officials proposed other rates, some with margins as wide as 5 per cent.

Whatever the relative merits of wider margins, Canada conformed to Fund requirements in May 1962, fixing its exchange rate at 92.5 US cents – a figure that was apparently Fleming's decision. In his explanation to the IMF's executive board on 2 May, Rasminsky said that the government wanted to make Canada an 'honest woman' once again, with an approved par value.[32] From 3 May, the government would maintain exchange rates within 1 per cent on either side of the fixed rate. As Rasminsky told the board, reading from his notes, the reasons were roughly as follows: 'Market seemed dominated by uncertainty; disorderly situation in exchange markets; international repercussions; had to make clear determination to defend a rate; the best way to eliminate uncertainty was to declare a par value.'

Rasminsky's announcement 'was warmly welcomed by the Board.'[33] Per Jacobsson, and the directors from Australia, Italy, and the United Kingdom made supportive statements, and none of them felt that the rate was too low. To the contrary, the board minutes point out that 'after hearing [Rasminsky's] explanation of how the rate was chosen, several Directors said that they were appreciative of the fact that the Canadian authorities had been aware of the temptation (always present in circumstances such as those which they were facing) of "playing it safe" and selecting a rate which was too low.' Indeed, the French director, Jean de Largentaye, thought that, given the continuing high rate of Canadian unemployment (5.5 per cent of the labour force), the dollar might be overvalued. The rate was unanimously approved.

However, confidence was not restored to the degree that Ottawa had hoped. Reports came in from many quarters, both in Canada and abroad, 'of widespread nervousness that exists in business and financial circles,' and the foreign exchange situation remained precarious. As a memorandum produced in the Department of Finance on 25 May noted, 'The outflow [of funds] could begin again in the weeks immediately ahead, and if it did, it would undoubtedly feed on itself, gathering momentum.'[34] If that happened, the government would then be faced with the task of defending the new rate on the basis of reserves that were already substantially depleted. The potential crisis related to continuing deficits in Canada. Investors were keeping their funds abroad because they feared for the basic value and integrity of the Canadian dollar and believed that its value could well be eroded.

In the meantime, a federal election had been called on 18 April, with the vote to be held on 18 June, and the resulting uncertainty made an unstable situation worse. The government was promising new programs and massive expenditures – not a happy circumstance for those charged with defending the external rate of the Canadian dollar. As the Finance memorandum of 25 May pointed out, 'While some government outlays, wisely deployed, can over time improve Canada's efficiency and international competitive position, most government expenditures, particularly those with the widest popular appeal, are almost certain to have the opposite effect. Announcements of such expenditure programs, on a large scale at this particular juncture, may precipitate, perhaps in a matter of days and in their most embarrassing form, the need for massive foreign borrowing to shore up an apparently shaky international position.'[35]

The international investment community knew that Canada was still running an international deficit on trade, tourism, and other current account of something like $1 billion per year. Obviously, it was not entirely convinced by the decision to peg the dollar or by other steps undertaken by the Diefenbaker government. Thus began the 1962 exchange crisis, as confidence in the Canadian dollar evaporated. Perhaps as a reflection of the growing difficulty of his job, Rasminsky asked Fleming to relieve him of the pressure of representing Canada as executive director at the IMF – a position that he had held since 1946. The September meeting of the Bank and the Fund was his last in that position.

There had been indications of a financial problem much earlier; Canada's holdings of gold and US dollars, which had stood at US$2.056 billion in January, had fallen to US$1.1 billion by June. The Dominion Bureau of Statistics drily noted in its publication 'The Canadian Balance of International Payments, 1961 and 1962' that persistent deficits on current account,

> varying with changing commodity trade conditions but based on an apparently intractable deficit from non-merchandise transactions, had exceeded the capital inflow in long-term forms each year after 1956. By mid-1960 the accumulated current account balance since the end of World War II exceeded the corresponding capital movement in long-term forms; over the period Canada had begun to borrow 'short'. The completion of some extended capital projects, unused capacity, and uncertainties arising at provincial and national levels added to the problems of the Canadian balance of payments.
>
> ... Measures to restore equilibrium were not fully effective in the situation which developed. Capital movements in long-term forms continued to contract, and in the second quarter of 1962 turned outwards. With growing uncertainty, outward private movements in short-term forms developed on a substantial scale. The pressure of a substantial net export of private capital from Canada combined with the current account deficit to exert heavy demands on official holdings of gold and foreign exchange.[36]

A memorandum prepared by Rasminsky had highlighted similar points. While by early 1962 the Canadian economy was in the midst of a marked upturn, there was a downside to it: 'The recovery which has been achieved has been associated with increasing Government expenditures entailing a large budgetary and over-all deficit and a considerable degree of monetary expansion. In the first nine months of 1961 Federal Government expenditures were 7 per cent higher than in the corresponding period of 1960.'[37] That growth in expenditure could not be matched by increased revenues, even under the prosperous conditions then prevailing. In 1961, 'there [had been] justification for taking the risks involved in these very expensive fiscal and monetary policies. The economy was in the doldrums and it was essential to get it started again.'

By 1962, the situation had changed, and Rasminsky believed that a government deficit of the same magnitude as 1961's would lead to a very difficult situation in financial markets, where the confidence of investors in Canada's financial stability might be impaired. 'If we run a large deficit in a period of high economic activity, investors and the public in general would be bound to ask themselves how huge the Government's borrowing requirements will be when the economy undergoes a cyclical set-back which, if past experience all around the world is any guide, will occur some time within the next two years. New public expenditures will then be undertaken in an effort to alleviate the situation, existing expenditures with a built-in growth factor will go on increasing, while revenues will fall off: the deficit would assume truly staggering proportions.' However great the price to be paid, political reality in the midst of an election campaign made a balanced budget impossible in 1962. Rasminsky hoped instead for some amelioration of the 1961 figure.

A critic could not blame the government for its unwillingness to take tough measures to deal with a deteriorating situation, while it was out on the hustings fighting for its political life. Aside from fixing the exchange rate, it chose to ignore the problem. As a result, Rasminsky saw the minister of finance in late May to tell him that the government would probably face a major financial crisis in the near future. He based his assessment on the behaviour of the exchange and bond markets, as well as some statements being made by at least one cabinet minister and also members of the financial community. The minister of agriculture, Alvin Hamilton, had raised temperatures on 8 June when he had told a Vancouver press conference that the 92.5-cent peg was a compromise and that he favoured a rate of 90 cents, which was more easily defensible. His comments suggested his basic lack of confidence in the government's determination to defend the Canadian dollar's exchange rate, which appalled businesspeople and some of his cabinet colleagues. Fleming managed to soothe the panic, but it was a blow to confidence.

The tempest caused by Hamilton only reinforced what many already believed – that the government was falling apart. There was intrigue among cabinet ministers and within the caucus; a Bank official, George Freeman, later described it as 'pretty well hopeless.'[38] Inertia had come to characterize the Conservatives. Robert Roosa had experienced it at first hand when discussing matters of mutual interest with Finance's Alan Hockin. He had not made any progress in pushing an American case because, he reported to US Treasury Secretary Douglas Dillon, '"The government" is not prepared to make any new decisions on controversial matters.'[39] The sentiments expressed in a British document sent to A.W. France of the British Treasury in June 1959, also remained apropos: 'The [Diefenbaker] Cabinet as a whole inspires very little confidence in banking and business circles and Mr. Diefenbaker none at all.'[40] Nor would the Liberals do anything to help. They believed that they had a good chance to become the government and were doing their best to demonstrate the futility of Conservative policy. They produced a '"Diefenbuck," a "dollar" with "92½¢" and Diefenbaker's wrinkled jowls upon it.'[41] Nor would they take the unpopular position of coming out in favour of higher interest rates, as the economic situation seemed to demand.

Despite his doubts that difficult decisions would be taken, the governor outlined a program that in all likelihood would have to be implemented immediately following the election. Among the items he proposed for consideration were:

- the government should announce that it would call the House into early session to pass a revised budget which would provide for a substantial reduction in the deficit;
- the government should announce it was setting aside $500 million of its present high Canadian dollar balances to be available only for the purchase of foreign exchange, and that it would raise money for its financial requirements through taxes or market borrowing without resort to these balances;
- the government take concrete steps to indicate that it gave very high priority to reducing the deficit on Canada's current account balance of payments by methods other than exchange rate depreciation. He urged that cabinet should consult with business and labour;
- the government should draw its gold tranche (about $175 million) from the IMF;
- the Bank of Canada would seek to arrange an exchange swap with the Federal Reserve Bank of New York for between $75 to 100 million.[42]

As the financial crisis worsened, Rasminsky suggested the unthinkable to Diefenbaker – that Pearson be brought in and given a full account of the exchange position and the government's program for dealing with the emergency. Why did he put that case to the prime minister? The *Montreal Daily Star* had a version. Rasminsky and the deputy minister of finance, Ken Taylor, had 'met with extreme reluctance on the part of the Government, and especially the prime minister, to take the course they urged as essential to save the Canadian dollar.' The newspaper account went on: 'The Prime Minister is reputed, on excellent authority, to have declared in effect that to follow [the] course [suggested by Rasminsky and Taylor] would be politically impossible and would immediately place him at the mercy of Mr. Pearson.'[43] Hence the proposed démarche to Pearson to convince him of the magnitude of the developing crisis.

To the governor's mind, the basic need to restore confidence went beyond political boundaries – a position that resonated in other countries. Indeed, Rasminsky's colleagues in foreign capitals believed that the serious financial emergency in Canada could be overcome only if there were a closing of ranks domestically. And Rasminsky had some influence; his opinions counted among his foreign colleagues, who believed that he was 'indispensable' in Ottawa. In short, his 'continued presence in the economic councils of [Canada was] necessary to assure international cooperation and confidence.'[44]

Rasminsky was blunt with the prime minister: 'In the circumstances, before I continue the discussions regarding foreign financial support, I must ask you to put me in a position to assure all those concerned that you propose to deal with the matter on a basis which seeks to avoid controversy and commands the support of all major elements of the community.'[45] If Pearson were apprised of the gravity of the exchange crisis, he might well be willing to give support to the government's program. From the governor's perspective, a Liberal attack on the methods being employed to deal with the crisis could impair the restoration of confidence and seriously aggravate the overall situation.

Diefenbaker's relationship with Pearson, however, was not amicable, and he refused to meet with the leader of the Opposition. But he did agree to the governor's request for permission to tell Pearson the full story of Canada's exchange losses and to answer fully any questions that he might pose. At Stornoway, Pearson's official home, Rasminsky put his case, impressing him with the seriousness of the situation. When the governor asked whether Pearson could support his program, the latter agreed, but only if Diefenbaker put it forward in a non-controversial way. Rasminsky reported Pearson's response to the prime minister.

That evening, the Liberal leader telephoned the governor to say that Walter Gordon, then a Liberal candidate in the 1962 election and Pearson's key adviser and fund-raiser, would be coming to see him around midnight concerning Canada's exchange position. Rasminsky had some very serious doubts about the propriety of seeing Gordon in that way. His meeting with Pearson that afternoon had been authorized by the prime minister, but there was no such blessing for one with Gordon. While the governor ultimately agreed, he would not give Gordon the same detail that he had Pearson. As Rasminsky describes it, 'Gordon arrived ... obviously in a poor frame of mind, and expressed views highly critical of the way the exchange position had been handled.' He went on to say that he did not see how the Liberal party could give any support to the government's program. Rasminsky 'did not attempt to persuade him, but merely said that [he] had Pearson's word for it that they would.' Gordon's response – 'We'll see' – alarmed the governor.[46]

Rasminsky found Gordon's position most unhelpful when the desperate need was to restore confidence. R.B. Bryce, secretary to the cabinet, had told Diefenbaker something about which Rasminsky was only too well aware – international investors felt that his government was 'not paying enough attention ... to "sound" financial policies ... Whether they are right or wrong is no longer the point – they are the ones whose opinion is important now and if we are to regain their confidence we have to demonstrate convincingly our intention to balance our budget within reasonable time and to improve the balance of our international income and expenditure, so that we are not dependent on imports of capital.'[47]

The economic muddle was in large part responsible for the Conservative crash in the June election, from 203 MPs to 116. They were, however, ahead of the Liberal's 99, and Diefenbaker stayed as prime minister, even if he had only a minority government. It also remained to him to deal with the economic crisis of June 1962, and on 24 June, following the precipitous decline in the country's official exchange reserves, he issued a statement 'that the Government were determined to defend the exchange value of the Canadian dollar at the level established in May, and that special measures designed to deal with the situation were being implemented immediately.'[48]

The 'special measures' were a program developed primarily by Rasminsky, with help from Ken Taylor. The exercise was reminiscent of his role in the 1947 exchange crisis. It was a difficult task, as the two had to walk a tightrope between showing that the government meant business and not throttling the economy. One thing was clear, however; the 'confidence of financial markets [could not] be secured under present conditions with a programme that is an easy and comfortable one or one that is confined solely to import measures.'[49] Certainly the Rasminsky–Taylor program was tough. It included among the list of special measures a temporary graduated surcharge on certain classes of imports, ranging from 15 per cent for less essential imports through 10 per cent on items such as imported automobiles to 5 per cent on about $2.5 billion worth of imports; a temporary reduction in the exemptions from customs duties accorded to Canadian tourists on goods brought back into Canada; reductions in government expenditures amounting to $250 million; and the earmarking of a portion of the government's cash balances for financing increases in the foreign exchange reserves. As well, Rasminsky arranged support from 'friends to put in the store window' in the form of cash and stand-by credits totalling to US$1.050 billion. This amount included Canada's $300-million tranche from the IMF, $250 million from the US Federal Reserve Board, $400 million from the Export–Import Bank, and $100 million promised by Lord Cromer at the Bank of England.[50]

If it was not going to be politically possible to implement a plan that would, Rasminsky hoped, restore confidence, then he believed that it would be 'pointless and imprudent to dissipate our reserves in defence of a fixed exchange rate which we should be forced to abandon very shortly.' In his cramped handwriting at the bottom of the seven-point, typed draft memorandum to the prime minister, Rasminsky wrote in as point number eight, 'I should again emphasize the extreme urgency of action on this matter.' And in the actual proposals submitted to the prime minister for his consideration, the last point made was that 'policy must be to err at first on being over-tough, and then relax. Opposite approach fatal.' Clearly the pressure was on the Conservatives to follow through with a tough program.

Nor did that pressure relent over the next few weeks. When rumours began circulating that the government was not going to publish any details regarding the $250-million reduction in expenditures, but would confine itself to the general statement that expenditures were being reduced by $250 million in a full fiscal year, Rasminsky sent a letter to Diefenbaker.[51] It was essential that the program should carry conviction, and a vague statement suggesting that $250 million would be cut 'may be received with scepticism and fail to create the confidence which all have agreed is necessary if this programme is to succeed.' Each point must be itemized, and the reductions spelled out, in order to achieve the objective. Ultimately, Diefenbaker agreed.

Following the plan's release to the press, Pearson issued a statement which recognized that there was an emergency but failed to indicate any degree of support for the government's program. Rasminsky felt betrayed, and the tenor of the Liberal response was 'distinctly unhelpful in the exchange market.' On 27 June, he met with Pearson, telling him that he was 'disappointed at the tone and character of the statement he had issued yesterday.'[52] The governor had two reasons: '1. There [was] still some chance that the programme itself, which [he] regard[ed] as urgently necessary in the national interest, could go forward successfully. 2. [He] had, probably unwisely, become deeply involved in the situation personally and if it misfired [he] would find [himself] in the middle of a political storm which would be damaging to the Bank ... and damaging to the effort to rebuild confidence.'

Nor was the prime minister especially pleased with the Liberal effort. Diefenbaker told Arnold Hart, president of the Bank of Montreal, that he was 'keen[ly] disappoint[ed] in Pearson's public statement.'[53] Rasminsky took that criticism to be an oblique reference to him. The only thing that could be done by the 27th that might serve to keep the whole situation from deteriorating further and help to keep the Bank out of politics was 'for the Liberal Party to issue a statement after its caucus today indicating that the measures announced, however regrettable, are necessary to meet the emergency and were being supported on that basis.'

According to the memo that Rasminsky wrote immediately following their meeting on 27 June, Pearson was supportive (as he had been following their first meeting), and it suggests a great deal about the leader of the Opposition and also the governor: '[Pearson] hoped that nothing harmful to the programme or confidence would come out of the Liberal caucus. [Rasminsky] interjected that [he] was hoping for something hopeful. [Pearson] said that he had the impression that the programme was not going badly. [Rasminsky] said that this was like a smallpox inoculation, that you had to wait some time to know whether it took and one could not yet say whether it had done so. Pearson then said that he hoped for something constructive from the caucus. [Rasminsky] then repeated that [he] thought the only constructive thing that could be done in the situation was to have the caucus issue a statement along the lines [he] had indicated.' Further, if things took a turn where Rasminsky became personally involved in political controversy, he would have to consider the right course of action for him to take, which in all likelihood included his resignation. However, that was unnecessary; on the 28th, Pearson issued another statement that satisfied Rasminsky.

The entire episode was quite extraordinary, complicated as it was by political considerations and personalities. As Walter Gordon's biographer, Denis Smith, notes in *Gentle Patriot*, Gordon's reaction to the news from Pearson of his visit with Rasminsky was immediate: 'I knew what his response would be, "Here's a proposal from a senior civil servant; of course we must accept it."'[54] Gordon did not want to do any such thing, believing that the whole package had been dictated to Canada by the IMF. When Smith's biography appeared in 1973, Rasminsky was stung by that assertion; it was simply not true. While the governor had been in consultation with Per Jacobsson, that was not out of the ordinary, given the situation. However, contrary to Gordon's assertion, Rasminsky later wrote that the managing director's 'consistent advice to me was not to press the Government too hard and to be aware of their political problems.'

Rasminsky suggested: 'It would be fruitless to speculate on the origin and nature of Walter Gordon's misinterpretation of these events and the part I played in them. The only thing I am certain of is that it could not have been based on my conversation with Pearson, as is suggested in the long quotation from *Gentle Patriot* [pages 107–8].' Rasminsky insisted that:

1. The decision of the Canadian Government to fix the exchange rate at 92½ US cents (or any other level) in May 1962 was not taken under any pressure from the Fund;
2. The programme to overcome the exchange crisis of 1962 was entirely worked out by Canadian officials and not dictated by the Fund;
3. The Fund (including the Managing Director) was not aware of all aspects of the programme until it was presented to them on June 23 along with the request for a $300 million drawing;
4. I was in frequent touch with the Managing Director ... during this period. The main subject of our conversation was our exchange losses and, in the final critical week after the election, the difficulties, as the Government considered the programme, in getting agreement on what cuts should be made in Government expenditures; and
5. At no time did [Rasminsky] mention the proposed [import] surcharge to Jacobsson.[55]

Jacobsson's biography supports Rasminsky's recollection on many of the points raised above.[56]

The deciding factor remained that Canada had limited freedom of action when confronted with an exchange crisis of this magnitude. The immediate impact of the stabilization program was favourable, however, and there was not any need to draw on the foreign credits. Despite the rather alarmist memoranda circulating in Ottawa in May and June, the crisis passed quickly. The Canadian dollar rose from the support level of 91.75 US cents to 92.64 US cents on 27 June, and the Bank of Canada was able to take reserves from the market as commercial buying of Canadian dollars was resumed. Nine months later, the import surcharges were withdrawn. Those were satisfying developments. However, the US Federal Reserve Board focused on the bleaker side of the program in its analysis of the Canadian situation. Clearly, the increase in the bank rate and the other restrictive measures announced would have had some effect on the 'lagging Canadian business recovery.'[57]

The pace of the Canadian recovery had been roughly comparable to that of the American, and the stabilization program incorporated several measures likely to restrain economic expansion – in particular, the cutback in federal spending, the rise in Canadian interest rates, and the higher cost of imported goods. As the memorandum from the 'Fed' noted, 'Those restrictive measures have been put into effect at a time when the business outlook in Canada has been clouded both because of the uncertain business outlook in the United States and because of the recent fall in stock prices.' The effect of the program would become evident over the next twelve months.

The memo also noted some effects of the program on the US balance of payments:

> The large US export surplus to Canada is likely to be reduced; our exports to Canada totalled US$3.6 billion in 1961, or about 17 per cent of total exports ... The United States balance of payments has benefitted ... during the second quarter by return flows to US capital from Canada and by ... shifts in 'leads and lags,' as evidenced by changes in the 'errors and omissions' item in the United States balance of payments. These shifts are likely to be reversed as confidence in present Canadian exchange rate is restored. Finally, Canadian interest rates have risen quite sharply since late April. In the past, a spread between the US and Canadian market rates has produced flows of US funds into Canadian securities; with a substantial gap, Canadian borrowings in this country have also tended to become substantial. Thus some increase in the flow of US funds both of a volatile and of an investment character to Canada is to be expected.[58]

In its rather technical language, the 'Fed' was reflecting a common sentiment among Americans with respect to the Canadian program. Certainly the US cabinet was not happy with it. President Kennedy, when briefed by Douglas Dillon, was told that North American relations might suffer as a result. In private discussions, US officials protested the surcharges. As Dillon told Kennedy, they would 'have a progressively corrosive effect in Canada and on US–Canadian economic relations. We will use every opportunity to impress on the Canadians the need for the replacement of the surcharges by a suitable substitute at the earliest possible moment.'[59] Similar criticisms were heard from Europe and the United Kingdom.[60]

Still, from Ottawa's point of view, desperate times called for desperate measures, and the rescue operation that Rasminsky spearheaded was successful. The pressure against the Canadian dollar had completely disappeared by early July, and the Bank of Canada was able to recoup some of Canada's exchange losses, though unknowns remained. In writing to the Earl of Cromer, the governor of the Bank of England, to thank him for his assistance during the crisis, Rasminsky observed: 'No one here thinks that we have done the trick through these emergency measures. They are essentially a crash programme which was designed to apply a tourniquet to the haemorrhage and give us time to work out more positive programmes to deal with out problems. The difficulties in this regard are ... pretty formidable, not least those resulting from the unsettled political situation.'[61]

As the financial and economic situation improved, the bank rate began a slow downward movement. By September, it had fallen to 5.5 per cent, signalling the end of the critical period, but not of unsettled conditions. Rasminsky explained the decline to the new minister of finance, George Nowlan. At 6 per cent, the prime rate was at a crisis level and 'justifiable only in terms of a situation as critical as that which faced us in June.'[62] Since then, conditions had improved to the point where government of Canada securities were selling well, official reserves had increased, and confidence generally was up. Still, there remained a large deficit to be financed in the immediate future, so interest rates had to be attractive to investors. It was important, so the governor believed, 'that the current small reduction in the Bank Rate should not be permitted to mislead people in this regard.' It was a fine balancing act.

Rasminsky also had some advice for Nowlan with respect to Canada's international-payments position. While he agreed that the new exchange rate would be very helpful in improving Canada's payments position, the country's deficit position was much too large to allow Ottawa to rely on the exchange rate alone. He suggested that additional, longer-term measures to reduce the country's current-account deficit were necessary in the interests both of Canada's external financial position and of its domestic economic welfare. There was a need to bring about a better balance in the government's budget, especially given the existence of the import surcharges, which were such an irritant for Canada's trading partners.

Nowlan would not have an opportunity to act on that advice. Another election in April 1963 returned a Liberal minority government, led by Lester Pearson, with Walter Gordon at Finance. Rasminsky would have the same counsel for it[63] – in short, the current-account deficit limited

Ottawa's freedom to enact certain measures, and reality should force it to shape certain policies accordingly.

Two developments in particular concentrated the new Liberal government's collective mind on the fragility of the Canadian condition. The first – construction of the budget of June 1963 – only tangentially involved Rasminsky. While he commented on certain aspects of it, and met with Pearson and Gordon at the Bank to discuss it, the budget, strictly speaking, fell under the purview of the Department of Finance. However, he played the lead in the second act – development of a Canadian response to the US Interest Equalization Tax, which is dealt with in chapter 9.

The first Pearson budget has been seen in either of two ways – as a clarion call to committed Canadians everywhere to take up the cause of repatriating control of the country's economy, or as a hopelessly misplaced and naïve attempt to penalize American business operating in Canada in the name of Canadian sovereignty. Rasminsky was a Canadian nationalist, but he also had responsibilities that made him less than supportive of the document. Because of the limitations on Canadian monetary sovereignty noted above, and because his job description included protecting the value of the Canadian currency, the governor disagreed with Gordon's approach.

He was opposed not to what the budget hoped to accomplish, but rather to the method by which it wanted to get there. His first, private, expression of discontent was made to his colleagues Robert Bryce, clerk of the Privy Council, Claude Isbister, at Trade and Commerce, and Simon Reisman of Finance. Peter Newman notes that they had 'a gloomy lunch together.'[64] He communicated his objections also to Prime Minister Lester Pearson, and on 31 May Pearson telephoned him and suggested that he, Gordon, and Rasminsky meet at the Bank over lunch to discuss the points of conflict.

What did the budget document contain that troubled Rasminsky? His notes, prepared for the meeting, ran to five pages.[65] Two measures stood out. The first was the revision of the 15 per cent withholding tax on dividends paid to non-residents. A reduced rate of 10 per cent would apply to companies that were more than 25 per cent Canadian-owned, while an increased rate of 20 per cent would be the lot of those not falling in that category. Gordon also levied a 30 per cent take-over tax on sales of shares in Canadian companies listed on Canadian stock exchanges by Canadian residents to non-residents and to companies controlled by non-residents.

As well, any Canadian company that was in the process of being sold to a non-resident company would be liable for the tax.

The economic expansion then under way was likely to continue into the next year. Several factors – the continuing effects of the devaluation of the Canadian dollar to 92.5 US cents, the prospect of a substantial increase in investment, and the confidence of the business community in the government following a number of years of increasingly erratic Conservative leadership – all augured well for the future. From the point of view of the government's concern with levels of unemployment, particularly during the coming winter, the most essential task was to keep the expansion going and to avoid any actions that would bring it to a premature end or induce reactions that would create unsettled economic conditions.

Against that background, there were several questionable aspects of the proposed budget. The first was its intention to raise the withholding tax on dividends of non-Canadian corporations. The government should, Rasminsky believed, reconsider its proposal; it could be 'unleashing forces whose magnitude [would be impossible] to measure.' If that step were interpreted as indicating a hostile view towards foreign investment (which it surely would be), it could result in massive liquidation of non-resident–owned investment in Canada and precipitate a new exchange crisis. The country's balance of payments was in no position to support large capital withdrawals, as Canada was still running a current-account deficit of $600 million to $800 million per year. Moreover, given that scenario, it was difficult to believe that Canada would be permitted to borrow large amounts in the New York market, making the ensuing exchange crisis more difficult to deal with than that of the previous year. As well, apart from exchange considerations, foreign-controlled companies accounted for about one-third of new private business investment in Canada, which amount could be reduced, with adverse effects on growth and employment.

The proposed tax also introduced the principle of discrimination based on nationality into the Canadian tax system. 'The position of the Government is stronger, and more in line,' Rasminsky thought, 'with the [recent Hyannisport] conversations between the Prime Minister and the President [of the United States] if this principle is expressed at the present time in the form of carrots for Canadians rather than sticks for Americans.'[66] If the carrots and a clear statement of government intention did not work, then the Liberals would be in a much stronger position in later budgets to bring out a few sticks.

Rasminsky also opposed the proposal to increase the tax on corporations. He thought that Canada's basic economic policy should be directed to increasing the efficiency and productivity of Canadian industry in general, and secondary industry in particular. That endeavour would produce jobs and improve the country's balance-of-payments position. An increase in corporate tax rates worked in precisely the wrong direction; it discouraged private investment and 'encouraged unnecessary and wasteful expenditure.' Ottawa should keep in mind the competitive situation in North America; US corporate taxes were to be reduced from the then-level of 52 per cent to a projected 47 per cent by 1965. Canada's rate was set at 52 per cent.

Rasminsky also argued, though not as strenuously, against the proposed surtax on personal income tax. At a maximum, it should be limited to 5 per cent. If implemented, it would make the marginal rates on the incomes of the professional class considerably higher than those prevailing in the United States. The proposed increase could result in intensified emigration southward by highly qualified people – the so-called brain drain could return with a vengeance.

There were a number of other features that he did not like; those proposals ran 'some risk of slowing economic expansion by changing the public's image of the government. [He] believe[d] that the business community regarded the government as competent, business-like, [and] anxious to address itself to [Canada's] basic economic problems. There [was] some risk that this view [would] be changed if the Government seem[ed] to go in for gimmicks which it might be thought are intended to create the appearance of action, but which are almost certainly going to be ineffective if not counter-productive.' Rasminsky pointed to the following points: '(a) the 36 per cent tax on certain take-overs. There were too many ways by which smart lawyers and operators [could] avoid this. It [did] not even set out to apply to non-list companies. The tax [was] of doubtful constitutionality. (b) the proposal to subsidize employment. This would inevitably result in the uneconomic unemployment of labour. (c) the $500 subsidy on winter-built houses. Apart from administrative difficulties, this [was] a costly method of compressing employment into certain periods of the year without contributing significantly to the total.' Thus Rasminsky's approach differed markedly from Gordon's (and, as events transpired, Pearson's as well).[67]

The governor had legitimate concerns about the budget's impact on the Canadian economy, especially with Canada's exposed economic position and its dependence on international investors, primarily American, to make up its current-account deficit. In short, he rightly believed that the country had limited freedom of action to pursue policies that potentially alienated the United States. If Ottawa wanted to undertake such a program, it had to put its own economic house in order; to do otherwise was to make it too vulnerable – a reality brought out starkly with the US Interest Equalization Tax of July 1963.

As Rasminsky later noted, however, the minister and, in this case, the prime minister were not interested in taking advice from him. In Pearson's defence, this subject was clearly out of his range of expertise. Walton Butterworth, the US ambassador in Ottawa, surely had it right when he told the US secretary of state that Pearson was 'basically uninterested in economic matters, even when they hurt.'[68] However, the budget's political implications should have been obvious. With respect to the document and with Gordon generally, Rasminsky was out of phase; only partly tongue-in-cheek, the governor has written that they spent more time talking about the employment of lawyers by Canada's Industrial Development Bank than about monetary policy during Gordon's time in office.

Rasminsky's reaction to the budget mirrored that of many others. It is arguable that it compromised Gordon's credibility and seriously damaged the reputation of the new government – a blow from which it did not soon recover. Opposition to the minister's method of reducing the amount of foreign ownership in the Canadian economy eventually forced Gordon to repeal the take-over tax.[69] The ensuing crisis also affected Pearson's relationship with his minister of finance, or so a conversation between the prime minister and Butterworth suggested. In November 1963, after disowning a recent statement by Gordon in the House of Commons that he would press on with policies of the sort laid out by the June budget, the prime minister, perhaps a bit disingenuously, told the ambassador: 'Gordon had already begun work on the next year's budget and he would have to take into account the views of other members of cabinet *or else he would have to go.* [Pearson] volunteered that not a mistake but a blunder had been committed [with the June budget]; that caught up as he was in the slipstream of "sixty days of decision," he had neglected to give consideration to the implications of the budget. I have discussed this problem at considerable length on a number of occasions with Pearson and this is the first time he has spoken in such categoric terms.'[70]

Perhaps that was why Gordon requested a pre-budget meeting with US Treasury Secretary Douglas Dillon and Undersecretary George Ball in early February 1964 as he prepared his next budget. Butterworth explained to Dillon: 'Canada follows British practice of complete budget secrecy before presentation to Parliament. Only once in recent years has FinMin made certain provisions known in advance to USG. Consequently, Gordon's approach indicates he must be concerned about US reaction to future measures or his unwillingness to alter measures to which US has objected. Moreover, domestic pressure for removal of discriminatory 1963 budget legislation probably also prompts Gordon to attempt to reach 'understanding' with US which could then be used to calm Canadian business community.'[71]

As the 1963 budget faded away like a bad memory, there were later Gordon budgets to which some officials at the Bank took exception. For example, his last as minister of finance in 1965, which held out the promise of tax cuts, Rasminsky labelled 'inappropriately expansionary.'[72] It collided with a Bank worry over inflation. The governor had contemplated an increase in interest rates, which would make monetary policy and fiscal policy work against each other. In the first half of that year, a document forecast rapid economic expansion and a drop in the unemployment rate, on a deseasonalized basis, to 4 per cent. The cost-of-living index had risen by 0.8 per cent from November to December 1964, which represented a substantial quickening of the rate of increase of prices, which stimulated concern over the possibility of inflation. A US Federal Reserve Board analysis clearly spelled out the dangers, of which Rasminsky was only too well aware: 'Symptoms of inflationary dangers have been increasingly evident in Canada in recent months. Through October, unemployment, seasonally adjusted, continued to fall (reaching 3.1 per cent compared with 3.6 per cent in September and 4.0 per cent in August); prices rose further (the general wholesale index moved up 0.4 per cent in October from its September level and was 3.2 per cent higher than in October 1964); and general loans outstanding at chartered banks moved up rapidly (the chartered banks' general loans outstanding in October 1965 were up 16.9 per cent higher than in October 1964, up from 16.2 per cent for the twelve months ending in September).'[73]

The Bank of Canada also criticized possible reductions in corporate taxes. While it remained very concerned about the competitiveness of Canadian industry, it questioned whether a tax break was the proper method to secure that result. From a certain perspective, the argument for decreasing business taxes was not a strong one. The 1965–6 outlook for capital investment in manufacturing was very strong; as the analysis suggested, the figure could go up by more than 30 per cent without any tax reduction.[74] Accordingly, it could be difficult to justify a mid-year corporate tax cut to stimulate capital expenditures. Moreover, the Bank's document asked, 'how important is a tax cut in stimulating capital investment?' Not very; the primary factors determining investment were sales growth and shortage of capacity.

In any event, the minister ignored the Bank's advice, pushing through cuts to both business and personal taxes. Tax reduction has always been well received by the public, and an election call was definitely in Liberal minds in mid-1965. They wanted a majority government and hoped that the vote, eventually called for 8 November 1965, would bring that result. It did not, however, and Pearson remained head of a minority government until he retired from politics in early 1968.

As the decade passed, the Bank's objections to some of the policies pursued by the government would become more focused. As is discussed below, Rasminsky's primary concern began to centre on what seemed to be the development of an inflation psychology among Canadians. As costly new government programs were developed and new expenditures entered into, the Bank was a lone voice preaching restraint. In the mid- to late 1960s, however, money (and prospects for the future) seemed limitless, and budgets reflected that perception. Increasingly, government lost control of the budgetary process, resulting in the inflationary disaster that came to characterize the late 1970s and the 1980s. Certainly, Rasminsky and the Bank of Canada did not oppose economic expansion; they were, however, opposed to uneconomic use of resources and to overly lavish wage settlements that were not matched in terms of productivity increases or enhanced Canadian competitiveness. That was a sound position, and one that governments ignored to their detriment.

Foreign ownership in Canada, which had been such a major issue in the 1963 budget, intruded into other areas connected with the Bank of Canada's responsibility. In the 1960s, the Mercantile Bank, then a Netherlands' subsidiary, was the only foreign-owned bank in Canada. The federal government had awarded it a charter in 1953, in part because it believed that competition among Canada's ten chartered banks was not strong enough. By the early 1960s, its Dutch owners were looking for a buyer, and the giant US First National City Bank of New York (Citibank) was interested in absorbing the Mercantile into its financial empire. The size of Citibank was a problem for both the minister of finance and the chartered banks, which were much smaller than the American behemoth.

Walter Gordon saw this issue as one of foreign ownership, and he had clearly laid out his position on that subject in his June 1963 budget. Indeed, the first inquiries made by Citibank about the possibility of expanding into Canada occurred at the same time as Gordon's budget was being savaged in Parliament. Rasminsky was sensitive to the political agenda of the day and also to the position of Canadian banks. R.P. Mac-Fadden, a vice-president of Citibank, had come to see him on 20 June to say that his bank had reached a purchase agreement with the Mercantile to acquire its stock. The American bank would wish to 'reconsider their decision' to come to Canada if Rasminsky or the minister of finance had strong adverse views.[75]

That decision lay within the purview of the Department of Finance, and the governor urged the American to talk to the minister before he went ahead. However, he did say that Citibank 'should know that there would be a much stronger reaction here to their coming in than there was to the Mercantile some years ago.' The governor told MacFadden: 'Since [the 1950s] the whole question of non-resident ownership had come much more in the public mind; the Mercantile was connected with distant Dutch banks which created less of a stir than [would] the First National City Bank coming in; moreover, they would be regarded as the forerunner of other American banks, one of which at least had shown strong interest from time to time in coming into Canada.'

Rasminsky was astonished that the Americans had not first cleared the proposed take-over with Ottawa or at least sounded out the Canadians on what their position might be. As he told them, 'Purchasers would be taking risk of unfavourable Canadian action' if Citibank proceeded without Canadian government approval.[76] That was not, strictly speaking, legally required, but it would be desirable, at least from Citibank's perspective. As well, was MacFadden aware, Rasminsky asked, 'of the views that the Minister of Finance had expressed regarding foreign ownership and control of Canadian chartered banks in the *Report of the Royal Commission on Canada's Economic Prospects?*' The governor read him the full text of paragraph 20 on page 93. MacFadden, knew of Gordon's views and reiterated that if strong opposition was encountered, the bank would reconsider its intention.

The bank's chairman and chief executive officer, James Stillman Rockefeller, accompanied by McFadden met with Gordon on 18 July. In anticipation of that meeting, the minister asked Rasminsky to set out the main technical considerations involved from the point of view of the Bank of Canada if the Americans were allowed to go ahead. The governor's reply ran to seven pages and set out the misgivings that he felt about Citibank's proposal; he had some difficulty with the idea of a large US bank establishing itself in Canada.

First, would Citibank improve the functioning of the country's financial system? The reasoning behind granting the Mercantile Bank a charter in Canada in the first place had been sound, and it remained so in 1963. Like former governor Graham Towers, Rasminsky believed that anything which increased competition among banks would yield dividends for the public. As he wrote, 'The degree of concentration that presently exists in Canada is disturbing: there are only eight banks in all, of which five account for 90 per cent of the business, and three for 70 per cent.'[77] But how much would First National effectively increase competition in Canada? Rasminsky thought not much; the American owners 'would be so anxious to soothe the ruffled feelings of the Canadian banks and maintain the valuable correspondent relationships they now have with them that they would be unlikely, for a period at any rate, to introduce more price competition into the Canadian banking system.' Competition would happen only if other US banks came into the country, and that would lead to pressure to transform the Canadian banking system into part of an integrated North American financial system, with integrated policies.

That prospect was most unlikely, at least in the forseeable future. But while the bank might not compete aggressively with its Canadian counterparts, Rasminsky thought that it would take a good chunk of business away from the latter. He told the minister: 'They would probably make a controlled drive on the branch plant business and they are, of course, with their US connections, in a good position to succeed ... The Canadian banks will ... complain that the new bank is skimming the cream of the business without bearing any of the overhead costs of running the branch banking system which provides the essential banking services for the country.'

Second, would the presence of a large US bank in Canada affect relations between the central and the chartered banks? Would it, the minister inquired, affect the way in which Rasminsky was 'able to talk to the banks and would it affect the degree to which [he could] influence their behaviour?' In the 1960s, relations were quite cordial; Rasminsky spoke frequently with bank chief executive officers on the telephone, as well as hosting regular meetings in Ottawa. There were many occasions when the two sides 'let their hair down' in discussing financial and exchange problems. Would Rasminsky do that if a representative of an American bank were present?

Probably not – he would certainly have to count on whatever was said being immediately passed along to Citibank's New York headquarters, which could be problematic. As long as the Mercantile was a Dutch bank, he had not felt inhibited, 'probably on account of the distance from Amsterdam and the fact that our relations with the Dutch are not of major importance.' As well, the control exerted by the central bank on monetary matters could conceivably be weakened by the presence of a large American bank. Such an institution would presumably have available to it the large US-dollar reserves of the parent bank, which it could use to build up its Canadian resources in periods of monetary stringency. It would be better able to operate against the trend of Canadian monetary policy than the domestic banks.

While Rasminsky responded fully to the minister's request for information, he did not want to become involved in the process of either granting or refusing a charter to Citibank. The reason lay in his Bank's recent history. As he correctly anticipated, Citibank would become a political issue, which he did not want to have reverberate in the Bank, especially so soon after the Coyne affair. His intention was to ensure that any negotiations took place with the Ministry of Finance – the relevant public office in this case.

Gordon's mind was made up, probably long before he received Rasminsky's memorandum; if Citibank proceeded, the minister told Rockefeller and MacFadden, he would introduce legislation to ensure that its efforts would be unsuccessful. MacFadden later told Rasminsky that 'the Minister of Finance had been fairly tough in indicating to them that he did not wish them to proceed with the transaction.'[78] In any event, after serious consideration, the Americans had gone ahead despite their previous commitment, buying 50 per cent of the Mercantile's shares. Their approach was later characterized as being like 'a bull in a china shop.'[79]

Gordon and Rasminsky had warned them about possible adverse consequences prior to the purchase, and so they could have no real complaint about retroactivity. An amendment to the Bank Act in 1966 severely limited the operations of any bank that was more than 25 per cent foreign-owned. Through many twists and turns over the next several years, Citibank eventually sold newly issued shares to Canadians, reduced its ownership to less than 25 per cent, and expanded as a 'Canadian' bank. In 1985, it was absorbed by the National Bank.

Why did the US government not retaliate in a substantive way against Canada's banking policy? Rasminsky had warned Gordon of that possibility in his memorandum, and Rockefeller had enlisted the support of the

US State Department in his campaign against the Canadian legislation. The counsellor of the US embassy in Ottawa had delivered a note of protest to the minister of finance, which Peter Newman later called, with some justification, 'one of the toughest diplomatic initiatives that has ever been directed at Canada by the US.'[80]

The relatively muted response probably had its roots in American banking legislation. The National Bank Act listed certain things that foreigners could not do. For example, a non-American could not become a director of Citibank. Washington was already attuned to the notion that banking might be one area that other countries might want to keep under domestic control. Further, as the *Journal of Commerce* suggested, 'American banks operate at least twice as many branches and agencies in other countries as foreign banks operate in the United States. If this country provokes retaliation by other nations against American banks, our banks would be much more vulnerable than would foreign banks operating here. Let's not look for trouble where none exists.'[81]

By 1961, Britain was in economic difficulty once again. That, of course, was nothing new to Rasminsky, as he had been one of the Canadians most concerned with the British situation during the 1950s; it seemed as if that country had stumbled from crisis to crisis since 1945. It ran true to form in the 1960s and experienced its first setback of the decade in July 1961, in the form of a crisis of confidence in sterling. The IMF's managing director, Per Jacobsson, asked Rasminsky to inform Donald Fleming that he would like to include Canada in the list of countries whose currencies were to be made available to the United Kingdom in the US$2-billion operation to support sterling. Canada's share was to total US$75 million.

Rasminsky was not thrilled by the request. As he told Jacobsson, Canada had a 'very large current account deficit. ... [I] said that I thought that the Fund should not expect a country which did not have a current account surplus to extend a large amount of credit abroad.' The managing director focused on other elements; 'he thought that the Fund was entitled to look at a country's over-all payments position and its reserve position, and not only the current account, and on this basis he thought we could afford to participate. ... Finally, he put the thought that on broad political grounds Canada might well regard it as desirable to participate in this international cooperative effort to help the United Kingdom; ... he thought that this would be very helpful from the UK point of view and that our participation was consonant with our position in the world.'[82] The minister agreed, and Canada got on board.

Three years later, Canada was involved again, along with the Americans and six European central banks, participating in a British rescue operation in November 1964 to the tune of US$50 million. Rasminsky attended the meeting at the Bank for International Settlements (BIS), in Basle, Switzerland, which arranged enough support to calm nervous markets. In September 1965 (renewed in June 1966), Canada, led by Rasminsky, joined in another aid-to-Britain operation, while in 1967, the Bank of Canada helped once again, obtaining authorization from the government to participate in an arrangement in November – the so-called Callaghan credits, named after the Labour chancellor of the exchequer.[83]

Despite the lengthy effort, sterling was devalued on 18 November 1967. It did not come as a great surprise, Finance Minister Mitchell Sharp told cabinet, 'since the United Kingdom was ... mortgaged to the hilt and had virtually no available foreign exchange reserves.'[84] London had negotiated for a $3-billion credit. Rasminsky had told Sharp that he was sceptical of success but had not wanted to hold out against the measure if other countries could be persuaded to contribute. However, his view remained that it was questionable whether such an operation would maintain the value of the pound, and if it did not work, then the loan would be tied up indefinitely.

He had also given some consideration to changing the value of the Canadian dollar; it was decided not to do so. To have done so would have added to the pressures on the American dollar and to the cost of living in Canada. In addition, Canada would not have obtained the necessary approval from the International Monetary Fund (IMF), since the Canadian reserve position was stong. Indeed, Rasminsky had spoken with the Fund's managing director, now Pierre-Paul Schweitzer, who had told him that he 'had taken it for granted that there was no question of a change in the Canadian rate.'[85]

British devaluation, combined with weakening of investors' confidence in the stability of the par-value system, helped to erode confidence in the Canadian dollar. To make the situation worse, there were some domestic factors to contend with. Concern was demonstrated 'about the outlook for Canada's current account position following the closing of Expo and other Centennial Year activities, and about the vulnerability of a country requiring continuing large capital inflows. The prices and costs performance of the Canadian economy was poor in relation to that of our chief competitors, and if this continued our competitive position in world markets would be eroded. There seemed to be little evidence that the Government was seriously concerned about this problem since some of the key wage settlements had been in negotiations in which the Government had been involved. Also, the Government's large borrowing requirements seemed to be adding to inflationary pressures.[86] When those ingredients were stirred into a mix to which the US Johnson program of January 1968 were added, an exchange crisis was precipitated in Canada, as is discussed in chapter 9.

Still, Canada was better off than the United Kingdom, and Ottawa renewed its facility to the United Kingdom in September 1968 and again a year later, until it expired at the end of March 1970. Even despite its own, significant problems experienced in early 1968, Canada, unlike Japan, did not withdraw its help to Britain. By late summer, Ottawa was one of twelve governments providing short-term deposits with the BIS of up to US$2 billion to be used to offset the effect on Britain's international reserves, which had declined from a level of £3.080 billion.[87] The shares of the participating countries were (in US dollars) Austria, $50 million; Belgium, $80 million; Canada, 100 million; Denmark, 20 million; Italy, 225 million; Japan, 90 million; Netherlands, $100 million; Norway, 20 million; Sweden, 35 million; Switzerland, $100 million; the United States, $650 million; and West Germany, $400 million. The total for countries that agreed to participate was $1,870 million. France was contributing nothing, and there remained to be allocated $80 million. By March 1970, the worst was over for Britain, at least for the 1960s. The trial for the United States, however, was only beginning, as will be seen in chapter 9.

The theme of this chapter – change, in global alignments, as seen through various British exchange crises, in American troubles with balance of payments; at the Bank of Canada itself; and between it and other agencies – and the fall-out from the Coyne affair must have made Rasminsky wonder at times if the job was worth it. But it was stimulating, with the stress and tension, the negotiations and the drama. He would leave the Bank only on retirement. But there was at least one source of flattering public speculation about another job – that of managing director of the IMF following the premature death in 1963 of Per Jacobsson.

The respected British periodical the *Economist* posed the challenge – to find a good man to replace Jacobsson: 'A bad or conservative choice now could spell stagnation for the difficult but vital movement towards a wider and more effective machinery of international finance. When new forms of organisation have to be developed in apposition to established centres of power, they are usually dependent on the vision and drive of one man;

and the world of official finance is more than usually studded with built-in resistances to change, not least when it appears to be imposed by an international authority.'[88] Where, the magazine asked, was the man of many talents to follow Per Jacobsson to be found?

It offered a list of candidates. Pierre-Paul Schweitzer from the Bank of France was said to be uninterested (though he was eventually appointed). The 'formidable' Wilfrid Baumgartner was a former governor of the Bank of France, had been a minister of finance, and was a Rasminsky friend. Guillame Guidney, an old acquaintance of Rasminsky's from the San Francisco UN negotiations, was at the BIS. Also listed were Robert Marjolin, vice-president of the European Economic Commission; J. Zijl-stra, the Netherlands' minister of finance; M.W. Holtrop, president of the Netherlands Bank; E. Van Lennep, a Dutch treasury official who had been chair of both the monetary committee of the EEC and of the payments subcommittee of the Organization for Economic Cooperation and Development; and Guido Carli, governor of the Bank of Italy.

However, there were doubts as to 'whether these able men would tackle the job in the widest way, and also whether they would put across their strictures on financial orthodoxy with Jacobsson tact.' As well, one did not associate with them 'the sense of adventure that is undoubtedly needed to make and keep the Fund an active force.' Who, then, would fit the bill? The *Economist* had the answer: 'An outstanding candidate from the American continent who could be counted on to develop the Fund in a positive way ... is Mr. Louis Rasminsky who in the past two years has been picking up the pieces at the Bank of Canada and earning new respect in the process.' He combined 'technical ability and economic expertise with notable personal qualities and is a popular figure ... It would be absurd if narrow and unnecessary ideas of geographical restrictions kept out the best man available for what should be the free world's number one economic job.' As flattering as the editorial's suggestion was, Rasminsky had no desire to leave the Bank.

Despite the domestic and international accolades, as mid-decade approached, there was one place in Ottawa where Rasminsky was not welcome. As a Jew, he was barred from joining the Rideau Club, the bastion of the establishment in the capital. While he had no desire to become a member then, a few friends and Rideau Club cardholders – Davey Dunton, Blair Fraser, Arnold Heeney, and Nik Monserrat – found that situation intolerable. In mid-1964, they approached four Jews, Rasminsky among them, and asked that they let their names stand. With the help of their four Jewish friends, they intended to smash those prejudiced rules.

While Rasminsky had some concerns about being viewed as a 'token' Jew, he agreed, but only after further discussion about the black-ball system of voting on the admission of new members. Members' votes were not identified – but if there was one dissenting voice, then the applicant was turned down. Anonimity allowed bigotry a free hand at the Rideau Club. Rasminsky's demand was that the system be changed; anyone who cast a negative vote must identify himself. Those members who harboured prejudices in private, it turned out, were not so ready to declare themselves in public. As a result, the club became a more open institution. Even after the success of the campaign, Rasminsky did not join the Rideau Club until after his retirement from the Bank.

Rasminsky's growing reputation, however, prompted Canadian universities to take a long, hard look at him as a possible recipient of one of their honorary degrees. He had been granted an honorary doctorate from the University of Toronto in 1953 and made an honorary fellow of the London School of Economics in 1959. Hebrew Union College in Cincinnati inquired in early January 1962 if he was available for its March convocation to receive an honorary degree (he was not), but he accepted an invitation from Hebrew Union College – Jewish Institute of Religion in Jerusalem to become a doctor of humane letters, on 2 June 1963. A doctor of laws from Queen's University in Kingston, Ont., followed in 1967; Bishop's, in Lennoxville, Que., honored him in 1968 (along with his good friend William Martin, chairman of the 'Fed'); and McMaster University, in Hamilton, Ont., followed two years later. At the 1973 convocation at Trent University in Peterborough, Ont., he received an honorary doctorate, and he did the same at the University of British Columbia in 1979.

As well, in mid-1964, he accepted an appointment from McGill's principal, Rocke Robertson, to sit on the consultative board of the new Centre for Developing-Area Studies. He also found that he could not refuse a 1965 request by Carleton University in Ottawa to sit on its board of governors – a task that he undertook with pleasure, until he retired from it in 1974. Also, in 1968 he received the Outstanding Achievement Award of the Public Service of Canada – the most significant honor that the government could present to a public servant. In his presentation, the governor general, Roland Michener, observed: 'Mr. Rasminsky's most valuable contribution to both Canada and the Western World will be his leading part in efforts to create an effective international monetary system.'[89] A prime ministerial letter elaborated: 'I have no doubt that one of the particular considerations in the Committee's decision was your remarkable role last March in the successful resolution of the serious difficulties facing Canada at that time. The importance of that achievement is now being re-emphasized by the current developments in international finance.'[90] That same year, he was appointed a companion of the Order of Canada.

Finally, there was a particularly special event offered to him by the IMF, which indicated clearly his place and prestige in international finance. He was asked to give the inaugural Per Jacobsson Lecture, sponsored by the Fund to honour its late managing director, and to be held at the Altieri Palace in Rome, headquarters of the Bank of Italy. The glitterati of international finance were there – Swiss bankers and others from Europe and North America; economic and financial correspondents from important newspapers and periodicals; BIS and IMF people, including the managing director, Pierre-Paul Schweitzer; and all the significant central bankers in the world, including the Americans Alfred Hayes and Charles Coombs, as well as Jacobsson's widow and daughter. He expounded on 'The Role of the Central Banker Today.' His forty-five-minute address was a huge success, and the Jacobsson Foundation was set on a firm footing. Rasminsky was at the top of his profession.

One of the subjects that he addressed in Rome became more and more of an issue as the decade waned. As he had said, 'It seems to me that what is needed is not to decide how much inflation can be tolerated but to concentrate on trying to find ways of making the economy work at satisfactory levels without rising price levels. It is clear that we have a lot to learn about living with prosperity without permitting it to degenerate into inflation.'[91] But degenerate it did in Canada, with a quickening pace by 1967. Percentage increases in credit to the public (10 per cent) and private (9 per cent) sectors told the story. As well, compared with the not-too-distant past, the value of money was depreciating with frightening speed. From 1955 to 1965, annual rates of inflation amounted to 1.8 per cent; in 1964–5, it was 2.3 per cent; in 1965–6, a staggering 4.1 per cent.

Increasingly, Raminsky spent his time and energy fighting inflation. As he noted, in its early stages inflation was popular, creating a feeling of ebullience and well-being, which 'did not tempt the community to ask too many questions about the future.' It was the job of the central banker to dampen that ebullience; 'Keynes once said that the perfect standard of good manners for a gentleman attending a party is to maintain precisely the same level of sobriety or inebriety as the rest of the company. If this is so, then central bankers cannot aspire to be gentlemen. Their role ... is rather the unpopular one of acting as the chaperon of the party who has to take away the stimulant just when the party is getting into high gear.'

He was reappointed as governor of the Bank of Canada for a second seven-year term on 24 July 1968; this mandate he directed primarily toward the fight against inflation. An acquaintance, John Exter, senior vice-president of the First National City Bank, was prophetic in his congratulations; his 'crystal ball show[ed] seven rather lean years ahead. Your life may not be easy.'[92] Nor was it.

Chapter Eight

Fighting Inflation: Second Term

The final few years of the 1960s were difficult ones for Rasminsky and for Canada. For his part, the governor could not maintain, like Keynes's fictional gentleman, 'precisely the same level of ... inebriety as the rest of the company' and proved an annoying chaperon as inflation became a very real problem. Canadians were drunk with the potential that seemed to stretch out endlessly into the future and the prosperity that characterized the present. More astute observers might say that the party was winding down but no one was yet willing to pay attention. Expo 67 in Montreal, the World's Fair celebrating Canada's one hundredth birthday in grand style, was a major success and had put the country on the map. It was a wonderful reflection of a developing English-Canadian nationalism that looked to neither Britain nor the United States for its measure.

Canadians, it seemed, could do anything, as could their new prime minister, Pierre Elliott Trudeau, who won the election on 25 June 1968 in convincing style, with 155 seats to the Conservatives' 72 and the New Democratic Party's 22. He personified the Canadian duality, with a French-Canadian father and an English-Canadian mother, speaking both languages with equal facility. Canada was no longer a cold, drab place in the north of the planet, governed by sober men in grey suits. Trudeau could make teenaged girls swoon and their mothers feel as if they had been reborn, such was the force of his charismatic personality. Canada was on the verge of a new era, or, as the *Globe and Mail* noted in an editorial on 26 June, the country was 'willing to adventure.'[1]

It was, but in a way that many did not like. Increasingly Canada was splitting into its English and French components. A question posed by anglophones was, 'What does Quebec want?' President Charles de Gaulle of France had partially answered that when he had responded favourably

TABLE 8.1
Canada's foreign exchange, 20 March 1968

Reserves/borrowings	Amount (US$million)
Reserves at end of 1967	2,500
Reserves lost in support operations	
to about 20 March 1968	−1,300
	1,200
Reserves recaptured since 20 March	430
Borrowings included in reserves:	
USFRB swaps	250
Swaps with market	330
IMF	190
Total published reserves	2,400

to a federal-government invitation to visit Canada in 1967. In Montreal, he had inflamed a Québécois crowd when he had shouted, 'Vive le Québec. Vive le Québec libre.' Not that any in Ottawa needed reminding, but Quebec separatism was becoming a potent force. And Pierre Trudeau seemed to be the man most capable of dealing with it, and any other problem that happened to come along.

Trudeau had been prime minister only since 6 April when he first met with Louis Rasminsky. On 1 May 1968, the governor walked over to the Centre Block of the Parliament Buildings for a lunchtime meeting in his office. As Rasminsky described it in an official summary, the conversation was pleasant, relaxed, and wide ranging.[2] Rasminsky quickly filled in the new prime minister on Canada's foreign-exchange position, telling him that the country had made considerable progress in recapturing the reserves that had been lost during the exchange crisis of March 1968 (discussed below in chapter 9) but that it 'still had a long way to go.' Rasminsky summed up the arithmetic in the way outlined in Table 8.1.

Liabilities to Canada were for the very short term, and, Rasminsky emphasized, it behoved the country to try to keep the exchange coming in. The confidence factor was important, and the governor expressed some apprehension about the possibility that things would be said in the course of the campaign for the upcoming election, called for June, which would be disturbing. When Trudeau pressed him on this point, Rasminsky suggested two things. The first was the danger 'of foolish statements [being] made by responsible people.' He stressed that he thought that it would be inappropriate 'in the present circumstances for any responsible person in Government to show anything except a determination to maintain and defend the present exchange rate – no flirtation, for example, with fluctuating exchange rates.' He had in mind Alvin Hamilton's remark to the Vancouver press corps in the 1962 election that the peg at 92.5 US cents was not a firm one, which had aggravated an already-unstable situation. The second point related to investors' confidence in Canada. The Bank of Canada had estimated that for the 1968–9 budget year there would be a deficit in excess of $400 million unless government expenditures were reduced. To Rasminsky's mind, it would be asking for trouble if it 'made a lot of expensive promises.'

Rasminsky recorded that 'Mr. Trudeau took this very well and said that it would influence him in the discussions that he had with his colleagues.' Indeed, the new prime minister told him 'that we had come to the end of the expensive universal social security programmes and that the public realized the connection between the high level of Government expenditures and some of the difficulties we had been experiencing, and that they did not really want any more universal programmes.'

The conversation ended with a brief foray by Trudeau into the question of regional disparities and the practicality of regional monetary policies. (Not very practical, Rasminsky assured him.)[3] As well, they had a brief discussion about the level of interest rates then prevailing; even though they were high (a result of the recent exchange crisis), the governor 'did not see any immediate prospect of reducing them materially through a Canadian initiative.' The rate was based on the need to defend the dollar and was influenced by that prevailing in the United States. 'One could only hope that the United States would take some of the weight off monetary policy, but until they did it would be asking for trouble for us to try to bring about any really significant contraction of the spread here.'[4] The Bank of Canada had not followed the US-Federal Reserve Board's lead the last time the latter had increased its prime rate, with the result that interest-rate spreads were relatively narrow in May 1968; latitude for independent action was very limited.

As Rasminsky had told John Diefenbaker and Lester Pearson before, the current-account deficit that plagued Canada should be dealt with; only by so doing would the country cease to be dependent on an inflow of capital from the United States. As the governor recorded:

> The Prime Minister wondered how much this would involve by way of reduction in our living standards, and I said that on a purely arithmetic basis what

was involved was that consumption would increase a bit less rapidly than it could if we were large net importers of goods and services. The problem was rather one of organization on how to bring about the desired result. The Prime Minister also wondered whether it was a nationalistic objective to seek to eliminate the current account deficit. I said that I did not think so provided that it was done by trying to become more efficient and competitive and not through import restrictions. In the present world, indeed, which was short of capital and where there were so many countries that needed external resources more than Canada, it was an open question whether we are morally justified in running our affairs year after year on a basis which made us large net users of external resources.

It was a good point, and one not lost on Trudeau, though through to 1984, his last year in office, he never dealt with it in a substantive way.

As the conversation ended, the prime minister asked Rasminsky to inform him if the governor felt that the Liberals were conducting the campaign in such a way as to cause the Bank of Canada difficulty. If that scenario developed, Trudeau urged him to phone and 'give them hell' without worrying that this would be regarded as interfering in their affairs in any way. Rasminsky 'undertook to do so.' The prime minister had been impressed enough with Rasminsky's wide-ranging intellect and clear exposition of the issues that he asked to meet on a quarterly basis, which they did.

The governor left the meeting with the feeling that much had been accomplished. Trudeau had not reacted at all negatively to the Bank's monetary policy, they had touched briefly on fiscal policy, and Rasminsky had gotten in his advice about the current-account deficit. However, as he was to learn, the new prime minister was not much interested in economic or financial affairs, and even reasoned argument did not necessarily persuade a politician. As he later remarked about his meetings with Trudeau, the latter 'had a very, very fine mind, very incisive and had a capacity for really going to the heart of an issue ... He would take things on board ... [However,] sometimes you would have the impression that your argument had been convincing, that it had prevailed without that necessarily ... resulting in a government policy which [reflected that position].'[5] To Rasminsky, Trudeau remained somewhat of an enigma, and the governor eventually concluded that on economic affairs the adviser offering the final piece of advice was often successful.

But it gradually became more important that Trudeau take note of what he was saying; quarter after quarter, as the two met to discuss trends and conditions, the economic situation began to deteriorate. Inflation, held at bay with the economic equivalent of garlic cloves (it never died), was becoming more of an issue, for the Bank of Canada at any rate. To Rasminsky, it was of particular concern especially from the autumn of 1968, when it had become apparent that inflationary pressure was not moderating.[6] John Harbron put the case succinctly in a series on inflation that he wrote for the *Toronto Telegram*: 'If you think prices are higher than ever, you are right. If you say we are going through one of the worst inflations in Canadian history, right again ... In man-in-the-street terms, the consumer price increase of 4.5 per cent in 1969 was the largest annual jump since 1950'[7] Hy Solomon of the *Financial Post* described the governor as 'a man walking a tight rope while juggling four or five balls.'[8] If interest rates remained high, it was because Rasminsky had all those balls to juggle – 'One wrong step and down we go into the inflationary net.'

For Rasminsky, there was no realistic alternative to bringing inflation under control. Only by so doing could the country maximize economic growth over the longer run. His belief was based not 'on any single-minded dedication to price stability as an end in itself but on the conviction that without it we will not be able to attain our potential output, employment and living standards in the future.'[9] Inflation distorted economic growth and hit certain people and sectors harder than others. He itemized a list of undesirable side-effects: 'a) Inequity – not everyone can adjust; b) distortion in allocation of resources; c) the lowering of standards of prudence and even ethics when everything is go-go; d) the international situation[;] e) the effects on capital markets – different borrowers can adjust themselves with more or less difficulty – bonds become second-class securities – the introduction of gimmicks and convertibles – but what gets left behind is social capital – provinces, municipalities, utilities and probably housing.'[10]

But Canada also had special problems, which every prime minister since Sir John A. Macdonald well knew. While politicians said that it was a difficult nation to govern, Rasminsky knew it to be 'a terribly difficult country in which to conduct economic policy.' The chief reason lay in its location – Canada was 'a small country [in economic terms] living side by side with the United States, the greatest economic power in the world.'[11] That was both a blessing and a disadvantage, with Canadians, noses pressed up against the window, wanting to live the American dream along with costly government services provided. However, as Rasminsky pointed out, a Canadian's 'average productivity [was] at least 20 per cent lower than [an American's].' As well, given the volume of trade with the neighbour to the south, some price inflation was imported, as US prices had been rising rapidly. Generally speaking, evidence that Canada was getting its inflation under control was disappointingly meagre.

Because of inflationary pressures, interest rates rose steadily from 6 per cent in September 1968 to 8 per cent by July 1969. Rasminsky was concerned that Canada's chartered banks follow his lead in this area and that those least able to defend themselves from high rates be protected as much as possible. For example, he told the annual meeting of the Canadian Bankers' Association that when the banks were unable to meet all loan demands on them from creditworthy borrowers, they should have special regard for the needs of: '(1) smaller businesses, which do not have alternative sources of credit; and (2) businesses in relatively depressed areas of the country, where there is no general pressure on the productive resources available.'[12]

He also told the bankers that it was clear that because of tight credit conditions and extremely high interest rates prevailing in other countries US subsidiaries and other foreigners were borrowing money in Canada 'for use abroad or to replace funds which would normally be obtained abroad. [He] expressed the view that Canadian bank credit should not be used for such purposes at a time when monetary restraints directed against inflation were making it difficult for our banks to meet all creditworthy demands from their Canadian customers.' When the flow of money, both to off-shore companies and in Canada, was not sharply staunched by the speech, Rasminsky followed it up with a letter to express his concern 'over the continued substantial rate of increase in outstanding bank loans.'[13]

His policy, which the chartered banks did not like, was straightforward – to slow the rate of increase in the money supply and to restrain the expansion of bank loans. In the summer of 1969, Rasminsky ran through the list of items that had been undertaken since October 1968 to accomplish this goal. A cash-reserve policy had resulted in a reduction of well over $750 million in the more liquid assets of the banks, and the ratio of those to bank assets was then at a low level. A further $250 million of liquid assets was immobilized by the increase in the secondary-reserve ratio from 7 to 8 per cent on 11 April. The Bank of Canada's rate was raised three times, and in the last two, with specific mention of bank credit. 'In circumstances where the signals have been so clear ... I find the response of the banks as a group disappointing.' As a result, Rasminsky asked that they report at month's-end the totals of authorized credits and of loans outstanding under lines of credit of more than $500,000. As well, the prime rate was increased again on 16 July. Rasminsky followed up his toughened policy assiduously. Faced with such determination, by the autumn of 1969 the banks were onside.

At every meeting with cabinet ministers, he spoke about the struggle against inflation and the results being obtained from the policies then employed. The Bank was waging its battle as part of a coordinated strategy with the Prices and Incomes Commission, headed by John Young, a University of British Columbia economist brought into government service. In a system designed to moderate the rise in prices and wages, compliance was voluntary, and it never really worked in the manner anticipated. One reason, as Rasminsky pointed out in a meeting with chartered banks' general managers, was that 'business capital expenditure seemed surprisingly impervious to restraints.'[14] As well, wage settlements continued to run at a high level, especially in the construction industry. While Rasminsky thought that he detected some continuing scepticism about inflation among the population at large, he told the general managers that there were 'no grounds for such skepticism in regard to intentions of monetary authorities.'

By November 1969, in view of a still-worsening situation, he reiterated his concern to bank officers; 'there seems little doubt that we are in for a difficult winter and it behooves those who think that present policies are right to do what they can to make them work and to be cautious about acting or talking in a way that will impair confidence in the effort that is being made to deal with inflation through fiscal or monetary policy.'[15] Rasminsky made the point emphatically because he had been surprised to see recent statements in the press from a few bankers to the effect that the Bank of Canada had embarked on its tight monetary policy only in the spring of 1969. That was not true; it had started taking liquid assets away from the banks more than a year earlier, and if the monetary screws had been tightened too gradually, then he could be accused of overoptimism. Maybe something more radical was necessary.

Perhaps the banks' perceptions had contributed to a developing trend that Rasminsky found disturbing. He thought that he detected a change in the way in which Canadians perceived inflation; an inflationary psychology was being fostered – a '"something for nothing" attitude.'[16] During the late 1960s, there had been a large increase in demand for borrowed funds, paralleled by declining confidence in the stability of money. Many Canadians had come to expect that prices would continue to rise at the rate of 3 to 5 per cent per year, and if those assumptions were realized, investors in bonds or mortgages whose marginal income-tax rate was 50 per cent would need to get a yield of 6 to 10 per cent to keep their capital intact in terms of purchasing power.

Investment dealers and officials of financial institutions seemed to be impressed with the risk of continuing inflation and uncertain about the success of methods to contain it. The senior deputy governor, Robert Beattie, who accompanied Rasminsky to a meeting of the cabinet committee on priorities and planning, told ministers that he and the governor believed that 'cynicism about tolerance of rising prices seems to be greater here than in the United States. One can believe ... that there is a large element of irrationality in this attitude but it is probably the most important factor in the present demoralized condition of the bond market. It means that the effort to put an end to inflation needs to be that much more strong and convincing.'[17]

Action was imperative; the long boom period that had begun in early 1960 had been possible at least partially because of low rates of inflation – while Canada's rate of growth in physical output had been among the highest in the world, averaging 6 per cent per year, the rate of increase in consumer prices had been among the lowest, averaging about 2 per cent per year. 'It was [no] accident,' Rasminsky had told the Joint Committee of the Senate and the House of Commons on Consumer Credit in 1966, 'that we simultaneously enjoyed markedly rising output *and relatively stable prices over this long period of expansion* ... I believe that our record of comparatively stable prices over most of this period ... made an important contribution toward maintaining a vigorous rate of economic expansion for such a long time. It protected our international competitive position and enabled us to avoid some of the distortions and imbalances in the internal structure of our economy which arise when prices are rising rapidly.'[18]

Unfortunately, the situation had changed dramatically, and increasing government expenditures were at least partly to blame. The claims of the public sector were rising more rapidly than those of the private sector. As Robert Bryce pointed out, 'The "all-items" component rose from a level of 109.5 in 1965, to 128.3 in 1969, or by 17.2 per cent. In contrast, the component for government purchases rose from 116.5 to 160.2, or by 37.3 per cent.'[19] Rasminsky supplied the prime minister with a table setting out the ratio of the consolidated total of public expenditures at all levels of government to gross national expenditures (GNE) over the past few years. Government expenditures (including transfers) as a propor-

TABLE 8.2
Major economic statistics (percentage of annual change)

	1963	1964	1965	1966	1967	1968	1969
GNP in current dollars	7.3	9.5	10.3	11.9	7.0	8.7	10.0
GNP in constant dollars	1.9	2.4	3.5	4.6	3.4	3.5	4.7
GNP implicit price index	5.3	6.9	6.6	7.0	3.5	4.9	5.0
Total employment	2.4	3.7	3.8	4.2	3.2	2.1	3.2
Unemployment rate	5.5	4.7	3.9	3.6	4.1	4.8	4.7

Source: LR76-551-29, Table A.

tion of GNE had been 31.2 per cent in 1964; 31.0 per cent in 1965; 32.3 per cent in 1966; 34.1 per cent in 1967; and 34.7 per cent in 1968.

But for politicians, however much of a concern inflation might be, there was also the problem of unemployment and, for some in cabinet, regional inequities. After all, inflation could not vote. While Rasminsky's approach was not unanimously endorsed by government, he remained committed, telling Trudeau that he knew 'it [was] not popular at a time when everyone is worried about unemployment to worry about the next inflation, but popularity [was] not the name of the game.'[20] His job, as set out by the Bank of Canada Act, was 'to control and protect the external value of the national monetary unit.' He certainly intended to do that.

Government outlays put a good deal of additional pressure on the economy at a time when private expenditures on capital and consumer goods and exports were rising strongly. Between 1964 and 1968, the total of the government's current and capital expenditures, including net loans and advances, rose by 62 per cent. Over the same period, gross national product (GNP) rose by 57 per cent in current dollars and 32 per cent in physical volume. The price index applicable to the GNP rose by 19 per cent. Over these five years, outlays totalled $53.1 billion, and revenues, $49.8 billion.[21] Table 8.2 demonstrates the change. Given the numbers, a team from the International Monetary Fund (IMF) that came to Ottawa in April 1970 for regular article-VIII consultations (where an IMF team was apprised of a member's monetary policy, fiscal policy, balance-of-payments situation, economic outlook and policies, wages policy, and exchange-rate policy), was not particularly impressed with Canadian resolve. 'Progress in dealing with inflationary pressures and expectations,' it thought, had been 'disappointingly small.'[22]

Rasminsky chaired the meetings with the team, asking the Department of Finance's William Hood to lead off. Hood spoke at length on capital investment in housing, on durables, on real demand, and on a restrictive monetary and fiscal policy. The forecast for the Canadian economy taken as a whole was for 2 per cent annual real growth, and prices were expected to rise annually at a rate of 4 per cent. Unemployment, the Bank's models showed, would grow throughout 1970. Though Rasminsky was unhappy over the prospect of increased unemployment, the projections were a plus from the perspective of international finance and the IMF: higher rates of unemployment meant lower rates of inflation – fewer people had less money to spend.

An IMF official responded – he had serious doubts about the Canadian program. Fiscal policy was 'expansive, not just less restrictive' as the Canadians had suggested. Moreover, the Bank's projections of a nominal rate of advance in GNP of 6 per cent per year obscured as much as it illuminated; it would 'involve a very large price component and a rather small volume change.' The Fund's team was interested in a sharper attack on inflation than seemed to be happening.

When Simon Reisman, the deputy minister of finance, complained about that narrow view, the IMF official was unmoved, pointing again to 'the meagre results of the anti-inflation effort thus far ... People lost sight of the fact that inflation tended to accelerate. As more people hedged against inflation, it would be found that in a short while the rate was running not at 5 per cent but nearer 25 per cent.' He realized that there was a political side to the problem that made it hard for governments to act:

> Among those of the Fund staff who were convinced that inflation was an evil, he was one of those most sympathetic to a gradualist approach. In 1969, the stance of policy in Canada, and in the United States, had been such that advances in the fight against inflation had been secured. But ... gradualism had its problems. It stretched out the fight, and was a severe test of the authorities' determination to persist. Alternatively, the shock approach had the advantage that it could resolve the problem quickly and facilitate a quick return to the long-run trend of growth ... Since fiscal policy in 1970 could not in any sense be considered as restrictive as in the year before, it seemed that because of the political difficulties, the government had not been able to continue longer than 18 months on the gradualist approach, and hence the shock approach became the only alternative.

Rasminsky did not necessarily disagree with the IMF analysis; indeed, he had been preaching it to politicians for a number of months. And he had been disappointed with the length of time that it had taken mone-

tary policy to take effect and the slowness of response of prices and costs
to economic developments. He certainly believed that in monetary policy
the stance should remain as tight as possible, balancing domestic against
international considerations.

The American price performance was a factor in rising prices in Canada
in 1970, but another factor, with both domestic and international implications, complicated the country's inflation problem – the strength of the
Canadian dollar. As has been seen, the currency was pegged in May 1962
at 92.5 US cents. Eight years later, almost to the day, the Canadian dollar
floated again, largely in response to external factors that were putting
enormous upward pressure on it. Did the float affect the country's economy? Yes, and the dollar appreciated quite considerably against its US
counterpart.

The background of the decision to allow the Canadian dollar to float
(and appreciate) was the strength that it was showing on the exchange
market and the weakness of the US currency. In order to maintain the
rate within 1 per cent of the par value of 92½ US cents, the Exchange
Fund operated by the Bank had purchased US dollars at an accelerating
rate in the preceding five months and the overall reserve position had
increased by more than US$1.2 billion. Slightly more than one-half of
that growth occurred in May. As a result, the Canadian government was
hard-pressed to purchase sufficient US dollars to keep Canada's
exchange rate from exceeding its par value by more than 1 per cent. As
well, the current-account position had improved, and the trade surplus
was now $600 million higher than it had been in the first four months of
1969.

The favourable current-account balance was partly the result of a surge
in grain exports from Canada following settlement of lengthy strikes by
grain handlers, and about one-third of that increase could be attributed
to the trade in automotive products with the United States, the result of
the Autopact signed in 1965. As a Bank of Canada memorandum prepared for Rasminsky noted,

> This strength in turn had reflected the underlying strength in the Canadian
> balance of payments. The current account had moved into surplus as a
> result of an unusually strong trade position. The inflow of short-term capital
> appeared to be continuing while the outflow of short-term funds was dimin-
> ishing as a result of the decline in Eurodollar interest rates. It appeared
> impossible to continue the defence of the fixed exchange rate without bring-

TABLE 8.3
Balances (receipts minus payments) in Can$million, 1965–70

	With all countries			With the United States		
Year	Merchandise trade	Services	Total current account	Merchandise trade	Services	Total current account
1965	+118	−1,248	−1,130	−1,041	−896	−1,937
1966	+224	−1,386	−1,162	−993	−1,024	−2,017
1967	+566	−1,065	−449	−655	−724	−1,379
1968	+1,376	−1,436	−60	+249	−1,041	−792
1969	+860	−1,611	−751	+367	−1,100	−733
1970	+3,002	−1,705	+1,297	+1,142	−1,109	+33

Source: Robert M. Dunn, *Canada's Experience with Fixed and Flexible Rates in a North American Capital Market* (Montreal: Private Planning Association of Canada, 1971), 68.

ing about a rate of monetary expansion *which would have undermined the efforts to contain inflation.* The decision to let the Canadian dollar float provided an escape from this dilemma without committing Canada to a new and higher exchange parity which would have been very difficult to select in view of the uncertainties about the future developments of the Canadian balance of payments and about the course of US and financial policy.[23]

Given this balance-of-payments situation, it became increasingly evident to the Bank that it would be difficult to maintain the existing exchange rate unless some action were taken to change the external-payments situation. Except in a floating of the dollar, that was a very difficult, if not impossible, task, as William Lawson explained to Working Party 3 (WP3) of the Organization for Economic Cooperation and Development, which had been established in 1961 to promote better international payments equilibrium. He was responding to a question about the inflow of long-term capital in the form of new issues abroad. Lawson's questioner had in mind the possibility of Ottawa's restricting the rate of provincial borrowing:

The difficulty with [meddling in provincial affairs] lies in the nature of the Canadian state. Under the Canadian federal system, the provinces have a good deal of autonomy, and their free access to new issue markets abroad to supplement their borrowing in Canada has never been challenged. The distribution of functions in Canada is such that the provincial governments have major responsibility in many of the areas in which expenditures are rising most rapidly – social capital, such as health, education, etc. Thus the financial requirements of provincial and local institutions are large and rising. In the current state of federal–provincial relations in Canada, intervention by the Government of Canada to restrict the access to foreign capital of the provinces would have been a political decision with repercussions far beyond the balance of payments.[24]

In short, that approach was a non-starter.

What about easing monetary policy, another wanted to know, which would serve two related purposes? It would make Canada a less attractive destination for short-term investment, and it would thereby help to eliminate upward pressure on the Canadian dollar. In theory, that might work, but it would surely increase the volume of IMF criticism. As Lawson told WP3, 'Inflation was far from being conquered in Canada and [a] more rapid easing [of interest rates] would undermine the government's anti-inflationary programme.' It was easily conceivable that such a policy would result in far greater difficulties for the Canadian economy in months to come.

Given the limited range of options, it was difficult to find an acceptable means of relieving upward pressure. A large increase in reserves could and would have been accommodated if it were not accompanied by speculation, but the growth in reserves itself had stimulated precisely those pressures that the Bank wanted to avoid. How far should this speculative surge that had increased the value of the dollar be allowed to develop? No further, Lawson thought. Why did Canada not propose a change in its par value to the IMF? Lawson answered with a question 'What change in its par value should it have proposed? What change would have been credible to the market in the very short run, and suitable over a longer period?' While a 97- or 98-cent US dollar might have been reasonable in mid-1970, what if the US economy slipped into a recession, as it had in 1958? Then an exchange crisis could result, and Canada's exporters could be faced with declining revenues.

However, there was also uncertainty as to the opposite – what if the US economy were to resume its previous inflationary growth path? Then, 'the resulting increases in the Canadian trade balance could make 97–98 too low and lead to a repetition of the events of early 1970.'[25] The various uncertainties made naming a new parity seem impossibly difficult. The decision to float was a decision to use the market to find a manageable and acceptable level for the Canadian dollar. Even in those relatively unsophisticated days, the appeal to 'market forces' must surely have recommended itself.

While the OECD could grudgingly accept the Canadian rationale, the IMF was most unhappy. It was, of course, concerned about its own future, especially as global monetary arrangements seemed to be less certain. If all countries followed the Canadian lead and floated their currencies, there would be no need for an international organization whose primary purpose was to ensure exchange stability. While in the mid-1970s the IMF would reinvent itself and, in the process, become a much more influential and powerful organization, such a course was not evident to Pierre-Paul Schweitzer, the managing director, and his staff in 1970.

Still, the Fund had discussed its *raison d'être* in 1969 and early 1970, focusing on the mechanism of exchange-rate adjustment to deal with the sort of situation that Canada was then experiencing. There was a sense within the IMF that change was necessary, as the comments of a number of executive directors made clear. While they thought that the main features of the Bretton Woods system should be retained, there were some, such as the United Kingdom's representative supported by Italy's, who favoured 'a general widening of the margins to 2 per cent.'[26] The Brazilian delegate was keen to amend the IMF's articles 'in order to legalize fluctuating rate regimes,' while Chile and the United States wanted more latitude to do as they wished. To that end, the Joint Economic Committee of the US Congress had recommended in its reports of 1964 and 1965 that 'the United States ... should give consideration to broadening the limits of permissible exchange rate variations,'[27] though the US secretary of the treasury in 1969, David Kennedy, was not in favour.[28] However, some Fund staff had also toyed with the idea of exchange-rate adjustment; the economic counsellor, Jacques Polak, had favourably examined this issue in a paper entitled 'The Mechanism of Exchange Rate Adjustment,' circulated in early 1970.[29] As well, there had been some discussion in academic circles about the pros and cons of floating versus fixed rates.[30] However, despite much time devoted to the subject both at the Fund and elsewhere, in the IMF report *The Role of Exchange Rates in the Adjustment of International Payments*, released in September 1970, the staff and executive directors decided that 'the par value system ... remained the most appropriate general regime to govern exchange rates in a world of managed national economies.'[31]

While Rasminsky stayed in Ottawa to attend a meeting of the cabinet committee on priorities to explain the float, Lawson and Steven Hand-field-Jones went to Washington to put the case to Schweitzer at the Fund and Paul Volcker at the US Treasury. At the Fund, Lawson told Rasminsky, 'we received a polite but unsympathetic hearing.'[32] The IMF expressed much concern about the effect of Canada's action on the stability of the international monetary system, which was 'showing signs of strain.' Earlier in the day, the managing director had told Rasminsky by telephone that he was 'not fully convinced about the need of doing something; hard to understand why movements of this size cannot be managed by domestic means; what taken place not enough to justify [this action].'[33] As well, 'the current-account surplus was of recent origin [and] ... it was premature to conclude that there was a fundamental disequilibrium.'[34] Rasminsky disagreed; the Bank of Canada had run models of various scenarios in mid- to late May, with some involving wider bands – for example, plus or minus 2.5 per cent – or pegging the dollar at a higher rate. But all had proved inadequate. As well, he thought that the situation as it had developed was here to stay.

Because of the managing board's disapproval, the IMF staff prepared a harsh statement condemning the Canadian initiative. Rasminsky had wanted something along the lines of the IMF's approval of the temporary German float of some months earlier. The critical paragraph in the German decision read as follows: 'At a meeting of the Executive Directors today, the Fund recognized the exigencies of the situation that have led the German Government to take the action described above. The Fund noted the intention of the German authorities to collaborate with the Fund to resume the maintenance of limits around par at the earliest opportunity. The Fund will remain in close consultation with the German authorities for the latter purpose.'

IMF officials told the Canadians that the phrase 'recognized the exigencies' was intended to indicate a considerable degree of approval for the German action; they also said that they would not use it in the Canadian case. The draft decision circulated to the executive committee was very critical: 'The Fund notes the current situation in Canada which has been described by the Canadian authorities. However, the Fund emphasizes the undertaking by members "to collaborate with the Fund to promote exchange stability, to maintain orderly exchange arrangements with other members, and to avoid competitive exchange alterations," and therefore requests Canada to remain in close consultation with the Fund with a view to the resumption of an effective par value at the earliest possible date.'

Robert Johnstone, Canada's alternate executive director, got the draft revised. He was helped in his campaign by three executive directors, who 'pressed very strongly for the addition of a third paragraph which would name a date at which the Executive Board would review its decision.' The rest of the board found their position so extreme that the three were isolated, they refrained from voting, and the offending words were removed. Still, the Fund believed that Ottawa should have continued to defend the old parity, but as a Bank of Canada memorandum pointed out, 'It has never been clear to us how this could have been done.'[35] In the context then prevailing, both in Canada and in the global financial community, that was simply not a possibility, which factor Rasminsky had emphasized to Schweitzer and to Frank Southard, the Fund's deputy managing director, when he had met them in August 1970. Then, Rasminsky had 'defended the need for a floating rate, while the Fund management continued to believe in the usefulness of measures to curb capital inflows and to alleviate their impact on the domestic economy.'[36]

Nor were the Americans very happy with Canada, as Lawson and Handfield-Jones discovered when they walked over to the US Treasury to speak with Volcker. On a decision of this magnitude, the US government expected some consultation – a position forcefully impressed on the Canadians. There was a possible domino effect to consider; what would happen to currency stability and to the IMF if other countries followed the Canadian lead? Arthur Burns, chairman of the board of governors of the federal reserve system and also present at the meeting, weighed in. He told the Canadians that the absence of consultation before the decision had been taken was unacceptable; it 'made a mockery out of consultative procedures such as the [US–Canada] Balance of Payments Committee that [Lawson] was attending.' Burns wanted Lawson to know 'that US foreign economic policy was determined by the financial people in Washington, and that they were not satisfied with bland exchanges of views or polite social gatherings.' The chairman was 'surprised that the Government of Canada could be so naïve as to suppose that it could make exchange rate decisions on a unilateral basis. Canada was lucky ... that cool heads had prevailed in Washington that week-end or we would have had reason to worry about our currency being too weak on the exchange market rather than too strong.'

Lawson put the case that the appreciation of the Canadian dollar that had taken place was a benefit to the United States in that it made Canadian exports more expensive while reducing the cost of import from the United States. That might be so, but Burns thought that 'the United

States could look after itself ... [Canada's] action was prejudicial to the interests of the international financial community. [Burns] said that failure to consult about exchange rate changes undermined the structure of international financial cooperation that the world had been developing in recent years.'

At the Bank for International Settlements (BIS) in Basel, Switzerland, Robert Beattie, representing Rasminsky, was shocked to realize that Canada's float was the only subject on the agenda for Sunday, 6 June. Generally, the commentary was not favourable. The Belgian Hubert Ansiaux reflected the prevailing sentiment, feeling strongly that 'the fault lay with Canada. He was critical of [its] monetary policy and lack of attempts at exchange control ... We should have put a tax on exports.'[37] The meeting adjourned after urging Beattie to report to Rasminsky and the minister of finance that the country should fix a new rate as soon as possible.

In the final analysis, and in spite of pressure put on Canada by the BIS, the IMF, and the United States, Canada never repegged its currency. It did, however, undertake periodic reappraisals of its policy during the following months, as did the Fund. The latter's studies on exchange-rate flexibility and widening of margins took on added urgency. The Fund initiated studies analysing the effects of greater exchange-rate flexibility, and the managing director circulated a statement to executive directors which suggested that, in the Canadian downturn of late 1969, 'a modest widening of margins might have been helpful ... to prevent the cumulative developments which ended in a crisis situation by the end of April.'[38] While IMF *principle* remained strong, there was increasing recognition of the possibility that some additional flexibility was required with respect to margins, at least until the uncertainties then plaguing the system had dissipated.

As events transpired, the Canadian action merely anticipated, perhaps in a more dramatic way, general exchange developments that would affect the global community. By early 1971, as Schweitzer had noted, monetary conditions were clearly deteriorating. The par-value system had been struck a mortal blow by world conditions, and it would never be fully re-established. Almost as soon as the managing director had issued his statement, Austria devalued its schilling, while the Germans, followed quickly by the Dutch, advised the IMF that, given the size of recent movements of foreign exchange, they could not ensure that rates for exchange transactions involving their currencies would be maintained within the margins hitherto observed. The flurry of activity ended with Richard Nixon's August 1971 announcement, which is discussed in chapter 9.

The float had some lingering effects on Canadian–American relations, though they were also coloured by the perceived anti-American approach that had been adopted by Trudeau's first government. Two years after the float, Arthur Burns told Marcel Cadieux, Canada's ambassador in Washington, that 'relations between [Canada and the United States were] bad and that our performance in the monetary field was the main cause.'[39] Burns would raise the issue with the new minister of finance, John Turner, and Rasminsky, when the two visited Washington in May 1972.

While the fall-out from the float lay in the future, Governor Rasminsky continued to have no illusions about the inflationary danger that confronted Canada in the present. Indeed, that was why the dollar had floated. Perhaps so draconian an initiative as a floating dollar would not have been necessary if policy-makers had 'been more alert to the dangers of inflation ... after 1963 and ... [had] done more to prevent it or alleviate it with fiscal and monetary measures.'[40] Over the previous decade, the seasonally adjusted unemployment rate had declined from 7.6 per cent in early 1961 to about 3.6 per cent in July 1965, and it had stayed there until March 1967. The average annual rate of increase in GNP between 1962 and 1966 was a healthy 7.2 per cent, while the privately held money supply grew at an average rate of 6.5 per cent per year. As well, there was a wage explosion by the spring of 1966 associated with Expo '67 construction, the high cost of the settlement to Seaway workers, who had gone on strike at a time when wheat shipments had to go forward, and sizeable public-service wage increases.

Hindsight is, of course, 20/20 vision, and in defence of what had not been done, it could be argued that it was impossible in 1964 or early 1965 to forecast the degree of growth of US military operations in Vietnam, which exerted an inflationary influence all around the world. Given the multi-faceted commercial and financial relationship between Canada and the United States, the US price performance was of vital importance to Canada. That fact that between 1968 and 1972 the United States experienced a substantially higher rate of inflation than did Canada was very worrying, as imported cost increases were added to the domestic variety.

That was scant comfort. How was it possible to reverse the situation now? Politicians and officials, however much they might agree that inflation was an evil, had different agendas and in a sense spoke different languages. The former had to be sensitive to the demands of the voting public and the problem of increasing unemployment. It was easier for the government to believe those economists who suggested that inflation was

not a problem than to enact policies that would reduce the rate of inflation but also increase interest rates, unemployment, and voter's hostility.

The Bank was concentrating on the problem of inflation. However,
that did not make it oblivious to unemployment; quite the contrary. In
extemporaneous testimony given before the Senate's finance committee
in June 1971, Rasminsky gave his *own* opinion, stressing that the Bank
attached great importance to the objective of full employment:

> It may seem odd that I should feel it desirable or necessary to make that
> statement, but I am well aware that the Bank is sometimes thought of as hav-
> ing a single-minded dedication to the goal of price stability and little con-
> cern with the great human misfortune of unemployment. This is simply not
> true. We are greatly concerned. If there is, in fact, any difference in this
> respect between us and some others, it is a difference of time perspective.
> We take the view that this country is going to be here for some time, and that
> our chances of achieving sustained growth and a sustained increase in
> employment will be considerably greater if we can manage to achieve a rea-
> sonable degree of stability in the value of money at the same time.[41]

Achieving full employment was difficult: 'One might think of Canada
as a collection of islands strung out over thousands of miles, with great
differences in the regional economies and considerable variations in economic conditions.'[42] Some evidence of Canadian disparities was provided
by the incidence of unemployment across the country. During the fourth
quarter of 1969, average unemployment was 4.3 per cent for Canada as a
whole, but it was more than 6 per cent in New Brunswick and Quebec,
and nearly 9 per cent in Newfoundland. In contrast, it was less than 3 per
cent in Alberta, Manitoba, and Ontario. Rasminksy was well aware that
the impact of anti-inflationary policies in so variegated an economy
raised peculiar difficulties.

Those difficulties were complicated by the sometimes-strained relations between federal cabinet ministers and senior officials in Ottawa.
The Bank of Canada could not always get across its danger-of-inflation
message. Sometimes, or so a Bank document noted, 'Governments got
unperceptive advice from some of their own [political] advisers.'[43] Jim
Davey, one of Trudeau's senior advisers, sent a memorandum on 28 May
to Gerald Bouey, then deputy governor of the Bank of Canada, intended
for Rasminsky as well, which spoke to the issue of minister–official mis-
communication. They were invited to a cabinet meeting, scheduled for
2 June 1970, that was to concentrate on an analysis of the economic situa-

tion. As Davey told Bouey, 'There should be the opportunity for Ministers to see, listen to, and put questions to the officials who advise the Government on economic policy. I believe it is most important that a feeling of confidence be generated by Ministers in these officials.'[44] The memo revealed the state of the relationship:

> It is equally important that a direct confrontation should be avoided between Ministers and officials. This can be achieved if the officials do not in any way seem to be trying to tell the Government what to do but rather, set out before it the alternative courses of action with their consequences and then ask the Government to make a choice. That choice should be made principally by the Minister of Finance and he should be the one who defends it.
>
> This situation is in contradistinction to the image that a number of Ministers have where:
> (i)   officials are deciding what should be done, and
> (ii) the Prime Minister is pushing that action.

Davey was suggesting that all was not well with ministers who contemplated with some unease the inflationary spiral that Canada seemed locked into. All of them believed that inflation was a problem, and all wanted to see the government in a situation of economic growth and stability by 1972, when an election was likely. However, at the same time, unemployment could not be allowed to rise. That meant quite an assignment.

The rest of the memorandum of 28 May reveals much about ministers' attitudes and the restrictions that they regarded as essential:

> (iii) Few if any Ministers would like to see the Government relax its current policy if that is an indication of weakness and backing away in the face of difficulty. If this were to occur, they believe that the Government would lose its credibility.
>
> (iv) Because inflation affects them both in terms of their regions and in terms of the operations of their department and because of its complexity, all of them would like to have a much better appreciation and understanding of what is going on. As has been pointed out above, there is considerable suspicion about the role of the economic advisers in the formulation of Government policy. As much as possible should be done to allay this suspicion.
>
> (v) While they are not sure what the Government ought to be doing, many

Ministers feel that we are not doing enough of whatever we ought to be doing. For this reason, many would probably be willing to support additional measures to produce some form of guidelines or wage restraint, [wage settlements had been running at about 9.2 per cent per year] particularly if this would bring about an end to inflation much more quickly.

Davey's recommendations of late May to Rasminsky and Bouey included maintenance of the restraints then in place, combined with the assurance to Canadians that it would not be the unemployed who bore the brunt of the fight against inflation (introduction of the new unemployment-insurance scheme would be seen as a measure of the government's 'concern'). In concert with that, some attempt to moderate wage settlements would be encouraged, and measures to relieve the burden on regions through public works would be implemented.[45]

Whatever the political situation, Rasminsky was not prepared in the early summer of 1970 to relax monetary policy. However, several months later, it seemed as if significant victories had been won. While anti-inflation policies continued, the fight was carried on with less force than in the immediate past because of success in moderating price increases in Canada. Opposed to that, 'the level of unemployment has caused deep and universal concern and the situation has been particularly worrying in parts of the country which chronically suffer from relatively high unemployment rates.'[46]

In an attempt to ameliorate this situation, the Bank lowered the prime rate from 8 per cent in mid-May to 6 per cent by November, creating easier credit conditions in the expectation of stimulating job creation. It was a propitious time to change tack, even slightly. There was certainly evidence of the increasing concern being shown over higher rates of unemployment, but there was also the crisis of October 1970 in Quebec, which helped to focus minds in Ottawa, and the Bank of Canada was not immune to demands that something be done to ameliorate conditions in Quebec.

For many people in the country, the October crisis was an unprecedented affair. The kidnapping of British Trade Commissioner James Cross and then of Quebec's minister of labour, Pierre Laporte, by the Front de Libération du Québec (FLQ), shattered the closed, comfortable world of many Canadians who thought that terrorism was something that happened elsewhere. The War Measures Act was invoked for only the third

time since August 1914. The Trudeau government asked all departments
of government and the Bank of Canada for suggestions about how to
help make the Quebec situation better. On 28 October, Rasminsky convened a meeting of chartered-bank presidents to discuss the economic situation in Quebec and its relation to the problem of national unity.[47]

Suggestions made during the discussions included examination of the
banks' own capital-investment programs in Quebec, such as construction
of new buildings, opening of new branches, and renovations. As well, Rasminsky suggested that the banks 'might find early opportunities for making public expressions of their confidence in the long-term future of the
Quebec economy.' He wanted the banks to take a 'tender view' of applications for credit in slow-growth regions of the province, to which measure they agreed. They would also increase the amount of mortgage
money available. The presidents pointed out, however, that in many of
those areas it was not bank policy that discouraged loan demand, but
rather lack of demand itself, which the banks could do little to change.
Rasminsky responded: 'The Bank of Canada feels the need for additional
information on this matter even though it is difficult to determine exactly
what kind of information would be the most useful. I pointed out that in
the discussion of economic policy in Ottawa, the Bank of Canada is in the
position of being asked what is happening to bank credit in slow-growth
areas and all that we can do is to repeat the assurances we have been
given by banks. It is awkward not to have any information at all to which
we can point, and I am not certain that this position can be maintained
much longer.' Rasminsky sent the record of the meeting with the bank
presidents to Gordon Robertson, the long-serving secretary to the cabinet and clerk of the Privy Council, who was heading the cabinet committee addressing the fall-out from the October crisis.

Following the Rasminsky démarche, the banks kept him apprised of
their 'projects.' The Royal Bank increased the amount on loan on the
province's $100-million line of credit from $27 million to $52 million. Its
chairman, Earle McLaughlin, told the governor: 'No other bank was
approached – nor did we ask that the other banks share this.'[48] His board
had 'unhesitatingly' accepted his recommendation. Arnold Hart of the
Bank of Montreal was a member of the General Council of Industry,
which had been formed by Quebec's (since-defeated) Union Nationale
government in March 1969 and focused on unemployment. The council
had sent a lengthy letter to Quebec's new minister of industry and commerce, Gérard Lévesque, which Hart had copied to Rasminsky, outlining
what it thought should be done to help. He also wrote that, while it was

'only a small step forward,' the bank had put what it called its Youth Project into operation in September 1969, designed to encourage the interaction of English and French.[49]

T.A. Boyles, deputy chairman and executive vice-president of the Bank of Nova Scotia, outlined four areas in which he thought his bank could help – personnel: get more francophones into its operations in Quebec; premises: put up 'quite a large new building in Quebec' and investigate how to refurbish its present branches throughout the province; new branch sites; and mortgage allotments: make arrangements to give Quebec a higher proportion than in the past of housing credits.

Allan Lambert of Toronto-Dominion (TD) also wanted a return to a fixed exchange rate, which Canada had abandoned the previous May. Such a move, he wrote, 'would improve national investment confidence and be of particular interest to Quebec whose mineral, forest and power intensive industries account for such a large part of the province's total exports.' What had the TD done? Its ratio of loans to deposit liabilities was higher in Quebec than in other parts of the country, it had opened more branches in the province than any of its larger competitors, it would increase its allocation of mortgage funds there and had purchased part of a capital issue of the City of Montreal, it was willing to get involved in urban renewal projects as part of a syndicate, and would be prepared to participate in a youth-training program.[50] Responses came also from the two Quebec banks – the Banque Canadienne Nationale and the Provincial Bank of Canada, which suggested special consideration to regional banks with respect to secondary reserves and loans from the Bank of Canada. And the Mercantile constructed new offices in downtown Montreal.

Still, prevailing sentiment had it that more should be done for Quebec, but it was difficult to know precisely what; unemployment remained high, and the economy seemed stalled. At a minimum, it was essential that the Bank of Canada continue its present expansionary monetary policy. Rasminsky took all the banks' suggestions offered and passed them along in summary form to the minister of finance, Edgar Benson. It would be up to the government to help implement suggestions. And while the banks were prepared to do their part in beating back the separatist threat, they also viewed the situation in Quebec as an economic opportunity – they would be able to make money from new government guarantees to the province.

While unemployment remained high in Quebec, recent evidence seemed to indicate that, when seasonal factors were taken into account, they suggested 'a pretty good recovery in economic activity.'[51] Rasminsky was not willing to assume the mantle of a prophet, but he did think that if the US economy behaved reasonably well, and if consumers in Canada had confidence enough to spend up to their incomes (which he thought they would), expansion in 1971 would be considerably greater and better balanced than that of 1970. On the inflation side, Canada had made good strides, to the point where Rasminsky was 'embarrassed at the congratulations of [his] confrères when [he went]·abroad and [was] told that we have solved all our problems.' While he did not agree with that assessment, there was a small light at the end of the tunnel. On 15 February 1971, the prime rate was reduced to 5¾ per cent; by late October, it was down to 4¾.

That approach continued: 'The emphasis of economic policy in [1971] has been placed on expanding output and creating jobs.'[52] But inflation, even though Canadian price levels had risen less than those of any other industrial country, did not go away. As Rasminsky pointed out, 'Despite almost two years of high unemployment and unused industrial capacity, a significant appreciation of the Canadian dollar [due to its float in May 1970], and the work of the Prices and Incomes Commission, there has not yet been enough moderation of costs to ensure a further slowing of price inflation. Indeed, some recent evidence ... seems to point in the other direction.' The governor accordingly asked for a regular weekly meeting with the new minister of finance, John Turner; as he pointed out, there was 'a need for close consultation at this time.'[53]

And so it was in 1972, Rasminsky's last full year as governor. A terse line in the *Annual Report* spoke volumes; 'The more rapid rise of prices in Canada in 1972 was disquieting.'[54] As the economy moved ahead, and with the government and the Bank stimulating economic activity to take up the slack, the governor sounded a warning with which his successor would have to deal: 'A situation of this character inevitably involves a risk that at a later stage of the expansion, aggregate demand may grow too strongly and cause general demand pressure on prices and costs to develop. As the expansion proceeds it will be important to guard against this danger. In Canada, as in other countries, there is already a certain amount of "built-in" inflation and this will not be easy to reduce even over a considerable period of time. It would be unfortunate indeed if instead the underlying rate of inflation were to be ratcheted up yet another notch.'

But that was happening. Rasminsky later recalled that the 1973 budget, tabled by Trudeau's minority government following the Liberals' near-defeat in the 1972 election, 'was not consistent with the view of the state of the economy that I had put forward not too long before ... It was clearly inappropriate with the general trend.'[55] Why governments would persist in such activity and why populations would accept it were the subjects of an address he gave at the Bank for International Settlements in Basle, Switzerland. In working to attain the objective of reasonable monetary stability, central bankers had to contend 'with a whole array of forces – governments who have to be re-elected, exaggerated expectations on the part of the public, academic economists whose thinking continues to have its roots in the Great Depression of the 1930s and have a single-minded devotion to expansion at any price. And recently, [the central banker] has also had to contend with some profound sociological changes which have affected the attitudes of people towards doing work ... The net result of all this is that we are again, at least in my opinion, threatened with a degree of inflation which can undermine the achievements of the past quarter century.'[56]

He elaborated on that sentiment to the Bank of England's Sir Leslie O'Brien: 'In a certain sense, I think it is really impossible to succeed at the job of being a central banker under today's conditions when economic arithmetic counts for so little and all the social and economic pressures favour inflation.'[57] Modern societies, Rasminsky remarked, did not 'have the stomach to push monetary and fiscal policies to the point where market conditions will bring [inflation] to an end.' The Bank of Canada had made a good effort, but 'once the unemployment rate got to 6 per cent or so, we had to ease off and divert policy in a stimulating direction even though it was obvious that cost inflation was still a problem.'[58]

Rasminsky believed that he had done as much as it was reasonable for a central banker to do in the pursuit of monetary stability. While, by comparison with other countries, his Bank's record was good, prices in Canada were still rising at a rate of 4 to 5 per cent per year. During 1973, the inflation rate climbed to 8 per cent. What else could have been done, or, more to the point, what else would have been politically possible? He did not know; indeed, he doubted whether any central banker knew how to cope with the situation then prevailing. As he later told an interviewer, 'He was unable to educate the public sufficiently for them to understand the role of the bank vis-à-vis monetary policy. There was not ... a choice between high inflation and low unemployment. This failure of perception led to expansionary government policy and, concomitantly paved the way for more inflation and greater unemployment – the twin ills of our era.'[59]

New attitudes and new instruments were needed to bring about the change that he believed necessary. In short, the Bank's attack against inflation was not successful. Inflation continued upward into the 1970s and 1980s and was wrestled to the ground only in the early 1990s. That war cost Canada dearly; unemployment created social unrest, and high rates of interest contributed to a sharp recession in the early 1980s and again in the following decade. Obviously, Bank attitudes, as well as those of the government, had changed. Rasminsky would retire on 1 February 1973, and it felt good to embark on a new career when he did.

Chapter Nine

Four Crises

Louis Rasminsky's tenure as governor of the Bank of Canada, from July 1961 to February 1973, was one that saw an increase in tension between the United States and the rest of the developed world, at least in economic and financial terms. As Europe and Japan recovered from the effects of the Second World War and the American share of world trade declined, the United States became more aggressive in pursuing its economic interest, which had an obvious impact on its policy development. Moreover, the US balance-of-payments condition deteriorated; as Robert Triffin has noted, there was a drain on US monetary reserves 'of a magnitude unprecedented in international monetary history: $23 billion in fifteen years. The gross reserves of the United States (gold, foreign currencies and the [International Monetary Fund, or IMF] gold tranche) fell from $26 billion at the end of 1949 to $16.7 billion at the end of 1964, while its indebtedness to the IMF and to foreign central banks climbed daringly – but precariously under the gold exchange standard – from $3 billion to $16.4 billion.'[1]

Year after year, those balance-of-payments deficits worried others. Per Jacobsson, managing director of the IMF, expressed the sentiments of the United States's industrial partners when he suggested at a luncheon meeting with the Committee for Economic Development in Washington, DC, in November 1960 that 'an over-all deficit of $3 billion per annum [the amount projected for 1960] can clearly not be allowed to continue forever.'[2]

Despite his relative distance from trade issues, the governor of the Bank of Canada was called on a number of times to facilitate the Canadian–American relationship, which was also hurt by prevailing conditions. This chapter investigates four of Rasminsky's interventions –

over (I) the implementation of the US Interest Equalization Tax (IET) in 1963, (II) the (Lyndon) Johnson guidelines of 1965, (III) the US balance-of-payments program of 1968, and (IV) the 'Nixon shock' of 1971.

I

The United States was concerned over its balance-of-payments situation, though in the first half of the 1960s its current-account position did improve markedly. Further, prospects looked relatively rosy, at least according to a study done in 1963 for the US government by a group of eminent economists from the Brookings Institution. That report 'projected that the US basic balance ... would improve from a deficit of $850 million in 1961 to a surplus of $2.7 billion in 1968.'[3] Of course, when the document was published in 1963, the extent of US involvement in Viet Nam was not foreseen.

However, while the US surplus on goods and services improved, many in the US administration came to view the outflow of private capital 'as exessive,' at least partly the result of an over-valued dollar, a problem that would not be addressed until the summer of 1971. Given the overall condition – that is, a growing current-account surplus, especially against western Europe, as opposed to the large outflow of investment dollars from the United States, at least in part taking advantage of higher European interest rates – it was not likely that continental European governments would contemplate a revaluation of their currencies against the US dollar. Therefore, in July 1963, in an attempt to deal with that problem, John Kennedy's administration imposed an investment-equalization tax (IET), designed to make it more expensive for foreigners (including Canadians) to borrow in the United States and thereby to show the outflow of investment money.

The US tax had the potential to damage Canada's economy. How did the tax work? In short, any American who wished to purchase a Canadian security had to pay a 15 per cent US tax on its price. In other words, if Ontario Hydro were to issue a bond in the United States with, for example, a face value of $1,000 and an interest rate of 8 per cent, the purchaser would have to pay $1,150 for that bond. The result was that the yield of the bond was not 8 per cent, but 8 divided by 115, or about 7 per cent. In turn, in order for Ontario Hydro to sell that bond in the United States instead of in Canada, Canada would need to have an interest-rate policy that would result in rates going up by practically a whole point in order to avoid an exchange crisis. And Canada needed foreign exchange to finance its annual current-account deficit. The practical implication was that the Bank of Canada would be forced to throw its monetary policy into reverse at a time when it was expansionary. The part that perplexed Rasminsky was that the Americans would not gain any benefit from application of the IET to Canada; indeed, given the two nations' very close economic and financial relationship, the United States itself would also be hurt.

Why would Washington deliberately set out (indirectly) to harm the United States, which would be the obvious result? There was some speculation at the time and later that it was a lesson administered to Ottawa for the Gordon budget of 13 June 1963, discussed above in chapter 7. American documents and the activities of certain officials and politicians do bear out that interpretation to a limited extent. Could it have been imposed out of inadvertence? Perhaps, though the Americans could not claim ignorance of their very close financial relations with Canada.

Their financial relationship had been the object of frequent conversations between the two nations, most recently in early May at the memorial service in Washington for Per Jacobsson, the recently deceased managing director of the IMF. Rasminsky believed in the power of repetition. As he had earlier remarked, 'It is perhaps inevitable that one becomes boring or appears doctrinaire if one continually enunciates a principle ... The question really is whether there is not a certain point in this. We should not underestimate the influence which Canada can wield ... In the White House the President ... is surrounded by advisers who must be open to political arguments, and it must be useful to remind these men from time to time of the way United States policies are viewed abroad.'[4]

At the Jacobsson service, Rasminsky had had a conversation on the state of Canadian reserves with Undersecretary of the Treasury Robert Roosa, who had then taken him to see the secretary, Douglas Dillon. The governor was only too happy to have the opportunity of talking about Canadian reserve policy with high-ranking Americans, 'as there was a great deal of misunderstanding and misinformation on the subject.'[5] He told Dillon that if one took all transactions into account, current and capital alike, Canada was a source of support to the US balance of payments. In effect, the country used part of its gold production and surpluses earned in third countries to cover the deficiency in its total-payments position with the United States. Further, so long as Canada had a current-account deficit, it would need to import capital or, Rasminsky said, experience another exchange crisis, probably worse than that of May and June 1962.

The most fruitful course for Canada would be to reduce further its current-account deficit and its dependence on the import of capital. 'But [Dillon] should realize,' the governor went on, 'that this would bring no benefits to the [US] balance-of-payments position; *since our current account deficit was entirely with them, it was reasonable to expect that a reduction in this deficit would take place mainly in our transactions with the United States.*'[6] In short, the United States could not hope to improve its balance of payments to any significant degree as a result of transactions with Canada. Moreover, Ottawa had not added to its official reserves in the first four months of the year; on the contrary, it had been a net exporter of private short-term capital, which was fine with Rasminsky, so long as its reserve position was safeguarded.

With respect to the size of Canada's reserves, Rasminsky commented that some Europeans 'had picked up in Washington that the Canadians were the "bad boys" in the US payments picture.' He was sensitive on this point. At a meeting of Working Party 3 (WP3) of the Organization for Economic Cooperation and Development (OECD) in Paris, Otmar Emminger, then a director of the Deutsche Bundesbank, had complained to Bill Lawson that the Bank of Canada 'was preoccupied with reserves' and that Canada 'would come in for severe criticism at the next meeting of the Working Party.' The governor had responded with a letter remarkable for its bluntness. Rasminsky had found it very difficult to follow Emminger's logic. Of course, it was quite possible 'that the experience of last summer when, at the height of the crisis, we were losing reserves at a rate which would have exhausted the remaining supply in a matter of days (not weeks, but days) has made me more than normally sensitive to the need for protecting Canada ... from a second ... exchange crisis.' Possible, but not likely. As to the level of the reserves themselves, Rasminsky was

interested in the view attributed to you that $2,500 million is adequate in our case. I wonder how you form a judgement of this sort: I myself find it very difficult to formulate any precise idea of what reserves we should have. Obviously the more flesh you have on your bones in the form of reserves the more importance you feel able to attach to other things, as is evidenced in our case by the monetary policy followed since last September. But if one compares the Canadian reserves with other relevant magnitudes and circumstances, I find it very difficult to see how one could possibly reach the conclusion that at $2,750 million they are excessive. We are still running a deficit of $600–800 million in our current-account transactions; our imports are running at a rate of $6,000–6,500 million a year; we are international debtors to the tune of $20,000 million, much of it in liquid form; we are more exposed to short-term capital flows than any debtor country in the world; we have no exchange controls, no import restrictions and no legal means of imposing them.[7]

Rasminsky rejected Emminger's position.

In his meeting with Dillon, Rasminsky covered many of the same points. He could not explain that attitude or how the Europeans could think that Canada was being less than fully cooperative with the United States in its payments problem. Canada's reserves were *not* high when compared with the volume of its international trade. All things considered, if Dillon could 'name an important industrial country participating in Working Party 3 whose reserves policies as regards amount and composition were more helpful to the United States than ours were, I would undertake to discuss with those concerned in Ottawa the possibility of Canada emulating this country.' The secretary could not; he took the point.

Those facts had also been clearly laid out in the Bank's *Annual Report* for 1962. They were well known to American technicians and had been repeated many times in WP3 and IMF meetings without provoking any adverse comment. It was true that Canada's continued ability to finance a large current-account deficit with the United States would be undermined if there were a sharp curtailment in the import of capital from the United States. It was also not reasonable to suppose that Canada would be able to effect a massive shift in its borrowing from the United States to other capital markets in order to finance the deficit. Rasminsky could have been only happy to learn that Roosa agreed. The American told the governor that 'he would bring the arithmetic of the position to the attention of other US Government agencies.'[8] Still, Rasminsky found in mid-July that he would have to make the same case following the US administration's announcement of the IET.

The governor first heard of the IET while salmon fishing in mid-July 1963 in the Gaspé with a small group of friends and acquaintances that included Quebec's premier, Jean Lesage. A telephone call from his senior deputy, Robert Beattie, had apprised him of the tax announcement in Washington; 'all hell had [then] broken loose on the Canadian market.'[9] Canada was 'losing exchange hand over fist, and prices of debt securities – of interest bearing securities – were plummeting. The 4½s of 1983, which was at that time a kind of bellwether long term issue, fell by three or three and a half points in a single day. This was ... part of the adjustment that the market recognized was needed in the circumstances to get our interest rates up.' The prime rate in May stood at 3.5 per cent.

Rasminsky immediately headed by car for Ottawa, where he found 'very profound depression.' Officials had been trying for two days to make the Americans see the harm that this decision would do to them as well as to Canada, but with no success. Certainly the Americans demonstrated no inclination to treat their northern neighbour differently from any other industrialized country, which was a surprise. More indicative of the normal US mindset, or so the Canadians believed, was for Washington to accord Canada a special place. In a conversation with Lester Pearson which demonstrated that principle, Walton Butterworth, the US ambassador in Canada, stated that the Americans were 'instinctively predisposed to treat Canada in a very special category.'[10]

There were only a few ways for Canada to deal with the crisis. The government could have followed the course pursued a year earlier and imposed more import restrictions to reduce the deficit in Canada's balance of payments that needed to be financed. It could also have let float the exchange rate, which had been fixed only in May 1962. Without question the rate would have fallen from its already low level, putting more strain on the economy. As well, that would have outraged the IMF's managing board. Nor were the governor and the government keen to fiddle with the exchange rate. As Rasminsky noted later, the rate that had been chosen was a good one; he thought that it 'played a large part in how well [Canada] did economically during the decade after that.'

Meanwhile, in his budget presentation of 13 June 1963, Walter Gordon had staked a certain amount of his credibility on the permanence of the pegged rate. He later made it clear that the government intended to maintain the peg at its present level, telling the House in early July: 'We are committed ... to a fixed exchange rate for the Canadian dollar. In my opinion it would be the height of irresponsibility to contemplate a second major devaluation of the currency. This government has stated that it will support the fixed rate for the dollar.'[11] The only feasible way of confronting the issue was to convince Washington that it should not levy the IET against Canada.

Understandably, the Americans had underestimated the likely Canadian response, especially given Gordon's recent budget, which had taken aim at American investment in Canada. Livingston Merchant stated the issue clearly; with respect to the tax 'Canada's interests had been taken into account [by Washington] and ... *the Canadians shouldn't object to this since it merely served to implement announced Canadian policy.*'[12] A more astute comment could not have been made, but three weeks later Rasminsky was in Washington on behalf of Ottawa as a supplicant, demanding that the Americans not cut their investment in Canada, or at least that part which the government did not want touched. Canada, Merchant suggested, had been hoisted on its own petard.

On Saturday, 20 July, Walter Gordon convened a meeting to discuss options to deal with the gathering crisis. After listening for some time, the governor suggested that the Canadian reaction should be not to accept it but to make another attempt to convince the Americans that it was against their interest. His observation was not well received; while officials had been jumping up and down attempting to attract American attention over the past few days, Rasminsky had been in hip-waders fishing for salmon. Now he was telling them what he thought they should do.[13] However, the minister eventually agreed, and Robert Bryce, the deputy minister of finance, called Robert Roosa and arranged for the governor to meet with Douglas Dillon. That afternoon, with Wynne Plumptre, the assistant deputy minister of finance, and Charles Ritchie, Canada's ambassador to the United States, Rasminsky flew to Washington to make the case for Canadian exemption from the IET.

Rasminsky was a good choice to send. He got along well with the Americans, having spent much time there since 1945, either on Canadian government or on IMF business, and he had developed an extensive network of contacts. Of some importance, the Americans admired him, considering him 'charming, urbane and sophisticated,' with a first-class mind.[14] As a result, they were perhaps more prepared to listen to him criticize US policy than they might be to other Canadian officials. Moreover, he was one of the reasons that Canada's contacts with the United States were generally close and friendly on financial matters. He worked at it – something the Americans appreciated.

In Washington, Rasminsky told Dillon that there was a strong basis for an exemption 'because the American action in imposing this tax ... really did put ... our balance of payments into an untenable position and confronted us with [the] very difficult choice ... of either getting up the domestic level of interest rates, which was contrary to the requirements of the domestic economy, or trying to deal directly with the balance-of-payments situation through import restrictions, or through exchange adjustment of some sort, including the possibility of a floating exchange rate.'[15] The prices of long-term bonds had fallen very sharply, and exchange losses on 19 July had exceeded US$100 million, with no sign of a let-up. The loss was far greater than anything that Canada had experienced in the worst days of 1962 and was equivalent to a gold loss by the Americans of US$1.5 billion in a single day. Nor would Rasminsky concede that the market reaction was overblown; as he told Dillon, 'It might indeed represent a fairly accurate appraisal of the true gravity of the situation to Canada if no relief was given.'[16]

The United States, he said, was making a mistake in applying the IET to Canada – it could not consider its payments position with Canada as imposing any burden on the country. While it was true that the United States was a large net exporter of capital to Canada, its net export of goods and services was even larger than the export of capital. Or, as Rasminsky told Dillon, 'in order to pay for our current-account deficit with the United States, we had to use not only all the capital that we imported from the United States, but all the money that we earned in third countries as well, such as Britain or continental Europe with which we had an export surplus, and all the capital that we imported from those countries ... In fact, if you look not at the capital account alone, but at the whole balance of payments, the United States gained foreign exchange as a result of the totality of its transactions with Canada.' If the country proved unable to pay its bills, the US balance of payments would not be improved, and a crisis, from which neither country would benefit, was bound to occur.

Dillon expressed some 'surprise' at the reaction in Canadian markets, which had been very strong. Surprise or not, the Americans had a good idea of what the Canadian response would be, as the papers of the assistant undersecretary of the treasury, James Reed, reveal.[17] Reed was with the president at Cape Cod when Dillon telephoned about the Canadian request for an exemption. As Reed remembered, 'It was interesting to see [Kennedy's] reaction. He was entirely familiar with the bill. He was entirely familiar with what the prospects were going to be ... if this bill was passed. He was entirely familiar with our relationship with Canada ... The President was anxious to have our relationship improved with the Canadians ... He had confidence in Secretary Dillon, so when the Secretary put the question to him, he said ... "If you think that's what is best under all the circumstances, that's all right with me."' Rasminsky was intrigued when he later learned of the telephone call: 'I was particularly interested in the evidence that the Americans had a pretty good idea how much the IET would hurt us before they clapped it on in July 1963. In my discussions with them they gave the impression that they were surprised at the sharp reaction in the bond and exchange markets.'[18]

Why then did the Americans plead ignorance of the effect of the IET on Canada? Certainly Canadian–American relations had been damaged by Walter Gordon's June budget, and barely a month later the minister of finance wanted Washington to take into consideration Canada's complaints about the effects of one of its policies. Still, Rasminsky was ambivalent about ascribing motive; as he later said, the tax itself was 'an attempt on the part of the United States, under a fair amount of European prodding, to take some concrete action to improve their balance of payments.'[19] However, he also conceded that it was 'quite likely that the budget of 1963 didn't predispose all Americans to focus on the Canadian position and ask themselves the question, "Is this going to do any harm to our good friends and neighbours, the Canadians?"' Indeed, it was probably the opposite. The Americans had followed the budget through Butterworth's reports and had not been pleased. In discussions about Ottawa's budget that followed, threats had flown like a flock of pigeons. As Plumptre had recorded following a meeting with US officials: 'Asked whether discriminatory taxes contravened Canada's international obligations?; Regretted "example" to underdeveloped countries of discriminatory tax treatment; Warned that this might cause difficulties in Canadians raising capital in New York – seemed to imply some veiled threat of official intervention; Doubts and questions regarding practicability of 30% tax on "takeover"; Is incidence of sales tax discriminatory against imports?'[20]

It seemed, however, as if many of the points that the Americans found noxious were already being addressed by cabinet, or so Basil Robinson, the Canadian chargé at the embassy in Washington, told senior US officials. He had been sent by personal order of the prime minister[21] to tell the Americans that 'the Pearson government was in deep trouble because of its handling of the budget and, given the general precarious [minority] situation in Ottawa, it might be overthrown ... There are pressures in and outside the Government in the direction of opposition to and modification of various aspects of the Budget. One example was the withdrawal of the takeover tax yesterday. Further modifications could be made in the future ... The way the United States feels about the Budget resolutions is already well understood within the Cabinet, where there is support for United States' views on these questions. The Prime Minister had asked Mr. Robinson to say that he hoped people in the US Government would realize that the points in the Budget about which the US would be concerned are already being made forcefully both outside and inside the Government.[22] The Pearson government had learned a valuable lesson in continental politics via the budget disaster.

Though the Americans had been provoked, it was also true that they had never intended to cut off the market entirely. However, they were very concerned about discriminating in Canada's favour. On the weekend of 20–21 July, Roosa offered a solution: 'You don't want to increase your exchange reserves, tell us how much you need to borrow in the United States, and we will give you a quota for whatever amount you think is reasonable.'[23] That suggestion did not meet Canadian needs, largely because the principal borrowers in the United States were the provinces, and Roosa's suggestion would have put Ottawa in a position of having to dole out a limited amount of access to the American capital market among the provinces. And even in the early 1960s, before the launch of intensive constitutional negotiations, that was a non-starter. As the governor explained, 'The broad political situation in Canada was such that that was a very, very difficult, perhaps even impossible, position for the [federal] government to be put in.'[24]

Rasminsky also told the Americans that weekend that he would monitor the possibility of third countries' borrowing in Canada and tell Canadian underwriters that the government did not want them to place any foreign issues in Canada. To relieve the Americans of fear of over-borrowing by Canadians, Rasminsky would talk to Gordon, and they could probably agree that if the country's reserves went up materially, then the two governments would talk. However, Roosa's attitude irritated Rasminsky, who was 'disturbed at [his] failure to recognize explicitly that the current-account deficit which Canada has to finance (in part) by borrowing in the United States is entirely with the United States. By saying that Canada has "to do some borrowing in the United States in order to cover its over-all current account deficit" he manages, whether by accident or design, to avoid making the point that the alternative would be to reduce our current-account deficit *with the United States*. The result is that the Canadian exemption is presented in effect as a concession to Canada rather than as an action taken in the interests of both Canada and the United States.'[25]

In the end, in return for receiving partial exemption, the Canadian government agreed not to increase the country's holdings of US dollars beyond $2.5 billion – what they had been on 30 June 1963. Rasminsky had argued against this proviso, but the Americans had been insistent. He thought it left Canadians 'with the feeling of a Damocles sword hanging over [their] head.'[26] Still, the agreement sold the Americans. Rasminsky talked with Gordon, who was overjoyed with the results. A few weeks later, the minister, perhaps believing that Canada was on a roll, asked Dillon for a complete exemption for Canadian securities. He had, he told cabinet, 'explained Canada's position in detail.'[27] The minister was a firm supporter of the agreement.

In making the announcement of the American exemption on the evening of Sunday, 21 July, Gordon said that it 'marked a major change of course by the US administration that would avoid an increase in Canada's whole interest rate structure which would have [had] a major impact on unemployment.' An editorial cartoon in the *Winnipeg Free Press* captured the minister's change of heart, with respect to the United States. It showed a hobo holding a sign with the words 'Yankee Stay Home'; the 'Stay Home' was scratched out, being replaced by 'Welcome.'[28] Like the *Free Press*, Rasminsky was surprised that Gordon welcomed the exemption so warmly. The minister's 'extreme nationalist views' would, he thought, have made the exemption unpalatable.[29]

The IET crisis had been overcome, but the underlying causes remained, and the situation had highlighted some unsettling indications in Canadian–American relations. As Rasminsky wrote to Pearson in late August, the implication of the American action was clear: 'Even in a situation where there is no conflict between our interests and the US interest, the US Administration may feel impelled to act in a way which is seriously injurious to our interest in order to serve some unrelated purpose, e.g. to appease uninformed European critics of US policy or forestall criticism from a congressional committee.'[30] In short, it seemed as if the Canadians could no longer 'count' on the Americans as they might have done in the past, and it behoved them to examine their international economic and financial condition and make some changes in the way in which they operated. There was another unsettling lesson; presidential discretion '[gave] the President of the United States enormous power over the Canadian economy: he has, in a sense, statutory power to create an exchange crisis in Canada, or slow down our growth rate, etc. whenever he chooses to exert it. We count, of course, on the President of the United States ... using his discretionary powers reasonably.'[31]

The main lesson was clear enough, however, as Rasminsky stressed to Prime Minister Pearson; 'Canada could not count on being able to import capital from the US in the amounts needed to cover the country's current-account deficit.'[32] If the country wanted to reduce its extreme exposure to the risk of recurrent and unpredictable shocks in the conduct of its economic affairs 'originating from the varying fortunes and attitudes of the United States, [it] must eliminate the remaining deficit in

[its] current-account balance of payments and [its] remaining dependence on net imports of capital from abroad.' Canada's first goal of
economic policy should be to become self-supporting internationally,
for only by so doing would it be able to achieve a reasonable degree of
independence.

Over the past number of years, the government had reduced the current-account deficit in its balance of payments by nearly two-thirds – from
$1.5 billion in 1959 to about $500 million in 1963. The lesson that Rasminsky had taken from the reduction was that the problem was much less
intractable than many had feared and that the remaining deficit could be
cleared up probably within a few years if public policy could attach real
importance to that objective. The government needed to encourage production of more goods and services for export and to displace imports,
and the country would then experience increased employment and economic growth.[33]

In order to achieve that goal without causing a sharp reduction in Canada's standard of living, Rasminsky thought two conditions had to be met:
'(a) The Canadian economy must become more competitive, particularly
in secondary industry where our imports are so large. This means, among
other things, that we must carefully watch our costs to be sure that they
do not advance as rapidly as those of our competitors; (b) Out of the
increased Canadian incomes that result from economic expansion there
must develop flows of Canadian financial savings adequate to replace the
foreign capital we are seeking to do without. In practice the problem
here will likely be that of finding adequate markets in Canada for Canadian long-term bonds and equities.'

What could public policy do to help in eliminating the imbalance in
Canada's international payments? Here the governor offered the prime
minister some advice that lay, strictly speaking, outside his realm. First,
the government should avoid action that had the effect of making it more
difficult for Canadians to 'stand on [their] own feet internationally.' An
example of this type of policy was the pension plan proposed by the Liberals and announced by Judy LaMarsh, the minister of national health
and welfare, after the 1963 election. The suggested model was an
unfunded, pay-as-you-go plan that would begin to pay benefits ten years
after it was implemented and which would not create a large pool of capital that Canadians could draw on for public investment projects.

The pension plan, financed as it is by a payroll tax, with benefits equal to tax
collections, offends ... the conditions [noted above]; the payroll tax will con-

stitute a substantial and growing addition to Canadian costs which will impair our international competitive position, and the so-called pay-as-you-go feature of the plan means that old age security is provided (and this, apparently on a scale higher than is done in the much richer and competitive US economy) without any of the intermediate accumulation of savings which would otherwise be achieved by plans which involve the accumulation of assets out of revenues paid in, and which are important sources of long-term financing. Thus the pension scheme will tend to make it more difficult for us (a) to be competitive enough to balance our international accounts, and (b) to find Canadian sources for the types of financial capital that we have been importing.

Rasminsky was not alone in encouraging the government to reconsider the pension plan, and it came under fire, for different reasons, from insurance companies, from social advocates, from the Conservative government in Ontario, and from the Liberal government in Quebec.[34] The federal government should concentrate its resources, the governor believed, in the continuing development of competitive secondary industry. He hoped that the new Department of Industry and the Economic Council of Canada would be addressing that need.

Rasminsky's was good advice on all counts, but it was never discussed. Walter Gordon had also been included in the discussion, and Rasminsky thought that he would be sympathetic to the idea of eliminating the deficit in the country's current account. After all, in 1962, when he had been a member only of the Liberal party and not of government, Gordon had rated bringing Canada's transactions with other countries 'more nearly into balance' second only to putting its finances in order and balancing the budget as the essential long-term policies required to restore a satisfactory annual growth rate and high levels of employment.[35] He had changed his mind, however.

If there was a negative aspect to the partial exemption given to Canada, it was the reserve agreement entered into as the quid pro quo. Did the Bank of Canada lose control of monetary policy as a result of this arrangement? Certainly Rasminsky and the Bank recognized the dangers involved in such an undertaking. At the same time, however, he never thought that he was under serious pressure from the United States to adhere strictly to a particular reserve level. Indeed, while the Bank had the reserve target in mind, it was only one of a number of issues taken into consideration when setting the prime rate. Of more importance were factors such as the state of the economy, the unemployment rate, the amount of unused industrial capacity, the movement of prices and interest levels, 'along with one's judgement of the probable behaviour of these and other variables in the future, and the lags involved in the impact of monetary policy.'[36]

Rasminsky later maintained that the influence of the reserve agreement on monetary policy was marginal at best, even though that was not always the American interpretation. For example, there was a meeting between Gordon and Dillon in mid-February 1964: 'Dillon felt they had made considerable progress in solving their problem in the United States. We discussed the accumulation of proposals in Canada to borrow in the United States and the problem this would entail as soon as the Interest Equalization Tax Bill is passed. Dillon referred to the understanding that we would not allow our exchange reserves to increase appreciably over present levels and said that he presumed that when the [IET] is passed [by Congress], the problem referred to could be handled if we narrowed the spread in interest rates between our two countries even further than it is at present.'[37]

Rasminsky was adamant that Dillon's interpretation was not consistent with discussions that he had had with the Americans on Canadian exchange reserves; the United States was reading more into the Canadian exemption than he thought was there. As well, it was not up to the minister of finance to make any commitments about monetary policy in Canada. Representations were made at once (February 1964) in Washington, and the Americans backed down.

Again, in December 1964, Dillon and Roosa met with Rasminsky regarding the scale of Canadian borrowing under the IET, which to them seemed overly large. The governor told them not to worry – temporary blips and anomalous situations would right themselves. The secretary told Rasminsky that his problem was with Congress, and it was a serious one. Dillon would be going back in the spring to ask legislators for an extension to the tax, and in his previous appearance he had 'rather unwillingly indicated a probable scale of Canadian borrowing under the proposed exemption – from US$300–$500 million.'[38] He would be 'embarrassed' to go before Congress with the fact that Canada had borrowed US$850 million in 1964, and it could be represented that Canada's reserves had gone up by more than US$300 million; Congress was capable, he warned Rasminsky, 'of irrational action.'

That did not faze the governor: 'Congress was not the only body capable of irrational action, and if they did act irrationally as regards Canadian access to the US capital market, then it was inevitable that this would provoke reactions in Canada which would be injurious to US as well as Canadian interests.' If Congress did something 'foolish,' there was a strong likelihood that Canadians would do likewise, 'because the fires of ultra-nationalism would be inflamed.' Rasminsky told Dillon: 'If it became necessary to take action to protect the Canadian dollar, he would act boldly.'[39] As the secretary well knew, Canada's fixed exchange rate, combined with a lack of foreign-exchange controls, meant that Canadian authorities could not achieve the kind of stability in the level of the country's reserves that Dillon seemed to be asking for; some fluctuation was to be expected.[40]

Moreover, Rasminsky told the American that he felt responsible for the undertakings into which he had entered in July 1963; he had 'not negotiated an agreement and then forgotten it ... If the agreement was not working, the difficulties should be ironed out in a joint effort.'[41] And so they were, to the point where, in 1968, when Secretary of the Treasury Henry Fowler visited Ottawa, the governor helped to draft an exchange of letters between two nations, stating that 'the understandings between the two countries do not require that Canada's reserve level be limited to any particular figure, and the United States recognizes Canada's need for flexibility with respect to reserve levels in order to accommodate the adaptation of monetary policy to the changing needs of the domestic economy, seasonal factors and other influences of a temporary nature.'

Canada remained exempt from the IET until the Nixon shock of August 1971, though the exemption became less important as the years passed. By early 1971, for example, Paul Volcker of the US Treasury could tell the Senate finance committee that the administration was carefully watching Canadian–American financial relations. Given that Canada's trade surplus with it neighbour had been $860 million in 1969 and $3 billion in 1970, the Senate committee 'might want to reconsider the Canadian new issue exemption.'[42] By that time, such American observations did not arouse the same jitters in Canada as they surely would have a few years earlier.

In conclusion, implementation of the Interest Equalization Tax in the summer of 1963 constituted an unpleasant dose of reality for the newly elected Pearson government. It might have been expected that Rasminsky's influence with the Liberals would rise; after all, he was the one who pulled many of their irons out of a raging inferno. While Walter Gordon remained minister of finance, however, his stock did not go up. Rasminsky later noted that when Mitchell Sharp succeeded Gordon as minister at the end of 1965, there was a change in the tone of his relations with the

minister: 'Sharp was by no means a "pushover" in the sense that he necessarily agreed with every idea that [Rasminsky] expressed, but he was
interested in hearing [his] views.'

II

The repercussions of the IET had no sooner worked their way through
the system than Canada was confronted with another plan, the Johnson
guidelines of 10 February 1965, designed to address a continuing adverse
US balance of payments.[43] They limited purchases of long-term foreign
securities by any American non-bank financial institution to 5 per cent of
the amount of its holdings on 30 September 1965 and permitted each
corporation an average rate of direct investment abroad in 1965–6 up to
135 per cent of its 1962–4 average. As direct investment in 1965 was
higher than that figure, the guidelines implied a cutback for 1966.[44] They
came at a particularly bad time for Canada, as its current-account deficit
increased by about $700 million to more than $1.1 billion in 1965; the
Canadian economy was expanding at a rapid rate, which meant that
imports were rising rapidly. Canada's current-account deficit with the
United States was therefore expected to be more than the record $1.8 bil-
lion of 1964.[45] And that was not helpful, at least from an American perspective, as Treasury Secretary Douglas Dillon told President Lyndon
Johnson. 'Canada,' he noted, 'has become a special problem of the
United States balance of payments position.'[46]

The guidelines encouraged repatriation of US-owned short-term financial assets held in Canada by American corporations. US corporations
affected could increase their credits, for example, via exports and earnings from foreign investments; repatriate capital; or reduce new investment. As the Bank of Canada's *Annual Report* noted, however, 'The effect
of these short-term capital withdrawals on our international position was
offset ... by a simultaneous inflow of banking funds from overseas which
was itself an indirect consequence of the guidelines.'[47] Still, the future
was shaping up to be difficult in terms of Canada's financial relationship
with the United States.

The Bank turned its attention to dealing with the chartered banks and
measures that would make it plain to the United States that Canada
would not be used as a channel to evade the emergency measures.
Indeed, there were a series of meetings among Bank officials and their
counterparts in the departments of finance and of Trade and Commerce,
senior exchange officials from the chartered banks, and US government

personnel to sort out how the banks would be monitored. Rasminsky drafted the letter that the minister of finance sent to bank presidents on 1 April requesting 'that while these US measures are in effect, you conduct your foreign currency operations in such a way that the net position in US dollars of your head office and Canadian branches vis-à-vis residents of the United States is not reduced below the position which existed on December 31, 1964.'[48] A week later, at Rasminsky's request, a senior officer from the international department of each of the chartered banks met with him to hear his proposals for guidelines for chartered-bank operations in foreign currencies as part of the government's steps to fulfil its obligations under the Canadian–US balance-of-payments agreement. Another meeting followed on 17 April.

As the year wore on, the US balance of payments continued to deteriorate. Indeed, the administration because very concerned by October 1965, as it could see no grounds for anticipating sufficient improvement to avoid an unfavourable last quarter. If it turned out to be as poor as it was shaping up to be, it could affect confidence in the dollar. As a result, the president and his advisers were considering possible further action to restore the momentum generated by the February announcement.

The US Treasury attributed much of the recent deterioration in the country's balance of payments to transactions with Canada. It had noticed that Canadian reserves plus Canada's creditor position in the IMF had improved by more than US$200 million in the third quarter. The Treasury also projected a further substantial growth in the fourth quarter of about US$800 million.[49] Given those numbers, more than a few rumours began to circulate that Washington was re-evaluating the necessity of the Canadian IET exemption. Those rumours were, an official believed, 'designed to prepare the ground for some discussion of this question on a mutually convenient occasion.'[50]

Ottawa was appalled that the Americans would even consider such a possibility, and Finance and the Bank turned their collective efforts to convincing the Americans that the exemption should remain. Supported by ammunition from Robert Bryce, the deputy minister of finance, and Rasminsky, Walter Gordon met in early November with Henry Fowler. With the data on his side, he managed to convince the secretary that Canadian reserves would fall after 1 January 1966. However, in order to ease an increasingly critical situation in the United States, Fowler asked if larger Canadian borrowers could delay receipt of their loans placed in the United States until after the end of the year. Rasminsky was instructed to investigate that possibility with corporations, while the federal govern-

TABLE 9.1
Scheduled US loans to large Canadian borrowers, as of autumn 1965

Borrower	Scheduled date of offering	Estimated amount (US$million)
Province of Ontario	17 November	$12.7
Province of New Brunswick	20 November	$10.0
City of St Catharines	Late November	3.4
Canadian Pacific Railway	1 December	$15–25
Bell Telephone	December (date unknown)	$10.0
Consolidated Paper	15 December	$7–12.5
Province of Saskatchewan	28 December	$1.2

Source: LR76-368-4, Fowler to Gordon, 3 November 1965.

ment would approach the provinces. The secretary had in mind the schedule laid out in Table 9.1, but with dates to be put back to early 1966. In addition, Bryce would try to learn more about two large issues – Pilkington Brothers ($23 million) and International Utilities Corp. ($36 million) – that also showed up on Fowler's list, scheduled for early December. It was in Canada's interest, he said, to be helpful.

By month's end, the US–Canada Balance of Payments committee, established the previous July for regular discussions, met to follow up the earlier ministerial meeting. The Canadian objective was to secure some undertaking that the 1963 exemption would remain and to try to convince the Americans that Canada needed further exemption from the Johnson guidelines. Rasminsky was especially firm, telling the Americans: 'If it became known that [the United States was] even considering proposals [to rescind the exemption, it was his] judgement that [that] would precipitate a major crisis in the Canadian bond market and security markets.'[51] The crisis would emerge from the fact that the US proposals created an 'unviable' situation for Canada, which would be unable to obtain the imports of capital necessary to pay its bills. If the Americans followed through, the governor forecast a crisis in exchange first, followed closely by one in bond prices as investors held off. That, he thought, would do the United States no good at all.

For his part, Bryce emphasized that the United States could not improve its overall balance of payments by changes vis-à-vis Canada except to the extent that the latter country could reduce its reserves, borrow elsewhere, or interfere with normal trade and payments with other countries. Moreover, Ottawa was 'already cooperating to check the capital outflow from Canada to other countries. We are sure that the US does not want to have us interfere with our current payments to the United States, reducing imports, for example, simply ... to reduce the capital flow necessary to finance them.'[52] And while Canada's current-account deficit with its neighbour had gone up quite considerably, the capital inflow was also less than the country's current-account deficit. Under the circumstances, it would be impossible to shift sources of borrowing.

With ministerial approval, the Bank and Finance had developed for non-banking financial institutions what they thought a satisfactory alternative to the US guidelines whereby Canada could keep a viable capital market while simultaneously accomplishing what the Americans had in mind. The proposal would permit unrestricted access to US markets for Canadian issues exempt from the IET, and US investors could buy such Canadian issues in accordance with normal market considerations.[53] If the Americans permitted this arrangement, Rasminsky said, Canada would undertake both to purchase from US holders enough Canadian securities held in the United States to keep their reserves to the agreed level and, in December 1965 and June 1966, to sell the United States $100 million worth of gold from its reserves. However, Bryce noted, 'It should be understood that we expect such a large deficit next year that it may be necessary in fact for the Government of Canada to borrow in the US to maintain its reserves rather than to have to carry out this repatriation proposed.' Not only should the Americans leave the IET exemption alone, but they should seriously consider exempting Canada from the Johnson guidelines. The Americans found these arguments persuasive and agreed, and by early December all was satisfactorily concluded, though not without some voluble criticism from at least one influential Canadian who was also a Quebec cabinet minister.[54]

As a result of the outcome, the Bank of Canada intensified its monitoring of the chartered banks in order to ensure that they adhered to the spirit of the agreement, though the arrangement was still regarded formally as a policy of moral suasion. Rasminsky met with their representatives on 5 January 1966 in order to discuss the possible effects of the Johnson guidelines on the demand for credit. He wrote to the presidents six weeks later: 'In view of recent developments, I believe that it has now become necessary to follow the situation more closely and I am therefore writing to ask each bank for a report as at the end of each month the total amounts of authorized credits and loans outstanding to subsidiaries of American companies with authorized lines of credit of at least $500,000. For purposes of comparison we would also like to have figures for the end of December 1964, March, June, September and December 1965 on the same basis.'[55] The regulatory net had just been tightened.

Crisis had again been averted, and the Bank of Canada's *Annual Report* for 1966 noted: 'By comparison with most recent years, 1966 was happily free of major difficulties in so far as Canada's external financial position was concerned ... Direct investment inflows of capital increased.'[56] Still, that did not mean that there had been clear sailing; there had been, for example, a brief flare-up concerning the nature of Canada's reserves and how they should be counted. The Americans had wanted the definition changed to include the net position of the chartered banks in foreign currency with non-residents, which would have added about US$500 million. Their justification for inclusion of the banks' positions 'was that it was a "rationalization" of their arrangements with Canada and would make it easier to defend these arrangements in Congress when the IET was extended this summer.'[57] However, Ottawa did not have access to those assets and could not consider them as reserves.[58]

The Americans eventually backed down, but it was another example of US muscle-flexing that could just as easily have complicated matters for Canada. Perhaps the US attitude was made easier by the fact that its situation seemed to be improving (though Robert Solomon later called it 'superficially favorable)';[59] in 1966, the United States had its first overall balance-of-payments surplus ($200 million) since 1957. Nevertheless, the Americans flexed their muscles again, as the guidelines were made more firm in 1968. As a result of another and tougher US program to help redress its balance-of-payments situation, combined with the uncertainty caused by sterling's devaluation in November 1967, Canada experienced an exchange crisis early in 1968.

III

The year 1967 witnessed the first signs of economic trouble, which erupted in full force in early 1968. The situation was marked by an erosion of confidence in several currencies and came to a head when the British, after several years of bolstering sterling with the help of other countries, including Canada, gave up the effort and devalued the pound (a move that demonstrated to the US president and his top advisers British 'ineptitude'), as was discussed in chapter 7 above. This move was accompanied by an attack on the US dollar by currency speculators, in the form of massive gold purchases in the unofficial market, which further destabilized the international monetary system.

As a memorandum prepared for President Johnson pointed out, with devaluation, 'it was as if the speculators – fresh, rich, and enthusiastic from their winnings in sterling – were now going to take on the dollar directly, or take on the dollar through gold or other currencies such as the Swedish kroner.'[60] It was clear to the Americans that sterling devaluation and the huge capital movements that it touched off would devastate US international accounts. Their preliminary figures suggested that the fourth quarter of 1967 would show a huge deficit, and Washington was worried that when all the relevant numbers were put together in final form and announced in February 1968, they would touch off a wave of speculation and shake the world's entire monetary system. The Americans felt that they had to implement a balance-of-payments program. This plan had a political purpose as well – to demonstrate that the United States had regained control of its balance-of-payments situation and therefore to cause the markets to discount the very poor figures for 1967, when they were announced. Secretary of the Treasury Henry Fowler met with President Johnson to discuss the program on 18 December.

Canada was caught up in the general speculative frenzy, and the crisis of confidence now affected all of North America. Many factors contributed to the perception of financial analysts that the Canadian dollar was weak, including their belief that Canada's balance of payments would deteriorate after the closing of Expo 67 and the resulting return home of so many free-spending tourists. The price and cost performances of the Canadian economy were also causing concern, and there was growing doubt that the government, whose borrowing requirements continued to be large and which had been a party to some very large wage settlements, was taking a serious enough view of the problem. With such unsettled conditions, the Bank of Canada raised the prime rate from 6 to 7 per cent to 'show [its] resolve.' As well, the government, realizing that monetary policy alone could not halt the rise in prices, passed a tough, anti-inflationary budget in November 1967.

Against this background, the announcement on 1 January 1968 of the US balance-of-payments program, designed to help redress a 1967 deficit of $3.4 billion, came 'as a severe jolt to Canada.'[61] The country was included in a group for which direct investment from the United States was to be limited to 60 per cent of the 1966 figure; however, there was no assurance that Canada would get any. A run on the Canadian dollar developed, and that month Canada lost US$350 million worth of reserves, or 15 per cent of the total. About US$120 million of that disappeared on one day, Friday, January 19, and indications were that the pressure would persist.

That situation was made worse by Washington's consideration of an import tax, which would apply to about $2 billion of Canadian commercial exports. A Canadian document noted: 'Apart from the obvious implications for our balance of payments, new barriers on our export trade are bound to have serious effects in terms of the production, investment and marketing plans of Canadian industry, particularly at a time when many producers were gearing up to take advantage of [the recently completed GATT] Kennedy Round opportunities.'[62]

Cabinet considered the problem and instructed officials to prepare a letter apprising the Americans of Canada's concern 'that any unilateral measures by the United States would trigger a cycle of action and retaliation which would undermine the structure of world trade and payments.'[63] If the United States followed through, Canada would be forced to take similar action. As well, Ottawa might have to limit certain freedoms of US subsidiaries. There had been a few reports that some had been shifting large amounts of money from Canada to their head offices, and that those transfers had resulted in some pressure on the Canadian dollar in the exchange market. Following discussions with the chartered banks, Rasminsky announced that they would discourage use of bank credit 'to facilitate abnormal transfers of funds abroad by Canadian subsidiaries of foreign companies and would also discourage the use of bank credit by such companies to meet requirements in Canada which have in the past normally been met by parent companies.'[64]

However, it was not the governor's intention to cut off all transfers. For a meeting with the bank presidents in mid-February 1968, he made a note to tell them that Canadian subsidiaries would have normal access to the capital market and would be able to patriate normal profits to their head office based on the 1966–7 average.[65]

As the crisis continued, Rasminsky had frequent meetings with the prime minister alone and with groups of other ministers. He was, he told Pearson and Sharp, 'very worried.'[66] The situation was potentially worse than 1962, and they were witnessing a 'partial breakdown of confidence.' However, there was little that the Bank could do. It had raised the prime rate to an almost-all-time-high of 7 per cent in an attempt to stabilize the dollar, and the problem was now one for the government. As Rasminsky said, 'We have shot our bolt and no more help is to be looked for from monetary policy ... The question for Govt. is can it restore confidence that its over-all policies will be coherently directed towards arresting erosion in value of money. Difficult but no soft options.'

The increase in the bank rate had been the subject of some discussion among a number of Rasminsky's colleagues in Europe. Hubert Ansiaux, the governor the the Banque nationale belgique, was nominated by European Economic Community central bankers to write a letter outlining their position; Ansiaux 'did not understand [the Canadian increase]. If all of us would do the same, the measures taken by the United States would have no chance to succeed.'[67] He went on: 'In order to help, we must see that our own internal expansion is free to develop. We must therefore be ready to substitute an internal expansion of liquidity for an increase deriving from a surplus in balance of payments originating from the US deficit and be prepared to lose reserves. If we don't do that, there is no chance for the USA to put their balance of payments in equilibrium and further, we run the risk of entering into a deflationary process which may lead to a world recession ... I do not know enough about your own internal problems, but I should like to understand, so I am asking you to let me know the paramount reasons which induced you to increase your rate to seven percent.'

In theory, Rasminsky did not disagree with Ansiaux's hypothesis. In a letter copied to all central bank governors in the Group of Ten (G-10), he explained: 'The first duty of all of us ... is to protect the external value of our own currencies.'[68] The obverse of the US payments deficit was the European payments surplus, which had to be reduced if the American program was to succeed. Canada, in contrast, was not a surplus country; 'at the end of 1967, our total reserves of gold and US dollars, including our net creditor position with the IMF, were lower than at the end of 1964. Canada has year after year a huge deficit in her current account balance of payments – about $1,000 million per year, which is covered by capital imports from the US.' Rasminsky did not think that Canada could find that sort of money in Europe, 'although I would naturally like to ... borrow as much in Europe as I [could].'

For those reasons, it was obvious that the United States could not significantly improve its balance-of-payments position at Canada's expense without this producing an exchange crisis in Canada. And, Rasminsky told Ansiaux, that seemed to be in the process of happening in January 1968:

There has ... been a good deal of uneasiness in exchange markets generally since the devaluation of sterling. The Canadian dollar was occasionally mentioned, but attention did not focus on us until after the publication of the new balance of payments program of the United States. Though it is extremely difficult to pin-point causes precisely when exchange pressure on a currency develops, I have no doubt that the severe pressure to which we were subjected in January was triggered off by large withdrawals of funds by Canadian subsidiaries of American companies, and attempts by some such companies to hedge their investment in Canada in the exchange market. Others joined in and there was a real devaluation scare.

Ansiaux and his colleagues could only agree with Rasminsky's explanation, especially as they knew that the Canadian situation was not improving. In view of that increasingly dismal reality, the governor met with ministers in late February. The dollar outflow, he told them, was the result of a mixture of external and domestic causes. The latter included the structural weakness in Canada's balance of payments – that is, the persistent current-account deficit. That necessitated a continuing reliance on foreign capital, a rise in costs, public perception that the government was not as concerned as it should be about the erosion of the value of money, and some lack of coherence in government policies.

At the February meeting Rasminsky had told Sharp that it was beyond question that 'the exchange position of the country [was] one of extreme peril.'[69] The reserve losses kept mounting despite the increase in the bank rate; in the first two months of the year, the Bank of Canada lost US750 million, or over 30 per cent of its gold and US-dollar reserves, in supporting the Canadian dollar in the exchange market. Canada could not continue to lose reserves at that rate: 'If no new elements are introduced, there is a very strong likelihood that exchange pressures will mount and that we will be faced with a forced devaluation or resort to a floating exchange rate.' While the government was considering 'new elements,' a domestic crisis could result. An increase in the cost of living and serious economic disorganization would follow. Internationally, devaluation of the Canadian dollar 'might well trigger off similar action by other currencies, and would almost certainly increase the pressure on the US dollar. The consequences [were] in fact unpredictable.'[70] Rasminsky went on: 'In thinking of the alternatives, and in considering the action that would have to be taken if the Canadian dollar is to be defended at its present value, it should be emphasized that the alternative courses of devaluing or floating will also require action in defence of the Canadian dollar. They are not themselves solutions to the problem, and there is no assurance whatever that confidence in Canada will be automatically restored if we devalue or float. The likelihood, indeed, is that we would have to mount a stronger domestic program than in the defence of the present rate, because the inflationary pressures would be greater and we would be less able to look to outsiders for assistance.'

What could the government do, given the erosion of confidence in the Canadian dollar? Rasminsky had some thoughts. Any strategy would have to address both the disturbed international currency situation following devaluation of sterling and the crisis that had to do with the new US balance-of-payments guidelines. On the domestic side, the governor was blunt, and he went in effect beyond his mandate. There were two main elements that had to be addressed. The first was the fiscal position of the government, and the other was 'the strong upward push of costs and prices, and the widely held view, despite the restrictive stance of monetary policy and steps recently taken to reduce the Government's net financial requirements, that the Government is not sufficiently concerned about inflation to take unpopular action designed to arrest it.' The American program had also raised doubts as to the basic viability of the Canadian situation. Would Canada be able to import enough capital to cover its current-account deficit? Only Washington could provide the necessary assurance that its guidelines would not stand in the way, but even the US government could not force American investors to place large amounts of money in Canada.

A possible program to defend the Canadian dollar, which Rasminsky laid out for Sharp, included domestic and external elements. On the domestic side, there should be a tax increase or – the only other possibility, he thought – a reduction in expenditures. With respect to monetary policy ('the only weapon,' according to Rasminsky, 'that has been used to deal with the situation since the acute exchange problem developed in January'), little room was left for manoeuvre. The bank rate was at an already-high 7 per cent, though an increase was possible but impracticable. On incomes policy, the governor believed that the government must agree that wages, salaries, and prices had been rising too rapidly and take steps at least to slow the rate of increase. Government action directed to restricting capital outflows by Canadians might also be considered.

Externally, Canada should work for revision of the Johnson guidelines. The US administration might be asked to change them so as to make it clear that it was not its intention to prejudice the viability of Canada's position. Rasminsky sought either complete exemption of Canada from the direct-investment aspects, including the requirement to repatriate earnings, or, less ideal, establishment of Canada as a separate category in the guidelines with a quota of 100 per cent of the base period. Canada would, much as it had in 1963, undertake as a quid pro quo that the US balance-of-payments position would not suffer on its account.

Rasminsky suggested also that the US government be asked for a very large line of credit. Ottawa would not necessarily use it, but it would be invaluable for confidence purposes. The Bank could plan to place a government-of-Canada issue in the US market as soon as conditions made it possible. As well, Canada could borrow in Italy and West Germany. However, the government should ensure that such borrowings, and its gold tranche from the IMF, were not counted in Canada's reserves for purposes of the agreement with the United States. It was, in sum, a well-rounded program, which covered all eventualities.

Rasminsky and Robert Bryce were sent to Washington in late February 1968 to tell the Americans how Canadian thinking had evolved. The prime minister had personally arranged the trip, and his anxiety and concern were evident from the tone of the letter he had sent: 'Under normal circumstances, I would suggest that appropriate Cabinet Ministers of the two governments should meet but, given the need to avoid public attention at a time of great sensitivity in the foreign exchange market, I propose to ask [Rasminsky and Bryce] to discuss the situation with Secretary Fowler and other appropriate officials.'[71] The Americans listened to the governor, who did most of the talking. A few days later, he would be back in Washington, authorized to enter into negotiations in a desperate attempt to preserve the country's foreign-exchange position. Obviously, Pearson had come to rely on Rasminsky's advice and negotiating skills.

On the governor's return, Gerry Stoner, at the Privy Council Office, gave Rasminsky a copy of a memorandum on the subject that he had produced for the prime minister and said: 'I would be grateful if you would avoid any reference specifically to this memorandum since it was intended for the Prime Minister only.'[72] The gist of the document had been suggested by Rasminsky and outlined a program to support the Canadian dollar. It concluded with a range of options to deal with the crisis and also with the recent defeat of the budget, Bill C-193, which had contained a tax increase – a 5 per cent surcharge on personal income taxes. Officials thought that the government should regroup and push through as strong a fiscal policy as had been in the defeated bill. In Stoner's view, that involved 'the strongest possible taxation measures acceptable of passage in Parliament and preferably measures affecting personal income. It should also involve further reductions in expenditures, at least in the order of $75 to $100 million and possibly include, at least for cosmetic purposes, some freeze on civil service recruiting and salaries.' Once agreement had been reached on a tax proposal, Stoner suggested that a small group of ministers meet with Pearson and Sharp in order to discuss the timing of an approach to the United States. Secrecy was important; it could be fatal to the Canadian dollar if it became known that Canada had approached the United States for concessions and had been turned down.

Following a few more private conversations with the prime minister, Rasminsky attended a crucial meeting on Sunday, 3 March, at 24 Sussex Drive, which included the minister of finance.[73] Sharp had just returned from Washington, where he had discussed with Fowler the impact on Canada of the 5 per cent surcharge planned by the United States on imports. However, Canada's exchange position had continued to deteriorate so rapidly that the minister had warned the American of the dire consequences for Canada if something were not done quickly. Rasminsky agreed with Sharp's interpretation, telling Pearson and Sharp that he was 'not at all convinced that [Canada's] basic position was in fact viable' if the Americans would not agree to certain measures. If they would not, then the Canadians had better know it soon, or Canada's reserves would be depleted to no good purpose. The governor asked the prime minister's permission to go to Washington to try to convince the Americans that it was not in their interest to see Canada experience a major exchange crisis. He proposed to ask them for complete exemption of Canada from the US direct-investment guidelines or, as plan B, establishment of Canada as a special category with a quota of 100 per cent of the 1965–6 average. In return, Canada would be prepared to offer: '(a) protection for the Americans against "pass through," i.e. the use of Canada as a channel for US corporations to export capital directly to third countries, which they could not do directly from the United States; and (b) to hold our reserves in a form which did not constitute a liquid claim on the United States under their definition, though we would have to have safeguards to ensure that the reserves would be immediately available to us if this was required to make payments.'[74]

The Bank of Canada would also make some commitments about the chartered banks' behaviour. In effect, it would police their foreign-exchange deposits, which would not be allowed to rise above foreign-currency claims on residents of countries other than Canada and the United States that existed as of 28 February 1968, unless an increase were accompanied by an equal increase in total foreign-currency liabilities to

TABLE 9.2
Canadian banks' holdings (Can$million) in third countries,
March 1968

	Assets	Liabilities	Net assets
Commerce	191	340	−149
Mercantile	21	32	−12
Montreal	260	323	−63
National	−	−	−
Nova Scotia	510	490	+20
Provincial	−	−	−
Royal	254	463	−209
Toronto Dominion	261	186	+75
Total	1,496	1,836	−340

residents of those third countries. (This particular promise resulted in copious documentation passing between the banks and the Bank of Canada over the next several years, as the situation evolved.)[75]

At the meeting of 3 March, the president of the Canadian Bankers' Association, Beverly McGill, proposed that the foreign-currency guidelines for chartered banks be amended so that the banks would maintain gross liabilities at least equal to their gross assets in third-country transactions, which would allow most of them some upward movement, as Table 9.2 demonstrates. Rasminsky rejected the request: 'Since the capital flows permitted by your proposal would constitute "pass-through," you are in effect proposing a revision of that agreement. We in the Bank of Canada would not want to propose opening that agreement to revision unless we were fairly sure that the balance of advantage of the likely changes in it would be in Canada's favour. We doubt that this is the case at the present time, and we, therefore, do not feel that we are in a position to recommend your proposal to the Government.' Much of the correspondence between the two sides involved tricky, difficult, and often technical interpretations of the agreement. The Bank monitored the banks' numbers so assiduously that rumours spread that some sort of foreign-exchange control was in the process of being drawn up. For the present, on 3 March the assembled ministers agreed that the effort along the lines suggested by Rasminsky should be made in Washington.

On 4 March, Rasminsky spoke to his friend Alfred Hayes, president of the Federal Reserve Bank of New York, who promised to discuss the Canadian situation with William Martin, chair of the Federal Reserve

Board's board of governors. As well, Pierre-Paul Schweitzer, managing director of the IMF, was called in by Rasminsky and told that Canada's overall position was $1,689 million to the bad and that the country was losing exchange. Schweitzer was sympathetic, and when the governor remarked on the difficulties that the Americans might feel in discriminating in favour of Canada, he responded 'that it would not hurt his feelings if they did so.' The Americans also met with Schweitzer, who, they told Rasminsky, 'was well informed and [who] had made some very constructive comments.' Indeed, the IMF official had told Washington that under the circumstances Canada could only devalue the dollar or return to a floating rate, which would not do anyone any good; 'Canadian devaluation at this time would shake the whole system. Other countries would follow and the run on gold could not be stopped. Schweitzer ... and Bill Martin agree that Canadian devaluation would be disastrous.'[76] The next day, Rasminsky was invited to Washington to see Fowler.

At 3:45 p.m. on 5 March, Rasminsky, Lawson, Finance's Allan Hockin, and the Canadian ambassador, Charles Ritchie, were ushered into Fowler's office. Across the table sat the secretary, Assistant Secretary John Petty, William Martin, and William Freed, from President Johnson's office. The governor outlined Canada's reserves situation and the reasons for their level. There was a difficult international environment, especially following British devaluation and numerous domestic problems. There were structural problems – the openness of the Canadian economy, the large volume of international transactions, the huge foreign investment in Canada, and continuation of a large current-account deficit. As well, the unstable political situation and the defeat of the tax bill on 19 February had thrown off the government's calculations. There was also concern about the fiscal situation, the large volume of government borrowing, large cost increases in the face of a lacklustre domestic economic situation, and the view held by some that the government was not sufficiently worried about the large price and wage increases to try to control them.

What had the Canadian government and the Bank of Canada done to respond? The former had introduced corrective fiscal action in November 1967, at the time of the British devaluation, and was determined to raise additional taxes, despite defeat of the tax bill in February. Ottawa was reducing its projected net borrowing requirements by over 50 per cent and was well advanced in planning for an incomes policy. On the domestic front, the government was doing what it reasonably could to restore confidence. Meanwhile, as noted above, the Bank had raised the prime rate to 7 per cent. That could not, by any stretch of the imagination, Rasminsky told the Americans, be described as a 'relaxed' monetary policy.

On the international side, trouble surrounded the Canadian government. Most important, there was basic doubt regarding the viability of Canada's position, resulting from the US balance-of-payments program. The country was 'in the unhappy position of having to import large amounts of capital from a reluctant lender, and people were wondering whether the United States was in the process ... of making it impossible for us to import capital on the scale needed to keep our heads above water.'[77] The Canadians wanted an indication from Washington that such a blockade would not happen. At the same time, Rasminsky emphasized that his program would not result in an undermining of the US balance-of-payments program. He then 'developed the idea of the package arrangement for the maximum possible exemption from the ... guidelines combined with protection against "pass through" and the undertaking to hold ... reserves, apart from working balances, in a form which did not constitute a liquid liability in the semantics of US balance of payments terminology, but which would nevertheless be available to us in case of need.' The give-and-take continued in Fowler's office until 3:00 a.m., with the secretary suggesting a number of alternatives, all of which Rasminsky rejected as inadequate.

Fowler finally agreed to a complete exemption for Canada, subject to the two conditions that Rasminsky had mentioned. The arrangement was not greeted with unanimous acclamation; a few officials from the (US) Council of Economic Advisors, and Robert Solomon of the 'Fed' 'thought that Fowler was going too far.'[78] However, an American account of the meeting pointed out the obvious – that the Canadian exemption 'would cost us relatively little in balance of payments terms because most capital flows to Canada come back to us in one form or another.' As well, 'the exemption is much less of a danger to us at this time than [Canadian] devaluation.'[79] Still, while some Americans thought the set-up too generous, so too might some Canadians, and Rasminsky told the Americans that the exemption might be problematic in Canada. While it was vital to the country's well-being, to some its negotiation would smack of a sell-out by Canada. There were political realities to be considered, and Rasminsky made it plain that the Canadians would not regard the offer as implying that Canada was 'harnessing [its] wheel firmly to the American chariot.' For example, if Fowler thought that in return for the exemption Canada would duplicate the US program, he was wrong.

In that case, Rasminsky would not recommend to the government that the offer be accepted.

An hour after the discussions had ended, Rasminsky was on the telephone to Gabriel Ferras, managing director of the Bank of International Settlements (BIS) in Basel, Switzerland. He wanted US$400 million from the BIS and asked if Ferras would call Karl Blessing of the German Bundesbank and Guido Carli of the Banca d'Italia in order to arrange a US$150-million infusion of money from them. By the time Rasminsky was back in his office in Ottawa at 8:00 a.m., he was able to announce the European package of central-bank credit, along with a US$500-million credit arranged by Canada's Department of Finance through the Export–Import Bank.

Sharp spoke to a waiting House of Commons on 7 March; Canada had its exemption, and the government would cut its borrowing requirements in half and appoint a Prices and Incomes Commission, to be headed by John Young, an economist from the University of British Columbia. On 15 March, the Bank rate was hiked to 7.5 per cent – to that point an all-time high. In effect, Rasminsky had pulled another rabbit out of a hat; the 1968 exchange crisis was over. However, the situation remained fragile, and the governor was very conscious that it could deteriorate at any moment.[80] Still, he could feel a certain amount of satisfaction. The Americans removed the guidelines in September 1974.

Since he had become governor in 1961, Rasminsky had obtained good results for Canada in crises with the Americans. Sometimes his hand had been bereft of cards as he sat opposite an opponent who could play from several decks. The agreements that opposite an opponent who could play from several decks. The agreements that he negotiated conformed to desperate Canadian need. Naturally, there was a quid pro quo demanded from the other sode of the table, and Canada was in no position to refuse.

The ceiling on Canadian reserves was one condition of the 1963 IET exemption, reaffirmed in 1968, that was under continual scrutiny in Ottawa. By the end of that year, it had become politically sensitive and was being used by some as an example of the American domination of Canada. It was not; rather, it was an indication of Rasminsky's skill in negotiation as well as of Canada's special relationship with its neighbour. It had been necessary in 1963 to give that undertaking, but by 1968 it had become a liability, both in developing monetary policy and politically, of which Rasminsky was only too well aware.[81]

By that year, Canada's money supply was expanding at an annual rate of 23 per cent, almost twice as fast as in 1967. This massive injection of money and credit had little to do with the financial needs of Canadian business or consumers and resulted instead from commitments, made in the dark days of July 1963, that the country would hold its foreign-exchange reserves below $2.55 billion. Higher levels, the Americans had thought, would unfairly deplete US reserves.

The ceiling was the subject of ongoing negotiation between the two nations, with Rasminsky taking a leading role on the Canadian side. It was also a target for the financial press, which now saw it as a hindrance to Canadian economic development and a suitable monetary policy. The Canadian price level rose at an annual rate of 4.2 per cent in the second half of 1968, which greatly exceeded rates between 1962 and 1966. The *Financial Times* ran an editorial entitled 'The Price of Concessions,' on 23 September 1968. As it pointed out, if Canada wanted continued access to the US money market, it had to acquiesce to US policy:

[Concessions] are part of the tribute to be paid for continuing exemptions from US balance of payments restraints. And the biggest part of this tribute is harmful, not only to the chartered banks and some Canadian companies, but to the economy as a whole. This is the $2.55 billion (US) ceiling on Canada's foreign exchange reserves which Canada has accepted to avoid Washington's interest equalization tax.

[John Coleman, vice-president and chief general manager of the Royal Bank of Canada, said:] In the summer and fall of 1967 the ceiling forced Canada to adopt a relatively easy monetary policy so as to keep interest rates down and reduce capital inflows. This was at a time when a tighter monetary policy and higher interest rates were called for ... Then, because the ceiling had prevented any build-up in Canadian reserves, it left Canada virtually no front-line defences to meet the attack on the Canadian dollar in January 1968. Canada was obliged to adopt a restrictive monetary policy and higher interest rates at a time when easier policies were more appropriate.[82]

The editorial demonstrated a short memory, but it was also an accurate assessment of conditions in the later 1960s. Rasminsky was aware of the problem. When the country's reserves were in the neighbourhood of the ceiling, the Bank of Canada had to expand the money supply to keep interest rates below the level that would attract undue quantities of US dollars. As the *Financial Times* pointed out, such action ran counter to the financial needs of the Canadian economy in 1968, making a strategy to fight inflation very difficult, if not impossible; a 25 per cent increase in holdings of government securities in one year put the chartered banks in a very liquid situation. They could increase their loan exposure, regardless of the wishes of the Bank of Canada. And fighting inflation increasingly preoccupied the governor; as the first line of the Bank's *Annual Report* for 1968 read, 'The performance of the Canadian economy last year was satisfactory in many ways, but it was marred by continuing inflation.'[83]

Rasminsky and Pierre Trudeau's minister of finance, Edgar Benson, had approached William Martin and Fowler, respectively, with a view to obtaining some relief from the ceiling provision of the agreement. The finance minister told Fowler that he was 'worried about the continuance of the reserve target of US$2,550 million. We are now just about at the target figure and there is a real risk that we would be forced into unsound financial policies if these had to be directed to making sure we did not exceed the target.'[84] Meanwhile, Lawson was active in Washington on Rasminsky's instructions, attempting to convince the Americans to relieve Canada of some of its obligations. John Petty, at Treasury, told him that if the Canadian government were 'pinned to the wall' it could say that it was well understood that the reserve figure 'was a target and not a ceiling.'[85] That was not news to the Canadians; it *was* Rasminsky's interpretation, but it still created difficulties.

Efforts took on added urgency following the defeat of the Democratic presidential candidate, Vice-President Hubert Humphrey, by the Republican Richard Nixon in the November 1968 US election. At the government's behest, Rasminsky raised the issue in a letter to William Martin; he was 'sorry to do so in the middle of such a difficult world currency situation,' but, as the chairman knew, he was 'most anxious that ... Secretary Fowler should deal with the problem while he [was] still in office.'[86] There were several reasons for addressing it now – Fowler was familiar with it, Rasminsky was afraid that it would 'be pretty low on the agenda of the new Administration,' and if it were not dealt with in the very near future, the reserve agreement could become a source of instability.

While it had played a useful role, the governor now thought that in the circumstances, 'where we hold all our foreign exchange assets, apart from working balances, in non-liquid securities of the US government, the agreement regarding a target on reserves has ... ceased to serve a useful purpose for the United States while doing positive harm to Canada.' Certainly it was bad for monetary policy, but it was now also bad politics, in an age that had become very sensitive to US influence in Canada. Mel Watkins's *Report on the Structure of Canadian Industry*, commissioned by the Liberal government and critical of American domination of Canada's economy, had just been presented to a ministerial committee. That concern, while not unimportant to Rasminsky, was not the only issue driving him; he remained very worried about the danger of inflation.

At a time when currency relationships in the world were unstable, he told Martin, it really was unwise to maintain an arrangement that contributed so materially to the instability of the Canadian dollar. Moreover, the Americans had nothing to fear 'from simply abolishing the present arrangements ... This will in no way change our attitude towards the amount of reserves we wish to accumulate and we would of course continue to hold our foreign exchange reserves ... in non-marketable securities of the US government.' Doing away with the target would benefit both countries; it would reduce agitation for a fluctuating exchange rate, and it would keep the United States from being blamed for inflation in Canada. Rasminsky's arguments won the day, and Fowler, in one of his last acts as secretary, agreed that Canada's reserve level need not be limited to any particular figure. That should have ended the campaign, but it did not. Rasminsky was forced to intervene again a month later, as the Americans had introduced the figure of US$2.55 billion for Canada's reserves. If that was the Treasury's view, the governor told John Petty, 'he was astonished that they should have failed to make their position clear to us.'[87] And if the Treasury must have a reference point, then it should be the level of Canadian reserves as of December 1968, when the arrangement had been made with Fowler – US$2.8 billion. In any event, the exchange of views proved academic, and no further Canadian action was needed.

Did the Johnson program help to ease the US balance-of-payments problem? Not really, though it seemed to work to the extent that, even with contraction of the surplus on current transactions to $750 million from more than $3 billion in 1967, the United States experienced an enormous improvement in its capital accounts, which produced an overall balance-of-payments surplus of $1.6 billion. However, the factors that improved the US capital account proved ephemeral, the result of temporary conditions. In 1969, the nation again experienced an overall surplus of $2.7 billion, but then things began to go wrong. The balance-of-payments deficit in 1970 was $9.8 billion. According to Solomon, 'The largest element in the reversal from 1969 was the switch from borrowing by US banks to repayment. Thus the veil that had kept attention from the deteriorating export surplus in 1968 and 1969 was lifted to reveal the brutal truth.'[88] As well, inflation was increasing, and the US economy seemed to be in a steady downward spiral.

Despite that, the United States remained by far the most influential country in the world, with much the largest economy. Moreover, its dollar remained tied to gold, and all other currencies were still linked to the greenback. So the American problem was of more than passing interest to the rest of the world, and it was discussed in various forums, such as the IMF, Working Party 3 of the OECD, and the Group of Ten. Still, governments were totally unprepared for the next round in the US attempt to reduce its deficit and arrest its economic deterioration.

IV

On 15 August 1971, US President Richard Nixon announced that the United States was untying its dollar from the gold standard and, more generally, changing the way it did business. This was yet another effort to set the US balance-of-payments condition on a more firm footing. What was the global context in which this initiative was launched? During the late 1960s the world had experienced rapidly growing trade and vastly increased integration of capital markes. That situation had contributed to the spread of inflation and to structural shifts in the relative competitiveness of major industrial economies. As well, short-term capital movements (reflective of interest-rate differentials), commercial hedging, and outright speculation had added to the uncertainty and 'to increasingly unsettled conditions in the international payments system.'[89]

Much of the change had hurt the United States, because of its central role in the global monetary system. By 1970, many observers hoped that those disruptions had worked themselves through and that that factor, together with the activation of the IMF's Special Drawing Rights (SDRs) developed over the 1960s and implemented in 1969, would create a new environment more conducive to order. However, some critics saw that outcome as unlikely, because Washington seemed unable or unwilling to take the hard decisions necessary to set things on the correct path. In part, or so Rasminsky told a Canadian cabinet committee in 1970, the United States was dealing with its problem 'by ignoring it and leaving it to other countries to adjust. Taking offensive by referring to need for other countries to pull more weight in defence arrangements and enlarging opportunities for US exports.'[90]

As a result, the ability of the US dollar to continue as the world's principal reserve currency came into question. More US dollars had moved into the hands of non-residents than they were prepared to hold, and the excess found its way into the official reserves of other countries. This whole process accelerated appreciably in 1970, when easier money conditions in the United States prompted massive repayments of earlier Eurodollar borrowings by US banks. The resulting heavy influx of funds into the Eurodollar market occurred at the very time that monetary policy outside North America generally was being tightened as an anti-inflationary measure. Not unexpectedly, therefore, residents of other countries began to tap the Eurodollar market to meet domestic financing requirements, and, as the proceeds of these Eurodollar loans were converted into local currency, foreign official holdings of US dollars skyrocketed.

By early 1971, this process was further speeded up by a deterioration of the US trade position and by a marked pick-up in speculation against the American dollar. The Canadian dollar had floated in 1970; during May 1971 the West German mark and the Dutch guilder did likewise, placing great stress on the internal structure of the EEC; and Austria and Switzerland revalued. West Germany was experiencing heavy speculative inflows during May, and by early summer so were Belgium, France, Japan, Switzerland, and the United Kingdom, which were all obliged to accumulate US dollars. Canada's position was protected by its floating regime, and the Dutch and German authorities minimized their exposure by allowing their floating currencies to move up sharply. On 3 August, France announced measures to prevent continued speculative inflows. As a result, the focus shifted to the Swiss franc, and Switzerland was forced to absorb large amounts of US dollars despite implementing measures to prevent that from happening.

That general unrest and US economic and financial policy provoked the Nixon program. It embraced both the domestic and the international economic problems facing the country. On the domestic front, the program entailed removal of the 7 per cent excise tax on cars; introduction of a 10 per cent tax credit for investment in new, American-produced machinery and equipment; acceleration to 1 January 1972 of the increased personal income-tax exemptions originally scheduled for 1 January 1973; a substantial cut in federal spending ($4.7 billion) and a 5 per cent cut in government employment; postponement of revenue-sharing and welfare reforms; renewed proposals for introduction of the DISC export incentive; and introduction of a temporary (ninety-day) freeze on prices and wages along with appointment of a cost-of-living council to help in the battle against inflation.

In the international field, convertibility of the dollar into gold was suspended, a 10 per cent surcharge on dutiable imports was applied, and US foreign economic aid was cut by 10 per cent. At the same time, the president announced that the United States would press for 'necessary reforms to set up an urgently needed new international monetary system.' Nixon's action in suspending convertibility removed the underpinnings of the Bretton Woods system and brought a need for fresh examination of the arrangements governing the conduct of international monetary transactions.

The formal breaking of the gold–dollar link merely gave official sanction to something that was already a reality. A 'dollar overhang' – an excess of US dollars held abroad over the value of US holdings of gold – had developed by the late 1960s. By mid-1971, the gold assets of the United States amounted to some $10 billion, while its liabilities to foreigners totalled about $53 billion.[91] If there had been a rush to convert dollars into gold, the par-value system would have ended earlier than 1971. However, Charles Coombs, president of the Federal Reserve Bank of New York, kept the Europeans in order by insisting that none should disrupt the international monetary system by asking for American gold. The only nations able to resist Coombs's blandishments were France and the United Kingdom. Louis Rasminsky later noted that the British 'did this for a long time after the United States was pretty obviously in trouble and this notwithstanding the help the United States had given them during the war and in the early post-war years.'[92] Aside from those two, 'the others were very docile and in some cases even entered into formal agreements with the United States not to ask for conversion into dollar balances.' The primary reason was that 'other countries didn't want to create monetary chaos in the world by seeing the United States go broke ... by putting the United States into default because the United States didn't have enough gold to meet its legal obligations to convert into gold.' The balance-of-payments improvement looked for by the United States was very large, and it would be difficult to negotiate a solution. The country had come, in the words of Paul Volcker, the undersecretary of the treasury for monetary affairs, 'to the end of the line.'[93]

On 15 August, the content of the program was unexpected even to some Americans, as the Canadian embassy in Washington reported: 'The package put together at Camp David seems to have come as a surprise even to senior USA officials left in Washington.'[94] World reaction was predictable, and most of it centred on US imposition of the 10 per cent surcharge, as countries attempted to assess the immediate adverse effects on their exports and economies. In Japan, stock-market values fell, and there was upward pressure on the yen, which trends the Americans applauded; they saw the Japanese as the key to reordering international trading and financial arrangements. As Sidney Katz, acting assistant secretary of state for economic affairs, told Peter Towe, Canada's alternate at the IMF, 'the surcharge could probably be removed quickly on the basis of a significant yen revaluation as this would pave the way for the alignment of other major currencies.'[95] The Americans were 'pleased at the shock effect the new program had produced on the Japanese.'

The Canadians believed that their exports to the United States would also be hard hit, and negotiations for an exemption were launched in Washington on 19 August by Benson and Jean-Luc Pepin, minister of trade and commerce, who headed a delegation that included Simon Reisman, deputy minister of finance, and a few other officials. However, the United States had adopted what to many in Ottawa seemed a very harsh attitude. Volcker told Reisman that Canada was a major contributor to US problems, which required world-wide adjustment: 'The strong Canadian external position was a major counterpart of the weak USA external problem.'[96]

The US secretary of the treasury, John Connolly, told the Canadian ministers that the United States would consider an exemption for Canada if there were 'an iron-clad case,' for it which, he thought, there was not.[97] Earlier, on NBC's *Today* show, Connolly had laid out his case in opposition: '[The Canadians are] going to come down and complain and ask that they be exempt from the imposition of the surcharge. We're certainly going to be cooperative ... but I'm going to point out that when they imposed a surcharge in 1962, we went up there to ask for relief for American products, they said no. I'm going to point out to them that in 1965 when they had real economic problems, we entered into an automotive agreement with them ... I must say that I don't think that their bargaining position is as strong as it might be.'[98]

Certainly the General Agreement on Tariffs and Trade (GATT) insisted on non-discrimination; for legal reasons, the United States could not discriminate in Canada's favour on trade measures, even if it had wanted to. It would, however, 'be more disposed to consider special problems created for "cooperative trading partners."'[99] The Canadian delegation had hoped for more positive results. The government, Reisman told the Americans, would have 'to look to its defenses and what Canada might have to do might not please the USA.' To make matters worse, a short while later Nixon identified Japan as America's largest trading partner. Canadians scrambled to point out that the province of Ontario alone did more business with the United States than did Japan.

Despite the adversarial tone of the meeting in Washington, Canada was still perplexed to find out that it did not fall into a special category. A (self-serving) memorandum prepared for Pierre Trudeau pointed out that 'Canada has more than met the tests of a good trading partner as outlined by your Government: Canadian dollar allowed to float freely since May, 1970, and value appreciated substantially (about 8%); Canada does not maintain any unfair or discriminatory trade restrictions against US; Canada accelerated final Kennedy Round cuts two years ago with no compensation from anyone.'[100]

The bitterness so obvious at the Washington meeting suggested the end of the so-called special relationship.[101] The Americans had been irritated by the defence and foreign-policy reviews that Trudeau's government had pushed through. It also seemed as if the new prime minister were contemptuous of the United States – a sentiment that probably contributed to Nixon's famous (or infamous) characterization of Trudeau as 'that asshole,' which did not augur well for continental relations.[102] The continental relationship had deteriorated to the point where, when Trudeau paid a visit to Washington, a Canadian briefing book baldly stated that its net effect should be 'to remove ... the charge that this government is anti-American or pro-Soviet.'[103]

Be that as it may, on 15 August 1971 the international monetary system was in a state of disarray as the dollar–gold link was severed and crisis erupted. Canada's interest in an early resolution was greater than that of almost any other country, as it would be particularly affected by a breakdown of the multilateral system of trade and payments. And it was also true that Canada was *not* the problem, despite Volcker's assessment. Even Connolly seemed to agree, in a calmer moment telling Benson that 'Europe is making more and more preferential arrangements which discriminate against us. The [EEC's] Common Agricultural Policy is an unconscionable evil. Japan does unbelievable things to keep our goods out.'[104] Canada did not act like that. However, to some extent the Americans were the authors of their own misfortune. Rasminsky later observed, 'I think that ... an important fundamental aspect of the answer to [the] question [of US problems] is that the United States never acquired the habit, or felt it necessary, to relate her domestic economic policies to her international position ... They preferred to try to deal with the[ir declining position] through measures of direct control that didn't affect the economy as a whole [such as the Interest Equalization Tax], but affected specific items in the balance of payments.'[105]

Whatever the reasons for the crisis, the future looked more clouded than ever. Only one thing, articulated by the Bundesbank's Karl Schiller,

seemed clear – under the stimulus provided by the 1971 US program and
the deterioration in international financial relations generally in the later
1960s and 1970s, the Group of Ten countries were 'moving away from
one another.'[106] At the IMF's twenty-sixth annual meeting, held between
27 September and 1 October, there was much talk of a 'collision course'
and a 'trade war.'[107] And that worried Ottawa.

John Connolly convened the so-called Smithsonian meetings in Washington in December 1971, to which all Group of Ten (G-10) countries were
invited. Ostensibly, they were an attempt to develop solutions to the issues
raised over the past number of months, but in reality they seemed
designed to allow Connolly to vent some steam and to force others' currencies to appreciate against the U.S. dollar. These discussions were the
last of the initial wave of post–15 August conferences to address the dollar
problem, which had included the G-10 finance ministers' meetings, held
in London on 15–16 September; the Commonwealth finance ministers'
conference at Nassau, Bahamas, 21–24 September; the IMF's annual
meetings in Washington late in the month; and more G-10 ministerial
meetings in Rome in late November. What had become clear from these
talks was an American penchant for unilateralism that many feared could
result in a return to the mentality that had characterized the 1930s.
Schiller spoke for the group when he observed: 'Any [monetary] realignment can only be successful if it is truly multilateral.'[108] Canada wholeheartedly subscribed to that sentiment, and, in the light of the relatively
hard line taken against the United States by others at these gatherings,
Edgar Benson, fearful of potential consequences for Canada if no agreement were negotiated, counselled compromise and conciliation; it was
'no longer fruitful to argue about the causes of the present disequilibrium' or to allocate blame. The only important issue to be resolved was
how to re-establish the situation on a firm foundation.[109]

Benson led the Canadian delegation to the Smithsonian meetings, with
Reisman as his second in command and Rasminsky in attendance to offer
advice when needed. The governor was a very good choice. Some diplomacy and tact, combined with a firm sense of what was required to
retrieve the situation, were required. Rasminsky knew precisely what was
expected and was the personification of diplomacy. And Benson needed
that kind of help; he 'was not one of the stars of the Trudeau cabinet, but
rather the accidental beneficiary [of the Ministry of Finance because] of
his early support of Trudeau for the Liberal leadership.'[110]

The conference was an attempt to create a new series of exchange rates

TABLE 9.3
Percentage changes from old parities, selected countries

| Country | Required changes for payments adjustment | | Actual changes as of 29 October 1971 |
	IMF	OECD	
Belgium	10.4	8.3	7.4
Canada	8.6	–	7.5
France	8.7	9.4	0.4
Italy	7.5	10.2	2.1
Japan	14.6	14.3	9.4
Netherlands	9.5	7.5	8.1
Sweden	6.9	–	3.0
Switzerland	11.9	9.3	6.9
United Kingdom	6.2	6.6	3.8
West Germany	11.3	9.7	9.7
Average	9.5	9.3	6.9

Source: LR PP, file 301, 'Discussion Paper,' 8 Nov. 1971.

that would, the Americans hoped, better reflect the global reality of the early 1970s. The United States had been demanding the upward revaluation of certain European currencies, primarily the mark, the French franc, the guilder, and the lira, on the basis that those countries had amassed extensive foreign exchange assets, largely as a result of their balance-of-payments surpluses, up from about US$5 billion in 1960 to US$34 billion at the end of 1973. However, many rates had already appreciated, as Table 9.3 illustrates. While a number of currencies had already moved a considerable distance towards new levels, the United States felt that these changes should be larger – an objective on which John Connolly set his sights.

In Washington, Rasminsky thought that Connolly 'conducted the meetings like a tobacco auction ... "Sold American!" He ran around the room saying "if Germany doesn't, etc. etc."'[111] The governor had never seen anything like it. The gathering had been preceded by a US investigation as to what would be the 'proper' structure of exchange rates – what would result in a solution to the problems of the US dollar over a period of time. As Rasminsky said: 'So the United States came into the meeting with concrete objectives in mind; not to have a nice quiet chat about the international monetary system ... One of the things that they wanted and apparently wanted very badly was not only that Canada should fix its exchange rate but fix the exchange rate at a level 6 per cent premium over the American dollar ... Well, we went around the table ... Whether by accident or design, Benson had to be in Ottawa for a crucial vote in the House of Commons the day that Canada had to defend her position. So, with Reisman's agreement, it fell to me to defend the Canadian position.'[112]

And defend it he did, emphasizing forcefully that it would be inappropriate to raise the value of the Canadian dollar by finding a new parity at a level 6.7 per cent above the May 1971 figure, as had been suggested by Paul Volcker. As well, for the time being, the best contribution that Canada could make to international monetary stability was to continue to allow its dollar to float. It had gone from 92.5 US cents in early 1970 to 100.5 US cents by December 1971, for an 8 per cent rise, meaning more expensive exports. And this shift, of course, had implications for Canada's domestic economy. The revaluation upward of the dollar did not fit in with the requirements of the Canadian economy, dealing as it was with higher rates of unemployment. It also remained that Canada was an importer of longer-term capital, and the current-account surplus had been falling continuously since the fourth quarter of 1970. By the third quarter of 1971, it was very close to balancing. With the exchange appreciation that had already taken place, further worsening of Canada's current-account surplus was a definite prospect. And now the Americans wanted the Canadian dollar to move to approximately US$1.05, for a further increase of 5 per cent. With some restraint Rasminsky said, 'There is nothing that the Canadian Government or its advisers can see in [Canada's] domestic position or international payments position to justify this proposal.'[113] The American position was 'completely unacceptable.' The session adjourned without much accomplished.

Benson returned to Washington later that day and received a message that Connolly would like to see him in his office in the Smithsonian. The minister was 'a pretty worried fellow and feeling the need of a bodyguard ... asked [Rasminsky] and Simon Reisman to go along with him.' Connolly asked: '"What contribution are you people going to make for settling this problem?" One of us said "We've already made a contribution of having a fluctuating exchange rate since 1970 which has risen in value and we feel that the countries that have already been behaving well in international things should get some credit for it and shouldn't be expected to make additional contributions, as you call it." And Connolly said, "Well, you Canadians are always looking for one thing or another, got your hand out for the automobile agreement or one thing or another, but when it comes to asking you to help out in any way, you aren't there.'"

Rasminsky took offence at Connolly's tone and demeanour and returned the latter's broadsides in the same way, interrupting him and certainly being less diffident and respectful than a Canadian official normally was when dealing with a powerful American cabinet secretary. Connolly eventually got up 'and stalked out of the room and called back to Volcker "Don't make any agreement of any sort with the Canadians without bringing it to me first."' Benson told Rasminsky when they were back in their own offices that that was 'the first time [he had] ever heard [Rasminsky] raise his voice.'[114]

When the formal sessions reconvened, Connolly went around the table, country by country, asking each to lay out its position. Canada's was 'that we [had] contributed to the working of the international system and we intend to remain on a fluctuating exchange rate, we don't intend to fix the par value.' Connolly then turned to the IMF's Pierre-Paul Schweitzer and asked him if the Canadian position was in accordance with the principles of the Fund. Of course it was not, and the managing director had no alternative but to point that out. As Rasminsky remembered, 'He said what he had to say as mildly as he could.' Still, it was a damaging criticism, that had to be dealt with as quickly as possible. Rasminsky conferred briefly with Benson, then raised his hand. When Connolly recognized him, he deferred to the finance minister, who put the question that Rasminsky had told him to ask: 'Was the rate of exchange proposed by the United States for the Canadian dollar an acceptable one or a rate likely to contribute to equilibrium?' Schweitzer's response was satisfying; 'No – the rate proposed is too high.' Valéry Giscard d'Estaing, the French minister of finance, looked over at Rasminsky following this exchange and 'smiled and winked.' However, Canada, with its floating rate, remained 'something of a pariah' in international money circles, though 'its decision to float appeared considerably more respectable later.'[115]

In Rasminsky's view, Connolly was little more than a bully, trying to squeeze out as much as he could. Even some Americans thought that; a senior Treasury official apologized to the governor after his meeting with the secretary. Rasminsky believed that the hard line came from Henry Kissinger, the secretary of state, and President Nixon. As he recalled, 'It certainly was a State Department view that was prevailing, because it was obvious that Connolly was antagonizing not only the Canadians, but ... his own people as well.' However, it was Kissinger who later salvaged the

TABLE 9.4
Exchange-rate relationships resulting from Smithsonian Agreement,
18 December 1971

| Country | Percentage | |
	Par value	In US dollars
Belgium	+2.76	+11.57
Canada	–	–
France	–	+8.57
Italy	−1.00	+7.48
Japan	+7.66	+16.88
Netherlands	+2.76	+11.57
Sweden	−1.00	+7.49
United Kingdom	–	+8.57
United States	−7.89	–
West Germany	+4.61	+13.58

Note: A plus sign indicates a revaluation, and a minus sign, a devaluation.
Source: Margaret de Vries, *The International Monetary Fund, 1966–71*,
vol. I (Washington, DC: International Monetary Fund, 1976), 555.

Canadian position, following a useful meeting between Nixon and Trudeau. Ultimately, the pressure to fix Canada's rate disappeared.

Following the impasse, which continued into the afternoon session, Nixon himself came to the meeting and spoke briefly. He then invited everyone to walk with him to the Air and Space Museum to meet members of the press, who had been waiting for two days among the exhibits. According to Rasminsky, it was all rather anti-climactic; Nixon 'made a nice little speech ... but it was the sort of thing you'd expect ... the cooperative effort and he was grateful to those who had contributed to a solution of this problem. Nobody knew that the problem was solved, because it was still basically the same statement in which Connolly had said it had not been solved.' Indeed, the cart was well before the horse; the press conference, with six hundred media people, was convened before there was any agreement. The decision to go ahead was Nixon's, 'because it was in the American interest to emerge with an agreement,' even though the reality was quite different. What was left to Connolly was to return to the meeting with the various delegations and draft up what had been said. That became the agreement.

Unquestionably, the United States had adopted a much harsher policy with respect to Canada than it had in the past. It could be that John Connolly was anti-Canadian (probable, given Trudeau's anti-Americanism) or that the United States, as Volcker had put it, was at the end of the line. Perhaps it was a bit of both. Volcker suggested as much in a speech entitled 'Canada and the US: The New Crunch' to American and Canadian executives at Johns Hopkins University. Rasminsky called it 'a very ill-tempered and tendentious piece.'[116] As the American declaimed, 'I must say I am confused and irritated when I see some reports from Canada that the whole program of ours, launched on 15 August 1971, seems to be aimed at stealing jobs from Canada. This was not exactly in the forefront of our minds, I assure you. The idea of the United States building its prosperity by stealing a few jobs from Canada hadn't quite occurred to me, but it seems to have added to the emotional tone of the arguments.'

Canadian–American relations were just bad in 1972, with Canada's performance in the monetary field, according to Federal Reserve Board chair Arthur Burns, 'the main cause.'[117] Burns felt that Canada 'had not been prepared to be helpful to the USA in its time of need [and] that as we were in surplus with the rest of the world we enjoyed more room to manoeuver than we were prepared to allow.' It was a rough new world that was emerging, and, while Louis Rasminsky's personal relationships with officials such as Burns remained good, institutional ones were increasingly problematic. It was that sort of change that encouraged him to resign on 1 February 1973, his sixty-fifth birthday.

The grind of the governorship was wearing him down, but more important, his wife had been diagnosed with cancer. Life now seemed too precious, and Rasminsky wanted to retire. The first of February became his target, even though his term as governor ran until 24 July 1975. Rasminsky had good reasons for contemplating retirement, though all paled to insignificance beside his wife's illness. The world was also becoming a more difficult place for a central banker, and his stress level had been rising. Inflation, unemployment, demands on his time, and the difficulty in implementing decisions in an increasingly globalized economy were also major considerations in his deciding on retirement.

Accordingly, Rasminsky wrote to the prime minister on 29 October 1972 to apprise him of his intention. Ever conscious of the need to keep the Bank out of politics, he sent his letter before the federal election, called for 30 October. He 'wished to make it perfectly clear that [his] decision was in no way affected by whatever the result of the election might turn out to be.'[118] His resignation was announced publicly on 8 November. He certainly appreciated Trudeau's reply: 'The last two or three years have been one of extraordinary difficulty for those who were responsible for financial or economic advice and policy. The Governor of the Bank has a position of unique responsibility and it must have constituted a very great burden to you at many times. It was a great advantage to the government to know that decisions in the extremely important financial matters with which you were charged were being taken by a person of such capacity, integrity and dedication to the public good.'[119]

Who would take over on 1 February 1973? Gerald Bouey and William Lawson were equally qualified to become governor, though Bouey had been appointed as the senior deputy on 1 January 1972 on Beattie's retirement. The board chose Bouey, perhaps because he was the domestic research and market man, as opposed to Lawson's dossier, which was international affairs. Lawson was appointed as the statutory deputy. With Rasminsky's retirement came the end of an era. Bouey and Lawson were both fourteen years younger than he and had grown up in a much different Canada. Their methods of dealing with situations were not the same.

A Bank of England memorandum offered an intriguing piece of speculation; 'Simon Riesman [sic], Deputy Finance Minister, has also been mentioned [as a successor to Rasminsky], but he is a Jew as is Rasminsky and there is some feeling (I do not know how widespread) that there could not be two in succession.'[120] That type of anti-semitism was dead in Canada, and the British official writing the report was mistaken. With some satisfaction, Rasminsky could look through the government of Canada telephone book and find many Jews in senior positions, among them Reisman; Herb Gray, the first Jew appointed to the federal cabinet; deputy ministers Alan Gottlieb and Jack Austin; and Sylvia Ostry, Canada's chief statistician. Retirement was looking better and better.

Retirement and Beyond

Louis Rasminsky had natural talents: a first-class mind; a commitment to work that had been encouraged by his parents, his religion, and his schools; and a personality that made people want to do their best for him. When he retired on 1 February 1973, he had accomplished his goal of becoming governor of the Bank, first given a focus with his application for the position of assistant deputy governor of the Bank of Canada in 1935. Moreover, he had not merely filled his last position; he could look back with satisfaction on his proactive record of eleven years and six months as governor. When he left, the Canadian economy was in an upswing, financial markets were functioning well, and, above all, he was 'leaving the Bank itself in good shape.'[1] He counted among his accomplishments that he had clarified what was once a *cause célèbre* in Canada – the respective responsibilities of the central bank and the government for monetary policy. He had also helped to have it recognized that monetary policy could not be judged in isolation and that what mattered in effecting the course and effects of total demand in the economy was the mix of monetary and fiscal policy.

However, his retirement also came at a good time, as the international system was soon confronted with a series of very difficult probles, including double-digit inflation, high interest rates, the oil shocks, the enormous growth of international indebtedness, the severe recession of 1982, huge government deficits, the disorder in international currency markets following breakdown of the Bretton Woods system, and the growth of protectionist sentiment in the United States.

He was a young sixty-five, and his life was not over with retirement from the Bank; while his time with Lyla would be short, he remained active. In among giving papers and commenting on other people's, he followed a sometimes-hectic schedule. For example, he was asked to give the keynote address at a dinner hosted by the British prime minister, Harold Wilson, on the occasion of Leslie O'Brien's retirement as governor of the Bank of England on 16 April 1973. A year later, he was awarded the Vanier Medal by the Institute of Public Administration of Canada; the letter informing him of it said: 'This Medal is awarded as a mark of distinction and exceptional achievement to a person who, in the opinion of a panel of independent judges, has shown distinctive leadership in public administration in Canada, or who, by his writings or other endeavours, has made a significant contribution in the field of public administration in Canada.'[2] Some of his old friends had been recipients, and the list was a distinguished one – Arnold Heeney, R.B. Bryce, John Deutsch, Marcel Cadieux, and Gordon Robertson. Also, he sat on a number of company boards, among them American Express, Bell Canada Enterprises, Boise Cascade Forest Products, and Shell Canada. There was also a lengthy list of social engagements to help fill in the time during the six-month 'cooling off' period from government service (and beyond) and his next task – becoming head of the International Development Resesrach Centre (IDRC) in September 1973.

Lester Pearson had been its first chair, appointed by Pierre Trudeau following the centre's inception in 1970. For Rasminsky it was an enjoyable four-year stint, which required hard work and a fair amount of international travel. It also it helped him to deal with the crushing blow of Lyla's death on 28 January 1976, following a long struggle with cancer. They had been married for forty-five years and had known each other for closer to fifty. She had been at his side through the ups and downs of his career, his sounding board and helpmate. One of the reasons that he had taken early retirement was to spend more time with her once the diagnosis was clear. He had the comfort of knowing that for the last few years of her life they had been together constantly.

The IDRC was a good organization to go to. Ably administered by David Hopper, it reflected Rasminsky's concern for economic development in the Third World and for human dignity. As well, it was at the end of what its president called the 'first phase of Centre development.'[3] Once Rasminsky was on board as the new chair, new policy initiatives would be developed and implemented. What was the IDRC's mandate? According to its act of establishment, it was to conduct research into the problems of the developing world and into the means of applying and adapting scientific, technical, and other knowledge to the economic and social advancement of those regions. In so doing, it was to enlist the support of Canadian natural and social scientists, to help build up research capabilities in less-developed countries (LDCs) and those institutions that were required to solve their problems, and to foster cooperation in research on development problems between the developed and developing regions. Rasminsky ensured that the centre was very responsive to the research needs of various developing countries. As a result, it gained a special place in the affections of LDC scientists for providing 'untied' assistance.

Following Lyla's death, Rasminsky worked also with the Canadian Jewish community. In the past, he had maintained an interest in it and had participated in various community causes, including the United Jewish Appeal, the United Israel Appeal, and the Hebrew University. While he was governor, however, his responsibilities had precluded closer identification. Now, that had changed, and he was free to immerse himself actively in Jewish causes; in short order, his calendar was filled with events in the Ottawa community. For their part, the capital's Jews honoured him.

In mid-1981, he gave testimony at a dinner for Chief Justice Bora Laskin to establish a chair in science teaching at the Weizmann Institute. Laskin, Rasminsky reminded his audience, had 'enriched our lives and given us all additional reason for taking pride in being Canadians and those of us who are Jewish, additional reason for taking pride in being Jews.'[4] Later that year, he was persuaded by Teddy Kolleck, mayor of Jerusalem, to sit as a Canadian board member of the Jerusalem Foundation, which provided funds devoted to improving the quality of life in that city. In 1983, there was a singular honour awarded him by the Canadian Association of the Ben-Gurion University of the Negev. Rasminsky had long been a supporter of Ben-Gurion and also of the Canadian Association, and the Ottawa branch asked if he would allow the association to use his name in its first fund-raising attempt. A special tribute dinner was held at the Château Laurier Hotel, with the objective of raising money to sustain the Louis Rasminsky Social Integration Endowment Fund. Word went out via his old friend Hy Soloway that charitable donations would be accepted and a dinner offered to celebrate Louis Rasminsky. The fund, capitalized at $300,000, was the first major undertaking for the newly established Ottawa link in a growing chain of Ben-Gurion associate organizations abroad. Almost two-thirds of that amount was raised the evening of 13 October, a result of donations by those attending the dinner. The list read like a who's who of Canadian finance – members of Parliament and senior civil servants, as well as a message sent by the prime minister. Ras-

minsky's stock remained high, even ten years after his retirement from
the Bank.

The income from the fund would be put to good use. When the university had suggested that it be directed towards ameliorating the condition
of Sephardic Jews, Rasminsky could only agree. Israel's ambassador to
Canada, Yaacov Avnon, had expressed some surprise at that; would not
research in some financial or economic subject be closer to Rasminsky's
heart? No – the decision 'to have the money used in specific action programs that were aimed at increasing the capacity of the less privileged sections of the population of the Negev (who tend to be the children of
immigrants from North Africa and the Arab countries) to make a positive
contribution to the community, to become part of the main-stream of
Israel's life and to do so without losing any of their pride in their
Sephardic origins' was very important to him.[5]

His choice 'was perhaps instinctive' and reflected the combination of
his Jewish heritage with some aspects of his Canadian life experience. He
told the dinner crowd: 'The Hebrew word for benevolence the giving of
charitable help is *Tzadakah*. In a way this is curious, since the root word
Tzadakah means a righteous man and the literal translation of *Tzadik* is
righteousness – doing what is right, doing good deeds, doing *Maasim
Tovim* and under Jewish tradition the most meritorious form of giving is
to give in a way that enables the recipient to become self-supporting so
that he does not continue to be dependent on you and risk losing his self-
respect. The programme to be financed by this Fund is to be based on
these principles.'[6] For the first number of years, the fund's resources were
directed towards helping Ethiopian youngsters by tutoring them in the
elementary schools of Beer Sheva. As well, they supported 'open apart-
ments' in Ethiopian housing projects in Beer Sheva, which were provided
rent-free to students who acted as counsellors, friends, social activists,
groups leaders, and role models for everyone in their neighbourhoods.

There was also one last task asked of him and his old friend William
Lawson in 1984 by the government of Canada. Michael Wilson, the minister of finance, inquired if they would investigate the advantages and disadvantages of initiatives to encourage development of Canada as an
international banking centre, then a serious topic in the federal government. In particular, the Conservatives were keen to attract Eurodollar
deposits to Canada. The report effectively finished off the idea; 'Neither
the costs nor the benefits of an initiative of this kind would be great,' it
said.[7] The government took the two men's advice.

That same year, following Laskin's death, Rasminsky agreed to act as honorary national chairman of the Bora Laskin Endowed Scholarship Fund of Yeshiva University, which hoped to raise $3 million in a national campaign to support Canadian students attending Yeshiva University in New York. The following year, he accepted an invitation to be honorary chairman of the Canadian Gathering of Jewish Holocaust Survivors and Their Children held in Ottawa. His address at the closing plenary session clearly expressed his anger and his sorrow, even forty years later, about what had happened to Jews in Europe. As he said, 'These past few days have been full of emotion, full of tears, as we thought of the six million Jews – two-thirds of the Jewish population of Europe – who were brutally and wantonly murdered in the Holocaust after first being put through unspeakably terrible suffering.'[8] His prominence in the Jewish community was such that for 1988 he was awarded the Past Chairmen's Award, presented annually to a member of the public service who had demonstrated exceptional service to Canada and to the Jewish community. That same year, he was made an honourary doctor of laws from Carleton University.

The pace slowed considerably over the past decade. The ailment that first affected him in Geneva some sixty years ago – spasmodic torticollis – continued to cause him some difficulty. A fracture of his spine some years ago affected his posture. In late 1996, he fell and fractured a hip. As throughout his career when confronted with a problem, he refused to accept defeat. What he now lacked in a physical sense was made up for by an alert and penetrating mind. Intellectual exercise was provided at weekly luncheon meetings at the Rideau Club of the Round Table, where twenty or twenty-five members gathered to discuss issues of public policy. Another group, which Rasminsky nicknamed 'The Sanhedrin,' fell into the habit of having lunch together at Le Cercle Universitaire d'Ottawa on Fridays, with no fixed agenda but also no lack of lively conversation. Another way in which Rasminsky kept in touch with the outside world was through his membership of more than fifty years in the Five Lakes Club, situated in the Gatineau Hills, an hour's drive from Ottawa. According to Rasminsky, when one reached the gravel road leading to the club, one left all cares behind.

His ability to maintain so active a social life in spite of his physical disabilities was truly remarkable. He said that it was largely the result of the encouragement that he received from his special friend, the artist Jerry Grey. His children, Michael (and Michael's wife, Judy Sklar) and Lola, were very supportive. Rasminsky clearly took great pride in them and in the promise shown by his grandchildren, Sonya and Abigail Rasminsky and Jonathan and Jeremy Weisstub.

On 1 February 1998, Rasminsky celebrated his ninetieth birthday while wintering at Longboat Key in Florida. His family, always close-knit, was there to participate, flying in from Canada (and in Abigail's case, from Mexico). As well, a number of long-time friends attended. Son Michael wrote a poem for the occasion, which reads in part:

> The statiticians have their ways
> Of naming aberrations,
> The far side of the bell curve that
> Confounds all expectations.
> Outliers that make their homes
> Beyond four standard deviations.
> And we are here to tell you why
> All these terms to Lou apply.
>
> Actuarially he's defied the odds
> And with indexation,
> The Bank of Canada pension fund
> Is demanding reparations.
> We hope he'll continue to break the bank –
> He's indifferent to inflation.
> A few years of this and don't you know,
> Not a penny left for Bouey and Crow.
> Our nonagenarian non-Alzheimarian,
> Never Rotarian or Rastafarian,
> Nonagenarian, soon centenarian Pa.

When he looked back over a life lived to the fullest, he must have felt a certain amount of satisfaction. He combined a loving and fulfilling home life with a professional life that was as varied as it was interesting. He was at the centre of some of the big issues of the 1930s and had a view of international affairs that was accorded very few other Canadians. His time in Geneva conditioned his perspective on problems that he encountered later in his life. For example, his conception of the International Monetary Fund reflected his concern over the unemployment that he had witnessed in the 1930s. Exchange stability would help to ensure the economic conditions vital to full employment. If at the end of the Second World War the view was a little too rosy, it does not diminish the strength of his commitment. In pursuit of that objective in the Fund negotiations, he sparred with some of the great intellects of the day, such as John Maynard Keynes and Harry White, and gained their respect. He was a Canadian first, but also always an internationalist. As he had learned at the League, and helped to put into practice during the war, international cooperation was necessary if the world were to live in peace.

At the same time, he was part of a seismic shift in attitudes in Ottawa, as government became more active in Canadian life, attempting to ensure that the conditions of the 1930s would not repeat themselves. His work at the Foreign Exchange Control Board was a reflection of that approach. It was only one of many wartime organizations designed to regulate the Canadian economy. He spent the war infringing, some might say, a basic right – but it was necessary to the war effort, and Canadians accepted the necessity of foreign-exchange control. A member of the small circle that comprised Ottawa's bureaucratic elite in the 1940s and 1950s, he also worked on other committees, both during the war and afterward, that saw regulation as a benefit. What worked internationally would work nationally.

The 1950s saw that agenda pushed ahead, with Rasminsky part of the movement. The decade was also, however, disappointing, at least in terms of his objective of becoming governor of the Bank. He wanted that job, but Jews, it seemed, were not viewed as appropriate at the top of that institution. Despite his formidable intelligence, his unparalleled network of international contacts, and his wide grasp of the intricacies of national and international finance, he was passed over as governor. Merit alone was not sufficient. However, he accomplished much with the Americans and the British and at the International Monetary Fund. And his time as governor came soon enough. Despite the disappointment of 1955, he was offered the job six years later, albeit under very difficult conditions. With his characteristic commitment, he made a success of that, too, and the Bank only benefited. His was an inspired appointment in 1961, and it represented the high point of a very long road that he had travelled against the odds.

Notes

CHAPTER 1   Montreal, Toronto, London

1 Gerald Tulchinsky, *Taking Root: The Origins of the Canadian Jewish Community* (Toronto: Lester Publishing, 1992), 231.
2 Bank of Canada Archives (hereafter BCA), Ottawa, Louis Rasminsky (hereafter LR) Personal Papers (hereafter PP). The Rasminsky Papers include letters, indicated below as, e.g., LR 84-31-5-2, Goldman to LR, 27 Oct. 1927. For a brief discussion of Zionism and how it affected the Canadian Jewish community (and also the Reform bent that characterized much of American Jewry), see Gerald Tulchinsky, 'The Contours of Canadian Jewish History,' in Robert J. Brym, William Shaffir, and Morton Weinfeld, eds., *The Jews in Canada* (Toronto: Oxford University Press, 1993), 5–21.
3 LR interview, June 1994. The idea of Zionism was also one against which most American Jews were ranged, given that it also demanded allegiance to a Jewish homeland.
4 LR PP, Harbord Collegiate Institute, Toronto, 'Term Report,' autumn 1924.
5 Ibid., Lionel Gelber to LR, 4 Sept. 1925.
6 Ibid., W.W. Pearse to LR, 16 Dec. 1925.
7 LR, ed., *Hadassah Jubilee* (Toronto: Toronto Hadassah Council, 1928), 177.
8 Ibid., 172.
9 LR PP, Bladen to LR, 11 June 1926.
10 LR interview, 5 Aug. 1997.
11 Vincent Bladen, *Bladen on Bladen: Memoirs of a Political Economist* (Toronto: Scarborough College in the University of Toronto, 1978), 42–3.
12 J.L. Granatstein, 'The Road to Bretton Woods: International Monetary Policy and the Public Servant,' *Journal of Canadian Studies* 16 (1981), 172.
13 For an account of Jackson's role in this area, see Ian M. Drummond with Wil-

liam Kaplan, *Political Economy at the University of Toronto: A History of the Department, 1888–1982* (Toronto: Faculty of Arts and Science, 1983), 69. Drummond suggests that this was almost part of Jackson's job, to try to find suitable places for some students, mainly from the commerce side of the department: 'Gilbert Jackson worked hard and knowledgeably at the task of supervising and placing the Commerce students ... He knew the capabilities of each man in the graduating class, and carefully considered where these men could best be placed.'

14 Allyn Young, *Economic Problems New and Old* (Boston: Houghton Mifflin, 1927). Some of the essay titles give a sense of what would fascinate Rasminsky – War Debts, External and Internal; The Structure and Policies of the Federal Reserve System; The Concentration of Wealth and Its Meaning; and The Trend of Economics as Seen by Some American Economists. The last, especially, evinced an iconoclastic spirit – '"It will be said, I suppose," Professor Tugwell observes in his Introduction, "that this book is a sort of manifesto of the younger generation; and in a sense it is that"' (232).

15 The course description comes from London School of Economics, *Calendar, 1928–29*. My thanks to one of University of Toronto Press's readers for mention of those calendars. The description of the course taught by Robbins in which Rasminsky participated read: 'The nature and significance of Economic Science. General conditions of Economic activity. Production and Distribution in an exchange economy. The legal framework of modern economic activity. Economic functions of states. Inter-local and international differences of productiveness.' Rasminsky also participated in the Robbins seminar, 'Economic Theory,' where admission was strictly by permission of the professor.

16 University of Toronto Archives, Department of Political Economy Records, vol. 7, 1929 file, LR to Innis, 26 Jan. 1929. My thanks to Jack Granatstein for this reference.

17 Ralf Dahrendorf, *LSE: A History of the London School of Economics and Political Science, 1895–1995* (Oxford: Oxford University Press, 1995), 187. Rasminsky would have also agreed with the Countess of Listowel (née Judith Marffy-Mantuano) that professors at LSE taught one 'to bury one's prejudices in order to find the causes of things' and 'that intolerance was both narrow-minded and uncivilized,' and 'they actively discouraged proselytizing.' 'I learnt that statements have to be based on facts, and I was taught how and where to look for them' (189).

18 LR interview, 28 July 1997.

CHAPTER 2 Geneva and the League of Nations

1 Wilfred Jenks, legal adviser of the International Labour Office, said that

among a number of special qualifications needed by members of an international staff, first was 'a distinctively international outlook.' Jenks also listed the qualities required of international officials, with which Rasminsky would have agreed – 'integrity, conviction, courage, imagination, drive and technical grasp.' See Egon F. Ranshoffen-Wertheimer, *The International Secretariat: A Great Experiment in International Administration* (Washington, DC: Carnegie Endowment for International Peace, 1945), 243.

2 Per Jacobsson, later managing director of the International Monetary Fund, wrote of Alexander Loveday when he first met him in 1920 that he was 'theoretically schooled and knowledgeable, very hard-working but a little pedantic as statisticians easily are.' See Erin E. Jacobsson, *A Life for Sound Money: Per Jacobsson, His Biography* (Oxford: Clarendon Press, 1979), 36.

3 LR interview, 10 May 1994. However, Rasminsky was never perfectly fluent in French.

4 LR PP, Gelber to LR, 9 March 1930.

5 LR PP, University of Toronto Correspondence, Jackson to LR, 13 Dec. 1930.

6 Ibid., Mackenzie to LR, 24 March 1930.

7 Ibid., Kennedy to LR, 17 July 1930.

8 LR interview. See also J.L. Granatstein, 'The Road to Bretton Woods: International Monetary Policy and the Public Servant,' *Journal of Canadian Studies* 16 (1981), 175.

9 Ranshofen-Wertheimer, *Secretariat*, 113; for a brief discussion of all the activities of the department, as well as its numbers, see 111–15.

10 League of Nations Archives (hereafter LNA), Geneva, file R.4383, Stencek to Abraham, 14 Feb. 1933.

11 Ranshofen-Wertheimer, *Secretariat*, 115.

12 Granatstein, 'The Road to Bretton Woods,' 174.

13 LR84-31-5-2, 'Memorandum on the League of Nations Economic Intelligence Work,' n.d.

14 Ranshoffen-Wertheimer, *Secretariat*, ix.

15 League of Nations, *The Course and Phases of the World Economic Depression* (Geneva: Secretariat of the League of Nations, 1931), 7; emphasis added.

16 LR PP, 'A Very Personal Piece' (hereafter AVPP), unpublished manuscript, 9.

17 LR PP, Kaldor to LR, 16 Aug. 1930.

18 Edward J. Nell and Willi Semmler, eds., *Nicholas Kalder and Mainstream Economics: Confrontation or Convergence?* (London: Macmillan, 1991), 13.

19 LR83-827, Kaldor to LR, 10 Oct. 1933.

20 Alfred E. Eckes, *A Search for Solvency: Bretton Woods and the International Monetary System, 1941–1971* (Austin, Tex.: University of Texas Press, 1975), 171.

21 Jacob Viner, as quoted in J. Keith Horsefield, *The International Monetary Fund,*

1945–1965: Twenty Years of International Monetary Cooperation, vol. I, *Chronicle* (Washington, DC: International Monetary Fund, 1969), 17. Viner went on to suggest 'a modified gold standard, under which, to prevent world-wide inflation or deflation, and also to permit orderly adjustment when needed of the exchange-parities of particular countries, changes in the monetary value of gold for at least the major countries would be permitted – or perhaps ordered – by an international body operating under general rules embodied in an international agreement.'

22 LR PP, LR to Lyla, 27 June 1939. LR interview, 10 May 1994.

23 John English, *Shadow of Heaven: The Life of Lester Pearson, 1892–1948*, vol. I (Toronto: Lester and Orpen Dennys, 1989), 177.

24 LR, AVPP, 3.

25 R.S. Sayers, *The Bank of England, 1891–1944* (Cambridge: Cambridge University Press, 1976), 350; on the establishment of the Gold Delegation, see 346–51. See also Erin Jacobsson, *A Life*, 39–46.

26 Sayers, *Bank*, 351.

27 LR PP, LR to Lyla, 1932.

28 LNA, 4635–1.32-1000, 'Copy of Certificate as to Grant of Annual Leave, 27 July 1932.'

29 LR, AVPP, 6. Pittman was chair of the US Senate Foreign Relations Committee and a man of some power in Washington. Hugh Brogan, in his delightful history of the United States, has this to say about him: '[Pittman] cared for nothing but the silver lobby: among his other disqualifications for the job was his habit of drinking himself into a stupor.' Hugh Brogan, *The Penguin History of the United States of America* (London: Penguin Books, 1985), 573–4.

30 LR84-17, Robertson to LR, 11 Aug. 1933. During the next examination of Canadian banking and finance, in 1962 and 1963 – the Royal Commission on Banking and Finance – Rasminsky testified as governor of the institution that the Macmillan Commission had recommended be established.

31 LR PP, Gelber to LR, 7 Aug. 1933.

32 LR83-883, Clark to LR, 5 Nov. 1933.

33 National Archives of Canada (hereafter NA), W.L. Grant Papers, vol. 9, O.D. Skelton to Grant, 3 Feb. 1934. My thanks to Jack Granatstein for the reference to this document.

34 LR PP, MacDonald to LR, 11 April 1935.

35 LR83-885, LR to Clark, 11 July 1934.

36 LR84-805, E.J. Urwick to LR, 7 Jan. 1932. None the less, Rasminsky is not mentioned as a possible candidate for a position; Ian Drummond with William Kaplan, *Political Economy at the University of Toronto: A History of the Department,*

1888–1982 (Toronto: University of Toronto Faculty of Arts and Science, 1983). Many other names were.

37 LR PP, Jackson to LR, 25 Oct. 1933. Jackson left the department for the Bank of England in 1935.

38 Ibid., MacGregor to LR, 21 Feb. 1934. However, Drummond suggests that a slightly different spirit animated the department; see *Political Economy,* 73–8.

39 LR PP, Laski to LR, 29 Nov. 1931.

40 Irving Abella, *A Coat of Many Colours: Two Centuries of Jewish Life in Canada* (Toronto: Lester and Orpen Dennys, 1990), 180. For a discussion of anti-semitism in Canada during the 1930s, see Irving Abella and Harold Troper, *None Is Too Many: Canada and the Jews of Europe, 1933–1948* (Toronto: Lester and Orpen Dennys, 1982); Lita-Rose Betcherman, *The Swastika and the Maple Leaf* (Toronto: Fitzhenry and Whiteside, 1975); David Rome, *Clouds in the Thirties: On Antisemitism in Canada, 1929–1939* (Montreal: Canadian Jewish Congress, 1977); and Arnold Ages, 'Antisemitism: The Uneasy Calm,' in Morton Weinfeld, William Shaffir, and Irwin Cotler, eds., *The Canadian Jewish Mosaic* (Toronto: Wiley, 1981), 383–95.

41 NA, W.L. Grant Papers, vol. 9, O.D. Skelton to Grant, 3 Feb. 1934.

42 Gerald Tulchinsky, *Taking Root: The Origins of the Canadian Jewish Community* (Toronto: Lester Publishing, 1992), 240.

43 See Cyril Levitt and William Shaffir, 'The Swastika as Dramatic Symbol: A Case-Study of Ethnic Violence in Canada,' in Robert J. Brym, William Shaffir, and Morton Weinfeld, eds., *The Jews in Canada* (Toronto: Oxford University Press, 1993), 80.

44 Toronto *Globe and Mail,* 17 Aug. 1933, 1. See also Cyril Levitt and William Shaffir, *The Riot at Christie Pits* (Toronto, 1987), 84–93.

45 Abella, *Coat,* 183.

46 LR PP, LR to Jackson, 15 Sept. 1932. Rasminsky's complaint is given credibility in Erin Jacobsson's biography of his father: 'There was an endless succession of meetings, technical committees of all kinds, of which the general public was unaware; but the political meetings of the Council, whether regular meetings or emergency sessions, drew journalists from all over the world. So did the Assembly, which was held in Sept. ... It commanded headlines around the world.'

47 The League of Nations Society was not very successful in Canada. As was noted by the League, 'The Canadian agency's activity ... is far from satisfactory ... Payments from Canada being very irregular and referring in the first place to subscriptions for the Monthly Summary, it is difficult to establish a comparison between this agency's activity and others. It may be said, however, that, as compared with India, China or Japan, the results are far from

satisfactory.' LNA, file R.5763, Publications and Printing Service, League of Nations, 9 June 1931.

48 LNA, 8A/31989/298, R.6013, LR to Loveday, 7 Oct. 1939.
49 LR PP, LR to Lyla, Jan. 1936.
50 Ibid.
51 Ibid.
52 Ibid.
53 Ibid.
54 LR PP, Wise to LR, 27 Oct. 1933.
55 LR83-829, Tirana to LR, Aug. 1937.
56 LR76-830, Condliffe to LR, 23 July 1937. The Italian question resulted in the recall of Canada's delegate to the League, Walter Riddell. His firm support of sanctions alarmed the prime minister, William Lyon Mackenzie King, who preferred to do nothing.
57 LR83-829, Tirana to LR, Aug. 1937.
58 LR PP, Rosamond Tirana to Lyla, 26 Sept. 1937.
59 LNA, 4635-1.36-1000, 'Copy of Certificate as to Grant of Annual Increment,' 23 July 1936.
60 See English, *Shadow of Heaven*, vol. I, 274–5.
61 LR PP, Warriner to Astor, 15 Sept. 1936.
62 LR84-15B, *Observer*, 2 Aug. 1936.
63 LR interview, 14 May 1994; LR, AVPP, 10.
64 LR84-15B, LN Information Section, 'The Food of the World,' 23 July 1936.
65 Ibid., *The Times*, 24 July 1936.
66 LNA, 4635-1.36-1000, 'Copy of Certificate as to Grant of Annual Increment,' 23 July 1936.
67 LR PP, Macdougall to LR, 10 July 1936.
68 Ibid., LR to Loveday, 30 July 1936.
69 LR84-15D, LR, 'The League and World Affairs.'
70 LR84-15, LR to Charron, 13 Nov. 1936.
71 Ibid., LR to Charron, 14 Nov. 1936.
72 Ibid., Charron to LR, 21 Nov. 1936.
73 Ibid., LR to Macdougall, 29 Dec. 1936.
74 Ibid., 'The League and World Affairs.'
75 Ibid., LR, 'Attitudes towards Meeting,' Dec. 1936.
76 Ibid., LR to Loveday, Memorandum, n.d.
77 *New York Times*, 4 Sept. 1937.
78 *New Statesman*, 4 Sept. 1937.
79 *The Times*, 2 Sept. 1937.
80 LR84-15, F.L. Macdougall, 'The Problem of Nutrition,' 1937. Queille, the French representative, also wanted wine included on the list of protective

foods. While he was eventually outvoted, he put up a stiff fight over an extended period. Rasminsky later wrote that 'had I shown the proper qualities of leadership, I would have suggested as a compromise that wine be classified as a "protective" foodstuff, provided it was of good quality, complemented the food with which it was consumed, and was served at the appropriate temperature.' LR, AVPP, 10.

81 LR76-15-1, 'Rep on the Nutrition of the Infant and Young Child,' 1938, 3.
82 LNA, 4635-1.37-1000, 'Copy of Certificate as to Grant of Annual Increment, 9 July 1937.'
83 LR76-827, Joseph to LR, 8 July 1937.
84 The list of those attending included Argentina, Bolivia, Brazil, Chile, Colombia, Cuba, Ecuador, Guatemala, Honduras, Mexico, Paraguay, Peru, the United States, Uruguay, and Venezuela. Also the Pan-American Health Office and the ILO sent observers.
85 LR84-17, Charron to LR, 11 Sept. 1939. See also LNA, R.4605, Charron to LR, 22 Sept. 1939: 'Knowing you as Love[day] and I do, we have no doubt whatever that you will make as big a success of the [mission] as anyone could in similar circumstances.'
86 LNA, 8A/31989/298, R.6013, Loveday to LR, 6 March 1940.
87 Abella and Troper, *None Is Too Many*, 3.
88 LR PP, 14 April 1939.
89 Ibid., LR to Lyla, 17 April 1939.
90 Ibid., LR to Lyla, 21 May 1939.
91 Ibid., LR to Lyla, 1 Aug. 1939.
92 LNA, Internal Circular 39.1939, Geneva, 20 April 1939.
93 LR PP, LR to Lyla, 11 May 1939.
94 Ibid.
95 Ibid., LR to Lyla, 30 April 1939. Distaste for Avenol ran deep at the League. Rasminsky told Lyla that Egon Wertheimer, another League employee and later author of a book commissioned by the Carnegie Endowment for International Peace, *The International Secretariat: A Great Experiment in International Administration* (Washington, DC: Carnegie Endowment for International Peace, 1945), had walked with Rasminsky for an hour, 'hating Avenol.' James Meade, the eminent British economist, was also furious with the secretary general. He noted: 'The more one hears of the S.G.'s little tricks, the more discouraging the outlook becomes.' Similarly, Rasminsky felt that there was a lack of leadership at the League among *all* top officials. He wrote: 'It is no wonder the League is where it is when its top officials are so utterly lacking in imagination and constructive ideas to say nothing of political judgement.' LR PP, LR to Lyla, 8 May 1939.
96 LR PP, LR to Lyla, 21 June 1939.

97 Ibid., LR to Lyla, 15 July 1939.
98 Ibid., LR to Lyla, 18 July 1939.
99 Ibid., LR to Lyla, 30 July 1939. Ranshoffen-Wertheimer records a similar impression. 'I remember walking to the new *Palais des Nations* early one afternoon with a friend ... It must have been 1938 or 1939. The day was dreary, the sky was overhung with a bleak veil and the work to which we were returning had assumed, in consequence of the deterioration of the international situation, an air of unreality. The road was uphill and we walked slowly. As we approached the Park Ariana, the *Palais des Nations* stood before us, monumental and as if erected for eternity. A solitary ray of sunlight was reflected on the marble walls of the Assembly building. I felt depressed, unwilling to work, possessed by a feeling of futility of my personal contribution in a world that was disintegrating.' Ranshoffen-Wertheimer, *Secretariat*, xi.
100 LR PP, LR to Lyla, 31 May 1939.
101 LR76-6-6, Memo by LR, 1939.
102 For the Brussels and Genoa conferences, see Sayers, *Bank of England*, 153–63, and, on the 1933 meeting, 453–7.
103 See, for example, LR84-6, Delegation on Economic Depresssions, 'Synthesis of Discussion at First Session on Recovery Policy, 30 Nov. 1938.' See also LNA, R.4605, LR to the Secretary General, 26 July 1939.
104 LNA, R.4650, Loveday to Secretary General, 25 July 1939.
105 LR 76-6-18, LR to Loveday, 30 May 1942.
106 LR76-6-6-3, Clark to LR, 6 Aug. 1941; Robertson to LR, 13 Aug. 1941.
107 LR PP, LR to Lyla, 24 June 1939.
108 LNA, 4635-1.39-1000, 'Copy of Certificate as to Grant of Annual Increment,' 26 Oct. 1939.
109 LR PP, LR to Lyla, 12 June 1939.
110 LR84-31-15-1, Loveday to LR, 25 Nov. 1939.
111 LNA, 8A/31989/298, R.6013, LR to Loveday, 7 Oct. 1939.
112 LR83-26, LR to Tirana, 4 Nov. 1939.
103 LR84-28, 'Report on Bolivian Mission,' 29 Dec. 1939.
104 LR84-31-17-3, LR to Loveday, 27 Nov. 1939.
115 LNA, LR to Loveday, 7 Oct. 1939.
116 LR84-31-24-1, Margery Pickett to LR, 6 Feb. 1940.
117 LR76-11-20, translation of LR's opening address.
118 LR84-31-17-4, LR to Loveday, 27 Nov. 1939. Loveday replied that he was 'not quite certain whether you do not attach too much importance to competence and work.' LR84-31-20-1, Loveday to LR, 16 Dec. 1939.
119 LR to Loveday, 27 Nov. 1939.
120 Ibid.

121 LNA, 10c/39921/2057, R.4590, LR to Deperon, 20 April 1940.

122 LR PP, LR to Lyla, June 1940.

123 LR76-11-15, LR to Carroll, 27 May 1940.

124 LNA, 10c/39921/2057, R.4590, Carroll to Loveday, 25 June 1940.

125 Ibid., LR to Deperon, 22 June 1940.

126 LR76-11-19, LR to Loveday, 30 Sept. 1940.

127 LR76-11-17, LR to Wrong, 20 April 1943.

128 LNA, LR to Loveday, 7 Oct. 1939.

129 LR76-16, Hilgerdt to LR, 14 March 1940.

130 LR84-31-26-1, LR to Loveday, 21 Feb. 1940.

131 LR84-31-26-2, LR to Loveday, 25 Feb. 1940.

132 LR84-31, Loveday to LR, 26 Feb. 1940.

133 LR84-31-3D, LR to Loveday, 26 Feb. 1940.

132 LR84-31-29, Loveday to LR, 6 March 1940.

135 LR83-143, LR to Loveday, 30 May 1940.

136 LR84-31, Loveday to LR, 9 July 1940.

137 LR84-31-31-1, Loveday to LR, 7 March 1940.

138 *New York Times*, 16 July 1940.

139 LR84-31, LR to Loveday, 26 July 1940.

140 LR84-31-43, A.S. to LR, 26 July 1940.

141 LR76-12, Loveday to LR, 21 Feb. 1941.

142 LR PP, Dec. 1942.

143 LR76-156-19, LR, 'Notes on Mr. Thompson-McCausland's Memorandum on Post-War Planning and Balance of Payments,' Aug. 1942.

144 LR PP, 6 July 1942.

145 Ibid., Lester to LR, 3 July 1943.

146 LR84-31, Loveday to LR, 28 June 1943.

CHAPTER 3   Ottawa and Wartime Controls

1 Much of the following comes from BCA, Rasminsky Papers, Sidney Turk, 'The Establishment of Foreign Exchange Control in Canada,' n.d. However, there are a number of sources that deal with Canada's situation and the operations of the FECB. See, for example, A.F.W. Plumptre, *Three Decades of Decision: Canada and the World Monetary System, 1944–1975* (Toronto: McClelland and Stewart, 1977), 90–4, and A.O. Gibbons, 'Foreign Exchange Control in Canada, 1939–1951,' *Canadian Journal of Political Science and Economics* 19 (1953), 35–54. For an account of the more gradual imposition of British exchange control, see R.S. Sayers, *Financial Policy, 1939–1945* (London: Longmans Green, 1956), 226–51.

2 R.D. Cuff and J.L. Granatstein, *Ties That Bind: Canadian–American Relations in Wartime from the Great War to the Cold War* (Toronto: Samuel Stevens Hakkert, 1977), 74.

3 LR76-150-74A-1, J.E. Coyne, 'Conservation of Exchange,' 8 Jan. 1941.

4 BCA, Graham Towers Papers (GTP), GFT75-8, Towers to Ilsley, 23 July 1940. See Sayers, *Financial Policy,* 321–62, for a discussion of Anglo–Canadian wartime financial and commercial relations. See also J.L. Granatstein, *Canada's War: The Politics of the Mackenzie King Government, 1939–1945* (Toronto: Oxford University Press, 1975).

5 Cuff and Granatstein, *Ties That Bind,* 74. For an analysis of the problem from the British side, see Sayers, *Financial Policy,* 323. 'These conditions underlying financial relations between Canada and Britain may be summarised as three lines of conflict. First, Britain sought from Canada supplies – eventually the utmost supplies – of men, munitions, materials and food, while Canada had to avoid over-burdening her economy to the point of disorganisation or the weakening of the will to war. Secondly, Britain had to minimise her payments in gold and US dollars, while Canada had to insist upon sufficient to pay her debts to the United States. Thirdly, Britain, keeping an eye on post-war problems, had to watch both the amount and the form of any residuary indebtedness, and was reluctant to part with all her investment connections in Canada, while Canada had to be careful lest her generosity left her too weak an economic neighbour for the United States after the war.'

6 Sayers, *Financial Policy,* 323.

7 Joseph Schull, *The Great Scot: A Biography of Donald Gordon* (Montreal: McGill-Queen's University Press, 1979), 39.

8 LR76-118-1, A.O. Gibbons, 'Foreign Exchange Control in Canada,' n.d.

9 LR76-179-14, R.H.Tarr, 'Post-War Control over Exports of Currency,' 16 Jan. 1945.

10 LR76-179-26, R. Lang, 'Examination of Mail,' 5 June 1945.

11 See LR76-128-28, Memorandum, 9 Jan. 1942.

12 LR76-173, Stone to LR, 7 Nov. 1940.

13 Ibid., LR to Stone, 13 Nov. 1940.

14 Ibid., Stone to LR, 23 Nov. 1940.

15 Ibid., LR to Stone, 5 Dec. 1940.

16 LR76-166, 'Special Border Permit,' 4 Dec. 1947.

17 LR76-127, LR to Gordon, 16 May 1941; emphasis added.

18 LR76-181-1, Kayalof to Turk, 15 Dec. 1951.

19 LR76-150, A.McD. McBain to M.W. Mackenzie, 16 April 1942.

20 For an account of the Hyde Park Agreement and its effect on Canada, see Cuff and Granatstein, *Ties That Bind,* 69–93.

21 LR76-165-6, LR to Coyne, 30 March 1943.
22 Plumptre, *Three Decades of Decision*, 67; Canada's year-end holdings (US$million) of gold and of US dollars were the following (p. 94):

Year's end (31 Dec.)	Gold	US dollars
1939	218.0	54.8
1940	136.5	172.8
1941	135.9	28.2
1942	154.9	88.0
1943	224.4	348.8
1944	293.9	506.2
1945	353.9	922.0

23 LR76-165-6, LR to Coyne, 30 March 1943.
24 LR76-142-7, Mackenzie to Bolton, 26 Nov. 1941.
25 LR76-142-34-2, LR to Ilsley, 4 July 1942.
26 Ibid.
27 NA, Department of Finance Records (hereafter DFR), vol. 3970, file 8-2-85, LR to Clark, 10 March 1943.
28 Ibid., LR to Clark, 10 March 1943.
29 Ibid., Acting Solicitor to the Treasury to Clark, 26 April 1943.
30 *Economist*, 18 Dec. 1943, 819. With respect to Mutual Aid, Robert Bryce of Finance told Rasminsky that it was 'somewhat clouded at the moment because of [the Australian's] reaction to the proposed article in the Mutual Aid agreement concerning the reaffirmation of the post-war international policy already undertaken in Article VII of the Lend-Lease agreements.' DFR, vol. 3970, file 8-2-85, Bryce to LR, 31 Jan. 1944.
31 LR76-160-5-3, Scott, Memorandum, 10 Sept. 1941.
32 LR76-16-5, LR, 'Price Ceiling,' 1941.
33 LR76-161, LR to Towers, 31 March 1942.
34 LR76-167, J.S. Lockie to LR, 5 Oct. 1944.
35 LR76-187-1, LR, 'Notes on Visit to Washington and New York, April 5–11, 1942.'
36 DFR, vol. 657, file 184-B, Seymour Harris, 'Conversation with Messers. Plumptre and Douglas ... ,' 23 Nov. 1942.
37 Ibid., LR to Donald Gordon, 1 Dec. 1942.
38 Ibid., Clark to LR, 4 Dec. 1942.
39 LR76-163-1, Gordon to LR, 9 March 1943.
40 LR76-109, LR, 'Notes for Discussion with Mr. Gordon,' 9 July 1941.
41 DFR, vol. 654, file 184, address, 'Report of FECB Study Group "B,"' 11 June 1942.

42 LR76-668A-32-1, LR to Lawson, 14 Feb. 1945.

43 LR76-179-1, LR, 'Outline of Study of Post-War Organization of FECB,' March 1944.

44 Canada, House of Commons *Debates*, 11 July 1944, 4737. Fred Rose, the Communist MP for Cartier, was eloquent in his denunciation of anti-semitism: 'Today's *Montreal Gazette* carries a very sad story. It told of 1,715,000 Jews who had been killed, exterminated, in gas chambers in upper Silesia. If some escaped being murdered are we supposed to say to them: Keep them out of this country. This is not humanity, this is cruelty. This question of refugees has been mixed up by certain political leaders with the problem of immigration. Certain papers are carrying cartoons on the subject. Here is a cartoon in *Le Moraliste*, Duplessis' sheet, showing Jews as did Streicher in the *Stürmer.* I think it is disgraceful ... Here is an article in the official organ of the Bloc Populaire, *Le Bloc*, of May 6, 1944. The article is headed "Canada, England's Garbage Dump," and ... gives its full front page to names of some of the refugees allowed into this country and makes sure to specify beside each name "Juif," "Juif," "Juif" – "Jew," "Jew," "Jew!" I am not a Christian myself, but that is un-Christian.' See Canada, House of Commons *Debates*, 3 July 1944, 4465.

Attacks on Rasminsky of an anti-semitic nature were renewed periodically throughout the rest of the decade, though they were not as overt. For example, between December 1947 and March 1948, Social Credit's Réal Caouette asked on a number of occasions what Rasminsky's nationality was. The third time was as obnoxious as the first: 'Is [Mr. Rasminsky] a Canadian by birth? If not, what is his country of origin?' See Canada, House of Commons *Debates*, 18 Dec. 1947, 441; 11 Feb. 1948, 1093; 24 March 1948, 2564.

45 Canada, House of Commons *Debates*, 11 July 1944, 4737–40.

46 LR PP, Michael Hicks, LR interview, 'Ottawa Decides, 1945–1971,' 1989.

CHAPTER 4   The Road to Bretton Woods

1 However, as Horsefield points out, from 1941 on there were many proposals in circulation for a postwar international economic and monetary mechanism. See J. Keith Horsefield, *The International Monetary Fund, 1945–1965: Twenty Years of International Monetary Cooperation*, vol. I, *Chronicle* (Washington, DC: International Monetary Fund, 1969), 16–18.

2 LR PP, 'Diary of 1942 Meetings,' Nov. 1942. Roy Harrod relates how, in the autumn of 1941, he had run into Keynes at the US Treasury. '"You must give up the bilateralist approach," I said, "and come down on the American side." "No," he said, "I must pursue both lines of thought ... *both*."' See Roy Harrod, *The Life of John Maynard Keynes* (New York: St Martin's Press, 1963), 527.

Not everyone in Britain took up the Keynes hymnbook. For example, perhaps as part of a bureaucratic 'turf war,' the Bank of England was neither pro-Keynes nor pro–Clearing Union. Siepmann was 'very deprecatory of Keynes who he says has influence because he has no administrative duties and has time to develop ideas which other people are too busy to tear apart.' As Rasminsky later reported of conversations at the Bank of England, 'The Governor and most other people in the Bank took a very dim view of the proposals for an International Clearing Union. The Governor and Siepmann were the most unequivocally opposed, and it seemed to me that their attitude was to some extent influenced by personal hostility to Keynes.' LR76-188-12-2, 'Report on Visit to London, October–November 1942.'

3 LR interview, 28 June 1994.
4 GTP, GFT, 75-10, Towers to Norman Robertson, 28 May 1942.
5 Bank of England Archives, London, Bank of England Records (hereafter BER), OV38/2, 50 cp=9, file L-11f, P.E.T. (42) 2nd Meeting, 'Post-War Economic Talks,' 26 Oct. 1942.
6 Harrod, *Keynes*, 541.
7 Ibid., 541–2.
8 LNA, file R.4605, LR, 'Report on Mission to England, July 12–24, 1939.'
9 LR, AVPP, 19.
10 DFR, vol. 3977, file E-3-1, LR, 'Meeting of Council on Foreign Economic Relations, New York,' 24 Jan. 1942.
11 Canadian Press report, 27 Oct. 1942.
12 BER, OV38/2-50 cp=9, P.E.T. (42) 1st Meeting, 'Post-War Economic Talks,' 23 Oct. 1942.
13 Ibid., 2nd Meeting, 26 Oct. 1942.
14 LR76-211-8-2, Memorandum for the Minister, 'Proposed Steps in the Future Discussion of the Clearing Union and Stabilization Fund Proposals,' June 1943.
15 LR PP, 'Diary of 1942 Meetings,' Nov. 1942.
16 He covered the gamut – for example, from asking Keynes about how the initial values of currencies were to be determined to expressing some misgivings about the proposal to make a charge of 1 per cent on excess credit balances. Always conscious of North American political realities, he pointed out with some understatement that the proposed charge 'might be a very difficult provision to explain to the United States Congress.' See BER, OV38/2-50, cp=9, 3rd Meeting, 27 Oct. 1942. According to Rasminsky, the Australians brought this argument to its most ludicrous conclusion. Roland Wilson of the Australian delegation insisted that 'if any country acquired a bancor balance in excess of its quota, it should be expelled from the Union!' LR76-188-19-12,

'Report of the Canadian Representatives at the Post-War Economic Talks Held in London between Oct. 23rd and Nov. 9th, 1942,' 9.

17 BER, OV 38/2-50, P.E.T. (42) 3rd Meeting, 'Post-War Economic Talks,' 27 Oct. 1942. The Australians were adamant about penalizing creditor countries. Their delegation proposed that any country that ran a consistent credit with the Clearing Union should be expelled.

18 J.L. Granatstein, 'The Road to Bretton Woods: International Monetary Policy and the Public Servant,' *Journal of Canadian Studies* 16 (1981), 178.

19 LR PP, 'Diary of 1942 Meetings,' Nov. 1942.

20 LR76-209-3, 'Report of the Canadian Representatives at the Post-War Economic Talks Held in London between Oct. 23–Nov. 9, 1942,' 5.

21 LR PP, 'Diary of 1942 Meetings,' Nov. 1942.

22 Ibid.

23 LR76-188-18-2, LR, 'Report on Visit to London, October–November 1942.' See also LR76-188-24, LR, 'Notes on Conversations at the Bank of England,' 11 Nov. 1942. See also Harrod, *Keynes*, 530, on the Bank of England.

24 LR PP, 'Diary of 1942 Meetings,' Nov. 1942.

25 Ibid., LR to Lyla, 6 Nov. 1942.

26 LR76-206-1-1, Harry White, 'Memorandum – A Stabilization Fund of the United and Associated Nations,' 16 Dec. 1942. This draft contained the scarce-currency clause which was so important later. Harrod, *Keynes*, 543–4.

27 LR76-206-2, 'Preliminary Draft of Proposal for a United and Associated Nations Stabilization Fund,' 24 Dec. 1942.

28 US National Archives (hereafter USNA), Washington, DC, Department of the Treasury Records (hereafter DTR), RG 56, box 8, H.D. White to Secretary Morgenthau, 'Lord Keynes' Plan for Post-War Monetary Control,' 11 Sept. 1942. For a brief comparison of the two plans, see Frederick A. Lutz, 'International Monetary Mechanisms: The Keynes and White Proposals,' Essays in International Finance, no. 1 (Princeton, NJ: International Finance Section, July 1943).

29 On this point, see Warren F. Kimball, *Churchill and Roosevelt: The Complete Correspondance*, vol. I, *Alliance Emerging, October 1933–November 1942* (Princeton, NJ: Princeton University Press, 1984), 3–10.

30 DFR, vol. 3977, file E-3-3, 'Anglo–American Antipathy,' discussions in Ottawa, 6 and 7 Feb. 1943. See also Harrod, *Keynes*, 539, and his description of 'the British,' whom he contrasts with 'the Americans.' Harrod's view can be described only as simplistic. See also Susan Howson and Donald Moggridge, eds., *The Wartime Diaries of Lionel Robbins and James Meade, 1943–1945* (London: Macmillan, 1990). Here, the diaries are peppered with references relating to the generally poor state of affairs between the Americans and the British. For

example, the entry for 15 June 1943 notes that Robbins 'asked [E.A. Golden-weiser, the statistical adviser to the US Federal Reserve Board] how he thought things were going. "I think Harry ... is doing very well and trying his hardest to be pleasant." ... I must have raised my eyebrows a trifle at this last, for he went on, "Of course Harry is the unpleasantest man in Washington"' (72). For 16 June, the diary records that Robbins met up with the Canadians, including Rasminsky, to consider the state of the June meetings: 'We discussed the present conference. I said that I could only explain it on two hypotheses – ineptitude or railroading; and that on the whole I was disposed to favour the former. It was interesting to see the eagerness with which they all pressed me to adhere to this view. "They're like this," said [Clifford] Clark, "and they'll never be any different. But there is no sinister intention. We know Harry very well." I am pretty clear that they are right' (73). However, the tone of the September–October meetings was better, at least according to James Meade.

See also Kimball, *Churchill and Roosevelt*, 10. As he writes, by mid-1943, at roughly the same time as the Robbins–Canadians conversation took place, the British were being forced by the Americans 'into the status of junior partner, a position that would inevitably tempt the United States to try to impose its own solutions to Anglo–American problems. In two such cases – British suppression of the rebellion against the Greek monarchy, and the negotiations over a postwar civil aviation agreement – correspondence ... indicates that both Churchill and Roosevelt came almost to the breaking point.' Certainly, that relationship had its ups and downs.

31 DFR, vol. 3977, file E-3-3, 'Anglo–American Antipathy.'
32 See LR76-207-1-3, Canadian Minister in the US to SSEA [Secretary of State for External Affairs], 12 March 1943. In speaking with Edward Bernstein about quotas and how they were to be set, A.F.W. Plumptre had ascertained the following: one of the factors influencing US officials about determination of quotas was the 'hard-headed attitude in Congressional and business circles which might demand that what each country could get out of the fund (indicated by its quota) should in some sense be proportioned to what it put in, and what it put in should be in proportion to what it was capable of putting in.' See also LR76-203-7, 'Excerpts from Survey US Press, Radio and Periodical Trends,' 19 April 1943. Even on this point, where the United States would clearly control the organization, the US conservative press was unhappy. The most common criticisms were that the United States must not play 'Uncle Sap' and that this was a further example of 'globaloney foolishness' – another plan for a world-wide New Deal. One or two extreme conservatives complained that the administration 'takes its guidance from London' and charged that the plan was not 'American' in character or purpose.

33 LR interview, 28 June 1994.
34 LR76-211-2-4, LR, 'United Nations Currency Stabilization and Clearing Fund,'
    24 March 1943.
35 LR76-207-2, 'Canada–United States Discussion of Stabilization Fund Propos-
    als, US Treasury,' 22 April 1943. This was Rasminsky's first exposure to Bern-
    stein, and, while their relationship was at first difficult, the two became life-
    long friends.
36 Bernstein interview, 16 Oct. 1994. As Bernstein later said, the fact that the IMF
    was located in Washington was meant to signify that the United States con-
    trolled the institution. At the meetings in Savannah, Georgia, in March 1946,
    Rasminsky wrote to his wife: '[The American] insistence on having the [head-
    quarters] site in Washington against the virtually unanimous wish of every
    other country' was a graphic demonstration of 'American domineeringness.'
    LR PP, LR to Lyla, 14 March 1946.
37 LR76-207-2, 'Canada–United States Discussion.'
38 Ibid., Meeting Thursday, 22 April 1943.
39 See LR76-207-18, Harry White to Clark, 1 Sept. 1943.
40 See LR76-207-3, 'Report on Discussion of US Stabilization Proposals, US
    Treasury, April 21–26, 1943,' 17 May 1943. This is also borne out by the Amer-
    ican record of the week of meetings. In a memorandum to Harry White sum-
    marizing the talks with the Canadians, the Americans agreed to give serious
    consideration to the following opinions expressed by Rasminsky, Mackintosh,
    Deutsch, and Plumptre: '1. That obligations of member countries should not
    form part of the Fund's assets; 2. That adjustment of exchange rates be made
    with the approval of less than four-fifths of the member votes during an initial,
    transitional period; 3. That provisions for basing voting power on creditor
    positions with respect to the Fund, as such, be substituted for the four-fifths
    voting requirements; 4. That reports to creditors be called for in circum-
    stances parallel to those applying to debtors; 5. That there be provision for a
    fixed amount of loans by each member country to the Fund that would
    become mandatory when the Fund needed the currency in question [a close
    approximation of the 1968 General Arrangements to Borrow and the later
    Special Drawing Rights]; 6. That the Fund be given larger resources than the
    minimum now contemplated, without proportionate increase in the drawing
    power of members; 7. That the devices for fixing exchange rates initially be
    explicitly made a matter of mutual agreement, and; 8. That the general pow-
    ers given in III(1) be explicitly made subject to the limitations of other
    sections.' See USNA, DTR, RG 56, box 21, file D4, no. 28, Memo to Mr.
    White, 20 May 1943. See also LR207-24, Henry Morgenthau to J.L. Ilsley,
    14 Sept. 1943.

41 BER, OV38/4/205, Washington to Foreign Office, 17 May 1943.

42 BER, OV38/4/261, cp=2, HCC to Secretary of State for Dominion Affairs, 11 June 1943.

43 BER, OV38/4/211, Foreign Office to Washington, 21 May 1943.

44 See United Kingdom, House of Lords *Debates*, 18 May 1943, 528–37.

45 DFR, vol. 3982, file M-1-7-4, Norman Robertson to W.C. Clark, 14 June 1943.

46 LR76-211-8, Memorandum for the Minister, 'Proposed Steps in the Future Discussion of the Clearing Union and Stabilization Fund Proposals,' 2 June 1943.

47 LR76-212-1-1, LR to Keynes, 3 June 1943. See also USNA, DTR, box 28, file: Comparison of White and Canadian Plans for an ISF, 'Memorandum of a Meeting on the International Stabilization Fund, Mr. White's Office,' 18 June 1943.

48 LR76-204-4, LR, 'Notes for Meeting on International Currency Plans,' 26 Aug. 1943.

49 BER, OV38/4/255, cp=2, Washington to Foreign Office, 8 June 1943; emphasis added.

50 LR76-222-29, Edward Bernstein to LR, 16 Sept. 1944. Bernstein echoed this sentiment, writing to Rasminsky: 'Banking opinion in New York has been firm against us from the start ... If we could get their support, or any other influential banking group, our chances [of getting the Bretton Woods Final Act passed by Congress] would be considerably improved ... There is so much respect for Canadian opinion in New York that it may be Mr. Towers and others could make an impression on the bankers.'

51 DFR, vol. 3982, file M-1-7-4, Secretary of State for Dominion Affairs to HCUK in Canada, 9 June 1943. The pressure on Ottawa not to publish the plan was intense. The British were clearly very concerned.

52 LR93 LR/Lyla 1943, LR to Lyla, 16 June 1943. See also USNA, DTR, box 28, file: Comparison of White and Canadian Plans for an ISF, 'Meetings,' 15 June 1943.

53 LR PP, LR to Lyla, 16 June 1943.

54 LR76-207-9, W.A. Mackintosh, 'Memorandum of a Meeting with Keynes,' 22 June 1943. See also Donald Moggridge, ed., *The Collected Writings of John Maynard Keynes*, vol. XXV, *Activities, 1940–1944, Shaping the Post-War World: The Clearing Union* (London: Macmillan, 1980), 298. Keynes wrote to D.H. Robertson: 'As you will have gathered from our telegram, we were much upset by the Canadian draft ... It all seems a great misfortune. The Canadian re-draft is, of course, a great improvement so far as it goes. All the changes are for the better and the drafting has been improved or made much clearer in many points of detail. But this makes one all the sorrier that it has been put in so definitely at this stage. For at a later date, and with some futher changes it might have been so easy for Canada to take a really decisive part of producing

a mediated scheme. As it is, they are wasting their ammunition. Really a most awful pity.'

55 The *Frankfurter Zeitung* of 29 July 1943 devoted a long article to the Canadian currency plan. See USNA, DTR, box 28, file: Comparison of White and Canadian Plans for an ISF, Memorandum from Mr. Ostrow to Mr. White, 'German Criticism of the Canadian and White Proposals for Currency Stabilization,' 20 Aug. 1943.

56 BER, OV38/4/273 cp=2, Washington to Foreign Office, 16 June 1943. See also LR76-212, Keynes to Rasminsky, 18 Sept. 1943. In London, Keynes told Mackintosh that 'a number of the Canadian points had been accepted.' See LR76-207-10-1, W.A. Mackintosh, 'Memorandum of Meeting at Treasury,' 23 June 1943. Lionel Robbins confided to his diary that, with respect to the reception that his plan had received, Rasminsky was 'somewhat sore and bewildered.' Howson and Moggridge, eds., *Diaries of Robbins and Meade*, 72.

57 LR PP, LR to Lyla, 18 June 1943.

58 Ibid., LR to Lyla, 16 June 1943.

59 LR76-208-1, Plumptre to Clark, 7 July 1943.

60 LR76-208-2, LR, 'Notes on Washington Conversations, Sept. 28–29.'

61 Ibid. See also LR76-212, Keynes to LR, 18 Sept. 1943.

62 BER, OV38/5/54, cp=2, Thompson-McCausland to Cobbold, 3 Oct. 1943. See also BER, OV38/6/189, cp=2, George Bolton, 'Memo,' 15 Dec. 1943. However, on 18 September 1943, Keynes had written to Rasminsky: 'The discussions [with White] are being thoroughly enjoyed.' Howson and Moggridge, eds., *Diaries of Robbins and Meade*, 340.

63 However, Keynes had those not entirely in agreement with him on his side. In writing to Cobbold, Thompson-McCausland noted: 'Monday's meeting produced nothing but another agendaless debating session without any opportunity for previous discussion on our side. As we have made it a point of discipline from the beginning not to disagree before the Americans, the result was that views were put forward [by Keynes] with which many of us did not feel at all happy ... I was given the not altogether enviable job of conveying to Keynes the general view of the rest of the delegation that a new approach was needed. The result was a tour de force of which few but Keynes would be capable.' See BER, OV38/5/73, cp=3,Thompson-McCausland to Cobbold, 10 Oct. 1943.

See also BER 38/5, 54, cp=2, Thompson-McCausland to Cobbold, 3 Oct. 1943. Harrod views the Keynes–White relationship differently. He suggests that it was a good one, with Keynes writing that White 'was a constructive mind.' Harrod, *Keynes*, 507. When Henry Morgenthau, secretary of the US Treasury, later told Harrod that Keynes 'was the best emissary [the British] could have chosen ... [and that] his sharp repartees were good rather than bad for personal relationships,' he must be misremembering. Harrod, *Keynes*, 508.

64 Harrod, *Keynes*, 559.

65 Howson and Moggridge, eds., *Diaries of Robbins and Meade*, 139.

66 USNA, DTR, box 21, file: Conferences in Mr. White's Office, 1943, D4, no. 28, 'Meeting in Mr. White's Office, Sept. 15, 1943.'

67 BER, OV38/5/73, cp=3, Thompson-McClausand to Cobbold, 10 Oct. 1943.

68 Canada, House of Commons Standing Committee on Banking and Commerce, Bill No. 238, *Minutes of Proceedings and Evidence*, 11 Dec. 1945, 6. Rasminsky's turn of phrase here – 'disagreement' – is revealing of the difficulties encountered.

69 The reason for the Bretton Woods location, according to Edward Bernstein, was that in the autumn of 1943 'Roosevelt wanted the Conference held in July in Portsmouth, New Hampshire. This place was chosen because it was the venue for the final arrangements of the Russian–Japanese Armistice in 1905 negotiated by Theodore Roosevelt. The Treasury and the State Department nearly tore Portsmouth to pieces to find adequate accommodation but failed. The President was adamant, however, about New Hampshire and that is the reason why we are marooned in this most beautiful bowl in the White Mountains completely out of touch with the outside world.' BER, OV38/9/76, cp=2, Bolton to Cobbold, 2 July 1944.

70 Raymond Mikesell, 'The Bretton Woods Debates: A Memoir,' Essays in International Finance, No. 192 (March 1994), 33.

71 LR PP, LR to Lyla, 27 June 1944.

72 Ibid.

73 BER, OV38/8, 45, cp=8, Bolton to Cobbold, 17 June 1943. Keynes did not disagree.

74 Howson and Moggridge, eds., *Diaries of Robbins and Meade*, 156.

75 As quoted in ibid., 158. Despite their difficulties, on 29 June the Americans accepted the British exchange clause redraft. Robbins thought that the Americans were behaving 'extremely handsomely' (165). Robbins certainly respected the judgment and intelligence of Rasminsky and a number of other Canadians. He wrote in his diary of 11 October 1945: 'In the afternoon we had another interview with the Dominions. Each delegation true to form – Canada first rate, South Africa debonair and friendly, New Zealand banal, Australia surly and unhelpful. Afterwards, [Sir Percivale] Liesching and I went along to the Canadian embassy to drink with Mike Pearson. How refreshing these Canadians are. My own private view is that if they rather than UK officials had the lead for the Commonwealth, policy all round would be much more effective and much more intelligent. What a wonderful flowering it is

which has produced Robertson, Wrong, Pearson, Mackintosh and Rasminsky. If only we could get Rasminsky for the Treasury' (233).

76 Jorge de Campos interview, 16 Oct. 1994. Campos later became a Brazilian cabinet minister and senator. As George Bolton noted, by late June Rasminsky had become 'a more passionate advocate of the Fund' than ever before. See BER Records, OV38/8/53, cp=2, Memorandum by George Bolton, 22 June 1944.

77 BER, Memorandum by George Bolton, 22 June 1944. See also DFR, vol. 3597, file DO3C no. 2, International Monetary Conference, 'Minutes of Second Informal Meeting,' 25 June 1944. But, as Edward Bernstein later claimed, if the United States demanded changes to the Britons' language, the latter would be accommodating; Keynes was 'perfectly willing to put in any obligation, provided there was also a loophole so that they could escape from it.' Edward Bernstein interview, 16 Oct. 1994. On this point, see also Public Record Office (hereafter PRO), London, Treasury Records (hereafter TR), T247 55, vol. 8326, 'The Problem of Our External Finance in the Transition,' 12 June 1944.

78 LR PP, LR to Lyla, 21 June 1944.

79 Howson and Moggridge, eds., *Diaries of Robbins and Meade*, 166.

80 LR76-222-19-2, 'Record of Instructions Given to Canadian Delegation, Bretton Woods, July 1, 1944.' The issue of quotas, while seemingly of not much importance, represented an 'insoluble problem.' As George Bolton wrote to Governor Cobbold, 'We have had a number of meetings with the Empire delegations and these have been most acrimonious. Australia and India are both pressing for a larger quota; India, in particular, demanding a permanent seat on the Fund Directorate, while Canada is torn between a desire to be regarded as a leader of the Dominions in the international field and her knowledge that she will never use the Fund. What will happen when the question of quotas is debated in the appropriate committee at Bretton Woods, I hardly like to prophesy.' BER, OV38/9/76, cp=2, George Bolton to Cobbold, 2 July 1944.

81 LR76-207-2, 'Canada–United States Discussion of Stabilization Fund Proposals, United States Treasury, April 21–26, 1943,' 23 April 1943.

82 BER Records, OV38/9/128, cp=2, Bolton to Cobbold, 10 July 1944.

83 LR76-222-25-1, LR to Tommy Stone, 31 July 1944.

84 LR PP, LR to Lyla, 5 July 1944.

85 Ibid., LR to Lyla, 9 July 1944.

86 LR interview, 28 June 1994. Williams wrote two articles for *Foreign Affairs* opposing the initiative. He and Rasminsky had corresponded in 1943, with the Canadian attempting to make Williams come around to his view. Clark at least

believed that Rasminsky had bested Williams. As the deputy minister told him, his letter to Williams was 'an excellent one and I am more than ever surprised that in his reply Williams does not really attempt to meet most of your points but rather switches the whole basis of the argument.' LR76-213, Clark to Rasminsky, 19 Aug. 1943.

87 LR, 'International Credit and Currency Plans,' *Foreign Affairs* (July 1944), 3. Rasminsky had given much thought to this issue in the late 1930s and earlier 1940s while with the League of Nations. See LR76-6-18, LR to Loveday, 30 May 1942; see also LR76-224-9, 'Opening Remarks of Mr. Harry D. White at the First Meeting of the Commission ... ,' 3 July 1944. Here, White echoed Rasminsky, noting that creation of full production and employment was possible only if 'military warfare was [not] followed by economic warfare – [in which] each country, to the disregard of the interests of other countries, battles solely for its own short-range economic interests.'

88 LR93 LR/Lyla 1944, LR to Lyla, 3 July 1944.

89 Ottawa *Citizen*, 5 Aug. 1944.

90 For example, there was an interesting drafting encounter with the Soviets, which Rasminsky could not explain. Harry White had suggested that they seek him out in order to arrange payment of a lesser gold subscription into the Fund, which, however much he might have wanted to (which he did not), he could not arrange. As Rasminsky said: 'One day after the articles of agreement had been accepted by the Fund Commission, my phone rang ... and it was ... Stepanov, the leader of the Russian delegation. He said there was a matter connected with the Fund agreement that he would like to discuss with me. I said to him "fine–where would you like to meet?" He said, "may I come to your room?" After a few minutes, there was a knock at the door and I opened it and there was a fairly statuesque and good-looking Russian blonde. She said that she had come to discuss the wording of the articles of agreement. I said that I preferred to discuss it with Mr. Stepanov. [She left] and in a few minutes Mr. Stepanov 'phoned and I said "let's meet downstairs." He said to me that he understood that I was the only person who could make any change in the draft articles of the agreement of the Fund and they had a minor change and they would be glad if I would make it. I asked what it was and he said "Well, we would like to see the provisions on the payment of gold in the Fund document changed to correspond to what they are in the Bank document," which was less. [Rasminsky said that he could not effect such a thing.] I asked him "What gave you the idea that I could make that change?" He said "Harry White told me that you were the only person who was authorized to make such a change."' White told Rasminsky that he realized that he could not make the change, but he wanted the Soviets 'off his back.' Rasminsky interview, 22 July 1994.

91 Edward Bernstein interview, 16 Oct. 1994.

92 Aron Broches interview, 16 Oct. 1994.

93 Burke Knapp interview, 17 Oct. 1994. The 'unwritten understanding in 1944 was that a European would head the IMF, while an American would be president of the World Bank.' Knapp was later an executive vice-president of the World Bank.

94 However, Towers was offered the position by Fred Vinson in early 1946.

95 LR76-222-25-2, LR to Tommy Stone, 31 July 1944. See also LR76-222-26, Stone to LR, 7 Aug. 1944.

96 LR PP, Tirana to LR, 30 Aug. 1944.

97 Bruce Macdonald, 'The Banker,' *Globe and Mail*, 5 Jan. 1963, 10. See also Canada, House of Commons *Debates*, 7 Aug. 1946, 4439–42. Speaking of Rasminsky, Jacques Pouliot, the Social Credit member for Temiscouta, told the House at the time of Rasminsky's defence of Bretton Woods that 'we can curb the powers of the foreign exchange control board. In the banking committee, members have been listening to Charybdis and Scylla in the form of Louis Rasminsky. He has a fine voice; he was listened to by all members, who said, "That gentleman has polished manners. We must believe him." That is not a reason. You can pick up a dude anywhere who has polished manners, who has a facial massage every day, who has scent, who has a shampoo every day; who is dressed up by the finest tailors in the country. That is not a qualification to put him in charge of the foreign exchange control board.'

98 Canada, House of Commons *Debates*, 15 March 1945, 1320.

99 Canada, Standing Committee on Banking and Commerce, *Minutes of Proceedings and Evidence*, 11–13 Dec. 1945, 130.

100 *Windsor Daily Star*, 7 Feb. 1950.

101 V. Orval Watts, 'The Bretton Woods Agreements: The Economic Consequences of Mr. Keynes,' *Economic Sentinel*, 3 (1945), vi. I am indebted to John MacPhail for drawing my attention to this document.

102 Alfred E. Eckes, *A Search for Solvency: Bretton Woods and the International Monetary System, 1941–1971* (Austin, Tex.: University of Texas Press, 1975), 168. Eckes's chapter, 'Selling the Magnificent Blueprint,' documents the approval process, both public and congressional.

103 BER, OV38/11, 115A, cp=2, Paul Barreau to George Bolton, 25 May 1945.

104 LR76-51-1-1, LR to Towers, 5 May 1945.

105 LR76-51, Bolton to LR, 11 Sept. 1944.

106 LR76-829-12, LR to Bolton, 21 Dec. 1944.

107 LR76-884, Lola Keynes to LR, 1 Sept. 1946.

108 LR76-823-81, Harry White to LR, 2 April 1947.

109 LR76-829-12, LR to Bolton, 21 Dec. 1945.

110 Ibid.

111 LR76-260-12, LR to Norman Robertson, 3 April 1946. See also NA, Reel C-9175, LR to Norman Robertson, 3 April 1946.

112 LR PP, LR to Lyla, 14 March 1946. Rasminsky told Keynes, indicative of his fear that the IMF would do nothing, that he had 'a night-mare of the Directors and Alternates studying trends (which we were told might be one of their more chronic duties) *and voting on them.*' See Donald Moggridge, ed., *The Collected Writings of John Maynard Keynes*, vol. XXVI, *Activities, 1941–1946, Shaping the Post-War World: Bretton Woods and Reparations* (London: Macmillan, 1980), 228.

113 Eckes, *Search*, 213.

114 Harrod, *Keynes*, 630. In his preference for Washington, Vinson was supported by the Federal Reserve Board, which was keen to strengthen its position against that of the Federal Reserve Board of New York. The latter, or at least its president and vice-president, Allan Sproul and John Williams, respectively, had not supported the Treasury's approach at Bretton Woods. See Eckes, *Search*, 176.

115 See also LR76-76-3, LR to Towers, 17 Jan. 1946. The British agreed with Canada on this point and later told Rasminsky that 'they thought they had ... an understanding [that executive directors would be part-time] with Harry White at Bretton Woods ... but that he is now going back on this.' For an account of the British view of Vinson, see Harrod, *Keynes*, 625–8, and Eckes, *Search*, 213.

116 Edward Bernstein interview, 16 Oct. 1994. See also BER, OV38/10, cp=5, George Bolton, 'The International Monetary Fund,' July 1944.

117 GTP, GFT75-9, Catto and Cobbold to Towers, 12 April 1946.

118 LR PP, LR letter, 9 March 1946.

119 GTP, GFT75-9, Towers to Catto, 16 April 1946.

CHAPTER 5   International Reconstruction

1 *Winnipeg Free Press*, 24 Nov. 1947, 15.

2 *Economist*, 27 March 1948, 361.

3 LR PP, LR to Lyla, 14 March 1946.

4 See Roy Harrod, *The Life of John Maynard Keynes* (New York: St Martin's Press, 1963), 631–2, for an account of the entire address.

5 LR PP, LR letter, 11 March 1946.

6 Peter Popham, 'Sad and Lonely 1950s Were Hardly a Great Golden Age,' *Independent*, as quoted in *Yomiuri Shimbun*, 27 Oct. 1996, 8(A).

7 LR76-56-2-2, Wrong to LR, 'Social and Economic Aspects of the Dumbarton Oaks Proposals, 8 March 1945.'

8 LR76-51-7-1, 'CBC Broadcast,' 13 May 1945. Earlier, Rasminsky had suggested that countries rethink economic relationships because old methods of 'doing business' were discredited. As he wrote to Alexander Loveday, his former chief at the League of Nations, 'The point of view which I think should be stressed is, in fact, incorporated at various places in the document and no doubt it will be brought out still more strongly in the chapter on the right to work ... You should include a "Statement of Policy." This ... should, in my view, be less an economic analysis than a manifesto. It should recognize what seems to be the basic fact which must condition the whole of our thinking about the economics of the post-war world, namely that this is in fact a revolutionary war and that the object of economic policy after the war will not be to make the institutions of a capitalist or semi-capitalist society work with a minimum of friction but to make sure that ... the fruits of production are widely distributed.' See LR76-6-18, LR to Loveday, 30 May 1942.

9 John English, *Shadow of Heaven: The Life of Lester Pearson, 1897–1948*, vol. I (Toronto: Lester and Orpen Dennys, 1989), 361

10 Ibid., 286. See also LR76-59-9-1, LR to Chair, 15 May 1945.

11 LR76-57-6-3, LR, 'Comparison of Canadian Redraft of Chapter IX and Chapter IX of Dumbarton Oaks Proposals,' 9 May 1945.

12 LR76-51-7, 'CBC Broadcast,' 13 May 1945.

13 LR76-51-11, LR to Sidney Turk, 17 May 1945.

14 LR76-51A-1-1, LR to Donald Gordon, 22 May 1945.

15 Ibid.

16 LR76-51-11, LR to Sidney Turk, 17 May 1945.

17 LR PP, LR to Clark, 20 June 1945.

18 LR76-68, LBP to Robertson, 7 Aug. 1945.

19 LR76-75-10, LR to Pearson, 30 Jan. 1946. See also Pearson's reply, LR76-75-11-1, Pearson to LR, 8 Feb. 1945. Pearson claimed that he 'always felt that there would be a European Secretary-General.' He was also convinced that no secretary general, 'whoever he may be, is going to be given a real chance to do his job as it should be done ... If Lie can cut through the tangle of Russian suspicion of and United States inexperience in international administration, he will be a very great man.'

20 For an account of this, see B.W. Muirhead, *The Development of Postwar Canadian Trade Policy: The Failure of the Anglo–American Option* (Montreal: McGill-Queen's University Press, 1992). See also R.D. Cuff and J.L. Granatstein, *American Dollars, Canadian Prosperity: Canadian–American Economic Relations, 1945–1950* (Toronto: Samuel-Stevens, 1978), 21–63.

21 GTP, GFT75-25, Memorandum, 9 Dec. 1947.

22 NA, Department of External Affairs Archives, Department of External Affairs Records, file 154 s, LR to Clark, 18 Sept. 1947.

23 LR interview, 10 May 1994.

24 Canada, House of Commons *Debates*, 12 Dec. 1947.

25 LR76-199B, LR to Gordon, 16 July 1949.

26 Erin E. Jacobsson, *A Life for Sound Money: Per Jacobsson, His Biography* (Oxford: Clarendon Press, 1979), 250.

27 LR76-199B-8, LR to Gordon, 9 July 1949.

28 GTP, GFT75-28, LR to Towers, 27 April 1949.

29 LR76-199B-20-1, LR to Gordon, 19 July 1949.

30 *Economist*, 12 July 1949, 876.

31 LR76-199B, LR to Gordon, 16 July 1949.

32 LR76-199A-19, 'Notes for Report on European Trip to Bank of Canada Directors, June 20, 1949.'

33 GTP, GFT75-28, LR to Towers, 6 May 1949.

34 It was true, too, that part of the British bureaucracy was working on a plan, ROBOT, that would introduce sterling convertibility. The Bank of England and Overseas Finance at the Treasury were enthusiastically in favour of letting the pound 'float at once ... blocking 80 percent or more of the sterling balances held by other countries, and making current earnings of sterling by non-residents of the sterling area (and such balances as were not blocked) freely convertible into gold or dollars.' This idea, which had been circulating since early 1952, was strongly opposed by a group led by Robert Hall, director of the Economic Section of the Cabinet Office, and an adviser to the chancellor of the exchequer, R.A. Butler. ROBOT was originally scheduled for implementation in the budget of 4 March 1952, but, given the opposition that it generated, it was dropped. Indeed, as Sir Alex Cairncross points out, 'What survived was a modified plan for combining early convertibility with a floating pound, provided a number of conditions were met, notably financial support from the United States and the IMF.' This became known as the collective approach to freer trade and currencies. See Sir Alex Cairncross, ed., *The Robert Hall Diaries, 1947–1953* (London: Unwin Hyman, 1989), 203.

35 LR76-658A-1-1, LR to Towers, 12 Jan. 1954.

36 LR PP, LR to Lyla, 8 Jan. 1954. Rowan, despite his reply to Rasminsky, had been one British official very much in favour of ROBOT.

37 LR76-836, LR to Mary and Leslie, 17 Nov. 1954.

38 LR PP, LR letter, 17 June 1956.

39 DFR, vol. 4180, file 8522/U575-1 (58), UKCCC (58), R.2, 20 June 1958.

40 A.F.W. Plumptre, *Three Decades of Decision: Canada and the World Monetary System, 1944–1975* (Toronto: McClelland and Stewart, 1977), 141.

41 LR PP, LR letter, 13 July 1947.

42 PRO, TR, T236, vol. 7859, Washington to Foreign Office, 10 Oct. 1946. See

also GTP, Memorandum no. 525, 23 Oct. 1946. For an American view of the IMF's organization, see Frank A. Southard, 'The Evolution of the International Monetary Fund,' Essays in International Finance, No. 135 (Princeton, NJ: International Finance Section, Dec. 1979), 1–7.

43 USNA, Department of State Records (DSR), box 4830, file 842.13/4-2751, Ottawa to Department of State, 21 June 1950.

44 Ibid., Ottawa to Department of State, 27 April 1951.

45 Southard, 'The Evolution of the International Monetary Fund,' 18.

46 PRO, TR, T236, vol. 7859, Washington to Foreign Office, 28 May 1946.

47 USNA, DSR, IMF box 1523, file 398.13/9-1350, Paris to Secretary of State, 13 Sept. 1950.

48 LR76-273-9-2, LR Memorandum, 'International Monetary Fund,' 18 Oct. 1949.

49 For an account of the tripartite talks, see Muirhead, *Development*, 39–40.

50 NA, Joseph Parkinson Papers, vol. 2, 'Thoughts on Canadian–American Collaboration on Change in Canadian Dollar,' Sept. 1949. See also LR76-275-2, LR to Bryce, 15 Oct. 1949. In a letter about the process of the devaluation, Rasminsky wrote to Bryce: 'The Western Europeans, and particularly the French, are very angry at the British for springing this on them and cutting as deep as they did. But behind their resentment lies the frustration of a plan to establish something that is jokingly referred to as a "European currency union," and which, so far as I can make out, consists mainly of an attempt to (a) knife the British in the back by having sterling quoted at a discount in most European countries, and (b) fool the US Congress into thinking that some big action towards economic liberalization was being taken on the European continent.' However, the decision to devalue was not taken lightly, or without opposition. C.D. Howe, the Canadian minister of reconstruction, was not in favour, because it would make machinery and equipment that Canadians were buying in the United States more expensive. Finance Minister Douglas Abbott convinced cabinet that it should be done. See Plumptre, *Three Decades*, 108.

51 NA, Parkinson Papers, vol. 2, 'Thoughts,' Sept. 1949.

52 J. Keith Horsefield, *Annals of the Fund, 1945–1965* (Washington, DC: International Monetary Fund, 1969), 188.

53 LR PP, LR letter, 12 Sept. 1950. Martin later became a good friend of Rasminsky's and chair of the board of governors of the US Federal Reserve Board.

54 See PRO, TR, T236, vol. 2808, B.W. (49) 5, 'Future of the Bretton Woods Organisations,' 23 Nov. 1949.

55 LR76, 'United States Attitudes in International Monetary Fund,' 1 Oct. 1949.

56 LR76-269-5, Gutt to LR, 6 Jan. 1949. See also USNA, Treasury Records (hereaf-
    ter TR), RG 56, Southard to Dillon Glendinning, 'Fund Board Action on Ad
    Hoc Committee Report on European Payments Problem, 5 Oct. 1949.'
57 LR83-269-1, Gutt to LR, 7 May 1950.
58 LR76-283-12, LR to E.J. Tarr, 27 Dec. 1946.
59 LR76-269-21-1, LR to Gutt, 7 May 1962.
60 See LR76-199A-19, 'Notes for Report on European Trip to Bank of Canada
    Directors, June 20, 1949.' For a brief account of the origins of the BIS, see
    Erin Jacobsson, *A Life*, 95–7.
61 PRO, Dominions Office, RG 35, vol. 8381, Kenneth McGregor, 'European
    Economic Affaairs, 5 Feb. 1960.' The full citation reads, 'Somerfelt [the Nor-
    wegian trade envoy in Ottawa] said he had known Rasminsky since 1947 as a
    dogged opponent of "European solutions," whether through the OEEC, or
    the EPU, of a Six plus Seven' (presumably the EEC and the seven-member
    European Free Trade Association).
62 LR PP, LR letter, 7 Sept. 1950.
63 LR76-115-13, 'A Method of Combining a Free Exchange Rate,' 31 Jan. 1949.
    For an IMF account, see J. Keith Horsefield, *The International Monetary Fund:
    Twenty Years of International Monetary Cooperation, 1945–1965*, vol. I, *Chronicle*
    (Washington, DC: International Monetary Fund, 1969), 270–5.
64 Paul Wonnacott, *The Canadian Dollar, 1948–1962* (Toronto: University of
    Toronto Press, 1965), 78. W.A. Mackintosh, 'A Note on the Canadian Dollar,'
    International Journal (1950–1), certainly believed that 'the strengthening of the
    Canadian dollar was wholly a matter of capital import.'
65 Plumptre, *Three Decades*, 142.
66 As quoted in Wonnacott, *Dollar*, 78.
67 Plumptre, *Three Decades*, 144.
68 Raymond Mikesell, 'The Emerging Pattern of International Payments,' Essays
    in International Finance, No. 18 (Princeton, NJ: International Finance Sec-
    tion, 1954), 18.
69 A.F.W. Plumptre, 'Exchange Rate Policy: Experience with Canada's Floating
    Rate,' Essays in International Finance, No. 81 (Princeton, NJ: International
    Finance Section, 1970), 6.
70 USNA, DSR, box 4830, file 842.13/4-2751, Ottawa to DS, 27 April 1951.
71 NA, Parkinson Papers, vol. 2, LR to Parkinson, 18 May 1951.
72 See Greg Donaghy, ed., *Documents on Canadian External Relations 1950* (hereaf-
    ter *DCER year*), vol. 16 (Ottawa: Department of Foreign Affairs and Interna-
    tional Trade, 1996), 696–711, for a series of memoranda on US and Fund
    reactions to Rasminsky's visit.
73 LR76-522-2, LR, 'Report on Washington Discussions,' 28–30 Sept. 1950. Only

partly tongue-in-cheek, Rasminsky told the Americans and the IMF that neither a fixed nor a floating rate suited Canada.

74 LR PP, LR letter, 9 Sept. 1950.
75 LR, 'Report on Washington Discussions.'
76 NA, Parkinson Papers, vol. 2, Parkinson to LR, 3 Oct. 1950.
77 USNA, DSR, box 4830, file 842.13/4-2751, Ottawa to Department of State, 27 April 1951. See also NA, Parkinson Papers, vol. 2, LR to Parkinson, 18 May 1951.
78 LR, 'Report on Washington Discussions.'
79 Ibid.
80 A.F.W. Plumptre to USSEA, 18 Oct. 1950, as quoted in *DCER 1950*, 707.
81 LR76-115-24, Graham Towers, 'Question of Continuing Foreign Exchange Control,' 12 Dec. 1951.
82 *DCER 1950*, 710.
83 LR76-272-31, LR to Abbott, 6 March 1952.
84 See, for example, LR76-518-1, LR, Memorandum to Fleming, 'Exchange Fund,' 19 July 1957.
85 LR76-518-9, LR, 'Exchange Fund Policy, 1950–57,' 16 Aug. 1957. See also S.I. Katz, 'Two Approaches to the Exchange Rate Problem: The United Kingdom and Canada,' Essays in International Finance, No. 26 (Princeton, NJ: International Finance Section, 1956), 18. Katz's essay compares the floating Canadian rate with the fixed British rate. His conclusion notes: 'The similar operating experiences of the two currencies suggest that a fixed and a fluctuating exchange system may not lead to such differences in day-to-day exchange variations and different operating techniques in the exchange market as economic theory would suggest.' With economic stabilization, 'it is not clear that there is a material difference between a fixed or fluctuating-rate policy; a strong, flexible currency may indeed prove to be about as stable as a fixed-rate currency.'
86 LR PP, LR to Lyla, 14 March 1946.
87 This quotation and the one in the next paragraph are in LR PP, LR, 'Notes of Conversation with Towers, 26.11.49.' However, rumours circulating in Ottawa had it that he was unacceptable to the cabinet because he was Jewish. I am indebted to Dr Michael Rasminsky for this document.
88 BER, OV58/6 38A, cp=11, 'Narrative Account of Tour of Canada, Nov. 1954.'
89 Dr Michael Rasminsky interview, 5 June 1995.
90 LR PP, Tom Kent to LR, 20 Nov. 1954.
91 Ibid., LePan to LR, 22 Nov. 1954.
92 Douglas Fullerton, *Graham Towers and His Times* (Toronto: McClelland and Stewart, 1986), 270.

93 BER, 'Narrative Account.'

94 Dr Michael Rasminsky interview, 5 June 1995.

95 LR PP, LR to James Meade, 13 Feb. 1953.

96 Ibid., Léger to LR, 23 Aug. 1955. The position was as minister.

97 USNA, IMF box 1523, Brussels to Department of State, 'Belgian Speculation on the Resignation of Camille Gutt from the International Monetary Fund,' 9 April 1951.

98 PRO, TR, T236, file 4546, I.M.F./I.B.R.D. Seventh Annual Meeting, I.M.F. Internal Organization, 18 Aug. 1952.

99 LR76-290A, 'Proposals for Changes in the International Monetary Fund,' 3 May 1961.

100 LR76-274-26, Parkinson to Rasminsky, 20 Dec. 1950. As well, in 1953, Canada opposed the US initiative to disallow Czechoslovak access to the Fund's resources. The counsellor at Canada's embassy in Washington, DC, Douglas LePan, accompanied by Rasminsky's alternate, Neil Perry, had visited the Department of State to protest. As a memorandum of conversation noted, 'The Canadians felt that the US position in the Fund had *political* overtones which disturbed them ... They did not wish to be associated with an effort to expel Czechoslovakia from the IMF.' The final act – the vote declaring Czechoslovakia ineligible – came up on 4 November 1953. The motion passed, with Canada voting in favour, and the country was expelled from the IMF on 31 December 1954. Still, Rasminsky remained very uncomfortable with the process and with Washington's attitude. See also USNA, DSR, IMF box 1524, file 398.13/11-253, Memorandum of Conversation, 2 Nov. 1953; emphasis added. For an account of the decision on Czechoslovakia, see Horsefield, *Annals of the Fund*, vol. I, 312.

As governments change, so too can policy, and John Diefenbaker's adopted a different approach to Communism than had the Liberals. Diefenbaker suggested in the House of Commons that the Fund's resources be used as a bulwark against the spread of international Communism. See Canada, House of Commons *Debates*, 25 July 1958, 2705. See also John Hilliker and Donald Barry, *Canada's Department of External Affairs: Coming of Age, 1946–1968* (Montreal: McGill-Queen's University Press, 1995), 158. As they note, Diefenbaker was firmly anti-Communist: 'One policy area to feel the effect of Diefenbaker's interest was East–West relations, on which he favoured a departure from the softer line favoured by the department.'

101 PRO, TR, T236, file 4546, I.M.F. Internal Organization, Jan. 1951.

102 Ibid., file 5716, Bolton to The Viscount Harcourt, 11 May 1955.

103 Ibid., file 4546, Sir H. Brittain, 'No. 32 Eager,' 7 Feb. 1951; see also 'Note,' 12 Feb. 1951. The British were not the only ones not to think highly of Overby.

Eugene Black, president of the IBRD, also thought his countryman a complete dud. In a general discussion of the IMF with Sir Edmund Hall-Patch, Black 'warned [Hall-Patch] of the delicate position of [managing director] Rooth. He was not popular with the Americans; he had not handled his own Board with conspicuous skill, and he was not a good administrator, but it was essential to keep him in his present position until a permanent home had been found for Overby. On present form, if Rooth left now, great pressure would be exercised to appoint an American as Managing Director: that American would be Overby. Black was quite clear that the appointment of Overby would be a disaster.' See ibid., vol. 5713, Hall-Patch to Brittain, 20 Aug. 1953.

104 Ibid., file 4546, Foreign Office to Washington, 5 March 1951.
105 Ibid., 'I.M.F. – Managing Director,' 24 Feb. 1951.
106 Ibid., M. Stevenson to Sir Herbert Brittain, 'IMF,' 11 Jan. 1952.
107 LR76-848, Cobbold to Towers, 22 Jan. 1952. The minister of finance, Douglas Abbott, had been asked by Cobbold for his opinion about Rasminsky; he 'thought it a good idea.'
108 PRO, TR, T236, file 4546, Foreign Office to Ambassador, Washington, 24 Jan. 1952.
109 Ibid.
110 Ibid., Washington to Foreign Office, 31 Jan. 1952.
111 Ibid., Washington to Foreign Office, 12 Nov. 1952.
112 LR76-284-2, Message from Minister of Finance to Chancellor of the Exchequer, 27 April 1956.
113 LR76-284-6, 'Appointment of Managing Director and the Canadian Proposals for Re-organization of the Executive Board,' 9 May 1956.
114 LR PP, LR letter, 11 June 1956. Rasminsky had been uncertain of Jacobsson's abilities, at least in the postwar period. He had written to Towers in May 1949, following his trip to Basle, Switzerland, for meetings at the Bank for International Settlements (BIS), that 'Jacobsson was rather incoherent – I never feel I really understand him.' See GTP, GFT75-28, LR to Towers, 11 May 1949.
115 LR PP, LR letter, 11 June 1956.
116 USNA, IMF, box 1469, file 398.13/7-2456, Burgess to Secretary Humphrey, 24 July 1956.
117 Bernstein interview, 16 Oct. 1994. For Jacobsson's insecurity regarding himself and the academic economists – 'the real economists' – see Erin Jacobsson, A Life, 259–60; for his recollection of his reception at the IMF, see ibid., 296–302.
118 LR76-284-8, 'Views of the Canadian Minister of Finance on the Organization

of the International Monetary Fund,' 31 May 1956. The minister's memorandum repeats arguments that Rasminsky had made to Harris on 20 April 1956. See LR76-284-1, LR, 'Functioning of the IMF,' 20 April 1956.

119 LR76-284-19, LR to Coyne, 16 June 1956.

120 LR76-284-4, Cobbold to Coyne, 2 May 1956.

121 LR76-284-30, Per Jacobsson, 'Canadian Proposals for Reorganiztion of the Executive Board,' 10 July 1957.

122 Erin Jacobsson, *A Life*, 299.

123 LR76-272-26, LR to Abbott, 15 May 1951.

124 LR76-284-1, LR, 'Functioning of the IMF,' 20 April 1956.

125 For an account of the Fund's financing problems, see Horsefield, *The International Monetary Fund*.

126 PRO, TR, T236, vol. 5718, 'International Monetary Fund,' 10 July 1957.

127 USNA, TR, RG 56, box 60, file f 6763-1, 'Requests for Special Quota Increases in the IMF,' 15 Dec. 1958.

128 Ibid., box 60, file F 6763-1, ? to Secretary of the Treasury, 18 Sept. 1958. See also LR76-427, 'International Monetary Fund,' 2 July 1958.

129 By 1961, the IMF had experienced heavy use of its resources, especially by the United Kingdom, which in 1961 took a $1.5-billion drawing and a $500-million stand-by credit in order to support sterling. Clearly, even with quota increases, the Fund's resources were too limited to respond adequately to new problems, even though, in his closing speech to the 1960 annual meeting, Per Jacobsson stated that 'there was no lack of international liquidity.' As well, there were associated issues with which the Fund was concerned relating to exchange stability and on which some important members took action. At the BIS in March 1961, the governors of the central banks of Belgium, France, Italy, the Netherlands, Sweden, the United States, and West Germany struck the Basle Agreement. As Margaret Garritsen de Vries describes it, 'They would hold each other's currencies to a greater extent than before, instead of converting them immediately into gold or dollars, and they would provide each other with short-term loans of needed currencies to help finance sudden flights of capital'; *The International Monetary Fund, 1966–1971: The System under Stress*, vol. I, *Narrative* (Washington, DC: International Monetary Fund, 1976), 14. As well, later that year, the Gold Pool was established, involving Belgium, France, Italy, the Netherlands, Switzerland, the United Kingdom, the United States, and West Germany. It would intervene when necessary in the London gold market in order to hold the market price of gold at, or close to, the official price of US$35 per ounce. See Horsefield, *The International Monetary Fund*, 482–5. Finally, the problem of international liquidity was tentatively settled in the 1960s, first with the General

Arrangements to Borrow, which came into operation on 24 October 1962 and which enabled the IMF to borrow up to US$6 billion in the currencies of ten of its industrial members – the so-called G-10 – which included Canada. The issue was finally settled in 1969 with development of the IMF's Special Drawing Rights (SDRs). For a full account of the setting up of the SDRs see de Vries, *The International Monetary Fund*, vol. I, 205.

130 See, for example, USNA, DSR, IMF box 1470, file 398.13/5-1457, Goldstein to Southard, 14 May 1956. See also USNA, TR, RG56, box 78, Frank Southard, 'IMF Policy on Discrimination,' 14 Oct. 1959, for Rasminsky's opinion.

131 Plumptre, *Three Decades*, 125–6.

132 LR76-274-352, Alan Hockin to LR, 8 July 1958.

133 PRO, Dominions Office Records, vol. 8679, UKCCC (59) 3rd Mtg., 3 July 1959.

134 See ibid., vol. 8679, Sir Frank Lee, 'The UKCCC Meetings on the 2nd/3rd July,' 8 July 1959. A few years earlier, Sir Leslie Rowan had told Rasminsky that the United Kingdom would continue to impose trade restrictions for one year after sterling became convertible. British policy had not changed. See LR76-274-15, LR to Warren, 12 Nov. 1954.

135 LR76-282-217, LR to Frank Hooton, 30 Jan. 1959.

136 LR76-282-229, LR to David Wilson, 17 Sept. 1959. See also LR76-274-392, C.L. Read to LR, 15 Sept. 1959.

137 LR76-274-387-3, IMF Board Meeting, 'Fund Position on Discrimination for Balance of Payments Reasons,' 14 Oct. 1959.

138 USNA, TR, RG 56, Secretary Anderson Papers, box 195, 'Article VIII–Article XIV: Preliminary Discussion in the Executive Board of the IMF,' 23 March 1960.

139 LR76-274-15, LR to Warren, 12 Nov. 1954.

140 USNA, TR, RG 56, Secretary Anderson Papers, box 195, 'Article VIII-Article XIV'; emphasis added.

141 For a representative sample of an article VIII consultation, see LR76-291-3, International Monetary Fund, 'Article VIII Consultations with Canada,' 21 Jan. 1964. Canada and the United States had proposed that all members of the Fund should consult annually, even though it was not a necessity once they had accepted the IMF's general obligations. Such consultations began in 1961.

CHAPTER 6   Into the Breach

1 USNA, DSR, box 4467 (1956–58), 842.14/4-357, Ottawa to Department of State, 3 April 1957.

2 Ibid., box 4466, 842.10/5-2059, Embassy Ottawa to Department of State, 20 May 1959.

3 William Lawson interview, 20 July 1994.

4 Many academic economists and other critics took issue with Coyne's policy of high interest rates and the damage that it did to the Canadian economy. Certainly the unemployment rate was increasing; it stood at 3.1 per cent of the workforce in 1957, 3.7 per cent in the first half of 1957, 4.8 per cent in August 1957, 6.2 per cent in December 1957, and 7.9 per cent in October 1958. Indeed, in 1958, unemployment was at its highest level of the 1950s, while the exchange rate vis-à-vis the US dollar stood at US$1.03 – a reflection of the relatively high interest-rate differentials between the two countries.

See, for example, H. Scott Gordon, *The Economists versus the Bank of Canada* (Toronto: Ryerson Press, 1961); Paul Wonnacott, *The Canadian Dollar, 1948–1962* (Toronto: University of Toronto Press, 1965), 223–39; A.F.W. Plumptre, *Three Decades of Decision: Canada and the World Monetary System, 1944–75* (Toronto: McClelland and Stewart, 1977), 155–64; Robert M. Dunn, *Canada's Experience with Fixed and Flexible Exchange Rates in a North American Capital Market* (Montreal: Private Planning Association of Canada, 1971), 61–2; Richard Caves and Grant Reuber, *Canadian Economic Policy and the Impact of International Capital Flows* (Montreal: Private Planning Association of Canada, 1969), 22–4; Robert A. Mundell, 'Problems of Monetary and Exchange Rate Management in Canada,' *National Banking Review* 2 (Sept. 1964), 77–86; Richard Caves, 'Flexible Exchange Rates,' *American Economic Review* 53, supplement (May 1963), 128.

The general criticism was that monetary policy between 1958 and 1960 was inappropriate. For example, Dunn (*Canada's Experience*) writes (61): 'In late 1958 the Bank of Canada overreacted to the potential inflationary effects of a large deficit by imposing an extremely tight monetary policy in the face of high unemployment. The Canadian money supply actually fell in 1959 and the recovery from the 1958 recession was completely stifled ... High Canadian interest rates attracted large flows of funds from the United States, sharply increasing [Canada's floating] exchange rate and greatly reduced the Canadian trade account. The loss of export and import competitive sales by Canadian firms deepened and prolonged the recession.' Plumptre notes (*Three Decades*, 157) that in 1957 the Canadian unemployment rate rose above the US rate for almost the first time since the war. The net annual inflow of long-term capital had been $698 million over the six years from 1950. Between 1957 and 1961 it averaged $1.1 billion. During those years, the Canadian dollar floated at a premium over the US dollar. 'As time went by,' Plumptre writes, 'it became increasingly clear that the high level at which the Canadian dollar continued to float ... was inappropriate in the relatively stagnant period from 1957 to 1961. It facilitated imports, it deterred exports, it depressed prices and it contributed to unemployment' (157–8). See Mundell, 'Problems,' and Caves, 'Flexible,' for similar analyses.

However, Rasminsky took issue with the implication in the IMF Report on the 1961 article VIII consultations with Canada that Canadian difficulties from 1955 onward had been largely the result of mistaken domestic policies. The governor communicated his reservations to the Fund's managing director, Per Jacobsson. See Erin E. Jacobsson, *A Life for Sound Money: Per Jacobsson, His Biography* (Oxford: Clarendon Press, 1979), 354.

5 Canada, House of Commons *Debates,* May 1959.

6 'Bank on Course,' *Regina Leader Post,* 1 Aug. 1961; emphasis added.

7 See GTP, Memorandum No. 490, 5 Sept. 1945. The proviso relating to the veto was given to Lord Keynes during the summer of 1945 as he was considering terms of legislation to nationalize the Bank of England. On the memo, Towers noted that he had 'urged use of Canadian pattern – Failed.'

8 Quoted in 'The New Broom,' *Halifax Chronicle Herald,* 3 Aug. 1961. Rasminsky echoed Dunning's sentiment of 1936 in his testimony of 1963 to the Royal Commission on Banking and Finance (Porter Commission, 1961–4).

9 Ibid.

10 For an account of this period, see J.L. Granatstein, *Canada 1957–1967: The Years of Uncertainty and Innovation* (Toronto: McClelland and Stewart, 1986), 70–83.

11 Donald M. Fleming, *So Very Near: The Political Memoirs of the Honourable Donald M. Fleming,* vol. II, *The Summit Years* (Toronto: McClelland and Stewart, 1985), 67–8.

12 See USNA, DSR, box 4467, 842.14/3-2158, Embassy Ottawa to Department of State, 21 March 1958.

13 BCA, interview with George Watts, 'The Coyne Years,' 8 April 1992.

14 George Freeman interview, 28 Jan. 1995.

15 BER, OV58/18, 111A, cp=2, Mulholland to George Bolton, 19 June 1961.

16 Ibid., 113B, Alexander to Bolton, 27 June 1961.

17 Lawson interview, 20 July 1994.

18 Freeman interview, 28 Jan. 1995.

19 The best account of this issue is Granatstein, *Canada, 1957–1967,* 74–83.

20 Ibid., 74.

21 Ibid., 75.

22 Simon Reisman interview, 19 Aug. 1994.

23 LR PP, Fleming to Plumptre, 11 June 1975. See also BER, Mulholland to George Bolton, 19 June 1961. The Bank of Montreal's president, Earl Mulhol-

land, raised the issue of the timing of the firing: 'I feel myself that something serious must have happened within the past month for Donald Fleming to ask for the resignation of Jimmy Coyne when all the former had to do was wait until 31st Dec. when the term of the appointment of the present Governor of the Bank of Canada would expire.'

24 Gerald Bouey interview, 21 July 1994. As an indication of how incorrect some outside observers of political processes can be, a member of the British High Commission staff in Ottawa told the Bank of England: 'It was generally accepted that in the present circumstances no candidate could be looked for from inside the central bank, although the appointment of Rasminsky would have been generally popular in spite of his lack of association with the home scene in recent years.' Instead, the diplomat believed that J. Douglas Gibson, the Bank of Nova Scotia's general manager, could be a likely candidate, as well as John Deutsch and J.T. Bryden, a member of the Bank of Canada's board. See BER, OV58/18, 114, cp=2, 'Bank of Canada – Governorship,' 28 June 1961.

25 Reisman interview, 19 Aug. 1994.

26 Privy Council Office (PCO) Records, Ottawa, 'Bank of Canada; Position of Governor,' 8 June 1961.

27 Reisman interview, 19 Aug. 1994. Reisman's opinion about why Rasminsky had taken this approach was that being passed over in 1955 for the governorship had hardened him, and he did not want to be disappointed again.

28 LR76-857-6-1, LR, 'Notes for Remarks to Directors, July 22, 1961.'

29 Peter Dempson, 'Found Room at the Top Despite Faith and Name,' *Toronto Telegram,* 25 July 1961.

30 LR PP, 'Discussion with Minister of Finance and Prime Minister re: Governorship, June–July 1961.' The US Federal Reserve Board encountered some of these issues a decade later. The chair of the Council of Economic Advisors, Paul McCracken, told President Nixon how he conceived of the appropriate relationship between the administration and the federal reserve system: '– that [the administration] respect the independent status of the Federal Reserve and its primacy of responsibility regarding monetary policy; – that [the President has] a legitimate interest in monetary policy stemming from the Employment Act of 1946; – that [the President's] interest is further justified, as monetary policy affects employment, production, and purchasing power; – things which you are held politically accountable for; and – that the distinction to be drawn is between the Federal Reserve's *primary responsibility* for monetary policy and [the President's] *legitimate concern.*' See USNA, Nixon, FG 131, Federal Reserve System, box 1, file 6/30/70, John Ehrlichman to the President, 16 Feb. 1970.

The debate between the 'Fed' and the adminstration over the respective powers of each continued into 1971, though in a quiet manner. For example, Arthur Burns and Nixon differed over their respective responsibilities, but the former would work with the latter to reach some sort of solution: 'On leaving Arthur again expressed his total dedication to you and your policies, and reiterated his desire to keep within the family any disagreements between the Administration and the Fed.' USNA, Nixon, FG 131, Fed. Res. System, box 1, file 1/1/71–12/31/71, Peter Flanigan to the President.

31 LR76-857-2-1, 'Memorandum,' July 1961.
32 PCO Records, Cabinet Conclusions, 8 June 1961.
33 Dr. Michael Rasminsky interview, June 1995. He remembers a similar 'repentance' by St Laurent later. See chapter 7 below.
34 *Ottawa Citizen*, 24 July 1961.
35 LR76-857-2-3, LR, 'Memorandum,' July 1961.
36 'Establishing Responsibility,' *Globe and Mail*, 2 Aug. 1961.
37 LR76-857-6-3, LR, 'Notes for Remarks to Directors, July 22, 1961.'
38 *Regina Leader Post*, 15 Aug. 1961.
39 Robert Moon, 'Canada's Banker Takes Over,' *Christian Science Monitor*, 16 Aug. 1961.
40 BER, OV58/18, 126, 'Mr. Rasminsky – Governor,' 25 July 1961.
41 Bruce Phillips, CBC news commentary, 25 July 1961.
42 For example, even as late as 1965, the Rideau Club, a bastion of the establishment, discriminated against Jews, routinely barring them from membership. Rasminsky was an unwitting part of a successful attempt to blast open the club's doors.
43 LR PP, 'Pension Fund Rule 17,' 11 Aug. 1961.
44 Ibid., LR to L. Patrick, 23 Nov. 1962.
45 A.C. Lamb interview, 22 July 1994.

CHAPTER 7   Rebuilding Confidence: First Term

1 Bank of Canada, *Annual Report of the Governor to the Minister of Finance for the Year 1961* (Ottawa: Queen's Printer, 1962), 6.
2 LR76-570-2-8, P.C. 1961–1484.
3 Gerald Bouey interview, 21 July 1994.
4 A.C. Lamb interview, 22 July 1994.
5 LR76-570-4-16, 'Notes for Royal Commission – Relations with Government,' 1961.
6 US Federal Reserve Board Archives, Washington, DC, Federal Reserve Board

Records (FRBR), Bodner to Holmes, 3 April 1963. Rasminsky also included his statement in Bank of Canada, *Annual Report for 1961*, 3–5.

7 See LR76-552-31-90, 'Proposed Substitute for Section 14,' 15 Oct. 1964.

8 Peter Stursberg's interview with LR, 1 June 1978.

9 'Economic Planning Stressed,' *Montreal Daily Star*, 26 Feb. 1964.

10 LR76-552-31-90, LR to Gordon, 10 March 1964.

11 Canada, House of Commons *Debates*, 14 March 1968, 7621.

12 LR76-552-115, LR to Sharp, 15 March 1968.

13 LR, 'Introductory Remarks,' in Bank of Canada, *Evidence of the Governor before the Royal Commission on Banking and Finance* (May 1964), 3. Rasminsky agreed with the comments of Marins Holtrop, president of the Netherlands Bank, to the Royal Commission on Banking and Finance. There he had stated that 'monetary policy does not consist only of the policy of the central bank. It includes that part of budgetary policy which is concerned with the choice between the financing of government expenditure in excess of income from taxation, out of capital-market or out of money-market resources. It also includes that part of debt-management policy which is concerned with the choice between consolidation or deconsolidation of outstanding debt.' See Marins Holtrop, *Monetary Policy in an Open Economy: Its Objectives, Instruments, Limitations and Dilemmas* (Princeton, NJ: International Finance Section, 1963), 16, 25–39. On the limitations of monetary policy, see also Sir Dennis Robertson, *A Memorandum Submitted to the Canadian Royal Commission on Banking and Finance* (Princeton, NJ: International Finance Section, 1964).

14 Bank of Canada, *Annual Report for 1961*, 4.

15 LR76-570-14-1, G.E. Freeman, 'The Six Percent Ceiling on Chartered Bank Lending Rates,' May 1964. See also Bank of Canada, *Evidence of the Governor*, 38.

16 LR76-570-14-13, 'The Case for Removal of the 6 Per Cent Rate Ceiling.'

17 When the House of Commons voted for removal in 1966, Mitchell Sharp was minister of finance, and Gordon, then an ordinary MP, was absent by arrangement. See Walter Gordon, *A Political Memoir* (Toronto: McClelland and Stewart, 1977), 236.

18 LR76-540-12, Management Committee Minute No. 58, n.d.

19 J.N.R. Wilson interview, 18 Aug. 1994.

20 Gerald Bouey interview, 21 July 1994.

21 LR76-552-31-90, Laing to Gordon, 31 May 1963.

22 Donald Fleming, *So Very Near: The Political Memoirs of the Honourable Donald M. Fleming*, vol. II, *The Summit Years* (Toronto: McClelland and Stewart, 1985).

23 A.F.W. Plumptre, *Three Decades of Decision: Canada and the World Monetary System, 1944–75* (Toronto: McClelland and Stewart, 1977), 165.

24 Canada, House of Commons *Debates,* 20 June 1961, 6639.
25 Donald Marsh, 'Canada's Experience with a Floating Rate, 1950–1962,' in George N. Halm, ed., *Approaches to Greater Flexibility of Exchange Rates: The Bür-genstock Papers* (Princeton, NJ: Princeton University Press, 1970), 341.
26 'Our Bouncing Dollar Bothers World,' *Toronto Daily Star,* 21 July 1961.
27 BCA, Bank of Canada Records (hereafter BCR), INT 4B-200, vol. 5, Washington to External, 9 Feb. 1962.
28 LR76-528-1, Hart to LR, 29 Aug. 1961; LR76-582-9-1, Hall to LR, 21 Dec. 1961. The Toronto-Dominion's general manager offered a unique suggestion; the dollar 'might be ... allow[ed] to float with the Treasury Bill rate most of the time, but ... fix[ed] ... at a specific level temporarily whenever the Bank of Canada thought it would be useful to give a more positive lead to the market[!]'
29 LR76-522-159, A.F.W. Plumptre, 'Exchange Rate Policy,' 23 Aug. 1961.
30 Plumptre, *Three Decades,* 168; Margaret Garritsen de Vries, *The International Monetary Fund, 1966–1971,* vol. II, *Documents* (Washington, DC: International Monetary Fund, 1976), 164.
31 Plumptre, 'Exchange Rate.'
32 LR76-522-177, LR, 'Fund Executive Board Meeting,' 2 May 1962.
33 LR76-522-178-3, IMF Board Meeting, 2 May 1962, 'Report to Mr. Rasminsky.' For a British account of the policy, see BER, G1/230-75, cp=2, M.H. Parsons to Sir Denis Rickett, 11 Dec. 1962. George Freeman, a former official at the Bank of Canada, tells a humorous story about this. When he was hired in 1950, one of his first tasks was to write a speech for Rasminsky to give to financial people in New York, explaining why the Canadian decision to float the dollar in October 1950 was 'not the end of the world.' When Canada fixed its exchange rate twelve years later, Freeman was instructed to write a speech for the governor to give in New York, explaining why that decision 'was not the end of the world.' George Freeman interview, 28 Jan. 1995.
34 LR76-522-176-4, Plumptre to LR, 25 May 1962.
35 Ibid.
36 Dominion Bureau of Statistics, 'The Canadian Balance of International Payments, 1961 and 1962' (Ottawa: Queen's Printer, 1963), 42.
37 LR76-552-7, LR, 'Memorandum,' 2 Jan. 1962.
38 Freeman interview, Jan. 1995.
39 John F. Kennedy Presidential Library (hereafter JFK), Boston, Mass., Kennedy Papers (hereafter KP), vol. 90, POF, 1/63, Memorandum, Dillion to JFK, 30 Jan. 1963.
40 PRO, Dominions Office Records, DO35, vol. 4376, 'Memorandum to A.W. France,' 18 June 1959.
41 John English, *The Worldly Years: The Life of Lester Pearson, 1949–1972* (Toronto: Alfred A. Knopf, 1992), 240.

42 LR76-523-24, LR, interview with Fleming, 31 May 1962.
43 *Montreal Daily Star,* 3 Oct. 1962.
44 *Barron's,* 2 July 1962, 7.
45 See LR76-523, LR to Diefenbaker, 21 June 1962.
46 LR, AVPP, 50.
47 LR76-523, RBB to Diefenbaker, 18 June 1962.
48 Bank of Canada, *Annual Report for 1962.*
49 LR76-523-40, 'Draft Covering Memorandum to the Prime Minister,' 12 June 1962.
50 See 'Dollar's Defense – A Study in Cooperation,' *American Banker* (Nov. 1963). Central bankers and others involved in the trade were 'friends.' 'The international system was characterized by highly personal relations, flexibility, and the speed of a long-distance phone call ... This kind of informality and cooperation is not unusual, for the money managers [in North America] and in Europe are on a first-name basis, visit one another's homes, and talk frequently by trans-Atlantic telephone.' During the 1962 crisis, for example, the letters exchanged between Rasminsky and other central bank governors began with 'Bill' [Martin of the FRB] or 'Rowley' [of the Bank of England] or 'Per' [Jacobbson]. A letter of acknowledgment from William Martin thanking Rasminsky for informing the 'Fed' of the measures adopted by the Canadian government had a hand-written line at the bottom, 'We are all for you.' In the aftermath of the 1962 exchange crisis, Rasminsky wrote to Jacobsson: 'Now that the dust has settled a bit, I write this line to thank you for the great help you gave me during the dark days of June ... I am thinking particularly of your own personal contribution – your immediate understanding of the need for the Fund to respond quickly and without complications, and the firm encouragement and wise advice you gave me at all times. It was a great comfort to be able to discuss my problems with you.' Finally, in the aftermath of the crisis, Rasminsky sent a telegram to the BIS in Basle in early July to thank central bank governors for their offers of help. It was a small club.
51 LR76-523, LR to Diefenbaker, 23 June 1962.
52 LR76-523-48, Rasminsky interview with Pearson, 27 June 1962.
53 LR76-523-31, LR, 'Memorandum,' 27 June 1962.
54 Denis Smith, *Gentle Patriot: A Political Biography of Walter Gordon* (Edmonton: Hurtig Publishers, 1973), 107.
55 LR, AVPP, 55-6. See also Plumptre, *Three Decades,* 171–2.
56 See Erin E. Jacobsson, *A Life for Sound Money: Per Jacobsson, His Biography* (Oxford: Clarendon Press, 1979), 355–7. 'Early in the afternoon of 1 May 1962 PJ received an urgent call from Rasminsky. What could be done about the exchange rate? No decision had been taken by the Cabinet, but there had been discussion about the rate of $Can 1 = $US 0.925. What did PJ

think? ... On the new rate, PJ declined to give advice, but assured Rasminsky that he could appreciate the reasoning for the choice of a rate of $US 0.925.'
57 FRBR, Paul Gekker to Board of Governors, 27 June 1962.
58 Ibid.
59 FK, KP, POF, box 89A, file Treas 7/16/62–7/31/62, Memorandum to President from Ball and Dillon, 17 July 1962.
60 LR76-523, Cromer to LR, 26 June 1962.
61 LR76-523-6, LR to Cromer, 3 July 1962.
62 LR76-552-23, LR to Nowlan, 12 Sept. 1962.
63 The Liberals had taken 128 seats, the Conservatives ninety-five, Social Credit twenty-four, and the NDP seventeen.
64 Peter C. Newman, *The Distemper of Our Times: Canadian Politics in Transition, 1963–1968* (Toronto: McClelland and Stewart, 1968), 16.
65 Much of the following comes from LR76-549, 'Some Comments on the Budget,' 31 May 1963. In this, he was not very different from Eric Kierans. See John McDougall, *The Politics and Economics of Eric Kierans: A Man for All Canadas* (Montreal: McGill-Queen's University Press, 1993), 43–7 and 241–5.
66 On 10–11 May 1963, Pearson had spent a day and a half with Kennedy at the president's family 'compound' at Hyannisport, Mass.
67 Mitchell Sharp was to say years later that his 'impression was that Walter Gordon did not have very general support for his extreme economic nationalism, either in the bureaucracy or in the country or in the Liberal Party.' He is surely incorrect. At that point, the prime minister supported his minister of finance. Sharp's belief that Gordon's views were not those of the Liberal party, and that if 'I opposed him, I won the arguments so that brand of economic nationalism never took over the Liberal Party during that time,' is also suspect. See LR PP, Michael Hicks, Mitchell Sharp interview, 'Ottawa Decides, 1945–71,' 1989. Newman, *The Distemper of Our Times*, 18, suggests that Pearson fully supported the budget: 'One reason for Gordon's self-confidence was the enthusiastic response the budget had prompted from the Prime Minister. He had been shown a preliminary draft on June 3 and the penultimate version on June 7. "He saw it all the way through," Gordon later recalled. "While they were my ideas, he knew all about them, and as a matter of fact, he thought it was a better budget than I did. The controversial takeover tax proposal, taken out of the budget and put back several times, finally stayed in when Pearson suggested it would give the budget some kick."'
68 JFK, KP, NSF, box 19, Canada, General, 11/9/63-12/2/63, Butterworth to Secretary of State, 15 Nov. 1963.
69 For an account of the budget and the more purely political crisis that fol-

lowed, see J.L. Granatstein, *Canada, 1957–1967: The Years of Uncertainty and Innovation* (Toronto: McClelland and Stewart, 1986), 278–9.

70 JFK, KP, Butterworth to Secretary of State, 15 Nov. 1963; emphasis added. The ambassador's perceptions of the situation would have been taken seriously in Washington, given his excellent reputation. In a memorandum to President Johnson prepared a few years later, as Butterworth was leaving Ottawa, John Macy wrote: 'Ambassador Walton Butterworth, Jr., is a grand old warhorse of the Foreign Service. These are his assets: – Excellent political analyst. His mind is acute. He quickly finds the heart of an issue. – Able advocate and negotiator. He is a diplomatic virtuoso – a one-man band. – Many of his oral and written communications are masterpieces of precision. – He is forceful, forthright, and persuasive. – At 63 he is still vigorous and imaginative. He has boundless self-confidence.' Later, Macy notes that Livingstone Merchant, Butterworth's predecessor in Ottawa and his long-time friend, said when the latter's appointment was announced: 'He's just the s.o.b. the Canadians deserve.' See Lyndon B. Johnson Presidential Library (hereafter LBJ), Austin, Tex., White House Central Files, 1963–69, Macy to President, 24 Aug. 1966.

71 LBJ, Canada Cables, vol. 1, Butterworth to Secretary of State, 8 Feb. 1964.

72 LR76-806-28, LR to William Twaits, 28 Nov. 1967.

73 FRBR, Hart to Board of Governors, 8 Dec. 1965.

74 LR76-54, Hood to LR, 18 Jan. 1965.

75 LR76-576-1-18, LR, 'First National City Bank of New York,' 23 June 1963.

76 Granatstein, *Canada, 1957–1967*, 215.

77 LR76-552-31-90, LR to Walter Gordon, 3 July 1963.

78 LR76-576-1-9, 'Notes of Telephone Conversation of Mr. MacFadden ... with Mr. Rasminsky on Friday, July 26, 1963. To the US ambassador in Ottawa, Rockefeller and MacFadden spoke of Gordon's "threats."' See JFK, NSF, box 19, Canada, General, 7/12/63-7/30/63, Butterworth to Secretary of State, 29 July 1963.

79 This description came from William Ogden, executive vice-president, and Francis Mason and Leo Martinuzzi, senior vice-presidents, of the Chase Manhattan Bank, in a visit with Gerald Bouey on 7 June 1972. These men told Bouey that their bank would not come into Canada if opposition was pronounced. See LR76-591-8, G.K. Bouey, 'The Chase Manhattan Bank – Operations in Canada,' 7 June 1972.

80 Peter Newman, 'Relations Threatened by Bank Bill,' *Ottawa Journal*, 1 Dec. 1966. See also PCO Records, 'Report on Visit to Washington by Minister of Finance, 7 Aug. 1963.'

81 'Let Foreign Banks in Our Midst Alone,' *Journal of Commerce*, 25 July 1966.

82 LR76-552-2, LR to Fleming, 27 July 1961. For accounts of British crises, see
Margaret de Vries, *The International Monetary Fund, 1966–71*, vol. I, *Narrative*
(Washington, DC: International Monetary Fund, 1976), 338–43 and 431-7;
Charles Coombs, *The Arena of International Finance* (New York: Wiley, 1976),
chap. 8; Robert Solomon, *The International Monetary System, 1945–1976* (New
York: Harper and Row, 1977), chap. 5; and Brian Tew, *International Monetary
Cooperation, 1945–1967* (London: Hutchison, 1967), 195–7 and 204–8.

83 For a discussion of this, see Brian Tew, T*he Evolution of the International Monetary System, 1945–1977* (New York: Wiley, 1977), 93–5.

84 PCO Records, Cabinet Minutes, 'Devaluation of Sterling,' 20 Nov. 1967.

85 Cabinet Minutes, 'Devaluation of Sterling,' 20 Nov. 1967.

86 LR76-525-77, E.M. Whyte, 'Canada's Foreign Exchange Crisis and Its Aftermath,' 4 July 1968.

87 See LR76-446-35-1, LR to Benson, 29 Aug. 1968.

88 *Economist*, 11 May 1963, 553.

89 Incentive Award Board, *News Bulletin* (April 1969).

90 LR76-813, Trudeau to LR, 26 Nov. 1968.

91 LR, 'The Role of the Central Banker Today,' The Per Jacobsson Memorial Lecture, 9 Nov. 1966.

92 LR76-806, Exter to LR, 24 July 1968.

CHAPTER 8   Fighting Inflation: Second Term

1 *Globe and Mail* editorial, as quoted in Robert Bothwell, Ian Drummond, and
John English, *Canada since 1945: Power, Politics, and Provincialism* (Toronto:
University of Toronto Press, 1993), 319.

2 LR76-525-75-1, 'May 2, 1968.'

3 This idea did not die, and the Department of Finance and the Bank of Canada
had discussions about it in 1970. Tom Kent, deputy minister of regional economic expansion, wrote to Robert Bryce, deputy minister of finance: 'The
Atlantic Development Council has made a proposal to my Minister as to how
the impact of "tight money" on the slow-growth provinces might be lessened.'
While government money for the region was requested, there was some discussion of variegated interest rates. See LR-806, Tom Kent to R.B. Bryce,
11 Feb. 1970.

4 US monetary policy affected Canada and the rest of the industrialized world.
Harry Johnson focuses the issue when he writes, perhaps optimistically: 'It will
be necessary to contrive some means of rendering the monetary policy of the
Federal Reserve system more responsible and responsive to the requirements
of the international economy as a whole, and less subordinate to the purely

domestic requirements of the United States. The troublesome current world situation of inflation and high interest rates is largely attributable to failures of United States economic management, which have thrust an excessive share of the burden of stabilisation policy on American monetary policy. The implications for the rest of the world have been strongly resented, and will be even more strongly resented if the rest of the world has eventually to recognise and live with the fact that it is on a dollar standard, and that the US Federal Reserve is in reality but not constitutionally the world's central bank.' Harry Johnson, *An Overall View of International Economic Questions Facing Britain, the United States, and Canada during the 1970's* (London: British–North American Committee, 1970), 6.

5 LR interview, 22 July 1994.

6 LR76-548-16, LR to Marshall Crowe, 15 Dec. 1969. See also LR76-548-10, LR to Cabinet Committee on Priorities, 22 April 1969, and LR76-548-12, LR to Cabinet Committee on Priorities, 23 Sept. 1969.

7 John Harbron, 'How Hard Is Inflation Hitting Us and How Much Can We Take?' *Toronto Telegram*, 23 Feb. 1970.

8 CBC Radio commentary, 3 Sept. 1970.

9 Bank of Canada, *Annual Report for 1970*, 10.

10 LR76-538-36, 'Notes for Brief for House of Commons Committee,' 3 July 1969.

11 LR76-539-3, 'Notes for Remarks on the Current Economic Situation by Louis Rasminsky,' 16 Feb. 1970.

12 LR76-581-12, LR to Chartered Bank Presidents, 27 June 1969.

13 LR76-581-13, LR to Chartered Bank Presidents, 10 July 1969. Part of the problem lay with the competition that existed among the banks. While the presidents took Rasminsky's warnings seriously, certain banks 'raided' the clients of others. Accordingly, given a more stringent Bank attitude by 1969, G.R. Sharwood, the chief general manager of the Canadian Imperial Bank of Commerce, proposed that the chartered banks meet to try to reach a 'no raiding' agreement. When Sharwood asked whether Rasminsky had any objection, the governor's response was that his sole concern was to bring loan expansion under control and that it was up to the banks to decide how best to do this. LR76-581-14, LR, 'Memorandum of Telephone Conversation,' 11 July 1969.

14 LR76-598-81, 'Meeting with General Managers,' 10 Sept. 1969.

15 LR76-599-83, 'Chief Executive Officers,' 29 Oct. 1969.

16 LR76-806-28, LR to William Twaits, 28 Nov. 1967.

17 LR76-548-9-3, Beattie, 'Discussion – Cabinet Committee,' 21 April 1969.

18 LR76-535-6, Statement by Louis Rasminsky prepared for the Joint Committee of the Senate and House of Commons on Consumer Credit, 'Monetary and Credit Conditions,' 13 Oct. 1966; emphasis added. A table published in the

March 1970 *Budget Papers* contrasts the rise in prices for 1961 to 1965 and for
1965 to 1969.

Components of price change, total economy, Canada: average annual percentage rate
of increase, 1961–5, 1965–9

	1961–5	Contribution to total increase	1965–9	Contribution to total increase
Wages and salaries per unit of output	2.0	1.1	5.8	3.1
Corporate profits per unit of output	5.9	0.7	0.2	n.s.*
Indirect taxes less of subsidies per unit of output	4.1	0.5	4.7	0.6
Other incomes per unit of output	0.2	ns	4.0	4.0
Total price change	2.3	2.3	4.0	4.0

*n.s.: not significant.
Source: N. Swan and D. Wilton, eds., *Inflation and the Canadian Experience:
Proceedings of a Conference* (Kingston, Ont.: Industrial Relations Centre, 1971), 229

19 Robert Bryce, 'Government Policy and Recent Inflation in Canada,' in N.
Swan and D. Wilton, eds., *Inflation and the Canadian Experience: Proceedings of a
Conference* (Kingston, Ont.: Industrial Relations Centre, 1971), 228.
20 LR76-551-33, Prime Minister's Briefing, 26 Feb. 1971.
21 LR76-548-20, 'Minutes of a Meeting Held with Canadian government and
Bank of Canada officials,' 15 April 1970.
22 LR76-291-7, J.R. Beattie, 'Memo for Governor,' 20 March 1969.
23 LR76-522-264, Memorandum to the Cabinet, 'Exchange Policy,' 24 March
1971; emphasis added. See also Robert M. Dunn, *Canada's Experience with Fixed
and Flexible Rates in a North American Capital Market* (Montreal: Private Planning
Association of Canada, 1971), 24. Dunn points out that '[Richard] Caves and
[Grant] Reuber conclu[de] that a one percentage point rise in Canadian
interest rates relative to those prevailing in the United States will raise short-
term capital inflows by eight to nine per cent, long-term portfolio capital
inflows by nine per cent, and direct investment inflows by 1.5 percent.' The
Bank of Canada wanted to raise interest rates to fight inflation, but this would
have had adverse effects on the exchange rate. For the IMF account of Canada's initiative, see Margaret Garritsen de Vries, *The International Monetary
Fund, 1966–1971: The System under Stress*, vol. I, *Narrative* (Washington, DC:
International Monetary Fund, 1976), 476–82.

24 LR76-522-257-2, Organization for Economic Cooperation and Development, 'The Canadian Exchange Rate Action,' 30 June 1970. However, the questioner had a point. In the 1960s, the financial requirements of provincial governments increased dramatically, and their total debt went up from $10 billion to $20 billion. As Gerald Wright and Maureen Appel Molot note, 'Massive social expenditures were undertaken to expand the role of assistance from that of an emergency palliative to that of a provider of universal security. Highway construction, university building, and the expansion of hydroelectric power utilities all made heavy financial demands.' Gerald Wright and Maureen Appel-Molot, 'Capital Movements and Government Control,' *International Organization* 28 (1974), 67.

25 Dunn, *Canada's Experience*, 69. He also writes: 'A higher fixed exchange rate would also represent a potential threat to the Canadian economy. If the US economy entered a recession, Canada would import that downturn through the trade account, as the combination of decreasing US aggregate demand and the effects of the higher fixed exchange rate led to a sharp reduction in Canadian exports. As suggested earlier, a flexible exchange rate breaks the linkage between the business cycles of the United States and Canada and provides Canada with incomplete but considerable protection from instability in the US economy. In light of these factors, *the Canadian decision to float the exchange rate seems almost obvious*, although it certainly did not appear so to the financial community in Canada or to the international central banking community on June 1.' Still, Plumptre is correct when he states: 'Canadian financial policy is not and can never be independent of financial conditions and financial policies abroad, particularly those in the United States. Its independence will always be a matter of degree. The freedom that flows from a floating rate exchange rate can be and often is exaggerated.' See A.F.W. Plumptre, *Three Decades of Decision: Canada and the World Monetary System, 1944–1975* (Toronto: McClelland and Stewart, 1977), 226.

26 LR76-522-235, Robert Johnstone, 'The Mechanism of Exchange Rate Adjustment – Report on Discussions in the Fund,' 7 April 1970. See also Robert Solomon, *The International Monetary System, 1945–1976: An Insider's View* (New York: Harper and Row, 1977), 171–2. There was no unanimity in the European Economic Community (EEC), however. At the IMF's 1969 annual meeting, French Finance Minister Valéry Giscard d'Estaing warned 'against abandoning the principle of "fixed rates" and stressed that EEC countries have a "need for maintaining the conditions for the working of the Common Market which cannot, obviously, survive daily fluctuations or crawling uncertainty."'

27 As quoted in George N. Halm, *Toward Limited Exchange Rate Flexibility* (Princeton, NJ: International Finance Section, 1969).

28 Solomon, *The International Monetary System*, 171. As Solomon notes, the US administration's approach to the issue 'was hardly a resounding expression of support for movement toward greater flexibility. The US perception was that, while work on greater flexibility should proceed actively with American support, it would not be constructive for the United States to adopt a *public* posture of activism on this matter.'

29 Lawson had commented on it, challenging Polak's proposition that it was desirable to introduce a greater degree of flexibility in exchange rates. He wrote: 'I am strongly in favour of what I take to be the underlying idea of the Fund's parity system, namely that it is both desirable and feasible that countries pick exchange parities and stay with them over long periods. This system accepts the need for a parity change if a country, for whatever reason, gets substantially out of line with other countries, but it is unsympathetic to the idea of parity changes based on short-run analysis ... If ... we went the whole way and adopted a floating system, we would reduce speculative flows, but we would have paid a price for it that many, including myself, are not ready to pay.' A few months later, Canada floated its dollar. Obviously, Lawson's reservations were overcome. See LR76-522-233, Lawson, 'The Mechanism of Exchange Rate Adjustment,' 6 March 1970.

30 See, for example, Anthony Lanyi, *The Case for Floating Exchange Rates Reconsidered* (Princeton, NJ: International Finance Section, 1969). Halm, *Flexibility*, 5, 7, and 11, discusses conflicting opinion on this issue. J. Marcus Fleming, *Guidelines for Balance of Payments Adjustment under the Par Value System* (Princeton, NJ: International Finance Section, 1968), 4, notes: 'With the recrudescence of payments problems in the later 1950s came a bifurcation or trifurcation of thinking on the process of balance-of-payments adjustment. First, an academic revolt against the par value system of Bretton Woods sought to achieve or preserve the freedom of international transactions through a general adoption of a flexible or floating rate of exchange. This school of thought, which probably predominates in academic circles, has more recently trimmed its sails somewhat toward an advocacy of a par-value system with wide exchange rate margins ... Bankers and officials, however, together with a proportion of the academic community, still adhere by and large to the Bretton Woods system of adjustment.'

See also John H. Wanson, *The Crawling Peg* (Princeton, NJ: International Finance Section, 1965), who favoured a crawling peg. See also the essays contained in George N. Halm, ed., *Approaches to Greater Flexibility of Exchange Rates: The Bürgenstock Papers* (Princeton, NJ: Princeton University Press, 1970). As Halm notes in his preface, in a poll taken of thirty-four conference participants following the meeting at Bürgenstock, Switzerland, 'only three favored making no change in the present system. Six favored a modest widening of the band by amounts ranging up to plus or minus 2½ per cent ... Eighteen participants voted for versions of a bank-and-crawl system with a width of the band up to plus or minus three per cent, and a maximum rate of annual parity changes up to 2½ per cent ... The seven remaining respondents ... favored even more flexibility in one form or another' (vi–vii). This finding was a surprise, as the questionnaire 'showed that a large majority of the participants of the Bürgenstock Conference favored a move toward greater flexibility of exchange rates.' The literature from the 1960s is voluminous. For example, many of the post-1968 essays in Princeton University's International Finance Section's Series of Essays in International Finance are devoted to this issue.

31 De Vries, *The International Monetary Fund*, vol. I, 512–3. The report is reproduced in Margaret Garritsen de Vries, *The International Monetary Fund, 1966–1971: The System under Stress*, vol. II, *Documents* (Washington, DC: International Monetary Fund, 1976), 273–330.

32 LR76-522-250, R.W. Lawson, 'Notes on a Visit to Washington on May 31, 1970 to Explain Canada's Exchange Rate Decision,' 1 June 1970.

33 LR76-522-247, 'Schweitzer – May 31, 1970.'

34 Frank A. Southard, 'The Evolution of the International Monetary Fund,' Essays in International Finance, No. 135 (Princeton, NJ: International Finance Section, Dec. 1979), 34. See also de Vries, ed., *The International Monetary Fund*, vol. I, 478–9.

35 LR76-522-266, IMF Consultation, 'Exchange Rate Developments and Policy.'

36 De Vries, ed., *The International Monetary Fund*, vol. I, 481.

37 LR76-522-253, 'Discussions re Canadian Exchange Rate at BIS, June 6-8, 1970.' Ansiaux claimed that this was Canada's third float. When Beattie objected, noting that the change in 1946 had been a 10 per cent appreciation to a new fixed rate, Ansiaux insisted that Canada had floated its currency in 1947.

38 LR76-522-272, Washington to Ottawa, 13 May 1971.

39 LR76-375-35, Washington to External, 1 May 1972. See also Samuel Katz, 'The Case for the Par Value System, 1972,' Essays in International Finance, No. 92 (Princeton, NJ: International Finance Section, 1972), 25–6. Also of concern to the Americans and others was what was seen as Canada's 'dirty float.' In such a float, the government intervenes in the market to influence the movement of its currency. Katz quotes R.W. Lawson, a Bank deputy governor, as saying that 'the most important question for a government in respect of exchange rate policy is not should the exchange rate be "fixed" or should it float, but what should the exchange rate be? ... I am aware that some people seem to believe that if the exchange rate is determined in a free market without official inter-

vention, it will inevitably be the right rate, but this view seems to me a considerable oversimplification ... Good exchange rate policy is ... a blend of economics and politics.'

40 LR76-551-29, 'Nov. 23, 1970.'

41 LR76-540-7, Senate Committee on National Finance, 'Notes for Everett Committee,' 17 June 1971.

42 LR76-539-2, 'Notes for remarks on Current Economic Situation by Louis Rasminsky ... ,' 16 Feb. 1970.

43 LR76-540-18, 24 Nov. 1970.

44 LR76-548-25, Davey to Bouey, 28 May 1970.

45 In the cabinet meeting, Eric Kierans, the postmaster general, took issue with some of his colleagues' positions, and certainly that of Davey. As he said, the focus of policy that was developing was the rate of unemployment, while the problem was still to fight inflation. He expected a recession if inflation continued unabated. Still, it was not possible to ignore labour's demands; his suggestion was that all three elements in society – labour, business, and government – cooperate. At the cabinet meeting, there was also some discussion of price and wage controls. From the vantage point of the 1990s, a surprising facet of the meeting was the concern demonstrated by ministers over the fate of the unemployed.

46 Bank of Canada, *Annual Report for 1970*, 5.

47 LR PP, 2 Nov. 1970.

48 Ibid., McLaughlin to LR, 10 Nov. 1970.

49 Ibid., Hart to LR, 4 Nov. 1970.

50 Ibid., Lambert to LR, 23 Nov. 1970.

51 LR76-599-108, 'Chief Executive Officers,' 20 Jan. 1971.

52 Bank of Canada, *Annual Report for 1971*, 10.

53 LR76-552-152, LR to Turner, 10 Feb. 1970.

54 Bank of Canada, *Annual Report for 1972*, 8.

55 LR interview, 22 July 1994.

56 LR76-866, Address to Bank for International Settlements, 6 Jan. 1973.

57 Ibid., LR to O'Brien, 7 Dec. 1972.

58 LR76-810-48, LR to A.J. MacIntosh, 2 Sept. 1971.

59 Sheldon Kirshner, 'Confidence Was Rasminsky's Stock-in-Trade,' *Canadian Jewish News*, 4 June 1981.

CHAPTER 9   Four Crises

1 Robert Triffin, *The Balance of Payments and the Foreign Investment Position of the United States* (Princeton, NJ: International Finance Section, 1966), 2. See also Robert Roosa and Fred Hirsch, *Reserves, Reserve Currencies and Vehicle Currencies: An Argument* (Princeton, NJ: International Finance Section, 1966).

2 International Monetary Fund, *International Monetary Problems, 1957–1963: Selected Speeches of Per Jacobsson* (Washington, DC: International Monetary Fund, 1964), 206.
3 Robert Solomon, *The International Monetary System, 1945–1976: An Insider's View* (New York: Harper and Row, 1977), 57.
4 LR76 Misc, 'Memorandum of Meeting with Mr. Heeney, July 1958.'
5 LR76-552-31-90, LR to Walter Gordon, 12 June 1963.
6 Ibid.; emphasis added.
7 LR76-556-2, LR to Emminger, 3 July 1963.
8 LR76-365, 'US Interest Equalization Tax,' 14 Aug. 1964.
9 LR interview with Peter Stursberg, 1 June 1978.
10 See JFK, NSF, box 19, Canada, General, 11/9/63–12/2/63, Butterworth to Secretary of State, 15 Nov. 1963; emphasis added. Action 'x' in this case was the automotive tariff rebate scheme.
11 Canada, House of Commons *Debates*, 2 July 1963, 1751.
12 See USNA, DSR (1964–66), RG 59, Econ Finance box 841, FN 12 Balance of Payments Can–US 1/1/64, Livingston Merchant, 'Memorandum for this File,' 9 Oct. 1964; emphasis added.
13 For Rasminsky's notes used on 20 July in Washington, see LR76-365, LR, 'Notes for Conversation with Dillon and Roosa.'
14 LBJ, Council of Economic Advisors, reel no. 44, file: Canada–US Committee on Trade and Economic Affairs, 1966, Reifman to Ackley, 4 Feb. 1966.
15 LR interview with Peter Stursberg, 1 June 1978.
16 LR, AVPP, 62.
17 JFK, KP, James A. Reed Oral History, 70-1.
18 LR PP, LR to J.L. Granatstein, 12 June 1979.
19 LR interview with Peter Stursberg, 1 June 1978.
20 LR76-541-6, Plumptre, 'US Preliminary Comments on Canadian 1963 Budget,' n.d.
21 JFK, NSF, box 18, Canada, General, 6/63, David Klein to McGeorge Bundy, 21 June 1963.
22 Ibid., William Brubeck, 'Memorandum for McGeorge Bundy,' 22 June 1963.
23 LR interview with Peter Stursberg, June 1978.
24 As an example, Jacques Parizeau, Quebec's deputy minister of finance, went to see Robert Bryce, federal deputy minister of finance, in November 1965. In that meeting, Parizeau 'emphasized the vital importance to the Provinces, particularly Quebec, of having reliable access to the New York market subject only to that market's own judgement on the provincial credit and how much it was prepared to lend to any particular borrower.' See LR76-368-17, Bryce to Sharp, 'Quebec's Proposals Concerning Information,' 15 Nov. 1965.

25 See LR76-365-13, LR to Plumptre, 20 Aug. 1963.

26 LR76-365, 'US IET,' 14 Aug. 1964. It also meant the end of an independent monetary policy for Canada.

27 PCO Records, 'Report on Visit to Washington by Minister of Finance, 7 Aug. 1963.'

28 *Winnipeg Free Press*, 22 July 1963.

29 Jamie Swift, *Odd Man Out: The Life and Times of Eric Kierans* (Toronto: Douglas and McIntyre, 1988), 139.

30 LR76-416-1, LR to Pearson, 27 Aug. 1963.

31 LR76-365, 'US Interest Equalization Tax,' 14 Aug. 1964. Harry Johnson writes: 'It will be necessary to contrive some means of rendering the monetary policy of the Federal Reserve System more responsible and responsive to the requirements of the international economy as a whole, and less subordinate to the purely domestic requirements of the United States.' See Johnson, *An Overall View of International Economic Questions Facing Britain, the United States, and Canada during the 1970's* (London: British–North American Committee, 1970), 6. Perhaps the indirect but powerful influence that the United States exerted on Canadian monetary policy suggests that Ottawa should attempt to improve the continental relationship. The ninth meeting of the Joint US–Canada Committee on Trade and Economic Affairs, held in Ottawa in April 1964, was devoted to that end. American cabinet secretaries Dillon, Freeman, Hodges, and Udall met with the Canadians, who included Walter Gordon, Paul Martin, and Louis Rasminsky. An American summary noted: 'The meeting was characterized by a far greater spirit of cooperation and understanding than had characterized our first meeting with the present Canadian Government in Sept. [1963]. The Canadians made the point both privately and publicly of improved relations with the United States.' See LBJ, Country File – Canada Memos, Douglas Dillon, 'Memorandum of the President,' 1 May 1964.

32 LR76-416-1, LR to Pearson, 27 Aug. 1963.

33 Ironically, given Cold War tensions, the sale of wheat to the Soviet Union provided welcome help in that way to Canada. As a Bank of Canada paper pointed out, 'The most important factor enabling us to get through the past year without serious exchange problems has undoubtedly been the fortuitous very large sales of grain for cash to the Soviet Union. Khrushchev substituted himself for the US capital market at a most opportune moment for Canada!' LR76-365, 'US Interest Equalization Tax,' 14 Aug. 1965. The current-account deficit for 1964 was about $500 million; a deficit of $1.5 billion with the United States was partly offset by a surplus of $1 billion with the rest of the world. The latter figure was unusually large because of the Soviet wheat sales.

34 See J.L. Granatstein, *Canada, 1957–1967: The Years of Uncertainty and Innovation*

(Toronto: McClelland and Stewart, 1986), 261–2. In this area, Quebec came up with its own plan, which was, Granatstein notes, 'better in virtually all respects than Ottawa's. [It] proposed to create huge amounts of capital through pension contributions, a total of $8 billion to $10 billion over years.' Rasminsky would have agreed with this approach. See also Penny Bryden, 'The Liberal Party of Canada: Organizing for Social Reform,1957–1966,' in Gustav Schmidt and J.L. Granatstein, eds., *Canada at the Crossroads? The Critical 1960s* (Bochum, Germany: Universitatsverlag Dr. N. Brockmeyer, 1994), 42–4.

35 LR, AVPP, 71.
36 Ibid., 73.
37 LR76-552-31-90, Plumptre to Roosa, 19 Feb. 1964.
38 LR76-365-31, Aide-Memoire, 'Conversation with Secretary Dillon, Dec. 3rd, 1964.'
39 Ibid., Memorandum of Conversation, 'Canadian Borrowing in the United States,' 4 Dec. 1964.
40 See DFR, vol. 3943, file 8522-U-585 (64), 'Joint US–Canadian Committee on Trade and Economic Affairs, Ottawa, April 29–30, 1964.'
41 LR76-365-31, Memorandum of Conversation, 'Canadian Borrowing in the United States,' 4 Dec. 1964.
42 LR76-365-54, Washington to External, 1 April 1971.
43 For a brief account of the twists and turns of US fiscal and monetary policy from 1965 to 1971, see Solomon, *The International Monetary System*, 100–9.
44 Bank of Canada, *Annual Report for 1965* (1966), 8–9.
45 LR76-367-44-2, 'Meeting between the Honourable W.L. Gordon and the Honourable H.H. Fowler, Friday, July 30, 1965.'
46 LBJ, B/P – Canada, Dillon to the President, 8 Feb. 1965.
47 Bank of Canada, *Annual Report for 1965*, 8.
48 LR76-367-30-3, Gordon to Arnold Hart, 1 April 1965.
49 LR76-367-48, Handfield-Jones to Bank of Canada, 22 Oct. 1965.
50 Ibid.
51 LR76-367-64, 'My Talking Notes on Points 4 and 7 of R.B. Bryce Memo of Nov. 22, 1965.' See also LBJ, Henry Fowler Papers, box 54, file: International Balance of Payments – Classified Material – Canada–US, Widman to Chuck, 18 Oct. 1965.
52 LR76-367-63, 'Notes for Discussion with US Nov. 22, 1965.'
53 Ibid.
54 See John N. McDougall, *The Politics and Economics of Eric Kierans: A Man for All Canadas* (Montreal: McGill-Queen's University Press, 1993), 85–92. McDougall outlines Kierans's objections to the American guidelines and how he chose to

communicate them to Fowler, via a 'strident' letter, which he then released to the press. The letter was apparently written after the minister had had 'a blunt exchange' with Rasminsky, which had gotten 'his dander up.' It was a public reaction to the conversation with the governor. This publicity irritated Rasminsky, who 'telephoned [Quebec Premier Jean] Lesage on his return from Florida and asked indignantly what right his minister had to intervene in the matter and, even worse, to purport to speak for all of Canada.' Lesage immediately disciplined Kierans. See also Peter C. Newman, *The Distemper of Our Times: Canadian Politics in Transition, 1963–1968* (Toronto: McClelland and Stewart, 1968).

55 LR76-581-6, LR to Chartered Bank Presidents, 18 Feb. 1966.

56 Bank of Canada, *Annual Report for 1966*, 6.

57 LR76-370-13, Lawson to LR, 11 Nov. 1966.

58 LR76-370-17, Lawson to LR, 12 Nov. 1966.

59 Solomon, *The International Monetary System*, 102.

60 LBJ, 1968 Balance of Payments Program, 'The Balance of Payments Program of New Year's Day, 1968,' n.d., Tabs 1–3. There were other reasons for the adverse American situation – among them, the memorandum pointed out, 'the growing foreign exchange costs of US military expenditures abroad arising out of Vietnam and the growing attraction of the Common Market as an area for US direct investment.'

61 LR, AVPP, 82.

62 LR76-525, Deputy Minister of Trade and Commerce to LR, 28 Feb. 1968. The Americans were not unanimous on this issue, as a discussion paper shows. See LBJ, 'The Balance of Payments Program of New Year's Day, 1968.' 'The most difficult issues to resolve were the trade and tourism proposals. Secretary Fowler recommended the imposition of a border tax equivalent to all indirect US taxes ... This would have amounted to a permanent export rebate and import surcharge of about 2½ per cent. His argument was that such action was permitted under the rules of the GATT and therefore could not be subject to retaliation. Other believed that retaliation would occur and argued for a temporary export rebate and import surcharge of perhaps 2–3 per cent, which would be applied after we had consulted with and obtained the agreement of our major trading partners on the need for such action ... Some favored only an import surcharge and still others preferred doing nothing in the trade field.'

63 LR76-525-6, Memorandum for the Prime Minister, 'USA Balance of Payments Programme,' 21 Jan. 1968.

64 LR76-590-6, R.W. Lawson, 'Further Notes on Guidelines for Canadian Banks,' 21 March 1968.

65 LR76-525-10, 19 Feb. 1968.

66 LR76-525-9, 'Meeting with P.M. and Ministers, Feb. 4th, 1968.'

67 LR76-296-10, Hubert Ansiaux to LR, 24 Jan. 1968.

68 LR76-297-9, LR to Ansiaux, 1 Feb. 1968.

69 LR76-552-112, LR to Mitchell Sharp, 26 Feb. 1968.

70 Ibid.

71 LR76-525-7, Pearson to Johnson, 27 Feb. 1968.

72 LR76-525-24, Stoner to Rasminsky, 1 March 1968.

73 LR76-525-52, Meeting of March 3rd.

74 Ibid.

75 See, for example, LR76-590-60, LR to Beverly McGill, 30 June 1970.

76 LBJ, Country File – Canada, vol. 5, Memorandum for the President, 'Canadian Dollar Crisis,' 7 March 1968.

77 LR, AVPP, 87.

78 LR76-525-52, Meeting of March 3rd.

79 LBJ, 'Canadian Dollar Crisis,' 7 March 1968.

80 An example of how acutely aware he was of the continuing delicacy of the exchange situation was his query to the Canadian Broadcasting Corporation (CBC) over a news report by Tim Ralfe. Rasminsky told George Davidson, the CBC's president, that Ralfe, in his report of the events of 7 March, injected editorial opinion that could be damaging to the rescue operation. He was not opposed to criticism but did object to the expression of personal opinion in a supposedly factual and objective news account. In his reply, Davidson told him: 'You may rest assured that it is our constant objective to base our News broadcasts firmly on reliable factual reporting – reserving expressions of editorial opinion for other types of broadcasts which are clearly labelled as such.' LR76-525-61-1, Davidson to LR, 21 March 1968.

81 See Robert M. Dunn, *Canada's Experience with Fixed and Flexible Exchange Rates in a North American Capital Market* (Montreal: Private Planning Association of Canada, 1971), 34. Dunn points out: 'Given the reserve ceiling and Canada's actual reserves, Canada's ability to deal with inflation through monetary policy was determined in Washington when the Federal Reserve System decided what interest rates would prevail in the United States.'

82 'The Price of Concessions,' *Financial Times of Canada*, 23 Sept. 1968. See also *Globe and Mail*, 27 Sept. 1968; *Financial Post*, 21 Sept. 1968.

83 Bank of Canada, *Annual Report for 1968*, 5.

84 LR76-371-11, 'Aide Memoire for Mr. Benson's Conversation with Mr. Fowler, October 1, 1968.

85 LR76-371-12, Lawson to Bryce, 4 Oct. 1968.

86 LR76-364-11, LR to Martin, 25 Nov. 1968.
87 LR76-371-33, 'Summary of Mr. Rasminsky's Comments to Mr. John Petty on the Telephone at 5:00 pm, Jan. 8, 1969,' 10 Jan. 1969.
88 Solomon, *The International Monetary System*, 104, 108.
89 LR76-293-1, G-10 Ministerial Meeting, London, 15–16 Sept. 1971, 'The International Monetary Situation,' 9 Sept. 1971.
90 LR76-551-42, 'Financial Situation,' n.d.
91 F. Boyer de la Giroday, 'Myths and Reality in the Development of International Monetary Affairs,' Essays in International Finance, No. 105 (Princeton, NJ: International Finance Section, 1974).
92 LR interview, 24 May 1974.
93 LR76-373-14, Washington, DC, to Ottawa, 26 Aug. 1971.
94 LR76-373-3, Washington, DC, to Ottawa, 16 Aug. 1971.
95 Ibid.
96 LR76-373-14, Washington to External, 26 Aug. 1971.
97 LR76-373-14, Washington, DC, to Ottawa, 26 Aug. 1971. See also J.L. Granatstein and Robert Bothwell, *Pirouette: Pierre Trudeau and Canadian Foreign Policy* (Toronto: University of Toronto Press, 1990), 65–7. Granatstein and Bothwell present a lively description of what transpired when Connolly and Volcker met with Benson and Pepin. They end by observing: 'The two teams parted on poor terms, though Reisman afterwards denied that he had really stubbed out his cigar on Connolly's elegant desk.' Obviously, relations were poor. As one US State Department official observed, 'In the 1960s the relationship between [Canadian and American] financial officials was so close that we were often shut out of policy. Now, their relations are so poor that they complicate policy.' Joseph Nye, 'Transnational Relations and Interstate Conflicts: An Empirical Analysis,' *International Organization*, 28 (1974), 968 n 16.
98 LR76-373-12, Washington, DC, to Ottawa, 19 Aug. 1971, 'Treasury Secretary Connolly on *Today* Show, NBC-TV.'
99 LR76-373-3, Washington to External, 16 Aug. 1971.
100 See LR76-374-2, 'Prime Minister's Meeting with the President of the United States of America,' 6 Dec. 1971.
101 Granatstein and Bothwell, *Pirouette*, 48.
102 Ibid., 50. As they also point out, 'Trudeau was a Liberal and ... Nixon was not.'
103 LR76-374-2, 'Prime Minister's Meeting with the President of the United States, Dec. 6, 1971.'
104 LR76-299-19, 'Notes of a Conversation between Mr. Benson and Secretary Connolly,' Sept. 1971.

105 LR PP, Michael Hicks, LR interview, 'Ottawa Decides, 1945–1971,' 1989.

106 LR76-299-27, LR's Notes of G-10 Meetings, Rome, 29 Nov. 1971.

107 Margaret Garritsen de Vries, *The International Monetary Fund, 1966–1971: The System under Stress*, vol. I, *Narrative* (Washington, DC: International Monetary Fund, 1976), 545.

108 LR76-299-13, Prof. Karl Schiller's Statement, 15 Sept. 1971.

109 LR76-301, 'Notes for a Statement by ... Benson,' 16 Sept. 1971. See also LR76-299-10, Statement by Mikio Mizuta, 15 Sept. 1971, and LR76-300, Reisman to the Minister, 6 Sept. 1971. As an example of hard attitudes, Japan's minister of finance, Mikio Mizuta, was adamant that 'the burden of adjustment should not be passed unduly to other countries.' Similarly, a report prepared by J. Zilstra, governor of De Nederlandsche Bank, suggested that the magnitude of the improvement being sought by the United States was 'very large and will not be accepted by other countries as a basis for negotiation.'

110 Granatstein and Bothwell, *Pirouette*, 66.

111 LR interview, 29 May 1974. Rasminsky's recollection is different from that of Solomon, who claims that 'Connolly, Burns and Volcker *skillfully* wheedl[ed] the various ministers to maximize the appreciation of their currencies relative to the dollar.' Solomon, *The International Monetary System*, 206; emphasis added.

112 LR interview, n.d.

113 LR76-299-35, LR's Statement, G-10 Meeting, Washington, DC, 17 Dec. 1971.

114 LR interview, 29 May 1974. Of course, the Americans pressed others to make concessions as well. In the case of Mikio Mizuta, this took on a personal dimension. While he agreed at the Smithsonian meetings to revalue the yen from ¥360 to ¥308 to the dollar (16.88 per cent), he had turned down the first US demand that the yen reach ¥305 to the dollar (more than 17 per cent). Mizuta knew that in 1932 Finance Minister Junosuke Inoue had been assassinated by a right-wing terrorist because he had agreed to a 17 per cent revaluation of the yen following foreign pressure. The stress of believing that he would be murdered in the streets of Tokyo made him quite ill, with violent diarrhoea. See interview with Takashi Hosomi, 'Entire Nation Is to Blame for Bubble Trouble,' *Yomiuri Shimbun*, 24 June 1997, 3.

115 Solomon, *The International Monetary System*, 208.

116 LR76-373-25-1, 'Transcript of Remarks Made by Volcker on 16 Feb. 1972 at Johns Hopkins.'

117 LR76-375-35, Washington to External, 1 May 1972.

118 LR76-806, LR to Trudeau, 29 Oct. 1972.

119 LR76-806, Trudeau to LR, 8 Nov. 1972.

120 BER, OV58/18, 143, 'Extract of Memo PHK Report of Visit, 4.5.72.' Neither
　　Rasminsky nor Reisman was aware of this speculation.

Epilogue　　Retirement and Beyond

1 LR76-866, LR to O'Brien, 7 Dec. 1972.
2 LR PP, J.F. O'Sullivan to LR, 12 Aug. 1974.
3 Ibid., 'Outline Statement by the President of the Board of Governors of the
　　IDRC, March 19, 1973.'
4 Ibid., 'Notes for Bora Laskin Dinner, June 17, 1981.'
5 Ibid., 'Draft Remarks for Ben-Gurion Dinner,' 11 Oct. 1983.
6 Ibid., 'The Louis Rasminsky Endowment Fund.'
7 *Canada as an International Banking Centre* (Ottawa: Department of Finance,
　　1986), 19.
8 LR PP, 'Holocaust Gathering, Closing Plenary Session, Arpil 30, 1985.'
9 LR interview, 25 June 1995.

Illustration Credits

Rasminsky Collection

Young Rasminsky; holidaying in Italy; United Nations San Francisco Conference; Abbott, Claxton, Rasminsky (Capital Press Service); IMF executive; en route to India (Graetz Bros. Limited); Rasminsky family (Paul Horsdal Ltd.); Bank meetings in Washington, DC (Capitol Photo Service, Inc.); Lyla and Louis Rasminsky (Photo Service di O. Gentili); Companion of the Order of Canada; Isaac Stern recital (Fernand R. Leclair); Fund for Social and Cultural Integration; the Round Table (Studio von Dulong); Louis Rasminsky and Jerry Grey

Bank of Canada Photographic Collection

Official Bank of Canada photograph of Rasminsky, BCP. 153-7; Gerald Bouey, BCP. 153-15

Index

Note: A page number followed by 'T' denotes a table.

Ball, George, 211
bancor, 86, 96
Bank Act, 185, 186–7; amendment (1966), 216
Bank for International Settlements (BIS), 126, 135, 154–5, 248; Canada's float, 240; European central-bank credit, 280; sterling crisis, 218–19
bank credit, and Canadian subsidiaries, 271
Bank of Canada: administrative reforms, 190–3; *Annual Report* (1961), 183–4, (1962), 254, (1965), 265, (1966), 269, (1968), 282, (1972), 247; building program, 193; and conflict with Finance, 167–71; francophones in, 191; language groups in, 192T; Pension Rule 17, 179–82; Rasminsky appointments, 20–1, 50, 98–9; and relationship with federal government, 186. *See also* inflation
Bank of Canada Act (1936), 168, 185; amendment (1967), 176, 186–7
Bank of England: opposition to Bretton Woods agreement, 109; opposition to Clearing Union, 87; on Rasminsky's appointment at Bank of Canada, 147–8, 179; relations with Canada, 67, 203, 207. *See also* sterling
Bank of Israel, 148
Bank of Montreal, 171, 204, 245
Bank of Nova Scotia, 246
bank rate, 205–6, 207, 244, 246–7; increase in, 270, 271–2, 278–9, 280
Banking and Finance Committee, 173
Banque Canadienne Nationale, 246
Baumgartner, Wilfrid, 156, 220

Beattie, Robert, 70, 146–7, 167, 171, 175, 177, 231, 240, 254
Belgium: nutrition research in, 32; and Stabilization Fund, 94
Bell Canada Enterprises, 298
Ben-Gurion, David, 299
Ben-Gurion associate organizations, 299–300
Bennett, R.B., 19
Benson, Edgar, 246, 282, 287–92
Bernstein, Edward, 92–3, 100, 107, 111, 141, 154
bilingualism, Bank of Canada, 192
Bill C-193, 275
Bill of Rights (Diefenbaker), 175
Bishop's University, honorary doctorate, 221
BIS. *See* Bank for International Settlements (BIS)
Bladen, Vincent W., 7–8, 149; wife of, 21
Blessing, Karl, 280
Boise Cascade Forest Products, 298
Bolivia, League work in, 44–5
Bolton, Sir George, 67, 105, 109, 124–5, 131, 151
Bora Laskin Endowed Scholarship Fund of Yeshiva University, 301
Bouey, Gerald, 185, 192, 242–3, 295
Boyles, T.A., 246
Brebner, J.B., 114
Bretton Woods (1944), 100, 102, 104–10, 237, 286; agreement, 107; opposition to, 109; preliminary meeting in Atlantic City (June 1944), 102–4
Britain. *See* United Kingdom
British Commonwealth Air Training Plan, 67, 120
Brittain, Sir Herbert, 151

American Diplomacy and the End of the Cold War

American Diplomacy and the End of the Cold War

An Insider's Account of U.S. Policy in Europe, 1989–1992

ROBERT L. HUTCHINGS

THE WOODROW WILSON CENTER PRESS
Washington, D.C.

THE JOHNS HOPKINS UNIVERSITY PRESS
Baltimore and London

Editorial offices:

The Woodrow Wilson Center Press

370 L'Enfant Promenade, S.W., Suite 704

Washington, D.C. 20024-2518

Telephone 202-287-3000, ext. 218

Order from:

The Johns Hopkins University Press

Hampden Station

Baltimore, Maryland 21211

Telephone 1-800-537-5487

2 4 6 8 9 7 5 3 1

All photographs courtesy the Bush Presidential Library

Library of Congress Cataloging-in-Publication Data

Hutchings, Robert L., 1946–

American diplomacy and the end of the Cold War : an insider's

account of U.S. policy in Europe, 1982–1992 / Robert L. Hutchings.

p. cm.

Includes bibliographical references and index.

ISBN 0-8018-5620-5 (cloth : alk. paper).— ISBN 0-8018-5621-3

(paper : alk. paper)

1. Europe—Foreign relations—United States.   2. United States—

Foreign relations—Europe.   3. Europe—Politics and

government—1989-   4. United States—Foreign relations—1981–1989.

5. United States—Foreign relations,—1989–1993.

I. Title.

D1065.U5H88 1997

327.7304—dc21

96-48308

CIP

For Kim

Contents

Preface

IN THE SPRING OF 1988, I gave a speech at the University of Virginia, where I had done my doctoral work a decade earlier. I argued five propositions: Soviet foreign policy had undergone an historic shift, Germany's role in Europe was changing fundamentally, the "European idea" was stronger than at any time since 1919, the United States was retreating from an active role in European affairs, and Eastern Europe would be the arena in which Europe's future would be decided, as it had been twice already in the century.[1] It was a forecast of impending major change in Europe and an appeal to American leadership.

Little did I suspect that just a year later I would be called on to play a role in these events as director for European affairs with the National Security Council. Still less could I have imagined how broadly these perspectives were shared at the senior levels of the incoming Bush administration, which set about acting on them with a decisiveness that belied my lament on declining U.S. leadership even while vindicating the other four propositions.

This is not to imply causality. I had no role in influencing the views of President George Bush, Secretary of State James Baker, or National Security Adviser Brent Scowcroft before Bush's inauguration as president in January 1989. As a nonpartisan professional, I was involved neither in the campaign nor with the transition team but rather was asked to join the NSC staff by virtue of my background in East European and German affairs.

I came to this field late, in my second year of graduate school, and almost by accident. A course in East European politics, taken mainly out of curiosity, piqued an interest that soon deepened. This field seemed where everything that mattered in international politics came together. It was where East met West, where liberal democracy confronted the communist experiment, where Karl Marx met John Stuart Mill. Moral questions were sharply defined; the human dramas were compelling. After graduate school I became deputy director of Radio Free Europe in Munich, diverted from an academic career by one of those opportunities too good to miss. For five years in the early 1980s I lived in divided Germany, among RFE's brilliant émigré communities, spending every working hour and many private ones totally absorbed in Central and Eastern European affairs. By the end of the 1980s, when Poland and Hungary stood on the threshold of revolutionary change, it was as if my whole career had been preparation for playing a role in Eastern Europe's liberation and Germany's unification.

So perhaps it was fate or destiny that brought me to the Bush White House in 1989. Or maybe it was just luck. It certainly was not political connections, because I had none. Indeed, it was emblematic of Bush's bipartisanship in foreign policy that in three and a half years at the White House, no one ever asked which political party I belonged to or for whom I voted in the 1988 election. I had reason to believe I would fit in with the Bush administration's general foreign policy orientation but was surprised—or rather, thrilled—to find how closely the thinking of Bush, Baker, Scowcroft, and others who mattered coincided with my own. More than once in doing the research for this book, I came across a Baker speech of which I had been unaware yet felt that I might have drafted it myself, so closely did it reflect my own views.

This book is part political memoir, part eyewitness account, and part scholarly analysis. I have gone over events and decisions twice, as it were—first as a participant or witness, second as a relatively detached scholar striving to understand and assess this period independent of my personal role in it. I have tried to combine the insider's unique perspective with the scholar's balanced judgment.

I was one of the dozen or so senior U.S. officials operating on the inside of policy making toward Europe and the Soviet Union at the end of the Cold War. Of course there were hundreds of officials involved in these policies and dozens more senior and influential than I. But only a handful of senior advisers around President Bush and Secretary Baker had a strategic vantage point and a direct role in formulating and implementing our broad strategies and policies toward Europe and the Soviet Union. On some issues—the diplomacy of German unification, for example—the "dozen or so" grew to perhaps twice that number as negotiations proceeded. On others, notably strategy toward Central and Eastern Europe after the revolutionary crowds had gone home and the first flush of enthusiasm had faded, the number dropped to fewer than a half dozen.

This book concentrates on aspects where I had personal, direct, and intense involvement: Central and Eastern Europe before, during, and after the revolutions of 1989, Germany during the period of unification and thereafter, and broad strategies toward Europe and the Soviet Union throughout the period. It also covers, but in less detail, aspects where my involvement was more peripheral: U.S.-Soviet relations, arms control, security policy, and trade relations.

This book thus encompasses the whole story of the end of the Cold War in Europe, but from a particular vantage point, one that was as good as any other and better than most for assessing the diplomacy of the period. It was arguably the *best* vantage point, if one believes, as I do, that the countries of Eastern Europe were the key to ending the Cold War and the key to the post–Cold War order in Europe. This is where the issues that had divided East and West for forty years came together; this was the arena of most intense activity during the period; this was where Soviet, West European, and American policies met and interacted.

This book's span of time coincides with my tenure with the National Security Council from early 1989 to mid-1992. It begins with the development of American strategy at the beginning of 1989, continues through the revolutionary developments of 1989–90 and the security issues arising therefrom, and concludes with the collapse of the Soviet Union at the end of 1991. Key events immediately thereafter, such as the deepening Yugoslav war, are dealt with selectively.

Roles and Perspectives

We NSC staffers liked to think of ourselves as advisers to presidents and secretaries of state, and so we were. We were expected to be the principal initiators of policy ideas, which were then approved, rejected, or amended at the political level. This was our main responsibility and the reason we took the job in the first place.

Yet the more prosaic tasks like note taking went with the territory, too. When the president met with foreign counterparts here or abroad, my role most often was to take notes. This was my admission ticket to hundreds of presidential meetings during the period. My policy role was played beforehand and afterwards. During the meetings themselves, I was rarely called on to offer an opinion. Like the model child of yesteryear, I was expected to be seen but not heard. Even more obscure was the role I played as note taker for presidential telephone calls, of which there were many under Bush. Typically, I would monitor and transcribe the calls from the White House Situation Room, with my telephone on receive only, so that I could be neither seen nor heard. (Occasionally, when the president made a call unexpectedly in the early morning or on weekends, it would be patched through to me at home so I could monitor from there. I had no capacity to mute the transmit side of my home phone, however, so foreign leaders were occasionally startled to hear the bark of my trusty German shepherd, Kazimierz—after King Kazimierz III, for you students of Polish history—in the background. He must have sounded like Millie, the Bush dog, on steroids.)

These prosaic functions were also important for the telling of this story. As note taking required only two or three brain cells, the rest were free to roam intellectually. I could observe and reflect, watching history unfold before my eyes. I imagine that I experienced more sheer joy and excitement in seeing history being made than did Bush, Baker, or Scowcroft, with their unending responsibilities.

Watching political leaders at close range is instructive. They are not like you and me. Their analytic capacities may not be as finely honed, but their political instincts and intuitive skills are much keener. They are trained to action, not reflection. They know how to size up situations, improvise, and make decisions under pressure. Their natural element is interaction with leaders who bear responsibilities comparable to their own. They understand the subtleties of political power in ways the rest of us could not possibly appreciate.

In discharging their daunting responsibilities, they look to their senior staff to provide the main ideas. They are used to relying on their staffs, but also distrusting them. Most of their best ideas have come from their staffs, but so have many harebrained or dangerous ones. They alone bear the responsibility to decide, usually on the basis of incomplete information; often they must do so under intense time pressure to act, with life-or-death consequences.

In writing this book I did not dwell on the internal debates within the administration. This was not due to squeamishness or timidity. In the relatively few instances of significant policy differences, I have analyzed the differing views in detail. Otherwise, I have employed the royal "we" to connote the broadly shared views among the senior foreign policy-makers in the Bush administration: the president and his national security adviser, the secretaries of state and defense, the chairman of the Joint Chiefs of Staff, and their most senior advisers. Thus "we in Washington," "we in the administration," or simply "we" stands as shorthand for the collective views of these senior officials. Where I have used "we" in some other sense, I have tried to make the distinction clear so as to avoid further ambiguity. It is not a perfect device, but it suits the purposes of this book. I was interested in the question "why" more than the question "how"—in policy rather than process. Besides, the Bush administration foreign policy team was about as collegial in style and like-minded on the major issues as one could imagine; a detailed accounting of the internal decision-making process would only divert attention from the larger story of how American diplomacy helped to end the Cold War.

The "we" should not be confused with "I." I claim no personal credit, except as part of a larger group of advisers to the president and his National Security Council. For the record, I was more right than most in seeing the coming collapse of East European communism, slower than many in recognizing the prospects for German unification, and somewhere in the middle of the pack in gauging Soviet intentions. Others lined up differently. No one was right on all the issues all the time. What mattered were the collective judgments that were translated into policy. Even where individuals erred in their forecasts, it was often for sound and valid reasons that helped shape effective policy. Besides, foreign policy decision making is not some sort of parlor game in which the grand prize is awarded to the most accurate forecaster. The proper measure of American policy was the extent to which our actions were consistent with the possibilities before us and our larger interests.

The temptation in a book of this sort to inflate one's own role is enormous, and I am conscious that I have not always resisted it. Thucydides set a standard that was hard to follow. Still, there were events for which I was the only witness, where my perspective was unique, or where a personal observation could lend verisimilitude. When in doubt about relating a personal event or perspective, I have tried to employ two criteria. Was the story essential for the larger one I am trying to tell? Was it necessary to tell it in my own voice?

The Perils of "Immediate History"

T. E. Lawrence, in the foreword to *Revolt in the Desert*, complained that his "interest in the subject . . . was exhausted long ago in the actual experience of it."[2] My feelings were rather the opposite. The period 1989–92 was so rich and complex that even those who lived with these events as they were happening and had a certain role in shaping them could not possibly absorb their totality. I could not be done with them until I had put them in such perspective as I could gain with the benefit of research and reflection.

The perils of writing "immediate history" are several. First is the matter of perspective: no one writing close on the heels of major events can possibly have the historical perspective that future generations will have. What is transitory is taken for permanent; what turns out to have been a trend of profound importance is missed altogether.

In the relatively few years since the collapse of the Soviet empire, already there have been several "paradigm shifts." A writer recounting the events of the preceding two years in Europe around the time of the Paris Summit of November 1990 would have been influenced by the then-prevailing euphoria over the seeming triumph of democracy. Six months later, the writer would have been less sanguine about democracy's prospects in the formerly communist countries but newly impressed by the military triumph of U.S.-led coalition forces in the Persian Gulf—and so might have seen the makings of a "new world order" in which the United Nations worked as its creators intended. A year after that, as Yugoslavia descended into the most egregious carnage Europe had seen since the defeat of Nazi Germany, any chronicler would have been affected by the deep sense of pessimism the international community felt because of its helplessness in the face of Europe's first post–Cold War crisis. The passage of a few years has lent a more balanced perspective, but no book written so soon after these epochal events can hope to capture their meaning in the broad sweep of history.

Second is the problem of sources. The great bulk of the official record of what transpired is still classified and inaccessible; no account based on memory, even supplemented by personal notes, interviews, and publicly available evidence, can substitute for the full documentary record. In that respect, the period 1989–92 was unusual in that some of the official documents are already in the public domain. The greatest number of these have come from the East German and Soviet archives, but some key U.S. documents, including presidential decisions on Soviet policy in 1989, have already been declassified.[3] Press accounts, interviews, and a burgeoning memoir literature also help fill out the historical record. Moreover, as modern diplomacy is conducted semipublicly, there is a vast and largely underutilized body of public documents on which this book relies. Every day, the White House and State Department issue reams of paper—press briefings, public statements, fact sheets, and the like. Most of it is forgettable, but among the trivial and routine are official statements that offer a reasonably good record of the thinking at the highest levels of government.[4]

I supplemented these sources with interviews with Soviet, German, French, British, and East European officials who had been involved in these events, but I deliberately avoided conducting extensive interviews with American officials. I occasionally sought information about a key event where I was not present or where memory failed, but I was wary of getting too close lest this book take on a corporate character as a kind of authorized account of Bush administration foreign policy. This is interpretive history, and I wanted to maintain a critical distance.

A third peril, specific to political memoirs like this one, is the temptation to engage in retrospective rationalization and self-justification. One is tempted to trumpet one's successes and disguise one's failures. As an honest and usually self-effacing sort of fellow, I had not expected this to be as great a problem as it turned out to be. Vanity is of course part of the explanation. So is the way one works through events as they are occurring, building up a set of rationalizations almost without knowing it. One does it in everyday life: the squabble with a coworker gets quickly rationalized, as one excuses or explains away one's own motives and behavior. For public officials, it is also a matter of conditioning: having been trained to defend government policies as part of the job, one instinctively continues doing so after leaving office. More than once in writing this book, I had to correct myself when I began to give the official explanation of an event or a policy as I had so often done as a member of the administration. I have tried to offset these tendencies by exposing my views to the no-holds-barred critiques of outside readers, documenting my assertions as thoroughly as was possible, and applying as much intellectual honesty as I could muster.

Although I could not hope to escape these perils entirely, the passage of time worked in my favor. The book took longer to write than I had expected, and this turned out to be a blessing (except for my long-suffering family). The historical perspective became somewhat clearer, significant new sources opened up to enrich the account, and my own role shifted more easily from participant to chronicler.

"Immediate history" has one great advantage over history produced at a greater distance from events. A biographer friend once complained that most biographies are written from the perspective of knowing how the life in question turned out in the end. The omniscient biographer thus tends towards condescension in treating the subject; to lend order, events that do not fit the biographer's pattern are discarded or minimized. Yet this is not how a life is actually lived. We confront issues and make choices not knowing how the next act of our personal drama will turn out. Confusion and occasional bewilderment come with the territory. So it is with history. Most historical writing suffers from what the French philosopher Henri Bergson called "illusions of retrospective determinism."[5] Knowing how the story turned out, the historian goes back in time and decides upon a certain structure, sifting out evidence that does not fit the pattern and marshalling all the political, economic, and social factors that drove history along its predetermined course. Yet this is not how history looks to those making it. They deal with confusion, contrary trends, and incomplete knowledge. The best of them may have foresight (in the sense of prudence, one of Bush's favorite terms), but they cannot have foreknowledge. They cannot turn the clock forward to see how their courses of action might influence future events.

Thus "immediate history," for all its demerits, can have the virtue of recapturing the moment and "humanizing" history, as it were, by restoring the sense that real choices were made by real people. This is the drama I have tried to capture in this book. It is how life is lived. It is how history happens.

Acknowledgments

AT THE WHITE HOUSE from 1989 to 1992 and the State Department in 1992 and 1993, I had the privilege of playing a role in the central drama of my generation. I was doubly privileged to have worked for two of the finest public servants our country has ever known—Brent Scowcroft and Larry Eagleburger—and to have served at one step removed under two others, George Bush and James Baker. Without the opportunity to serve under their leadership, there would be no book.

A Woodrow Wilson Center fellowship in 1993 and 1994 afforded me a full year of uninterrupted research and writing in as congenial a setting as one could imagine. It is a better book for the company I kept, particularly the long discussions over lunch in the fellow's dining room on the fourth floor of the Smithsonian Castle. I learned more from a Ghanaian philosopher, an Indian journalist, a historian of sixteenth-century England, and other scholars with whom I shared my fellowship year than from specialists in my own field.

Another year at the Woodrow Wilson Center filling in as director of its international studies program enabled me to finish the book only a year or so behind schedule. My thanks and affection go to all my colleagues there, particularly the Center's deputy director, my friend Sam Wells. I am grateful to the Woodrow Wilson Center Press, especially to Joe Brinley, director, and Robert Poarch, editor, for shepherding the manuscript through its final stages, and to my research assistants, led by Sabina Crisen, for their invaluable support and unfailing good humor along the way. Many colleagues were kind enough to read all or part of the manuscript: Jim Brown, David Gompert, Peter Mulrean, Jan Nowak,

Joe Rothschild, Brent Scowcroft, Paul Shoup, Gale Stokes, Steve Szabo, Ron Tiersky, and Greg Treverton should be specially mentioned.

My deepest thanks go to my family, which endured my chaotic schedule during my time at the White House and then had to live through this period a second time as I wrote this book. I am grateful to my mother, Ruth Hutchings, and my mother-in-law, Pauline Schwartz, for helping out on the home front during my frequent trips abroad. My son, Jonathan, to whom my last book was dedicated, was a constant inspiration and a daily reminder that what really matters is right here at home. Most of all, I am indebted to my wife, Kim, whose love and support are the wind beneath my wings. This book is for her, in more ways than one.

American Diplomacy and the End of the Cold War

Introduction

WITHIN A FEW MONTHS in late 1989, communist regimes fell in Poland, Hungary, East Germany, Czechoslovakia, Bulgaria, and Romania. Less than a year later, Germany was reunited. A year after that, the Soviet state collapsed, returning Russia to the preimperial boundaries of sixteenth century Muscovy. Thus the end of the Cold War was also the culmination of the processes of imperial dissolution that spanned the entire century. Never in modern history, not even during the French Revolution, had changes of such magnitude occurred except as a consequence of major war.

The swift and largely peaceful course of these revolutionary developments tended to lend them a false air of inevitability and obscure the enormity of the changes left in their wake. Epochal changes that few would have thought possible in 1989 were by 1992 too easily taken for granted, as was America's pivotal role during the period.

There was nothing inevitable about the dramatic course of events beginning in 1989. The Berlin Wall would not have fallen in November 1989 but for the successful challenge to communist rule in Poland earlier in the year. Even after the fall of the Berlin Wall, there were enormous obstacles—beginning with Soviet opposition—to the successful unification of Germany with no restrictions on its sovereignty. Nor was the disintegration of the Soviet Union the inevitable consequence of the conflicts that raged through that country for most of 1991. There were several possible outcomes to the crisis of Soviet communism, not just one.

U.S. policy obviously did not *cause* these developments. They were deeply rooted in history and driven by the heroic efforts of democratic opposition leaders in Central and Eastern Europe. Former Soviet presi-

dent Mikhail Gorbachev deserves credit, too, for legitimizing change in
the Soviet empire and for refusing to resort to forcible suppression even
as those changes went far beyond anything he had considered at the
outset.

Yet American policy exerted a strong, sometimes decisive, influence
on the peaceful end of Europe's postwar division and the collapse of
the Soviet empire. As German foreign minister Hans-Dietrich Genscher
said with regard to the unification of his country, "If America had so
much as hesitated, we could have stood on our heads" and gotten
nowhere.[1] Although policy was at times reactive—given the pace and
scope of change, it could hardly have been otherwise—it was also informed, to a greater degree than has so far been credited, by a grand
strategy for ending the Cold War and laying the foundations of a new
order.

Strategy is a term often associated with military campaigns. *Grand*
strategy, however, is chiefly related to diplomacy. It is a higher type of
strategy that aims at integrating policies and power toward achieving
national objectives short of war.[2] The term is apt for describing American diplomacy at the end of the Cold War.

During forty years of Cold War, the United States and its allies had
mobilized as if for war and came more than once to the brink of armed
conflict with the Soviet Union. History suggested that so deep-seated a
confrontation between great powers could only end violently. As Paul
Kennedy noted in *The Rise and Fall of the Great Powers,* "The triumph
of any one Great Power . . . or the collapse of another, has usually been
the consequence of lengthy fighting by its armed forces."[3] That the
Cold War ended peacefully and on Western terms was an achievement
without parallel in modern history.

This book examines the sources, assumptions, and conduct of American foreign policy with respect to the revolutionary developments that
began in Central and Eastern Europe in 1989. It reconstructs the relevant environment that confronted policymakers here and in Europe and
illustrates the choices available at key junctures; it describes assumptions and judgments made on the basis of inevitably incomplete knowledge and critically examines choices made and not made in the light of
what we now know. The book also explores the interactions among the
major powers, particularly the United States, the Soviet Union, Germany, Great Britain, and France, as well as the countries of Central and
Eastern Europe.

A leitmotif that runs throughout the book is the tension between strategic goals and tactical necessity. Effective policy called for both strategic rigor and tactical flexibility in devising and implementing plans with clear objectives, subjecting those plans to constant reassessment, and revising them, often radically, as yesterday's bold initiative was overtaken by today's new reality. Every day brought with it new and unexpected problems that had to be overcome for strategic goals to be realized, yet the process of dealing with these problems risked undermining the main goals being pursued in the first place. For example, achieving the dual goal of uniting Germany and assuring that it remained a full member of NATO required Soviet acquiescence to German unification. Yet gaining Soviet assent involved the risk that Moscow would pressure Germany to relinquish its NATO membership as the price of unity.

Under such circumstances, the diplomat had to be both fox and hedgehog. The fox, in Isaiah Berlin's essay, "knows many things" and pursues "many ends, often unrelated and even contradictory," while the hedgehog "knows one big thing" and keeps his sights fixed on "a single central vision" and organizing principle.[4]

In 1989, that "one big thing" was that Eastern Europe, where the Cold War began, was also where it had to end. This judgment, which contradicted the then-conventional wisdom that the United States needed to "meet Gorbachev halfway" and reach an "understanding" on the future of Eastern Europe, formed the basis of an American grand strategy that served us well in navigating the challenges at the end of the Cold War. This organizing principle and its corollaries—self-determination in Eastern Europe, deep reductions in Soviet forces, and the internal transformation of the USSR itself—lent a singleness of purpose that helped steer policy through a period of profound, often chaotic, change.

American diplomacy achieved great successes in 1989 and 1990, as the objectives we had set for ourselves were met and far exceeded. Our policies were less successful thereafter, as the multiple challenges of German unification, the Gulf War of early 1991, and a disintegrating Soviet Union diffused our strategic vision and undercut efforts to build a "new world order." This should not be surprising. Policy at the beginning of the period, while skillfully executed, was the culmination of four decades of consistent foreign policy through Democratic and Republican administrations alike. The changes with which American policy had to deal were revolutionary, but they fit a familiar Cold War frame of reference. Those reference points exploded with the precipitous collapse of the Soviet empire in 1990 and 1991.

We and our Western allies were conscious of certain parallels with the Versailles conference of 1919, which, among its other deficiencies, vastly underestimated Russian power on the morrow of the October Revolution and hence erected a postwar settlement that was never rooted in the realities of power.[5] In 1991 as in 1919, Russia was weak enough to ignore but had enormous latent power that would have made its exclusion short-sighted in the extreme. Thus the post–Cold War order we sought to build was one in which Russia would not be isolated but rather welcomed into the interstate system.

Although the concept of a "new world order" deserved closer study than it received, it ultimately failed to persuade—not so much for any conceptual deficiencies as for the inherent difficulty of defining America's place and role in a new era whose contours were only beginning to make themselves apparent. Operationally, then, the "central vision" of American policy for the immediate post–Cold War period was, perhaps inevitably, a more limited and transitional one. It sprang from the conviction that the United States had to remain in Europe to balance Russian power, lend a general stability, and help organize a durable post–Cold War order in which former adversaries were brought into a new system of cooperative security.

This orientation toward a post–Cold War order was not without its flaws. In placing such a high premium on military power, and specifically American military power, it accorded less weight to the political, economic, and other attributes of power and influence in a world that would no longer be dominated by hostile bipolar competition. To build secure democracies on the ruins of communist rule, the prime requirement of a viable post–Cold War order in Europe, was a task for which the traditional instruments of security policy were largely irrelevant. Nor was the traditional focus on armed aggression by one state against another of much use in dealing with threats arising *within* states among parties to a civil war. Iraq's aggression against Kuwait in 1990 fit the first category; the Yugoslav crisis that erupted about the same time belonged to the second.

The failures of U.S. and other Western policies toward a disintegrating Yugoslavia underscored how far Europe was from a secure post–Cold War order. Coming so soon on the heels of the U.S.-led coalition to defeat Iraq in the Gulf War, the Yugoslav conflict also seemed to call for an undiminished level of American engagement in the post–Cold War world, thus opening up a gap between the leadership we asserted and that which we were actually ready to provide. Above all, it raised doubts about the nature of America's post–Cold War role, absent the threat that had lent focus and coherence to American policy for forty years.

Still, the hedgehog's focus on certain sound, if imperfect, principles helped steer policy through a period of chaotic change, in which the dangers were great of conceding larger strategic objectives in the interest of tactical expediency. In this regard, American steadiness of purpose was itself an important stabilizing factor in a period of profound disorientation for virtually all of Europe, to say nothing of the republics of the former Soviet Union.

I

American Grand Strategy

THE BUSH ADMINISTRATION entered office in January 1989 predisposed to major change—to "dream big dreams," as the president put it, and to think unconventionally.[1] Though not quite the hostile takeover of government that characterized the transition from President Jimmy Carter to President Ronald Reagan in 1980, the Reagan-to-Bush transition was abrupt. At the first NSC staff meeting, Reagan administration holdovers were politely told that their services were no longer required. An entirely new team came in, representing foreign policy approaches fundamentally at odds with those of the Reagan administration. At the White House and the State Department, where the transition was equally abrupt, these changes were soon reflected in major shifts in policy—quite different from the image of continuity that the public at large perceived. There was no such thing as a "Reagan-Bush" foreign policy. Before 1989 there was Reagan; afterwards there was Bush.

At the NSC, the abruptness of the transition was made vivid in a physical sense. Along one corridor in the offices of the European and Soviet directorate on the third floor of the Old Executive Office Building was a long row of file cabinets—all empty, their contents having been packed up and sent off to the Reagan library. This was standard White House procedure, but it was one that astonished foreign officials whose parliamentary systems favored stability and continuity. It meant that we were unburdened with the policies of the administration just departed, but also that we had to start from scratch in developing our approaches. As it turned out, the events and issues with which we were confronted were so revolutionary that the file of "business as usual" policy papers and analyses would have been of little use

6

anyway. There was no drawer labeled "in case of German unification, open file and follow instructions," nor were there any policy papers on "what to do if the Soviet Union disintegrates." We were entering uncharted waters.

In Europe and the Soviet Union, revolutionary change was in the air. Yet the *annus mirabilis* of 1989 began quietly enough. For all the hopeful trends associated with Soviet president Mikhail Gorbachev, fundamental change remained potential, not yet actual. Soviet military power was undiminished, one-party rule was intact in the USSR, the countries of Eastern Europe were ruled by governments that owed their existence to Soviet power, and half a million Soviet troops were still stationed in the center of Europe.

Gorbachev's early policies of *glasnost* (openness) and *perestroika* (economic restructuring) after coming to power in the spring of 1985 were cautious and incremental; only as these policies failed to produce the desired results did he consider more radical measures. The new openness he espoused had paved the way for organized political opposition, including national independence movements, while the economic half-measures associated with *perestroika* only deepened the economic crisis and eroded Gorbachev's domestic standing. In the West, however, his star was still rising, and a steady stream of Soviet arms proposals—advanced under the rubric of "new thinking" in Soviet foreign policy[2]—had caused public expectations to race well ahead of the real changes in Soviet international conduct.

Yet change was surely coming, most rapidly and irresistibly in Eastern Europe, where prolonged economic crises had given rise to mounting social pressures. Communist rule in Poland and Hungary was under assault—spurred by organized opposition groups and supported by reform-minded figures within the ruling establishments. The winds of change blowing from Moscow served further to heighten pressure on the communist regimes of Eastern Europe for more sweeping measures. Just as Metternich, after the election of Pius IX, reportedly said that he had "bargained for everything except a liberal Pope,"[3] the East European communists were ill-equipped to handle the consequences of a reform-minded Soviet leader. The more dogmatic among them found it hard to rule with the same ruthlessness, and even those predisposed to reform were unable to stay ahead of public demands for more sweeping change.

It was also apparent that, just as Gorbachev's reforms in the USSR encouraged and legitimized the far more radical efforts in Poland and

Hungary, successful challenges to communist rule in Eastern Europe would eventually blow back on the Soviet Union, particularly among its restive nationalities. This was the assumption of American policy from the earliest days of the Cold War, dating to NSC (National Security Council report) 58/2 of December 1949, which considered Eastern Europe to be the "weakest link" of the Soviet empire.[4] Indeed, it is hard to imagine the Soviet enterprise unraveling in any other sequence than it ultimately did. Under conditions of relaxation of control from the imperial center, the empire broke apart first in Central and Eastern Europe, next among the Baltic states, then in Ukraine and other republics, and finally in Russia itself.

Although a myth has developed that the world was caught unprepared for the events of 1989, many of us, inside government and out, had concluded already that communist rule in Eastern Europe was in deep crisis and that the "end of an era" was at hand.[5] If Soviet suppression of the Hungarian Revolution of 1956 and the Prague Spring of 1968 had killed communist ideology and the belief that it could be reformed, the crushing of the Solidarity trade union movement in Poland in 1981 had made it clear that Soviet power, or the threat of its application, was the sole remaining prop for the communist regimes of Eastern Europe. By the end of the 1980s, Soviet policy under Gorbachev had called into question that last prop, even as the example of his domestic innovations was fueling pressures from below in Eastern Europe for sweeping change.[6]

The question was not whether revolutionary upheaval was coming, but whether it would lead to catastrophe or liberation, and the answer hinged on Soviet attitudes. Was the "Brezhnev Doctrine," whereby Moscow claimed the right to intervene to preserve communist rule in Eastern Europe, still in force? Was the Soviet Union prepared, "new thinking" notwithstanding, to use military force if that alone could rescue an East European client regime? What were the limits of Soviet tolerance in its eroding East European empire?

Those of us responsible for U.S. policy put the questions in active voice: What could we do to expand the scope of Soviet tolerance? How could the United States, together with its Western allies, facilitate self-liberation in Eastern Europe and the end of Europe's division?

Two Events   Two events crystalized thinking in the early months of the administration. The first was Gorbachev's December 1988 announcement, before the United Nations General Assembly, of a unilateral reduction of five hundred thousand Soviet forces, with nearly half coming from Eastern Europe and the western military districts of the USSR. The pledge signaled for the first time Soviet acceptance, born in part of the urgent need to reduce defense spending, of the principle that a viable new military equilibrium in Europe demanded much deeper reductions on the Eastern side than on the Western. Thus it not only heralded the prospect of reducing Soviet military power in the center of Europe but also suggested how this might be achieved.

This initiative, more than any other step taken or proposed under Gorbachev up to then, went to the root of the Cold War and Europe's division. One could imagine an essentially unreformed Soviet Union withdrawing from Afghanistan or negotiating deep mutual reductions in strategic arms, but not relaxing its grip on Eastern Europe. On this point, Gorbachev also declared that the "use or threat of force cannot be and should not be an instrument of foreign policy. . . . Freedom of choice is . . . a universal principle, and it should know no exceptions. . . . This applies to both the capitalist and the socialist systems."[7] This was not quite the categorical renunciation of the Brezhnev Doctrine one might have wanted, but it went well beyond any prior Soviet assurances and, more importantly, put the pledge against the use of force in the context of the changes under way in Poland and Hungary.

Soviet officials later criticized the United States for focusing on the arms reduction initiative in the UN speech but ignoring this "turning point in Gorbachev's new thinking."[8] The fact is that while we in the Bush administration paid considerable attention to the passage in question, we did attach greater significance to the prospect of real force reductions, which would give substance to declaratory policy. What we probably underestimated was the extent to which Gorbachev's rhetorical shift was meant, for internal Soviet consumption, to prepare the ideological ground for radical departures yet to come in Soviet foreign policy.

The second event was the April 1989 Polish Roundtable Agreement between Solidarity and the communist authorities, which called for free and authentic parliamentary elections, albeit with certain prior guarantees for the ruling Communist party. It was clear then that the Roundtable Agreement, if fully implemented, was the beginning of the end of communist rule in Poland. And if communism was finished in Poland, it was finished everywhere in Eastern Europe, including East Germany, which in turn meant that German unification had just leapt onto the international agenda.[9]

These, of course, were very large "ifs"; our appreciation of the potential for such sweeping change was by no means a prediction that it would actually occur, much less that it could occur within the year. Indeed, the very logic of the proposition, which we assumed was evident to Soviet leaders as well,[10] underscored how much was at stake in Poland's tenuous agreement, as well as in the similarly hopeful process then under way in Hungary.

For all the uncertainties ahead, we nonetheless perceived an unparalleled, and perhaps short-lived, opportunity to promote the self-liberation of the countries of Eastern Europe and so begin the process of ending Europe's long division. It was toward these goals that American foreign policy had to be harnessed with a single-mindedness seldom seen in peacetime.

Four Prerequisites There were, however, four prior requirements, without which American leadership would not have been up to the task. Execution of these tasks inevitably caused a delay in the presentation of the new administration's foreign policy approach, a lag for which President Bush took considerable criticism; it also comported with a deliberate decision to defuse public pressure for a quick American response to Soviet peace initiatives and to develop instead a series of proposals that would test the seriousness of Gorbachev's "new thinking."

The first task was to restore foreign policy bipartisanship and overcome the deep divisions in the Congress, particularly over Nicaragua and the Iran-Contra scandal. President Bush made this one of his highest priorities, as symbolized by the bipartisan accord on Central America that Secretary of State James Baker negotiated with the congressional leadership in March 1989.[11] It is as remarkable as it was essential that, aside from differences over the level of aid to Eastern Europe and the agonizing vote over U.S. military engagement in the Persian Gulf, virtually every foreign policy initiative during the turbulent period of 1989–92 was undertaken with broad bipartisan consensus.

The second was to restore executive branch coherence, following a period in which government departments were pursuing what seemed to be independent foreign policies, much to the confusion of allies and adversaries alike. Toward that end, President Bush ordered a series of wide-ranging strategy reviews that helped establish agreement on major objectives and bring coherence to policies that had been scattered and uncoordinated. These were not insignificant achievements. Otherwise,

however, these protracted sessions served mainly to demonstrate to anyone who needed further proof that effective policy cannot be made by
committee.

The third requirement was to restore cohesion and common purpose
among our European allies, whose confidence in American leadership
had been badly shaken by the oscillations in U.S. policy from "evil empire" to the Strategic Defense Initiative and the alarming proposals at
the 1986 Reykjavik Summit, initiatives undertaken with little or no consultation with allies.[12] Europe's discontent, accentuated by antinuclear
demonstrations and the impact of Soviet "peace initiatives," had
opened a wide transatlantic divide and had revived the Gaullist (*cum*
leftist) rallying cry for the "Europeanization of Europe." Secretary
Baker's February 1989 trip to every NATO capital, whirlwind and substantively thin though it was, signaled U.S. commitment to closer consultation with allies, while President Bush's early assurance that American forces would remain in Europe "as long as they are wanted and
needed" helped restore confidence in American staying power.

The fourth and related task was to shift the international agenda away
from Gorbachev's "common European home" toward a new and radical
agenda for ending the Cold War. This was no mere public relations competition nor petulant reaction to "Gorbymania." Fundamental issues
were at stake. The "common home" was flawed not because it excluded
the United States—this Gorbachev quickly corrected—but because it proposed to validate and stabilize a status quo that was inherently unacceptable and unstable. As both Gorbachev and his foreign minister, Eduard
Shevardnadze, made clear at the time, their vision demanded Western
"respect for differing social systems" and disavowal of any attempt to
"undermine" the Warsaw Pact.[13] It was also dangerous, because the attraction of "helping" a less aggressive and more accommodating Soviet
leadership had made Western publics, including our own, vulnerable to a
vision that would have eased Europe's division superficially without addressing any of its root causes. Thus the concepts of "beyond containment" toward a "Europe whole and free" that Bush would later present
had psychological purposes in addition to their substantive content.

European Perspectives

For all the euphoria associated with "Gorbymania" among European
publics, especially in West Germany, in the early part of 1989, European

governments were cautious and circumspect. Their chief concerns were with the corrosive effects of Soviet public diplomacy on domestic attitudes and ultimately on Western cohesion, particularly in the absence of a persuasive Western answer to Gorbachev's initiatives. With the partial exception of the Bonn government, West European leaders were not much swayed by the argument that the West needed to "help" Gorbachev. In one form or another, all sought instead a coordinated Western approach that would test Soviet intentions without exciting further expectations among their own publics for sweeping arms reductions.

Analytically, our major European partners saw events in the East much as we did, with the British the most skeptical and the Germans the most hopeful. Yet the Germans, too, were circumspect: Chancellor Helmut Kohl had said as late as 1988 that he did not expect German unification in his lifetime.[14] The policy implications they drew from these events were quite different, however. Where the Germans saw new opportunities in the East and were eager to exploit them, the British saw new dangers for the West and were at pains to offset them, while the French saw new opportunities for "overcoming Yalta" but doubted their capacity to contain a newly resurgent Germany.

"A Well-Stocked Hat Full of Well-Armed Rabbits"   British perspectives were informed by a deep, enduring skepticism of the reformability of communist systems, whether in the Soviet Union or among the countries of Eastern Europe.[15] Prime Minister Margaret Thatcher turned this perspective into a paradox: these systems must change but cannot. They must change, given the manifest superiority of liberal democracy and the conspicuous failures of Soviet-type systems; yet they cannot do so from within, because the same rigidities that produced failure also engendered a reactionary immobilism in the ruling apparatus.[16] While believing these systems were doomed to collapse in the longer term, she had little sense of *how* this might occur—save, one assumes, through revolutionary upheaval—and was therefore more impressed than most with their staying power in the short term. Meanwhile, her focus was on ensuring the cohesion of the Western alliance during what was likely to be a prolonged and skillful Soviet "peace offensive"; her worry was that a lax and irresolute West, above all West Germany, would be seduced by high-sounding but empty Soviet peace initiatives.

As Thatcher's foreign secretary, Sir Geoffrey Howe, put it in a speech in January 1989, "We must not confuse hope or even expectation with reality. . . . The Soviet Union has a well-stocked hat full of well-armed rabbits and . . . will be able to go on surprising us by drawing rabbits from that hat for many years to come."[17] Similarly, in her banquet speech during Gorbachev's visit to London in April, Thatcher lectured the Soviet leader on the steps necessary to translate words into deeds, adding that "one thing we shall never do . . . is base our policies on wishful thinking rather than on reality."[18] Ironically, though, Thatcher's assertion that Gorbachev was "a man we can do business with" contributed to the very "Gorbymania" she feared.

As to Eastern Europe, British policy in the 1980s was not unlike our own, combining expanded economic and political contacts with a strong commitment to human rights, strictly linking Western assistance to internal political reforms. While Thatcher was later to argue, in the context of German unification, that the East European countries were "Britain's natural allies,"[19] British policy never had the push behind it to constitute a separate *ostpolitik* (eastern policy) capable of offsetting German influence in the region. Even well into 1989, the British were skeptical that fundamental change was imminent and more doubtful still that Moscow would allow any substantial relaxation of its grip on Eastern Europe. As Foreign Secretary Howe put it shortly after the Roundtable Agreement in Poland, the East Europeans "may be on a longer leash, but it is a leash all the same."[20] By July, one of his ministers acknowledged that "reforms in parts of Eastern Europe have moved further and faster than anyone could have imagined," but warned that "it would be a grave mistake to believe that Europe's postwar divisions can be swept away at once."[21]

British analysis coincided neatly with British interests, for the United Kingdom had less reason to want to disrupt the status quo than most of its continental partners. Its preoccupations were with managing a difficult process of adjustment with the European Community in ways that preserved British freedom of maneuver, while maintaining the integrity of the Western alliance and the "special relationship" with the United States. It is not quite right that the British "never developed a grand design for Europe," as one writer suggested.[22] The design, offering consistency if not imagination, was status quo in the West and "status quo plus" in the East, where the hope was that gradual political liberalization would lead to a more secure, though essentially conflictual, East-West relationship. Execution of this design hinged on U.S. leadership; hence Thatcher's impatience with the Bush administration's slowness to engage Gorbachev, which she felt was eroding Western resolve and common purpose. Her efforts to mediate between the two leaders were reminiscent of similar attempts by previous British prime ministers, from Harold Macmillan on, to serve as "honest broker" between Washington and Moscow. (The unstated premise of this postwar pattern was that the British were fit to lead the alliance but lacked the power; the Americans had the power but were wanting in leadership and needed periodic prods to exercise the role that came so naturally to a British prime minister.)

If Thatcher betrayed occasional impatience with the United States, her real antagonism was directed at the West Germans, whom she believed had "gone wobbly" on security and were caving in to public antinuclear pressures. The immediate issue of contention—Bonn's push for early negotiations to reduce short-range nuclear forces (SNF)[23]—was part of a larger worry that another "zero option" of elimination of this category of theater weapons would lead to the complete denuclearization of Europe. This would leave Western Europe hostage to Soviet conventional preponderance and undermine the bedrock of nuclear deterrence. Not incidentally, such a process also threatened to involve British and French nuclear forces and thus raised the most sensitive issues of membership in the "nuclear club." British adamancy against an SNF "zero option" fueled German fears of being singularly exposed—as in "the shorter the range, the deader the Germans." Britain's attitude contributed to a chaotic breakdown of alliance consensus in the spring of 1989, reaching a crescendo at the time of Thatcher's semipublic row with Chancellor Kohl at their meeting at Kohl's home in Deidesheim in late April.[24]

British thinking in early 1989, in short, saw few prospects for meaningful change in the East and many dangers for the cohesion of the West. The main task for British diplomacy was to prod the Americans into organizing a cogent, coordinated Western response to Gorbachev that would both test the seriousness of Soviet "new thinking" and rein in those, like the Germans, who might be tempted down the garden path of denuclearization.

"Germany's Hopes Are France's Fears"   France, where "Gorbymania" had never caught on in the same way as in Germany or Italy, in many ways shared British skepticism about the prospects for change in the East and certainly shared its concerns about further denuclearization.

Having launched early on a campaign of "disintoxication" to cleanse the French Left of delusions about Franco-Soviet friendship, President François Mitterrand had remained cool to Soviet blandishments even after Gorbachev chose Paris for his first official visit to a Western country. Additionally, he worried that further nuclear force reductions would diminish the significance of France's independent *force de frappe*. Meanwhile, a more fluid situation in Central Europe threatened to upset the vision of an EC-centered Europe under French and German coleadership. As one French analyst put it in late 1988: "De Gaulle's France of the mid-1960s was a revisionist power, intent on modifying the existing European security system. Today France is, at heart, a status-quo power, whereas Germany's deepest hope must be to transcend the division of Europe between East and West. . . . As long as Germany's hope remains France's fear, . . . the French-German nucleus of Europe will . . . remain central but inadequate."[25]

To consider France in 1989 a "status quo power" makes sense only in the context of two seemingly contradictory factors: undiminished French ambitions to "overcome Yalta" and the substantial evolution in French strategic thinking, particularly during the 1980s, toward fusing France's future with "Europe."[26] As President Mitterrand put it in a November 1988 interview, "Yalta is the symbol of the division of Europe into zones of power and influence between the Soviet Union and the United States. I cannot make do with it. My dream is of a reconciled and independent Europe."[27] Yet, in French thinking, this ambition had to be deferred until "European construction" was complete, and this was still a long way off. Thus, while remaining deeply dissatisfied with the status quo in this larger sense, France was even more hesitant than Great Britain to disturb it in the near term, lest rapid change in the East undermine EC integration before Germany had been safely tied up in a more federalized Europe.[28]

Eastern Europe had little place in this strategic vision, except as part of the distant goal of a Europe free of the superpowers. Indeed, so inert had France become in this region that one French analyst began a 1989 article with the question, "Does French policy toward Central and Eastern Europe still exist?"[29] French disregard for the region had been expressed most notoriously in Foreign Minister Michel Debré's characterization of the 1968 invasion of Czechoslovakia as a "traffic accident on the road to detente." Then there was Prime Minister Pierre Mauroy's defense of the French decision to conclude a natural gas deal with the

Soviet Union just after the imposition of martial law in Poland in late 1981: "Let us not add to the sufferings of the Polish people those of the French people lacking gas." Leaving aside the callousness of the remarks, they reflected a strategic judgment that France's interests did not lie in separate links to the smaller countries of Eastern Europe but rather in the multiple relationships among Moscow, Washington, Bonn, and Paris. As late as July 1989—after the opening of the Hungarian-Austrian border, after the Polish elections—former French president Valéry Giscard d'Estaing could still maintain that "our relations with Eastern Europe do not differ essentially from those we will continue to have with other parts of the world. Physical proximity does not lend them any special quality."[30]

This orientation was understandable enough before 1989, but it made less sense thereafter, particularly in that the oldest tenet of French diplomacy was the *alliance de revers*, making common cause with the neighbors and rivals of one's potential enemy.[31] If German power was the concern, would it not have made sense for France to cultivate relations with the countries to Germany's east, particularly Poland? We in Washington certainly would have welcomed a stronger French role in the region, as a counterweight to what risked becoming excessive German economic and political influence. Given France's historic ties to the region and its ability to play balance of power politics more cynically and skillfully than the United States, such a role would have been natural. Yet Mitterrand had declined to accept Kohl's 1988 suggestion that France and Germany develop a joint *ostpolitik*, and when he belatedly decided to engage in the region, he chose, unaccountably, to begin with Bulgaria, where nothing interesting was happening, rather than one of the "lands between" Germany and Russia.

This would not be the last time that some of us in the U.S. administration were frustrated at French unwillingness to act in what seemed to us France's own interests. That French aims were in some respects antithetical to America's was something we could understand and live with; that France would fail to develop a strategy consistent with its own manifest interests was harder to credit.[32]

Strategic myopia may be part of the answer, for it did seem that events in the East were fast overtaking France's EC-centered strategy, but it is evident that French leaders were aware that the stakes were high in Eastern Europe. In a March 1989 radio interview, Foreign Minister Roland Dumas was asked why France was not playing the active role that West Germany was in Central and Eastern Europe. His answer was a lament, suggesting strategic fatigue more than myopia: "I am personally sorry that France, which also enjoys certain historic advantages and a certain prestige in that region, has not been able, over the past few years, to do equally well out of that situation; which is why we have fallen behind. . . . We had fallen so far behind that anything we win back will be welcome."[33] Mitterrand, asked roughly the same question a few months before, replied with a none-too-subtle criticism of West German *ostpolitik*: "While we kept our distance for moral rather than political reasons, other countries were brushing aside considerations of that sort and establishing themselves in East European markets. I think that, although we were not wrong, we should be there too."[34]

Morality, one can say with confidence, was not the deciding factor in French policy. Inability to keep pace with German economic and political involvement, along with an exaggerated sense of inferiority in the face of resurgent German power, was perhaps more to the point. There was a strategic purpose buried in this *agitation immobile*,[35] however: it was the deliberate aim of decelerating the process of change in the East while accelerating integration in the EC. This approach had much to recommend it from the point of view of French interests, but it presumed vastly more influence than France actually had to retard history's course. It was a race against time, and France was losing.

"Let's Take Mr. Gorbachev at His Word" The West Germans, meanwhile, were not to be restrained. Their attitudes had been expressed in Foreign Minister Genscher's controversial speech in Davos in 1987, entitled "Nehmen Wir Gorbatschows 'Neue Politik' beim Wort." It is interesting that the title—literally, "Let's Take Gorbachev's 'New Policy' at Its Word"—was rendered in the foreign ministry's official English translation as "Let's Put Mr. Gorbachev's 'New Policy' to the Test." The latter, tougher-sounding title was actually closer to the sense of the text, which did not imply that Gorbachev should be taken at face value but rather called on the West to take his policies seriously and challenge him to translate his words into concrete actions. This, of course, is what the United States was proposing by early 1989, albeit with a more demanding set of challenges. It was the more provocative "at his word" that took hold, however, and gave rise to fears that the Federal Republic had succumbed to "Gorbymania." (Much was made of opinion polls showing that only 24 percent of the West German public considered the So-

viet Union a military threat,[36] but polls in Italy, the United Kingdom, and even the United States yielded similar results.)

To understand German approaches in terms of an assessment of Gorbachev is to get the analytic cart before the strategic horse. Policy toward the Soviet Union was part of a larger German *ostpolitik,* which in turn was driven by *Deutschlandpolitik,* aimed at expanding ties with the "other" Germany. Facilitating the ultimate goal of German unity, or at least doing nothing to retard it, was the determining objective. *Ostpolitik,* as it had evolved, pursued "change through rapprochement": its logic was that reassuring Moscow would allow it to relax its grip on Eastern Europe, giving reformers there greater leeway to pursue gradual change. Regime-led reform, in turn, would produce greater stability and confidence, which would encourage Eastern Europe and Moscow alike to undertake further steps toward reform. The result of this "virtuous circle" of reassurance and reform would be an easing of the division of Europe, making possible eventual rapprochement between the two German states.

Thus, West German policy was not wedded to "stability," any more than France's was wedded to the status quo. The German aim, in best dialectical fashion, was stable change, born of the belief that positive change could occur only under conditions of stability. The gamble inherent in this approach, as one French scholar put it, was that it is not clear "whether this increased self-confidence [on the part of the East European regimes] is supposed to bring the elites to lower their guard and to promote an unwitting . . . structural change, thereby working against their own real interests, or whether [the goal is] real stabilization which would allow them to keep their domination but dispense with the more pathological measures born out of insecurity."[37] Further, as a matter of policy born of geographic proximity and of their own history, the Germans had always been suspicious of change generated spontaneously from below, preferring regime-managed reform from above. This was particularly true of the Social Democrats, who had made it a habit to snub Lech Wałęsa and other Solidarity leaders during visits to Poland,[38] and to a lesser extent of Foreign Minister Genscher's Free Democrats, who tended to cultivate regime exponents of "reform Communism."

Germans of this persuasion backed the wrong horse, as subsequent events would show. *Ostpolitik* did not encourage the East European regimes to liberalize; to the contrary, by offering a degree of legitimation and considerable economic assistance, it helped them stabilize their rule without reform.[39] As it turned out, it did not matter much, so quickly did the events of 1989 sweep away the so-called reformers in Eastern Europe. There was also a certain complementarity between Bonn's closer relations with the East European regimes and Washington's (and London's) more consistent support for democratic opposition groups. And of course both we and the West Germans recognized that reform had to be led from above as well as pushed from below; U.S. policy, too, had long pursued a dual track, engaging East European regimes as well as regime opponents.

Three elements of *ostpolitik* need underlining. First, there were significant, though sometimes overstated, differences of approach between Kohl and Genscher. Kohl and his CDU (Christian Democratic Union) were products of West Germany and the tradition of Konrad Adenauer; their approaches toward the East proceeded from a profoundly Western orientation and conviction. Genscher and the FDP (Free Democratic Party) had their roots in East as well as West Germany; the integrity of the Western alliance was, for them, not the goal but the instrumentality for achieving the larger ambition of overcoming the division of Germany and of Europe. But to state the differences in this fashion is to overstate them; they were differences more of degree and nuance. To be sure, there were some in the Bush administration (though fewer than in the Reagan administration) who shared Thatcher's view of "Genscherism."[40] By the same token, there were many who shared the general perception in the Federal Republic that Genscher had a much keener sense of the historic moment. The two views were not, of course, mutually exclusive.

In any case, to the extent that "Genscherism" affected U.S. policy, it was rarely in the sense of "demonizing" the foreign minister, as was sometimes alleged[41]; rather, it was simply that Kohl was seen as more reliable than Genscher when it came to the integrity of the Western alliance and that it was therefore in American interests to support and strengthen the chancellor's foreign policy role. This perspective, attributable more to the NSC than to the State Department, never interfered with the administration's ability to establish relations of trust with both Kohl and Genscher; indeed, it invited a natural division of labor between the White House and the State Department that served us well, particularly during the diplomacy of German unification.

Second, German strategy depended on reassurance, gradualism, and predictability: West German goals, as Kohl put it in early 1988, were "long-term stable cooperation with the Soviet Union" and its emergence as a "more predictable security partner."[42] In this conception, too much detente was as risky as too little, for rapid change could be seen as threatening to East European and Soviet leaders and risked converting the "virtuous cycle" into a "vicious cycle" of revolt and repression.[43] (This predisposition stood in marked contrast to the approach, favored in American conservative circles, of doing nothing to help or reassure the East European and Soviet regimes, but rather letting them be hoist by their own petards.)

Finally, although some on the West German Left had argued in the 1980s for the "divisibility" (*trennbarkeit*) of East-West detente, meaning that European detente should proceed despite the cooling of U.S.-Soviet relations, both Kohl and Genscher proceeded from the conviction that *Deutschlandpolitik* and *ostpolitik* could not be divorced from broader Western approaches toward the East. As Horst Teltschik, Kohl's national security adviser, put it in June 1989,

> The West German government knows . . . that its freedom of action with respect to the Soviet Union or the other Warsaw Pact countries basically depends on the superpowers' relationship to one another. The better and more constructive the relationship between the USA and the USSR, the greater the freedom the small and mid-size countries in Eastern and Western Europe to cultivate relations with the leading power of the other alliance and among each other.[44]

Hence German ambitions required bringing the Americans and their European partners around to a new, coordinated pattern of engagement. Kohl's meeting with Gorbachev in Moscow in October 1988 and Gorbachev's reciprocal visit to Bonn in June 1989 were designed to accomplish just that. The centerpiece was a German-Soviet joint declaration, which Kohl considered a "sensational" document for its affirmation of the "right of all peoples and states to self-determination" and its commitment to "overcoming the division of Europe."[45]

In Washington, anticipation of the Gorbachev visit and the joint declaration, together with Horst Teltschik's admonition that "we ought not to ask too much of Gorbachev,"[46] lent urgency to the articulation of our own approaches toward Gorbachev. Indeed, between German eagerness, British skepticism, and French ambivalence, there was ample room for an American approach that could weld a coordinated Western approach toward Gorbachev and test the limits of Soviet "new thinking."

The Strategy Reviews: A Few Words on Process

It was against this backdrop that President Bush had ordered a series of wide-ranging strategy reviews. Aimed at prodding the foreign policy bureaucracy toward new thinking, with a view toward the longer term, the reviews instead demonstrated the difficulty of trying to craft policy by committee. Their essence seemed to have been anticipated nearly seventy years before by the estimable F. M. Cornford, writing in a different context. His droll observations are worth quoting at some length:

> There is only one argument for doing something; the rest are arguments for doing nothing. . . . [All] important questions are so complicated, and the results of any course of action so difficult to foresee, that certainty, or even probability, is seldom, if ever, attainable. It follows at once that the only justifiable attitude of mind is suspense of judgment. . . . At this point the arguments for doing nothing come in; for it is a mere theorist's paradox that doing nothing has just as many consequences as doing something. . . .
>
> As soon as three or more alternatives are in the field, there is pretty sure to be a majority against any one of them, and nothing will be done. . . . [A] few bad reasons for not doing something neutralize all the good reasons for doing it.

Cornford then explains the "Principle of the Wedge," through which action is inhibited by adducing all manner of implied, potential, or unforeseeable consequences. (Today this is known as the "thin end of the wedge," meaning that a small opening can be made larger.) On the "Principle of Unripe Time" (as in "the time is not yet ripe"), he observes that time "has a trick of going rotten before it is ripe." Finally:

> The Principle of the Dangerous Precedent is that you should not now do an admittedly right action for fear you, or your equally timid successors, should not have the courage to do right in some future case, which, *ex hypothesi,* is essentially different, but superficially resembles the present one. Every public action which is not customary, either is wrong, or, if it is right, is a dangerous

precedent. It follows that nothing should ever be done for the
first time.[47]

Translated into the world of Policy Coordinating Committees
(PCCs)—renamed Interagency Working Groups, or IWGs, in the Clinton administration—the policy process looked something like this.
Meetings would be chaired by the cognizant assistant secretary (or his
or her principal deputy) of the lead agency—the Department of State
for most political issues. The NSC staff representative, serving as executive secretary, typically joined the State chair in trying to move the meeting to action (on which they had usually agreed in advance). Representatives of other agencies assembled on either side of a long conference
table. Around the periphery of the room were assorted and anonymous
"strap-hangers," whose function, one presumed, was to report back to
their superiors what epochal decisions had been reached—or perhaps
just to enjoy a brief diversion from their daily routines.

When it came time for decision, most representatives, especially from
the economic agencies, came armed with a mandate to defend at all
costs their particular bureaucratic sacred cows. But otherwise they were
unwilling to support any policy decision, in which they took no interest
and voiced no opinion. No one from Treasury could speak for anyone
else. The Department of State would be represented by as many as ten
or fifteen separate offices or bureaus, each claiming primacy within the
department on at least a part of the action. Representatives of OSD (Office of the Secretary of Defense) and JCS (Joint Chiefs of Staff) typically
engaged amiably in the debate but then refused to commit (or "reserved") on any decision or even to disclose what course of action their
superiors might wish to see adopted. The intelligence community's role
was to demonstrate that any possible course of action was fraught with
danger or otherwise doomed to fail, while advancing the seemingly inconsistent view that events in the outside world were driven by deep im-
personal forces not susceptible to human intervention.

These patterns, though offered tongue-in-cheek, represented very real
concerns. They applied at every level but were particularly destructive
of policy making at assistant secretary level and below, where not even
the most senior participants could speak authoritatively for their departments or agencies on large issues. The absence of a crisis or action-
forcing event could be paralyzing even at cabinet level. This problem
was sometimes overcome by recasting the issue in a way that eliminated

the do-nothing option and isolated those known to prefer inaction. Of course, sheer numbers inhibited action, which is why interagency Policy Coordinating Committees rarely served as vehicles for decision. So much for policy making by committee. Thereafter, policy making was conducted mainly among National Security Council principals, deputies, and their immediate advisers.

This is as good a place as any to say a few words about the decision-making process in the Bush administration. Formally, there were three tiers. The first consisted of NSC principals. The president, the vice president, the secretary of state, and the secretary of defense were statutory members. The chairman of the Joint Chiefs and the director of Central Intelligence were statutory advisers, and the president's national security adviser managed the NSC system.[48] Second was the Deputies Committee (DC), chaired by the deputy national security adviser and attended by deputy or undersecretaries from the same agencies. Third were the many Policy Coordinating Committees.

Full NSC meetings were common during the first six months of the administration, when principals were settling in and basic lines of policy were being drawn, but relatively rare thereafter. DC meetings proved to be the better venue for decision: they were efficiently chaired (by Deputy National Security Adviser Bob Gates) and easier to convene, given the crowded schedules of NSC principals, yet still at sufficiently senior level for decisions to be reached on the spot. PCCs generally met either to consider issues below the threshold of principals or deputies or to prepare issues for referral to the Deputies Committee. There were also various ad hoc committees such as the European Strategy Steering Group, which were devoted more to strategic planning than operational decision making.

The "NSC system," however, was much broader than the sum of its formal meetings: it embraced the whole pattern of interaction among the key agencies at every level. For issues of the greatest import, often there was no substitute for face-to-face discussions among principals or deputies, but the vast majority of decisions were reached outside the formal structure of NSC meetings, through a sequence of vertical (i.e., within-agency) and horizontal (interagency) deliberations. The day began with a series of staff meetings held within agencies and a round of telephone calls among agencies at several levels; it ended, usually well into the night, with another round of telephone calls to reach final agreement on issues that had to be decided by "COB," or close of business. In between, for each staff officer, were several rounds of meetings in each agency, perhaps one or more interagency meetings, and many dozens of telephone conversations.

Important cables to the field were handled by a "crosshatch" system of interagency clearance, with the cognizant NSC staff officer the last to clear, often from secure telephone at home in the small hours of the morning. (Even cables on which there was no substantive disagreement took the whole day to wend their way through the State Department's maze of internal clearances by COB. The NSC's COB was a few hours later, when the cable had been processed by the State Department operations center and sent to the White House Situation Room for NSC clearance.) Speeches by administration officials, briefing material for their meetings with foreign counterparts, initiatives undertaken by U.S. officials abroad, and all the other elements that went into the making and execution of policy were likewise subject to interagency clearance. All these steps were part of the "NSC system" in this broader sense.

Typically, the making of major policy decisions would begin at senior staff level, on the initiative of one or more of a relatively small group of senior officials at the NSC staff, State, and the Pentagon (plus Treasury and other agencies, depending on the issue). They would develop a proposed course of action and then go separately to their respective superiors, who would approve, disapprove, or amend, consulting among themselves as they saw fit. For large issues, the process usually was accompanied by formal memoranda; more often, it was done face to face or by telephone. The process was interactive: initiatives from staff level did not spring from a void but rather from daily, informal contact with cabinet principals, whose views were in turn shaped by their key staff members.

The system worked well, owing to the insistence of the president and his national security adviser, Brent Scowcroft, on cabinet government and the disciplined, orderly presentation of issues for decision. That meant, among other things, that the views of all relevant agencies, and especially of cabinet officers, were to be fully and faithfully represented in any memorandum for the president's decision. (One early casualty on the NSC staff paid with his job for trying to advance his favored policy outcome by circumventing the known views of a key cabinet officer.) It was also a tight and compartmentalized system, based on strict "need to know" access, so that decision-making circles were kept as compact as possible. The main lines of policy were of course widely circulated, but sensitive issues like negotiations with So-viet leaders were tightly held.[49]

The system was not leak-proof, but there were relatively few in-stances in which information was leaked to the media inadvertently. Leaks were supposed to have a purpose. Secretary Baker was the undis-puted master of the art, and the discerning reader of dispatches from the State Department press corps may have noticed that an anonymous and voluble "senior administration official" seemed always to be at Baker's side. (It was, of course, usually Baker himself.) Relations with the media were closely guarded, not so much to manipulate or cast cer-tain officials in favorable light (though such efforts were not unknown) as to avoid ceding the agenda and obliging the administration to react to the notoriously transitory issues and preferences of the media.[50]

It was, at the same time, an almost unfailingly collegial and coopera-tive interagency process, owing mainly to the tone and example set by General Scowcroft, Secretary Baker, and Secretary of Defense Dick Cheney.[51] Their weekly breakfast meetings and regular telephone com-munication helped resolve interagency disagreements before they could fester. (Sometimes the weekly breakfasts were used for decision making, a practice that caused more than a little confusion, in that none of the three was in the habit of briefing his staff on the results of these ses-sions.) Rivalry there was among agencies, along with tough policy fights, but there was almost none of the backbiting and turf warfare that had characterized other administrations. If this sounds too good to have been true, suffice it to say the NSC system under President Bush and Brent Scowcroft worked the way it was supposed to work.

In relations between the NSC staff and the State Department, Secre-tary Baker's well-known pattern of relying on a small circle of close ad-visers made matters easier. In the ceremony held upon his appointment as ambassador to the Court of St. James (the United Kingdom), Ray Seitz disputed this characterization, however, saying that he never felt excluded from an "inner circle." "It was more like a trapezoid," he said, as an amused Baker looked on. Circle or trapezoid, the pattern as-sured maximum focus on the key strategic issues, so that bureaus, even if cut out from the decision process, could be harnessed to priority ob-jectives that fully commanded the secretary's attention. It gave a coher-ence and single-mindedness to policy, rather than allowing the agenda to be routinized by the constant flow of issues large and small that char-acterizes the normal work of a bureau.

Like any model, it had its flaws; like most, its virtues were also its liabilities. This one worked particularly well through 1989 and to the end of 1990, when a confined set of the most vital issues related to Europe and the Soviet Union demanded, and received, priority attention. It worked less well thereafter, when a wider range of important but unrelated issues—including Iraqi intentions in the Persian Gulf—needed, but failed, to penetrate the inner circle. The closeness and congeniality among the key cabinet officers and their deputies, including particularly Deputy Secretary of State Lawrence Eagleburger, also had the effect of narrowing the range of opinions and options that found their way into the policy debate. The antidote to this danger is a more vertical process, with assistant secretaries and other senior staff officers accorded greater, and more nearly equal, access to key decision makers, but this then risks routinizing policy and obscuring larger strategic goals.[52] No model is perfect. Whichever is chosen should be done with an awareness that the process affects the issues, and the issues affect the process.

To return to the strategy reviews: although their results came to be characterized, with some justification, as "status quo plus," they nonetheless served certain purposes. Most obviously, they signaled a break from the past, in that the president had given a strong mandate to engage in a thorough-going review of every aspect of policy, without deference to the policy preferences of the administrations in which he had served as vice president for eight years. These interagency meetings had a very different tone from those held just a few weeks earlier, even though many of the participants were the same.

The reviews also helped restore interagency coordination by ensuring that at some minimum level there was an understood baseline of agreed policy. They facilitated policy coherence by bringing together offices and agencies that were focusing more or less independently on different aspects of much larger issues and tieing these strands together in a general statement of policy. They also helped reestablish the proper role of the National Security Council staff in foreign policy making and coordination, rather than as independent executors of policy. The reviews exposed some of the existing but unarticulated fault lines of policy and helped clarify what needed resolution, whether by persuasion or command decision, before anything innovative could be expected. On occasion, they surfaced some interesting ideas that ultimately found their way into policy, even if not into the formal review documents. In this regard, NSC staff members could be retailers as well as producers of policy, lifting ideas from their agencies of origin, where they had no chance of prospering, and putting them into circulation at cabinet level in a context that might produce action.

The Debate over Grand Strategy

The reviews also brought to the surface several issues that had been held over from the Reagan administration, chief among them an understanding of Gorbachev's reforms in the Soviet Union, the implications of Soviet "new thinking," particularly for Eastern Europe, and the consequences of these trends for U.S. strategy. The policies that ensued departed sharply from those of the Reagan administration, particularly in rebuilding support for nuclear deterrence and radically revising Soviet policy away from a narrow focus on arms control, toward a much more ambitious political agenda. Indeed, the foreign policy shift under the Bush administration in 1989 was as stark in substance (though not in style or rhetoric) as the change from Carter to Reagan in 1981.

The strategy reviews, disappointing though their results were, informed the more serious and substantive debate at the highest levels of the administration in early 1989,[53] leading up to a comprehensive presentation of U.S. strategy in five major speeches delivered by President Bush in April and May. Indeed, the speeches were not only the vehicles for articulating policy but also the means through which major policy decisions were reached in the first place. When the president said it, it became policy; thus there was nothing like the draft of a presidential speech to focus the mind and force decision.[54] Before turning to the speeches themselves, it is worth exploring in some detail the debates from which they derived.

Arms Control and Dilemmas of Nuclear Deterrence In light of the long-standing public fixation on nuclear arms reduction as the principal measure of U.S.-Soviet relations, it is perhaps surprising that arms control issues generated little controversy within the administration. Rather, this public perception *was* the issue: how to make the case for nuclear deterrence to an American public whose views had been conditioned by the nuclear freeze movement, the television docudrama "The Day After" and the specter of "nuclear winter," the INF (Intermediate Nuclear Force) Agreement, and President Reagan's proposal at Reykjavik for the elimination of all strategic nuclear weapons. These, together with the false promises of SDI (the Strategic Defense Initiative, or "Star Wars"), contributed to the perception that these evil weapons could be, if not eliminated or frozen in place, rendered harmless by a protective antinuclear umbrella. In Europe, meanwhile, and especially in West Germany, the INF Agreement had accentuated fears that the continent had been made "safe" for war waged by short-range tactical nuclear weapons.

It is probably true that some quarters of the Bush administration harbored an excessive enthusiasm for nuclear weapons (akin to Thatcher's, although one or two more closely resembled Dr. Strangelove, the movie character who "learned to love the bomb"). This zeal was born of the mistaken, monocausal view that nuclear weapons, rather than a combination of many factors, had, in the oft-repeated mantra, "kept the peace in Europe for 40 years." But the main effort was to restore public support for the principle of nuclear deterrence, including extended nuclear deterrence. This meant, while negotiations on START (Strategic Arms Reduction Treaty) proceeded, avoiding further denuclearization in Europe and maintaining the coupling of our nuclear deterrence to Europe's defense.[55] Above all, it meant shifting the prevailing logic away from nuclear arms control for its own sake and focusing on the massive conventional imbalance in Europe. If negotiators, through the conference on Conventional Armed Forces in Europe (CFE), could equalize the number of conventional weapons held by each side, then and only then would it be possible to negotiate reductions on tactical nuclear weapons. Finally, CFE was seen in political as much as military terms as a vehicle for relaxing Soviet pressure on its Warsaw Pact allies and so facilitating political liberalization in Eastern Europe.

As President Bush was to put it in his first foreign policy address, "Arms are a symptom, not a source of tension. The true source of tension is the imposed and unnatural division of Europe."[56] It was a judgment that consciously echoed the views of then-political prisoner (and future Czechoslovak president) Václav Havel: "The cause of the danger of war is not weapons as such but political realities in a divided Europe. . . . No lasting, genuine peace can be achieved simply by opposing this or that weapons system, because such opposition deals only with consequences, not with causes."[57]

Dealing with a More United Europe As to U.S. attitudes toward Western Europe, there had been little agreement and substantial ambivalence about the process of European unity. Certainly, our European partners perceived U.S. hostility toward the ambitions of "1992," the European Community's target date for creating a single European market. They felt that the United States supported European unity as an abstract ideal but not as an imminent reality. They were not wrong. Strategically, there was substantial, though not universal, support for the proposition that a more united Europe was profoundly in American interests: we wanted a strong, more cohesive Europe as our main partner in world affairs, and we were prepared to lend our support and encouragement toward that end. In this sense, the Bush administration was genuinely supportive of European unity, and certainly more disposed than its recent predecessors. But these abstract judgments still begged the question of what *kind* of Europe. Most immediately, there was the danger that "1992" would lead to a closed, heavily subsidized EC internal market and a protectionist "Fortress Europe," at least during the early stages of creating a single market.

Over the longer term, economic and monetary union inevitably would give new impetus toward European political union, with ambiguous implications. If political union were achieved, we could expect a more cohesive, stronger European partner, but one that was also more exclusionary and potentially in competition with the Atlantic alliance. Already there were signs that Franco-German security cooperation was tending toward a European security and defense identity that would be independent of, rather than integral to, the transatlantic alliance. Having linked our own security to Europe's for forty years, we were adamant that the United States not be excluded from decisions on core issues of European and transatlantic security. NATO would then become the "alliance of last resort," involved via its European members at the eleventh hour in conflicts for which neither NATO nor the United States had assumed responsibility or leadership. Under such conditions, the American public could hardly be expected to support a continued U.S. military presence in Europe.

The greatest concern, however, was not that efforts toward political union would succeed but that they would fail, yet in the trying would accentuate the pattern whereby decisions were reached within closed EC councils. These decisions would then become immutable, as none of the twelve member countries would wish to reopen issues that had been resolved after much internal bloodletting. This would be the worst of several worlds. We were prepared to deal with twelve interlocutors or with just one, but we could see ourselves being left with no reliable European partner. None of the twelve individually could negotiate, because they were bound by (or chose to hide behind) collective decisions already reached. Nor could the EC as a collective be a partner. The EC presidency country, rotating among the twelve every six months; the "troika" of past, present, and future presidency countries; and the EC Commission all lacked the power to negotiate reliably on behalf of the twelve. (This was precisely the pattern we confronted in negotiations over the Uruguay Round of the General Agreement on Tariffs and Trade, or GATT, when we were obliged to deal with multiple EC representatives, none of whom could speak authoritatively for the others.)

It was nonetheless clear that closer European unity, in the political as well as the economic arena, was coming whether we liked it or not and that U.S. policy therefore had to come to grips with a more cohesive and assertive European Community. A more supportive U.S. stance and the development of more regular U.S.-EC consultations would enhance our ability to shape the Community's development in ways consistent with U.S. interests. There was a current of opinion, particularly in the State Department, that enthusiastically and optimistically supported European unity, but the majority view remained, perhaps inevitably, supportive in principle but skeptical in practice. (My own view was that a strong Atlantic alliance was essential for European unity and that a stronger and more united Europe was essential for the future of the alliance, but I found more support for the first half of the proposition than for the second.)

The strategy review devoted to U.S.–European Community relations[58] had advanced policy in one small step. We moved from the position that the United States "supported European unity *but*," meaning that our endorsement was contingent on resolution of major concerns we had over protectionist trade practices and the exclusionary process of EC political consultations. Instead we took the view that we "supported European unity *and*," meaning that we intended to defend energetically America's commercial interests and push the EC to open up its decision-making process so that meaningful U.S.-EC policy coordination could take place. That U.S. support was qualified remained implicit in this new formulation, but the rhetorical shift also implied that the onus was on the United States as well as the EC to see that things came out right.

West Germany was the key, and there was general agreement that a greatly strengthened, more substantive U.S.-German relationship would be essential to U.S. interests and to what was later referred to as a "more mature" U.S.-European relationship. (The U.S.-German dialogue at that time was surprisingly thin and formalistic, vastly different from the frank, highly substantive discussions we always had with the British.) While Prime Minister Thatcher, in her memoirs, overstated the strength of America's intention to abandon Britain in favor of Germany as its principal European partner, she correctly perceived an early shift of emphasis.[59] A closely held NSC memorandum to the president in March 1989 put it bluntly:

> Today the top priority for American foreign policy in Europe should be the fate of the Federal Republic of Germany. . . . Even if we make strides in overcoming the division of Europe through greater openness and pluralism, we cannot have a vision for Europe's future that does not include an approach to the "German question." Here we cannot promise immediate political reunification, but we should offer some promise of change.[60]

It was from these basic judgments that the notion of the United States and Germany as "partners in leadership" emerged and ultimately found its way into President Bush's speech in Mainz in May 1989 (discussed below). Although the term came to be seen, in a kind of sentimental light, as a bestowal of American approval, it arose in the more neutral context of our recognition of the Federal Republic's emergence as the dominant European power, particularly in relations with the East. It also expressed our hopes that the Federal Republic's economic and political weight could be harnessed to greater leadership and responsibility.

"Testing" Gorbachev's New Thinking   The most important issue with which the administration grappled in early 1989, of course, concerned policy toward the Soviet Union. There was, in the first place, a calculated decision to undertake what Soviet leaders came to deride as the *pauza*: the "pause" was deliberate, aimed not just at giving the administration time to chart a strategy for the longer term but also at altering the psychology of U.S.-Soviet relations. Instead of the tit-for-tat pattern whereby Western leaders were expected to react to every Soviet "peace initiative," no matter how specious and self-serving, with their own (equally specious and self-serving) counterproposals, we wanted a rela-

tionship built on seriously considered Western interests, carefully coordinated among the major allies. Rather than being stampeded into hastily concocted initiatives for the sake of waging a public relations campaign, there were strategic as well as tactical reasons to let relations cool for a while.[61]

Opinions within government largely mirrored informed thinking outside. At one extreme were the hard-liners who felt any Western gesture would only abet a skillful adversary and encourage what they saw as a neutralist drift in Europe, especially in West Germany. For them, the Reykjavik Summit had shown the dangers of trying to beat Gorbachev at public diplomacy: there was always the risk that this Soviet leader might say *da* instead of *nyet*. Related to this perspective was a more widely held view that Western pressure, which had forced the Soviet leadership to undertake internal reforms, should be maintained, not relaxed, so as to compel further internal liberalization. At the other end of the spectrum were those who felt that Gorbachev was approaching the limits of tolerance of his hard-line critics and that U.S. policy should aim at ensuring Gorbachev's political survival. In this view, tangible signs of Western reciprocation, of "meeting Gorbachev halfway," were necessary to give him the mandate to continue down the path of reform and "new thinking."

Among senior administration officials, one of the more skeptical views came from Deputy National Security Adviser Bob Gates, who predicted in an April 1 speech in Brussels a period of "prolonged turbulence" in the USSR. Secretary of Defense Dick Cheney went a step further in an April 29 CNN television interview, predicting that Gorbachev was likely to fail and be replaced by someone "far more hostile" to U.S. interests.[62] It should be noted that the latter was an ad-libbed response to a question posed by the interviewer; Cheney's response to a similar query at an April 4 press conference had been more circumspect.[63]

The negative fallout from these remarks, particularly in Europe, persuaded Secretary of State Baker to issue a corrective and offer a more comprehensive statement of U.S. policy than had emerged up to then. Speaking at the Center for Strategic and International Studies on May 4, he rejected the view of "some who say that we don't need to do much of anything because the trends are so favorable to us. Their counsel is to sit tight and simply await further concessions." Stressing that the United States wished *perestroika* to succeed but noting that its reality had been both "promising and problematic," Baker suggested, in conscious evocation of West German foreign minister Genscher's 1987 speech in Davos, taking Moscow "at its word" and "testing" Soviet new thinking to see if its promise would be "translated into enduring action."[64]

These differences within the administration, while real enough, should not be overplayed. Analytical judgments about what one or another senior official expected to happen were one thing; policy was another. (In his memoirs, Secretary Baker noted that he did not disagree with the substance of Cheney's analysis, only with the wisdom of airing it publicly.[65]) Scholars and analysts outside government exaggerated the significance of these differences precisely because they tended to judge policies by the extent to which they conformed to their analysis, whereas policymakers crafted policies not to advertise their analysis but to advance their policy objectives. It is an altogether different optic, which helps explain why the policy-making and scholarly communities often talk past each other.

Policy toward the Soviet Union in early 1989 was developed not on the basis of predictions, which would have been a risky business indeed, but on the basis of interests and objectives. To be sure, policy was informed—or circumscribed—by a range of alternatives deemed more or less plausible, but no one predictive line dominated. Indeed, believing that we were entering a period of profound and essentially unpredictable change, we felt it all the more important to be absolutely clear on first principles and main objectives. Nor were we about to assume responsibility for the fate of *perestroika*, much less of Gorbachev's political future. The fundamental choices would be made within the USSR itself: while we hoped to nudge the process in directions congenial to U.S. interests, we were under no illusions that we could make the Soviet Union's choices for it.[66]

A secret cable from Jack Matlock, U.S. ambassador to the Soviet Union, dated February 22, 1989, put it this way:

> We have an historic opportunity to test the degree the Soviet Union is willing to move into a new relationship with the rest of the world, and to strengthen those tendencies in the Soviet Union to "civilianize" the economy and "pluralize" the society. U.S. leverage, while certainly not unlimited, has never been greater. That leverage should be used not to "help" Gorbachev or the Soviet Union, but to promote U.S. interests.[67]

The idea of "testing" Gorbachev was a common denominator that appealed to all but the most extreme policy advocates here and in Europe. The skeptics saw this approach as a way of calling his bluff and silencing the Gorbachev enthusiasts among Western publics, while the optimists saw this as a way of bringing to fruition the benevolent intent of Gorbachev's policies. The dominant view in Washington, however, was that those policies had the *potential* to cause significant change, whose scope was still to be determined. Soviet "new thinking," according to this perspective, was still an empty vessel that awaited filling; U.S. and other Western policy could exert a significant, perhaps decisive, influence on what substance might eventually find its way into the vessel. As vice president, George Bush had embraced the idea from his very first meeting with Gorbachev in 1985: "The challenge is not to 'help' him but to put forward U.S. interests in a way that affects his policy the way we want."[68]

But what kind of "test," and how ambitious should it be? Horst Teltschik, Chancellor Kohl's national security adviser, cautioned that we "should not ask too much of Gorbachev." Within the U.S. administration, our view was that "we should not ask too little, either."[69]

The greatest mistake would have been to accept the existing Soviet agenda as the starting point for our own approaches, which would have vindicated the view that nuclear arms reductions were the essential yardstick of East-West relations.[70] This, indeed, was stated explicitly in a report issued in December 1988 by a panel of 31 distinguished American experts: "An American strategy for developing its relations with the Soviet Union must take the present state of the relationship as its point of departure. It must also be grounded in the political realities of the situation in the Soviet Union."[71] Much like Genscher's Davos speech, its "agenda for the future" stressed arms control, confidence-building measures, expanded economic relations, and scientific and technical cooperation. The best that can be said of such a menu is that it was one to which Moscow would have agreed readily.

Acceptance of putative "political realities" was also the premise of a Trilateral Commission report issued by Valéry Giscard d'Estaing, Yasuhiro Nakasone, and Henry Kissinger,[72] and of articles by several American academics.[73] Although stressing the need to redress the problem of the preponderance of Soviet conventional forces in Europe, these various proposals gave pride of place to nuclear arms control and were nearly silent on the *sources* of East-West conflict. They said next to nothing about Eastern Europe: the Trilateral Commission report, for example, concluding that "the Soviet Union is not yet willing to implement in Eastern Europe the principle of nonintervention," proposed nothing more than that the countries of Central and Eastern Europe be given a special category of "association" with the European Community.[74]

Administration policy, soon to be unveiled publicly in the second of the president's major speeches, was delineated authoritatively in National Security Directive 23, classified secret, on "United States Relations with the Soviet Union."[75] Drafted and debated in April and May, NSD 23 stressed that "we will not react to reforms and changes in the Soviet Union that have not yet taken place, nor will we respond to every Soviet initiative." While applauding changes in Soviet declaratory policy, it called for words to be translated into deeds:

> A new relationship with the international system cannot simply be declared by Moscow. Nor can it be granted by others. It must be earned through the demilitarization of Soviet foreign policy and reinforced by behavior consistent with the principles of world order to which the Soviet Union subscribed in 1945 but has repeatedly violated since. . . . The United States will challenge the Soviet Union step by step, issue by issue and institution by institution to behave in accordance with the higher standards that the Soviet leadership itself has enunciated. Moscow will find the United States a willing partner.

The document then delineated specific conditions that would lead to a new cooperative relationship, including "deployment of a force posture that is smaller and less threatening," internal democratization to "establish a firm Soviet domestic base for a more productive and cooperative relationship with the free nations of the world," and adherence to the principle of "self-determination for the countries of East-Central Europe" and renunciation of the Brezhnev Doctrine.

Eastern Europe: Self Determination or Yalta II?   The future of Eastern Europe was a matter of first importance. The assumption behind the Trilateral Commission report, among others, was that the United States and the West must renounce Eastern Europe as a precondition for better relations with the Soviet Union—and avert another "traffic accident on the road to détente," as it were. One could make the case, as a tactical

matter, that addressing Eastern Europe's predicament had to await a period of warming and reassurance in Western relations with Moscow;
this, indeed, was among the long-standing premises of West German
ostpolitik. (*Wandel durch Annäherung*, or "change through rapprochement," was a tenet advanced from the early 1960s. It also implied that
one had to "accept the status quo in order to change it.") The best that
could be said of this view in early 1989 was that it was based on a
flawed assessment of trends already well advanced in Poland and Hungary, where revolutionary pressures were not about to await Western
convenience. But more was implied than tactics in at least some of these
proposals: they advanced, as a basis of Western grand strategy, acceptance and legitimation of a Soviet sphere of influence in Eastern Europe
as a necessary precondition for improved East-West relations.

It was in this context that the so-called Kissinger Plan for a U.S.-
Soviet "understanding" on Eastern Europe was mooted.[76] The issue actually arose from the more prosaic question of whether Eastern Europe
should be added to the U.S.-Soviet agenda, along with such hardy
perennials as strategic arms, regional conflicts, and human rights. Given
all that was happening and about to happen in Poland and Hungary,
there was little disagreement that we ought to begin talking seriously
with the Soviet leadership about American interests and perspectives in
this region. We also agreed that the prospects for hopeful change could
be enhanced by assuring Moscow that we had no intention of exploiting events in Eastern Europe for unilateral advantage. The Kissinger
Plan implied something else altogether: a Yalta-like agreement by the
superpowers over the heads of the East Europeans. This idea was never
on the agenda, nor ever given serious consideration by any senior administration official.[77]

The administration's position could not have been more different
from these attitudes. Eastern Europe was not some sort of shared
"problem" that had to be overcome before we could get on to the serious business of improving East-West relations; Eastern Europe was
what it was all about. Here was the perspective, which Cold War revi-
sionists can take on if they wish: The Cold War was not, in its essence, a
set of misunderstandings, mistakes, and miscalculations. It was the
product of Soviet conduct, above all Soviet domination of Eastern Europe and the forward deployment of more than half a million Soviet
troops in the heart of Europe. The Cold War began in, and because of,
Eastern Europe, and it was there that it had to end. Eastern Europe,

therefore, was the key "test" of whether Soviet "new thinking" would lead to a fundamental amelioration of the Cold War division of Europe.

"Eastern Europe" thus was shorthand for several related objectives: self-determination in this region, Soviet military withdrawal from the heart of Europe, a shift toward more cooperative Soviet international behavior, and above all an end to a worldview that demanded a ring of "satellite" states on key Soviet borders. Additionally, events in this region were closely tied to changes inside the Soviet Union: just as Gorbachev's policies had encouraged and legitimized reform in Eastern Europe, the far more radical changes envisioned in this region, if realized, would ultimately "blow back" on the Soviet Union itself. Policy toward Eastern Europe was therefore closely tied to how we wished to see the Soviet Union evolve.[78]

Eastern Europe had been at the center of President Bush's thinking well before his inauguration. Asked about his attitude toward Gorbachev during the election campaign, in his first television debate with Governor Michael Dukakis, Bush observed that "the interesting [question], one of the things that fascinates me about *perestroika* and *glasnost,* is what's going to happen in Eastern Europe."[79] After the inauguration, the "interesting question" became what he was going to do about it.[80]

The U.S. policy of "differentiation" had for many years meant "rewarding," mainly through trade concessions or political gestures, East European countries that either (a) distanced themselves from Soviet tutelage or (b) embarked on a path of internal liberalization. (It was George Bush himself, as vice president, who spelled out this hitherto classified policy in great and ill-advised detail in a 1983 speech in Vienna, much to the alarm of the reform-minded Hungarian leadership.[81]) With Mikhail Gorbachev in the Kremlin, the first half of the differentiation formula had become counterintuitive and counterproductive—were we to reward East European hard-liners for distancing themselves from Soviet new thinking? The focus then shifted to internal liberalization, with Poland and Hungary being the two cases in point in early 1989.

In the bureaucratic trenches of the administration, this spawned a furious internal battle, which seemed in retrospect like debating how many angels could dance on the head of a pin, but which was serious enough at the time. The question was whether the United States should offer economic incentives to support *political* liberalization absent any significant movement toward economic reform.[82] The economic agencies, mindful of the mountains of credits Poland squandered in the

1970s, argued strongly against this approach. They were joined by adherents to "the worse, the better" school, who felt that economic deterioration had compelled Polish and Hungarian leaders to enact reforms and that more misery would produce further reform. Against these views were those holding that a political opening would have to *precede* economic reform and that carefully conditioned U.S. assistance could facilitate first political, then economic liberalization. Those of us advocating this concept within the administration were joined by leaders of the democratic oppositions in Poland and Hungary, with whom we maintained close contact,[83] and, of greater political relevance, by President Bush and Secretary Baker. We were given a mandate to draw up a set of U.S. economic initiatives toward Poland and Hungary.

Far more important than any economic assistance package was the effect of American leadership. This was the point that the British historian and journalist Timothy Garton Ash, but few others, correctly perceived: "At this crucial juncture, the United States linked the development of its relationship with the Soviet Union to Soviet conduct in East-Central Europe."[84] Indeed, this may have been the single most important contribution the United States made to the events of 1989. Rather than seeking a strategic partnership with a reform-minded Soviet leadership, the United States, in effect, held its bilateral relationship with the Soviet Union, and East-West relations generally, hostage to the end of Soviet domination of the countries of Eastern Europe.

However obvious it may look in hindsight, this strategic judgment was by no means widely shared at the time. Nor was it without risks. Had Gorbachev been removed from power during the course of 1989, there would have been no shortage of second-guessing that U.S. intransigence had contributed to the downfall of the best Soviet leader that system was likely to produce. The administration, and above all the president himself, was acutely conscious of the risks, beginning with the danger that self-determination in Eastern Europe might be more than the market could bear in the Kremlin. Indeed, the very prudence with which the president pursued these aims caused many to miss just how ambitious the central vision was.

Five Speeches: American Grand Strategy "Beyond Containment"

American grand strategy for ending the Cold War was elaborated in five major speeches delivered by President Bush in April and May of 1989.[85]

They were developed as a package, each building on the other and culminating with a summation in the May 31 speech at Mainz, West Germany.

Eastern Europe The first, delivered in Hamtramck, Michigan, on April 17, elevated Eastern Europe to the top of the agenda: "The Cold War began in Eastern Europe, and if it is to end, it will end in this crucible of world conflict." In response to the Polish Roundtable Agreement, the president offered a set of economic assistance measures—including preferential trade treatment, investment promotion, and debt relief—designed to "recognize the reforms under way and to encourage reforms yet to come." Noting that "if Poland's experiment succeeds, other countries may follow," he pledged that further U.S. and other Western assistance would come "in concert with [political and economic] liberalization" and articulated a "vision of the European future":

We dream of the day when Eastern European peoples will be free to choose their system of government and to vote . . . in regular, free, contested elections. We dream of the day when Eastern European countries will be free to choose their own peaceful course in the world, including closer ties with Western Europe. And we envision an Eastern Europe in which the Soviet Union has renounced military intervention as an instrument of its policy—on any pretext. We share an unwavering conviction that one day all the peoples of Europe will live in freedom.

Stressing that "these are not bilateral issues between the United States and the Soviet Union," the president put them in the context of the future of Europe and pledged also to make them the centerpiece of the following month's NATO Summit. The final message was directed to Moscow:

As East and West now seek to reduce arms, it must not be forgotten that arms are a symptom, not a source, of tension. The true source of tension is the imposed and unnatural division of Europe. . . . The United States . . . has never accepted the legitimacy of Europe's division. We accept no spheres of influence that deny the sovereign rights of nations. . . .

The Soviet Union should understand . . . that a free, democratic Eastern Europe as we understand it would threaten no one and no country. Such an evolution would . . . imply and reinforce the further improvement of East-West relations in all its dimensions— arms reductions, political relations, trade—in ways that enhance the safety and well-being of all of Europe. There is no other way.

So much for "Yalta II"! Eastern Europe, ever history's object, was now its subject, and self-determination in this region was, for the United States and its allies, the principal requirement for improved East-West relations. (Yugoslavia, it should be noted, was a blind spot from the beginning. To the extent it entered into our strategic thinking, it was in the context of a general liberalization in the region. We saw the warning signs of impending disintegration but drew no lessons from them.[86])

The Soviet Union   The second speech, delivered at Texas A&M's commencement on May 12, called for moving "beyond containment" in U.S.-Soviet relations:

Wise men—Truman and Eisenhower; Vandenburg and Rayburn; Marshall, Acheson and Kennan—crafted the strategy of containment. They believed that the Soviet Union, denied the easy course of expansion, would turn inward and address the contradictions of its inefficient, repressive, and inhumane system. And they were right. . . . Containment worked. . . .
    We are approaching the conclusion of an historic postwar struggle between two visions. . . . Our goal is bold, more ambitious than any of my predecessors could have thought possible. . . . It is time to move beyond containment. . . . We seek the integration of the Soviet Union into the community of nations.

This was a conceptually new idea. The containment strategy had assumed that the U.S.-Soviet relationship was essentially conflictual. So did the policy of détente, which sought to carve out areas of cooperation and ease tensions, but within what was still a basically conflictual relationship. If the notion of containing Soviet power no longer carried the same weight as in the early days of the Cold War, the other premise of containment remained—namely, that the nature of the Soviet system had to change for the relationship to change fundamentally. It was this fundamental systemic change, rather than a superficial amelioration of the tone or atmosphere of East-West relations, that "beyond containment" sought to effect.

Arguing (along the lines of his NSD 23) that "a new relationship cannot be simply declared by Moscow or bestowed by others," the president delineated five conditions that would determine whether the vision could be fulfilled. He called for deep reductions in Soviet forces to less threatening levels as well as Soviet support for self-determination in Central and Eastern Europe (and "specific abandonment of the Brezhnev Doctrine"). He also stipulated that positive Soviet efforts to resolve regional conflicts were required, along with cooperative efforts in addressing environmental and other global challenges. And he called for respect for political pluralism and human rights within the USSR itself.[87] (These were the "tests," although the word was not used. They were also the yardsticks against which we would gauge the U.S.-Soviet relationship during the coming turbulent months.) While acknowledging the "hopeful, indeed remarkable" changes that had already taken place and expressing a "sincere desire to see *perestroika* succeed," he also stressed that "the national security of America and our allies is not predicated on hope. It must be based on deeds. We look for enduring, ingrained, economic and political change."

It was a tough, demanding speech, considering that it was delivered against the backdrop of Gorbachev's enormous popularity in early 1989.[88] Instead of "meeting Gorbachev halfway," it called on him to come the rest of the way to meet us; instead of "helping Gorbachev" stabilize the status quo, it asked him to infuse "new thinking" with substantive content and address the entire range of issues that had divided East and West for forty years.[89]

The Future of Europe   The third speech, which the president delivered in the company of French president Mitterrand at Boston University's commencement on May 21, aimed at conveying America's unambiguous support for European unity and its readiness to develop a new pattern of cooperation with the European Community as it moved toward closer economic and political unity. It did so through a characteristic blend of Wilsonian liberalism and a form of realism that embraced the power factor in world affairs, but without its balance of power assumptions:

The postwar order that began in 1945 is transforming into something very different. Yet certain essentials remain because our Alliance with Western Europe is utterly unlike the cynical power alliances of the past. It is based on far more than the perception of a common enemy. It is a tie of culture and kinship and shared values. . . .

Now a new century holds the promise of a united Europe. . . . The United States has often declared it seeks a healing of old enmities, an integration of Europe. At the same time, there has been an historical ambivalence . . . [to which] has been added apprehension at the prospect of 1992. . . . [But] this Administration is of one mind. We believe a strong, united Europe means a strong America. . . . We are ready to develop, with the European Community and its member states, new mechanisms of consultation.

The speech also outlined what Secretary Baker would later elaborate as the "New Atlanticism," welcoming West European efforts toward closer defense cooperation both bilaterally, particularly between France and Germany, and through the Western European Union. At the same time, it cautioned against letting hopes of a more benign Soviet Union outrace real changes, or accepting at face value "Soviet new thinking that has not yet totally overcome the old." On East-West relations, it laid principal stress on conventional arms reductions, "on negotiating a less militarized Europe" and building "a real peace . . . not a peace of armed camps."

Hardly noticed in the United States, the speech was well received in Europe, among those who were looking for, and found, a signal of U.S. readiness to build a more balanced transatlantic partnership with a more united Europe. While the results of this overture would be mixed, it at least had the effect of stimulating new forms of U.S.-EC consultations and new efforts to encourage and accommodate a European defense and security identity within the Atlantic alliance.[90]

Arms Control   The fourth speech, given May 24 at the Coast Guard Academy's commencement, returned to the "beyond containment" theme in the context of the changing security landscape. It recapitulated the key elements of the unfolding strategy:

We are witnessing the end of an idea—the final chapter of the communist experiment. . . . But the eclipse of communism is only one-half of the story of our time. The other is the ascendancy of the democratic idea. . . . There is an opportunity before us to shape a new world.

What is it we want to see? It is a growing community of democracies anchoring international peace and security, and a dynamic free market system generating prosperity and progress on a global scale. . . .

As to the Soviet Union, "We want *perestroika* to succeed. And we want to see the policies of *glasnost* and *perestroika*—so far, a revolution imposed from top down—institutionalized within the Soviet Union. We want to see *perestroika* extended as well."

This was the least successful of the five speeches, partly because the main impending initiative—a new U.S. conventional arms reduction proposal—was being hotly debated within the administration and could only be hinted at in the speech.[91] The main thrust of the arms control portion of the address aimed at restoring public support for nuclear deterrence and refocusing the East-West arms control agenda on the Soviet Union's massive advantage in conventional forces in Europe, which "far exceeds the levels needed to defend the legitimate security interests of the USSR. . . . The USSR has said it is willing to abandon its age-old reliance on offensive strategy. It's time to begin."

The president's positive reference to the unilateral reductions Gorbachev promised at the UN presaged his CFE (Conventional Armed Forces in Europe) initiative, unveiled a week later at a NATO Summit in Brussels, for further mutual reductions in NATO and Warsaw Pact forces to a level 20 percent below current NATO totals.[92] The obvious strategic aim was to seize the opportunity for deep and asymmetrical force reductions implied in Gorbachev's proposal. More important, the initiative had the political objective of facilitating a Soviet retreat from Eastern Europe by demonstrating that Soviet reductions, whether made voluntarily or under the pressure of a deteriorating economy and demands from Eastern Europe, would be met by corresponding Western reductions down to common ceilings.

Ending the Cold War The final speech, delivered May 31 in Mainz, West Germany, offered a summation of the various elements of the strategy for ending the Cold War. It began with the call for the United States and Germany to become "partners in leadership." (Our German friends were as flattered by this as they were nonplussed by the sentence that followed: "Of course, leadership has a constant companion—responsibility.") The president then laid out the vision of a "Europe whole and free," which he held out as "the new mission of NATO":

> The Cold War began with the division of Europe. It can only end when Europe is whole. Today, it is this very concept of a divided Europe that is under siege . . . not by armies, but by the spread of ideas. . . . A single powerful idea—democracy . . . is why the communist world, from Budapest to Beijing, is in ferment. Of course, for the leaders of the East, it is not just freedom for freedom's sake. But whatever their motivations, they are unleashing a force they will find difficult to channel or control. . . . Nowhere is this more apparent than in Eastern Europe, the birthplace of the Cold War.
>
> As President, I will continue to do all I can to help open the closed societies of the East. We seek self-determination for all of Germany and all of Eastern Europe. . . . When I visit Poland and Hungary this summer, I will deliver this message. . . . And I will take another message: the path of freedom leads to a larger home—a home where West meets East, a democratic home—the commonwealth of free nations.

The president then laid out a series of proposals. He suggested ways to strengthen and broaden the Helsinki process[93] to promote free elections and political pluralism in Eastern Europe. He proposed ways to bring down the Berlin Wall and promote new cooperation between the two halves of the city as well as extend Western assistance for environmental remediation in the East. He also sought to create "a less militarized Europe" through several arms initiatives, including the new U.S. proposal for deeper reductions in conventional forces. As to the Soviet leaders, "Our goal is not to undermine their legitimate security interests. Our goal is to convince them, step by step, that their definition of security is obsolete, that their deepest fears are unfounded." Finally:

> Growing political freedom in the East, a Berlin without barriers, a cleaner environment, a less militarized Europe—each is a noble goal, and taken together, they are the foundation of our larger vision: a Europe that is whole and free and at peace with itself.
>
> A few years ago, [this vision] would have been too revolutionary to consider. And yet today, we may well be on the verge of a

more ambitious agreement in Europe than anyone considered possible.

Competing Visions of the European Future   Leaving aside the rhetorical excesses and strained metaphors that come from overwritten presidential addresses, the kind of European future the United States was proposing contrasted starkly with the Soviet vision outlined by President Gorbachev in his speech to the Council of Europe in Strasbourg a few weeks later. According to Gorbachev: "I know that many in the West see the presence of two social systems as the major difficulty. But the difficulty actually lies elsewhere—in the widespread conviction (sometimes even a policy objective) according to which overcoming the division of Europe means 'overcoming socialism.' But this is a policy of confrontation, if not worse. No European unity will result from such approaches."

As one writer later observed, "Gorbachev did not say that there were many social systems in Europe. . . . He said that there were just two, East and West, 'socialist' and not. By implication, the common European home should be built around, and in spite of, this central difference."[94] This, indeed, went to the nub of the matter: a Europe "whole and free" or a Europe based on the permanence of the "two social systems"; an end to the division of Europe or an East-West accommodation based on Western acceptance of "political realities" in the East.

Bush's vision also contrasted with the dominant European perspective, articulated most clearly by West German foreign minister Hans-Dietrich Genscher. The difference between these two perspectives was made vividly clear in speeches given ten days apart in April 1989. Here is an excerpt from Bush's Hamtramck speech of April 17: "Victor Hugo said, 'An invasion of armies can be resisted, but not an idea whose time has come.' My friends, liberty is an idea whose time has come in Eastern Europe."

On April 27, speaking before the West German parliament, Genscher also cited Hugo, but without attribution:

Nothing is more powerful than an idea whose time has come. This is the idea of eliminating hostility from East-West relations. It is is the idea of demilitarizing East-West relations. It is the idea of de-ideologizing East-West relations. It is the idea of dialogue and co-operation . . . , of developing new peace structures. These are the topics for the forthcoming summit of the Western Alliance.[95]

"Liberty" or "new peace structures"? Freedom or "dialogue and cooperation"? Ending the Cold War or "de-ideologizing East-West relations"?

At the beginning of 1989, there had been three competing visions of Europe's future—Gorbachev's, Bush's, and Genscher's. By the time of the May 1989 NATO Summit to which Genscher referred, there was one. Gorbachev's had been overtaken by our much more ambitious vision, around which the Western alliance had rallied. Here is how the NATO Summit communiqué put it: "Now, more than ever our efforts to overcome the division of Europe must address its underlying political causes. . . . In keeping with our values, we place *primary* emphasis on basic freedoms for the people of Eastern Europe. . . . Our goal is a sustained effort geared to specific tasks which will help . . . promote democracy within Eastern countries and thus contribute to the establishment of a more stable peace in Europe."[96]

With that, the United States had reversed the logic of the international agenda and offered a Western vision of Europe's future that helped expose the limitations of Gorbachev's "common European home" even as it sought to extend the potential of Soviet "new thinking." More important, it had put in place a strategy for ending the Cold War division of Europe, within the context of our relations with the Soviet Union and what we hoped that state could become.

To recapitulate, American grand strategy involved a sequence of steps. The first was to alter the psychology of East-West relations away from an accommodation based on existing "political realities" toward a much more radical vision of Europe's future. The second was to restore the cohesion of the Western alliance—beginning with a resolution of the SNF dispute at the upcoming NATO Summit and articulation of a common Western strategy—and to begin building a new transatlantic partnership that encouraged and accommodated a stronger, more united Western Europe. The third was to place Eastern Europe at the top of the international agenda and to engage American leadership on behalf of political liberalization and independence. Then, as U.S.-Soviet relations had been put on hold while the first three steps were being carried out, the fourth was to challenge the Soviet leadership to respond to specific proposals. These proposals were consistent with the spirit and promise of Gorbachev's "new thinking" but went well beyond its practice to date; they would address the sources rather than the consequences of East-West conflict. The ultimate aim was to end the Cold War and the division of Europe through the peaceful, democratic transformation of its eastern half.

Little did we know how quickly this ambitious agenda would be achieved, then exceeded. Our most hopeful expectation in the early part of the year was that Poland and Hungary were headed toward a two- or three-year period of power-sharing between the Communist parties and democratic oppositions, during which time democratic change would advance in those countries and spread beyond. We got the pattern of change right and correctly judged the potential for communism's collapse throughout the region, but we certainly did not see it coming so fast. Astonishing event followed astonishing event—the successful June elections in Poland were followed by the opening of the Hungarian border and the installation of Tadeusz Mazowiecki as Poland's first noncommunist prime minister in four decades. Then swarms of East Germans occupied West German embassies in Prague and Budapest seeking to flee from East Germany to freedom. Only as we witnessed these breakthroughs and above all, the breach of the Berlin Wall on the night of November 9, did we dare hope that the scenario we had imagined earlier in the year might actually be accomplished so swiftly and peacefully.

2

The Revolutions of 1989

IT WAS LATE IN THE AFTERNOON of December 21 that Adrian Moruzi lost his fear. He had gathered with a few dozen others in the main square in Braşov, Romania, in sympathy protest for the demonstrators killed in Timişoara four days before. Securitate forces arrived and sprayed bullets over their heads. Moruzi and the other protestors dropped to the ground. But after thirty seconds or so, they began rising, one by one, to face their assailants. These were acts as much of desperation as of bravery: if they were to be gunned down on that square that day, so be it, but they would no longer be cowed. As it turned out, the security forces held their fire, having lost their nerve or perhaps their sense of duty for attacking their own countrymen gathered in peaceful protest against an unspeakably cruel regime. At that moment, something fundamental changed in Romania. Moruzi told me his story over dinner in Braşov in May of 1992, shortly after he had become the city's first democratically elected mayor.[1] Pockmarks from the bullets fired that December day were still visible on building facades.

Moruzi's story must have been replayed ten thousand times in cities and towns across Eastern Europe in the fall of 1989, albeit without the brutality of the Romanian regime.[2] Other stories of 1989 were more prosaic: a blue-collar worker in another city recalled thinking, when student protestors across the street yelled at him to join them, that the curb on which he hesitated was the dividing line between onlooker and participant. He crossed his personal Rubicon, and the authorities were soon faced down by a swelling crowd of defiance.

These events, from the heroic to the mundane, marked the end of fear as an agent of political authority in communist Eastern Europe.

They also signaled the ruling elite's loss of confidence in its own right to rule, which also belongs to the dynamic of revolutionary change, as Alexis de Tocqueville showed more than a century ago in his study of the French Revolution. As de Tocqueville put it, in terms as relevant to 1989 as to 1789, this phenomenon helped explain "why it was that an uprising of the people could overwhelm so abruptly and decisively [a regime] that . . . had seemed inexpugnable even to the men who were about to destroy it."[3]

In the summer of 1989, free elections in Poland led to the installation of Eastern Europe's first noncommunist prime minister since the imposition of communist rule, and roundtable negotiations in Hungary reached agreement on a multiparty system and fully free parliamentary elections. In September and October, tens of thousands of East German refugees made their ways via Hungary and Czechoslovakia to West Germany. Spontaneous demonstrations spread throughout East Germany, leading to the opening of the Berlin Wall on the night of November 9. The next day, veteran Bulgarian party leader Todor Zhivkov was replaced by a new leadership that announced the end of one-party rule and soon opened negotiations with a new "Union of Democratic Forces." In late November, spiraling public demonstrations in Czechoslovakia obliged the regime to open negotiations with opposition forces led by Václav Havel. Also in late November, Romanian leader Nicolae Ceauşescu was unanimously reelected president amidst the usual official accolades; a month later, he was deposed, sentenced to death, and executed by firing squad. Finally, on December 29, Havel, who had been imprisoned earlier in the year for political activities, was unanimously elected president by parliamentary vote. As a White House press release of that day put it, "In a year of astonishing events, none is more astonishing that the election of this playwright–political prisoner as president of Czechoslovakia."[4]

That these events occurred so quickly and peacefully defies satisfactory explanation, even in retrospect. The very speed of change was part of the dynamic, as was the cross-border impact of successful challenges to communist authority.[5] There were obvious linkages, such as the impact on the GDR (German Democratic Republic) of the Hungarian decision to open its borders to East German refugees and the July 1989 visit by Polish opposition leaders to Prague for meetings with Czech dissidents. Another was the presence of Hungarian dissidents in Czechoslovakia to help commemorate the August anniversary of the 1968 War-

saw Pact invasion.[6] But there were also more subtle ones, as successful
defiance in one country emboldened opposition forces elsewhere even as
it discredited and demoralized their ruling parties.

Of course, Soviet action—or, rather, inaction—was the permissive
cause. When it became evident, after the Polish elections and especially
after the opening of the Berlin Wall, that Soviet power was no longer at
the disposal of the East European regimes, there was nothing to retard
the headlong surge to freedom. The discredited and enervated East European regimes, now thrown on their own resources to preserve their
grip on power, proved no match for peaceful democratic revolutions led
by organized opposition movements—or even disorganized ones, as in
Bulgaria and Romania. The ruling parties lacked the credibility to retain
power by embracing pseudodemocracy; as it turned out, they lacked the
will, or perhaps the capacity, to muster the coercive power required to
subdue virtually their entire populations.

The first half of the year called to mind the interplay between Hungarian and Polish reform movements in 1956; the second half evoked
the 1848 "springtime of nations," as national independence movements
spread from city to city with astonishing speed and unexpected success.[7]
It was as if generations of history were compressed into a few months.

Indeed, the very swiftness of these changes tended to impart, after the
fact, an air of irreversibility to the process and inevitability to the outcome, contributing to Bergson's "illusions of retrospective determinism."[8] It was an irresistible temptation for scholars and political pundits, having failed to anticipate these events, to go back to find the
evidence they had missed and then, by way of atonement, to adduce a
powerful body of evidence purporting to show how and why things had
to come out as they did. To make order out of chaos, the formula was
simple: draw a straight line backwards in time, then go back to some
convenient date and follow the line forward, showing all the social, economic, political, and other forces that drove history ineluctably along
its predestined course.

This is not how it looked at the time; this is not how it was. It was a
period of great uncertainty and was so perceived by protagonists in
West and East alike; the Hungarians and Poles in particular had bitter
memories of failed revolutions, both ancient and recent. (Those who
followed the Polish events of 1980–81 at close range remember well
how firmly many believed, right up to the moment that martial law was
declared and Solidarity outlawed, that the Solidarity-led social revolu-

tion could no longer be reversed.[9]) Within the Polish opposition in the spring of 1989, few believed that Solidarity would win the election, and fewer still thought that the Wojciech Jaruzelski regime would honor such an outcome.[10]

Evocations of 1848 or of the French Revolution (captured in banners proclaiming, "1789–1989") were meant to exhilarate, but they also served to remind how quickly repression can follow liberation. Indeed, had the Polish opposition not decided to support General Jaruzelski's election as president—ultimately secured by the margin of a single vote—the history of the next several months might have been one of retreat and repression rather than democratic triumph. As if to underscore the point, the first round of the Polish elections was held on the day of the massacre in Beijing's Tiananmen Square. Similarly, in Leipzig on October 9, had maestro Kurt Masur not persuaded local authorities to issue a joint appeal for nonviolence, the huge street demonstrations that day might have led, not to triumph, but to disaster.[11]

Even later in the year, no one could be sure how Moscow would react: it was one thing for Gorbachev to countenance, even encourage, greater liberalization and autonomy in Eastern Europe, quite another for the Soviet leadership to preside over the dissolution of an East European empire. This clearly was never Gorbachev's intent; his assumption was that replication in Eastern Europe of his own policies of *glasnost* and *perestroika*, together with the advent of new leaders who were reasonable facsimiles of himself, would produce, somehow, a revitalized socialism. As late as July, in his speech at Strasbourg, Gorbachev continued to express his belief in the viability of East European socialism. Soviet foreign minister Shevardnadze seems to have understood better the bankruptcy of communist rule in Eastern Europe. So, ironically, did Gorbachev's hard-line critics, who knew only too well that force, and the willingness to use it, undergirded their authority. To his credit, though, Gorbachev never signaled that he was prepared to restore order through repressive means; at every critical juncture, he not only acquiesced but actively encouraged the process of change he had unwittingly helped to unleash.

U.S. Policy

A successful democratic transformation in Central and Eastern Europe was the highest priority for U.S. foreign policymakers, yet these were events effectively beyond our ability to influence, except indirectly. In this sense, the U.S. role, like that of the Germans and the Western allies collectively, was marginal. Foreign policy, even for a superpower, is usually made in the context of broad historical forces that can at best be nudged in one direction or another. Yet policy so conducted can make a difference, sometimes a decisive one.

U.S. policy was instrumental in five respects. First, following Yogi Berra's dictum, we made no "wrong mistakes" that might have threatened the hopeful course of events and sparked a reaction. Second, we elevated Eastern Europe to the top of the international agenda and made self-determination in this region the prime test of Soviet "new thinking." Third, we were unambiguous on principles: our goals were democracy and independence, not "reform communism" and "Finlandization." Fourth, recognizing that reform had to be led from above as well as pushed from below, we provided incentives for the Polish and Hungarian communist leaders to move along the path of political liberalization. Fifth, we worked to persuade Soviet leaders that democratic change in Eastern Europe could be accomplished without undermining legitimate Soviet security interests—and helped them redefine what constituted "legitimate" interests.

After the Roundtable Agreement in Poland, our near-term aim was to lend support to the process of political opening and, more immediately, to facilitate the faithful implementation of the accords. The Hamtramck speech of April 1989 had set the basic strategic goals and offered several modest initiatives designed to encourage the Polish and Hungarian regimes along the path of political and economic liberalization. And the NATO Summit and Mainz speech of late May had articulated a coordinated Western approach toward the region.[12] There remained the task of dramatizing U.S. leadership.[13] What better way than for President Bush to visit both Poland and Hungary, and to use the announcement of the visit as leverage for continued reform movement in both countries?

There were signs of change elsewhere in the region, as well, in the spring of 1989. In Bulgaria, the independent trade union Podkrepa (Support) joined an informal "Club for the Support of *Perestroika* and *Glasnost*," the environmental group "Ecoglasnost," and other pro-democracy movements as the seeds of organized opposition. In Romania, six former Communist party leaders sent an open letter to Ceauşescu accusing him of "discrediting socialism," and veteran human rights activist Doina Cornea sent several open letters charging him, more pointedly, with crimes against human dignity.[14] A small but defiant group of asylum-seekers marched in Leipzig, demanding exit visas to West Germany. In Prague, Václav Havel was released from prison, halfway through his eight-month sentence, following public and international calls for his release. Shortly thereafter, he issued a petition entitled "Several Sentences"[15] calling for democratic reforms and for the regime to open a dialogue; its original 1,800 signatories were soon joined by thousands more.

In the Soviet Union itself, voters swept aside several prominent Communist party leaders in favor of independent candidates, including Boris Yeltsin, the former Moscow party leader whom Gorbachev had fired in 1987, for the new Congress of People's Deputies. Indeed, these elections, the freest in the history of Soviet rule, gave further impetus for democratic change in Poland and Hungary. If relatively free elections could be held in the USSR, why not in Poland and Hungary? Yet the Poles and Hungarians were at the leading edge of reform, and it was their progress, more than events in the USSR, that was seen elsewhere in Eastern Europe as the real test of Soviet intentions.[16]

U.S.-Soviet Relations   Managing the U.S.-Soviet relationship through this period was the most important and complicated aspect of policy. By mid-1989 we were clearly dealing with a Soviet Union in retreat, and a Soviet leadership beset with internal as well as external challenges to its authority. Our task was to help secure Soviet acquiescence without humiliation, so that Moscow would have a stake and a place in the emerging order and see its legitimate security concerns addressed. These political and diplomatic efforts, including arms control initiatives that helped Gorbachev save face while also meeting Soviet security concerns, were widely and favorably reported. Less well understood among Western publics, particularly the American public, was the importance of the uses of power, including its personal and psychological dimensions.

Here, President Bush understood the requirements better than clever pundits or advisers. His approach toward his counterpart in the Kremlin ran roughly as follows.[17] Soviet leaders, including Gorbachev, understood power and the "correlation of forces," and they also drew conclusions when power—not only military power—was arrayed against them. They certainly understood in the fall of 1989 that they were playing a losing hand. Yet they also knew, and knew that we knew, that they had a trump card—more than half a million troops in the heart of Europe and a military capacity that could threaten Europe for many decades to come, no matter the evolution of political events. Gorbachev and Shevardnadze, and indeed others within the Soviet leadership, were intelligent and imaginative men. While their position was too weak to deploy a grand strategy in Europe, neither were they unwitting dupes as one communist regime after another fell in Eastern Europe. Once these events were well advanced in the fall of 1989, they knew perfectly well what the game was and were fully capable of playing a weak hand well, as indeed they did. They needed to be treated with the utmost seriousness and respect, as indeed they were.

Securing Soviet acquiescence to the loss of empire would require the mobilization of diplomatic, political, military, economic, and, not least, psychological power toward this end. At the same time, as leaders in retreat can react unpredictably, even irrationally, power must be exercised with subtlety and sensitivity. Finally, just as the tsar consolidated power in the Kremlin when threatened at one of its imperial borders, a Soviet leader facing losses abroad would be more likely to guard jealously his personal power at home.

This venture into psycho-history may help explain some of the more controversial aspects of President Bush's approach: his initial slowness to engage Gorbachev in serious dialogue (while mobilizing the requisite power) and his reluctance to confront Gorbachev directly over the crackdown in the Baltic states. It may also explain his sensitivity to Gorbachev's domestic standing even after the Soviet leader's star was clearly waning.[18]

Another case in point was the president's May 1989 CFE (Conventional Armed Forces in Europe) initiative. It was designed to help Gorbachev find a way toward a less militarized Europe consistent with Soviet security interests. But it also made it plain what the alternative was: a united NATO, fully prepared to maintain and continue modernizing its forces into the indefinite future, leaving Moscow to cope on its own with an eroding empire and bankrupt economy. Appealing to Moscow's better instincts and showing the way to a more cooperative future was important, but so too was backing this vision with power and creating a new reality that made a return to "old thinking" a less plausible option.

Engagement in Eastern Europe   These strands came together in President Bush's visit to Poland and Hungary in July 1989. With events in those countries already moving in hopeful directions, we wanted to facilitate further democratic change without inadvertently provoking a backlash. Another failed revolution could have set the clock back a decade in Eastern Europe and derailed Soviet reform for perhaps a generation; as we were in no position to assure success or come to the rescue if things went awry, it was important that American intentions not be misunderstood. Operationally, we wanted to lend strength to the dominant forces of moderation within the Polish and Hungarian oppositions, as well as to reform-minded regime figures, and give the fire-breathing fringes no grounds for action.[19] (Our engaging of communist leaders willing to support reform, or at least not oppose it, was born partly of the assumption that they would be participants in the process for some years to come.) At the same time, we wanted the fact of the visit, along with the symbolism and substance of key events, to make it clear that our agenda for democratic change went far beyond the modest concessions made so far by the ruling establishments.

In May, I went to both countries to advance the president's trip. This, technically, was the "pre-advance" trip, in which we made tentative arrangements for what the president would do, where he would go, and whom he would see. Later, once our tentative arrangements had been approved, the "advance" team would go for a longer stint to prepare the logistics of the visit in excruciating detail, eventually to be incorporated into the "event book" everyone would carry on the trip. I have the Polish event book before me as I write; a single day in Warsaw runs to nearly a hundred pages. The "pre-advance" was the substantive trip, designed to ensure that the visit furthered our policy objectives.

In Warsaw, we had lunch at Ambassador John Davis's residence with key Polish opposition leaders and "independents," using the opportunity to compare notes on strategy and tactics. I reminded Solidarity adviser Bronisław Geremek that when last we had met, in April 1988, he had explained the strategy behind Solidarity's readiness to enter into an "anticrisis pact" with the Jaruzelski government. Now, a year later, that opening had produced the Roundtable Agreement, but the same dilemmas remained for Solidarity. The regime wanted to co-opt and eventually discredit the opposition by making it coresponsible for the painful economic austerity measures to come while retaining for the Communist party the essential levers of political power. Solidarity, having been created a decade before on the premise that opposition to communist rule had to come from independent social organizations operating outside, and parallel to, the ruling establishment, was now prepared to gamble for a share of political power to help arrest the virtual collapse of the Polish economy. Solidarity was by no means certain that its strategy would prevail over a regime that still had powerful instruments of control at its disposal.

On the regime's intentions, the "Soviet factor," and all the other fundamentals, our analyses were almost identical with those of Solidarity strategists. We also agreed that a frontal assault by regime opponents was less likely to succeed than the careful course which Solidarity had undertaken in the Roundtable Agreement. Beyond that, Solidarity's strategy was not for us to decide; we only needed to know how the United States could be helpful. What was needed, we were told, was U.S. moral support and leadership, a coordinated approach by the West, further incentives for the Polish regime to fulfill its pledges, and an approach toward Moscow that was firm on principles while avoiding any hint of gloating or triumphalism.[20] This guidance coincided with our own thinking and, *mutatis mutandis,* with that of Hungarian opposition figures as well. In a May 1 paper, which I had with me on the trip, the dissident Hungarian philosopher János Kis echoed the thinking of his Polish counterparts. One paragraph in particular was pertinent:

> The *Ostpolitik* which consisted in cooperating with governments only is to be rejected. But, in cases where there is a significant chance for negotiated transition, the Cold War attitude which involved a complete rejection of serious talks with governments should also be abandoned. What Western governments ought to support is not one side against the other but the making of a social contract between the two. This, however, must not mean abandoning the opposition to the good will of the so-called reformist wing of the Communist party leadership. By recognizing the de facto pluralism of the political arena, Western governments could contribute to its consolidation and further development.[21]

Against this background, the U.S. delegation began official negotiations with our Polish counterparts.[22] Some events, they informed us, were *de rigueur*: an arrival ceremony, wreath-laying ceremony at the Tomb of the Unknown Soldier, a meeting with General Jaruzelski, and a state dinner. The Polish government also assumed, rightly, that President Bush would go to Gdańsk to see Solidarity leader Lech Wałęsa. Everything else was open. Indeed, we left all the Polish proposals open and refused to commit to any of them, even the "required" events, until we had secured Polish agreement to our main objectives, at that point unknown to them.

The first issue was the venue for a speech. We wanted President Bush to be the first foreign leader to address the first freely elected East European parliament since the onset of communist rule, and to use the announcement of this event to exert pressure on the Polish authorities to ensure that free and fair elections were held as promised. Understandably, our broaching of this idea evoked horrified looks on the faces of the Polish foreign ministry officials with whom we were dealing. They had no way of knowing whether the Polish government had any intention of allowing the elections to proceed as agreed, no way of knowing what the outcome would be, and no way of knowing whether the Polish authorities would honor the outcome if Solidarity won. They threw up a blizzard of objections and a host of alternative proposals. We remained adamant, making it clear that the trip itself might be in jeopardy unless we were assured that the president would speak to the Polish parliament. Ultimately they relented, but only after General Jaruzelski's personal intervention.

Our second main objective was to arrange the president's visit to Gdańsk and meeting with Wałęsa in ways that made it plain that our sympathies were with the democratic aspirations of the Polish people. First, we wanted a speech that would be emotional and symbolic, in contrast to the cooler and more analytical address to the Polish parliament. We wanted it out of doors, with huge crowds . . . in front of the Lenin Shipyard in Gdańsk. Here our own Secret Service showed greater concern than did the Polish authorities, but in the end they relented. What about the meeting with Wałęsa? We thought it would be a nice touch, after the stiff setting of a state dinner in Warsaw, for the President and Mrs. Bush to join the Wałęsas in their home for a private luncheon, accompanied only by interpreters. I do not know that President Bush ever heard how this was done; he might be amused to learn how we angled an invitation. Lech Wałęsa was out of the country, so we arranged to meet his wife, Danuta, together with a Solidarity adviser, at the Wałęsa home. Sitting around their small dining room table as assorted Wałęsa children walked in and out, we broached the idea of a small private luncheon, to which they were receptive. We suggested that Mrs. Wałęsa might want to send back with us a handwritten invitation to President and Mrs. Bush, which we thought would be literally an offer the president could not refuse. Mrs. Wałęsa agreed, worked out a text with her adviser, and the deal was done.

The last remaining issue, a logistical one with substantive implications, was what to do about General Jaruzelski. He, understandably, did not wish to be in Gdańsk for Solidarity's events. Neither would his sense of protocol allow him to have President Bush leave Poland without his being there to send him off. Nor, given Jaruzelski's pivotal role in overseeing a process of political liberalization, was it in our interests to snub him. Yet the president's schedule was too tight for him to fly back to Warsaw before going on to Budapest. Finally it was agreed that Jaruzelski would fly to Gdańsk after the luncheon and the speech, accompany the president to Westerplatte, site of the opening shots of World War II, and then see his plane off from Gdańsk. We were not thrilled with this second set of Gdańsk events that returned the spotlight to the Polish regime, but we were prepared to agree if all our other objectives, including the Polish parliament speech, were accepted.

These logistical issues may seem small, and indeed the other issues with which we dealt were smaller still, yet they had a substantive dimension as well. Even grand strategy is implemented in small steps.

In Budapest, where the political distance between the regime and its opponents was not so great, our task was much simpler. Our main interest was finding two sites for presidential speeches—one outdoors and emotional, another indoors but with a symbolically rich setting. Our first choice for the outdoor speech was Batthány Square, which memorialized Hungary's prime minister who was executed after the 1848 Revolution and which had become, in 1989 as in 1956, a symbol of protest and democratic defiance. This site the Secret Service ruled out for security reasons, the square being surrounded by close-in apartment buildings with countless windows. Ultimately, we settled on Kossuth Square just behind the Hungarian parliament building, with the president standing just under the statue of Lajos Kossuth, Hungary's great national hero of 1848.

The second speech venue came to us easily. We had already decided to take a look at Karl Marx University, whose reputation for espousing free market principles offered a nice philosophical juxtaposition. When we saw the reception hall with a huge bust of Marx, beneath which the president could speak about economic liberty, the choice was made. Otherwise, our main tasks were to see that the president met with the right balance of regime figures, which was a matter mainly for the Hungarian side to sort out, and representatives of the democratic opposition, which we accomplished via a large—and, as it turned out, not very successful—meeting with independent political leaders in the ambassador's residence.

One small vignette reinforced our general impression of impending major change. I was invited to a dinner in Budapest in honor of visiting Hungarian-Canadian industrialist George Sarlos (not to be confused with the Hungarian-American financier and philanthropist George Soros). Present as a speaker was Hungarian Communist party leader Károly Grósz. His remarks were bland enough; what was remarkable was the open criticism and condescension to which he was subjected by several Hungarians in the audience. Even in Hungary, this kind of treatment of a communist leader would have been hard to imagine a year earlier. If Hungary was indeed moving toward a multiparty system and free elections, I recall thinking, Grósz and his party are finished.

Poland and Hungary: Events Accelerate   By the time of the president's visit in early July, the Polish elections had returned a stunning victory for Solidarity candidates. In the freely contested elections for the new upper house, the Senate,[23] they won 99 of the 100 seats. In the lower (but more powerful) house, the Sejm, they won 160 of the 161 seats available to them, the remaining 65 percent having been reserved for the communist bloc.[24] No one inside Poland or out had expected such a landslide; indeed, many in the Polish opposition had thought it a blunder to agree to elections with only two months to prepare. Wałęsa himself had complained: "None of us wants these elections. They are the terrible, terrible price we have to pay to get our union back."[25] As the election results began to come in, the Warsaw Citizens' Committee of Solidarity watched, in stunned disbelief, from its informal headquarters in a place aptly called "Cafe Surprise."[26] Having succeeded beyond their wildest expectations in challenging communist rule in Poland, Solidarity now had to prepare for the unanticipated consequences of its success: assuming responsibility for the formation of the new Polish government. As Wałęsa put it, "I face the disaster of having had a good crop."[27] This was Wałęsa's usual overstatement, but it conveyed his sense of the unexpected challenges ahead.

In Hungary, meanwhile, there had been a similar acceleration. In May, portions of the Iron Curtain between Hungary and Austria were dismantled, symbolizing an open door to the West that would soon acquire even greater importance as the route of choice of thousands of East German asylum-seekers. In mid-June, government-opposition roundtable talks reached agreement on fully open parliamentary elections and other political reforms; at the same time, the long-awaited reburial of Imre Nagy, prime minister during the 1956 Revolution, touched off vast demonstrations in tribute. A week later, Károly Grósz, whose political future turned out to be even shorter than it appeared in May, was forced to share party leadership within a new presidium of four that included leading progressives Imre Pozsgay, Prime Minister Miklós Németh, and veteran economic reformer Rezsö Nyers.[28]

The timing of President Bush's visit thus turned out to be even more pivotal and delicate than we had imagined. The Hungarian government-opposition roundtable negotiations would be ongoing. In Poland, he would arrive in the midst of deliberations over the shape and composition of the new government. The position of his official host, General Jaruzelski, was now in doubt. The Roundtable Agreement had stipulated that the new president would be elected by the two houses of parliament, but Solidarity's sweeping victory called into question whether the power-sharing arrangement it had concluded with the communist regime could in fact be honored.[29]

Behind all this was the larger question of Soviet attitudes, which the president addressed in a *Washington Post* interview in early June.[30] His remarks, which combined insistence on the rights of the Poles and Hungarians to chart their own course with reassurance that the United States would not exploit these developments for unilateral advantage, evidently resonated well in Moscow. Georgi Shakhnazarov, Gorbachev's chief adviser on Eastern Europe, read the text carefully and told an American visitor that it was "extremely important and positive" and that, as far as he was concerned, "all of Bush's conditions can be fulfilled."[31]

Gorbachev's speech to the Council of Europe in Strasbourg,[32] delivered just a day before the president's departure from Washington for Poland, was another positive signal, and a seemingly conscious response to U.S. calls for a renunciation of the Brezhnev Doctrine. "Social and political orders in one or another country have changed in the past and may change in the future," Gorbachev said. "This is exclusively the affair of the peoples themselves. . . . Any interference in internal affairs and any attempts to restrict the sovereignty of states—either friend and allies or anyone else—are inadmissable." These remarks were studied closely in Washington. This was the most categorical statement yet that the Soviet Union would not intervene to save an allied regime. It was also the first time a Soviet leader had ever implied that a "socialist" country could choose "capitalism" and that—Marxist orthodoxy notwithstanding—history's wheel could turn the other way round.

In effect, Gorbachev had repudiated the Brezhnev Doctrine by which Moscow had claimed the right to intervene in a "fraternal" state if "socialism" were threatened. Indeed, two days later, at a Warsaw Pact meeting in Bucharest, Hungarian foreign minister Gyula Horn declared "the so-called Brezhnev Doctrine is over once and for all."[33]

Yet, here again, "illusions of retrospective determinism" come in. One can look back on this period and selectively assemble a powerful body of evidence putatively demonstrating that in public remarks as well as private deliberations, Soviet leaders had already reconciled themselves to the loss of empire and even to the prospect of eventual German unification. What was all the fuss about? But to reach these judgments is to neglect countervailing evidence that clouds the historical picture, and certainly clouded the picture that we were able to perceive at the time. Gorbachev's Strasbourg speech was not the only thing being said or written by Soviet officialdom at the time. Coverage by the official Soviet dailies *Pravda* and *Izvestia* of the events in Poland and Hungary was replete with ominous warnings of anti-Soviet and antisocialist activities,[34] code words reminiscent of Soviet commentaries during the Hungarian Revolution of 1956, the Prague Spring of 1968, and the rise of Solidarity in Poland in 1980–81. Which was the authentic, definitive Soviet position—Gorbachev's speech before a Western audience in Strasbourg or the line taken by the official Soviet press? The answer was probably both . . . and neither: Soviet attitudes were still in evolution and far from uniform.

From the point of view of U.S. policy, the most that could be safely assumed was that Moscow welcomed democratic changes in principle but remained wary about them in practice. It was against this backdrop of mixed Soviet signals that President Bush prepared to travel to Poland and Hungary. The goals of the trip were sketched out in a background briefing to the press by a "senior administration official"[35] on the eve of the president's departure:

We seek to overcome the division of Europe and bring Eastern European countries into the commonwealth of free nations. . . . Conceptually, this is a newly-vivid goal for American policymakers. In the past, the desire for an end to Europe's unnatural division seemed unapproachably distant. Recent events have now brought this ambitious objective into view. . . .

The historical symbolism of the President's trip to Poland and Hungary and the power of a simple restatement of what we stand for will, we think, tap a great well of popular sentiment in these two countries. . . . Memories, symbols, ideas all count in Eastern Europe to a very great degree. And that is why the very fact of the American President standing in these countries at this particular time and talking about their place in history and about freedom, about Western involvement in their future, is so important.[36]

The President's Trip to Poland and Hungary   With these objectives in mind, the president arrived in Warsaw on July 9 for a trip that would take him to Gdańsk, Budapest, Paris (for the G-7, or Group of Seven, Summit), and the Netherlands. In his speech to the newly elected Polish parliament, he sought to capture the essence of the moment, urging Poles "to forge a rare alloy of courage and restraint": "The future beckons with both hope and uncertainty. Poland and Hungary find themselves at a crossroads. Each has started down its own road to reform, without guarantee of easy success. . . . The way is hard. But the moment is right, both internally and internationally, for Poland to walk its own path. . . . Poland is where the Cold War began, and now the people of Poland can help bring the division of Europe to an end [and] redeem the principles of the Atlantic Charter."[37]

On East-West relations, his focus was on "greatly reduced levels of arms" and insistence that reductions in military forces must "take place in parallel with political change."[38] The president then cited Gorbachev: "Universal security rests on the recognition of the right of every nation to choose its own path of social development and on the renunciation of interference in the domestic affairs of other states. A nation may choose either capitalism or socialism. This is its sovereign right."[39] This was meant for multiple audiences: for Gorbachev, to turn his words back on him as the standards to which we meant to hold him; for the Polish regime, to convey that democratic change should have no arbitrary limits, nor any imposed by the putative bounds of Soviet tolerance; and for the Polish population at large, to encourage them to seize the moment.

Building on the "Hamtramck package" of economic assistance initiatives,[40] the president announced an additional set of measures and pledged to use U.S. leadership at the forthcoming G-7 Summit to galvanize coordinated Western assistance to Poland and Hungary. Of the new assistance measures, the most important was the capitalization of a new Polish-American Enterprise Fund, which would provide start-up loans and technical assistance to new Polish private business. Although we settled on the name literally on the eve of the president's departure, the Enterprise Fund concept was the product of much discussion and analysis. These efforts led us to the conclusion that Poland's newly emerging private economic sector, particularly small and medium-sized enterprises, would be the principal source of economic dynamism and growth during the initial transition toward a market economy. This was also the sector most likely to be neglected by the World Bank, as the loans involved would be too small for its usual programs, and the one where we could make the most difference.[41] Finally, as the fund would provide support directly to the emerging private sector, it was an approach that allowed us to help Poland's economy without having that assistance pass through its still-communist bureaucracy.[42]

The direct assistance measures were modest in the extreme, useful more as a symbol of American involvement than for their tangible economic benefits. They were meant to help lead Poland, including its communist leadership, along a path of reform that had not yet begun in the economic sphere. The administration (particularly the Treasury Department), recalling the gross misuse of Western credits in the 1970s by the regime of Edward Gierek, was perhaps overly concerned that our aid might be squandered or, worse, manipulated by the current regime to prop up its own rule. These were fair enough concerns at the time, but the paucity of the U.S. assistance package weakened the symbolic effect we hoped to achieve and, as will be seen, set the wrong example for our G-7 partners. We should have done more, and we certainly should have corrected our mistake later in the year, when political and economic reforms sweeping the region justified much greater financial assistance.

In his meetings with Jaruzelski, the president's aims were to establish a relationship of trust with the Polish leader, appeal to his patriotism,[43] and help persuade him to play a role in overseeing, or at least acquiescing in, a process of political liberalization. Bush argued that a political opening, based on acceptance of the results of the Polish elections, was the only way out of Poland's economic and political crisis. If Jaruzelski was prepared to support such an opening, he could count on U.S. help. The United States aimed to "assist in a process, an evolution," not enter into a contest with the Soviet Union over Poland. "We are not asking you to choose between East and West," the president told the visibly relieved Polish leader.[44]

Polish prime minister Mieczysław Rakowski, in his memoirs, summed up Bush's visit this way:

> It is quite certain that Bush did not choose the [timing of his visit] without consideration. He came to Poland in the middle of the process of shaping a new political balance, after the parliamentary election . . . and during ongoing negotiations on the presidency, government, etc. In my view he came with the idea of giving moral and political support to Jaruzelski, whom he described as "one of the leading political reformers in the countries of Eastern Europe." Undoubtedly that was a very deliberate statement.[45]

Rakowski's last sentence showed that he got the point. The statement was indeed deliberate. We did not believe Jaruzelski to be one of the leading reformers, but we wanted to turn Bush's assertion into reality by a combination of flattery and conditionality, to help Jaruzelski play the role we hoped he had the capacity to play.[46] Both Rakowski and General Czesław Kiszczak, the regime's chief negotiator during the Roundtable talks, later argued that Bush's visit was critical in persuading Jaruzelski to run for the presidency.[47]

The U.S. approach toward General Jaruzelski was based on the judgment, shared by most of the Solidarity leadership,[48] that his role (under the above conditions) was essential. He was needed to fulfill the commitments of the Roundtable accords and reassure Moscow that events in Poland, however unexpected or unwelcome they might be, were proceeding in an orderly and peaceful fashion. Like Solidarity's leaders, we believed that political liberalization in Poland had to be led, at least nominally, from above even as it was being pushed from below, and that this would be a multiyear process extending at least through the next scheduled elections in 1993. Indeed, Solidarity's assumed timetable was for a gradual transition to full democracy over a six-year period until Jaruzelski's term expired in 1995. Even after that point, they foresaw a Polish political system that retained strong elements of central control by the communist bureaucracy.[49]

The next day's visit to Gdańsk was designed to demonstrate America's solidarity with the aims and aspirations of Poland's democratic opposition, and to reinforce the theme of "courage and restraint" in navigating the difficult transition to democracy. The discussion over lunch was pure Wałęsa, as all of his meetings tended to be. He observed, rightly, that the direct U.S. assistance being offered was meager, though he underestimated (as he continued to do after becoming president of Poland a year and a half later) the importance to Poland's economy of the market-opening and investment-promotion measures being proposed. But the president's visit, as Wałęsa well knew, was not about economic measures but about the symbolic importance of American leadership and support at a critical juncture, dramatized by their joint appearance before a huge, emotional crowd in front of the Workers' Monument at the gates of the Lenin Shipyard.

In Budapest, as if in answer to Wałęsa's appeal for greater U.S. assistance, a homemade poster that was displayed when President Bush arrived at Kossuth Square read, in English: "Don't give money to the communists."[50] Well, we didn't give them much. The assistance measures the president announced were a scaled down version of the Polish package, along with the creation of a regional environmental center in Budapest and inauguration of a Peace Corps program in Hungary, the first ever in Eastern Europe.

Otherwise, the character of the Budapest visit was quite different from Warsaw and Gdańsk. Internally, the situation was in rapid flux but not nearly as delicate as in Poland. The Hungarian leadership, after the elevation of Pozsgay and Nyers to the party presidium, was vying with opposition figures to see which could control the reform process; the question was not whether reform would proceed, but on whose terms. And internationally, Hungary's room for maneuver was much greater than strategically pivotal Poland. Here, with echoes of 1956, was the interplay between Polish and Hungarian events: when Poland, with its geostrategic weight in Soviet thinking, got away with some new step toward political liberalization, the Hungarians saw this as a green light for themselves. And Hungary, precisely because it was strategically less critical, had more leeway than Poland to test the limits of the possible, in the process setting new standards to which the Poles could aspire.

The president's public remarks in Budapest were accordingly more aggressive, aimed at accelerating the process of change lest half-reforms by the party leadership overwhelm an opposition that was much less unified than Poland's. In his major speech at the Karl Marx University, the president applauded the beginning of limited Soviet troop withdrawals from Hungary, adding, "As those forces leave, let the Soviet leaders know they have everything to gain, and nothing to lose or fear, from peaceful change. . . . The United States believes in the acceleration of productive change, not in its delay. So this is our guiding principle: the United States will offer assistance not to prop up the status quo, but to propel reform."[51]

The official meetings likewise reflected the more nuanced relationships unfolding in Hungary's "negotiated revolution."[52] In a meeting with Nyers, Grósz, and Németh—as well as in a separate meeting with Pozsgay, the fourth member of the new party presidium—the president reassured them that "we are not going to complicate things for you. We know that the better we get along with the Soviets, the better it is for you." Repeating the line he had employed with Jaruzelski, he assured them the United States is not going to force you to "choose between East and West."[53]

That evening, the president met with ten leaders of the principal opposition parties and organizations, including the Hungarian Democratic Forum, the Alliance of Young Democrats, and the Free Democratic Party. Despite the perception in Hungary that the United States favored the Budapest intellectuals associated with the Free Democrats,[54] the president was at pains to distance himself from a partisan position in the Hungarian political debate.[55] Like Secretary Baker's subsequent (February 1990) meetings in Sofia and Bucharest with representatives of all the major opposition parties, the meeting was not very successful. The format encouraged participants to vie with one another for attention and vent their partisan grievances, rather than present a cogent overall strategy on which all could agree. Still, the impression of the meetings, along with the tumultuous public response to this first ever visit by an American president, reinforced the sense that Hungary was moving rapidly toward multiparty democracy. The impression was conveyed symbolically when the president was presented with a piece of the barbed wire that had been removed a few weeks earlier from the Hungarian-Austrian border.

The impact of Bush's visit was electric. Among ordinary citizens in both countries, it helped replace public cynicism with a sense that meaningful democratic change might indeed be possible and worth struggling for. It is impossible to demonstrate the precise impact on Polish voters, but the anticipation of Bush's impending visit surely contributed to the stunning turnout in favor of Solidarity candidates. During the election campaign in Poland, a prominent Solidarity poster showed the American movie actor Gary Cooper, in a scene from *High Noon*, striding through town wearing, instead of his sheriff's star, a Solidarity badge. *That* was the image we were trying to project.

In both Poland and Hungary, Bush's visit almost certainly had the effect of advancing the political agenda well beyond what had been contemplated in the earlier negotiations between the regimes and opposition forces. Among the Western allies, the visits greatly strengthened the president's ability to command attention at the G-7 Summit and so elevate Eastern Europe to first place on the international agenda.

Concerted Western Action   The Paris Summit meeting of the Group of 7 was held to coincide with the commemoration of the two hundredth anniversary of the French Revolution, a fact that fit nicely with the aim of making democratic change in Eastern Europe the centerpiece of the meeting. The summit's first document was a "Declaration on Human Rights" adopted, in deference to our hosts, almost verbatim from the admirably concise French draft. (Never one to err on the side of deference, Prime Minister Thatcher took the occasion to remind her hosts, in a *Le Monde* interview on the eve of her departure from London, that "human rights did not begin with the French Revolution."[56])

Of course, G-7 summits were supposed to be about the state of the world economy,[57] but this one was dominated more than most by political events, above all change in the East and its implications for East-West relations. It was an occasion to compare notes on several recent encounters with leaders in the East. In addition to the president's just-completed trip to Poland and Hungary, Thatcher had recently hosted Jaruzelski in London, Mitterrand had visited Warsaw and hosted Gorbachev in Paris, and Kohl had just received Gorbachev for a state visit to the Federal Republic. During this visit the two leaders signed a broad joint declaration affirming, *inter alia*, "the rights of all peoples and states to self-determination."[58]

One divisive note in an otherwise shared G-7 perspective was the July 5 announcement that Chancellor Kohl was postponing once again his long-planned visit to Poland. The trip was hostage to an acrimonious conflict over the status of the German minority in Poland and the

German-Polish border,[59] punctuated by West German finance minister Theo Waigel's public hints of continuing German territorial claims against Poland.[60] Kohl's deference to his right-wing constituency on these issues, a pattern that was to continue through the early stages of German unification, did not help in demonstrating Western solidarity with the Polish cause. Kohl's electoral difficulties—there seemed always to be another Land election to which Bonn had to give priority— seemed an insufficient excuse to snub the Poles at this critical moment.

Nonetheless, there was general agreement on the president's proposal for developing "concerted Western action" in support of Polish and Hungarian reforms. The obvious motives behind our approach were to mobilize greater Western assistance, coordinate Western efforts so that they would be complementary rather than competitive, and ensure that assistance was conditional upon real movement toward political and economic reform. There was an equally important political objective, as well: we wanted to lift Western engagement of Eastern Europe out of the traditional zero-sum logic of East-West, especially U.S.-Soviet, relations. "These are not bilateral issues between the United States and the Soviet Union," the president had said in his Hamtramck speech in mid-April. The aim at Paris was to place U.S. engagement in Eastern Europe, which might have been seen in Moscow as an effort to destabilize, within a broader multilateral framework that would allay rather than excite Soviet fears.

Our initial suggestion, broached by the president in letters to his G-7 counterparts before departing from Washington, had been to establish a multinational conference under the aegis of the G-7 itself. As some had predicted they would, the French rejected any "institutionalization" of the G-7 process. With a stalemate developing during the plenary meeting devoted to the topic, Chancellor Kohl proposed, and President Bush and other leaders readily agreed, that the EC Commission be assigned the coordinating role.[61] So it was that the commission took the lead in organizing what came to be called the G-24, or Group of 24, industrialized democracies pledged to provide assistance to Poland and Hungary and ultimately to other countries of the region.

Another option would have been to assign the task to the OECD (Organization for Economic Cooperation and Development), which had much to recommend it from our perspective: it included all 24 of the countries that ultimately joined the assistance effort, and our membership would have given us greater influence over the coordinating process. The EC Commission, however, had better organizational capacity through its existing Brussels bureaucracy across most of the areas relevant to the tasks of economic transition. As association with, or eventual membership in, the EC was a common aspiration among democratic reformers in Eastern Europe, it also made sense for the Community to take the lead role in shaping the transition strategies of countries embarking on political and economic reform. Besides, the EC wanted to take the lead, and our larger European strategy looked to the Community's assuming a constructive leadership role in a more united Europe.

There was another compelling reason for allowing the EC to take the lead. As Willie Sutton put it when asked why he robbed banks, that was "where the money is." Our view from the beginning was that the West Europeans should assume the principal financial assistance burden; it seemed right that the recipients of Marshall Plan aid should take the lead in extending its benefits eastward, fulfilling the Marshall Plan's original pan-European vision.[62] Beyond these lofty considerations was the more prosaic fact that we were unwilling to come up with a significant U.S. financial commitment. Therein lay the principal weakness of our approach. No one questioned that Western Europe should bear the larger burden, but U.S. leadership was essential in helping define the scope of Western commitment. At Paris and even afterwards, when democratic change accelerated all across Eastern Europe, we made it clear that the United States was not prepared to consider assistance even approaching Marshall Plan dimensions. Absent such an American commitment, the European Community never rose to the challenge.

After Paris, the president made a one-day trip on July 17 to the Netherlands—which, like Hungary, had never before been visited by an American president. His speech at the Pieterskerk [St. Peter's Church] in Leiden, the home of Dutch freedom and the site from which many pilgrims departed for the New World, was the ideal venue for linking the Old World and the New and embedding Eastern Europe in this vision. It began with a strong reiteration, building on the Boston University speech two months earlier, of America's support for "a stronger Europe, a more united Europe" as "a natural evolution within our Alliance—the product of true partnership 40 years in the making." The president then turned to "the 'other Europe'—the Europe behind the Wall" and focused on extending the Atlantic idea eastward to embrace all of Europe. The speech summed up both strategic goals and tactical approaches:

Our hope is that the unnatural division of Europe will now come
to an end—that the Europe behind the wall will join its neighbors
to the West, prosperous and free. . . .

We will never compromise our principles. We will always speak
out for freedom. But we understand as well how vital a carefully
calibrated approach is in this time of dynamic change. . . . The Soviet Union has nothing—nothing—to fear from the reforms that
are now unfolding in some of the nations of Eastern Europe. We
support reform—in Eastern Europe and in the Soviet Union. . . . I
want to see the Soviet Union chart a course that brings it into the
community of nations.

We will play a constructive role in Eastern Europe . . . and in
creating an international climate in which reform can succeed.
And that is why America's relations with the Soviet Union are so
important. Improved relations with the USSR reduce the pressure
on the nations of Eastern Europe, especially those on the cutting
edge of reform.

The new world we seek is a commonwealth of free nations
working in concert—a world where more and more nations enter
a widening circle of freedom. . . . Here in Leiden, where the pilgrims dreamed their new world, let us pledge our effort to create a
new world in Europe, whole and free, a new world now within
our reach.

Finally, citing Winston Churchill's 1946 speech at the same pulpit in the
Pieterskerk, the president foreshadowed the belated vindication of
Churchill's vision and its extension to all of Europe: "The great wheel
has swung full circle. . . . Let freedom reign."[63]

With that, American grand strategy for ending the Cold War had
been fully deployed, except for direct engagement with the Soviet Union
at the highest level. With events in Eastern Europe moving faster than
anyone had foreseen when the strategy was launched in April, a Bush-
Gorbachev summit acquired new urgency. Accordingly, aboard Air
Force One en route back to Washington, the president drafted an invitation to Gorbachev for an informal meeting to precede the formal summit planned for 1990.

Secretary Baker reiterated the invitation in a July 29 meeting with Soviet foreign minister Eduard Shevardnadze in Paris, using the occasion
to discuss the revolutionary developments in Eastern Europe.[64] Though

brief, it was an important meeting—not quite a meeting of the minds, but a convergence of thinking on several essentials. Shevardnadze's concern was not with the prospect of sweeping change per se; it was with the danger that the process could lead to a general "destabilization" that "could be catastrophic." His appeal to Baker, therefore, was that the United States act responsibly and not exploit the situation for unilateral advantage. Baker concurred. However, he added that the United States would continue to support democratic change in the region, which we believed did not endanger Soviet security, and that the use of force by the Soviet Union to suppress such changes would have the most severe consequences for U.S.-Soviet relations. Shevardnadze agreed that "it was up to these countries and their peoples to decide for themselves" and assured Baker, though not quite as categorically as we might have wished, that Moscow would not use force against them.[65]

Shortly thereafter, it was vacation time in Washington. The president was off to Kennebunkport, Secretary Baker went to Wyoming, and most of the rest of government scattered.

From Reform to Revolution

Meanwhile, events in Eastern Europe and the Soviet Union were accelerating rapidly. Movement among the Baltic states was particularly dramatic. On July 17, I met in my office with Vytautas Landsbergis, president of the independent Lithuanian popular front organization Sajudis. (Landsbergis was elected president of Lithuania in March 1990, so this, as it turned out, was the first of a series of meetings I had that year with opposition leaders who soon became presidents, prime ministers, or foreign ministers after the collapse of communist rule.) Sajudis, Landsbergis assured me, was unanimous in pressing for Lithuania's full independence and had no interest in some lesser form of autonomy or semi-independent status within the Soviet Union. The goal of Lithuanian independence was beyond question; the only debate was over tactics, and he put himself toward the moderate, gradualist end of the spectrum. His assessment, which I had no reason to disbelieve, was dramatic enough, but events on the ground in Lithuania were moving even faster. A month later, on the fiftieth anniversary of the Hitler-Stalin pact, the Lithuanian parliament declared the Soviet annexation of the Baltic states to be invalid, and Landsbergis issued a public call, in Sajudis's name, for a "free Lithuania."[66] The next day, more than a million people formed a "human chain" across Lithuania, Latvia, and Estonia condemning the Nazi-Soviet pact and demanding freedom and independence.[67] In Georgia, Armenia, Azerbaijan, and Ukraine, where proindependence groups staged a march through Kiev in early September, nationalist demands were also on the rise.

It was around this time that I wrote a memorandum for the president predicting that Czechoslovakia, where three thousand protesters defied the regime's prohibition to commemorate the August 21 anniversary of the 1968 invasion, could not resist the pressures for change much longer. It would be the next to go, and we should begin stepping up our engagement so as to be in a position to influence events as they unfolded. I recall writing that communist rule would be toppled within a year, then hedging my bet in the final draft to "within two years." It took about three months. And Bulgaria "went" even sooner: its veteran communist leader Todor Zhivkov was removed from power on November 10, the day after the night the Berlin Wall fell. (Thereafter my predictive capacities improved. When Alan "Punch" Green, our ambassador-designate to Romania, met with me in late October, shortly before leaving for Bucharest, I told him the Ceaușescu regime had no more than three months. Even then, I was too cautious by a month. The Ceaușescus were executed on Christmas Day.)

Poland Elects a Noncommunist Prime Minister   In Poland, meanwhile, a postelection crisis over Jaruzelski's election as president was resolved by the tactical decision of Solidarity leaders to secure the victory of the same general who had banned their union and thrown many of them into prison less than eight years before. It was a controversial decision within the opposition, achieved by the abstention of several Solidarity deputies and the deliberate invalidation of ballots by seven others. While the United States did not presume to offer specific advice on the issue, the president's public remarks in Warsaw and Gdańsk made it clear that we favored compromise ("a rare alloy of courage and restraint") and adherence by both sides to the terms of the Roundtable Agreement, including Jaruzelski's election as president.

In retrospect, this still seems to have been the right stance for the United States and, more to the point, for the Polish opposition, which bore primary responsibility, to have taken. At this early stage of the revolutions of 1989, Jaruzelski's defeat, and the loss by the communists of the defense and interior ministry portfolios, might have caused a reaction to begin crystallizing in Moscow. Even if these losses did not lead to anything so drastic as military intervention, they might well have prejudiced Soviet attitudes toward revolutionary events only beginning to unfold elsewhere, particularly East Germany. We will never know for sure. We know what Shevardnadze and his closest aides say they were thinking at the time,[68] but we cannot know what they might have *done*, much less what others in the Soviet ruling elite might have pressed on them.

Jaruzelski's election, by the margin of a single vote, cleared the way for negotiations over the composition of the new government. Having obliged on the question of the presidency, Solidarity was less inclined to do so on the composition of the government. If it was to assume coresponsibility for the fate of the Polish economy, Solidarity needed decisive influence over economic policy, including international economic policy. After nearly a month's tense negotiations, during which time two Jaruzelski nominees for prime minister were rejected, the regime and Solidarity ultimately settled on a broad coalition government headed by Catholic intellectual and veteran Solidarity adviser Tadeusz Mazowiecki. The Communist party retained the defense, interior, and transportation ministry portfolios but relinquished most others to Solidarity leaders or nonparty independents.[69] (In a last minute telephone call to Gorbachev by Mieczysław Rakowski, who had succeeded Jaruzelski as Polish Communist party leader, the Soviet leader refrained from involving himself in the composition of the new government aside from reaffirming his support for Jaruzelski.[70]) So it was that Eastern Europe's first noncommunist prime minister in more than four decades was confirmed by the Polish Sejm on August 24. As Wałęsa put it, what Solidarity had hoped to accomplish in four years, it had been obliged to do in four weeks.[71]

Of all the contributors to the peaceful revolutions of 1989 and the end of the Cold War, Tadeusz Mazowiecki ranks among the most important. It is hard to imagine Poland more responsibly led at this critical moment. Together with the key members of his government—Foreign Minister Krzysztof Skubiszewski, Finance Minister Leszek Balcerowicz, and Labor Minister Jacek Kuroń—and the heroic Bronisław Geremek, newly elected leader of the Solidarity group in the Sejm, Mazowiecki conveyed the right combination of resolve and conciliation. This is not to denigrate Wałęsa's indispensable role. Indeed, his decision to forego direct participation in the new government also contributed to its success, by removing himself as a potential lightning rod for hard-line opposition in Poland and, one presumes, Moscow as well. Besides, he was needed as an above-politics symbol of legitimation for the coalition government.

Mazowiecki's first speech to the Sejm was masterful: in direct, honest language that Poles had not heard from their government for a very long time, he outlined his main goals of restoring "a market-oriented economy," the "rule of law," and "freedom of conscience." Above all, while declaring that "we separate ourselves from the past with a thick line," Mazowiecki offered reassurance at home and abroad:

> The principle of struggle . . . must be replaced by the principle of partnership. . . . I want to be the prime minister of all Poles, regardless of their views and convictions, which must not be a criterion for dividing citizens into categories. . . . Poles themselves have to solve Polish problems. . . . The world is watching the transformations taking place [in Poland] with sympathy and hope. . . .
>
> Poland can fulfill an important role in the political, economic, and cultural life of Europe. . . . Europe is one, including the East as well as the West. . . . We desire to maintain good-neighborly, friendly relations with the Soviet Union. . . . We understand the significance of obligations resulting from the Warsaw Pact. To all its members, I state that the government that I will form will respect this treaty.[72]

Most of us dealing with these issues in the United States or in Europe had our epiphanies, our moments of realization that the end of Europe's division might actually be at hand—not just as an aspiration for the 1990s but as an imminent reality. For many it came with the opening of the Berlin Wall on November 9; others may have had premonitions already in early 1989 (although surely not as many as later claimed such prescience). Mine came with the election of Tadeusz Mazowiecki and the early steps taken by his government. The United States was working hard to persuade the Soviet Union that self-determination in Eastern Europe could be achieved in a manner consistent with legitimate Soviet security interests; now, in Poland, the Mazowiecki government was living proof of that contention, offering an early glimmer of what post–Cold War Europe might look like. (To be sure, even the most optimistic scenario for this transition was still being measured in years, not months.)

Polish Shock Therapy and the Stabilization Fund   The new government wasted little time in addressing its most immediate problem: the collapsing Polish economy. In late September, Finance Minister Leszek Balcerowicz visited Washington to present his economic restructuring plan to International Monetary Fund and administration officials.[73] American Embassy Warsaw had cabled an advance copy, which was quickly reviewed at the NSC, State, and Treasury. It was ambitious but conceptually sound, receiving high marks even from the most skeptical Treasury officials. Embedded in the plan, and crucial to its success, was a $700 million IMF loan and a $1 billion currency stabilization fund to be financed by additional Western contributions. (The fund was meant to provide a reserve in the event that the devaluation of the Polish *zloty* precipitated a run on the banks. The hope, which ultimately was fulfilled, was that the mere existence of this fund would be sufficient assurance and that it would not actually have to be drawn down.) When Balcerowicz met with General Scowcroft on September 26, he made it plain that Poland looked to the United States to take the lead in assembling the stabilization fund. The general, as was his wont, was sympathetic but noncommittal.

At staff level, we went to work to develop a plan. Our starting point was that the United States must take the lead, as the Poles asked us to do. To win West European and other backing, the United States had to make the first commitment. Although the Poles had not specified the form of the stabilization fund, we concluded it should be in the form of grants rather than loans or lines of credit, as the latter would only add to Poland's enormous debt burden. This, in turn, would require congressional approval, so we needed to decide what our fair share would be and what would be acceptable on Capitol Hill. In an informal meeting with the NSC legislative staff, I proposed that our contribution be $250 million, or one fourth of the total; others felt a $200 million proposal had a better chance of success. So it was decided, and we began lining up bureaucratic support for the proposal, which ultimately gained approval at a full NSC meeting the next month. We had also established a kind of precedent: from that point on, 20 percent became the informal benchmark for America's fair share of the Western commitment to East European assistance. (Over the next year, as more and more East European countries began to line up for scarce resources, particularly for major balance of payments support, we began to fall in arrears of our "fair share.")

On October 4, we announced our $200 million contribution, and President Bush then sent letters to his G-7 counterparts asking that they pledge the remaining 80 percent.[74] The Europeans moved equally rapidly. On October 24 the European Community announced a $300 million assistance program for Poland and Hungary; West Germany and France followed suit with bilateral programs. At a specially convened summit in Paris on November 18, the EC announced further assistance measures, including creation of a European Bank for Reconstruction and Development.[75]

At a G-24 meeting in Brussels on December 13 (the first such meeting at ministerial level), Secretary Baker noted we were "close to our target" for the stabilization fund, with G-7 pledges totalling around 90 percent of the required $1 billion, and successfully appealed to others to make up the difference. (Except for our contribution and Great Britain's $100 million grant, all the other contributions were in the form of loans and lines of credit, a pattern that was to continue through the G-24.[76]) With that, we had successfully assembled a $1 billion Stabilization Fund—just in time for the January 1, 1990, launching of Poland's ambitious economic restructuring program.

When he visited Washington in mid-November 1989 to receive the Presidential Medal of Freedom and give an historic address before a joint session of Congress, Lech Wałęsa expressed his thanks for U.S. support but called also for a Marshall Plan for Eastern Europe as "an investment in freedom, democracy, and peace." The appeal galvanized congressional action for a substantial increase in U.S. assistance but failed to produce any serious consideration of aid of Marshall Plan dimensions. In addition to trying to prod the United States and other Western countries to "let deeds follow words," Wałęsa also addressed himself to Soviet sensibilities. Echoing Mazowiecki's remarks of two months before, Wałęsa's tone was conciliatory:

Is there any sensible man understanding the world around him who could now say that it would be better if the Poles kept quiet because what they are doing is jeopardizing world peace?. . . Could we not say that stability and peace face greater threats from countries . . . which do their best to preserve the old, disgraced ways of government contrary to the wishes of their societies?

Things are different in Poland. And I must say that our task is viewed with understanding by our eastern neighbors and their leader Mikhail Gorbachev. This understanding lays the foundation for new relations between Poland and the U.S.S.R., much better than before.[77]

The Walls Come Tumbling Down

By the time of Wałęsa's visit to Washington in mid-November, the changes he spoke of were becoming an avalanche that would soon engulf all of Eastern Europe. In the early fall, Poland and Hungary were well advanced down the path of democratic transformation, but elsewhere communist regimes were resisting any steps in that direction. By the end of the year, all were gone, swept away by revolutionary upheavals scarcely imaginable just a few months before. Particularly after the opening of the Berlin Wall on November 9–10, events proceeded with such bewildering speed that U.S. and other Western policies could not hope to keep pace. It was in the first half of the year that U.S. policies had helped create the international context in which peaceful democratic transformation in Eastern Europe could occur; by late fall, as one communist regime after another succumbed to popular demands for democratic change, we in Washington often found ourselves in the role of thrilled, not to say astonished, onlookers.[78]

Hungary Opens the Floodgates   In Hungary, reform communism was fast losing ground to multiparty democracy. Lajos Für, leader of the opposition Hungarian Democratic Forum (and later to become Hungarian defense minister), had assured me during a meeting in my office on August 31 that the regime was finished and that the Democratic Forum would win the elections scheduled for March 1990. In separate meetings a week before, Balint Magyar and József Szajer, leaders of the other main democratic opposition parties,[79] had taken a different view, accusing the Democratic Forum of striking a Faustian bargain with the reformist wing of the Communist party, led by Imre Pozsgay. Indeed, the alleged tacit agreement whereby Pozsgay would become president, with the indirect support of the Democratic Forum, quickly fell apart, as the other opposition parties mounted a successful referendum in September calling for the president to be elected by the forthcoming parliament, rather than by the public directly.[80]

The Hungarian roundtable agreement of mid-September attracted less attention than its Polish counterpart in March–April, partly because the free elections it scheduled were still half a year away. It also lacked the drama of the long-running Polish struggle for power between two sworn enemies. In Hungary the contest was more diversified and, well, polite. How could a revolution be so civilized? Yet the results of the Hungarian roundtable were revolutionary indeed, heralding a political opening even more far-reaching than Poland's: opposition political parties, already operating in complete freedom, were to compete in fully open parliamentary elections, with no prior assurances for the ruling party. Hungarians were acting as if their country were already a multiparty democracy. Meanwhile, the party and state leadership scrambled to keep up with rapidly escalating public expectations, abandoning orthodox Marxism from the party platform, changing its name to the Hungarian Socialist party, and proclaiming a new Republic of Hungary (dropping the word "socialist") in which "the values of bourgeois democracy and democratic socialism are equally recognized."[81] It may not have been too little, but it was certainly too late.[82]

Waging a losing battle inside the country, Hungarian leaders took to the road looking urgently for external legitimation. In a mid-September visit to Washington, Mátyás Szürös, speaker of the Hungarian parliament, gave an interview in which he referred to Hungarian neutrality as an imminent possibility.[83] His purpose for coming, however, was to assure the U.S. administration that the new emigration legislation, on which we had insisted as a precondition for extending permanent Most Favored Nation (MFN) trade status, was forthcoming. Armed with that assurance, the president sent the required congressional notification on September 19.[84]

Indeed, Hungarian emigration policy was shifting in ways that were shaking the entire region. In mid-August, nearly two hundred East German "vacationers" in Hungary occupied the West German embassy in Budapest seeking emigration visas, with many more making their ways out illegally via the porous Hungarian-Austrian frontier. In early September, following intense consultations with Bonn, Hungary formally annulled its travel agreement with the GDR and opened its borders to East German emigration.[85] By the end of September, another forty thousand East Germans had emigrated via Hungary, an opening for which Hungary was soon rewarded with U.S. permanent MFN status and a one billion Deutsche Mark credit from Bonn.[86]

Fall of the Berlin Wall   Far from relieving the pressure within the GDR, the existence of this escape valve only increased it. Thousands of

East German emigration-seekers were soon massed in the West German embassy in Prague, with at least one and a half million more back in the GDR having formally applied to emigrate.[87] Within the GDR, opposition activists formed an umbrella movement called the "New Forum" to catalyze organized demands for democratic reform (and also to help defuse pressures for mass emigration by creating a mechanism for promoting internal change). Pressure was mounting outside the country as well: at the UN General Assembly in New York in late September, West German Foreign Minister Hans-Dietrich Genscher and Secretary Baker met separately with the Soviet, Czechoslovak, and Hungarian foreign ministers to urge them to try to effect a relaxation of GDR emigration policy. The Erich Honecker regime tried to resolve the impasse through a "dual track" approach. They permitted East German "squatters" in Prague to travel via GDR territory to West Germany (a decision which Genscher announced in an emotional balcony speech in Prague), then tried to slam the door on further such problems by reimposing exit visa requirements for travel even to Czechoslovakia.[88] These combined signs of regime vulnerability and intransigence were all that were needed to excite further public demands for free emigration and democratic change within East Germany.

It is tempting to say that the GDR's fate was sealed at that moment, as some Bonn politicians later claimed to have concluded by late September.[89] Yet here again, "illusions of retrospective determinism" (and perhaps hindsight embellishing memory) come into play. I was in Berlin from October 1 to 3 for an Aspen Institute conference on "Strategic Directions for the Federal Republic of Germany in the 1990s," attended by prominent American, French, British, and German scholars and officials. The papers and my handwritten notes of the sessions make for instructive rereading. Much of the discussion focused on prospects for deployment of the follow-on to the Lance missile (FOTL), the topic du jour of the transatlantic security debate. While East German instability was on people's minds, no one was yet talking of regime collapse or of German unification, except as a long-term possibility. The most daring held out the scenario of an all-German parliament within a five- to ten-year period, but they stopped short of predicting such sweeping change. Nor did my official discussions in East Berlin and then Bonn give a premonition that Germany would be united in exactly one year; the preoccupation was on Honecker's October 3 decision to slam the door on emigration, a move which seemed to herald further repression and spiraling instability in the GDR. (One notable exception was Ambassador

Vernon ["Dick"] Walters, who was already on record as predicting early unification, much to the consternation of official Washington.[90])

Nor did Gorbachev see unification coming when he visited East Berlin October 7 for the GDR's fortieth anniversary celebrations, despite his prophetic warning to East Germany party leader Erich Honecker that "life punishes those who come too late."[91] Of course, Gorbachev's widely quoted remark was itself part of the subsequent dynamic. He was no mere observer of the East German scene but a protagonist in the unfolding drama, and this comment, as well as his public pledge that "all walls . . . will fall,"[92] signaled unmistakably to the East German populace that Soviet power would not rescue the discredited GDR regime. Within days, demonstrations erupted in Leipzig, Dresden, Berlin, and other cities, with a bloodbath in Leipzig October 9 narrowly averted by the last-minute agreement among demonstration leaders and local authorities.[93] Neither Honecker's ouster on October 18 nor the frantic efforts of his successor, Egon Krenz, could stem the torrent. On November 9, through what Krenz would later call a "slight mistake,"[94] a vaguely worded politburo decision to liberalize procedures for emigration and "private trips abroad" was translated by harried border guards into free access through the Wall into West Berlin. Within days, the Berlin Wall was being physically as well as symbolically dismantled.

Bulgaria: From Coup d'État to Revolution   Just a few hours after the opening of the Berlin Wall, Bulgarian party leader Todor Zhivkov unexpectedly resigned in favor of Foreign Minister Petŭr Mladenov, thus ending a 35-year reign that was, as J. F. Brown pointed out, the longest in Bulgarian history—longer even than Tsar Simeon's 34-year reign in the late tenth and early eleventh centuries.[95] Although not fully apparent at the time, opposition to Zhivkov within the party leadership had been building for several years. Georgi Atanasov, Bulgaria's prime minister from 1986 to 1990, later told an interviewer that he and Mladenov spoke in July 1988 about making changes to the party central committee. By July 1989 they and others in the top leadership, including Andrei Lukanov and Defense Minister Dobri Dzhurov, were actively conspiring to bring Zhivkov down.[96]

The opportunity presented itself in October, when a CSCE (Conference on Security and Cooperation in Europe) environmental meeting in Sofia sparked public demonstrations by Ecoglasnost and other nascent opposition groups. While in the meeting hall, the Bulgarian regime was subjected to harsh Western criticism over its brutal repression of its ethnic Turkish minority. Indeed, in response to the mass expulsions of Bulgarian Turks in May 1989, we had recalled our ambassador and sent cables to West European capitals asking whether, or on what terms, Western countries should agree to attend the Sofia meeting. After further debate within the administration, the United States agreed to participate because the subject matter of the conference was both important and directly pertinent to Bulgaria's most significant opposition group, but we also insisted that Western representatives miss no opportunity to hammer the Bulgarian regime over its treatment of ethnic minorities.[97]

Otherwise the U.S. role in these events was nil. When word reached us at the White House of Zhivkov's resignation, my NSC colleague Condi (Condoleezza) Rice and I looked at each other in utter bemusement. We had been so totally preoccupied with Germany—this being the day after the night the Berlin Wall fell—that we had not even thought about Bulgaria for weeks and certainly had no premonition of impending change.

The direct Soviet role was likewise minimal. Atanasov revealed that the Soviet ambassador in Sofia had been informed on November 4 that Zhivkov would be replaced at the November 10 Central Committee plenum. For the next week, Moscow was silent as members of the Bulgarian party's Politburo, coming singly and in groups, went to Zhivkov and urged him to resign. Finally persuaded that he had support neither in Sofia nor in Moscow, Zhivkov relented and announced his resignation to the Central Committee on November 10.[98]

The new Bulgarian leadership, like the Hungarian before it, moved quickly to try to get into step with history. Petŭr Mladenov, the new party leader, promptly announced the end of one-party rule, called for free elections the following spring, and proclaimed full observance of civil liberties on the road to a democratic Bulgaria. It was, as Gale Stokes observed, an "amazing" performance "for a man who had been at the center of single-party Communist power for almost twenty years."[99] "Incredible" might have been a better word: the new leadership had stolen the march on the fledgling democratic opposition, coopting its agenda and embracing the vocabulary, but not the substance, of pluralistic democracy.

It was as good a strategy as any; all it lacked was authenticity and plausibility. There were, to be sure, many within the party leadership who understood that Bulgaria could no longer be governed in the old way and who were ready to embrace *glasnost* and *perestroika* on the road to a more humane, but still socialist, Bulgaria. It was harder to credit that the hearts of committed democrats had been beating within their breasts through long years of service to the Zhivkov regime, nor did their sudden conversion seem entirely believable.

The early, skillful steps by the new Bulgarian leadership did, however, galvanize the main opposition movements to concerted action through a new Union of Democratic Forces, formed December 10 under the chairmanship of dissident philosopher Zhelyu Zhelev. By year's end, a more cohesive party and a more united opposition were preparing for formal roundtable negotiations on Bulgaria's political future, particularly the terms of the forthcoming elections.

The "Velvet Revolution"   After the fall of the Wall, nearly everyone expected Czechoslovakia to be the next to experience a democratic breakthrough. Yet, there had been no movement toward reform from its dogmatic communist regime. In 1988, I was in Prague with a congressional delegation led by Senator John Glenn. When Glenn asked his regime interlocutor, the hard-liner Vasil Bil'ak, why Czechoslovakia did not emulate Soviet reforms, Bil'ak replied, "You Americans used to accuse us of being Soviet puppets, of slavishly following the Soviet model. Now you accuse of us not following the Soviet model closely enough!" It was a good line, but Bil'ak was still a thug.

The Czechoslovak regime nonetheless had been obliged to make some modest concessions to pressures for reform. In December 1987, Gustáv Husák, who had been installed as party leader after the 1968 Soviet invasion, was replaced by Miloš Jakeš; a year later Bil'ak was dropped from the party leadership. Jakeš was a long way from being a reformer, but he and his regime began to adopt the vocabulary of *glasnost* and *perestroika* (or *přestavba,* the Czech version of economic "restructuring"). None of these measures produced real reform, but they had the effect of further weakening the regime's authority. It would not reform, but neither could it continue the ruthless repression which alone could secure its continuation in power. The regime's hesitancy, in turn, prompted dissident and religious activists to begin probing the limits of the possible.

Yet even after the Zhivkov's ouster in Bulgaria, eerily little was happening in Czechoslovakia. On November 13, foreign correspondents contrasted the faint signs of protest in Prague with the vast demonstrations held the month before in Leipzig, only 160 miles away.[100] Jiří Dienstbier, one of the founders of the human rights group Charter 77 (and soon to become, improbably, his country's foreign minister), spoke plaintively to an interviewer a week after the breach of the Berlin Wall: "What surprised everybody was the quick unraveling of things in East Germany. . . . The next step? I hope it's Czechoslovakia. . . ."[101] By the time the interview was published on November 18, Dienstbier's hope was turning into reality.

On November 17, a small, officially sanctioned student demonstration grew spontaneously to an estimated thirty thousand protestors, several thousand of whom broke off from the authorized route and headed for Wenceslas Square, where they were stopped and brutally beaten by riot police. This, as Garton Ash put it in his vivid firsthand account from the revolution's chaotic command center in the Magic Lantern theater, was "the spark that set Czechoslovakia alight."[102] The next day, a gathering of opposition groups convened by Václav Havel formed a "Civic Forum" to serve as spokesman for the democratic aspirations of society at large; the day after, Slovak intellectuals led by the artist Ján Budaj and the prominent movie actor Milan Kňažko[103] met in a Bratislava art gallery to create a similarly inspired organization called "Public Against Violence." Armed with videotapes of the November 17 assault, student supporters went to factories and farms across the country to widen the base of support. An alliance of intellectuals and workers began to form, of the kind that had long existed in Poland but never in Czechoslovakia, not even during the Prague Spring.

On November 20, another demonstration took place on Wenceslas Square, this time gathering hundreds of thousands of ordinary citizens. As demonstrations continued, Havel was joined in Wenceslas Square for a dramatic joint appearance with Alexander Dubček, prime minister during the Prague Spring, providing a powerful symbol of historical continuity and (Dubček being Slovak) national solidarity.

The resignation of Jakeš and the rest of the party leadership on November 24 did nothing to slow the momentum of protest. When virtually the entire country joined in a two-hour general strike on November 27, just ten days after protests had begun, the tide had shifted decisively to the democratic opposition, who correspondingly escalated their demands to include a voice in the composition of a new coalition government. The proposal by new prime minister Ladislav Adamec for a sham "coalition" government with almost no opposition figures was rejected out of hand by Civic Forum. Adamec himself resigned almost as soon as he had been appointed, replaced by Marián Čalfa, an obscure Slovak communist who left the party in early 1990.

As with Bulgaria, the direct American role in these events was negligible. We did, however, exert considerable indirect influence where it counted most—with the Soviet leaders. On December 1–3, during the most delicate phase of negotiations between Civic Forum and the communist regime, Presidents Bush and Gorbachev met off Malta for their first summit.[104] The success of the summit, covered extensively by Czechoslovak television, served to embolden opposition leaders and the populace at large, just as Gorbachev's subsequent meeting with Warsaw Pact leaders in Moscow served to persuade Czechoslovakia's communist regime that its time was up.[105]

The new Czechoslovak government, with noncommunists in the majority, was sworn in on December 10. At month's end, Dubček was named chairman of the Federal Assembly, which then elected Václav Havel president of Czechoslovakia. *Havel na Hrad!*—Havel to the Castle!—had gone from daring chant to improbable reality in a matter of a few thrilling weeks.

Romania: From Revolution to Coup d'État   Ever the maverick, Romania had so far resisted the changes sweeping the region. Indeed, because the Ceauşescu regime had made a career of distancing itself from Moscow, and of developing its own elaborate system of internal security rather than relying on Soviet power, it was less directly affected than others by Gorbachev's reforms. These same factors also made it a more brittle regime, incapable of ruling in any fashion other than the repression that had grown increasingly brutal as conditions in Romania worsened and public restiveness grew. Whether Ceauşescu and his wife and coruler, Elena, were oblivious to these conditions or all too aware of their political implications—one could adduce evidence on both sides of the ledger—hardly mattered toward the end. After the collapse of communist regimes elsewhere in the fall of 1989, all that was needed was an event to trigger a revolution to unseat the Warsaw Pact's last and most truly evil leader.

It began in Timişoara, with Romanians and Hungarians from this multiethnic community joining in protest against the expulsion of Hungarian reformed pastor László Tökés from his home and parish. Following several days of growing protests, army units arrived December 17 to crush the demonstration in a massacre that left nearly a hundred dead, though widely reported estimates at the time placed the number in the thousands.[106] Within days, as Brown put it, "the Timişoara rioting had become the Romanian Uprising."[107] As demonstrations erupted throughout the country and army units began to join the protestors, Ceauşescu cut short a visit to Iran and returned to Bucharest, making what proved to be his last public appearance before a huge crowd in Palace Square on December 21. And a bizarre one it was: television cameras captured Ceauşescu's bewilderment as ritual cheers from the combined "official" and spontaneous crowd below turned to shouts of derision, before Elena ushered him off the balcony and the television screens went blank in Romania. The next day, a group of former party officials, joined in the course of the afternoon by well-known dissidents, appeared on Romanian television as leaders of a self-proclaimed National Salvation Front, declaring itself the new provisional government and pledging to establish full democracy.

Here is how a White House statement of that day put it: "Today, December 22, 1989, a terrible burden appears to have been lifted from Romania: the burden of despotic dictatorial rule. . . . The United States salutes the decision by representatives of the Romanian Government to order a cessation of the brutal police repression and to bring a merciful end to the Ceauşescu dictatorship. . . . We hope the Romanian Government will now move quickly to respond to the demands of its people for democratic change."[108] The verb "appears" turned out to be well chosen, for the events of the next few days were confusing in the extreme.

With most of official Washington away for the holidays, an interagency working group had been formed to coordinate U.S. policy during the crisis, through daily teleconferences and frequent telephone calls.[109] We were not lacking for information: television coverage, along with a constant flow of cables from Embassy Bucharest and other posts (reporting reactions of key foreign governments) allowed us to follow these events, responding as necessary, literally as they unfolded. In this case as in others, the glut of information was itself one of the problems of crisis management: keeping up with the mountains of reporting, essential though it was, also threatened to intrude on the more pertinent business of producing sensible policy.

After December 22, our main aims were to throw U.S. support behind the provisional government, discredit as "outlaws" the remaining

Ceauşescu loyalists, and help end the bloodshed by underscoring the futility of further resistance by those forces. We also sought to ensure the widest possible support for those positions among foreign governments, including the Soviet. Given the uncertainties surrounding the Front and its intentions, as well as the ambiguous roles played by Securitate officials, we were at pains to link our support to the popular mandate for democratic change and the Front's expressed commitments to that end. Together with other Western countries, we also made it clear that we would extend economic assistance to the new government as and if it proceeded down the path of political and economic reform. Whatever our misgivings about the Front and its early, mysterious behavior, this course of action was clearly preferable to remaining neutral and waiting for the dust to settle.

One event bears explanation. On December 24 Secretary Baker was quoted as supporting a Soviet intervention in Romania on behalf of prodemocracy forces. It was an unfortunate comment, but one that was not quite as egregious as it seemed.[110] The context was this. The day before Baker made his remark, officials of the provisional government appealed to Moscow and the West for help, claiming they were running out of ammunition and feared being overwhelmed by the well-armed Ceauşescu loyalists. Responding to this appeal, French Foreign Minister Roland Dumas offered to send a brigade of volunteers and said he would welcome Soviet assistance as well, without specifying whether he meant sending fresh supplies of ammunition or rendering more direct "assistance." It was in response to a question about Dumas's position that Baker made his statement. The desire not to offend his French counterpart may be part of the explanation, but Baker evidently was swayed by the argument that Soviet intervention on the side of prodemocracy forces, in response to their specific appeal for help, would be preferable to seeing the revolution fail and the Ceauşescus returned to power. It was an argument that had a few adherents at staff level during those chaotic days, during which a successful counterrevolution by Ceauşescu loyalists seemed a real danger; however, the dominant view was that the United States could not legitimize Soviet intervention in Eastern Europe, no matter the circumstances. This position was made clear the next day in a White House "clarification" of the secretary's remarks, expressly opposing any Soviet intervention in Romania.[111]

The unfortunate irony of this episode was its juxtaposition with the ongoing U.S. intervention in Panama. After Moscow had politely declined the offer to intervene in Romania, the image seemed to be that of one superpower disdaining the role of forcible arbiter of its neighbors' disputes, while the other continued to reserve the right to do so. A Soviet foreign ministry official suggested bitterly that Moscow had ceded the "Brezhnev Doctrine" to the United States.[112]

By Christmas Day, the question was moot as far as Romania was concerned, as word of the capture, trial, and execution of the Ceauşescu pair reached the outside world. The episode nonetheless helps recapture the enormous confusion and uncertainty surrounding the Romanian Revolution and its aftermath. Was it a revolution or a palace coup? That spontaneous revolts broke out in several Romanian cities is indisputable. That prior contacts existed among disaffected or former officials of the Ceauşescu regime is likely but undocumented, nor do we know the scope of any organized or semiorganized coup-plotting among those who emerged as leaders of the National Salvation Front. These and many other mysteries of the events of December 1989 in Romania will have to be sorted out by future historians.

Available evidence and informed analysis to date suggest that this was a revolution followed immediately by (or coincident with) a coup d'état. Yet the role of the National Salvation Front remained controversial. Did it rescue the revolution by stepping in to fill a vacuum of power, or was the revolution "hijacked" and its democratic goals betrayed by the Front and its supporters?[113] From the perspective of U.S. policy, these were issues not to be judged a priori but rather demonstrated by the subsequent deeds of the NSF-led provisional government. We viewed its mandate, pending the free elections it had pledged, to derive from the democratic aspirations of the popular revolution (the "spirit of Timişoara") and its expressed commitment to democracy. Thus, from our perspective, the Romanian Revolution, like those that preceded it in the fall of 1989, was an authentic democratic revolution.

A Summing Up   The superficial similarities of the revolutions of 1989 were striking: spiraling mass demonstrations, creation of umbrella opposition movements with similar names (New Forum, Civic Forum, Democratic Forum) that even their organizers sometimes confused,[114] regime crackdowns followed by vacillation and then concessions, and formal roundtable negotiations leading to eventual regime capitulations. Yet the processes at work were much more differentiated than they first appeared. Poland and Hungary followed expected paths, albeit with un-expected results, consistent with the long history of their experience under communist rule. Yet if these were both "refolutions," to borrow Garton Ash's term for a combination of reform from above and revolution from below, then the accents were different: more on reform in the Hungarian case, more on revolution in the Polish. Bulgaria's evolution came closest to what might have been expected for the region as a whole: communist leaders jettisoning the hard-line leadership and seizing the mantle of democratic reform, using their considerable material and organizational resources to divide and co-opt opposition groups. That Romania would be the exception was predictable: it would have been hard to imagine a regime in which power and position were linked so personally to the ruling family, relinquishing power through peaceful negotiation.

The two most surprising cases were the East German and the Czechoslovak, for few would have predicted that such cynical and hardened party leaderships would have thrown in the towel so quickly. In retrospect, one can perhaps see why this happened. When public demands exploded in the fall of 1989, there were three basic options for the East European communist leaderships: capitulation, brutal repression, and temporizing negotiation. The third option, tried by the Polish, Hungarian, and Bulgarian leaders (Romania again being a case apart), was unavailable to the Czechoslovak and East German regimes. The former lacked credibility because of its role as liquidator of the Prague Spring reforms, while the latter could not embark on democratic reform without calling into question the GDR's raison d'être as a separate German state. As an East German party official put it in an August 1989 interview, "What right to exist would a capitalist GDR have alongside a capitalist Federal Republic?"[115]

For these regimes, therefore, there were but two options,[116] and both regimes, it should be noted, pursued repression as the preferred course of action before their ultimate capitulation. Even at the eleventh hour, when force on a massive scale would have been required, a "Chinese solution" (referring to the June 1989 massacre in Tiananmen Square) was actively considered. As has been seen, the Honecker regime in fact ordered such a crackdown on October 9;[117] similarly, as late as November 24, the day before the entire party leadership resigned, the Czechoslovak defense minister's proposal for a massive military crackdown was narrowly defeated by the party's central committee.[118]

The metaphors one grasps to describe these events—tumbling walls, avalanches, and sparks that ignited, to say nothing of falling dominos—point to the difficulties of analyzing any one of these revolutions in isolation from the others, or outside the larger international context. (It is for these reasons that the burgeoning literature on "regime change" falls wide of the mark in trying to explain the revolutions of 1989.[119]) The Velvet Revolution would not have happened—at least not in 1989—had not the Berlin Wall fallen, and that would not have occurred save for the prior, successful challenges to communist rule in Poland and Hungary. And none of these events would have transpired—not so soon nor so peacefully—had not there been a Soviet leadership that had undertaken a fundamental redefinition of Soviet security interests and which was further redefining those interests as wholly unexpected events transpired. Much of this redefining was attributable to Mikhail Gorbachev and Eduard Shevardnadze, and much of it was born of the necessity imposed by an eroding empire and a deteriorating economy.

Yet Soviet attitudes were shaped by the international context and by the efforts of the United States and its Western allies to rally firmly behind democratic change in Eastern Europe and to conduct themselves in ways that helped persuade Gorbachev and Shevardnadze that these changes could be accommodated on a radically new basis. Publicly and privately, President Bush and Secretary Baker must have said a hundred times that the changes unfolding in Eastern Europe "did not threaten legitimate Soviet security interests." It was hard to disentangle truth from tactics in this assertion: we believed the Soviet Union could find its security in ways other than a ring of client states around its borders, but there was no gainsaying the loss of Soviet power and influence that these events portended. It was obviously in our interests to push this line, just as the notion of a "Europe whole and free" served certain immediate interests, even though its ultimate meaning was obscure.

The scope and speed of change likewise made it difficult for Moscow to arrest the process, even if such had been its intent. As an NSC briefing paper put it just before President Bush's December 1–3 meeting with Gorbachev off the coast of Malta, "The Soviets had lost control of their policy toward Eastern Europe. They had not anticipated current developments [and] were now reacting to events day to day."[120] Indeed, by the time of this long-awaited meeting between the two leaders, Soviet attention and ours already had moved from democratic change in Eastern Europe to the prospect of a headlong rush toward German unification.

3

The Diplomacy of German Unification

AFTER THE ACHIEVEMENT of German unity in the fall of 1990, many Germans, beginning with Chancellor Kohl, were effusive in their gratitude for U.S. support, saying that unification could not have happened without us. For American officials who had worked so hard for German unity, those were nice words to hear. But they were not quite accurate. Unification could have occurred without us, all right, but it could only have been consummated as a result of a separate German-Soviet arrangement. If the United States had joined the French and British in opposing unification, what choice would the Germans have had but to strike whatever deal they could with Moscow, which held the key by virtue of its military occupation of East Germany? Who could have blamed the Germans, if they had been abandoned by their closest allies at the moment that their deepest national aspiration was at hand? And if Bonn had been left alone to deal with Moscow, what kind of terms would the Germans have been obliged to accept, with what infringements on German sovereignty, and with what implications for the future of European security?

U.S. support was essential, not so much for German unification itself, but for ensuring that the process came out right—with Germany enjoying full sovereignty from the moment of unification; with all of Europe, including the Soviet Union, accepting and supporting this outcome; and with the essential structures of European and transatlantic security intact and ready to adapt to radically changed circumstances. Although our West German counterparts never fully grasped this fact, the United States had as much at stake in the process of unification as they did. Our diplomacy during this period was harnessed to securing, not German, but American interests and to broader considerations of European stability and security. Happily, American and German interests, though not identical, converged to a large degree; indeed, U.S.-German relations during the period, while more complex and difficult than has been recorded to date, achieved a remarkable level of coordination in successful pursuit of our common goals.

An account of American diplomacy during the period should in no way detract from Bonn's masterful role in overseeing economic and political union between the two German states in less than a year, and in managing its delicate relationship with Moscow. These aspects of the story have been well told by key West German participants in the process.[1] Yet the successful conclusion of German unification also required close U.S.–West German cooperation, and there was nothing foreordained about the extraordinarily close coordination that was achieved in 1989 and 1990. Foreign Minister Hans-Dietrich Genscher later put it this way: "If America had so much as hesitated, we could have stood on our heads" and gotten nowhere.[2]

Nor was it foreordained that Moscow, whose role was of course crucial, would assent to unification and to Germany's remaining in the Atlantic alliance. Timothy Garton Ash was right in concluding that by mid-1990 Gorbachev "was weak enough to feel he had to concede German unification within the Western Alliance but still strong enough to push this through at home," but Garton Ash too quickly ascribed this state of affairs to the handiwork of "Lady Luck."[3] To be sure, the deterioration of the Soviet internal situation was the product of forces beyond U.S. influence. But it was "no accident" (as the Marxists used to say) that Gorbachev by mid-1990 was confronted with a solid international consensus in support of Germany's unification within the alliance and so was in a weaker position to try to oppose this outcome. This international solidarity was the product, in large measure, of strenuous American diplomatic efforts from the beginning, based on a dual strategy of isolation and reassurance. We also assigned a high priority to strengthening Gorbachev's position internally—not, as some pundits argued, out of nostalgic allegiance to a Soviet leader whose star was already waning, but because we felt that Gorbachev's continued foreign policy authority was essential to gaining Soviet acceptance of German unification within the alliance.

Alexander Moens, in his crisp analysis of American diplomacy during the period, identified four pivotal points in which it was decisive:

"First, it shielded Chancellor Kohl in early December 1989, when he jumped ahead of other world leaders on the unification issue. Second, it committed France, the UK and the USSR to the Two-Plus-Four negotiating framework in February 1990. Third, it forged a common Western position on German membership in NATO in late February. Fourth, it brokered a package of guarantees in May and June that led the USSR to accept the idea of a united Germany being in NATO."[4]

To these should be added one prior consideration that made our initial steps more surefooted than those of the British, French, Soviets, and indeed the Germans themselves: namely, that German unification was on our agenda long before the opening of the Berlin Wall on November 9, 1989. This prospect was embedded in our thinking by the time of President Bush's May 31 speech in Mainz, in which he advanced the idea of the United States and Germany as "partners in leadership." In his memoirs, Bush recounts a long discussion about German unification that he initiated with French President Mitterrand during a meeting in Kennebunkport on May 20.[5] While we, like the rest of the world, were caught by surprise by the speed of the process, we nonetheless had seen it coming, had considered our options in the context of a broader strategic review, and were better prepared than others to respond creatively to the tumultuous events beginning in the fall of 1989.

It was an extraordinarily complex period. In the spring and early summer of 1990, according to one count, President Bush and Chancellor Kohl met four times, Secretary Baker and Foreign Minister Shevardnadze ten times, Baker and Foreign Minister Genscher 11 times, and Genscher and Shevardnadze eight times in May and June alone.[6] Added to these were many NATO, European Community, and Conference on Security and Cooperation in Europe (CSCE) meetings, others associated with the Two Plus Four process, and countless telephone conversations and messages. Owing partly to the speed of events, it was a period in which pure diplomacy, unencumbered by the usual domestic political processes, played a central role more reminiscent of nineteenth- than twentieth-century international relations. Karl Kaiser was not overstating the case in calling this the "most intensive phase of bilateral and multilateral diplomacy in European history."[7]

The present chapter cannot do full justice to this rich diplomatic history, still less to the complex set of Two Plus Four negotiations so skillfully led on our side by Secretary Baker. It focuses instead on the most critical issues involved, chiefly but not exclusively from the American perspective. Its judgments do not depart radically from those already offered by West German participants in the process and by scholars with access to American and other policymakers,[8] but it depicts a much more complex set of relationships—between the United States and Germany, particularly—than has so far been described. With all due consideration of the gravity of the issues involved, the diplomacy of the period had the character of a complex, high stakes chess match—or, rather, if the metaphor will stretch this far, of multiple, interrelated chess matches in which moves on one board simultaneously affected the play on other boards.

Opening Moves

This was not the way it was supposed to happen. German unification was supposed to be a *consequence* of the end of the division of Europe, not one of its driving forces. This logic and sequence were embedded in West German *ostpolitik* from the time of Willy Brandt onward. Germans and non-Germans alike had thought that the *German question* would arise within the context of an already much transformed European scene, following a period in which the prospect of a reunited Germany could be debated, its future contours shaped, and the new reality gradually (perhaps grudgingly) accommodated.

Yet, as West German president Richard von Weizsäcker once put it, "A question does not seek to exist merely because no one has an answer for it."[9] When the question arose in the fall of 1989, a consequence of East Germany's peaceful, democratic revolution, it caught most of the world by surprise. This unpreparedness helps explain the confused and highly emotional reactions on the part of the French, British, Soviet, and other leaders, who sought first to dismiss the prospect altogether and then to defer it to some distant, more convenient date (preferably long after their terms in office had expired).[10] There is no doubt that initial American reactions were more measured and sensible than those of our French, British, and Soviet counterparts, and no amount of retrospective rationalization on their part can explain away the clumsiness of their early steps. (The French would have us believe that Mitterrand's early meeting with Gorbachev in Kiev was designed to help German unification along; Shevardnadze later said he saw it coming from the beginning and was only trying to secure the best possible terms; and so on.) Yet there was more method to their seeming madness than has so far been credited.

The chess metaphor is apt, for the policies of key leaders immediately following the opening of the Berlin Wall are better understood if one thinks of this period as the opening stage of a chess match, in which players are trying to establish a position in the middle of the board. These moves were not yet directed toward an ultimate strategy; rather, they were designed to establish a strong position against any possible countermoves. The players would then wait to see how the game developed before acting more boldly. Dropping the metaphor—and not a moment too soon!—the efforts of the key participants in this early period were to establish their influence over the process of German unification. The West Germans were as determined to establish their primacy as others were to make it known that German unification affected their interests as well and that they meant to defend those interests, even at the risk of giving offense.

Soviet Warnings   Helmut Kohl later termed his June 1989 heart-to-heart talk with Gorbachev in the chancellor's bungalow overlooking the Rhine "the decisive moment" in securing Gorbachev's acceptance of German unification. Moreover, he saw the German-Soviet joint declaration issued during that visit as a "sensational" document for its affirmation of the "right of peoples to self-determination."[11] These are extravagant judgments. They may capture the evolution of Gorbachev's thinking on Germany and especially his hopes for Soviet-German cooperation, but they go much too far in implying that the Soviet leader had by that time accepted German unification as an imminent reality.

When President von Weizsäcker raised the question of German unity during a visit to Moscow in mid-1987, Gorbachev went so far as to acknowledge that history would decide what would happen in a hundred years—an interval that von Weizsäcker was able to halve by gaining Gorbachev's agreement to the proposition, "or perhaps fifty."[12] By the time of his meeting with Kohl in Bonn two years later, events in Poland and Hungary had pushed the issue closer to the fore. But it was still sufficiently remote, or so it seemed, to permit Gorbachev to ruminate about future possibilities, comfortable in the belief that no action was required on his part to arrest the process. Foreign Minister Shevardnadze's *post facto* contention that he saw German unification as "inevitable" as early as 1986 belongs in the same category, as does a far-reaching presentation on "ending the division" (of Europe and of Germany) reportedly was made by Vyacheslav Dashitschev to an advisory council of the Soviet foreign ministry in November 1987. As Garton Ash put it,

> There is enough retrospective and circumstantial evidence to suggest that by 1987, in the context of a general questioning and rethinking of all the basic positions of Soviet foreign policy, even the question of eventually overcoming the division of Germany into two states was privately discussed at a high and even at the highest level in Moscow. But there is no evidence whatsoever that this was translated into operative policy. Quite the contrary. Dashitschev himself says that his speculative proposals were roundly repudiated by virtually the whole foreign policy apparatus of the Soviet party-state.[13]

As the spiral of events in the late summer and early fall of 1989 brought the German question into sharper relief, Soviet policy hardened considerably. In a speech to the UN General Assembly in late September, even as he was working with Secretary Baker and Foreign Minister Genscher to enable East German asylum-seekers to reach West Germany via Hungary and Czechoslovakia, Shevardnadze issued a blistering assault on "national selfishness" and warned against those who would "ignore the interests of other peoples": "Fascism, which started the war, is the extreme and ugliest form of nationalism and chauvinism. German Nazism marched under the banner of revanchism. Now that the forces are again becoming active and are seeking to revise and destroy the post-war realities in Europe, it is our duty to warn those who, willingly or unwillingly, encourage those forces."[14]

A few days after the opening of the Berlin Wall, Shevardnadze warned more pointedly about the "attempt of some circles in [West Germany] to place the question of the reunification of Germany on the agenda."[15] Gorbachev, in a speech of the same day, declared German unification "no issue of current policy."[16] Both warned visiting French foreign minister Roland Dumas that talk of German unification was causing "great anxiety" and also sent frantic messages to Western leaders calling for urgent Four Power consultations. Later on, as if reciting the mantra could make it so, the Soviet foreign ministry spokesman repeated the official attitude toward German unification: "It is not on the agenda."[17]

An "Anglo-French Axis"? French, British, and other West European leaders were scarcely less determined to push the German question off the immediate agenda and into the indefinite future.[18] Just after the fall of the Berlin Wall, French president Mitterrand undertook a series of steps that belied his earlier protestation that he was "not afraid of unification"—convening an urgent EC summit in Paris, publicizing the fact of a long telephone conversation with Gorbachev about the German situation, and, without consulting Kohl, announcing an early visit to East Germany.[19] At the Paris Summit on November 18, Mitterrand and other EC leaders were at pains to relegate German unification to the distant and indefinite future. As Prime Minister Thatcher put it at the close of the session (as well as in a message to President Bush just before her departure for Paris), "The question of borders is not on the agenda. They should stay as they are."[20]

At the time, we in the U.S. administration knew very well of the antipathy of the British and French, to say nothing of the Soviets, toward unification and suspected they would seek to derail or at least postpone the process. The reality was worse than we knew. In her memoirs, Thatcher recounts having discussed her opposition to unification with Gorbachev in Moscow in September, and even earlier with Mitterrand.[21] At the EC Summit in Strasbourg in December, in two private talks with Mitterrand arranged at the latter's suggestion, the two leaders agreed on what she termed an "Anglo-French political axis" to "check the German juggernaut," later working out specific joint measures to try to slow down German unification.[22]

While Thatcher later laid the blame on Mitterrand for "the fact that little or nothing in practical terms came of these discussions,"[23] it was in fact the French who proved the more determined and effective in using their not inconsiderable influence to retard the process. They seized the diplomatic initiative within the EC, exploited the Polish border issue to disrupt the Two Plus Four process, and worked separately with Moscow and East Berlin to try to build a constituency against early unification before finally abandoning this rear guard effort in the spring of 1990. The British foreign office, meanwhile, never translated the prime minister's tough position into consistent policy. To the contrary, although British negotiators could be tough on key points, their drafting skills more often than not facilitated the Two Plus Four negotiations.

However emotional the response and clumsy the execution, both leaders successfully (perhaps only semiconsciously) conveyed another message: we may not be able to stop unification or even slow it appreciably, but we can certainly make life difficult unless our concerns are taken into account as participants in the process. It was a message that Bonn and Washington alike had to take seriously.

American Support for Unification   American support for unification was as swift and unequivocal as British and French reactions were grudging and, at best, ambivalent. The reasons, as has been seen, were several, and more complex than the seemingly automatic U.S. expression of support might have suggested. Not everyone in the U.S. administration shared former secretary of state Henry Kissinger's conviction that unification was "inevitable" as of mid-November 1989, or Ambassador (to the FRG) Vernon Walters's earlier prediction that unification would come quickly.[24] For one thing, the leaders of the East German revolution were at that moment declaring themselves in favor of a separate, democratic, and "socialist" GDR. While this "third road" seemed no more likely to succeed than previous efforts elsewhere in Eastern Europe toward "reform communism," we did not then know how quickly these figures and their political platform would be eclipsed by a headlong rush to unity. Nor had the full magnitude of the East German economic collapse yet made itself manifest. Our view, rather, was that the process of internal change in the GDR was "inexorable," as President Bush put it, and that unification was the likely, but not the inevitable, result.[25] Not even the boldest forecasters saw it coming within the year.

Thus, while surprised by the speed of events, we had nonetheless seen unification coming sooner than others, including the Germans themselves, and had thought through our position well in advance—even before the president's May 31 call in Mainz for the United States and Germany to become "partners in leadership."[26] We had seen this potential at the time of the Polish Roundtable Agreement in the spring of 1989,[27] worked to build a strong partnership with Bonn in anticipation of this prospect, and made clear our unequivocal support for German unification well before November 9. From the perspective of core interests, we did not have the British and French worry of strategic loss and indeed had much to gain from the prospect of a strong, democratic, and united Germany, whose security would no longer require such a massive investment of American resources.

Our support, therefore, was genuine, consistent with our principles, and based on careful consideration of our interests. Yet along with this positive endorsement was the consideration that the United States could not be seen as opposing German unification, or even showing hesitancy: if it were coming, as we believed likely, it would come whether we willed it or not. Moreover, active U.S. support would be required to ensure that it occurred in a manner consistent with European stability and our own interests. This meant, among other things, that we needed to forge the closest possible coordination with Bonn during the process of unification and lay the foundations for a strong German-American partnership thereafter. The German question, after all, was not only about unification but about how, or whether, Germany could fit into a secure and stable European order. Mindful of Kissinger's earlier judgment that Germany was "too big for Europe, too small for the world," we held the conviction that a strong U.S. link was needed both to balance the weight of a united Germany in Europe and to encourage this new entity to play an active and constructive global role.

Given the outspoken opposition of the British, French, and especially of the Soviets, it was imperative to move from rhetorical U.S. support to active U.S. leadership. Accordingly, we worked quickly to arrange a series of key meetings before and after President Bush's Malta Summit with Gorbachev, which had been announced at the end of October. These included meetings with Genscher in Washington on November 21, with Thatcher at Camp David on November 24, with the NATO allies at a summit in early December (just after Malta), and, finally, with Mitterrand at St. Martin in mid-December.

During Genscher's discussions with President Bush and Secretary Baker, both sides agreed that events in the GDR were pushing unification closer to the fore, perhaps at a faster pace than anyone had been expecting. They felt that there was a danger that the growing chorus of international opposition would prejudice the prospects for German unification before the process had even begun. Both sides also saw a need to lend some stability to the process, in order to avert a chaotic breakdown of order and possible violent backlash in the GDR, whether deliberate or unintended, that could set back the prospects for eventual unification.[28] As he had done with Kohl in two earlier telephone conversations, the president assured Genscher that the United States would lend its active support to unification. More specifically, he would use the forthcoming meetings with his British, French, and Soviet counterparts to avert early intrusion of the Four Powers in a process that should be a "matter for the Germans" to decide.[29]

Kohl's Gambit: "Ten Points"   A week later, Kohl made his own dramatic move to preempt Four Power involvement, as well as regain the initiative domestically, in a speech to the West German parliament outlining a ten-point, stage-by-stage process toward eventual German unification. It called for urgent humanitarian and other economic assistance to the GDR and the development of "confederative structures" between the two Germanies (after the holding of free elections in the GDR). The eventual goal would be the "reattainment of German state unity" within the context of European integration and the overcoming of the division of Europe.[30] The speech was an exercise in political brinkmanship, aimed at setting the terms and pace of German unification before British, French, and Soviet efforts to arrest the process had been fully formed.

The "ten point" speech was nearly as much of a surprise, though not quite the bombshell, in Washington as it was in London, Paris, and Moscow[31]—the key difference being that we shared Kohl's main objectives while the others did not. We could also understand Kohl's reasons, as he explained them in a telephone call to President Bush the next day, for keeping the speech secret even (or especially) from his own foreign minister. And while some of us at staff level saw it as a "clear breach" (to borrow Prime Minister Thatcher's characterization[32]) of the spirit of close coordination we thought had been agreed upon, we could not help but admit that Kohl had pulled off a tactical coup, which we might have tried ourselves had we been in his shoes.

I also figured, although no German official ever said so, that it was meant to send a signal not only to Paris, London, and Moscow, but also to Washington—virtually on the eve of the president's meeting with Gorbachev off Malta—that Bonn intended to assert primacy on the German question and not defer leadership on this issue to the Four Powers individually or collectively.[33] On that point, there was no disagreement in Washington. Nor did Kohl's speech, irritating though it was to have it sprung on us, prevent the establishment of the exceptionally close American–West German coordination that characterized the entire process of German unification. It did, however, underscore that points of tension, competition, and, on some issues, real political differences existed beneath the surface harmony of our bilateral cooperation.

The Evolution of American Strategy

Our immediate concern was that Kohl's brinkmanship might backfire and provoke a hardening of British and French attitudes or even an instinctive, potentially dangerous Soviet effort to prop up a failing East German regime. Accordingly, it was important for the United States to weigh in with a policy statement that renewed our support for unification while also offering some reassurance to Moscow and others that the process was not spinning out of control. (Was this the reaction Kohl hoped to provoke from his American friends? If so, his gambit worked to perfection.) This U.S. position, then, would be the basis for President Bush's discussions with Gorbachev at the Malta Summit and, at a NATO Summit in Brussels immediately thereafter, for gaining allied endorsement of a set of generally shared Western principles on unification.

The day after Kohl's speech, Secretary Baker previewed "four principles" on German unification that the president would advance in Malta and Brussels: (1) "self-determination should be pursued without prejudice to its outcome"; if there is to be unification, it should occur (2) "within the context of Germany's continuing alignment with NATO and an increasingly integrated European Community" and (3) as a "peaceful, gradual, . . . step-by-step process"; and (4) following the principles of the Helsinki Final Act (of the Conference on Security and Cooperation in Europe), the inviolability of existing borders should be respected.[34] Two of these four dealt specifically with what we considered crucial elements missing from Kohl's ten points: NATO membership and the border issue (meaning the permanence of the existing German-Polish border).[35] Thus, while offering strong American support to German unification in the face of sharply negative international reactions to the Kohl speech, the principles were designed to superimpose an American agenda over and above the points the chancellor had outlined. By stressing gradualism and a controlled process, the principles also aimed at building a firm Western consensus and assuaging British, French, and especially Soviet concerns about what seemed a runaway unification train.

Crisis Contingencies   Soviet attitudes, like ours and Bonn's, were also preoccupied with the mounting instability in the GDR and the danger of confrontation that might involve East German and Soviet military forces. These concerns reached a peak in early December, with renewed street demonstrations (prompted by revelations that Stasi [East German state security] files were being systematically purged) and confrontations, or near-confrontations, at East German and Soviet military installations. What appeared in the open press was but a fraction of the reports, most of them fragmentary and inconclusive, that we were receiving through official channels. That many of the incidents smacked of Stasi provocation—i.e., events either manufactured or greatly magnified to provide a pretext for a crackdown—only heightened our concern, particularly in light of evidence, such as that emerging from Gera on December 9, that some Stasi officials were inciting their units to armed resistance.[36]

Soviet intentions were difficult to gauge. Soviet military forces in the GDR were placed on higher alert status, ostensibly to protect Soviet military bases and nuclear weapons depots, and we were warned by Soviet officials that these units "would be obliged to use force" if the security situation got out of control.[37] While we judged these measures to be defensive, we could not exclude the possibility that they might be preparatory to a Soviet-led effort to impose martial law and restore communist rule.

Here a brief digression is in order, examining such evidence as has so far emerged. Well after this period, Shevardnadze spoke of pressures within the Soviet establishment for military intervention to rescue the East German regime. In an interview with *Literaturnaya Gazeta* in April 1991, four months after his resignation as foreign minister, Shevardnadze said that "we" (presumably himself and Gorbachev) "were urged fairly actively to apply force" in Eastern Europe in 1989. By whom? Shevardnadze does not say. We know that Romanian party leader Nicolae Ceauşescu was actively pushing for such steps as late as the December 1989 Warsaw Pact Summit, shortly before his own ouster and execution. We do not know whether Shevardnadze was referring to Ceauşescu or to unspecified figures within the Soviet establishment.

As to the GDR specifically, Shevardnadze said during the same interview that "our opponents" were urging that the Soviet Union "start the tank engines."[38] In defending his German policy in a June 1990 *Pravda* interview, he argued that the only alternative to a negotiated settlement would have been "to use our half-million troops in the GDR to block unification," implying but not saying directly that this option was being actively pushed.[39] Shevardnadze also mentioned this military option in his memoirs, but wrote that he learned of this pressure only after the fact and went on to assert categorically: "The question of our interference in the G.D.R. or anywhere else was not posed, nor will it be."[40]

Until further evidence becomes available, we cannot know how much weight or credence to attach to Shevardnadze's cryptic and somewhat contradictory statements on the subject. One reading would be that while there may have been pressures for military intervention, and perhaps specific planning (of which Shevardnadze learned only later) for military action in the GDR, these questions were never "posed" in the sense of being actively considered by the top Soviet leadership. Other interpretations are also possible. And of course Shevardnadze's *post facto* accounts cannot be accepted uncritically. He may have exaggerated these pressures as an exercise in *post facto* self-vindication, or he may have downplayed them, feeling it was too early for a full revelation. We do not know. As future historians sift through new evidence, it will be worth considering whether calls for military intervention, to the extent they in fact constituted a real danger at the time, might have acquired greater weight had the United States and its Western partners behaved differently in late 1989 and early 1990. The fact that the military option was not used does not mean that it *might* not have been under different circumstances. (Such are the "illusions of retrospective determinism.")

To return to the period at hand: not knowing how the story would come out as we were living through it (and indeed being protagonists in the unfolding drama), we in the U.S. administration were obliged to take seriously the danger of Soviet military action or, more plausibly, a ratcheting up of tensions that could lead to unintended but potentially uncontrollable confrontation in the GDR. During this period, I was involved in preparation of a contingency paper examining various crisis scenarios. It recommended U.S. actions in response to border incidents, uncontrolled emigration, confrontations at Soviet military installations, provocations there or along Berlin access routes, and attempts by East German or even Soviet authorities to impose military rule. Mercifully, the paper was consigned, unneeded, to the files (under the category, one might say, "in case of emergency, break glass and remove instructions").

Publicly, we revealed none of our concerns lest they create a climate that could make them self-fulfilling. Indeed, to dampen media speculation of an impending crisis that might prompt Soviet intervention, Secretary Baker cited, during a press briefing, the conclusions of a classified cable from the U.S. embassy in East Germany: despite the "disorder born of change, . . . demonstrations continue peacefully amidst rumors of potential violence."[41]

It was in the context of these concerns that we reluctantly acceded to urgent Soviet appeals for a meeting of the Four Power ambassadors, held in Berlin on December 10, as a means of reassuring Moscow that its voice would be heard and averting a situation in which it might take some unilateral step to assert its "rights and responsibilities" in and around Berlin. (The British and French had been nearly as eager as the Soviets to reaffirm Four Power prerogatives. As one French official said after the meeting, "The purpose was to remind the Germans who is in charge of Berlin."[42]) We had insisted, however, that the December 10 meeting have a restricted agenda[43] that did not include consideration of the German question itself, and we refused to agree to follow-up meetings.

The Malta Summit   The Malta Summit of early December 1989 made no great breakthrough in Soviet attitudes toward unification, nor was one expected. President Bush's main aims, which he previewed by telephone with Chancellor Kohl just before leaving for Malta, were to reiterate our "four principles," without any expectation that Gorbachev would sign on to them at this early date. He wanted to lay primary stress on the rights of the German people to self-determination, which Gorbachev himself had affirmed in principle several months before.[44] From this it followed that the next essential step was for free and fair elections to be held in the GDR—the first ever in that state's history—so that its people could express their wishes in what would amount to a referendum on unification. Meanwhile, it would be inappropriate for the Four Powers to intrude or interfere in the process. (In addition to being consistent with logic and lofty principle, this sequence also comported with our strategy of deferring external involvement until the German "process" was well advanced.) Finally, the president sought to begin—only to begin—shifting Soviet thinking away from unification per se, which we insisted was a matter for the Germans to decide, toward consideration of the future security situation that might arise in the context of unification, which was indeed a legitimate subject of U.S.-Soviet and broader international dialogue.

For his part, Gorbachev stressed "the reality" of two German states as the "decision of history" and warned against "any artificial acceleration" of relations between the two Germanies, yet his reactions were not as categorically negative as we had expected. (In President Bush's briefing material for the meeting was a paper I had drafted as "Gorbachev's Talking Points on Germany"—i.e., the main arguments I judged that the Soviet leader would make in the meeting, designed to help the president anticipate the tenor of the discussion. As it turned out, Gorbachev's line was milder than my draft had anticipated.[45]) The great surprise was Gorbachev's unsolicited assertion that U.S. military forces should remain in Europe as a stabilizing factor. Apart from contradicting decades of Soviet declaratory policy,[46] this position revealed the extent to which Gorbachev already was considering the implications for Soviet security of a confederal, perhaps even a united, Germany. He seemed, in other words, already to be thinking of a continued, if reduced, American military presence as a useful counterweight to a newly powerful Germany.

The Malta Summit, as both leaders were later to confirm, was a turning point in U.S.-Soviet relations and in the relationship between Presidents Bush and Gorbachev in particular.[47] It was important mainly for the intangibles of U.S.-Soviet relations—building a degree of trust and understanding between the two leaders, including the shared confidence that each was prepared to take the other's security concerns into account. It also helped establish an agenda, even if not yet fully endorsed by the Soviet side, that would facilitate Gorbachev's finding his way through the seemingly intractable dilemmas for Soviet security and prestige posed by German unification.

Malta did not, however, overcome the enormous differences between the two positions on the core issues of German unification. (Indeed, the president had not pressed as hard as we on his staff would have liked, judging that it was too early to engage Gorbachev frontally on the German question. His political instincts were probably more sound than those of his impatient advisers.) Just three days later, Gorbachev told Mitterrand during their meeting in Kiev that if Germany were reunited "there would be a two-line announcement that a Marshal had taken over my position."[48] Then, briefing his Central Committee on the results of the Malta meeting, Gorbachev issued an assurance to the GDR and a veiled threat to Bonn: "We firmly declare that we will see to it that no harm comes to the GDR. It is our strategic ally and a member of the Warsaw Treaty. It is necessary to proceed from the post-war realities—the existence of the two sovereign German states, members of the United Nations. Departure from this threatens with destabilization in Europe."[49]

Of course, one needs to "deconstruct" these statements and conversation fragments, considering not only what was said but to whom, in what context, and for what political purpose. The first was given to and disclosed by a French president who, as Gorbachev subsequently revealed to Kohl and Genscher, urged the Soviet leader during the meeting to prevent unification[50]; the second, to a gathering of Communist party officials already alarmed by the imminent collapse of the Warsaw Pact. There were also different levels of meaning to consider, as in Gorbachev's following his seemingly ironclad assurance to the GDR with an escape clause—"*to proceed from* the post-war realities"—that seemed to hold the door open to an alteration of those realities. Still, there was no mistaking Moscow's rejection of unification as an issue for the immediate future. This message was underlined when Gorbachev and Shevardnadze, meeting with Genscher in Moscow during this same period, denounced Kohl's ten points as a *diktat* and an "attempt to annex the GDR."[51]

Gaining Allied Support for the "Four Principles"   Immediately after Malta, the NATO Summit in Brussels endorsed President Bush's "four principles." Symbolically, the president's private dinner with Kohl on the eve of the summit made it clear that the United States stood firmly behind unification. (As he recalls in his memoirs, the president's "gut feeling" was that Kohl would push for the earliest possible unification.[52])

The aim during the summit itself, as with Gorbachev at Malta, was to override opposition to unification per se by addressing related issues of concern, both procedural and substantive. Affirmation of a united Germany's continued membership in NATO and a more integrated European Community were of course key for Britain and France respectively, points the president underscored in his separate meetings with Thatcher and Mitterrand.

By advancing principles around which all of the alliance could rally, the president helped circumscribe the opportunities for unilateral actions by any one member—meaning not only France and Britain but also Germany and, for that matter, the United States. Yet this by no means eliminated French and British divisiveness, nor prevented Prime Minister Thatcher during the summit meeting from insisting that German unification would have to wait another ten to fifteen years. Instead, the principles provided a reference point of agreed allied policy through which we and the West Germans could begin isolating and neutralizing first British, then French objections.

As Margaret Thatcher put in her memoirs, the NATO Summit made it clear "there was nothing I could expect from the Americans as regards slowing down German reunification."[53] Precisely so. Neither the

British nor even the French would find it easy publicly to depart from the shared allied support for unification, which meant that the Soviet Union would find itself increasingly isolated should it continue down that path. The strategy, in other words, was to isolate those who would obstruct unification, while also assuring all concerned that the process would occur in an orderly way, within a broader European and transatlantic context.

As we had hoped, the NATO Summit evoked a positive Soviet response. In a December 19 speech at the European parliament,[54] Shevardnadze said the Soviet leadership was giving "careful and scrupulous study" to the NATO communique, which "differ[ed] greatly from previous documents of its type." We in Washington paid similarly scrupulous attention to the Shevardnadze speech, whose jarring mixture of truculence and conciliation, we now know, was the product of two competing drafts from within the Soviet establishment.[55] Our main focus, however, was on two related elements of the speech. First was the assertion that "we [in the USSR] . . . do not want to set ourselves at odds with the legitimate interests of the Germans," followed by a seeming openness to finding a solution "through the mutual agreement of all parties concerned." Second was a list of what Shevardnadze termed "seven questions" that would arise in the context of German unification, including recognition of existing borders, the future status of German armed forces and troops stationed on German soil, the place of a united Germany in Europe's "military-political structures," and (twice) the national security interests of other states. While these struck us more as "seven demands," they also amounted to an agenda—in places problematic, but as a whole reasonable—for finding the "mutual agreement" of which Shevardnadze spoke.

Like the British and French, the Soviets had gone a long way from the assertion that German unification was "not on the agenda" toward reluctant acceptance of this prospect, so long as it occurred within an orderly, step-by-step framework. At year's end, we in Washington and our counterparts in Bonn could take some satisfaction in having helped create an atmosphere more conducive, or at least less resolutely obstructionist, to unification.

"The Faster, the Better"   By this time, however, we in Washington already had abandoned the notion of a "gradual, step by step" process, as had the government in Bonn.[56] Secretary Baker's meetings with the new

GDR leadership in Potsdam December 13 and Chancellor Kohl's tumultuous reception in Dresden December 19 already indicated the impo-
tence of the East German regime.[57] In early January, East German prime
minister Hans Modrow's clumsy attempt to revive the hated Stasi and
revelations of the full state of the East German economic collapse,[58]
coupled with the rising emigration tide to an estimated two thousand
daily, persuaded Bonn and Washington alike that the prospect of an orderly movement toward unity over a period of years was rapidly being
overtaken by the virtual implosion of the East German state.

The German question, in short, was not only "on the agenda," it demanded a prompt answer, whether the world was ready with one or
not. Chancellor Kohl's ten-point plan, which had caused such a furor in
late November, now seemed tame indeed. From that point on, the assumptions from which we developed our strategy were that unification
was inevitable and was coming very fast; that faster was better, given
that the alternative of a separate, democratic GDR was now foreclosed,
and that a more rapid pace of unification would offer fewer opportunities for obstruction and delay. Strong and agile U.S. leadership would be
required for unification to be achieved successfully and in a manner
consistent with European stability and our own security interests.

Legally, the four wartime Allies—the United States, Britain, France,
and the Soviet Union—had residual rights and responsibilities that had
to be disposed of before unification could be finalized. Politically, there
was every danger that Soviet intransigence, coupled with misgivings or
worse on the part of Britain, France, and others, could lead in any of a
number of uncontrollable directions: an international peace conference
amounting to open season for any country with a grievance, a protracted Four Power regime to oversee a semisovereign Germany, and/or
a disorganized process that would leave Germany vulnerable to Soviet
blackmail. It was not a process that the Germans could manage alone.
Indeed, the United States had to be more attentive to German sovereignty than the Germans themselves, lest the pressures, especially from
Moscow, induce them to accept a settlement that would prejudice the
structure of European security for generations to come.

While few harbored "Rapallo fears" of a separate Soviet-German
peace or worried that the Germans would be swayed by a repetition of
the 1952 Stalin offer of a reunited but neutralized Germany, there was
considerable concern that Moscow might press Germany to accept any
of a number of lesser infringements on its sovereignty. The possibilities

included, if not exclusion from NATO, then a ban of nuclear weapons on German soil, withdrawal of stationed forces, limits on the size of the German army, and acceptance of a special status for East German territory. If one or more of these conditions were seen by the Bonn leadership as the necessary price for German unification, its capacity to resist would be sorely tested, particularly if some of Germany's neighbors allowed their own anxieties to become tacit endorsement of Soviet demands. If the Germans were abandoned by their Western allies at the moment when unification was within reach, could they be blamed for cutting a separate deal with Moscow to achieve their goal? And if the choice were between unity and alliance, could any German leader's answer be in doubt? One key concern for American diplomacy was to ensure that the question was never posed in that fashion.

Our strategy was to recast the issue in Soviet calculations by lining up preponderant international support for a fully sovereign Germany. We would then direct Soviet attention away from the issues of unification and NATO membership, which we insisted were matters for the Germans to decide, toward broader considerations of what kind of Europe was emerging, with what kind of security structures and what kind of role for the United States and the Soviet Union. Process and sequence were crucial. It was important to resist early invocation of Four Power rights. Then, after the East German people had expressed their will through free elections, we would insist that the role of the Four Powers be strictly confined to the tasks of relinquishing all remaining rights and responsibilities and restoring full sovereignty to a united Germany.

Meanwhile, practical steps taken between the two Germanies toward unification would constitute a series of faits accomplis that Moscow could oppose only at great and increasing cost. (Here is where the speed of the process would work to our advantage.) We would also work to address and, where possible, anticipate legitimate Soviet security concerns: President Bush's proposal, in his State of the Union Address in late January, for further conventional force reductions down to 195,000 on each side, for example, was designed to show that as Soviet troops were being pushed out of Eastern Europe, including potentially the GDR, the United States would voluntarily draw down its own forces as well.

The strategy, in short, combined isolation and reassurance: we wanted to make it harder for the Soviet leaders to say *nyet*, while working to resolve their security concerns so they would find it easier to say *da*. As Soviet deputy foreign minister Yuli Kvitsinky later put it, "from day to day, we had lost one trump card after another."[59]

Beyond the immediate task of winning Soviet acquiescence, we were also looking to the larger question of a viable European order after unification had been achieved. It was imperative to avoid a Versailles-like settlement that left Europe divided once again between victors and vanquished. All parties, above all the Soviet Union, needed to accept the settlement and have a stake in the emerging order. Reconciling this longer term strategic objective with the tactical exigencies of the process of German unification was neither easy nor always successful, however. History probably will record that we achieved more success with the latter than the former. Let it also record that, aware of these larger responsibilities, we tried to do both.

The Bonn-Washington Nexus   The first task was to ensure the closest possible cooperation with Bonn. There is ample testimony from Kohl, Genscher, and many others to the extraordinary degree of coordination, at all levels, between Washington and Bonn throughout the period of German unification. And so there was. This was all the more remarkable given what was at stake: for Germans, the unification of their country; for Americans, the future U.S. role and presence in Europe; for both, the future structure of European security and of their relations with the Soviet Union. Our main objectives and interests were in close harmony, but they were not identical—nor could they be, given that one was a global power with global interests and responsibilities while the other was a continental power with more parochial interests. The U.S.–West German relationship during the period was thus more complex than the image of "seamless" cooperation to which Genscher later alluded.[60]

The interplay between Kohl's "ten points" and Bush's "four principles" already implied a process of mutual adjustment between Washington and Bonn. We would lend full support to unification, which entailed considerable latitude for Bonn's separate diplomacy toward that end. They in turn would line up unequivocally behind the future integrity of the Western security system. This meant that unification would not be pursued at the cost of Germany's continued membership in NATO. By early January, this process of adjustment was under way but not yet complete. The positions needed to be brought into even closer harmony if we were to achieve the level of coordination needed to see the unification process through to successful conclusion.

Such coordination was all the more important in that the diplomacy of German unification demanded a certain division of labor. In mobilizing Western consensus in support of unification, Bonn would need to play the major role in securing the support of France and the European Community, while Washington's role would be more important with Great Britain and within the Atlantic alliance. (That Bonn would take the lead in relations with the GDR and in managing the internal aspects of unification was of course understood from the beginning.) Only after developing a solid international consensus would the way be clear to begin securing Soviet concurrence. This, too, required a division of labor. Dealing with the many bilateral issues arising from the removal of Soviet forces from the then-GDR necessarily would be Bonn's responsibility. Here U.S.-German coordination was not always compatible with the requirement that there had to be an historic settling of differences between Bonn and Moscow, a process in which we could not be full participants. By the same token, there were many areas of Soviet concern that only the leader of the Western alliance could address; some would have to be addressed through U.S.-Soviet arms negotiations to which the FRG was not party.

Given these numerous opportunities for slippage, it was essential that there be solid agreement between ourselves and Bonn on principles and main goals. Accordingly, with Genscher already scheduled to meet with Secretary Baker in Washington, Deputy Secretary of State Lawrence Eagleburger and Deputy National Security Adviser Robert Gates traveled to Bonn on January 29 to consult with Kohl and also arrange for the chancellor to hold extended talks with the president at Camp David in late February.[61]

Meanwhile, the drive to unification was accelerating much as we had envisioned. On January 28, just before departing for a meeting with Gorbachev in Moscow, East German prime minister Modrow had been obliged by the government-opposition roundtable to advance the timetable for parliamentary elections, which had been scheduled for May, to March 18. In Bonn, Chancellor Kohl had quietly formed a "Unity Committee" within his cabinet to prepare the way for unification and avert an avalanche of East German emigration. As Kohl put it, "If the DM [Deutsche Mark] doesn't come to Leipzig, then the Leipzigers will come to the DM."[62]

Soviet Questions, German Answers Soviet thinking was also adjusting to the new realities. While *Pravda* continued to rumble that "destabilization of the situation in the GDR is fraught with unpredictable consequences, . . . above all for the Germans themselves,"[63] Gorbachev was taking a more forthcoming posture, remarking to journalists just before Modrow's arrival that "no one ever cast doubt in principle on the unification of the Germans."[64] Gorbachev also declined to endorse Modrow's call for "treaty-based association" between the two Germanies as a step toward eventual confederation, suggesting that the Soviet leader realized that events already had passed that point.

In his extended public comments on the Modrow visit, Foreign Minister Shevardnadze expressed the evolving Soviet attitude. Leaving aside the occasional rhetorical bouquet thrown to hard-line elements in his own leadership (such as his rejection of "aggressive neo-Nazi actions in the FRG and the GDR"), Shevardnadze's presentation was substantively consistent. He supported "the eventual creation of a united, peace-loving and democratic Germany" but insisted that unification was not the affair of the Germans alone and that the process must be "gradual and pass through certain stages." He also repeated the "seven questions" from his December 19 speech to the European parliament, this time adding (though not specifically endorsing) Modrow's call for the two German states to declare "military neutrality."[65]

Of course, Shevardnadze's insistence on gradualism, at a time when he and Gorbachev must have realized that events were moving rapidly, may have been designed to increase Soviet leverage (as well as assuage his hard-line critics). The call for military neutrality, as if united Germany could be turned into a somewhat larger Switzerland, may have been influenced by similar considerations, as Gorbachev and Shevardnadze groped for some answer to the question of a united Germany's security position. If such was their aim, they did not have long to wait.

In a major speech at the Tutzing Academy on January 31, Foreign Minister Genscher asserted, without consulting any of his allies (or, for that matter, Chancellor Kohl), that "proposals for incorporating the part of Germany at present forming the GDR in NATO's military structures would block intra-German rapprochement." Nor was this all. Speaking not about the GDR but about Poland, Czechoslovakia, and Hungary, Genscher added: "What NATO must do is state unequivocally that whatever happens in the Warsaw Pact there will be no expansion of NATO territory eastward."[66] Preemptive capitulation as regards the GDR was one thing, arguably within the purview of the foreign minister–presumptive of a united Germany; preemptively sacrificing the future security of the new democracies of Central Europe on the altar of German unification, quite another.

Of course, Genscher may have advanced these positions purely for Soviet consumption, with no intention of binding NATO or himself to them, as a means of conditioning Moscow to Germany's continued membership in NATO. The speech nonetheless underscored the danger that, left to themselves, the Germans might pay—and make others pay—an unacceptable and unnecessary price to win Soviet acceptance of unification.

Forging a Western Consensus

By late January, the administration's aim of deferring Four Power involvement was in any case becoming harder to sustain. We had agreed reluctantly to the December 10 meeting of the Four Power ambassadors, as has been seen, but we had since rebuffed repeated Soviet demands for further meetings. Already there had been half a dozen such entreaties, including two separate messages from Shevardnadze in the space of ten days. A stream of other proposals recommended deferring settlement of the German question to the conclusion of a postwar peace treaty, placing it on the agenda of the ongoing, 35-nation Vienna talks on confidence building measures, and subjecting the question to an "all-European referendum" (in which the United States and Canada would also participate).[67]

The French and British, too, were increasingly insisting on Four Power involvement to slow down the process and, as Prime Minister Thatcher put it, ensure that Germany's "narrow nationalist goals" were subordinated to the broader interests of European security.[68] Indeed, Shevardnadze's January 10 message to Secretary Baker asserted that as a result of recent Soviet contacts with the United States, Great Britain, and France, "a consensus is emerging about the desirability of maintaining within the 'Big Four' an exchange of views on German affairs." As we had joined no such "consensus," it evidently was a Franco-British-Soviet one.[69]

Creation of the Two Plus Four   We on the NSC staff and at the State Department had already been thinking of the best strategy for bringing the other powers into the process. As we learned when the Genscher entourage arrived February 1, the West Germans had been thinking along the same lines and had reached similar conclusions. Months before, Genscher had told President Bush that in the 1940s and 1950s the Four Powers had met to decide Germany's future, while the Germans had been relegated to the *katzentisch,* or side table. He made it clear that the Germans did not want to be on the *katzentisch* again.[70] Nor did we want them there. For reasons of principle, we believed from the outset that the two Germanies should take the lead in deciding their future; as a matter of strategy, we did not like the political arithmetic of a Four Power process that was stacked three against one, with the United States the only defender of German unification.

From this emerged the concept of the Two Plus Four—the two German states plus the United States, Great Britain, France, and the Soviet Union—an idea we had already broached in outline form to British foreign secretary Douglas Hurd. Even there the mathematics were potentially unmanageable, so it was equally critical to delimit the scope of activities of the Two Plus Four process. Here, too, we and the West Germans were in full agreement. The internal aspects of unification—that is, whether and in what fashion Germans east and west chose to live together in one state—were strictly up to the Germans, pending only the forthcoming elections in which the people of the GDR would express their wishes. The Two Plus Four were to deal only with the external aspects of unification—and only those aspects required to return full sovereignty to a united Germany. Questions such as alliance membership, military forces, and future European security arrangements were beyond its purview. The role of the Four Powers was solely to discharge and then relinquish all residual rights and responsibilities in Berlin and Germany as a whole.

The question of timing was important as well. We did not want the Four Powers involved until the Germans had sorted out their future, and certainly not until formation of a new GDR government following the March 18 elections. Yet there was also a risk of leaving Soviet entreaties unanswered, particularly in light of Chancellor Kohl's planned visit to Moscow in mid-February. Hence the State Department in particular wanted to reach agreement on the Two Plus Four framework as soon as possible, so that Gorbachev and Kohl did not feel pressure (or see an opportunity) to turn their meeting into a "One Plus One" deal on Germany's future.

With Baker having reached agreement with Genscher on all these points, we then undertook the usual double-tracking with Chancellor

Kohl. (This was still only two days after Genscher's Tutzing speech, in which he spoke on the most sensitive issues of German foreign policy without so much as an advance warning to Kohl.) It was tedious always to have to reach agreement with Kohl and Genscher separately. However, the fact that there was virtually total agreement between the State Department and the White House (and constant coordination and communication between the two) meant that sometimes we could supply Bonn with the policy coordination it lacked. Knowledge being one of the currencies of power, it also gave us added leverage in dealing with Bonn, in that we occasionally knew more about where Kohl or Genscher stood on an issue than either of them knew of the other. To return to the point at hand, Kohl was in full agreement on the Two Plus Four formula, so the way was clear to work toward securing agreement among the other parties.

Secretary Baker then took to the road to sell the Two Plus Four idea. He secured the reluctant agreement of French foreign minister Dumas during a refueling stop at Shannon Airport[71] and then shopped (but did not yet sell) the idea to Gorbachev and Shevardnadze in Moscow before continuing on to Ottawa for a meeting of NATO and Warsaw Pact foreign ministers.[72]

Ottawa was a three-ring circus. Shevardnadze held five separate talks with Baker and three with Genscher, and also met individually with Hurd, Dumas, and Polish foreign minister Krzysztof Skubiszewski, all in a single day. In his memoirs, Shevardnadze also recalled that while he could see Two Plus Four turning into Five Against One—"and it was not hard to guess that the Soviet representative was the 'one' "—he was persuaded that this mechanism, coupled with assurances Moscow could gain bilaterally with Bonn and Washington, offered the best leverage available to secure Soviet interests.[73] Shevardnadze no doubt had a premonition of what actually transpired. Each Two Plus Four was preceded by a "One Plus Three" meeting to forge agreement among West Germany, Britain, France, and the United States.[74] These key gatherings, supplemented by Bonn's bilateral diplomacy with East Germany, turned out to be instrumental in forging a five-way consensus that Moscow found hard to resist. Nonetheless, the nonstop bilateral diplomacy at Ottawa—between and among Baker, Genscher, and Shevardnadze, particularly—led to unexpectedly swift agreement. The two Germanies and the Four Powers created what came to be known as the Two Plus Four mechanism "to discuss external aspects of the establishment of German unity, including the issues of security of the neighboring states."[75]

The Polish Border Issue Among these issues was the question of borders, with the Polish-German border being the case in point. This complicated issue can only be outlined here.[76] Chancellor Kohl, wanting to handle the issue in a way that did not alienate politically important constituencies (above all, the organizations of German expellees from the immediate postwar period), took the firm position that as a legal matter the issue could not be settled except by an all-German parliament, which did not yet exist. There seems little doubt that Kohl genuinely believed this to be the case under international law, but it was convenient to his political purposes as well.[77] The Poles, understandably worried that a new, postunification German parliament might take a very different line, demanded firm guarantees beforehand. There is nothing like having one's country wiped off the map of Europe for 125 years, as Poland was after the partitions of the late eighteenth century, to engender a certain suspicion of the assurances of benevolent intent from one's neighbors.

There was a further danger that concerned me and some at the State Department. We worried that Kohl's motivations may have included one that he could not say openly: namely, that he did not want to go down in history as the chancellor who gave up Germany's "eastern territories" once and for all. It was not that Kohl harbored aggressive intentions against Poland—far from it—but that he wanted to leave this issue open for resolution by future generations. That, we felt, would only encourage right-wing irredentist dreams in Germany and excite fear and anxiety in Poland. German-Polish relations could never be mended so long as this issue was left open. Once it was closed, Germans and Poles could leave this legacy behind them and begin building a new relationship. (This perspective was shared in some quarters at the State Department, but it was a minority view at the NSC, which tended to take Kohl's assurances at face value.)

The border issue pitted Kohl against nearly everyone else, including his foreign minister and the other five countries of the Two Plus Four. The immediate American concern, shared even by those who accepted unreservedly Kohl's repeated private assurances that the question would be unambiguously resolved at the time of unification, was that the border issue could seriously complicate the Two Plus Four process, with the

French and others championing the Polish cause as a means of slowing unification.[78]

Our many discussions with the Bonn government on this issue aimed at urging Kohl to find a way to resolve the issue quickly, and to Poland's satisfaction. This task was complicated by another compelling objective: to strengthen Chancellor Kohl's position internally so as to enhance his leadership role in the unification process. On issues of European security and particularly the question of NATO membership, as will be seen shortly, we wanted Kohl's voice, not Genscher's, to be decisive.[79] Having set about consciously to strengthen the chancellor's position, we were prepared to defer to his judgment on the tactical handling of the border issue so long as it did not begin poisoning the Two Plus Four negotiations.

President Bush had listed "inviolability of existing borders" as one of his "four principles" of November–December 1989 and reaffirmed them privately and publicly during his Camp David meeting with Kohl in late February 1990 (discussed below). The visit to Washington of Polish prime minister Tadeusz Mazowiecki in late March provided the occasion for the president's direct mediation between the Poles and the Germans. This Bush did directly with Mazowiecki in Oval Office meetings on March 21 and 22, as well as in telephone calls to Kohl before, during, and after Mazowiecki's visit.[80]

Ultimately an acceptable formula was found whereby the parliaments of the two German states issued simultaneous resolutions recognizing Poland's western border to be final (with the text of this passage agreed to beforehand by the Poles and Germans) and calling for a binding treaty between Poland and a united Germany. Within the Two Plus Four process, it was agreed that the Polish foreign minister would participate in the meeting where borders were discussed.[81] While the episode left a bitter aftertaste, especially for the Poles, it nonetheless led to a satisfactory legal resolution of the border issue, and it was managed in a way that solidified U.S.-German coordination on the increasingly complex set of issues related to unification.

Overcoming Opposition to Unification   This increasingly close U.S.-German cooperation was most crucial during the intense round of diplomatic negotiations in February 1990. Just before Kohl's arrival in Moscow on February 8 for his first meeting with Gorbachev since the opening of the Berlin Wall, the chancellor received two messages. One was from Secretary Baker, reviewing his just-concluded meetings with Gorbachev and Shevardnadze and the progress he had made toward gaining Soviet agreement to unification and the Two Plus Four formula. The second was a long and intimate letter from President Bush, which Kohl later termed "one of the most important documents in the history of U.S.-German relations."[82] It not only reaffirmed full U.S. support for German unification but detailed specific steps the United States was prepared to take to counter possible Soviet efforts to impede unification, restrict the sovereignty of a united Germany, or prejudice the future of the Atlantic alliance by seeking to limit Germany's role therein.[83] The immediate political objective of the letter, coupled with the February 7 announcement of Kohl's forthcoming trip to Washington, was to stiffen Kohl's resolve and strengthen his hand for his meetings with Gorbachev.

Indeed, the Kohl visit to Moscow achieved a breakthrough that complemented the Ottawa agreement on Two Plus Four. Immediately after his meeting with Gorbachev, Kohl announced their agreement "that the Germans themselves must resolve the question of the unity of the German nation and themselves decide in what kind of state system, in what time frame, at what speed, and under what conditions they wish to bring about this unity."[84]

This was all the assurance Kohl needed to move aggressively to build a pro-unification coalition of East German conservative parties,[85] called "Alliance for Germany," and help it score a resounding victory in the March 18 elections. At Kohl's urging, the new East German prime minister, Lothar de Maizière, had already committed himself and his party (CDU-East) to rapid unification via Article 23 of the "Basic Law" (the West German constitution). This meant in effect that the states (*länder*) of East Germany would simply vote themselves into the existing Federal Republic of Germany. The alternative route was via Article 146, which would have amounted to a merger of two separate states and the creation of a new legal entity, requiring a new constitution and renegotiation of existing treaties and other legal commitments. Although not, strictly speaking, our business, Article 23 was our preference as well, in that it created fewer new issues to be settled and meant that Germany's relationships with the EC, NATO, and other institutions need not be renegotiated. In subsequent interviews, Soviet officials noted that they, too, saw unification via Article 23 as tantamount to an "*anschluss*" (annexation) of the GDR, which they rightly feared would make NATO membership a virtual fait accompli.[86] Indeed, the point was quickly confirmed, as negotiations began immediately toward economic and social union, and then full political union, between the two Germanies.

Among their other consequences, the results of the East German elections prompted a sharp reversal in French thinking—away from the vain hope of slowing unification. Instead they formed a new strategy of using the relatively brief interval of maximum influence on Bonn to secure firm German commitment to accelerate the process of European integration. The West Germans, having asserted repeatedly that unification would not hinder but rather strengthen "European construction," were vulnerable to subtle French blackmail on this subject. Any hesitation on Bonn's part would be read, or at least portrayed, by its neighbors as confirmation of their worst fears about a united Germany's propensity to *alleingang* (going it alone). Hence, whatever private reservations Kohl or the *Bundesbank* (German federal bank) may have had, the chancellor acceded quickly to Mitterrand's proposal for a joint letter to their EC counterparts in mid-April, calling for an accelerated timetable for reaching EC economic and political union by 1993.[87]

Germany and NATO   The concern, then, was not with whether unification could be achieved—by early 1990 the momentum had become irresistible, as all the participants had come to acknowledge—but with what kind of Germany would emerge from the process, and with what the implications would be for the future of Europe and the transatlantic link. Even after German unification was well advanced, few experts outside government held out continued NATO membership by a fully sovereign Germany as a plausible outcome of the unification process or a realistic goal of American policy. Some in the United States and West Germany even argued that U.S. support for united Germany's NATO membership constituted an obstacle, perhaps a deliberate one, to unification. Voices on the West German Left argued that "a unified Germany and NATO membership are mutually exclusive."[88] Even the most respected commentators and analysts here and in Europe advanced various schemes for a united Germany that would be disarmed or demilitarized, temporarily or permanently bifurcated through dual membership in NATO and the Warsaw Pact, or consigned to some other form of semisovereignty.[89] One such commentator, saluting Gorbachev's statesmanship, lamented the lack of "parallel subtlety of understanding on the Western side" and called on the United States to abandon its support for Germany's NATO membership.[90]

Within the administration, we considered these outcomes unacceptable. In early February, I drafted a paper for internal consideration, listing some 17 different security outcomes for a united Germany, beginning with a fully sovereign Germany with its alliance relationships intact and ending with a demilitarized and neutralized Germany cut adrift from its NATO and EC partners.[91] In between were permutations and combinations regarding nuclear weapons, stationed forces, the size and status of the German military, and membership in various political or security institutions. One did not have to go far down the list before European security began to unravel. Most obviously, if German membership in NATO or the presence of U.S. forces were sacrificed on the altar of unification, the fundamental transatlantic security link would have been severed, leaving a post–Cold War jungle not unlike that described in Mearsheimer's widely read *Atlantic* article.[92] Whether NATO could or should be replaced at some future date was another matter; our concern was that the sole functioning European security institution not be jettisoned in the midst of rapid and unpredictable change. As a matter of principle as well as policy preference, we also refused to accept that a democratic, united Germany should be denied full sovereignty, including the right to choose its own alliance relationships.

The U.S. position, spelled out in countless public statements during the course of 1990 and closely coordinated with Bonn, was that a united Germany should be fully sovereign from the moment of unification, with no new discriminatory constraints on its sovereignty. Germany should also remain a full member of NATO, including its integrated military structure, and substantial U.S. forces should remain in the country. Our conviction was that there was no reason, 45 years after the war, for a united, democratic Germany to be singled out for special status. Of course, we had no way of knowing whether, or to what extent, these ambitious objectives could be realized. (As it turned out, what emerged from the Two Plus Four process was the second of 17 outcomes on our list, with German sovereignty limited only by the special security status accorded the territory of the former GDR. But this successful outcome seemed distant indeed in the early months of 1990.) What we did know was how much was at stake in the outcome; we knew, as well, that the United States had to remain absolutely clear about its main objectives and harness policy single-mindedly to those ends. Our task, then, was to secure Moscow's acquiescence to a state of affairs that successive Soviet leaders would have considered a reversal and betrayal of the USSR's great historic gain of World War II—the emasculation of German power.

Mixed Signals from Bonn   While trying to condition the Soviet leadership to this prospect, as President Bush did at Malta and Secretary Baker did in his February visit to Moscow, our main effort was to weld a united Western position behind Germany's NATO membership. The first requirement was to secure an unambiguous commitment from the West Germans, whose public statements to date had been muddy at best. These concerns were not pulled out of thin air. Devotees of original sources, we at the NSC staff made a practice of studying the texts of major speeches by foreign leaders. Having noted with more than passing interest that Chancellor Kohl's "ten point" speech omitted reference to NATO, we also focused on this summing up in Foreign Minister Genscher's Tutzing speech: "We want to place the process of German unification in the context of EC integration, of the CSCE process, the West-East partnership for stability, the construction of the common European house and the creation of a peaceful European order from the Atlantic to the Urals."[93]

To be sure, Genscher affirmed German membership in NATO—a more political, less military NATO—earlier in the speech, but the alliance did not figure in this key passage in his final paragraph. An oversight? Here was Genscher's almost identical formulation two months later, in a major address to the Western European Union: "We seek the process of German unification in the context of EC integration, the CSCE process, East-West partnership for stability, the construction of the common European house and the creation of a pan-European peaceful order."[94]

Tired speechwriters? Perhaps, but not too tired to insert a conspicuous addendum when Genscher presented the now-familiar formulation in a speech before a U.S. audience in early April: "We want German unity *as a member of NATO,* in the context of the integration of the European Community and in the CSCE process. We want it as a contribution to the development of a partnership between West and East based on stability, to the construction of the common European house, and to the establishment of the peaceful order spanning the whole of Europe."[95]

This kind of textual analysis can be carried too far, and perhaps we have carried it too far already. But words matter, as veteran politicians know well. They use major speeches to affirm priorities and signal intent, often indirectly. What is *not* said can be as important as what is. It was for these reasons that *our* words, and the words we urged visiting Western leaders to utter at every opportunity, laid stress on united Germany's remaining "a full member of NATO, including participation in its integrated military structure" (a phrase I must have written into draft remarks a hundred times during the spring of 1990). They were words meant for Moscow's attention, and also for the attention of certain German politicians who might be inclined to allow NATO membership to become a bargaining chip. They were words meant to rally the Western alliance in support of Germany's continued membership in NATO as a vital element of European stability and security.

Clearly, these differences were primarily about tactics. Genscher feared that raising the NATO issue at this early date might provoke a negative Soviet reaction and a premature hardening of the Soviet position. He thought that even his qualified references to NATO in the Tutzing speech put Germany on "thin ice."[96] Better to tread lightly on the issue until Moscow had been conditioned to react more favorably. Our concern was that this approach risked leaving the impression that Germany's future membership in NATO was subject to discussion and negotiation. It was an invitation for Soviet probing of German resolve.

While our concerns were mainly over tactics, we were also conscious that Genscher already had offered a unilateral and uncoordinated concession on the future status of GDR territory within the alliance. What other concessions might he be prepared to make? It is important to be precise here. The general view in Washington was that Genscher hoped and expected that united Germany would remain in NATO and that he was working with us toward that end. Yet many also saw Genscher as a Europeanist first and an Atlanticist second, a characterization that Genscher surely would not have disputed. Because NATO membership ranked lower on his list of priorities than on Kohl's or ours, he was more likely than the chancellor to concede on issues we considered vital to the future of European security.

Rallying International Support   We therefore attached great importance to Chancellor Kohl's joining President Bush in affirming these points publicly when the two met at Camp David on February 24 and 25. We at staff level wrote our standard formulation—"[Chancellor Kohl and I] share a common belief that a unified Germany should remain a full member of the North Atlantic Treaty Organization, including participation in its military structure"—into the draft statement President Bush would read after their meeting. We then ran it by Horst Teltschik, the chancellor's security adviser, who readily agreed to its inclusion. Later, Kohl expressed irritation at the implication that his fidelity to the alliance was in doubt, asserting that he had stressed the need for Germany to remain in NATO in a hundred speeches before the Camp David meeting.[97] Perhaps. But it is worth noting that it took the U.S. side to say so publicly at Camp David; Chancellor Kohl's statement at the same press conference referred only to "the security link between North America and Europe,"[98] an essentially meaningless formulation. And in their private talks at Camp David, Kohl had floated—and Bush rejected—the idea of a "French solution," whereby united Germany would remain in NATO's political alliance but not in its integrated military structures. Bush's reply was that "we can't let the Soviets clutch victory from the jaws of defeat."[99]

If Genscher's reticence on NATO membership was primarily tactical, that of the committed Atlanticist Helmut Kohl was almost entirely so. But too much was at stake to allow this ambiguity to persist. Besides, it was easier for the United States to speak forcefully and often on the issue than it was for West Germany, which was in the position of *demandeur* with respect to Moscow. And it was important that we do so, lest Western circumlocutions on this key issue lead Moscow to question Western resolve or exploit perceived differences. After Camp David, it was clear that there were no such differences to exploit between Bonn and Washington.

Indeed, by the time of his meeting with Mitterrand in Key Largo on April 19, President Bush could claim virtually Europe-wide agreement: "President Mitterrand and I both believe that a united Germany should remain a full member of NATO, as called for by Chancellor Kohl. All of our allies and several Eastern European countries share this view as well."[100] This two-line assertion represented the conclusion of strenuous U.S. diplomatic efforts throughout the spring of 1990.

Among the allies, France's position was of course the most problematic. On the one hand, the French favored a continuing U.S. military presence in Germany and wanted united Germany to be wrapped in a warm multilateral embrace; on the other, they were loath to accept the revitalization of NATO's role that was required to make either of those goals possible. The Key Largo meeting was therefore an occasion for blunt talk as well as compromise, with the U.S. side making it clear that a continued American presence in Europe demanded French acceptance of a continuing strong role for NATO. We made it plain that American troops would not stay in Europe as mercenaries if a more united EC cut the United States and NATO out of key decisions on issues of European security.[101] At the same time, Mitterrand was reassured that the United States did not oppose but in fact welcomed a stronger European security and defense identity, as a natural evolution in the EC's movement toward economic and political unity.

We also attached considerable importance to the positions of the new East European leaders and their influence within the still existing, if rapidly eroding, Warsaw Pact. The Poles and Hungarians were enthusiastic supporters of NATO, and German membership therein, from the outset. Czechoslovakia was more problematic. Its new president, Václav Havel, had carried from his days in opposition the conviction that both "military blocs," NATO and the Warsaw Pact alike, should disband and be replaced by a new "pan-European peace order," with the CSCE (Conference on Security and Cooperation in Europe) evolving into a new system of collective security. Given Havel's tremendous moral authority and his ability to influence thinking well beyond his own country, we considered it important to help him understand why the United States felt that while the CSCE should indeed take on new roles, it could not replace NATO as an agent of European security. Secretary Baker had made these points to Havel during a visit to Prague in early February—the same trip that took Baker to Moscow and on to Ottawa—and President Bush amplified them during Havel's official visit to Washington later that month.[102] Official Czechoslovak thinking shifted markedly as a result of these efforts and the surprisingly close personal affinity between Presidents Bush and Havel—one a man of the world and the other a man of the intellect.[103] By late spring, Havel had joined his Polish and Hungarian counterparts as an outspoken, if still hesitant, supporter of NATO; shortly thereafter he was clamoring for Czechoslovak membership in the organization.

The final East European recalcitrants were newly elected GDR prime minister Lothar de Maizière and Foreign Minister Markus Meckel. Their views were akin to Havel's initial position but much more troublesome, in that the East Germans had a seat at the Two Plus Four table. Even late in the Two Plus Four process, Meckel was advancing various uncoordinated initiatives for "pan-European security struc-

tures" and even for a Central European demilitarized zone encompassing Germany, Poland, and Czechoslovakia. Kohl and Genscher naturally took the lead in averting East German divisiveness in the Two Plus
Four setting, resorting to arm-twisting when diplomatic persuasion
failed. Ours was a supporting role: in addition to Secretary Baker's
diplomacy with Meckel, President Bush hosted de Maizière on an official visit to Washington (the first and last such visit by a GDR leader) in
early June. I recall beginning the president's briefing memorandum by
noting that "Lothar de Maizière presides over a government whose
chief function is to negotiate itself out of existence," but adding that he
nonetheless pursued his role with a sense of great responsibility. Bush's
personal diplomacy secured de Maizière's public support for "the continuing vital role of the alliance and of U.S. forces stationed in Europe
as guarantors of stability and security."[104]

Securing Soviet Consent:
"Seven Questions," "Nine Assurances"

By late spring, the essential work of developing a strong international
consensus was complete. If there was to be a skunk at the Two Plus
Four picnic, it would be Moscow alone, with all that implied for the future of German-Soviet relations and the future of Europe if a united and
powerful Germany were cut adrift from its key alliance relationships.
Already Moscow had come a long way toward the view that if unification was inevitable, NATO and the U.S. military presence were important instruments for containing a newly powerful Germany. Gorbachev
and Shevardnadze increasingly came to understand that permanent neutrality was not really an option for a country of Germany's geostrategic
weight. For them, the prospect of a reconstituted German general staff
and German military doctrine, two logical consequences of a Germany
cut adrift from its NATO allies, must have evoked vivid memories.
(Certainly, we missed no opportunity to drive these points home.)

Moscow and the NATO Issue   Yet the prospect of united Germany's remaining in NATO was more than the Soviet leadership was yet prepared
to accept, not just for security reasons but also because of internal political resistance. As Shevardnadze told Baker in late March, unification is
coming "too fast": "We don't want to see a neutral Germany. We want
to see your troops remain. But we have a problem with NATO." The

problem, he continued, was the short-term one of appearances and selling the idea domestically—"It would look like you had won and we had
lost"—and the longer-term problems for Soviet security.[105] Subsequently,
Shevardnadze argued that he and Gorbachev delayed giving consent to
Germany's NATO membership in order to "bring Soviet public opinion
around," exact Western concessions on NATO's transformation, and resolve other Soviet security concerns.[106] There is undoubtedly considerable truth in those assertions, though they have to be weighed against
the element of retrospective rationalization in Shevardnadze's strained,
and not altogether convincing, explanation of why "our starting position
differed substantially from our finishing one."[107]

While signs of a softening of Soviet attitudes were evident as early as
the Malta Summit and Secretary Baker's visit to Moscow in February,
we in Washington also had to reckon with the prospect that Gorbachev
and Shevardnadze, whatever their own predilections, might be unable
to overcome opposition elsewhere in the Soviet establishment. Nor does
the fact that both were probing for ways to deal with the NATO issue
mean that their ultimate acceptance was a foregone conclusion. Certainly, the official statements issued at the time by Gorbachev and Shevardnadze showed little flexibility. In a March 6 interview with West
German television, Gorbachev replied categorically to the question of
united Germany's remaining in NATO: "We will not agree to that. That
is absolutely excluded."[108] Shevardnadze repeated the point during a
visit to Washington in early April: "What is unacceptable to us . . . is
united Germany's remaining in NATO."[109]

At the first Two Plus Four ministerial meeting, held in Bonn on May
5, Shevardnadze's statements reflected the mounting pressures that he
and Gorbachev faced, both externally and internally. The international
community was as united in support of Germany's continued NATO
membership as the Soviet establishment was adamantly against it. In a
very tough speech, Shevardnadze reiterated the conditions first advanced
in his "seven questions" address at the European parliament and proposed, more ominously, that "a decision on the internal and external aspects of German unity should not necessarily coincide in time." "Even
after the creation of a single parliament and government in Germany," he
continued, there would remain in force "over a certain number of years
. . . certain measures related to decisions on external aspects of the settlement."[110] My copy of the speech has this apt marginal notation made at
the time by one of my NSC colleagues: "Unity without Sovereignty!"

This, as we feared, was the new tactical approach: if Soviet security concerns were not addressed by the time of unification, then some form of Four Power supervision should be continued into the indefinite future. It was a recipe for protracted difficulties between a semisovereign Germany and a defeated, embittered Soviet Union. Europe had seen these ingredients in combination once before, had it not? They had contributed, in E. H. Carr's characterization of the period, to the "twenty years' crisis" between the two world wars.[111] It was precisely to avert a latter-day "twenty years' crisis" that we continued to insist that Germany should be fully sovereign from the moment of unification and that legitimate Soviet security concerns should be addressed before that time rather than be projected into an uncertain future.

At the Two Plus Four meeting, Secretary Baker stood fast against Shevardnadze's proposed "decoupling" of the internal and external aspects of German unity, a formula to which Genscher was ready to subscribe until being overruled by Kohl (after a quick Kohl-Bush telephone call). Once again delivering the result we needed, Baker gained agreement that the Two Plus Four process should be limited to external issues arising directly from unification, rather than becoming an open forum for discussion of all manner of extraneous security matters.[112] At the same time, as Shevardnadze later recalled approvingly, Baker stressed that "we must find a solution where there won't be any winners and losers, but where everybody wins."[113]

On the question of NATO membership, Shevardnadze reiterated the Soviet Union's "negative attitude" but also offered an opening: "Both we and you speak about the prospects of transforming the two blocs. [But] when will this happen, and will it happen at all? No guarantees in this regard have yet been developed." As important as his substantive positions were Shevardnadze's several allusions to the internal political pressures that gave rise to them. "Our political flexibility is severely limited," he asserted. "This is a fact of our real life . . . [that] neither the current nor any other Soviet leadership will be able to disregard. . . . The population of our country . . . is uncompromisingly against the idea of including a united Germany in NATO. . . . These are also the sentiments of our Supreme Soviet. We cannot ignore this."

Conflicts over Baltic Independence   In his private conversations with Secretary Baker in Bonn, Shevardnadze distanced himself further from the positions he had taken in the speech, explaining the pressures he and Gorbachev were under from their conservative critics on German policy and the gathering drive for independence among the Baltic states. Indeed, much of their discussion was on the economic embargo Moscow had imposed on Lithuania in response to the latter's recent declaration of independence. Baker sought and received Shevardnadze's assurance that force would not be used, but the secretary also made it clear that concluding a U.S.-Soviet trade agreement (to which the Soviet side attached great importance) by the time of the Washington Summit in late May would be "very difficult" unless there were serious negotiations toward Baltic independence.[114]

The soft U.S. line on the Baltics, for which the president took much criticism, needs to be understood against this backdrop. Our main effort was to press for private assurances that force would not be used against the Baltic states, in the belief that a peaceful process of change would create a new reality of de facto independence that Moscow ultimately would have to recognize. Our public posture, however, was deliberately restrained, in order to give Gorbachev and Shevardnadze the breathing space to find a peaceful, negotiated solution. The question we asked ourselves was not which approach would have been more satisfying rhetorically—a ringing call for "freeing the captive nations" would have made all of us feel better—but which was most likely to achieve the goal of independence for the Baltic states. In the end, the goal was achieved, albeit a year and a half after the Baltic states declared their independence. Even with the benefit of hindsight, it seems doubtful that a more strident (some would say, "more principled") approach would have achieved a quicker or more satisfactory result.

A more serious question is whether Washington and Bonn subordinated the aspirations of the Baltic peoples to German unification. This, certainly, was the view of Lithuanian prime minister Kazimiera Prunskiene during her meetings in early May with President Bush in Washington and Chancellor Kohl in Bonn. As Kohl related in a telephone call to the president after Prunskiene's visit, he took a "brutal" line, telling her that the Lithuanians had done "everything wrong" and risked upsetting all the positive developments in Europe—beginning, of course, with the prospect of German unification.[115] It is no small irony that Prime Minister Thatcher had admonished the Germans, about the same time and in similar terms, for insisting that "German reunification should take priority over everything else" and urged them to put a "longer view of Europe's needs before their more narrow, nationalist goals."[116]

The Germans, then, were probably guilty as charged of placing their unification above Baltic aspirations. So, to some extent, were we, though we tended to see Baltic and German aspirations as part of the same problem of imperial dissolution, both demanding sensitivity to Soviet security concerns and to the delicacy of the Soviet internal situation. As President Bush put it, "I don't want people to look back 20 or 40 years from now and say, 'That's where everything went off track. That's where progress stopped.'"[117]

U.S.-Soviet Relations at Endgame   Here, then, was the context of U.S.-Soviet relations in late spring 1990. Following the February 27 Supreme Soviet vote granting sweeping new presidential powers, Gorbachev and Shevardnadze had unprecedented authority over foreign policy,[118] and both demonstrated openness toward a solution on German unification that would restore Germany's full sovereignty and affirm its continued membership in NATO. To deliver, they needed our help (and Bonn's) in strengthening their hands against conservative critics at home,[119] yet our ability (and willingness) to provide that help was prejudiced by the crackdown in the Baltic states. We therefore aimed to find a way through these cross-pressures in order to secure our objectives for German unification. Additionally, the restricted mandate of the Two Plus Four process (on which we had insisted from the outset) meant that it would be up to U.S. and West German bilateral diplomacy to address some of the many concerns Gorbachev and Shevardnadze had raised.

We had already been working to address legitimate Soviet security concerns. In his State of the Union Address in late January, President Bush had announced a new initiative on CFE (Conventional Armed Forces in Europe), calling for U.S. and Soviet force reductions down to a level of 195,000 each. As with the May 1989 initiative, this was designed to make it easier for Moscow to accept what was being forced on it anyway (by East European calls for Soviet troop withdrawals) and to show that even the prospect of the removal of Soviet forces in the GDR would be accompanied by reciprocal cuts on the American side. (The president was also careful to place a floor on U.S. reductions and to begin "delinking" U.S. and Soviet troop withdrawals, lest the principle of reciprocity be taken to mean that if all Soviet forces eventually left Europe then all U.S. forces should do so as well.)

In a major speech at Oklahoma State University on May 4, President Bush called for an early summit meeting of NATO leaders to undertake a wholesale review of the alliance's military and political missions, proposing also that CSCE be strengthened as a forum for helping to overcome the division of Europe. He also called for accelerated negotiations toward a CFE treaty, to be followed by U.S.-Soviet negotiations on short-range nuclear forces, and announced the unilateral cancellation of the follow-on to the Lance missile (FOTL) and of NATO's nuclear artillery modernization program.[120] These initiatives aimed at a substantially transformed Atlantic alliance—the "transformation of the blocs" that Shevardnadze had called for in Bonn.

During a visit to Moscow two weeks later, Secretary Baker listed these initiatives among what became known, almost biblically, as the "nine assurances" the United States and its Western allies were providing to address legitimate security concerns arising from German unification:

(1) agreements to limit the size of the German armed forces;
(2) commitment to negotiate on short-range nuclear weapons;
(3) reaffirmation of Germany's nonnuclear status;
(4) revisions of NATO strategy to make it less threatening;
(5) a pledge not to deploy NATO forces in the former GDR;
(6) a transitional period for Soviet forces in Germany;
(7) renunciation of any future German territorial claims;
(8) strengthening the CSCE and the Soviet role therein; and
(9) extensive German economic assistance to the USSR.[121]

Coordinating U.S. and West German Approaches As the "nine assurances" involved a combination of U.S., West German, and broader Western initiatives, it was important to establish the closest possible coordination between Bonn and Washington as both sides pursued their bilateral diplomacy with Moscow. Accordingly, a large West German delegation headed by Kohl and Genscher arrived in Washington on May 17 for a general stocktaking and coordination of initiatives toward Moscow as the Two Plus Four process entered its most critical stage. Several events were key: the just-concluded trip to Moscow by Kohl's foreign policy adviser, Horst Teltschik, in which he presented a variety of economic assistance measures; Baker's trip to Moscow; the forthcoming Bush-Gorbachev summit in Washington at the end of the month; and the subsequent NATO summit that the president had called for in his Oklahoma State speech.

The summary I wrote immediately after the meeting is worth ex-
cerpting at some length, in that it captures the sense of the moment and
the tenor of U.S.–West German relations:

> Atmosphere. Couldn't have been better. Kohl particularly, but
> all the Germans, were effusive in their gratitude for U.S. support.
> What a contrast to a year ago, when our mutual trust and confi-
> dence were slipping badly.
> Unification and Two Plus Four. Continuing broad agreement on
> the essentials:
> —Germany should remain a full member of NATO, including par-
> ticipation in its integrated military structure.
> —NATO's security guarantee should apply to all the territory of
> the united Germany. [Germans less explicit than we.]
> —U.S. military forces should remain stationed in the united Ger-
> many and elsewhere in Europe. [Kohl was particularly strong
> on this.]
> —The Two Plus Four talks should terminate Four Power rights
> and responsibilities at the time of unification, with no new con-
> straints on German sovereignty. [Germans seemed more solid on
> this than we might have expected.]
> —Two Plus Four should not decide issues like German member-
> ship in NATO, the status of stationed forces, or the size of the
> Bundeswehr. [Germans agree in principle but not as explicit as
> we.]
> [The Germans want to conclude Two Plus Four before the CSCE
> Summit. We also think that by pressing ahead toward a settle-
> ment, Moscow will find it harder to maintain a position in
> which the USSR alone wants to retain occupation rights after
> unification.]
> Soviet troops in the GDR. The Germans said they could accept
> Soviet forces remaining for a transitional period but only that.
> The President . . . worries that the longer Soviet troops remain,
> the more there will be a perception of "parallelism" with U.S.
> forces. . . .
> Timing of unification. Germans want to finish the job before
> the CSCE Summit. They expect to sign the treaty on economic and
> monetary union next week. Kohl expects a "big noise" when this
> is submitted to the Bundestag.

Helping the Soviet economy. Kohl painted a dark picture of the Soviet economy and was looking for ways we and the Germans could help Gorbachev. . . .

U.S.-Soviet Summit. . . . The Germans particularly wanted the President to present our position on unification and Two Plus Four. Kohl also thought it important that Gorbachev be treated—and be seen to be treated—as an equal. The President agreed. [Kohl is more concerned than we that we do all possible to keep Gorbachev in the saddle.]

NATO Summit. The President reviewed his proposal that the Summit launch a wide-ranging strategy review. . . . There wasn't much discussion, though the Germans fully support the idea. [Genscher made the point that the Soviets were mounting a campaign domestically to remove NATO's "demonic image."]

Despite this close convergence of views, one of our overriding concerns by this time was that Gorbachev or Shevardnadze might come to the Germans with their final offer or, in Washington parlance, their "bottom line." They would say, in effect, "We have said we can accept German unification. We can even accept your remaining in NATO. But you must understand the implications of these developments for our security. . . ." Then would follow the Soviet conditions, which might have included withdrawal of U.S. as well as Soviet forces, removal of all nuclear weapons from Germany, withdrawal of all stationed forces, total demilitarization of GDR territory, or some other mix of Soviet demands. (According to Kohl's security adviser Horst Teltschik in subsequent conversations, the "deal" was never proffered. If such an offer had been made, what would the German answer have been? Teltschik could not say, though he admitted that "some members of the government would have said that we have to accept it. Others would have resisted, but for how long?"[122]) While there was nothing we could do about it directly if Bonn were prepared to accept such a deal, recognition of this danger underscored the importance of our efforts. The United States needed to resolve Soviet security concerns lest Gorbachev and Shevardnadze look to the West Germans for answers.

The Washington Summit　　The Bush-Gorbachev Summit thus emerged as the most important U.S.-Soviet meeting ever held.[123] It was a summit essentially unlike any that had gone before. The issues under discussion went to the root of Cold War conflict: the division of Germany and of Europe, significant reductions in the Soviet military threat to the West, and the transformation of the U.S.-Soviet relationship toward one of genuine cooperation. In this regard, the two presidents' long, informal discussions at Camp David the next to the last day of the summit turned out to be more important than any of the formal White House events or even the agreements that were signed. Yet Gorbachev's preoccupation was with his own deteriorating domestic situation. Boris Yeltsin, now a serious rival, had been elected the day before as parliamentary leader of the Russian republic, and Gorbachev was due to face a restive party congress in early July. For the U.S. side, therefore, the task was both to achieve a breakthrough on the key security issues—arms control as well as Germany—and to help Gorbachev answer his domestic critics. Nor could the two tasks be separated: if Gorbachev did not survive the party congress with his political power intact, whatever other breakthroughs we might have achieved could quickly be reversed. Gorbachev needed a successful summit, and we meant to give him one.

While there were differences within the administration as to how far we should go to give Gorbachev the help he felt he needed, there was general agreement, certainly as far as the president and Secretary Baker were concerned, that we should do what we could to build Gorbachev up for his forthcoming party congress. For Gorbachev and Shevardnadze, the most important result was the signing of a U.S.-Soviet trade agreement, a point to which both kept returning as a crucial symbolic vindication of their foreign policy line. Technically, our pursuit of a trade agreement hinged on Soviet emigration policy and passage of accompanying legislation then pending in the Supreme Soviet. Politically, the issues were Soviet intransigence on Baltic independence and ongoing economic sanctions against Lithuania, points we felt as strongly about as Congress did. Although the Soviet side was not yet in a position to resolve these issues to our satisfaction, the president sought and received Gorbachev's renewed commitment to resolve Baltic independence demands through peaceful dialogue. At Gorbachev's urging, the president reluctantly agreed not to make an explicit link between the trade agreement and Lithuania. Instead, he announced simply that he would sign the trade agreement but would not send it to Congress for approval until the Supreme Soviet passed its emigration law.[124] (Whether a different course would have hastened or hindered Baltic independence is debatable. The president's judgment, for which he knowingly took considerable criticism from the Baltic-American community and others, was that the course he chose to take was the one most likely to secure German unification *and* Baltic independence.)

More than a dozen other separate agreements were signed, including critical ones on nuclear testing, chemical weapons reductions, and especially strategic arms (affirming near-agreement on a START treaty). From the U.S. perspective, however, the most important was an agreement to accelerate negotiations toward a CFE treaty, so as to make sure that agreed military reductions kept pace with and reinforced the breakneck pace of political change. We did not want to approach the final stages of German unification with the question of future agreed force levels in Europe left undetermined, particularly in light of ongoing discussions between Bonn and Moscow on limiting the size of the future German armed forces. With so much in flux, a few fixed points of reference were needed. We therefore attached particular importance to the joint statement in which President Bush and President Gorbachev declared that they considered a CFE agreement "the indispensable foundation" of European security and "committed themselves to intensifying the pace of the negotiations in Vienna and to reaching rapid agreement on all outstanding issues."

On the question of Germany's NATO membership, Gorbachev returned to the idea of united Germany's being simultaneously a member of both NATO and the Warsaw Pact. Recalling President Bush's naval background, he offered the view that "if one anchor is good, two anchors are better." Yet it was clear that he was still casting about for a solution.[125] Ultimately, by shifting the logic of the discussion from outcome to process, the president gained Gorbachev's reluctant agreement that sovereign states should be accorded the right to choose their own alliance relationships. Thus, with Soviet consent, we were able to insert the following key passage into the president's public statement at the close of the summit: "President Gorbachev and I . . . are in full agreement that the matter of alliance membership is, in accordance with the Helsinki Final Act, a matter for the Germans to decide."[126] It was a major breakthrough.

Equally important, discussion of the issue was framed in the right way—not on NATO membership per se, but on the broader questions of what kind of Europe was emerging, with what kind of security structures and what kind of roles for the United States and the Soviet Union.

While this was precisely what we had been working for many months to achieve, it also placed the burden squarely on our shoulders to demonstrate that NATO was indeed transforming itself in ways that Moscow should find reassuring. It was a point that was reinforced a few days later at a CSCE foreign ministers' meeting in Copenhagen, where Shevardnadze told Baker privately that the Soviet Union could accept united Germany's membership in NATO if the "nine assurances" could be codified.[127]

Our first opportunity came immediately thereafter, at a meeting of NATO foreign ministers in Turnberry, Scotland, on June 7 and 8. In his speech on the first day of the meeting, Secretary Baker called on NATO "to accelerate the alliance's ongoing process of reassessment and renewal" and to "look beyond the narrower task of preventing war to the broader one of building the peace."[128] That evening, in one of those surreal experiences of this period in which all the old rules were changing, several of us were called away from dinner to draft a response to a communiqué just issued by Warsaw Pact foreign ministers (then meeting in Moscow), who had declared an end to hostility between the two alliances. Accordingly, the 16 delegations prepared a "Message from Turnberry" in which NATO "extend[ed] to the Soviet Union and to all other European countries the hand of friendship and cooperation." The main communiqué was pretty thin gruel, however.[129] It called on the alliance to "adapt . . . to the enormous changes now taking place" and endorsed the initiatives in President Bush's Oklahoma State speech. Owing partly to the reluctance of Prime Minister Thatcher (who, as host, opened the meeting) to countenance any weakening of nuclear deterrence policy, it offered nothing further of substance as regards the promised "wide-ranging strategic review."

It was therefore up to the United States to lead NATO in a substantially new direction and to articulate a new common vision by the time of the London Summit, now less than a month away. The pivotal importance of this summit was underscored at the second Two Plus Four foreign ministers' meeting, held in Berlin on June 22. Although less strident than in the first meeting, Shevardnadze's official position had not moved much. He called for a five-year transitional period during which the Four Powers would continue to oversee semisovereign Germany and would reciprocally reduce their forces stationed there down to no more than "token contingents." During this transition, Germany would remain simultaneously bound—doubly anchored, as it were—to NATO and the Warsaw Pact. Secretary Baker and British foreign secretary Hurd forcefully rejected these proposals, which Shevardnadze himself disavowed in his private discussions with Baker. Explaining that his presentation was a "Politburo document" that had been forced on him and Gorbachev, Shevardnadze made it plain that their ability to prevail depended on the outcome of the NATO Summit.[130]

The London Summit: A Transformed NATO It is not often that policymakers—or historians, for that matter—can trace the lines of policy from conception through execution to demonstrable impact. The "London Declaration on a Transformed North Atlantic Alliance" was one such case. The NSC staff took the lead in drafting, coordinating (i.e., with the Departments of State and Defense), and gaining the president's approval for a bold, plain-language text, which was then passed via presidential message to allied leaders and revised on the basis of their comments. At the London Summit, allied leaders approved a final version, identical in most respects to our original text though somewhat diluted, which Secretary Baker sent in advance draft form to Shevardnadze while the Soviet party congress was in session. Aboard Air Force One en route back from London, the president also sent Gorbachev a message highlighting the ways the declaration addressed Soviet concerns. Thus when the declaration was released in London, Gorbachev and Shevardnadze were able to react promptly and positively before hard-line critics were able to weigh in. Both later stressed publicly as well as privately that the London Declaration was critical to their acceptance of German unity within the alliance and to their ability to override domestic political opposition.[131]

The declaration pointed to a transformed alliance in four main areas. First, it set as its new political mission the development of cooperation and partnership with former adversaries. The alliance pledged never to be the first to use force, proposed a nonaggression pact with members of the Warsaw Pact, and invited those governments to establish diplomatic liaison missions at NATO headquarters in Brussels. Second, it called for changing the character of conventional defense by moving away from the doctrine of "forward defense" and relying increasingly on more mobile, truly multinational forces. The summit also proposed follow-on conventional arms control negotiations (after the conclusion of a CFE treaty) to further limit offensive military forces in Europe. Third, it announced a new NATO nuclear strategy, modifying "flexible response" to reduce reliance on nuclear weapons and "making nuclear forces truly weapons of last resort." Fourth, it proposed strengthening the CSCE process by giving it a new mandate to promote democratic institutions, operational capacity in the area of conflict prevention, and, for the first time, institutional expression through a new secretariat and other bodies.[132]

Agreement on these proposals came through a combination of compromise and duress, both within our own government and among the allies. "Institutionalizing" the CSCE process was anathema to some in Washington who feared that the organization would eventually undermine NATO or felt that the CSCE, because of its diverse membership and rigid procedures, was inherently incapable of playing a real security role. The modification of "flexible response" was adopted over the strenuous objections of Prime Minister Thatcher, who insisted that the "last resort" formulation be preceded by the statement that there are "no circumstances in which nuclear retaliation to military action might be discounted."[133] The French, always the most problematic, opposed any expansion of NATO's role eastward and objected, with some justification, to launching the "new" NATO via the old pattern of having a "made in USA" draft thrust on them at the last moment. (We paid a price for our heavy-handedness, in the form of hardening French attitudes toward the alliance and what they saw as continued, unalterable American dominance of the organization. Yet this aggressive approach was perhaps the only one that could have produced the desired result at the London Summit, which had to go beyond the usual mush that comes from communiqués drafted by committee.)

When one rereads the London Declaration some years after the fact, the document seems much less dramatic than it was at the time.[134] It went about as far as allied leaders were prepared to go, but not far enough in preparing NATO for a radically different role in a Europe undergoing revolutionary change. Indeed, early in the drafting stage, we played around at staff level with proposing that NATO's name be changed—to "Euro-Atlantic Treaty Organization" or some such—to mark a symbolic break with the past and underscore the alliance's intent to transform itself fundamentally. Although this controversial idea never made it beyond the level of informal discussions, mainly at staff level, it was emblematic of our recognition, even at that early stage, that NATO's survival would require a far more wrenching adjustment than anything envisioned in the London Declaration.[135] Still, the declaration was bold enough to enable the alliance to stay a step ahead of the enormous changes then unfolding. And it was forthcoming enough to pass the immediate test, which was to satisfy Soviet concerns sufficiently to pave the way for agreement for a united Germany within the alliance. Together with the Washington Summit and the U.S.-Soviet trade agreement, the London Summit helped Gorbachev to emerge from his party congress with his political authority intact. Moreover, these measures provided the essential backdrop for the dramatic meeting in the Caucasus between Kohl and Gorbachev.

Two Plus Four Adds Up to One Germany

Since the first Two Plus Four ministerial (held in Bonn on May 5), the West Germans had been working virtually nonstop to address Soviet security concerns and extend emergency economic assistance. As this part of the story has been recounted by German officials who were directly involved, its key elements can be reviewed in telegraphic form here. In mid-May, following a visit to Moscow by the chancellor's security adviser, Horst Teltschik, Bonn offered to assume all East German economic obligations to the USSR and to extend the country a $3 billion credit as part of a package of agreements linked to German unity. Meanwhile, in four separate meetings with Shevardnadze in May and June, Genscher offered compensation for the costs of maintaining Soviet forces in Germany during a transitional period. He also sought to answer Soviet demands for limitations on the future level of the German armed forces, assurances on the military status of GDR territory, and renunciation by Germany of weapons of mass destruction. With these issues close to resolution, Chancellor Kohl traveled to the Soviet Union in mid-July for meetings with President Gorbachev in Moscow and then at Gorbachev's home near Stavropol in the Caucasus.

"V-E Day II": Agreement in the Caucasus　While expecting further progress during the visit, neither we nor the Germans dared hope that the result would be as stunning as it was. By the end of the visit on July 16, the two sides had reached agreement on all major issues. Germany would remain in NATO, with Four Power rights terminated at the time of unification. Soviet forces would remain for a transitional period of three to four years, during which time NATO structures would not be extended into GDR territory. United Germany would renounce produc-

tion or possession of nuclear, biological, and chemical weapons and would reduce its military forces to a level of 370,000.

Some journalists termed it "Stavrapallo," combining Stavropol and Rapallo (site of the signing of a separate peace treaty between Germany and the USSR in 1923) and implying that it was another bilateral deal struck over the heads of other powers. Given the intensity of the coordination between Bonn and Washington, this was hardly our view. At the NSC, not normally known for its party-like atmosphere, we celebrated over champagne (agreeing that German *sekt* would have been better). In private, we termed July 16, 1990, "V-E Day II," signifying the belated liberation of the continent, nearly two generations after the Allied victory in Europe in 1945.

From that point on, the terms of German unification were effectively set. The third Two Plus Four foreign ministers' meeting, held in Paris the day after the agreement in the Caucasus, reached agreement on the Polish-German border and on an outline of a final agreement on German unification. To be sure, there were a vast number of issues still to be resolved and substantive disagreements still to be overcome. At a "One Plus Three" political directors' meeting I attended in London in August, we listed some 25 separate issues, many of them complex and contentious, that needed to be resolved—in just over a month—in order for German unification to be finalized. Yet the main political battles had been won. The rest was anticlimax.

NATO's future role in East Germany was the last significant unresolved issue when the Two Plus Four political directors met in Moscow in early September to agree on a treaty text. That the GDR should have "special status" had been agreed on long since.[136] Yet the Soviet side insisted that, even after the withdrawal of their forces from GDR territory, non-German forces could neither be stationed nor "deployed" in that territory. So, for a time, did the Germans, tabling language that allied forces "shall not cross a line" into this territory except for access to Berlin.[137] Even after the Germans backed away from this formulation, important questions remained. Could NATO forces conduct maneuvers in eastern Germany? Could they discharge their treaty responsibilities in the event (however remote or unlikely it may have seemed at the time) of some future military threat to Germany? Would, in other words, Germany be partly in NATO and partly not?

Ultimately, these concerns were resolved by the device of an "Agreed Minute" to the treaty, stipulating that "any questions with respect to the application of the word 'deployed' . . . will be decided by the Government of the united Germany in a reasonable and responsible way."[138] It was a remarkable formulation and indeed may have constituted a unique case in international law, whereby the interpretation of an element of a multilateral treaty is left solely to the discretion of one signatory. Equally remarkable was that the Soviet side, in what can only have been an oversight by their negotiating team, agreed to this blanket formulation in the following article (Article 6): "The right of the united Germany to belong to alliances, with all the rights and responsibilities arising therefrom, shall not be affected by the present Treaty." As we read the two formulations, NATO's role in Germany was undiluted, and Germany would freely render a decision when questions arose. We could hardly ask for more than that. With that issue behind us, the way was clear for agreement.

"The Treaty on the Final Settlement with Respect to Germany" was signed by the Two Plus Four foreign ministers in Moscow on September 12.[139] German unification was formally consummated on October 3, welcomed by President Bush during his visit to the united Germany November 18, and blessed by the 34 members of the CSCE at the Paris Summit from November 19 to 21. What had seemed a remote aspiration scarcely a year before had become reality.

Final Reflections on the "Final Settlement"   The American role in helping secure German unification surely will be recorded as one of the most successful diplomatic endeavors in the history of American statecraft. Nearly all our main goals were achieved. Germany was united "in peace and freedom," enjoying full sovereignty from the moment of unification. It remained a full member of the North Atlantic alliance and an active proponent of a more united Europe. German unification was endorsed by all of Europe, including the Soviet Union, and, in the end, was genuinely welcomed by most. It was achieved within the context of an emergent democratic order in Europe and the transformation of its key institutions. The United States remained in Europe as a factor of stability, its continued political, economic, and military presence not only tolerated but actively encouraged. Our successes were attributable to a coherent strategy and to the single-mindedness with which we pursued our objectives, even when the chances of fulfilling them seemed remote. They were attributable also to President Bush's statesmanship and political judgment, Secretary Baker's skills as strategist and negotiator, and the close coordination between the National Security Council staff and the Department of State, as well as between Washington and Bonn.

Our broader objective of embedding German unification within a stable new European order proved more elusive. Given the revolutionary flux in the East and the imminent disintegration of the Soviet Union itself, this goal may well have been unattainable. Still, with the benefit of a few years' hindsight, some questions persist. First, was Prime Minister Thatcher really so wrong in protesting that the rush to unity was threatening the future of European security? Did the priority we attached to the unification process cause us to neglect other objectives that would have helped "synchronize" Germany's unification with Europe's? Second, did our cooperation with Bonn during this period establish, as we hoped it would, the United States and Germany as "partners in leadership"? Were we right in seeing the U.S.-German relationship at the center of a future European and transatlantic order, and did we succeed in laying the foundations of future partnership? Had we, finally, helped achieve German unity without answering the German question? It is obviously far too early to pass historical judgment on these issues, but a few preliminary thoughts can be ventured.

As to the speed of the process, our assumption (and Bonn's) that we needed to move rapidly, while we still had a Soviet leadership able and disposed to compromise, seemed less compelling after the breakup of the Soviet Union and the advent of Boris Yeltsin's government in Russia. Perhaps we did not need to work so feverishly to "get the hay in the barn before the storm comes," as Chancellor Kohl put it, or set German unification so far above other objectives, such as supporting the democratic transformation of Central and Eastern Europe. Yet we did not have the opportunity in 1990 to turn the clock forward to see what the next few years would hold in store. (Nor, of course, would there have been any guarantee that this putative "future" would have been the same had we not acted as we did.) Moreover, while a more measured, step-by-step pace of German unification might have been preferable for the sake of future stability, the virtual implosion of the GDR made this option elusive and perhaps unattainable. It is not clear that the East German state could have been propped up even if all concerned had sought to do so. Even if inter-German rapprochement had been pursued via the stages envisioned in Kohl's ten points, the reality would have been very rapid merger, whether labeled "confederation," "treaty-based association," or something else.

As to the future U.S.-German relationship, "partners in leadership" may have set an unrealistically high standard, which not even our close cooperation during unification could fulfill. Some in Washington presumed that German "gratitude" for U.S. support would translate into political capital. They were soon, and predictably, disappointed, notably by Germany's failure to act decisively in resolving U.S.-EC disputes over the Uruguay Round of the GATT (General Agreement on Tariffs and Trade).[140] We should not have expected gratitude for actions that were in our interests as well, nor should we have sought to build a new relationship on this transitory sentiment. Many of us also tended to extrapolate from the unification period an exaggerated convergence of U.S. and German interests and, by the same token, to underestimate the extent to which the "partners" concept collided with Germany's relations with its EC partners, especially France. Indeed, when German president von Weizsäcker later paid a state visit to the United States, President Bush sought to answer these concerns: "A united Germany, champion of a more united Europe, stands as our partner in leadership. . . . Strong German-American cooperation is fully compatible with development of a more united Europe, a goal that the United States has consistently supported over the years, just as unequivocally as we supported German unity."[141]

While "partners in leadership" led to extravagant expectations springing from our close cooperation in 1989 and 1990, its initial conception was not based on a sentimental or naive view of future U.S.-German relations. It proceeded from our anticipation of the emerging reality in pre- and postunification Europe and our recognition that U.S.-German relations would be key to realization of important U.S. interests in Europe and beyond. The relationship that came out of the unification period was a sound one, built on the foundation of successful cooperation toward shared goals. Yet just as that cooperation was the product of a complex and sometimes difficult process of mutual adjustment during unification, its extension into the new era could not simply be assumed.

The German question was never about unity alone but about fitting a powerful Germany into a stable and secure European order. In 1990, the question was not so much about Germany but about the European order into which it needed to fit. Germany's democracy and its European and Atlantic credentials were no longer in doubt, but the country's moment of unification occurred in the midst of profound turbulence that could only complicate its settling into a stable new role. Within the European Community, unification had been accompanied by renewed commitment on the part of Germany and its partners to economic and political union and to the realization of the Community's early vision of a broader unity that spanned the continent. The Atlantic alliance, again with Germany's strong support, had undertaken a process of renewal, also aimed at helping overcome Europe's division. Whether these efforts would succeed hinged on the progress of postcommunist transformation in the East and the gradual integration of these emerging (or aspiring) democracies into a broader democratic community.

The German question, in short, was still open, but this time it was not the fault of the Germans. Linked as always to the European question, it was in any case not amenable to final and definitive resolution. For this historical moment, the answer to the German question had to be found within a still-elusive post–Cold War European order.

4

Toward a Post–Cold War Order

WHEN PRESIDENTS and prime ministers from all of Europe and North America convened in Paris in November 1990, it was a moment of triumph for the principles and values that had animated Western policies for four decades and more. In the glowering presence of Soviet defense minister Dimitri Yazov, a symbol of an era now drawing to a merciful conclusion, the Paris Summit codified the decisive end of the Cold War and of Europe's long division. (When Hungarian Prime Minister József Antall delivered a speech calling for the dissolution of the Warsaw Pact, I happened to be sitting behind Antall and directly across the table from Yazov. The latter's look of now-impotent malevolence seemed as good a symbol as any of the passing of the old order.[1]) Its stunning achievements would have been hardly imaginable a year before: acknowledgement of German unification, conclusion of an agreement for deep military reductions, issuance of a joint declaration of friendship between members of NATO and the soon to be defunct Warsaw Pact, and publication of a "Charter of Paris" heralding a new era of European peace and comity.

Yet the triumphalism of the Paris Summit was already being overshadowed by the sober realities of the post–Cold War world: the Iraqi invasion of Kuwait in August 1990, the looming crisis in Yugoslavia, and the growing fragmentation of the Soviet Union. These were but the most egregious portents of a wider instability. There were fears of resurgent German power, of failed democratic experiments in Eastern Europe, of revived national conflicts and border disputes, all arising outside the confines of the known bipolar system, without the galvanizing element of a common threat.

The end of the Cold War, it seemed, was also the end of the "long peace" in which nuclear deterrence had inhibited conventional war as well.[2] And the institutions and policies of the bygone era were showing themselves inadequate for the one now upon us. As Macauley had written in a different context, "The revolution [eliminated] one class of evils, but had at the same time—such is the imperfection of all things human—engendered or aggravated another class of evils which required new remedies."[3] Among these were the tasks of transforming Western institutions to meet radically new challenges, building a new order in which the Soviet Union and the states of Eastern Europe would find a secure place, and dealing with new threats to European security arising from the ashes of communist rule.

Even more fundamental was the task of democratic consolidation in the East, without which no amount of "architectural" innovation or conflict resolution mechanisms among European institutions would have any prospect of success. Democratic development in Central and Eastern Europe, then, was preeminently a security issue. More than that, it was *the* preeminent security issue for post–Cold War Europe. It was a challenge for which Western policies and institutions were ill-prepared. Indeed, the daunting tasks of postcommunist transition served as a reminder that the end of the Cold War had reopened the *Eastern question* that had preoccupied Europe at Yalta, Versailles, and the Congress of Vienna.[4]

If averting another Versailles-like German settlement had been an urgent priority of the diplomacy of German unification, so too was preventing the emergence of a latter-day Weimar Republic, this time in the form of an embittered, defeated Soviet Union. We did not want Russia any more than Germany to be "singularized" or isolated in the emerging order. Thus, the strenuous efforts to address Soviet security concerns during 1990 had been aimed not only at facilitating German unification but also at creating conditions that would permit the Soviet Union to assume a strong and secure place in the international community. In form as well as substance, these measures sought to build a pattern of relations that would carry over to a post–Cold War world of concerted action among former adversaries. The losers had to have a stake in preserving the settlement, just as the winners needed to find ways of sustaining their cooperation into the new era. As one writer put it, "The diplomacy that preceded unification was reminiscent of concert diplomacy in the nineteenth century except that the big powers [were] no longer the sole arbiters of Europe's fate. The principle [was] the same: concerted policies are likely to protect the interests of each state better than unilateral action."[5]

The "New World Order"

Elements of this conception were to be found in the efforts to articulate and shape a "new world order." The concept, it must be admitted, failed to persuade, partly because the term betrayed an unfortunate American proclivity toward universalism and grandiosity. Then there was the "Holy Roman Empire" analogy of seeming to its critics to be none of the three—in this case, neither new in concept, worldwide in application, nor orderly in practice. Outside the European context, particularly in the Middle East, the term suffered from what was seen as an incongruity between principles and interests. Was it high principle that led us to oppose the Iraqi invasion of Kuwait, or was it oil? The obvious answer—that it was both, along with regional stability and weapons of mass destruction—never satisfied the domestic need for moral clarity, so the term took on the crusading rhetoric of a "Pax Americana" that was never intended. And it was held to the impossibly high standard that its principles should find universal adherence and the order it promised guarantee perpetual peace.

Although the concept later acquired ambitious theoretical and institutional trappings, the "new world order" proceeded from a simple idea. President Bush and General Scowcroft were fishing off the Bush compound in Kennebunkport, Maine, in August 1990, just after Secretary Baker and Foreign Minister Shevardnadze had issued a joint condemnation of the Iraqi invasion of Kuwait and shortly before Bush and Gorbachev were to meet in Helsinki to issue a similar joint statement. If the United States and the Soviet Union could find common cause in opposing aggression waged by a longstanding Soviet client state, Bush and Scowcroft thought, then perhaps there were opportunities to translate the successes in Europe into a framework of global cooperation in which the United States and its traditional allies were joined by the Soviet Union itself. This was the foundation of the concept: not an aggrandized United Nations or a U.S.-Soviet strategic partnership but rather the pragmatic notion that the Soviet Union might now become an active contributor to the resolution of global problems, particularly in cases of international aggression. This, indeed, had been embedded in Bush's thinking from the time of the Texas A&M speech in May 1989,[6] but the events of the intervening 16 months had made the aspiration newly vivid.

Conceptually, the "new world order" deserved closer study than it received. Its principles were drawn from the most basic American values and interests—democracy, free markets, the rule of law—which were also to be found in the United Nations Charter and the Helsinki Final Act.[7] It combined the realist's appreciation of the permanence of the power factor in world affairs with the liberal internationalist's recognition that democracies make better partners than dictatorships in building a secure order.[8] It offered a reasonable structure, with the Western allies at the core of an expanding democratic community, facilitating the gradual development of a modern version of the nineteenth-century concert system in which the major powers calibrated and coordinated their actions with due consideration for the interests of all.[9] It looked to a revitalized United Nations and other institutions, such as a strengthened CSCE, to legitimate and facilitate common action. It called on a secure, prosperous, and more united Europe, in which the new democracies of the East joined our traditional allies, to assume new responsibilities as our main partners in global leadership. In this sense, it was meant to be both a challenge to Europe and a point of reference for the American public in the post–Cold War world.

The "new world order" was articulated first in September 1990. Bush and Gorbachev had just met in Helsinki, where the two leaders issued a joint statement insisting that "Iraq's aggression must not be tolerated. No peaceful international order is possible if larger states can devour their smaller neighbors." Using this as his point of departure, the president invoked the prospect of a new world order in a September 11 address before a joint session of Congress:

> We stand today at a unique and extraordinary moment. The crisis in the Persian Gulf, grave as it is, also offers a rare opportunity to move toward a historic period of cooperation. Out of these troubled times . . . a new world order can emerge . . . , a world where the rule of law supplants the law of the jungle, a world in which nations recognize the shared responsibility for freedom and justice, a world where the strong respect the rights of the weak.
>
> This is the vision that I shared with President Gorbachev in Helsinki. He and other leaders from Europe, the Gulf, and around

the world understand that how we manage this crisis could shape the future for generations to come. The test we face is great—and so are its stakes. This is the first assault on the new world that we seek, the first test of our mettle.

America and the world must defend common vital interests. . . . Vital issues of principle are at stake. Saddam Hussein is literally trying to wipe a country off the face of the earth. . . . Vital economic interests are at stake as well. . . . An Iraq permitted to swallow Kuwait would have the economic and military power . . . to intimidate and coerce [neighboring countries] that control the lion's share of the world's remaining oil reserves. We cannot permit a resource so vital to be dominated by one so ruthless. . . . Iraq will not be permitted to annex Kuwait. That is not a threat; that is not a boast; that is just the way it is going to be.[10]

The concept fared best when extrapolated from the European context, as in the president's November 1990 Prague speech, which made explicit the goal of seeking to replicate on a global scale that which was already being approximated in Europe. The speech was meant to weave into a coherent whole several disparate strands: the realization of a Europe "whole and free," in the context of the president's visit to Czechoslovakia and then to united Germany en route to the Paris Summit as well as the threats to this new order posed by the Iraqi invasion of Kuwait and the gathering Yugoslav crisis. (As will be seen, we had wanted to make Yugoslavia a major theme at Paris, but found little support or interest in Europe for a topic that might put a damper on the festivities.[11]) The president's speech was at once a celebration, a challenge, and a warning:

Europe, east and west, stands at a threshold of a new era—an era of peace, prosperity, and security unparalleled in the long history of this continent. Today, Europe's long division is ending. . . . Working together, we can fulfill the promise of a Europe that reaches its democratic destiny—a Europe that is truly whole and free. . . .

Europe's celebration of freedom brings with it a new responsibility. Now that democracy has proven its power, Europe has both the opportunity and the challenge to join us in leadership—to work with us in common cause toward a new commonwealth of freedom . . . , a moral community united in its dedication to free ideals . . . , a world in which the use of force gives way to a shared respect for the rule of law. . . . That is why our response to the challenge in the Persian Gulf is critical. [It] is a warning to America as well as to Europe that we cannot turn inward, somehow isolate ourselves from global challenges. . . .

More and more, the Soviet Union is demonstrating its commitment to act as a constructive force for international stability. More and more, the United Nations is functioning as its creators intended—free from the ideological confrontation that frustrated collective action. . . . From this first crisis of the post–Cold War era comes an historic opportunity . . . to draw upon the great and growing strength of the commonwealth of freedom and forge for all nations a new world order far more stable and secure than any we have known.[12]

It was a complex set of ideas—too complicated for a twenty-minute speech. Perhaps the most difficult was the linkage between democracy and international relations. Those of us who were developing the idea of a "new world order" did not require or expect that all states be democratic, nor did we assume that a world of democracies was the answer to all the ills of humankind. Rather, the concept rested on the proposition that democratic principles observed *within* states could inform an order *among* states which could, over time, induce more states to adhere internally to these broader norms. As more countries embraced the principles, the international order would gain strength, which in turn would encourage yet more states to adapt domestically to principles they might otherwise flout. And so on, in a happy Wilsonian virtuous cycle.

This might seem implausibly idealistic coming from practical men like Bush, Baker, Cheney, and Scowcroft. But this progression approximated what had just happened in Europe, as the principles undergirding the Western democracies established, via CSCE and elsewhere, international norms to which the communist regimes of the East ultimately succumbed. As more states embraced democratic values, the international community was able to strengthen and elaborate a set of international principles based on human rights, democratic values, free market economies, and the rule of law. Expanded to the global scale, the "new world order" thus conceived did not require that every state be democratic but only that democratic norms increasingly inform an international order. (The logical extension of this in the Middle East would have had the Saudi monarchy ultimately yielding to pressures for democratic change or at least toward greater political participation for its citizens, but we could not very well say that—another reason that the concept seemed so cynical in application.)

The problems with the "new world order" were several. Most obviously, it was caught up in the euphoria of a unique moment of democratic ascendancy in the wake of the Cold War, in which it was all too easy to mistake the transitory for the permanent. It was hard to resist the Wilsonian temptation to believe that the principles themselves were so compelling that no one dared flout them. Those who did—like the Serbian leadership—were branded outlaws from this new order, as if that would move them to alter their behavior.[13] It was also a state-centered approach that may have been useful for addressing clear cases of military aggression like the Iraqi invasion of Kuwait, but which had no answer to conflicts springing from impoverishment, civil disorder, or ethnic nationalism. The concept was focused on international aggression, the predominant threat to the international order but by no means the only source of conflict. The Wilsonian panoply of policies—moral suasion, economic sanctions, and, as a last resort, military force in the name of collective security—were hard enough to invoke against sovereign states. They had little or no utility when directed against parties to a civil war.

In the final analysis, however, the deficiencies of the "new world order" were not so much conceptual as political: the term involved not just the articulation of a set of principles but a statement about American readiness to defend an "order" whose contours were only beginning to make themselves apparent and a set of interests that remained elusive. It demanded a domestic political constituency that had yet to be molded—a challenge that the administration never took seriously enough. Thus, when it came to assuming new burdens, the "new world order" conflicted with public expectations of a handsome post–Cold War "peace dividend" that would enable us to eschew foreign commitments and focus on pressing needs at home. Nor was the United States alone in groping for its role and purposes in the new era: our major partners and especially our former adversaries faced even greater uncertainties, which made calculations of a new order premature at best.

Competing Visions of the New Europe

Political leaders are animated as much by their visions of the future—
intellectual constructs about the desired or assumed future state of affairs—as by dispassionate analysis of present and likely future trends. In
short, visions matter, and they can be impervious to inconvenient realities. If the American administration was moved by thoughts of a new
transatlantic partnership as the foundation of an emergent global order,
politicians in Paris, Brussels, and elsewhere were equally bent on seizing
the moment to create a more united, post-Yalta Europe that ended the
continent's dependency on American power. Others wanted to scrap existing institutions and create out of whole cloth a new post–Cold War
European order. Indeed, although political commentators decried the
lack of "vision" on the part of statesmen on both sides of the Atlantic,
the problem was not a dearth of new ideas but a surfeit of competing,
unreconciled visions. At least four distinct conceptions, with overlapping adherents, were evident at the time of the Paris Summit.

First was the Atlanticist vision, advocated most forcefully by the
United States and Great Britain, of a permanent American political and
military presence in Europe and a seamless transatlantic security community, albeit with a new balance of U.S. and European roles to accommodate an increasingly assertive European Community. U.S. power, in
this conception, was required to balance continuing, if diminishing, Soviet military preponderance, serve as a counterweight to a newly powerful Germany, and lend a general stability. Its adherents saw the world as
still a dangerous place, in which the requirement for traditional military
security was reduced but still substantial. NATO, as the institutional expression of this vision, was required to continue performing its traditional functions as well as help fill the security vacuum developing in
the East as Soviet power receded and the Warsaw Pact collapsed.

Second was the Europeanist vision, championed by the French and
"Brussels" (meaning the burgeoning EC bureaucracy there, in Strasbourg, and elsewhere), of a more united, cohesive European Community,
moving resolutely to build economic and political union among the
twelve member countries even as it widened its scope to accept new
members. Advocates of this vision presumed and desired a continuing but
gradually diminishing American role during a transitional period until
"Europe" had developed the capacity to assume full responsibility for its
own security. Security, in this conception, was defined less as a traditional

military concern but rather in terms of economic interaction, common values, and shared history and tradition. As these were more relevant than NATO's military might to the problems of the eastern half of the continent, it was argued, the European Community had the responsibility to take the lead in ending the division of Europe and realize the initial vision of Jean Monnet and Robert Schuman of a fully united Europe.

Third was the "Vancouver-to-Vladivostok" vision of a pan-European, CSCE-based security community, advocated with differing motivations by the Russians, Czechoslovaks, and others. They foresaw the CSCE supplanting both NATO and the Warsaw Pact and developing new institutions and capacities for collective action. Cooperative security was their watchword. The CSCE, it was argued, was an inclusive institution embracing all of Europe and North America and hence was uniquely suited to bring together former Cold War adversaries. In the most ambitious conception, the CSCE was to become the institutional expression of a "pan-European peace order" that would impel Europe toward perpetual peace and harmony. Even the more limited conception of the CSCE as a forum for political consultation and an umbrella over existing institutions was burdened with the usual problems of collective security arrangements. The most demanding requirement was that states find common purpose and undertake joint action against threats, wherever they might arise, to the stability and integrity of the system—in this case a region encompassing Europe, Eurasia, and North America. "Indivisible security"—a concept that German politicians in particular liked to invoke—meant that every state's security was linked to the security of all others. It was an assumption likely to be proven false the first time it was tested.

Fourth was a "Europe of the States," a vision embraced openly only by Prime Minister Thatcher but shared privately or even unknowingly by many others, not least the French. It was, in fact, a neo-Gaullist conception, which gave primacy to preserving national sovereignty and thus favored bilateral relations and traditional diplomacy. (In her memoirs, Thatcher concluded with her familiar injunction "to shift the emphasis in Europe back toward the original Gaullist idea of a *Europe des Patries*."[14]) Existing multilateral institutions like NATO, the EC, and the CSCE would continue to function and could even take on new responsibilities—but strictly in the service of their sovereign member states. Although conceptually the least ambitious of the four visions, it was as a practical matter nearly as demanding as the others, placing the major powers at the center of a latter-day concert system, whereby each would calibrate its policies and actions in service of the broader international order.

Few of the 34 delegations represented at Paris would have accepted this four-way division of their various aspirations for the future, and fewer still would have recognized how contradictory they were. Indeed, judging from the interminable speeches delivered by every head of state or government,[15] nearly everyone subscribed to the first three combined. The Germans in particular saw no difficulty in adhering equally to the first three—and, privately, to the fourth as well. German diplomats had a slogan, usually dialectical, to reconcile every contradiction and, as a political matter, to avoid taking sides on contentious issues at the moment of their national reunification.

Yet the differences among these visions were profound—and ultimately irreconcilable. There were differences of geography. "The French Europe," as a Danish writer put it, "is necessarily *Western* Europe," with Eastern Europe entering this picture not as an integral part but "as the *mission,* as the *task* for Western Europe."[16] The Atlanticist vision, by contrast, saw the western borders of "Europe" extending across the ocean and so was in theory, though not always in practice, more open to its eastward extension as well. If the United States described itself as a "European power," as we did, we could hardly quibble about the "Europeanness" of countries east of the old Cold War divide. In this, "Atlantic Europe" found an echo in Gorbachev's increasingly desperate plea for a "common European home" that would avert Soviet Russia's exclusion and marginalization. The new democracies of Central and Eastern Europe harbored similar fears but proffered different remedies: Europe's western boundary should stretch across the Atlantic to cement a Euro-Atlantic community, but "Europe" should stop at their eastern frontier. They would be in; Soviet Russia would be out. The notion of "Central Europe" also came to be used as a way of defining geographically who should be in and who out of the new Europe. The Bulgarians in particular resented the exclusivity of the Visegrád club (discussed below), which they saw as a device to ensure their marginalization.

There were different assumptions about the role of the state. For the French (and "Brussels"), the centralized state was to be replicated at the level of Europe, and intrusive, supranational institutions would wrest sovereignty from constituent states. The British, voicing what many others privately endorsed, insisted that sovereignty be retained by states, whose cooperation would be intergovernmental rather than supranational. Common policies would be the sum total of what member states agreed to undertake—nothing more, nothing less. The Germans, and to some extent their eastern neighbors, aspired to a "Europe where borders have lost their meaning"—which they saw as a consequence not of European federalism but of increasing economic, social, and cultural interaction beneath the level of formal political structures.[17] Although the French and German positions sometimes sounded alike when uttered in the argot of EC diplomacy (known irreverently as "Eurospeak"), the conceptual and practical differences between the two perspectives—between French supranationalism and German subnationalism—were vastly greater than either side saw fit to admit.

There were of course different institutional preferences. For the French, the European Community was at the center. For the United States and Britain, it was NATO. The Germans, as usual, wanted both; yet there were internal divisions between Kohl, who wanted both equally, and the foreign ministry, which gave priority to the EC. The Russians favored the CSCE, for the simple reason that they had a seat at the table. The Central and Eastern Europeans wanted to join both NATO and the EC—meaning that their support was genuine but qualified by the prospect of their admission—and, in the interim, placed a high premium on the CSCE for the same reason as the Russians. And there were differences among the Central Europeans: the Poles were the most ardent Atlanticists, because their historic concerns about German and Russian power could be met only through NATO, while the Hungarians, despite the genuine Atlanticism of their prime minister, focused more on the EC owing to their lesser concerns about Russia and Germany.

The coexistence of so many differing perspectives was an inevitable and in some ways a healthy consequence of the precipitous collapse of the old order. A degree of experimentation was necessary in the transitional period toward an uncertain future. Yet there was a danger that the simultaneous pursuit of multiple, competing visions would ensure the failure of all, in the process hollowing out existing institutions, weakening Western coherence and resolve, and disorienting the embryonic democracies to the east.

U.S. Strategy

With a "new world order" more an ambition than a goal that could be achieved in the near term, American diplomacy aimed instead to achieve a set of more practical and specific immediate objectives. Of necessity, they were built on points of convergence in the competing visions of Europe's future, and would become the basis of a coherent strategy that could gain broad, though not universal, adherence. U.S. approaches proceeded from the guiding principles that the United States had to remain in Europe to balance Russian power and provide stability so that a more united Western Europe could extend its zone of democratic stability eastward. Our presence was also needed to help organize a durable post–Cold War order in which former adversaries were brought into a new system of cooperative security. From these core principles several axioms followed.

First, NATO had to survive the demise of the threat it was formed to counter, for it remained the institutional link binding European and North American security and the only institution capable of providing for the collective defense. This, in turn, meant that U.S. forces had to remain in significant, though much reduced, numbers. Second, NATO's role in post–Cold War Europe called for its radical transformation—internally, toward a new balance of European and American roles and responsibilities; externally, by extending the Atlantic community eastward; and existentially, by adapting itself to the newly emerging security challenges in Europe. Third, the radical reduction of nuclear and conventional forces in Europe had to be accomplished in a way that did not introduce new instabilities and insecurities, so that Russian forces did not become, perversely, even more preponderant in a less militarized Europe and so that European military capacity and readiness were appropriate to new kinds of threats on the horizon. Fourth, the United States needed to embrace European unity, including the development of a common foreign and security policy, while also maintaining the indivisibility of transatlantic security—two competing tasks that proved easier to reconcile in principle than in practice. Fifth, the CSCE (Conference on Security and Cooperation in Europe) needed the institutional and operational capacity to play a stronger political role and assume new security responsibilities, particularly in the areas of conflict prevention and crisis management.

This orientation was largely transitional, aimed at creating a provisional new order for the challenges immediately ahead. It looked to proven institutions like NATO and the EC, rather than an aggrandized CSCE, to provide the essential leadership, relying on their ability to adapt to radically changed circumstances and indeed fulfill their original visions of a more united Europe.[18] We resisted efforts to leapfrog over this transitional stage, disband NATO along with the Warsaw Pact, and move immediately to create what the Czechs and others called a "pan-European peace order" in which the CSCE would be transformed, somehow, into a new system of collective security. If we saw more clearly than the Czechs how illusory such a new order was, and how reminiscent of the pious legalisms of the 1920s, however, they may have understood better the insufficiency of existing structures for the new requirements of European security.

Policy and Process   Policy was hammered out chiefly through a European strategy steering group, also known as the "Gates Group" after Deputy National Security Adviser Bob Gates, who chaired the sessions in the White House Situation Room. Created during German unification but extended to consider issues thereafter, the group met regularly at undersecretary level from the NSC, State, and Defense, including the Joint Chiefs of Staff. (International economic policy was handled by an interagency group chaired by the Treasury Department at undersecretary level.) It was essential to have a regular forum such as this, because cabinet principals were by this time preoccupied with events outside Europe. The president and General Scowcroft were consumed by the Gulf War, as of course were Secretary of Defense Dick Cheney and General Colin Powell. As the war wound down in the late spring of 1991, Secretary Baker devoted most of his energies to the Middle East peace process. And after the failed August coup against Gorbachev, all were focused on a rapidly disintegrating Soviet Union. European policy no longer commanded the undivided attention of NSC principals the way it did in 1989 and 1990, and policy became somewhat more disjointed— or, to be more precise, the follow-through on policy became less consistent and focused.

There were very few policy differences at the highest levels. Indeed, the "inside story" of foreign policy decision making in the Bush administration was not one of ferocious battles of the kind that had characterized most recent administrations, but of almost total agreement on the main lines of policy. Baker was the most sympathetic toward European aspirations—a disposition manifest in his more forthcoming attitudes toward the CSCE, the EC, and NATO's transformation—but within a generally shared strategic perspective. Bush, Baker, Scowcroft, Eagleburger, Treasury Secretary Nicholas Brady: all were men of similar age, experience, and outlook.[19] Cheney, Powell, and Gates, though younger, were men of like disposition. Among this group, with the partial exception of Baker, there was hardly a foreign policy difference of any moment. Firm internationalists, they believed in American leadership and the use of power, especially military power, in foreign policy. Theirs was a state-centered view of the world, in which military aggression conducted by one sovereign entity against another posed the chief challenge to global peace and security. Although they had shown great imagination and creativity in devising an American grand strategy for ending the Cold War, they did so from the familiar post–World War II frame of reference—and appropriately so. But it was a frame of reference less congenial to the brave new world we were about to enter.

The attributes that served U.S. policy so well in 1989 and 1990—the substance of policy as well as the collegial decision-making style—served us less well thereafter. Some of the virtues became liabilities: the commitment to American leadership of the free world, which had been indispensable to forging a Western consensus in 1989–90, carried over afterwards to a rigid insistence on an undiminished American role and made it harder to cede leadership gracefully to the Europeans. Instinctively, we clung to a role we were no longer ready to play.

And some of the preexisting biases that did us little harm in 1989–90 became serious liabilities in 1991–92. A somewhat antiquated suspicion of the European Community and exaggerated, although not altogether fanciful, fears of European protectionism complicated efforts to build up the U.S.-EC bond as part of a new transatlantic relationship. And the view the principals had of the EC remained ambivalent: was it European unity we feared, or European disunity?[20] The similarly outdated and ambivalent image of the CSCE—as a feckless debating club at best and, at worst, as a snare and a delusion or even a threat to NATO's primacy—obscured the organization's potential for bridging the two halves of Europe and taking the lead on "soft" security issues like conflict prevention and resolution. Baker, who took more interest in the CSCE, was able to overcome much of this resistance and put the United States in the lead on several key initiatives, but it was an uphill struggle that never enjoyed the full support of the administration. Finally, their collegiality evolved, by the midpoint of the administration, into a closed and self-contained decision-making circle, increasingly impervious to new and unconventional ideas at the very time that unconventional thinking was most needed.

These liabilities were replicated at senior staff level. Those of us who had been with the administration from the beginning had become more skillful implementors of policy by 1991, but our thinking was not as fresh and less open to ideas from outside.[21] We were running out of gas, and our batteries were low, but the journey was so compelling that we failed to notice.

The United States in Europe The overriding focus on keeping the United States in Europe needs underlining. In terms of Isaiah Berlin's fox and hedgehog distinction,[22] this was the hedgehog's "one big thing"—our central vision and key organizing principle. It was the driving force behind the European strategy group and the main reason it had been created in the first place. No idea was more strongly and deeply held in the upper levels of the administration than the core conviction that the American presence was indispensable to European stability and therefore to vital American interests. This can be illustrated by passages from two speeches delivered a day apart in mid-May 1990 by Czechoslovak foreign minister Jiří Dienstbier and Secretary of State Baker. First, Dienstbier:

> We . . . hear the objection that NATO must be preserved at any price. We have nothing against NATO. It has successfully played its role and will continue to play it for a certain period of time. . . . Another objection against the replacement of the old bloc structures . . . is that it would mean the American departure from Europe. Well, for how long do we want the American people to pay for our freedom, for our inability to settle the conditions in Europe?[23]

Now, Baker:

> The visible reduction in the Soviet threat has led some to assume that our only reason for being in Europe over the last 40 years was to contain that threat. Beyond containment, in their view, lies the end of the American role. And so as the alleged "single cause" of America's involvement—fear of Soviet aggression—recedes, America's position in Europe should recede with it.
> This would be the most profound strategic mistake of the generation. We must leave not only the cold war behind but also the

conflicts that preceded the cold war. The reduction of the Soviet threat need not cause Europe to revert to an unsteady balance of power or a fresh outbreak of national rivalries and ethnic tensions.[24]

Dienstbier's was an argument not to be dismissed. Indeed, the great majority of Europeans and Americans alike would have seconded his sentiments unless their own political leaders could offer persuasive arguments to the contrary. President Bush and Secretary Baker were preoccupied with this concern. Privately as well as publicly, Bush came back to it again and again; he saw it as his chief foreign policy responsibility to hold back the inevitable pressures for disengagement, if not isolationism, by creating the conditions for an active and continuing American role.[25] Here is Bush speaking at Aspen in August 1990, just after the Iraqi invasion of Kuwait:

> The U.S. will keep a force in Europe as long as our allies want and need us there. . . . We will remain in Europe to deter any new dangers, to be a force for stability—and to reassure all of Europe, east and west, that the European balance will remain secure. . . .
> The brutal aggression launched last night against Kuwait illustrates my central thesis: Notwithstanding the alteration in the Soviet threat, the world remains a dangerous place with serious threats to important U.S. interests *wholly unrelated to the earlier patterns of the U.S.-Soviet relationship.*[26]

The case for continued American engagement had to reckon not only with the decline of the Soviet threat but also with the advent of a more united Western Europe, eager to assume responsibility for European stability and security. During the course of German unification, we had worked—so far with success—to delink the American military presence in Europe from Soviet troop withdrawals. Now we had also to delink the American presence from the process of European integration. The importance of the American role, we believed, transcended Europe's achievement of greater economic and political unity; it had to do with semipermanent factors of power and geography.

We knew where it should come out in the end: a permanent American presence that would facilitate European unity and so reduce the burden on ourselves, yielding a new transatlantic balance of roles and responsibilities. But getting there would require a careful balancing act. We wanted to encourage European unity, but not so effusively as to cause our own public to conclude our presence was superfluous. We wanted to reduce American preponderance via NATO in European affairs, but not so rapidly as to cause Europeans to believe we lacked staying power. There was a delicate balance between the short-term, tactical requirements of flexibility and the longer-term, strategic necessity of sticking to core principles: too much flexibility would jeopardize ultimate goals, and too much rigidity would prevent the experimentation needed to revamp the institutions and habits of forty years of transatlantic relations.

The American presence we had in mind had an economic as well as a security dimension and indeed was acquiring an increasingly economic logic and rationale. As the military dimensions of security receded, trade issues loomed larger—and now would be played out without the galvanizing element of the Soviet threat. It was, as Bush put it in a speech in the Netherlands just before the Maastricht Summit, "the danger that old Cold War allies will become new economic adversaries— cold warriors turned to trade warriors."[27]

Indeed, the Uruguay Round trade negotiations loomed at least as large as security matters in U.S.-European relations after 1990. The negotiations toward a new, more open worldwide trading regime involved all members of the General Agreement on Tariffs and Trade, or GATT. Once agricultural subsidies were identified as the key stumbling block, however, the talks centered on differences between the United States and the European Community. Having sought and received from Congress special one-year negotiating authority, Bush spent more time on the Uruguay Round in 1991 than on any other foreign policy issue save the Gulf War and Soviet policy. He feared—rightly, as it turned out— that the EC's unwillingness to reduce agricultural subsidies in the face of French (and other) protectionism would prevent a Uruguay Round agreement from being concluded and dash his hopes for the development of a more open world trade system. At a personal political level, it would be Bush who would pay the price in the 1992 presidential election for having bucked domestic protectionist sentiment and failing to deliver an agreement on account of EC intransigence.

Moreover, the negotiating style we encountered in the Uruguay Round talks confirmed everyone's worst fears about the post–Cold War EC. We negotiated bilaterally with Kohl, John Major, Mitterrand, and all the other EC heads of state or government, and we dealt in their "collective" capacities with the EC's designated negotiators, the commission, the presidency country (which changed every six months), and the "troika" of past, present, and future presidency countries. None could deliver or speak authoritatively for the Community as a whole; all invoked the EC's consensual decision-making rules to explain or excuse their inaction. The Germans, whose interests ran clearly in the direction of freer trade, were particularly disappointing. Kohl would expound at length about his commitment to free trade (which we had no reason to doubt) but did little to alter the EC position, choosing to treat this as a U.S.-French political problem that Washington was supposed to solve. Genscher did even less, choosing to forget that besides being foreign minister he was also vice chancellor and leader of the free-trading FDP (Free Democratic Party) and so had broader responsibilities for ensuring the success of GATT negotiations. On the substance of the negotiations, to be sure, there was plenty to criticize on both sides; Bush himself had plenty of frustrations with his own negotiating team. But whatever the complaints EC leaders had about substantive positions taken by the United States, they cannot have had the same frustrations as we with the way the negotiations were conducted.[28]

Thus these two realms—the economic/commercial and the political/security—interacted and overlapped after 1990. Conflict over the first-ever U.S.-EC declaration was a portent of difficulties ahead. Responding to overtures made by Bush as early as the Boston University speech of May 1989 and by Baker in his December 1989 Berlin speech, the Germans took the lead in proposing such a document so as to give U.S.-EC relations a more intense and regular character, cemented by common principles. They also sought to allay American misgivings as the Community worked toward economic and political unity. The two sides had worked out a text to be issued at the time of the Paris Summit, seeing this venue as a good one for affirming the "new European architecture." It was a nice, four-page document, mostly hortatory but with a few specific commitments inserted at our insistence over French objections.[29] Inauspiciously, however, U.S.-EC Uruguay Round negotiations hit an impasse over agricultural subsidies on the eve of the Paris Summit. Bush and Scowcroft were loath to sign a lofty agreement whose spirit, they felt, was being violated by unyielding European protectionism. It was only after eleventh-hour negotiations on the margins of the Paris Summit that the U.S.-EC declaration was issued—so quietly that it passed unnoticed. The White House did not even publish a copy or issue the customary press release, lest the embarrassing contradiction between word and deed be pointed out by the media.

All this of course reinforced preexisting biases within the Bush administration about the EC and helps explain the ambiguity of our approaches. On the one hand, we wanted a more united and capable Europe and knew in any case that American policy had to take into account the reality of a more ambitious EC. On the other, we did not like the kind of EC that seemed to be emerging and so adopted policies that seemed to oppose the Community at every crucial turn. It was not that American policy was duplicitous—that would be too easy an historical judgment—but rather that the two strands of thinking were equally strong and frequently in conflict. The concern, put in simplest terms, was that the United States would be shut out of the new Europe, both economically and politically, and that we would be dealing with a Europe that was protectionist, exclusivist, inward-looking, and difficult to deal with. State Department counselor Robert Zoellick, in a September 1990 speech, posed the question whether the new Europe would be "insular, itinerant, or international"—that is, internally preoccupied; globally engaged but wandering as an independent force; or, as we hoped, internationally engaged in a new partnership with the United States.[30]

The hope, as expressed in President Bush's Prague speech and elsewhere, was that the end of the Cold War would create the conditions not only for a continued transatlantic relationship but a stronger and more natural one. American military preponderance in European affairs was a requirement thrust upon both sides by the exigencies of the Soviet threat in the heart of Europe. The American presence had provided the shield that enabled Europe to build greater unity and prosperity, but it also stifled the full realization of Europe's aspirations. In this sense we in the administration—some of us at least—were sympathetic to the French complaint. Freed from this unnatural imbalance of roles and responsibilities, we saw new possibilities for U.S.-European relations. We looked to Europe—as well as to other allies, notably Japan—as our main partner in world affairs and in solving global problems that we had neither the desire nor the capacity to tackle alone.[31]

President Bush made the point during German president Richard von Weizsäcker's state visit in early 1992. The reference was to Germany but the sentiment applied equally to Europe as a whole:

Just as Germany has transcended and triumphed over its past, so has the German-American relationship shed the burdens that were history's legacy. A united Germany, champion of a more united Europe, now stands as our partner in leadership. Together, we have achieved our common goal of a Germany united in peace and freedom.

But our partnership did not end with that. To the contrary: now that we are free of the dangers and divisions of Europe's Cold War confrontation, the German-American partnership has really just begun.[32]

For "Germany," substitute "Europe"—meaning not just a Europe of the twelve EC member countries but a Europe widening to embrace the new democracies of the eastern part of the continent—and you have the essence of what we were trying to achieve in and through our transatlantic relations after 1990.

Strategy   From our core interests and objectives we developed a multipronged strategy. Conceptually, we tried to develop a new consensus around our basic aims, building on the major goals of the key players and shaping them into a workable structure of security. To reaffirm NATO's continuing role and lead its more radical transformation, we relied on the firmly Atlanticist British, Dutch, and others, as well as NATO's able secretary-general, former German defense minister Manfred Wörner. We embraced European unity, forging more intense and frequent contacts with the European Community, including commission president Jacques Delors, with whom President Bush met bilaterally on several occasions. And we championed a stronger CSCE, which we aimed to shape in ways that did not vitiate NATO but rather enhanced CSCE's role as a forum for political dialogue and agent of conflict resolution.

In his two Berlin speeches—December 1989 and June 1991—Secretary Baker developed the theme of "interlocking institutions" with flexible and complementary roles.[33] Warning in the first speech that "a Europe undivided may not necessarily be a Europe peaceful and prosperous," Baker proposed "a new architecture for a new era." The term was designed to appeal to West European political elites in the midst of their own "architectural" debate. Calling for a "fundamentally different approach to security," especially in nonmilitary dimensions, he proposed a set of new and complementary relationships among the key European and transatlantic institutions—NATO, the EC, the CSCE, the Council of Europe, and others. In particular he wanted to develop a much strengthened U.S.-EC relationship, "whether in treaty or some other form." The second Berlin speech updated and expanded on these ideas in the context of the challenge "to extend the trans-Atlantic Community to Central and Eastern Europe and to the Soviet Union":

> As we extend the Euro-Atlantic architecture to the east, we need to be creative about employing multiple methods and institutions. . . . CSCE will contribute by creating the political, economic, and security conditions that may defuse conflict. . . . [NATO] provides a foundation of stability within Europe as a whole. . . . The EC, the Council of Europe, and OECD are creating a network of political and economic support [that] both strengthens the new market democracies internally and signals any would-be threat that these nations are part of a larger community with a stake in their success.

Operationally, we worked mainly through NATO to keep the respective roles of key institutions in plausible harmony (to borrow Somerset Maugham's nice turn of phrase). As the communiqué of the June 1991 meeting of NATO foreign ministers rather awkwardly put it, "Our common security can best be safeguarded through the further development of a network of interlocking institutions and relationships, constituting a comprehensive architecture in which the Alliance, the process of European integration, and the CSCE are key elements."[34] In this effort, we had reasonably good success with NATO and the CSCE, much less with the EC.

The strategy was played out in our key bilateral relationships as well. Our conspicuous (if ambivalent) support for European unity also aimed at pushing a reluctant Britain toward "Europe," because British participation was critical for realization of the EC agenda. Additionally, we wanted Britain's global and Atlantic perspective to influence the outlook of an increasingly cohesive Europe: we needed a more Europeanized Britain because we wanted a more Anglicized Europe. Thatcher had more reservations about our approach than did John Major, who succeeded her as prime minister in the fall of 1990. We took a position on European unity at variance with the British government not because we valued Britain's role less but because we knew we would need its involvement even more as Europe moved toward closer economic and political unity. The Anglo-American "special relationship," in other words, was as important as ever but it would hinge less on a global partnership than on Britain's position in Europe. Our approach was only partly successful: British policies on key issues were almost always congenial to U.S. interests, but British influence remained limited by its reluctance to embrace European unity before and after the Maastricht Summit of late 1991.

With the French, we worked intensely in late 1990 and early 1991 to arrive at a formula that would permit creation of a European security and defense identity that did not undermine but rather strengthened NATO and might pave the way for France's drawing closer to the alliance, a prospect for which there was sympathy in some French quarters. In a post–Cold War world no longer dominated by superpower competition, we judged, NATO without France was probably doomed. To have a chance of bringing France fully back into NATO, we were banking on the close Franco-American cooperation that had developed in the Gulf War, as well as on President Bush's good personal relations with President Mitterrand. (Baker's relationship with French foreign minister Roland Dumas, to put it mildly, never warmed.) The aim was not a complete meeting of minds, which was out of the question, but a shared understanding, at the most basic level, that a continued U.S. role in Europe (via NATO) was essential and that it need not conflict with the goal of a more united Europe. The French connection, as it turned out, was the least successful dimension of our European strategy. Bush worked extremely hard at cultivating Mitterrand—and Delors as well—but could not overcome the deep-seated suspicions that Mitterrand and especially his foreign ministry continued to harbor.

Among the Western allies, Germany was key. France was a driving force in the EC but not in NATO; Great Britain was influential in NATO but much less so in the EC; Germany exercised substantial influence in both. And of all the major players, Germany had an agenda and set of interests that were closest to ours, particularly with respect to Western engagement of Central and Eastern Europe and the Soviet Union. Accordingly, we sought to forge the closest possible ties with the Federal Republic both before and after unification. Whenever possible, we gave tangible expression to being "partners in leadership" by issuing joint declarations, cosponsoring initiatives on the eve of important

NATO or CSCE meetings, and working to see that there was little or no daylight between U.S. and German positions on any of the major issues. Baker's relationship with Genscher was as strong as Bush's with Kohl, and these close ties were replicated easily and naturally at senior staff level. The relationship worked well, but it was frequently in conflict with the Franco-German partnership. It was easy to say to the Germans, as we often did, that we fully understood the importance of Franco-German cooperation and were not asking them to "choose between Washington and Paris," but there was no getting around this tension when it came down to cases like the Uruguay Round or development of a common European foreign and security policy. In both cases, what we wanted was precisely what France did not.

The Eastern Conundrum: A Europe "Whole and Free"?

"Central and Eastern Europe and the Soviet Union," Baker said with breathtaking understatement in his second Berlin speech of June 1991, "are the still incomplete pieces of our architecture." With Moscow, our aim of bringing our erstwhile adversary into new patterns of cooperation ran up against the inescapable realities of diminished Soviet influence and deepening internal strife that vitiated many a well-intended initiative. As to the new democracies of Central and Eastern Europe, the prospect of entering or reentering Western institutions was an indispensable point of orientation for societies in the midst of such wrenching change. This was also the essence of the integrationist strategy we had embraced in 1989, with the ultimate goal of overcoming the postwar division of Europe—not just as a formal or rhetorical matter but as one embedded in the economic, political, and social life of the continent.

Regional Cooperation   Between isolation and integration was the important intermediate stage of enhanced regional cooperation. This was a conscious aim of Western policy from the beginning, especially among the more advanced Central European countries. Western policymakers had the dual aim of encouraging cooperation to fill the void left by the discredited institutions of the past (the Warsaw Pact and Comecon[35]) and to ameliorate some of the conflicts that had plagued this region in the past. Secretary Baker had addressed this issue directly in a February 1990 speech in Prague:

In a region that has suffered so greatly from the distortion of national interest and from international isolation, I am encouraged by the first signs of coordination and possible new association among the newly democratic states . . . [and efforts] to build international civil society and overcome old animosities. . . . We welcome recent discussions [among] Hungary, Poland, and Czechoslovakia, including a possible free trade agreement. . . . The purpose of such closer ties should not be to isolate the countries in association from others. . . . The choice of whether to associate and in what form is, of course, entirely yours to make.[36]

The formulations on regional cooperation had been the subject of internal debate in the administration, as well as with our Western partners, that continued on the secretary's plane during the flight to Prague. Should we take a leaf out of the Marshall Plan and oblige the Central and East European governments to work out their own common strategies, with regional integration an explicit political goal? Should we make Western assistance conditional upon these steps toward regional integration? Would this be an important means of helping these countries transcend the national antagonisms that had torn this part of the world apart in the past? Could this cooperation be a stepping stone for their eventual integration into "Europe"—much as EFTA (the European Free Trade Area) had been, for some West European countries, a kind of preparatory stage for entry into the European Community? Or was such an approach inappropriate for countries at such different stages on the road to political and economic reform?

Did we risk slowing down Polish reforms by insisting that Poland synchronize its policies with Hungary and Czechoslovakia? Was it wise to promote regional integration when there were already-functioning Western institutions like NATO, the EC, and many others to which the Central and Eastern European countries could gradually adhere? These were the terms of our internal debate, which we had also broached, in almost precisely those words, in informal discussions with the British and Germans. Internal EC debates mirrored this transatlantic dialogue.

We and our West European partners settled on the middle ground reflected in Baker's speech. The postcommunist transformations would be hard enough without our imposing new requirements for access to Western assistance, particularly in light of the modest levels of aid being proposed. These countries were trying to escape the Warsaw Pact and Comecon and had no desire to create successor organizations. They had just rid themselves of one "Big Brother" in the form of the USSR and did not need another telling them how to live their lives. Emerging from nearly half a century of foreign domination, they needed some breathing space to establish and consolidate democratic rule before deciding what forms of external cooperation they might choose to undertake.

Our approach, rather, was to do all we could to encourage these new governments to adopt common strategies and cooperative regional arrangements and to offer inducements toward that end, short of making Western assistance conditional on an explicitly regional approach or the creation of new regional institutions. As a practical matter, the most important inducement was not aid but membership in Western institutions—particularly the EC and NATO but also the Council of Europe, the Organization for Economic Cooperation and Development (OECD), and others. Accordingly, we and our Western European partners agreed that Poland, Hungary, and Czechoslovakia, as the most advanced of the postcommunist states, should be treated as a group and encouraged to synchronize their policies and approaches toward affiliation and perhaps eventual membership in some or all of these institutions.

The new democratic leaders of the region were thinking along the same lines, and it was to their spontaneous cooperation that Baker referred in Prague. In an address to the Polish Sejm in late January, Czechoslovak president Václav Havel had called for Central European regional cooperation, warning that "to return to Europe individually . . . would certainly take much longer and be much more complicated than acting together."[37] A logical extension of the contacts among Polish, Czech, and Hungarian dissidents in the 1980s, regional cooperation thus conceived aimed at hastening their entry into "Europe" and ameliorating the national antagonisms that lay just beneath the surface. These sentiments, echoed by others in the region, led to an informal and largely symbolic "summit" in Bratislava in March 1990.

(A second, more ambitious summit was held in February 1991 at Visegrád, a castle on the Danube just north of Budapest, in conscious evocation of an earlier summit meeting of Polish, Czech, and Hungarian leaders on that site. [The year was 1335; the leaders were Kings Kazimierz III of Poland, John of Bohemia, and Charles Robert of Hungary. Their cooperation helped usher in one of the brightest periods in the history of east-central Europe.] The 1991 Visegrád Declaration, signed by Presidents Wałęsa of Poland, Havel of Czechoslovakia, and Árpád Göncz of Hungary, as well as Hungarian prime minister József Antall, proclaimed that the three countries were pursuing "essentially identical goals," affirmed "the rights of each nation to express its own identity," and advanced an extensive but vague common agenda.)

Our notion, and theirs, of the "Visegrád process" was never that it should be an end in itself or accompanied by elaborate institutions. Rather it should serve to coordinate their main foreign policy programs and facilitate joint action when it made sense, such as in promoting free trade and thus enlarging their respective markets. Although this cooperation was to founder after the split of Czechoslovakia in January 1993, it proved of great utility in strengthening their hands in negotiations with Moscow, particularly with regard to the withdrawal of Soviet forces, and coordinating approaches toward the West. Cooperation via other groupings like the "Pentagonale" and "Alpe-Adria," which included Austria and Italy,[38] also contributed to a web of overlapping and mutually reinforcing ties. Like the Visegrád process, we saw these ties not as substitutes for joining the European mainstream but stepping stones in that direction.

Integration into Western Institutions   In his Prague speech of February 1990, Secretary Baker also proposed a step-by-step process of integration into European and transatlantic institutions. The proposals were cautious, proceeding from the reality of the Warsaw Pact's continued existence and the presence of substantial Soviet forces still deployed in the region. On European security, Baker noted President Bush's recent CFE (Conventional Armed Forces in Europe) proposal for deeper force reductions, which "should minimize and deter the threat of any army of invasion and end the unjust presence of any army of occupation." NATO and the U.S. military presence should continue "for as long as our allies desire it," serving "to reassure the nations of Europe, large and small, that we will stand by them to resist invasion, intimidation, or coercion." Presaging initiatives that the president would unveil at NATO's July 1990 London Summit, Baker said that the alliance "must evolve to assume new missions" and "help address old and new European animosities and fears—outside and inside NATO." Then, in a line he was to repeat many times, he warned that "we must leave behind not only the Cold War but also the conflicts that preceded it."

In addition to NATO's new opening to the East,[39] Baker focused on the need to "integrate the new market democracies into the international economic system" via the international financial institutions, the OECD, and the newly created European Bank for Reconstruction and Development. He proposed that the latter be located in Prague as a sign of Europe's center of gravity shifting eastward. He also called on Western countries to open their markets to East European trade and facilitate those countries' access to high technology through a liberalized COCOM (Coordinating Committee for Multilateral Export Controls). Finally, Baker held out the prospect of a "special relationship with the EC, the nations of EFTA, or the United States" toward Central and Eastern Europe's gradual integration into European and transatlantic institutions. "No longer," he said, "should the circumstances of this continent subject you to characterization as 'the lands between.'"

Yet in their efforts to "return to Europe," the Central and Eastern Europeans were aiming at a moving target. Hungary and others considered applying for membership in the European Free Trade Area (EFTA),[40] only to find that EFTA countries were lining up to join the European Community. By the same token, Central European hopes of joining the EC were pushed off to the distant future as they were obliged to take their places behind the economically more advanced "EFTAns." Finally, as the Central Europeans shifted gears to focus on negotiating the "association agreements" the EC had promised in November 1990, they found a newly protectionist Community that resisted any opening in "sensitive" sectors like agriculture, textiles, and steel— where Central Europe could have been competitive immediately. The EC sought even to raise tariffs in areas where they had been generous in 1989 and 1990. It was only after the failed coup attempt in Moscow in August 1991 that the EC gave the process a new push, culminating in the signing of the "Europe agreements" with Poland, Czechoslovakia, and Hungary in December 1991.[41]

Indeed, Western approaches toward the East after 1990 took place against the backdrop of growing conflict verging on chaos in the Soviet Union that made coherent planning elusive. Soviet foreign minister Shevardnadze's abrupt resignation on December 20, 1990, coincided with tangible actions that seemed to bear out his warning of incipient "dictatorship."[42] The influx of hard-line military and KGB officers into the top leadership was evident in every aspect of Soviet policy: efforts to broker a separate peace with Saddam Hussein on the eve of Operation

Desert Storm, violations of the freshly signed CFE treaty, and a new truculence at home. Since mid-1990, Gorbachev had beat a steady retreat from democratization and opened a wide rift with radical reformers led by Boris Yeltsin, leader of the Russian Federation. Most ominous were military crackdowns against Baltic independence movements in the two "Bloody Sundays" of January 13, 1991, in Vilnius, Lithuania, and January 20 in Riga, Latvia. Nor did Gorbachev's rambling and implausible denial of personal responsibility help matters. As Soviet ambassador to the United States (and soon to be Shevardnadze's successor as foreign minister) Aleksandr Bessmertnykh confided to Deputy Secretary Eagleburger, "The situation is almost out of control."[43]

Although the immediate crisis abated, the situation continued to deteriorate as Gorbachev sought to carve out a middle ground between hard-liners and reformers, in the process alienating both and facilitating the coup attempt against him in August 1991. Thereafter, the ascendancy of Russian Federation president Boris Yeltsin and the collapse of the Soviet Communist party led to recognition of the independence of the Baltic states and, by year's end, the disintegration of the Soviet Union itself.

Gorbachev's early boast that he would deprive the West of a threat was taking on an existential meaning that he surely did not intend. The burden was therefore intense on Western governments, especially ours, to reach out to the newly independent states while also preserving the transatlantic security community without the threat it had been created to counter. At the same time, the Central and Eastern Europeans, at the front line of a Soviet Union that seemed on the brink of violent or at least chaotic disintegration, were clamoring for a more forthcoming Western response to their security concerns.

Not everyone in Central and Eastern Europe shared Lech Wałęsa's sense of "deadly danger" to Poland or took seriously Russian Federation foreign minister Andrei Kozyrev's warning that "if the forces of darkness prevail in the Soviet Union, Central Europe is next on their agenda,"[44] but all feared a set of lesser threats. Short of military aggression, which seemed unlikely given the chaotic state of the Soviet leadership, there were more plausible, indeed actual, dangers arising from curtailment of essential energy supplies, collapse of foreign trade generally, or waves of refugees fleeing economic and social disorder. Moscow was also adopting a tougher posture about the withdrawal of Soviet forces from Central Europe, dragging its feet on dissolving the military arm of the Warsaw Pact, and exerting pressure on the Central and Eastern Europeans to sign new bilateral treaties that would have given the Soviet Union a kind of *droit de regard* in the region.

The countries of Central Europe were indeed "the lands between," and not only in the geographic sense. Of the West but not in it, in the East but not of it, they still belonged to a security organization—the Warsaw Pact—that offered only insecurity. Yet with Soviet forces still on their territory, they could not yet aspire openly to the one organization—NATO—that could provide real security. Central and Eastern European leaders generally recognized that the answers to the threats they faced lay mainly in strengthening their own internal stability through a deepening of democracy and market-based economic systems. But they saw these imperatives as linked to their countries' external situation, for the collapse of the Soviet market and the growing chaos on their eastern borders had generated new economic and social instabilities in their own countries. What these countries sought from the West, at a minimum, was a perspective for the future—a strategic plan that assured them of their eventual, gradual integration into Western institutions as they consolidated democratic rule at home.

The Soviet Factor   The calls were urgent, reasonable, and consistent with U.S. interests in enlarging Western Europe's "zone of stability." Indeed, the ardently pro-American and pro-NATO Poles, Czechs, and Hungarians were essential to our larger vision of a new Euro-Atlantic community. Yet Western policies had also to consider the danger of strengthening hard-line sentiment in Moscow by what might have seemed a provocative acceleration of the integration of Moscow's erstwhile allies into Western security structures. In the often repeated phrase of the day, we did not want to "draw new lines in Europe" that left the Soviet Union on the other side, defeated, embittered, hostile.

The dilemma for Western policy was acute. In 1990 it had been fairly easy to adopt a gradualist approach toward opening Western institutions to association with the East, putting the Soviet Union and the Eastern European countries on roughly the same footing. Now there was greater urgency among Eastern Europeans to have their countries brought in more rapidly and integrally, and greater merit to their contention that their progress toward stable democratic rule warranted sharper differentiation from an unstable and more authoritarian Soviet Union. As to the latter, while not wishing to isolate or alienate Moscow, we and our Western partners were finding its leadership increasingly difficult to deal with constructively (in contrast to our extremely good bilateral relations with Poland, Czechoslovakia, and Hungary).

The Western Europeans took a similar position, sympathetic to the Eastern Europeans but preoccupied with Moscow as well as their own internal negotiations toward European union. The Germans were the most consistent advocates of an accelerated integration strategy, but they, too, attached first priority to relations with Moscow in the context of the protracted withdrawal of Soviet forces from eastern Germany. The French were at the other extreme, opposing any opening to the East that might upset their strategy of building European union and so containing Germany with a tight European embrace. Mitterrand's early proposal of a "European confederation" was rightly seen as a device to keep Central Europe out of the European mainstream, as was Delors's proposal for a "European Economic Space."[45]

U.S. and other Western approaches therefore had to balance Central and Eastern European insistence on inclusion against Soviet and then Russian fears of exclusion. In NATO, for example, we aimed to find a formula that would treat all former Warsaw Pact members equally as a formal matter but would in practice be highly differentiated in favor of the new democracies of Central and Eastern Europe. This was no mere diplomatic compromise but a sober calculation of the existing and potential distribution of power in Europe. In 1919, the Versailles conference had vastly underestimated Russian power on the morrow of the October Revolution and hence erected a postwar settlement that was never rooted in the realities of power.[46] Again in 1991, Russia was weak enough to ignore but with enormous latent power to have made its exclusion shortsighted in the extreme.

Such was the thinking at the highest levels of the administration, and it was a sound basis for long-term strategic engagement of a Russia in the midst of another "time of troubles." The problem was with the execution of this strategy in the short run. No amount of Western largesse could alter the plain facts that the Soviet empire was lost, its political and economic system in profound crisis, and, for the immediate future, its global role negligible. The burden on the U.S.-Soviet (and later the U.S.-Russian) relationship was particularly heavy. With arms control an issue largely of the bygone era and economic cooperation foundering because of Gorbachev's refusal to embrace internal reform, we had to grope for other ways to engage Moscow and embed a disintegrating Soviet Union in a cooperative international order. The efforts of the United States and its Western partners to facilitate Soviet and later Russian participation in the G-7, the IMF and World Bank, and the Middle East peace process made good strategic sense, albeit in a largely symbolic way. When it came to the transformation of European and transatlantic institutions, however, deference to Soviet/Russian sensibilities amounted to a self-imposed veto over steps needed to help secure the new democracies of the East and overcome the continent's division.

Although a minority in Washington pushed consistently for accelerated efforts to integrate the new democracies into Western institutions, we and our Western partners erred almost always on the side of Soviet sensibilities. This cautious approach was reasonable enough at the time, given how much was at stake in a successful Soviet transition. The hitch was that a go-slow approach could always be justified, no matter the course of events in Moscow. If reformers were ascendant, they needed our support to vindicate their approach. If hard-liners were pushing their way to the fore, we had to be careful not to provoke or embolden them. And if things were stable, why rock the boat?

The same administration that had judged wisely in 1989 that we could not make the Soviet peoples' choices for them or allow the Soviet agenda to dictate our own began to forget its own lessons, greatly exaggerating our ability to influence the Soviet internal dynamic and international role. As President Bush had said way back in his Texas A&M speech—was it really less than two years before?—"a new relationship cannot be simply declared by Moscow, or bestowed by others." At Mainz in May 1989, Bush sought to convince the Soviet leaders "that their definition of security is obsolete, that their deepest fears are unfounded." By 1991, reacting to the most atavistic forces in Moscow, we were discarding some of our core principles on U.S.-Soviet relations, in the process missing an opportunity to assist consolidating democratic rule in Eastern Europe, where we *could* make a difference. In our understandable preoccupation with Soviet Russia and the Western security system, we were neglecting the "lands between." In 1989 we had rightly judged that Eastern Europe was the key to ending the Cold War, but we failed to see that this region was also the key to the post–Cold War order in Europe.

President and Mrs. Bush with Solidarity leader Lech Wałęsa in front of the Lenin Shipyard in Gdańsk, July 1989. Bush's electrifying visit helped Poland awaken to the possibility of genuine independence and democracy.

White House departure ceremony for Czechoslovak president Havel, February 20, 1990. Havel is holding a portrait of Thomas Masaryk, Czechoslovakia's first president, a gift from Bush.

President Havel and the new Czechoslovak government meet President Bush in the Cabinet Room, February 20, 1990.

The President and President Göncz of Hungary in the Oval Office, May 18, 1990. The genial, intelligent Göncz was one of Bush's favorites.

Presidents Bush and Gorbachev at the Washington Summit, May 31, 1990, about to begin negotiations that would pave the way to Soviet acceptance of German unification

West German and U.S. leaders get ready for the last phase of German unifica-tion, May 17, 1990, in the Cabinet Room. Chancellor Kohl, in the middle on the right, is flanked by Foreign Minister Genscher, to his right, and Defense Minister Stoltenberg; Bush, by Vice President Quayle and Deputy Secretary of State Eagleburger.

Bush cracking wise on the way into the Oval Office from the Rose Garden in June 1990, flanked by Scowcroft and Gates, with the author just behind.

The President and Polish Prime Minister Mazowiecki enjoy a light moment in Bush's suite at the Waldorf Astoria during the UN General Assembly, September 29, 1990. Polish Foreign Minister Skubiszewski, gazing upwards, does not seem to be amused.

French President Mitterrand prepares to open the Paris Summit of the CSCE (Conference on Security and Cooperation in Europe), November 1990, signaling the end of the Cold War. Baker and Bush are at left, next to Genscher and Kohl, with Gorbachev and Shevardnadze on the right.

Presidents Bush and Havel signing a U.S.-Czechoslovak declaration of principles in the Cabinet Room, October 22, 1991. Havel was signing on behalf of a
country to disappear from the map of Europe just over a year later.

NATO leaders pose for their "class photo" at the November 1991 Rome
Summit, where they approved NATO's "new strategic concept." Bush stunned
his allied counterparts by demanding to know that if Europe intends to
organize its security without the United States, "Tell me now!"

Presidents Bush and Gorbachev sign bilateral agreements—including, later in the day, the START treaty reducing strategic arms—at Gorbachev's *dacha* in Moscow, July 31, 1991, with Secretary Baker and Foreign Minister Bessmertnykh looking on. Three weeks later hard-liners staged a coup attempt against Gorbachev.

Presidents Bush and Yeltsin at Camp David in February 1992, where they issued a joint statement declaring "Russia and the United States do not regard themselves as potential adversaries."

5

The Challenges of
Postcommunist Transition

THE DAY AFTER THE BREACH of the Berlin Wall, Lech Wałęsa had a premonition that Poland would "pay the price" for this event because of German preoccupation with the challenges of unification.[1] Indeed, all the countries of Central and Eastern Europe paid a price because of Western preoccupation first with German unification, then with the Iraqi invasion of Kuwait in August 1990, and finally with the disintegration of the Soviet Union after the failed coup of August 1991. Eastern Europe continued to engage U.S. and other Western attention, but never with the priority and focus that it commanded in 1989 and 1990. The leadership that the United States provided in Eastern Europe during this early period would in any case have been hard to sustain, as the revolutionary drama gave way to the more prosaic challenges of structurally transforming these political, economic, and social systems.

In 1989 and through 1990, the United States and the European Community responded swiftly and appropriately, if not always generously, to the urgent needs of the new democracies of Central and Eastern Europe. The major Western and transatlantic institutions—NATO, the European Community, the Conference on Security and Cooperation in Europe, the Western European Union, and the Council of Europe—all moved quickly to help integrate the new democracies, as did the newly created Group of 24. By the end of 1990, all these countries had joined or rejoined the General Agreement on Tariffs and Trade (GATT), the International Monetary Fund, and the World Bank, and most were admitted as associate members of the Organization for Economic Cooperation and Development (OECD). A series of reciprocal market-opening measures implemented with the EC as well as the United States in early

1990 helped enable Hungary and especially Poland to register trade surpluses with the West in their first difficult year of economic transition.

It was at the beginning of 1991 that Wałęsa's premonition manifested itself, for the West's growing neglect coincided with a sharp deterioration within the region. A combination of factors were at work: the growing number of countries joining Poland and Hungary on the road to reform and competing for scarce Western resources; a sharp downturn in regional trade, owing to the disappearance of the East German market and virtual collapse of the Soviet market; and the severe (and uncompensated) impact of international sanctions against Iraq and later Yugoslavia. Most serious, as has been seen, was the growing fragmentation of the Soviet Union, which generated urgent calls from Central and Eastern Europe for integration into Western structures. Yet at the very time that a renewed Western commitment and an updated strategy were most urgently needed, the United States and Western Europe alike were elsewher e preoccupied, their strategic vision diffused and resources stretched by the costs of the Gulf War and the burgeoning assistance needs of the Soviet Union. Additionally, a Western recession, aggravated by the high cost of German unification, constricted Western markets and fueled new protectionist measures against East European products. Western markets that were opened to them in 1990 were slammed partially shut in 1991. This was hardly the economic and political chaos of the 1920s, but neither was it an international economic environment conducive to economic recovery and growth.

First Encounters

In early 1990 the countries of Central and Eastern Europe were poised uncertainly between the old order and the new. Elections had been held only in Poland, and even there the power-sharing stipulations of the Roundtable Agreement had assured communist control of the presidency, as well as the key defense and interior ministries, and 65 percent of the seats in the Sejm (the lower, and more important, of the two houses of the Polish parliament). Elsewhere, the revolutions of 1989 had produced stunning changes of power at the top, but these new leaders presided over political and economic systems that were essentially unaltered. This jarring duality was brought home on a trip by Secretary Baker to Prague, Sofia, and Bucharest from February 7 to 11, 1990, rendered here in a series of impressions and vignettes.

With Havel and Kafka in Prague   Accompanying Secretary Baker to Prague in early February 1990, just a few weeks after the "Velvet Revolution," was a surreal experience. Prague Castle, where I had been not so many months before with a congressional delegation led by Senator John Glenn for meetings with some of the worst of the East European communist leaders, was now occupied by the flower children around President Václav Havel. The world, it seemed, had been turned upside down. Or had it? This was, after all, Kafka's castle; his book of that title was written just around the corner.² Havel's aides recounted an event that occurred a few days before we arrived. Havel, it seemed, needed to communicate with President Gorbachev by telephone but was not sure how this could be done. As they were discussing the matter in a corridor, a hidden door opened from one of the walls and out came a security official with a telephone wired into the Warsaw Pact circuit. They had not known about the circuit, the hidden room, or the man behind the wall, who evidently had been waiting patiently for his services to be required by his new superiors. The story made one wonder how many other ghosts from the past were lurking behind the walls of postcommunist Eastern Europe.

There was something Kafkaesque, too, about the ubiquitous *Havel na Hrad!* (Havel to the Castle!) posters. I spotted one miniature in a working-class beer hall that I used to frequent during my student days in Prague in the late 1970s and had revisited a couple of times since. It was just above the cash register, in exactly the same spot that a picture of communist leader Gustáv Husák once hung. Surely this time the image was placed out of real conviction! (Havel would have appreciated the irony, for he had begun his celebrated essay "The Power of the Powerless" with the story of the conformist, and therefore culpable, greengrocer who dutifully displayed regime propaganda slogans in his shop window.) And surely the federal assembly had voted its conscience in electing Havel president without a single vote against. Of course, this was the same federal assembly (give or take a few changes pushed through during the Velvet Revolution) that shortly before would approve, also unanimously, anything sent to it by the communist regime, including vitriolic denunciations of that infamous "enemy of the people" Václav Havel, but never mind.

The meetings took place in a gilded chamber of Hradčany Castle. Havel, looking uncomfortable in a new suit and tie, spoke in long, complex monologues that his interpreter struggled heroically to follow. I recognized her from my last trip to Prague, when she was interpreting the rather simpler stock phrases of Vasil Bil'ak and other egregious exemplars of Czechoslovakia's communist leadership. Like the man behind the wall, her presence was a jarring link with a past whose legacy would persist for a long time to come. Chain-smoking and looking down at his hands, glancing up furtively every so often as if embarrassed to find others in the room with him, Havel spoke in a low monotone that obliterated the usual sing-song of Prague-style Czech. His main lines of thought, familiar from his many essays published abroad, bore interestingly but not always wisely on his unexpected new political responsibilities. He spoke eloquently about the moral and political devastation of his country. Introducing morality into Czechoslovak foreign policy was among his priorities, and he felt that his small country had a particular mission to help overcome Europe's division into two hostile blocs. He saw the Conference on Security and Cooperation in Europe (CSCE) as the foundation of a new "pan-European peace order" that would supplant the two military alliances.

Our concern was that Havel's ethical compass would prove an untrustworthy guide for the difficult world his country was entering. With exquisite politeness, Secretary Baker observed that we did not see the United States and the Soviet Union, NATO and the Warsaw Pact, as two sides of the same coin. Nor did we believe that the CSCE could replace the North Atlantic alliance as a reliable security organization. NATO, as a defensive alliance of democracies and the institutional link that bound the United States to European security, should be preserved as a factor of stability. This was no abstract matter. Baker was headed the next day for Moscow, where he hoped to begin persuading Gorbachev and Shevardnadze to accept continued membership in NATO by a united Germany.[3] Against this backdrop, we worried that Havel, in all innocence and with the best of intentions, could do considerable harm, including to his own country, by placing his hopes in, and lending his considerable moral authority to, an elusive and illusory peace order.

Secretary Baker's major speech, discussed below, was delivered at Charles University, in the same hall where my graduation ceremonies had been held from the university's Summer School of Slavonic Studies in 1977. Nowhere in view were the miserable party hacks who had taken over the university under the so-called normalization following the 1968 invasion; instead, Baker was introduced by Radim Palouš, who had been dismissed after 1968 but had been quickly reinstated as

Charles University's new rector. Building on his December 1989 Berlin speech, which had been devoted to "the new Europe, the new Atlanticism," Baker focused his remarks on "how we might promote, perpetuate, and protect Europe's democratic revolutions."[4]

Czech-Slovak Dissonance   After Prague, Secretary Baker continued on to Moscow for discussions on German unification and our proposal for a Two Plus Four process, ultimately agreed to at the conclusion of the trip in Ottawa. (Indeed, for all the drama associated with the Velvet Revolution, the trip was dominated by German events: the usual careful background briefings to the traveling press on the secretary's plane dealt almost exclusively with Germany.) Inasmuch as my NSC colleague Condoleezza Rice was responsible for the Moscow leg of the journey, I remained behind in Prague—waiting for the Baker entourage to decide whether he would visit Bulgaria and Romania after Moscow. Romania was the stumbling block. Given our misgivings over the actions and intentions of the National Salvation Front since the December 1989 Revolution, there was a debate as to whether a visit by the secretary of state would advance democratic change. Or would it provide undeserved legitimation of a government that had yet to demonstrate its democratic bona fides? Ultimately the secretary decided to stay a full day in Sofia but stop only for a few hours in Bucharest, using the opportunity to press a democratic agenda on the ruling establishment and lend support to the fledgling opposition parties.[5]

With time on my hands, I arranged to visit Civic Forum headquarters in Prague and then travel to Bratislava, the Slovak capital, to give a talk at an academic institute and meet with officials of Public Against Violence (Civic Forum's Slovak counterpart) in their new headquarters. The energetic staff at Civic Forum—headquartered near the Magic Lantern theater, Havel's "command post" during the Velvet Revolution—offered the remarkable revelation that none of them had been to Slovakia since December, so preoccupied had they been with organizing at the grass roots in the Czech lands of Bohemia and Moravia. Yet Bratislava was only a three-hour drive, and two months was an eternity given the rapidity of political change in the country. It was an early indication that the long-suppressed differences between Czechs and Slovaks might resurface sooner rather than later; indeed, the symbolic solidarity between Havel, a Czech, and Alexander Dubček, a Slovak, that had helped spark the Velvet Revolution already seemed a dim memory.

These fears were borne out in Bratislava. The political and economic agendas of Civic Forum and Public Against Violence were already diverging, and resentment was building among Slovaks that they were being ignored and taken for granted by the Czechs. Their complicated relationship with the Czechs also translated into an unexpected wariness tinged with mistrust of American intentions. For one thing, Slovak perceptions of the United States for the most part had been filtered through the distant and suspect prism of Prague. In this respect, there was a certain similarity with East Germany, where attitudes were shaped via the Federal Republic and thus similarly distorted. It was not hostility but rather a philosophical distance and disconnectedness that contrasted sharply with the easy familiarity and instinctive pro-Americanism one encountered among the Poles, Czechs, and Hungarians.[6]

A brief tour of Bratislava revealed another surprise.[7] In the hills in which the former communist *nomenklatura* resided was one particularly imposing villa—still occupied by Vasil Bil'ak. The policy of conciliation espoused by Havel and others—of giving officials of the former communist regime a dignified exit—was going to be harder to apply in the case of a man like Bil'ak. He was among the anti-Dubček conspirators in 1968 and one of those who had requested the Soviet invasion.[8] Such questions presaged the difficult battle over the Lustration (*Lustrace*) law of bringing to light the crimes of the communist period. They also foretold the special difficulties Slovakia would have in ridding itself of the remnants of the old guard. Precisely because the latter days of communist rule had not been as repressive in Slovakia as in the Czech lands, the break with the past was less decisive, more ambiguous.

Bulgaria Arriving in Sofia on February 9, a day ahead of the Baker entourage, I arranged through our embassy to visit the headquarters of the Union of Democratic Forces (UDF) and have separate meetings with several of its leaders, who would also meet with Secretary Baker. It was a pivotal time in Bulgaria. The Bulgarian Communist party, in an extraordinary congress a few days before, had changed its name to "Socialist," and a stormy roundtable meeting with the opposition had set a date for early national elections. The UDF, having finally secured office space from the still-communist Bulgarian government (which remained the country's sole landlord as well as its sole employer), had just moved in the week before to a dilapidated building with just one telephone and no copiers, fax machines, or computers. The dim lighting illuminated one or two bearded, Tolstoyesque figures. Despite its meager infrastructure, the UDF had managed to produce the first edition of the newspaper *Demokratsia* and was trying to weld a cohesive political movement out of a congeries of disparate personalities and agendas.

A meeting with several opposition leaders that afternoon in my hotel room was a preview of what Baker would encounter the next day. Sofia being one of those cities where everyone knows everyone else, these opposition leaders knew well what the regime was up to. They spoke with precision about the regime's strategy and what would have to be done to counter it. The regime had co-opted their agenda and called for early elections, confident that it could sufficiently restrict the opposition's ability to organize and publicize its campaign. They needed maximum international pressure to have a fighting chance in the elections, and they needed to hold together despite the disparity of their political orientations. It was a diverse group, held together in plausible harmony by the self-effacing and conciliatory UDF chairman Zhelyu Zhelev.[9] A former dissident philosopher, Zhelev had now become an unlikely but effective political leader, if only because his ego was smaller than those of other UDF leaders. The next time I saw him he was visiting the White House as president of Bulgaria, the first Bulgarian head of state or government ever to do so.

Baker arrived the next day, fresh from a small breakthrough with Gorbachev and Shevardnadze on the Two Plus Four concept.[10] It was the first visit to Bulgaria by an American secretary of state. The main official meeting was bizarre: it was around an enormous round table in a cavernous room, with the Bulgarian side represented by Petǔr Mladenov and Alexander Lilov, who had succeeded Todor Zhivkov as president and party leader respectively, and new prime minister Andrei Lukanov. Mladenov, who did most of the talking, was a nonentity; Lilov, an *apparatchik* who looked vaguely familiar. Lukanov was a smooth talker who knew how to strike the right themes with Western leaders. "Lukanov the *lukav*," meaning unprincipled and crafty, was how Bulgarian critics saw him. Baker saw him, rightly, as the one to do business with.

Baker was blunt. Although he must have been preoccupied with German affairs and the diplomatic challenge facing him in Ottawa the next day, the secretary had mastered his brief in consummate lawyerly fashion. He knew before the meeting began exactly what he wanted to achieve. He meant to push these officials a few steps further down the road of supporting democratic change by making it clear that the United States was not about to support sham democracy or reform communism. They could expect our help if and only if the new government took further, demonstrable steps toward political and economic liberalization; otherwise, we would cut them off from G-24 and IMF assistance. In what I came to learn was his standard operating procedure, Baker quickly cut through their thundering generalities to focus on the specific, tangible, and measurable. In Sofia (and, the next day, Bucharest), it was the parliamentary elections scheduled for early summer. He pressed them on electoral laws and procedures, campaign financing and organization, media access, and impartial election observers. The presentation was direct to the point of lecturing, even bullying.

This was the first time I had seen Baker at work in a confrontational setting, the meeting with Havel having been a love-fest. I was taking mental notes, from which I later drew when thrust into the unfamiliar role of dealing with ministers, prime ministers, and presidents on my own. Somehow, his bearing, courtesy, mastery of detail, and seriousness of purpose enabled him to say the most undiplomatic and demanding things without giving offense. Or perhaps it was that his manner did not allow his interlocutors to show offense. (One of Havel's chief advisers later remarked that when Bush or Baker entered the room it was as if the entire history and power of the United States entered with him.[11] Perhaps these Bulgarian officials were similarly awed.) Of course, he knew, and knew that they knew, that they were the ones who needed something and we were the ones who needed to have our concerns met. He was not going to waste his time or theirs with diplomatic niceties; he wanted to let them know precisely what we wanted to see happen. They got the message. What they would do with it remained to be seen.

The secretary's meeting with opposition figures was less successful. Like President Bush's meetings with opposition leaders in Budapest in July 1989, this was a setting that invited posturing. There was little of the strategic precision of the day before; instead, speakers seized the occasion to curry favor with the American secretary of state, generally at the expense of other opposition leaders. Zhelev sat in bemused silence, intervening only occasionally for the purpose of gently steering the conversation away from partisan backbiting. Baker did his best, shifting from the role of secretary of state to former manager of four presidential election campaigns, three of them successful. He spoke of building and maintaining electoral unity in order to topple the communists,[12] making it clear that while the United States would be formally neutral, our sympathies and support were for parties of the democratic opposition. It was a point Baker made emphatically in addressing a small but enthusiastic rally awaiting him at our hotel after the day's events.

Romania   If Prague had been surreal, Bucharest was eerie. Otopeni Airport, the presidential palace, and University Square were pock-marked with bullet holes. It was like a war zone, as indeed it had been just six weeks before. We traveled in what must have been the world's longest motorcade. For some reason, no vans or buses had been laid on for the Baker party and the traveling press, so the whole crowd went in cars, the motorcade snaking its way to meetings in three separate locations in three hours—with the new government headed by Prime Minister Petre Roman of the National Salvation Front, with NSF Chairman Ion Iliescu, and with key opposition and independent figures.

Since the December revolution, the self-proclaimed provisional government of the National Salvation Front had made a series of retreats from its initial agenda. Elections would be held as promised, but instead of acting as caretaker and then stepping aside, Iliescu, around whom a Ceauşescu-like personality cult was already forming, had announced that he would run for president. The Front, instead of playing a temporary function as facilitator of democratic elections, was hunkering down for a permanent role. The authors of the revolution, meanwhile, were growing increasingly disenchanted with a ruling team that looked too much like the one they thought they had just got rid of. Student activists declared Bucharest's University Square a "communist-free zone" and were soon to establish a tent city in permanent protest.

Baker's pitch was much the same as in Sofia, adjusted to reflect our greater concerns about the political evolution in Romania. His focus was again on elections, particularly on the widest possible participation of election observers. Because we feared that the elections would be neither free nor fair, we wanted to be sure to have unambiguous evidence with which to mobilize continued international pressure. The secretary must have repeated a dozen times that we looked to the new Romanian leadership to issue public invitations for the CSCE and other institutions to send election observer missions. This, too, was typical for Baker: the more skeptical he was of progress, the more specific his demands. Inviting election observers may not have been much, but at least it was tangible, verifiable, and directly related to our larger objectives. While assuring Iliescu and Roman of our continued willingness to provide emergency humanitarian assistance, the secretary made it clear that other forms of economic assistance would be conditioned on real progress toward market democracy, of which there was scant evidence so far. Restoration of most favored nation status, which they sought as a symbol of American approval, would be forthcoming only in response to significant progress.

With Iliescu I experienced a sense of déjà vu: his manner and physical appearance were similar to Alexander Lilov's. And now I placed whom Lilov had reminded me of: Károly Grósz, Hungarian party leader in 1988 and early 1989, who in turn bore a resemblance to Miloš Jakeš, Czechoslovakia's communist leader up until the Velvet Revolution. A year later, traveling with Baker in Tirana, I added Albanian communist leader Ramiz Alia to the list. Iliescu, Lilov, Grósz, Jakeš, Alia: all were gray men, short of stature, with bland visages and impenetrable eyes. They came across as clever but unimaginative. These were the archetypical second generation East European communist leaders: not as evil as their predecessors and not as ideological, either, they were careerists, survivors, opportunists. They personified the banality of East European communism after its revolutionary fire had burned out. Veterans of many a leadership reshuffle or policy "new course" during the communist era, they were thoroughly creatures of the party-state bureaucracy from which they were spawned. Iliescu, it should be noted, had been purged by Ceaușescu for allegedly harboring reformist sentiments and so may have possessed an independence of mind, perhaps even a degree of personal courage.

After the official encounters with the National Salvation Front, we repaired to the ambassador's residence for meetings with opposition leaders. The residence was once the home of Ana Pauker, a first generation Romanian communist purged in 1952 by Gheorghe Gheorghiu-Dej, Ceaușescu's predecessor, but not before she had added a grand indoor swimming pool to provide the "vanguard of the proletariat" respite from its revolutionary labors. After a private meeting with Reverend László Tökés, whose defiance touched off the December revolution, Baker met in another large roundtable setting with some thirty opposition leaders. This was even more a shambles than the meeting in Sofia. For all their well-founded criticism of the Front's antidemocratic behavior, they evinced no shred of strategy for combating it. Baker lectured them on the need to stay together and mount a common electoral strategy if they hoped to defeat the NSF, but his words were falling on deaf ears. We left Bucharest more pessimistic than we had arrived.

In Prague, "the man behind the wall" suggested that the communists and their vestiges would be hard to expunge. In Romania, they were still running the country. The "spirit of Timişoara"—the revolutionary impulse as well as the manifesto of democratic reform embodied in the Timişoara Declaration of December 1989—served as a reminder that "democracy, market, Europe" were the aspirations of the revolution's true authors, but these brief first encounters in postcommunist Central and Eastern Europe were portents of the enormity and complexity of the challenges ahead.

"Democracy, Market, Europe"

For most of its modern history, Eastern Europe had been a collection of weak, multiethnic, unprotected lands between two large and powerful neighbors—Germany and Russia. Allowing that the generalization would need qualification to hold universally, it nonetheless captures the essence of the East European problem, and the problem Eastern Europe posed for a wider stability. The dilemma was therefore threefold: economic and political weakness, a legacy of bitter national conflict, and, to put it mildly, an international system that did not make room for the smaller nations of Eastern Europe. These three together dashed the hopes of East Europeans after 1848, when virtually the entire region rose in revolt against Habsburg rule; again after 1919, when most of these nations gained or regained their independence; and of course after 1945, when the entire region fell under Soviet domination.

1990 was a long way from 1848, but the same threefold dilemma of weakness, conflict, and exclusion were still evident. The similarities of the revolutions of 1989 were often superficial—spiraling public demonstrations leading to the swift and, with the exception of Romania, peaceful capitulation of the existing regimes, and their replacement by leaders of anticommunist umbrella movements with virtually identical democratic agendas. They tended to mask the much more complex and differentiated processes at work. So, too, did the commonality of the first phase of political and economic transformation, which included preparing the legal and political ground for the first round of free elections and establishing the constitutional foundations for democratic rule. It also involved embarking, under the guidance of the International Monetary Fund, on programs of macroeconomic stabilization, whether of the "shock" or gradualist varieties. These early steps were necessarily led from above by the new democratically elected governments, with little public debate or involvement. Thereafter began the much more variegated, intensely political, structural transformations of the political and economic systems, each with its own logic born of specific national circumstances.[13] The revolutions had just begun.

From the Balkans to the Baltic, "democracy, market Europe!" was the rallying cry, with "Europe" meaning not only integration with a prosperous, secure West but also replication of Western Europe's postwar success in overcoming destructive nationalism. To be "European," for Eastern Europe's new leaders, was, as one writer put it, "to think beyond their frontiers, to transcend the provincial and destructive terms of traditional debates."[14] The task confronting the peoples of the region and their new leaders was unprecedented, for they were undertaking three simultaneous, overlapping revolutions in the political, economic, and social spheres.

In prior cases of transition from authoritarian rule, at least some elements of a market economy or liberal democracy were already in place—an existing market-based economic system, for example, or a stable ruling elite. Among the postcommunist countries, everything had to be changed in one way or another, and everything was related to everything else. New elections had to be held even while constitutions were being revised and wholesale economic restructuring undertaken. Society at large, meanwhile, had to acclimate itself to new responsibilities, for, as de Tocqueville said with regard to the French Revolution, "Political freedom had been so long extinct . . . that people had almost entirely forgotten what it meant and how it functioned."[15]

The postcommunist transitions inevitably would be messy, intensely political processes, unlikely to conform to prescriptions hatched in Western social science laboratories or advanced by visiting teams of "expert advisers." The very term "transition" was misleading, implying movement from one fixed point to another "post-transition" destination.

There were, of course, alternative models of transition from authoritarian rule. General Augusto Pinochet's Chile and General Chun Doo-Hwan's South Korea were two models commonly adduced and sometimes studied in the region. Yet for the countries of Central and Eastern Europe, the "Korean model" of capitalist development undertaken by a still-authoritarian government was not what was being espoused or pursued by the new governments and their populaces. Their aspiration was democracy *and* the market. The alternative, and the danger, was authoritarianism pure and simple, not some new "model" that combined political authoritarianism and economic liberalism. It was probably true that the "Korean model" was inherently flawed, containing the seeds of its own destruction, in that free market systems inevitably generate internal pressures toward an eventual loosening of authoritarian rule. (The Chilean, South Korean, and Taiwanese examples supported the point, as each government was obliged eventually to bow to pressures for greatly expanded economic and political participation, though such was not the initial intent of the ruling establishments.) This was certainly true for postcommunist Central and Eastern Europe, whose populaces were not likely to be satisfied with economic freedom alone (nor shoulder its attendant burdens) if their hard-won political liberties were denied.

In this sense, it was reassuring that "democracy, market, Europe" were inseparable aspirations for most of the new Central and Eastern European leaders and the standards to which they were held by their publics. Political, economic, and social change under these circumstances could not be separated or pursued sequentially. Suspending the economic transformation in order to consolidate democratic rule or suspending democracy to push through painful economic reforms were recipes for achieving neither.

The political, economic, and social spheres interacted in complex ways. The Polish sociologist Jadwiga Staniszkis cited a former Polish minister of industry as saying, "I represent interests that do not exist yet."[16] It was a provocative thought. The minister did not say the interests were not yet articulated; he said they did not even exist. Of course, something related to "industrial interests" could be identified, but they amounted to the bureaucratic, monopolistic interests of an as yet unreformed managerial class, not those of an economically vibrant industrial sector manifesting itself in ways conducive to market-based economic competition. To be real in this sense, industrial interests had to be backed by social and economic power; to be politically relevant, they had to be accompanied by a devolution of power and creation of new avenues of political participation. To take another example: Most of the countries of the region had political parties that could be called "liberal" in the European sense of the term. Yet how could a European-style liberal party exist without a politically active entrepreneurial class wielding real economic power? Without these social and economic roots, the embryonic "parties" were more political "clubs" organized around a set of personalities and political orientations, a consideration that may explain why the "liberals" in Central and Eastern Europe soon lost their initial popularity and support.

One paradox was that the new, democratically elected governments were obliged to create the conditions for their own demise. Replacing the intrusive role of the state in social, economic, and political life was among their most important tasks, yet it required an exceptional concentration of governmental authority to destroy the old command system and replace it with less intrusive, regulatory government. They had, in short, to amass power in order to dispose of its excesses. The economic monopoly of the state had to be broken for democracy to take root, just as democratic legitimacy (and a measure of governmental efficiency) were required for structural economic transformation.

Over the longer term, the key to secure democracy would be civil society. The building, or rebuilding, of democratic civil society required economic empowerment and democratic devolution, as well as the cultivation of all the institutions and habits that go into making democracy work from the bottom up.[17] This would entail the democratization of public policy: devolution of power to lower levels, rebalancing legislative and executive authority, and, above all, enhancing public participation in the policy process through the development of private voluntary organizations (PVOs), nongovernmental organizations (NGOs), and other intermediate institutions that were leveled under the Stalinist *gleichschaltung* four decades before. These measures were not just adjuncts of democratic and market development; they were integral to the overall process of postcommunist transition. Their successful accomplishment would demand an awareness, as one writer put it, "that civil society and the market are vital to democracy—that there can be no democracy without a civil society, and no civil society without a market."[18]

In the economic realm, there were certain necessary and irreducible steps—price liberalization, macroeconomic stabilization, foreign trade liberalization, currency reform, small-scale privatization, and private sector promotion—that all of these countries undertook, albeit with differing levels of conviction and commitment.[19] These were the essentials of "marketization," which was often but wrongly equated with "privatization." The key elements of a market-based economy could be introduced relatively quickly and successfully, even if large areas of the economy remained under state ownership. Over the longer term, it was essential—for democracy as well as a market economy—to reduce the state's economic monopoly; thus a rational plan for mass privatization needed to be part of a longer-term (say, decade-long) strategy of economic restructuring. (Here again was the paradox of the government's crucial role in managing the economic transformation in a way that reduced its own role in managing the economy.) Yet this was also the politically most difficult task, for it raised the specter of mass unemployment of workers in hitherto protected positions. The task for the new governments of the region was not to privatize overnight but rather to put in place a rational and politically tenable process of mass privatization. Subsidies had to be reduced in order to control inflation and free up scarce resources for critical investments, a measure of market discipline was needed so as to reduce inefficiency, and conditions had to be created that would attract urgently needed foreign investment. Even that limited agenda would prove hard to fulfill.

During the initial period of economic restructuring, while much of the state-owned sector remained unreformed and unprofitable, it would be the new private sector that generated economic growth and provided new jobs. It would be imperative to nurture this sector, so that fledgling small businesses could prosper and expand—first in the service sector and then into light manufactures and other productive sectors. Improved access to Western markets was essential both for private sector growth and the attraction of foreign investment. Creation of new capital markets was also crucial, requiring financial reform and bank privatization as well as the creation of private pension funds and other new sources of indigenous capital.

Even under the best of circumstances, these economic measures were sure to spawn social discontent and generate new inequalities, among the populations at large as well as regionally. The diamond-shaped socioeconomic structure associated with advanced industrial democracies, with small upper and lower classes and a large middle class bulge, would be years in the creation. Nor would opportunities for social mobility emerge quickly. Instead, these transitions were likely to produce pyramidal socioeconomic structures, with a vast and resentful underclass and a small but conspicuously wealthy group at the top. Lacking the social welfare benefits that the East Germans acquired as a result of unification with a prosperous Federal Republic, the rest of Central and Eastern Europe had little capacity to redress these burgeoning social and economic inequalities and the political dangers associated with them. Absent external underwriting of costly social safety net programs, the only available answers were to be found in economic growth and job creation, along with a streamlining of existing welfare systems. These would take time.

Meanwhile, the burden would fall on the new political leaders of the region, whose inexperience called to mind Edmund Burke's characterization of the leaders of the French Revolution: "Among them . . . I saw some of known rank; some of shining talents; but of practical experience in the state, not one man was to be found. The best were only men of theory."[20] The tasks in 1989 as in 1789 were immense for, as Burke elsewhere put it, "To make a government requires no great prudence. . . . To give freedom is still more easy. . . . But to form a free government; that is, to temper together these opposite elements of liberty and restraint in one consistent work, requires much thought. . . ."[21] These reflections were echoed in 1990 by the Polish historian Adam Michnik, who stressed that "the victory of freedom has not yet meant the triumph of democracy": "Democracy is something more than freedom. Democracy is freedom institutionalized, freedom submitted to the limits of the law, freedom functioning as an object of compromise between the major political forces on the scene."[22]

New democracies, as Samuel Huntington observed, face an inevitable dilemma: "lacking legitimacy they cannot become effective; lacking effectiveness they cannot develop legitimacy."[23] Throughout Central and Eastern Europe there were debates over measures to strengthen governmental authority via a powerful presidency or electoral laws that aimed at limiting the number of small parties, for example by requiring parties to gain more than 4 or 5 percent of the popular vote to qualify for seats in the parliament. With or without these special measures, governments throughout the region were obliged to retreat in one fashion or another from radical reform measures in the face of popular backlash. As a long-term proposition it may be true, as Huntington argued, that public disillusionment is not only inevitable but salutary, in that "the lowered expectations it produces are the foundation of democratic stability,"[24] but in the short term it would prove a source of *in*stability and indeed, in some instances, of protracted governmental crisis.

Ralf Dahrendorf put it succinctly. "The issue is how to establish the constitution of liberty and anchor it firmly. The heart of the problem lies in the incongruent time scales of the political, the economic, and the social reforms·needed to this end."[25] Free elections and a democratic constitution could be effected in a matter of months, while structural economic transformation demanded a period of years, with the result that passage through the inevitable "valley of tears . . . will always take longer than the lifetime of the first parliament and . . . engender a degree of disillusionment which will threaten the new constitutional framework along with the economic reforms."[26] During the still longer process of building a civil society rooted in democracy, with much of the old managerial class still in place, these societies would remain vulnerable to what Václav Havel would later call the "post-communist nightmare" of authoritarian ultra-nationalism.[27]

Laying the Foundations

But to tell the story this way is to get too far ahead of events and the circumstances in which U.S. and other Western policy was actually made. At this time—that is, early 1990—General Jaruzelski was still president of Poland, Václav Havel sat atop an essentially unaltered political system, and "reform communists" or newly minted "democrats" of dubious authenticity ruled in Romania, Bulgaria, Hungary, and East Germany. Not counting the open but circumscribed June 1989 elections in Poland, free and fair democratic elections had yet to be held anywhere in the region. Stalin-era constitutions were still in place, as were the main institutions of the discredited but not yet dismantled communist party-state. In the economic sphere, only Poland (and, under different circumstances, Yugoslavia) had embarked on serious programs of market reform. It was probably too late for die-hard communists to turn the clock back, but neither could the clock be turned forward to reveal secure democracies throughout the region.

The essential task for Western policies was to consolidate the gains of the 1989 revolutions by facilitating the prompt withdrawal of Soviet troops and other elements of Soviet control and influence, promoting free and fair elections, and supporting the nascent democratic forces against the still formidable power of the ruling establishments. We could also provide emergency assistance where needed so as to avert a chaotic breakdown of order and assist with the transition from a rapidly collapsing system of central planning toward market-based economies. It was important, too, to establish an international consensus on the principles that should guide these unprecedented transitions and ensure that the governments of Central and Eastern Europe, as well as the Soviet leadership, endorsed them.

The traditionally cool U.S. attitude toward the Conference on Security and Cooperation in Europe (CSCE) was being revised rapidly, as the demise of East European communism pointed to a whole range of functions that an invigorated CSCE was well placed to perform. As early as his Mainz speech in May 1989, President Bush had called for adding free elections to the CSCE's mandate, an initiative later endorsed by the November 1990 Paris Summit. The CSCE at this point had no institutional character aside from the periodic conferences held under its purview, the most recent being the Vienna conference that concluded in January 1989. It needed to develop an institutional and operational capacity to fulfill what was now becoming its new mandate—the consolidation of democracy in Eastern Europe. Toward that end, the CSCE needed to agree on and establish a set of principles, building on but going far beyond the general precepts codified in the Final Act of the 1975 Helsinki conference.

A "Magna Carta of Free Enterprise"   The March–April 1990 Bonn conference on the economic dimensions of security—the so-called second basket of the 1975 Helsinki agreement of the CSCE—provided the right venue for reaching agreement on the principles of the transition from centrally planned toward market-based economic systems. The conference grew out of a 1987 West German proposal that the United States had reluctantly supported (at the Vienna review conference ending in January 1989) despite misgivings about offering economic concessions to unreformed Eastern economies.[28] This was the familiar West German preference for East-West contacts against the American (and British) insistence on conditionality. By early 1990, the circumstances were radically different, and we saw the Bonn conference as an ideal opportunity to affirm the principles that should guide the postcommunist economic transformations and on which the conditionality of Western assistance should be based. (While the Germans doubtless would argue that they were once again at the leading edge of history while the Americans only belatedly caught up, it was the circumstances more than U.S. attitudes that had changed.) We therefore attached a significance to this conference that may have surprised our European partners, long accustomed to American suspicions of the CSCE debating club. It was the beginning of a new U.S. look at the CSCE and its possibilities.

Accordingly, at the opening of the session, the U.S. delegation proposed ten principles that were ultimately accepted in the conference's concluding document. Affirming the link "between political pluralism and market economies," the principles included, with unusual specificity for a document of this kind, "fiscal and monetary policies that . . . enhance the ability of markets to function efficiently," "international and domestic policies aimed at expanding the free flow of trade," "free and competitive market economies where prices are based on supply and demand," and "protection of all types of property including private property." The declaration called special attention to the "particular importance of small and medium sized enterprises" and "the introduction of undistorted internal pricing." Finally, it called for "an efficient price mechanism and for progress toward convertibility," laying particular stress on "reform of the banking system, introducing a money market, reform of the investment laws, transformation of public enterprises, taxation, structural adjustment policy, [and] organization of a labor and capital market as well as a foreign exchange market."[29]

It was, as one commentator put it, a document that amounted to a "Magna Carta of Free Enterprise."[30] This was not an abstract exercise in declaration-drafting. Real choices lay ahead for postcommunist Eastern Europe as well as for the Soviet Union, with direct relevance for Western efforts to provide support and assistance. Poland's "shock therapy," which was to achieve remarkable if painful results in its first year, was being watched with a mixture of interest, skepticism, and disdain elsewhere in the region. The new leadership in Prague spoke of a "soft landing" on the way to a mixed economy, while Hungarian economists continued to debate a "third road" between capitalism and socialism. The Bulgarians and Romanians had not even begun to dismantle the old system of central planning.

While we did not intend at Bonn or elsewhere to dictate how the peoples of the East should organize their economic lives, we did consider it vitally important to reach agreement on the basic elements of market-based economic development and the terms on which these countries could expect Western help. Politically, we also wanted to support those forces in the East that genuinely wanted to build democracy and make it harder for the die-hards to legitimize their continued rule through some pseudodemocratic authoritarian rule.

The Bonn conference was followed in June 1990 by a conference in Copenhagen devoted to human rights, now called, in the argot of "Eurospeak," the "human dimension." As with the Bonn conference, we had expressed reservations about this series of meetings, particularly a planned 1991 meeting in Moscow. At Vienna, we and the British had bowed to the CSCE consensus on this issue but made it clear that our attendance hinged on significant improvements in the Soviet human rights record. (Little could we have known that the Moscow session ultimately would be held just after the failed hard-line coup attempt of August 1991 and the imminent collapse of the Soviet state, or that this would be the meeting that formally admitted into the CSCE the Baltic states of Lithuania, Latvia, and Estonia as sovereign, independent states.) Our attitude had shifted markedly by the time of the Copenhagen meeting, however.

Copenhagen began with the admission of Albania into the CSCE. This event, poignant to those of us who had followed Albania's self-imposed isolation on the Adriatic and listened to Radio Tirana's vitriolic English-language broadcasts, was accomplished in an odd fashion. Danish foreign minister Uffe Ellemann-Jensen, chairing the session, began by reading a letter from his Albanian counterpart formally petitioning to attend the conference as an observer. Ellemann-Jensen then said, "I assume there are no objections?" paused for a millisecond, and then moved on to the next item on his agenda. There was confused whispering among the delegations, with no one quite sure what had just transpired. At the first break, it became clear that Ellemann-Jensen, believing that Paragraph 54 of the Helsinki Final Act guaranteed observer status to all European states (plus the United States and Canada), had accepted the proposal without submitting it to a vote or even a debate.

Our concern, like that of many delegations, was with establishing a framework and set of procedures for Albania's eventual membership that would place an onus on that country to adhere to the democratic principles enshrined in the Helsinki Final Act and subsequent documents. In other words, we wanted to use the admission process for political purposes. We had in mind not just Albania but potential future applicants—not suspecting just how many there would be within the next two years!—for admission into a body that was now acquiring a much more ambitious character than anyone envisioned when the Final Act was signed. We insisted, for example, that applicants affirm their intention to abide by "Helsinki principles" and accept an initial observer mission to review the extent to which it met or deviated from those standards before membership was accorded. These procedures, later adopted at the Paris Summit of the CSCE in November 1990, proved useful indeed in dealing with the new states that emerged from the Soviet Union upon the latter's dissolution at the end of 1991.

Toward a CSCE "Constitution"   Secretary Baker's speech at the opening of the Copenhagen conference, one of his best, aimed at breathing new life into the CSCE, which he called "the conscience of the Continent," and signaling a new American approach toward it:

> We are present at the creation of a new age of Europe. It is a time of discussion of new architectures, councils, committees, confederations, and common houses. These are, no doubt, weighty matters. But all these deliberations of statesmen and diplomats, scholars and lawgivers, will amount to nothing if they forget a basic premise. This premise is that "all men are created equal, that they are endowed by their Creator with certain inalienable Rights, that among these are Life, Liberty, and the pursuit of Happiness." It is "to secure these rights [that] Governments are instituted among them, deriving their just powers from the consent of the governed." *That* is why we are here. . . .
>   Three challenges lie before us. First, we must ensure that the freedoms so recently won are rooted in societies governed by the rule of law and the consent of the governed. Second, we must ensure that all peoples of Europe may know the prosperity that comes from economic liberty and competitive markets. And third, we must ensure that we are not drawn into either inadvertent conflict or a replay of the disputes that preceded the Cold War.[31]

Among the specific U.S. proposals Baker advanced for the next CSCE Summit (held in Paris in November 1990) were ones to endorse the Bonn Principles of Economic Cooperation, strengthen the CSCE's role in conflict resolution (with specifics to be worked out at a meeting to be held in Valletta, Malta, in January 1991), and expand CSCE political consultation through annual foreign ministers' meetings and biannual review conferences. He also called for the CSCE to develop, as a first step toward its "institutionalization," mechanisms for promoting and monitoring free elections and to adopt at Copenhagen a concluding document that set forth "the elements of democratic society operating under the rule of law."

Baker also had raised this issue in his February 1990 Prague speech, echoing President Bush's call (at the 1989 Paris Summit of the G-7) for adding free elections to the human rights obligations of all members of the Conference on Security and Cooperation in Europe. Anticipating the round of elections scheduled in virtually every East European country between March and June of 1990, Baker proposed that all CSCE member states join with the United States in sending observing delegations. Previewing the message he would carry with him to Sofia and Bucharest a few days later, Baker added that "we are troubled by indications that some of the governments in the region have engaged in practices that will obstruct truly free and fair elections. . . ." There may not have been much we could do directly to guarantee that the Bulgarian and Romanian elections would be freely conducted, but we did have the capacity to raise the international stakes on those regimes and provide further encouragement elsewhere.

The Copenhagen document, whose final shape owed much to the work of the American delegation led by Ambassador Max Kampelman, was even more remarkable than the Bonn document in its programmatic detail.[32] Its commitments on election procedures were precise: "The participating States [i.e., the 35 members of the CSCE] will hold free elections at reasonable intervals, as established by law; permit all seats in at least one chamber of the national legislature to be freely contested by popular vote; . . . ensure that votes are cast by secret ballot or by equivalent free voting procedures . . . ; provide that no legal or administrative obstacle stands in the way of unimpeded access to the media . . . ; [and] invite observers from any other CSCE participating States and any appropriate private institutions and organizations who may wish to do so to observe the course of their national election proceedings."

The document went on to affirm fundamental freedoms and the rule of law, including commitments to specific practices that would give practical and measurable content to rights too often observed in the breach:

A clear separation [should be created] between the State and political parties; in particular, political parties will not be merged with the State. . . .

No one may be deprived of his property except in the public interest and subject to the conditions provided for by law and consistent with international commitments and obligations. . . .

Everyone will have the right to freedom of expression, the right of association . . . [and] the right to freedom of thought, conscience and religion. . . . [States will] ensure that individuals are permitted to exercise the right of association, including the right to form, join and participate effectively in nongovernmental organizations . . . , including trade unions and human rights monitoring groups.

The imposition of a state of emergency must be proclaimed officially, publicly, and in accordance with the provisions laid down by law; . . . such measures will not discriminate on the grounds of race, colour, sex, language, religion, social origin, or belonging to a minority. . . .

The participating States will protect the ethnic, cultural, linguistic and religious identity of national minorities on their territory and create conditions for the promotion of that identity. . . . [They] clearly and unequivocally condemn totalitarianism, racial and ethnic hatred, anti-semitism, xenophobia and discrimination. . . .

As one commentator put it, "Concepts such as a 'pluralist democracy' and 'the rule of law' had not been previously mentioned in CSCE documents. . . . True, these are merely words, but no such words have been allowed into any CSCE document between 1975, when the Helsinki Final Act was signed, and June 1990, when the [Document of the Copenhagen Meeting] was adopted." This "landmark international charter," he continued, "in its political scope and significance, is unmatched by other international human rights instruments."[33] Munich's *Süddeutsche Zeitung* offered the headline, "The CSCE States Adopt a Constitution." Like the Bonn document before it, the Copenhagen declaration had direct practical significance—in affirming the main goals of postcommunist transformation, establishing the conditions of Western assistance, and informing a broadly shared assistance strategy.

Western Assistance Strategies

The aspirations to "democracy, market, Europe" formed the basis of Western assistance strategies, which included emergency aid for the immediate tasks of the transitions toward democratic rule and sustained technical and financial assistance for creating the foundations of market-based economic systems. Western leaders also undertook multilateral efforts to support the integration of these economies into the broader European and global economy. To coordinate these activities, as has been seen, G-7 leaders had created a new forum for "concerted Western action" that became the Group of 24 industrialized democracies (G-24) under the chairmanship of the Commission of the European Community.

The common assumption during the heady days of 1989 was that a three- to five-year burst of external assistance—balance of payments and structural adjustment support from the international financial institutions, bilateral technical assistance programs coordinated through the G-24, and facilitation of foreign trade and investment—would propel these countries toward integration into the global economy. This assumption proved much too optimistic, and Western assistance efforts had to adjust to the longer term challenges of postcommunist transformation.

The U.S. Assistance Program   Eastern Europe figured prominently in President Bush's State of the Union Address in late January 1990: "There are singular moments in history—dates that divide all that goes before from all the comes after. . . . The events of the year just ended [mark] the beginning of a new era in world affairs. . . . Today, with communism crumbling, our aim must be to ensure democracy's advance . . . to take the lead in forging . . . a great and growing commonwealth of free nations."[34]

The next day, in his presentation to Congress of the administration's foreign affairs budget request, including $300 million for the SEED (Support for East European Democracy) Act, Secretary Baker offered a cautionary note:

> The old world of dogmatic dictatorships is on its way out. But the new world of secure, prosperous, and just democracies is not yet here. It will not arrive automatically. If we fail to support the principles that brought us this far, we could end up living in a future that resembles the past—the past of the Cold War and the conflicts that preceded it. Too many nations have won the war only to lose the peace. We cannot afford to let that happen now. The stakes are too high and can only get higher.[35]

And indeed Eastern Europe enjoyed priority attention for a time. At the end of 1989, the president had named Deputy Secretary of State

Lawrence Eagleburger as his coordinator for East European assistance, responsible not only for all programs administered under the SEED Act but for other assistance-related activities as well. It was a choice we on the NSC staff had pushed. Other options that we presented for the president's consideration were, in our view, clearly inferior. Letting the Agency for International Development (AID) run it was out of the question, as AID had no presence in the region and a developmental ethos ill-suited to the urgent needs of relatively advanced Central and Eastern European countries. Besides, at the senior levels of the administration there was a visceral aversion to AID that persisted even after the agency acquitted itself well and imaginatively in Central and Eastern Europe. Putting the NSC in charge was better, but Scowcroft felt (rightly) as a matter of principle that the NSC should not take on such a highly operational role.[36] Treasury lacked the strategic perspective that was needed, and a joint State-Treasury program (among the options offered) would only confuse lines of authority. State was the right agency to oversee the process, and the deputy secretary was the right level of seniority. This particular deputy secretary also knew the region well and exercised a degree of authority even beyond his rank.

At the same time, we wanted this to be a multiagency effort, so as to draw on the specific strengths of Treasury, Labor, the Environmental Protection Agency, Energy, and others, as well as to produce the widest possible backing within the administration. Given the active role being played in the region already by Labor Secretary Elizabeth Dole and other powerful cabinet officers, it was going to be multiagency regardless. (As it turned out, departments and agencies that could not be kept out of the action in 1989 and 1990 were by 1991 and 1992 invisible. Eastern Europe had become yesterday's news.) Under any arrangement, Treasury's role would be indispensable: it was, by long tradition, the lead agency with respect to policy on international debt, the international financial institutions (the IMF and World Bank), and other issues that bore directly on the postcommunist transitions. Accordingly, the president named Deputy Treasury Secretary John Robson, together with Council of Economic Affairs Chairman Michael Boskin, as Eagleburger's deputy coordinators. They were later joined by a third deputy, AID Administrator Ronald Roskens.

The day-to-day direction of the East European assistance program was devolved to Eagleburger's special adviser for East European assistance (a position I held in 1992 and 1993[37]), who chaired an interagency working group of State, NSC, Treasury, and AID (replicating, more or less, the coordinator and deputy coordinators) and an expanded group that included all of the 18 agencies engaged in the assistance effort. All assistance activities by any government agency—every trip to the region, each initiative or proposal, every dollar spent or promised—had to be coordinated with and approved by Eagleburger. The dynamics of the group evolved over time. Treasury's role diminished somewhat as the main lines of macroeconomic policy were established in the region; in contrast, AID's role expanded as assistance moved from the conceptual phase to implementation and monitoring. After the first year or so, the State/NSC/Treasury/AID working group became the venue of policy making, and AID became the lead implementing agency, all under the direction of the coordinator.[38]

The organization of U.S. assistance involving multiple agencies was a model of how to get things done. This was no interagency debating club; it was a operational body that made quick and authoritative decisions, whether at the level of the deputy secretary or his special adviser. It was the most efficient, streamlined, and collegial interagency effort anywhere in government. It was also a model of foreign assistance well suited for an era of budgetary stringency. It engaged the strengths of multiple agencies, including those charged with advancing U.S. commercial interests; embedded foreign assistance in a larger strategic design that was linked to domestic policy as well; and created innovative and cost-effective partnerships with the American private sector, business and nonprofit alike. It was, as well, woefully underfunded, though this liability made itself felt only later, as Poland and Hungary were joined by Czechoslovakia, Bulgaria, Romania, and others in competition for scarce resources.

In his February 1990 "From Revolution to Democracy" speech in Prague, Secretary Baker had laid out the main elements of the strategy, designed to "promote, perpetuate, and protect Europe's democratic revolutions." First was short-term emergency aid—food, medicine, disaster relief—of the kind we had already delivered in large quantities to Poland and Romania. This had logical priority, both to meet urgent immediate needs and to avert a chaotic breakdown of public order that would undermine economic and political reforms before they had really begun. Second were bilateral and multilateral (i.e., through the international financial institutions) efforts to facilitate debt restructuring and support macroeconomic stabilization programs so as to reduce hyperinflation and provide a stable economic environment conducive to growth and market development.

Third were various forms of technical and financial assistance. In the economic arena, our efforts focused on promotion of foreign investment, which would bring in capital, know-how, and new jobs, and on seed money and technical assistance for local private ventures so that a new and dynamic private sector could emerge. Later, as several countries embarked on programs of structural economic transformation, we also provided considerable assistance for the privatization of large-scale enterprises and banking systems. Finally, there was a wide variety of programs, albeit of modest scope, to help build the foundations of democratic rule through constitutional and electoral reform, assistance to nascent political parties, and others aimed at the reconstruction of civil society. (One specific program Baker announced in Prague was an International Media Fund to provide capital, equipment, and technical assistance to independent media, both print and electronic.)

In an address delivered in mid-February 1990, just ten days after Baker's Prague speech, Deputy Secretary Eagleburger spoke more operationally, in his new capacity as the president's coordinator for East European assistance:

> We can no longer think of Eastern Europe as a bloc. We must now think of each country in the region in its own light, with its unique history, aspirations, and potential. . . . Our efforts should be focused on projects where we can make a difference, not dispersed over so many programs that none in the end will have a substantial impact. . . .
>
> There have been calls . . . for a new Marshall Plan for Eastern Europe. . . . [But] we are not dealing with a situation similar to postwar Western Europe, where we had to help rebuild a region that was physically devastated but which still possessed the technical skills, public institutions, and market experience to recover quickly. In Eastern Europe, which is emerging from a 40-year time capsule and which lacks those skills and institutions, our strategy must be different. . . . Our primary goal, at least in the early stages, must be to provide the democratic institution-building skills and entrepreneurial know-how without which the privatization of the Eastern economies simply will not succeed.[39]

These tasks called for engagement of the American private sector and creation of a public-private partnership to use scarce public funds as a catalyst for much greater private engagement. President Bush focused on this aspect in his commencement address at the University of South Carolina in May 1990, in which he announced creation of a Citizens Democracy Corps as a "center and clearinghouse for American private sector assistance and volunteer activities in Eastern Europe."[40] Like the Enterprise Funds and the International Media Fund, the CDC had a private board of directors, announced but not formally appointed by the president, that made decisions with a minimum of governmental oversight, our idea being that eminent private Americans were better able than bureaucrats to take swift, effective action. The Enterprise Funds, with their mixed boards of Americans and citizens of the country in which they operated, proved particularly successful in providing loans and technical assistance to local businesses, serving also as catalysts for American investors. The Polish and Hungarian Funds, created after the president's July 1989 trip, were followed by Czechoslovak and Bulgarian Enterprise Funds in 1990 and 1991, respectively.[41]

Most other programs in the U.S. assistance effort were in the same spirit of public/private partnership—from the Peace Corps (whose Polish program soon became its largest) to the American Bar Association's Central and East European Legal Initiative (CEELI).[42] This program combined public funds with pro bono legal services provided by private American lawyers. In this way, we could use scarce public funds to leverage substantial assistance and also create self-sustaining programs that could continue even after Central and Eastern Europe no longer commanded priority attention. Indeed, by 1992 we faced the unanticipated problem that some of the Enterprise Funds actually turned a profit. Hence we had to amend their bylaws so that provision was made for disposing of their assets when the time came to close them down.

The U.S. program naturally evolved over its first three years. As I put it in congressional testimony in early 1993,

In 1989 and 1990, we sought "targets of opportunity" and put a premium on getting programs up and running as quickly as possible. It was politically essential to do so—to show U.S. engagement at that critical moment. In 1990 and 1991, we put in place the "building blocks" of the program. These included the four Enterprise Funds, partnership programs in various sectors, and large institutional contracts [in areas like privatization] that are administered regionally but deployed according to each country's specific needs. [In 1992] we developed more detailed country strategies—tightly argued, real-world statements of our priority objectives and the programs we have or intend to advance those objectives. . . .

In that thrilling fall of 1989, when our assistance program began, no one knew what lay ahead. . . . We engaged as fast as we could and learned as we went. We were willing to take risks because of the importance and urgency of the task at hand, and we adapted the program to changing circumstances. Now $3\frac{1}{2}$ years later, we are wiser, perhaps, but no more able to predict what the next few years will bring. These countries are still in the midst of profound and essentially unpredictable change; the economic transitions are in some cases well advanced, but the revolutionary transformation of these societies is only beginning.[43]

A program that was adequate to the requirements of 1989 and 1990 was by early 1991 eclipsed by the advent of new Eastern European claimants for scarce resources and a much deteriorated international economic environment. By March 1991, when Lech Wałęsa visited Washington as Poland's new president,[44] the administration had put together one further assistance package. In addition to a U.S.-brokered international agreement to reduce Poland's external debt burden by more than half, there were three new initiatives aimed at the region as a whole.

First was a Trade Enhancement Initiative (TEI), substantially opening the U.S. market to Central and Eastern European exports, including politically sensitive ones like steel, textiles, and agricultural products. The result of intense internal negotiations among USTR (Office of the U.S. Trade Representative), the Commerce and Agriculture Departments, and others, the TEI also expanded duty-free benefits under the U.S. Generalized System of Preferences (GSP). Even allowing that the United States was not going to be a major destination of most Central and Eastern European exports, this was a major market-opening measure that had the additional advantage of putting pressure on the Western Europeans to follow suit: "The President is challenging the European Community, Central and Eastern Europe's largest market, with the largest potential for trade expansion, to redouble its efforts to open its markets to Central and Eastern European countries and to open all sectors (including agriculture) for liberalization under the free trade area agreements now under negotiation with Poland, Hungary, and Czechoslovakia."[45]

Second was an American Business Initiative (ABI), a $45 million program carried out by the Agency for International Development (AID), the Department of Commerce, the Overseas Private Investment Corporation (OPIC), and the U.S. Trade and Development Program (TDP). Its purpose was to help the countries of the region promote U.S. trade and investment in key sectors: agriculture and agribusiness, energy, environment, telecommunications, and housing.[46] Although the ABI was to have uneven results in practice, owing partly to Commerce's slow implementation of its part of the package, some of its more successful programs helped Central and Eastern European countries take advantage of hundreds of million dollars in export and investment insurance programs administered by OPIC, the Export-Import Bank, and TDP. (When Polish prime minister Bielecki visited the White House in September 1991, President Bush announced a new housing loan guaranty program to promote the private housing sector in Poland and other countries of the region.[47])

Third was the president's decision to include in his budget a 50 percent increase in U.S. assistance to Central and Eastern Europe, from the $300 million authorized in 1989 to $470 million for the fiscal year beginning in October 1991. Originally intended for three countries in Central Europe, the SEED program was by 1991 stretched to cover more than a dozen from the Balkans to the Baltic, with a combined population of some 135 million. But Congress, which had trebled the president's 1989 request for Eastern Europe, was by this time in a different frame of mind and reduced the president's request to $400 million. Caught between a penny-pinching Republican minority and a Democratic majority flexing its muscles in anticipation of election year 1992, the president was not inclined to buck the political tide again.

Coordinating International Assistance   After its creation in July 1989, the G-24 sprang into action quickly, meeting in August, September, November, and again in December to garner financial pledges from member countries, organize the first shipments of food and other humanitarian aid to Poland, and begin developing an overall strategy of assistance. Given the enormity of the tasks ahead of the new democracies and the modesty of Western financial assistance pledged or contemplated, it was important to be clear about where and how Western support could make a difference. Aside from the example of Western economic and political success, the most important thing Western assistance could do was to encourage the Central and Eastern European governments to pursue policies that would promote continued democratic and free market development. In other words, the G-24 countries, individually and collectively, needed to provide economic incentives, technical assistance, and political suasion to help these new governments pursue the policies they should have been pursuing anyway. Beyond that, Western assistance could show the way and offer targeted assistance in key areas, but the chief burden would fall on these countries themselves, no matter the scope of outside aid.

"None of us should underestimate the difficulty of the work ahead," Baker had stressed in his February 1990 Prague speech. It was a warning that President Bush, Secretary Baker, and their Western European counterparts repeated at every occasion, but it always seemed to fall on deaf ears, so eager were the peoples of this region to believe that liberation would lead swiftly to prosperity.[48] While American and other Western leaders may have contributed to that impression by emphasizing that prosperity would eventually be theirs if they stayed the course of market reform, no one ever said the process would be easy or that it could be accomplished quickly.[49] For most in Central and Eastern Europe, West Germany's postwar "economic miracle" was their aspiration, their inspiration, their expectation. They failed to recall that the *wirtschaftswunder* was more than a decade in the making and was achieved under economic circumstances that were, relatively speaking, less difficult than Eastern Europe's economic, political, and social devastation after four decades of communist misrule.

The G-24 did well to affirm the conditions of Western assistance, a role that was particularly important in the early, chaotic period of postcommunist transition. On the American side, these proceeded from what Secretary Baker, in his Prague speech, called a "new democratic differentiation": "Because the circumstances of each nation differ considerably, it would be a mistake to apply a mechanistic assistance formula. . . . Any backsliding in the movement to create legitimate governments will isolate a nation from the support we can provide." In addition to the obvious practicality of offering support only to those countries in a position to make good use of it, this formula was meant as a warning to those resisting reform and a boost to the struggling democratic oppositions, particularly in Bulgaria and Romania. Through the PHARE (Poland/Hungary Aid for Restructuring of Economies) program, the European Community adopted essentially the same set of standards, linking its assistance to compliance with IMF-endorsed economic stabilization programs and continued movement toward democracy.[50]

There was broad agreement that the problems facing these countries were unlike those of traditional underdevelopment, but rather of severe, sometimes bizarre "mis-development." The Central European countries in particular had highly educated populations, skilled work forces, and existing, albeit decrepit, industrial bases, which meant that well-targeted external assistance often could achieve wonders by helping open up the inherent potential of these economies and societies. On the other hand, the legacy of some four decades of communist misrule meant that virtually every aspect of political, economic, and social life had to be reformed in one way or another.

Progress would be neither uniform nor orderly: some changes might be implemented from the top down, but most would proceed from the bottom up in the helter-skelter of daily efforts to make things work. These countries were in the midst of revolutionary flux, with the old system of central planning collapsing before anything could be created to replace it, and most were led by new and inexperienced leaders from the democratic opposition who faced extravagant popular expectations that the democratic revolutions would produce instant prosperity. In addition to direct financial support for macroeconomic stabilization programs, what was needed was the transfer of knowledge and the diversity of Western experience across the full range of political, economic, and social life.

Although a cumbersome and overly bureaucratic institution, the G-24 played an important role in coordinating overall approaches among the 24 participating countries, each with its own legal and bureaucratic structure and often a separate agenda. Its key achievement can be put this way: when the EC Commission's chair—Jacques Delors for ministerial-level meetings, Franz Andriessen for "senior officials" meetings—offered an introductory overview of the countries of the region and their assistance priorities, there was rarely a word of disagreement. It was not unusual for Andriessen's main points to be almost identical to those in the U.S. delegation's (and presumably other) briefing books. Achieving that level of consensus among so disparate a group was no mean feat. The commission also provided an important element of continuity and consistency as governments changed and attention was diverted elsewhere. We in Washington sometimes railed at the EC bureaucracy, but these particular "Eurocrats" became the close allies of all those in G-24 governments trying to keep priority attention focused on the ever-changing, ever-increasing needs of the Central and Eastern Europeans.

The G-24 also offered a forum for coordination with the international financial institutions and working out a certain division of labor. The IMF and the World Bank took the lead in macroeconomic stabilization and sectoral transformation.[51] Their standards, rigorously and indiscriminately applied at first, became more sensitive to the special circumstances surrounding the postcommunist transitions. The OECD proved particularly helpful in analyzing, in close consultation with the governments concerned, the structural changes required for market-based development.[52] Through its Center for Cooperation with Economies in Transition, established in 1990, and a "Partners in Transition" program, created in 1991 at U.S. initiative as a halfway house toward full membership, the OECD developed detailed sets of recommendations with candidate countries, beginning with Poland, Hungary, and Czechoslovakia. On the political side, the Council of Europe served, as it were, to translate CSCE principles into practical steps toward democratic governance and the rule of law; its "Demosthenes" program played a particularly useful role in helping bring the new democracies into conformity with wider European legal and human rights practices.[53] Other institutions, too numerous to name here, also fit into the general mosaic.

Among donor countries, a division of labor also developed, half by design and half spontaneously. The U.S. program focused on economic growth, private sector development, and civil society, whereas the EC's preference was for "social market" programs in public infrastructure, industrial restructuring, and social welfare. The difference between the two perspectives was more pragmatic than philosophical. The U.S. approach, favored also by the British, had nothing to do with "Reaganomics" or Thatcherism: It derived from the view that we should do what we could to help these countries produce wealth so that they could make their own choices. Since no one in the West was about to come up with the billions of dollars needed to underwrite social safety nets, finance major infrastructure projects, or clean up the environmental devastation, we wanted to help these countries develop as quickly as possible the financial wherewithal to address these problems themselves. This, we believed, was preferable to promulgating grandiose plans without providing any external resources toward their realization. Besides, it made sense for the United States to draw on its natural strength—a vibrant and diverse private sector—and leave most of the government-to-government programs to the European Community, to whose standards and norms the Central and Eastern Europeans needed to adapt anyway. (When the Office of Management and Budget and General Accounting Office lobbied to organize assistance programs, many of us bridled at the idea of transferring our own suffocating bureaucracy to our new friends in Central and Eastern Europe. Let the Western Europeans take on that task.)

Yet the G-24 never supplied the kind of strategic, operational coordination of assistance envisioned at its inception. Perhaps it never could have done so, given its close links to the EC bureaucracy and the jealously guarded national prerogatives of G-24 member countries, including the United States. The haphazard nature of Western approaches was acceptable during the initial phase of the postcommunist transitions, when Central and Eastern European governments were disorganized and when a degree of experimentation was inevitable. But the duplication of effort and competition among G-24 countries became increasingly costly as the Central European reform programs progressed. Over time, we in Washington developed close and surprisingly cordial cooperation with the EC Commission, as well as with the IMF, World Bank, and OECD, but there was little operational coordination, with the result that a great deal of duplication and competition persisted among donor countries.

The European Bank for Reconstruction and Development (EBRD) was a case in point. It was proposed in October 1989 by President Mitterrand without prior consultation and had more to do with French ambitions for wresting control away from the World Bank, which they saw as too much the creature of Washington, than with the needs of its nominal beneficiaries, the Central and Eastern Europeans. Despite skepticism on the part of the Dutch, Italians, British, and Germans, EC countries approved the proposal at the December 1989 EC Council meeting in Strasbourg, leaving the details for further negotiations.[54] From late 1989 into 1990, there was strenuous behind-the-scenes wrangling and horse-trading over the location and leadership of the bank. We had proposed Prague, with Vienna our second choice, so as to situate the bank in the region of its intended activities, and we wanted it led by a distinguished international financier already conversant in multilateral lending operations. We were outflanked from the beginning, however, and could do no more than help effect a compromise of sorts, whereby the bank would be headquartered in London rather than Paris under the presidency of Mitterrand's key foreign policy adviser, the flamboyant Jacques Attali.[55]

More substantive were disputes over the question of Soviet membership in the EBRD, which France supported but we opposed on grounds that Eastern Europe's needs would be eclipsed by the virtually unlimited needs of an essentially unreformed Soviet economy. A related dispute was whether the EBRD should lend chiefly to governments, as France proposed, or to private businesses, which we favored on grounds that these new firms were in greater need and likely to show greater promise as generators of jobs and financial profit. Both issues came to compromise: the USSR would join but with strict limits on its borrowing rights (so as not to deplete resources meant for Eastern Europe),[56] and lending rules were established that permitted both public and private borrowing but stipulated that at least 60 percent of loans must be to private business. After an excruciatingly slow start, the EBRD gradually acquired expertise that helped shift its initially statist, highly politicized agenda toward a more balanced one that had some relevance to the needs of the countries it ostensibly had been created to assist.

Why No Marshall Plan?   The G-24's chief failure was the paucity of aid offered by its members. By early 1992, the cumulative total of Western assistance to Central and Eastern Europe, according to the G-24 "scoreboard," was around $37.5 billion (30 million ECU),[57] a figure which included lines of credit and "commitments" and so was vastly greater that the amount actually received. Even allowing that the slowness of disbursements was often due to recipient countries' failure to meet the minimum appropriate conditions attached to assistance, the claimed total was wildly inflated. Nearly two-thirds was in the form of loans or lines of credit (often at prevailing world market rates) that the heavily indebted countries of Central and Eastern Europe could never draw on. Of the remaining third, many of the grants were total commitments for programs that would be funded over the course of several years, if at all. Yet everything was thrown into the hopper for the G-24's running scoreboard.

The U.S. share was 17 percent of the overall total but 32 percent of the total grant aid; Germany's was 20 percent of the overall and 22 percent of grants. The EC PHARE program and European Investment Bank contributed 12 percent and 10 percent respectively; all others were far behind.[58] The U.S. preference was for grant assistance, on grounds that it made little sense to offer loans at unfavorable rates to Central and Eastern European countries already laboring under huge debt burdens. This was a matter of principle but also of necessity, for U.S. credit reform (legislated in the wake of the savings and loan crisis of the late 1980s) required that every foreign loan have a budgetary offset pegged to the foreign country's creditworthiness. For most of Central and Eastern Europe, that meant up to fifty cents on the dollar. A $100 million loan, in other words, had to be backed by $50 million in the administration's already strained assistance budget. EC member countries had no such constraint; their governments could simply undertake a loan commitment without budgetary impact. These policy differences often led to acrimony in G-24 meetings in 1990 and into 1991, but by the end of that year the increasingly exposed Europeans joined the United States in showing caution before extending further loans.

Among the more onerous tasks the G-24 was obliged to perform was to solicit contributions for IMF-led stabilization programs. The typical pattern was for the IMF to come up with a funding level short of that actually needed and then to look to the G-24 to provide an additional amount of up to $1 billion. These were known in G-24 parlance as "gap-filling exercises," which produced heated exchanges between the United States and its Western partners. As has been seen, the United States led the effort to amass the $1 billion Polish stabilization fund, but we did so with $200 million in grant funding that we could not replicate thereafter. When it came time to support similar funds for Hungary and Czechoslovakia, we were able to offer only much smaller grants of $10 and $15 million respectively, leaving the EC to bear the lion's share of the burden. When Bulgaria and Romania joined the queve, neither we nor the EC met the IMF's targets, leaving those two countries to pursue macroeconomic stabilization programs that were seriously underfunded.[59]

By the beginning of 1991, the inadequacy of G-24 assistance levels had become all too apparent. Resources had not increased to meet the growing number of recipient countries, much less offset severe new external shocks to these nascent democracies. The virtual collapse of the East German and Soviet markets, together with the high cost of sanctions against Iraq and later Yugoslavia, contributed to a region-wide recession. In 1991, gross domestic product (GDP) declined by 8–10 percent in Poland, 10 percent in Czechoslovakia, 7–9 percent in Hungary, 9 percent in Romania, and a staggering 25 percent in Bulgaria.[60] During the winter of 1991–92, as will be seen, Albania came perilously close to extinction as a functioning society[61]—this at the very time that the Yugoslav civil war was threatening a wider Balkan conflagration.

This was the time for a new burst of Western assistance, supported by an entirely new Western strategy to deal with a situation in Central and Eastern Europe that had deteriorated markedly since Western leaders last gave the region serious attention in 1989–90. Yet no such effort was undertaken, as Western leaders were preoccupied with other concerns. Worse, existing resources increasingly were diverted to providing emergency aid to the Soviet Union in the form of subsidized Western food shipments that directly undercut Central and Eastern European exports. By 1991, G-24 meetings occasionally turned into name-calling affairs, with the EC criticizing the overall low levels of U.S. contributions and the United States reminding the Europeans that their claimed assistance levels were vastly inflated. The deeper truth was that neither we nor the European Community rose to the challenge of providing the levels of help needed for countries in the midst of profound economic transformation. Which side was the more culpable was hardly the relevant question.

We in Washington looked increasingly to our Western European partners to take the lead, and to some extent they did, but there was no replacing U.S. leadership when it came to setting and implementing a post–Cold War European and transatlantic agenda. The Marshall Plan offered little in the way of a model, except as a demonstration of the scope of American commitment. It was, as George Kennan, one of its principal architects, stressed, directed at the specific problems associated with postwar reconstruction in Western Europe,[62] almost none of which applied to the postcommunist states of Eastern Europe. The main problems they faced—creation of a new private sector and managerial class, mass privatization of thousands of state enterprises, and establishing the foundations of democratic civil societies—were not the work of a few years, no matter the scope of external assistance.

The inaptness of the Marshall Plan analogy and the unprecedented character of postcommunist transformation had the perverse effect of forestalling among Western governments a serious, ongoing review of the appropriate levels of Western assistance. (It also prejudiced subsequent debate over aid to Russia and the other states of the former Soviet Union, as Western governments settled on similarly insufficient levels of support.) While assistance on the scale of the Marshall Plan would not have yielded a commensurate increase in the probability of success in Central and Eastern Europe, nor appreciably reduced the social pain these populations had to endure, a strong case could have been made for a doubling or tripling of Western assistance as an investment in the stability of post–Cold War Europe.[63] Such an increase was not forthcoming nor even seriously debated here or in Europe.

There is no satisfactory explanation for Western failure to provide adequate resources for Eastern Europe. On the American side, a partial explanation was that the internal decision-making process continued to treat these issues as matters of foreign assistance rather than national security.[64] If the consolidation of democracy in Central and Eastern Europe was among our highest national security priorities, as it was, the expenditure of an additional $500 or $600 million toward that end should have been obvious and should not have required special pleading before cabinet officers. It was a modest sum relative to a defense budget running in the hundreds of *billions* of dollars.

As it turned out, the naming of a coordinator for East European assistance had the unintended effect of removing East European assistance issues from the ongoing, active agendas of cabinet officers. After Eagleburger's appointment, not a single meeting of the National Security Council (i.e., formal sessions chaired by the president), nor even of the NSC Deputies Committee, was devoted to East European assistance strategy. Of course, Eagleburger talked to Baker and Scowcroft, both of whom talked to the president, but that was not the same thing. Thus, instead of elevating Eastern Europe in the bureaucratic scheme of things, the coordinator's position had the effect of marginalizing the region from broader strategic considerations. A deputy secretary of state, especially one as effective and respected as Larry Eagleburger, is a powerful figure, but not powerful enough to single-handedly deliver cabinet officers. When it came to tough choices—garnering more money for assistance, bucking domestic lobbies in efforts to open U.S. markets to East European imports, and the like—Eagleburger was left without the ongoing support of Bush, Baker, and others. Perhaps the most telling fact is that Baker, in his memoirs running to 687 pages, does not refer once to the East European assistance program.[65]

There were at least three respects in which the Marshall Plan offered lessons that should have been applied in Central and Eastern Europe. First, responsibility for devising economic recovery programs should have rested more firmly with the peoples and governments concerned, just as it had in Western Europe under the Marshall Plan. Too much time, energy, and money were spent on issues like the launching of the EBRD, which had more to do with competing Western ambitions than with assisting countries in transition; too little attention was paid to supporting the first new democratic governments, which bore the full brunt of public disapproval. Second, encouragement of regional cooperation should have been a more explicit strategic goal of foreign assistance. While there was no need for strict conditionality to promote regional institutions, more could have been done to support and indeed insist upon cooperative efforts among Poles, Hungarians, Czechs, and Slovaks. Those in Prague or Budapest hoping to outrace their neighbors into the European Community should have been made to understand that membership in Western institutions entailed responsibilities that began with one's immediate neighborhood, and Western governments should have adopted a strategic design and backed it with financial inducements. Finally and most important was the strategic priority of the task: support for this region, like postwar Western Europe, was a matter not of foreign assistance but of European stability and security. It was a lesson that became vividly clear with the violent disintegration of Yugoslavia and the risks this posed for spreading instability.

6

The United States and Eastern Europe

IT WOULD BE HARD to exaggerate U.S. influence among the peoples of Central and Eastern Europe and their new political leaders in 1990 and 1991. They looked to us as the victor of the long Cold War against their chief oppressor, the champion of the ideals that had animated their own democratic revolutions, and, with our swift military triumph in the Gulf War in early 1991, the world's sole and unchallenged superpower. Wildly inflated though they often were, these perceptions gave us, during this early period, enormous influence over attitudes and policies in the region. At the same time, they gave rise to extravagant expectations of U.S. readiness to provide security for these embryonic democracies and provide levels of direct assistance that would propel them on the path to prosperity. Later on, as the drama of revolution gave way to what President Bush liked to call "the hard work of democracy" and our own attention wandered, U.S. influence correspondingly diminished, and the countries of Central and Eastern Europe gravitated naturally toward their immediate Western neighbors. But during this early period, U.S. influence was enormous—easily as great as that of the countries of Western Europe combined.

Yet the authority we commanded did not always translate into meaningful influence over the course of the postcommunist transitions. These hinged on fundamental changes well beyond the influence of the United States or even of the West collectively. It was all too easy to confuse the two: to mistake the influence we seemed to have with that which we were able to turn into tangible results. Our chief influence, naturally, was on the international context in which these democratic experiments played out. We were instrumental in securing the completion of Soviet military withdrawal and ending the vestiges of Moscow's imperial dominion, as well as in drawing these countries into a cooperative international system. U.S. leadership was instrumental in creating an international framework of assistance and laying the conceptual foundations for the postcommunist transitions in Central and Eastern Europe, as well as in pointing the way for the embryonic transitions farther east.

The United States also exerted substantial influence over the policies these new governments adopted—their foreign political orientations as well as their domestic reform programs—though our influence varied greatly by country. It was strongest in Poland, where we were consistently and actively engaged, much weaker in Hungary or Bulgaria, where high-level American interest was more episodic. Throughout the region, our main efforts were to engage the new leaders of the region on their most urgent security concerns, lending our support to those committed to building democracy and keeping the pressure on the recalcitrants, like the Romanians, to follow the same path.

The following surveys of U.S. bilateral relations with the countries of Central and Eastern Europe cannot do full justice to the extraordinarily rich and complex evolution of these countries in their first few years of postcommunist existence.[1] Inasmuch as they are told from the American perspective, this being a book about U.S. foreign policy, they may also tend to magnify the American role and hence should be seen against the backdrop of broader Western engagement in the region and the multiple dramas being played out in the Central and Eastern European countries themselves.

Poland: The Special Relationship

U.S. policy from the beginning had focused on Poland, owing to that country's geostrategic weight, the importance for the entire region of its trailblazing program of economic "shock therapy," and the friendly pressure exerted by the large and effective Polish-American community. The Balcerowicz plan of rapid "marketization" achieved swift results after its introduction on January 1, 1990: after prices were liberalized and the economy opened to foreign trade, empty shelves were soon filled with goods, albeit at prices beyond the reach of many Poles, and a vibrant new private sector began to spring up. Forecasts of severe winter food shortages had prompted a massive external assistance effort, but the fears proved largely groundless. For all the uncertainties ahead, the early results of the economic reforms were encouraging.

Prime Minister Mazowiecki in Washington   Although President Bush had exchanged long messages with Tadeusz Mazowiecki and had dispatched high-level investment missions to Poland, we and the Poles had agreed that an official visit to the United States by the prime minister should come only after the Polish reform program was launched. We thought we could do more to lend him support if he had already established his own program and agenda. Accordingly, the White House announced in late January that Mazowiecki would visit in mid-March 1990. Having successfully mobilized international support for the $1 billion Polish Stabilization Fund and (thanks to Senator Paul Simon and other leading Democrats in Congress) tripled our initial assistance package for Poland, our aims now were to throw our weight behind Mazowiecki and his reform program. We also intended to strengthen his hand in securing Poland's full independence and lay the groundwork for Poland's integration into the Western community of nations. Because there were no new assistance measures announced, the media, especially the resolutely superficial White House press corps, failed to grasp how important this visit was for Poland's transition to democracy and full independence.

In their meetings—following the usual formula of arrival ceremony, one-on-one meeting in the Oval Office, and expanded meeting in the Cabinet Room[2]—Mazowiecki detailed Poland's experiment in "shock therapy," which had progressed as well as could have been hoped in its first three months. He and Foreign Minister Krzysztof Skubiszewski then turned to their international agenda. They reiterated Poland's unambiguous support for German unification, arguing that a country that had been partitioned for 125 years could do no less than support the right of self-determination for its neighbor, even for a country that had destroyed Poland's independence more than once. Their concern, however, was with securing the finality, as a legal matter, of the German-Polish border as the two Germanies moved swiftly toward unity.[3] Their other concerns lay in the complex of issues related to the future of the Warsaw Pact, the withdrawal of Soviet troops from Poland, and, more fundamentally, measures that would enhance Poland's newly won, but still precarious, independence within a broader European and transatlantic community.

Privately and in his public remarks, the president echoed those themes and referred prominently to Poland's border:

America wants to help Poland succeed. We want to welcome Poland as a full partner in the community of free nations [and help it] achieve its full measure of democracy and independence. . . . At this time of great and turbulent change . . . the United States will remain a European power—a force for freedom, stability, and security. . . . We see a new Europe in which the security of all European states—and their fundamental right to exist secure within their present borders—is assured.[4]

Bush and Mazowiecki connected well personally.[5] In a follow-up meeting the next day arranged at Bush's invitation, Mazowiecki focused particularly on the question of Soviet troops and the more general difficulty he was having of persuading Soviet officials of Poland's independence. Bush asked if there was anything else that he could say or do that would be helpful. Mazowiecki said that a statement affirming Poland's positive role in building the future of Europe would be helpful. After the meeting, Bush repaired to a prescheduled press conference dealing mainly with Central America. Before any of us could get to him to remind him of Mazowiecki's request, Bush ad libbed a reference to their meeting, noting that "we discussed questions of European security and Poland's place in a new Europe. And I told the prime minister that we see an important role for a free, democratic and independent Poland as a factor for stability in Europe." Later in the press conference, asked about Soviet troops in Poland, the president stated, perhaps too plainly, that "there isn't any need for Soviet troops in Eastern Europe, and the sooner they get out of there, the better."[6] (We on the NSC staff cringed whenever Bush got asked the question, because he always went for the blunt rather than the diplomatic response.)

Breakdown of Solidarity   Back at home, Mazowiecki's honeymoon with the Polish people was short-lived. After his domestic popularity plummeted, it became fashionable, within Poland and outside, to blame Mazowiecki and Finance Minister Leszek Balcerowicz for failures of leadership. This was unfair. To be sure, they might have done better in explaining to the population what was coming and why, as Labor Minister Jacek Kuroń tried to do in his weekly television spots, and it may also be true that Mazowiecki was too much the aloof intellectual to play that role. But the Polish leadership was trying to rescue an economy that had been in steep decline for a decade and more. No amount of inspired leadership could have altered the fundamental facts that the needed economic reform measures would hit hardest the average Polish worker, Solidarity's main constituency, and that tangible benefits for the bulk of the Polish population would take years to be realized.

Nor were Polish attitudes to be changed overnight. Most Poles might have conceded the need for sweeping economic change, but they were uncertain what this might entail and impatient for quick results. It is hard to imagine any Polish leadership successfully undertaking essential reform measures, and the economic dislocation inevitably attending them, while also retaining popular support. Mazowiecki and Balcerowicz deserve great credit for doing the first while others were pandering to public grievances without advancing a credible alternative. Along with Foreign Minister Skubiszewski, they also built up tremendous support for the Polish cause among Western countries, above all the United States, as well as skillfully managing relations with Moscow.

Two figures loomed in the background in mid-1990: Lech Wałęsa, on the political sidelines for the first time in a decade, and President Wojciech Jaruzelski, an embarrassing reminder that Poland's once-radical political reforms had been eclipsed by democratic elections elsewhere in the region. Jaruzelski posed a problem for us as well, particularly after Wałęsa decided to break the Roundtable Agreement and challenge Jaruzelski in new presidential elections. During his July 1989 visit, President Bush had invited Jaruzelski to pay a reciprocal visit to the United States some time in 1990. A year later, the circumstances surrounding that invitation had been wholly overtaken by events. President Bush, who believed deeply that breaking commitments of this kind would be both unethical and a dangerous breach of the trust on which political leaders have to rely, would not hear of our suggestion at staff level that he renege on the invitation, so we resorted instead to having Embassy Warsaw make periodic queries to see whether Jaruzelski was still planning to come. The invitation was of course still in force, we stressed; we just wondered whether the visit was still on in light of the new circumstances. Ultimately, Jaruzelski decided not to run for president and, taking our repeated hints, to cancel the U.S. visit—two further signs of dignity, perhaps even patriotism, on the part of this man of ambiguous legacy.[7]

Wałęsa's motives in challenging Jaruzelski for the presidency ostensibly were to effect a political acceleration.[8] Feeling the brunt of worker discontent, he argued that the economic reform program, directed largely from on high, was stifling democratic development. Leaving aside matters of personal ambition, Wałęsa had hit on one of the dilemmas of the postcommunist transitions: whether to maintain political solidarity, meaning in effect a suspension of full democratic participation, in order to pursue essential but painful economic reform measures, or to give priority to democratic expression even knowing that this would result in an antireform backlash. Another dilemma was buried inside this one: whether to enhance the power and efficiency of the executive, through a strong presidency or electoral laws that erected barriers to small parties (e.g., by requiring that a party gain 4 or 5 percent of the votes cast to qualify for seats in parliament), or whether to strengthen political participation even if it meant a plethora of squabbling microparties. These were not, strictly speaking, dilemmas but rather questions of balancing competing objectives, and Poland experimented with various formulas in its early postcommunist transition. Indeed, Wałęsa himself jumped to the other side of the argument soon after becoming president, pushing for sweeping presidential powers in order to drive through further economic reforms.

Our view in Washington was that the Poles would be making a mistake to break ranks less than a year into their economic reforms, but the choice was Poland's to make, and we would support whatever was decided so long as it was done democratically. We were determined to keep ourselves out of Poland's internal affairs, despite pressures from some Polish quarters to discourage Wałęsa from challenging the new political set-up so early in Poland's postcommunist transition. Not for the last time, we focused instead on the broader issues of Poland's democratic and free market development. Given Wałęsa's highly ambivalent public statements on the economic reforms—sometimes he argued they were moving too slowly, other times he would say that "if we try to move to the market in one jump, we will break both our legs"[9]—we used our still considerable influence to stress how crucial it was for the Poles to stay the course of an economic reform program that was working. This was our consistent line through the terms in office of two Polish presidents and six prime ministers from 1990 to 1992. It was this steadiness of purpose and support, more than any specific policies or assistance measures, that was the greatest American contribution to the Polish cause during this turbulent period.

Wałęsa won the December 1990 presidential elections, disposing of Mazowiecki handily but needing a runoff ballot to beat back an unexpected challenge from a bizarre émigré businessman named Stanisław Tymiński.[10] Wałęsa's initial steps were reassuring, owing partly to behind the scenes advice, coordinated with the administration, from the Polish-American Congress.[11] He retained Balcerowicz as finance minister, though demoting him from his position as deputy prime minister. For the successor to Mazowiecki as prime minister, Wałęsa overrode parliamentary pressures in favor of former Solidary lawyer Jan Olszewski, a critic of "shock therapy," and pushed through as his personal choice Jan Krzysztof Bielecki, a respected proponent of market reform.[12] The prematurely gray Bielecki was to turn grayer still in the coming year.

Wałęsa's State Visit   We and the Poles set about promptly to arrange an early trip to Washington by Wałęsa in his new capacity, agreeing on a full protocol state visit in March 1991. High on their agenda was the signing of a bilateral treaty, which they saw as a counterweight to one they were negotiating with Moscow and an adjunct to the other such documents with which they were littering the European landscape. (Czechoslovakia's new leaders were even more fascinated than the Poles with these pieces of paper. The spectacle was reminscent of the "spirit of Locarno" in the 1920s, when Europeans east and west produced dozens of bilateral and multilateral treaties—none of which did anything to arrest or deter Hitler's aggression.) While open to such a document, we wanted it to be an informal political declaration rather than a formal treaty.[13] On that basis, we drafted a notional text and negotiated it with Wałęsa's representatives in the weeks leading up to the visit.[14]

The U.S.-Polish "Declaration of Principles" was a nice two-page document that recalled the past close association between the two countries and peoples, "which survived even during the long periods when Poland's independence and liberty were denied." Its thrust was toward the future, however, affirming the principles and policies that would guide U.S.-Polish relations in the years ahead. The Poles had wanted an ironclad security guarantee but settled for this more general formulation, which was as far as we were then prepared to go: "The United States attaches great importance to the consolidation of Poland's democracy and independence, which it considers integral to the new Europe, whole and free."

The declaration was prepared at Poland's request, but there were also elements we insisted on, including codification of Poland's, especially Wałęsa's, commitment to free market democracy: "Poland and the United States share the conviction that the development of a market economy in Poland is essential to its stability and security. . . . Poland's firm commitment to an economic reform program that enjoys the endorsement and support of the International Monetary Fund has made possible the mobilization of substantial new financial and other economic assistance from the international community."[15]

Although overshadowed by the liberation of Kuwait less than a month before and a wave of independence declarations by Soviet republics, Wałęsa's visit was an almost complete success. At staff level, we had been working feverishly to conclude several new initiatives to support Poland's economic transition and further cement Wałęsa's commitment to it. The first and most important measure was agreement on reduction of Poland's official debt burden by more than half. Although this had been under negotiation for many months among Poland's official creditors in the Paris Club, Wałęsa's visit gave the Treasury Department added impetus to finish the deal quickly—a task that was facilitated by a series of messages and telephone calls by President Bush to each of his G-7 counterparts. Under terms of the agreement, creditors were also permitted to reduce bilateral debt by as much as 70 percent—which we did, using the additional debt relief to finance a new environmental foundation in Poland.[16]

The other measures, covered in the preceding chapter, included a Trade Enhancement Initiative and American Business Initiative—aimed at promoting trade and investment and challenging the European Community to follow suit—and a 50 percent increase in U.S. assistance to Central and Eastern Europe. They were directed at the region as a whole and were meant to give new impetus to postcommunist reforms that had been severely complicated by external reversals, notably the international sanctions against Iraq and the collapse of trade with the Soviet Union and the now defunct East Germany. As President Bush put it in the arrival ceremony welcoming Wałęsa, "Today we rededicate ourselves to the success of free market democracy in Poland and throughout Central and Eastern Europe."[17]

Wałęsa was at his most gracious and statesmanlike. Whereas he had been known to criticize the West for its niggardliness, he used his arrival statement publicly to thank the United States and President Bush personally for their "political, economic and, above all, moral" leadership. In his toast at the state dinner that night, Wałęsa described Bush as "the most popular politician in Poland"—a tribute that was literally true according to recent public opinion polls there.[18] Wałęsa opened the official meetings by saying that Bush had anticipated and met all of the requests for help that he had planned to make. As his advisers said privately later on, the Poles were ecstatic about the visit, both for the tangible initiatives and for the symbolic boost it gave Wałęsa.

Wałęsa reaffirmed his commitment to an accelerated pace of economic reform and increased U.S. investment, but with typical ambivalence. In a meeting later in the day with American business leaders, arranged by the Department of Commerce, Wałęsa warned of wholesale instability in Poland if increased investment were not forthcoming. As an NSC colleague quipped, it was like the cover of a back issue of the American humor magazine *National Lampoon*, which showed a man holding a pistol to the head of a puppy with the caption "Buy this magazine or I will shoot this dog." Wałęsa's was precisely the wrong message to send to corporate leaders, who needed reassurance about Poland's stability and his own commitment to the market, not an invitation to invest their resources in a country on the edge of an abyss.[19]

Wałęsa also made clear his political agenda at home: a new constitution that secured strong presidential powers, a new electoral law that would exclude minor parties and so facilitate a stable governmental coalition, and new elections for the Polish parliament, whose current members were elected in June 1989 as a result of the Roundtable Agreement that guaranteed heavy communist representation. He was stymied on all counts in the spring of 1991. New elections would be held, but not until October and on the basis of the existing system; in addition, Wałęsa's growing chorus of critics in the Sejm (the lower, and more powerful, of the two houses of parliament) blocked his efforts to amass new presidential powers.

Political Fragmentation As a frustrated Wałęsa hinted darkly at declaring emergency powers, one of his key advisers, Jarosław Kaczyński, visited Washington to test the American attitudes toward such a step.

When he called at the NSC on July 8, we were prepared for him, having been forewarned of his agenda by Embassy Warsaw. If the Polish president were to use his constitutional authority to exercise exceptional economic powers, we told him, there would be no objection from Washington, so long as this were done legally and democratically. But if this were done unconstitutionally, or had the effect of suspending democracy, neither the administration nor Congress would understand or support such measures. Under such circumstances, we would have to review the overall relationship and curtail most U.S. assistance. The message was blunt, and the trial balloon was never floated again. We never knew whether, or to what extent, Wałęsa was aware of this probe, but just in case Ambassador Thomas Simons delivered a similar message to him in Warsaw.

Whether the Polish economy was doing well or ill was open to debate as Poland prepared for parliamentary elections in October 1991. Statistics were often misleading. Trade liberalization and small-scale privatization had yielded full shelves and a burgeoning service sector, but wage restraints meant that most Poles could not avail themselves of these benefits. Poland registered a trade surplus in 1990, but much of this was accounted for by selling surplus goods at less than market value. On the other side of the ledger, unemployment was up, but a large share of it was made up of those actually employed in the new private sector but not declared (so that they could continue receiving unemployment payments and their employers could avoid paying taxes and benefits).

What was not debatable was that the majority of Poles felt, and probably were, worse off than they had been under communist rule, and they vented their anger at convenient targets like Balcerowicz, Bielecki, and the IMF. And of course when times are tough in this part of the world, conspiracy theories flourish. One of the prevalent ones was that a secret arrangement had been struck during the 1989 Roundtable Agreement to permit the exiting communists to acquire economic power and privilege under the new system. It was the fallacy of *post hoc, ergo propter hoc*—of an antecedent event being mistaken for a causal one. It was indisputable that a kind of "*nomenklatura* capitalism" had emerged, whereby former communist officials used their political connections (and, to be fair, their acumen as well) to acquire economic power, but it was simply preposterous to conclude that people of the stature of Wałęsa, Bronisław Geremek, and Adam Michnik had betrayed their country in the spring of 1989. Equally preposterous was a "Malta equals Yalta" conspiracy theory—also in vogue at the time—holding that the United States had reached some sort of understanding with Moscow allowing the latter to preserve a sphere of influence in Central and Eastern Europe. (Readers may refresh their memories of the unassailable evidence to the contrary in Chapters 1 and 2.)

The question of "decommunization" is more complex. What Solidarity leaders had done—with the full support of the United States and its Western partners—was to offer the communists a graceful, nonpunitive exit, on grounds that this conciliatory strategy was more likely than one based on vengeance to induce them to hand over power peacefully. It was the right strategy, for ethical as well as practical political reasons. Yet it made it possible for the most able among the former communists to acquire economic power and bide their time for another run at political power. How they would wield that power hinged on the depth and speed of democratic consolidation and perhaps on the redemptive power of the politics of conciliation—though one might not want to put too much faith in the latter.

The decommunization dilemma arose throughout Central and Eastern Europe in the early 1990s, with special bitterness in Poland, Czechoslovakia, and Bulgaria. With the benefit of a few years' hindsight, it is evident that advocates of conciliation, east and west, underestimated the danger that remnants of the old guard would pose for these fragile new democracies. Yet the alternatives proffered to this approach were even more dangerous: they came almost entirely from the radical Right and aimed at expunging communist influence through means that were vindictive, antidemocratic, and often unconstitutional.

In Poland, the issue was a powerful one that politicians of the Right played upon with considerable success in the October 1991 elections. The last vestiges of unity among the post-Solidarity political leaders were shattered: more than 60 parties fielded candidates, and 29 gained representation in the Sejm, leading to a government crisis that lasted nearly a year. In December 1991, protracted negotiations yielded a fragile center-right coalition headed by Prime Minister Jan Olszewski—the same Olszewski whose candidacy Wałęsa had successfully opposed at the end of 1990. The new cabinet reflected an antireformist, anticommunist, anti-Russian bias—the latter immediately evident in a newly aggressive Polish stance in negotiations over the withdrawal of Russian forces. Our counsel was to be firm on principle but flexible on tactics, giving the Russian leadership enough breathing space to find a solution. This was the approach we had adopted to good effect in winning Moscow's compliance with the CFE agreement.

It was a delicate moment for Poland, with the economic reform program under siege at the very time that the economy was poised for sustained growth. Again to show support and help Poland keep on the straight and narrow, we at staff level quickly went to work to arrange a visit by Olszewski, making it clear that we expected Poland's new prime minister to stay the course of political and economic reform. Indeed, when Olszewski visited in early April 1992[20]—the fourth Polish prime minister whom Bush had met in less than three years[21]—he was at pains to profess his commitment to continued reform. The White House press release captured the main lines of the discussion, including our specific push for Poland's IMF compliance and our efforts to increase American private investment in Poland:

> The President reaffirmed his strong support for the pioneering transformation to democracy and a free market in Poland, whose success is all the more important in light of the revolutionary changes farther east. . . .
>
> Prime Minister Olszewski outlined his government's economic policies and its commitment to working with the IMF on an agreed reform program . . . and welcomed the President's offer, made in a recent letter to President Wałęsa, to send a mission of U.S. business leaders to visit Poland with the aim of facilitating some of the many U.S. private investment projects now under negotiation.[22]

In the end it was not Russian policy or the economy but his own decommunization crusade that was Olszewski's downfall, as the Sejm forced his resignation in June 1992 in the wake of a series of scandals, including a crude and unsuccessful campaign to incriminate Wałęsa himself. After another month of negotiations, the Sejm approved a seven-party coalition headed by Prime Minister Hanna Suchocka, a little known but well respected lawyer who enjoyed support in Solidarity and church circles alike.

The President's Second Visit to Poland   At staff level, we had been working for months to see whether the president could add a stop in

Warsaw to his July 1992 trip to Munich for the G-7 Summit and to Helsinki for another CSCE summit. We even had an initiative up our sleeves. The Stabilization Fund the United States had helped create in the fall of 1989 had now run its course, and we proposed to convert our $200 million share to new uses and exert leverage on other contributors to make the remaining $800 million similarly available to Poland—and to make the entire amount contingent upon Poland's remaining in compliance with the IMF. The stakes were high, for the Paris Club debt reduction agreement, as well as hundreds of millions of dollars in World Bank loans, hinged on Poland's staying with an economic program that met IMF standards.

Despite significant election year pressures to curtail his European trip, the president agreed to pay a brief visit to Poland en route to the G-7 Summit in Munich. In the run-up to the visit, we worked with the Poles on a strategy for the Stabilization Fund, each side approaching the other G-7 members to join the United States in committing their shares to Poland's uses, with details to be worked out in Munich. There was also a highly significant symbolic event attached to the visit. The remains of the celebrated pianist, and independent Poland's first prime minister in 1919, Ignacy Paderewski, were returned to Poland fifty years after he had been interred in Arlington Cemetery to rest temporarily, in the words of President Roosevelt, "until Poland would be free."

Departing Washington on July 4, President Bush arrived the next morning in Warsaw—his third visit in five years and his second as president. His meetings with Wałęsa and Prime Minister–Designate Suchocka were important occasions to preview issues at the G-7 and CSCE Summits. But the real import of the visit was symbolic: the historic ceremony in which Presidents Bush and Wałęsa solemnly accompanied Paderewski's coffin to St. John's Cathedral and the tonic-like effect on an exhausted Poland of seeing the two men standing before a huge and exuberant crowd in Castle Square.[23] With his enormous personal popularity in Poland, Bush aimed at rallying Poland to the further challenges ahead:

It was here in Poland that the Second World War began. It was here in Poland that the Cold War first cast its shadow. And it was here in Poland that the people at long last brought the Cold War to an end. . . . Today, Poland stands transformed. Your bold economic reforms have earned the world's admiration, and what is more, they are working. . . .

Reaching your dreams will be difficult, and I know that the sheer volume of new voices can sometimes be deafening, but from the clamor of new voices must come democracy, a common vision of the common good. Of course, in many places and for many people there is more pain than progress. But we must take care to separate cause from consequence. Poland's time of trial is not caused by private enterprise, but by the stubborn legacy of four decades of communist misrule. Make no mistake: the path you have chosen is the right path. . . .

America shares Poland's dream. America wants Poland to succeed, and we will stand at your side until success is guaranteed to everyone.[24]

The president announced that the United States would make its $200 million contribution to the Polish Stabilization Fund available to Poland for new uses and would call on his G-7 counterparts, during their summit meeting in Munich the next day, to follow the U.S. example, so that the entire $1 billion would remain committed to Poland. Although we did not advertise the fact, the initiative did not involve new financial help but rather was a recycled grant that we never expected back in the first place. It was like giving the sleeves from our vest, but the Poles did not seem to mind. Even those in the media who caught on to the gambit nonetheless understood that the importance lay in this further example of U.S. leadership on Poland's behalf. As the independent *Nowa Europa* put it, "Bush's support for Poland during the upcoming summit of the world's richest nations in Munich is worth more than a billion dollars. It is a statement of the consistency of American policy in Central and Eastern Europe."[25]

Czechoslovakia: The Velvet Annulment

In late February 1990, just two weeks after Secretary Baker's visit to Prague, President Bush received President Václav Havel and the new Czechoslovak government at the White House. The purpose was largely symbolic—to show U.S. engagement and lend support to Czechoslovakia and to Havel personally. Though celebrated in Western intellectual circles, Havel was in his own country either unknown or regarded as something of a curiosity, a Don Quixote tilting futilely at the windmills of communist Czechoslovakia after the post-1968 "normalization" and the general apathy it engendered. His name had become familiar during the Velvet Revolution, of course, but he remained an enigmatic figure. A meeting with the American president, therefore, was important in building up Havel's credibility and authority at home. Given the responsibilities that had fallen his way, he was going to need plenty of both.

It was symptomatic that the Czechs had failed to consider Slovak sensibilities in arranging the logistics for the visit. Only eight Slovaks were on the delegation of more than two hundred, and the only one appearing on their proposed lists for the White House meetings was Prime Minister Marián Čalfa, who only recently had left the Communist party and so lacked authenticity. It was only at my insistence that more Slovaks—still not enough—were added. These instincts were later confirmed: "Bush and a bunch of Czechs" is what Slovak viewers saw on Czechoslovak television, as one Slovak official told me. In his memoirs, another Slovak official bitterly recounted these events as the first of many examples of Slovaks being excluded from official delegations.[26]

The discussions, as with Baker, were at a fairly high level of generality. Havel spoke, as he did in his moving address to a joint session of Congress,[27] of the need to help Gorbachev effect economic reforms in the Soviet Union. Havel's appeal to Congress that "you can help us most of all by helping the Soviet Union" was particularly welcome in light of the task then before the administration of persuading Moscow to accept the demise of the Warsaw Pact and the unification of Germany. As to his own economy, the Czechoslovaks were divided as to how to proceed. Finance Minister Václav Klaus advocated sweeping market reforms, but Deputy Prime Minister Valtr Komárek abjured Polish-style "shock therapy" in favor of a gradual approach toward a mixed economy, and Havel himself spoke of a "soft landing" for the Czechoslovak economy. As if to dissociate themselves from their neighbors, they sought "trade, not aid" from Western countries. (It was a formulation they continued to favor even after their reforms were launched and their list of requests for assistance became very long indeed.[28])

At the departure ceremony after their meetings,[29] President Bush surprised Havel with a portrait of Tomáš Masaryk, Czechoslovakia's first president. The portrait had been offered to the president for the occasion by Fred Starr, president of Oberlin College. Behind it lay a nice story:

> This portrait was done at Prague Castle and kept by President Masaryk until his death, when he gave it to his successor at Charles University's Department of Philosophy, Jan Kozak. In

1939, at the time of the Nazi invasion, Professor Kozak had two hours to pack his belongings and to flee Czechoslovakia. Among the items he took with him was this portrait of his friend. Professor Kozak settled in Ohio at Oberlin College, and so did the portrait . . . until today. Now [in keeping with Kozak's bequest], with freedom returning to Czechoslovakia, so too should this portrait. . . ."[30]

At the president's invitation, Havel returned to the Oval Office the next day for an unscheduled, informal talk.[31] After hearing what was on Havel's mind—mainly his recounting of his address to Congress—Bush spoke for a long time on the U.S. role in Europe and why he saw NATO as the mechanism that would keep the United States engaged as a stabilizing force. It was a remarkable, even moving, performance from a man not noted for his eloquence, and it clearly made a powerful impression on Havel. The meeting cemented the personal chemistry between Bush and Havel, as did their emotional private talk in the Lincoln Bedroom in the White House, which they visited at Havel's request.[32]

The Bush Visit to Prague   By the time of President Bush's visit to Prague in November 1990, on the first anniversary of the Velvet Revolution, the international climate had altered radically. German unification was complete; agreement had been reached on the withdrawal of Soviet forces from Czechoslovakia and Hungary (though negotiations with the Poles were held up over transit procedures for Soviet forces scheduled to leave Germany). And all of Europe was preparing to revel in freedom's triumph and the Cold War's end at the Paris Summit of the CSCE, November 19–21. In the Persian Gulf, however, Iraqi forces had invaded and occupied Kuwait in August, and President Bush was mobilizing an international coalition to repel the Iraqis and restore Kuwait's sovereignty. The Prague visit—preceding a stop in Germany to celebrate unification with Chancellor Kohl en route to Paris—thus acquired a significance well beyond Central Europe.

There were several compelling reasons to visit Prague: to show the flag in the region, try to ameliorate the growing strains between Czechs and Slovaks, and lend support as the country prepared to launch a radical reform program. Czechoslovakia, victim of the Munich Agreement in 1938, was also the ideal venue to underscore why aggression far from home bore on Western freedoms as well. In his main address, the president made the connection explicitly, warning against seeing Kuwait's plight as "just a quarrel in a faraway country, between a people of whom we know nothing." It was Neville Chamberlain's dismissive line from 1938, which helped seal Czechoslovakia's fate at the hands of the Third Reich. Although delivered without attribution to avoid offending the British, it was of course instantly recognized by the president's audience in Czechoslovakia's federal assembly.[33]

The president's schedule reflected the delicacy of the internal balancing act among federal, Czech, and Slovak political leaders and institutions. Following an arrival ceremony at the airport and motorcade to Hradčany Castle, Bush met with (1) President Havel privately, (2) Havel and members of the federal government, (3) Prime Minister Čalfa, (4) Czech Republic premier Petr Pithart and parliamentary leaders, (5) Slovak Republic premier Vladimír Mečiar and National Council chairman František Mikloško, and, over lunch, (6) Havel and company again. It was a moveable feast, or perhaps the Mad Hatter's tea party, as we moved from one mirrored chamber to another. Even the hyperkinetic Bush was showing signs of fatigue, but his schedule was far from over. The president then paid a courtesy call on the aged František Cardinal Tomášek, met with federal assembly chairman Alexander Dubček, delivered his major speech at the federal assembly, and spoke before a tumultuous crowd that more than filled the enormous Wenceslas Square, where he pledged that "America will not fail you at this decisive moment."[34] It was a deeply moving event, made doubly so for the American delegation, especially those of us of a certain age, when a Czech folksinging group led hundreds of thousands singing, in English, the civil rights song "We Shall Overcome."

In his official meetings and public remarks, President Bush stressed the difficulty of the road ahead. He announced a package of economic assistance measures similar to those already in place in Poland and Hungary: an American enterprise fund, preferential trade treatment, technical assistance in various sectors, and substantial environmental assistance, to be delivered chiefly through the IMF and the World Bank. Privately, he also returned to issues of European security, assuring Havel that the United States did not accept a European future that left Czechoslovakia as a "buffer zone" or "no man's land" between a secure, prosperous West and a chaotic East. He stressed again the importance of NATO and the U.S. role before President Havel and Foreign Minister Dienstbier, whose early enthusiasm for a "pan-European peace order" had given way to a sober reappraisal of their country's real and prospective security situation. At the same time, Bush stressed that we did not see a military threat to Czechoslovakia's security; rather, we saw the main tasks as repairing the country's economy, consolidating democracy, and building a stable new relationship among Czechs, Slovaks, and other national groups in the region.

It was a more somber Havel than Bush had met in Washington six months before. In the spring, the Slovaks had led a bitter battle to change the country's name from Czechoslovak Republic to the infelicitous "Czech and Slovak Federative Republic," and the huge turnout in Bratislava during Pope John Paul II's visit lent further strength to those who embraced—and manipulated—the Slovak national cause. In the Czech lands and Slovakia alike, the June elections had surfaced a number of charges against former communists and collaborators, real or alleged. These revelations marked the beginning of an ugly debate over a *Lustrace* law to expose misdeeds of the communist era and the end of the spirit of tolerance Havel had espoused. Now Havel was embroiled in a Czech-Slovak conflict over a new constitution that threatened to erode the basis of the federal state. Indeed, he used his speech in Wenceslas Square to cite the *Federalist Papers* and urge his fellow citizens to follow the American example in overcoming a constitutional crisis and agree on a strong federal system.[35] The president had been urged to speak directly about the issue by a prominent American lawyer advising Havel on the constitution. Instead, Bush spoke more generally about the need to put the newly free country on a firm legal foundation, a point to which he also alluded in a radio address to the Slovak Republic.[36] (Less subtle was the advance team's distribution of copies of the Constitution and Bill of Rights to members of the federal assembly before Bush's speech.)

Czechs versus Slovaks: Lurching toward Divorce   Political differences were exacerbated by Slovak opposition to elements of the emerging, "made in Prague" economic reform plan. In September 1990, Finance Minister Klaus, having wrested control over economic policy,[37] won approval in the federal assembly for his "Scenario for Economic Reform,"[38] to be implemented beginning in January 1991. Its program of currency reform, price liberalization, and opening to foreign trade was as radical as Polish "shock therapy," albeit in a country whose economic crisis was not so deep as Poland's. In a way, the relative health of the Czechoslovak economy made the political task more difficult: the population at large felt little of the urgency their Polish counterparts did, at least at the beginning. And the parts of the economic system most in need of reform—including large and privileged defense plants concentrated in Slovakia—were the most resistant to change. At the same time, because Klaus had staked his career on the reform program, his subsequent dealings with the Slovaks undoubtedly were conditioned by the imperative of economic success in the Czech lands. This is not to imply that Klaus encouraged the division of his country for the sake of his reform plan but rather that the higher priority he attached to the latter made him less amenable to compromise with the Slovaks on matters he deemed economically essential.

The launching of Czechoslovakia's economic reform program in January 1991 coincided with the opening of debates over a new constitution and consideration of Havel's proposal for a referendum to determine whether Czechs and Slovaks wished to continue living in a common state. How had things come to this pass? As Havel put it in his "Summer Meditations" of 1991, "Most Czechs had no idea how strong was the longing of the Slovaks for autonomy and for their own constitutional expression." Acknowledging some of his own failures in that regard, Havel did profess to understand one thing: "the aversion the Slovaks feel to being governed from elsewhere." The judgment Havel rendered was perhaps harsh—and Slovaks doubtless found it typically Czech—but it does capture the Slovak mood in 1991 and 1992 and helps explain how easily it was exploited and manipulated by Slovakia's political leaders: "For many Slovaks, whether they are governed well or badly, with their participation or without it, with their interests in mind or without them, is less important than the bare fact that they are governed from somewhere else."[39]

Slovak economic fears, not without foundation, were the most easily manipulated. Although the macroeconomic stabilization plan succeeded in liberalizing prices, controlling inflation, and preparing for the transition to a market economy, there was no hiding its uneven impact on the two republics. Slovakia's less diversified economy, with many towns and regions dependent on a single large factory or defense complex, made it more vulnerable than the Czech lands to huge dislocations associated with economic reform. The inconvenient fact that Slovak politicians failed to mention was that many if not most of these factories were doomed for reasons unrelated to the reform program. If

factories were producing goods for which there were no buyers, owing
to the collapse of Soviet trade and the shrinking international arms
market, whether the factory was "reformed" or "unreformed" was
hardly the point. Yet the "made in Prague" reform program, together
with Havel's early pledge to curtail arms sales on ethical grounds,
made for handy scapegoats.

When Czechoslovak foreign minister Jiří Dienstbier visited the
United States in mid-April 1990, his agenda was almost wholly economic, and almost wholly related to Slovak concerns. At the White
House, he used a brief meeting with the president to talk about . . .
cheese quotas. (Had he done his homework, he would have known that
almost any other trade item would have had better prospects of success
than cheese imports, which were regulated according to an elaborately
worked out set of quotas affecting all importing countries.) With General Scowcroft, he also previewed what became known as the "Dienstbier Plan" for Western underwriting of a multibillion dollar payments
system to revive trade and spur investment in the former Comecon
area.[40] The plan never got off the ground, not only for want of money
but for serious doubts here and elsewhere about its efficacy—particularly its reliance on dubious administrative measures rather than the
market to shape trade relations in the region.

"Defense conversion" was next on Dienstbier's agenda, his plea
being for U.S. assistance in converting Slovak defense industries to viable commercial use. His aim was mainly political—to demonstrate to
Slovaks that the Prague leadership was trying to find answers for their
economic problems. Though skeptical, we wanted to be helpful and so
worked with our counterparts at the Pentagon to arrange for a defense
conversion mission led by Deputy Secretary of Defense Donald Atwood.
In retrospect, the mission was a mistake: it contributed to the illusion
that "defense conversion" was a task susceptible to quick fixes and that
solutions could be found through political or military channels rather
than on the basis of commercial viability. It took us another year to get
this issue back in the commercial domain where it belonged, and longer
still before we could show even modest results. (As late as the fall of
1992, when I led an interagency assistance delegation to Bratislava,
some Slovak ministers were still treating the issue as one that required
only an act of political will on our part. Even later, NATO ambassadors
were proposing a defense conversion "data bank," as if bureaucrats in
Brussels could solve the problem.)

The political climate in Czechoslovakia continued to deteriorate. Civic Forum and Public Against Violence had both split—the latter abandoned by populist prime minister Vladimír Mečiar, who formed a new party called Movement for a Democratic Slovakia (HZDS). When Mečiar himself was forced to resign the prime ministership on charges springing from the *Lustrace* campaign, he set about systematically to foment and exploit Slovak national grievances. His party as well as the new Slovak National party demanded sweeping changes to the federal constitution; their aims ranged from loose confederation to outright independence, though the latter was rarely articulated openly.[41] Instead, Mečiar and others spoke of "autonomy," "confederation," or "international subjectivity," with the result that ordinary Slovaks, in supporting those who seemed most attuned to their grievances, never quite knew what agenda they were backing.

The U.S. Position By late summer 1991, we in Washington were viewing these developments with growing concern. Bush and Havel, who had communicated often at the time of the failed August coup against Gorbachev, would have a chance to discuss matters when Havel paid a state visit planned for October, but we at staff level felt the issue needed to be discussed with the Slovaks as well. So in mid-October, I hived off from an investment mission to Poland (led by Commerce Secretary Robert Mosbacher) to visit first Bratislava and then Prague, conveying U.S. attitudes and policies regarding the possible breakup of Czechoslovakia and, relatedly, to advance the notion of turning the "Visegrád Three" into the "Visegrád Four" (or at least "three and a half") so as to give Slovakia the status it seemed unable to find in federation with the Czechs.[42]

Having failed to prepare adequately for the disintegration of Yugoslavia,[43] we tried to apply sounder policy to the imminent collapse of the Czecho-Slovak federation. I therefore had drafted and gained interagency approval for a set of principles to guide our relations. Taking about a minute to recite, they boiled down to this: the United States, while not indifferent to the fate of Czechoslovakia and believing that the interests of its citizens would be best served in a common state, would accept any solution democratically and peacefully agreed to by the people of Czechoslovakia. Moreover, the United States would continue to base its relations and policies on enduring American interests in democracy, free markets, human rights, minority rights, and cooperative

regional and international relations. Although those of us who cared
deeply about this country considered taking a stronger position in support of the federation, it was clear for practical as well as ethical reasons that this decision was not ours to make or impose.[44] We judged it
was better to focus on first principles than preferred specific outcomes,
and to do what we could to promote minority rights and regional cooperation among the Visegrád Three—or Four.

I conveyed the U.S. position in a series of meetings on October 13
and 14 with Slovak politicians across the spectrum,[45] culminating in a
private luncheon with former (and future) Slovak prime minister
Vladimír Mečiar.[46] They considered it a reasonable position and felt
that the Visegrád process was an important means of averting Slovakia's
marginalization, particularly if the federation were to be dissolved. The
ease with which many of these politicians lapsed into theories of conspiracy and betrayal, moreover, strengthened my conviction that the
U.S. line was the right one. (Indeed, in early 1993, as the first senior
American official to visit independent Slovakia, I was the first beneficiary of this policy. Our relations, although strained because of certain
antidemocratic practices of the Mečiar government, nonetheless proceeded from a reasonably sound foundation, unburdened by a futile effort to try to hold together a doomed Czechoslovak state. Instead, I was
able to return, credibly and authoritatively, to the same agenda we had
advanced in 1991.[47])

Over lunch, Mečiar treated me to a disquisition on "international
subjectivity" and criticized Havel for turning the Czech-Slovak debate
into one of federation or separation, arguing that there were several intermediate possibilities. Brushing aside my suggestion that the European
Community's notion of "subsidiarity" would give the smaller nations of
Europe room for autonomy and self-expression, Mečiar countered that
a confederal relationship with the Czechs was required lest the Slovaks,
as he put it, become "lost in a European sea." One option that he advanced was a Slovak declaration of independence followed immediately
by a new, confederal association with the Czechs. The idea was that Slovakia's moment of independence—literally a moment, in this conception—would enable the two sides to renegotiate their relationship on
the basis of equality. The Czechs, of course, were having none of this.

The next day in Prague, I met with Foreign Minister Dienstbier to
convey the same message to him and brief him on my conversations in
Bratislava. Dienstbier was by this time resigned to the inevitability of a

split, noting that most Czechs—starting with himself?—had put up with enough and were saying the Slovaks could "go to hell." I ventured that the United States did not want to meddle, but we were prepared to help where we could—by promoting the "Visegrád Four" notion or helping the Slovaks realize their "international subjectivity" through cultural exchanges and the like, adding impertinently that we in Washington could not detect anything resembling a strategy for addressing Czech-Slovak problems but rather a series of ad hoc initiatives that only made matters worse.

Havel's State Visit   While in Prague, I devoted half a day to previewing President Havel's impending visit to Washington with Havel's foreign policy adviser, Saša Vondra, and press spokesman Michael Žantovsky.[48] We finished negotiating a U.S.-Czechoslovak "declaration of principles," modeled on the U.S.-Polish declaration of a few months before, for the signature of the two presidents. Although their preference was for a treaty-like document rather than the informal statement we insisted on, it was a negotiation among friends that was wrapped up in less than an hour.

Havel's state visit, in late October 1991, was overshadowed by the drama in the Soviet Union following the failed August coup. Unlike Havel's first visit just eighteen months before, this one passed almost unnoticed beyond official circles. Central Europe's moment of world prominence had passed; its problems now seemed prosaic, if not ugly. And Havel's country, which he had hoped would contribute to a broader democratic stability, had become, as he lamented, a source of instability because of its imminent disintegration. In the expanded meeting in the Cabinet Room, Havel began by noting that his ministers around the table were mostly the same as when he had first visited in February 1990, but now they represented different parties and would be vying for office in the elections scheduled for June 1992. Finance Minister Václav Klaus, who distributed sample privatization vouchers in explaining his program of mass privatization of Czechoslovakia's state-owned enterprises, was leader of the Civic Democratic party, while Dienstbier led the Civic Movement, another offshoot of Civic Forum.

Security, or rather insecurity, was on Havel's mind. Although the withdrawal of Soviet forces from Czechoslovakia had been completed in May 1991, the failed anti-Gorbachev coup in the Soviet Union raised the prospect of new dangers arising in the East, not so much from naked aggression as from the spillover of a chaotic breakdown of order. Havel welcomed NATO's recent creation of a North Atlantic Cooperation Council[49] to bring in members of the now defunct Warsaw Pact but made it clear that Czechoslovakia's aim was eventual full membership in the alliance. In his public remarks as well as privately, Havel attached great importance to the joint declaration that the two presidents signed just before their meeting. Although not a binding document, it expressed the two countries' shared perspective on key elements of European security:

> The United States . . . considers [Czechoslovakia's] security and independence integral to the new Europe, whole and free. . . . Czechoslovakia and the United States will help to build a new system of cooperative security in Europe . . . which will complement NATO and its indispensable role. . . . The United States and the Czech and Slovak Federal Republic reaffirm the importance of cooperative regional ties [among] the states and peoples of Central Europe [which] will help them overcome historic national antagonisms and will advance their integration into Europe.[50]

It was perhaps a fitting irony that the declaration was not even issued in Czech but rather in English and Slovak only. This was the inadvertent consequence of my suggestion, in Prague, that the document be issued in English, Czech, and Slovak so as to assuage Slovakia's sense of exclusion and reflect its desire for "international subjectivity." Not wanting to set a precedent that might mean every future international agreement would have to be issued in both Czech and Slovak, Havel's advisers decided instead to issue it in Slovak only. So it was that my Czech friends negotiated a declaration on behalf of a state soon to disappear, in a language not their own. Kafka lives!

The Velvet Divorce   Over the next year, negotiations over a new constitutional arrangement were stalemated. The Slovaks insisted on a loose confederal system, which the Czechs rejected as tantamount to full separation, and neither side could agree to the country-wide referendum Havel proposed. When Havel met with visiting Secretary of Defense Dick Cheney in mid-December 1991, he was optimistic that the coming June 1992 elections would create the basis for a "new state" that nonetheless would preserve the federation. Slovak minister of international relations Pavol Demeš, an able young scholar who stood throughout as a voice of reason and moderation, similarly offered Cheney his personal view that the Czecho-Slovak state would survive. Foreign Minister Dienstbier, however, would venture only that Czechoslovakia would be "no Yugoslavia" and expressed concern, which we shared, that a split of the federation would jeopardize the status of the six hundred thousand Hungarians in Slovakia and further complicate Hungarian-Slovak relations. And in side discussions with me, Havel's key advisers, Vondra and Žantovsky, offered scenarios that supported Dienstbier's fatalism more than their president's optimism.[51]

The June 1992 elections brought coalition governments headed by Klaus in the Czech lands and Mečiar in Slovakia. Despite Klaus's protestation that he had no mandate to negotiate the dissolution of the country, he and Mečiar began doing precisely that. Public opinion polls in both republics continued to show a majority opposed separation, but Mečiar's campaign for a loose confederation (tantamount to destruction of the federal state) and the Czech backlash thereto created a momentum that neither Havel nor anyone else could arrest. Three years after the Velvet Revolution, the Czechoslovak federation was headed, now ineluctably, toward a "velvet divorce" that was, to many Slovaks, more an annulment of a union that never quite took. To stretch the metaphor perhaps to excess, those who had helped create the marriage—the United States and Great Britain—could only watch wistfully as it dissolved. It was destroyed in the first instance by two headstrong personalities of limited vision, but the differences between Czechs and Slovaks were far deeper and perhaps, for this moment in history, irreconcilable. Once the Slovaks made the first moves toward independence, Czech attitudes underwent a sea change, and sentiment in favor of the federal state was soon overtaken by biases just below the surface that association with Slovakia was dragging Czech culture and civilization eastward and backward. By the end, Czechs were more adamant than Slovaks that the federal state was finished.

When Havel met Bush briefly during the July 1992 CSCE Summit in Helsinki, he explained that the federation was lost and that he would soon resign as president in keeping with his pledge not to preside over the dissolution of the federal state—adding, however, that he would be available to serve as president of an independent Czech Republic. Observing this denouement to Havel's presidency and his country, it struck me as an uncharacteristically careless interpretation of his pledge from a man for whom words mattered so deeply. I was thinking in particular of Havel's essay "A Word about Words," which concluded with this: "[This] is not just a linguistic task. Responsibility for and toward words is a task which is intrinsically ethical."[52] Havel, no doubt, was thinking of the moral obligation to which he referred in his eloquent address to a joint session of Congress in February 1990: "Intellectuals cannot go on forever avoiding their share of responsibility for the world and hiding their distaste for politics under an alleged need to be independent."[53]

Hungary: From Euphoria to Disillusionment

U.S.-Hungarian relations after 1990 had little of the intensity or urgency that characterized our interaction with Poland and Czechoslovakia. It was not that Hungary was neglected entirely. Certainly, there was no shortage of American visitors, official and private. Indeed, so many American officials were finding excuses to visit Budapest and imposing on already harried Hungarian officials that Deputy Secretary Eagleburger's office had to issue an edict that sharply curtailed such visits, and blocked any that smacked of tourism dressed in official garb. But policy issues related to Hungary alone—that is, discounting region-wide policy initiatives—rarely commanded cabinet-level attention after 1989.

Hungary's political system was stable, perhaps too stable, after the March 1990 election of a coalition government headed by Prime Minister József Antall. Its gradualist economic reform—so gradual as to be sometimes imperceptible—did not occasion the political battles that characterized those farther north, though the social backlash was just as great. Hungary in 1990 had seeming advantages over its neighbors: an economy that was already semireformed and able to compete in Western markets and a geostrategic position that made it less buffeted by turmoil in the Soviet Union. In addition, the peaceful, negotiated revolution of 1989 had produced a stable governing coalition with a respectable opposition. Yet these assets were also liabilities, permitting the Hungarians to defer painful austerity measures, for which the population at large saw little justification, and contributing to a political style that made democracy mainly a matter for Budapest politicians.[54] Hungary also suffered from the success of its own propaganda, as Western governments tended to take at face value the claim of Hungarian politicians that their country was well ahead of the pack among the emerging democracies of the region. And again the matter of geopolitics: Hungary did not command quite the same sustained engagement as Czechoslovakia or especially Poland, the "lands between" Germany and Russia.

Nor did the Hungarians look so much to us for help. Antall was a committed Atlanticist, but his first priority was Europe and, within Europe, Germany. Although heavily indebted, the Hungarians (wisely) chose to repay rather than reschedule their debts so as to maintain a favorable international credit rating and so did not look to us for special help. Our dialogue on economic matters, though lively, was conducted largely at working level. At the highest levels, U.S.-Hungarian relations focused more on international issues: Hungary's integration into the Western community, the plight of Hungarian minorities in Romania and Slovakia, and, after conflict erupted in Yugoslavia, Hungary's exposed position as a front-line state with compatriots across the border in Serbian Vojvodina.

None of this is to denigrate Hungary's key role in setting a standard for the region as a whole, through its bold foreign policy initiatives as well as its economic and political reforms. Its elections of March 1990 were a model of democratic propriety that set a standard for the entire region. Given that these were the first fully free and open elections in postcommunist Central Europe, it is a tribute to the authors of Hungary's "negotiated revolution" that we felt no need to dispatch a Presidential Mission to observe the elections (as we did for those in Romania and Bulgaria), relying instead on observer teams arranged through CSCE and the American party institutes (the National Democratic Institute and the International Republican Institute).

First Encounters in Washington The president's May 18 meeting with newly elected Hungarian president Árpád Göncz was mainly ceremonial, in keeping with Göncz's limited authority under the Hungarian constitution; the event was meant to demonstrate symbolically U.S. support and commitment to Hungary's new leaders.[55] The genial, intelligent Göncz was not shy about speaking his mind, though, and he and Bush got on well, engaging in a long discussion about the Soviet Union and the conflict then raging between Moscow and Lithuania. Indeed, Bush was sufficiently impressed to pencil in a reference to his meeting with Göncz in his commencement address at the University of Texas the next day.[56] (The next meeting between the two, a year later at the White House, was equally successful, as an unusually animated President Bush began immediately to probe Göncz's thinking on everything from GATT to Gorbachev.[57])

Budapest continued to set the pace in foreign policy among the Central Europeans. Having reached agreement with Moscow for the removal of Soviet forces from Hungary by June 1991, the Antall government began preparing for Hungary's withdrawal from the Warsaw Pact. Hungary's new foreign minister, Géza Jeszensky, had earlier said that Hungary would remain a member of the pact "as long as necessary, but not one day longer," and at a Warsaw Pact meeting in Moscow in June 1990 gave notice that Hungary planned to withdraw by 1991.[58] As an alternative, Antall floated the idea of an "East-Central European Union,"[59] modeled on the Western European Union, to complement such emerging regional groupings as the Visegrád troika and the "Alpe-Adria," a loose association of substate regions of northern Italy, Bavaria, Austria, Hungary, Slovenia, and Croatia. Antall, it should be added, was too much the realist to place much stock in such arrangements. They were designed to camouflage his real aim of extricating Hungary from Moscow's grip and preparing the way for its integration into the European and transatlantic mainstream as quickly as possible. Hungarian neutrality, another idea that was sometimes mooted, was but a way station on the road west.

Antall's official visit to Washington in October 1990, a few days after German unification and less than a month before the CSCE Summit in Paris, similarly had a foreign policy focus. Indeed, in their several meetings and numerous telephone conversations, Antall and Bush hardly talked about Hungary. Their topics were the Soviet Union, European security, the Atlantic alliance, Yugoslavia, or whatever was hottest on the international agenda. Most of their discussion during this visit was about Iraq, about which Antall was as knowledgeable as he was hawkish. Although the two men never developed the personal chemistry that Bush had with Havel and Mazowiecki, the president came to value Antall's thoughtful, if long-winded, views. (In preparing talking points for the president's telephone conversations with Antall, I began to think that "Hello" and "Good-bye" were all that Bush needed for a half-hour call. Antall would take care of the rest.)

On this first visit to the White House, Antall wanted, and received, further U.S. assistance and increased support from the IMF and World Bank, but his main political objective was to gain American public recognition of Hungary's sovereignty and independence. This, too, he received. As Bush put it, with some overstatement, in his remarks during the arrival ceremony, "Hungary is no longer an emerging democracy; Hungary is a democracy. The government you head is a sovereign, pluralistic, democratic European state. . . . Hungary has taken its natural place as a valued member of the commonwealth of free nations."[60]

The president delineated several economic initiatives, including $47.5 million in credits for food grains to compensate for the effects of Hungary's severe drought that year. Recognizing the high economic price Hungary and others in the region were paying for their resolute support of UN sanctions against Iraq, he also announced that the United States would "ask the IMF to increase its lending to the countries of the region by as much as $5 billion and urge the World Bank to accelerate its assistance in the energy field, drawing on the $9 billion now committed." These pledges did not involve new U.S. resources, as the Hungarians knew well, but the commitment of American leadership in the "IFIs" (international financial institutions) was welcome. Antall—like Göncz and Jeszensky—an historian, delivered a thoughtful brief speech at the same ceremony, including this reference to warm the heart of an NSC adviser: "You, Mr. President, have spoken about all those matters that I could have also mentioned here when presenting my requests. . . . I think this is an indication of the fact that we have come here as friends. . . . And we are being received by friends who can perhaps read our minds."

"Gradualism" and Its Consequences The confidence Hungary projected seemed vindicated for a time. Shortly after his return to Budapest, Antall was able to enlist the support of the socialist opposition in parliament to defuse a taxi drivers' strike that seemed destined to spread to other sectors and threaten the government's survival. A privatization law was passed, well ahead of any other country in the region; price liberalization and market regulatory measures were efficiently implemented; and foreign direct investment increased impressively. Despite ongoing conflicts over the respective powers of the president and prime minister, constitutional reforms implemented already in 1989 put Hungarian civic life on a more secure foundation than elsewhere. In recognition of these steps, in November 1990 Hungary became the first East European country to join the Council of Europe.

Yet the Hungarians succumbed to the temptation of deferring the toughest decisions. Because the modest reforms of the János Kádár era had introduced a degree of market rationality into pricing, Polish-style "shock therapy" was not required to bring the macroeconomic system into balance. New economic measures would be introduced in "separate bundles," Antall promised, warning that more radical changes could lead to a catastrophe.[61] To avert a social backlash, the government declined to cut the huge subsidies provided to state enterprises or to move forward with a mass privatization program. Antall's government based its program on recommendations of a prestigious Blue Ribbon Commission report of April 1990, but in erring on the side of caution failed to heed one of its cardinal warnings: "Deciding on a quantum leap is also a matter of political efficiency. Slowness can cause the early consensus supporting the government's program to collapse before implementation is completed and results become evident, because interest groups have time to mobilize and drag down the program."[62]

Once the opportunity for early, decisive action had been lost, a kind of paralysis set in. Antall's coalition was strong enough to resist pressures for more rapid change coming from the opposition Free Democrats and especially FIDESz (Alliance of Young Democrats), which were in any case too busy vying with one another to advance a unified alternative.[63] But the coalition was itself internally divided and increasingly preoccupied with issues of Hungarian nationalism, both on domestic policies and on matters affecting Hungarian minorities abroad.

Nationalism on the Rise   When Antall met with the president at the White House in early October 1991, his focus was almost entirely on Yugoslavia, where Serbian forces were launching brutal assaults on Croatian towns and villages in the aftermath of the Slovenian and Croatian declarations of independence. Antall got to the nub of the matter, as he had in two or three recent telephone calls to Bush: Serbia had to be confronted with the credible threat of force, and only a U.S.-led NATO effort could do the job, as the European Community was not up to it. This was wise counsel, but U.S. policy had become more inert than Antall knew since Secretary Baker's ill-fated visit to Belgrade in June.[64] The Hungarians looked to us for more leadership than we were prepared to provide; instead they got vacillation from the West Europeans, as they had feared. Antall's greatest concerns were the threat to the Hungarian minority in Vojvodina, across the border in Serbia, the influx of refugees into Hungarian territory, and the mounting domestic pressures on his government to galvanize stronger international engagement.[65]

Visiting Budapest in mid-December 1991 as part of a developing bilateral security dialogue with each of the Central European countries, Secretary Cheney heard these concerns in graphic detail in separate meetings with Antall, Foreign Minister Géza Jeszensky, International Economic Relations Minister Béla Kádár, and especially from our Hungarian host, Defense Minister Lajos Für. Whereas the security concerns Cheney had heard from his Polish and Czechoslovak counterparts were abstract and potential, arising from fears of resurgent Russian power, Hungarian concerns were actual. Serbian aircraft had violated Hungarian air space a few months before, and the Hungarians were without the minimum requirements of territorial self-defense. The mainstay of its air force was aged MiG-21s, which had been introduced in the USSR in the late 1950s and provided to Hungary a decade later, and half of them had to be cannibalized just to keep the others operational. Hungary lacked even detection and early warning capacities, the entire Warsaw Pact air defense system having been withdrawn to Moscow along with Soviet forces.

The domestic repercussions of the Yugoslav war within Hungary were strong indeed—particularly on top of continuing tensions with Romania and Slovakia over treatment of their Hungarian minorities. Another cause of tension was the long-standing dispute over Slovak plans to complete the Gabčikovo-Nagymaros dam along the Danube (despite the well documented evidence that it would cause environmental damage). Antall had proclaimed himself early on to be prime minister not only of the ten million Hungarians within Hungary's borders but also, in a spiritual sense, of the five million living outside.[66] And Antall was a force for moderation within his Democratic Forum: Jeszensky and Für spoke pointedly and often about their government's responsibility for the fate of Hungarians abroad. To be sure, they denied harboring current territorial claims, but their public comments tended to reflect popular nostalgia for "Greater Hungary."

The Yugoslav tragedy had the effect of pushing the Hungarian political climate further in the "national" direction. Antall, having earlier maneuvered to secure the removal of the outspoken nationalist József Torgyán from the leadership of the Independent Smallholders party, in coalition with the Democratic Forum, also faced a growing, and increasingly assertive, nationalist faction within the Forum itself. This erupted in August 1992, when Forum vice chairman István Csurka published a neofascist, anti-Semitic diatribe—and did so in the Forum's weekly *Magyar Forum*.[67] Although Antall later secured Csurka's removal as he had Torgyán's, he could not entirely remove the sources from which these views sprang. The familiar urban-rural split in Hungarian political culture—between the Western-oriented Budapest intellectuals and neo-Populists with roots in the countryside and a romantic attachment to Hungarian village life—was reasserting itself. Among the latter grouping, anti-Semitism was the familiar surrogate for attacking the patriotism of political opponents.

Economic and Political Malaise   In economic policy, these political trends manifested themselves in several ways. Proponents of a Hungarian "third road"—between capitalism and socialism, with special measures to protect traditional rural life—were joined by those, mainly on the Left, who wanted to shield the working class and state bureaucracy from the painful effects of the market. Privatization was slowed and skewed by these twin forces, with the nationalists warning of a foreign takeover and remnants of the old managerial class trying to preserve their privileged economic position. Thus while small-scale privatization proceeded apace, privatization of large state-owned enterprises, as well as the banking sector, hardly began. Hungary's considerable head start in attracting foreign direct investment also slowed, with many prospective investors complaining that deals would be concluded, only to be reversed by a nationalist backlash in the parliament and held in abeyance by the State Property Agency. Large-scale privatization everywhere in Central and Eastern Europe was an intensely political affair, but in Hungary this was true to a marked degree. It was almost all politics, and foreign investors and private Hungarians alike complained that transactions were conducted behind closed doors on the basis of political favoritism or outright kickbacks.

Prime Minister Antall's rapidly failing health deprived the government of the coherent leadership it needed as the domestic situation deteriorated. His flagging energy was devoted almost entirely to foreign policy and fending off nationalist challenges within the coalition. The failures of his government to tackle the state sector made it harder to constrain subsidies, balance the budget (while also meeting onerous debt repayment schedules), and promote greater efficiency and profitability. Hungary's gross domestic product declined by nearly one-fifth between 1989 and 1992,[68] and sharply increased prices, even for basic foodstuffs, undermined living standards for most of the population and dissipated what little support remained for further reform. To be sure, much had been achieved in three short years in laying the foundations of a market economy, but the reality for most Hungarians was continuing economic decline with no visible prospect of improvement.

U.S.-Hungarian relations underwent a similar decline, as public sentiments ranged from disappointment (at failures, real or imagined, of American leadership) to outright anti-Americanism (among those who felt American business was exploiting Hungarian economic weakness for unilateral advantage). More important than whether we were liked was whether we could have done more to advance Hungary's democratic transition, and with it our own interests. The inadequacy of our overall assistance budget meant that our direct aid could do little more than facilitate change at the margins. Even granted those limitations, this was not an easy country to help: its hesitancy to embrace large-scale privatization and financial sector reform led us to deploy our scarce resources to Poland and Czechoslovakia, where reforms were being pursued with more determination and where our help could be effectively used.[69] Still, U.S. assistance to Hungary was never as large or successful as in Poland, owing partly to our failure to join other G-24 countries in providing significant balance of payments support in 1990 and 1991. That is when Hungary, like most of the rest of the region, was being hard hit by the loss of key foreign markets and the severe (and uncompensated) impact of economic sanctions against Iraq and Yugoslavia. Equally damaging was the failure of the United States and its Western partners to engage meaningfully in the Yugoslav conflict, whose spillover lent strength to ultranationalist forces and diminished the Western community as a magnet and point of reference. Thus, Hungary's transition to free market democracy, which had seemed so promising in early 1990, seemed to have stalled by 1992, with much of the populace disenchanted with their new political leadership and feeling that their lives had been better under the communists.[70]

Romania: "Diplomacy of the Absurd"

Although Romanians, particularly officials of the ruling National Salvation Front (NSF), accused the United States of neglect during their difficult transition after the December 1989 revolution, in fact we devoted a great deal of attention to Romania. We also delivered more assistance, mainly humanitarian aid, to this country than to any other in the region save Poland. The outpouring of American private assistance, together with more than $100 million in government aid, during the winter of 1989–90, was testimony to America's desire to help Romania overcome the immediate legacies of Ceauşescu's misrule and begin developing the foundations of liberal democracy.

The problem was not lack of attention so much as the sharply differing judgments we and the NSF leadership drew from postrevolutionary developments in Romania.[71] Our relations with the Front, to borrow the subtitle from a book about U.S.-Romanian relations at the end of the Ceauşescu era, was another episode in "diplomacy of the absurd."[72] Oddly, some leaders of democratic opposition parties, loosely allied under the Civic Alliance and later the Democratic Convention, also argued that we failed to give them sufficient support. This contention is best consigned to the file of theories of conspiracy and betrayal, and to the tendency—not unique to Romania, but particularly acute there—to blame others for one's own failings. If anything, the United States erred on the side of partisanship in favor of democratic opposition parties, both by rendering electoral assistance and by withholding support from the ruling NSF. Indeed, it was precisely those opposition leaders from the Civic Alliance who constantly urged us to withhold MFN status and other assistance so as to keep the pressure on the Front. They can hardly blame us for the consequences of their own political strategy. Scapegoating, like charity, ought to begin at home.

Of all the postcommunist countries of Central and Eastern Europe, Romania worried us the most. (Nor were we alone among Western countries: as late as 1993, the Council of Europe continued to deny admission to Romania for failing to meet its democratic standards.[73]) In the run-up to the May 1990 elections, the NSF had backtracked from its early promises and was using its grip on power to skew the electoral campaign in its own favor. During his February visit, Baker had gained Iliescu's agreement to welcome election observers, and we used the intervening time to mobilize as much outside involvement as we could. We also provided quick financial and technical assistance to the many independent newspapers and radios springing up around the country. In addition to the international observer teams already in the country, we (i.e., NSC staff and State) proposed, and the president agreed, to name a presidential mission to monitor the elections. This, we hoped, would ratchet up the pressure on the NSF and help document electoral abuses if, as we feared, they occurred. As it turned out, the presidential mission—whose composition, unfortunately, was left to the office of presidential personnel and selected on domestic rather than foreign policy grounds—gave a much more generous report than did any other observer team, including those representing European socialist and social democratic parties.[74] Consequently, in commenting officially on the fairness of the elections, we downplayed the presidential mission's statement. Instead, like our West European partners, we stressed the consensus judgment of the many other observer teams: while the elections were, with some notable exceptions, technically free and fair, the electoral campaign preceding them had been characterized by a pattern of media manipulation and local intimidation.[75]

The NSF won the May 1990 elections handily, and no doubt would have done so even if the electoral campaign had been fully free and fair. Iliescu retained the presidency with a landslide 85 percent, and with the Front's two-thirds of the seats in the new parliament, Petre Roman was easily elected prime minister. The most prominent opposition leaders, Radu Câmpeanu of the Liberal party and Ion Raţiu of the Peasant party, had both spent decades in emigration. Although decent and civilized men, their programs and personae were too dated to have much resonance beyond Bucharest intellectual circles. (Both visited Washington in early 1990, and I recall a conversation with Câmpeanu in which he outlined an agricultural policy derived straight from the Liberal party's program of the 1920s.)

Our concerns about the direction of Romanian politics were amply confirmed a month later, when some ten thousand miners from the Jiu Valley, pressed into service by the Front itself, swept through Bucharest's University Square, bludgeoning student protestors and ransacking the Liberal and Peasant parties' headquarters nearby. Clearly, the miners did not need much encouragement, and their rampage was probably a mixture of spontaneity and governmental instigation. Whether President Iliescu ordered, incited, or merely condoned the miners' assault was unclear, but his complicity was evident from his own public statements and actions.[76] The White House and State Department issued sharp rebukes, and our ambassador in Bucharest was recalled to Washington for consultations.

One vignette will serve to illustrate the tenor of U.S.-Romanian relations at the time. On June 20 and 21, veteran Romanian human rights activist Doina Cornea, together with Petre Bacanu, editor of the independent newspaper *România liberă*, visited Washington for meetings at the NSC and State Department. They had just come from Western Europe and Canada, conveying the message that the West should withhold assistance until the National Salvation Front demonstrated its commitment to democracy and human rights. Back in Bucharest, several parliamentarians demanded that the two be stripped of their Romanian citizenship if they persisted with this line in Washington, and the Romanian government suggested that these two not be received by U.S. officials. Not much liking the idea that Romanian officials could blackmail their own citizens and presume to tell the United States government whom it should see and not see, we worked at staff level on a ministrategy to counter this provocation. The idea was to ratchet up their official meetings in Washington and call public attention to them, so that any subsequent harassment of these two would constitute a slap at the United States as well. Deputy National Security Adviser Bob Gates readily agreed to meet Cornea and Bacanu in his office in the West Wing of the White House, as did Deputy Secretary Eagleburger at the State Department. We then drafted a couple of paragraphs of State Department press guidance, stressing that these high-level White House and State Department meetings demonstrated the importance the United States attached to such meetings with Romanians defending basic human rights. As press guidance of this sort goes into the daily briefing book but is used only in response to a query from the press, I called a journalist friend and made sure the question got asked. Once this was in the public domain, Cornea and Bacanu had no trouble in ensuring that it was widely quoted in Romania, providing them a measure of insurance against harassment upon their return.

On July 4, at a meeting of G-24 foreign ministers in Brussels, Secretary Baker restated U.S. insistence on "democratic differentiation," a policy first enunciated in his Prague speech in February 1990. He argued that Bulgaria, despite our continuing concerns, had met the basic conditions set by the G-24 and should be admitted conditionally into the G-24 process, joining Poland, Hungary, and Czechoslovakia. As to Romania, he minced no words:

> Romania has not yet met the conditions required for G-24 support. The Iliescu regime's complicity with the miners' violent repression of demonstrators and the arrest of the political opposition raised serious questions about its commitment to democratic reform and basic human rights. We look forward to the day when

we can include Romania in the G-24 process. However, we will require demonstrable progress on both political and economic reform and respect for human rights before that day can come.[77]

At staff level, we set about to specify what "demonstrable progress" we had in mind. Beginning with two Policy Coordinating Committee meetings (PCCs) on June 26 and 27, we worked out what came to be known as the "benchmark cable" (to Bucharest) delineating four main areas of concern—free and fair elections, democratic control over the Securitate, independent media, and equal treatment of minorities. We also described, with as much specificity as we could muster, the steps that would be required before we could consider any forward movement in our bilateral relations.[78] It was important to put this in writing, in a document that the Romanians could retain and to which we could refer as the standard to which they would be held. As the United States had adopted the toughest position toward Romania of all the G-24 countries, we also sent the cable to West European capitals so that their governments would know the bases of our position and understand what we expected to see before we were prepared to relent. Otherwise, it was entirely foreseeable that six months later we would be told by the French and others that the situation in Romania had "improved." This cable gave us a standard against which to measure "improvement."

This approach helped us exercise pressure but did not yield much in the way of tangible results. The hated Securitate was reorganized and partially purged (under the new Romanian Intelligence Service, or SRI) but not disbanded, and rumors persisted of direct links between Iliescu and a Securitate-type force within the SRI. The status of the Hungarian minority improved substantially, but anti-Hungarian incidents and invective flourished, some with the implicit or explicit endorsement of Prime Minister Roman and other leading government officials.[79] Independent newspapers operated in relative freedom, but the government used its control of newsprint and distribution to repress those it found troublesome, going so far as to propose (and then withdraw under pressure) a highly restrictive press law in the fall of 1990. Television remained largely under government control.

Romania was nonetheless moving haltingly toward political and economic liberalization, and U.S.-Romanian relations began to thaw in early 1991. There was an explosion of new political parties. Five leading democratic opposition parties, including the Hungarian Democratic Union of Romania, coalesced in November 1990 under the Civic Alliance. Yet extremist parties also flourished: on the far Right, the quasi-fascist party of Romanian National Unity, part of the much larger movement *Vatră Românească* (Romanian Cradle), gained strength and organization, including reputed links to the ruling NSF. On economic policy, Roman announced a bold, if hastily prepared, reform plan that enabled him to sign a "letter of understanding" with the International Monetary Fund in April 1991, paving the way for IMF loans and credits, entry into the G-24 process, and an eagerly sought meeting with Secretary Baker in Washington.[80] The meeting with Baker was also meant to reward Romania for its considerable help, during its period as a member of the UN Security Council in 1990 and 1991, in securing a succession of UN resolutions against Iraq after the latter's invasion of Kuwait. Seeking to capitalize on Baker's largesse, the Romanians mounted a diplomatic offensive for U.S. restoration of Romania's MFN status and the symbolic blessing they believed it would confer.[81]

Just as Washington's attitudes were softening, relations took another nosedive when Jiu Valley miners returned to Bucharest in September 1991. They were widely believed to have been brought in by Iliescu, this time to give a pretext for securing the resignation of Prime Minister Roman, whose competition with Iliescu for leadership of the Front had become increasingly open and bitter. Indeed, the many Romanian officials who visited Washington to lobby the NSC and the State Department for restoration of MFN status had been urging us to throw our support behind Iliescu, who was said to be striving to build democratic rule over the constant obstructions of Roman. If the visitors' loyalties were on the other side, then they urged us to support the genuinely democratic but misunderstood Roman against the unreconstructed Iliescu. (On one occasion, an American businessman returning from Bucharest sought me out to deliver a personal message from Iliescu for President Bush, the brunt of which was to discredit Roman and seek to forge a Bush-Iliescu understanding. It was not explained why Iliescu chose a private American to deliver the message rather than the many official channels available to him.) Endlessly conspiratorial, these visitors could not be persuaded that we had neither the time nor the inclination to involve ourselves in their internal machinations.

Opposition leaders like Nicolae Manolescu, leader of the Civic Alliance party, were nearly unanimous in arguing against restoration of MFN.[82] As the thoughtful and straightforward Manolescu commanded considerable respect in Washington, we made it clear after this second miners' rampage that MFN would not be considered until after the holding of the long-promised local and parliamentary elections. Although only 18 months had passed since the May 1990 elections, Romanians and outsiders alike felt that new elections were needed—as they had been in most of the rest of the region—to extend a new mandate and build legitimacy in a country still undergoing revolutionary transformation.

When local elections in February 1992 produced a democratic breakthrough, with parties of the Civic Alliance winning Bucharest and other major cities, we in the administration decided on a two-stage process toward restoring MFN. We would sign a bilateral trade agreement as a first step, thus recognizing the progress made already, but would defer granting MFN itself until after free and fair country-wide elections were held so as to retain some leverage over their conduct. Even those of us who had advocated a firm position—withholding support until the concerns detailed in our "benchmark cable" had been met—largely had come to the view that our use of the MFN issue had run its course and that we could extract no further policy benefits from it.[83] MFN had always been a blunt instrument, useful for extracting one concession but not able to be so finely calibrated as to extract several as an ongoing element of policy. With Romania, this was the most hopeful period since the June 1990 miners' rampage, and we wanted to marshal what influence we retained for the one purpose of ensuring that these parliamentary elections would be held as promised and that they would be freely and fairly conducted.

Armed with this mandate and responding to a long-standing invitation from Romanian foreign minister Adrian Nastase, I traveled to Bucharest in early April 1992 to detail the further steps that would be required for the United States to restore MFN. The message, worked out through interagency meetings and approved at cabinet level, was generally positive. The United States was encouraged by the February local elections and, as Romania prepared for new parliamentary and presidential elections, was prepared to take further steps to advance the bilateral relationship, including restoration of MFN. The question of whether MFN would be withheld until after the nationwide elections was still unresolved within our own government, so this had to be left vague. On the other main electoral issue—whether parliamentary and presidential elections should be held together or sequentially—we took no position.

Together with Ambassador John Davis,[84] we made these points, expanding on the political and economic steps we hoped to see, in a series of meetings with Foreign Minister Nastase, new prime minister Teodor Stolojan, and President Iliescu. Over dinner, we spoke at greater length with leaders of the principal opposition parties, including Petre Roman, who had broken with Iliescu to form a new party, and Ion Raţiu, who had come to play a moderating and civilizing influence on Romanian politics since abandoning his hopes for the presidency.

With Nastase, we stressed the importance of passage of two pending pieces of legislation, one governing (and liberalizing) radio and television broacasting and another providing for domestic election observers. Nastase agreed, noting that he had gotten assurances on the latter issue from Iliescu the previous day. But Nastase's preoccupation was Moldova, where he was flying, literally within the hour, for a quadripartite meeting of Soviet, Ukrainian, Romanian, and Moldovan foreign ministers. Their agenda was to discuss the crisis provoked by Soviet intervention in the Transdniester region, a military action ordered by Moscow ostensibly to protect ethnic Russians there but more broadly to counter the separatist movement in this predominantly Romanian republic. The U.S. position, as conveyed in a State Department statement a few days earlier, was on Romania's side in the dispute, but we advised the Romanians to show flexibility until the Soviet leadership could sort out its policy.

Prime Minister Stolojan, easily the most impressive of these Romanian leaders, was an able and self-effacing technocrat serving as caretaker until the coming parliamentary elections. Under next to impossible circumstances, he had kept inflation under control, made progress on macroeconomic policy, and, by dint of his own quiet authority, strengthened public confidence and external support for Romania's economic reform. He had also taken a courageous public stance against anti-Semitism and national chauvinism, at a time when neofascist journals like *România mare* (Great Romania) and ultranationalist political leaders like Cluj's new major Gheorghe Funar were commanding considerable support. Stolojan agreed on the need for new elections to break the current political impasse, but the irony was that new elections meant the end of his caretaker government and the loss to Romania of its most competent political leader.

The meeting with Iliescu was arranged unexpectedly at his request. It was emblematic of the importance Romania attached to U.S. support that the president of the republic would seek out a visiting NSC staffer for a private meeting. There were just four others—two Iliescu aides, an interpreter, and the deputy chief of mission of the U.S. embassy[85]— in a cavernous room in the gloomy presidential palace, which seemed nearly deserted in contrast to the hubbub of activity that always prevailed at the White House. Iliescu was at his most statesmanlike, confining his criticism to the dry observation that the United States had extended MFN status to Romania under Ceauşescu's despotic rule but was withholding it now under conditions that, however imperfect, were by any standards an improvement.[86] I acknowledged that the standards had changed but said that our current policy of "democratic differentiation" had been articulated clearly by Secretary Baker and was being consistently applied. Others had met and exceeded the standards; Romania had not, though we were confident that with free and fair elections Romania would qualify for MFN and a full range of U.S. assistance.

As it turned out, these meetings were but a dress rehearsal for a visit a month later (May 1992) by a large U.S. delegation headed by Deputy Secretary Eagleburger.[87] Eagleburger's foreign policy priority was to press for Romanian compliance with international sanctions against Serbia, on which he got correct but vague assurances. On internal Romanian matters, he delivered the same message that I had carried, obviously with much greater authority and import. Eagleburger pressed particularly hard for the holding of early parliamentary elections.

The elections were eventually held in September and October 1992, yielding another victory for Iliescu and the Front, which formed a coalition dominated by Iliescu's "Democratic National Salvation Front." Even before that, the administration proceeded, over the objections of those who wanted to wait until after the elections, to recommend the restoration of Romania's MFN status, only to have that recommendation overwhelmingly defeated in Congress in September 1992.[88] Nearly three years after the December Revolution, U.S.-Romanian relations, like the Romanian political scene itself, were characterized by the same ambiguities and suspicions that had plagued them throughout.

Bulgaria: Island of Stability?

U.S.-Bulgarian relations were in some respects a victim of bad timing. When we were engaged and ready to help, the political and economic standoff in Bulgaria made it difficult for us to do more than offer indirect support from outside. By the time the opposition had seized the reins of power in late 1991, our own crowded agenda and badly stretched assistance funds prevented us from rendering the kind of support Bulgaria needed. And the Bulgarians, beginning with the ardently pro-American President Zhelyu Zhelev, looked to us for a degree of political intimacy that we were not prepared to provide.

Yet, as a tactical matter, our timing was exquisite. Partly by design and partly through sheer luck, U.S. policy was a step ahead of the major political turning points in Bulgaria's rocky road toward democracy in 1989 and 1990. Already in 1989, U.S. and other support for Bulgaria's "Ecoglasnost" protestors during the CSCE environmental conference in Sofia strengthened the nascent domestic opposition that led to the peaceful revolution a month later. The pattern continued in 1990, as U.S. initiatives anticipated by precisely one month each subsequent breakthrough. The March roundtable agreement that created the framework for new elections was signed a month after Baker's visit to Sofia. UDF (Union of Democratic Forces) chairman Zhelev ascended to the presidency a month after Baker led the call for Bulgaria's admission into the G-24. Finally a broad-based coalition replaced the Socialist government in November–December, a month after Zhelev visited Washington and signed a comprehensive U.S.-Bulgarian trade agreement.

It would be too much to suggest that U.S. policy caused these events, but neither were they purely coincidental. Our reading from the beginning was that democratic progress in Bulgaria would have to be pushed from below, with public (and we hoped peaceful) protests obliging the regime to make concessions it otherwise would have withheld. Given the enormous influence of U.S. policy during this period of Cold War triumph, we needed to provide incentives for further progress, rewarding the regime for each step in the right direction, however ambiguous its purpose, and emboldening the opposition to continue pressing its case. In this sense, our approach resembled the ones we had taken toward Poland and Hungary in early 1989 and, as will be seen, toward Albania in 1991.

Following up on Secretary Baker's strong push for election observers, made during his February 1990 visit to Sofia, we assembled a presidential mission to reinforce the many international delegations already in the country and provided technical assistance to the newly created Bulgarian Association for Fair Elections.[89] The results of the elections, which were won by the Socialists (the renamed Communist party) with a near majority, were not so egregiously distorted as those of the Romanian elections held the month before, but were sufficiently flawed as to prompt significant criticism. The presidential mission expressed its "deep concern about significant inequities," including the "overwhelming imbalance of resources and widespread intimidation" but noted that "the major political parties have agreed to accept the election results and take their places in the new Assembly."[90] The White House and State Department took the same line, as did most West European governments, giving a qualified vote of confidence to Bulgaria's progress toward multiparty democracy. At the G-24 ministerial in Brussels two weeks after the Bulgarian elections, Secretary Baker had made this support tangible but conditional: "We have expressed our deep concern about the fairness of the recent elections. Nevertheless, pending formation of the new Bulgarian Government, and assuming continued democratization, we believe that progress toward reform has been sufficient for Bulgaria to be eligible for G-24 assistance."[91]

We did not have long to wait for our assumption to be vindicated. Two days later, Mladenov resigned the presidency, his position having become untenable because of public airing of an aside caught by television cameras during a December 1989 demonstration in Sofia: "The best thing to do is to bring in the tanks." After two weeks of contentious debate, spurred from the streets by a semipermanent encampment of protestors called the "City of Truth," the grand national assembly elected as president of Bulgaria the former dissident philosopher and political prisoner, now UDF chairman, Zhelyu Zhelev.[92]

President Zhelev's visit to Washington in late September for the annual World Bank/IMF meeting offered an opportunity to take another step in our bilateral relations and strengthen Zhelev's position at home. Bulgarian politics were still poised between the old order and the new, with Zhelev facing a Socialist-dominated parliament and government headed by Andrei Lukanov. Nonetheless, we decided to accelerate negotiations toward an ambitious bilateral trade agreement that extended MFN treatment and made Bulgaria eligible for Export-Import Bank, OPIC, and GSP (Generalized System of Preferences) benefits.[93] We finalized the package at a September 17 PCC (Policy Coordinating Com-

mittee), just in time for President Bush to announce the initiative in an
Oval Office meeting with Zhelev on September 29. Zhelev was impressive in his laconic way, assuring Bush that Bulgaria was becoming an
"island of stability" in a turbulent Balkan sea and wanted to be a close
and reliable partner for the United States in the region.[94] It was an historic meeting—the first visit to the White House by a Bulgarian president—but one that was overshadowed by a cavalcade of other events.

It is worth digressing for a paragraph to enumerate the events of the
week of Zhelev's visit, as they illustrate the enormity of President Bush's
agenda during the period. After addressing the World Bank/IMF annual
meeting and holding a signing ceremony for the transmittal to the Senate of the treaty on German unification, the president departed for New
York, where he addressed the World Summit for Children (attended by
more than seventy presidents and prime ministers, the largest summit
meeting ever held). Later he spoke before thirty-five foreign ministers at
a CSCE ministerial (the first ever on U.S. soil), addressed the UN General Assembly, and held no fewer than 27 separate bilateral meetings
with foreign leaders in his suite at the Waldorf Astoria.[95] He ended his
New York stay to return to Washington for an historic (and, as it
turned out, politically disastrous) "budget summit" in which he and
congressional leaders agreed on "revenue enhancement" (read: tax increase) measures. Upon returning to Washington, he hosted a Rose Garden reception on October 3 to celebrate German unity and taped a tele-
vised message to the German people. Small wonder that Bulgaria got
neglected in the shuffle.

The Zhelev meeting, though brief, served the purpose of lending tangible U.S. support to the democratic process in Bulgaria. Once again the
push came from below. Nationwide strikes in November and December
forced the resignation of Lukanov's government, ushering in a broad
coalition government headed by the political independent Dimitur
Popov and committed to a new constitution (ultimately issued in July
1991) and new elections in 1991. Meanwhile, the new government,
with the UDF controlling the key economic ministries, began the belated reform of an economy in deep crisis. The political struggles of the
previous year had precluded creating any coherent governmental program, even as the economy was being hard hit by the collapse of the Soviet market, which had accounted for 60 percent of Bulgaria's foreign
trade, and the impact of sanctions against Iraq. The new reforms
achieved early successes, bringing inflation down from an estimated 300

percent annually to below 5 percent per month and gaining some control over the runaway state budget. With U.S. support, the IMF announced in mid-March a $500 million loan package, Paris Club official creditors declared a two-year moratorium on debt repayments, and the World Bank began preparing an additional $250 million loan.[96] We also assembled a package of bilateral U.S. assistance measures, concluding in April the trade agreement that was initialed during Zhelev's visit and, in July, launching a $50 million Bulgarian-American Enterprise Fund.[97] It was a respectable package within the constraints of our overall assistance budget, but it was paltry indeed compared to the magnitude of Bulgaria's problems.

The UDF in Power   The UDF, managing just enough cohesion to hang together for the September 1991 elections, won a narrow victory over the Socialists, many of whom were only too glad to let someone else take responsibility for the economic shambles. The new prime minister, Filip Dimitrov, was committed to deep economic reform but faced a still strong and obstructionist Socialist opposition. Nor was his own government and parliamentary majority cohesive. Dimitrov himself betrayed a radical anticommunism that set him apart from much of the UDF, including Zhelev.[98] In response to President Bush's congratulatory message, Dimitrov had written back to ask for the president's help in locating and liquidating communist-owned assets in the United States. Although mystified by the request, we replied through diplomatic channels—i.e., not using the president's imprimatur—that we were ready to provide appropriate assistance but could not involve ourselves in a partisan political struggle. Here again was the problem of how to deal with the decommunization issue. Had the matter been broached by more responsible political forces, we might have been more supportive; the fact that it smacked of a witch-hunt made it harder to do so.

With the new government showing signs of bogging down before it had a chance to address Bulgaria's huge economic problems, we at staff level wanted to dispatch a senior American delegation to show the flag and deliver friendly but pointed messages to the new government. But with the Soviet Union in a state of advanced disintegration and a virtual civil war raging in Iraq, no one of cabinet rank could undertake such a trip. (An oft-postponed trip by Eagleburger and his deputy assistance coordinators ultimately took place the following May.) Accordingly, one of Eagleburger's advisers and I took on the assignment, hiving off from meetings in Brussels and Berlin for a whirlwind 24-hour stay in Sofia, November 13–14, for meetings with the prime minister and all the major political leaders save President Zhelev, who was out of the country visiting NATO headquarters.[99]

In addition to conveying U.S. support and delineating what the new government could expect of us, our main efforts were to solidify political support behind continued economic and political reform.[100] In the manner of a Dutch uncle—having learned my lessons from Baker perhaps too well—I explained that we had seen a recurrent pattern in post-communist Central and Eastern Europe: no sooner had leaders of the democratic opposition defeated the communists than they began drawing long knives against one another. A degree of this was inevitable and indeed healthy for democratic development, but given the parlous state of the Bulgarian economy and the fragility of its democratic institutions, Bulgarians across the political spectrum needed to find ways to keep their divisions from paralyzing further economic and political reform.

With leaders of the powerful trade union Podkrepa, we stressed the larger responsibility they had for supporting the essential elements of economic reform even as they discharged their responsibilities to Bulgarian workers.[101] Among the latter, it was important that Podkrepa continue to include members of the large ethnic Turkish minority (roughly 10 percent of Bulgaria's population of 10 million) in its leadership and rank-and-file, lest they feel their only avenue of political action was via the Turkish-based Movement for Rights and Freedom (MRF). It was a point we reiterated in meetings with MRF and UDF leaders, adding that it was crucial that the MRF continue to be primarily a democratic party, allied with other democratic forces in the country, and only secondarily a Turkish party.[102] On the delicate issue of the constitutional prohibition of ethnically based parties, the United States stood firmly behind freedom of association, so we were uneasy with this provision. Yet we felt that the UDF, the MRF, and others had so far managed to interpret it in a reasonable way, as the MRF was represented in parliament where it had a substantial say in governmental decisions even though its members did not hold cabinet positions.

The Bulgarian Socialist party (BSP), whose leaders we met separately, was cynically exploiting anti-Turkish sentiment and positioning itself, incredibly, as the defender of Bulgarian national interests.[103] Our message, delivered mainly to George Pirinski, who subsequently became Bulgarian foreign minister under the Socialist government, was blunt: the United

States was prepared to develop cordial and constructive relations with the BSP, as it had with West European socialist and social democratic parties, but would have nothing to do with a party embracing chauvinistic and antidemocratic principles, as the BSP showed signs of doing. The aim was not to sway the hard core of the BSP, which was hardly likely to be impressed by this peroration from visiting American officials, but to influence, for the record, the internal debate then raging within the BSP over the party's future orientation.

Prime Minister Dimitrov was even more low-key than his president— the only Bulgarian, I later joked to Bulgaria's ambassador in Washington, who could make Zhelev look charismatic by contrast. In a separate meeting, we urged him to develop a public relations strategy to explain to the population at large what steps were being taken to transform the economy and why, and to set benchmarks that would allow the government to claim credit for each achievement. The conferring of MFN status and creation of the Bulgarian-American Enterprise Fund, for example, were tangible benefits for which he and his government could take credit. Dimitrov outlined his economic plan and the huge political obstacles in front of him. He seemed to have the economics right, but not the politics.

These had been evident the night before in what the embassy reporting cable termed "the Balkanization of a dinner." Dimitrov was all but drowned out by the sharp exchanges among four other key political leaders[104] in a debate focused mainly on Yugoslavia and Macedonia (and well lubricated with strong Bulgarian wine). The Bulgarians were unanimous in criticizing EC efforts to mediate between Serbia and Croatia, and the more nationalistic among them argued that the West was proceeding from the flawed results of Yalta and Versailles. Since no state frontier in Central and Eastern Europe predated Versailles, I observed, reopening these border issues was a recipe for endless conflict. They took the point and affirmed that Bulgaria had no territorial claims, but their disillusionment with Western policies was profound— and, as subsequent events proved, well-founded. They also solemnly vowed that Bulgaria would follow the international consensus on the question of Macedonia, a pledge that they promptly broke when Bulgaria became the first to recognize Macedonian independence. As for the internal scene, the atmospherics of the dinner made it plain that Bulgaria's new political power brokers were not about to set aside their differences and rally behind their young new prime minister.

Back in Washington, we began working on an early visit by Dimitrov, setting the stage in a mid-January meeting at the NSC with new Bulgarian foreign minister Stoyan Ganev. Despite his preoccupation with the conflict in Yugoslavia, which rendered strategic planning elusive, Ganev laid out an intelligent strategy of creating a base of strong bilateral relations with Bulgaria's neighbors and a gradual framework for multilateral Balkan cooperation. Apart from its precipitous recognition of Macedonia, a step that only hardened Greek intransigence, Bulgaria had pursued an exemplary foreign policy and had developed particularly good relations with neighboring Turkey.

Dimitrov's visit in mid-March focused more on Bulgaria's political and economic reforms. His Oval Office meeting with President Bush was not particularly successful, in that he missed an opportunity to drive home a short list of priorities for which he sought American support. Instead, he rambled, making the cardinal mistake of not knowing before a meeting began what specifically he hoped to achieve from it. The administration nonetheless did what it could to make the visit a success. As Deputy Secretary Eagleburger put it in addressing a Trade and Economic Conference held during the visit,

> When Americans think of the revolutionary changes in Europe over the past several years, they tend to remember the fall of the Berlin Wall and the heroic struggles of Lech Wałęsa in Poland and Václav Havel in Czechoslovakia. What until now they perhaps have not sufficiently appreciated is the fact that the Bulgarian revolution has traveled the furthest distance of any throughout the region; it has struggled against the greatest odds; and against all odds it has remained peaceful and democratic.

Eagleburger went on to warn that "destructive hatreds lie not far from the surface," adding that "the enemies of democracy within Bulgaria may try to exploit those emotions to thwart economic change which threatens their interests." This, of course, was a message aimed mainly at the Bulgarian Socialist party. Next came a message for the government: "We would like to see Bulgaria accelerate the pace of economic reforms. . . . Clinging to the remnants of the old system, . . . however comforting they may seem, is a recipe for permanent economic decline."[105]

These warnings, as we feared, fell on deaf ears. Zhelev won the January 1992 presidential elections, but by the time of Eagleburger's visit in May 1992, political infighting within the UDF-led government was well advanced. So, too, was the growing influence of organized crime, a danger delineated over dinner by a Bulgarian deputy prime minister.[106] Criminal elements, with patrons in government and among the security services, were putting down deep roots under the conditions of freewheeling entrepreneurship and lax regulation. After a spate of government crises over the summer, Dimitrov's government fell in October, just a year after gaining power, largely as a result of a showdown needlessly provoked by the prime minister himself. The successor "government of experts" headed by independent economist Lyuben Berov was destined to be a transitional one, giving the newly revived Socialists the opportunity they had sought to prepare for a return to power.[107]

Albania: Of Bunkers and Tree Stumps

Three images stand out. First was the tumultuous welcome Secretary Baker had received on his visit to Tirana in June 1991. Hundreds of thousands were massed in Skanderbeg Square, more than Tirana's entire population. They came by train, by bus, and on foot to see the American secretary of state and this tangible symbol of American presence and support. Security broke down entirely. The motorcade crept through masses of well-wishers pressing against the cars. They held up banners and placards, one reading "Baker-Messiah!"—an excess for which not even Baker's press secretary Margaret Tutwiler could have been responsible.

Second were the bunkers, tens of thousands of them, radiating in some fifty concentric circles from Tirana, defending that city from . . . what? They had been built, not in wartime, but in the 1960s and 1970s to protect Albania against, variously, the Soviets, the Americans, the British. They stood in mute testimony to Albania's compulsive isolation, longtime communist leader Enver Hoxha's paranoid delusions, and above all to the lengths to which his regime was prepared (or obliged) to go to justify the exigencies of a war economy and siege mentality.

Third were the tree stumps. With Baker in 1991, the motorcade had traveled the 15 kilometers from the vast civilian-military airport to the city square on a crude two-lane road bordered most of the way by trees spaced at close intervals. A year later, traversing the same route with

Deputy Secretary Eagleburger, we passed 15 kilometers of tree stumps, every one of those trees having been cut down for fuel during the intervening winter.

Diplomatic Relations   The United States restored diplomatic relations with Albania on March 15, 1991, two weeks before the country's first free elections and a month after prodemocracy demonstrators had toppled Hoxha's massive statue in Skanderbeg Square. There had been a debate within the administration as to the proper timing, with some arguing that diplomatic recognition before the elections would enable the Labor party (the renamed Communist party) of Ramiz Alia to take credit and others worrying that further delay on the issue would put us too much in the middle of Albania's elections. Besides, if Labor won, we would be hoist by the petard of a too clever strategy: as we could hardly withhold recognition indefinitely, we would eventually be obliged to bestow it on a new Labor government, thus conferring a symbolic blessing we did not intend. We therefore decided to hedge our bets, exchanging diplomatic recognition in a State Department ceremony with Foreign Minister Muhamet Kapplani but sharing the credit with Sali Berisha, presidential candidate of the opposition Democratic party, whom we had invited to Washington on a private visit. So ended a 53-year hiatus in U.S.-Albanian diplomatic relations.

If we had faced unrealistic expectations of U.S. support on the part of many new Central and Eastern European leaders, with the Albanians the case was extreme. In a meeting with Berisha and party vice chairman Gramoz Pashko at the State Department, we at staff level tried in vain to dampen their conviction that a Democratic party victory in Albania would propel that country to U.S.-bankrolled prosperity. Indeed, upon their return to Tirana, Pashko declared publicly that there would be a U.S. "blank check" if the Democratic party won the election. They were, nonetheless, an impressive pair, with Berisha's charisma complemented by Pashko's more analytical turn of mind. American eagerness to satisfy at least some of their extravagant expectations led to excesses of our own: our charge d'affaires in Tirana had to be reminded that appearing on the same platform with Berisha during his campaign stops was a step too far.

Following a pattern similar to those of Romania and Bulgaria a year before, Albania's first free elections, held on March 31, were won by the

Labor party (the renamed Communist party) with two-thirds of the vote. Labor dominated the countryside, where its campaign of intimidation was conducted largely outside the purview of foreign election observers. Ramiz Alia, who had led the cautious policy of opening Albania to the outside world and of internal liberalization, was elected president despite the indignity of losing his Tirana constituency. Berisha's Democratic party was strong in the cities and towns, however, and, like the UDF in Bulgaria a year before, it controlled the streets. "Controlled" is not quite the word for the mass demonstrations, verging on civil war, that followed the March elections, but the political agenda was being set by the masses of Democratic party followers in defiance of regime repression. Amidst social and economic chaos, tens of thousands of Albanian "boat people" floated to Italy, with a similar number fleeing across the border to Greece.[108] It was an alarming exodus for so small a country.

The Baker Visit It was against this backdrop that Baker made his triumphal visit in late June. The aim, as in his visits to Sofia and Bucharest in February 1990, was to lend support to a peaceful, step-by-step process of democratization. He did this by extending American moral backing to the democratic opposition and providing inducements for the political leadership of Ramiz Alia and the multiparty government headed by Prime Minister Ylli Buffi (with Gramoz Pashko of the Democratic party as deputy prime minister). In his speeches, Baker noted that he was visiting at the invitation of Berisha, who was at his side throughout. Speaking to the newly elected assembly, he pledged U.S. humanitarian and economic assistance but also sounded a warning to Alia and the hated Sigurimi (security services) still at his disposal:

> Just as there is no turning back on the road to a new Albania, there is no place along that road for violence, no place for intimidation, no place for the use of force. . . . Let us see an end to all fear in Albania. This is a new Albania, and you are members of a new Europe. You have joined the nations that have pledged to uphold the standards of CSCE—standards that govern a state's behavior toward other nations and toward its own people. You have made a solemn compact with Europe and with yourselves. Do not forsake it.

He concluded with a long agenda for Albania's future:

> freeing all political prisoners . . . , full respect for religious and
> minority rights . . . , the opening of the media to genuine plural-
> ism . . . , eliminating repressive security organs and bringing legiti-
> mate police functions under democratic controls . . . , depoliticiz-
> ing and developing civilian control over the military . . . , freeing
> the factories, farms, and mines from political controls and mis-
> management . . . , instituting a fair and open judicial process . . . ,
> pursuing democratization at every level of government and soci-
> ety . . . , [and] holding free and fair elections at both the national
> and local level—elections that include a fair campaign as well as
> equal allocation of state resources, and fair media access to all
> parties. For these are the challenges of your new freedom, and the
> elements of lasting legitimacy.[109]

At Skanderbeg Square, overflowing with an estimated four hundred
thousand joyous Albanians,[110] Baker gave an address that began "Free
citizens of Albania. . . ." In contrast to his lecture to the parliament,
Baker was emotional and personal:

> I have not come here today to instruct you on the virtues of free-
> dom or democracy. You know how inhuman are the ways of total-
> itarianism. You know how difficult is the yoke of tyranny. And
> you know how it is to be cut off from the wider world. . . .
>   I want you all to know we understand how hard you have
> toiled and we are anguished by the pain you have endured. . . . As
> I stand with you in this square at this historic time, I want for a
> moment to remember those of your countrymen who endured Al-
> bania's long winter but did not live to see the spring. Your long
> march to freedom owes a great debt to their suffering and their
> courage. . . .
>   You will not be alone as you travel freedom's road. . . . For I
> have come to bring you a message from another free people—the
> American people. . . . You are with us, and we are with you.[111]

None of us—not even Baker, veteran of many a political rally—had
ever experienced anything like it.[112] President Bush's speeches in
Gdańsk in July 1989 and Prague in November 1990 were as emotional,

but they did not equal Tirana for sheer exuberance. Even the most cynical journalists (if that is not a redundancy) among us were moved by the wild enthusiasm for the United States—and this after 45 years of the most relentless anti-American propaganda on earth. (German foreign minister Hans-Dietrich Genscher, who visited Tirana shortly before Baker, received a warm reception, but nothing like this.) Some of us on the trip later encountered dozens of Albanians who, never having traveled abroad or taken formal English language training, had taught themselves nearly flawless English from VOA and BBC broadcasts.[113] Hoxha's elaborate propaganda machinery—accessible to outsiders via Radio Tirana's vitriolic short-wave broadcasts—had backfired exquisitely. Because they assumed that the domestic media absolutely lied, Albanians tended to believe the polar opposite, with the result that official anti-Americanism helped foster a wildly exaggerated pro-Americanism.

Baker's meeting with President Alia conjured up images from his meeting eighteen months before with Iliescu in Romania. The rough physical resemblance of the two leaders has already been mentioned. Similar, too, were the reception rooms: while those in Albania's presidential "palace" were much more modest than their counterparts in Bucharest, they had the same eerily inhuman character. There was not a single work of art or piece of furniture to connect the inhabitants with the human experience. Albert Camus had described interiors that evoked feelings such as these. How communist leaders led their daily lives and even how they furnished their official quarters—from the Wandlitz compound in East Berlin to Brezhnev's dachas and the third-worldly meeting rooms in Tirana—were not just eerie but terrifying, symbolic of the fundamental inhumanity of these regimes and part and parcel of the violence they so casually perpetrated on their countrymen.

Alia, in retrospect, might seem to have been at his historic vanishing point, rendered irrelevant by the tide of emotion on the streets. Yet as the clashes of a few months before had demonstrated, the Sigurimi retained the capacity to wreak considerable vengeance in one last spasm of violence. Secretary Baker reiterated much of what he had said publicly, combining pledges of U.S. assistance with warnings against further resort to violence. Knowing that Alia's political strategy placed high priority on creating an opening to the West, beginning with the country's admission into the CSCE process, Baker laid particular stress on CSCE principles. At U.S. insistence, Albania's acceptance of a CSCE observer mission had been made a precondition for its membership. Our approach, and that of the observer mission, was facilitated by the specific provisions that had been endorsed at CSCE's Bonn and Copenhagen conferences a year before. As will be seen,[114] this general approach—of linking our bilateral relations to CSCE's specific provisions regarding political pluralism and free market economies—proved even more critical in managing our relations with the newly independent states of the former Soviet Union. Invoking CSCE principles was no guarantee that they would be observed, of course, but they gave us an opportunity to press an agenda of internal reform as a condition of American diplomatic recognition, political support, and economic assistance.

The Baker visit gave a boost to Albania's prodemocracy forces and to Berisha personally. (The ubiquitous Berisha had insinuated himself into Baker's motorcade, in the car just behind mine, and I watched as Berisha, waving and giving the victory sign, turned the event into a campaign swing past hundreds of thousands of newly enfranchised Albanian voters.) The visit may also have deterred remnants of the communist regime from resorting to major violence, but it did not avert a precipitous breakdown of order.

Back from the Brink   As disorder turned to chaos in Albania in the fall of 1991, the Democratic party pulled out of the government in October and negotiated a caretaker government pending new elections. Berisha visited Washington on November 5 and was received by Secretary Baker, who took the occasion to announce new humanitarian and other assistance programs aimed first at averting a humanitarian and social catastrophe in Albania and second at strengthening Berisha's hand. Baker had ordered these new programs literally on the plane returning from Tirana, along with the instruction that he would tolerate no delay in implementation. More importantly, he had intervened personally to throw U.S. weight fully behind Albania's immediate entry into the G-24, IMF, and World Bank, so that substantially greater assistance would be available than our limited bilateral efforts. Among the latter, our programs focused particularly on emergency food and medical assistance and on providing inputs (including such prosaic essentials as fertilizers and cotton) to jump-start the collapsed agricultural and textile sectors on which the Albanian economy depended.

These measures, together with similar efforts undertaken by the European Community and American private donors, did not prevent the catastrophic Albanian winter of 1991–92, but they did avert even greater human suffering and set the stage for a spectacular recovery of the agricultural and textile sectors the following year. They may also have helped the Democratic party to pull off a landslide 66 percent victory in the elections of March 22, 1992. The ever ebullient Berisha was elected president by the new parliament the next month, in time to receive Deputy Secretary Eagleburger and his large entourage for a brief visit in May 1992.[115]

Thousands of tree stumps on the drive from the airport were testimony to the enormity of Albania's challenge, yet the country had survived a test that nearly destroyed it as a functioning society. Its embryonic democracy was alive, the economy was flickering back to life, and the alarming depopulation of the country had abated. Perhaps national survival was the essential point.

A final image: Eagleburger and Berisha sipping coffee on a balcony of Skanderbeg's castle near Kruje, an hour's drive from Tirana, as the two looked down from the Albanian highlands and discussed the country's future. As it must have seemed to Skanderbeg, Albania's national hero, after he turned back the Turks from this castle in the mid-fifteenth century,[116] the miracle was that the Albanians still had a future to discuss.

A Summing Up

In mid-1992, two and a half years after the glorious revolutions of 1989, most of Central and Eastern Europe was mired in recession, with rising unemployment and social tensions threatening the political consensus behind these painful transitions. Yet there were spectacular successes as well: a dynamic new private sector in Poland, an upsurge in Western investment in Czechoslovakia, and an impressive expansion of Hungary's trade with new partners in the West. Free elections had been held and the results honored, and constitutional government was in place. In the Balkans, progress was more halting and uneven, owing partly to the spillover of the conflict in the former Yugoslavia; yet Bulgaria, Albania, and Romania largely maintained their commitment to democracy under difficult circumstances.[117]

Conditions varied substantially by country, but certain general patterns could be identified after 1989. The broad-based democratic coalitions of that year held together long enough to oust the communists, win the first free elections, and form the first governments. (In the

Balkans, the democratic parties generally lost the first elections but then pushed their way into government on the strength of public demonstrations.) Then they splintered, giving way to a proliferation of parties with no roots, organized around prominent personalities whose aversion to compromise made it hard to form stable ruling coalitions (the old us/them mentality being hard to shake). The introduction of the market produced successes that would prepare the way for a wider prosperity, but its initial impact was to generate new inequalities, with a small but conspicuously wealthy group at the top and a large and resentful underclass. Public impatience had fueled pressures for a retreat from painful austerity measures, further divided the erstwhile democratic coalitions, and created fertile ground for demagogues and would-be authoritarians. Civil society, the ultimate guarantor of secure democracy, was developing, but slowly, through the gradual strengthening of independent media, judicial systems, nongovernmental organizations, and all the other institutions and habits that go into making democracy work from the bottom up.

The most obvious generalization of the first two to three years of postcommunist experience was that building a stable democracy would take longer and be both harder and more complex than was assumed during the heady days of 1989 and early 1990. Yet the growing pessimism that had set in by 1991 was also misplaced, a reaction against the earlier inflated expectations of a swift transition to democracy and prosperity. Just as Wagner's music is said to be better than it sounds, the embryonic democracies of Central and Eastern Europe were more promising than outward appearances might have suggested. Gale Stokes offered an historian's perspective:

Totalitarian states hide their weaknesses and present a surface of unity, efficiency, and strength. Pluralist societies hide their strengths and present a surface of disarray, confusion, and weakness. . . . The East Europeans have brought all of their problems to the surface at once, and they are severe. There is no hope that the new regimes will solve them all right away or even ever. But at least they are now available for solution. Each country in its own way will solve something here, something there, and when it does, the new arrangements will enter into a structural strength of that society, creating a new political culture and a new style of economic behavior.[118]

For all the disarray and disillusionment attending these transitions, the countries and societies of the region largely stayed the course of economic and political reform. The Poles and Czechs, who had kept moving steadily forward despite nearly continuous political upheaval, were well advanced toward secure democracy. So were the Hungarians and Slovaks, though their respective nationalistic preoccupations had diverted them from what should have been their main goals. In the Balkans, the embryonic forces of democracy faced powerful and relatively cohesive remnants of the communist old guard, economies in deep recession, and political cultures that retained strong authoritarian elements. Yet these were now pluralistic societies, vastly more open, humane, and free than they had been in 1989. Great uncertainties and questions surrounded the future of these newly liberated countries. For perhaps the first time in their modern histories, however, the answers were to be found within rather than imposed from outside.

U.S. policy was instrumental in helping these countries navigate the first difficult months of postcommunist transition and in creating an international environment conducive to their peaceful extrication from Soviet domination and their gradual integration into a larger democratic community. Our influence varied substantially by country. With Poland it was substantial throughout, sometimes to decisive effect. In Czechoslovakia, we helped shape the early foreign policy thinking of the new leadership and later exerted useful, if limited, influence over the dissolution of the federation. Our influence on Hungary was less significant, owing partly to neglect and partly to the higher priority it assigned to Germany and the EC. With Romania, our role was important in the negative sense of establishing firm rules of conditionality, but in the process we failed to engage this country around any positive agenda. Bulgaria looked to us for a level of support and intimacy that we failed to provide, even as a reformist government faced a severe economic recession and a powerful postcommunist opposition. With Albania, by contrast, our influence was timely and decisive in galvanizing international support at the moment of greatest danger to the country's survival.

The chief failure of American policy was its growing neglect of these countries after the enormous commitment of American leadership we made in 1989 and 1990. The new version of Europe's age-old Eastern question could be simply put. Would the forces of fragmentation on the loose in the East overwhelm the confidence, cohesion, and ultimately the institutions binding the Western democracies? Or would the Western community be able to extend its zone of democratic prosperity eastward, vindicating the vision of a united, free, and democratic Europe and creating a wider transatlantic community?

7

Europe in Search of Security

THERE WAS WISDOM in George Kennan's admonition, in early 1990, to observe a three-year moratorium on changes to European security structures.[1] Yet there was no stopping the disintegration of the Warsaw Pact, notwithstanding a brief Soviet effort to keep it alive as a forum for political dialogue, and Western leaders were under pressure from the East as well as their own publics to transform Western institutions to accommodate radically new realities. The luxury did not exist of creating a new strategic design in cloistered contemplation, free of the political exigencies of a world still in the midst of profound flux toward unknown ends.

These challenges would soon be put to the test. After the November 1990 Paris Summit of the Conference on Security and Cooperation in Europe, three other crucial meetings loomed. A NATO summit to be held in Rome in November 1991 was to present the alliance's "new strategic concept" and complete the vision of a "transformed alliance" heralded at the July 1990 London Summit. The following month, in December 1991, the EC was to meet in Maastricht, the Netherlands, to complete the "single European market" and point the way to European economic and political union. And in July 1992, a CSCE summit in Helsinki was to fulfill the Paris mandate to give the CSCE operational and institutional capacity for overcoming Europe's division and dealing with new threats to European security.

Dutch foreign minister Hans van den Broek, during the period of the Dutch presidency of the EC in late 1991, called Maastricht "a race against history."[2] Indeed it was. Not only were the key European and transatlantic institutions challenged to keep a step ahead of the profound forces of change unleashed by the end of the Cold War; they were also racing against one another to try to shape the post–Cold War order in Europe. Secretary Baker had touched on this point in his December 1989 Berlin speech: "As Europe moves toward its goal of a common internal market, and as its institutions for political and security cooperation evolve, . . . we want our transatlantic cooperation to keep pace."[3] Thus the three summits, and the competing visions underlying them, lent focus, urgency, and occasional acrimony to European and transatlantic diplomacy through 1991 and into 1992.

The European security debate after the Paris Summit was couched in language more akin to engineering and the construction industry than the art of diplomacy: reinforcing structures, variable geometry, multiple speeds, bridges, linkages, and pillars. Sorting out the respective roles of key institutions—NATO, the EC, and the CSCE—was essential, but this debate tended to preempt more fundamental challenges. Chief among these was to preserve the institutions binding the Western democracies as the new era dawned and to bring former adversaries into the European and transatlantic community. Capacities for dealing with new threats to European stability and security also needed to be developed. As President Bush put it at NATO's November 1991 Rome Summit,

> We are not here as engineers but as trustees of democracy. . . . We must provide answers to four defining questions:
>
> First, in this uncertain world, how can we be sure that every ally can be safe from any threat of any sort?
>
> Second, how should we answer the calls of Europe's new democracies to join us?
>
> Third, how should we respond to the disintegration of Soviet power?
>
> And lastly, how should we relate to each other as Europe travels toward union?[4]

While American and European diplomats debated these questions, real threats to European stability and security were erupting. Like the violent disintegration of Yugoslavia, they were threats of a more ambiguous and intractable character, for which traditional military responses were insufficient. Originating not in outright military aggression mounted by one state against another, they sprang instead from social and economic upheavals and ancient ethnic animosities. Thus there emerged a wide gap between the furious but abstract debate over security policy on the one hand and the passivity and confusion of Western responses to actual threats that were erupting in the wake of the Cold War.

The "New European Architecture"

Well-publicized U.S.-French differences captured part of the transatlantic debate, which was by no means confined to two countries alone. Animated by the vision of an EC-centered Europe, rather than uneasy reliance on Anglo-Saxon power in its losing effort to retain preeminence over a resurgent Germany, France aimed to accelerate European integration while it still had political leverage over newly united Germany. This meant deferring consideration of new EC members lest they "dilute" the Community before the movement toward economic and political union had become irreversible. The "European construction" required a security organization to complement the Community's political and economic institutions. But French efforts to reinvigorate the Western European Union (WEU) or create a "Eurocorps" became locked in "zero-sum" competition with NATO. The French believed, with some justification, that the Americans wanted to preserve a NATO-centric European security order while (so they believed) gradually disengaging from an active role in European security. Hence efforts to transform NATO and develop new approaches toward the East were always viewed with suspicion in Paris, just as we were wary of French-led efforts to set up what appeared to be free-standing European security institutions in competition with NATO.

The debates that ensued were increasingly theological, with the British closer to our position and the Germans trying to straddle the middle but hazy about their own priorities—and increasingly divorced from the real world of post–Cold War Europe. The fact was that everyone was reducing military forces at a rapid clip, making it essential to rationalize and combine efforts to meet multiple new threats to European stability rather than set up competing centers of decision making. U.S., French, and British joint action in the Gulf War demonstrated that such cooperation could work in practice, yet we found it hard to replicate this in the loaded debate over the new "European architecture." For our part, it must be said, we found it easier to support the European defense identity in principle than deal with the reality of diminished American authority. Indeed, the Gulf War example cut both ways: it demonstrated the ability of the Western allies to cooperate in the first post–Cold War crisis, but it also made vivid European dependence on American power and reinforced the determination of our European partners to develop a capacity for joint action independent of the United States.

France and NATO   The pressure was particularly felt in Paris, prompting a reappraisal in some French quarters of France's relationship to NATO and the United States after German unification and the collapse of the Warsaw Pact. In the French defense ministry and at the Elysée (the presidential palace) in particular, there was a current of thinking that favored drawing closer to NATO lest France be marginalized in post–Cold War Europe.[5] These sentiments were reciprocated on our side: France's withdrawal from the military side of the alliance, which we had learned to live with after 1966, now acquired new significance in a Europe where the political and economic dimensions of security were ascendant. We needed France in NATO and indeed wondered whether the alliance could survive absent French participation.

Even before the Paris Summit, we had made overtures to the French, chiefly through Mitterrand security adviser Admiral Jacques Lanxade and his American counterparts, General Scowcroft and the NSC senior staff, about France's rejoining the military side of the alliance. At Paris, Scowcroft and Lanxade happened to share a taxi and used the long ride to discuss in some detail the prospects for France's drawing closer to the alliance. In a series of secret meetings thereafter, we explored what changes would need to be made for this to be possible. These were serious discussions but also exploratory, not yet involving Mitterrand directly and kept far away from the foreign ministry at the Quai d'Orsay, where hostility toward the idea was a given. When Lanxade and French defense minister Pierre Joxe visited Washington in early February 1991, they explained that the minimum requirement on the French side would be NATO's fundamental transformation and in particular the reform of its integrated military command. The existing structure, they felt, guaranteed an unacceptable level of American domination and in any case had lost much of its military rationale with the precipitous withdrawal of Soviet forces from Europe. The proposition seemed, in the new security environment, reasonable and interesting. General Scowcroft promised the United States would give it serious consideration.

What might have been an historic reformation of the alliance did not materialize.[6] Discussions broke down on both sides. On ours, the uniformed military, supported by Secretary Cheney, were adamantly opposed to a fundamental change to command arrangements that had served the alliance for forty years. It was, many of us felt, a shortsighted position: NATO's hallowed integrated command would not be of much use if the alliance failed to make the political transformation needed for its survival. But the Pentagon was not to be moved from the view that "if it ain't broke, don't fix it." On the French side, meanwhile, Lanxade could not overcome opposition from the foreign ministry nor bring Mitterrand around. This became evident at the Bush-Mitterrand meeting in Martinique in mid-March 1991, when the French president slammed the door on the idea, arguing that Europe had to develop the capacity to defend itself because American disengagement was only a matter of time.[7]

This was a prophecy that threatened to become self-fulfilling: If the Europeans, anticipating our eventual withdrawal, took steps to develop a security organization that excluded us, the case for our staying would indeed be harder to sustain. If the American public felt that Europeans preferred to organize for their own defense, they would be only too happy to oblige by withdrawing U.S. forces, whose role and mission absent a direct Soviet threat was in any case less compelling. Besides, Mitterrand's argument that Europe had to prepare for the inevitable American disengagement was only part of the story. If his many calls for "overcoming Yalta" were to be taken seriously, he was at least equally moved by the desire to extricate Europe from what he saw as American domination. The French were not aiming at the destruction of NATO, which they neither desired nor thought likely, but rather at keeping it from retaining the dominant role it had played during the Cold War. French behavior during this period therefore needs to be understood partly as a reaction to U.S.-led efforts to infuse the alliance with new missions and to strike a new strategic partnership with Germany.

Transatlantic Discord   Failure to find a way to bring France back into the NATO fold meant that even more was at stake in ensuring that the EC's efforts to build a European security identity did not undermine NATO. Already transatlantic conflicts were erupting over several European proposals issued in the context of an EC Intergovernmental Conference (IGC) launched in Rome in December 1990 with the mandate to produce a draft treaty on European political union in time for consideration at the Maastricht Summit a year later.[8] The phoenix-like Western European Union was convened at foreign-minister level a few days before the Rome IGC to see what role that body might play in the new security environment.

There was a frantic and ill-considered series of European diplomatic initiatives in late 1990 and early 1991. First, Kohl and Mitterrand circulated a letter to their EC and Western European Union (WEU) counterparts the first week of December proposing the European Community's eventual absorption of the WEU, which would become the EC's security and defense arm. Italian foreign minister Gianni de Michelis likewise called for an early "merger" of the two institutions, also without saying how this new entity would relate to the Atlantic alliance. WEU secretary general Willem (Wim) van Eekelen volunteered that the WEU might serve as a "temporary bridge" between the EC and NATO.[9]

EC Commission president Jacques Delors went further, proposing that the WEU's mutual defense commitment be inserted into the EC's political union treaty, without explaining how this new commitment would relate to the existing NATO Article 5 mutual defense guarantee. As Delors put it in summarizing the commission's draft treaty, "What we are proposing is a single [security] Community as a logical extension of the ambitions of European union." Asserting that there was broad agreement within the Community that "a common defence policy must be built on . . . the Western European Union," Delors called for the WEU to become "a melting-pot for a European defence embedded in the Community." What that meant, exactly, we did not know, but it seemed to have no connection to NATO or the United States. Delors concluded by acknowledging that "there is no point in concealing the fact that these plans, even in outline, have caused concern across the Atlantic."[10]

Mindful of Josef Joffe's characterization of the WEU as "the sleeping beauty of European security—often kissed but never awakened,"[11] we in Washington nonetheless saw considerable danger in these initiatives, which in effect would have created a separate, competing European security community. Moreover, France insisted on the narrowest possible definition of NATO's role, whereby Article 5 would apply only to full-scale aggression against a member state and not to any lesser or more ambiguous threats to European stability and security.

The French had long opposed NATO's assuming "out of area" responsibilities, but now they interpreted this to apply not only to the Middle East or North Africa but also to Central and Eastern Europe. If NATO had no role in this region, in our view, it had no role at all except as an insurance policy against a latent Soviet threat. NATO would be marginalized as an agent of European security.

From our perspective in Washington, however, we could see the United States becoming involved at the eleventh hour in such "out of area" European conflicts over which we had no influence because they had been handled in Europe-only channels. NATO would become the "alliance of last resort" rather than the mechanism for joint political and military action on the part of all members of the North Atlantic community.

The U.S. reaction was swift and sharp. A February 22 démarche to all allied capitals—dubbed the "Bartholomew message" because it happened to be signed out in the absence of both Baker and Eagleburger by Under Secretary of State Reginald Bartholomew in his capacity as acting secretary—warned against creating a European caucus in NATO and, worse, a separate European security organization in competition with NATO. The message provoked angry rebuttals from many quarters in Europe. It was criticized even by some who supported our posture as being too blunt and unyielding—needlessly so, given the extreme unlikelihood that the Europeans would actually create an independent defense identity. Better, they argued, to take a relaxed attitude while the Europeans experimented and to weigh in only later, as intentions clarified. Perhaps. But fundamental issues were at stake, and the drift in Europe was, we felt, toward a formula that ultimately would destroy NATO and undermine the basis for an enduring American presence, whereas there were any number of approaches that could have created a European defense capacity that actually strengthened the alliance.

Nor were we alone in our views. Indeed, our démarche was aimed precisely at influencing the debate among and within EC governments before positions hardened irretrievably. The British, supported by the Dutch and others, accepted the need for closer European coordination in foreign and security policies via the WEU but wanted the latter firmly tied to NATO.[12] British foreign secretary Douglas Hurd, speaking in Berlin in early December (en route from the WEU meeting in London to Rome for the Intergovernmental conference), came down hard and helpfully in favor of a "single collective structure based on multinational units comprising both American and European forces," proposing also that the WEU be transferred to Brussels so as to "build bridges to the [EC] Twelve as well as becoming truly the European pillar within the Atlantic Alliance."[13]

There were divisions within European capitals as well, particularly where coalition governments were in power. In Bonn, the defense ministry and the chancellery were closer to our view than was the foreign ministry, but the latter's influence had become much stronger after the resignation in late 1990 of the redoubtable Horst Teltschik as Kohl's foreign policy adviser.[14] In Rome, the Christian Democratic prime minister Giulio Andreotti and his security adviser, Umberto Vattani, were likewise closer to our position than his Socialist foreign minister, the flamboyant Gianni de Michelis.[15]

With the issues now exposed, the transatlantic debate in late spring and early summer 1991 focused on reconciling the competing perspectives. With the British and Dutch, along with NATO secretary general Manfred Wörner and WEU secretary general Wim van Eekelen, we worked out a "dual hatting" proposal, whereby European forces could be assigned either to WEU or to NATO command depending on the circumstances. The WEU, following Hurd's proposal, would be relocated from London to Brussels, so that NATO ambassadors could simultaneously be ambassadors to the WEU. Colocating NATO, the WEU, and the EC would also help coordination among organizations whose membership was overlapping but not identical. (The Danes and Greeks were in the EC and NATO but not the WEU, the Irish were in the EC but not NATO or the WEU, and the Turks, like us, were in NATO but not the EC or the WEU.) The formula was not hard to come by and had, from our perspective, much to recommend it, allowing for a European defense capacity that was simultaneously the EC's security arm and NATO's "European pillar." By the same token, it was anathema for the French, who felt that colocation could only mean the WEU's subordination to NATO, so the idea simply withered away. The critical point for us, however, was not who wore which hat but that there be one overarching transatlantic security organization—the Atlantic alliance—and not two competing ones. That was precisely the arrangement France did not want.

Germany in the Middle   The Germans were anxious to close the rift between Washington and Paris before the Rome and Maastricht Summits, but they had so far been wandering between the two positions without expressing their own. In a January 30 speech before the Bundestag, for example, Kohl had come down squarely on both sides of the issue: "In the field of security policy we aim to strengthen the European pillar of the Atlantic Alliance, which has proved its worth. President Mitterrand and I have suggested that the intergovernmental conference on political union consider how [the WEU] might be strengthened and ultimately incorporated in the European union."[16]

Although we could understand that leaders of the newly united Germany needed to show themselves to be both good Atlanticists and good Europeanists, this studied German ambiguity was weakening our case among other NATO members, notably Spain and Italy. We therefore had to secure a clearer expression of German support, being careful as a tactical matter to assure the Germans that we were not asking them to "choose between Washington and Paris" but merely to take a stand on an issue that should have been as important to them as it was to us. In early May, shortly before two crucial NATO meetings, Genscher and Kohl visited Washington on separate trips, and we at the NSC and State began working on draft statements that might be issued in the context of each.[17] The Germans were receptive. In a joint statement issued after their meeting, Genscher and Secretary Baker proposed a set of new measures to open the alliance to the new democracies of the east and strengthen CSCE institutions (discussed below). They then turned to the "European security identity and defense role":

> In their meeting today, Secretary Baker affirmed that the United States is ready to support arrangements the European Allies decide are needed for the expression of a common European foreign, security, and defense policy. Minister Genscher affirmed that . . . a European security identity should be reflected in the development of a European pillar within the Atlantic Alliance. They both agreed that to ensure this development will strengthen the integrity and effectiveness of the Atlantic Alliance, NATO should be the principal venue for consultation and the forum for agreement on all policies bearing on the security and defense commitment of its members under the North Atlantic Treaty.[18]

Inclusion of this last essential principle, which had become dogma for us, facilitated its adoption by the alliance as a whole in communiqués following the May 29 Defense Planning Committee (defense ministers and military commanders) meeting and the June 6–7 North Atlantic Council (foreign ministers) meeting. The latter statement also called for "appropriate links and consultation" among NATO, the WEU, and the EC.[19] The French, who participated in the NAC but not the DPC, were isolated but unaltered in their position, despite Secretary Cheney's talks with Mitterrand in Paris en route to Brussels for the DPC meeting.[20]

Ten days after Genscher, Kohl arrived on his first visit since unification. Although the president made little headway with him on the EC's position on the GATT round, there was progress on the European security identity. In a speech in Washington just after his meeting with Bush, the chancellor took on the issue, beginning on a disingenuous note but finishing well:

Deliberations with respect to a common European foreign policy—and in the long term a common defense policy as well—are being closely followed in Washington and, here and there, they evoke criticism—not all of which I understand. Let me make two things unequivocally clear:

My government does not want to see the long-standing Atlantic Alliance in any way weakened, still less replaced by a European structure.

My government is adamantly opposed to any suggestion that responsibility in some areas be divided. That would run counter to the principle of the indivisibility of our collective security and would only lead to the dissolution of the transatlantic security link.[21]

The issue was by no means closed, however, for the prevailing draft of the EC's political union treaty continued to use the preferred French position, with some concessions to the British.[22] Indeed, scarcely a month after his meeting with Bush, Kohl met with Mitterrand and the two vowed to reconcile their differences over the common foreign and security policy.[23] The French had been playing diplomatic hardball with the Germans for some time—particularly in the context of negotiations over a formula that would permit the continued presence of French forces in the Federal Republic. In a fit of pique just before unification, the French had hastily, and unwisely, declared that their forces in Germany would be withdrawn. It was one of several French diplomatic fumbles during Mitterrand's prolonged disorientation after the fall of the Berlin Wall. They were now having second thoughts, and the Germans were eager to oblige them so as to ground united Germany securely among its EC and NATO partners.

From this aim there developed the idea of a "European corps." The political objective was one we fully endorsed, for our own continued presence in Germany would be greatly facilitated if other countries also remained, but we saw considerable room for mischief in an October 1991 proposal by Mitterrand and Kohl for a Franco-German corps that would be open to other European forces as well in a new "Eurocorps." What would be the command arrangements of such a corps? we asked. Would it be in NATO or outside? We got no answers.[24] The Germans would tell us not to worry, that the Eurocorps was a means of bringing the French closer to NATO, but its evolution so far suggested that the French, via the Eurocorps idea, were taking Germany farther away.

The Rome Summit In his address to NATO's summit in Rome in early November, the president took these issues head-on:

> The alliance is not an American enterprise nor a vehicle of American power. We never sought preponderance, and we certainly do not seek to keep it. Nor do we claim a monopoly on ideas for the alliance. If we did, none of us would be sitting here today, for the idea of the Washington treaty [establishing NATO] was Europe's. . . .
>
> The United States has been, is, and will remain an unhesitating proponent of the aim and process of European integration. This strong American support extends to the prospect of a political union—as well as the goal of a defense identity. . . .
>
> Even the attainment of European union, however, will not diminish the need for NATO. . . . We support the development of the WEU because it can complement the alliance and strengthen the European role in it. . . . But we do not see the WEU as a European alternative to the alliance.[25]

Behind closed doors, Bush was more blunt: "If Western Europe intends to create a security organization outside the Alliance, tell me now!" As his stunned counterparts shifted nervously in their seats, Bush explained that he would stake his presidency, if necessary, on the continued American commitment to European security via NATO, but he could not do so if America's closest allies were prepared to undermine and divide the alliance at the moment of its crowning success.

The Rome communiqué adopted compromise language that resulted from tough bargaining with the French. We got our formulation on NATO's role as "the essential forum for consultation among its members and the venue for agreement on policies bearing on the security and defence commitments of Allies under the Washington Treaty," papering over the huge differences in interpretation of what those commitments entailed. And the French got some of their favored formulations, including this labored sentence ending with a Delphic phrase that all sides could interpret as they wished: "We welcome the perspective of a reinforcement of the role of the WEU, both as the defence component of the process of European integration and as a means of strengthening the European pillar of the Alliance, bearing in mind the different nature of its relations with the Alliance and with the European Political Union."[26]

Neither Rome nor Maastricht settled these fundamental questions bearing on the future of the Western security community. Nor was the disposition of the still-emergent "Eurocorps" settled until the Germans—principally General Klaus Naumann, head of the armed services—finally noticed that the existing blueprint called for German integration with French forces into an entire corps operating outside NATO structures. It was in early 1992 that General Naumann, Admiral Lanxade, and the American SACEUR (Supreme Allied Commander, Europe), General John Shalikashvili, met quietly to work out the arrangement that should have been adopted at the outset: German forces assigned to NATO could be seconded to a Franco-German or European corps operating outside the alliance for purposes other than Article 5 security commitments. And the decision for such deployment should be made within the alliance. The issue was settled, more or less, of which forces were committed to which organization, and when. But this begged the question for which no one had an answer: for what purposes would these forces be used?

Even at the time, these debates seemed overwrought. With the benefit of hindsight, they appear shockingly detached from the real issues of security confronting Europe after 1990. Our own NATO-centered approach was right in principle but mistaken in practice. It would have been sound and sustainable if we were prepared to undertake the kind of fundamental restructuring of the alliance that some in Paris were urging on us. But we could not have it both ways—preserving a level of American dominance that was anathema to the French (as well as the Spanish and Belgians) while also insisting that any European effort be made within the alliance framework. The French position was the mirror image of ours. They wanted a European security capacity but systematically undermined efforts to transform NATO in ways that might have made their ambition feasible.

Both the French and American conceptions, and indeed those of the Germans as well, were, in any case, fast being overtaken by growing fragmentation in the East. The French were more transparent: the notion of a "European confederation" was rightly seen as a device to consign the East Europeans to an outer circle of European security, while they constructed what amounted to "Fortress Western Europe." Our approach, while conceptually more sound, proved too timid in practice. In particular, the rhetoric of NATO's lead role in European security was belied by the institution's passivity with regard to the unfolding war in the former Yugoslavia. Our acute ambivalence with regard to taking direct action in security threats to the East caused us to retreat, in fact if not in principle, to the mentality of "Fortress Transatlantica." Preserving NATO took precedence over adapting it or answering the hard question of how we proposed to use it. The notions of "Fortress Western Europe" or "Fortress Transatlantica," however attractive they might have seemed to war-weary Western publics, were built on the same false premise that the Western community could be preserved and even strengthened in the new era without addressing the main problems that threatened it.

Integrating the East

In his eloquent opening address to the November 1990 CSCE conference, French president François Mitterrand set the tone: "The Paris Conference, I hope, will be an anti-Congress of Vienna, since round this table we have neither victors nor vanquished, but 34 countries equal in dignity."[27] They were noble sentiments, echoed with evident sincerity by most Western leaders in their interventions at Paris. Yet their Eastern counterparts shared an unease tinged by distrust. Their misgivings were captured best by Polish prime minister Tadeusz Mazowiecki in his address:

We must all face the question [of] whether the borderline of the old Yalta-based division of Europe is not for a long time going to mark a civilizational division. Our common future may be darkened by the sinister clouds of the resurging conflicts of bygone days, unless the split into a rich and poor Europe, an 'A' class and a 'B' class Europe, is overcome. . . . This is the key to the unity of Europe as a whole; it is a fundamental issue . . . for which [a] determined and consistent solution cannot be delayed indefinitely.[28]

With the Warsaw Pact fast disintegrating, the countries of Central and Eastern Europe, and indeed the Soviet Union as well, looked to the CSCE as the sole institution where they sat on equal footing with the rest of Europe and North America. By design or simply for want of other institutional alternatives, they offered proposals to expand CSCE's scope and mandate to turn it, over time, into the preeminent political and security organization bridging the two halves of Europe.

Institutionalizing the CSCE The Paris Summit itself had been a Soviet idea, coming from President Gorbachev's initiative in Rome in late 1989, just before his summit meeting with President Bush off Malta. Shortly thereafter, Polish prime minister Mazowiecki had proposed creation through CSCE of a "permanent council of European coöperation."[29] At Paris, Gorbachev came back to the idea, calling for an "All-European Security Council."[30] Still more ambitious was the proposal of Czechoslovak foreign minister Dienstbier, which envisioned, as a first step, creation of a "European Security Commission" among CSCE member states that would serve as a bridge between NATO and the Warsaw Pact. The second stage, in Dienstbier's conception, would be "establishment, on a treaty basis, of an Organization of European States, including the United States and Canada," leading, in the third and final stage, to a "confederated Europe of free and independent states."[31]

This, surely, was a bridge too far. We and most other CSCE members rejected such ambitious designs and aimed instead toward an evolutionary development of the CSCE in ways that would complement existing institutions like NATO and the EC. And we did not want to burden the CSCE with the false promise of collective security, with which Europe and America had recent and bitter experience through the League of Nations. (It will come as no surprise that the interpretation one found in

the Bush administration was that the league's failure was only incidentally related to the U.S. refusal to join; it had much more to do with inherent and irremediable flaws in collective security systems of this sort.)

Based on initiatives advanced by NATO at its summit in London in
July 1990, the Paris Summit had taken the first steps toward institutionalizing the CSCE as a forum for political dialogue between the two
halves of Europe. They included creating a Council of [Foreign] Ministers, which would meet at least annually; a Committee of Senior Officials to convene regularly in the interim; and a parliamentary assembly,
which, like the Council of Ministers, would meet at least once a year. To
these were added a small permanent staff, located in a new secretariat
in Prague, to provide administrative support and disseminate information to member governments, an office for free elections in Warsaw, and
a conflict prevention center in Vienna.

Yet to list the new bodies in this fashion is to exaggerate their importance at this early stage. They did not yet exist and were in any case
quite modest in conception. Some, like the parliamentary assembly,
were still the subject of heated debate within CSCE, and between Congress and the administration in our own country. (We at the NSC staff
had championed the Council of Europe's parliamentary assembly as the
model for the new assembly but were obliged to beat a hasty and hum-
ble retreat after several irate members of Congress made plain their
preference for the known venue of the North Atlantic Assembly.)

This modest approach may have been a sensible one for institutions
so new, but the pressure was great and expectations high to turn the
CSCE overnight into an institution that could bear a large share of the
weight of overcoming four decades of division. Having rejected the
more extravagant proposals for the CSCE's expansion, we and most
other members nonetheless shared the view that the CSCE urgently
needed to take on new tasks and functions. Developing regular forums
for political dialogue was the first task: having met but intermittently in
the past, in formal, highly stylized East-West encounters, the CSCE now
needed to become the premier venue for serious discussion among all
the states of Europe and North America.

The CSCE's role as a forum for political dialogue should not be undervalued, even allowing for the seemingly innate capacity of Europeans—but not Americans!—to sit endlessly in plenary session, listening
to mind-numbing, content-free orations. Yet for the new democracies of
Central and Eastern Europe, this was the *only* forum in which they

could discuss the issues that concerned them most, and do so as equals around the table with all the countries of Europe and North America. There was plenty to talk about. In particular, there was a strong push to erect new mechanisms for conflict prevention and crisis resolution in the midst of the gathering storm in Yugoslavia. The first meeting of the Council of Ministers, set for June in Berlin, was to report progress on creation of these new institutions and mechanisms, which were to be finalized by the time of the next summit, scheduled for the summer of 1992 in Helsinki.

Events in the East quickly outpaced these evolutionary efforts through the CSCE. Soviet foreign minister Shevardnadze's resignation in December 1990, Gorbachev's cultivation of hard-line military and KGB officers, the crackdown against Baltic independence movements, and disputes over Soviet troop withdrawals all served to heighten security concerns in Central and Eastern Europe. Polish president Lech Wałęsa, as has been seen, warned of "deadly danger" to Poland emanating from what Lithuania's foreign minister called the "mad generals" in Moscow.[32] Another ominous note was sounded when, the day after the second "Bloody Sunday" in the Baltic states, Polish, Czechoslovak, and Hungarian foreign ministers were consulting in Budapest and calling for the early dissolution of the Warsaw Pact's military apparatus. In Moscow, *Pravda* warned about their efforts to set themselves "against the Soviet Union . . . as if the *troika* wanted to determine common approaches . . . without the participation of the remaining members of the Warsaw Pact."[33] Undeterred, the "troika" met at summit level in Visegrád, Hungary, on February 15, agreeing to strengthen political and military cooperation among the "Visegrád group," as it increasingly came to be called.

Although the immediate crisis passed with the resumption of talks on Baltic independence and Gorbachev's agreement to disband the Warsaw Pact's military arm,[34] continuing conflict in Moscow and among the republics leading up to the August 1991 coup attempt against Gorbachev kept Central European security concerns at a high pitch throughout 1991. Czechoslovak president Václav Havel, who had placed so much hope in the CSCE as the centerpiece of a pan-European peace order, now looked for more substantial and immediate security assurances, on grounds that "we cannot dream of the future only." In Brussels in late March for visits to NATO and the European parliament, Havel warned against leaving the region in a security "no man's land" or "zone of instability," and called for early membership in the EC and closer association with NATO.[35] Polish foreign minister Skubiszewski spoke in similar terms:

> Europe should be treated as a homogeneous security area. This is the approach of the Paris Charter of a New Europe, adopted by the CSCE Summit of 1990. In particular, central Europe cannot become a gray, buffer, or neutral zone from the point of view of security. . . . The North Atlantic Alliance is integral to European security and thus cannot remain indifferent to a threat to international security in any part of the Continent. . . . It is necessary to seek a certain fusion of the CSCE system with NATO.[36]

Even as the CSCE was struggling to implement the Paris Summit initiatives through regular meetings of the new Committee of Senior Officials, the pressure was shifting to the EC, WEU, and NATO as the institutions to draw the new democracies into a larger zone of security and stability. The EC's launching of two intergovernmental conferences in December 1990—one on economic and monetary union, the other on political union—had made it plain that its internal transformation took precedence over the prospect of new members. The "deepeners," led by France, were ascendant over the "wideners." Nonetheless, the EC Commission had been authorized to negotiate association agreements—formally called the "Europe Agreements"—with Czechoslovakia, Hungary, and Poland. Ultimately signed in December 1991, the agreements provided for political consultations as well as significant market-opening measures (except in sensitive areas like agriculture).[37]

As to the Western European Union, Secretary General van Eekelen visited Warsaw to explore "ways in which the security needs of these countries might be addressed by the WEU."[38] But neither these initiatives nor the EC's Maastricht Treaty opened the door to full membership or provided a timetable toward that end. The French in particular were at pains to push prospective membership off into the indefinite future, notably in Mitterrand's dismissive remark in June 1991 that the new democracies might have to wait "decades" to join the EC because of the dilapidated state of their economies.[39]

NATO's Opening to the East Meanwhile, NATO's first steps toward reaching out to the East had about run their course. These measures, adopted at NATO's July 1990 summit in London, included invitations to Warsaw Pact member governments to establish regular diplomatic liaison missions at NATO headquarters. NATO extended invitations to Gorbachev and the Central and Eastern European leaders to address the North Atlantic Council and intensified military-to-military contacts, including visits by NATO military commanders to Eastern capitals. NATO's opening also legitimized and provided a framework for various steps taken bilaterally, including Secretary Cheney's visits to Poland, Hungary, and Czechoslovakia in the course of 1991, which capped extensive military contacts at lower levels. Similar visits were made by his allied counterparts. A number of nonbinding bilateral agreements also were concluded, such as the U.S.-Polish declaration of March 1991 and the French-Polish friendship treaty of April 1991, and bilateral military-to-military programs were becoming more regular and extensive.

With the hardening of Soviet policies in early 1991, we in Washington began developing initiatives to strengthen and formalize the NATO liaison relationships. Inasmuch as the French were working hard to block even the modest measures agreed to at London, it was clear that we would need German cosponsorship of any new measures to develop NATO's outreach to the East. Then, working bilaterally with other key allies, particularly the British, Italians, and Dutch, we could build a NATO consensus and so isolate the French when it came time for a decision.

To pave the way for the NATO foreign ministers' meeting scheduled for June in Copenhagen, Secretary Baker and Foreign Minister Genscher proposed a long list of initiatives to strengthen the CSCE process and expand NATO's links with the East.[40] Although watered down by the French, most of the initiatives were endorsed by the Copenhagen meeting. The ministers expanded the liaison function through political visits and military exchanges at all levels, a strengthened security dialogue, and participation by Soviet and Eastern European officials in certain NATO activities. One such activity was cooperation in "airspace management," a handy euphemism that enabled us to address Central and Eastern European calls for assistance in air defense without unduly alarming the Soviet military.

The Copenhagen communiqué also established a new principle for the alliance, anticipating NATO's "new strategic concept" being readied for the Rome Summit in November: "Our own security is inseparably linked to that of all other states in Europe. The consolidation and preservation throughout the continent of democratic societies and their freedom from any form of coercion and intimidation are therefore of direct and material concern to us."[41]

The Rome Summit took place against the backdrop of epic events in the Soviet Union: the failed hard-line coup against Gorbachev, the ascendancy of Russian president Boris Yeltsin, and the collapse of the Soviet Communist party. Recognition of the independence of the Baltic states was accompanied by the growing disintegration of the Soviet state. NATO's promised "new strategic concept" acquired new urgency, to put it mildly.

In September, President Bush had already announced a series of dramatic, unilateral arms reduction measures and challenged Moscow to reciprocate. These measures included elimination of all U.S. ground-launched short-range nuclear weapons, artillery shells, and short-range ballistic missile warheads as well as removal of all tactical nuclear weapons from U.S. surface ships and attack submarines. The president also announced a standing down from alert status of all U.S. strategic bombers and intercontinental ballistic missiles and termination of several nuclear weapons programs.[42] Gorbachev did indeed respond in kind, but by this time he was presiding over a state on the brink of extinction.

The burden was therefore intense on NATO to demonstrate its relevance in a world without the threat it had been created to counter. At the same time, the Central and Eastern Europeans, at the front line of a Soviet Union that seemed on the brink of violent or at least chaotic disintegration, were clamoring for a more forthcoming NATO response to their security concerns.

During the period of the Soviet coup, Western leaders instinctively extended such reassurances as they could to Eastern Europe. The day of the coup attempt, when its outcome was still in doubt, President Bush spoke by telephone with Wałęsa, Havel, and Antall, noting in a press conference the next day that he had assured them "that the democratic processes in their countries cannot be reversed."[43] Western European leaders did likewise, pledging also to accelerate negotiations on EC association agreements. NATO placed the three leaders' concerns high on the agenda of an emergency foreign ministers' meeting in Brussels in late August, with Secretary Baker calling on the alliance to consider "further concrete ways in which we can bolster the processes of economic and political reform in Central and Eastern Europe."[44]

With NATO's initiatives once again wholly overtaken by events in the East, we began working with the Germans, British, and others on a more radical approach toward opening the alliance to the new democracies of the East. Foreign Minister Genscher's planned visit to Washington in early October, on the first anniversary of German unification, provided an ideal opportunity for another joint statement, this one aimed at influencing NATO's Rome Summit. A visit to the White House by Chancellor Kohl two weeks earlier had been an even better occasion, for which we at the NSC had prepared a draft statement; however, the president, preoccupied with the Middle East in the aftermath of Operation Desert Storm, returned the draft two or three times for shortening before finally electing not to use it at all.[45] We therefore looked to the Genscher visit to carry the message.

The objective was to bring the new democracies of Central and Eastern Europe, particularly the Visegrád group, closer to the alliance, while also providing a forum for more regular interaction with the Soviet Union. Instead of irregular visits and exchanges, we had in mind an entirely new institution that would bring NATO allies and former Warsaw Pact adversaries together in a forum for political consultation and defense cooperation. Trying to square the circle between Soviet sensibilities and Central and Eastern European nervousness, we devised a formula that would treat all former Warsaw Pact members equally as a formal matter but would in practice be highly differentiated in favor of the new democracies.

Creation of the North Atlantic Cooperation Council   Toward that end, Secretary Baker and Foreign Minister Genscher issued a joint statement after their October 2 meeting in Washington, calling for the upcoming summits of NATO, the EC, and the CSCE and the "fundamental transformations" they heralded to be "complementary and interdependent." As to NATO, new initiatives called for direct participation by the Central and Eastern European countries and the Soviet Union in meetings of NATO's Political and Economic Committees and establishment of NATO information offices in Eastern capitals. More important, they also called for creation of a new "North Atlantic Cooperation Council" to bring the countries of Central and Eastern Europe, as well as Baltic states and the Soviet Union, together with NATO in regular consultations at ambassadorial or foreign minister level.[46] The initiative was welcomed within hours in a joint statement issued by the "Visegrád" foreign ministers of Poland, Czechoslovakia, and Hungary.[47]

Creation of the North Atlantic Cooperation Council, or NACC, at the Rome Summit marked a reasonably successful conclusion to a year's intense effort to transform the alliance in ways relevant to the new security situation in the eastern part of the continent. As Bush had put it shortly after the failed August coup, "The world has changed at a fantastic pace, with each day writing a fresh page of history before yesterday's ink has even dried."[48] Banal, perhaps, but it conveyed something of the difficulty of keeping NATO's transformation more or less in step with history.

Although the NACC served some immediate objectives, it fit uneasily into the alphabet soup of existing European and transatlantic institutions. In particular, it seemed to vitiate efforts to strengthen the role of the CSCE. If the NACC, bringing together the most powerful countries of Europe and North America, was to meet regularly at foreign minister level to discuss matters of European security, what role did that leave for the CSCE? The French disliked the NACC from the outset, seeing it as an American effort to undermine the CSCE process by usurping its mandate under a new institution susceptible to American control. Relatedly, the inclusion of NATO and former Warsaw Pact members in the NACC meant exclusion of European neutrals and the nonaligned, notably Finland and Austria. Where did they fit in? If they were invited to participate, as eventually they were, did not this accentuate the NACC's duplication of the CSCE's membership and mission?

The NACC's most serious deficiency was that it fell between two stools: in trying to balance Central and Eastern European insistence on inclusion in Western security organizations against Soviet fears of exclusion, it wound up meeting neither objective and satisfying no one. The Soviet Union, and later Russia, did not see it as an institution worthy of a great power, even an enfeebled great power. The Central and Eastern Europeans felt that participating alongside the Russians in a NATO-related institution could only mean their own marginalization and indeed defeated their purpose in associating with NATO in the first place. They would join—what choice did they have?—but with their security concerns unanswered.

The fatal blow to the NACC came at its second meeting, held in March 1992, shortly after the disintegration of the Soviet Union. The first question to be answered in arranging the meeting was whom to invite among the newly independent states of the former Soviet Union. The Baltic states, whose independence we had recognized some months before, were already in. But what other countries should participate? All of them? Russia only? Russia and Ukraine? The nuclear states— Russia, Ukraine, Belarus, and Kazakhstan? A minority of us in Washington favored the latter solution, but we were quickly overruled by the senior levels of the administration as well as by nearly all the allies, who insisted that all the states of the former Soviet Union be invited and indeed encouraged to join the NACC.

The same issue arose in the CSCE and was handled in the same way, but with different implications. As an inclusive institution based on shared principles, the CSCE was an appropriate instrument for bringing the newly independent states into a larger community of values. There we had a positive interest in their association, which we rightly urged on them and then utilized to leverage their adherence to CSCE principles. In early 1992, as will be seen, Secretary Baker did just that, traveling to each of the newly independent states, armed with a long list of CSCE principles that he linked to the establishment of U.S. diplomatic relations. As an operational matter, the advent of so many new members made CSCE decision making even more cumbersome and tedious than it had been before, but these liabilities did not vitiate the organization's purpose.

The NACC, by contrast, was meant to be a security organization; the hasty and indiscriminate invitation to new members thousands of miles beyond the traditional NATO area only served to muddle the nascent institution's purpose. The argument in favor of this course—that the successor states to the Soviet Union should not be discriminated against—was hard to refute as a matter of principle, but as a matter of policy it preempted whatever role the NACC might have played in helping overcome the division of Europe. Secretary Baker, in his intervention at the NACC ministerial meeting, gamely put it this way: "Today we welcome the new states of the former Soviet Union into the NACC. Their presence expands our horizons."[49] In truth, our horizons were expanded to the NACC's vanishing point. At the first expanded meeting of the NACC,[50] the manifest lack of interest in NATO issues on the part of the newly independent states of Central Asia, and the consequent neglect of a focused agenda relevant to countries like Poland and Ukraine, made it plain that the NACC was already irrelevant. And if the NACC was irrelevant, what of NATO itself?

New Threats to Security

At the Rome Summit, NATO approved the alliance's "New Strategic Concept." As the summit communiqué explained it,

> We no longer face the old threat of a massive attack. However, prudence requires us to maintain an overall strategic balance and to remain ready to meet any potential risks to our security which may arise from instability or tension. . . . Our new strategic concept . . . allows us, within the radically changed situation in Europe, to realise in full our broad approach to stability and security encompassing political, economic, social and environmental aspects, along with the indispensable defence dimension. . . .
>
> Our military forces will adjust to their new tasks, becoming smaller and more flexible. Thus, our conventional forces will be substantially reduced as will, in many cases, their readiness. They will also be given increased mobility to enable them to react to a wide range of contingencies, and will be organized for flexible build-up, when necessary, for crisis management as well as defence. Multinational formations will play a greater role within the integrated military structure. Nuclear forces committed to NATO will be greatly reduced. . . .[51]

The summit also reaffirmed NATO's four new "core functions" that had been agreed on at the Copenhagen meeting of foreign ministers in June 1991. The second, third, and fourth of the four core functions were the familiar ones of dialogue, deterrence and defense, and preserving the strategic balance. What was new was the first: "to provide one of the indispensable foundations for a stable security environment in Europe, based on the growth of democratic institutions and commitment to the peaceful resolution of disputes, in which no country would be able to intimidate or coerce any European nation or to impose hegemony through the threat or use of force."

General Colin Powell, chairman of the Joint Chiefs of Staff, put it more succinctly: "NATO's original purpose—providing security for the West—is still very relevant. NATO's new, added purpose is to help build stability in the east and, in turn, stability in all of Europe."[52]

This was, of course, the right orientation for NATO in the new era—indeed the only one for it to adopt if the alliance were to be relevant to

the new threats to European security. The creation of a NATO rapid reaction force was an appropriate adaptation of the alliance to new challenges, as were similar efforts taken by the Western Europeans via the
WEU and the new "Eurocorps." But "instability," "tension," and "uncertainty" were elusive enemies, for which NATO was not well suited.
Taken together with the solemn reaffirmation that "the Alliance is the
essential forum for consultation among its members and the venue for
agreement on policies bearing on the security and defence commitments
of Allies under the Washington Treaty," the Rome Summit had assigned
NATO a potentially open-ended set of responsibilities for exorcising the
demons unleashed with the end of Cold War rigidities.

CSCE's Role in Conflict Resolution   It was in this context that the alliance, following the lead of the Baker-Genscher joint statements, looked
to a strengthened CSCE as "the organ for consultation and cooperation
among all participating States, capable of effective action in line with its
new and increased responsibilities . . . for effective crisis management
and peaceful settlement of disputes." The Rome declaration called on
the forthcoming Helsinki Summit to strengthen the roles of the Committee of Senior Officials, Conflict Prevention Center, and Office of Free
Elections, as well as to establish organizational and operational links
among the CSCE, NATO, the EC, and other institutions. It further proposed that CSCE decision-making rules, which required unanimous
consent, be amended to what came to be known as "consensus minus
one," whereby action could be taken against a state in "cases of clear,
gross, and uncorrected violations of relevant CSCE commitments, if
necessary in the absence of the consent of the state concerned."
    Since the Paris Summit, the CSCE had been grappling with two sepa-
rate dimensions of these problems: the rights of national minorities and
mechanisms for the peaceful settlement of disputes. The first effort
aimed at developing a set of principles and procedures that would help
prevent or contain ethnic conflict before it erupted into violent confrontation; the second sought to develop a full array of conflict resolution mechanisms from arbitration and mediation through sanctions,
peacekeeping, and potential peacemaking (i.e., imposing and enforcing
a peace between two combatants).
    Minority rights had been one of the most contentious issues at
CSCE's Copenhagen conference of June 1990, which made little headway and so devolved discussion to a separate meeting of experts, con-

vened in Geneva in July 1991. This meeting, too, reflected sharp divisions and essentially irreconcilable positions. There were definitional and conceptual problems. Which "minorities" are covered—national, religious, territorial? Do minorities have rights as individuals, derived from citizenship in states adhering to international human rights conventions, or do they have collective rights derived from their belonging to an identifiable group? Relatedly, should states be obliged simply to ensure equal rights and equal protection under the law on a nondiscriminatory basis, or should they take active measures to promote those rights, extending preferential treatment to disadvantaged minority groups?

Hungary wanted extensive, internationally supervised rights accorded to the millions of Hungarians living outside its borders; Romania opposed such measures as infringements on its sovereignty. A Hungarian draft proposal, for example, listed some twenty separate rights of national minorities, including the "right to an appropriate form of self-government," and would have enjoined participating states to "guarantee the protection as well as *the possibility for the effective exercise* of the rights of national minorities."[53] At Geneva, the head of the Hungarian delegation added that "special measures, including legal guarantees, should be adopted to ensure genuine equality and compensate for [minorities'] disadvantages."[54] Few countries were prepared to go that far, but most wanted to go beyond the language of existing international documents in recognizing group as well as individual rights.

As a statement of common principles, the Geneva conference report was a great success, by far the most extensive delineation of minority rights ever produced in an international document. As an operational document, however, it failed to establish specific commitments that could be invoked by the international community in cases of violations of the rights of national minorities or disputes arising therefrom.[55] The 11-page document began with the existing United Nations formulation of "rights of persons belonging to national minorities," but added that "peace, justice, stability and democracy require that the ethnic, cultural, linguistic and religious identity of national minorities be protected, and conditions for the promotion of that identity be created." The conference thus acknowledged the collective rights of minority groups while giving precedence to individual rights.

The document also distinguished between cultural rights, which were given extensive and precise treatment, and political rights, which were treated much more gingerly. Thus the report presented a long list of the rights of national minorities, including development of their ethnic, cultural, linguistic, and religious identities free from involuntary assimilation. It also specified the freedom to use one's mother tongue, establish institutions and associations, participate in public affairs, and engage in contacts across national frontiers. The report provided examples of specific political arrangements such as local and autonomous administration, commissions of mixed nationalities, and special provisions for minority representation in parliamentary bodies. But these were in no way binding on the signatory states and indeed were prefaced by the disclaimer that "the diversity and varying constitutional systems among them . . . make no single approach necessarily generally applicable."

Similar, but more damaging, limitations beset efforts to devise new mechanisms for conflict resolution, which was the mandate of an experts meeting held in Valletta, Malta, in January and February 1991. The meeting report, like that from Geneva, was long on principles and short on commitments.[56] It presented a reasonable set of measures for the peaceful settlement of disputes (known in CSCE jargon as the PSD), expanding the roles of the CSCE's Committee of Senior Officials and Conflict Prevention Center and establishing links with existing bodies like the International Court of Justice and Permanent Court of Arbitration. It also created a new facility, darkly termed "the mechanism," that specified a series of measures that could be invoked, including a list of mediators from CSCE members whose services could be drawn upon.

Yet none of these steps could be made binding on recalcitrant states. Under the heading "strengthening of commitments," each particular was prefaced by a qualifying phrase like "endeavor to," "to the extent possible," and, six times in a list of eleven measures, "consider" doing this or that. The entire document, moreover, was limited by an exceptions clause inserted at the end (Section XII) that prohibits use or continuation of "the mechanism" if any party considers that the dispute "raises issues concerning its territorial integrity, or national defence, title to sovereignty over land territory, or competing claims with regard to the jurisdiction over other areas."

Valletta's results were exasperating to those of us back in Washington who had been working to find ways and means to resolve the growing crisis in Yugoslavia. Every delegation at Valletta, including ours, made certain that nothing was agreed to that might potentially be invoked against its own country. The United States even shared responsibility for the meeting's failure to specify a CSCE lead institution for "the mechanism," so even the meager provisions agreed to remained inoperative. For reasons known only to the State Department's hardy band of experts, who had been steeped in the arcana of the CSCE process during the Cold War period but were not ready temperamentally to adapt the organization for new purposes, the U.S. delegation was instructed to oppose the EC's preferred institution, the Conflict Prevention Center. Other delegations were similarly staffed with CSCE hands of the old school—the "CSCE Jesuits," as I called them—which made innovation elusive.

It was a particularly egregious lack of diplomatic consistency, for, as the following chapter reveals, we had been littering Europe with cables urging concerted action to avert an impending crisis in Yugoslavia—yet we had failed to empower our own delegation at Valletta to make the CSCE an effective instrument toward that end. The reason for our inattention was that at the same time, in February 1991, the United States was preparing half a million coalition troops for the air and ground assault against Iraqi forces in Operation Desert Storm. Under the circumstances, one could hardly expect Secretary Baker—the only top administration official who paid attention to CSCE matters—to focus on the goings-on in Valletta.

By the time of the CSCE ministerial in Berlin in June, the senior levels of the administration were reengaged, having prepared the way with initiatives contained in the Baker-Genscher statement of the month before. This German-American coordination was especially useful, for Genscher, as foreign minister of the host country, was in the chair at Berlin and ran the proceedings with an efficiency not seen before in the CSCE. Like the Germans, we wanted to use Berlin, the first meeting of the Council of Ministers since the body had been approved at the Paris Summit, to strengthen the CSCE's conflict prevention capacities, with the Yugoslav crisis the case in point. Indeed, as will be seen, the main import of the Berlin meeting was the behind-the-scenes negotiations on Yugoslavia, to which Baker was flying immediately after the meeting.

Baker quickly overrode his experts and supported the EC in designating the Conflict Prevention Center as the lead institution for the peaceful settlement of disputes mechanism. With Baker and Genscher taking turns bluntly pointing out that history would not treat kindly ministers who failed to adopt measures relevant to the crisis in Yugoslavia, the Berlin meeting created a mechanism for calling emergency meetings on the demand of at least 12 countries, a number that could be easily come by if needed but sufficiently high to prevent frivolous or purely partisan convocations.[57] It was a small achievement, to be sure, but the fact that no such procedure existed before was illustrative of how urgently we were scrambling to give the CSCE even the rudiments of an operational capacity. Indeed, this new mechanism was used twice within two weeks, as we and others called for emergency meetings of the Conflict Prevention Center and Committee of Senior Officials to deal with the outbreak of violence in Yugoslavia. Finally, the Berlin conference endorsed mechanisms providing, in theory at least, an unprecedented level of intrusiveness in the internal affairs of a member state whose actions were seen as jeopardizing security and stability.

Under pressure from the unfolding crisis in Yugoslavia, the next CSCE meeting—the long-scheduled Moscow human rights conference, the last of a triad that began in Paris in 1989 and continued in Copenhagen in 1990—took further steps in this direction. Meeting in September and October 1991, the Moscow conference, in addition to admitting the three Baltic states as CSCE members, approved a "human dimension mechanism" to monitor human and minority rights commitments.[58] It authorized a progression of steps, beginning with a request by any CSCE member state for a human rights observer mission to be sent to any other state to investigate possible abuses and continuing with procedures incrementally more intrusive and mandatory. Under the mandatory procedure, one state seconded by nine others could direct that human rights observers be sent to any other state, immediately and without right of refusal. For the CSCE, since its inception in 1975 governed by the principle of voluntary consent, the adoption of mandatory procedures was revolutionary indeed. Even more so was Foreign Minister Genscher's call for the CSCE to employ collective sanctions against a member state in serious violation of CSCE principles, without that state's consent.

The Helsinki Summit of the CSCE   By the time of the Helsinki Summit of July 1992, culminating three and a half months of negotiations at Helsinki, CSCE had indeed acquired the institutional capacity for imposing sanctions, as well as for peacekeeping.[59] It had established itself as a regional organization under Chapter VIII of the UN Charter and forged institutional linkages with the EC, NATO, the WEU, the NACC, the Council of Europe, and other organizations, as well as with nonmembers like Japan. Its organizational structure was tightened through such measures as the formation of a "troika" of past, present, and future host country foreign ministers. It had created a CSCE "Forum for Security Cooperation" to deal with all European arms control issues, along with various fora devoted to economic development, migration problems, and the like.

New procedures had been elaborated to prevent any one state or group of states from preventing action by the others. Indeed, so extensive were the provisions under the human dimension mechanism (HDM) and peaceful settlement of disputes (PSD) mechanism, that the State Department's European bureau prepared a large spreadsheet, in small type, to keep track of the various mechanisms and modalities now available. The Helsinki Summit created the position of high commissioner on national minorities, as the CSCE's highest permanent official, whose mandate was early warning, conflict management, and crisis prevention. CSCE also had created a full array of mechanisms for dealing with conflict: early warning, political consultation and suasion, fact-finding and observer missions, mediation and arbitration, sanctions, and peacekeeping operations, including the capacity to call on NATO, the NACC, or the WEU to mount peacekeeping operations under the CSCE's mandate.

NATO's peacekeeping role had been the most contentious issue in the run-up to Helsinki. The French, clinging to their position that NATO's responsibilities should be strictly limited to Article 5 security commitments involving direct attack against an allied state, had opposed any role whatever in "out of area" peacekeeping. They sought instead to invest the CSCE alone with that mandate, leaving NATO and the NACC on the sidelines. Nearly every other CSCE member disagreed, seeing no point in creating a separate CSCE peacekeeping capacity when such capacities already existed elsewhere. Neither we nor any other state wished NATO to arrogate unto itself sole responsibility in this area: we not only accepted but actively supported a flexible approach that would allow the CSCE to call on any of several institutions or ad hoc coalitions of states, depending on the circumstances. At the opening of the Helsinki review conference in March, a large majority of states favored this approach; by the July Summit ending the session, France was outnumbered 51 to 1. Finally persuaded of the futility of opposing a NATO role that Russia, the Vatican, and every other European state welcomed, the French relented on the last day. In this instance at least, the "new European architecture" made good sense.

Although the CSCE's role in the Yugoslav conflict was much criticized, the deficiencies of international action were not institutional or architectural; they had to do with the more pertinent question of how national governments proposed to deal with the new threats to European security. Two problems were paramount and did not lend themselves to easy solution. The first was the problem of dealing with conflicts arising within rather than between states. Neither institutions nor their member states found it easy to engage with sufficient resolve in the internal affairs of another state until the problem had in fact moved from conflict prevention to crisis management. At that point the problem of mobilizing force against local conflicts arose.

Germany was constrained for historical and constitutional reasons from engaging directly in such military operations. The French and British had recent memories of the postcolonial conflicts in which they had been embroiled, and our own country had long been allergic to messy military entanglements. It was President Wilson who said, in trying to reassure the American public about the League of Nations, "If you want to put out a fire in Utah, you do not send to Oklahoma for the fire engine. If you want to put out a fire in the Balkans, . . . you do not send to the United States for troops."[60]

The CSCE could serve to filter out conflicts in which we had no desire to involve ourselves and refer those in which we did have a stake to NATO or the UN, where we could consider joining a multinational force, or the WEU, where we could perhaps take on a support role. But such modalities could not answer the questions of which conflicts involved important U.S. interests and whether we and other CSCE states were prepared to act decisively when such interests clearly were at stake, as in Bosnia.

8

The Return of History

JUST AS THE SECOND WORLD WAR was a continuation of the conflicts that had produced the First, the end of the Cold War summoned forth issues that had arisen at the beginning of the century from the breakup of the multiethnic Turkish, Austrian, German, and Russian empires. The disintegration of the first two was complete; on their ruins came a set of weak new states, some of them, notably Yugoslavia, the artificial constructs of the peacemakers at Versailles. The third great empire, the German, had its brutal revival under the Third Reich but ended with Germany defeated and divided.

Only the fourth empire, the Russian, survived. It was a close call. For much of 1919, the Red Army controlled little more than the territory of sixteenth-century Muscovite Russia.[1] Ukraine was not conquered until late 1920. The Caucasus, Central Asia, and eastern Russia were not subdued for two years more. So fractious and artificial was the new Soviet empire that only totalitarian dictatorship could hold it together. Yet survive it did, not only withstanding the German onslaught in World War II but emerging from the war with its territory enhanced by the annexation of the Baltic states and Bessarabia. The survival of such a state for nearly seventy years, and its acquisition of military power second only to the United States, was enough to impress even the staunchest adversaries with its staying power.

Yet the nature of totalitarian rule made it hard to detect the deep crisis in the empire of Soviet Russia. Causes had no effects: social and economic pressures that should have had profound consequences for the Soviet system produced none, at least none that could be discerned. Recurrent agricultural crises led not to agrarian movements and land re-

form but to a perpetuation of the agricultural system that had brought
about the crises in the first place. The failures of central economic planning caused barely a ripple in the regime's economic strategy. Conflicts
arising from the dispersed nationalities of this multiethnic empire were
resolved with ruthless dispatch. "Kremlinologists" were reduced to investigating political struggles among the handful of top party leaders, as
if those were the true manifestations of seventy years of history of a
transcontinental power.

Inasmuch as the Turkish, Austro-Hungarian, and German empires
broke apart with extreme violence, it had been assumed throughout the
Cold War that the Soviet empire could only end violently.[2] It was an expectation reinforced by the history of another strange artifact of the
century's first war—Yugoslavia. The semivoluntary "Kingdom of the
Serbs, Croats, and Slovenes" proclaimed at the end of World War I had
become a decade later a Serb-dominated dictatorship beset with separatist pressures, principally from the Croats. Under the conditions of
German occupation, these national conflicts boiled over into a civil war
that claimed over a million lives between 1941 and 1945. The unity imposed under communist rule initially followed the Soviet "model," but
recurrent nationalist challenges led to a series of concessions to republican autonomy. By the time of Marshal Josip Tito's death in 1980, Yugoslavia was neither centralized enough for effective leadership in Belgrade nor decentralized enough for genuine federalism to take hold.
And the galvanizing element of a Soviet threat was fast disappearing.

It should not have been surprising that the most artificial and tenuous of the states arising out of imperial breakup at the time of the First
World War—Yugoslavia and the Soviet Union—were the first casualties
of the post–Cold War era. They were anachronisms, lacking a raison
d'être other than the authoritarian rule that had held them together for
most of the century. So, to a lesser degree, was Czecho-Slovakia, another artifical construct of Versailles and the third early casualty of the
new era.

Yet the disintegration of these states did catch the outside world by
surprise. Of course, we could see the evidence of disintegration as
events unfolded, but our frame of reference did not allow for a full appreciation of what these trends portended. We were intellectually prepared for the liberation of the countries of Central and Eastern Europe,
including the Baltic states, as we were for German unification. The
swiftness and scope of change may have been unexpected, but not the

events themselves, for they fit our Cold War frame of reference. But the disintegration of the Soviet Union and Yugoslavia belonged to an entirely different logic, whose antecedents were to be found not in the period of Cold War but in the era of imperial dissolution at the beginning of the century.[3]

The end of the Cold War was not the "end of history" and the final triumph of liberal democracy, as Francis Fukuyama had argued in his controversial essay.[4] It was, rather, the *return* of history in the sense that the lifting of authoritarian control had opened the way for the interplay of competing forces through which history became possible. More than one observer reached for the metaphor of the deep freeze. It was apt. The warming of East-West relations had thawed out historical problems that had been frozen not only during the Cold War but, in the Soviet and Yugoslav cases, for most of the century.[5]

Well before the revolutions of 1989, Eastern European dissidents warned that powerful social pressures were waiting "under the ice" and that the seemingly powerless dissident movement would become the "icebreaker with a kamikaze crew."[6] These brilliantly jarring metaphors would prove all too prophetic with regard to the coming self-destruction of Yugoslavia.

The Yugoslav Tragedy

The bloody disintegration of Yugoslavia, and the helplessness of the international community in the face of it, revealed how far post–Cold War Europe was from a secure and peaceful new order. The failures of Western policy proceeded in part from the fact that this was the first major challenge to the emerging order and, in particular, the first test in this new era of the ill-defined concept of "self-determination" arising in a multiethnic state. If anything positive came of the conspicuous failure of efforts to hold together a fragmenting Yugoslav federation, it was that we applied these bitter lessons in our approach toward the (relatively uncomplicated) split of Czechoslovakia and, with greater success than has so far been credited, to the much more critical challenge of dealing with a disintegrating Soviet Union.

Yugoslavia was a portent of the post–Cold War era in another sense. At the heart of the problem for Western governments lay the judgment, reached early on in Washington and most European capitals, that Yugoslavia no longer mattered much because it was no longer likely to be an arena of East-West conflict. As Warren Zimmermann, the last U.S. ambassador to Yugoslavia, noted in his memoirs: "[Deputy Secretary of State] Eagleburger and I agreed that in my introductory calls in [in early 1989] in Belgrade and the republican capitals, I would deliver a new message: Yugoslavia no longer enjoyed the geopolitical importance that the United States had given it during the Cold War."[7]

From this flawed premise—a case of applying yesterday's strategic logic to tomorrow's problems—flawed policies ensued. As the conflict deepened, policy was caught between lofty principle and uncertain resolve. As it threatened to spread, Western policy awakened to the fact that this region did indeed matter, but for an entirely different set of reasons than had been assumed and internalized during the long years of Cold War in Europe.

Democracy versus Unity   The error was not that the administration failed to see it coming.[8] Well before 1989, it was clear that Yugoslavia was in deep crisis,[9] owing to the collapse of central authority (under the system of collective leadership Marshal Tito left behind) and to a Serbian campaign to overturn what a notorious 1986 memorandum of the Serbian Academy of Sciences argued was an anti-Serb conspiracy in federal Yugoslavia. It is probably true, as Zimmermann argued, that Serbian leader Slobodan Milošević was motivated by considerations of political power and not by ideology, but he quickly seized nationalist demagoguery as the vehicle to election as Serbian president in 1987 and to his consolidation of power thereafter.[10] As other republics, especially Slovenia, distanced themselves from Serbian-dominated federal institutions, the political agenda in Serbia turned increasingly toward creation of a "greater Serbia" inspired by its medieval kingdom and embracing Montenegro, most of Bosnia-Herzegovina, and perhaps Macedonia as well.[11]

Yet in the cavalcade of events in the fall of 1989, one passed almost unnoticed: the mid-October visit to Washington by Yugoslav prime minister Ante Marković, for meetings with President Bush and officials of the International Monetary Fund. In retrospect, we and our European partners should have paid more attention to Marković's efforts to forge a new Yugoslav consensus on economic and political reform. As it turned out, his visit was like the sound of one hand clapping: he got a polite hearing and words of encouragement, but no tangible economic or political support. After the U.S.-led "Friends of Yugoslavia" economic assistance effort in the early 1980s and the futile attempts to support the on-again, off-again economic reform program of Marković's predecessor, Branko Mikulić, we were wary of committing ourselves to another effort to support a Yugoslav leader who had yet to demonstrate his authority among the country's disparate republics.

Was Marković Yugoslavia's last hope, or was he already marginal to the real political struggle over the future of the federation? If the former was true, then we should have lent him all possible support. If the latter, we should have concluded that Yugoslavia was already doomed and begun preparing for its dissolution. Yet in the early fall of 1989, preoccupied as we were with the dramatic events taking place in Central Europe, we failed to translate our worry over Yugoslavia into meaningful policy.

By the spring and early summer of 1990, as the rest of Central and Eastern Europe was moving rapidly toward democratic rule, we were viewing events in Yugoslavia with growing alarm. Prime minister Marković's program of economic "shock therapy," launched in January 1990, produced encouraging initial results, but these were already being overshadowed by the steady disintegration of the federation. That same month the Yugoslav Communist party (the LCY, or League of Communists of Yugoslavia) adjourned in acrimony from its party congress, never to reconvene. Marković's hopes for Yugoslav-wide democratic elections were preempted by a series of elections in individual republics, beginning with Slovenia and Croatia in April and May.

With Yugoslav federal institutions crumbling, the political dynamic shifted to the republics. The question became whether the process of democratization within republics could produce leaders who would use their newly acquired legitimacy to negotiate among themselves a democratic arrangement for the Yugoslav state, reconstituted along looser federal or confederal lines. Indeed, had the democratic tide washed more evenly over the Yugoslav republics, such an arrangement might have been feasible—and consistent with Marković's economic and political reforms. As it was, embryonic democratic forces in Serbia were no match for the nationalistic hatreds unleashed and manipulated by Serbian president Slobodan Milošević. The newly elected presidents of Slovenia and Croatia, Milan Kučan and Franjo Tudjman, moved quickly to distance their republics from an increasingly repressive Serbia and the federal institutions it dominated. By July Slovenia had severed political and economic ties with the federal government, declaring itself a sovereign republic whose laws took precedence over those of the federation. Croatia, meanwhile, had effectively disenfranchised its large Serbian minority by launching a propaganda barrage—particularly in areas like Krajina, where Serbs held a local majority—and proclaiming the republic "the national state of the Croatian nation."[12]

By this time, it was evident that Yugoslavia was in the advanced stages of disintegration. It was also clear that a breakup would be contested and violent. This, indeed, was the essence of a national intelligence estimate prepared during this period and leaked to the *New York Times* upon its release in November 1990.[13] No one in the policy community disagreed with the main thrust of these judgments—only with the smug finality with which they were rendered. Yet the estimate had little impact, for it was so unrelievedly deterministic that it suggested no possible avenue for American policy that might avert or at least contain the violence attending Yugoslavia's seemingly inevitable disintegration. Even when the intelligence community gets it right, as it did in this case, it can get it wrong by being too detached from the exigencies of policy making.[14]

The failures were not of analysis but of policy. Partly it was that the crisis we saw coming was too catastrophic to accept. Senior staff are always prone to the hubris of believing they can change history's course by dint of their own exertions and the farsightedness of their ideas. These extravagances were accentuated in the Yugoslav case, for the crisis unfolded at the very moment of the democratic liberation of Central and Eastern Europe. With democracy ascendant everywhere, it was hard to credit what our dispassionate analysis told us: that the peoples of Yugoslavia would choose this moment once again to reach for the long knives.

When the foreign policy archives of this period are opened, the unfolding of Western approaches toward Yugoslavia in 1990 and the first half of 1991 will present an exquisitely well-documented case study. Thereafter, as the senior levels of government considered what to do as Yugoslavia descended into civil war, the story became more opaque, and much of the informal decision-making process was not recorded in the official records. But in this initial period, nearly the full story was laid out in a series of diplomatic exchanges between Washington and every European capital, all carried via State Department cables. If the future historian wants to know the official position of Norway, Romania, or the Vatican at the moment of Yugoslavia's breakup—as well as the British, French, German, and Soviet positions—it will be laid out with a thoroughness and transparency rarely available in the annals of modern diplomacy.

In late summer 1990, we sent lengthy cables to every European capital, explaining, along the lines of the national intelligence estimate then being prepared (but issued a couple of months later), that our government believed that events were propelling Yugoslavia toward disintegration, that the disintegration would be bloody, and that this course of events no longer could be averted by the protagonists themselves. Strenuous, concerted engagement by the international community, the cable continued, would be required if catastrophe were to be averted. The cables did not propose a specific set of policies, but focused on such critical elements as a common international position on recognition of breakaway states and on the use of force to suppress independence movements. They also raised the issue of internationally supervised guarantees for national minorities—particularly the Serbian minority in Croatia. As this was preeminently a matter of European stability, we looked to Europe to take the lead in mobilizing the international community. The Yugoslavia crisis, the cables concluded, should be the subject of urgent consultations in NATO and at the CSCE Summit in Paris in November.

The replies that trickled in over the next few weeks were shockingly irresponsible. Only the Austrians and Hungarians, as I recall, fully endorsed our views. The Germans and British said that they shared some of our concerns but that we were overreacting and that it was certainly premature to consider the steps we proposed. The French likewise accused us of "overdramatizing" the situation, rejected NATO consultations, and warned that if we tried to raise this at the Paris Summit, they would consider it a "summit-breaker"—meaning that its inclusion was for them, as hosts, out of the question. More reasonably, several respondents argued that the international community should await the results of the remaining republic-level elections and particularly the Serbian elections in December 1990. With the senior levels of the U.S. administration preoccupied with Iraq and unwilling to press matters on Yugoslavia, we reluctantly agreed to wait. It was a mistake.

Absent a Western consensus, the State Department issued a statement on October 19 that carried a formulation we would repeat many times over the next year: "The US firmly supports unity, democratic change, respect for human rights, and market reform in Yugoslavia. We believe that democracy is the only enduring basis for a united, prosperous and voluntary Yugoslav union. . . . We would strongly oppose any use of force that would block democratic change in Yugoslavia."

By the beginning of 1991, the Yugoslav crisis had deepened. Serbia had become more truculent with the reelection of Slobodan Milošević as president. Slovenia, in its December 23 referendum, had voted overwhelmingly for independence, agreeing only to defer actual implementation for six months. With the clock ticking, we sent another round of cables to European capitals in January 1991. The replies from European capitals this time were more receptive, though the French and others who had argued in September that international involvement was premature now said it was too late!

The international community had missed a critical six-month period during which it might have organized for coordinated engagement of the Yugoslavs. As it turned out, it was only after the Serbian walkout from the Yugoslav presidential council in March—blocking the looser federal structure agreed to by the other republics and prompting Croatia to follow Slovenia in declaring its independence[15]—that the Europeans belatedly took up the challenge. A common strategy of sorts was hammered out then between the United States and the European Community.

The decision to keep NATO in the background was another mistake. It made some sense at the time, in that the EC had more immediate leverage over the Yugoslav protagonists—via a $4 billion economic aid package and the prospect of eventual association or even membership. But it was the wrong institution to exert credible pressure on the combatants once armed conflict erupted. Only NATO could do that, and NATO could do it only if the United States were prepared to lead. We were not. The upper levels of the administration overruled recommendations at staff level that NATO take the lead under CSCE mandate. Worse, the Department of Defense and the Joint Chiefs were at pains to exclude the military option a priori and, fresh from the military triumph in the Gulf, their opinions carried even more weight in administration councils than usual. In early June, for example, NATO's SACEUR (Supreme Allied Commander, Europe), General John Galvin, was quoted in a Belgrade daily as saying that "NATO [would] not intervene in Yugoslavia" because it was "not within NATO's defense zone."[16]

The European Community, newly committed to building political union, was eager to demonstrate its capacity for concerted action in foreign policy; Washington, having just led the international coalition to defeat Iraq in the Gulf War and still tied down with its messy aftermath, was eager to let the Europeans take the lead this time. In June, the EC dispatched commission president Jacques Delors and Prime Minister Jacques Santer of Luxembourg (in its capacity as EC presidency country on six-month rotation) to Belgrade. Shortly thereafter, Luxembourg's foreign minister Jacques Poos, speaking for the "troika" of EC foreign ministers, declared (in a line reminiscent of Neville Chamberlain's "peace in our time"), "This is the hour of Europe. It is not the hour of the Americans."[17]

U.S.-EC coordination worked well for a time. Secretary Baker and his EC counterparts conferred intensely on the margins of a CSCE foreign ministers' meeting in Berlin in late June, building support for the Community's taking the lead on behalf of the CSCE. The declaration issued at the end of the meeting "expressed friendly concern and support for the democratic development, unity, and territorial integrity of Yugoslavia" and called for continued dialogue among all parties "without recourse to the use of force and in conformity with legal and constitutional procedures."[18] It was a limp statement that came down too hard on the side of unity, but it was the best we could do, given that CSCE resolutions required unanimous consent. Yugoslav foreign minister Budimir Lončar agreed to this much only after intense lobbying in Berlin by Baker and EC foreign ministers, who also agreed that the secretary should convey their common position directly to Yugoslav leaders.

The Baker Visit to Belgrade　Armed with a CSCE mandate of sorts and having coordinated with his EC counterparts, Baker flew from Berlin to Belgrade to make a last-ditch try at bringing Yugoslavia's leaders back from the brink. The visit—which I, among others, had recommended—was a mistake. Baker himself had misgivings, which were amply confirmed in Belgrade. For one thing, it came too late by several months at least. Positions among republics were all but fixed: Slovenia was already determined to declare its independence, and Croatia, not wishing to be left behind in a Serb-dominated Yugoslavia, was sure to follow. For another, in trying to avert disaster and embracing various formulae (advanced by federal prime minister Marković, Macedonian president Kiro Gligorov, and Bosnian president Alija Izetbegović) for a "new, democratic unity" with substantially greater autonomy for republics, we put ourselves in a position of equidistance between the

Slovenes and the Serbs. Worse, by warning equally against unilateral declarations of independence and the use of force to hold the federation together, we seemed to be sanctioning the latter if the Slovenes and Croats resorted to the former.

Baker tried heroically. In a 12-hour marathon he met first with Marković and Lončar, then with Kosovar Albanian leader Ibrahim Rugova,[19] throughout the afternoon and early evening with each of the six republic presidents, and finished with another meeting with Marković and Lončar over dinner. Zimmermann and I alternated as note-takers.[20] Baker's message was that the United States would support any future arrangement among the peoples of Yugoslavia that was reached consensually and peacefully; we would oppose any unilateral secession as well as the use of force or incitement to violence.[21] "If you force the United States to choose between unity and democracy," he said, "we will always choose democracy."[22] Tactically, he pressed hard to effect a mini-compromise, whereby the Serbs and Montenegrins would unblock the federal presidency (thus preserving an interrepublic negotiating forum, however weak) and the Slovenes would declare their independence but take no precipitous steps to implement it (thus preserving a possibility, however slim, for continued dialogue and negotiation).

Baker was disciplined, focused, persistent, and blunt—all to no effect.[23] His interlocutors were not to be moved. Milošević was a consummate dissembler and ruthless leader who might have been impressed by real military power but not by diplomatic overtures. Tudjman was a romantic lost in dreams of a glorious Croatian past that never was. Kučan, the Slovenian president, was a seemingly decent man who nonetheless was prepared to leave the Bosnians and Croatians to a bloody inferno that he knew his country would escape. Montenegrin president Momir Bulatović was a young rogue whose vote to block the rotation of the federal presidency gave him a role in history disproportionate to his meager attributes. Among the republic leaders, the only reasonable ones were Gligorov and Izetbegović, who had little to gain and much to lose by Yugoslavia's disintegration. But like Marković and Lončar, they were by this point marginal to the drama unfolding among the Serbians, Croatians, and Slovenians.

Baker summed up his meetings in a statement to the press based on a text that his staff and I had hastily drafted. Although noting that his interlocutors had expressed support for his appeals for dialogue and nonuse of force, he was pessimistic:

We came to Yugoslavia because of our concern about . . . the dangers of a disintegration of this country [which] could have some very tragic consequences. . . . The 34 other countries of the CSCE . . . have all expressed, along with us, our collective concern. . . . I have conveyed these very serious concerns about the future of this country in the meetings I have been privileged to have. In all candor, ladies and gentlemen, what I heard today has not allayed my concerns. Nor, I suspect, will it allay the concerns of others when we give them a readout of these meetings.

In all of these meetings, I stressed the importance of respecting human and minority rights, of continuing the process of democratization, and of continuing a dialogue to create a new basis for unity. In particular, I emphasized the need to move ahead on the constitutional rotation of the federal presidency, as well as the need to avoid unilateral acts that could preempt the negotiating process. . . .

We will be consulting with the European Community and other interested members of the international community. Based on these discussions today, I am very hopeful that notwithstanding all of the difficulties, there is some prospect for continued dialogue. . . . But in the end. . . , it is really going to be up to the people of Yugoslavia whether or not these problems are overcome.

In response to a question from the press, Baker asserted that the United States would not recognize Slovenia's forthcoming declaration of independence "because we want to see this problem resolved through negotiation and dialogue and not through preemptive unilateral actions." He then amplified what we meant by Yugoslav "unity" in the new circumstances: "a new basis for the unity of Yugoslavia" based on "the devolution of additional authority, responsibility, and sovereignty to the republics of Yugoslavia."[24]

Because Baker was silent on the question of possible military or other reprisals in the event of violent suppression of independence movements in Yugoslavia, the visit was later interpreted to have given Milošević and the Yugoslav national army (JNA) a "green light" to resort to force. This contention needs careful analysis. It is true that if Baker did not signal a green light, he did not flash a red one either. Had we concluded beforehand that trying to restrain the Slovenians and Croatians was at this point futile, we would have been better advised to devote all our energies to warning the Serbs and the Yugoslav military against the use of force, leaving open the possibility of Western military reprisals if they failed to heed the warning. Yet the question ultimately was whether we were prepared to *use* force, not whether we were prepared to threaten to do so—and certainly not what Baker said or failed to say in Belgrade. There would be endless opportunities for testing American resolve, so a mere bluff would not have deterred the aggression that followed. One therefore should not exaggerate the impact of the Baker visit on the main protagonists: the conflict would have unfolded pretty much as it did had Baker not gone. At best, the visit was worth the try, even though it failed. At worst, it was simply irrelevant.

The real impact of the visit was on U.S. policy, because the intractability of the conflict and the bloody-mindedness of republic leaders led Secretary Baker and others to wash their hands of whole mess. "We got no dog in this fight" was thenceforth the watchword of American policy.

Spreading Violence   Events moved rapidly thereafter. Within days of Baker's visit, Slovenia and Croatia declared their independence, the former seizing control of customs posts in one of the escalating steps Baker had urged them to forego. When Yugoslav army units moved in and armed conflict began, Slovenia declared a "state of war" and appealed for international assistance. Within a week, the EC troika had mounted three separate missions to Yugoslavia, two at foreign minister level, and the CSCE convened twice to condemn the use of force. Brandishing the threat of economic sanctions, the EC brokered the July 5 Brioni Agreement providing for the withdrawal to barracks of the Yugoslav army and the disarming of the Slovenian militia.[25] But the skirmish in Slovenia, which Milošević was never interested in fighting for anyway, was just the prelude to the real battles over Croatia and Bosnia-Herzegovina.

The Croatian leaders, surprised by Slovenia's successful defiance (which they had conspicuously failed to support), hastily moved to implement their own independence declaration—prompting Serb-dominated Krajina to declare its independence from Croatia. That move in turn led the largely Croatian city of Kijevo within Krajina to repudiate the latter's authority and declare *its* allegiance to Croatia. "Self-determination" at work! Serb-Croat clashes erupted and intensified in July and August. Cease-fires were repeatedly broken. JNA forces moved en masse from Serbia into Croatia in preparation for full-scale war. Like Milošević , the army had been prepared to see Slovenia go, but Croatia was another matter entirely. As Zimmermann put it in his memoirs: "The fighting in Croatia began with the illusion of evenhandedness. The Yugoslav army would step in to separate the Serbian and Croatian combatants. During the summer of 1991, however, it soon became clear that the JNA, while claiming neutrality, was in fact turning territory over to Serbs. The war in Croatia had become a war of aggression."[26]

While technically a civil conflict, the Yugoslav war had in fact become a "war of aggression," in that Milošević and the JNA were acting not to preserve but to dismember the federal state—not to restore order and protect the citizenry but to seize territory and expel non-Serbs in an effort to create an ethnically homogeneous "Greater Serbia." For its part, the EC condemned the "illegal" use of force, threatened further sanctions, and invoked an "arbitration procedure" (which later became the Badinter Commission). They then convened a peace conference, under the chairmanship of former British foreign secretary Lord Carrington, that took place in the Hague on September 7.[27] With these efforts showing no signs of success the action moved to New York, as the UN Security Council, having deferred so far to the EC, finally met in late September. Secretary Baker, in his address at the UN, condemned "outright military intervention against Croatia":

> The apparent objective of the Serbian leadership and the Yugoslav military working in tandem is to create a "small Yugoslavia" or "greater Serbia" which would exclude Slovenia and a rump Croatia. It would be based on the kind of repression which Serbian authorities have exercised in Kosovo for several years. This entity would also be based on the use of force—well underway in Croatia, and beginning to take shape in Bosnia-Herzegovina—to establish control over territories outside Serbia. The aggression within Serbia, therefore, represents a direct threat to international peace and security.[28]

Despite the tough rhetoric, U.S. policy was by this time inert. To be sure, the UN secretary-general's designation of former secretary of state Cyrus Vance as his personal envoy gave an American dimension to the EC-led mediation efforts, but this was the limit of our involvement. Even as Serbian aggression turned into the indiscriminate shelling of

civilian populations in the Croatian cities of Dubrovnik and Vukovar—
in the latter case, with the aim of forcibly expelling its entire population—the only U.S. policy option given serious consideration was to
continue our perfunctory support for the Vance-Carrington peace plan.

Any proposal for military action to halt the slaughter ran up against
the presumed lessons of Vietnam and the Persian Gulf War: unless the
mission was clear, commitment strong, and victory sure, as in Operation
Desert Storm against Iraq, any U.S. military engagement was depicted as
leading to a Vietnam-type quagmire. The superficially attractive idea of
a reversal of Desert Storm roles, with the United States providing airlift
and logistical support to a predominantly European effort, was rightly
rejected at the upper levels of the administration as militarily ineffectual.
But so, too, were more limited proposals, notably the use of combined
U.S., European, and other naval power (whether under NATO, WEU, or
some other command) to halt the shelling of Dubrovnik. Nor were they
prepared to use air power to interdict the long tank convoys rolling
along the highway from Serbia to support the leveling of Vukovar and
other cities. These limited missions, justifiable on grounds that shelling
civilian populations is a war crime, would not have demanded an open-
ended commitment to defend Croatia or defeat Serbia. Yet such proposals were rejected precisely because their advocates could not demonstrate a strategy guaranteeing ultimate victory.

This "in for a penny, in for a pound" philosophy was to haunt U.S.
policy thenceforth. Any initiative that surfaced from staff level was dismissed out of hand at the highest levels of the State Department and especially the Pentagon as being pointless unless we were prepared to see
the project through to its potential worst-case conclusion. Unless we
were prepared to commit hundreds of thousands of U.S. ground forces,
the argument ran, we should take no military action whatever.[29] And
since such a military commitment was ruled out a priori, no initiative
whatever was given serious consideration. Those of us advocating military options did so all too timidly, cognizant of the fact that the burden
was entirely on us to demonstrate their efficacy over the known opposition of NSC principals.

Thus the United States offered no alternative to the German-led campaign to recognize Slovenia and Croatia in order to "internationalize"
the conflict and better support them. We and most of the European
Community opposed the idea on grounds that it would ensure the
spread of the war to Bosnia-Herzegovina without addressing any of the

root causes of the conflict in Croatia. To "internationalize" the conflict would have made sense only if the Germans or others had developed an international strategy to deal with it. They had none, invoking instead the "right of self-determination"—as if that solved anything. Absent a credible military alternative that the United States was willing to propose and then support, however, we had no answer to the German argument that recognition was preferable to passivity in the face of brutal aggression.

On December 20, 1991, three days after the EC decided to move toward recognizing Slovenia and Croatia, Bosnia-Herzegovina declared its independence and requested international recognition. Bowing to EC insistence, the Izetbegović government held a referendum on the question in late February 1992, with 64 percent voting in favor but with most Serbs boycotting and moving instead to create a "Serbian Republic of Bosnia-Herzegovina." The United States supported Bosnia's call for recognition, which we linked to our recognition of the other two breakaway republics. Like the German position on Slovenia and Croatia, we invoked high principle but offered no strategic plan. How, we asked, could the international community deny recognition to Bosnia-Herzegovina, which had followed all the rules? Also like the Germans, we had no strategy to accompany the "internationalization" of the conflict—only the vague belief, or vain hope, that this course was preferable to denying recognition and consigning Bosnia-Herzegovina to the tender mercies of Milošević in a rump Yugoslavia.[30]

Sometime in March, Bosnian foreign minister Haris Silajdžić visited Washington, as he had in early January, urgently asking of the U.S. government two things: diplomatic recognition and protection against the inevitable attack on his new state by the well-armed Bosnian Serbs. My meeting with him in my office in the Old Executive Office Building was the most painful of my career. We were prepared to offer recognition but nothing more, though I knew he was right in saying that the attack on his country would commence within days. How, he asked, could we and the Europeans recognize a country and then permit it to be destroyed at the moment of its birth? How indeed?

Recognition of Bosnia-Herzegovina by the United States and most European countries came in early April. The only "protection" we could muster was modest indeed: a token contingent of the UN Protection Force (UNPROFOR) then arriving in Croatia was diverted to Mostar, and its headquarters was established in Sarajevo. Neither measure did anything to prevent the systematic and brutal dismemberment of Bosnia.

Serbian attacks began almost immediately. The systematic removal of Bosnian Muslims from towns and villages—so-called ethnic cleansing, in the grotesque term of Bosnian Serb leaders like Radovan Karadžić— was accomplished through brutal and inhuman means not seen in Europe since the defeat of the Third Reich. In May and June, we began receiving reports of Serbian atrocities—death camps, torture, and gang rape—that came to public light in a series of well-documented press reports in early August.[31] After a few weeks of hesitation owing to lack of independent verification, the administration confirmed the reports and called for an international tribunal to investigate war crimes.[32] As evidence continued to mount in the fall of 1992, Eagleburger—by then secretary of state[33]—issued a detailed accounting in December 1992 and named those, including Milošević and Karadžić, who bore responsibility as war criminals.[34]

The London Conference   The August 1992 London conference on Yugoslavia was perhaps the last chance to restore Western resolve before Bosnia-Herzegovina was destroyed irreparably. The Vance-Carrington effort was going nowhere, and the parties to the Yugoslav war were unmoved by Western inducements. This was the time to shift from negotiation to pressure and to pass responsibility from the EC to NATO, acting under CSCE mandate. As the *New York Times* put it in an editorial on the second day of the conference: "The U.S. and Europe have a number of military options short of limitless ground war. They can lift the arms embargo on Bosnia. They can use air power to silence the Serbs' big guns that still pound Sarajevo and other cities, and to attack military installations, arm-making plants, and air bases in Serbia."[35]

Instead, the London conference offered lofty rhetoric and uncertain resolve. The principles solemnly advanced were the right ones, but they could be upheld only through concerted international action. Inasmuch as the Serbian and Croatian leaders were continuing to wage war in defiance of international condemnation, effective international engagement would entail a readiness to use military force to punish and deter. But no such action plan was advanced. Participating states, represented by foreign ministers, almost universally proclaimed that they would "never recognize territory seized by force" and reaffirmed the "territorial integrity of Bosnia-Herzegovina," but without any hint of how the ongoing dismemberment of that country, and the genocide waged against its Muslim inhabitants, might be arrested.

The proceedings were as bizarre as they were tragic. Karadžić roamed the halls chatting amiably with members of various delegations even as he and Milošević (also in attendance) were being linked with "ethnic cleansing" and "crimes against humanity" in speeches by Eagleburger, German foreign minister Klaus Kinkel, and others.[36] Next door to our delegation's offices was the room assigned to the delegation of the rump Serbian-Montenegrin "Yugoslavia" and its new premier, a Serbian-born California businessman named Milan Panić. One of their advisers was a former U.S. ambassador to Yugoslavia, who had to pass the suite of the American delegation—headed by Eagleburger, another former ambassador to Yugoslavia—on his way to his adopted delegation.

This dual role of Karadžić—potential peacemaker or archvillain?—was emblematic of the growing tension between the international community's twin goals of mediation and enforcement. The former effort called for neutrality and impartiality, the latter, for sanctions and other punitive measures in a conflict that had passed from civil war to a war of aggression. The incompatibility of these two orientations was manifest at every level. An arms embargo imposed against all the parties had the effect of rewarding the well-armed Serbian aggressors and punishing their victims, the Bosnian Muslims. UNPROFOR, whose rules of engagement precluded entering the conflict as a protagonist, wound up abetting aggression by trying to uphold successive cease-fire lines, each determined by the aggressor. International mediators, insisting that they would not reward aggression, wound up doing just that by using these new territorial lines as the basis for the next round of negotiations, which they would supervise with strict impartiality. Humanitarian relief convoys carrying food and medicine had to pay tribute to Bosnian Serb forces controlling the supply route; forcing their way through would only have meant the closure of the corridor the next day and the complete cutoff of supplies to the besieged enclaves they were trying to assist. Operations mounted by the UN high commissioner for refugees (UNHCR) fell into the same pernicious logic of indirectly abetting "ethnic cleansing" by helping relocate Bosnian Muslims driven out their homes and villages by Serb forces.

None of this is to denigrate the heroic work done by UN bodies and nongovernmental relief organizations, nor is it to suggest that there are easy answers to these dilemmas. It was Western governments, including

our own, that left these incompatibilities wholly unresolved. The international community could not produce a peace and would not confront
aggression, yet it could not bring itself to admit either of those realities.
In trying to pursue both mediation and enforcement, we adopted a set
of policies so riddled with contradictions that both objectives were
doomed to fail.

Who Lost Yugoslavia?   The European Community? NATO? The UN?
CSCE? The United States? Some in Washington pointed the finger at the
West Europeans, who pointed theirs back at us. The question, of
course, presumes that Yugoslavia was someone else's to lose.

Ambassador Warren Zimmermann, in his valedictory cable—a stylis-
tic masterpiece entitled "Who Shot Cock Robin?"—laid the blame at
.the atavistic forces of ethnic nationalism unleashed by the collapse of
central authority and manipulated by unscrupulous politicians led by
Slobodan Milošević. Many on both sides of the Atlantic took that view
a step further: the conflict, however tragic, was born of age-old Balkan
conflicts beyond American influence and remote to our interests. This
contention was analytically dubious as well as conveniently exculpatory
of American policy.

Hindsight is rarely 20/20, and some critics of American policy during
the period surely exaggerated our ability to influence events for good or
ill.[37] Indeed, hindsight could lead to judgments worse than those that
were reached because these retrospective conclusions were based on an
awareness of outcomes that seemed—but may not have been—the inevitable consequences of policies actually pursued. Like second-guessers
after a football game, critics too easily assumed that the loss was a result of the coach's bad decisions. And of course second-guessers never
see the consequences of their recommendations. They simply assume
that their alternatives, had they been adopted, would have won the
game. As the Yugoslav crisis deepened, everyone inside and especially
outside government seemed to know what should have been done *before*, but no one seemed to know what to do *next*.

With those caveats in mind, there were three junctures in 1989–91
where a different approach might have made a difference. First was at
the beginning: had we thrown our weight fully behind Marković and
lent him all possible support, including substantial economic assistance,
Yugoslavs might have rallied around a new blueprint for a democratic

federal state. It would have been a slim chance, so far advanced were
the forces of disintegration, but it would have been worth taking. Indeed, this was the approach the European Community adopted in early
1991, but by that time it was too late.

Second was the period from late 1990 to mid-1991, when Slovenia
and Croatia were preparing their independence declarations. Had we
focused not on formulae for preserving the federal state but on the
modalities of its dissolution *and* backed this approach with massive international engagement, we might have helped avert the armed conflict
that erupted almost immediately thereafter. This Western strategy
should have been developed even earlier—by the summer of 1990[38]—
and deployed immediately after Slovenia's December 1990 independence referendum, when Western leverage was highest. In fact, we and
the EC did advance principles and conditions for recognition, including
all the right ones—steps toward independence should be taken legally,
constitutionally, peacefully, and consensually, with clear guarantees for
the rights of national minorities. But we did so too late and too timidly.
Indeed, to enforce these principles would have required highly intrusive
international involvement, including tens of thousands of UN or CSCE
peacekeeping forces (this even before a single shot had been fired in
anger). It also would have required international supervision of conflicted areas like Serb-dominated Krajina. And the international community would have had to provide substantial economic assistance to
cushion the disruptions, assist fledgling governments, and provide inducements to follow Western strictures. As a practical matter, it is always difficult for democracies to galvanize public support for engagement on that scale before conflict has broken out—by which time it
may be too late. "Conflict prevention" is easier said than done.

The third juncture was in the fall of 1991, when Serb-sponsored JNA
forces were shelling civilian populations in Vukovar, Osijek, Dubrovnik,
and other Croatian cities. Tanks and other heavy weapons were being
deployed in long convoys from Serbia into Croatia. Whatever the character of the conflict before that time, it had now become a war of Serbian aggression. Instead of allowing Germany to bring the EC to endorse the ill-advised recognition of Slovenia and Croatia, we had a
chance to lead the international community in an altogether different
direction by gaining consensus around a policy of threatening and, if
need be, carrying out military reprisals specifically targeted at Yugoslav

naval units and tank convoys. Whatever its merits, the military option certainly had better chances at this juncture, before JNA forces were already redeployed and dispersed.

Would any of these courses of action have made a difference? It is of course impossible to demonstrate a counterfactual, but it seems clear that each of them offered better chances of success than the policies actually pursued. The second and third, however, carried with them substantial American responsibilities against doubtful prospects. At any given point after hostilities began, it was always easier to "kick the can down the road" and defer tough decisions for a few weeks—by which time the options had gotten even worse. The administration's Balkan task force, which had been meeting via teleconference nearly daily since the conflict began, soon fell into a routine. As no one who mattered was prepared to support a serious policy initiative, the task force produced instead recommendations for the next 24 hours that amounted to little more than diplomatic busywork. Worse, participants began succumbing to the temptation of serving up what they believed their masters wanted to hear: that the hollow strategies we and our European partners were concocting might actually achieve their stated objectives.[39]

These considerations bring us back to the cardinal error of U.S. and other Western policies: We never decided whether important U.S. interests were at stake. We never decided whether Yugoslavia mattered enough to invest considerable American leadership and, if need be, to place substantial numbers of American men and women in harm's way to halt or at least contain the conflict.[40] Absent such clarity of purpose, any course of action—including the three alternatives outlined above— was doomed to fail. As my NSC colleague David Gompert put it in his incisive critique of Western policies: "Western leaders did not see—or if they saw, did not translate into public support and purposeful policies— that the crisis, in Bosnia especially, was setting the worst possible precedents for the new era. They did not appreciate the importance of defeating this case of fiendish nationalism before it had metastasized elsewhere in the former communist world."[41]

For all the policy failures in Yugoslavia, Western leaders remained largely faithful to core principles. (It was later in the conflict that Western leaders began succumbing to the perverse "tribal logic" then prevailing in the Balkans—that the only solution lay in segregating ethnic nations and building high walls between them, with UN "blue helmets" patrolling the perimeters.) It was critically important not to confuse the difficulty of enforcing basic democratic principles with the continuing validity of the principles themselves. In Yugoslavia, several of these principles came together in applying the slippery concept of "national self-determination," for which a brief digression is in order.

"Self-Determination" in Yugoslavia and the Soviet Union

Small wonder that President Wilson, reflecting at the end of the First World War on the chaos engendered by the principle of self-determination he had so uncritically embraced, soon had misgivings: "You do not know and can not appreciate the anxieties that I have experienced as the result of these many millions of peoples having their hopes raised by what I have said."[42] His secretary of state, Robert Lansing, anticipated these consequences even as Wilson was championing self-determination at the Paris Peace Conference of 1919: "The phrase is simply loaded with dynamite. It will raise hopes that can never be realized. It will, I fear, cost thousands of lives. . . . What a calamity that the phrase was ever uttered! What misery it will cause!"[43]

We in government at the end of the Cold War had reason to echo those sentiments. Although Wilson's name is the most closely identified with the quintessentially American concept of "national self-determination," it was a principle the United States had invoked regularly, and carelessly, since. For most of the post–World War II period, the United Nations had applied the concept exclusively to cases of decolonization, i.e., the pursuit of independence by European colonies, chiefly in Africa and Asia.

During the Cold War, the United States also used the term with reference to the Baltic states and other countries of Central and Eastern Europe, but with a different meaning. When successive U.S. administrations said "self-determination," they really meant "independence" or "liberation" from Soviet domination of countries in Central and Eastern Europe whose existence we already recognized. But these terms, like "captive nations" and "rollback," sounded too provocative and retrograde, so we invoked the more high-sounding principle of self-determination—imbuing it with a status that we would have reason to regret. For understandable tactical reasons, we allowed ourselves to be identified as champions of a principle of dubious legality or practicability.

What was meant by "self-determination"? In the spring and summer of 1991, we asked the State Department's Office of Legal Affairs to research the matter thoroughly. International law is ambiguous. To begin with, there is no agreement on who is the "self" in self-determination. Article 1, Section 2, of the United Nations Charter affirms the principle of "self-determination of peoples." But what is a people? Is it a nation, a state, a constituent republic of a federal state, or communities of people however constituted? In a multinational, federal state, who has the right to self-determination—the totality of the federation, the federal units, or the nationalities dispersed among these units? International law does not say.[44]

Nor is it clear what is meant by "determination," except that the term seems to refer to a process rather than an outcome—a right to seek but not necessarily to achieve a desired state of affairs such as statehood. It certainly does not imply the right of state independence. United Nations and CSCE documents affirmed the sanctity of existing borders but also allowed for the possibility of border changes so long as they were accomplished peacefully and consensually. The tension between sovereignty and self-determination is left unresolved. What if border changes are neither peaceful nor consensual? What if independence declarations are contested? International law is silent.

The Political Declaration of the G-7 (Group of 7) Summit in London in July 1991 offered this cumbersome interpretation of these principles with regard to Yugoslavia:

> We will do whatever we can, with others in the international community, to encourage and support the process of dialogue and negotiation in accordance with the principles enshrined in the Helsinki Final Act and the Paris Charter for a new Europe, in particular respect for human rights, including rights of minorities and the right of peoples to self-determination in conformity with the Charter of the United Nations and with the relevant norms of international law, including those relating to territorial integrity of states.[45]

The criteria for statehood are more straightforward, though still subject to interpretation. To qualify for recognition, states must possess a defined territory, a permanent population, a government capable of speaking and acting for its citizens, and the capacity to enter into relations with other states.[46] With respect to the disintegration of Yugoslavia and the Soviet Union, both the United States and the European

Community added a set of more demanding criteria derived from the UN Charter and various CSCE documents.

On September 4, 1991, the U.S. administration issued a set of principles that would guide its policy toward recognition of new states emerging from Yugoslavia, the Soviet Union, and elsewhere. The would-be states, we said, must

— support internationally accepted principles, including democratic values and practices and the principles of the Helsinki Final Act;

— respect existing borders, both internal and external, with change through peaceful and consensual means consistent with the principles of the Conference on Security and Cooperation in Europe (CSCE);

— support the rule of law and democratic processes;

— safeguard human rights, including minority rights; and

— respect international law and obligations, especially the provisions of the Helsinki Final Act and the Charter of Paris.[47]

The EC's guidelines, issued three months later and amplified through the work of the Badinter Commission, were nearly identical:

— respect for the provisions of the Charter of the United Nations and the commitments subscribed to in the Final Act of Helsinki and in the Charter of Paris, especially with regard to the rule of law, democracy, and human rights;

— guarantees for the rights of ethnic and national groups and minorities in accordance with . . . the CSCE;

— respect for the inviolability of all frontiers, which can only be changed by peaceful means and by common agreement;

— acceptance of all relevant commitments with regard to disarmament and nuclear non-proliferation as well as to security and regional stability;

— commitment to settle by agreement, including where appropriate by recourse to arbitration, all questions concerning state succession and regional disputes.[48]

As a practical matter, the United States, while invoking essentially the same principles, made a sharper distinction than did the EC between recognition and the establishment of diplomatic relations. The former, in our view, was a legal act and therefore subject to the narrower criteria for statehood, while the latter was a political act to which we attached much more stringent considerations.

These stipulations presented one further conceptual difficulty that arose in both Yugoslavia and the Soviet Union: namely, that the "self" invoking self-determination was not always the same "self" that sought recognition. As one writer put it, "The 'self' entitled to claim the right of self-determination [under the UN system] was limited to territorial entities under colonial rule or international trusteeship, and no other 'self' was recognized as a potentially legitimate claimant."[49] When Croatia declared its independence, this was done by and on behalf of Croatians within that republic, yet this territory was under the jurisdiction of the Republic of Croatia as a whole, and the vehicle for seeking recognition was the government of that republic. Thus, in Croatia, Bosnia, Ukraine, and elsewhere, the international community was obliged to deal with claimants that spoke for only part of the "peoples" within their borders.

Where self-determination and sovereignty collided, the relevant political pressure almost always came in support of the former. Americans tend to be Wilsonian. Our revolutionary origins and successive waves of immigrants fleeing oppression brought us down on the side of "the little guy." With the media and political commentators, this disposition was even stronger. It was easier to construct a morality play around David than Goliath.

In international law, the principles of self-determination and sovereignty are parallel to the concepts of change and stability. On that score as well, Americans tended instinctively to favor change and view the existing international order with disdain; Europeans, however, for reasons of geography and history, were more apt to equate change with a chaotic breakdown of order. The analytical predisposition of Americans also tended to see change as the natural order, or disorder, of things. To support the status quo was to be out of step with the hoofbeat of history.

It was against this backdrop, and with violent conflict in Yugoslavia unfolding before our eyes, that we addressed the potentially much graver prospect of a disintegrating Soviet Union. It was easy for Western publics, especially our own, to overlook how much mischief could be caused by abandoning the principle of sovereignty. The power of sovereign states may well have been dwindling at the end of the Cold War, but states nonetheless were the units of such international order as we had. They controlled the armies and the weapons—in the Soviet case, nuclear weapons capable of rendering the planet uninhabitable. There was nothing like the prospect of human annihilation to focus the mind. Such were some of the considerations that made the Bush administration less eager than its critics to revel in the prospect of a dismembered Soviet Union.

The End of the Soviet Union

After the crackdown against the Baltic states in mid-January 1991, the CIA's *National Intelligence Daily* offered a prescient summary: "Gorbachev has started a conflict without a visible program and with scant prospect of long-term success. He will not easily escape the predicament for which he is largely responsible, and he may become its principal casualty."[50] At about the same time, Polish president Lech Wałęsa reminded a *Figaro* interviewer that he "was the first political person to say that there existed only one solution for the Soviet Union—to dissolve itself."[51]

From Crisis to Crisis For the rest of the year, Gorbachev beat one retreat after another, none gaining him the upper hand, each inviting further challenges to his authority. One week after the "Bloody Sunday" in Riga, Latvia, Gorbachev dispatched his new foreign minister (and former ambassador to the United States) Aleksandr Bessmertnykh to Washington to assure Bush and Baker that the use of force was "not presidential policy" and would not be repeated.[52] On the strength of this assurance and in deference to Gorbachev's plea for understanding, Bush, in his State of the Union Address the next day, withheld direct criticism of Gorbachev. But he noted that he had been given "representations" which, "if fulfilled, would result in the withdrawal of some Soviet forces, a reopening of dialogue with the republics, and a move away from violence."[53]

From the beginning, Gorbachev would have been better advised to have conceded Baltic independence, concentrating his energy and political capital on measures to hold together the rest of the union. The man who had leapt over history up until 1990 was now constantly trying to catch up to it—always too late and too timidly to shape it. Even allowing for the enormous pressure under which he was laboring, his handling of the crisis only served to embolden hard-line critics and strengthen secessionist movements elsewhere—without doing more than momentarily slowing drives for independence in the Baltic states.

The narrow public endorsement of a March 17 referendum on preserving the Soviet Union did nothing to arrest the growing disintegration of central authority. Six republics—Moldova, Armenia, Georgia, and the three Baltic states—boycotted the referendum and pressed ahead with preparations for full independence. They did so with the blessings of Boris Yeltsin, soon to be elected president of the Russian federation,[54] who had interposed himself as champion of the republics in their several struggles with the center. In late March he demonstrated his own independence by holding a huge rally near the Kremlin in defiance of police and interior ministry forces.

Once again obliged to retreat, Gorbachev met at his country house (dacha) on April 23 with leaders of the nine republics that had not boycotted the March 17 referendum to hammer out the terms of a new union treaty. The "Dacha Agreement," also known as the Nine Plus One, devolved substantially greater authority to the republics and also provided more workable modalities for secession. It was a formula that might have facilitated creation of a voluntary union, or reunion, among these republics, but it came so late that attitudes among the main protagonists were already hardened.

In trying to steer down the middle of the road, Gorbachev was being hit by traffic coming from both directions. Against the intransigence of hard-line opponents on center-republic relations and economic reform, Gorbachev could muster nothing more than belated half-measures— which only emboldened republic leaders to go their own ways. Yet the concessions they were able to wring from him further antagonized a growing hard-line faction of disaffected party, military, and KGB officials. Thus even as republic leaders, led by Yeltsin, were pulling the country apart from the periphery, hard-liners were conspiring to bring Gorbachev down and restore authoritarian control.

A secret CIA analysis of "The Soviet Cauldron" issued April 25 warned of the growing likelihood of a coup attempt but also judged that "the long-term prospects of such an enterprise are poor, and even short-term success is far from assured."[55] By late June, the agency's clandestine service had specific reports of an imminent attempt to strip Gorbachev of his presidential authority via a "constitutional coup d'état." President Bush sent a letter to Gorbachev warning him that a

coup attempt would be mounted against him on June 21.[56] Secretary
Baker, alerted to the threat while attending a CSCE ministerial in Berlin
(just before his trip to Belgrade), conveyed the same message to Foreign
Minister Bessmertnykh, also in attendance at Berlin.[57]

Such was the situation in the Soviet Union as two important summits
loomed in mid- and late July. London was to be the site of a G-7 summit, to which Gorbachev had managed to get himself invited and where
he was sure to lobby for substantial economic aid. The long-delayed
Bush-Gorbachev Summit would take place in Moscow, where the two
leaders were expected to sign a START agreement codifying further deep
reductions in strategic nuclear weapons. They also hoped to resolve outstanding issues arising from Soviet backtracking from key provisions of
the CFE (Conventional Armed Forces in Europe) treaty. The two summits framed the issues before U.S. policy: economic and political engagement of a Soviet Union in the midst of profound turmoil, and the conclusion of key agreements with the embattled leader of that country to
"lock in" Soviet reductions in nuclear and conventional forces.

The relevant options for U.S. policy—and those pressed on us from
various quarters—were basically threefold. First, we could begin distancing ourselves from Gorbachev and cultivate Yeltsin and other republic leaders, with the conscious aim of encouraging the dismemberment, full or partial, of the Soviet Union. This was the course urged on
us by Yeltsin and the Baltic states, as well as independence-minded leaders in other republics, and it had support in some quarters of the administration, chiefly in the Pentagon. (The CIA and many outside pundits
also favored this course but not necessarily the political objective; they
merely wanted U.S. policy to conform to what they saw as the emerging
reality.) Second, we could lend as much support as possible to Gorbachev in order to avert a hard-line coup and potentially a descent into
civil war. This is of course what Gorbachev wanted from us, and it was
supported by Chancellor Kohl and most of our other European allies,
who feared above all a chaotic breakdown of order in the Soviet Union.
Third, we could support Gorbachev conditionally, using our leverage to
push him further down the path of economic and political reform. This
was the premise of a "Grand Bargain" proposal advanced by two Harvard academics and former policymakers, in which the United States
would assemble a three-year international assistance package of $15–20
billion a year in return for deep and sustained reform of the Soviet
economy.[58]

Each of these courses of action had its liabilities. The first, by further weakening Gorbachev, would have undercut efforts to secure nuclear and conventional arms reductions and would have put us squarely in the middle of delicate and dangerous relations between republics and a diminished central authority in Moscow. The second presented the difficulty that there was precious little to "support," except rhetorically, so we risked backing a losing horse. Similarly, the third option presumed that there was a power or combination of powers in the Soviet Union that could deliver on its part of the bargain. There was not. It was not just that Gorbachev lacked the will to reform; he had by this time made pacts with so many devils that he lacked the political capacity to do so.

As it turned out, we tried a bit of option one by "diversifying" our relations with Soviet, republic, and local leaders and a bit of option three by advancing a modest set of economic assistance measures aimed at spurring reform, but we essentially came down on the side of the second option of supporting Gorbachev. However weakened, he was still the "linchpin" between the center and the republics and was the "communications node between the extremes," as one of my NSC colleagues put it.[59] Without him, it was hard to see what institutions or processes could facilitate negotiations among the rival centers of power. But the most important considerations derived from American interests: inasmuch as we lacked the capacity to determine the future of Soviet reforms or relations between the center and the republics, we acted to take care of issues that manifestly were in our interests—particularly in controlling and reducing Soviet nuclear and conventional forces.

Our Western allies felt much as we did. Chancellor Kohl was the most eager to provide economic assistance, owing chiefly to his urgent desire to secure the timely removal of Soviet forces from eastern Germany, but even he was loath to throw good money after bad. Accordingly, the G-7 Summit in London in mid-July was long on good wishes but, in the absence of any Soviet economic reform plan, short on new assistance measures. The G-7 leaders agreed to support the Soviet Union's "special associate status" in the International Monetary Fund, but even that fell short of Gorbachev's plea for full membership.[60] The main achievement at London, from our perspective, was resolution of the last issues on the START treaty,[61] clearing the way for its signature by Presidents Bush and Gorbachev at the Moscow Summit two weeks later. In the weeks leading up to London, President Bush had used his leverage with Gorbachev toward that end, withholding agreement to attend the Moscow Summit until the Soviet side had agreed to the terms of the CFE and START treaties. This was the bargain we pursued—not as grand as the other, but it had the virtues of being achievable and directly related to our vital interests.

The Moscow Summit at the end of July contrasted sharply with the Washington Summit of May–June 1990. In 1990, Gorbachev was embattled but still in charge, his role essential to the conclusion of German unification, the CFE treaty, and other key issues. A year later, there was no disguising his loss of power at home and abroad. Thus the Moscow Summit was anticlimactic, quite irrelevant to the real issues facing the Soviet state. Apart from the START treaty, the only achievement to which Gorbachev could point was President Bush's decision to send to Congress the U.S.-Soviet trade agreement, but this was merely the consummation of a document the two leaders had signed in Washington (and which Bush had held in abeyance pending passage of Soviet emigration legislation).[62]

The major event of the summit came not in Moscow but in Kiev. The reason for the president's stop there was to show understanding for the aspirations of Ukrainians and others; the purpose of the president's speech to the Ukrainian parliament was to promote the ongoing negotiations between Gorbachev and republic leaders toward the new union treaty. Neither objective was achieved. His address backfired because it persuaded his audience of American hostility toward Ukrainian self-determination. Quickly dubbed the "Chicken Kiev" speech,[63] it conveyed a useful distinction between liberty and state independence—the former being an aspiration that the United States unreservedly supported; the latter, a more complex matter to which peoples did not have an automatic right. Had the speech been given in Zagreb or Ljubljana, it might have served as a corrective to the indiscriminate invocation of the "rights of self-determination." As it was, Bush's condemnation of "local despotism" and "suicidal nationalism" was taken, understandably, as gratuitously offensive to the Ukrainian people and their leaders.

From Coup d'État to Coup de Grâce   As the CIA's analysis had warned, the prospective conclusion of the new union treaty prompted the anti-Gorbachev coup-plotters to make their move. On August 18, just a few days before Gorbachev and nine republic presidents were to begin signing the treaty, a self-proclaimed "State Emergency Committee" seized Gorbachev, imposed a "temporary" state of emergency, and named Vice President Gennady Yanayev president in Gorbachev's stead.[64]

Among the limited options at our disposal, President Bush chose the right ones. Alone among Western leaders, he observed from the outset that "coups can fail."[65] Far from being the offhand intuitive remark it seemed, this judgment was the product of careful, ongoing analysis beginning with the CIA's April 25 report on "The Soviet Cauldron." While some of his counterparts, notably French president Mitterrand, were busily accommodating themselves to the new situation, Bush ensured that the outside world would rally behind a policy of nonrecognition that stressed the illegitimacy of the coup and its leaders.[66] (Had the coup succeeded, the United States eventually would have found ways to deal with the new leadership, but the president was not about to capitulate preemptively.) At the height of the crisis, Secretary Baker travelled to Brussels for an emergency NATO ministerial to hammer out an allied consensus on responding to developments in the Soviet Union.[67] As events unfolded, Bush's strong support for Boris Yeltsin, even while maintaining solidarity with Gorbachev, compensated for whatever slights he may have inflicted on the Russian leader before. Thus when the coup failed, the United States was well positioned to deal with Gorbachev and Yeltsin alike.

In the immediate aftermath of the coup, it was plain to all save Gorbachev that de facto political leadership had passed to Yeltsin.[68] In his first television appearance, Gorbachev called for the "renewal" of the Communist party; within a week he was forced to step down as its leader and acquiesce to Yeltsin's demand that party activities be banned altogether. Ukraine, Belarus, and five other republics promptly declared their independence. The Baltic states sought and received international recognition by most European states and, after a brief delay to spare Gorbachev needless humiliation, the United States as well. As Bush put it, "When history is written, nobody will remember that we took 48 hours longer than Iceland." Unfortunately, the line was so provocative that it would be cited in every contemporary account, including this one, assuring that "history" would indeed remember, at least for a while.[69]

American policy from that point on focused on the prospect of a radically altered and perhaps dismembered Soviet Union. Our concerns were with the modalities for negotiating the future relations among the republics and with the issues arising therefrom, chiefly the disposition of nuclear weapons in Russia, Ukraine, Belarus, and Kazakhstan, the four republics on whose territories nuclear weapons were deployed. An internal State Department memorandum of late August concluded that "the Center and its institutions continue to exist . . . largely at the indulgence of the republics," which "will try to sweep the Center aside and find a new vehicle through which to work out their relations" unless Gorbachev, implausibly, seized from Boris Yeltsin the agenda of radical reform.[70]

As Gorbachev's authority continued to diminish over the next few weeks, so did prospects for renegotiation of the union treaty. By late October, it was evident that, as a State Department policy paper put it, "The Soviet Union as we know it no longer exists. What matters now is how the breakup of the Soviet Union proceeds from this point onward. Our aim should be to make the crash as peaceful as possible."[71]

The differences within the administration by this time were not so much about the likelihood of disintegration nor even its desirability, but about the proper course of U.S. policy. For Secretary Cheney and the uniformed military, the possibility of the dissolution of the Soviet Union presented an opportunity that U.S. policy should exploit. We could do this by lending our support to independence movements among the republics and according prompt recognition to republics declaring their independence.[72] The president, Secretary Baker, and others were not so sure. The disintegration of our Cold War adversary was arguably in American interests, but it depended . . . on what kind of new states emerged from this process, and what kind of hands were on the nuclear trigger. As has been argued, we lacked the capacity either to save or destroy the Soviet state, so our better course was to tend to our own business, trying where we could to ensure a peaceful, negotiated outcome and working to ensure the responsible disposition of nuclear weapons.

We had said that "the Soviet Union *as we know it* no longer exists"; that formulation left room for the renegotiation among key republics, with Gorbachev nominally in the center, of the terms of a radically restructured Soviet Union. It was a possibility that we, as a matter of policy, neither promoted nor excluded; we simply kept it among the universe of possible outcomes as we engaged key leaders. President Bush's view was that if we were not certain of the outcome—and we were not—we should take a step back from the process and try to manage those aspects that bore immediately on American interests.

In early September, Secretary Baker had announced five principles that would guide our approaches toward the republics: self-determination consistent with democratic principles, respect for existing borders, support for democracy and the rule of law, human rights and the rights of national minorities, and respect for international law and obligations.[73] The other main line of policy was to press Gorbachev and key republic leaders on nuclear weapons issues: compliance with the START treaty, control over nuclear weapons, and adherence to the nuclear nonproliferation treaty. In late September, as has been seen, the president announced several unilateral initiatives on nuclear arms and proposed immediate discussions with the Soviet Union on nuclear command and control and warhead security.[74] Baker then pushed this agenda along with the "five principles" in a series of visits to every Soviet republic beginning with a long-scheduled CSCE human rights conference in Moscow in September.[75] Negotiations on nuclear issues were particularly arduous, stretching throughout 1991 and into 1992.[76]

It was a confluence of forces—some deeply rooted, others accidental—that brought about the disintegration of the Soviet state. If the Soviet Union were to survive as a voluntary association of republics and peoples, its very essence needed to be transformed. Such an outcome might have been possible had it not been for the rivalry between Gorbachev and Yeltsin *and* the structures of the institutions they led. Had there been a weak, mainly ceremonial Soviet presidency, as there was for most of the USSR's history, Yeltsin might have seen his way clear to retaining a much looser union with himself as first among equals. Or, had Gorbachev moved some months earlier, rather than in the immediate aftermath of the August 1991 coup, to resign the Communist party leadership and so separate the power of the party from the power of the presidency, Yeltsin might simply have challenged him for that position and felt no need to detach Russia from the union. So much for "what ifs." Suffice it to say that there were several plausible outcomes to the political struggle of the fall of 1991, not just one.

As it was, the irreconcilability of the issues at play between Gorbachev and Yeltsin made it impossible to transform the center in ways that might have induced key republics to remain. On December 1, Ukrainians voted overwhelmingly for independence. A week later, Yeltsin, newly elected Ukrainian president Leonid Kravchuk, and Belarusian president Stanislav Suskevich met in Minsk, Belarus, to declare that the Soviet Union had ceased to exist and to announce a new "Commonwealth of Independent States." Secretary Baker promptly undertook another trip to Moscow for meetings with Yeltsin and Gorbachev, traveling also to Ukraine, Belarus, and Kyrgyzstan, pressing the "five principles"—for which he sought and received specific commitments.[77]

On December 25, 1991, Mikhail Gorbachev formally declared the end of the Soviet Union. President Bush simultaneously announced immediate U.S. recognition of the independence of the 12 new states and the immediate establishment of diplomatic relations with six: Russia, Ukraine, Belarus, Kazakhstan, Armenia, and Kyrgyzstan. In keeping with the distinction we made between recognition, a legal act, and diplomatic relations, a political one that was subject to more stringent conditions, the president withheld the establishment of diplomatic relations with the remaining new states "until they have made commitments to responsible security policies and democratic principles, as have the other states we recognize today."[78] In February 1992, following Secretary Baker's visit to the remaining new states—except Georgia, then engulfed in civil turmoil—the United States established diplomatic relations with Moldova, Azerbaijan, Tajikistan, Turkmenistan, and Uzbekistan.[79] Finally, with Eduard Shevardnadze's assumption of the interim presidency of Georgia and Secretary Baker's visit there in May, we established relations with the last of the newly independent states.[80]

Yet in our zeal to be helpful to the struggling new states, we got off on the wrong foot. In an otherwise well-conceived speech at Princeton University in December 1991, Secretary Baker noted that "the opportunities are historic: We have the chance to anchor Russia, Ukraine, and other republics firmly in the Euro-Atlantic community and democratic commonwealth of nations. We have the chance to bring democracy to lands that have little knowledge of it. . . ."[81] The trouble was that neither "we" the United States nor "we" the Western community had any such chance. That chance belonged to the Russian people, and it was our responsibility to see that the opportunity was extended to them—but not to imply that democracy and integration into the Western community were gifts we could bestow. What may have begun as a careless rhetorical flourish soon became embedded in policy, setting the United States on a course toward objectives that were well beyond our capacity to deliver.

At a huge "coordinating conference" arranged in Washington in January 1992, President Bush made the sounder observation that "ultimate success or failure rests squarely with the efforts and wisdom of the peoples of Russia and the Ukraine and the Caucasus and Central Asia."[82] But the fact that the conference took place conveyed the impression that the United States and its Western partners bore the chief responsibility. Because the objectives were so extravagant, participating countries, beginning with the United States, wildly inflated their projected levels of assistance and disguised the conditions under which their assistance would be offered. When the levels of assistance actually extended fell far short of what seemed to have been promised, Russians increasingly believed that they had been misled by a Western community bent on weakening, not assisting, their country.

The administration moved quickly to engage the leaders of the newly independent states. Russian president Boris Yeltsin visited Washington and Camp David in early February. In early April, the president submitted to Congress the "Freedom Support Act" for assistance totalling $24 billion, a wildly misleading figure that mixed together old and new, U.S. and non-U.S., bilateral and multilateral, loans and grants, all in an understandable but ill-advised effort to impress.[83] Ukrainian president Leonid Kravchuk and Kazakhstan's president Nursultan Nazarbayev visited Washington in May, each signing with President Bush a declaration on bilateral relations.[84] Yeltsin followed in June with a full state visit, during which he and President Bush issued a "Charter for American-Russian Partnership and Friendship" and no fewer than 31 other agreements and joint statements.[85] Several of these were key, particularly those concerning weapons of mass destruction, but for sheer dramatic effect none matched the opening of the "Camp David Declaration" issued by Presidents Bush and Yeltsin during the latter's February 1992 visit: "Russia and the United States do not regard each other as potential adversaries."[86]

American Policy Revisited   The peaceful disintegration of the Soviet state was among the most remarkable developments in modern history. How much credit should go to American diplomacy? Our "five principles," after all, were essentially the same ones we had advanced to no avail with leaders of the Yugoslav republics. Did our approaches toward a disintegrating Soviet Union make a difference?

In the first place, our approaches were undertaken with the right frame of mind: in his meetings with leaders of every new state of the former Soviet Union, Secretary Baker presented the principles on which we and the rest of the CSCE community insisted. He also made it clear that our future relations would be based on these principles, and placed the onus on republic leaders to adhere to them. We had helped to establish a framework through which the international community could deal with independence declarations by Soviet republics, based on a shared set of principles and procedures. And the principles were the right ones, even though we could not compel compliance among the Soviet republics any more than we could in Yugoslavia. We pressed them with greater urgency, and with a stronger international consensus, in the Soviet case, but in the end it was the behavior of the protagonists themselves rather than outside pressure that made the difference. If our influence over the process of German unification was decisive, and our early engagement in Eastern Europe instrumental in paving the way for the revolutions of 1989, our influence, though important, was considerably less over the process of Soviet dissolution.

The most common critique was that the Bush administration held on too long to Gorbachev and "the center" and failed to engage leaders like Yeltsin and others among the republics. This assertion needs to be "deconstructed." It is true that the upper levels of the administration exaggerated the strength and staying power of the apparatus of the Soviet state—such is the tendency of leaders accustomed to dealing with other world leaders. Relatedly, our contacts with and understanding of the Soviet Union were Moscow-centric. One could count on one hand the number of experts within government on the non-Russian republics. It is also true that President Bush, having developed a relationship of trust with Gorbachev, went the extra mile to avoid embarrassing his Soviet counterpart.[87] It is true, finally, that the administration erred on the side of caution in dealing with independence movements among the republics.

Analytically, then, pundits outside government and some analysts within may have been closer to the mark than the senior levels of the Bush administration in divining the coming breakup of the Soviet state. Yet "illusions of retrospective determinism" come into play once more. The disintegration of the Soviet Union was not inevitable: had it not been for the power struggle between Gorbachev and Yeltsin, which was only distantly related to center-periphery relations, the Soviet Union might well have held together. The Baltic states would have left regardless, perhaps joined by Georgia, Moldova, and Armenia, but the "Slavic core" of Russia, Ukraine, Belarus, and Kazakhstan could well have renegotiated the terms of their union—as indeed they were doing in the spring and again in the fall of 1991.

More importantly, because the Soviet Union's disintegration occurred in a peaceful and orderly way, it was easy after the fact to come to the judgment that the United States should have acted more boldly in support of independence movements among the republics. Yet an aggressive American policy might well have precipitated reckless actions among the republics and galvanized a much more determined hard-line backlash in Moscow. It was what we refrained from doing, as much as what we did, that mattered.

It has already been mentioned here that scholars and pundits like to see policy conform to their analysis, whereas policymakers develop policies to advance their objectives. Those who argued loudest for a different American approach may have had it right analytically, but their policy prescriptions were unpersuasive. What, exactly, should the United States have done differently, and to what end? It was said we should have cultivated influential republic leaders, as well as the reformist mayors of Leningrad, Moscow, and other cities. But why, precisely? To "establish contact"? This was too woolly a prescription for serious policymakers. To "build up influence"? This was the working-level perspective of the State Department, which saw the world as a bank account into which the United States must make regular deposits—in order to increase its influence—but never make a withdrawal. U.S. interests did not require that we ingratiate ourselves with the up and comers among the republics. We might have done more, but our neglect cost us nothing.

Even the Kiev speech, which virtually everyone later agreed was a mistake, probably did little harm. Would history have turned out differently had Bush given a different speech? A safer, middle-of-the-road speech would have been better than the one Bush actually delivered, but events would have transpired pretty much the same. There is no evidence that it influenced the coup plotters one way or another. Arguably, however, had he delivered a fire-breathing call for Ukrainian independence, this might have energized hard-line opponents of Gorbachev and created a stronger constituency behind the August coup attempt. If he had to err, better to err on the side of caution before seeming to advocate the dissolution of a state bristling with nuclear weapons.

A stronger case was that the United States should have engaged the republics in order to influence the likely, even if not inevitable, dissolution of the Soviet state. This, as was argued above, was an option we should have pursued with regard to Yugoslavia. Yet interposing ourselves between the center and the republics would have been a risky strategy, more likely to backfire by provoking republics into precipitous action. It was arguably justifiable in the Yugoslav context, where we had reason to believe that the breakup would be contested and violent, but it was fraught with dangers in the Soviet case, where negotiations were proceeding well enough without us. The physician's counsel was good for diplomats as well: first, do no harm.

The harshest criticism was reserved for the administration's policy toward the Baltic states. The basic tone was set in the spring of 1990, when President Bush said that he did not want history to judge that this was where "everything went off track" and "progress stopped."[88] Instead of openly challenging Gorbachev on this issue, we worked behind the scenes to gain his assurance that force would not be used against the Baltic states and pushed him toward dialogue and negotiation. We held key Soviet desiderata—like a bilateral trade agreement—hostage to Soviet compliance with these stipulations. We took essentially the same position a year later, after the "Bloody Sundays" in Riga and Vilnius.

One can question the premises of this approach but not its results: the objectives, as we had framed them, were realized fully and with less bloodshed than we feared. The independence of the Baltic states was an aim from which we never wavered, but it was one that we balanced against other key objectives. Even had Baltic independence been the sole objective of American policy during the period, it is not clear that another course of action would have been more successful or succeeded more rapidly. Baltic leaders felt otherwise, however.

At the Helsinki Summit of July 1992, the president met with the three Baltic delegations. It was my last day on the job, as I would take up my new assignment under Deputy Secretary Eagleburger immediately upon returning to Washington. In the course of a discussion about difficulties with Moscow over the withdrawal of Russian troops, Tamas Meri, Estonia's former foreign minister and future president, noted offhandedly that he hoped the United States would not make the same mistakes with Yeltsin that it had made with Gorbachev. Before the president could reply, another of the Baltic leaders tactfully tried to change the subject; Bush, however, despite being preoccupied with his coming election struggle, was having none of it. "Wait! I want to finish this!" Asked what he meant, Meri opined that when the West showed understanding or tried to accommodate Russian concerns, this only lent strength to the hard-liners, whereas a tough posture would demonstrate resolve and so isolate hard-line opponents. As I was taking notes of the conversation, I was thinking that this was a preposterous bit of cheek given all the Bush administration had been through with Moscow over the past three years: the strategic and tactical planning, the measured use of power as an instrument of policy, the carefully calibrated approaches that combined firmness on principles with flexibility on tactics, and, not least, the successes. The liberation of Eastern Europe (including Estonia!), the unification of Germany, and the collapse of Soviet communism, all achieved peacefully and on Western terms: did Meri think all of this occurred by accident? Bush was as hot as I had ever seen him. He reviewed our approaches briefly but forcefully, coming as close as I had ever seen him to immodesty: "We like to think we know a thing or two about dealing with Russian leaders." Indeed.

Conclusion: Beyond the Cold War

"AFTER A LONG WAR, it is impossible to make a quick peace."[1] Harold Nicolson's judgment on the 1919 Versailles conference ending World War I is worth recalling in the aftermath of a far longer war. Indeed, the Cold War had gone on so long that it was easy to forget what it was all about in the first place—the stability of Europe, rather than the Soviet threat. With Soviet acquisition of nuclear weapons capable of destroying us and our allies, the Cold War and the Soviet threat became virtually synonymous. Our interests were seen almost wholly in terms of countering this threat, which helps explain our diminished sense of strategic purpose as that threat receded. Yet what animated American policy in the immediate postwar period was defense of interests that had not diminished with the disappearance of the threat.

From the Truman Doctrine to the Marshall Plan and the formation of the Atlantic alliance, our postwar strategy was to shield Western Europe so that it could recover economically, build democracy, and overcome its national rivalries. In the process it would become a more cohesive bulwark against further Soviet expansion and a magnet that would ultimately draw the countries of Central and Eastern Europe into its field. The Cold War was also a struggle over Germany and with the irreconcilable differences of the *German question*. While the resulting division of Germany was a de facto solution that survived for more than a generation, U.S. policy aimed from the beginning to overcome the postwar division of Germany and of Europe.[2]

These combined strategies were brilliantly successful but not yet complete, nor could their achievements in Western Europe be taken for granted. The great unresolved problem for European stability lay in the

East. It was, in the first instance, much the same *Eastern question* that preoccupied the peacemakers at Yalta and Potsdam, Versailles, and indeed the Congress of Vienna in 1815: how to deal with the breakup of the multiethnic empires in Europe's eastern reaches.[3] As before, it remained linked to the German question, which seemed finally to have been answered in 1990 with the achievement of unity "in peace and freedom" but which could be reopened if democratic stability remained elusive among Germany's eastern neighbors. Already the war in the former Yugoslavia had exposed deep fissures in the European Community and undermined its confidence in continued movement toward European unity. And of course there was the still larger Eastern question posed by Russia, Ukraine, and the other newly independent states of the former Soviet Union. The daunting challenges they faced served to dramatize how far we remained from a secure new order.

Much like 1919 and 1945, the mood at the end of the Cold War was the triumphalist expectation that the values that had won the war would now produce the peace. As before, triumphalism gave way to disillusionment and disorientation, both here and in Europe, as these sanguine expectations inevitably were shattered.

"Why this sudden restlessness, this confusion?" asked the Greek poet Cavafy, writing early in this century about the Roman senate before the fall of the Roman empire. His answer bore also on the challenge of finding America's place and role in the post–Cold War world, absent the threat that had lent focus and purpose to U.S. policy for four decades:

> Because night has fallen and the barbarians have not come.
> And some who have just returned from the border say
> there are no barbarians any longer.
>
> And now, what's going to happen to us without barbarians?
> They were, those people, a kind of solution.[4]

American Diplomacy at the End of the Cold War

American diplomacy in the period 1989–92 had exercised decisive leadership though the end of the Cold War, dealt reasonably well with the challenges immediately in its wake, and laid the foundations, incomplete though they were, of a viable post–Cold War order. The objectives which we had set for ourselves in early 1989—self-determination in

Eastern Europe, reduction of Soviet forces to less threatening levels, Soviet cooperation in solving regional disputes, and the liberalization of
the USSR itself—had been met and far exceeded. Our successes in this
period were attributable to the early recognition of an historic chance
for ending the Cold War, the forging of a grand strategy appropriate to
the challenge, the skill and coherence of the Bush administration's foreign policy, and the single-mindedness with which we grasped what we
knew could be a fleeting opportunity.

Lady Luck played a role as well, for we were dealing at the end of
the Cold War with a Soviet leadership still strong enough to override
hard-line opponents domestically but too weak to offer effective resistance to the precipitous loss of empire. Still, Americans could take pride
in the fact that at a critical moment, their government was on the right
side of history and successfully pursued policies that were consistent
with our principles and our interests. Lest these judgments seem unduly
self-congratulatory, it should be added that the policies we pursued
were not the work of a single administration but rather the extension of
four decades of American leadership under Republican and Democratic
presidents alike.

Our policies for the transitional period of the post–Cold War order
were less successful. NATO was intact but slow to adapt itself to radically new circumstances. A new balance of American and European responsibilities was beginning to emerge, but transatlantic relations were
beset by sharply divergent conceptions of the future "architecture" of
European security. Among the postcommunist countries, progress toward democracy was well advanced in Central Europe but much more
problematic farther East, and the integration of former adversaries into
a stable new order remained a distant vision. The deepening conflict in
the former Yugoslavia seemed to herald not a "new world order" but
old world disorder.

Partly it was a failure of foresight. John Lewis Gaddis recalled the
awkward silence that ensued when he inquired, at a meeting of foreign
policy experts convened in Washington in early 1985, whether it might
be useful to consider the possibility that the Cold War could end some
day and to begin thinking about what kind of order might replace it.[5]
By 1989, such thinking was indeed taking place, but the very sudden-
ness of the revolutionary upheavals that began that year meant there
was little opportunity to engage in a thorough assessment of the
post–Cold War order and the American role in it.

Perhaps it was just as well. Prior examples of this kind of planning for a postwar peace were not particularly auspicious. The "Inquiry" launched by President Woodrow Wilson as early as 1913 did little to inform a post–World War I order; its underestimation of the force of nationalism was as naive as Wilson's belief that he could tame the beast through the principle of self-determination.[6] Similarly, the "Advisory Committee for Post-War Planning," created by President Franklin Roosevelt in 1939, exerted little influence until it was transformed into a much more limited and operational body toward the end of the war.[7]

In both cases, planning suffered from the inherent difficulties, vastly greater than the participants realized, of divining the real power relationships that would emerge once the conflict was over and postwar reconstruction complete. Their recommendations, to the extent they penetrated the consciousness of the political leaders they served, tended to reinforce the belief that a properly designed new status quo could be sustained by reconstituting the wartime coalition as the defender of the postwar order. Both committees also ran up against the danger of trying to affirm in advance the precepts and attendant responsibilities that would bind the country in the postwar order. Roosevelt understood this better than Wilson and indeed may have learned the lesson too well. His assumption of renewed isolationist sentiment after the war led him to eschew considerations of a postwar political settlement in favor of a United Nations organization that would cement continued American engagement via a perpetuation of the wartime coalition. (At the end of the Cold War, as has been seen, the Bush administration looked to NATO in much the same way—as an institutional means of ensuring America's continued postwar engagement.)

During the two world wars, visions of the future peace also animated thinking outside of government, from democratic idealists to world federalists to balance of power realists. All three conceptions found adherents at the end of the Cold War; their ranks waxed and waned with each shift in the still emergent post–Cold War world. The democratic revolutions of 1989 and the triumphalism of the November 1990 Paris Summit led commentators to see an expanding "zone of peace" among ascendant liberal democracies.[8] By 1991, with democracy's outlook looking less bright in the postcommunist world but with the fresh success of the international coalition in the Persian Gulf, the focus had shifted to a revitalized United Nations and regional security organizations as the foundations of a new world order.[9] The messy aftermath of the Gulf War, together with the bloodletting in the former Yugoslavia, in turn, gave fresh impetus to balance of power realism and the hitherto forgotten virtues of spheres of influence. While some stuck to their conceptual guns throughout, the weight of political commentary during the period tracked exquisitely with these phases, sometimes with the same commentator shifting from one to another.[10]

The loss of focus at the end of the Cold War was accentuated by the manner in which it ended—not with military victory, demobilization, and celebration but with the unexpected capitulation of the other side without a shot being fired. We had mobilized as if for war and were mercifully spared the conflict that many saw as inevitable. The grand struggle had ended not with a bang but a whimper.

Americans of an earlier generation knew when V-E Day and V-J Day were; there were dates on the calendar marking victory in Europe and victory over Japan in 1945. But the Cold War ended on no certain date; it lacked finality. The exhilaration Americans felt at the fall of the Berlin Wall was real but somehow distant and abstract; it was detached from our own intense role in the city's history since 1945. The end of the Cold War thus evoked among the American public little sense of purpose fulfilled—and even less of responsibility for the tasks of postwar construction.

Instead of celebrating a stunning victory that vindicated our principles and filled us with new confidence for the tasks ahead, Americans seemed to feel that we had prevailed in a war of attrition but had exhausted ourselves in the process. It was as if we and the Russians were two punch-drunk boxers, equally spent after 15 rounds. The fact that one was still standing seemed almost beside the point.[11]

President Bush tried to counter this perspective in what turned out to be his last State of the Union Address in January 1992. But his assertion that "the Cold War didn't 'end'—it was won"[12] was misinterpreted as an attempt to gain personal credit during a presidential election year rather than a serious effort to get Americans to think positively about the role their country had played and needed to play in the future. Against the danger of post–Cold War disengagement, it was meant to be a call to continued American leadership. It was not a message Americans were ready to hear. The key to our future, they seemed to be saying in the 1992 election, lay within—in the regeneration of the domestic economy and the pursuit of a long agenda of pressing domestic problems deferred during the long years of the Cold War. It was a public mood that helped propel Bill Clinton to the presidency, but it also conditioned his administration to eschew foreign policy leadership in favor of an almost exclusively domestic agenda.

In short, the scope and rapidity of change after 1989, and the loss of a galvanizing threat, caused our ship of state to slip its strategic moorings. We were adrift, searching for the lodestar that would help us find our bearings.

In Search of the National Interest

In 1994 and 1995, the Council on Foreign Relations undertook a 15-month study, culminating in a two-day conference among some thirty foreign policy experts from around the country, to identify vital American interests after the Cold War.[13] The results were literally all over the map. Only one of the 12 "vital interests" on the final list enjoyed unanimous support: the physical defense of U.S. territory. Everything else was contested. As remarkable were items that did not make the final cut, notably the stability of Europe and the incorporation of Russia and China into a cooperative international order. The results of this commendable effort, in short, only confirmed the sense of strategic confusion that afflicted post–Cold War American foreign policy.[14]

Four decades of Cold War seemed to have robbed us of the capacity to think in terms of a foreign policy based on a set of core American interests that commanded broad public support. The Cold War tended to conflate principles and interests. Both, the American people overwhelmingly believed for nearly two generations, were threatened by a hostile adversary, against which the use of American power enjoyed broad domestic consensus. So the essential elements of foreign policy—principles, interests, threat, and power—all seemed to coincide in a balance that evoked relatively little opposition, but also little discriminating public debate, during the long years of Cold War.

The post–Cold War world looked much different. Of these four elements of policy, the threat had receded dramatically, and the currency of power had shifted markedly toward its nonmilitary dimensions. But our principles had not changed, or so one hoped, and our interests, to paraphrase Lord Palmerston, should have been more or less permanent. It was to these first principles and core interests that we needed to turn to find our way in the post–Cold War world.

Instead of carefully considering our interests, balancing them against our capacity and determination, and developing a strategy for advancing those interests, there was a tendency to conjure up new threats or to find a new catch-all for America's international role. Presidents Bush and Clinton both tried to define the new threats to American security and well-being as "uncertainty" and "instability." But those were elusive enemies, and a threat-based foreign policy in an era of multiple but lesser dangers was too diffuse and open-ended. So were approaches that tried to define America's role in terms of a single guiding principle, such as "democratic enlargement" or the "new world order."

The evolution of the "new world order" idea was instructive. Among its other deficiencies, as has been seen, the term suffered from what was seen as an incongruity between principles and interests. Was it high principle that led us to oppose the Iraqi invasion of Kuwait, or was it oil? The obvious answer—that it was both—never satisfied the domestic need for moral clarity, so the term began to migrate, each new formulation a bit more grand than the last. By the end, the Gulf War had become the moral equivalent of a holy war, and Saddam Hussein had been demonized as the spiritual heir of Adolf Hitler. When applied to the UN and to Europe—and imbued with the Wilsonian euphoria of the triumph of democratic principles—the term took on the crusading rhetoric of a "Pax Americana" that was never intended.

The concept of "national interests" was always difficult for Americans, for reasons of history, political culture, and the simple geographic fact of having two large oceans separating us from any potentially hostile power.[15] Considerations of national interest seemed to fly in the face of American exceptionalism—the belief that our country was not like any other. We had a moral mission, if not to save the world, at least to redeem it by our example. Thus, this "national interest" seemed to belong to an age of cynical balance of power politics that was inconsistent with our values and principles. For some, it conjured up images of gunboat diplomacy and a reckless disregard for the rights of others; the pursuit of narrow and transitory self-interest, it was argued, redounded ultimately to our own detriment.

Yet setting up interests against principles was a false dichotomy: promotion of core values and principles was part and parcel of our interests. We needed to uphold basic norms of international conduct for our own well-being, and we needed to support fundamental human rights—if only because the world was more dangerous when leaders of potentially hostile powers were not accountable to their own people. But principles alone were an insufficient guide in a world where the number of problems needing solution vastly exceeded the resources we had at our disposal for addressing them. They led either to an open-ended set of responsibilities that Americans in the end would be unwilling to shoulder or to the arrogance of believing we could and should impose our grand design on the rest of the world.

An interest-based foreign policy, by contrast, should bear some relation to capability—a consideration that would help set priorities and impose limits on our ambitions. Far from being immoral or illiberal, such a foreign policy would recapture a spirit of tolerance, respect for the legitimate interests of others, and a certain caution against intruding into other people's business unless it impinged on our own.

Lessons for the Post–Cold War Era

From the beginning of the Bush administration, we pursued an interest-based strategy. We resisted the pressures to "meet Gorbachev half-way"—to reciprocate Soviet peace initiatives and strike a strategic bargain with Gorbachev and so strengthen his staying power in Moscow. Embracing the Soviet agenda of half-measures or helping Moscow prop up a crumbling empire was not what we had in mind. We deliberately put U.S.-Soviet relations on a slow track, so as to build down public expectations of reciprocal U.S. steps on Soviet terms. We also undertook a systematic review of our interests that led to a grand strategy for ending the Cold War. We advanced our own agenda of deep reductions in Soviet conventional forces in Europe, Soviet acceptance of peaceful democratic change in Eastern Europe, and Soviet cooperation in solving regional conflicts. It was a remedy that went to the causes rather than just the symptoms of the Cold War division.

American foreign policy at the end of the Cold War—the largely successful approaches that guided American policy through the Eastern European revolutions of 1989, the unification of Germany, and the disintegration of the Soviet Union—offered lessons for the immediate future. Yet these lessons were not always grasped, even by those who crafted the policies in the first place.

At least five straightforward lessons could be drawn from this period. The first was that a secure, stable, and prosperous Europe was vital to our own security and well-being. That seemingly obvious proposition needed restating in light of tendencies among the American public to turn inward and among the political elites to become enraptured by our growing commercial interests along the Pacific rim. But Europe went to the core of our political, military, and economic security (to say nothing of our national identity) in ways that Asia did not. We had fought two hot wars and one cold one already; our presence in Europe had become so pervasive that it risked being taken for granted. As a practical matter, there were any number of challenges around the world that bore on important American interests, yet we had neither the capacity nor the desire to solve them alone. Where to turn for help? Naturally, to those countries that shared our values and our interests and with whom we had developed habits and patterns of cooperation—notably Europe and Japan.

If the stability of Europe was a vital American interest, what endangered that stability after the end of the Cold War? The answer was less obvious than in 1947, when most of Europe lay in ruins, with communist parties in Italy, France, Greece, and elsewhere exploiting economic and social unrest. At the end of the Cold War, the issue seemed to have become a contest between the forces of integration and of disintegration. Would Western Europe be able to extend its zone of democracy, security, and prosperity eastward, or would the forces of fragmentation on the loose in the East undermine the self-confidence, cohesion, and ultimately the institutions binding the Western democracies?

Thus a second lesson was that Eastern Europe, the key to ending the Cold War, was also the key to the post–Cold War order in Europe. In 1989, we elevated Eastern Europe to first place on the international agenda and, in effect, held U.S.-Soviet relations hostage to Moscow's acceptance of peaceful democratic change in this region. This was arguably the most important single thing the United States did in helping bring about the end of the Cold War. Of course, the United States did not cause the revolutions of 1989: those sprang from deep historic, economic, and political roots. But we did help create an international environment conducive to their success.

The success of the postcommunist transitions in Central and Eastern Europe—particularly the lands between Germany and Russia—should have been the highest priority for the new security order in Europe. Yet after the first flush of enthusiasm in 1989 and 1990, the United States and its Western partners devoted little attention and few resources to this task. As a matter of security rather than of foreign aid, what was needed was more assistance for countries attempting to make these un-precedented transitions, as well as greater market access and a more rapid integration into Western institutions. The bleak alternative was being played out before our eyes in the former Yugoslavia, and the Western response, timid though it was, proved much more costly than the total of our foreign assistance to Central and Eastern Europe.

A third lesson was that the German question was still open, and American leadership was still required to ensure it was answered in a way consistent with our interests. In 1989 we saw, earlier and more clearly than the Germans themselves, that the German question was on the international agenda and that U.S. leadership was required to ensure that it was answered in ways consistent with European security. Thus our seemingly instinctive support for German unification—at a time when Britain, France, and of course the Soviet Union were bitterly op-posed—was actually the product of a careful consideration of U.S. in-terests. This thinking was embedded in American policy during Presi-dent Bush's visit to Germany in May 1989, long before the fall of the Berlin Wall.

We did not cause German unification any more than we did the revo-lutions of 1989. Unification was coming whether we willed it or not. But if we had joined the British, French, and Russians in opposing Ger-man unification—or if we had merely remained passive—the Germans would have had no choice but to cut the best deal they could with Moscow. So we were looking not only to the process of German unifi-cation but to the future structure of European security and to Ger-many's role in a more united Europe.

The German question was never about unity alone but about whether a powerful Germany could be accommodated within a secure and stable European order. That question was still open, though this time it was not the fault of the Germans. For forty years, Germans across the political spectrum knew that their deepest national aspira-tion—the unity of their country—could be achieved only in cooperation with their Western partners. That situation changed objectively after the achievement of German unity. On some issues it became evident that German interests were better secured by going it alone—as indeed Ger-many threatened to do in order to drag the European Community into premature recognition of Croatia and Slovenia in the fall of 1991.

In the aftermath of unification, the Germans bent over backwards to prove themselves good Europeans and Atlanticists, more often than not subordinating or adjusting their particular interests to the larger interests of the cohesion of the European Union and the Atlantic alliance. But for how long? Just as American diplomacy in 1989 and 1990 worked to ensure that the Germans were never asked to choose between unity and alliance, the task afterwards was to ensure that Germans did not have to choose between alliance and their fundamental interests.

If, as Henry Kissinger once said, Germany was too big for Europe, too small for the world, the U.S. role was indispensable in both respects. We stood as a friendly counterweight to German power in Europe, and as a partner in other parts of the world that could help Germany play a global role commensurate with its economic and political weight. An integral part of this effort was to ensure that Germany play this new role in concert with its European partners, which in turn required a more united Europe, capable of assuming larger responsibilities.

Thus a fourth lesson was that European unity was even more important to us in the post–Cold War era and, somewhat paradoxically, could not be achieved without American leadership. Despite our constant assurances in 1989–91, Europeans believed we were ambivalent about a more united Europe, supporting it in principle but often opposing it when it came to specific steps being considered. They were right. The ambivalence derived from consideration of our interests, which made some conceptions of European unity congenial and others less so. The interests we pursued were the right ones: we wanted a Europe that strengthened rather than weakened the Atlantic alliance, and we wanted to see the Europeans develop a greater capacity for common action, especially in the East. In practice, however, we continued to cling instinctively to a dominant role that we were no longer ready to play and so found it difficult to cede leadership gracefully to the Europeans. And of course the Europeans did not make it easy, for American policy was obliged to deal with a highly ambitious conception of a federal Europe, driven by the French and "Brussels," that masked deep misgivings among the Europeans themselves. Moreover, the European Community's attempts to exert leadership in Yugoslavia—which we were only too ready to endorse—demonstrated how far the EC was from developing a serious capacity for concerted action in foreign policy.

It was also evident that our own ability to stay engaged in Europe required a more united, cohesive, and capable European Community. But what kind of unity? The United States could not be agnostic on so vital a question. For one thing, it was futile to support a vision of Europe that could not be fulfilled. We needed to recognize, as most Europeans privately did, that the grandiose objectives enshrined at the 1991 Maastricht Summit of European political, economic, and monetary union could not be achieved any time soon, and that continuing to pay lip service to these goals only distracted Europe and the United States from more urgent business. The main danger to the future of Europe lay in the postcommunist East, and that should be Europe's priority. The Community's reaching out to the new democracies via the "association agreements" was a step in the right direction, but much more weight needed to be attached to full accession by these countries according to clear criteria and timetables for membership. Debates within the European Union, as it was ambitiously and misleadingly called after Maastricht, between "deepening" (among existing members) and "widening" (to include new ones) proved a distraction from the more urgent practical tasks in the East.

The Atlantic alliance's debate over whether to accept new Central European members was likewise diverted, in NATO's case because the issue came to be seen as an act of hostility toward Russia. It was one thing to take seriously Russian fears of exclusion, quite another to give credence to the argument of Russian politicians that NATO constituted a threat to Russian security. One way of escaping this impasse was to return to the simple concept of alliance, which could be *for* as well as against something. Originally formed to counter a hostile Soviet Union, NATO was being turned to new purposes: pooling scarce military resources, integrating national military structures, strengthening shared values and interests, and enhancing the capacity to act on behalf of those interests, as in Bosnia. The North Atlantic Treaty had 14 articles; only one of them—Article 5—entailed mutual defense commitments. Article 1 involved the peaceful settlement of disputes, Article 2 concerned strengthening free institutions, Article 4 provided for political consultation. Article 10 nicely captured the logic of enlargement: "The parties may, by unanimous agreement, invite any other European State in a position to further the principles of this Treaty and to contribute to the security of the North Atlantic area to accede to this Treaty."[16]

Turning finally to Russia, a fifth lesson was that "a new relationship cannot simply be declared by Moscow, or bestowed by others." So said President Bush in his May 1989 commencement address at Texas A&M.[17] It was wise counsel then, and it was wise counsel even after the breakup of the Soviet Union. In 1989, rather than "meeting Gorbachev halfway," we instead challenged him to come the rest of the way to meet us. To begin with, we refused to allow ourselves to be held accountable for the fate of Soviet reforms, much less Gorbachev's personal fate. These were events well beyond our influence, except at the margins. The peoples of the Soviet Union had great, wrenching choices ahead of them. We could hope to nudge them toward policies congenial to our interests, but we were under no illusions that we could make the Soviet peoples' choices for them. Our focus was on Soviet international behavior, where our influence was much greater and which was a more legitimate focus for our policy anyway. Bush and Secretary of State Baker got considerable credit for their diplomatic and arms control initiatives that avoided humiliating a Soviet leadership in the midst of imperial breakup, but what was not as well understood was their sophisticated use of power—not only military power—toward those ends. As German unification proceeded, we mobilized an international consensus that made it harder for Soviet leaders to say *nyet*, even as our other initiatives made it easier for them to say *da*.

Yet by the end, the Bush administration had forgotten some of its own lessons, vastly exaggerating our ability to influence the Russian internal dynamic and embarking on a self-defeating strategy that had us intruding too deeply in Russia's domestic affairs. Worse, in our zeal to avert Russia's exclusion from the emerging international order, we allowed the Russian agenda to dictate our own and put ourselves in the position of trying to compensate Russia for lost influence. In the process, we inadvertently lent strength to the extremist forces we meant to oppose. We seemed to be legitimizing and accommodating ultra-nationalist demands that sprang from an obsolete definition of security based on spheres of influence and territorial control.

The Clinton administration accentuated these mistakes by elevating Russia's internal transformation to first place in our global agenda. As if to underscore the strategic confusion, a January 1996 essay in *Time* magazine criticized the Clinton administration's Russia policy as "outdated." But the essay nonetheless concluded that "the proper goal of American policy toward its former cold-war rival remains in 1996 what it was in '93: a peaceful, democratic, prosperous Russia fully integrated into the international community."[18] It was a widely shared view in and out of government, but it was misguided. The happy state of affairs it described was the proper goal of *Russian* policy, not American. Clearly, a democratic, peaceful, and cooperative Russia would be in America's interest and indeed in everyone's interest, but that outcome was so far beyond our capacity to deliver as to constitute mere wishful thinking or, worse, dangerous arrogance. When the United States intruded directly into the Russian political process in support of "reformers," we were more likely to generate anti-American sentiment than we were to advance the cause of reform.

In an article a few years earlier, John Gaddis had defined our objectives more modestly: "rehabilitate defeated adversaries and invite them into the international state system."[19] There was a world of difference between this formulation and the one just cited from *Time*. It was right to help "rehabilitate" the Russian economic and political system so that the Russian people could have the chance to decide on a democratic future. Whether they seized that chance, however, was beyond our capacity to decide. As regards Russia's involvement in the international system, "invite" was a better verb than "integrate." "Integrate" suggested that it was within America's capacity and indeed our responsibility to bring Russia in; "invite" was more in keeping with our real capabilities and also kept the onus where it belonged—on the Russians themselves. It also would have freed us from the task of trying to tell the Russians what their interests were and enabled us to focus on our own instead.

Countering the emergence of a hostile power capable of threatening the United States and its allies certainly belonged on a short list of American vital interests. So did controlling and reducing weapons of mass destruction. Both dangers arose in the Russian case, and they argued for a long-term, sustainable strategy—one that did not rest so heavily on the dubious proposition that we could influence Russian behavior by dint of our own good intentions. There was also the old-fashioned way of influencing a state's behavior by altering the international context in which that state operates. In this sense, it was worth considering the remainder of the passage cited above from Bush's Texas A&M speech of May 1989:

> The national security of America and our allies is not predicated on hope. It must be based on deeds. We look for enduring, ingrained economic and political change. . . . As we seek peace, we must also remain strong. The purpose of our military might is not to pressure a weak Soviet economy, or to seek military superiority. It is to deter war. It is to defend ourselves and our allies, and to do something more—to convince the Soviet Union that there can be

no reward in pursuing expansionism—to convince the Soviet Union that reward lies in the pursuit of peace.

Substitute "Russia" for "Soviet Union," and this was a set of principles that would serve us well for the post-Soviet era. Of course, the stress on military power was dated, but the uses of power more generally—meaning the economic, political, moral, and psychological aspects as well as the military—were not. Lest this seem unduly confrontational, it was worth recalling that we did not hesitate to play power politics with our friends, notably Japan, yet we tended to shrink from doing so with Russia. In the end, this would prove a more sound and durable basis for American policy, just as the advent in 1995 of a more tough-minded Russian foreign policy promised to yield, paradoxically, a relationship more solidly grounded in Russian national interests—and ours.

Perhaps the most compelling argument for an interest-based foreign policy derived from the evolution of U.S. policy toward a disintegrating Yugoslavia. At the heart of the problem for Western governments, as has been seen, was the judgment, reached early on in Washington and most European capitals, that Yugoslavia no longer mattered much because it was no longer likely to be an arena of East-West conflict. Even as Yugoslavia descended into the most brutal conflict Europe had seen since World War II, the Bush administration could not decide whether important U.S. interests were at stake. Did Yugoslavia matter enough to invest considerable American leadership and, if need be, commit American military forces to peacekeeping or peacemaking efforts? It was argued that the American public, eager for a post–Cold War "peace dividend," was unprepared to support such action, yet the case was never made in terms the public could understand and weigh. We even began to lose faith in our principles, succumbing to the perverse Balkan "wisdom" that peace could be built on the foundation of ethnic nationalism.

In 1993, the Clinton administration assumed office full of criticism for the failures of its predecessor but was similarly unprepared to make a case for American leadership. It was only after Croatia's military breakthrough in the fall of 1995 that the administration began to make its case for the dispatch of U.S. military forces as part of a NATO-led UN mission to Bosnia.

Finally, four years after the outbreak of hostilities in the former Yugoslavia, a serious debate had been joined over American policy—and it was a debate framed in the right way. What was at stake in Bosnia was the stability of the Balkans, and potentially of Europe as a whole. Also of grave concern was the precedent that might be set for authoritarian ultranationalism elsewhere in Eastern Europe and the former Soviet Union. The conflict was thus at the intersection of the Cold War division between East and West, and the manner of its resolution bore on our vital interests across two continents. Honorable men and women could and did come down on different sides of the debate over the proper role of the United States in this conflict, but it was a debate that finally could be conducted on the sound bases of American national interests and fundamental principles. Regaining the capacity to think about our international involvement in that way may have been the beginning of wisdom in the post–Cold War world.

For all the challenges ahead, the circumstances for American policy at the end of the Cold War were much more auspicious than in 1945 or 1919. There was no large external threat on the horizon. There was a functioning, if sluggish, global economy. A prosperous, democratic, and integrated Western Europe was a magnet and point of reference for the emerging East European democracies. The main European and transatlantic institutions were intact. Above all, the United States had not retreated across the ocean, as it had after World War I.

Just as the Cold War order and the strategy of containment took the better part of a decade to put in place, creation of a post–Cold War order was not to be the work of a few months or years. Yet long years of Cold War, and the success of strategies for ending it, had demonstrated a few simple truths: that the indivisibility of transatlantic security needed to be preserved into the indefinite future, that Europe's future depended on the fate of democratic transformation in its eastern half, and that American leadership would be as essential in the new era as it had been in the last.

Chronology

Jan. 16: Václav Havel is arrested in Prague.

Jan. 18–19: French president Mitterrand visits Bulgaria.

Feb. 6: Roundtable talks in Poland between Solidarity and regime begin in Warsaw; adjourned to mid-March.

Feb. 11: Group of Bulgarian intellectuals and artists applies to register an independent trade union called Podkrepa (Support).

Feb. 12: Hungarian Socialist Workers party abandons one-party rule.

Feb. 16: Slovenian Democratic Alliance and Social-Democratic Alliance hold founding conventions calling for democracy.

Feb. 20–21: New Hungarian constitution omits "leading role of the Communist party."

March 9: Tentative Roundtable Agreement is reached in Poland on political reform.

March 11: Six once-prominent Romanian Communist party members send an open letter criticizing party leader Nicolae Ceauşescu.

March 13: Hundreds demonstrate in Leipzig demanding exit permits.

March 16: Yugoslav federal assembly endorses new prime minister, Croat Ante Marković.

March 26: In elections to the new Congress of People's Deputies, the freest in Soviet history, voters reject several prominent communist leaders in favor of Boris Yeltsin and other independents.

April 5: Polish roundtable talks end with agreement on political reform; free parliamentary elections scheduled for June.

April 6: Radio Budapest announces that a partial withdrawal of Soviet troops from Hungary would begin on April 25.

April 9: Soviet troops break up a Georgian nationalist demonstration in Tbilisi.

April 17: The independent Solidarity trade union is restored to legal status.

Soviet Union announces that withdrawal of ten thousand troops and a thousand tanks from the GDR will begin on May 11.

May 2: Part of the Iron Curtain between Hungary and Austria is dismantled.

May 8–9: Hungarian Socialist Worker Party relieves former general secretary János Kádár of posts as party president and Central Committee member.

May 19–20: Thousands of ethnic Turks stage protests in Bulgaria.

May 25: Gorbachev is elected head of state.

May 30–31: NATO Summit in Brussels endorses President Bush's CFE (Conventional Armed Forces in Europe) proposal for deep mutual reductions by 1990; Bush meets with Chancellor Kohl in Mainz, delivers a programmatic speech on ending the division of Europe.

June 2–7: Bulgaria expels hundreds of ethnic Turks.

June 4: The first round of Polish elections is held.

Peaceful demonstrators are massacred in Beijing's Tiananmen Square.

June 6: Solidarity wins 99 of 100 seats in the new Polish senate and 160 of 161 available seats in the Sejm.

June 13–15: President Gorbachev visits West Germany.

Government-opposition roundtable talks convene in Hungary.

June 16: Former prime minister Imre Nagy is reburied, with vast demonstration in tribute at Budapest's Heroes' Square.

July 6: Hungarian supreme court legally rehabilitates Nagy.

Gorbachev addresses Council of Europe in Strasbourg.

July 7–8: Warsaw Pact Summit, in Bucharest, affirms the right of member states to choose own domestic policies without interference.

July 9–12: President Bush visits Poland and Hungary, announces economic assistance measures.

Soviet miners begin strike.

July 15: In Paris, G-7 leaders issue declaration supporting economic and political freedom in Eastern Europe and call for an international conference to coordinate aid.

July 17: European Community foreign ministers meet in Brussels to discuss a coordinated aid program for Poland and Hungary.

July 19: General Wojciech Jaruzelski is elected president of Poland by the margin of a single vote.

Aug. 3: East Germans occupy West German mission in East Berlin and West German embassy in Budapest, seeking emigration visas.

Aug. 21: Large mass demonstration is held in central Prague on the anniversary of the 1968 Warsaw Pact Invasion.

Aug. 22–23: Lithuanian parliament declares the 1940 annexation of the Baltic states illegal; human chain across the Baltic republics marks the fiftieth anniversary of Hitler-Stalin pact.

Aug. 24: Tadeusz Mazowiecki becomes Poland's first noncommunist prime minister in forty years.

Aug. 25: Hungarian prime minister Németh visits West Germany.

Sept. 21–22: Prime Minister Shevardnadze and Secretary of State Baker meet in Wyoming.

Sept. 25: In the biggest spontaneous demonstration in the GDR, thousands march in Leipzig, calling for political reforms.

Sept. 29: Polish finance minister Balcerowicz presents economic "shock therapy" plan.

Oct. 5: More than seven thousand East German refugees are transported to West Germany.

Gorbachev attends the GDR's fortieth anniversary celebrations.

Oct. 7–9: Demonstrations erupt in East Berlin, Dresden, and other cities.

Oct. 10: Hungarian Socialist Workers party changes its name to Hungarian Socialist party.

Oct. 16: One hundred thousand East German protesters march through Leipzig.

CSCE conference opens in Sofia amidst demonstrations by Bulgarian "Ecoglasnost."

Oct. 18: Erich Honecker is replaced by Egon Krenz as East German Communist party leader.

Oct. 23: Three hundred thousand march in Leipzig and other cities.

A new Hungarian republic is proclaimed.

Oct. 24: West Germany announces aid package for Poland.

EC pledges $300 million to assist Poland and Hungary.

Oct. 25: France announces aid plan for Poland.

Oct. 26–27: At Warsaw Pact meeting in Warsaw, new Polish foreign minister Skubiszewski pledges to maintain friendly ties with the Warsaw Pact allies "on the principle of equal rights."

Oct. 30: Three hundred thousand march in Leipzig; protest spreads to other cities.

Nov. 3: Demonstrations break out in Bulgaria.

Nov. 4: One million demonstrate in East Berlin.

Nov. 7–8: Entire East German council of ministers and Politburo resign, with Krenz continuing as party leader.

Nov. 9–14: Kohl visits Poland (interrupted for trip to Berlin).

Nov. 9: The Berlin Wall is opened.

Nov. 11: Bulgarian Communist party leader Todor Zhivkov is replaced by Petŭr Mladenov.

Demonstration in Prague is suppressed by police.

Nov. 11–12: Foreign ministers of Hungary, Austria, Italy, and Yugoslavia meet in Budapest and pledge regional cooperation.

Nov. 13: Two hundred thousand protesters in Leipzig demand free elections and an end to one-party rule. Hans Modrow is appointed prime minister of the GDR.

Nov. 15: Lech Wałęsa speaks to joint session of U.S. Congress.

Nov. 16: Hungary applies to become the first East European member of the Council of Europe.

Nov. 18: EC leaders meet in Paris to discuss Eastern Europe.

Nov. 19–23: Spiraling demonstrations in Prague and Bratislava call for democracy. Václav Havel meets with prime minister Adamec. Alexander Dubček makes his first public speech in 21 years.

Nov. 23–27: Mazowiecki makes official visit to the Soviet Union.

Nov. 24–25: Miloš Jakeš resigns as Czechoslovak Communist party leader. Hundreds of thousands rally in Prague to listen to Havel and Dubček.

Nov. 27: Workers stage two-hour general strike throughout Czechoslovakia. Two hundred thousand East Germans demonstrate in Leipzig.

Nov. 28: Kohl announces a ten-point plan for German unification.

Dec. 2–3: Presidents Bush and Gorbachev meet at Malta.

Dec. 3: East German Politburo, including Krenz, resigns.

Dec. 4: NATO Summit in Brussels supports the goal of German unification as a "gradual, step-by-step process."

Dec. 4–5: Hundreds of thousands of demonstrators rally in Prague.

New Czechoslovak cabinet is formed; the majority is noncommunist.

Dec. 6: Krenz resigns as chairman of the National Defense Council.

Mitterrand meets Gorbachev in Kiev.

Dec. 7: In Bulgaria, independent organizations join to form the Union of Democratic Forces (UDF), with chairman Zhelyu Zhelev.

Czechoslovak prime minister Adamec resigns. First Deputy prime minister Čalfa named to form new government.

Dec. 8–9: EC Summit in Strasbourg supports German unification so long as it is embedded in European integration.

Dec. 10: Prodemocracy demonstrators in Sofia, organized by the Union of Democratic Forces, call for roundtable talks.

Dec. 16–17: Police and demonstrators clash in Timişoara, Romania, after police tried to evict pastor László Tökés from his home.

Dec. 18–20: Clashes continue in Timişoara, extend to other cities.

Yugoslav prime minister Ante Marković unveils economic and political reform package.

Lithuanian communists declare independence from the Soviet party leadership.

Dec. 20–21: Mitterrand pays state visit to GDR.

Dec. 22: State of emergency is declared in Romania. National Salvation Front declares itself the new government while clashes erupt between armed NSF supporters and Ceauşescu loyalists.

Dec. 25: Nicolae and Elena Ceauşescu, having been tried by a military tribunal and sentenced to death, are executed by firing squad.

Dec. 26: NSF appoints Ion Iliescu its president.

Dec. 29: Václav Havel is elected president of Czechoslovakia.

1990

Jan. 11: Gorbachev visits Lithuania in an effort to halt the proindependence movement.

Jan. 15: Gorbachev dispatches troops to Azerbaijan after anti-Armenian riots.

Jan. 31: In his State of the Union Address, President Bush proposes deeper conventional force reductions down in Europe to 195,000 on each side.

Feb. 10: Chancellor Kohl meets President Gorbachev in Moscow.

Feb. 12–17: Ethnic riots erupt in Tajikistan.

Feb. 13: American, Soviet, British, French, and German foreign ministers agree on Two Plus Four talks during meeting in Ottawa.

Feb 24–25: Kohl and Bush meet at Camp David.

Feb. 25: Demonstrations throughout USSR signal growing opposition to Gorbachev on both the Right and the Left.

March 11: Lithuania declares independence; Gorbachev denounces the move as "illegitimate and invalid."

March 13: The Soviet Congress of People's Deputies repeals the Communist party's monopoly on political power.

March 18: In East German elections, voters back the prounification party allied with Kohl's Christian Democratic Union.

March 25: József Antall and his Hungarian Democratic Forum win plurality in the Hungarian elections.

March 30: Estonia proclaims its independence.

April 9: Havel, Wałęsa, and Antall meet in Bratislava to discuss trilateral cooperation.

April 13: Gorbachev threatens an embargo of Lithuania.

April 28: EC Summit in Dublin prepares the integration of East Germany into the European Community.

May 4: The Latvian parliament declares independence and is branded illegal by Gorbachev.

May 5: First Two Plus Four meeting is held in Bonn.

May 18: Treaty on Economic, Monetary, and Social Union between the two German states is signed.

May 20: National Salvation Front led by Ion Iliescu wins elections in Romania.

May 29: Yeltsin is elected leader of the Russian parliament.

May 30–June 2: Bush-Gorbachev Summit is held in Washington and Camp David; arms control and trade agreements signed; Gorbachev concedes it is "up to the German people" to decide on NATO membership.

June 10–17: The Bulgarian Communist party wins over prodemocracy parties in national elections.

June 12: Russia declares its sovereignty.

June 14–15: Student protests in Bucharest are violently suppressed.

June 22: Second Two Plus Four meeting is held in East Berlin.

June 25–26: EC Summit in Dublin supports German unification.

July 1: Economies of the two German states are unified.

July 2–15: Twenty-eighth Soviet party congress is held in Moscow; Yeltsin resigns from the Communist party.

July 5–6: NATO Summit issues "London Declaration on a Transformed North Atlantic Alliance," invites Gorbachev and East European leaders to visit NATO headquarters and establish liaison missions.

July 9–11: G-7 Summit is held in Houston.

July 16: Gorbachev and Kohl, meeting in the Caucasus, agree that the united Germany will belong to NATO.

Ukraine declares its sovereignty.

July 17: Bulgarian roundtable discussions begin with UDF.

Third Two Plus Four meeting is held in Paris.

Aug. 2: Iraq invades Kuwait.

Following demonstrations, Zhelev is elected Bulgarian president.

Aug. 3: Árpád Göncz is elected president of Hungary.

Sept. 9: Bush meets with Gorbachev in Helsinki to discuss Iraq.

Sept. 12: Treaty on German unification is signed at fourth and final Two Plus Four meeting, in Moscow.

Oct. 3: East and West Germany unite.

Oct. 27–28: In Rome, EC decides that transition to second stage of economic and monetary union will take place on January 1, 1994.

Nov. 9: USSR and Germany sign treaty of friendship and cooperation.

Nov. 19–21: At CSCE Summit in Paris, European and North American leaders sign "Charter of Paris"; CFE agreement, NATO–Warsaw Pact nonaggression pact, and U.S.-EC declaration are also signed.

Nov. 23: Gorbachev proposes new union treaty that will loosen ties between the central Soviet government and the 15 republics.

Nov. 27: UN Resolution 678 authorizes use of force against Iraq.

Dec. 9: Lech Wałęsa is elected president of Poland.

Slobodan Milošević is reelected president of Serbia.

Dec. 11: Albania abandons one-party rule.

Dec. 20: Shevardnadze resigns, warning of a hard-line dictatorship.

Dec. 20–21: EC begins negotiations with Czechoslovakia, Hungary, and Poland on new association agreements.

1991

Jan. 1: Jan Krzysztof Bielecki is named prime minister of Poland.

Jan. 2: Soviet troops seize buildings in Vilnius.

Jan. 13: Fifteen are killed in a "Bloody Sunday" in Lithuania.

Jan. 16: Military action against Iraq begins.

Jan. 20: Four demonstrators are killed in a "Bloody Sunday" in Latvia.

Feb. 15: Wałęsa, Havel, and Antall sign "Visegrád Declaration" on regional cooperation among Poland, Czechoslovakia, and Hungary.

Feb. 20: Slovenian and Croatian parliaments propose the dissolution of the Yugoslav confederation into separate sovereign states.

Feb. 25: Military structures of Warsaw Pact are dissolved.

Feb. 27: Kuwait is liberated.

March 15: The United States recognizes Albania after 53-year hiatus.

March 17: Soviet citizens vote in favor of the union treaty, but six republics boycott.

March 31: In Albania's first free elections, the (ex-Communist) Labor party wins two-thirds of the vote.

April 9: The Georgian parliament unanimously declares independence.

April 15: European Bank for Reconstruction and Development opens.

April 23: Gorbachev, Yeltsin, and the presidents of eight other republics sign treaty of union.

May 29: Croatia declares its sovereignty.

June 4: Coalition government is formed in Albania.

June 12: Yeltsin is elected to the newly created Russian presidency.

In Prague, Mitterrand proposes European confederation.

June 25: Croatia and Slovenia declare independence.

June 27: The Yugoslav army intervenes in Slovenia.

July 6: Civic Alliance party is formed in Romania.

July 15–17: G-7 Summit in London announces six-point assistance plan for the USSR.

July 30–31: Moscow Summit is held between Presidents Bush and Gorbachev; START (Strategic Arms Reduction Treaty) is signed.

Aug. 18–19: Hard-liners stage coup attempt against Gorbachev. Boris Yeltsin calls for general strike and civil disobedience.

Aug. 24: Gorbachev, following failed coup attempt, resigns as head of the Communist party.

Ukrainian and Byelorussian parliaments declare independence.

Aug. 26–Sept. 5: Vukovar, Okucani, Danuvar, Dubrovnik, and other Croatian cities are shelled.

Aug. 29: The Soviet parliament bans Communist party activities.

Sept. 2: The United States recognizes the independence of the Baltic states.

Sept. 27: President Bush announces a series of unilateral arms control measures and calls on Soviet Union to reciprocate.

Oct. 15: UDF and ethnic Turkish Movement for Rights and Freedom (MRF) win Bulgarian elections.

Oct. 16: Bosnia-Herzegovina declares independence.

Oct. 27: Polish elections produce fragmented parliament, leading to protracted government crisis.

Nov. 7–8: NATO Summit in Rome adopts "new strategic concept" and invites countries of the former Warsaw Pact to join a new "North Atlantic Cooperation Council."

Dec. 1: Ukrainians vote for independence.

Dec. 8: Yeltsin and the leaders of Ukraine and Belarus declare the formation of a "Commonwealth of Independent States."

Dec. 11–12: EC Maastricht Summit convenes and treaty is signed.

Dec. 16: EC's "Europe" agreements with Poland, Hungary, and Czechoslovakia are signed.

Dec. 17: EC agrees to recognize Croatia and Slovenia as independent states by January 15, 1992.

Dec. 24: Germany recognizes Croatia and Slovenia.

Dec. 25: Gorbachev resigns. The USSR ceases to exist.

Notes

Preface

1. The scenario was not quite right: I did not foresee German unification but rather much closer ties between two independent German states, which would increasingly act together out of their shared interests. The speech itself was never published, but I developed elements of the argument in an essay written later in the year and published as "Soviet Dilemmas in Eastern Europe," in Richard F. Staar, ed., *U.S.–East European Relations in the 1990s* (New York: Crane Russak, 1989), pp. 15–34, esp. 30–31.

2. T. E. Lawrence, *Revolt in the Desert* (London: The Folio Society, 1986), p. 13. [An abridgment of Lawrence's *Seven Pillars of Wisdom*, *Revolt in the Desert* was first published by Jonathan Cape, London, 1927.]

3. Many of these documents will be printed and analyzed in a forthcoming (1997) issue of the Woodrow Wilson Center's Cold War International History Project *Bulletin*.

4. Before and after important events, it is common for senior officials to give background briefings to the press; Secretary Baker was the unrivaled master of the art. Of course they are incomplete and are sometimes used to give the administration's particular "spin" on events, but the overriding motivation is to inform. Sometimes political leaders need to maintain absolute secrecy on operational plans; much more often they want to keep the press informed, lest their initiatives fall on deaf ears. They want the media to understand the intent behind a major speech or foreign policy initiative; they would rather have their policies criticized on their merits (or demerits) than have them misinterpreted or ignored altogether.

5. Cited in Timothy Garton Ash, *In Europe's Name: Germany and the Divided Continent* (New York: Random House, 1993), p. 44.

Introduction

1. Elizabeth Pond, *Beyond the Wall: Germany's Road to Unification* (Washington, D.C.: The Brookings Institution, 1993), p. 186.

2. See, e.g., the three definitions presented in Chas. W. Freeman, Jr., *The Diplomat's Dictionary* (Washington, D.C.: National Defense University Press, 1994), pp. 364–65.

3. Paul Kennedy, *The Rise and Fall of the Great Powers* (New York: Random House, 1987), p. xv.

4. Isaiah Berlin, "The Hedgehog and the Fox," in Isaiah Berlin, *Russian Thinkers*, ed. Henry Hardy and Aileen Kelly (New York: Viking Press, 1978), p. 22.

5. On this point, see Keohane and Nye in their introduction to Robert O. Keohane, Joseph S. Nye, and Stanley Hoffmann, eds., *After the Cold War: International Institutions and State Strategies in Europe, 1989–1991* (Cambridge, Ma.: Harvard University Press, 1993), p. 16.

Chapter 1

1. Bush's admonition came even before the inauguration, along with tentative planning by his transition team. See James A. Baker, III, with Thomas M. DeFrank, *The Politics of Diplomacy: Revolution, War and Peace, 1989–92* (New York: G. P. Putnam's Sons, 1995), p. 40.

2. See, e.g., Mikhail Gorbachev, *Perestroika: New Thinking for Our Country and the World* (New York: Harper & Row, Publishers, 1987).

3. As cited in J. F. Brown, *Surge to Freedom: The End of Communist Rule in Eastern Europe* (Durham, N.C.: Duke University Press, 1991) p. 4.

4. "Report to the President by the National Security Council (NSC 58/2): United States Policy Toward the Soviet Satellite States in Eastern Europe," December 8, 1949, in *The Foreign Relations of the United States, 1949*, Vol. 5 (Washington, D.C.: U.S. Government Printing Office, 1976), pp. 42–54.

5. In an article written in the fall of 1988 and published in 1989, I concluded that "the advent of the Gorbachev leadership . . . heralded the end of an era in Eastern Europe. . . . Eastern Europe is entering a period of flux more profound than at any time since the immediate post-Stalin period. The Gorbachev era may not be so explosive, but it is likely to introduce changes more fundamental and lasting." (Robert L. Hutchings, "Soviet Dilemmas in Eastern Europe," in Richard F. Staar, ed., *U.S.–East European Relations in the 1990s* [New York: Crane Russak, 1989], pp. 16 and 30.) See also Lincoln Gordon et al., eds., *Eroding Empire: Western Relations with Eastern Europe* (Washington, D.C.: Brookings Institution, 1987) and William E. Griffith, ed., *Central and Eastern Europe: The Opening Curtain?* (Boulder, Co.: Westview Press, 1989).

6. For background, see Robert L. Hutchings, *Soviet–East European Relations: Consolidation and Conflict* (Madison: University of Wisconsin Press, 1983; rev. paperback ed., 1987).

7. *Current Digest of the Soviet Press*, January 4, 1989, p. 3.

8. Anatoli Chernyayev, speaking at a Princeton University conference devoted to "A Retrospective on the End of the Cold War," Session III, February 26, 1993.

9. In an interview with Don Oberdorfer in early May, William Hyland offered the same judgment: "If there is some kind of new order in Hungary, Poland and perhaps Czechoslovakia, with less of a Soviet presence, a substantial reduction of troops and liberalization inside the countries with multiparty elections and so on, then the question is whether that can be applied to East Germany. And if it is, aren't you just a step away from the unification of Germany?" (Don Oberdorfer, *The Turn: From the Cold War to a New Era* [New York: Simon and Schuster, 1991], p. 346.)

It was the same logic back in 1980–81 that caused East German party leader Erich Honecker to conclude that if Solidarity prevailed in Poland, East Germany was finished.

10. Indeed it was, though we had no way of knowing it at the time. According to Sergei Tarasenko, Shevardnadze had concluded after considering the results and implications of the Polish elections in June 1989 that Eastern Europe would probably "go." Cited by Timothy Garton Ash, *In Europe's Name: Germany and the Divided Continent* (New York: Random House, 1993), p. 124.

11. Baker, *Politics of Diplomacy*, pp. 47–60. See also Jay Winik, "The Quest for Bipartisanship: A New Beginning for a New World Order," *The Washington Quarterly* (Autumn 1991): 123 ff.

12. Prime Minister Thatcher described her concerns over SDI's possible impact on nuclear deterrence and the "earthquake" caused by President Reagan's proposal at Reykjavik for the complete elimination of U.S. and Soviet strategic nuclear weapons. See Margaret Thatcher, *The Downing Street Years* (New York: HarperCollins, 1993), pp. 462–73.

13. See, e.g., Gorbachev's July 1989 speech in Strasbourg, discussed at the end of this chapter.

14. Angela Stent, "The One Germany," *Foreign Policy* No. 81 (Winter 1990/91): 60.

15. Edwina Moreton, "The View from London," in Gordon et al., ed., *Eroding Empire*, p. 246.

16. Thatcher, *Downing Street Years*, pp. 452–53.

17. "Alliances in a Changing World: How to Manage the Thaw," speech given at the Wehrkunde conference in Munich, January 28, 1989, Verbatim Service VS010/89, London Press Service. See also Howe's similar remarks in speeches given at the close of the CSCE human rights meeting in Vienna, January 17 (VS005/89) and the opening of the Conventional Forces in Europe Conference, also in Vienna, March 6 (VS023/89).

18. Speech at a dinner given for President Gorbachev at No. 10 Downing Street, April 6, 1989, Verbatim Service VS031/89, London Press Service release of April 7.

19. Thatcher, *Downing Street Years*, p. 770. See also the discussion of her 1984 visit to Hungary, pp. 455–58, and her 1988 trip to Poland, pp. 777–82.

20. "Europe's Role in NATO's Fifth Decade," speech at the Royal United Services Institute, London, April 11, 1989, Verbatim Service VS033/89, London Press Service.

21. "Change in Eastern Europe and the Response of the West," speech given by the Honorable William Waldegrave, minister of state for foreign and commonwealth affairs, at the Great Britain/East Europe Center, London, July 6, 1989, Verbatim Service VS067/89, London Press Service.

22. Moreton, "The View from London," p. 246.

23. Sometimes termed, in the arms control acronym of the day, Short-Range Intermediate Nuclear Forces, or SRINF.

24. Thatcher, *Downing Street Years*, p. 786. Margaret Thatcher termed the meeting "acrimonious . . . behind [its] stage-managed friendliness" and, with an instinct for the jugular, characterized the chancellor as "deeply uncomfortable, as any politician will be whose instincts and principles push him one way while his short-term political interests push him the other" (p. 747).

25. Dominique Moïsi, "The French Foreign Policy: The Challenge of Adaptation," *Foreign Affairs* Vol. 67 (Fall 1988): 157–58.

26. Steven Philip Kramer, "The French Question," *The Washington Quarterly*, Autumn 1991, pp. 83–96; and Samuel F. Wells, Jr., "Mitterrand's International Policies," *The Washington Quarterly*, Summer 1988, pp. 59–75.

27. *Libération*, November 23, 1988.

28. Ronald Tiersky, "France in the New Europe," *Foreign Affairs* Vol. 71, No. 2 (Spring 1992): 131–46.

29. Dominique Moïsi, "French Policy Toward Central and Eastern Europe," in William E. Griffith, ed., *Central and Eastern Europe: The Opening Curtain?* (Boulder, Co.: Westview Press, 1989), pp. 353–65.

30. Valéry Giscard d'Estaing, "The Two Europes, East and West," Speech to the Royal Institute of International Affairs, London, July 1989, *International Affairs* Vol. 65, No. 4 (Autumn 1989): 657.

31. Pierre Hassner, "The View from Paris," in Gordon, ed., *Eroding Empire,* pp. 191–3; and Moïsi, "French Policy Toward Central and Eastern Europe," p. 354–5.

32. Thatcher evidently harbored similar sentiments. See *Downing Street Years,* pp. 796–98.

33. Interview with Radio France *Internationale,* March 26, 1989, *Service de Presse et d'Information, Ambassade de France a Londres* (Sp.St/LON/36/89), April 3, 1989.

34. *Libération,* November 23, 1988.

35. For a discussion of de Tocqueville's characterization of *agitation immobile* as a recurrent theme in French policy, see Hassner, "The View from Paris," p. 231.

36. *Economist,* May 27, 1989, p. 47, citing a 1988 West German poll.

37. Pierre Hassner, "Western European Perceptions of the USSR," *Daedalus* (Winter 1979), p. 145.

38. The stance of the SPD toward Solidarity was egregious from the beginning. Snubbing Wałęsa showed more timidity than was asked of the SPD, even by General Jaruzelski.

39. These conclusions are argued persuasively in Garton Ash, *In Europe's Name,* esp. pp. 362–71. As he notes, West German policy had the unintended effect of making these regimes more brittle by helping them avoid internal reform, but there is no evidence of such a fiendishly clever intent in the considerable documentary record of *Ostpolitik.*
    For their part, the East European regimes, beginning in the early 1970s, pursued a strategy of using Western trade and credits as a means of avoiding domestic reform and its attendant risks. See Hutchings, *Soviet–East European Relations,* pp. 10–11 and 192–205.

40. One colleague who harbored such concerns traced them to a speech he had heard Genscher deliver, in which the foreign minister had spoken for an hour about the FRG's past and present without once mentioning the United States or the Atlantic alliance.

41. There were a few in the Bush administration who harbored the worst suspicions of Genscher, but there was nothing like the broad anti-Genscher sentiment of the Reagan administration.

42. Speech at the 25th International *Wehrkunde* conference, February 6, 1988, as cited in Günter Müchler and Klaus Hofmann, *Helmut Kohl, Chancellor of German Unity: A Biography* (Bonn: Press and Information Office of the Federal Government, 1992), pp. 144–45.

43. Joffe, "The View from Bonn," pp. 151–53.

44. Horst Teltschik, "Gorbachev's Reform Policy and the Outlook for East-West Relations," *Aussenpolitik* Vol. 40, No. 3 (June 1989): 210.

45. Müchler and Hofmann *Helmut Kohl: Chancellor of German Unity,* p. 167; and Teltschik, "Gorbachev's Reform Policy," p. 212.

46. Teltschik, "Gorbachev's Reform Policy," p. 203.

47. F. M. Cornford, *Microcosmographia Academica* (Chicago: University of Chicago Press, 1945; first published in Great Britain by Bowes and Bowes, Cambridge, 1922), pp. 19–24. Another of his observations (p. 8), too impolitic to place in the main text of the present volume, also evokes the strategy reviews: "A caucus is like a mousetrap; when you are outside, you want to get in; and, when you are inside, the mere sight of the other mice makes you want to get out."

48. This was the "full NSC," in which other cabinet members participated depending on the issues under consideration. The "Principals Committee" was the same group without the president.

49. As an example, when I traveled as part of Secretary Baker's delegation, he usually invited me to attend his meetings with European counterparts—those being my NSC responsibility—but almost never with Soviet interlocutors.

50. The White House press corps was particularly prone to gossipmongering and trivialization, partly because they dealt with the whole range of domestic and foreign issues and partly because their stories almost always focused on personalities. Unless a speech or other policy initiative was backgrounded in advance, it was a given that its substance would be missed. The State Department press corps was much better.

51. See also Baker, *Politics of Diplomacy*, pp. 21–27.

52. Indeed, the Clinton administration opted initially for this model, particularly at the State Department, but soon found that they had paid a price in policy coherence.

53. The NSC staff's role in this period was particularly strong, owing not only to the president's activist foreign policy leadership but to the more prosaic fact that NSC staff members, unlike most of our counterparts at State and Defense, did not require Senate confirmation and hence were in place much earlier. Owing to the defeat of the Tower nomination, the Defense Department was at a special disadvantage: Secretary Cheney was not nominated until March, and many of his senior staff were not confirmed or even nominated until much later.

54. This was one of the all-too-rare periods when the NSC staff seized control of the drafting, coordinating (i.e., among other agencies as well as among White House offices), and revising of speeches. As the White House speech-writing staff had responsibility for all presidential speeches, foreign and domestic, the more common pattern on foreign policy addresses was a dog fight between NSC staff, which had responsibility for substance, and the speechwriters, who had responsibility for presentation. It was a muddy distinction that virtually guaranteed conflict and sometimes led to the chaotic situation of two versions of the same speech, one produced by the NSC and the other by the speechwriters, wending their way to the president at the same time. (At the State Department, by contrast, foreign policymakers, usually in the policy planning staff, wrote the speeches.)

55. In early 1989, as will be seen in Chapter 3, the main issue of contention in the "coupling" debate concerned FOTL, the Follow-on to the Lance missile.

56. Speech delivered at Hamtramck, Michigan, April 17, 1989, excerpted below in the present chapter.

57. Václav Havel, "An Anatomy of Reticence," in *Václav Havel, or Living in Truth*, trans. Jan Vladislav (London: Faber and Faber, 1986), p. 186.

58. The overall review was directed by Assistant Secretary of State (for European and Canadian Affairs) Rozanne Ridgway; the working group on U.S.-EC relations was chaired by Felix Block, whose laconic performance was perhaps explained by the fact that he was then under investigation on espionage charges and left the department shortly thereafter.

59. Thatcher, *Downing Street Years*, esp. pp. 768–69 and 813–14.

60. Memorandum from Brent Scowcroft to President Bush entitled "The NATO Summit," March 20, 1989, as cited in Philip Zelikow and Condoleezza Rice, *Germany Unified and Europe Transformed: A Study in Statecraft* (Cambridge: Harvard University Press, 1995), p. 28.

61. Cf. Michael R. Beschloss and Strobe Talbott, *At the Highest Levels* (Boston: Little, Brown and Co., 1993), pp. 7–71 *passim*, who offer persuasive evidence that the *pauza* was a deliberate, conscious policy decision, yet continue to imply that failure to engage Gorbachev was somehow a product of dithering.

Jack Matlock, U.S. ambassador to the Soviet Union at the time, makes a similar assertion in his memoirs but offers no argument to support his chapter title, "Washington Fumbles," except for vague and unpersuasive calls for economic engagement. (Jack F. Matlock, Jr., *Autopsy on an Empire: The American Ambassador's Account of the Collapse of the Soviet Union* [New York: Random House, 1995], pp. 177–200.) It was an oddly defensive complaint, particularly in that Matlock's main recommendations, as will be seen below, were endorsed in the president's policy of "testing" Gorbachev.

62. One prominent Kremlinologist predicted over the course of several years that Gorbachev would be out of office "within six months." Eventually he was proved right.

63. *American Foreign Policy Current Documents 1989*, ed. Nancy L. Golden and Sherrill Brown Wells (Washington, D.C.: U.S. Department of State, 1990), pp. 354–56.

64. "Address by Secretary of State Baker before the Center for Strategic and International Studies, May 4, 1989," Department of State *Bulletin*, July 1989, pp. 36–39.

65. Baker, *Politics of Diplomacy*, p. 70.

66. These points were also made in Baker's CSIS speech, esp. pp. 38–9.

67. This long cable, entitled "U.S.-Soviet Relations: Policy Opportunities," was declassified and made available by the National Security Archive, Washington, D.C., along with two other Matlock cables dated February 3 and 13, as a briefing book for a conference on "Cold War Endgame," Princeton University, March 29–30, 1996. See also Matlock's account in *Autopsy on an Empire*, pp. 186–90.

68. Beschloss and Talbott, *At the Highest Levels*, p. 8.

69. Michael Mandelbaum was asking exactly the same question at this time. See his prescient "Ending the Cold War," *Foreign Affairs* Vol. 68 (Spring 1989), p. 19.

70. It is interesting that Gorbachev's principal adviser, Anatoli Chernyayev, subsequently criticized Gorbachev on precisely these grounds, for seeing U.S.-Soviet arms negotiations as the essence of East-West relations.

71. "U.S.-Soviet Relations: An Agenda for the Future," A Report to the Forty-first President of the United States, Foreign Policy Institute, School of Advanced International Studies, The Johns Hopkins University, Washington, D.C., December 1988, p. 4.

72. Valéry Giscard d'Estaing, Yasuhiro Nakasone, and Henry A. Kissinger, *East–West Relations: A Report to the Trilateral Commission* (New York: Trilateral Commission, 1989). An adapted version of the report was also published in *Foreign Affairs* Vol. 68 (Summer 1989): 1–21.

73. Mandelbaum's "Ending the Cold War" is a notable exception, which holds up better than any of its contemporaries in the light of all that transpired since its publication in spring 1989. His diagnosis that "the core of the Cold War in Europe is Soviet domination of Eastern Europe," as well as his prescription of self-determination in that region, were precisely those being reached in the upper levels of the Bush administration at the

time. So was his judgment that "the division of Germany will be the last part of the cold war in Europe to be liquidated." We were both wrong on that point.

74. Giscard d'Estaing et al., *East–West Relations*, pp. 7 and 13.

75. National Security Directive 23 (SECRET), "United States Relations with the Soviet Union," The White House, September 22, 1989; declassifed November 1, 1995. Released under the Freedom of Information Act, copy courtesy of National Security Archive, Washington, D.C. (Although not signed until September, the document was drafted and approved in substance in the spring of 1989.)

76. The "plan," together with Secretary Baker's rejection of any U.S.-Soviet "arrangement" for Eastern Europe, is described in Thomas L. Friedman, "Baker, Outlining World View, Assesses Plan for Soviet Bloc," *New York Times*, March 27, 1989.

77. Although Baker flirted with Kissinger's idea of engaging the Soviets directly on Eastern Europe, the idea of cutting a deal with Moscow was never considered. See the accounts in Baker, *Politics of Diplomacy*, p. 40, and Matlock, *Autopsy on an Empire*, p. 190–92.

78. This was among the conclusions of the president's February 12, 1989, meeting with Soviet experts in Kennebunkport, as described in Beschloss and Talbott, *At the Highest Levels*, pp. 22–3.

79. Oberdorfer, *The Turn*, p. 330.

80. In his memoirs, written with Brent Scowcroft, President Bush notes that Eastern Europe figured prominently in their daily strategy sessions during January 1989. Scowcroft, in the same memoirs, called the emerging policy toward Eastern Europe one of "gentle rollback." (Forthcoming from Alfred A. Knopf, Inc.; draft manuscript shared with the author in July 1996.)

81. On Hungarian reactions to the speech, see Thatcher, *Downing Street Years*, p. 455.

82. Beschloss and Talbott, *At the Highest Levels*, pp. 53–4.

83. Through Ambassador John Davis and others in Embassy Warsaw, our contacts with Solidarity were particularly close. My own contacts during the period included meetings in Warsaw with, among others, Bronisław Geremek, the courageous and brilliant adviser to Solidarity, in early 1988, at the time of the so-called anti-crisis pact that led to the roundtable talks, and again in May 1989, when Polish strategists were worrying about how to translate the Roundtable Agreement into an action plan.

84. Ash, *In Europe's Name*, p. 123.

85. The speeches were compiled in *Beyond Containment: Selected Speeches of President George Bush on Europe and East-West Relations, April 17–June 2, 1989* (Washington, United States Information Agency, 1989). See also *American Foreign Policy Current Documents 1989*.

86. See Chapter 3 below for a thorough review of the administration's failed policies toward Yugoslavia.

87. This was a more ambitious version of the approach advocated by Graham Allison in "Testing Gorbachev," *Foreign Affairs* Vol. 67, No. 4 (Fall 1988): 19–32.

88. The only specific offers on the U.S. side were to explore once again Eisenhower's "Open Skies" proposal for aerial overflights and a pledge to work toward extending most favored nation trade status if Soviet emigration laws were codified and implemented in accordance with international standards. Although the American media predictably focused

on the "initiatives," or lack thereof, these were peripheral to what was meant to be a conceptual speech articulating U.S. policy for the longer term.

89. This is precisely how Shevardnadze saw the speech: "Are the Americans willing to do *nothing* to help us? Are *we* the ones who have to make all the moves? We take these huge steps and all we hear from Washington is, '*More! More! You must do more!*'" Cited in Beschloss and Talbott, *At the Highest Levels,* p. 60.

90. These often contentious aspects of U.S.-European relations after 1989 are covered in Chapters 4 and 7.

91. For details of the debate, see Beschloss and Talbott, *At the Highest Levels,* pp. 74–80.

92. See Chapter 3.

93. This refers to the Conference on Security and Cooperation in Europe (CSCE) and the process begun at the 1975 Helsinki Summit of 35 European and North American leaders.

94. Garton Ash, *In Europe's Name,* p. 3. Garton Ash, again getting the point that others missed, also draws the contrast between the Gorbachev and Bush speeches.

95. Speech to the West German Bundestag, embassy of the Federal Republic of Germany, London, April 27, 1989, as cited in Lawrence Freedman, ed., *Europe Transformed: Documents on the End of the Cold War* (New York: St. Martin's Press, 1990), p. 281.

96. "Declaration of the Heads of State and Government Participating in the Meeting of the North Atlantic Council in Brussels (29th–30th May 1989)," NATO Press Service, May 30, 1989, pp. 6–8. Emphasis added.

Chapter 2

1. In November 1987, brutal repression ensued in Braşov after several thousand workers marched to the center of the city and sacked the local party headquarters. Moruzi, a naturally ebullient man, recounted how he went into an almost clinical depression during these years, as hopeful events transpiring elsewhere in the region contrasted starkly with the deepening repression in his own country.

2. Poland and Hungary were exceptions, in that fear had long since lost much of its grip. Yet even in those countries, there was fear of losing one's job, of being denied travel opportunities, and of having one's children denied entrance into university.

3. Alexis de Tocqueville, *The Old Regime and the French Revolution,* trans. Stuart Gilbert (Garden City, N.Y.: Doubleday & Doubleday, Inc., 1955), p. 204.

4. Statement by the Press Secretary, White House Press Office, December 29, 1989.

5. J. F. Brown, *Surge to Freedom: The End of Communist Rule in Eastern Europe* (Durham, N.C. and London: Duke University Press, 1991), pp. 1–5.

6. Ronald D. Asmus, J. F. Brown, and Keith Crane, *Soviet Foreign Policy and the Revolutions of 1989 in Eastern Europe* (Santa Monica, Ca.: The RAND Corporation, 1991), pp. 134–36.

7. Michael Howard, "The Springtime of Nations," *Foreign Affairs* Vol. 69, No. 1 (Winter 1989–90): 17–32.

8. Garton Ash, *In Europe's Name,* p. 44.

9. I was Deputy Director of Radio Free Europe at the time, and remember vividly being called to the office in the early morning hours of December 13, 1981, where I lis-

tened in stunned disbelief to General Jaruzelski's 6:00 a.m. speech explaining that Solidarity had been outlawed and its leaders imprisoned.

10. Timothy Garton Ash, "The Empire in Decay," *New York Review of Books* Vol. 35, No. 14 (September 29, 1988): 53–60, and the other two articles (in Nos. 15 and 16, October 13 and 27, 1988) in his three-part series on Eastern Europe. See also David K. Shipler, "Letter from Budapest," *New Yorker,* November 20, 1989, pp. 74–99.

11. Timothy Garton Ash makes this point in *The Magic Lantern: The Revolutions of '89 Witnessed in Warsaw, Budapest, Berlin and Prague* (New York: Random House, 1990), p. 68.

12. See Chapter 1.

13. Michael Beschloss and Strobe Talbott, *At the Highest Levels: The Inside Story of the End of the Cold War* (New York: Little, Brown and Company, 1993), pp. 80–81, quote Chief of Staff John Sununu as saying the "game plan" was to "whip Western Europe into line, then turn everyone's attention to Eastern Europe." It might have been stated more elegantly, but that was the general idea.

14. Gale Stokes, *The Walls Came Tumbling Down* (New York: Oxford University Press, 1993), pp. 146 and 162; Brown, *Surge to Freedom*, pp. 191 and 211.

15. The text is reprinted in Bernard Wheaton and Zdeněk Kavan, *The Velvet Revolution: Czechoslovakia, 1988–91* (Boulder, Co.: Westview Press, 1992), pp. 196–97.

16. Western observers made more of the demonstration effect of Soviet reforms. For most East Europeans, what was happening in the USSR was remote; it might or might not have any significance for them. Poland and Hungary were different: their progress, meaning their ability to implement democratic change without reprisal from Moscow or their own regimes, was seen as much more directly relevant to Czechoslovakia, Bulgaria, Romania, and the GDR.

17. For an interesting assessment of President Bush's approach (drawn partly from George Bush with Victor Gold, *Looking Forward* [New York: Doubleday, 1987]), see Joseph G. Whelan, *Soviet Diplomacy and Negotiating Behavior, 1988–90*, U.S. Congress, Committee on Foreign Affairs, Vol. III (Washington, D.C.: U.S. Government Printing Office, 1991), pp. 149–211.

18. These aspects of power evoked—to this staffer, at least—passages from Thucydides. Bush as Pericles?!

19. Among these were the Confederation for an Independent Poland (KPN, in its Polish acronym) and "Fighting Solidarity," which was calling for a violent showdown with the communist regime.

20. Beschloss and Talbott, *At the Highest Levels*, p. 85.

21. János Kis, "The Challenge of Democracy in Eastern Europe," paper presented at a conference on democratic revolution organized by the National Endowment for Democracy, Washington, D.C., May 1, 1989.

22. The leader of the Polish team was Vice Foreign Minister Jan Majewski, with whom I was to have subsequent (not altogether pleasant) experience negotiating the first ever U.S.-Polish "Declaration of Principles," signed by Presidents Bush and Wałęsa during the latter's March 1991 state visit to the United States.

23. The Roundtable accords provided for the restoration of the senate, an institution which had existed from 1919 to 1939 and was abolished by the postwar government after a fraudulent referendum in 1946. See Abraham Brumberg, "Poland: The Demise of Communism," *Foreign Affairs* Vol. 69, No. 1 (Winter 1989/90), pp. 79–80.

24. I.e., the Polish United Workers party and its "satellite" or "bloc" parties, the United Peasants party and the Democratic party.

25. Lawrence Weschler, "A Grand Experiment," *New Yorker,* November 13, 1989, p. 65.

26. Garton Ash, *The Magic Lantern,* p. 29. As Garton Ash notes, pp. 29–32, the elections embraced three related but separate surprises: the Communists lost, Solidarity won, and the Communists acknowledged that Solidarity won.

27. Cited in Stokes, *The Walls Came Tumbling Down,* p. 127.

28. Nyers, architect of Hungary's New Economic Mechanism launched in 1968, went on to succeed Grósz as party leader in October 1989.

29. In addition to the near sweep by Solidarity candidates, the traditional "bloc" parties (nominally independent but in fact aligned with the communists), the Democratic party and the United Peasants party, were evincing a new-found independence and refusing to support Jaruzelski's presidential nomination.

30. Oberdorfer, *The Turn,* pp. 351–2.

31. Beschloss and Talbott, *At the Highest Levels,* pp. 81–2.

32. *The Current Digest of the Soviet Press* Vol. XLI, No. 27, (1989), p. 6.

33. Hungarian television, July 9, 1989, as cited in Vladimir V. Kusin, "Mikhail Gorbachev's Evolving Attitude to Eastern Europe," *Radio Free Europe Research,* RAD Background Report/128, July 20, 1989, p. 4.

34. In the runup to the Polish elections, for example, *Izvestia* warned that "the election campaigns for the Sejm and senate have taken on the undertones planned by the secret orchestrators of anti-socialism and anti-Sovietism. It is no accident that the disturbances have broken out precisely at a time of favorable prospects for change in Poland and for Polish-Soviet relations." (*Izvestia,* May 21, 1989, *Current Digest of the Soviet Press,* Vol. XLI, No. 20 [1989], p. 20.) *Pravda,* commenting on the reburial of Imre Nagy in Hungary, likewise warned of "anti-Soviet attacks" and quoted FIDESz leader Viktor Orbán as calling for "smashing the communist dictatorship." (*Pravda,* June 17, 1989, *Current Digest of the Soviet Press,* Vol. XLI, No. 24 [1989], p. 27.) See also Garton Ash, *The Magic Lantern,* p. 41, on how Solidarity strategists in Poland viewed the mixed signals emanating from Moscow.

35. This was the usual formulation for "on background" briefings to the press when the speaker did not wish to be named. In this case, the "senior administration official" was Ambassador Robert Blackwill, NSC senior director for Soviet and European affairs.

36. "Background Briefing by Senior Administration Official," Office of the Press Secretary, The White House, July 7, 1989.

37. "Remarks by the President at Joint Session of Parliament, The Sejm, Warsaw," Office of the Press Secretary, The White House, July 10, 1989. The reference to redeeming the Atlantic Charter was of course particularly poignant to the Poles, for it was precisely those principles, they believed, that were sacrificed at Yalta.

38. This congruity was soon to acquire significance in the opposite sense, as we sought to launch arms control initiatives that would enable military reductions to keep pace with the breakneck speed of political change.

39. Mikhail Gorbachev, *Perestroika: New Thinking for Our Country and the World* (New York: Harper & Row, Publishers, 1987), p. 143. I recall looking long and hard for that quote on the eve of the president's departure. It would have been even better to have used a line from Gorbachev's Council of Europe speech, delivered just two days before the president spoke in Warsaw.

40. These included preferential trade access through the generalized system of preferences, authorization for OPIC (Overseas Private Investment Corporation) operations in Poland, support for World Bank loans, debt-for-equity swaps, and generous Paris Club rescheduling of Polish official debts.

41. As will be seen in Chapter 5, the Enterprise Funds, for which the Council of Economic Advisers deserves the most credit, turned out to be the most successful of all U.S. assistance efforts.

42. We had in mind the example of former Polish party leader Edward Gierek's exploitation of Western loans and credits for political ends.

43. This is not to say we had reached definitive judgment on the longstanding debate as to whether Jaruzelski was "Polish patriot or Soviet stooge," but it was in our interests, and Poland's, to accentuate the former aspect. It was a matter not of analysis, but of policy.

44. Oberdorfer, *The Turn,* pp. 359–60; and Beschloss and Talbott, *At the Highest Levels,* p. 89.

45. Mieczysław F. Rakowski, *Jak to sie stało?* [How did it happen?] (Warsaw: Polska Oficyna Wydawnicza "BGW," 1991), p. 238.

46. Rakowski got the point; Beschloss and Talbott (*At the Highest Levels,* pp. 87–89), did not. They asserted, wrongly, that President Bush was trying to "prop up" Jaruzelski and favored "familiar processes and gradual, orderly change, even at the sacrifice of democratic ideals."

47. Rakowski, *Jak to sie Stało?,* p. 240; and Witold Beres and Jerzy Skoczyslas, *General Kiszczaks Mowi . . . Prawie Wszystko* [General Kiszczak tells us . . . almost everything] (Warsaw: Polska Oficyna Wydawnicza "BGW," 1991), p. 272.

48. Garton Ash, *The Magic Lantern,* pp. 37–9; and Stokes, *The Walls Came Tumbling Down,* pp. 127–28.

49. Garton Ash, *The Magic Lantern,* pp. 36–7.

50. *Népszabadság* and *Magyar Hirlap,* July 12, 1989, as cited in *Radio Free Europe Research,* Hungarian Situation Report/13, August 18, 1989, p. 19.

51. "Remarks by the President at the Karl Marx University of Economics," Office of the Press Secretary, The White House (Budapest), July 12, 1989.

52. The apt term comes from László Bruszt, "Hungary's Negotiated Revolution," *Social Research* 57 (1990): 365–87.

53. Beschloss and Talbott, *At the Highest Levels,* p. 90.

54. A year later, having developed close relations with the government of Prime Minister Antall, leader of the Hungarian Democratic Forum, we were perceived as having thrown our support behind the center-right. It was hard to persuade the highly partisan Hungarian political elite that the United States really did not much care whether it was the center-right, center-left or some other configuration that governed Hungary, so long as the country was moving toward democracy and free markets.

55. Some of the particulars of the meeting were reported by Reuters, AP, and UPI, July 12, 1989.

56. Thatcher, *Downing Street Years,* p. 753.

57. The long Economic Declaration was confined mainly to broad general commitments, including a long section on environmental issues, and hortatory language such as calling for "further substantial progress in the Uruguay Round [of the General Agreement on Tariffs and Trade] in order to complete it by the end of 1990." The summit documents

were reprinted in the Department of State *Bulletin,* Vol. 89, No. 2150 (September 1989), pp. 1–3 and 13–17.

58. Horst Teltschik, "Gorbachev's Reform Policy and the Outlook for East-West Relations," *Aussenpolitik* III/89 (June 1989): 201–14; and Günter Müchler and Klaus Hofmann, *Helmut Kohl: Chancellor of German Unity* (Bonn: Press and Information Office of the Federal Government, 1992), pp. 158–61 and 167–71.

59. Horst Teltschik, "The Federal Republic and Poland—A Difficult Partnership in the Heart of Europe," *Aussenpolitik* I/90 (January 1990): 3–14; and Müchler and Hofmann, *Helmut Kohl,* pp. 162 and 172–80. See also *Keesing's* Record of World Events, News Digest, July 1989, p. 36830.

60. *New York Times,* July 7, 1989, I, 3:3.

61. This agreement was affirmed in the summit's "Declaration on East-West Relations," in which the G-7 countries pledged "to work along with other interested countries and multilateral institutions to concert support for the process of reform underway in Hungary and Poland" and called for a "meeting with all interested countries . . . in the next few weeks." Seconding the concept of "testing" Soviet intentions, the declaration also called "upon the Soviet Government to translate its new policies and pronouncements into further concrete action at home and abroad."

62. Poland, Czechoslovakia, and other countries had been invited to participate in the Marshall Plan but were denied that possibility by Stalin.

63. "Remarks by the President to the Residents of Leiden," The Pieterskerk, Leiden, The Netherlands, July 17, 1989, White House press release of that day.

64. James A. Baker, III, with Thomas M. DeFrank, *The Politics of Diplomacy: Revolution, War and Peace, 1989–92* (New York: G. P. Putnam's Sons, 1995), pp. 135–42.

65. *Ibid.,* pp. 140–1. These points of agreement were further cemented during Baker's three-day meeting with Shevardnadze at Jackson Hole, Wyoming, September 21–24, 1989. See Baker's account in *ibid.,* pp. 144–52.

66. *New York Times,* August 22, 1989.

67. Oberdorfer, *The Turn,* p. 399.

68. Garton Ash, *In Europe's Name,* p. 124, cites Sergei Tarasenko as saying that Shevardnadze had concluded after the Polish elections that Eastern Europe would probably "go."

69. Garton Ash, *The Magic Lantern,* pp. 39–45. (The transportation ministry was critical to Moscow because of the transit routes between the USSR and East Germany.)

70. This was not quite the specific intervention by Gorbachev that was widely reported at the time. See Stokes, *The Walls Came Tumbling Down,* pp. 129–30.

71. *Deutsche Presse Agentur,* August 28, 1989, as cited in Brown, *Surge to Freedom,* p. 57.

72. Associated Press, August 27, 1989, as reprinted in Gale Stokes, *From Stalinism to Pluralism: A Documentary History of Eastern Europe since 1945* (New York: Oxford University Press, 1991), pp. 240–42.

73. The plan, involving radical measures to halt hyperinflation, stabilize the Polish *zloty,* decontrol prices, and create the foundations of a market economy, was drawn from the reform strategy of Harvard economist Jeff Sachs, as outlined in Jeffrey Sachs and David Lipton, "Poland's Economic Reform," *Foreign Affairs* Vol. 69, No. 3 (Summer 1990): 47–66. For a more detailed description, see David Lipton and Jeffrey Sachs, "Creating a Market Economy in Eastern Europe: The Case of Poland," *Brookings Papers on Economic Activity,* 1990:1.

74. Statement by the Press Secretary, The White House, October 4, 1989. The statement, which began, "The world has watched with wonder . . ." included an invitation to both Mazowiecki and Jaruzelski to pay separate visits to the United States "at times convenient to each of them." Mazowiecki came on a state visit in March 1990; a Jaruzelski visit was postponed several times before being canceled altogether.

75. On the EC's assistance program, including the controversy over the European Bank, see Chapter 5.

76. There was a political dimension to this as well. Most of our West European partners could extend loans and lines of credit by executive decision, while we, because of credit reform, had to have a budgetary offset requiring congressional approval for every loan. These offsets ran to 50 percent and more of the loan amount for countries with credit ratings as low as the East Europeans' then were.

77. *New York Times*, November 15, 1989, A22.

78. As is described in Chapter 8, the rush of events caused us to neglect one that would soon come back to haunt us: a mid-October visit to Washington by Yugoslav prime minister Ante Marković, desperately seeking economic and political support.

79. These were SzDSz (Free Democratic party) and FIDESz (Confederation of Young Democrats), respectively.

80. Für was the MDF's initial presidential candidate in October but ultimately made way for the Free Democrats' Árpád Göncz, elected as a result of a compromise with the MDF.

81. *New York Times*, October 19, 1989, I, 3:5; and Ash, *The Magic Lantern*, pp. 58–9.

82. By the time Imre Pozsgay met with General Scowcroft in Washington November 2, it was clear that the reform wing of the newly renamed Hungarian Socialist party had been eclipsed, along with Pozsgay's presidential ambitions.

On December 15, I met with József Antall and Géza Jeszensky, who were already looking beyond the scheduled March elections toward their new responsibilities as leaders of a democratic Hungary. Antall's firm Atlanticism, despite his reputation of being a Germanophile, was already firmly entrenched in his thinking in December 1989. (When I next met with them in the course of 1990, I observed that they had gone from being obscure Hungarian opposition figures to prime minister and foreign minister, respectively, while I was still in the same job.)

83. *Washington Post*, September 19, 1993. Here again was the interplay between Hungarian and Polish events: had a Polish official spoken openly about neutrality, this might well have provoked a reaction in Moscow, yet a Hungarian official's doing so strengthened the hand of the new Mazowiecki government in its evolving relationship with Jaruzelski's presidency.

84. Szürös met with General Scowcroft at the White House on the 19th. Following the required notification period, the United States formally extended permanent MFN status to Hungary in a White House ceremony on October 4.

85. The sequence of events was as follows. Hungarian prime minister Németh and foreign minister Horn visited West German Foreign Minister Genscher in Bonn on August 25. Horn flew to East Berlin September 1 to suspend the bilateral travel agreement. On September 10, in Budapest, Horn announced that Hungary's borders were open to any GDR citizens wishing to leave for West Germany via Austria.

86. *New York Times*, September 15, 1989, I, 10:1; and Elizabeth Pond, *Beyond the Wall: Germany's Road to Unification* (Washington, D.C.: The Brookings Institution, 1993), p. 96.

87. *New York Times,* August 14, 1989, I, 3:1.

88. Pond, *Beyond the Wall,* pp. 97–98. Honecker's decision to oblige asylum-seekers to return to the GDR before proceeding to West Germany only fueled popular discontent.

89. E.g., Elizabeth Pond's interview with Genscher, as cited in *Beyond the Wall,* p. 98.

90. "Walters: German Unity Soon: U.S. Ambassador Envisions an Early Reunification," screamed the front page of the *International Herald Tribune,* The Hague, Monday, September 4, 1989. The same story quoted East German foreign minister Oskar Fischer as warning that anyone who tries to redraw the map of Europe "plays with fire."

91. Garton Ash, *In Europe's Name,* p. 594, explains that Gorbachev's remark, delivered behind closed doors in a meeting with the East German party leadership, was somewhat differently phrased and did not explicitly refer to the situation in the GDR. Yet it was the shorthand version that stuck and had the political impact.

92. Speech at the GDR fortieth anniversary celebration, as cited in Michael J. Sodaro, *Moscow, Germany, and the West* (Ithaca, N.Y.: Cornell University Press, 1990), p. 377.

93. Pond, *Beyond the Wall,* pp. 112–20.

94. Sodaro, *Moscow, Germany, and the West,* p. 379.

95. Brown, *Surge to Freedom,* p. 181.

96. Stokes, *The Walls Came Tumbling Down,* pp. 147–48, and Professor Stokes's transcript of the interview, which he generously made available to me.

97. A similar debate within the administration took place at this time over U.S. participation in a CSCE human rights conference scheduled for Moscow in 1991. The outcome of the debate was provisional agreement to participate, subject to ongoing review of the Soviet human rights record. By the time of the conference, which we did attend, our reservations had long since been overtaken by events.

98. Stokes, *The Walls Came Tumbling Down,* pp. 147–48.

99. *Ibid.,* p. 148.

100. On November 13, the *New York Times* reported from Prague on the small turnout of ten thousand for a demonstration in Wenceslas Square; a week later, it was recounting a massive gathering of two hundred thousand in the same square. See Bernard Gwertzman and Michael T. Kaufman, eds., *The Collapse of Communism* (New York: Times Books, 1990), pp. 200–201 and 229–32.

101. *New York Times,* November 18, 1989, I, 6:1.

102. Garton Ash, *The Magic Lantern,* p. 80.

103. Kňažko, who later became Slovakia's foreign minister, bore a striking resemblance to the American actor Glenn Ford in the latter's younger days. A charismatic figure with a sense of irony more common in Czechs than Slovaks, he would be my chief interlocutor in Slovakia when I directed the U.S. assistance program in 1992 and 1993.

104. For details of the summit, see below in the present chapter and in Chapter 3.

105. Garton Ash, *The Magic Lantern,* p. 122.

106. Nestor Ratesh, *Romania: The Entangled Revolution* (New York: Praeger Publishers, 1991), p. 78.

107. Brown, *Surge to Freedom,* p. 219.

108. White House press release, December 22, 1989.

109. I well recall spending nearly all of Christmas Day on the secure phone at home, at one point calling (via pager) Bob Gates out of a movie theater with his family.

110. The most extravagant interpretations went so far as to link Baker's remark to a U.S.-Soviet conspiracy to unseat Ceauşescu and install the NSF. (See, e.g., Andrei Codrescu, *The Hole in the Flag* [New York: William Morrow and Co., Inc., 1991], pp. 205–6.) The reality was more prosaic. We had no prior knowledge of the Romanian Revolution or of any coup-in-the-making, nor were we in any way colluding with Moscow before, during, or after these events. Our contacts with Moscow as the revolution unfolded were much like our contacts with Bonn, London, Paris, and other capitals, with whom we compared notes and tried to ensure coordinated international support on behalf of prodemocracy forces. With Moscow as with others, there was a broadly shared desire to see Ceauşescu loyalists defeated, the bloodshed ended, and the democratic "spirit of Timişoara" vindicated, as well as agreement that the outside world should lend its qualified support to the NSF-led provisional government.

111. *New York Times,* December 24 and 25, 1989; Statement by the press secretary, the White House, December 25, 1989.

112. Beschloss and Talbott, *At the Highest Levels,* pp. 170–1. In his memoirs, President Bush recounts that Gorbachev told him during their meeting off Malta that "some are saying the Brezhnev Doctrine is being replaced by the Bush Doctrine." (Forthcoming from Alfred A. Knopf, Inc.)

113. For thorough accounts of these events, see Ratesh, *Romania: The Entangled Revolution,* esp. pp. 80–119; Martyn Rady, *Romania in Turmoil* (London: I. B. Taurus & Co., Ltd., 1992); and Matei Calinescu and Vladimir Tismaneanu, "The 1989 Revolution and Romania's Future," *Problems of Communism* (January–April 1990), pp. 42–59. For an exposition of the "hijack" theory, see Trond Gilberg, "Romania: Will History Repeat Itself?" *Current History* (December 1990), pp. 409–12.

114. Garton Ash, *The Magic Lantern,* p. 97, recounts that one of the drafters of a Civic Forum declaration in late November inadvertently wrote "Democratic Forum," before saying, "Oh, sorry, I was thinking of Hungary."

115. Radio GDR II interview with Otto Reinhold, rector of the party's Academy of Social Sciences, August 19, 1989, as cited in Brown, *Surge to Freedom,* p. 125,

116. A third, not very plausible option for the GDR would have been to strike a deal with Bonn, presumably to avert a chaotic breakdown of order.

117. That there was serious consideration, in Moscow as well as East Berlin, of a military crackdown long after October 9 is likely but so far undocumented.

118. From the "Report of the Commission of Enquiry on the Events Surrounding November 17," published in October 1990, as cited in Wheaton and Kavan, *The Velvet Revolution,* p. 72.

119. See, e.g., Samuel Huntington, *The Third Wave* (Oklahoma City: University of Oklahoma Press, 1991); Terry Lynn Karl and Philippe C. Schmitter, "Modes of Transition in Latin America, Southern and Eastern Europe," *International Social Science Journal* Vol. 128 (May 1991): 273–84; and Juan J. Linz, "Transitions to Democracy," *The Washington Quarterly,* Summer 1990, pp. 143–64.

120. Memorandum from Brent Scowcroft (drafted by Condoleezza Rice) to President Bush entitled "The Soviets and the German Question," November 29, 1989, cited in Philip Zelikow and Condoleezza Rice, *Germany Unified and Europe Transformed: A Study in Statecraft* (Cambridge: Harvard University Press, 1995), p. 125.

Chapter 3

1. On the diplomacy of German unification from key advisers to Chancellor Kohl and Foreign Minister Genscher respectively, see Horst Teltschik, *329 Tage: Innenansichten der Einigung* (Berlin: Siedler Verlag, 1991); and Frank Elbe and Richard Kiessler, *Ein Runder Tisch mit Scharfen Ecken* (Baden-Baden: Nomos Verlags Gesellschaft, 1993). The internal aspects are authoritatively covered by then West German interior minister Wolfgang Schäuble, *Der Vertrag: Wie Ich Über die Deutsche Einheit Verhandelte* (Stuttgart: Deutsche Verlags-Anstalt, 1991).

2. Elizabeth Pond, *Beyond the Wall: Germany's Road to Unification* (Washington, D.C.: The Brookings Institution, 1993), p. 186.

3. Timothy Garton Ash, *In Europe's Name: Germany and the Divided Continent* (New York: Random House, 1993), p. 363.

4. Alexander Moens, "American Diplomacy and German Unification," *Survival*, Vol. XXXIII, No. 6 (November/December 1991), p. 531. (The Two Plus Four talks, as is explained below in the present chapter, involved the two German states and the four World War II Allies—the United States, the Soviet Union, France, and Britain.)

5. Forthcoming (with Brent Scowcroft) from Alfred A. Knopf, Inc.; draft manuscript shared with the author in July 1996.

6. Moens, "American Diplomacy," p. 538.

7. Karl Kaiser, "German Unification," *Foreign Affairs*, Vol. 70, No. 1 (1991), p. 179.

8. In addition to Teltschik and Elbe, see Pond, *Beyond the Wall*; Stephen F. Szabo, *The Diplomacy of German Unification* (New York: St. Martin's Press, 1992); James A. Baker, III, with Thomas M. DeFrank, *The Politics of Diplomacy: Revolution, War and Peace, 1989–92* (New York: G. P. Putnam's Sons, 1995); and Philip Zelikow and Condoleezza Rice, *Germany Unified and Europe Transformed: A Study in Statecraft* (Cambridge: Harvard University Press, 1995).

Baker's memoirs and the book by my NSC colleagues Zelikow and Rice both came out after this chapter was written (during my 1993–94 fellowship year at the Wilson Center). Neither caused me to revise my text. The sole exception is a passage dealing with the Polish-German border issue: I had forgotten the extent of Bush's personal mediation, even though I was notetaker for all the relevant conversations, and so changed the account thanks to Zelikow and Rice. Otherwise, I have not changed a word of the text but rather have confined the relatively few points of difference to the notes.

9. Richard von Weizsäcker, "Only Cooperation Can Create Peace," *Die Zeit*, September 30, 1983.

10. These hopes were supported by a British foreign office analysis of the German question prepared in late October 1989, as cited in Zelikow and Rice, *Germany Unified*, p. 97.

11. "Joint Declaration of the Federal Republic of Germany and the Soviet Union, June 13, 1989," Embassy of the Federal Republic of Germany, Washington, D.C., June 13, 1989, in Lawrence Freedman, ed., *Europe Transformed: Documents on the End of the Cold War* (New York: St. Martin's Press, 1990), pp. 317–21.

12. Garton Ash, *In Europe's Name*, p. 108.

13. *Ibid.*, p. 109.

14. Cited in Freedman, ed., *Europe Transformed*, p. 340. (On the diplomatic activity at the U.N., see Chapter 2.)

15. *Pravda*, November 15, 1989.

16. Cited in Teltschik, *329 Tage*, p. 37.

17. *Washington Post*, November 30, 1989, p. A53.

18. That French official thinking was unprepared for unification, both analytically and emotionally, was demonstrated by the sharply negative reaction to an article written in late September 1989 by the French scholar Dominique Moïsi, in which he anticipated rapid movement toward German unity and warned of "the futility of any attempt to prolong an unwarranted division." (*International Herald Tribune*, September 25, 1989.)

19. *New York Times*, November 15, 1989.

20. *Washington Post*, November 20, 1989; Margaret Thatcher, *The Downing Street Years* (New York: HarperCollins Publishers, 1993), pp. 792–3.

21. Thatcher, *Downing Street Years*, p. 792.

22. *Ibid.*, pp. 796–97. Mitterrand, according to British officials, felt even more strongly that urgent joint actions were needed: "Mitterrand told Mrs. Thatcher that this was the worst crisis in fifty years, and in times of great crisis Britain and France have been together. He seemed to want to revive the *entente cordiale*." (Cited in John Newhouse, "The Diplomatic Round," *New Yorker*, August 27, 1990, p. 81.)

23. *Ibid.*, p. 798.

24. *New York Times*, November 16, 1989; *International Herald Tribune*, September 4, 1989.

25. In early September 1989, President Bush also predicted, in an interview with David Frost, that the Berlin Wall would come down during his presidency. (*New York Times*, September 6, 1989; *Public Papers of the Presidents of the United States: George Bush, 1989* [Washington, D.C.: U.S. Government Printing Office, 1990], p. 1593.)

26. Baker, *Politics of Diplomacy*, p. 159, describes his very specific discussion of the prospects for German unification in a conversation with President Bush over lunch at the White House on May 17, 1989.

27. See, e.g., the March 20 NSC memorandum for the president that stressed that "our vision for Europe's future" must include "an approach to the 'German Question,'" as cited in Chapter 1. (Zelikow and Rice, *Germany Unified*, p. 28.)

28. Two days before the fall of the Berlin Wall, National Security Adviser Brent Scowcroft alluded to "reversals that could throw the entire development back by decades." (Remarks made on November 7, 1989, as cited in *Die Welt*, July 11, 1990.) Similarly, the *International Herald Tribune* of December 1, 1989, cited unnamed U.S. officials as worrying that "something very violent and very ugly" could derail the process of democratic change in the GDR.

29. These views were contained in my memoranda to Scowcroft (conveying the recommendations of an interagency working group) of November 11 and 20, as cited in Zelikow and Rice, *Germany Unified*, pp. 112–13, 404–32, and 405–35. See also Szabo, *Diplomacy*, p. 41.

30. "Speech by Chancellor Kohl to the Bundestag on Intra-German Relations," November 28, 1989, in Freedman, ed., *Europe Transformed*, pp. 372–76.

31. In Moscow, Foreign Ministry Spokesman Gennadi Gerasimov issued a terse statement: "Realities have to be respected. One is that Europe is divided into two military alliances, NATO and the Warsaw Pact. The second is that frontiers stand as confirmed in Helsinki and the third is that there are two Germanies." (*International Herald Tribune*, November 30, 1989.)

The British and French were incensed that they had not been apprised of the speech in advance. (When a French embassy officer asked me whether the U.S. government had been so apprised, I said that of course our German friends had given us an advance copy but told us, whatever we did, not to share it with the French. After letting him dangle for a while, I owned up to the fact that we had not been informed, either.)

32. Thatcher, *Downing Street Years*, p. 795.

33. Indeed, there were those in Washington, particularly at the Pentagon, who were perhaps overly eager to assert American rights as one of the Four Powers—not out of opposition to German unification but from the instinctive desire to exert control over what seemed a runaway process.

34. "Statement by Secretary of State Baker, November 29, 1989," in *American Foreign Policy: Current Documents, 1989*, ed. Nancy L. Golden and Sherrill Brown Wells (Washington, D.C.: Department of State, 1990), pp. 346–7.

35. Oddly, neither Baker in his memoirs nor Zelikow and Rice in *Germany Unified* explained or even noted the secretary's direct contradiction of Kohl on these two crucial elements. It is an important point, because it places the "quid pro quo" (active American support for unification in return for West German backing on NATO) to which Zelikow and Rice refer at the beginning, not in late January, as they assert (p. 173).

36. Pond, *Beyond the Wall*, p. 147.

37. *Washington Post*, December 8, 1989.

38. *Literaturnaya Gazeta* (Moscow), No. 14, April 10, 1991 (trans. in Foreign Broadcast Information Service/Soviet Union, April 12, 1991, p. 32).

39. *Pravda*, June 26, 1990, trans. in *Current Digest of the Soviet Press*, Vol. XLII, No. 33 (1990), pp. 19–20.

40. Eduard Shevardnadze, *The Future Belongs to Freedom*, trans. Catherine A. Fitzpatrick (New York: The Free Press, 1991) pp. 134 and 146.

41. *Washington Post*, December 8, 1989, pp. A21–22.

42. *International Herald Tribune*, December 12, 1989.

43. Although we consented to hearing Soviet concerns, the agenda was limited to review of the 1987 U.S. "Berlin Initiative" aimed at improving communications and contacts in and around Berlin. The meeting was also coordinated in advance with the West Germans through the "Bonn Group" (the FRG, United States, Britain and France).

44. This was the recommended approach I forwarded to General Scowcroft in my November 20 memorandum on "Handling the German Question at Malta and Beyond," as cited in Zelikow and Rice, *Germany Unified*, pp. 113 and 405 n. 35.

45. See also Zelikow and Rice, *Germany Unified*, p. 131.

46. Whether Moscow, even at the height of the Cold War, really wanted U.S. forces out of Europe is another matter. It seems more likely that Soviet aims were to see NATO weakened and divided but not so divided as to prompt the Europeans, especially the Germans, to mobilize seriously for their own defense.

47. In his memoirs, President Bush gives a detailed account of the Malta meetings in the strengthening of his personal relationship with Gorbachev. (Forthcoming from Alfred A. Knopf, Inc.; draft manuscript shared with the author in July 1996.)

48. Teltschik, *329 Tage*, p. 109. It was a one-liner that the French ostentatiously publicized.

49. "General Secretary Mikhail Gorbachev's Speech to the Central Committee, 9 December 1989," in Freedman, ed., *Europe Transformed*, p. 385. In a subsequent message to Kohl, Gorbachev made the threat more explicit. (Garton Ash, *In Europe's Name*, p. 596.)

50. Teltschik, *329 Tage*, p. 109; Newhouse, p. 81. Gorbachev also told the Germans of a similar British overture, presumably the one made by Thatcher during her September 1989 visit to Moscow.

51. Teltschik, *329 Tage*, p. 69; *"Die Siegermachter warnen Bonn," Der Spiegel*, December 11, 1989, p. 17.

52. Forthcoming from Alfred A. Knopf, Inc.; draft manuscript shared with the author in July 1996.

53. Thatcher, *Downing Street Years*, pp. 795–96.

54. *Pravda* and *Izvestia*, December 20, 1989, *Current Digest of the Soviet Press* Vol. XLI, No. 51 (1989), pp. 9–12.

55. Interview by the American scholar Dan Hamilton with Soviet foreign ministry official Sergei Tarasenko, from Hamilton's manuscript on German unification and cited with his permission. The interview describes the contest between the Americanists around Shevardnadze and the "Berlin Wall" of Soviet foreign ministry Germanists.

56. Zelikow and Rice, *Germany Unified* (pp. 154–55, 159–60, 415 n. 9, and 417 n. 17), cite two memoranda that I drafted and forwarded to Scowcroft through Robert Blackwill, NSC senior director for Soviet and European affairs. The first, in mid- to late December, called for a slowing down of the process lest Moscow take precipitous steps to try to derail it altogether. The second, dated January 19, 1990, reflected our change of view toward "the faster, the better." Though I could be wrong, I recall the change of heart coming in a meeting with Blackwill in his office some time toward the end of the Christmas holidays—i.e., the end of December. The memo may have been the first formal written record of a new line we had already conveyed orally to Scowcroft. The substantive point was that the progression in our thinking corresponded precisely to the progression of thought in Bonn.

57. Although Baker's visit to Potsdam had been opposed by some within the administration as conferring an unintended legitimacy to the Modrow government, its aim was not to imply U.S. preference for a "two-state" solution but to secure Modrow's public commitment to setting a date for new elections and to avert precipitous regime collapse in the meantime. Some, nonetheless, considered the visit an exercise in "grandstanding" that could have the effect, even if unintended, of weakening U.S. support for unification. See Baker's account in *Politics of Diplomacy*, pp. 174–76, in which he describes his conviction at that point that "there will be de facto economic unification between the GDR and FRG in any event." See also Pond, *Beyond the Wall*, p. 169, and Szabo, *Diplomacy*, p. 44.

58. See, e.g., *Neues Deutschland*, January 11, 1990. Meanwhile, the resignation of the East German communist leadership on December 3 had left the party "headless and almost irrelevant," in the words of an American embassy cable. (Cited in the *Washington Post*, December 8, 1989, p. A21.)

59. Julij A. Kwizinskij [in German transliteration], *Vor dem Sturm: Erinnerungen eines Diplomaten*, trans. Hilde and Helmut Ettinger (Berlin: Siedler Verlag, 1993), p. 39.

60. Cited in Pond, *Beyond the Wall*, pp. 185–86.

61. Teltschik, *329 Tage*, p. 117.

62. Cited in Pond, *Beyond the Wall*, p. 172.

63. *Pravda*, January 31, 1990, *Current Digest of the Soviet Press* Vol. XLII, No. 5 (1990), p. 22. *Pravda* went on to express Soviet "concern over aggressive neofascist actions in the GDR and attempts by external right-wing radical forces to stir up and fan neo-Nazi sentiment" and condemned "the interference in the GDR's affairs by circles that are fomenting tension."

64. ADN wire service, February 1, 1990, as cited in Pond, *Beyond the Wall*, p. 171.

Two days after Modrow's visit, Gorbachev received Gregor Gysi, head of the renamed communist party ("Socialist Unity Party of Germany—Party of Democratic Socialism"), and acknowledged that "in the context of the European process and in the building of a common home in Europe, the question of German national unity can also be resolved." (*Pravda*, February 3, 1990, in *Current Digest of the Soviet Press*, Vol XLII, No. 5 (1990), p. 23.)

65. *Pravda*, February 3, 1990, *Current Digest of the Soviet Press*, Vol. XLII, No. 5, pp. 23–4.

66. "German Unity within the European Framework," Speech by Foreign Minister Hans-Dietrich Genscher at a conference at the Tutzing Protestant Academy, January 31, 1990, *Statements and Speeches* Vol. XIII, No. 2, February 6, 1990, German Information Center. Teltschik, *329 Tage*, pp. 123 and 151, notes Kohl's extreme displeasure at having had no advance notice of the "Genscher Plan."

67. These Soviet proposals came mainly from Shevardnadze's December 19 speech at the European parliament and his February 3 statement in Moscow after the Modrow visit. Shevardnadze's messages to Baker came on January 1 and 10; President Bush also spoke with Gorbachev by telephone on January 31.

68. Interview with the *Wall Street Journal*, January 26, 1990, p. A12. This was shortly after the two Thatcher-Mitterrand meetings in Paris, discussed above, in which the two leaders agreed on an "Anglo-French axis" to slow unification.

69. Thatcher, *Downing Street Years*, pp. 792–98, hints at just such a meeting of the minds among Mitterrand, Gorbachev, and herself.

70. Genscher's reference to the "cat table" came during his November 21, 1989, meeting with President Bush in the Oval Office.

71. To illustrate the problems of reliable "insider" accounts, it is worth mentioning that my role at Shannon was to wander around the duty-free store while Baker and his advisers made history with Dumas. I was usually included in Baker's meetings with European leaders (though not with the Soviets), but the secretary wanted maximum secrecy during this round of negotiation.

72. Reflecting on his meetings with Gorbachev and Shevardnadze, Baker (*Politics of Diplomacy*, p. 205) made the trenchant observation that "Gorbachev seemed to believe that the Soviet Union would always be a preeminent power in Europe. I began to think that possibly Shevardnadze saw the future more clearly, and was wary of codifying Soviet decline."

The Ottawa meeting was called to discuss the "Open Skies" proposal that President Bush issued in his Texas A&M speech in May 1989. The other important stops on Baker's trip—Prague, Sofia, and Bucharest—will be discussed in Chapter 5.

73. Shevardnadze, *The Future Belongs to Freedom*, pp. 136–37.

74. There were actually two such "One Plus Three" groups—one of political directors, the other of legal advisers.

75. The NSC staff was opposed to moving so quickly—not because of any difference over the Two Plus Four formula (which was a joint State/NSC initiative) but for fear that Moscow would seize the mechanism to intrude prematurely in the unification process. Indeed, it was the final line of the Ottawa statement that caused the most concern: "Preliminary discussions at the official level will begin shortly." State's view, which turned out to more sound, was that the risk of Soviet mischief-making would be reduced if they were brought into an appropriate multilateral framework. There was also some concern at the NSC that Kohl might object to this early invocation of Four Power prerogatives—the deal

at Ottawa was struck by foreign ministers, after all, and the poisonous relationship between Kohl and Genscher was hardly a state secret. As it turned out, a quick call from the president to the chancellor showed these concerns to be groundless. (See Baker's account in *Politics of Diplomacy*, pp. 198–99.)

76. For background, see Garton Ash, *In Europe's Name*, pp. 216–31, esp. pp. 222–31.

77. It is harder to extend this generous assessment of Kohl's motivations to his linking the border issue to the status of the German minority in Poland and Poland's renunciation of reparations claims against the GDR—points that Germany pressed through rough bilateral negotiations.

78. President Mitterrand hosted Polish prime minister Mazowiecki and Foreign Minister Skubiszewski in early March and spoke of a Four Power role in guaranteeing the boundary. Prime Minister Thatcher, in a March 26 interview with *Der Spiegel*, termed resolution of the border issue a "precondition" for German unification. (Pond, *Beyond the Wall*, p. 196.) Even after Kohl had moved substantially to resolve the issue to Poland's satisfaction, the French continued to obstruct, arguing at a "One Plus Three" legal advisers' meeting at the end of May that France would not sign an agreement on German unity until after a border treaty had been signed and ratified by a united German parliament. All this suggests that while the French may have supported the Polish cause out of principle as well, their main interest was in complicating the unification process.

79. There was a certain division between the NSC staff and the State Department on this point, owing partly to somewhat different judgments on Genscher's reliability on security issues and partly to institutional biases in favor of our chief counterparts in Bonn (the chancellery and the foreign ministry, respectively).

80. Zelikow and Rice, *Germany Unified*, pp. 219–22. Bush, as I recall, went beyond the talking points I had prepared on the subject (constrained as I was by the general NSC inclination to go easy on Kohl), so Baker must have gotten to the president directly to recommend a more active mediating role. It was a good thing if he did (though Baker says nothing about it in his memoirs).

81. The resolutions were passed by the two German parliaments on June 21, and Polish foreign minister Skubiszewski attended the third Two Plus Four meeting in Paris on July 17. Shortly after German unification, Chancellor Kohl and Polish prime minister Mazowiecki agreed to negotiate a border treaty, which was signed on June 17, 1991, following difficult negotiations over the status of Poland's German minority.

82. Michael R. Beschloss and Strobe Talbott, *At the Highest Levels: The Inside Story of the End of the Cold War* (Boston: Little, Brown and Company, 1993), p. 188.

83. Zelikow and Rice, *Germany Unified*, pp. 186–87.

84. TASS (Moscow), February 11, 1990, as cited in Günter Müchler and Klaus Hofmann, *Helmut Kohl: Chancellor of German Unity* (Bonn: Press and Information Office of the Federal Government, 1992), pp. 185–86. It is worth noting that the Genscher-Shevardnadze joint statement issued at the same time was much less forthcoming than the Kohl-Gorbachev agreement. Both texts are translated in Freedman, ed., *Europe Transformed*, pp. 472–73 and 474–75.

85. These included the East German sister parties of Kohl's CDU (Christian Democratic Union) and its Bavarian coalition partner CSU (Christian Social Union), as well as the East German "Democratic Awakening."

86. Interviews by Dan Hamilton with Sergei Tarasenko and Nikolai Portugalov, cited with permission of the interviewer.

87. For Prime Minister Thatcher's reaction to the "Franco-German juggernaut," see *Downing Street Years*, pp. 761–63.

88. Remarks by SPD (Social Democratic party) adviser Egon Bahr at the Wehrkunde Conference, Munich, February 1990. See also Szabo, *Diplomacy*, p. 44, and Pond, *Beyond the Wall*, pp. 174 and 317.

89. Some of these proposals by Western analysts are cited in Pond, *Beyond the Wall*, pp. 188–89.

90. McGeorge Bundy, "From Cold War to Trusting Peace," *Foreign Affairs*, Vol. 69, No. 1 (Winter 1989–90), p. 205.

91. Zelikow and Rice, *Germany Unified*, p. 422–58.

92. A fuller version of his August 1990 *Atlantic* article is John J. Mearsheimer, "Back to the Future: Instability in Europe After the Cold War," *International Security* Vol. 15, No. 1 (Summer 1990): 5–56.

93. "German Unity within the European Framework," Speech by Foreign Minister Hans-Dietrich Genscher at a conference at the Tutzing Protestant Academy, January 31, 1990, *Statements and Speeches* Vol. XIII, No. 2, February 6, 1990, German Information Center.

94. Speech by Foreign Minister Hans-Dietrich Genscher at the meeting of the Western European Union, Luxembourg, March 23, 1990, *Statements and Speeches* Vol. XIII, No. 8, March 30, 1990, German Information Center, New York.

95. "The Future of a European Germany," speech by Foreign Minister Hans-Dietrich Genscher at the Conference of the American Society of Newspaper Editors, Washington, April 6, 1990, *Statements and Speeches* Vol. XIII, No. 9, April 10, 1990, German Information Center, New York. (Emphasis added.)

96. Kiessler and Elbe, *Ein runder Tisch mit scharfen Ecken*, p. 80.

97. Pond, *Beyond the Wall*, p. 319 n.19.

98. Both texts are carried in full in *Public Papers of the Presidents: George Bush, 1990* (Washington, D.C.: U.S. Government Printing Office, 1991), pp. 264–66.

99. Teltschik, *329 Tage*, p. 162. The president's remark is cited in his memoirs (forthcoming from Alfred A. Knopf, Inc.).

100. "News Conference of President Bush and President François Mitterrand of France in Key Largo, Florida, April 19, 1990," in *Public Papers of the Presidents: George Bush, 1990*, p. 523.

101. Pond, *Beyond the Wall*, p. 212.

102. Havel's February 1990 visit to Washington is discussed in Chapter 5.

103. On the Bush-Havel relationship, see Chapter 6.

104. "Statement by the Press Secretary on the President's Meeting with Prime Minister Lothar de Maizière of the German Democratic Republic, June 11, 1990," in *Public Papers, 1990*, p. 810.

105. Shevardnadze's remarks during a meeting with Secretary Baker in Windhoek, Namibia (where both were attending that country's independence celebrations), March 20, 1990, as cited in Beschloss and Talbott, *Highest Levels*, p. 198.

106. Shevardnadze, *Future Belongs to Freedom*, pp. 132, 136.

107. *Ibid.*, p. 133. In fact, Shevardnadze acknowledges that even he is not satisfied with his explanation: "I must admit that I reread these statements now with mixed feelings. It seems that not even three months went by and we turned our attitude around 180 degrees. (*Ibid.*, p. 138.)

108. ARD television, March 6, 1990, as cited in Teltschik, 329 *Tage*, p. 168.

109. *Izvestia*, April 7, 1990, as translated in *Current Digest of the Soviet Press*, Vol. XLII, No. 14 (1990), p. 9.

110. *Izvestia*, May 6, 1990, as translated and condensed in *Current Digest of the Soviet Press*, Vol. XLII, No. 18 (1990), pp. 10–12.

111. Edward Hallett Carr, *The Twenty Years' Crisis, 1919–1939* (New York: Harper and Row Publishers, 1964).

112. Pond, *Beyond the Wall*, p. 214; Szabo, *Diplomacy*, p. 83; and Serge Schmemann, "German Coalition Leaders Split on Soviet Proposal for Unification," *New York Times*, May 9, 1990.

113. Shevardnadze, *The Future Belongs to Freedom*, p. 139.

114. Beschloss and Talbott, *At the Highest Levels*, pp. 207–9.

115. In press coverage of the visit, much was made of the fact that Prunskiene's entry into the White House grounds was delayed for several minutes, which reporters insisted on interpreting as a deliberate snub. For the record: the gate was really stuck.

116. Interview with the *Wall Street Journal*, January 26, 1990, p. A12; and Thatcher, *Downing Street Years*, p. 797.

117. Oberdorfer, *The Turn*, p. 404.

118. Soviet defense minister Dimitri Yazov, one of the leaders of the August 1991 coup attempt, later complained that "Gorbachev often traveled abroad in recent years, and frequently we had no idea what important issues he discussed. . . . Take Gorbachev's report to the [July 1991] G-7 meeting in London—none of us knew what was said there." (*New York Times*, October 7, 1991, p. A7.)

119. See, e.g., Shevardnadze's remarkable interview with *Literaturnaya Gazeta*, April 19, 1990, in which he warned of the "death of perestroika" and the advent of dictatorship and chronicled the growing internal attacks against himself and Gorbachev. (*Foreign Broadcast Information Service*, FBIS-SOV-90–181, 26 April 1990, pp. 5–11.)

120. "NATO and the U.S. Commitment to Europe," Address by President Bush at the Oklahoma State University commencement, Stillwater, Oklahoma, May 4, 1990, in *Public Papers (1990)*, pp. 625–29.

121. See, e.g., Thomas Friedman, "U.S. Will Press the Soviets to Accept Plan on Germany," *New York Times*, June 5, 1990, p. A17.

122. Remarks during a question-and-answer session following Teltschik's presentation at the American Institute for Contemporary German Studies, Washington, November 26, 1991.

123. For a wonderfully detailed examination of the Washington Summit, see Joseph G. Whelan, *Soviet Diplomacy and Negotiating Behavior—1988–90*, Committee on Foreign Affairs Special Studies Series, Vol. III (Washington, D.C.: U.S. Government Printing Office, 1991), pp. 291–418.

124. For a blow-by-blow account, see Beschloss and Talbott, *At the Highest Levels*, pp. 215–24, and Bush's account in his memoirs (forthcoming from Alfred A. Knopf, Inc.).

125. A few days earlier, in a meeting with Mitterrand in Moscow, Gorbachev had explored the idea of a "French solution" whereby Germany would be politically but not militarily integrated into NATO. (Teltschik, 329 *Tage*, pp. 243–48.)

126. "Press Conference by the President and President Mikhail Gorbachev," June 3, 1990, Office of the Press Secretary, The White House. Baker, *Politics of Diplomacy*, notes that Gorbachev was leaning in this direction during the secretary's visit to Moscow in

mid-May (p. 252) and that as far back as February Kohl had predicted that "Gorbachev will make that concession [on Germany's NATO membership] to the President of the United States" (p. 231).

127. Beschloss and Talbott, *At the Highest Levels*, p. 230; Pond, *Beyond the Wall*, p. 216. This was another of those historic events at which I was there but not there. I was invited to sit in on most of Baker's meetings at Copenhagen but not the Shevardnadze "bilat" (bilateral meeting with a foreign leader).

128. "The NATO Alliance and the Future of Europe," intervention by Secretary Baker before the North Atlantic Council meeting, June, 7, 1990, Turnberry, Scotland, United States Department of State, Current Policy Document No. 1284 (June 1990).

129. "Ministerial Meeting of the North Atlantic Council at Turnberry, United Kingdom, 7th–8th June 1990," NATO Press Service, Communiqué M-1 (90) 29, June 8, 1990.

130. Szabo, *Diplomacy*, p. 88; Beschloss and Talbott, *At the Highest Levels*, pp. 232–33.

131. The NSC draft of the declaration was done by Philip Zelikow. For his detailed account, see Zelikow and Rice, *Germany Unified*, pp. 303–24. See also Szabo, *Diplomacy*, pp. 95–97, 106 and Shevardnadze, *The Future Belongs to Freedom*, pp. 140–42.

132. "London Declaration on a Transformed North Atlantic Alliance, Issued by the Heads of State and Government participating in the meeting of the North Atlantic Council in London on 5th–6th July 1990," NATO Press Service, Communiqué S-1 (90) 36, July 6, 1990.

133. Thatcher, *Downing Street Years*, pp. 811–12. As she put it (p. 811), "I found myself at odds with the Americans and indeed with the NATO Secretary-General [Manfred Wörner] about how we should approach the NATO Summit." (Wörner, a former West German defense minister, played a critically important role in encouraging NATO's transformation and building consensus around a new vision for the alliance.)

134. I recall being asked by academic specialists and think-tankers just before the London Summit what initiatives we had in mind. Since I was not at liberty to say, I challenged them to offer some ideas. They had plenty with regard to CSCE, many of which were in fact already in our draft declaration, but almost none with respect to the alliance itself.

135. I later learned from senior German officials that similar discussions were going on in Bonn. On the European security debate after German unification, see Chapters 4 and 7.

136. It is an open question whether even this concession, made preemptively by Genscher at the beginning of the process, could have been averted.

137. This language was tabled by the FRG representative to the August 23 One Plus Three political directors' meeting in London and prompted me to write a memorandum for Scowcroft ("German Unification: New Problems at End-Game") warning that differences over this issue "cast serious doubt on the agreement we thought was at hand for the united Germany's remaining a full member of NATO." From the way the Germans broached the subject, it seemed to me and others on the American delegation that a prior arrangement to that effect had already been worked out between Bonn and Moscow.

138. British foreign secretary Hurd's insistence on clarifying this point at Moscow was not, as some have interpreted it, a last-ditch British effort to derail the Two Plus Four agreement. We were as adamant as the British that all of united Germany, including the territory of the former GDR, be fully within NATO's sphere of competence. We were sat-

isfied that this was already assured under the draft treaty, and the Agreed Minute provided further clarification.

139. The text is reprinted in Szabo, *Diplomacy*, pp. 131–34.

140. After the December 1990 all-German elections, with no state (*Land*) elections scheduled for nearly two years, we felt that this was the ideal time to build U.S.-German cooperation and coleadership on key issues like GATT. For all their protestations to the contrary, there was scant evidence that the Germans lifted a finger to try to broker an EC compromise.

141. Office of the Press Secretary, The White House, April 29, 1992. These nuances, ignored in the media coverage of the visit, were immediately picked up by the von Weizsäcker entourage and cabled back to Bonn.

Chapter 4

1. As will be seen as Chapter 8, however, Yazov performed a last malevolent act in helping lead the anti-Gorbachev coup attempt in August 1991.

2. John Lewis Gaddis, *The Long Peace: Inquiries into the History of the Cold War* (New York: Oxford University Press, 1987).

3. Lord [Thomas] Macauley, "The Earl of Chatham," in *Critical and Historical Essays* Vol. IV (London: Longmans, Green, and Co., 1895), p. 274.

4. The "Eastern question" traditionally refers to the protracted decline of the Ottoman empire in the nineteenth and early twentieth centuries. Yet it is related as well to the Polish question, Czech question, and others that arose in Central and Eastern Europe in the context of the collapse of the Habsburg, Russian, and Ottoman empires. In short, the term connotes the dilemmas, past and present, posed by the break up of multiethnic empires in the entire region from the Baltic Sea to the Balkans.

5. James Goodby, "Commonwealth and Concert: Organizing Principles of Post-Containment Order in Europe," *The Washington Quarterly*, Summer 1991, p. 78. See also Stanley Hoffmann, "Balance, Concert, Anarchy, or None of the Above," in Gregory F. Treverton, ed., *The Shape of the New Europe* (New York: Council on Foreign Relations Press, 1992), pp. 194–220; and Philip Zelikow, "The New Concert of Europe," *Survival*, Summer 1992, pp. 12–30.

6. See Chapter 1.

7. The Helsinki Final Act was issued at the 1975 summit meeting of the Conference on Security and Cooperation in Europe.

8. Joseph S. Nye, Jr. ("What New World Order?" *Foreign Affairs* Vol. 71, No. 2 [Spring 1992], pp. 83–96) was not quite right in arguing that the Bush administration "thought and acted like Nixon, but borrowed the rhetoric of Wilson and Carter." In fact, the two strands were more nearly balanced in both action and rhetoric, albeit with a realistic tilt, until public discomfort with this dual explanation for American action in the Persian Gulf (as if a country could not have interests in principles of international conduct as well as in secure oil supplies) pushed the rhetoric toward moralism and universalism.

9. See Goodby, "Commonwealth and Concert," as well as Richard Rosecrance, "A New Concert of Powers," *Foreign Affairs* Vol. 71, No. 2 (Spring 1992), pp. 64–82.

10. "Toward a New World Order," Address by President Bush before a Joint Session of the Congress, September 11, 1990, Current Policy No. 1298, Bureau of Public Affairs, U.S. Department of State.

11. See Chapter 8.

12. "Remarks by the President to the Czechoslovak Federal Assembly," November 17, 1990, White House press release of that day.

13. This frame of mind was much like that of the peacemakers at Versailles in 1919. There were other parallels to which we should have been more alert, such as Baker's discerning genuine democrats among some of the warmed over despots from Kazakhstan or other points east, just as Wilson had done three generations before. "Why, they are just like us!" was the wishful thought that crowded out hard reason.

14. Margaret Thatcher, *The Downing Street Years* (New York: HarperCollins Publishers, 1993), p. 815.

15. Ever the gentleman, President Bush sat through each one, though heads of other delegations absented themselves from time to time for the many "bilats" (bilateral meetings with other leaders) held on the margins of the summit. When it came time to prepare for the next CSCE summit, held in Helsinki in July 1992, our first requirement at staff level was that the session be orchestrated so that presidents and prime ministers were not obliged to be present for interventions by each of the countries represented (by then totalling 52).

16. Ole Waever, "Three Competing Europes: German, French, Russian," *International Affairs*, Vol. 66, No. 3 (1990): 481. Waever's breakdown of the competing European visions differs from mine, but it captures the same contradictions and incompatibilities.

17. *Ibid.*, 480.

18. These visions were spelled out, e.g., in the 1967 Harmel Report, which affirmed NATO's ultimate goal as the achievement of "a just and lasting peaceful order in Europe," and the Treaty of Rome, which called on the European Community to "eliminate the barriers which divide Europe" and "lay the foundations for an ever closer union among the peoples of Europe."

19. Bush was born in 1924; Scowcroft, in 1925; and Baker, Brady, and Eagleburger, in 1930.

20. On this point, see Hoffmann, "Balance, Concert, Anarchy, or None of the Above," p. 212.

21. In truth, the advice coming from outside was rarely helpful. The inside-the-Washington-Beltway think tanks tried to replicate what we were doing inside government but could not do it as well, and scholars and thinkers farther removed from Washington usually offered insights too abstract and detached from the exigencies of policy making. The difference was that early in the administration we made the effort to tap the best and most relevant thinking, but by mid-term—whether from weariness, overwork, or sheer hubris —we rarely did so.

Another point that needs making—without naming names—is that the mid-term turnover at State produced a marked deterioration in policy making, especially from the European bureau. From both the conceptual and operational perspectives, the falloff was dramatic.

22. See the Introduction.

23. Jiří Dienstbier, "Central and Eastern Europe and a New European Order, Address at Harvard University, May 15, 1990, reprinted in Tim Whipple, ed., *After the Velvet Revolution: Václav Havel and the New Leaders of Czechoslovakia Speak Out* (New York: Freedom House, 1992), p. 120. (The citation here is from the as-delivered copy I got from the Czechoslovak embassy. The wording differs slightly from Whipple's version.)

Dienstbier's speech echoed the 1985 "Prague Appeal," which he and other Charter 77 signatories sent to the fourth Amsterdam conference on disarmament.

24. "The Common European Interest: America and the New Politics Among Nations," address by Secretary Baker upon receiving the Hans J. Morgenthau Award, New York City, May 14, 1990, Current Policy No. 1278, Bureau of Public Affairs, U.S. Department of State.

25. I heard Bush ask Kohl at least a dozen times whether Germans would still want an American military presence after unification and the departure of Soviet troops. Though equally worried about American public attitudes, he felt he could make the case so long as European developments did not conspire to push U.S. forces out.

26. "Remarks by the President at the Aspen Institute Symposium," The Aspen Institute, Aspen, Colorado, August 2, 1990, Office of the Press Secretary, The White House. Emphasis added.

27. "Remarks by the President at Luncheon Hosted by Prime Minister [Ruud] Lubbers," Binnenhof, The Hague, The Netherlands, November 9, 1991, Office of the Press Secretary, The White House.

28. Negotiating positions taken by the USTR had to be approved by the president and so were not always as authoritative as the Europeans might have wished, but our decision-making system was simplicity itself compared to the EC's cumbersome process.

29. "Declaration on US-EC Relations," Rome, Brussels, and Washington, November 23, 1990. The French fought against any commitments at all, ultimately agreeing only to stipulations for biannual consultations at head-of-state level, additional biannual consultations at foreign-minister level, and somewhat strengthened contacts between the United States and the EC Commission.

30. Robert B. Zoellick, "The New Europe in a New Age: Insular, Itinerant, or International? Prospects for an Alliance of Values," address before a conference on U.S.-EC relations, Annapolis, Maryland, September 21, 1990, *Current Policy* No. 1300, Bureau of Public Affairs, U.S. Department of State.

31. Zoellick, in *ibid.*, put it this way: "The United States, the European Community, and Japan are colleagues in pursuit of common ends. The three of us together could, however, accomplish a great deal more. We can be the catalysts and major contributors toward addressing the post–Cold War problems. We can draw other nations into existing or new international structures that support our common interests and objectives."

32. "Remarks by President Bush and President von Weizsäcker of Germany in Exchange of Toasts," The State Dining Room, The White House, Office of the Press Secretary, April 29, 1992. As was noted in the chapter on German unification, these remarks, though offered at a social occasion, did not pass unnoticed by the German delegation, which immediately faxed the texts back to Bonn.

33. "A New Europe, A New Atlanticism: Architecture for a New Era," Address by Secretary of State James A. Baker, III, to the Berlin Press Club, Steigenberger Hotel, December 12, 1989, U.S. Department of State, Office of Public Affairs; and "The Euro-Atlantic Architecture: From West to East," Address to the Aspen Institute, Berlin, Germany, June 18, 1991, U.S. Department of State *Dispatch,* June 24, 1991, pp. 439–43.

34. "Partnership with the Countries of Central and Eastern Europe," Statement issued by the North Atlantic Council meeting in ministerial session in Copenhagen on 6th and 7th June 1991, NATO Press Service, Brussels, June 6, 1991.

35. Comecon, the Council for Mutual Economic Assistance, was the Soviet-directed trading bloc with Eastern Europe.

36. "From Revolution to Democracy: Central and Eastern Europe in the New Europe," Charles University, Prague, Czechoslovakia, February 7, 1990, U.S. Department of State, Bureau of Public Affairs, Current Policy No. 1248. (Baker's visit to Prague is discussed in Chapter 5.)

37. Cited in Bernard Wheaton and Zdeněk Kavan, *The Velvet Revolution: Czechoslovakia, 1988–1991* (Boulder, Co.: Westview Press, 1992), p 149.

38. The "Pentagonale" originally included Hungary, Czechoslovakia, and the northern republics of Yugoslavia (Slovenia and Croatia) and was later expanded to include Poland and renamed the Central European Initiative. The less ambitious "Alpe-Adria" involved regional cooperation among sub-national units (republics, Länder, autonomous regions) of Italy, Austria, Yugoslavia, Hungary, and, as an observer, the German Free State of Bavaria. (See Paolo Perulli, "The Political Economy of a 'Mid-European Region,'" in Colin Crouch and David Marquand, eds., *Towards Greater Europe* [Cambridge, Ma.: Blackwell Publishers, 1992], pp. 154–69.)

39. The security aspects of Western integration strategies will be explored in Chapter 7.

40. EFTA at this time consisted of Austria, Norway, Sweden, Switzerland, Finland, and Iceland.

41. Kalypso Nicolaidis, "East European Trade in the Aftermath of 1989: Did International Institutions Matter?" in Robert O. Keohane, Joseph S. Nye, and Stanley Hoffmann, eds., *After the Cold War: International Institutions and State Strategies in Europe, 1989–1991* (Cambridge, Ma.: Harvard University Press, 1993), pp. 207–10 and 220–27. For more on the "Europe agreements," more commonly known as the "association agreements," see Chapter 5.

42. For the text of the rambling, emotional resignation speech, see Eduard Shevardnadze, *The Future Belongs to Freedom* (New York: The Free Press, 1991), pp. 223–26.

43. Michael R. Beschloss and Strobe Talbott, *At the Highest Levels: The Inside Story of the End of the Cold War* (Boston, Ma.: Little, Brown and Company, 1993), p. 302.

44. Quoted by Charles Gati in the *New York Times*, February 14, 1991.

45. On Mitterrand's proposal, see *Le Monde*, December 31, 1989; Delors's was carried in the *Financial Times*, October 16, 1989. Mitterrand held out the prospect of a confederation that would "associate all the states of our continent in a common organization," but this was to be the second of two stages, followed by a protracted period in which the priority would be for the European Community to "reinforce its structures."

46. On this point, see Keohane and Nye in their introduction to Keohane, Nye, and Hoffmann, eds., *After the Cold War*, p. 16.

Chapter 5

1. Comment made to Chancellor Helmut Kohl in Bonn, November 10, 1989, as cited in Horst Teltschik, *329 Tage: Innenansichten der Einigung* (Berlin: Siedler Verlag, 1991), p. 16.

2. Although Kafka wrote the book literally in the shadow of Hradčany, the castle on which his was modeled was another one, situated some miles from Prague.

3. See Chapter 3, as well as Baker's account of his meeting with Havel, in James A. Baker, III, with Thomas M. DeFrank, *The Politics of Diplomacy: Revolution, War and Peace, 1989–92* (New York: G. P. Putnam's Sons, 1995), pp. 200–1.

4. "From Revolution to Democracy: Central and Eastern Europe in the New Europe," Charles University, Prague, Czechoslovakia, February 7, 1990, United States Department of State, Bureau of Public Affairs, Current Policy No. 1248.

5. See Baker's account, in *Politics of Diplomacy*. He argues that security concerns were the reason for the delayed decision to visit, but at least some among his staff believed there was a policy debate involved as well.

6. Slovak wariness was evident in a question-and-answer session following a lecture I gave at the institute of my host, Dr. Jozef Kučerák. While polite and curious, the questions nonetheless betrayed a reserve about the United States that differed sharply from my encounters with others from Central and Eastern Europe.

7. My tour guide was my other cohost in Bratislava, Public Against Violence official Andrej Bartosiewicz.

8. This was later confirmed. When Havel called Boris Yeltsin in early 1992, shortly after the collapse of the Soviet Union, Yeltsin told him that he had found in his—until recently, Gorbachev's—office in the Kremlin a sealed letter marked "Never to be opened." (Kafka in Moscow?) Yeltsin of course had opened it promptly and told Havel what he had found inside: the notorious "letter from the Czechoslovak comrades" which Soviet leader Leonid Brezhnev had invoked in justifying the Soviet-led Warsaw Pact invasion of 1968. Most of us in the West doubted that such a letter actually existed, but here it was—signed by five senior Czechoslovak communist officials, including Vasil Bil'ak.

9. In addition to Zhelev, the group included UDF Spokesman Rumen Vodenicharov, Petŭr Beron of the environmental movement Ecoglasnost, Yanko Yankov of the Social Democratic party, and Father Christopher Subev, chairman of the Committee for Human Rights—joined, we presumed, by an unseen, uninvited functionary at the other end of a listening device installed in the room.

10. See Chapter 3.

11. This official went on to note that their successors evoked no such feelings of awe.

12. The strategy of forming a united front against communist rule was probably justified for these first elections, when it was essential to break the ruling parties' monopolistic grip on power, but it may have arrested the natural development of a stable party system by forcing such diverse political bedfellows into largely artificial coalitions like the UDF.

13. David Stark, "Path Dependence and Privatization Strategies in East Central Europe," *East European Politics and Societies* Vol. 6, No. 1 (Winter 1992), pp. 17–54.

14. Tony Judt, "*Ex Oriente Lux?* Post-Celebratory Speculations on the 'Lessons' of '89," in Colin Crouch and David Marquand, eds., *Towards Greater Europe?: A Continent without an Iron Curtain* (Oxford and Cambridge, MA: Blackwell Publishers, 1992), p. 94.

15. Alexis de Tocqueville, *The Old Regime and the French Revolution*, trans. Stuart Gilbert (Garden City, NY: Doubleday and Doubleday, Inc., 1955), p. 161.

16. Jadwiga Staniszkis, *The Dynamics of the Breakthrough in Eastern Europe: The Polish Experience* (Berkeley: University of California Press, 1991), xii.

17. Bronisław Geremek, "Postcommunism and Democracy in Poland," *The Washington Quarterly*, Summer 1990, p. 129, set this task—what he called "building local democracy from the bottom up"—among the highest priorities for Poland's postcommunist transformation.

18. Giuseppe Di Palma, "Why Democracy Can Work in Eastern Europe," *Journal of Democracy*, Vol. 2, No. 1 (Winter 1991), p. 28.

19. Among the many excellent analyses of the challenges of the postcommunist economic reforms, see especially the country and sectoral surveys in Paul Marer and Salvatore Zecchini, eds., *The Transition to a Market Economy* (Paris: Organization for Eco-

nomic Cooperation and Development, 1991); Vittorio Corbo, Fabrizio Coricelli, and Jan Bossak, eds., *Reforming Central and Eastern European Economies* (Washington, D.C.: The World Bank, 1991); U.S. Congress, Joint Economic Committee, *East-Central European Economies in Transition* (Washington, D.C.: U.S. Government Printing Office, 1994); and many excellent articles in the journal *East European Politics and Societies*.

20. Edmund Burke, "Reflections on the Revolution in France," in *Edmund Burke*, The Harvard Classics, ed. Charles W. Eliot (New York: P. F. Collier and Son, 1909, 1937), p. 179.

21. *Ibid.*, p. 375.

22. Adam Michnik, "The Two Faces of Eastern Europe," *The New Republic*, November 12, 1990, p. 23.

23. Samuel P. Huntington, *The Third Wave: Democratization in the Late Twentieth Century* (Norman and London: University of Oklahoma Press, 1991), p. 258.

24. *Ibid.*, p. 263.

25. Ralf Dahrendorf, *Reflections on the Revolution in Europe* (New York: Times Books, Random House, 1990) p. 78.

26. *Ibid.*, p. 84.

27. "Address by Václav Havel, President of the Czech Republic, at the George Washington University, Washington, April 22, 1993," press release of that day by the embassy of the Czech Republic.

28. For background, see "The Bonn CSCE Conference on Economic Cooperation in Europe," in *From Vienna to Helsinki: Reports of the Inter-Sessional Meetings of the CSCE Process* (Washington, D.C.: Commission on Security and Cooperation in Europe, 1992), pp. 53–66; and Vojtech Mastny, *The Helsinki Process and the Reintegration of Europe, 1986–91: Analysis and Documentation* (New York: New York University Press, 1992), pp. 215–22.

29. *Document of the Bonn Conference on Economic Cooperation in Europe of the CSCE* (Washington, D.C.: Commission on Security and Cooperation in Europe, 1990). The text is excerpted in Mastny, *The Helsinki Process*, pp. 222–28.

30. Mastny, *The Helsinki Process*, p. 222.

31. "CSCE: The Conscience of the Continent," Remarks by Secretary of States James A. Baker, III, at the CSCE Conference on the Human Dimension, Copenhagen, Denmark, June 6, 1990, Department of State, Office of the Assistant Secretary/Spokesman. The full text is also carried in Samuel F. Wells, Jr., ed., *The Helsinki Process and the Future of Europe* (Washington, D.C.: The Woodrow Wilson Center Press, 1990), pp. 185–94.

At Copenhagen, Baker also met with Soviet foreign minister Shevardnadze to build on the progress made in the Bush-Gorbachev Washington Summit of the previous week and to further move Soviet thinking toward acceptance of united Germany's remaining in NATO. From there, Baker's party went directly to Turnberry, Scotland, for a NATO foreign ministers meeting, where we advanced a radical agenda for transforming the Atlantic alliance.

32. *Document of the Copenhagen Meeting of the Conference on the Human Dimension of the CSCE, June 1990* (Washington D.C.: Commission on Security and Cooperation in Europe, 1990).

33. Thomas Buergenthal, "The Copenhagen CSCE Meeting: A New Public Order in Europe," *Human Rights Law Journal* 11 (1990), as excerpted in Mastny, *The Helsinki Process*, pp. 246 and 252.

34. "State of the Union Address," The U.S. Capitol, Washington, D.C., January 31, 1990, Office of the Press Secretary, The White House. Earlier the same day, the White House had announced that President Havel would pay an official visit in late February, followed by Polish prime minister Mazowiecki in March.

35. "U.S. Foreign Policy Priorities and FY 1991 Budget Request," February 1, 1990, United States Department of State, Bureau of Public Affairs, Current Policy Bulletin No. 1245. Baker's remarks included a reminder of the limits of U.S. influence: "Ultimately, we believe that the staggering task of transforming the Soviet Union and the East European countries into democratic, prosperous societies depends on the decisions freely made by the people themselves and the extent to which [their leaders] have the consent and confidence of the governed."

36. In fact, we at the NSC staff—principally my colleague Adrian Basora—had been managing the assistance programs since the president's July 1989 trip to Poland and Hungary, but the job was getting much too large for this arrangement to continue.

37. I succeeded Ambassador Robert Barry, who ably directed the assistance program from 1990 to 1992.

38. The State/A.I.D. relationship, although difficult at times, developed into an effective partnership, with State providing the strategic vision and political direction, and A.I.D. bringing the developmental perspective and sectoral knowledge that State lacked.

39. "America's Opportunities in Eastern Europe," Remarks by Deputy Secretary Lawrence S. Eagleburger before American Chamber of Commerce's International Forum, Washington, D.C., February 16, 1990, United States Department of State, Bureau of Public Affairs, Current Policy No. 1250.

40. "Citizens Democracy Corps Proposed for Eastern Europe," Commencement Address by President Bush at the University of South Carolina, May 12, 1990, U.S. Department of State, Bureau of Public Affairs, Current Policy No. 1277. The president's speech, one of his best on Eastern Europe, addressed "the landscape of moral destruction . . . , the tragic consequence of four decades of communist rule. . . . Fortunately, the moral destruction . . . was not complete. Individuals somehow managed to maintain an inner strength. . . . They did so, as Václav Havel put it, by the simple act of 'living in truth.' They created 'flying universities' where lecturers taught in private homes. They formed underground publishing houses and groups to monitor human rights—an authentic 'civil society' beyond the reach of the ruling establishment. . . ."

41. Romanian, Baltic, and Albanian Funds were created in 1993–94.

42. These programs spanned virtually every sphere of political, economic, and social activity, from health care partnerships linking American and East European medical centers to local agrobusiness ventures relying on American volunteers.

43. Robert L. Hutchings, "US Aid to Central and Eastern Europe: A Call for Imagination," U.S. Department of State *Dispatch*, Vol. 4, No. 17, April 26, 1993, pp. 292–94. The testimony also noted that "G. K. Chesterton once said that anything worth doing is worth doing badly, by which he meant that there are some things so important, some tasks so urgent, that we should be prepared to take risks and be prepared to make mistakes."

44. See Chapter 6.

45. "Fact Sheet: Trade Enhancement Initiative for Central and Eastern Europe," Office of the Press Secretary, The White House, March 20, 1991.

46. "Fact Sheet: American Business and Private Sector Development Initiative for Central and Eastern Europe," Office of the Press Secretary, The White House, March 20, 1991.

47. Statement by the Press Secretary and Fact Sheets, Office of the Press Secretary, The White House, September 11, 1991.

48. Welcoming Havel to Washington two weeks after Baker's speech in Prague, President Bush repeated the point: "We know there is no room for illusions. Difficult work lies ahead. The damage of four decades of fear and repression cannot be repaired in a day." ("Remarks by the President and President Havel of Czechoslovakia Upon Departure," February 20, 1990, Office of the Press Secretary, The White House.)

49. Having heard the charge so often from my academic friends that U.S. officials led East Europeans to believe that prosperity would come quickly if only they would embrace "the market," I scoured the record of public and private statements in 1989–91 and could find not a single statement, public or private, implying that prosperity was just around the corner. What we *did* say was that prosperity could only follow some essential, and inevitably painful, steps toward economic restructuring and that the sooner these steps were taken, the sooner this painful period would be over.

50. Commission of the European Communities, "Operation PHARE: A Legal Basis for the Community's 'Action Plan,'" Information Memo P–63, Brussels, 26 October 1989, and "EC-Eastern Europe Relations," ICC Background Brief, Brussels, 19 January 1990.

51. Corbo, Coricelli, and Bossak, eds., *Reforming Central and Eastern European Economies.*

52. See, e.g, Marer and Zecchini, *The Transition to a Market Economy,* as well as the OECD's series of detailed country surveys.

53. See, e.g., "Cooperation and Assistance Programmes with Central and Eastern European Countries," Annual Report for 1991, Council of Europe, Directorate of Political Affairs, Strasbourg, 6 January 1992.

54. Stephan Haggard and Andrew Moravcsik, "The Political Economy of Financial Assistance," in Robert O. Keohane, Joseph S. Nye, and Stanley Hoffmann, eds., *After the Cold War: International Institutions and State Strategies in Europe, 1989–91* (Cambridge, Ma.: Harvard University Press, 1993), pp. 265–72.

55. Our reservations about Attali's qualifications were muted by the prospect of his removal from Paris and away from Mitterrand's ear, where we worried that his influence would make it harder to forge a Franco-American understanding on the basic elements of a new European and transatlantic order.

56. For the first three years, Soviet borrowing was limited to the level of its paid-in capital (roughly $216 million). After the dissolution of the USSR, the rule was eliminated, but with the understanding that the main focus of the bank would remain on Central and Eastern Europe.

57. All figures are from the "Scoreboard of G-24 Assistance" published by the Commission of the European Communities, Brussels, 8 April 1992.

58. The attentive reader may recall from Chapter 2 that 20 percent had become our informal benchmark dating from our assembling of the Polish Stabilization Fund in the early fall of 1989. We in fact exceeded that percentage in 1990–91 but then began to fall behind.

59. For a survey of the stabilization funds mounted for Poland, Czechoslovakia, Hungary, Bulgaria, and Romania, see "Progress Report on the G-24 Medium-Term Financial Assistance Initiative for Central and Eastern European Countries," Commission of the European Communities, Brussels, 6 April 1992.

60. *Ibid.*; and Organization for Economic Cooperation and Development, *Reforming the Economies of Central and Eastern Europe,* p. 23.

61. See Chapter 6.

62. George F. Kennan, *Memoirs 1925–50* (Boston: Little, Brown and Company, 1967), pp. 352–53.

63. I advanced several such plans in 1991 and 1992—my target being a round $1 billion—but was singularly unsuccessful in winning support at the cabinet level.

64. In his memoirs (written with President Bush), Scowcroft found the Treasury Department resolutely "tone deaf" to any agreement in favor of increased aid to Eastern Europe. (Forthcoming from Alfred A. Knopf; draft manuscript shared with author in July 1996.)

65. Baker (*Politics of Diplomacy*, pp. 45–46) does, however, refer to a "tacit division of labor with our Western allies, whereby Germany and others would focus on economic assistance to the East Europeans and Soviets, while we would focus more . . . working to demilitarize Soviet foreign policy and push Gorbachev on political reform." This does not explain why we were unable to come up with an aid level for this entire region that was no more than what we once offered Costa Rica alone.

Chapter 6

1. The best of the books so far on this early period are J. F. Brown, *Hopes and Shadows: Eastern Europe after Communism* (Durham, N.C.: Duke University Press, 1994), and Gale Stokes, *The Walls Came Tumbling Down: The Collapse of Communism in Eastern Europe* (New York and Oxford: Oxford University Press, 1993), but even these admirable volumes seem almost telegraphic to those who followed the postcommunist transitions in all their detail and complexity.

2. The Cabinet Room meetings normally included, on our side, the president, vice president, secretary of state, national security adviser, chief of staff, and one or two senior staff members each from the State Department and NSC. In photographs of these sessions, the NSC staff note-taker can be identified as the one with head down concentrating on the note pad.

3. Skubiszewski had made essentially the same points to Baker in their bilateral meeting at Ottawa the month before. See James A. Baker, III, with Thomas M. DeFrank, *The Politics of Diplomacy: Revolution, War and Peace, 1989–92* (New York: G. P. Putnam's Sons, 1995), pp. 210–11.

4. "Remarks by the President and Prime Minister Tadeusz Mazowiecki of Poland Upon Arrival," The White House, Office of the Press Secretary, March 21, 1990. The reference to secure borders referred in particular to Polish concerns over the disposition of Germany's borders after unification, as did the president's assurance earlier in his remarks that "in any decisions affecting the fate of Poland, Poland must have a voice."

5. In preparing the president's talking points for a telephone call to Chancellor Kohl the next day, I emphasized Mazowiecki's concern over the Polish border issue, his commitment to radical economic reform, and then, having to surmise the president's personal view of Mazowiecki, ventured that "I liked the man." Bush, who followed his scripts only when he believed them, used the line, so it must have been so.

6. Press Conference by the President, The White House, Office of the Press Secretary, March 22, 1990.

7. In a gracious message to Jaruzelski, President Bush renewed the invitation for Jaruzelski to visit in a private capacity.

8. Lech Wałęsa, *The Struggle and the Triumph: An Autobiography* (New York: Arcade Publisher, 1992), pp. 278–9.

9. Wałęsa used almost precisely those words as late as October 1991, speaking to an investment mission to Poland led by Commerce Secretary Robert Mosbacher.

10. A self-confessed "zombie," Tymiński claimed to have had several out-of-body experiences while living in Peru. He had also amassed a small fortune and was able to project himself to Polish voters as a self-made man (or zombie) capable of leading his country to a capitalist promised land.

11. The NSC staff and the State Department's European bureau compared notes and strategy regularly with the Polish American Congress, particularly its Washington-based vice president, the indefatigable Jan Nowak.

12. See, e.g., Jan Krzysztof Bielecki, "Problems of the Polish Transformation," *Communist Economies and Economic Transformation*, Vol. 4, No. 3 (1990). I later came to know and respect Bielecki as my Polish point of contact when I directed the U.S. assistance program for Eastern Europe in 1992–93.

13. General Scowcroft was reluctant to accede even to an informal document, on grounds that virtually every country around the world was eager to codify a bilateral security relationship with the United States—security being what we provided and others accepted—and that Poland could set a precedent. We at staff level ultimately won his agreement to an informal political declaration that did not contain language implying a security commitment, forewarning him that we could expect a similar request from Czechoslovakia when Havel arrived six months later on an already scheduled state visit.

14. I hammered out the final text at the Polish embassy in Washington shortly before Wałęsa's arrival, but only after Polish ambassador Kazimierz Dziewanowski and Professor Tadeusz Ziółkowski, a genial former academic seconded to service in the Belevedere (Poland's presidential palace), overruled Deputy Foreign Minister Jan Majewski, whose negotiating style was a product of his long and mindless service to the communist regime.

15. "Declaration of Principles Between the United States of America and the Republic of Poland," signed by President George Bush and President Lech Wałęsa, March 20, 1991, and released that day by the Office of the Press Secretary, The White House.

16. The precise formulae applied were complex in the extreme. The details are explained in "Fact Sheet: The Reduction of Poland's Debt," Office of the Press Secretary, The White House, March 20, 1991.

17. "Remarks by the President and President Wałęsa of Poland During Arrival Ceremony," The South Lawn, Office of the Press Secretary, The White House, March 20, 1991. In an interview with the Polish press agency just before Wałęsa's visit, President Bush had put it this way: "We are full of admiration for the courage and tenacity with which Poland has pursued [its] unprecedented economic transformation. We believe it is the right course and have supported it wholeheartedly, and we expect it to succeed. Its success is crucial, not only to Poland but to the other new democracies in the region. Because Poland was the first to take this bold step and because of Poland's important role in Europe, others are watching the reform closely."

18. Office of the Press Secretary, The White House, March 20, 1991. (Pope John Paul II was of course the most popular public figure, but Bush was the most popular politician.)

19. I had discussed precisely this issue with Jan Nowak, vice chairman of the Polish American Congress, who had briefed Wałęsa personally on the appropriate line to take. Wałęsa got it right with Bush but reverted to type later on.

20. During the Bush-Olszewski meeting in the Oval Office, I was seated across from Zdzisław Najder, a noted biographer of Joseph Conrad who had become adviser to the prime minister. Just eight years before, we had been together at Radio Free Europe in Munich. Najder was director of the Polish service while I was RFE's acting director. Little could we have imagined. . . .

21. For those who have lost count, they were: Mieczysław Rakowski during Bush's July 1989 visit, Mazowiecki in March 1990 at the White House (as well as at the UN General Assembly in September 1990 and in Paris for the November 1990 CSCE Summit), Bielecki at the White House in September 1991, and now Olszewski. Bush's meeting with Prime Minister Hanna Suchocka in Warsaw during his July 1992 visit made five in three years. (In November 1995, Wałęsa was defeated in his bid for reelection. He was succeeded by Alexander Kwasniewski of the Left Democratic Alliance, an offshoot of the communist party.)

22. "Statement by the Press Secretary," April 13, 1992, Office of the Press Secretary, The White House.

23. Such also was the judgment of veteran Solidarity adviser (and speaker of the Sejm) Bronisław Geremek, with whom I stood just below the dais from which the two presidents spoke.

24. "Address by the President at Castle Square," Warsaw, Poland, July 5, 1992, Office of the Press Secretary, The White House.

25. *Nowa Europa* (Warsaw), July 6, 1992. The commentary began by noting, "George Bush has no new money, because this is an election year. The mood in America is bad because of the lingering recession, record unemployment, the trade deficit and the budget deficit. The world's expectations exceed America's ability to meet them. . . ."

26. Juraj Mihalík, *Velvet Failures* (Bratislava, 1993), pp. 11–12.

27. *New York Times*, February 22, 1990. The text is also carried in Tim D. Whipple, ed., *After the Velvet Revolution: Václav Havel and the New Leaders of Czechoslovakia Speak Out* (New York: Freedom House, 1992), pp. 69–80.

28. By 1992, when I was directing the East European assistance program from the Department of State, Václav Klaus, by then prime minister, and Economic Minister Karel Dyba would visit Washington to tell members of Congress that they sought no assistance and indeed thought it worthless, repeating the same line for media consumption, and then repaired to the Department of State where they would unveil a long list of assistance requests.

29. The protocol for an "official working visit" by a head of state called for the following sequence: one-on-one meeting in the Oval Office, expanded meeting in the Cabinet Room, small working lunch in the Old Family Dining Room of the White House, and departure ceremony.

30. "Remarks by the President and President Havel of Czechoslovakia Upon Departure," February 20, 1990. The White House, Office of the Press Secretary.

31. In addition to the two presidents and their interpreters, there were just six of us: Secretary Baker, Chief of Staff John Sununu, and myself on our side and Havel advisers Alexander (Saša) Vondra, Michael Žantovsky, and Milan Kňažko (a key Slovak leader during the Velvet Revolution—invited to the meeting at my insistence) on theirs. For me, it was the beginning of a close friendship with Vondra, later the number two in the Czech foreign ministry, and Žantovsky, who succeeded Rita Klimova as Czech ambassador in Washington. Vondra, a delightfully disheveled man then in his late twenties, was an activist in the younger generation of Czech dissidents. A signer of Charter 77 and by 1989 its spokesman, he was one of the cofounders of the Civic Forum movement during the

Velvet Revolution. Žantovsky's career took him by a different route to a similar destination. Trained in clinical and social psychology, he migrated to literature, translating into Czech such writers as James Baldwin, Norman Mailer, and Joseph Heller. A founding member of the Czech chapter of the international writers organization P.E.N., he was another cofounder of Civic Forum and, by December, its spokesman. Possessed of a wonderful Puckish sense of humor, Žantovsky was at that time forty but looked years younger. One could not ask for better or more congenial colleagues—for that is what we were—than these two men at the elbow of Václav Havel. Kňažko, a popular movie actor who resembled the young Glenn Ford, later became my chief interlocutor in Bratislava when he was Slovak foreign minister and I directed the U.S. assistance program for Eastern Europe.

32. The president later described how Havel was moved to tears in thinking about freedom's return to Czechoslovakia while standing in the room where Lincoln signed the Emancipation Proclamation. ("Remarks by the President in University of Texas Commencement Address," The White House, Office of the Press Secretary, Austin, Texas, May 19, 1990.)

33. When the president delivered the line to the hushed assembly hall, someone in the audience gasped audibly. It was the appropriate punctuation mark.

34. "Remarks by the President at Wenceslas Square," Prague, November 17, 1990, The White House, Office of the Press Secretary. I recall that on an early draft of the speech, General Scowcroft had written "Too much?" in the margin next to the "we shall not fail you" line. With memories of the Western failures (betrayals?) of 1938, 1948, and 1968, I left the line in—more out of ardent hope than sound judgment.

35. Citing Alexander Hamilton but having Slovak premier Vladimír Mečiar in mind, Havel warned against "the perverted ambition of another group of people determined to profiteer from the confusion prevailing in the country."

36. As the president's tight schedule did not permit a visit to Bratislava, we arranged for his radio address to serve as a kind of surrogate. The president also used this venue to announce the reopening of the American consulate in Bratislava.

37. Valtr Komárek was dropped from the Council of Ministers in June 1990.

38. Brown, *Hopes and Shadows*, pp. 133–34.

39. Václav Havel, *Summer Meditations*, trans. Paul Wilson (New York: Alfred A. Knopf, 1992), pp. 26–7.

40. The plan, elaborated on at Harvard a month later, is explained in Jiří Dienstbier, "Central and Eastern Europe and a New European Order," Address at Harvard University, May 15, 1990, reprinted in Whipple, ed., *After the Velvet Revolution*, pp. 115–25.

41. For more on the period, see Wheaton and Kavan, *The Velvet Revolution*, pp. 175–86.

42. The "Visegrád Four" initiative was one that we had developed at staff level, and the senior levels of the administration were too preoccupied with more pressing business in the Persian Gulf either to endorse or overrule it. In Warsaw, the foreign ministry was also thinking along these lines and welcomed an American initiative in Bratislava and Prague.

43. See Chapter 8.

44. Interestingly, some who had accused the United States of clinging too long to the Yugoslav federation now urged us to pull out all the stops to keep Czechoslovakia intact. We in the administration made mistakes, but we didn't usually make the same one twice.

45. These included dinner with František Mikloško, chairman of the Slovak parliament (the Slovak National Council), and four members of the foreign relations committee representing the Slovak National party (SNS), the Movement for a Democratic Slovakia (HZDS), and the Christian Democratic party (KDH); breakfast with Minister of International Relations Pavol Demeš; and separate meetings with the deputy prime minister and deputy chairman of parliament.

46. Reminiscent of Franz-Josef Strauss, the late minister-president of Bavaria (whom I used to see occasionally in Munich's Tivoli restaurant), Mečiar had the same rude populist appeal, bluff manner, and personal magnetism—a kind of Franz-Josef Strauss without the brains.

47. In March 1993, traveling from Prague, where I was deputy head of the U.S. delegation to a CSCE economic forum, I arrived in Bratislava during a political crisis. Mečiar had fired his foreign minister and political rival, Milan Kňažko, and the case had been referred to the president, Michal Kováč. Indeed, it was in the middle of my meeting with Kováč in Bratislava Castle that he was interrupted to sign the order finalizing Kňažko's dismissal.

48. My other purpose in Prague was to join up with a U.S. Defense Department delegation for two days of meetings with Czechoslovak counterparts, headed by Defense Minister Luboš Dobrovský.

49. The NACC will be discussed in the next chapter.

50. "Joint Declaration of the United States of America and the Czech and Slovak Federal Republic," October 22, 1991, Office of the Press Secretary, The White House.

51. The main purpose of the Cheney visit, which also took him to Budapest, was an extended bilateral discussion with Czechoslovak defense minister Luboš Dobrovský on general security issues and U.S.-Czechoslovak military-to-military exchanges and programs.

52. The essay, a speech read in Havel's absence to the October 1989 German Booksellers Association in acceptance of its Peace Prize, was carried in *The New York Review of Books*, January 18, 1990.

53. *New York Times*, February 22, 1990. Havel was elected president of the Czech Republic in January 1993. In June 1996, Václav Klaus was reelected Czech prime minister. In Slovakia, Prime Minister Mečiar and his cabinet were ousted after a no confidence vote in March 1994, only to be reelected the following fall.

54. See, e.g., László Bruszt, "1989: The Negotiated Revolution in Hungary," *Social Research*, Vol. 57, No. 2 (Summer 1990), pp. 365–87; and Rudolf Tőkés, "Hungary's New Political Elites: Adaptation and Change, 1989–90," *Problems of Communism*, November–December 1990, pp. 44–65, esp. pp. 56–8.

55. Technically, Göncz was "Acting President" at this time, pending the formality of parliamentary enactment of the new election laws.

56. Office of the Press Secretary, The White House, Austin, Texas, May 19, 1990.

57. A statement and brief transcript of remarks to the press were issued by the Office of the Press Secretary, The White House, May 23, 1991.

58. Bennett Kovrig, *Of Walls and Bridges: The United States and Eastern Europe* (New York: New York University Press, 1991), p. 326. This was the same Warsaw Pact meeting that sent a message of friendship to the NATO foreign ministers meeting in Turnberry, as described in Chapter 3.

59. *Ibid.*, p. 358.

60. "Remarks by the President and Prime Minister Antall of Hungary Upon Arrival," The South Lawn, October 18, 1990, Office of the Press Secretary, The White House.

61. Judith Pataki, "Hungary: New Government Prefers Cautious Changes," *Report on Eastern Europe*, Vol. 1, No. 28, Radio Free Europe Research, July 13, 1990, p. 24.

62. *Hungary in Transformation to Freedom and Prosperity: Economic Program Proposals of the Joint Hungarian-International Blue Ribbon Commission* (Indianapolis, Ind.: Hudson Institute, 1990), p. 14.

63. We maintained regular contact with the opposition parties as well. During this period, for example, I met with FIDESz chairman Viktor Orbán on December 6, 1990, and SDS leader and Budapest mayor Gabor Demszky on April 15, 1991.

64. For a rundown on U.S. policy at the time, see "U.S. Efforts to Promote a Peaceful Settlement in Yugoslavia," Statement before the Senate Foreign Relations Committee by Ralph Johnson, principal deputy assistant secretary of state for European and Canadian affairs, October 17, 1991, U.S. Department of State *Dispatch*, October 21, 1991.

65. Gyula Kodolanyi, Antall's able foreign policy adviser and a trusted friend throughout the period, expanded on these issues in meetings at the NSC and State Department in early November.

66. FBIS-EEU-90-107, June 4, 1990, 42, as cited in Stokes, *The Walls Came Tumbling Down*, p. 209.

67. *Magyar Forum*, August 20, 1992. For the sordid details of the article and its political spillover, see Judith Pataki, "Istvan Csurka's Tract: Summary and Reactions," *RFE/RL Research Report*, No. 40, October 9, 1992.

68. Brown, *Hopes and Shadows*, p. 139.

69. These issues were high on the agenda of an interagency assistance delegation I led to Budapest in the fall of 1992. We explained that we had substantial privatization assistance funds notionally allocated for Hungary's use, but disbursement hinged on Hungary's implementing a serious program.

70. The Hungarian Socialist party, in coalition with the Free Democratic party, took power following the elections of May 1994, and Gyula Horn, former foreign minister in the communist regime, became the new prime minister.

71. For two brief accounts of U.S.-Romanian relations during the period, see Roger Kirk, "The U.S. and Romania: Facing a Difficult Future," The Atlantic Council of the United States *Policy Paper*, April 1991; and Sergiu Verona, "Romanian Political Developments and U.S.-Romanian Relations," *CRS Issue Brief*, Congressional Research Service, The Library of Congress, April 14, 1993.

72. Roger Kirk and Mircea Raceanu, *Romania Versus the United States: Diplomacy of the Absurd, 1985–1989* (New York: St. Martin's Press, 1994).

73. In a visit to Bucharest in April 1993, Belgian prime minister Wilfried Martens made precisely this point, focusing particularly on Romania's policies toward national minorities. (Reuters, April 13, 1993.)

74. The Presidential Mission, headed by a Republican governor, spent only a few days in Romania and somehow failed to gain an understanding of the context in which these elections were held. Such are the risks in dispatching a high level mission: the assets of senior political leadership weigh against the lack of control over its findings.

75. See, e.g., the report by Thomas Carothers, a member of the election monitoring team organized by the National Democratic Institute, in Larry Garber and Eric Bjornlund, eds., *The New Democratic Frontier* (Washington, D.C.: National Democratic Institute for

International Affairs, 1992), pp. 75–94. See also *The May 1990 Elections in Romania* (Washington, D.C.: National Republican Institute for International Affairs and National Democratic Institute for International Affairs, 1991).

76. For some of these events, see Nestor Ratesh, *Romania: The Entangled Revolution* (New York: Praeger Publishers, 1991), pp. 131–36; and Martyn Rady, *Romania in Turmoil* (London, IB Tauris & Co., Ltd., 1992), pp. 186–89.

77. "Remarks by Secretary of State Baker at the G-24 Ministerial Meeting, Palais D'Egmont, Brussels, Belgium, July 4, 1990," Current Policy No. 1289, Bureau of Public Affairs, U.S. Department of State, July 1990.

78. This calls to mind an earlier "benchmark" message to the Romanians, in the form of a 1988 letter from Deputy Secretary of State John Whitehead to Ceauşescu, explaining what the United States expected of Romania before it was prepared to restore most favored nation status.

79. In December 1990, Român himself booed Hungarian participants in a ceremony held in Alba Iuliu. See Brown, *Hopes and Shadows*, pp. 196–97.

80. David Binder, "Slight Thaw is Detected in U.S.-Romania Ties, *New York Times*, April 18, 1991.

81. My appointment book during the period is peppered with references to office calls by Romanian ambassador Constantinescu, a decent man given a bad hand to play. He understood that Romania's isolation was of its own making but was obliged to push the line that Washington was pursuing a discriminatory policy.

82. Manolescu visited Washington in late September 1991, for meetings with Eagleburger and others, during which I had two extended conversations with him.

83. There was still a holdout or two in the Department of State's policy planning staff, but the rest of the department and all of us on the NSC staff were ready to move forward with MFN.

84. This was the same John Davis who had been ambassador in Warsaw during the revolutionary year of 1989. If he now succeeded in bringing democracy to Romania, I warned him, the president would probably send him to Pyongyang next.

85. One of the Romanians was Ioan Mircea Pascu, whom I had met (together with Professor Dan Nelson, who sent a wide variety of visiting Romanians my way) in my office a month before.

86. One of the legacies of the Ceauşescu era, especially for Romanian politicians like Iliescu, was a belief that U.S. policies were entirely cynical. To the end, Ceauşescu and his coterie never believed that we were serious about human rights. That we would reward him for upsetting Warsaw Pact unity was something he could understand, but when we raised human rights issues, he always felt this was a smoke screen for some hidden agenda.

87. The Eagleburger entourage, including also Deputy Treasury Secretary John Robson and senior officials from several other agencies, traveled the same route as Baker had taken in February 1990—Prague-Moscow-Sofia-Bucharest—and continued on to Tirana, which Baker had visited in June 1991.

88. Verona, "Romanian Political Developments and U.S.-Romanian Relations," pp. 13–16. The next month (October 1992), Iliescu won reelection as president, naming Nicolae Vacaroiu, a nonpartisan economist, the new prime minister.

89. Vermont governor Madeleine Kunin, for example, participated in a sixty-member international delegation led by Iceland's prime minister Steingrimur Hermannsson. The

U.S. Presidential Mission was ably led by Oklahoma governor Henry Bellmon. For a detailed examination of the June 1990 elections, see Larry Garber, "Bulgaria," in Garber and Bjornlund, eds., *The New Democratic Frontier*, pp. 135–60.

90. "Focus on Central and Eastern Europe," No. 19, July 18, 1990, Bureau of Public Affairs, U.S. Department of State.

91. *Ibid.*

92. Stokes, *The Walls Came Tumbling Down*, pp. 177–78.

93. The agreement, formally initialed on October 5, is detailed in "Focus on Central and Eastern Europe," No. 27, October 31, 1990, Bureau of Public Affairs, U.S. Department of State.

94. When we were leaving the Oval Office after his meeting with Bush, I reminded Zhelev that I was the author of the "island of stability" line—which I used in an August 8 meeting with our ambassador to Bulgaria, Ken Hill, who in turn had conveyed it to Zhelev. I added that I would gladly cede all rights to the phrase, so long as I could be a footnote to history. This is it.

95. The series of bilats was a one-ring circus, with presidents and prime ministers ushered in and out in assembly-line fashion, allowing just enough time to change flags. Although they managed to get some diplomatic business done, Bush, Baker, and Scowcroft were punch-drunk by the time they had received a couple of dozen assorted world leaders. (In a similar marathon on a different occasion, Secretary Baker, ten minutes into an animated discussion with a foreign minister counterpart, handed a note to his nearest aide: "Who is this guy?")

96. Duncan M. Perry, "Bulgaria: A New Constitution and Free Elections," *RFE/RL Research Report*, Vol. 1, No. 1, January 3, 1992, esp. p. 79; and Marvin Zonis and Dwight Semler, *The East European Opportunity* (New York: John Wiley & Sons, Inc., 1992), pp. 307–10.

97. "New U.S.-Bulgarian Agricultural Fund Established," Statement by the Press Secretary, The White House, July 22, 1991.

98. See Brown, *Hopes and Shadows*, pp. 111–12, for a discussion of Dimitrov's "dark blue" faction in the UDF.

99. I was accompanied by Deputy Secretary Eagleburger's senior adviser Kenneth Juster, who had also been on the Eagleburger delegation for a G-24 ministerial in Brussels and a gathering of European ambassadors in Berlin.

100. These main lines of policy were of course worked out in advance in interagency discussions back in Washington, approved in outline form by Scowcroft and Eagleburger, and coordinated via cable with Embassy Sofia.

101. Its fiery leader, Konstantin Trenchev, was out of the country, so the meeting was with Podkrepa deputies Radoslav Nenev and Boyko Proichev.

102. MRF spokesman Yunal Lyufti was particularly determined that MRF be a mainstream democratic party. He opposed seeking local autonomy, for example, on grounds that this would only result in MRF's marginalization from the larger issues of economic and political reform.

103. Our other interlocutor was Filip Bokov, who was at that time the Socialist party's shadow foreign minister.

104. They were National Assembly chairman Stefan Savov, UDF leaders Alexander Yordanov and Mikhail Nedelchev, and MRF spokesman Yunal Lyufti.

105. "Remarks by Deputy Secretary of State Lawrence S. Eagleburger to the Bulgar-

ian-U.S. Trade and Economic Council Conference on 'The Future of Democracy and Economic Transition in Bulgaria,' March 4, 1992," Bureau of Public Affairs, U.S. Department of State.

106. Eagleburger's huge delegation, with three deputy secretaries and numerous other senior officials, had broken up into different parties with separate schedules.

107. The Bulgarian Socialist Party won the December 1994 elections, naming Zhan Vlednov prime minister.

108. Louis Zanga, "Albania: Between Democracy and Chaos," *RFE/RL Research Report* Vol. 1, No. 1, January 3, 1992, pp. 74–7.

109. "Address by Secretary of State James A. Baker, III, to Members of the Assembly, Tirana, Albania, Saturday, June 22, 1991," U.S. Department of State, Office of the Assistant Secretary/Spokesman.

110. In June 22 dispatches from Tirana, Reuters estimated four hundred thousand; AP, "hundreds of thousands." AP also noted that the crowd chanted "Bush, Bush" in addition to "Baker, Baker"—a point I was at pains to stress back at the White House.

111. "Remarks by Secretary of State James A. Baker, III, at Skanderbeg Square, Tirana, Albania, June 22, 1991," U.S. Department of State, Office of the Assistant Secretary/Spokesman.

112. A deeply moved Baker used exactly those words with Prime Minister Buffi just afterwards (State Department press release, June 22, 1991).

113. Elez Biberaj, head of VOA's Albanian broadcast service, was known to virtually every Albanian and regarded as a national hero.

114. These issues, as well as the circumstances surrounding Albania's admission into the CSCE, are discussed in Chapter 7.

115. Berisha was returned to the presidency in June 1996 in elections marred by widespread fraud and intimidation.

116. Skanderbeg—sometimes spelled Skenderbeg or Scanderbeg—took the name after converting to Islam, with the "beg" denoting the military rank to which he rose. (His victory at Kruje gave way to full Ottoman domination in the next century, but our historical analogy need not be carried all the way to that sad end.)

117. Robert L. Hutchings, "Five Years After: Reflections on the Post-Communist Transitions and Western Assistance Strategies," in *East-Central European Economies in Transition*, Joint Economic Committee, Congress of the United States (Washington, D.C.: U.S. Government Printing Office, 1994), pp. 176–90.

118. Stokes, *The Walls Came Tumbling Down*, p. 259.

Chapter 7

1. United States Information Service, January 18, 1990, as cited in Bennett Kovrig, *Of Walls and Bridges: The United States and Eastern Europe* (New York: New York University Press, 1991), p. 361.

2. EC Commission president Jacques Delors made a similar point in 1990: "The Community once again faces the same choices as it did in the 1950s and 1980s: rapid progress or gradual disintegration." (Jacques Delors, "Europe's Ambitions," *Foreign Policy* No. 80 [Fall 1990]: 27.)

3. "A New Europe, A New Atlanticism: Architecture for a New Era," Address by Sec-

retary of State James A. Baker, III, to the Berlin Press Club, Steigenberger Hotel, Berlin, December 12, 1989, U.S. Department of State press release of that date.

4. President Bush, "A Time of Decision for the NATO Alliance," Intervention at the NATO Summit, Rome, Italy, November 7, 1991, U.S. Department of State *Dispatch*, November 11, 1991, p. 823.

5. The Elysée was also dropping hints in the press of a possible rapprochement between Paris and Washington. See, e.g., "French-U.S. Relations Blossom Amid Desert Storm," *Washington Post*, February 26, 1991.

6. The plan, premature in 1990 and 1991, came to fruition in December 1995, when Jacques Chirac, Mitterrand's successor as French president, announced France's rapproachement with NATO's military institutions. For a good analysis, see Ronald Tiersky, "A Likely Story: Chirac, France-NATO, European Security, and American Hegemony," in *French Politics and Society*, Vol. 14, No. 2 (Spring 1996): 1–8.

7. U.S.-French discussions on NATO had been kept so well hidden from the media that not a single question during the extensive press conference touched on the issue but rather focused almost entirely on the Gulf War. (Office of the Press Secretary, The White House, March 14, 1991.)

8. For background on these disputes, see Peter Ludlow, "Europe's Institutions: Europe's Politics," in Gregory F. Treverton, ed., *The Shape of the New Europe* (New York: Council on Foreign Relations Press, 1992), pp. 77–79; and Hans Binnendijk, "The Emerging European Security Order," in Brad Roberts, ed., *U.S. Foreign Policy After the Cold War* (Cambridge, MA: MIT Press, 1992), pp. 41–44.

9. Cited in Binnendijk, "European Security Order," p. 42.

10. Jacques Delors, "European Integration and Security," Alastair Buchan Memorial Lecture, International Institute for Strategic Studies, London, March 7, 1991.

11. A keen political analyst, Josef Joffe is senior editor with Munich's *Süddeutsche Zeitung*.

12. Unpublished UK paper on foreign policy and security issues, February 1991, as cited in Ludlow, "Europe's Institutions," p. 79.

13. "European Defense and Security in the 1990s," Transcript of the Speech given by the Foreign Secretary, Mr. Douglas Hurd, to the Berlin Press Conference in Berlin on Monday, 10 December 1990, copy provided that date by the British Embassy, Washington.

14. Teltschik's successor was Peter Hartmann, later German ambassador to London. As a career diplomat, he lacked Teltschik's independence from the foreign ministry, which meant that relations between the chancellery and the ministry were not as hostile, but also that the latter's views predominated unless Kohl weighed in personally. To make matters worse, the chancellery adviser (under Hartmann) responsible for these issues was an ardent Europeanist whose views were much closer to the French than to ours.

15. Vattani and I discussed these issues over a private dinner on May 7, and I recall being gratified at how close our perspectives were.

16. "Policy Statement by Herr Helmut Kohl, Chancellor of the Federal Republic of Germany, in the German Bundestag on 30 January 1991," facsimile copy transmitted that day to the White House by the Federal chancellery in Bonn.

17. Some weeks before the Genscher visit, we at the NSC staff had come up with the idea of a joint statement and had sketched out what it might include—only to find, when we broached the idea, that Secretary Baker's senior staff had been thinking along the same

lines and indeed had developed an almost identical working draft for negotiation with the Germans.

18. "U.S.-German Views on the New European and Trans-Atlantic Architecture," Joint Statement by Secretary Baker and German Foreign Minister Genscher, May 10, 1991, U.S. Department of State *Dispatch*, May 13, 1991, p. 346.

19. The full texts were reprinted in U.S. Department of State *Dispatch*, June 10, 1991. Both documents likewise reaffirmed NATO's integrated command, reflecting our decision not to accede to French overtures.

20. *Washington Post*, May 28, 1991, p. A15.

21. "The Agenda of German Politics for the Nineties," Speech by Dr. Helmut Kohl, Chancellor of the Federal Republic of Germany, in Washington, D.C., on May 20, 1991. Text provided by the German embassy, Washington, D.C.

22. This was the 95-page draft, or "non-paper," assembled in April 1991 by Luxembourg, as EC presidency country.

23. *Washington Post*, June 26, 1991, p. A13.

24. Indeed, the following January, when I traveled to Bonn mainly to mend fences over the issue of recognition of breakaway Yugoslav republics, I was misled by Kohl's security advisers. No decisions had been taken, I was assured, but the United States would be fully informed. Yet a few weeks later, another Franco-German proposal called for creation of a "Eurocorps," again with the preferred French formulation.

25. President Bush, "A Time of Decision for the NATO Alliance," Intervention at the NATO Summit, Rome, Italy, November 7, 1991, U.S. State Department *Dispatch,* November 11, 1991, p. 824.

26. "Rome Declaration on Peace and Cooperation Issued by the Heads of State and Government participating in the meeting of the North Atlantic Council in Rome on 7th–8th November 1991," NATO Press Service, November 8, 1991.

27. "Opening Address by Mr. François Mitterrand, President of the Republic, At the Conference on Security and Co-operation in Europe," Paris, Kleber Conference Center, November 19, 1990. Text distributed at the Paris Summit.

28. "Address by Mr. Tadeusz Mazowiecki, Prime Minister of the Republic of Poland, to the CSCE Summit of the Heads of State and Government," Paris, November 20, 1990. Text distributed at the summit.

29. Speech to the Sejm, January 1, 1990.

30. "Remarks by Mikhail S. Gorbachev before the Paris CSCE Summit Meeting, November 19, 1990," unofficial Soviet translation distributed at the summit.

31. "Memorandum on the European Security Commission" by the government of Czechoslovakia, Prague, April 6, 1990. Text provided by Mr. Dienstbier.

32. See Chapter 4.

33. *Pravda* (Moscow), January 25, 1991.

34. Gorbachev had signaled his willingness to disband the pact's military organization on the eve of the Visegrád Summit, and the measure was formally agreed on at a contentious February 25 meeting of Warsaw Pact foreign and defense ministers in Budapest. (*Washington Post*, February 26, 1991, p. A16.)

35. Unclassified reporting cable from American Embassy Brussels, dated March 21, 1991. During his meetings with Havel in Prague in November 1990, President Bush had used almost precisely the same image in saying that the United States did not want to see a security vacuum or "no man's land" in the region—an answer, in part, to Henry

Kissinger's proposal, in a June 1990 lecture in Prague, for a "neutral belt" in Central Europe.

36. "Statement by Minister for Foreign Affairs Prof. Krzysztof Skubiszewski to the Polish Sejm, 14 February 1991." English draft provided by the Polish embassy. Skubiszewski also threatened to revoke the 1956 treaty legitimizing the stationing of Soviet forces unless troop withdrawal negotiations were concluded promptly.

37. The "Europe Agreements" were summarized in press releases of the EC Commission in Brussels on November 22, 1991, and March 26, 1992, and printed in full by the Delegation of the Commission of the European Communities, Washington, D.C., on April 16, 1992.

38. *Time*, February 25, 1991, as cited in Vladimir V. Kusin, "Security Concerns in Central Europe," *Radio Free Europe Research*, February 26, 1991, p. 20:

39. William Drozdiak, "France Clouds EC Prospects; Mitterrand Urges Confederation Plan," *Washington Post*, June 13, 1991, p. A31.

40. "US-German Views on the New European and Trans-Atlantic Architecture."

41. "Partnership with the Countries of Central and Eastern Europe," statement issued by the North Atlantic Council meeting in ministerial session in Copenhagen, NATO Press Service, June 6, 1991.

42. "New Initiatives to Reduce Nuclear Forces," Address to the Nation, Washington, D.C., September 27, 1991, U.S. Department of State *Dispatch*, September 30, 1991, pp. 715–18.

43. "Press Conference by the President, The Rose Garden, August 20, 1991," Office of the Press Secretary, The White House.

44. Secretary Baker, "Conflict in the Soviet Union," excerpts from remarks during a meeting of the North Atlantic Council, Brussels, Belgium, August 21, 1991, U.S. Department of State *Dispatch*, August 26, 1991, pp. 632–33.

45. The president had taken the latest, shortest draft from his pocket at the joint press conference in the Rose Garden but, gauging his audience, put it back in his pocket unread. As he must have anticipated, the questions put to him and Kohl by the media did not touch at all on European issues, so the statement would have gotten no media play anyway. ("Press Conference by the President and Chancellor Helmut Kohl," The Rose Garden, September 16, 1991, Office of the Press Secretary, The White House.")

46. "U.S.-German Joint Statement on the Transatlantic Community," Joint Statement by Secretary Baker and German Foreign Minister Hans-Dietrich Genscher, Washington, D.C., October 2, 1991, U.S. Department of State *Dispatch*, October 7, 1991, pp. 736–37.

47. On a trip to Warsaw, Bratislava, and Prague a few days later, I learned from Zbigniew Lewicki, the amiable and able former professor who headed the Americas department in the Polish foreign ministry, how the Visegrád group managed to reply so quickly. As soon as the Poles read the Baker-Genscher statement, Polish foreign minister Skubiszewski instructed Lewicki to draft a reply and coordinate by facsimile with Prague and Budapest. The sequence took but a few hours and enabled the three countries to set a positive tone before Moscow or others had a chance to react to the contrary.

48. Bush, "New Initiatives," p. 16.

49. Secretary Baker, "Intervention at the North Atlantic Cooperation Council (NACC) ministerial meeting," Brussels, March 10, 1992, U.S. Department of State *Dispatch*, March 16, 1992, p. 201.

50. It was the NACC's second meeting overall but the first in which new members from the East participated.

51. "Rome Declaration," November 8, 1991.

52. Colin Powell, "The American Commitment to European Security" (text of the Alastair Buchan memorial lecture, delivered April 7, 1992 in London), *Survival*, Summer 1992, p. 5.

53. "Proposal on National Minorities submitted by the delegations of Austria, Czechoslovakia, Hungary, Italy and Yugoslavia," as reprinted in "International Protection of National Minorities: Memorandum for the Copenhagen Meeting on the Human Dimension," Hungarian Human Rights Foundation, June 1990. [Emphasis added.]

54. "Statement delivered by Mr. Géza Entz, Head of the Hungarian Delegation, at the opening session of the CSCE Expert Meeting on National Minorities," July 2, 1991. (Text provided by Mr. Entz.)

55. "Report of the CSCE Meeting of Experts on National Minorities," Geneva, July 1991. For excerpts and analyses, see Vojtech Mastny, *The Helsinki Process and the Reintegration of Europe, 1986–91* (New York: New York University Press, 1992), pp. 42–43 and 298–306; and the Commission on Security and Cooperation in Europe, *From Vienna to Helsinki: Reports on the Inter-Sessional Meetings of the CSCE Process* (Washington, D.C.: U.S. Congress, Commission on Security and Cooperation in Europe, April 1992), pp. 133–49. Focusing on principles, Mastny (p. 42) termed the conference "heartening"; looking for specific commitments, the Commission (pp. 133 and 144) found its achievements "modest."

56. "Report of the CSCE Meeting of Experts on Peaceful Settlement of Disputes," Valletta 1991, issued in Valletta, Malta, February 8, 1991. See also Commission on Security and Cooperation in Europe, *From Vienna to Helsinki*, pp. 111–23.

57. "Berlin Meeting of the CSCE Council, 19–20 June 1991: Summary of Conclusions." (The issuance of a matter-of-fact summary rather than a tortuous declaration was another innovation designed to move CSCE from the hortatory to the operational.) See also Mastny, *The Helsinki Process*, pp. 41–42 and 311–13.

58. Commission on Security and Cooperation in Europe, *From Vienna to Helsinki*, pp. 151–75; Mastny, *The Helsinki Process*, pp. 320–28.

59. The 68-page declaration was issued as "CSCE Helsinki Document 1992: The Challenges of Change," Helsinki, July 1992. For excerpts and a summary of the negotiations, see "The Helsinki Follow-Up Meeting of the Conference on Security and Co-operation in Europe, March 24–July 8, 1992," report prepared by the staff of the Commission on Security and Cooperation in Europe, United States Congress. (A ministerial meeting in Prague, January 30–31, 1992, prepared the way for the Helsinki Summit, as did another foreign ministers' meeting in Helsinki at the opening of the review conference. Baker attended the former, and Eagleburger the latter, in a memorable forty-hour over-and-back trip to Helsinki.)

60. Ray Stannard Baker and William E. Dodds, eds., *The Public Papers of Woodrow Wilson: The New Democracy*, 2 vols. (New York: Harper, 1926), 2:351.

Chapter 8

1. David Reynolds, "Thawing History: Europe in the 1990s and Pre–Cold War Patterns," in Colin Crouch and David Marquand, eds., *Towards Greater Europe* (Oxford and Cambridge, Ma.: Blackwell Publishers, 1992), p. 28.

2. E.g., the second paragraph of the introduction to Paul Kennedy's *The Rise and Fall of the Great Powers* (New York: Random House, 1987), p. xv: "The triumph of any one Great Power . . . or the collapse of another, has usually been the consequence of lengthy fighting by its armed forces."

3. It is perhaps emblematic of this "paradigm shift" that in 1990 I brought from home my undergraduate historical atlas and kept it close at hand in my office in the Old Executive Office Building.

4. Francis Fukuyama, "The End of History?" *The National Interest*, No. 16 (Summer 1989): 3–18. The article by Fukuyama, deputy director of the State Department's policy planning staff at the beginning of the Bush administration, was more sophisticated than his critics credited, but the debate took on a life of its own. For an elaboration of his thesis, see Francis Fukuyama, *The End of History and the Last Man* (New York: Avon Books, 1992).

5. Reynolds, "Thawing History," p. 9.

6. Mark Brandenburg [pseudonym], "Under the Ice," *New Republic* 190 (April 23, 1984): 13–15.

7. Warren Zimmermann, "The Last Ambassador: Memoirs of the Collapse of Yugoslavia," *Foreign Affairs*, Vol. 74, No. 2, March/April 1995, p. 2.

8. For two authoritative accounts of the Bush administration's approaches toward Yugoslavia, see Zimmermann, "The Last Ambassador," and David Gompert, "How to Defeat Serbia," *Foreign Affairs*, Vol. 73, No. 4, July/August 1994, pp. 30–47.

9. In an article written in 1988 and published in early 1989, I described a Yugoslavia in deep crisis: "Before 1980, central authority was provided by the Communist party and Tito himself. Now there is no Tito, and hardly any party, to hold the country together." (Robert L. Hutchings, "'Leadership Drift' in Communist Systems," *Studies in Comparative Communism*, Vol. XXII, No. 1 (Spring 1989): 7–8.)

10. Zimmermann, *Last Ambassador*, p. 5.

11. For discussion, see J. F. Brown, *Hopes and Shadows: Eastern Europe After Communism* (Durham, N.C.: Duke University Press, 1994), pp. 238–52; and Gale Stokes, *The Walls Came Tumbling Down* (New York and Oxford: Oxford University Press, 1993), pp. 232–41.

12. Stokes, *The Walls Came Tumbling Down*, pp. 241–49.

13. David Binder, "Yugoslavia Seen Breaking Up Soon," *New York Times*, November 28, 1990, p. A7.

14. There is obviously a danger that an overly cozy relationship with the policy community would compromise the intelligence community's critical distance and analytic integrity, but the much more common failing was a hands off approach that rendered intelligence analysis abstract and often unusable. Besides, the "politicization" of intelligence sprang less often from policy advocacy than from a kind of corporate mind-set that foreclosed lines of analysis that went against the grain. This latter problem was more likely to be ameliorated by involvement in the give-and-take with the policy community than in cloistered seclusion.

15. London *Times*, March 19, 1991, p. 7; and *The Independent* (London), March 19, p. 11. On May 19, Croatia overwhelmingly endorsed independence in a referendum widely boycotted by Serbs.

16. *Politika*, June 2, 1991, in *Foreign Broadcast Information Service* Daily Report, Eastern Europe, June 3, 1991, p. 43.

17. *New York Times*, June 29, 1991. The "troika" consisted of past, present, and future EC presidency countries in their six month rotational system.

18. London *Times*, June 20, 1991. See also Richard Weitz, "The CSCE and the Yugoslav Conflict," *Radio Free Europe/Radio Liberty Research Report*, Vol. 1, No. 5, January 31, 1992, p. 24.

19. A member of Rugova's small delegation, having studied Baker's speech in Berlin the day before, discoursed knowledgeably about the secretary's view of the principle of "subsidiarity"—making for an oddly academic discussion under the circumstances.

20. Mercifully, the State Department's reporting cables required only that we summarize the discussions rather than record them verbatim as was required for presidential "memcons" (memoranda of conversation). The sessions were nonetheless grueling. Baker may have been the only one of the exhausted American delegation to stay awake throughout.

21. My recollection of the meetings tracks precisely with Zimmermann's, in *The Last Ambassador*, pp. 11–12. Secretary Baker's account in his memoirs, because it accentuates his warnings against the use of force in his several conversations, may tilt the overall message toward greater toughness than was perceived by his interlocutors. (James A. Baker, III, with Thomas M. DeFrank, *The Politics of Diplomacy: Revolution, War and Peace, 1989–92* [New York: G. P. Putnam's Sons, 1995], pp. 478–83.)

22. Zimmermann, *The Last Ambassador*, p. 12.

23. Baker said as much in his message to President Bush that night: "Frankly, I'm dubious about the effect." (Baker, *Politics of Diplomacy*, p. 483.)

24. Secretary Baker, "U.S. Concerns about the Future of Yugoslavia," Excerpts from Remarks at the Federation Palace, Belgrade, Yugoslavia, June 21, 1991, U.S. Department of State *Dispatch*, Vol. 2, No. 26, July 1, 1991, p. 468.

25. For a blow-by-blow account, see Marc Weller, "The International Response to the Dissolution of the Socialist Federal Republic of Yugoslavia," *American Journal of International Law*, Vol. 86, No. 3 (July 1992): 569–607.

26. Zimmermann, *The Last Ambassador*, pp. 12–13.

27. Weller, "International Response," pp. 575–77.

28. "Violent Crisis in Yugoslavia," Address by Secretary Baker before the UN Security Council, New York City, September 25, 1991, in U.S. Department of State *Dispatch*, Vol. 2, No. 39, September 30, 1991, p. 723.

29. In his memoirs, Secretary Baker explained that "there was never any thought at that time of using U.S. ground troops" with reference to the two world wars and the Cold War (Baker, *Politics of Diplomacy*, pp. 635–36), yet there were many military options that stopped far short of open-ended commitment. Indeed, Baker also notes his endorsement, a year later, of a "game plan" (which was never implemented) for Bosnia-Herzegovina that involved a naval blockade and limited air strikes (pp. 648–50).

30. In a March 5 letter sent to the European allies, as well as Carrington and Vance, Secretary Baker posed but did not resolve the problem: "We have wrestled with the question of whether recognition of Bosnia-Herzegovina's independence would contribute to stability in that delicately balanced republic or encourage efforts by the large Serbian minority to destabilize the situation." (Baker, *Politics of Diplomacy*, p. 641.)

31. These were reported in a series of articles by Roy Gutman in *Newsday*, August 2, 3, 5, 6, and 9, 1992.

32. The State Department initially confirmed the reports through its spokesman, then retracted the statement in congressional testimony the next day, stressing that we had no

independent confirmation. Critics within the State Department—including the acting Yugoslav desk officer, who resigned in protest over U.S. passivity in the face of genocide—felt that the administration was deliberately suppressing what it knew so as to avoid being pushed to take stronger action.

I was not directly involved in this issue, having moved from the NSC the month before to direct the U.S. assistance program for Eastern Europe, but my sense was and is that there was no conspiracy of silence. It was, rather, a difference of judgment as to whether we had at that time sufficient corroborated evidence to confirm the press reports. The department may have been overcautious in its public statements and less than zealous in trying to draw out of the intelligence community the evidence it needed, but there was not, to my knowledge, a deliberate effort to suppress or conceal.

33. Secretary Baker had moved to the White House to help direct the president's re-election campaign, and Eagleburger served as acting secretary and then secretary.

34. Eagleburger issued these charges in a December 16 speech before the Geneva conference. (*New York Times*, December 17, 1992.)

35. *New York Times*, August 27, 1992, p. 22.

36. *New York Times*, August 27, 1992; and "Material Relating to the London Conference (August 26–27, 1992) and the Crisis in the Former Yugoslavia," U.S. Department of State *Dispatch* Vol. 3, Supplement No. 7, September 1992.

37. Foreign policy officials are accustomed to hearing from their academic and journalistic counterparts that when something good happens in the world, the United States was not a factor, but when something bad happens, we were responsible for it.

38. This is about the time that we sent our urgent cables to all European capitals. Our instincts were right, but our follow-through was weak.

39. By the time of the London conference, I took it as my main mission—given my conspicuously ineffectual role hitherto—to ensure that policy papers destined for NSC principals were scrupulously honest about the likely effect of a given policy option. Although I disagreed with the policies we were pursuing, I fully respected the fact that the president and other NSC principals had life and death responsibilities that I could only dimly imagine. Yet it was no service to mislead them into believing they could have their cake and eat it too—that they could avoid risky policies yet still achieve our stated objectives. If half-measures were likely to fail, we owed it to them to say so.

40. Long after leaving office, Baker addressed this point directly: "Does the United States have an interest in stopping the humanitarian nightmare . . . [and] supporting the territorial integrity of Bosnia? Of course. But are our interests in either sufficiently vital to warrant the introduction of ground forces into a potential military quagmire? The answer is clearly no—as it has been from the beginning." (*Los Angeles Times*, June 25, 1995.) Baker went on to argue that U.S. interests lay in containing the conflict and averting a broader Balkan war.

In his memoirs, Secretary Baker asserted again that "our vital interests were not at stake." (Baker, *Politics of Diplomacy*, p. 636.) But this begged the question of whether there were *any* important interests involved. Thus, his explanation of U.S. policy toward Yugoslavia (pp. 634–51) tends to frame the issues so starkly as to obscure the wide range of policy choices between passivity and Armageddon in a conflict that impinged on important, though arguably not "vital," American interests.

41. Gompert, "How to Defeat Serbia," p. 42.

42. Meeting between Wilson and Frank P. Walsh and Edward F. Dunne, Paris, June 11, 1919, as cited in Daniel Patrick Moynihan, *Pandaemonium* (Oxford: Oxford University Press, 1993), p. 85.

43. Lansing's Confidential Diaries, as cited in *ibid.*, p. 81.

44. For detailed discussion of the concept, see *ibid.*, pp. 63–106, esp. pp. 66–71, and Kamal S. Shehadi, *Ethnic Self-Determination and the Break-up of States*, Adelphi Paper 283 (London: International Institute of Strategic Studies, December 1993), pp. 4–10.

45. "Political Declaration: Strengthening the International Order," London Economic Summit 1991, July 16, 1991. Text distributed at the summit.

46. James Crawford, *The Creation of States in International Law* (Oxford: Clarendon Press, 1979), pp. 31–128, esp. pp. 36–48.

47. "U.S. Approach to Changes in the Soviet Union," Statement by Secretary of State James A. Baker, III, in U.S. Department of State *Dispatch*, Vol. 2, 1991, p. 667.

48. "Guidelines on the Recognition of New States in Eastern Europe and in the Soviet Union," Declaration of the European Community, Brussels and the Hague, December 16, 1991. The EC also stipulated that "The Community and its Member States will not recognize entities which are the result of aggression."

49. Shehadi, *Ethnic Self-Determination*, p. 21.

50. Cited in Michael R. Beschloss and Strobe Talbott, *At the Highest Levels: The Inside Story of the End of the Cold War* (Boston: Little, Brown and Company, 1993), p. 317.

51. *Figaro*, February 11, 1991.

52. Beschloss and Talbott, *At the Highest Levels*, p. 323; Baker, *Politics of Diplomacy*, p. 391. See also Anatoly Chernyaev's first-hand account of Ambassador Jack Matlock's meeting with Gorbachev on January 24, 1991, in A. S. Chernyaev, *Shest' let s Gorbachevym* [Six Years with Gorbachev] (Moscow: Progress Publishers, 1993), pp. 416–19. Gorbachev said that he had told Baltic leaders that "if you've decided to leave, then leave, but legally, constitutionally" and also asked Matlock to assure President Bush that "I will act as we agreed. . . . I will do everything."

53. "Address by the President on the State of the Union," The U.S. Capitol, Washington, D.C., January 29, 1991, Office of the Press Secretary, The White House.

54. Yeltsin was elected Russian president on June 12, 1991, with 57 percent of the vote against just 17 percent for Gorbachev's preferred candidate, former Soviet prime minister Nikolai Ryzhkov.

55. "The Soviet Cauldron," Report of the Office of Soviet Analysis, Central Intelligence Agency, April 25, 1991, declassified and approved for release, November 1994, from "Briefing Book for Cold War Endgame," documents compiled by the National Security Archive for a conference at Princeton University, March 29–30, 1996.

56. See Chernyaev's account of Matlock's meeting with Gorbachev to deliver the letter, as well as verbatim excerpts of Bush's subsequent telephone conversation with Gorbachev, in Chernyaev, *Shest' let*, pp. 451–55.

57. For Baker's account, see *Politics of Diplomacy*, pp. 470–71.

58. Graham Allison and Robert Blackwill, "America's Stake in the Soviet Future," *Foreign Affairs* Vol. 70, No. 3 (Summer 1991): 77–97.

59. Such were the conclusions of my NSC colleague Condoleezza Rice in her valedictory memo before returning to the Stanford faculty. (Beschloss and Talbott, *At the Highest Levels*, pp. 345–46.)

60. On the G-7 decisions, see U.S. Department of State *Dispatch*, Vol. 2, No. 29, July 22, 1991, pp. 519–27.

61. For background on the START and CFE negotiations in the spring and early summer of 1991, see Beschloss and Talbott, *At the Highest Levels*, pp. 362–73 and 402–6.

62. On the summit documents and agreements, see U.S. Department of State *Dispatch*, Vol. 2, No. 32, August 12, 1991, pp. 591–98; and various fact sheets distributed by the White House's Office of the Press Secretary, July 30 and 31, 1991.

63. The text was reprinted in *ibid.*, pp. 597–99. It was indelibly dubbed the "Chicken Kiev" speech by William Safire in the *New York Times*, August 29, 1991.

64. In addition to Yanayev, the leaders of the coup were Defense Minister Dmitri Yazov, KGB chairman Vladimir Kryuchkov, Interior Minister Boris Pugo, Prime Minister Valentin Pavlov, and three others.

65. See Baker's detailed account, in *Politics of Diplomacy*, pp. 514–23.

66. In principle, our line was quite similar to that we had taken in Romania in the midst of the December 1989 revolution.

67. Bush's various statements are carried in U.S. Department of State *Dispatch*, Vol. 2, No. 33, August 19, 1991, pp. 615–17. See also Secretary Baker's press briefing en route to Brussels, issued by the Office of the Assistant Secretary/Spokesman, U.S. Department of State, August 20, 1991.

68. For Gorbachev's account, see Mikhail Gorbachev, *The August Coup: The Truth and the Lessons* (New York: HarperCollins, 1991).

69. See, e.g., Beschloss and Talbott, *At the Highest Levels*, p. 444. (The point, which administration critics ignored, was that recognition by a small European country was one thing, recognition by the United States quite another.)

70. Cited in Baker, *Politics of Diplomacy*, pp. 524–25.

71. *Ibid.*, p. 558.

72. In his memoirs, General Powell, chairman of the Joint Chiefs, described his strong support for the nuclear reductions package that Bush announced in late September and criticized the opposition from the "Reagan-era hard-liners" on the civilian side of the Pentagon. But he failed to disclose his thinking on the prospect of the dissolution of the Soviet Union. See Colin Powell, *My American Journey* (New York: Random House, 1995), pp. 540–41.

73. "US Approach to Changes in the Soviet Union," opening statement at a news conference, Washington, D.C., September 4, 1991, U.S. Department of State *Dispatch*, September 9, 1991, p. 667.

74. See Chapter 7. See also Bush's address to the nation, Washington, D.C., September 27, 1991, U.S. Department of State *Dispatch*, Vol. 2, No. 39, September 30, 1991, pp. 715–18.

75. For background to the Moscow CSCE conference, see Chapter 7. On the margins of the conference, Baker met with the Russian leadership and then traveled to Kazakhstan and the three Baltic states.

76. Baker, *Politics of Diplomacy*, pp. 659–65 and 668–71.

77. *Ibid.*, pp. 564–83.

78. President Bush, "US Welcomes New Commonwealth of Independent States," Address to the nation, Washington, D.C., December 25, 1991, U.S. Department of State *Dispatch*, December 30, 1991, pp. 911–12.

79. Baker, *Politics of Diplomacy*, pp. 614–33.

80. *Ibid.*, pp. 665–68. The establishment of diplomatic relations actually came on April 23, just before Baker's visit.

81. "America and the Collapse of the Soviet Empire: What Has to Be Done," Address

by Secretary of State James A. Baker, III, at Princeton University, December 12, 1991, U.S. Department of State, Office of the Assistant Secretary/Spokesman.

82. "Remarks by the President in Address to International Conference on Humanitarian Assistance to the Former USSR," U.S. Department of State, Washington, D.C., January 22, 1992, Office of the Press Secretary, The White House.

83. "Multilateral Financial Assistance Package for Russia," Office of the Press Secretary, The White House, April 1, 1992. It was inadvertent but perhaps appropriate that the document was released on the American "April Fool's Day."

84. "Declaration on U.S.-Ukrainian Relations and the Building of a Democratic Partnership, by President Bush and President Kravchuk," May 6, 1992, Office of the Press Secretary, The White House, May 6, 1992; and "Declaration by President Bush and President Nazarbayev on Relations between the United States and Kazakhstan," Office of the Press Secretary, The White House, May 19, 1992.

85. Press releases and fact sheets issued by the Office of the Press Secretary, The White House, June 17, 1992.

86. "Camp David Declaration on New Relations, by President Bush and President Yeltsin," Camp David, Maryland, Office of the Press Secretary, The White House, February 1, 1992.

87. This personal relationship also redounded to our benefit. See, e.g., Bush's vivid account, in his memoirs, of the very close relationship with Gorbachev that was cemented in their June 1990 meeting at Camp David. (Forthcoming from Alfred A. Knopf, Inc.; draft manuscript shared with the author in July 1996.)

88. Quoted in Don Oberdorfer, *The Turn: From the Cold War to a New Era* (New York, Simon and Schuster, 1991), p. 404.

Conclusion

1. Harold Nicolson, *Peacemaking 1919* (London: Constable and Peter Smith, 1943), pp. ix–x.

2. David Reynolds, "Thawing History: Europe in the 1990s and Pre–Cold War Patterns," in Colin Crouch and David Marquand, eds., *Towards Greater Europe?* (Oxford and Cambridge, Ma.: Blackwell Publishers, 1992), pp. 16–17.

3. Robert Hutchings, "The 'Eastern Question' Revisited," *Problems of Post-Communism* (Fall 1994), pp. 45–49.

4. "Waiting for the Barbarians," in C. P. *Cavafy: Collected Poems*, ed. George Savidis, trans. Edmund Keeley and Philip Sharrard (Princeton: Princeton University Press, 1975; rev. ed. 1992), p. 18.

5. John Lewis Gaddis, *The United States and the End of the Cold War* (New York and Oxford: Oxford University Press, 1992), p. vii.

6. William L. Neumann, *After Victory: Churchill, Roosevelt, Stalin and the Making of the Peace* (New York: Harper and Row, 1967), pp. 33–38.

7. *Ibid.*, pp. 38–44; and Lynn Etheridge Davis, *The Cold War Begins: Soviet-American Conflict over Eastern Europe* (Princeton, N.J.: Princeton University Press, 1974), pp. 70–74. The organization and charter of the advisory committee are described in Harley Notter, *Postwar Foreign Policy Preparation, 1939–45* (Washington, D.C.: U.S. Government Printing Office, 1949).

8. See, e.g., Richard N. Gardner, "The Comeback of Liberal Internationalism," *The Washington Quarterly*, Summer 1990, pp. 23–39; Richard H. Ullman, "Enlarging the Zone of Peace," *Foreign Policy* No. 80 (Fall 1990), pp. 102–20; and Francis Fukuyama's often misrepresented "The End of History," *The National Interest*, Summer 1989, pp. 3–18.

9. In the European context, see, e.g., Stephen Van Evera, "Primed for Peace: Europe After the Cold War," *International Security*, Vol. 15, No. 3 (Winter 1990/91), pp. 7–57; and W. R. Smyser, "Vienna, Versailles, and Now Paris: Third Time Lucky?" *The Washington Quarterly*, Summer 1991, pp. 61–70.

10. Mearsheimer, "Back to the Future"; Charles Krauthammer, "The Unipolar Moment," *Foreign Affairs*, Vol. 70, No. 1 (Winter 1990/91), pp. 23–33; and John Lukacs, *The End of the Twentieth Century and the End of the Modern Age* (New York: Ticknor and Fields, 1993). See also Stanley Kober, "Revolutions Gone Bad," *Foreign Policy* No. 91 (Summer 1993), pp. 102–20, which, as he acknowledges, contrasts sharply with his earlier "Idealpolitik," *Foreign Policy* No. 79 (Summer 1990).

11. In Moscow in May 1992, Secretary Eagleburger delivered a speech—meant to show empathy, presumably—whose message was basically that: "We both sacrificed dearly and suffered greatly. . . . [We] squandered [our] energies and wasted precious resources in the colossal folly which was the Cold War." ("A Democratic Partnership for the Post-Cold War Era," address before the Trade and Economic Council's annual meeting, the Kremlin, Moscow, Russia, May 27, 1992, U.S. Department of State *Dispatch*, Vol. 3, No. 23, June 8, 1992, p. 441.) The speechwriters had distributed the draft too late for those of us on the delegation to suggest a different tone than that of "colossal folly," but the speech, mercifully, was ignored by the traveling press.

12. President Bush, State of the Union Address, January 28, 1992, excerpted in U.S. Department of State *Dispatch*, February 3, 1992, p. 73.

13. Council on Foreign Relations, Conference on "US National Interests After the Cold War," Wye Center, Queenstown, Maryland, December 14–16, 1995, summarized in a Council Memorandum on "Vital US Interests," dated January 8, 1996.

14. Robert L. Hutchings, "Rediscovering 'The National Interest' in American Foreign Policy," Occasional Paper, Woodrow Wilson International Center for Scholars, Washington, D.C., March 1996.

15. Kissinger puts it well in Henry Kissinger, *Diplomacy* (New York: Simon & Schuster, 1994), pp. 19–25.

16. "The North Atlantic Treaty," in *NATO Handbook* (Brussels: NATO Office of Information and Press, 1992), pp. 143–46.

17. See Chapter 1.

18. Michael Mandelbaum, "Our Outdated Russia Policy," *Time*, February 5, 1996, p. 39.

19. Gaddis, *United States and the End of the Cold War*, p. 211.

Bibliography

Books

Allison, Graham, and Gregory F. Treverton, eds. *Rethinking America's Security: Beyond Cold War to New World Order.* New York: W. W. Norton and Co., Inc., 1992.

Asmus, Ronald D., J. F. Brown, and Keith Crane. *Soviet Foreign Policy and the Revolutions of 1989 in Eastern Europe.* Durham, N.C.: Duke University Press, 1991.

Baker, James A., III, with Thomas M. DeFrank. *The Politics of Diplomacy: Revolution, War and Peace, 1989–92.* New York: G. P. Putnam's Sons, 1995.

Baranczak, Stanisław. *Breathing Underwater and Other East European Essays.* Cambridge, Ma.: Harvard University Press, 1990.

Batt, Judy. *East Central Europe: From Reform to Transformation.* New York: Council on Foreign Relations Press, 1991.

Behr, Edward. *Kiss the Hand You Cannot Bite: The Rise and Fall of the Ceauşescus.* New York: Villard Books, 1991.

Beres, Witold, and Jerzy Skoczyslas. *General Kiszczaks Mowi . . . Prawie Wszystko* [General Kiszczak tells us . . . almost everything]. Warsaw: Polska Oficya Wydawnicza "BGW," 1991.

Bertram, Christoph. *Europe in the Balance: Securing the Peace Won in the Cold War.* Washington, D.C.: Carnegie Endowment for International Peace, 1995.

Beschloss, Michael R., and Strobe Talbott. *At the Highest Levels: The Inside Story of the End of the Cold War.* Boston: Little, Brown and Company, 1993.

Boldin, Valery. *Ten Years That Shook the World: The Gorbachev Era as Witnessed by his Chief of Staff.* New York: Basic Books, 1994.

Brandon, Henry, ed. *In Search of a New World Order: The Future of U.S.-European Relations.* Washington, D.C.: The Brookings Institution, 1992.

Brown, J. F. *Surge to Freedom: The End of Communist Rule in Eastern Europe.* Durham, N.C.: Duke University Press, 1991.

———. *Hopes and Shadows: Eastern Europe after Communism.* Durham, N.C.: Duke University Press, 1994.

Brown, J. F., Robert D. Hormats, and William H. Luers. *Western Approaches to Eastern Europe.* New York: Council on Foreign Relations Press, 1992.

Brzezinski, Zbigniew K. *The Grand Failure: The Birth and Death of Communism in the Twentieth Century.* New York: Collier Books, 1990.

Bush, George, and Victor Gold. *Looking Forward.* New York: Doubleday and Co., 1987.

Carrere d'Encausse, Helene. *The End of the Soviet Empire: The Triumph of the Nations.* New York: Basic Books, 1993.

Chase, James. *The Consequences of Peace: The New Internationalism and American Foreign Policy.* New York: Oxford University Press, 1992.

Chernyaev, A. S. *Shest' let s Gorbachevym* [Six years with Gorbachev]. Moscow: Progress Publishers, 1993.

Chirot, Daniel. *The Crisis of Leninism and the Decline of the Left: The Revolutions of 1989.* Seattle: University of Washington Press, 1991.

Codrescu, Andrei. *The Hole in the Flag.* New York: William Morrow and Co., 1991.

Corbo, Vittorio, Fabrizio Coricelli, and Jan Bossak. *Reforming Central and Eastern European Economies: Initial Results and Challenges.* Washington, D.C.: World Bank, 1991.

Crawford, James. *The Creation of States in International Law.* New York: Oxford University Press, 1979.

Crouch, Colin, and David Marquand, eds. *Towards Greater Europe? A Continent without an Iron Curtain.* Cambridge, Ma.: Blackwell Publishers, 1992.

Dahrendorf, Ralf. *Reflections on the Revolution in Europe.* New York: Random House, 1990.

Dawisha, Karen. *Eastern Europe, Gorbachev, and Reform.* Cambridge: Cambridge University Press, 1988.

Echikson, William. *Lighting the Night: Revolution in Eastern Europe.* New York: William Morrow and Co., 1990.

Elbe, Frank, and Richard Kiessler. *Ein Runder Tisch mit Scharfen Ecken* [A round table with sharp corners]. Baden-Baden: Nomos Verlags Gesellschaft, 1993.

Fischer, Stanley, and Alan Gelb. *Issues in Socialist Economy Reforms.* Washington, D.C.: The World Bank, Country Economics Department, 1990.

Frankland, Mark. *The Patriot's Revolution: How Eastern Europe Toppled Communism and Won its Freedom.* Chicago: I. R. Dee Publishers, 1992.

Freedman, Lawrence, ed. *Europe Transformed: Documents on the End of the Cold War.* New York: St. Martin's Press, 1990.

Gaddis, John L. *The Long Peace: Inquiries into the History of the Cold War.* New York: Oxford University Press, 1987.

———. *The United States and the End of the Cold War.* New York: Oxford University Press, 1992.

Garton Ash, Timothy. *The Uses of Adversity; Essays on the Fate of Central Europe.* New York: Random House, 1989.

———. *The Magic Lantern: The Revolutions of '89 Witnessed in Warsaw, Budapest, Berlin, and Prague.* New York: Random House, 1990.

———. *In Europe's Name: Germany and the Divided Continent.* New York: Random House, 1993.

Gates, Robert M. *From the Shadows: The Ultimate Insider's Story of Five Presidents and How They Won the Cold War.* New York: Simon and Schuster, 1996.

Gedmin, Jeffrey. *The Hidden Hand; Gorbachev and the Collapse of East Germany.* Washington, D.C.: AEI Press, 1992.

Gelb, Alan H., and Cheryl W. Gray. *The Transformation of Economies in Central and Eastern Europe: Issues, Progress and Prospects.* Washington, D.C.: The World Bank, 1991.

Glenny, Misha. *The Rebirth of History: Eastern Europe in the Age of Democracy.* London: Penguin Books, 1990.

———. *The Fall of Yugoslavia: The Third Balkan War.* New York: Penguin Books, 1992.

Golden, Nancy L., and Sherrill Brown Wells, eds. *American Foreign Policy: Current Documents*. Washington, D.C.: Department of State, 1990.

Goldfarb, Jeffrey C. *After the Fall: The Pursuit of Democracy in Central Europe*. New York: Basic Books, 1992.

Gomułka, Stanisław, and Anthony Polonsky. *Polish Paradoxes*. New York: Routledge, 1991.

Gorbachev, Mikhail. *Perestroika: New Thinking for Our Country and the World*. New York: Harper and Row Publishers, 1987.

———. *The August Coup: The Truth and the Lessons*. New York: HarperCollins Publishers, Inc., 1991.

Gordon, Lincoln, et al. *Eroding Empire: Western Relations with Eastern Europe*. Washington, D.C.: The Brookings Institution, 1987.

Griffith, William E., ed. *Central and Eastern Europe: The Opening Curtain?* Boulder, Co.: Westview Press, 1989.

Gwertzman, Bernard, and Michael T. Kaufman, eds. *The Collapse of Communism*. New York: Times Books, 1990.

Haftendorn, Helga, and Christian Tuschhoff. *America and Europe in an Era of Change*. Boulder, Co.: Westview Press, 1993.

Hankiss, Elemer. *East European Alternatives*. New York: Oxford University Press, 1990.

Havel, Václav. *The Power of the Powerless: Citizens Against the State in Central-Eastern Europe*. New York: M. E. Sharpe, Inc., 1985.

———. *Disturbing the Peace: A Conversation with Karel Hvizdala*. First American ed. New York: Alfred A. Knopf, 1990.

———. *Summer Meditations*. New York: Alfred A. Knopf, 1992.

Heisenberg, Wolfgang. *German Unification in European Perspective*. Washington, D.C.: Brassey's, Inc., 1991.

Heller, Agnes, and Ferenc Feher. *From Yalta to Glasnost: The Dismantling of Stalin's Empire*. Cambridge, Ma.: Blackwell Publishers, 1991.

Hewett, Ed A., and Victor H. Winston, eds. *Milestones in Glasnost and Perestroyka: Politics and People*. Washington, D.C.: The Brookings Institution, 1991.

Hill, Ronald, and Jan Zielonka. *Restructuring Eastern Europe: Towards a New European Order*. Brookfield, Vt.: Edward Elgar Publishers, 1990.

Hobsbawm, E. J. *Nations and Nationalism since 1780: Programme, Myth, Reality*. New York: Cambridge University Press, 1992.

Huntington, Samuel. *The Third Wave: Democratization in the Late Twentieth Century.* Norman, Ok.: University of Oklahoma Press, 1991.

Hutchings, Robert L. *Soviet–East European Relations: Consolidation and Conflict.* Madison: University of Wisconsin Press, 1983; rev. paperback ed., 1987.

James, Harold, and Marla Stone. *When the Wall Came Down: Reactions to German Unification.* New York: Routledge, 1992.

Jarausch, Konrad H. *The Rush to German Unity.* New York: Oxford University Press, 1994.

Jarausch, Konrad H., and Volker Gransow. *Uniting Germany: Documents and Debates, 1993–1994.* Translated by Allison Brown and Belinda Cooper. Providence, R.I.: Berg Publishers, 1994.

Kaiser, Robert. *Why Gorbachev Happened: His Triumphs and His Failures.* New York: Simon and Schuster, 1991.

Kennedy, Paul. *The Rise and Fall of the Great Powers: Economic Change and Military Conflict from 1500 to 2000.* New York: Random House, 1987.

Keohane, Robert O., Joseph S. Nye, Jr., and Stanley Hoffman, eds. *After the Cold War: International Institutions and State Strategies in Europe, 1989–91.* Cambridge, Ma.: Harvard University Press, 1993.

Kirk, Roger, and Mircea Raceanu. *Romania versus the United States: Diplomacy of the Absurd, 1985–1989.* New York: St. Martin's Press, 1994.

Kornai, János. *The Road to a Free Economy.* New York: W. W. Norton and Co., 1990.

Kovrig, Bennett. *Of Walls and Bridges: The United States and Eastern Europe.* New York: New York University Press, 1991.

Kraljic, Matthew A., ed. *The Breakup of Communism: The Soviet Union and Eastern Europe.* New York: H. W. Wilson, 1993.

Krause, Axel. *Inside the New Europe.* New York: HarperCollins, 1991.

Kwizinskij, Julij A. *Vor dem Sturm: Erinnerungen eines Diplomaten* [Before the storm: A diplomat's memoirs]. Translated by Hilde and Helmut Ettinger. Berlin: Siedler Verlag, 1993.

Lederer, Ivo. *Western Approaches to Eastern Europe.* New York: Council on Foreign Relations Press, 1992.

Legters, Lyman H., ed. *Eastern Europe: Transformation and Revolution, 1945–1991.* Lexington, Ma.: D. C. Heath and Company, 1992.

Lesourne, Jacques, and Bernard Lecomte. *After Communism: From the*

Atlantic to the Urals. Chur, Switzerland: Harwood Academic Publishers, 1991.

Levine, Robert A. *Toward a Stable Transition in Europe: A Conservative/Activist Strategy for the United States.* Santa Monica, Ca.: The RAND Corporation, 1990.

Ligachev, E. K. *Inside Gorbachev's Kremlin: The Memoirs of Yegor Ligachev.* New York: Pantheon Books, 1993.

Lukacs, John. *The End of the Twentieth Century and the End of the Modern Age.* New York: Ticknor and Fields Books, 1993.

Lundestad, Geir. *The American "Empire" and Other Studies of US Foreign Policy in a Comparative Perspective.* New York: Oxford University Press, 1990.

Lynn-Jones, Sean M., ed. *The Cold War and After: Prospects for Peace.* Cambridge, Ma.: The MIT Press, 1991.

Marer, Paul, and Salvatore Zecchini. *The Transition to a Market Economy.* Paris: Organization for Economic Cooperation and Development, 1991.

Mason, David S. *Revolution in East-Central Europe: The Rise and Fall of Communism and the Cold War.* Boulder, Co.: Westview Press, 1992.

Mastny, Vojtech. *The Helsinki Process and the Reintegration of Europe, 1986–1991: Analysis and Documentation.* New York: New York University Press, 1992.

Matlock, Jack F., Jr. *Autopsy on an Empire: The American Ambassador's Account of the Collapse of the Soviet Union.* Cambridge, Ma.: Harvard University Press, 1995.

Menges, Constantine C. *The Future of Germany and the Atlantic Alliance.* Washington, D.C.: AEI Press, 1991.

Merkl, Peter H. *German Unification in the European Context.* University Park, Pa.: Pennsylvania State University Press, 1993.

Moynihan, Daniel P. *On the Law of Nations.* Cambridge, Ma.: Harvard University Press, 1990.

———. *Pandaemonium.* Oxford: Oxford University Press, 1993.

Müchler, Günter and Klaus Hofmann. *Helmut Kohl, Chancellor of German Unity: A Biography.* Bonn: Press and Information Office of the Federal Government, 1992.

Murrell, Peter. *The Nature of Socialist Economies: Lessons from Eastern European Foreign Trade.* Princeton, N.J.: Princeton University Press, 1990.

Nye, Joseph S., Jr. *Bound to Lead: The Changing Nature of American Power.* New York: Basic Books, 1990.

Oberdorfer, Don. *The Turn: From the Cold War to a New Era.* New York: Simon and Schuster, 1991.

O'Donnell, Guillermo, Phillippe C. Schmitter, and Laurence Whitehead, eds. *Transitions from Authoritarian Rule: Tentative Conclusions about Uncertain Democracies.* Baltimore: John Hopkins University Press, 1986.

Organization for Economic Cooperation and Development. *Transition to a Market Economy in Central and Eastern Europe.* Paris: OECD, 1991.

———. *Reforming the Economies of Central and Eastern Europe.* Paris: OECD, 1992.

Pinder, John. *The European Community and Eastern Europe.* London: The Royal Institute of International Affairs, 1991.

Pond, Elizabeth. *Beyond the Wall: Germany's Road to Unification.* Washington, D.C.: The Brookings Institution, 1993.

Powell, Colin. *My American Journey.* New York: Random House, 1995.

Przeworski, Adam. *Democracy and the Market: Political and Economic Reforms in Eastern Europe and Latin America.* New York: Cambridge University Press, 1991.

Rady, Martyn C. *Romania in Turmoil: A Contemporary History.* New York: IB Tauris, 1992.

Rakowski, Mieczysław F. *Jak to sie stało?* [How did it happen?] Warsaw: Polska Oficyna Wydawnicza "BGW," 1991.

Ratesh, Nestor. *Romania: The Entangled Revolution.* Washington, D.C.: Center for Strategic and International Studies, 1991.

Roberts, Brad, ed. *U.S. Foreign Policy After the Cold War.* Cambridge, Ma.: MIT Press, 1992.

———. *U.S. Security in an Uncertain Era.* Cambridge, Ma.: MIT Press, 1993.

Rostow, Eugene. *Toward Managed Peace: The National Security Interests of the United States, 1759 to the Present.* New Haven: Yale University Press, 1993.

Rupnik, Jacques. *The Other Europe: The Rise and Fall of Communism in East Central Europe.* New York: Schocken Books, 1989.

Schäuble, Wolfgang. *Der Vertrag: Wie Ich Über die Deutsche Einheit*

Verhandelte [The Treaty: How I Negotiated German Unity].
Stuttgart: Deutsche Verlag-Anstalt, 1991.

Schöpflin, George, and Nancy Wood, eds. In Search of Central Europe.
Cambridge: Cambridge University Press, 1989.

Shehadi, Kamal S. Ethnic Self-Determination and the Break-up of
States. Adelphi Paper 283. London: International Institute of Strategic Studies, 1993.

Shevardnadze, Eduard A. The Future Belongs to Freedom. New York:
Free Press, 1991.

Simons, Thomas F., Jr. The End of the Cold War? New York: St. Martin's Press, 1990.

———. Eastern Europe in the Postwar World. New York: St. Martin's
Press, 1991.

Sodaro, Michael J. Moscow, Germany, and the West from Khrushchev
to Gorbachev. Ithaca, N.Y.: Cornell University Press, 1990.

Staar, Richard F. U.S.–East European Relations in the 1990s. New
York: Crane Russak, 1989.

Staniszkis, Jadwiga. The Dynamics of the Breakthrough in Eastern Europe: The Polish Experience. Berkeley: University of California Press,
1991.

Stokes, Gale. From Stalinism to Pluralism: A Documentary History of
Eastern Europe since 1945. New York: Oxford University Press, 1991.

———. The Walls Came Tumbling Down: The Collapse of Communism in Eastern Europe. New York: Oxford University Press, 1993.

Szabo, Stephen F. The Diplomacy of German Unification. New York:
St. Martin's Press, 1992.

Teltschik, Horst. 329 Tage: Innenansichten der Einigung [329 Days: An
Insider's View of Unification]. Berlin: Siedler Verlag, 1991.

Thatcher, Margaret. The Downing Street Years. New York: Harper-
Collins Publishers, 1993.

Tismaneanu, Vladimir. In Search of Civil Society: Independent Peace
Movements in the Soviet Bloc. New York: Routledge, 1990.

Treverton, Gregory F. America, Germany and the Future of Europe.
Princeton, N.J.: Princeton University Press, 1992.

Treverton, Gregory F., ed. The Shape of the New Europe. New York:
Council on Foreign Relations Press, 1991.

van Brabant, Josef M. The New Eastern Europe and the World Economy. Boulder, Co.: Westview Press, 1993.

Verdery, Catherine. *National Ideology under Socialism: Identity and Cultural Politics in Ceauşescu's Romania.* Berkeley: University of California Press, 1991.

Volten, Peter M. E. *Bound to Change: Consolidating Democracy in East Central Europe.* New York: Institute for East-West Studies, 1992.

von Weizsäcker, Richard. "Speeches for Our Time, May 8, 1985–December 13, 1991." *German Issues* 1992.

Wałęsa, Lech. *The Struggle and the Triumph: An Autobiography.* New York: Arcade Publishers, 1992.

Wheaton, Bernard, and Zdeněk Kavan. *The Velvet Revolution: Czechoslovakia, 1988–1991.* Boulder, Co.: Westview Press, 1992.

Whelan, Joseph G. *Soviet Diplomacy and Negotiating Behavior, 1988–1990: Gorbachev-Reagan-Bush Meetings at the Summit,* vol. 3. Washington, D.C.: Committee on Foreign Affairs, U.S. Congress, 1991.

Whipple, Tim D., ed. *After the Velvet Revolution: Václav Havel and the New Leaders of Czechoslovakia Speak Out.* New York: Freedom House, 1991.

Wolchik, Sharon. *Czechoslovakia in Transition: Politics, Economics, and Society.* New York: Pinter Publishers, 1991.

Yakovlev, A. N. *The Fate of Marxism in Russia.* New Haven: Yale University Press, 1993.

Zelikow, Philip, and Condoleezza Rice. *Germany Unified and Europe Transformed: A Study in Statecraft.* Cambridge, Ma.: Harvard University Press, 1995.

Articles

Adelman, Irma. "Should There be a Marshall Plan for Eastern Europe?" *Review of Black Political Economy* 19 (Fall 1990): 17–42.

Adomeit, Hannes. "Gorbachev and German Unification: Revision of Thinking, Realignment of Power." *Problems of Communism* 39 (July–August 1990): 1–23.

Allison, Graham. "Testing Gorbachev." *Foreign Affairs* 67, no. 4 (Fall 1988): 19–32.

Allison, Graham, and Robert Blackwill. "America's Stake in the Soviet Future." *Foreign Affairs* 70, no. 3 (Summer 1991): 77–97.

Ardito-Barletta, Nicolas. "Democracy and Development." *The Washington Quarterly* 13, no. 3 (Summer 1990): 165–75.

Asmus, Ronald. "Evolution of Soviet–East European Relations under Mikhail Gorbachev." *Radio Free Europe Research,* RAD Background Report 153 (August 22, 1989): 1–25.

Banac, Ivo. "Yugoslavia: The Fearful Asymmetry of War." *Daedalus* 121, no. 2 (Spring 1992): 150.

Bialer, Seweryn. "Interview: Aleksandr Yakovlev—Redefining Socialism at Home and Abroad." *Journal of International Affairs* 42, no. 2 (Winter 1988/89): 333–55.

Bielecki, Jan Krzysztof. "Problems of the Polish Transformation." *Communist Economies and Economic Transformation* 4, no. 3 (1990).

Breslow, Aimee. "Monitoring Eastern Europe's Transition." *The Washington Quarterly* 14, no. 4 (Autumn 1991): 205–18.

Brumberg, Abraham. "Poland: The Demise of Communism." *Foreign Affairs* 69, no. 1 (America and the World: 1989/90): 70–88.

Brus, Włodzimierz. "From Revisionism to Pragmatism: Sketches Towards a Self-Portrait of a 'Reform Economist.'" *Acta Oeconomica* 40, no. 3 (1989): 204–10.

Bruszt, László. "Hungary's Negotiated Revolution." *Social Research* 57, no. 2 (Summer 1990): 365–87.

Brzezinski, Zbigniew. "Post-Communist Nationalism." *Foreign Affairs* 68, no. 5 (Winter 1989/90): 1–25.

———. "Selective Global Commitment." *Foreign Affairs* 70, no. 4 (Fall 1991): 1–20.

Bunce, Valerie. "Rising above the Past." *World Policy Journal* 7, no. 3 (Summer 1990): 395–430.

Bundy, McGeorge. "Chronology 1989: From Cold War Toward Trusting Peace." *Foreign Affairs* 69, no. 1 (America and the World: 1989/90): 197–212.

Burley, Anne-Marie. "The Once and Future German Question." *Foreign Affairs* 68, no. 5 (Winter 1989/90): 65–83.

Butler, William E. "International Law, Foreign Policy and the Gorbachev Style." *Journal of International Affairs* 42, no. 2 (1988/89): 363–75.

Chernoff, Fred. "Ending the Cold War: The Soviet Retreat and the U.S. Military Buildup." *International Affairs* 67 (January 1991): 111–26.

Connor, W. R. "Why Were We Surprised?" *The American Scholar* 60, no. 2 (Spring 1991): 175.

Dahrendorf, Ralf. "Roads to Freedom: Democratization and its Problems in East and Central Europe." *Institute for East-West Security Studies Occasional Paper* no. 16 (1990).

Dashichev, Vyacheslav. "The Soviet Perspective." *Problems of Communism* 37 (May–August 1988): 60–7.

de Montbrial, Thierry. "Die Aussenpolitik Frankreichs." *Europa Archiv* 44 (May 25, 1989): 283–90.

Deak, Istvan. "Uncovering Eastern Europe's Dark History." *Orbis* 34 (Winter 1990): 51–65.

Delors, Jacques. "The Meaning of 1992." *Harvard International Review* 11 (Summer 1989): 23–7.

———. "The Two Europes, East and West." *International Affairs* (London) 65 (Autumn 1989): 653–58.

———. "Europe's Ambitions." *Foreign Policy* (Fall 1990): 14–27.

Di Palma, Giuseppe. "Why Democracy Can Work in Eastern Europe." *Journal of Democracy* 2 (Winter 1991): 21–31.

Diamond, Larry. "Beyond Authoritarianism and Totalitarianism: Strategies for Democratization." *The Washington Quarterly* 12 (Winter 1989): 141–63.

Frank, Andre G. "Europe from Helsinki to Finlandization." *Review of International Affairs* 41 (February 20, 1990): 16–18.

Fukuyama, Francis. "The End of History." *The National Interest* no. 16 (Summer 1989): 3–18.

———. "The Beginning of Foreign Policy: America Confronts the Post–Cold War World." *The New Republic* (August 17, 1992): 24–25.

Gardner, Richard. "The Comeback of Liberal Internationalism." *The Washington Quarterly* (Summer 1990): 23–39.

Garton Ash, Timothy. "The Empire in Decay." *New York Review of Books* (September 29, 1988): 52–60.

———. "The German Revolution." *New York Review of Books* (December 21, 1989): 14–19.

Gati, Charles. "East-Central Europe: The Morning After." *Foreign Affairs* (Winter 1990–91): 129–45.

———. "From Sarajevo to Sarajevo." *Foreign Affairs* 71, no. 4 (Fall 1992): 64–78.

Genscher, Hans-Dietrich. "Let's Put Mr. Gorbachev's 'New Policy' to the Test." Ministry of Foreign Affairs, Federal Republic of Germany. *Reihe: Berichte und Dokumentationen* (February 1, 1987).

Geremek, Bronisław. "Postcommunism and Democracy in Poland." *The Washington Quarterly* 13, no. 3 (Summer 1990): 125–31.

Giscard d'Estaing, Valéry, Yasuhiro Nakasone, and Henry A. Kissinger. "East-West Relations." *Foreign Affairs* 68, no. 3 (Summer 1989): 1–21.

Gligorov, Vladimir. "Balkanization: A Theory of Constitution Failure." *East European Politics and Societies* 6, no. 3 (Fall 1992): 283–302.

Gompert, David. "How to Defeat Serbia." *Foreign Affairs* 73, no. 4 (July/August 1994): 30–47.

Goodby, James. "Commonwealth and Concert: Organizing Principles of Post-Containment Order in Europe." *The Washington Quarterly* (Summer 1991): 71–90.

Hacker, Jens. "The Berlin Policy of the USSR under Gorbachev." *Aussenpolitik* 3 (1989): 232–50.

Hartley, Anthony. "After the Thatcher Decade." *Foreign Affairs* 68, no. 5 (Winter 1989/90): 102–18.

Hassner, Pierre. "Europe Beyond Partition and Unity: Disintegration or Reconstruction?" *International Affairs* 66 (July 1990): 461–75.

Hendrickson, David C. "The Renovation of American Foreign Policy." *Foreign Affairs* 71, no. 2 (Spring 1992): 48–63.

Hoagland, Jim. "Europe's Destiny." *Foreign Affairs* 69, no. 1 (America and the World: 1989/90): 35–50.

Hoffman, Stanley. "The European Community and 1992." *Foreign Affairs* 68, no. 4 (Fall 1989): 27–47.

———. "A New World and Its Troubles." *Foreign Affairs* 69, no. 4 (Fall 1990): 115–22.

Horelick, Arnold P. "U.S.-Soviet Relations: The Threshold of a New Era." *Foreign Affairs* 69, no. 1 (America and the World: 1989/90): 51–69.

Hormats, Robert D. "Redefining Europe and the Atlantic Link." *Foreign Affairs* 68, no. 4 (Fall 1989): 71–91.

Howard, Michael. "The Springtime of Nations." *Foreign Affairs* 69, no. 1 (America and the World: 1989/90): 17–32.

Hutchings, Robert L. "The 'Eastern Question' Revisited." *Problems of Post-Communism* (Fall 1994): 45–9.

———. "Five Years After: Reflections on the Post-Communist Transitions and Western Assistance Strategies." In *East Central Europe in Transition*, 176–90. Joint Economic Committee, U.S. Congress. Washington, D.C.: Government Printing Office, 1994.

———. "Rediscovering the 'National Interest' in American Foreign Policy." Occasional Paper. Woodrow Wilson International Center for Scholars (March 1996).

Janos, Andrew C. "Social Science, Communism, and the Dynamics of Political Change." *World Politics* 44 (October 1991): 81–112.

Kaiser, Karl. "German Unification." *Foreign Affairs* 70, no. 1 (America and the World: 1990/91): 179–205.

Kirk, Roger. "The U.S. and Romania, Facing a Difficult Future: Policy Recommendations." The Atlantic Council of the United States *Policy Paper* (April 1991).

Klaus, Václav. "Transition—An Insider's View." *Problems of Communism* 41 (January–April 1992): 73.

Kligman, Gail. "Reclaiming the Public: A Reflection on Creating Civil Society in Romania." *East European Politics and Societies* 4, no. 3 (Fall 1990): 393–439.

Kober, Stanley. "Idealpolitik." *Foreign Policy* 79 (Summer 1990): 3–24.

Kohl, Helmut. "East-West Relations and Arms Control: Challenges for the Future." *Harvard International Review* (Summer 1989): 46–52.

Kovács, János M. "From Reformation to Transformation: Limits to Liberalism in Hungarian Economic Thought." *East European Politics and Societies* 5, no. 1 (Winter 1991): 41–72.

Kramer, Mark. "Beyond the Brezhnev Doctrine." *International Security* 14, no. 3 (Winter 1989/90): 25–67.

Kramer, Steven P. "The French Question." *The Washington Quarterly* 14, no. 4 (Autumn 1991): 83–96.

Krauthammer, Charles. "The Unipolar Moment." *Foreign Affairs* 70, no. 1 (Winter 1990/91): 23–33.

Kusin, Vladimir. "Mikhail Gorbachev's Evolving Attitude to Eastern Europe." *Radio Free Europe Research,* RAD Background Report 128 (July 20, 1989): 1–12.

Kux, Ernst. "Revolution in Eastern Europe—Revolution in the West?" *Problems of Communism* 40 (May–June 1991): 1–13.

Larrabee, Stephen F. "Long Memories and Short Fuses: Change and Instability in the Balkans." *International Security* 15, no. 3 (Winter 1990/91): 58–91.

Legvold, Robert. "The Revolution in Soviet Foreign Policy." *Foreign Affairs* 68, no. 1 (America and the World 1988/89): 82–98.

Levy, Jack S. "Preferences, Constraints, and Choices in July 1914." *International Security* 15, no. 3 (Winter 1990/91): 151–86.

Lewis, Flora. "Bringing in the East." *Foreign Affairs* 69, no. 4 (Fall 1990): 15–26.

Linz, Juan J. "Transitions to Democracy." *The Washington Quarterly* 13, no. 3 (Summer 1990): 143–64.

Lynch, Allen. "Changing Contours of Soviet–East European Relations." *Journal of International Affairs* 42, no. 2 (1988/89): 423–34.

Mandelbaum, Michael. "Ending the Cold War." *Foreign Affairs* 68, no. 2 (Spring 1989): 16–36.

McNeil, William H. "Winds of Change." *Foreign Affairs* 69, no. 4 (Fall 1990): 152–75.

Mearsheimer, John. "Back to the Future: Instability in Europe after the Cold War." *International Security* 15 (Summer 1990): 5–56.

Millar, James R. "The Conversion of the Communists: Gorbachev's Legacy." *Soviet Union/Union Sovietique* 16, nos. 2–3 (1989): 201–10.

Moens, Alexander. "American Diplomacy and German Unification." *Survival* 33, no. 6 (November–December 1990): 531–45.

Moïsi, Dominique. "Mitterrand's Foreign Policy: The Limits on Continuity." *Foreign Affairs* 60, no. 2 (Winter 1981/82): 347–57.

———. "French Foreign Policy: The Challenge of Adaptation." *Foreign Affairs* 67, no. 1 (Fall 1988): 151–64.

Newhouse, John. "The Diplomatic Round: Sweeping Change." *The New Yorker* (August 27, 1990): 78–89.

Nitze, Paul H. "America: Honest Broker." *Foreign Affairs* 69, no. 4 (Fall 1990): 1–14.

Nixon, Richard. "American Foreign Policy: The Bush Agenda." *Foreign Affairs* 68, no. 1 (America and the World 1988/89): 199–219.

Nye, Joseph S., Jr. "What New World Order?" *Foreign Affairs* 71, no. 2 (Spring 1992): 83–96.

Pond, Elizabeth. "A Wall Destroyed: The Dynamics of German Unification in the GDR." *International Security* 15, no. 2 (Fall 1990): 35–66.

———. "Germany in the New Europe." *Foreign Affairs* 71, no. 2 (Spring 1992): 114–30.

Powell, Colin. "The American Commitment to European Security." *Survival* (Summer 1992): 3–11.

Prybyla, Jan S. "The Road from Socialism: Why, Where, What, and How." *Problems of Communism* 40 (January–April 1991): 1–17.

Rosecrance, Richard. "A New Concert of Powers." *Foreign Affairs* 71, no. 2 (Spring 1992): 64–82.

Rubinstein, Alvin Z. "The USSR in Turmoil: Views from the Right, Center, and Left." *Orbis* (Spring 1991): 267–84.

———. "Soviet Client-States: From Empire to Commonwealth." *Orbis* (Winter 1991): 69–78.

Sachs, Jeffrey, and David Lipton. "Poland's Economic Reform." *Foreign Affairs* 69, no. 3 (Summer 1993): 47–66.

Schwartz, Herman. "Constitutional Developments in East Central Europe." *Journal of International Affairs* 45, no. 1 (1991/92): 71–89.

Shipler, David K. "Letter from Budapest." *The New Yorker* (November 20, 1989): 74–99.

Smith, Geoffrey. "Britain in the New Europe." *Foreign Affairs* 71, no. 4 (Fall 1992): 155–70.

Smyser, W. R. "Vienna, Versailles, and Now Paris: Third Time Lucky?" *The Washington Quarterly* 14, no. 3 (Summer 1991): 61–90.

Snyder, Jack. "Averting Anarchy in the New Europe." *International Security* 14 (Spring 1990): 5–41.

Sorensen, Theodore C. "America's First Post–Cold War President." *Foreign Affairs* 71, no. 4 (Fall 1992): 13–30.

Stark, David. "Path Dependence and Privatization Strategies in East Central Europe." *East European Politics and Societies* 6, no. 1 (Winter 1992): 17–54.

Stent, Angela. "The One Germany." *Foreign Policy* 81 (Winter 1990/91): 53–70.

Surovell, Jeffrey. "Ligachev and Soviet Politics." *Soviet Studies* 43, no. 2 (1991): 355–74.

Tarrow, Sidney. "Aiming at a Moving Target: Social Science and the Recent Rebellions in Eastern Europe." *Political Science* (March 1991): 12–20.

Teltschik, Horst. "Gorbachev's Reform Policy and the Outlook for East-West Relations." *Aussenpolitik* 3 (1989): 201–14.

———. "The Federal Republic and Poland: A Difficult Partnership in the Heart of Europe." *Aussenpolitik* (January 1990): 3–15.

Tiersky, Ronald. "France in the New Europe." *Foreign Affairs* 71, no. 2 (Spring 1992): 131–46.

Tismaneanu, Vladimir. "The Quasi-Revolution and Its Discontent." *East European Politics and Societies* 7, no. 2 (Summer 1993): 309–48.

Tismaneanu, Vladimir, and Matei Calinescu. "The 1989 Revolution and Romania's Future." *Problems of Communism* 40 (January–April 1990): 42–59.

Tökés, Rudolf L. "The Science of Politics in Hungary in the 1980s." *Südosteuropa* 37 (January 1988): 8–32.

Treadgold, Donald W. "Mikhail Sergeevich and the World of 1990." *Soviet Union/Union Sovietique* 16, nos. 2–3 (1989): 211–20.

Tucker, Robert W. "1989 and All That." *Foreign Affairs* 69, no. 4 (Fall 1990): 93–114.

Ullman, Richard H. "Enlarging the Zone of Peace." *Foreign Policy* 80 (Fall 1990): 102–20.

"U.S.-Soviet Relations: An Agenda for the Future," a report to the 41st president of the United States, Foreign Policy Institute, School of Advanced International Studies, the Johns Hopkins University, Washington, D.C., (December 1988).

Van Evera, Stephen. "Primed for Peace: Europe After the Cold War." *International Security* 15, no. 3 (Winter 1990/91): 7–57.

Vardary, Tibor. "Collective Minority Rights and Problems in Their Legal Protection: The Example of Yugoslavia." *East European Politics and Societies* 6, no. 3 (Fall 1992): 260–82.

Waever, Ole. "Three Competing Europes: German, French, Russian." *International Affairs* 66 (July 1990): 477–93.

Wandycz, Piotr S. "Poland's Place in Europe in the Concepts of Pilsudski and Dmowski." *East European Politics and Societies* 4, no. 3 (Fall 1990): 451–68.

Weller, Marc. "The International Response to the Dissolution of the Socialist Federal Republic of Yugoslavia." *American Journal of International Law* 86, no. 3 (July 1992): 569–607.

Wells, Samuel F., Jr. "Mitterrand's International Policies." *The Washington Quarterly* 11, no. 3 (Summer 1988): 59–75.

Weschler, Lawrence. "A Grand Experiment." *The New Yorker* (November 13, 1989): 65.

Winik, Jay. "The Quest for Bipartisanship: A New Beginning for a New World Order." *The Washington Quarterly* 14, no. 4 (Autumn 1991): 115–30.

Yankelovich, Daniel. "Foreign Policy after the Election." *Foreign Affairs* 71, no, 4 (Fall 1992): 1–12.

Zelikow, Philip. "The New Concert of Europe." *Survival* (Summer 1992): 12–30.

Zielonka, Jan. "East Central Europe: Democracy in Retreat?" *The Washington Quarterly* 14, no. 3 (Summer 1991): 107–20.

Zimmerman, Warren. "The Last Ambassador: Memoirs of the Collapse of Yugoslavia." *Foreign Affairs* 74, no. 2 (March/April 1995): 2–20.

Index

437

342; in Bosnia, 353; and CSCE,
298, 299; in East Germany, 138–39;
and France, 29, 122, 136, 164–65,
273–78, 282–83, 299–300, 408n6;
"French solution" to Germany's
participation in, 122, 389n125; and
German unification, 92, 98, 100,
105, 109, 111–12, 116–26, 128,
130, 133–35, 137–39, 177; integration of Eastern Europe into, 167,
171, 174, 287–90; *meetings of:* in
Ottawa, 114–15, in Turnberry
(Scotland), 133; new mission for,
44, 135, 142, 157, 168, 293–94,
341, 350; proposals for transformation of, 130, 154, 396n31; *Summits
of:* Brussels, 39, 43, 46, 52, 100,
105–6; London, 135–37, 168, 271,
285, 288, 390n131; Rome, 271–72,
281–83, 288–91, 293–94; views of
role of, in new Europe, 150–51,
153, 290, 294; and Warsaw Pact,
133–35, 143, 172, 236; and Yugoslavian crisis, 242, 283, 289, 307,
308, 316
Naumann, Klaus, 282
Nazarbayev, Nursultan, 334
Nelson, Dan, 405n85
Németh, Miklós, 60, 66
Nenev, Radoslav, 406n101
Netherlands, 69–70, 159
"New Forum" movement (East Germany), 79
"new world order," xiv, 3, 4, 145–49,
153, 343, 345
Nicaragua, 10
Nicolson, Harold, 339
Nine Plus One. *See* "Dacha Agreement"
North Atlantic Assembly, 285
North Atlantic Cooperation Council
(NACC), 236, 280, 285, 288,
290–92, 298, 299
North Atlantic Treaty Organization. *See*
NATO
Nowak, Jan, 400nn11, 19
NSF. *See* National Salvation Front (Ro-
mania)
nuclear freeze movement, 27
nuclear weapons, 14–15, 27–28, 34,
135–36, 330–32. *See also* military

forces; short-range nuclear forces
Nyers, Rezsö, 60, 65, 66

OECD (Organization for Economic Cooperation and Development), 68,
163, 167, 169, 174, 206, 207
Office of Management and Budget
(U.S.), 207
Office of the Secretary of Defense, 22
Office of the U.S. Trade Representative,
202
oil (as motivation in Gulf War), 145,
147, 345
Olszewski, Jan, 219, 223–24, 401n21
"One Plus Three" meetings, 114, 138,
387n78
Operation Desert Storm. *See* Gulf War
OPIC (Overseas Private Investment Corporation), 203, 255
opposition groups, 87; in Albania, 262,
263; American support for, 190,
392n13; in Bulgaria, 50, 80–82,
179–82, 205, 254, 256; in Czechoslovakia, 83; in Hungary, 7–8, 38,
49–50, 56, 66, 89, 238; in Lithuania, 71; in Poland, 7–8, 38, 49–50;
in Romania, 50, 85, 183–84, 205,
246, 247–51. *See also specific
groups and parties*
Orbán, Viktor, 404n63
Organization for Economic Cooperation
and Development. *See* OECD
OSD. *See* Office of the Secretary of Defense
ostpolitik, 13, 16–20, 36, 56, 93,
370n39
Ottawa, 114–15, 117, 178
Overseas Private Investment Corporation (OPIC), 203, 255

Paderewski, Ignacy, 225
Palmerston, Lord, 344
Palouš, Radim, 177–78
Panama, 86–87
Panić, Milan, 317
Paris Charter, 143, 287, 322, 323
Paris Club, 220, 225, 257
Paris Peace Conference (1919), 321
Paris Summit (of CSCE), 147, 194, 228,
271, 272, 283–87; apparent tri-

Robson, John, 198

Roman, Petre, 182–83, 247, 249, 250, 252

Romania: American concerns about, 85–87, 178, 190, 214, 245–53, 267, 269; anti-Semitism in, 252; Baker's visit to, 178, 182–84; communist regime's demise in, 1, 48, 52–53, 72, 84–88; desire of, for Most Favored Nation status, 250–51, 253; Eagleburger's visit to, 253; economic assistance to, 209, 245–46, 248; economic crisis in, 210; elections in, 182, 195, 239, 246–47, 249, 251–53, 255; Hungarian minority in, 84, 239, 242, 243, 249; and Iraq, 250; miners' riots in, 247–48, 250–51; on minority rights, 295; opposition groups in, 50, 85, 183–84, 205, 246, 247–51; Securitate in, 86, 249

Romanian Intelligence Service (SRI), 249

Romanian National Unity party, 250

Roosevelt, Franklin D., 225, 342

Roskens, Ronald, 198

Rugova, Ibrahim, 310

Russia, 8, 301, 330, 333, 335, 340. *See also* Soviet Union

Ryzhkov, Nikolai, 415n54

Sachs, Jeffrey, 378n73

Sajudis (Lithuanian opposition group), 71

Santer, Jacques, 309

Sarlos, George, 59

Savov, Stefan, 406n104

Schuman, Robert, 151

Scowcroft, Brent: and Eastern Europe, 232, 373n8, 399n64; and European trade, 160, 211; and France, 274; and Gulf War, 155; meetings of, with Polish officials, 75; as national security adviser, ix, x, xii, xvii, 24, 25, 198, 400n13; and "new world order" concept, 145

SDI (Strategic Defense Initiative), 11, 28

security: American concern for legitimate Soviet interests regarding, 52, 89, 104, 126, 128, 129–31; Ameri-

can concerns about European, 116, 144, 150, 339, 346–47, 354; concerns about, in post-Cold War Europe, 4–5, 170–71, 213, 235–36, 242–43, 271–300, 341, 346–47, 354; economic dimensions of Eastern European, 171, 191–93, 204, 211, 212, 220, 221, 230; Franco-German cooperation as alternative to NATO, 29; French views of European, 150–51. *See also* military forces; NATO; nuclear weapons; Warsaw Pact

SEED (Support for East European Democracy) Act, 197–98, 203

Seitz, Ray, 25

self-determination: Bush's speech on, in Ukraine, 329; international law on, 321–24; movements for, in Baltic states, 71–72, 321; in multiethnic states, 303, 311–12, 315, 321–25; as principle of American grand strategy, 3, 35, 37, 40, 41, 44, 52, 74, 100, 103, 340–41; by republics of former Soviet Union, 324–38; Soviet endorsement of, 20, 60–62, 67, 71, 94; Wilson's view of, 342. *See also* nationalism

Serbia, 239, 242, 305; Antall on, 242–43; attacks on Croatia by, 259, 312–13, 319; elections in, 307–8; international sanctions against, 253; and the United States, 310. *See also* Serbs

Serbian Academy of Sciences, 304

Serbs: atrocities by, 316; in Bosnia-Herzegovina, 315, 316; in Croatia, 306, 307, 312. *See also* Serbia

Shakhnazarov, Georgi, 60

Shalikashvili, John, 282

Shevardnadze, Eduard, 11, 73; on American policy toward Soviet Union, 374n89; and Baker, 70–71, 114, 117, 124–27, 134–35, 145, 180, 396n31; on Eastern Europe's future, 51, 101–2; and German unification, 92–94, 105, 106, 111, 112, 114, 124, 128, 132, 134, 135, 137, 369n10; as legitimizer of change in Soviet empire, 89; as president of Georgia, 333;